All About Old Buildings

THE WHOLE PRESERVATION CATALOG

All About Old Buildings

THE WHOLE PRESERVATION CATALOG

Edited by Diane Maddex
National Trust for Historic Preservation

THE PRESERVATION PRESS

The Preservation Press
National Trust for Historic Preservation
1785 Massachusetts Avenue, N.W.
Washington, D.C. 20036

Initial development of this book was supported in part by a grant from the National Endowment for the Arts, a federal agency.

Research and Writing Staff:

Patricia Leigh Brown
Jennie B. Bull
Richard A. Crocker
Sarah Gleason
Carol Hallman
Ellen Horowitz
Carolyn Hufbauer
Wendy A. Jordan
Margaret Johnson
Sandra Kashdan
Patricia Kelley
Anne Marie Kelly

Diane Maddex
Ellen R. Marsh
Shirley Maxwell
Eileen McGuckian
Mary Anne O'Boyle
Constance Ramos
Candace Reed
Gail Rothrock
Andrea Schoenfeld
Stephen H. Snell
Kathleen Swiger
A. Elizabeth Watson

Printed in the United States of America
89 88 87 86 85   5 4 3 2 1

Library of Congress Cataloging in Publication Data

All about old buildings.
    Includes index.
    1. Buildings—United States—Conservation and restoration. 2. Buildings—United States—Remodeling for other use. I. Maddex, Diane. II. National Trust for Historic Preservation in the United States.
NA106.A44 1985   363.6'9'0973   85-9286
ISBN 0-89133-107-7 (casebound)
ISBN 0-89133-108-5 (paperbound)

Designed by Meadows and Wiser, Washington, D.C.

Preface

I do not know any reading more easy, more fascinating, more delightful than a catalogue.

Anatole France, *The Crime of Sylvestre Bonnard.* 1881.

If you are a lover of old buildings, you'll probably agree with Anatole France—especially as far as catalogs about old buildings are concerned. This whole preservation catalog represents an enormous ambition: to capture not just the facts and figures but also the overriding vitality of preservation efforts today. This landmark undertaking required many years of research, and the result is a unique resource for everyone who cares about all the buildings that surround us.

All About Old Buildings is a point of reference. It shows what to look for, where to go, who to see. It also has its share of fascinating reading: excerpts from listed sources and quotations from a variety of observers in addition to organizations to contact, books to read, articles to consult, illustrations of examples and outlines of preservation steps. For the most part, we have chosen to let these sources speak for themselves, to give voice to the far-ranging and sometimes divergent views that help make preservation a vital movement. Trying to keep up with this fast-changing field is like chasing a ball rolling down hill, as eminent preservationist Robert E. Stipe has observed. The ball is still rolling, as new groups form, new books are published, new issues arise and new preservation solutions are found.

A few notes should help guide readers: Entries are generally listed in order of preference or importance, except where geographical order makes more sense. The absence of a price on a book usually indicates that it is out of print but still recommended as a good source to be located in a library. Complete information on a book usually is provided only once in a chapter.

No book of this scope could be published without the aid of scores of dedicated people. Brian L. Stagg first suggested to the National Trust that preservationists needed a catalog of their own resources if they were going to save at least the architectural portion of the earth. Up until his untimely death in 1976, he showed the special dedication common to so many preservationists in his work to revive the historic town of Rugby, Tenn. *All About Old Buildings* is dedicated to him.

The core of the book is based on research conducted by A. Elizabeth Watson, Sandra Kashdan and Carolyn Hufbauer, who ambitiously took the first steps to locate all the resources that affect preservation—more than could possibly be bound between two covers. In later stages, various chapters and sections were updated by Ellen R. Marsh, Patricia Leigh Brown, Eileen McGuckian, Gail Rothrock, Sarah Gleason, Kathleen Swiger, Candace Reed, Shirley Maxwell, Wendy A. Jordan and Stephen H. Snell. Illustration research was

aided by Carol Hallman, Constance Ramos, Mary Anne O'Boyle and Ellen Horowitz. Interns who assisted with small sections included Margaret Johnson, Andrea Schoenfeld, Patricia Kelley, Anne Marie Kelly and Richard A. Crocker.

Two people in particular made uniquely dedicated contributions. The challenge to design such a complex book was eagerly assumed by Robert Wiser, and his creative and professional efforts to meet deadlines have helped us produce another book we feel sure is built to last. The final updating, in the last weeks before going to press, could not have been accomplished without the thorough and faithful work of Ellen Marsh.

Encouragement has been provided by Trust executives beginning with the former publisher, Terry B. Morton, Hon. AIA, and former senior vice president, Russell V. Keune, AIA, through Robert H. Angle, vice president for development and communications, and J. Jackson Walter, president. The National Endowment for the Arts and Robert H. McNulty also provided a needed early impetus. The staffs of nearly every National Trust office and regional office shared information and advice, as did many of the organizations and publishers included here and countless other preservationists. Among Trust staff readers of manuscript sections were Stephen Dennis, John Frisbee, Frank Gilbert, Peter Hawley, Rob Mawson, Henry McCartney, Mary C. Means, Susan Shearer and Rex Wilson; Anne E. Grimmer and Kay D. Weeks of the National Park Service provided helpful advice as well. Patient library staff have included Alyce Faye Morgan, Brigid Rapp, Laurie Beyer, Trish Orr and Cary Schneider. Support also has come from preservationists William J. Murtagh, Robert R. Garvey, Jr., Margaret E. Sweeney, Donald B. Myer, AIA, Richard M. Candee, Louise M. Merritt and Richard Kearns; and Andre Schiffrin, Barbara Plumb and Betsy Amster of Pantheon Books.

Editorial work was aided by the able Preservation Press staff, including Gretchen Smith, Melanie Dzwonchyk, Helen Cook and Jennie B. Bull. Manuscript typing was carried out by Cyna Cohen, Susan Krueger, Katherine E. Irvin, Marcia Cole, Miranda Sims, Jane Schneider and Mary Gaffney. Robert Wiser first designed the book under the direction of Barbara Charles of Staples and Charles Ltd and later worked in coordination with Marc Meadows of Meadows and Wiser to produce another award-winner; John Crank assisted with several chapters. Credit also is due the staffs of Carver Photocomposition, Inc. and Collins Lithographing and Printing for extraordinary service.

To these and all preservationists who have made *All About Old Buildings* a reality, the National Trust extends its sincere appreciation.

Diane Maddex, Editor
Preservation Press Books

Contents

Introduction

Preservation, as a Savannah teacher likes to tell her charges, is a "great big old word." Being a good teacher, she finally makes that big word a part of the children's everyday vocabulary. In the same way, the National Trust for Historic Preservation has been working for three and a half decades to make preservation a part of Americans' everyday lives. It may seem like a big word to those who are unfamiliar with it, but preservation is a simple concept: In short, it means saving architecturally and historically distinguished places, caring for them and putting them to good uses that will enrich all our lives. The word is not nearly as big as all the activities and the possibilities that preservation encompasses.

Preservation is increasingly viewed as one of the best hopes for managing the constant change in our environment. In a country as diverse and constantly on the move as ours, the maintenance of a common identity is particularly important. Physical reminders of a shared past—old buildings, neighborhoods, Main Streets—play a critical role in defining and reinforcing a uniquely American identity. These places also provide sheer visual delight and add variety to our streets and towns. How they do this, and how we can preserve them, is explained in irrestible detail in the following pages. This book is literally all about old buildings, encapsulating and reflecting all the wonderfully varied pursuits that today fall under the rubric of historic preservation.

As the chapters here show, Americans are rehabilitating their houses and renovating their workplaces, revitalizing neighborhoods and bringing back Main Streets. They are finding new uses for old buildings, and they are also finding that some of the old uses still work very well, even after 50 or 150 years. Other people are involved in preserving parts of our heritage that not long ago were ignored. They are saving old McDonald's and Apollo launch towers and 20th-century bungalows, using creative negotiations (and, when necessary, old-fashioned picketing and lawsuits). Homeowners who maintain their old houses with loving care, developers who recycle warehouses, historians who accurately restore a landmark, educators who teach tomorrow's generation, mayors who save their old city halls, lawyers who win battles in court and legislatures, bankers who help find the wherewithal to make it all possible—these are all preservationists, and all these activities are preservation.

Preservation makes all kinds of sense, including dollars and cents, as National Trust research has documented. In recent years, $21 billion has been invested annually in rehabilitating buildings more than 50 years old. Compared to new construction, rehabilitation tends to cost less, takes less time, saves energy, reuses scarce materials and provides jobs. Visiting historic sites is Americans' fourth most popular recreational activity. An important factor in this economic revitalization has been the federal tax incentives offered for rehabilitation of historic buildings since 1977 and expanded in 1981. Private investors are now putting more than $2 billion annually into rehabilitating historic buildings and have undertaken some 10,000 projects using the tax benefits. These rehabilitations have added thousands of new housing units, including renovated spaces for low- and moderate-income residents. Preservation is not just a nice idea. It is a needed answer to many problems the country faces in providing housing, saving energy, protecting our environment, creating jobs and building more stimulating surroundings for all of us.

This fact has not gone unnoticed. Today, an estimated two million people are involved in preservation activities in the United States, either in caring for their own old homes, taking a turn on the front lines of preservation campaigns or just being members of local preservation and historical groups. They have succeeded in obtaining recognition in the National Register of Historic Places for some 37,500 properties, including almost 4,000 historic districts representing more than a quarter million individual buildings; creating almost 1,000 local preservation commissions; operating some 2,500 house and history museums; running 4,000 state and local preservation organizations; reviving Main Streets in hundreds of small towns across the nation; and receiving 30,000 answers to preservation problems from the National Trust in one year.

But that is why the National Trust was established— to guide and lend support to all these activities that go under the name of preservation. And that is why we have published this catalog, which we intend to be a source both of information and of the inspiration that is so vital for finding creative solutions to save historic buildings. This whole preservation catalog is meant to be an idea book and a wish book as well as a handbook to be used whenever an answer to a preservation question is needed. If you started out asking if it is possible that the preservation movement is so broad and so deep as to require a sourcebook of more than 400 pages, 400,000 words, 6,500 entries, 850 illustrations and countless bits of useful and just entertaining information, the answer is not only yes. It is that there is even more out there waiting to be enjoyed and discovered about old buildings and, we hope, more people ready to join in.

J. Jackson Walter, President
National Trust for
Historic Preservation

City Hall (1892–94, Wesley Lyng Minor), Brockton, Mass., a Richardsonian Romanesque landmark that has been restored for continued use by the city. From *America's City Halls*. (Peter Vanderwarker)

Fugitive Places

1

The places that we have known belong now only to the little world of space on which we map them for our own convenience. None of them was ever more than a thin slice, held between the contiguous impressions that composed our life at that time; remembrance of a particular form is but regret for a particular moment; and houses, roads, avenues are as fugitive, alas, as the years.

Marcel Proust, *Swann's Way*. Translated by C.K. Scott Moncrieff. New York: Random House, 1970.

"We will probably be judged not by the monuments we build but by those we have destroyed."

Editorial. *New York Times,* October 30, 1963.

"When the first European settlers set foot on the American continent, they began to destroy as surely as they began to build a new civilization. In the act of building, they eroded the wilderness. And in their quest for more land, they first disrupted and then destroyed the man-made traces of the aboriginal civilizations that preceded theirs."

Constance M. Greiff, *Lost America: From the Atlantic to the Mississippi*

"To what end, pray, is so much stone hammered? . . . Most of the stone a nation hammers goes toward its tomb only. . . . I love better to see stones in place."

Henry David Thoreau, *Walden: or, Life in the Woods*. 1854.

Demolition in 1966 of the Richardsonian Romanesque-style National Presbyterian Church (1889, J. C. Cady), Washington, D.C. (Matthew Lewis, *Washington Post*)

"Not since the War of 1812 has the United States suffered any serious loss of its buildings through foreign military action. Yet in the second half of the twentieth century we suffer an attrition of distinguished structures which has the aspect of a catastrophe. . . . "

George Zabriskie, "Window to the Past." In *With Heritage So Rich*. 1966. Reprint. Washington, D.C.: Preservation Press, 1983.

"We do not use bombs and powder kegs to destroy irreplaceable structures. . . . We use the corrosion of neglect or the thrust of bulldozers. . . . Connections between successive generations of Americans . . . are broken by demolition. Sources of memory cease to exist. . . . We ourselves create the blank spaces by doing nothing when the physical signs of our previous national life are removed from our midst."

Albert Rains and Laurance G. Henderson, Preface. *With Heritage So Rich*

"Remove not the ancient landmark, and enter not into the fields of the fatherless."

Proverbs 22:28

Saltair (1926, Ashton and Evans), at Great Salt Lake, Salt Lake City. The second pavilion on the site, this followed the fate of its predecessor: It burned, in 1970, after being abandoned. (Utah State Historical Society)

"Safe upon the solid rock the ugly houses stand: Come and see my shining palace built upon the sand!"

Edna St. Vincent Millay, "Second Fig." *A Few Figs From Thistles*. In *Collected Poems, Edna St. Vincent Millay*. Norma Millay, ed. New York: Harper and Row, 1975.

"Since demolition is irreversible, special care should be taken to err on the side of preservation."

Andrew Gold, "The Welfare Economics of Historic Preservation." In "Perspectives on Historic Preservation." *Connecticut Law Review,* vol. 8, no. 2, Winter 1976.

"My old block in Grand Island [Nebraska] is now mostly a parking lot. The first time I went back there I turned the corner breathlessly, expecting to see the old playhouse, swing on the old swing, and so on, and suddenly everything was out of proportion. There was all this asphalt, and a big supermarket. It was like seeing the aftermath of a bombing. I felt like they'd wiped out my past without asking my permission."

Dick Cavett, *Cavett*. With Christopher Porterfield. New York: Harcourt Brace Jovanovich, 1974.

"How people feel about a place is very important to their psychic health. It is very important to their physical health. Some of the old people who lived in [a demolished neighborhood] died shortly thereafter. I don't exaggerate when I say the loss of that area . . . was a contributing factor to their ill health and eventual rapid death."

Chester Hartman. In *Living With Seismic Risk: Strategies for Urban Conservation*. Washington, D.C.: American Association for the Advancement of Science, 1977.

The Harral-Wheeler House (1846, A. J. Davis), Bridgeport, Conn., torn down in 1958 despite appeals to the city council.

The Language of Destruction

abandonment. The relinquishment of ownership or control of property. "With the exception of the bulldozer, the most fatal hazard of all structures is abandonment, which accelerates deterioration." (Orin Bullock. In *Preservation and Conservation: Principles and Practices*. Washington, D.C.: Preservation Press, 1976.)

bulldozer. A broad, blunt ram propelled by a heavy tractor and used to demolish small buildings.

demolition. The deliberate and systematic disassembly or destruction of a structure.

destruction. The partial or complete loss of a structure, generally connoting a sudden or unplanned occurrence such as fire, earthquake or accident, as opposed to overt demolition.

deterioration. A worsening of a structure's condition, generally attributable to exposure to weather, normal wear and tear, aging or lack of maintenance.

dismantle. To take apart a structure piece by piece, often with the intention of reconstructing it elsewhere.

11th hour. Last-minute attempts to preserve a building threatened with demolition, often through a court-ordered injunction or solicitation of funds for purchase.

headache ball. Synonym for *wrecking ball*.

raze. To demolish; destroy to the ground. "We raise and raze buildings. In between, we merely use them." (William Marlin, *Inland Architect*, December 1969.)

wrecking ball. A heavy ball of concrete suspended from the boom of a crane and swung against or dropped on a structure to demolish it. They vary in weight, averaging several tons.

Adapted from *Landmark Words: A Glossary for Preserving the Built Environment*, National Trust for Historic Preservation. Forthcoming.

City Hall (1884–88, Elijah E. Myers), Grand Rapids, Mich., seen through an Alexander Calder sculpture. (William Andrews)

Demolition began in 1969 under an urban renewal plan. (Colorama)

Attempts to spare the city hall tower failed. (Colorama)

The loss of the Grand Rapids City Hall occurred under the city's urban renewal contract with a local bank despite a suit by preservationists. (Colorama)

Ruins of the Honoré Block, burned in the Great Chicago Fire of 1871.
(Chicago Historical Society)

Why Landmarks Are Lost

The question of why landmarks are lost should be asked at the outset. Why are fine old buildings torn down? Why are they allowed to decay so that they have to be torn down? Or why, as often happens, are they "modernized" in such a fashion that one wishes they had been torn down?

These are hard questions that cannot be dismissed lightly. It may be comforting to imagine that some malign fate, some diabolical plot, is working against efforts to preserve our architectural heritage. But such comforting fancies do not save buildings. The facts are real and, if buildings are to be saved, the facts must be squarely faced.

First, preservationists must accept certain inexorable realities. Buildings, like people, grow old. The repair or deferred maintenance of an old building is usually expensive. The uses for which a structure was originally designed can become obsolete. The people who originally used a building may die or move away. Fashions change. Urgent new needs compete for limited amounts of land. And most people like to make money; in particular, they expect a fair return on their investments. There is nothing inherently evil about any of these facts. They are simply the inescapable elements of a very real problem. No amount of hopeful thinking can wish them away.

In addition, there are the factors of ignorance, indifference and inertia to be faced. Many people know little about architecture or history; of those who do know something, most are preoccupied with other concerns. Of the few who both know and are concerned, a great number, unfortunately, feel that circumstances are so unfavorable for preservation that the loss of old buildings is inevitable.

Harmon H. Goldstone, FAIA,
"Administrative, Legal and City
Planning Aspects of Historic
Preservation Programs." In
*Preservation and Conservation:
Principles and Practices*

Looking down California Street from Nob Hill following the 1906 San
Francisco earthquake. From *San Francisco: Creation of a City.*

The Four Horsemen of Destruction

Fire   War
Disaster   Man

"Four Horsemen of Destruction."
Historic Preservation, no. 3, 1961.

"There is no art as imperma-
nent as architecture. All that
solid brick and stone mean
nothing. Concrete is as evanes-
cent as air. The monuments of
our civilization stand, usually,
on negotiable real estate; their
value goes down as land value
goes up. . . .

In addition to land economics, buildings, even great ones,
become obsolete. Their functions and technology date. They
reach a point of comparative
inefficiency, and inefficiency today is both a financial and a
mortal sin.

It would be so simple if art
also became obsolete. But a
building that may no longer
work well or pay its way may
still be a superb creative and
cultural achievement . . . and
therein lies the conflict and
dilemma of preservation."

Ada Louise Huxtable, "Anatomy
of a Failure." *Will They Ever
Finish Bruckner Boulevard?* New
York: Times Books, 1970.

"One of the major mistakes of
the Modern movement, in its
compulsion to sweep away the
clutter of Victorian substyles
and Art Nouveau, was to sweep
away the good with the bad. In
their espousal of the automated
machine as the ideal of the
contempoary artisan, early
Modernists rejected handcraft
and ornamentation—not only
for themselves but also retroac-
tively for other periods of architecture and design."

C. Ray Smith, *Supermannerism:
New Attitudes in Post-Modern
Architecture.* New York: E. P.
Dutton, 1977.

"There is one threat to buildings that has nothing to do with
demolition crews, urban renewal
schemes or bulldozer-style development. That is the seldom
discussed threat of neglect. Ig-
nore any building long enough
and time will take its toll,
eventually rendering the wrecking ball unnecessary."

"Demolition by Neglect." Editorial, *Preservation News*, March
1978.

"Nature has used elements of
architecture as objects, just as
art takes as object elements of
Nature."

Paul Zucker, *Fascination of Decay. Ruins: Relic-Symbol-Orna-
ment.* Ridgewood, N.J.: Gregg
Press, 1968.

"Pennsylvania Station succumbed to progress at the age
of fifty-six, after a lingering
decline. The building's facade
was shorn of its eagles and
ornament. The last wall went
not with a bang, or a whimper,
but to the rustle of real estate
stock shares. The passing of
Penn Station was more than the
end of a landmark. It made the
priority of real estate values
over preservation conclusively
clear."

Ada Louise Huxtable, "A Vision
of Rome Dies." *Will They Ever
Finish Bruckner Boulevard?*

Removal of the eagle sculptures
from Pennsylvania Station before
demolition. (*New York Times*)

Ruins from New York City's Pennsylvania Station (1906–10, McKim, Mead
and White) were trucked to Secaucus Meadows when it was razed in 1966
for the new Madison Square Garden. (Edward Hausner, *New York Times*)

Remains of a gate made from the
Old War Department in Washington,
D.C. (David Blume)

Windsor, near Port Gibson, Miss.,
in ruins from neglect. From the
cover, *Lost America.*

Charleston, S.C., in April 1865,
bearing the effects of the Civil War.
(Library of Congress)

Razing of Loew's Palace (1918), Washington, D.C., in 1978 as part of the
new construction activity under the Pennsylvania Avenue development plan.
(Bob Burchette, *Washington Post*)

Evans Hotel, Hot Springs, S.D.,
burned during renovation. (© 1979
Charley Najacht, *Hot Springs Star*)

The Roster of the Dead

Those buildings which are gone but not forgotten are legion. Those portions of older cities, waterfronts, fine residential areas, handsome early office buildings, old mills, great churches and all other storied places of our past that now form a roster of our architectural dead, form a formidable and heart-breaking list, too long to be recounted. . . .

The personality of any city is not just dependent on its great buildings and great places but is created by the total complex of large and small, important and minor, the individual and the mass. . . .

Minor buildings, in the aggregate, create the major urban scene. They are the body of any city. The body is being rapidly carved up bit by bit and sometimes in whole chunks. . . . History is dead in such a city just as though it had never existed, although there is still perhaps a bone or two lying around bleaching.

> Carl Feiss, "Our Lost Inheritance." In *With Heritage So Rich*

Art Deco facade of the Studebaker Service Building, Chicago, built in the 1920s but lost in the mid-1960s. (Hedrich-Blessing)

Electrical Building at the 1933 Chicago Century of Progress Exposition. (Hedrich-Blessing)

Round House (c. 1865, Christopher Southwick), Middletown, R.I., razed for an airport in 1952. (SPNEA)

Club House at Washington Park Race Track (Solon S. Beman), Chicago, in 1896; it was gone by 1908. (Chicago Historical Society)

The second Cliff House (1896, Adolph Sutro) on San Francisco Bay survived the earthquake but burned in 1907.

Haumont Soddie, Custer County, Neb., in 1887, lost to neglect. (Nebraska State Historical Society)

Forestry Building (1904, Whidden and Lewis), Portland, Ore., a fire victim. (Oregon Historical Society)

Church of the Unity (1869, H. H. Richardson), Springfield, Mass. (Cervin Robinson, HABS)

Cherokee Female Seminary (1852), Park Hill, Okla., burned. (Oklahoma Historical Society)

The Fair Store, Chicago, decorated in 1899 for the arrival of President McKinley. (Chicago Historical Society)

Bradbury Mansion (1888, Sam and J. C. Newsom), Los Angeles, demolished after serving as a rooming house. (Henry E. Huntington Library)

Waiting room of the Boston and Albany Railroad Station (1884, H. H. Richardson), Wellesley, Mass. (HABS)

Pell's Fish House (1881), Denver, with its stained-glass windows and stamped-tin cornice. (Western History Department, Denver Public Library)

Spectators watching the demolition of houses on Capitol Hill in Washington, D.C. (John J. G. Blumenson, NTHP)

A wrecking ball and crane drawn by 5-year-old Kelly Hamlin of Alliance, Ohio, after seeing a local high school demolished.

The Wrecking Business

There's nothing quite like a good house-wrecking. Come one, come all. You are cordially invited to a demolition-watching. It's a great performance of a kind being given with increasing frequency. . . . one that could replace the 'happening' as the most chic of avant-garde anti-cultural events.

Watch an architectural landmark demolished piece by piece. Be present while a splendid building is reduced to rubble. See the wrecking bars gouge out the fine chateau-style stonework. Hear the gas-powered saws bite into the great beams and rafters. Thrill to destruction. Take home samples. Hurry to the show.

On second thought, don't hurry. There will be many more performances.

> Ada Louise Huxtable, "The Architectural Follies." *Will They Ever Finish Bruckner Boulevard?*

"You just take a crane and ball and beat it down. It's strictly a case of smashing it down and carting it away."

A Wrecker

Satisfaction

" 'Doesn't the thought of a ball coming down and smashing things strike you as the epitome of violence—in a power sense?' asked Bernard Duval of Arlington. 'It's a reducing thing—with such little ado.'

Andrea Clanchette, an intern on Capitol Hill who was out jogging, also was fascinated by it. 'I like powerful things and that's pretty powerful,' she said. 'And it's changing all the time.' . . .

'It's such a large powerful thing which one man can completely destroy by himself. They must get a lot of satisfaction. Like Moses parting the Red Sea.'

In fact, wreckers do get satisfaction. 'That's the most exciting part—just tearin' something up,' said 10-year veteran wrecker Albert Beckford of Lanham, who was in charge of the razing yesterday.

Wrecking isn't easy, according to Beckford. 'It's more difficult than just picking up [girders and beams] and setting them down. To be a good wrecking man takes two to three years,' Beckford said.

But 'this job is fascinating. There's never a dull moment. You're never bored. Every building you wreck is different.' . . . "

> Caryle Murphy, "Power in Wrecker's Ball Awes Watchers." *Washington Post*, October 17, 1977.

Building Wrecking: The How and Why of a Vital Industry. Jean Poindexter Colby. New York: Hastings House, 1972. 96 pp., biblio., index. $7.95 hb.

An attempt to teach children about the ways in which buildings are razed, the workers, the process, the growth of the industry and the reasons behind demolition. A dispassionate effort by the author of more preservation-oriented books, concluding that building wrecking is little more than "making way for tomorrow."

How to Wreck a Building. Elinor Lander Horwitz. New York: Pantheon, 1982. 56 pp., illus. $9.95 hb.

A tale told from a child's viewpoint as he watches the demolition of his 71-year-old Baltimore school, which was "tall and fancy," unlike its "low and square" replacement. Why the old school must go is never asked or answered. Even the teacher agrees when a student suggests, "Time moves on and so must we."

Unbuilding. David Macaulay. Boston: Houghton Mifflin, 1980. 80 pp., illus., gloss. $12.95 hb.

A 1989-era fantasy (or so preservationists hope) in which the Empire State Building is dismantled for shipment to the Arabian desert, there to be reerected as headquarters for a petroleum institute. The landmark is lost at sea, however, adding a new peril for the preservation cause.

'The Wrecking Business Isn't What It Used to Be'

"Just as many construction men take great pride in the way they put up buildings, there are those who take just as much pride in tearing them down. . . . These men of the wrecking business revel in the tales of old buildings others have long forgotten. . . . These days, however, the wrecking business isn't what it used to be. Sure, they're still tearing down those old buildings to make way for new ones. But the wreckers don't use hand labor anymore. Today it's the three-ton steel ball, the bulldozer, the crane claw and dynamite. . . . 'There have been many changes in this business, but few improvements,' says [Bernie] Gittleson, who operates Federal Wrecking with his brother Nate. . . . 'Now, because of the high prices paid for these old buildings, people want the land as fast as possible. Today we're working against time.' . . . 'They are cheaper to take down than to put up,' adds [Marvin] Stickman, 'and they all come down easily . . . .' 'It's either feast or famine,' according to Gittleson. 'When the building business is good, so is the wrecking business.' . . . "

> Lew Sichelman, "Building Wreckers Recall Better Days." *Washington Star*, April 22, 1977.

"It's exhilarating to have such tremendous, awesome power at your fingertips."

John Loizeaux

Timed sequence views of the dynamiting of the Traymore Hotel (1906–14, William L. Price) on the boardwalk in Atlantic City, N.J. (Jack E. Boucher, HABS)

The Family That Topples Skyscrapers

"Jack Loizeaux (pronounced La-Wah-Zo), his wife Freddie, and their sons Mark and Doug run a company called Controlled Demolition, Inc. (CDI) from their home in Towson, Md., a suburb of Baltimore. . . .

Mark . . . has been helping his father since he was old enough to hold a stick of dynamite at the age of 8. . . .

With the help of four employees, they demolish buildings, bridges, smokestacks and other structures with explosives without blowing themselves and half of downtown to Kingdom Come. . . .

Their biggest in total size so far is the 21-story, 600-room Traymore Hotel that covered most of a square block in Atlantic City, N.J. The prime demolition contractor estimated it would take 11 months to bring down the Traymore by the conventional method of beating it slowly to death with a 4000-pound 'headache ball' swung from a crane. CDI took 10 seconds with 550 pounds of explosives. . . .

Explosive demolition, Jack Loizeaux figures, can be accomplished at half the cost or less of conventional methods and often with major side benefits. . . .

The Loizeauxs don't blow buildings up, they coax them down. . . .

Although CDI insists it is 'not in the entertainment business,' the spectacular work invariably draws large crowds and the local news media, bringing instant celebrity. . . . Sometimes when a shot doesn't go off on time, crowds get angry when they have waited hours for a view. . . ."

Michael Stachell, "The Loizeaux Family: They Get Paid for Precision Bombing." *Parade*, June 18, 1978.

See also:
"The Demolition Family: Bringing Down the House," Hal Hellman. *Geo*, October 1979.

The Fall of a 'House of Cards'

ATLANTIC CITY, N.J., June 23, 1972— "Nine seconds. It took nine seconds to reduce the 18-story Traymore Hotel in Atlantic City to an unrecognizable pile of rubble about 20 feet high. I saw it and I still don't believe it.

The dynamite blast that was designed to level the 65-year-old Art Deco landmark was scheduled for 7:00 a.m. I had been in position with my camera atop a 13-story hotel two and a half blocks away since dawn, in case the demolition experts decided to do their thing early. Those things happen when a historic landmark faces destruction and there is substantial opposition. . . .

In nine seconds it was all over. The steel-reinforced, poured concrete frame, massive brick structure had folded like a house of cards. When the dust cleared only the north and south towers remained, as had been planned by the demolition crew for later demolition. The towers reminded me of a headstone and footstone at a grave."

Jack E. Boucher, Historic American Buildings Survey

A Bad Gamble

"Several years ago some people at Loews Corp. made a costly error—they decided to tear down their old 575-room Traymore Hotel in Atlantic City, N.J., and convert the property into a parking lot.

That's the reason Loews wasn't the first firm with a highly profitable palatial gambling casino on the Boardwalk. . . .

[Preston Robert] Tisch, president of Loews, was asked about the decision by a reporter the other day during an interview. 'I wish you had talked me out of tearing it down,' he said."

Donald Saltz, "Hotel Traymore Razing Called a Costly Error." *Washington Star*, November 15, 1978.

Execution Squad

They've been called the "building execution squad," and these are some of the notches on their cranes: Chicago's McCormick Place and Robert Todd Lincoln mansion; New York's Polo Grounds; Brooklyn's Ebbets Field; Spokane's Great Northern Railway depot—and Peyton Place, Prince Valiant's castle and the Red Sea, the latter all part of a 20th Century-Fox movie set in Hollywood. The squad even has wrecked a number of its own offices. Although it has no offices in Cleveland, the Cleveland Wrecking Company is a landmark among wreckers. More than 85,000 structures have felt the weight of its ball and claw since Cleveland started in 1910. "When the work is done there is nothing to show for it. Who would enter such a business? . . . " asks Jim Szantor in the *Chicago Tribune*. "For the demolition contractor, there is little room for nostalgia and only slight allowance for esthetic appreciation. To the men who swing the 6,000-pound steel demolition ball (or 'skullcracker') the only welcome sight is rubble and bare ground."

Jim Szantor, "Piles of Rubble Monuments to Wreckers' Art." *Chicago Tribune*, August 30, 1974.

The Wrecking Game

"You, as operator of the toy . . . can also imagine that you are wrecking old buildings to make way for a new and better country."

William Fenning, President, Cleveland Wrecking Company. Instructions for playing the Cleveland Wrecking Company Game

Shelby and Patrick Haller playing the Cleveland Wrecking Company Game. (Grant Haller, *Seattle Post-Intelligencer*)

"COAST TO COAST"

CLEVELAND WRECKING COMPANY

AMERICA'S FOREMOST DEMOLITION CONTRACTOR

Public Comfort Station (1910, Foltz and Parker), Indianapolis, Ind., torn down in 1963. (Bass Photo Company)

The Lost Generation

A type of book began to evolve in the 1960s as part of the movement to catalog the wave of destruction sweeping over cities everywhere: the Lost *book. From London to Montreal, from Boston to New Orleans all the way to the Pacific coast, these books survey the most respected, most loved and sometimes most idiosyncratic of the places lost. They are not, of course, the complete record—who could presume to finish this? They do share a number of attributes: They are pleas for an end to irrational destruction, attempts to awaken the public to the measure of the loss and available mechanisms for preservation. The books generally carry an interpretive introductory essay, organize photographs and drawings of lost sites by use or structural type and include captions identifying and assessing the buildings portrayed. Beyond this, the books are as different as the cities and places featured, and as much the same as destruction anywhere.*

Art Deco detail from the Richfield Building (1929, Morgan, Walls and Clements), Los Angeles, replaced with a larger skyscraper. (Marvin Rand, HABS)

Lost America

"This is a sad book. It is meant to be. It represents only a small sample of the rich and diverse delights that have vanished from the American scene. Some were major monuments. Some were examples of interesting types, illuminating the contributions made to American life by differing cultures and disciplines. Some were buildings of no particular architectural distinction, but were deeply woven into the fabric of their communities. Not all of them, on sober reflection, could have been or should have been saved. But far too many, even of the minor structures, were destroyed heedlessly, for insufficient reasons, and were replaced with structures or, in the case of parking spaces and vacant lots, nonstructures that have diminished the quality of the man-made environment. . . .

We are losing not only identity in place, but in time. The buildings that have gone and the ones that are threatened constitute a valuable historic and artistic testimonial, recorded in brick and mortar rather than in ink, of what America has been and what it is becoming. We need our old buildings as a point of reference, not just to tell us about the past, but to help place the present and future in perspective"

Constance M. Greiff, *Lost America: From the Atlantic to the Mississippi*

Lost America: From the Atlantic to the Mississippi. Constance M. Greiff, ed. Foreword by James Biddle. Princeton: Pyne Press, 1971. 242 pp., illus., index.

Lost America: From the Mississippi to the Pacific. Constance M. Greiff, ed. Foreword by James Biddle. Princeton: Pyne Press, 1972. 243 pp., illus., index.

Lost New York

"If architecture is, as I believe, not the art of beautiful buildings, but the art of human use, then conservation of good use is a matter of concern for everyone, in the present and future, and conservation is not 'obstructionist' but wise. That is the point of this book, and the aspect of *Lost New York* best remembered. . . . I had hoped that someone else later might write a *New Lost New York*— much shorter I hope."

Nathan Silver, *Lost New York*

Lost New York. Nathan Silver. 1967. New York: Crown, 1983. 242 pp., illus., index. $9.98 pb.

National Cash Register Building, 1939 New York World's Fair. (Museum of the City of New York)

Fifth Avenue, New York City, in 1898. (Byron, Museum of the City of New York)

Marshall Field Wholesale Store (1887, H. H. Richardson), Chicago. (Chicago Historical Society)

Gen. Noble Tree House (c. 108 B.C.), built 1892, moved to Washington, D.C., 1894, destroyed 1940. (W. R. Ross)

Salem, Ore., with the Marion County Courthouse (1873, William W. Piper) and State Capitol (1873, Justus M. Krumbein). (Oregon State Library)

Removal of the cornice from the Old Stock Exchange (1894, Adler and Sullivan), Chicago, during demolition in 1972 for a new office building. (Richard Nickel)

Dumbarton Theater (1913, William Nichols), Washington, D.C., now remodeled. (Robert A. Truax Collection)

Lost Chicago

"The supreme magic of Chicago was always the sheer physical presence of the city, the unequaled splendor of its architecture. For me, growing up was coincidental with becoming aware of that architecture. . . .

After college, when I moved away, every trip back to Chicago was a revelation of monuments fallen: the Mecca, the Palmer castle, the Garrick Theatre, the Federal Building, the long bar of the Auditorium, the Stock Exchange, Diana Court. Even lesser landmarks, the places that had given the city its special personality, were not spared: the Paradise Theatre, Henrici's, the Chez Paree, the Lindbergh Beacon, and, unbelievably, the Stock Yards themselves. Their owners had not saved them. They were an incomparable heritage mindlessly squandered, pieces of gold minted by the fathers and thrown away by the sons. I could not save them in their concrete form, but I was determined that somehow I would preserve their spirit. I would do it in the one way I could, by writing a book that would reveal them and their architectural predecessors in all their glory. Perhaps, by showing the splendor which has been lost, I might, in some small way, help to preserve that splendor not yet departed."

David Lowe, *Lost Chicago*

Lost Chicago. David Lowe. 1975. New York: Crown, 1985. 241 pp., illus., index. $9.98 pb.

Lost Boston

"Change, the narrative of Boston's buildings shows, can be a creative act: It can be a manifesto of the joy in city-making. The eighteenth century gave way to a still more splendid Boston in the nineteenth, for Victorian builders responded to the city and its citizens. Our twentieth-century builders do not: When nineteenth-century architecture falls, it falls for naught. We of the twentieth century seem most adept at paving paradise to put up a parking lot."

Jane Holtz Kay, *Lost Boston*

Lost Boston. Jane Holtz Kay. Boston: Houghton Mifflin, 1980. 320 pp., illus., biblio., index. $24.95 hb, $12.95 pb.

Province Street (formerly Governor's Alley), Boston, about 1890, before it was widened in the 20th century. (Bostonian Society)

Lost Washington

"In one generation, since World War II, Washington has lost a large number of architecturally significant buildings, ranging from Federal structures of the 1790s to art moderne landmarks from the 1930s. Demolition resulted from a multitude of factors, including government expansion, private real-estate development, urban renewal, freeways, commercial growth, and the enlargement of institutions such as universities, hospitals, and churches. . . . I have included many examples of lost federal and municipal buildings, as a means of providing a context within which the presentation of so many private buildings will not lead the reader to forget the origin and life of Washington as a public place."

James M. Goode, *Capital Losses*

Capital Losses: A Cultural History of Washington's Destroyed Buildings. James M. Goode. Washington, D.C.: Smithsonian Institution Press, 1979. 464 pp., illus., append., index. $37.50 hb, $19.95 pb.

Francis Scott Key Mansion (c. 1802), Washington, D.C., razed in 1948 for Key Bridge. (Leet Brothers)

Wreckage of the Houghton House, Austin, Tex., torn down for a parking lot. (Steve Hultman)

Caryatids being temporarily removed for a 1920s remodeling of the Dividend Office (1818–23, John Soane), Bank of England, London. (Bank of England)

St. John Red Lion Square (1874, J. L. Pearson), London, bombed in WWII, later disassembled and finally demolished. (Greater London Council)

Lost New Orleans

"When the English-born American architect, Benjamin Henry Latrobe, came to New Orleans in 1819 he was greatly impressed by the French character of the city. . . . He correctly predicted that 'it would be a safe wager that in 100 years not a vestige will remain of the buildings as they now stand, excepting perhaps a few public buildings and of houses built since the American acquisition of the country.' Of the public buildings that he saw, only the Cabildo and the Presbytère on Jackson Square and the old Ursuline convent farther down Chartres Street have survived, along with a mere dozen or so other eighteenth-century houses. Latrobe's predictions were largely correct, due not only to 'American notions of right and wrong,' but also to natural disaster: fire, hurricane, and the deleterious effect of wet soil and a humid climate."

Samuel Wilson, Jr., FAIA, Foreword. *Lost New Orleans*

Lost New Orleans. Mary Cable. 1980. New York: Crown, 1984. 256 pp., illus., biblio., index. $8.95 pb.

Lost Texas

"Any history of Texas architecture based solely upon a survey of extant buildings must be incomplete. . . . Even while this book was in press the historic structure in which the Texas A&M University Press offices were located was virtually destroyed by flames (and subsequently demolished)."

Willard B. Robinson, *Gone From Texas*

Gone From Texas: Our Lost Architectural Heritage. Willard B. Robinson. College Station: Texas A&M University Press, 1981. 316 pp., illus., gloss., biblio., index. $29.95 hb.

Lost in Utah

Saltair. Nancy D. McCormick and John S. McCormick. Salt Lake City: University of Utah Press, 1985. $14.95 pb.

Lost Colonials

"To turn these pages is to realize the depth of our artistic and historic loss through the destruction of old buildings by war, by fire, by revolutions of taste, and by the ruthless march of urban improvement. *Quod non facerunt barbari, fecerunt Barberini* . . . .

Much as we deplore the destruction, we must not think its extent peculiar to our own country and time. It has always and everywhere accompanied life and vital growth. Raphael's palaces in the Borgo were swept away after a century to make way for the colonnades of St. Peter. The old quarters of Paris fell before the grandiose *percements* of the Napoleons. We should be more concerned that so little of what has taken the place of our colonial buildings shares their merits of honesty, dignity and beauty."

Fiske Kimball, Introduction. *Lost Examples of Colonial Architecture*

Lost Examples of Colonial Architecture: Buildings That Have Disappeared or Been So Altered as to Be Denatured. John Mead Howells. 1931. Reprint. New York: Dover, 1963. 248 pp., illus., index.

Lost Baltimore

"Sadly, Baltimore shares with other historic centers the erosion of its physical heritage, never, perhaps, in as drastic a form as Detroit or St. Louis or Boston, but still with major wounds. Baltimore business and government has traditionally used far too lenient a hand in shaping the city physically, except where capitalizing land or taxes for the city treasury or friendly powers has been concerned. The result has been that many a choice structure on the periphery of the inner city has gone to rack and ruin or been taxed or milked out of existence, while perfectly sound things have been bulldozed over in areas where land values and location counted."

Carleton Jones, *Lost Baltimore Landmarks*

Lost Baltimore Landmarks: A Portfolio of Vanished Buildings. Carleton Jones. Baltimore: Maclay and Associates (P.O. Box 16253, 21210), 1982. 64 pp., illus. $7.95 pb.

Market Day at Place Jacques Cartier, Montreal, about 1890; the city hall burned in 1922. (Notman Photographic Archives, McGill University)

Demolition workmen taking a bow for their work on the Stanton Theater, Baltimore, during demolition in 1966. (La Force, *Baltimore Sun*)

Montreal harbor in 1863, showing the Convent of the Dames de la Congregation. (Notman Photographic Archives, McGill University)

Lost Bar Harbor

"The decade of the 1880s saw more cottages built than any other period in Bar Harbor history, and they were no longer simple. . . . Within a few years, there were some 175 cottages in Bar Harbor, occupied during the summer by their owners, the elite of New York, Boston, Philadelphia, Washington, Chicago (in that order), and lesser cities,"

G.W. Helfrich and Gladys O'Neil, *Lost Bar Harbor*

Lost Bar Harbor. G.W. Helfrich and Gladys O'Neil. Camden, Maine: Down East Books, 1982. 136 pp., illus., biblio., index. $8.95 pb.

Lost London

"In 1928, Osbert Sitwell could write of a 'devastation of London more serious and widespread than the havoc caused by the Great Fire'; if to this we add the damage caused by the Blitz and the post-war reconstruction, then it is clear that the face of London has been more altered than that of any other comparable Western European capital in the same period. . . . This is not to declare war on all redevelopment. This could only be done by someone ignorant of the history of London, which has included wave after wave of necessary and interesting rebuilding. . . .

In many instances, indeed, the way in which a series of fine buildings has occupied the same site almost gives the lie to the preservationist case. On the other hand, how much richer would London be today, if some control had been exercised over demolition in the past hundred years."

Hermione Hobhouse, *Lost London*

Lost London. Hermione Hobhouse. 1971. Boston: Houghton Mifflin, 1972. 250 pp., illus., index.

Lost Montreal

"Over twenty years ago Gerard Morisset cautioned that 'There are two ways to spoil a country. Either get rid of its monuments one by one, those that are worthy of interest, its crown, or bury them amid a mass of architectural mediocrity to hide them from view; or detract from their architectural qualities by cluttering up their surroundings.' In choosing the first of these approaches to our environment—destruction—Montreal has irresponsibly achieved some kind of immortality. It once possessed architecture that was among the oldest and richest in North America."

Luc d'Iberville-Moreau, *Lost Montreal*

Lost Montreal. Luc d'Iberville-Moreau. Toronto: Oxford University Press, 1975. 183 pp., illus.

Lost Toronto

"*Lost Toronto* is not meant to be a depressing tale of woe and destruction. It is rather a filling-in of the gaps in our streets and the blanks in our understanding of the city. . . . (Changes in taste have led to the disappearance of more of the buildings illustrated here than functional obsolescence—the usual and almost always specious argument put forward to justify demolition—or even fire.)"

William Dendy, *Lost Toronto*

Lost Toronto. William Dendy. Toronto: Oxford University Press, 1979. 206 pp., illus., index.

Boom town of Mercur, Utah, about 1910, when gold ore was reduced at the Golden Gate Mill. (Utah Power and Light Company)

Mercur in 1971, when the town had been abandoned and only ruins remained. (HAER)

Evolution

One thing hastens into being, another hastens out of it. Even while a thing is in the act of coming into existence, some part of it has already ceased to be. Flux and change are forever renewing the fabric of the universe just as the ceaseless sweep of time is forever renewing the face of eternity. In such a running river, when there is no firm foothold, what is there for a man to value among all the many things that are racing past him?

Marcus Aurelius, *Meditations*
(VI, 15)

St. Paul's Historic Summit Avenue. Ernest R. Sandeen, with Margaret Redpath and Carol Sawyer. St. Paul: Living Historical Museum, Macalester College, 1978. 110 pp., illus.

An unusually systematic attempt to record a century of change on one street. A "Table of Razed and Moved Houses" shows as graphically as an accountant's chart the high points and low points of erosion of the avenue's character. "With only seven exceptions, the houses razed before 1929 were replaced by new houses which in every case were more expensive, in most cases were better designed and more interesting than the houses they replaced, and which certainly added vigor and vitality to the avenue. . . . Thus, until 1929 the process of demolition, even though quite extensive, cannot be viewed simply as a negative force but, rather, as part of a complex process of decay and further growth on the avenue."

East India Marine Hall: 1824–1974. Christopher P. Monkhouse. Drawings by Philip Chadwick Foster Smith. Foreword by Walter M. Whitehill. Salem, Mass.: Peabody Museum (161 Essex Street, 01970), 1974. $3.25 pb.

"The Metamorphosis of East India Marine Hall," Philip Chadwick Foster Smith. *Historic Preservation*, October–December 1975.

A chart of the metamorphosis of a landmark and its neighbors seen from the perspective of a century and a half. The sketches, says Smith, "form a picture in motion of a small strip of New England street frontage as it slipped from a residential zone into a commercial one and, finally in our day, into entirely institutional use. Perhaps similar exercises involving other sections of the United States would serve as a useful reminder of how rapidly an isolated environment can change."

The Changing Countryside. Portfolio of 7 color paintings by Jörg Müller. 1973. New York: Atheneum, 1977. $11.95.

The Changing City. Portfolio of 8 color paintings by Jörg Müller. 1976. New York: Atheneum, 1977. $11.95.

This is environmental evolution seen whole, through the eyes of an artist. The same section of an idealized city and countryside is drawn at approximately three-year intervals, the countryside during 1953–72, the city during 1953–76. "One watches with horror the advancing tide of disruption." (Grady Clay, "Compelling, Fascinating Gaze Into Urbanization." *Landscape Architecture*, January 1978)

1825

1867–1890

1930–1943

1974

Evolution of East India Marine Hall (1825, Thomas Waldron Sumner) and its changing neighbors on Essex Street, Salem, Mass., over 150 years. (Philip Chadwick Foster Smith)

Main Street, Los Angeles, in 1885. From *Views of Los Angeles*. (Title Insurance and Trust Company Collection)

Main Street in 1978, when only three buildings remained: the Pico House (1869), Merced Theatre (1870) and Masonic Hall (1858). (Gernot Kuehn)

On top of Bunker Hill, Los Angeles, in 1900. The San Gabriel Mountains are behind the residential neighborhood, built in the 1880s; the old courthouse is at right. From *Views of Los Angeles*. (L.A. County Natural History Museum)

Bunker Hill in 1978, following the grading of the hill in the 1960s. The Criminal Court Building (dark tall building at center) stands on the old courthouse site. (Gernot Kuehn)

Found Again

Lost places can be found again—on paper if not in brick and mortar—in a variety of publications and other places. Among them: surveys of a town or region's architectural development; local histories, particularly illustrated volumes; books of old engravings or "early views"; catalogs or treatises on the work of particular architects, especially those whose buildings have suffered heavy losses; guides to archeological sites; pictorial, especially photographic, books focusing on a place, period or photographer; surveys of specific architectural styles and building types; social studies of towns that almost refused to die; surveys of "early homes" or "early architecture"; books of old town plans; before-and-after explorations of places; historical society journals; personal reminiscences; histories of photography; state histories such as the 1930s WPA guidebooks; photographic archives; collections of architectural drawings; and catalogs of the Historic American Buildings Survey. For more on all of these, see Building Roots.

Views of Los Angeles. Gernot Kuehn and William L. Burnett. 1978. 3rd ed. Los Angeles: Portriga Publications (P.O. Box 36759, 90036), 1979. 138 pp., illus., index. $24.95 hb, $14.95 pb.

L.A. in the Thirties: 1931–1941. David Gebhard and Harriette Von Breton. Salt Lake City: Peregrine Smith, 1975. 165 pp., illus., biblio., index.

Suddenly San Francisco: The Early Years of an Instant City. Charles Lockwood. A California Living Book. San Francisco: San Francisco Examiner, 1978. 176 pp., illus., chron., biblio., index. $17.50 hb, $9.95 pb.

San Francisco As It Is, As It Was. Paul C. Johnson and Richard Reinhardt. Foreword by Herb Caen. Garden City, N.Y.: Doubleday, 1979. 240 pp., illus., index.

San Francisco: Creation of a City. Tom Moulin and Don DeNevi. Millbrae, Calif.: Celestial Arts, 1978. 177 pp., illus.

The Great Chicago Fire in Eyewitness Accounts and 70 Contemporary Photographs and Illustrations. 1915. Rev. reprint. David Lowe, ed. New York: Dover, 1979. 94 pp., illus. $4 pb.

The Great Chicago Fire. Paul M. Angle. Chicago: Chicago Historical Society, 1971. 122 pp., illus. $7.50.

Boston Then and Now: 65 Boston Sites Photographed in the Past and Present. Peter Vanderwarker. New York: Dover, 1982. 128 pp., illus. $6.95 pb.

New York Then and Now: 83 Manhattan Sites Photographed in the Past and Present. Edward B. Watson and Edmund V. Gillon, Jr. New York: Dover, 1976. 192 pp., illus. $7.95 pb.

Rothco. © Punch

"I'm sure it constitutes no clear and present danger, but it comes off as one helluva psychological threat." (Henry Martin. © 1971 *Saturday Review*)

Gallows Humor

Over the years, even the most liberal cartoonists have tended to regard innovation and change with a reserve and skepticism that gives them a natural sympathy for the goals of the preservation movement. . . . Cartoons . . . have been recognized and employed as potent persuaders for more than 200 years. . . . Perhaps the only real common denominator lies in the relentless application of humor to mankind's singularly unfunny propensity for lopping off its roots and fouling its nests.

Draper Hill, *"I Feel I Should Warn You . . ."*

"I Feel I Should Warn You . . ." Historic Preservation Cartoons. Terry B. Morton, ed. Essay by Draper Hill. Washington, D.C.: Preservation Press, 1975. 112 pp., illus., index. $6.95 pb.

A collection of preservation cartoons that have nipped and nudged to keep the wreckers at bay for more than 150 years. The book "makes us hurt only when we laugh," says architecture writer Martin Filler. "Its humorous approach to one of our great national disgraces . . . is a two-edged sword that should puncture our complacency far more readily than any 'serious' book."

"Save the Capitol! Save the Robie House! What about me?" Alan Dunn. From *Architecture Observed.*

b. 1962
d. 1962?

"The way they build and tear down buildings in New York City, we've decided it's not too early to start a Save Lincoln Center Committee. We know this venerable hall is almost a week old, but there is still a lot of life left in her. . . . Just because a building has been used once is no reason to decide it's served its function and that we must now make way for something new. . . . There is still time to beat the demolition teams if you *Act Now.* A lot of people may say we're unnecessarily worried, and that Lincoln Center may still be with us next year. That may be so, but on opening night we saw William Zeckendorf and his son in front of the hall with surveying tools, and everybody in New York knows what that means."

Art Buchwald, "Save Lincoln Center." *New York Herald Tribune*, 1962. Reprinted in *Historic Preservation*, October–December 1962.

Hunting Licenses

"It was very helpful of the Government to produce Statutory Lists of Buildings of so called 'Special architectural or historical interest.' This enables us to pinpoint the action spots."

David Sturdy, *How to Pull a Town Down.* 1972. Reprinted in *Historic Preservation*, April–June 1973.

On Becoming a Parking Lot

"Having slipped behind somewhat in its effort to preserve beautiful old homes and other buildings downtown, Dayton now is considering a new approach to take advantage of the Gem City's remaining assets. Dayton is applying to be designated as a National Register parking lot. . . .

Many young people now doubt the existence of pre-1913-flood Dayton, just as historians doubt the pre-Noah-flood existence of Atlantis and Lemuria. Some local revisionist historians, studying under a research grant by PMI, now argue that Dayton was founded in 1915 as a parking lot for Columbus residents who were driving to Cincinnati for a ball game but ran out of gas and needed to leave their cars somewhere."

Hap Cawood, *Dayton Daily News.* 1976. Reprinted in *Preservation News*, March 1976.

"The real jest is that I am in earnest."

George Bernard Shaw

The Oldtron Bomb

"At last—the heritage bomb: we knew all along Dr. Strangelove wouldn't let us down.

From its incorporation in 1973, Heritage Canada has maintained a firm stand concerning nuclear holocausts: we are solidly against them. Quite apart from the annoying disruptions a holocaust would bring to our staff's holiday schedule, the thought of all the world's old buildings blowing away in a mushroom cloud really got our dander up. Now, at last, however, we can relax. Word has it the geniuses among us have developed a neutron bomb. That's the bomb, you'll recall, that, when dropped, destroys all human life but doesn't do a speck of damage to surrounding buildings. Well, we here at H.C. think that's just great: it's just the bomb we're dying to see. We're so pleased with its heritage value, in fact, that we're thinking of renaming it the oldtron bomb."

Heritage Canada. *Heritage Conservation*, Fall 1977.

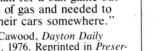

Rothco. © Punch

A graffiti artist who passed by while the old Panamanian Legation (c. 1893), Washington, D.C., was being demolished in 1972 had listened to the Joni Mitchell song "Big Yellow Taxi." (John J. G. Blumenson, NTHP)

A Prologue

To have a building torn down can be a terrible setback and it can make you despondent, which is perfectly normal. But then just look around your neighborhood or city and see what's still there.

St. Clair Wright. *American Preservation*, April–May 1979.

"Perhaps preservationists can learn at least as much from a resounding failure as from a brilliant success."

Dianne Newell, *The Failure to Preserve the Queen City Hotel, Cumberland, Maryland*. Washington, D.C.: Preservation Press, 1975.

"What's past is prologue. . . ."

William Shakespeare, *The Tempest*, Act II, sc. i.

Alan Dunn. From *Architecture Observed*. (© 1971 Architectural Record Books)

The remains of the Chamber of Commerce Building (1886–88, H. H. Richardson), Cincinnati, were recycled into sculpture by University of Cincinnati students. (Mimi Fuller)

Preservation

2

The basic purpose of preservation is not to arrest time but to mediate sensitively with the forces of change. It is to understand the present as a product of the past and a modifier of the future.

John W. Lawrence, Dean, School of Architecture,
Tulane University, April 24, 1970.

The great potential contribution of preservation to American life is not in the saving of structures per se but in the transformation of the values by which we live.

Roderick S. French, "On Preserving America:
Some Philosophical Observations." In
Preservation: Toward an Ethic in the 1980s

A long-neglected link with the past that is in need of preservation.

Old and new landmarks that shape the Boston skyline, including the Exeter Street Theatre (1884) and John Hancock Tower (1976, I. M. Pei). (© 1980 Peter Vanderwarker)

Why Preserve?

If most preservationists were honest, they would admit that they seek to preserve ancient buildings and sites because these add to the variety and beauty of a life that is daily more mechanized and stereotyped. Yet too often conscience enters in and makes them feel that they must scrabble about and discover some high purpose that will justify their preoccupation.

Walter Muir Whitehill, "The
Right of Cities to Be Beautiful."
In *With Heritage So Rich*

Old buildings . . .

1. Are physical links to the past
2. Give a sense of national and personal identity
3. Provide environmental diversity
4. Have intrinsic value as art
5. Continue to be useful
6. Are more economical than new construction
7. Contribute to urban revitalization
8. Represent scarce resources
9. Further energy conservation
10. Stimulate edification and education
11. Lend psychological stability
12. Serve as sources of recreation
13. Encourage patriotism
14. Fulfill nostalgic instincts

Memory

"We may live without her [architecture], and worship without her, but we cannot remember without her."

John Ruskin, *The Seven Lamps of Architecture.* 1849.

"Architecture is an art whose masterpieces cannot be stored away like paintings or reproduced centuries later like poetry or music. The art lives on in used buildings; they alone can carry it. Without them we are perpetual juveniles, starting over and over, a nation of children, a people without a memory."

Douglas Haskell, "Is There Preservation Planning for the City of Tomorrow?" *Historic Preservation*, vol. 13, no. 4, 1961.

A Louisiana mansion evokes memories of the past. (Library of Congress)

Stowe Alley on Nantucket, Mass. (Jack E. Boucher, HABS)

California-bound migrants near Muskogee, Okla., bidding farewell to their familiar surroundings in 1939. (Russell Lee, Library of Congress)

Towers of the Idanha Hotel (1901, Walter S. Campbell), Boise, Idaho, reflected in a new glass-walled neighbor. (D. Nels Reese)

"A nation can be a victim of amnesia. It can lose the memories of what it was, and thereby lose the sense of what it is or wants to be."

Sidney Hyman, "Empire for Liberty." In *With Heritage So Rich*

"I have come to believe that the 'urge to preserve' is less rooted in high-style cultural soil than in a more fundamental, even biological, need all of us have to try to reduce or moderate the pace and scale of change itself. What we are really trying to preserve, I think, is 'memory.' It is an attempt to keep a mental grip on familiar and accustomed environments that make us feel comfortable and secure whether or not they are aesthetically pleasing or historically credentialed. The real issue is not whether we will have change, but how great it will be, how quickly it will happen, and how shattering its impact will be."

Robert E. Stipe, "A Decade of Preservation and Preservation Law." *North Carolina Central Law Journal*, vol. 11, no. 2, April 1980.

Continuity

"[It has] become apparent that human life is not limited to a single lifespan but goes far beyond. It is as impossible to sever its contacts with the past as to prevent its contacts with the future. Something lives within us which forms part of the very backbone of human dignity: I call this the demand for continuity."

Sigfried Giedion, *The Beginnings of Architecture: The Eternal Present*. Princeton, N.J.: Princeton University Press, 1957.

"Society has many built-in time spanners that help to link the present generation with the past. Our sense of the past is developed by contact with the older generation, by our knowledge of history, by the accumulated heritage of art, music, literature and science passed down to us through the years. It is enhanced by immediate contact with the objects that surround us, each of which has a point of origin in the past, each of which provides us with a trace of identification with the past."

Alvin Toffler, *Future Shock*. New York: Bantam Books, 1971.

"The women sat among the doomed things, turning them over and looking past them and back. 'This book, my father had it. He liked a book. *Pilgrim's Progress*. Used to read it. Got his name in it, right here. Why, here's his pipe—it still smells rank. And this picture—an angel. I looked at it before the first three children came—didn't seem to do much good. Think we could get this china dog in? Aunt Sadie brought it from the St. Louis fair. See—it says right on it. No, I guess we can't take that. Here's a letter my brother wrote the day before he died. Here's an old-time hat. These feathers—I never got to use them. No, there isn't room. . . . How can we live without our lives? How will we know it's us without our past?"

John Steinbeck, *The Grapes of Wrath*. 1939. New York: Penguin Books, 1976.

"The architect should be regarded as a kind of physical historian, because he constructs relationships across time: civilization in fact."

Vincent Scully, *American Architecture and Urbanism*. New York: Praeger, 1969.

Familiarity

"The destruction of things that are familiar and important causes great anxiety in people. So keeping some familiarity, often even token familiarity, is needed."

Margaret Mead. In "Mainstream: An Interview with Margaret Mead," *American Preservation*, February–March 1978.

"Preservation has become the best carrier of that moral force architecture needs if it is to have value beyond shelter. Preservation is capable of projecting a vision of new possibilities, of hope for our own future, which functionalist modern once claimed for itself and which has now fled from that style. The existing context—city neighborhoods, streets, individual examples of older architecture—in which people have lived their lives and in which they place whatever sense of private wholeness and connection with society that remains to them, has become a primary symbol of our 'humanness.'"

Robert Jensen, "Design Directions: Other Voices." *AIA Journal*, Mid-May 1978.

The new Boston City Hall (1968, Kallmann, McKinnell and Knowles), contrasts with the old Faneuil Hall (1762–63, 1805–06, Charles Bulfinch).

Richly detailed sandstone facade of the former Petty Building (1893) in Hot Springs, S.D. (James L. Ballard, NTHP)

"Individuals feel both more secure and more purposeful when they recognize that they exist as part of an historical continuum. Personal death is viewed with less fear, and a life devoted to more-than-just-immediate pleasures seems more warranted. . . . Our firmest physical link with the past is our architecture."

> Joyce Brothers, "Landmark Battle: History Needs Symbols to Point Up Our Past." *Historic Preservation*, May–June 1965.

"In some cases, it is when a historic heritage is threatened that its value is brought into focus. . . . The dilemma in rebuilding war-ravaged European cities [after World War II] was whether to reconstruct selected historic buildings or to use the limited resources available to build more efficiently anew. The recovery of traditional values was considered important to local morale, and thus many historic structures that symbolized these values were rebuilt or restored."

> Eugene George, "Tradition and Progress: A Creative Partnership." *Historic Preservation*, October–December 1974.

Diversity

"Cities need old buildings so badly it is probably impossible for vigorous streets and districts to grow without them. By old buildings I mean not museum-piece old buildings, not old buildings in an excellent and expensive state of rehabilitation—although these make fine ingredients—but also a good lot of plain, ordinary, low-value old buildings, including some run-down old buildings."

> Jane Jacobs, *The Death and Life of Great American Cities*. New York: Random House, 1961.

"A great deal of the force of the preservation movement comes from contemporary architecture's failure to build well, its failure to build in a style that satisfies the needs of our cities and the needs of our senses. A lot of our belief in preservation comes from our fear of what will replace buildings that are not preserved; all too often we fight to save not because what we want to save is so good but because we know that what will replace it will be no better."

> Paul Goldberger, "New Directions: Architecture and Preservation." In *Preservation: Toward an Ethic in the 1980s*

"The prospect of a city made up entirely of mirrored facades, blindly reflecting back and forth into each other and into infinity, is not without its charm, especially if you happen to be the fairest one of all—i.e., the one and only building in a neighborhood that boasts a real facade, and can therefore see itself reflected ad infinitum in all directions."

> Peter Blake, *Form Follows Fiasco: Why Modern Architecture Hasn't Worked*. Boston: Little, Brown, 1974.

"Many remarkable buildings exist all round us, invisible under a shroud of grime and familiarity. Their rediscovery will give us both profit and pleasure, and their civilizing influence may help to counteract our present excesses. In the context of our cities even a third rate old building becomes a masterpiece when seen beside a modern commercial development.

We need those monuments, all of them, and many, many more."

> Theo Crosby, *The Necessary Monument: Its Future in the Civilized City*. Greenwich, Conn.: New York Graphic Society, 1970.

Tangibility

"Soon there'll be nothing left to preserve. And we'll enter that dangerous area of distortion of fact. We'll have to take the historian's word for what existed instead of seeing it for ourselves."

> Robert Redford. Interview, *Publishers Weekly*, March 6, 1978.

"Not only structures, but also the artifacts of daily life—tools, implements, household utensils—reflect the meaning of living patterns which grow increasingly distant from ours, in both time and manner. From these we can learn the conditions of life close to nature and the soil, in which the individual is also the means of production. Yet very often in these archaic things we discover patterns—both esthetic and technic—which can be employed to enrich our own lives."

> Christopher Tunnard, "Landmarks of Beauty and History." In *With Heritage So Rich*

Contemporary use of the Cleveland Arcade (1888–90, John Eisenmann and George H. Smith), built as a shopping center and offices, continues to make economic sense. (Library of Congress)

Drayton Hall (1738–42), near Charleston, S.C., a National Trust property open to the public. (Carleton Knight III, NTHP)

"Americans were once afraid of their history—or overwhelmed by it. We tried to make it sacred and we called our monuments shrines. . . . [Now] we have begun to call our monuments landmarks. In the very term, we accept them as a part of our environment—we can walk around them, touch them, and live in them—they are everywhere, they are for everybody."

Gordon Gray, "Decade of Decision." Annual Report, National Trust for Historic Preservation, 1965–66.

Orientation

"The Congress finds and declares—

(a) that the spirit and direction of the Nation are founded upon and reflected in its historic past;

(b) that the historical and cultural foundations of the Nation should be preserved as a living part of our community life and development in order to give a sense of orientation to the American people; . . ."

National Historic Preservation Act of 1966

"Our monuments and . . . the more modest works of architecture and town-planning of the past . . . continue to provide the setting for our everyday lives. Beyond any special meaning they have acquired through their history, they shelter us as well as modern structures while bringing us that subtle but basic element in architecture—*the dimension of time*. Time and memory, memory and continuity: vital concepts to help man from being lost in the present."

Raymond M. Lemaire, Introduction. *Monumentum*, vol. XIII, 1976.

Education, Recreation and Inspiration

"Historic preservation has existed, in its traditional sense, for three purposes. The first is education. Historic preservation supplements the written word. In a properly interpreted historic house museum, a person gains insight into the life and times of previous individuals and groups. It is, in effect, a three-dimensional learning experience.

Secondly, historic preservation exists for the purpose of recreation. It is fun to visit historic sites, to see the unusual, quaint and often difficult ways in which people lived in an earlier age.

Thirdly, historic preservation exists for inspiration. Patriotism, in its truest sense, is instilled and strengthened by gaining a better insight into who we are as a people and nation, whence we came, and where we are headed. Historic preservation can help instill and strengthen these concepts.

There is today a fourth reason for historic preservation. This is the putting of historically and architecturally valuable sites and buildings to economically viable uses. Such uses are often different from, and yet compatible with, the original function of the structure. This is perhaps the greatest challenge and most important work of the historic preservationist. It requires careful planning, creativeness, extra effort and, most important of all, a state of mind that will seek alternatives to the obvious one of demolition."

David N. Poinsett, "What Is Historic Preservation?" *Preservation News,* July 1973.

Proxemics and Economics

"In addition to the old 'cultural memory' and 'antique texture' bases, three new arguments for preservation have been pinpointed by Peirce Lewis, a professor of geography at Pennsylvania State University: successful proxemics, environmental diversity, and economic gain. . . . Successful proxemics, says Lewis, concerns the very livability of cities, the relationships between people and things such as buildings that create a space and a society that work. The argument for environmental diversity is that everything need not and perhaps should not be alike, that preservation of elements of the past can create environments that offer alternatives to much of modern society. Finally, the argument of economic gain is used by preservationists to convince skeptics that preservation of old buildings can be a profitable venture."

National Trust et al., "Our Hidden Inheritance." In *America's Forgotten Architecture*

"Historic preservation has traditionally focused on the value of the aesthetic, historic and cultural aspects of buildings. But buildings are also workplaces; when we preserve an older building we are preserving not only a cultural and visual asset but an economic asset as well. . . .

Older and historic buildings make up at least one-fourth of all buildings in the United States today. They represent an important part of our nation's stock of existing buildings. These older buildings defined as more than 50 years old represent a substantial national investment and constitute a major national resource. The replacement value of the U.S. building stock is estimated . . . to be about $5.5 trillion. The replacement value of buildings more than 50 years old is estimated to be at least $1.5 trillion."

Betsy Chittenden, with Jacques Gordon, *Older and Historic Buildings and the Preservation Industry.* Washington, D.C.: National Trust for Historic Preservation, 1984.

Visual pollution from unrestrained urban signage. (Phil Stitt, *Arizona Architect*)

A monotonous suburban development, a contrast to the architectural variety found in many older neighborhoods. From *God's Own Junkyard*. (William Garnett)

An incongruous juxtaposition of 20th-century technology and 19th-century architecture in Jackson, Miss. (Marion Cost Wolcott, Library of Congress)

To replace the Silver Dollar Saloon (1893), Nashville, Tenn., would require the energy equivalent of 42,200 gallons of gasoline. (NTHP)

Energy

"In the days of cheap energy, it might have made a kind of short-sighted economic sense to destroy old structures, but that era ended forever with the oil embargo of 1973. . . . The preservation and renovation of residential, commercial and industrial structures will itself be a major industry within a few years. The force behind this emerging industry is the philosophical transition away from a throwaway society based on an illusion that resources are unlimited—toward a new kind of civilization grounded in permanence, balance and order. Through historic preservation's leadership, it will be made obvious to all that two vital social goals—energy conservation and historic preservation—are self-reinforcing."

> John C. Sawhill, "Preserving History and Saving Energy: Two Sides of the Same Coin." In *New Energy from Old Buildings.* National Trust for Historic Preservation. Washington, D.C: Preservation Press, 1981.

Quality of Life

"The problem now is to acknowledge that historic conservation is but one aspect of the much larger problem, basically an environmental one, of enhancing, or perhaps providing for the first time, a quality of human life. Especially is this so for that growing number of people who struggle daily to justify an increasingly dismal existence in a rapidly deteriorating urban environment. . . . The importance of our nostalgic, patriotic and intellectual impulses cannot be denied, but they are no longer a wholly sufficient motivation for what we are about. . . .

Basically, it is the saving of people and lives and cities—not just buildings—that are important to all of us. We have before us an unparalleled opportunity, if we are sufficiently determined, to contribute significantly to the upgrading of the quality of human existence. If we can achieve this, to some extent at least, the architecture and the history will fall into place."

> Robert E. Stipe, "Why Preserve Historic Resources?" In *Legal Techniques in Historic Preservation.* Washington, D.C.: National Trust for Historic Preservation, 1972.

Frugality and Responsibility

"Urban conservation . . . is one of government's legitimately expanding fields of endeavor. The value of beautiful wilderness parks and scenic rivers is vitiated if our daily environment is one of cancerous *schlock*. The economic benefits of spectacular corporate monuments likewise are diluted when the American economy simply discards older buildings and neighborhoods and then finds itself paying the enormous costs of resulting social problems. Urban conservation is not just a romantic indulgence in nostalgia. It is a physical restatement of the long-hallowed American values of frugality, good craftsmanship and community responsibility."

> Bruce Chapman. In "Adaptive Use: A Survey of Construction Costs." Advisory Council on Historic Preservation *Report*, June 1976.

A mid-19th-century slave cabin on the Georgetown, Ky., farm of George W. Johnson, Confederate governor of Kentucky, reflects the Greek Revival preference of the era. (Ann Bevins)

What's Worth Saving?

The bottom line for architectural preservation must ultimately be what is and what is not saved.

Margaret H. Floyd, *Architectural Preservation Forum* (SAH), February 1979.

The 1828 church is part of Fort Ross, Calif., once the largest Russian fur trading center south of Alaska.

"In preservation, there must always be selection; everything old cannot be saved just because it is old. There will always be doubts, disagreements and regrets. In addition, as time goes on, as more research is done, and as changes are made to structures, new and perhaps contradictory evidence will come to light. There are, however, a few simple rules to lend guidance.

The first of these is the one applied by Noah: Save a couple of good working models of each creature. Secondly: It is better to preserve by selection what has already been well preserved by chance and by use than to reconstruct by conjecture that which has been neglected beyond the point of reasonable recovery. Thirdly: Grace of architectural form has a value in itself but its greatest value comes when its presence and setting suggest its uses and charms for its earliest owners. . . . In most cases the best solution is to provide for appropriate and productive continuing use for that which has proved its value in the past."

> Ipswich Historical Commission, *Something to Preserve: A Report on Historic Preservation by the Acquisition of Protective Agreements on Buildings in Ipswich, Massachusetts.* Ipswich: Ipswich Historical Commission, with Ipswich Heritage Trust and U.S. Department of Housing and Urban Development, 1975.

"The objective of preservation is the retention of the full range of styles, sensations and references that record the city's history and achievements visually and environmentally to keep them in the city's vital mainstream."

> Ada Louise Huxtable, *Will They Ever Finish Bruckner Boulevard?* New York: Macmillan, 1970.

"There are many humble structures in which 'George Washington never slept' that form an important part of our visual surroundings. They represent fine craftsmanship, unique architectural character, perhaps also a picturesque quality that are not likely to be produced again in this day of mass production."

> William C. Shopsin, AIA, "Adapting Old Buildings to New Uses." In *Workbook,* New York State Council on Architecture, 1974.

"As a nation's monuments tell of its past, so they also tell much of its citizens. What a people select from the tangible national patrimony to keep for themselves and their posterity, and why and how they keep it, express what they value both in the past and in themselves. . . .

Americans save an extraordinary variety of evidences of their forebears' mark on history and on the land. Among the preserved evidences are: dwellings of all kinds, from the palatial residences of 19th-century captains of industry to rude cabins along the successive stages of the westward advancing frontier, from prehistoric Indian pueblos to blocks of urban row houses spanning the past two centuries, public buildings ranging from obscure county courthouses and railroad stations to the Philadelphia, Pennsylvania, Independence Hall, birthplace of the nation; religious buildings erected by colonial ancestors and later by constituent nationalities—Swedish churches in the state of Delaware, Irish and Polish churches in Cleveland, Ohio, Spanish missions in the Southwest, Russian churches in the state of Alaska; the battlefields and fortifications of colonial wars, the War for Independence, internal struggles and defenses against foreign attacks, factories, commercial buildings, bridges, dams, canals and other engineering works that were landmarks of our material development and are often preserved through continued or adaptive use; and whole districts of these and other elements in combination."

> Robert M. Utley and Barry Mackintosh et al., "Historic Preservation in a Democracy." *Monumentum,* vol. XIII, 1976.

"LITTLE ROCK, Sept. 8 (AP)—Little Rock Central High School, which marks its 50th anniversary this year, has been approved for listing in the National Register of Historic Places. . . .

This year also marks the 20th anniversary of desegregation at Central. In 1957, nine black students entered the high school under protection of federal troops. The confrontation has come to symbolize the beginning of the end of dual school systems in the South."

> "School in Ark. 'Historic Place'." *Washington Post,* September 9, 1977.

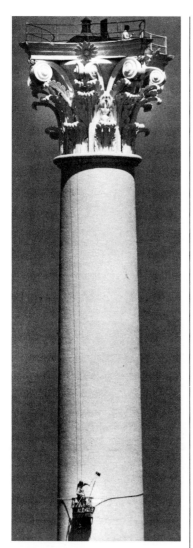

At 154 feet the world's tallest Corinthian column, the Grand Avenue Water Tower (1871, George I. Barnett), St. Louis, is listed in the National Register.

"The mansion on the hill was an important part of American life, but so were the workers' houses, transportation system, factory, churches and all else that made up the town. The plantation house is understandable only with the slave quarters, the dependencies and the fields. . . . Preservation is the domain of no individual locale and must represent all peoples in all geographic areas.

History is an ongoing process. A broad spectrum of time as well as of people and place is essential if the vitality of the historic and cultural environment is to be preserved. For example, the significant places of the civil rights movement and the space age should be of particular interest to future generations."

"Goals and Programs: A Summary of the Study Committee Report to the Board of Trustees, the National Trust for Historic Preservation." Washington, D.C.: National Trust, 1973.

Kinishba Ruins in Arizona, built by Native Americans in the 13th century, 250 years before Columbus arrived. (Arizona State Parks)

National Register Criteria
"The quality of significance in American history, architecture, archeology, and culture is present in districts, sites, buildings, structures, and objects that possess integrity of location, design, setting, materials, workmanship, feeling, and association, and:

(a) that are associated with events that have made a significant contribution to the broad patterns of our history; or

(b) that are associated with the lives of persons significant in our past; or

(c) that embody the distinctive characteristics of a type, period, or method of construction, or that represent a significant and distinguishable entity whose components may lack individual distinction; or

(d) that have yielded, or may be likely to yield, information important in prehistory or history."

National Register of Historic Places, U.S. Department of the Interior, Washington, D.C.

"Preservationists, some believe, soon will have completed their work since, those same people say, everything worth saving will be saved. Nothing could be further from the truth. The job of preservation has barely begun; the inventories now being undertaken to determine what is worthy of preservation and laws established to assure the protection of that cultural patrimony are but the first steps in an unending process. One hundred years from now, preservationists will be working to save buildings not yet even on the drawing boards."

"Planning Ahead," Editorial. *Preservation News,* November 1977.

"Some estimate that the National Register of Historic Places is only 10 percent complete, and the number of eligible properties discovered each year as the result of surveys in advance of construction tends to confirm the belief that many thousands more could be added in future years."

Richard H. Jenrette. In *Advisory Council on Historic Preservation: Report to the President and the Congress of the United States, 1978.*

"The appreciation of architecture operates under a grandfather clause, or perhaps it might be more accurate to say a great-grandfather clause. Aesthetically, the generation gap has been with us for a long time. We tend to denigrate the tastes of the generation or two immediately preceding our own at the same time that we are attracted to the life style of their predecessors, first, perhaps, as merely amusingly quaint, and then as the object of serious study and admiration."

Constance M. Greiff, *Lost America: From the Atlantic to the Mississippi.* Princeton: Pyne Press, 1971.

"The National Register criteria for evaluation accept the nomination of properties that have achieved significance within the last 50 years only if they are exceptionally important or if they are integral parts of districts that are eligible for listing in the Register. That principle serves as a safeguard against listing properties of contemporary, faddish value and ensures that the Register will be a Register of Historic Places. . . ."

Marcella Sherfy and W. Ray Luce, "How to Evaluate and Nominate Potential National Register Properties That Have Achieved Significance Within the Last 50 Years." Washington, D.C.: U.S. Department of the Interior, 1979.

Occidental Mine, Comstock Historic District, Nev. (Martin Stupich)

"The more modern milestones do not even have the tenuous protection of the national landmarks legislation. . . . Even where [legislation] does not have an age limit, the lack of interest in the potential problems of recent buildings has created a de facto cut off point—somewhere around 1940. But where is it written that art and history stopped having milestones after this date?"

Bradford Perkins, "Preserving the Landmarks of the Modern Movement." *Architectural Record,* July 1981.

The Value of Hindsight, or Oh, What a Difference a Half Century Makes
"So far no voice has been raised against the Golden Gate Bridge on aesthetic grounds. Yet discriminating persons believe that such a structure would prove an eye-sore to those now living and a betrayal of future generations, for whom the present generation is a trustee. A bridge of the size projected—the plans call for towers 800 feet high—would certainly mar if not utterly destroy the natural charm of a harbor famed throughout the world."

The Wasp (San Francisco), May 2, 1925.

San Francisco's Golden Gate Bridge (1933–37, J. B. Strauss). (Carleton Knight III, NTHP)

Neighborhoods in Detroit shrink beside the highways that fuel the Motor City's livelihood. From *God's Own Junkyard.* (Elliott Erwitt, Magnum)

Preservation Is Not . . .

To begin with, we must understand that preservation and destruction are not *equivalent alternatives, and that conservation is progressive, not reactionary.*

> William Morgan, "The Urban Environment." *Louisville Courier-Journal and Times,* April 20, 1975.

"Historic preservation is not shrines or pilgrimages to 'hallowed ground.' Shrines should be left to religion, where matters of faith and subjectivity belong. . . . The shrine concept has often been viewed as an aspect of preserving our heritage. Whatever it may be, it is not historic preservation. . . .

Historic preservation is not guides in 'period costume' leading people through dusty, musty rooms, pointing out odds and ends of memorabilia that are more interesting to the guide than to the viewer. . . .

Historic preservation is not new structures that are 'colonial' in style. With 13 original colonies, each having several indigenous styles of architecture, there can be no single 'colonial style.' . . .

Historic preservation is not saving everything. It makes no more sense to save everything than it does to tear everything down. The value of the good sites, buildings and structures will be diluted in direct proportion to the number of unworthy ones that remain. . . .

True historic preservation is objective in its attitude. That is, it regards all periods and styles as inherently equal for learning about our past. . . .

Historic preservation is mainly a state of mind, an attitude that says those who lived before have left us not only written history, not only laws and customs, traditions and a way of life, but also specific physical remains in the form of buildings, structures, objects and the sites where great events took place. Historic preservation is a state of mind that says we should save the best of the past as it relates to our national, state and local heritage. Such retention of our historic patrimony in its physical form gives people a feeling of time and place."

> David N. Poinsett, "What Is Historic Preservation?" *Preservation News,* July 1973.

Egyptianesque-style former headquarters of the Penn Mutual Life Insurance Company (1838, John Haviland), Philadelphia, before and after its incorporation into the new Penn Mutual Tower (1975, Mitchell/Giurgola Architects), a type of "preservation" called "facadism." (Rollin R. La France)

Durham, N.H., obtained more space for town offices by recycling two 1920s houses and joining them with a contemporary link. (Richard Bonnarigo)

South Street Historic District, Kalamazoo, Mich., one of more than 1,000 local historic districts established throughout the United States.

Preservation Is . . .

Preservation is an overt act in response to a threat; conservation is the continuing love that forestalls the need for preservation.

> Norval White, *The Architecture Book*. New York: Knopf, 1976.

In the days before the health of the national economy depended on planned obsolescence, preservation was not a movement but was synonymous with conservation: necessary maintenance and a stewardship of resources. . . . Architectural preservation meant keeping houses, barns and outbuildings, meetinghouses, town halls, and churches in repair, painting them regularly and replacing window sashes when necessary. Preservation was making sure that fence lines held and that streets were at least passable. When things were preserved, it was because saving was necessary to surviving, and continued maintenance meant saving. "Waste, not, want not" was not merely a quaint legend to be cross-stitched on a sampler.

> National Trust et al., *America's Forgotten Architecture*

"I believe we might describe this basic movement as the evolution towards a more 'conserving society.' . . . What we may be doing as a nation is to re-evaluate the importance of growth over stability, mobility over a sense of place, sprawling urbanization as opposed to planned and bounded cities, to consider the value of historical properties over the additions of square footage of commercial space."

> Richard C. Collins, "Historic Preservation and the Politics of Growth." In *Historic Preservation and Public Policy in Virginia*. Boston, Va.: Mouseion Press, 1978.

A San Francisco McDonald's found a tasteful home in a converted building. (Carleton Knight III, NTHP)

"There are marked contrasts between the objects and purposes of associative and environmental historic preservation. Associative properties, whether maintained as patriotic shrines or tourist attractions, exist outside the mainstream of contemporary life. . . . They are a kind of museum, and their guardian fences, gates and ropes are the equivalent of glass cases.

Environmental properties, on the other hand, while sometimes sharing associative values, are preserved more for their enhancement of the contemporary environment. . . .

Environmental historic preservation concentrates on structures and districts of historical, aesthetic, or other cultural value that may be retained in modern functional use. Total restoration to bygone periods is not attempted; while unsympathetic facade modifications may be reversed, interiors are customarily adapted to serve current needs. Attractive but decaying apartment buildings may be converted to modern condominiums or offices. Factories may be adapted to housing. Railroad stations, underutilized or abandoned by the thousands, may be rehabilitated as retail shops. Neighborhoods of special architectural, ethnic or cultural character may be revitalized without losing old identities that give them their distinctive sense of place."

> Robert M. Utley and Barry Mackintosh et al., "Historic Preservation in a Democracy: The Partnership Between Government and the Private Sector in the United States." *Monumentum*, vol. XIII, 1976.

"Preservation—a word most frequently preceded by 'historic'—has taken on new dimensions in the United States in recent years. Most preservationists would just as soon drop the all too frequent modifier 'historic' in describing the broad-based preservation movement underway in this country today. . . . The preservation movement has gone populist—restoring old market places for the enjoyment of people, such as the newly restored and popular Quincy Market in Boston . . . ; turning cast iron buildings and lofts into apartments in New York City; restoring inner city neighborhoods for *existing* residents, rather than displacement. Smaller cities and villages are also sprucing up Main Street, peeling off layers of siding to rediscover old brick and rich architectural details. Preservation in America today is an exciting and dynamic field. Key word associations are conservation, rehabilitation, recycling, restoration."

> Richard H. Jenrette. In *Advisory Council on Historic Preservation: Report to the President and the Congress of the United States, 1978.*

"Historic preservation has become perhaps the highest form of planning for the man-made environment because it looks at the whole fabric of society, including amenities and even the traditions of the people."

> "A Structure for the Nation's Program of Historic Preservation: A Working Paper for the Advisory Council on Historic Preservation," April 1977.

The Lawn of the University of Virginia (1822–26, Thomas Jefferson), Charlottesville, Va., with the Jeffersonian-style Rotunda, voted the "proudest achievement of American architecture over the past 200 years." (University of Virginia)

Terminal and tower at Dulles International Airport (1962, Eero Saarinen) outside Washington, D.C. (U.S. Department of Transportation)

Johnson Wax Building and Laboratory Tower (1939, Frank Lloyd Wright), Racine, Wis.

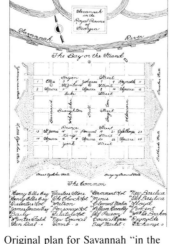

Original plan for Savannah "in the Royal Province of Georgia" (c. 1735, James Oglethorpe).

Seagram Building (1957, Ludwig Mies van der Rohe and Philip Johnson), New York City, an International Style landmark that spawned a plethora of "glass box" skyscrapers throughout the world. (Philip Johnson Collection)

What Makes a Landmark?

In a Bicentennial pulse-taking, the AIA Journal *in 1976 asked a group of architects, historians and critics to nominate up to 20 of what they considered "the proudest achievements of American architecture over the past 200 years." The results of the informal poll showed some expected answers—and some unexpected ones: More than half of these landmarks were built within the last 50 years—indicating that time may be speeding up when it comes to evaluating what's worth preserving.*

"Probably the first such poll took place in 1885, when the American Architect and Buildings News *asked its readers to nominate the 10 most beautiful buildings now existing in the United States," wrote Mary E. Osman.*

"At that time, the 75 respondents named 175 buildings. First place went to Henry Hobson Richardson's Trinity Church in Boston, also a leader in our poll. Those in sixth through 10th place also were by Richardson, then 48 years old. Only five of the 10 leading buildings in the 1885 survey showed up in our canvass."

"Highlights of American Architecture," Mary E. Osman, ed.
AIA Journal, July 1976.

Trinity Church (1877, Henry Hobson Richardson) on Boston's Copley Square, mirrored in the new John Hancock Tower (1967–76, I. M. Pei and Partners). (Carleton Knight III, NTHP)

200 Years of Architectural Landmarks

29 votes
University of Virginia Campus, Charlottesville, Va. (1822–26). Thomas Jefferson

22 votes
Rockefeller Center, New York, N.Y. (1940). Reinhard & Hofmeister; Corbett, Harrison & MacMurray; Hood & Fouilhoux

17 votes
Dulles International Airport, Chantilly, Va. (1962). Eero Saarinen & Associates
Fallingwater, Bear Run, Pa. (1937). Frank Lloyd Wright

16 votes
Carson Pirie Scott Building, Chicago, Ill. (1899). Louis H. Sullivan

15 votes
Seagram Building, New York, N.Y. (1957). Ludwig Mies van der Rohe and Philip Johnson
Philadelphia Saving Fund Society, Philadelphia, Pa. (1932). George Howe and William Lescaze

12 votes
New City Hall, Boston, Mass. (1968). Kallman, McKinnell & Knowles; Campbell Aldrich & Nulty; Le Messurier & Associates
Trinity Church, Boston, Mass. (1877). Henry Hobson Richardson

11 votes
Lever House, New York, N.Y. (1952). Skidmore, Owings & Merrill
Brooklyn Bridge, New York, N.Y. (1883). John A. and Washington Roebling
Robie House, Chicago, Ill. (1909). Frank Lloyd Wright
Johnson Wax Company's Administration Building and Laboratory Tower, Racine, Wis. (1939). Frank Lloyd Wright
Ford Foundation Building, New York, N.Y. (1967). Kevin Roche, John Dinkeloo Associates

10 votes
Grand Central Terminal, New York, N.Y. (1903–13). Reed & Stem; Warren & Wetmore
Johnson Glass House, New Canaan, Conn. (1949). Philip Johnson

9 votes
Gateway Arch, St. Louis, Mo. (1967). Eero Saarinen & Associates
Plan of Savannah, Ga. (c. 1735). James Oglethorpe
Monticello, Charlottesville, Va. (1769–70, 1796–1809). Thomas Jefferson
Monadnock Building, Chicago, Ill. (1891). Burnham & Root

8 votes
Wainwright Building, St. Louis, Mo. (1891). Adler & Sullivan
Reliance Building, Chicago, Ill. (1895). Daniel H. Burnham & Company
Salk Institute of Biological Studies, La Jolla, Calif. (1965). Louis I. Kahn

7 votes
Central Park, New York, N.Y. (1859–76). Frederick Law Olmsted, Sr., and Calvert Vaux
Plan of Radburn, N.J. (1929). Clarence Stein and Henry Wright
Unity Temple, Oak Park, Ill. (1906). Frank Lloyd Wright

6 votes
Taliesin West, Scottsdale, Ariz. (1938). Frank Lloyd Wright
Guggenheim Museum, New York, N.Y. (1959). Frank Lloyd Wright
U.S. Capitol, Washington, D.C. (1793–1875). William Thornton, Benjamin H. Latrobe, Charles Bulfinch, Robert Mills, Thomas U. Walter, Frederick Law Olmsted, Sr.
Lincoln Memorial, Washington, D.C. (1922). Henry Bacon
Plan for Washington, D.C. (1792). Pierre Charles L'Enfant
Illinois Institute of Technology, Chicago, Ill. (1945–52). Ludwig Mies van der Rohe and Ludwig Hilberseimer; Friedman, Alschuler & Sincere; Holabird & Root; Pace Associates

Pennsylvania Academy of the Fine Arts, Philadelphia, Pa. (1876). Furness & Hewitt
John Hancock Center, Chicago, Ill. (1969). Skidmore, Owings & Merrill
Marshall Field Wholesale Warehouse, Chicago, Ill. (1887). Henry Hobson Richardson
Lovell "Health" House, Los Angeles, Calif. (1929). Richard Neutra
Richards Laboratory for Research in Medicine, Philadelphia, Pa. (1960). Louis I. Kahn

Crown Hall (1945–46, Ludwig Mies van der Rohe), Illinois Institute of Technology, Chicago, Ill. (Hedrich-Blessing)

A plantation house that survived the years as a result of "poverty, plutocracy and privacy." (Library of Congress)

Preservation's Past: History of the Movement

The story of the historic preservation movement in America is not a long one. Since the birth of the United States, there have been those who have understood the need to save some tangible evidence of our cultural and historical heritage, but only recently has the critical need to remember "where we came from" [Carl Sandburg, Remembrance Rock*] become obvious to many of us. Only now are we beginning to see how greatly our future depends on an awareness of our past.*

James Biddle, Foreword. *The History of the National Trust for Historic Preservation, 1963–1973*

The first plant where the soft drink Dr. Pepper was manufactured in Waco, Tex., now restored as a museum.

"The great historical preservatives in America have been poverty, plutocracy and privacy. It was poverty that protected (if that is the proper word for the results of the Civil War among those who lost it) the great architectural treasures of Charleston and Beaufort, S.C., and Savannah, where nothing, literally nothing, had happened since the Civil War to change the framework or alter the old structures built before and after the Revolution. . . . Old buildings weren't torn down. They fell down. . . .

On the other hand, and in quite another part of the nation, it was plutocracy that created, maintained and preserved the Newports, the Bar Harbors, the Tuxedo Parks and the wealthy suburbs of such cities as Baltimore. . . .

And finally, the third great preservative—privacy and isolation. As I run through my mind and check my notes on remarkable townscapes and landscapes that are still memorable and visitable today, many are so because they are isolated from the juggernaut of progress—either as islands of plutocratic power with strength to keep all others away, or as places so deliberately or accidentally removed from the thrust of development, so protected from the Iron Law of Progress, that they remain beautiful and well preserved."

> Grady Clay, "Townscape and Landscape: The Coming Battleground." *Historic Preservation*, January–March 1972.

"The popularity of historic preservation in the 1970s has tended to obscure the fact that the guardians of America's historical and architectural heritage have struggled for many years against the forces of 'progress' and apathy. The massive federal and state surveys, the National Register of Historic Places, the matching grants, and the growing National Trust for Historic Preservation were only visionary dreams in the 1930s and 1940s. If it can be said that preservation history had a heroic phase, that phase probably came during the quarter century that separated the birth of the Williamsburg Restoration from the chartering of the National Trust in 1949."

> Charles B. Hosmer, Jr., *Preservation Comes of Age: From Williamsburg to the National Trust, 1926–1949*

Presence of the Past: A History of the Preservation Movement in the United States Before Williamsburg. Charles B. Hosmer, Jr. Foreword by Walter Muir Whitehill. 1965. Washington, D.C.: Preservation Press, 1974. 386 pp., illus., biblio., index. $12.95 hb.

A lively account of the early movement and its landmark achievements—Mount Vernon and Monticello among them. "It is the first of its kind. Historic preservation in the United States is a little more than a century old, yet this is the first record of its history in broad terms, the first study of the varied aspirations of the people who began to save buildings of the American past for the present and future." (Walter Muir Whitehill, foreword)

Preservation Comes of Age: From Williamsburg to the National Trust, 1926–1949. Charles B. Hosmer, Jr. Charlottesville: University Press of Virginia, 1981. Published for the National Trust. 1,291 pp., illus., biblio., chron., index. 2 vols. $37.50 hb.

"In *Preservation Comes of Age,* Charles Hosmer . . . has produced the definitive history of American preservation from 1926 . . . to the chartering of the National Trust for Historic Preservation. . . . This handsomely printed, thoroughly researched, and very readable monumental study is clearly the standard reference work on the subject, and it should be required reading for preservationists." (William Morgan, review. *Christian Science Monitor,* March 9, 1981)

The History of the National Trust for Historic Preservation, 1963–1973. Elizabeth D. Mulloy. Washington, D.C.: Preservation Press, 1976. 315 pp., color illus., appends., index. $9.95 hb.

The story of preservation's rise in the 1960s as well as a record of the National Trust's role. Retraces the work of the Trust to its founding.

Monumentum, vol. XIII. International Council on Monuments and Sites. Terry B. Morton, ed. Washington, D.C.: US/ICOMOS, 1976. 128 pp., illus. $10 pb.

Several essays discuss the history of the preservation movement in this overview of the past, present and future of preservation in the United States.

With Heritage So Rich. Special Committee on Historic Preservation, U.S. Conference of Mayors. Albert Rains and Laurence C. Henderson, eds. 1966. Rev. reprint. Washington, D.C.: Preservation Press, 1983. 232 pp., illus., appends., index. $18.95 pb.

Preservation history, including European antecedents, is presented in this classic study.

History of the National Trust for Historic Preservation, 1947–1963. David E. Finley. Washington, D.C.: National Trust for Historic Preservation, 1965. 115 pp., illus., appends., index. Available only in microfilm, hardbound and paperbound editions (no. 2004589) from University Microfilms, 300 North Zeeb Road, Ann Arbor, Mich. 48106. Prices available on request.

A record of the National Trust's formation and its early activities, summarized in the later *History of the National Trust* (Mulloy).

The United States Government in Historic Preservation: A Brief History of the 1966 National Historic Preservation Act and Others. Robert R. Garvey and Terry B. Morton. 1968. Rev. ed. Washington, D.C.: National Trust for Historic Preservation, 1973. 40 pp., illus., biblio.

A succinct history of the major federal legislation affecting preservation from 1906 to 1973.

Historic Preservation Today: Essays Presented to the Seminar on Preservation and Restoration, Williamsburg, Virginia, 1963. National Trust for Historic Preservation and Colonial Williamsburg Foundation. Charlottesville: University Press of Virginia, 1966. 265 pp., index.

A review of the history and philosophical basis of the American preservation movement, plus a 1960s era discussion of its future.

Historic Preservation Tomorrow. National Trust for Historic Preservation and Colonial Williamsburg Foundation. Charlottesville: University Press of Virginia, 1967. 64 pp., illus. Available only in microfilm, hardbound and paperbound editions (no. 2004590) from University Microfilms, 300 North Zeeb Road, Ann Arbor, Mich. 48106. Prices available on request.

"The History Museum." In *Museums in Motion: An Introduction to the History and Functions of Museums.* Edward P. Alexander. Nashville: American Association for State and Local History, 1979. 308 pp., illus., biblio., index. $13.50 pb.

A brief survey of the history of preservation and history museums, including outdoor villages, historic house museums and historical societies.

Parks, Politics and the People. Conrad L. Wirth. Norman: University of Oklahoma Press, 1980. 450 pp., illus., index. $24.95 hb.

A history of the national park movement based on Wirth's 36-year involvement, including 12 years as National Park Service director in the 1950s and 1960s. The book documents the development of historic sites especially during the Depression growth period. Coverage is devoted to the New Deal programs, CCC and other emergency period programs, including the Historic Sites Act of 1935 and the Historic American Buildings Survey.

Conservation Histories

Witnesses to a Vanishing America: The Nineteenth-Century Response. Lee Clark Mitchell. Princeton: Princeton University Press, 1981. 320 pp., illus., biblio., index. $23 hb.

Traces the roots of conservation in the 19th century: the artists and photographers who recorded the images, the citizens who became interested in local history and the drives to preserve parks and wilderness areas.

Voices for the Earth: A Treasury of the Sierra Club Bulletin, 1893–1977. Ann Gilliam, ed. Introduction by Harold Gilliam. San Francisco: Sierra Club Books, 1979. 592 pp., illus. $19.95 hb.

Chronicles conservation battles and related environmental history, drawn from 70 years of environmental writing.

Earthworks: Ten Years on the Environmental Front. Staff of Friends of the Earth. Mary Lou Vandeventer, ed. Andover, Mass.: Brick House Publishing, 1980. 224 pp., illus. $8.95 pb.

The best of *Not Man Apart*, the organization's newspaper.

John Muir and His Legacy: The American Conservation Movement. Stephen Fox. Boston: Little, Brown, 1981. 436 pp., illus., biblio., index. $19.95 hb.

A history of the conservation movement focusing on the zealous amateurs who gave it shape, beginning with its founder.

National Leaders of American Conservation. Richard H. Stroud, ed., Natural Resources Council of America. Washington, D.C.: Smithsonian Institution Press, 1985. 540 pp. $24.95 pb.

Biographical sketches of important past and present conservationists.

Duke of Gloucester Street, Williamsburg, Va., in 1928 before restoration was begun, showing the current site of Raleigh Tavern. (Colonial Williamsburg Foundation)

Rev. W. A. R. Goodwin meeting with John D. Rockefeller, Jr., behind the Wythe House to discuss plans for the Williamsburg restoration, funded by Rockefeller. From *Preservation Comes of Age.* (Colonial Williamsburg Foundation)

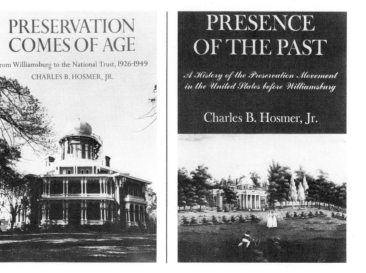

River side of Mount Vernon in 1855, before restoration work had begun. (Mount Vernon Ladies' Association of the Union)

Shelter built to stabilize the adobe ruins of the Great House at Casa Grande National Monument in Arizona. (George A. Grant, National Park Service)

Preservation USA: A Chronology

The United States experience in historic preservation can be seen in terms of three major kinds of motivation—patriotic, cultural, and environmental. . . . Patriotic motivations emerged first, in the early years of the nineteenth century; broader cultural motivations came on the scene in the later nineteenth century; and environmental motivations became apparent in the second quarter of the present century. . . .

The national historic preservation program is essentially an environmental planning program, although it has taken nearly a decade for that philosophy to be generally recognized.

Robert B. Rettig, *Conserving the Man-made Environment: Planning for the Protection of Historic and Cultural Resources in the United States.* Washington, D.C.: National Park Service, 1975.

Independence Hall (1732–56), Philadelphia, restored as the figurehead of Independence National Historical Park. (National Park Service)

The Grand Canyon at Yellowstone, established in 1872 as the first national park. (M. Woodbridge Williams, National Park Service)

1749 An old Philadelphia log cabin reportedly preserved as a "relic of early days."

1816 Independence Hall, threatened with demolition, sold by the state to the city of Philadelphia; steeple rebuilt by William Strickland in 1829.

1828 Touro Synagogue, Newport, R.I., restored; perhaps the first restoration in the U.S.

1850 Hasbrouck House, George Washington's headquarters in Newburgh, N.Y., purchased by the New York legislature as the nation's first historic house museum.

1853 Efforts initiated to purchase and restore Mount Vernon; restoration begun in 1859.

1856 Purchase of The Hermitage, Andrew Jackson's home near Nashville, authorized by the Tennessee legislature.

1872 Yellowstone National Park established as first national park.

1876 Old South Meeting House, Boston, rescued from demolition.

1888 Association for the Preservation of Virginia Antiquities formed, first large private preservation group in South after Civil War.

1889 Congress authorizes Casa Grande reservation in Arizona to save prehistoric adobe ruins; first example of federal responsibility for cultural resources on public property.

1890 Chickamauga Battlefield, Ga., authorized as first national military park; soon followed by Gettysburg and Shiloh.

1891 Trustees of Public Reservations (Mass.) incorporated; inspires English National Trust (1894) and American National Trust (1949).

1905 Paul Revere House, Boston, restored as one of the first thoroughly professional restorations.

1906 Antiquities Act, first major federal preservation legislation, passed to preserve prehistoric sites.

1910 Society for the Preservation of New England Antiquities incorporated.

1916 National Park Service established, taking over nine existing national monuments.

1918 Massachusetts adopts constitutional amendment authorizing condemnation of property for preservation.

1924 First Vieux Carré Commission (New Orleans) formed but later disbanded; new commission created in 1936 with power to assure preservation.

1926 Williamsburg restoration begun under a plan by W.A.R. Goodwin and funding by John D. Rockefeller, Jr.

Greenfield Village (Dearborn, Mich.) established by Henry Ford.

1931 First local historic district ordinance in U.S. passed in Charleston, S.C.

1933 Battlefields and other historic federal property transferred to National Park Service, strengthening its preservation responsibilities.

Historic American Buildings Survey begun.

1935 National Historic Sites Act passed authorizing Interior Department to survey sites and acquire historic property.

1940 Society of Architectural Historians and American Association for State and Local History founded.

Henry Ford and "Lincoln" in 1929 at the Postville Courthouse, which Ford moved from Illinois to Greenfield Village. (Ford Archives, Dearborn, Mich.)

Lookout Mountain at Chicamauga Battlefield and Chattanooga National Military Park. (M. Woodbridge Williams, National Park Service)

1947 National Council for Historic Sites and Buildings, predecessor of National Trust, organized.

1948 Congress authorizes Independence National Historical Park, Philadelphia.

1949 National Trust for Historic Preservation chartered by Congress.

1952 National Trust magazine *Historic Preservation* begun.

1954 National Council merged into single National Trust.

1959 Providence, R.I., College Hill Demonstration Study is the first to combine preservation goals with urban rehabilitation.

1960 Limited register of nationally significant landmarks, predecessor of National Register of Historic Places, initiated by National Park Service.

1961 National Trust newspaper *Preservation News* begins.

1964 First graduate course in preservation inaugurated at Columbia University School of Architecture.

1966 National Historic Preservation Act establishes an expanded National Register of Historic Places, an Advisory Council on Historic Preservation and grants to the states.

Department of Transportation Act declares policy of preservation of natural and historic sites on highway routes.

Demonstration Cities and Metropolitan Development Act redirects urban renewal to recognize and fund preservation projects.

First local law granting tax credits for scenic open space preservation passed in Prince George's County, Md.

1967 First scenic easement donated to U.S. under Historic Sites Act of 1935 (to preserve Tudor Place, Washington, D.C.)

American Revolution Bicentennial Commission appointed.

First members of Advisory Council on Historic Preservation appointed.

Office of Archeology and Historic Preservation established in National Park Service; state historic preservation officers requested; first Keeper of National Register appointed.

1968 Association for Preservation Technology founded.

"How Will We Know It's Us?" released by National Trust and HUD as first national preservation film.

First local law permitting transfer of development rights for preservation enacted in New York City.

1969 Historic American Engineering Record established.

Interior Department makes first preservation grants to the states.

National Environmental Policy Act stresses federal preservation responsibility and creates environmental impact statements.

1970 First Earth Day celebrated.

1971 U.S. Supreme Court considers environmental provisions of federal highway statutes for the first time in the case of *Overton Park v. Volpe*.

Executive Order 11593 directs federal agencies to preserve, restore and maintain their cultural properties.

First national conference on preservation law sponsored by National Trust.

National Trust opens Western Regional Office as first of six regional offices.

Society for Industrial Archeology founded.

1972 Transfer of surplus federal property to local public agencies for preservation authorized by Congress.

1973 First National Historic Preservation Week held.

Wilmington, Del., begins first urban homesteading program.

Virginia and Oregon become first states to adopt building codes sympathetic to preservation.

New York City's Landmarks Preservation Commission is authorized to designate historic interiors.

1974 Constitutionality of historic district ordinances upheld by Federal District Court in New Orleans case.

National Trust creates fund for endangered properties.

Preservation Action formed as national citizens lobby for preservation.

1975 National Trust establishes the Preservation Press and legal service program for landmarks commissions and sponsors first national conference on economic benefits of preservation.

1976 American Revolution Bicentennial strengthens interest in preservation.

Tax Reform Act of 1976 provides the first major preservation tax incentives for certified income-producing properties.

Public Buildings Cooperative Use Act encourages restoration and adaptive use of historic buildings for federal use.

Main Street project undertaken by National Trust.

1978 U.S. Supreme Court rules in first major preservation case (Grand Central Terminal) that New York City's preservation law is constitutional.

1979 National Trust sponsors conference, "Preservation: Toward an Ethic in the 1980s," to chart future directions of preservation.

1980 Amendments to National Historic Preservation Act strengthen federal agency responsibilities and broaden local government participation in preservation.

1981 Federal historic preservation funding for 1982 cut but partially restored after national lobbying effort.

Economic Recovery Tax Act provides significant new investment tax credits for rehabilitation.

1982 Proposed elimination of federal preservation grants for the states and National Trust fought successfully through nationwide campaign.

1983 Preservationists led by the National Trust save the West Front of the U.S. Capitol and the Apollo launch tower.

1985 A revitalized Pennsylvania Avenue in the nation's capital is unveiled for Inauguration visitors.

For other chronologies, see also:

"Historic Preservation U.S.A.: Some Significant Dates," Charles E. Peterson. *Antiques,* February 1966.

Preservation Comes of Age: From Williamsburg to the National Trust, 1926–1949.

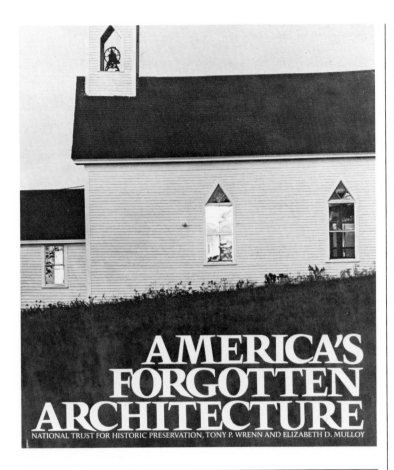

AMERICA'S FORGOTTEN ARCHITECTURE
NATIONAL TRUST FOR HISTORIC PRESERVATION, TONY P. WRENN AND ELIZABETH D. MULLOY

Preservation Primers

In the past, books about historic preservation written for general readers tended to be one of two types. Either they were coffee-table volumes, lavishly illustrated with artful photographs of famous and historic houses . . . or they were tales of lament, full of speckled documentary photos or stark mugshots of venerable old buildings pictured in mid-demolition, their insides hanging out after the onslaught of a wrecking ball. Both approaches serve a purpose: the first, to inspire appreciation of major landmarks of beauty and historical importance, the second, to anger building-lovers to the point of taking action to save them.

America's Forgotten Architecture

America's Forgotten Architecture. National Trust for Historic Preservation, Tony P. Wrenn and Elizabeth D. Mulloy. New York: Pantheon, 1976. 312 pp., illus., biblio., appends., index. $12.95 pb.

An overview of preservation today, surveying what is worth saving and how to do it. Photo essays trace eight major building types. Other chapters examine preservation history and techniques, legal and funding programs and the variety of new uses to which old buildings are being put. "Extraordinary work . . . a kind of handbook on what the preservation movement is all about." *(Chicago Tribune)* "The book is powerfully instructive." *(Newsweek)* "For a one-volume library on the importance of historic architecture, there can be no better book." *(New York Times)*

With Heritage So Rich. Special Committee on Historic Preservation, U.S. Conference of Mayors. Albert Rains and Laurence G. Henderson, eds. 1966. Rev. reprint. Washington, D.C.: Preservation Press, 1983. 232 pp., illus., appends., index. $18.95 pb.

A classic compilation of photographs and essays by noted preservationists that spurred passage of the landmark National Historic Preservation Act of 1966. It examines the heritage of the United States reflected in its buildings, lost and extant, and compares American preservation efforts to "the older vision" of Europe. Included are recommendations that largely have been translated into preservation practice and law today.

Historic Preservation: Curatorial Management of the Built World. James Marston Fitch. New York: McGraw-Hill, 1982. 434 pp., illus., index. $34.95 hb.

An overview of worldwide preservation issues and techniques by a leading preservation educator. Covered are the history and theory of preservation, economic rationales, adaptive use, restoration techniques, museums and interpretation, landscapes, documentation and training, with examples from the U.S. and abroad.

Preservation in American Towns and Cities. Nathan C. Weinberg. Boulder, Colo.: Westview Press, 1979. 233 pp., illus., index. $26.50 hb.

Analyzes preservation practices in a variety of contexts—districts, neighborhoods, towns and cities—and offers a concept of preservation as a social movement. First examining the development of the preservation movement in Europe and the U.S., the book then addresses such issues as urban neglect and speculation, revolving funds, tourism, community involvement and the conflict between preservation and development.

Monumentum, vol. XIII. International Council on Monuments and Sites. Terry B. Morton, ed. Washington, D.C.: US/ICOMOS, 1976. 128 pp., illus., biblio. $10 pb.

Leading preservationists look at preservation in the U.S.—past, present and future—in this concise introduction to the subject. Among the topics: preservation in a democracy, preservation and the national mythology, the impact of law, urban neighborhoods, commerce and preservation, tourism and leisure, taming technology for preservation and preservation as a national goal.

Readings in Historic Preservation. Norman Williams, Jr., Edmund H. Kellogg and Frank B. Gilbert, eds. New Brunswick, N.J.: Center for Urban Policy Research (P.O. Box 489, Piscataway 08854), 1983. 400 pp. $20 hb.

An anthology of published articles addressing a wide range of issues—history, preservation philosophy, preservation criteria, restoration, adaptive use, planning and preservation's effect on the poor and minorities.

The Brown Book: A Directory of Preservation Information. Diane Maddex and Ellen R. Marsh. Washington, D.C.: Preservation Press, 1983. 160 pp., illus., biblio., index. $17.95 pb.

The first concise directory of the names, addresses, telephone numbers, facts, figures and step-by-step techniques preservationists need almost daily in their work. The 34 sections, arranged alphabetically, cover the Advisory Council on Historic Preservation through tax incentives.

Information: A Preservation Sourcebook. National Trust for Historic Preservation. Washington, D.C.: Preservation Press, 1979–85. 800 pp., illus., biblios. $39.95 binder.

A compilation from the Information Series of 34 publications on basic preservation issues including rehabilitation, financing, preservation, economic benefits, adaptive use, state laws, tax incentives, rural areas and special topics such as schools, theaters and churches.

The Historic Preservation Yearbook. Russell V. Keune, ed. Bethesda, Md.: Adler and Adler (4550 Montgomery Avenue, 20814), 1984. Published in cooperation with the National Trust for Historic Preservation. 590 pp., appends. $78 hb.

A comprehensive reference providing the laws governing preservation as well as innovative annual developments in areas such as legislation, federal laws, historic districts and policy issues.

Conservation of Historic and Cultural Resources. Ralph W. Miner, Jr. Chicago: American Planning Association, 1969. PAS Report 244. 56 pp., illus., biblio.

An early but still useful survey of the reasons for, history of and techniques involved in preservation.

Historic Preservation: A Guide to Information Sources. Arnold L. Markowitz, ed. Detroit: Gale Research, 1980. 295 pp., append., index. $55 hb.

Topics covered include financial, legal and planning aspects, districts, ensembles, neighborhoods and towns; the physical fabric: materials and technology; renovation, restoration and reuse of existing buildings; interpretation of history through buildings, objects and sites; specialized preservation areas; natural landscape; losses.

Where to Find It: A Guide to Preservation Information. Advisory Council on Historic Preservation. Washington, D.C.: GPO, 1982. 88 pp., illus., appends., index. $5.50 pb. GPO stock no. 052-003-00879-3.

A narrative bibliography surveying preservation literature on all related subjects.

Architectural Preservation in the U.S., 1941–1975: A Bibliography of Federal, State and Local Government Publications. Richard N. Tubesing. Reference Library of the Humanities, vol. 61. New York: Garland Publishing, 1978. 452 pp. $53.

Annotated listings for the full range of government publications from posters, tourist brochures and maps to state historic preservation plans and federal agency annual reports.

Preservation Periodicals

Alert
Preservation Action
1700 Connecticut Avenue, N.W.,
Suite 401
Washington, D.C. 20009

APT Bulletin and *Newsletter*
Association for Preservation
Technology
P.O. Box 2487, Station D
Ottawa, Ontario K1P 5W6,
Canada

Architectural Record
McGraw-Hill
1221 Avenue of the Americas
New York, N.Y. 10020

*ARCHITECTURE: The AIA
Journal*
American Institute of Architects
1735 New York Avenue, N.W.
Washington, D.C. 20006

Historic Preservation and
Preservation News
National Trust for
Historic Preservation
1785 Massachusetts Avenue, N.W.
Washington, D.C. 20036

Museum News
American Association of
Museums
1055 Thomas Jefferson Street, N.W.
Washington, D.C. 20007

History News
American Association for State
and Local History
708 Berry Road
Nashville, Tenn. 37204

Landscape Architecture
American Society of
Landscape Architects
1733 Connecticut Avenue, N.W.
Washington, D.C. 20009

The Victorian
The Victorian Society in
America
219 South Sixth Street
Philadelphia, Pa. 19106

Old-House Journal
69A Seventh Avenue
Brooklyn, N.Y. 11217

Planning
American Planning Association
1313 East 60th Street
Chicago, Ill. 60637

Progressive Architecture
600 Summer Street
Stamford, Conn. 06904

SIA Newsletter and *IA Journal*
Society for Industrial
Archeology
National Museum of
American History
Room 5020
Washington, D.C. 20560

*Society of Architectural
Historians Journal, Newsletter*
and *SAH Forum*
1700 Walnut Street
Suite 716
Philadelphia, Pa. 19103

Conservation Abroad: A Sampler

The American preservation movement has . . . borrowed from the European at several critical junctures in its history. . . . In many respects preservation programs here and abroad are more remarkable for their similarities than for their differences.

Robert E. Stipe, Introduction.
*Historic Preservation in Foreign
Countries*

"Europe . . . gives greater emphasis to the aesthetic values of its historic buildings and places; the United States gives greater weight to historical associations. Most of Europe is prepared, in the last analysis, to override purely personal interests in the interests of the community; in the United States personal property rights remain well-nigh sacred and inviolable. In one or two countries, heritage conservation has always formed an integral part of the land use planning system; in many more it has fallen to a Ministry of Fine Arts or its equivalent. . . ."

Michael Middleton, Foreword.
Historic Preservation in Foreign Countries

Historic Preservation in Foreign Countries Sèries. Robert E. Stipe, ed. Vol. I: France, Great Britain, Ireland, Denmark, the Netherlands. Antony Dale. Vol. II: Austria, Switzerland, Federal Republic of Germany. Margaret Thomas Will. Washington, D.C.: US/ICOMOS (1600 H Street, N.W., 20006), 1983. 150 pp., illus. $11 pb each.

Our Past Before Us: Why Do We Save It? David Lowenthal and Marcus Binney, eds. London: Temple Smith, 1981. 253 pp., illus., index. $12.95 pb. Available from Preservation Resource Group, 5619 Southampton Drive, Springfield, Va. 22151.

The Future of the Past: Attitudes to Conservation, 1147–1974. Jane Fawcett, ed. Nikolaus Pevsner, John Betjeman, Osbert Lancaster, Jane Fawcett, Mark Girouard et al. New York: Whitney Library of Design, 1976. 160 pp., illus., index. $15.95 hb.

Without Our Past? A Handbook for the Preservation of Canada's Architectural Heritage. Ann Falkner. Toronto: University of Toronto Press, 1976. 242 pp., illus., appends., biblio. $15 hb, $7.50 pb.

Architectural Conservation in Europe. Sherban Cantacuzino, ed. New York: Whitney Library of Design, 1975. 144 pp., illus., index. $20 hb.

The Conservation of European Cities. Donald Appleyard, ed. Cambridge: MIT Press, 1979. 308 pp., illus., index. $39.95 hb.

Architectural Conservation in Europe: A Selected Bibliography of Publications in English. Margaret Thomas Will. Monticello, Ill.: Vance Bibliographies, 1980. A-251. 28 pp. $3.50 pb.

The Face of the Past: The Preservation of the Medieval Inheritance in Victorian England. Charles Dellheim. New York: Cambridge University Press, 1983. 232 pp., illus., biblio., index. $29.95 hb.

Flower market on the baroque building-lined Grand Plaza in Brussels, Belgium. (Paul Elson, Belgian National Tourist Office)

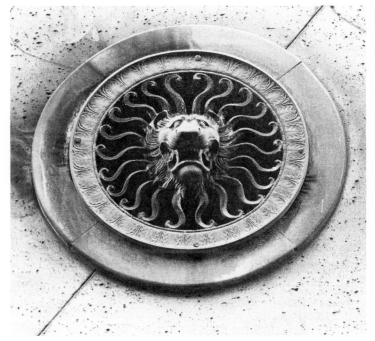

Decorative lion's head air vent made of iron on Chestnut Street in Philadelphia. (B. Clarkson Schoettle)

Stone grave marker surrounded by ornate cast-iron fence in an old Silver City, Nev., cemetery. (Martin Stupich)

The Past in the Future

It is time to move historic preservation from a movement of enthusiastic proponents to a national ethic.

Carlisle H. Humelsine, Fore-word. *Preservation: Toward an Ethic in the 1980s*

Downtown New Haven, Conn., seen from the clock tower of its old city hall. From *Vital Signs—Connecticut*, Connecticut Trust. (Tom Zetterstrom)

Preservation: Toward an Ethic in the 1980s. National Trust for Historic Preservation. Washington, D.C.: Preservation Press, 1980. 248 pp., append. $8.95 pb.

An agenda for preservation during what has been called "the decade of preservation." Goals and recommendations charted by leaders of the movement are presented for such areas as objectives and organizations, standards and practices, avocational and vocational involvement, education, communications, information resources, funding and legislation. Specific concerns addressed include the economics of preservation, neighborhood conservation, criticisms of preservation, endangered building types, a national legislative agenda and public policies toward preservation. Among the contributors are John Kenneth Galbraith, Sen. Patrick Leahy, Michael Middleton, Arthur P. Ziegler, Paul Goldberger and James M. Fitch. The recommendations synthesize two conferences held in 1978 and 1979 to examine the future directions of preservation in the United States.

Controversies in Preservation: Understanding the Movement Today. Pamela Thurber, ed. Preservation Policy Research Series. Washington, D.C.: National Trust for Historic Preservation, 1985. 60 pp. $8 pb.

A collection of thought-provoking papers on various critical aspects of the field—perceptions of preservation from within and without the movement, what is preserved, the National Register, house museums, planning, business and tax incentives and future directions.

A Challenge

"Success and power often breed new problems. . . . Many still see preservation as an elitist effort; although its orientation has changed from a preoccupation with historic house museums, it is nonetheless considered a vocation or avocation for a limited segment of the population. Even though the preservation movement's participants and concerns are increasingly diverse, there is an increasing backlash, justified or unjustified, against preservation when it comes into conflict with other important national, state and local social, economic and political goals.

Questions to be considered:

Has the growth of the preservation movement caused it to extend itself beyond legitimate boundaries? Has historic preservation become a source of social and economic displacement or is it used as a scapegoat for other sources of displacement? Is the nomination process for inclusion in the National Register of Historic Places abused? Are current methods adequate for determining whether preservation, or some other development alternative, provides for the greater public good?. . . . What are the proper limits of modification to historic buildings to meet the requirements of the handicapped and the aged? . . . Is the movement as elitist today as it was in the past or was that a distorted perception?"

"Preservation's Backlashes." In *Preservation: Toward an Ethic in the 1980s*

Decorative wrought-iron security fencing at Mar-a-Lago (1923–27, Marion Sims Wyeth), Palm Beach, Fla. (Jack E. Boucher, HABS)

Vernacular 1939 house in Corpus Christi, Tex., covered with recycled license plates. (Russell Lee, Library of Congress)

"The preservation movement has achieved one of the greatest, fastest victories of any environmental movement in American history. The victory has been the result of many factors: energy crunches, a distrust of modern design, a general swing to conservatism, a natural turning away by one generation from the ideals, newness and mobility of its parents.

But much has also been due to the heroic efforts of the preservationists themselves. After such a triumph one could forgive smugness. What is exciting is that none exists. It's healthy and encouraging, and surprising to find the leaders of the movement today more inquiring and critical than ever, more committed than before to moving the nation toward a sane, fad-free ethic in which we will see ourselves as caretaking tenants of all our built worlds."

Robert Campbell, "Preservationists: Underdogs Are Suddenly the Top Dogs." *Boston Globe*, October 1978.

"Given the present economic and environmental conditions, preservation is no longer a matter of taste but a mandatory expression of basic social responsibility. Urban conservation in particular should be seen not as a private endeavor in behalf of one's heirs but as the maintenance of a legacy for the species."

Roderick S. French, "On Preserving America: Some Philosophical Observations." In *Preservation: Toward an Ethic in the 1980s*

"The preservation of historic buildings and sites has now become a part of the larger job of creating and managing complex environments. Preserve one building and you preserve one building. Preserve the setting and the larger environment, and you keep open a thousand doors and opportunities for a better life for the entire community."

Grady Clay, "Townscape and Landscape: The Coming Battleground." *Historic Preservation*, January–March 1972.

"The aggressive pursuit of a firm public commitment to a new conservation ethic is no longer a matter of luxury or self-indulgence. In these closing years of the twentieth century, it has become a matter of urgent social necessity which is essential to the survival of the human spirit and personality."

Robert E. Stipe, "The Conservation of Place." In *Carolina Dwelling: Towards Preservation of Place*. Doug Swaim, ed. Raleigh: North Carolina State University, 1978.

"Preservation is only one part of the complex debate currently in progress on how clean air and water, open space, scenic features, and other desirable amenities can be preserved for the public good without unduly restricting individual rights or sacrificing economic development. . . .

The debate has just started."

Robert Bruegmann, "What Price Preservation?" *Planning*, June 1980.

The 1950 "waterfall" marquee of the DuPage Theatre (1927), Lombard, Ill., spared by exemption from a local sign ordinance barring flashing signs.

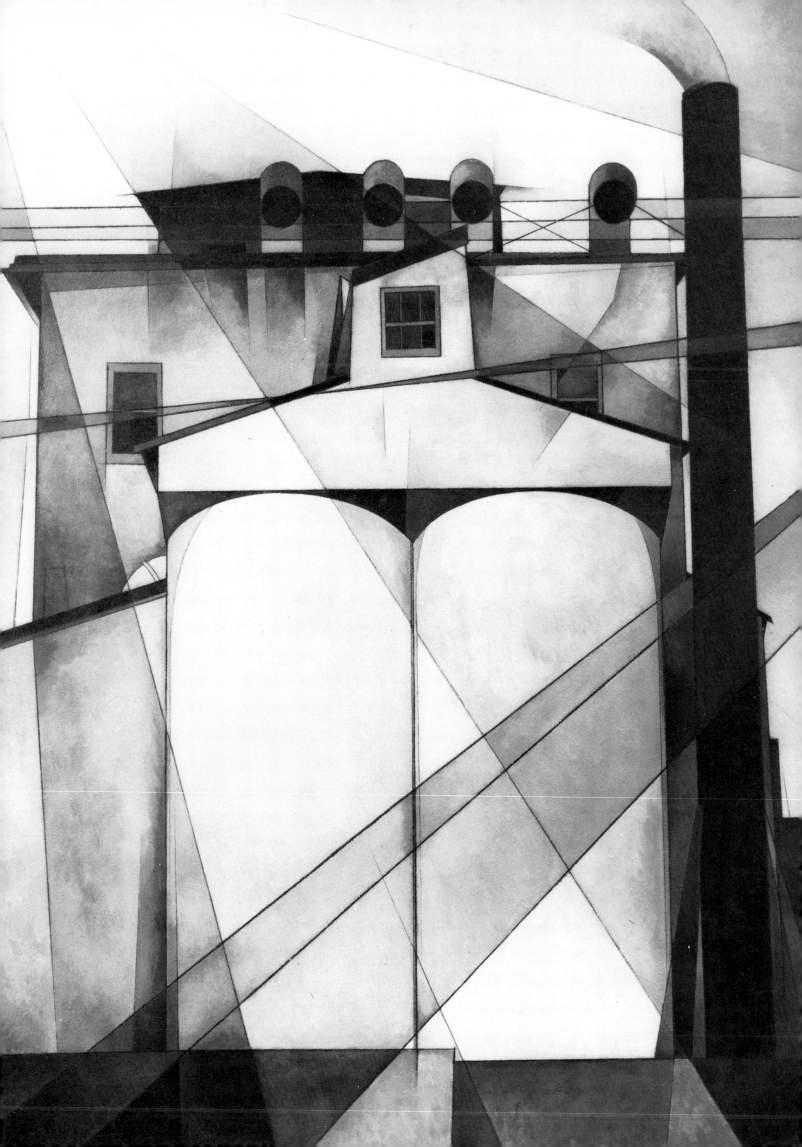

Looking at the Built Environment 3

*T*he way to understand the built environment is what may be called the Holmesian method: looking at the elements—closely, inquisitively, suspiciously, thoroughly.

National Trust et al., *America's Forgotten Architecture.* New York: Pantheon, 1976.

*L*earning to look is a pleasure; the buildings will embrace your eyes.

Judith Lynch Waldhorn, *A Gift to the Street*

Looking Around

Si monumentum requiris circumspice. (If you would see his monument, look around.)

Inscription to Sir Christopher Wren (1675–1710), St. Paul's Cathedral, London

Varied forms and materials in historic Crested Butte, Colo. (Tom Huth)

My Egypt (1927) by Charles Demuth (1883–1935), oil on canvas. (Collection of Whitney Museum of American Art, New York)

"Fixing up deteriorated environments cannot possibly come to anything until the people involved learn to see them first, and one of the facts that came through clearly was that visual illiteracy, not billboards and dumps, was the central problem."

George Nelson, *How to See: Visual Adventures in a World God Never Made*

"Any inhabited landscape is a medium of communication."

Kevin Lynch, *Managing the Sense of a Region.* Cambridge: MIT Press, 1976.

Environmental Encounter: Experiences in Decision-Making for the Built and the Natural Environment. Joanne Henderson Pratt, James Pratt, Sarah Barnett Moore and William T. Moore. Dallas: Reverchon Press (P.O. Box 1964, 75219), 1979. 168 pp., illus., index. $14.95.

A series of learning exercises intended "to reveal the unseen relationship between people and their environment." Topics include sensory perception, texture, light, movement, scale, public spaces and taking responsibility for the environment.

Hinsdale House and Holiday Inn Tower, Raleigh, N.C.

How to See: Visual Adventures in a World God Never Made. George Nelson. Boston: Little, Brown, 1977. 233 pp., illus. $8.95 pb.

More accurately, "How *I* See," as the author concedes. This witty, perceptive primer examines the interrelationships and meanings of everyday elements around us, from highways to hydrants.

Abandoned coal pocket, Lowell, Mass. (© Randolph Langenbach)

Federal Home Loan Bank Board, Washington, D.C. (GSA)

Spiraling International Rotunda at the Mission Inn (1902–32, Arthur B. Benton), Riverside, Calif. (Jim Edwards)

Environmental Planning: Perception and Behavior. Thomas F. Saarinen. Boston: Houghton Mifflin, 1976. $14.95 pb.

Looks at the facets of urban symbolism, how the built environment acquires symbolic meanings and how these images influence people. Covered are individual elements, streets, special areas, suburbs, neighborhoods, central business districts.

Images of the Urban Environment. Douglas Pocock and Ray Hudson. New York: Columbia University Press, 1978. 181 pp., biblio., index. $24 hb.

A multidisciplinary examination of the nature of environmental perception.

Meaning and Behaviour in the Built Environment. Geoffrey Broadbent, Richard Bunt and Tomas Llorens, eds. New York: John Wiley, 1980. 372 pp., index. $62.95 hb.

A scholarly study of "the vague and yet pervasive notion of 'meaning' . . . the basis of culture." The editors,and authors look at the built environment as a cultural product. "When we refer to the 'meaning' of buildings therefore, we refer to all those things which *relate* those buildings, beyond the 'face value' of their physical properties, to all those other things in life which people attach significance and value. . . ." A companion book is *Signs, Symbols, and Architecture.* Geoffrey Broadbent, Richard Bunt and Christopher Jencks, eds. New York: John Wiley, 1980.

The Semiotics of the Built Environment: An Introduction to Architectonic Analysis. Donald Preziosi. Bloomington: Indiana University Press, 1979. 116 pp., illus., biblio. $17.50 hb.

An investigation of the analysis and description of the built environment as a semiotic system—a system of meaningful signs. It seeks to establish some of the principal ways in which "architectonic systems" are similar to and different from other forms of human symbolic communication.

Spaces: Dimensions of the Human Landscape. Barrie B. Greenbie. New Haven: Yale University Press, 1981. 335 pp., illus., index. $50 hb, $16.95 pb.

A visual exploration of how the built environment—houses, fences, neighborhoods, cities, parks—affects human behavior.

The Sense of Place. Fritz Steele. Boston: CBI Publishing Company (51 Sleeper Street, 02210), 1981. 225 pp., illus., biblio., index. $21.50 hb.

A look at how the sense of place affects people, how they create their own sense of place and the interaction between people and their settings.

The Psychology of Place. David Canter. New York: St. Martin's, 1977. 200 pp., illus., index. $22.50.

A multidisciplinary study of environmental perception and the sense of place, with practical applications for decision making.

No true secrets are lurking in the landscape, but only undisclosed evidence, waiting for us. No true chaos is in the urban scene, but only patterns and clues waiting to be organized. . . . A city is not as we perceive it to be by vision alone, but by insight, memory, movement, emotion, and language. A city is also what we call it and becomes as we describe it.

Grady Clay, *Close-Up: How to Read the American City*

Oil refinery in Texas, 1949. (Russell Lee, University of Louisville Photographic Archives)

Old St. Louis County Courthouse (1839–64), one of the few surviving historic buildings in the waterfront area, reflected in the Equitable Building. (William Clift, Seagram County Court House Archives)

Looking at Architecture

The art of building, or architecture, is the beginning of all the arts that lie outside the person.

> Havelock Ellis, *The Dance of Life*. 1923.

Architecture is an art—but it is the art of architecture, not sculpture or painting. The most fundamental difference is that architecture is an art—the only form of art—intended for human habitation.

> Donald Canty, "The Art of Architecture." *AIA Journal,* April 1980.

"It is not enough to *see* architecture; you must experience it. You must observe how it was designed for a special purpose and how it was attuned to the entire concept and rhythm of a specific era. You must dwell in the rooms, feel how they close about you, observe how you are naturally led from one to the other. You must be aware of the textural effects, discover why just those colors were used, how the choice depended on the orientation of the rooms in relation to windows and the sun."

> Steen Eiler Rasmussen, *Experiencing Architecture*

Experiencing Architecture. Steen Eiler Rasmussen. 1959. 2nd ed. Cambridge: MIT Press, 1962. 244 pp., illus. $5.95 pb.

A fundamental and highly readable classic on how we perceive our architectural surroundings, designed to "tell people outside our profession [architecture] what it is that we are engaged in." Surveys solids and cavities, color, scale and proportion, rhythm, texture, daylight and "hearing architecture."

Body, Memory and Architecture. Kent C. Bloomer and Charles W. Moore. New Haven: Yale University Press, 1977. 145 pp., illus. $9.95 pb.

A whimsically illustrated, provocative book tracing the significance of the human body from its role as the organizing principle in the earliest built forms to its virtual elimination from modern architectural thought. The authors draw on contemporary models of spatial perception as well as on body-image theory in arguing for a return of the body to its place in architecture.

The Architecture of Humanism: A Study in the History of Taste. Geoffrey Scott. 1919. Reprint. New York: W.W. Norton, 1974. 196 pp. $6.95 pb.

A classic treatise on why buildings are designed the way they are. It analyzes the theories behind 19th-century architecture, the classical tradition and the role of the human body in that tradition.

Dimensions: Space, Shape and Scale in Architecture. Charles Moore and Gerald Allen. 1976. 2nd ed. New York: Architectural Record Books, 1977. 182 pp., illus. $19.95 hb.

Explores the application (or misapplication) of space, shape and scale. Moore and Allen define "dimensions" as "not just the familiar ones of height, width and depth but any variable which can be changed without affecting any of the others."

Detail from a house on Delores Street, San Francisco. "Once you start to notice, you will find faces everywhere, tucked into a transom, glaring from a gable, pouting over a portico. . . ." From *A Gift to the Street*. (Carol Olwell)

Architecture and the Human Dimension. Peter F. Smith. Forest Grove, Ore.: ISBS/Eastview, 1979. 240 pp., illus. $18.50 hb.

Develops a value system for architectural design by exploring the psychological basis for the artistic experience. The author contends that, apart from performance, architecture's chief aim should be to give delight. He shows a range of buildings and how they work on the mind.

Architecture as Space: How to Look at Architecture. Bruno Zevi. 1957. Rev. ed. New York: Horizon, 1974. 310 pp., illus., biblio., index. $14.95 pb.

"If we really want to teach people *how to look at architecture*, we must first of all establish a clarity of method." Zevi establishes space as his methodology and looks at how it has been used from antiquity to the modern period.

Architecture and You: How to Experience and Enjoy Buildings. William Wayne Caudill et al. New York: Whitney Library of Design, 1978. 176 pp., illus., gloss., biblio., index. $14.95 pb.

Although weighted toward modern buildings, usefully analyzes the basics of design—space, form, site, color, light—in examples ranging from the Taj Majal to the local shopping center.

How Architects Visualize. Tom Porter. New York: Van Nostrand Reinhold, 1980. 120 pp., illus., biblio., index. $16.95 hb, $9.95 pb.

Written primarily to aid the architectural student in learning how to draw, the book is intended to provide a basic understanding of the nature of space "through an experience of its many constructs and structures." Included are a brief history of spatial representation, the elements governing spatial perception and an assessment of the ways of externalizing spatial ideas.

Anatomy of Architecture. George Mansell. New York: A&W Publishers, 1979. 192 pp., illus. $19.95 hb.

An introductory, down-to-earth guide to the elusive qualities that make certain buildings "great architecture": structure, form, proportion, decoration, balance, rhythm, etc. Covers medieval walled cities through modern skyscrapers.

The Shapes of Structure. Heather Martienssen. New York: Oxford University Press, 1976. 166 pp., illus., biblio. $6.95 pb.

Philosophical essays on the historical development of architectural design, including a view of structures in terms of their form, the art of building, architecture as art, building plans, the architect as artist and engineer, the engineer as architect and anonymous architecture.

The Aesthetics of Architecture. Roger Scruton. Princeton: Princeton University Press, 1979. 302 pp., illus., biblio., index. $22 hb, $8.95 pb.

Analysis of the romantic, functionalist and rationalist theories of design as well as the Freudian, Marxist and semiological approaches to aesthetic value.

Architecture as Art: An Esthetic Analysis. Stanley Abercrombie. New York: Van Nostrand Reinhold, 1984. $24.95 hb.

Archabet: An Architectural Alphabet. Photographs by Balthazar Korab. Washington, D.C.: Preservation Press, 1985. 64 pp., illus. $12.95 hb.

A visual exploration of letter shapes found on, in and around buildings. Korab, recipient of the AIA Architectural Photography Medal, helps find new ways of looking at the built environment from A to Z.

A Psychology of Building: How We Shape and Experience Our Structured Spaces. Glenn Robert Lym. Englewood Cliffs, N.J.: Prentice-Hall, 1980. 155 pp., illus., index. $4.95 pb.

A Pattern Language: Towns, Buildings, Construction. Christopher Alexander et al. New York: Oxford University Press, 1977. 1,169 pp., illus. $45 hb.

According to the authors, ". . . the second in a series of books which describe an entirely new attitude to architecture and planning. The books are intended to provide a complete working alternative to our present ideas about architecture, building, and planning—an alternative which will, we hope, gradually replace current ideas and practices." The others: *The Timeless Way of Building.* Christopher Alexander et al. New York: Oxford University Press, 1979. $37.50 hb. *The Oregon Experiment.* Christopher Alexander et al. New York: Oxford University Press, 1975. $25 hb.

The Brutalistic rhythms of the Transamerica Pyramid (1972, Wm. Pereira), San Francisco. (Carleton Knight III, NTHP)

Three perceptions of Oxford's covered market: eye and brain image of a freehand sketch and retinal images of a perspective and a camera. From *How Architects Visualize*. (Mike Jenks photo)

Shuttered and arcaded building providing shade in the Lower Garden District, New Orleans. (Carleton Knight III, NTHP)

Brick-paved, geometrical entrance plaza flows up and into the new Boston City Hall. (1963–69, Kallmann, McKinnell and Knowles)

Stone gutter, brick pavement and decorative cast-iron fence near the Shrewsbury House, Madison, Ind. (Jack E. Boucher, HABS)

Looking at Streetscapes

In a city the street must be supreme. It is the first institution of the city. The street is a room by agreement, a community room, the walls of which belong to the donors, dedicated to the city for common use. Its ceiling is the sky.

Louis I. Kahn. In *Between Silence and Light: Spirit in the Architecture of Louis I. Kahn*

The street—particularly in the center city—is among the greatest of our cultural legacies. It is the river of city life. It gives the city continuity and coherence. It defines its scale. But it is under attack.

William H. Whyte, Jr., "The Humble Street: Can It Survive?" *Historic Preservation,* January–February 1980.

"Buildings in combination with one another create a sum that is greater than their parts. A structure can echo its neighbor's color or contrast its massiveness with delicacy, absorbing its partner's best characteristics or lending some of its own. Building groups in combination with other constructed elements, landscaping and the street furniture—paving, fences, benches, lampposts, mailboxes, utility poles, chute covers, transit shelters, kiosks, street signs, and commercial signs—create a streetscape. . . .

In evaluating a streetscape these questions can be asked: Does it invite human interaction? Are buildings set too far back from the street to be readily experienced? Are they set at a distance that permits comfortable walking? Are there surprising and interesting vistas that appear as the pedestrian passes? Are there gaps caused by poor design or by demolition? Do the things that help tie buildings together into a total environmental unit—landscaping (trees, shrubbery, parks, open green areas) and street furniture—add or detract? Do they, in other words, pull everything together or apart?"

National Trust et al., *America's Forgotten Architecture*

"It was on the street, with our feet shuffling on the courthouse square, that America discovered its identity and concentrated its drives. It seems impossible to think of any city or town in pioneering America that did not depend on at least one street as its 'living room.' The squares of Savannah or of New England, the wrought-iron balconies of New Orleans, the recessed arcades of Santa Fe, the narrow lanes of Boston's Beacon Hill all bring to mind the function of streets as places where values, not just vehicles, intermingle. Even the western settlers curled their Conestoga wagons into a circle around the campfires for company as well as protection—thereby creating an instant 'public space' as historically vivid and valid as the most resplendent, urbane esplanade."

Raquel Ramati, *How to Save Your Own Street.* With Urban Design Group, New York Department of City Planning. Garden City, N.Y.: Doubleday, Dolphin Books, 1981.

Streets for People: A Primer for Americans. Bernard Rudofsky. 1969. New York: Van Nostrand Reinhold, 1982. 351 pp., illus. $10.95 pb.

An early attempt to focus attention on streets as part of a city's architecture. In contrasting American and Western European attitudes toward streets, it calls for humaneness in scale and respect for the pedestrian over the auto.

On Streets. Stanford Anderson, ed. Institute for Architecture and Urban Studies. Cambridge: MIT Press, 1978. 416 pp., illus., biblio. $55 hb.

An examination of streets as spatial structures, including essays on streets in the past; streets as "communications artifact"; the anthropology and sociology of streets and human dimensions in urban design.

The Social Life of Small Urban Spaces. William H. Whyte, Jr. Washington, D.C.: Conservation Foundation, 1980. 125 pp., illus., appends. $9.50 pb.

A paen to the restoration of life to streets. "This book is about city spaces, why some work for people, and some do not, and what the practical lessons may be." Its architectural components include plazas, sitting space, indoor spaces and concourses and megastructures.

Dramatic street wall of the Everett Mill, Lawrence, Mass. (© Randolph Langenbach)

Urban Spaces. David Kenneth Specter. Greenwich, Conn.: New York Graphic Society, 1974. 279 pp., illus.

Calls on city observers to identify and then to manipulate these tangible and intangible elements: "the power of anticipation and surprise, the mystery of lighting, the pull of the waterfront, the excitement of arcades, the appeal of people-watching, the surfaces and objects of the city." Specter's photo essay, accompanied by brief descriptions, illuminates these elements using international examples.

Alleys: A Hidden Resource. Grady Clay. Louisville, Ky.: Grady Clay (330 Wildwood Place, 40206), 1978. 60 pp., illus., biblio., index. $9.95 pb.

A plea to look beyond the street and behind the facades of buildings to another neglected resource: alleys. "The alley could once again become a special world. . . . It offers one of the few urban rather than suburban or rural 'retreats,' an enclave just off the busy streets, a step away from the hurly-burly."

Livable Streets. Donald Appleyard. Berkeley, Calif.: University of California Press, 1981. 364 pp., illus., appends., biblio., index. $14.95 pb.

Written in the belief that streetlife can be reclaimed for people, this analysis of British and American efforts to cure excessive traffic in residential neighborhoods includes surveys of residents' attitudes toward use of their streets.

Streets Ahead. Design Council, with Royal Town Planning Institute. London: Design Council, 1979. 111 pp., illus.

Examines the individual components that make up the streetscape, in addition to addressing more detailed planning concerns. Mostly European in orientation.

See also: Cities

Townscape by moonlight. (Tom Engeman, NTHP)

Looking at Townscapes

If I were asked to define townscape I would say that one building is architecture but two buildings is townscape.

Gordon Cullen, *The Concise Townscape*

Floodlit tower of Philadelphia City Hall (1871–1901, John McArthur, Jr., and Thomas U. Walter). (City of Philadelphia)

"As an artificial world, the city should be so in the best sense: made by art, shaped for human purposes. On home grounds, we may begin to adapt the environment itself to the perceptual pattern and symbolic process of the human being. . . . These elements are the building blocks in the process of making firm, differentiated structures at the urban scale. . . ."

Paths: the city's circulation routes.

Edges: linear elements either not used or considered as paths.

Districts: medium-to-large sections of the city distinguished from one another by a set of common characteristics.

Nodes: central points of reference.

Landmarks: external points of reference, usually a single physical object, like a church spire or bridge.

Kevin Lynch, *The Image of the City*

"There is no universal and everlasting right way for cities to present themselves to us. Each reflects the ideas, traditions, and energies available to its citizens in past centuries, as well as at this moment. Each landscape and townscape is an intricately organized expression of causes and effects, of challenges and responses, of continuity and, therefore, of coherence. It all hangs together, makes sense, fits one way or another—for good or bad, loosely or tightly. It has sequences, successions, climaxes. It reveals patterns and relationships forming and reforming."

Grady Clay, *Close-Up: How to Read the American City*

"Any historic environment has a network of pivotal or focal buildings as its foundation. . . . Upon this framework hangs a series of anonymous structures—anonymous in their average aesthetic quality and limited associative values. Together, whether contiguous or separated by alleys or gardens, these linkages of anonymous structures provide the walls of continuity that create the definitive quality of the area. . . . Thus, the buildings, the spaces between them—whether parks, streets, walkways or gardens— and such street furniture as sculpture, lighting fixtures and directional signs together create the total identity of place that can be visually observed. Such sense of place is created not only by the integral parts of the units and their interrelationships but by the interplay of time, tradition and continued mutual existence."

William J. Murtagh, "Aesthetic and Social Dimensions of Historic Districts." *Historic Districts: Identification, Social Aspects and Preservation.* Washington, D.C.: National Trust for Historic Preservation, 1975.

The Image of the City. Kevin Lynch. Cambridge: MIT Press, 1960. 194 pp., illus. $20 hb, $5.95 pb.

Lynch's classic planning treatise analyzes the visual image of three cities: Boston, Jersey City and Los Angeles. The book entered such new concepts as paths, edges and nodes into the language of looking at townscapes.

The Concise Townscape. Gordon Cullen. New York: Van Nostrand Reinhold, 1961. 199 pp., illus. $7.95 pb.

A planner's guide to seeing, but through fundamental concepts that can enlarge anyone's town view. With sensitivity, Cullen defines basic design principles as well as more subtle qualities: "fluctuation," "intricacy," "entanglement," "nostalgia." "The typical town is not a pattern of streets but a sequence of spaces created by buildings . . . it is the stimulation of our sense of position through moving from the wide to the narrow and out again into some fresh space."

Mansions of the South Battery in the Old and Historic District, Charleston, S.C. In the background are early 18th- to late 19th-century houses.

Close-Up: How to Read the American City. Grady Clay. 1973. Reprint. Chicago: University of Chicago Press, 1980. 192 pp., illus. $7.95 pb.

"Mr. Clay believes that cities can tell us what they are and what they are becoming if we have eyes to see and a vocabulary capable of telling it like it is. . . . He speaks of fronts, guerilla suburbia, beats, fragging, DMZs, turf. It's a tough, but useful, vocabulary for describing urban change." (Constance Greiff. Review in *Historic Preservation*, January–March 1974)

Cities. Lawrence Halprin. 1963. Rev. ed. Cambridge: MIT Press, 1973. 160 pp., illus. $9.95.

The urban scene through a photographer's eye—color, texture, form, function and interrelationships. The accompanying thumbnail essays are enriched by forgotten historical tidbits.

How to Look at Your Town. Historic Landmarks Foundation of Indiana. Indianapolis: Author (3402 Boulevard Place, 46208), 1975. 4 pp., illus.

A concise guide to looking at towns. Questions and learning exercises provide tricks of townscape watching.

Skylines: Understanding and Molding Urban Silhouettes. Wayne Attoe. New York: John Wiley, 1981. 128 pp., illus., biblio., index. $41.95 hb.

An exploration of the role of the skyline in cityscapes—as collective symbols, social indexes, utilitarian objects, aesthetic contributors, indicators of social behavior and cultural icons.

Townscape as a Philosophy of Urban Design. William M. Whistler and David Reed. Chicago: Council of Planning Librarians, 1977. No. 1342. $2.40 pb.

See also: Cities

Rockefeller Center (1940, Reinhard and Hofmeister; Corbett, Harrison and MacMurray; Hood and Fouilhoux), New York City, a virtual city within a city occupying 24 acres. (Thomas Airviews)

The Artist's Eye

It is the artist's function to examine, digest, and interpret our surroundings, to give us ways in which to react to them, evaluate them, and, in various ways, to come to terms with them. The artist can point out beauty where there seems to be none, can intensify moods or qualities that reveal the means to see, enjoy, and appreciate our conditions. The artist can help us to digest or grasp the welter of confusing and diverse forms that our increasingly built-up environment throws at us.

Donald Stoltenberg, *The Artist and the Built Environment*

The Artist and the Built Environment. Donald Stoltenberg. Worcester, Mass.: Davis Publications, 1980. 158 pp., color illus., biblio., index. $18.95 hb.

Images of American Architecture. Robert Miles Parker. 1981. New York: Van Nostrand Reinhold, 1982. 144 pp., illus. $10.95 pb.

America Observed. Drawings by Paul Hogarth. Text by Stephen Spender. New York: Clarkson Potter, 1979. 128 pp., illus.

Richard Haas: An Architecture of Illusion. Richard Haas. Introduction by Paul Goldberger. New York: Rizzoli, 1981. 160 pp., color illus. $35 hb.

Dayton Sketchbook. Drawings by Craig MacIntosh. Text by Robert Frame. Dayton, Ohio: Landfall Press, 1977. 168 pp., illus. $7.95 pb.

Sketches of Nebraska. Robert Hanna. Lincoln: University of Nebraska Press, 1984. 128 pp., illus., index. $12.95 hb.

Through the Photographer's Lens

"I can only hope that my pictures will in some way help us to see elements in our surroundings that we have up to now ignored, and in seeing them, we may react to them."

David Plowden, *The Hand of Man on America.* Washington, D.C.: Smithsonian Institution Press, 1971.

An American Chronology: The Photographs of David Plowden. Introduction by David McCullough. New York: Viking, 1982. 160 pp., illus. $45 hb.

Photographs of Architecture: Philip Trager. Photographs by Philip Trager. Middletown, Conn.: Wesleyan University Press, 1977. 60 pp., illus., index. $24.95 hb.

Philip Trager: New York. Middletown, Conn.: Wesleyan University Press, 1980. Foreword by Louis Auchincloss. 120 pp., illus. $45 hb.

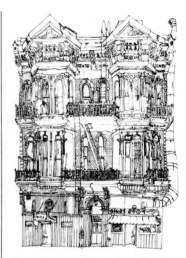

From *Images of American Architecture.* (Robert Miles Parker)

Observations on American Architecture. Ivan Chermayeff. Photographs by Elliott Erwitt. New York: Viking, 1972. 143 pp.

Architecture: Theory. New York: Lustrum Press, 1985. 132 pp., illus. $17.95 pb.

Decorative sawn-wood porch on a house (c. 1890), Litchfield Avenue, Torrington, Conn. From *Photographs of Architecture.* (Philip Trager)

Woodbury County Court House (1918, William L. Steele and Purcell and Elmslie), Sioux City, Iowa. (Bob Thall, Seagram Archives)

Paving stones, Washington, D.C. (Jack E. Boucher, HABS)

Olana (1874), Church Hill, N.Y. (HABS)

The Language of Looking

amenity. A building, landscape feature, etc., that makes an aesthetic contribution to the environment, rather than one that is purely utilitarian.

archiphobia. Fear of architecture—a malady of those who fear to look at or understand the built environment.

background buildings. Buildings that may lack exemplary character but that are nonetheless essential in maintaining a sense of place.

balance. A principle of visual order analogous to physical balance; elements of a building's design can be said, visually, to have weights supported or distributed evenly around a central axis, i.e., fulcrum. Balance is also the harmonious integration of elements that lends a building visual character and appeal.

fabric. The physical material of a building, structure or city, connoting an interweaving of component parts.

genus loci. The prevailing spirit of a place, implying the conscious art of developing the character of a given place rather than imposing a foreign character on it.

human scale. A combination of qualities in architecture or the landscape that provides an appropriate relationship to human size, enhancing rather than diminishing the importance of people.

landscape. The totality of the built or human-influenced habitat experienced at any one place. Dominant features are topography, plant cover, buildings or other structures and their patterns.

massing. The combination of several volumes to create a total building volume; also, the organization of the shape of a building, as differentiated from wall treatment, fenestration, etc.

proportion. The relation of one dimension to another (e.g., width to height, front area to side depth), often described as a numerical ratio. In architecture, proportions determine the creation of visual order through coordination of shapes in a design.

rhythm. A visual movement characterized by regular recurrence of elements in alternation with opposite or different elements.

scale. A measure of the relative or apparent size of a building or any architectural element in relation to other elements, structures, open spaces, or—usually—the dimensions of the human body.

sense of place. The sum of attributes of any place that give it a unique and distinctive character.

street furniture. Municipal equipment placed along streets, including light fixtures, fire hydrants, police and fire call boxes, signs, benches, kiosks.

streetscape. The distinguishing and pictorial character of a particular street as created by width, degree of curvature and paving materials, design of the street furniture and forms of surrounding buildings; a smaller version of townscape.

style. A definite type of architecture, distinguished by special characteristics of structure and ornament; also, a general quality of distinctive character.

townscape. The relationship of buildings, shapes, spaces and textures that lends a town or area its distinctive visual atmosphere or image.

visual pollution. Anything that is offensive to the sense of sight based on its concept, from garbage dumps to garish neon—a subjective matter.

Adapted from *Landmark Words: A Glossary for Preserving the Built Environment,* National Trust for Historic Preservation.

The View of the Green in 1800, New Haven, Conn., by William Giles Munson. (New Haven Colony Historical Society)

Architectural Histories

Buildings nearly always say something, even their bones speak when disintered after centuries, while standing ruins and ancient structures still in use retain the impress of the emotions, beliefs, fears and pleasures of their makers.

John Gloag, *The Architectural Interpretation of History.* New York: St. Martin's, 1975.

American Architecture, 1607–1976. Marcus Whiffen and Frederick Koeper. Cambridge: MIT Press, 1981. 576 pp., illus., biblio., index. 2 vols. $10.95 pb each.

A new survey that focuses on the environmental and social factors in the development of American architecture.

Texas State Capitol, 1888. (State Library and Archives Commission)

A Concise History of American Architecture. Leland M. Roth. New York: Harper and Row, 1979. 400 pp., illus., gloss., biblio., index. $11.95 pb.

An overview of the shaping of the American built environment from the arrival of the Europeans to the present, exploring "the pluralism that has complicated and enriched American architecture from the beginning."

American Buildings and Their Architects

Vol. 1. *The Colonial and Neoclassical Styles.* William H. Pierson, Jr. Garden City, N.Y.: Doubleday, 1970. 503 pp., illus., gloss., index. $10.95 pb.

Vol. 2A. *Technology and the Picturesque. The Corporate and the Early Gothic Styles.* William H. Pierson, Jr. Garden City, N.Y.: Doubleday, 1978. 500 pp., illus., gloss., index. $10.95 pb.

Vol. 3. *Progressive and Academic Ideals at the Turn of the Twentieth Century.* William H. Jordy. Garden City, N.Y.: Doubleday, 1972. 448 pp., illus., gloss., index. $10.95 pb.

Vol. 4. *The Impact of European Modernism in the Mid-Twentieth Century.* William H. Jordy. Garden City, N.Y.: Doubleday, 1972. 496 pp., illus., gloss., index. $10.95 pb.

A series spanning the colonial period to the 1960s, rich in historical background and descriptions of representative building types and styles.

America Builds: Source Documents in American Architecture and Planning. Leland M. Roth. New York: Harper and Row, 1983. 666 pp., illus., index. $38.50 hb, $21.75 pb.

An anthology of documents on architecture, planning and landscape architecture from Capt. John Smith (1624) to Robert A.M. Stern (1980)—letters, essays, selections from books, articles and journals covering specific projects and building types. Provides an introduction to the ideas of architects and clients in their historical context.

American Building 1: The Historical Forces That Shaped It. James Marston Fitch. Boston: Houghton Mifflin, 1966. 350 pp., illus., biblio., index. $15 hb. Rev. ed. New York: Schocken Books, 1973. $7.95 pb.

An analysis of the European antecedents, philosophical and social forces and literary romanticism that determined the American architectural development.

American Building 2: The Environmental Forces That Shape It. James Marston Fitch. Boston: Houghton Mifflin, 1972. 349 pp., illus., index. $20 hb. 2nd ed. New York: Schocken Books, 1975. $9.95 pb.

An environmental approach to architecture and design, including chapters on lighting, temperature and noise and how they have influenced architectural and planning decisions.

Architecture: Nineteenth and Twentieth Centuries. Henry-Russell Hitchcock. 1958. 1963. 2nd ed. Reprint. New York: Viking Penguin, 1977. 510 pp., illus., biblio., index. $16.95 pb.

Features primarily English and European architecture but includes noteworthy coverage of American development—the rise of commercial architecture, the detached house and masters such as Richardson and McKim, Mead and White.

In Search of Modern Architecture: A Tribute to Henry-Russell Hitchcock. Helen Searing, ed. Cambridge: MIT Press, 1983. 375 pp., illus., index. $45 hb.

Essays on 18th- to 20th-century architecture by noted scholars.

American Architecture and Urbanism. Vincent Scully. New York: Praeger, 1969. 274 pp., illus.

The history of American architecture from an urbanistic and sociological point of view, based on the premise that "there is no difference between architecture and city planning; all must now—or, rather, again—be treated as one."

Roots of Contemporary American Architecture. Lewis Mumford, ed. 1959. Reprint. New York: Dover, 1972. 470 pp., illus., index. $6 pb.

Essays by 37 architects and theorists from the mid-19th century on, prefaced by a discussion of the impact of American writers and architects.

Sticks and Stones: A Study of American Architecture and Civilization. Lewis Mumford. 1924. Reprint. New York: Dover, 1955. 238 pp. $3.50 pb.

A critique emphasizing the influence of the medieval tradition and the importance of vernacular architecture.

The Brown Decades: A Study of the Arts in America, 1865–1895. Lewis Mumford. 1931. Reprint. New York: Dover, 1955. 266 pp. $3 pb.

A noted work that points up the significance of 19th-century architects, Richardson in particular.

Architecture in America: A Pictorial History. G. E. Kidder Smith. Introductions by Marshall B. Davidson. New York: American Heritage Publishing Company, 1976. Distributed by W. W. Norton. 832 pp., illus., index. 2 vols.

A pictorial review of the American architectural landscape designed to capture the spirit of America's great structures and its little-known regional and vernacular examples. Arranged state by state by region.

Architecture in America: A Photographic History from the Colonial Period to the Present. Wayne Andrews. Introduction by Russell Lynes. 1960. Rev. ed. New York: Atheneum, 1977. 182 pp., illus., index. $8.95 pb.

A cross section of building types and regional styles, by period, including lost structures and documentation of their demise.

Space, Time and Architecture: The Growth of a New Tradition. Siegfried Giedion. 1941. 5th ed. Cambridge: Harvard University Press, 1972. 897 pp., illus. $35 hb.

A collection of critical analyses of the development of worldwide architecture and planning in relation to emerging industrialization.

View of the Upper Village of Lockport, Niagara County, N.Y. by W. Wilson. (Library of Congress)

The Architecture of America: A Social and Cultural History. John Burchard and Albert Bush-Brown. Boston: Little, Brown, 1961. 592 pp., illus., notes, biblio., index.

A survey sponsored by the American Institute of Architects for its centennial, this social history highlights architecture between the two world wars.

Images of American Living: Four Centuries of Architecture and Furniture as Cultural Expression. Alan Gowans. 1964. Reprint. New York: Harper and Row, 1976. 516 pp., illus., index. $12.95 pb.

A study of cultural and social attitudes viewed through architecture and the decorative arts, including architect-client relations and the role of builders from the Stone Age to the modern age. Organized thematically, its subject range from the classical spirit to folk traditions.

The Architecture of Choice: Eclecticism in America, 1880–1930. Walter C. Kidney. New York: Braziller, 1974. 178 pp., illus., notes, index. $5.95 pb.

An evaluation of eclectic architecture from Eastlake and Talbert's "Domestic Revival" through the "lean years" of World War II. The author predicts a comeback for eclecticism.

The Rise of an American Architecture. Edgar Kaufmann, Jr., ed. New York: Praeger, 1970. 241 pp., illus., biblio.

A quartet of essays by Henry-Russell Hitchcock, Albert Fein, Winston Weisman and Vincent Scully on the contributions of 19th-century America to the history of architecture and city planning.

Architecture and the Aesthetics of Plenty. James Marston Fitch. New York: Columbia University Press, 1961. 304 pp., illus.

Articles on 200 years of American architecture, surveying the domestic revolution, comparing Jefferson and Wright, engineering, the effect of affluence and "What is 'American' in American architecture?"

The Evolution of American Taste: The History of American Style from 1607 to the Present. William Peirce Randel. New York: Crown, 1978. 212 pp., illus., index.

Chronicles the transformation of America from a style "importer" to a style "creator," featuring architecture as a prominent factor.

A Choice Over Our Heads: A Guide to Architecture and Design Since 1830. Lawrence Burton. Forest Grove, Ore.: ISBS/Eastview Editions, 1979. 191 pp., illus. $15 hb, $9.95 pb.

A survey of the United States, Europe and Britain, with an annotated guide to more specialized reading.

A History of Architecture: Settings and Rituals. Spiro Kostof. New York: Oxford University Press, 1985. 800 pp., illus. $45 hb.

A major survey examining the built environment from four premises basically calling for a comprehensive and contextual understanding of architecture.

People and Spaces: A View of History Through Architecture. Anita Abramowitz. New York: Viking, 1979. 207 pp., illus., biblio., index. $14.95 hb.

Discusses the effects of social, cultural and economic changes on the look, use and feel of a building.

Architecture of the Western World. Michael Raeburn, ed. New York: Rizzoli, 1980. 304 pp., color illus., biblio., index. $37.50 hb.

Traces the evolution of Western architecture in the contexts of social history, urban planning, construction and aesthetic movements, from Greece to the modern movement.

The Story of Western Architecture. Bill Risebero. New York: Scribner's, 1979. 272 pp., illus., biblio., index. $12.95 hb.

A survey of 1,500 years of Western architecture, America's contribution being just a small part of the story. Numerous specially drawn, full-page illustrations show selected periods, styles, building types and buildings at a glance.

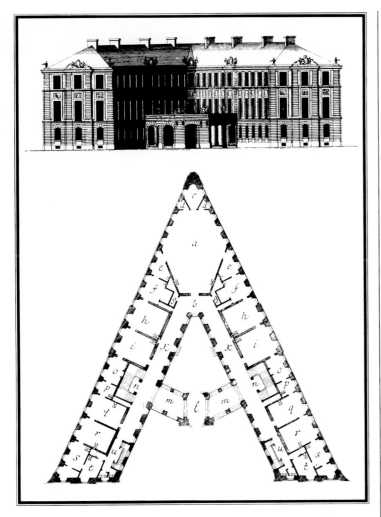

From *Architectural Alphabet* (1773) by Johann David Steingruber. (Courtesy George Braziller)

Sourcebooks and Bibliographies

To relish architecture is both an intellectual and intuitive emotional affair. . . . Art collector Vincent Price said succinctly: 'I like what I know.' Know architecture, both in mind and feelings, and your experience of it may become exalted. The beginning of such understanding can be gained through knowledge of the words and people of architecture.

Norval White, *The Architecture Book*

Arts in America: A Bibliography. Vol. I: *Art of the Native Americans, Architecture, Decorative Arts, Design, Sculpture, Art of the West.* Vol. 4: *Index.* Archives of American Art, Smithsonian Institution. Bernard Karpel, ed. Washington, D.C.: Smithsonian Institution Press, 1979.

Section B, "Architecture" (Charles B. Wood III, ed.) in vol. I includes annotated references for architectural histories, 19th-century styles and building materials, building types, architectural commentary, landscape gardening, the 19th- and 20th-century city, 20th-century architecture, geographical studies and architects' biographies.

Encyclopedia of American Architecture. William Dudley Hunt, Jr. New York: McGraw-Hill, 1980. 612 pp., illus., index., biblio. $43.95 hb.

Covers subject matter in roughly seven categories: individual architects and firms, the building industry, building types, components and systems of buildings, history of architecture, construction materials and the practice of architecture. Each entry includes a guide to related information and reading.

The Architecture Book. Norval White. New York: Knopf, 1976. 343 pp., illus.

An irreverent and witty reference to practitioners, periods and terms.

The Book of Buildings. Richard Reid. Chicago: Rand McNally, 1980. 448 pp., illus., gloss., index.

Topographical guide to architecture in Europe and North America, grouped by period, geographic region and building type.

American Architecture and Art: A Guide to Information Sources. David M. Sokol. Detroit: Gale Research, 1976. 480 pp., index. $44 hb.

An annotated bibliography of general reference sources as well as entries on specific topics—architectural histories and surveys, city planning, aesthetics, regional architecture, architects and the decorative arts.

"General Reference Works on American Architects and Their Architecture." In *American Architects. I: From the Civil War to the First World War.* 1976. 343 pp. *2: From the First World War to the Present.* 1977. 305 pp. Lawrence Wodehouse, ed. Art and Architecture Information Guide Series. Detroit: Gale Research. $44 hb each.

A brief survey with annotations of major architectural history reference books covering the two periods.

Bibliography of Early American Architecture: Writings on Architecture Constructed Before 1860 in the Eastern and Central United States. Frank J. Roos, Jr. 1943. Rev. ed. Urbana: University of Illinois Press, 1968. 389 pp., index. $75.90 hb.

An early bibliography of more than 4,000 entries that served as the base for the Gale Art and Architecture Information Guide Series.

American Architectural Books: A List of Books, Portfolios, and Pamphlets on Architecture and Related Subjects Published in America Before 1895. Henry-Russell Hitchcock. 1946. Rev. ed. Reprint. New York: Da Capo, 1975. 130 pp. $21.50 hb.

A bibliography of the major works arranged alphabetically by author and indexed by subject.

Encyclopedia of Architectural Technology: An Encyclopedic Survey of Changing Forms, Materials, and Concepts. Pedro Guedes, ed. New York: McGraw-Hill, 1979. 313 pp., illus., index.

An inclusive international survey with sections on architectural styles, building types, structure and construction, mechanical and environmental systems, building materials and tools, techniques and fixings. The emphasis is more British and Continental, but American examples are used.

Pediment detail with steer and Driskill Hotel (1885) namesake, Austin, Tex.

Catalog of the Avery Memorial Architectural Library, Columbia University. 2nd ed. Adolf K. Placzek, Librarian. Boston: G.K. Hall, 1968. 19 vols. Fourth Supplement, 1980.

Catalogs (in reprint form) of the holdings of America's finest architectural library.

Avery Index to Architectural Periodicals, Columbia University. 2nd ed. Boston: G.K. Hall, 1973. 15 vols. Second Supplement, 1977.

Reproduces the card catalog to periodicals in the Avery collection. A broad range of related subject matter is covered—archeology, decorative arts, interior design, landscape architecture, city planning and housing.

Books on Architecture: A Selected Bibliography. Mary Vance, ed. Monticello, Ill.: Vance Bibliographies (P.O. Box 229, 61856), 1979. A-60. 62 pp. $6 pb.

One in a series of architectural bibliographies covering architects, history of architecture, design and other preservation-related subjects. "List of Bibliographies in Print" available from Vance Bibliographies.

Encyclopedia of World Architecture. Henri Stierlin. New York: Van Nostrand Reinhold, 1982. 416 pp., illus. $16.95 pb.

A detailed overview of buildings of all major cultures from ancient to modern.

Dictionaries and Glossaries

To fully appreciate this environment, we need to know its language. Many of us know only that a certain building or structure is capable of making us feel a certain way: nostalgic, uneasy, alienated, significant, forgotten. Words like 'vermiculated' and 'quoin,' 'mullion' and 'mansard,' 'lintel,' 'balustrade,' 'fenestration,' and 'setback' are almost a foreign language, although these things affect our moods and attitudes every day. A familiarity with the basic terminology of the components of the built environment provides a common language with which to share the experiences and translate our feelings about these structures. When the images and reactions are broken down into verbal terms, a new-found vocabulary enables us to communicate feelings and concerns about the built environment, including the importance of preserving it.

National Trust et al., *America's Forgotten Architecture*

The Penguin Dictionary of Architecture. John Fleming, Hugh Honour and Nikolaus Pevsner. 1966. Rev. ed. Baltimore: Penguin Books, 1973. 247 pp., illus. $5.95 pb. *A Dictionary of Architecture.* John Fleming, Hugh Honour and Nikolaus Pevsner. Rev. ed. Woodstock, N.Y.: Overlook Press, 1976. 554 pp., illus. $25 hb.

Definitions of terms plus biographical notes by these leading architectural historians. Unlike the original, the Overlook edition is generously illustrated with photographs and drawings.

Dictionary of Architecture and Construction. Cyril M. Harris, ed. New York: McGraw-Hill, 1975. 553 pp., illus. $42.50 hb.

A comprehensive reference covering every stage of building from planning to painting, intended for nonspecialists.

Dictionary of Architecture. Henry H. Saylor. 1952. Reprint. New York: John Wiley, 1963. 221 pp., illus. $11.95 pb.

Pocket handbook with brief definitions and pronunciations.

Illustrated Dictionary of Historic Architecture. Cyril M. Harris, ed. 1977. New York: Dover, 1983. 581 pp., illus. $14.95 pb.

Five thousand years of architectural history in definitions of terms and line drawings, arranged alphabetically.

Illustrated Glossary of Architecture, 850–1830. John Harris and Jill Lever. 1966. Reprint. Salem, N.H.: Faber and Faber, 1979. 314 pp., illus. $9.95 pb.

Definitions in words and illustrations of details shown in relation to the whole facade, with photographs arranged chronologically.

A Dictionary of Building. John S. Scott. 1964. Rev. ed. Baltimore: Penguin, 1975. 392 pp. $4.95 pb.

A guide to terms on materials, methods and masters of the building trade.

Architecture and Building Trades Dictionary. R. E. Putnam and G. E. Carlson. 1950. 3rd ed. New York: Van Nostrand Reinhold, 1983. 510 pp., illus., gloss. $18.50 hb.

Directed more to nuts-and-bolts than style, emphasizing technical and engineering definitions, with a section on legal terms.

A Dictionary of Architecture and Building: Biographical, Historical and Descriptive. Russell Sturgis. 1902. Reprint. Detroit: Gale Research, 1966. 1,607 pp., illus., biblio. 3 vols. $79 set.

An early comprehensive and well-illustrated dictionary emphasizing the classical tradition.

Glossary of Art, Architecture, and Design Since 1945. John A. Walker. 1975. 2nd ed. Hamden, Conn.: Shoe String Press, 1977. 240 pp. $19.50 pb.

Terms and labels describing movements, styles and groups, derived from the vocabulary of artists and critics.

An Illustrated Dictionary of Ornament. Maureen Stafford and Dora Ware. New York: St. Martin's, 1975. 246 pp., illus., biblio., index. $12.95 pb.

A guide to classical architectural details and terminology.

The Grammar of Ornament. Owen Jones. New York: Van Nostrand Reinhold, 1972.

Classical and modern ornament, described in scholarly fashion.

Landmark Words: A Glossary for Preserving the Built Environment. National Trust for Historic Preservation. Forthcoming.

A comprehensive reference covering all preservation-related subjects— styles, building types and parts, aesthetics and design, preservation, restoration, planning, neighborhoods, economic development, adaptive use, law.

Periodicals

Progressive Architecture
600 Summer Street
Stamford, Conn. 06904

Architectural Record
McGraw-Hill
1221 Avenue of the Americas
New York, N.Y. 10020

ARCHITECTURE: The AIA Journal
American Institute of Architects
1735 New York Avenue, N.W.
Washington, D.C. 20006

Society of Architectural Historians Journal, Newsletter and *SAH Forum*
1700 Walnut Street
Suite 716
Philadelphia, Pa. 19103

Blueprints
National Building Museum
440 G Street, N.W.
Washington, D.C. 20001

Landscape Architecture
American Society of Landscape Architects
1733 Connecticut Avenue, N.W.
Washington, D.C. 20009

Harvard Architecture Review, Perspecta: The Yale Architectural Journal, Oppositions and *Places*
MIT Press
28 Carleton Street
Cambridge, Mass. 02142

Journal of Architectural Education
Association of Collegiate Schools of Architecture
1735 New York Avenue, N.W.
Washington, D.C. 20006

Skyline
c/o Rizzoli Publications
597 Fifth Avenue
New York, N.Y. 10017

Metropolis
207 West 25th Street
New York, N.Y. 10001

Local AIA Chapter Magazines
c/o American Institute of Architects
1735 New York Avenue, N.W.
Washington, D.C. 20006

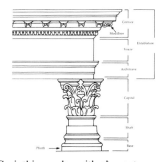

Corinthian order with elements composing a column. From *What Style Is It?*

Contacts

American Institute of Architects
1735 New York Avenue, N.W.
Washington, D.C. 20006

Society of Architectural Historians
1700 Walnut Street
Suite 716
Philadelphia, Pa. 19103

National Building Museum
440 G Street, N.W.
Washington, D.C. 20001

Institute for Architecture and Urban Studies
8 West 40th Street
New York, N.Y. 10018

Project for Public Spaces
875 Avenue of the Americas
Room 201
New York, N.Y. 10001

American Society of Civil Engineers
345 East 47th Street
New York, N.Y. 10017

Society for the History of Technology
Department of History
University of California
Santa Barbara, Calif. 93106

Archives of American Art
Smithsonian Institution
Washington, D.C. 20560

Canadian Centre for Architecture
418 Rue Bonsecours
Montreal, Quebec H2Y 3C4
Canada

International Confederation of Architectural Museums
c/o Museum of Finnish Architecture
SF-00140
Helsinki 14, Finland

The Master Builders

The case for architects should not be hard to make. What should be clear to anyone . . . is the truth that every community is more permanently marked, its character more surely delineated and its future more ordered by the products of its forgotten architects than by a host of local immortals. . . . In a nation of heroes and villains, architecture must claim human identification if it is to change the present public apathy.

John D. Baker, "Anonymity and American Architecture." *Historic Preservation,* July–September 1972.

Bibliographies and Writings

American Architects. 1: From the Civil War to the First World War. 1976. 343 pp. *2: From the First World War to the Present.* 1977. 305 pp. Lawrence Wodehouse, ed. Art and Architecture Information Guide Series. Detroit: Gale Research. $44 hb each.

American Association of Architectural Bibliographers' Papers. Vols. 1–11. Charlottesville: University Press of Virginia, 1965–75. William B. O'Neal, ed. Vols. 12–13. New York: Garland Publishing, 1977, 1979.
Vol. 1. 1965. Includes *Walter Gropius* (Carol Shillaber); *Philip C. Johnson* (William B. O'Neal). $10.
Vol. 2. 1966. Includes *Holabird and Roche* (William Rudd). $10.
Vol. 3. 1966. Includes *Walter Gropius.* $10.
Vol. 4. 1967. $10.
Vol. 5. 1968. Includes *Calvert Vaux* (John D. Sigle). $10.
Vol. 6. 1969. Includes *Jefferson as an Architect* (William B. O'Neal). $10.
Vol. 7. 1970. Includes *Sir Nikolaus Pevsner* (John R. Barr). $10.
Vol. 8. 1972. $10.
Vol. 9. 1972. Includes *Walter Gropius* (Ise Gropius); *Benjamin Henry Latrobe* (Paul F. Norton); *Frank Lloyd Wright in Print 1959–1970* (James Muggenberg). $10.
Vol. 10. 1973. $12.50.
Vol. 11. 1975. *Index to Papers 1–10.* $12.50.
Vol. 12. 1977. Frederick D. Nichols, ed. Includes *Louis Kahn* (Jack Perry Brown). $23.
Vol. 13. 1979. David A. Spaeth, ed. Includes *Ludwig Mies van der Rohe* (David A. Spaeth). $36.

Index to Information on Individual Architects in a Select List of Books. Susan Brookes, ed. Monticello, Ill.: Vance Bibliographies, 1979. A-132. 39 pp. $4.50 pb.

Biographies

Macmillan Encyclopedia of Architects. Adolf K. Placzek, ed. New York: Macmillan, 1982. 2,750 pp., illus., biblio., gloss., index. $275 hb (4 vols).

Master Builders: A Guide to Famous American Architects. Diane Maddex, ed. National Trust for Historic Preservation. Washington, D.C.: Preservation Press, 1985. 192 pp., illus., biblio., append., index. $9.95 pb.

The Architecture Book. Norval White. New York: Knopf, 1976. 343 pp., illus.

Who's Who in Architecture: From 1400 to the Present. James M. Richards, ed.; Adolf K. Placzek, American consultant. New York: Holt, Rinehart and Winston, 1977. 368 pp., illus. $19.95 hb.

Three Centuries of Notable American Architects. Introduction by Vincent Scully. New York: American Heritage, 1981. 348 pp., illus.

Avery Obituary Index of Architects and Artists. Adolf K. Placzek. Boston: G.K. Hall, 1963. 338 pp.

Biographical Dictionary of American Architects (Deceased). Henry F. Withey and Elsie Rathburn Withey. 1956. Reprint. Los Angeles: Hennessey and Ingalls, 1970. 678 pp. $28.50 hb.

Contemporary Architects. Muriel Emanuel, ed. New York: St. Martin's, 1980. 933 pp., illus. $70 hb.

Architectural Firms

ProFile: The Official AIA Directory of Architectural Firms. Henry W. Schirmer, ed. Topeka, Kans.: Archimedia, 1983. 295 pp. $86 pb nonmembers.

Directory of Historic American Architectural Firms. Committee for the Preservation of Architectural Records. Washington, D.C.: American Institute of Architects Foundation (1799 New York Avenue, 20006) and Committee for the Preservation of Architectural Records, 1979. 44 pp. $3.

"An Architectural Family Tree That Traces the Paths to Fame," Roxanne Williamson. *AIA Journal,* January 1978.

Great American Architects Series: The Architectural Record, Nos. 1–6, May 1895–July 1899. I: McKim, Mead and White. II: Adler and Sullivan. III: Daniel H. Burnham. IV: Henry I. Cobb. 1895–99. Reprint. New York: Da Capo, 1977. 750 pp., illus. $65.

Architects in Practice, New York City 1840–1900. Committee for the Preservation of Architectural Records. New York: Author (c/o AIA New York Chapter, 457 Madison Avenue, 10022), 1980. $5.

A Preliminary Checklist of the Records of Pre-1970 Architectural Firms of Greater Boston. Cambridge: Massachusetts Committee for the Preservation of Architectural Records (P.O. Box 129, 02142), 1980. 30 pp.

Albany Architects. Historic Albany Foundation. Albany, N.Y.: Author (300 Hudson Avenue, 12210), 1979. $4.

Who Built Alexandria: Architects in Alexandria, 1750–1900. Penny Morrill. Alexandria, Va.: Carlyle House Historic Park, Northern Virginia Regional Park Authority, 1979. 43 pp.

The Architects of Norton. Curtis Dahl. Norton, Mass.: Norton Historical Society (Box 1776, 02766), 1978. 20 pp. $2.

Charles L. Thompson and Associates: Arkansas Architects 1885–1938. F. Hampton Roy, Quapaw Quarter Association. Little Rock: August House (1010 West Third, 72201), 1983. 128 pp., illus., append., index. $17.95 hb.

Smith, Hinchman and Grylls: 125 Years of Architecture and Engineering, 1853–1978. Thomas J. Holleman and James P. Gallagher. Detroit: Wayne State University Press, 1978. 240 pp., illus., biblio., index. $19.95.

Architectural Practice

The Image of the Architect. Andrew Saint. New Haven: Yale University Press, 1983. 191 pp., illus., index. $19.95 hb.

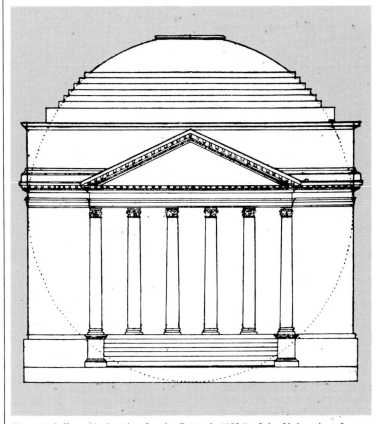

Thomas Jefferson's drawing for the Rotunda (1824) of the University of Virginia, Charlottesville, Va., based on classical Roman proportions. (University of Virginia)

The Architect: Chapters in the History of the Profession. Spiro Kostof, ed. New York: Oxford University Press, 1976. $35 hb.

The Making of an Architect 1881–1981. For the Centennial of the Columbia School of Architecture. Richard Oliver, ed. New York: Rizzoli, 1982. 271 pp., illus. $30 hb.

Architect? A Candid Guide to the Profession. Roger K. Lewis. Cambridge: MIT Press, 1985. 278 pp. $17.50 hb, $9.95 pb.

Architects and Firms: A Sociological Perspective on Architectural Practice. Judith R. Blau. Cambridge: MIT Press, 1984. 200 pp. $19.95 hb.

The Architect and His Client Through the Ages: A Bibliography of Books and Articles. Carole Cable. Monticello, Ill.: Vance Bibliographies, 1979. 17 pp. $1.50 pb.

Charrettes on Architects

Conversations with Architects. John W. Cook and Heinrich Klotz. Introduction by Vincent Scully. New York: Praeger, 1973. 272 pp.

Philip Johnson, Kevin Roche, Paul Rudolph, Bertrand Goldberg, Morris Lapidus, Louis Kahn, Charles Moore, Robert Venturi and Denise Scott Brown.

American Architecture Now. Barbaralee Diamonstein. New York: Rizzoli, 1980. 253 pp., illus.

I.M. Pei, Hugh Hardy, Cesar Pelli, Richard Meier, John Portman, Frank O. Gehry, Charles Moore, Michael Graves, Richard Weinstein, Jonathan Barnett, Robert A.M. Stern, Charles Gwathmey, James Stewart Polshek and Edward Larrabee Barnes.

Analysis of Precedent: An Investigation of Elements, Relationships, and Ordering Ideas in the Work of Eight Architects. Roger Clark, Michael Pause and Students. Student Publication, Vol. 28. Raleigh: School of Design, North Carolina State University, 1979. 229 pp.

Alvar Aalto, Louis Kahn, Charles Moore, James Stirling, Mitchell/ Giurgola, Le Corbusier, Andrea Palladio, and Venturi and Rauch.

Five California Architects. Esther McCoy. 1960./New York: Holt, Rinehart and Winston, 1982. 200 pp., illus. $12.50.

Bernard Maybeck, Irving Gill, Henry M. Greene and Charles S. Greene and Rudolph Schindler.

Drawing by Alexander J. Davis for Lyndhurst (1838, 1864–65), a National Trust property in Tarrytown, N.Y. (Louis H. Frohman, NTHP)

On the Edge of the World: Four Architects in San Francisco at the Turn of the Century. Richard W. Longstreth. Cambridge: MIT Press, 1983. 350 pp., illus. $40 hb.

Bernard Maybeck, Ernest Coxhead, Willis Polk and A.C. Schweinfurth.

Architects on Architecture: New Directions in America. Paul Heyer. 1966. Rev. ed. New York: Walker, 1978. 416 pp., illus., biblio., index. $14.95 pb.

The architectural theories and practices of 41 leading architects and firms from tape-recorded interviews.

Global Architecture Series. Yukio Futagawa, ed. Tokyo: A.D.A. Edita Tokyo Company, Ltd. (3-12014 Sendagaya, Shibuya), 1970–.

Several series from Japan on the work of the modern masters: *Global Architecture.* $15 pb each. *Global Architecture Interiors.* $22.50 pb each. *Global Architecture Houses.* $22.50 pb each. *Global Architecture Details.* $15 pb each.

On Architects: A Selection
Charles Bulfinch

The Architecture of Charles Bulfinch. Harold Kirker. Cambridge: Harvard University Press, 1969. Illus. $20.

Daniel Burnham

Burnham of Chicago: Architect and Planner. Thomas S. Hines. New York: Oxford University Press, 1974. 445 pp., illus. $35 hb. Chicago: University of Chicago Press, 1979. $6.95 pb.

Daniel H. Burnham, Architect, Planner of Cities. Charles Moore. 1921. Reprint. New York: Da Capo, 1968. 498 pp., illus. $55.

Frank Furness

Architecture of Frank Furness. James F. O'Gorman and George E. Thomas. Philadelphia: Museum of Art, 1973. 212 pp., illus.

Cass Gilbert

Cass Gilbert, 1859–1934. Lamia Doumato. Monticello, Ill.: Vance Bibliographies, 1980. 10 pp.

Bertram Grosvenor Goodhue

Bertram Grosvenor Goodhue. Richard Oliver. Cambridge: MIT Press, 1983. 297 pp., illus. $30 hb.

Greene and Greene

Greene and Greene: Architecture as a Fine Art. Randell L. Makinson. Salt Lake City: Peregrine Smith, 1977. 288 pp., illus. $19.95 pb.

A Guide to the Work of Greene and Greene. Randell L. Makinson. Salt Lake City: Peregrine Smith, 1974. 65 pp., illus.

The Firm of Greene and Greene and Its Impact on California Domestic Architecture: A Selected Bibliography. Robert B. Harmon. Monticello, Ill.: Vance Bibliographies, 1980. 13 pp.

A Greene and Greene Guide. Johann Strand and Gregory Cloud. Pasadena, Calif.: Gran Dahlstrom/Castle Press, 1974. 112 pp., illus. $8.

Greene and Greene: Architects in the Residential Style. William R. and Karen Current. Dobb's Ferry, N.Y.: Morgan, 1974. 128 pp., illus. $10.95 pb.

Walter Gropius

"Walter Gropius, A Bibliography," Caroline Shillaber. Vol. 1, 1965. "Walter Gropius, A Bibliography of Writings By and About Walter Gropius," William B. O'Neal, ed. Vol. 6, 1966. "A Supplement to the Bibliography of Walter Gropius," Ise Gropius and William B. O'Neal, eds. Vol. 9, 1972. *American Association of Architectural Bibliographers' Papers.* Charlottesville: University Press of Virginia. $10 each.

Walter Gropius. James Marston Fitch. New York: Braziller, 1960.

Holabird and Roche

"Holabird and Roche, Chicago Architects." J. William Rudd, ed. *American Association of Architectural Bibliographers' Papers,* vol. 2. Charlottesville: University Press of Virginia, 1966. $10.

Richard Morris Hunt

Richard Morris Hunt. Paul R. Baker. Cambridge: MIT Press, 1980. 588 pp., illus. $49.95 hb.

Benjamin Henry Latrobe's drawings of the entrance hall, Decatur House (1818), Washington, D.C. (Library of Congress)

Thomas Jefferson

"Jefferson as an Architect," William B. O'Neal, ed. *American Association of Architectural Bibliographers' Papers*, vol. 6. Charlottesville: University Press of Virginia, 1969. $10.

Mr. Jefferson. Architect. Desmond Guinness and Julius Trousdale Sadler, Jr. New York: Viking, 1973. 177 pp., illus.

Thomas Jefferson, Architect. Fiske Kimball. 1916. Reprint. Introduction by Frederick D. Nichols. New York: Da Capo, 1968. 348 pp., illus. $85.

Thomas Jefferson Landscape Architect. Frederick D. Nichols and Ralph E. Griswold. Charlottesville: University Press of Virginia, 1977. 196 pp., illus. $4.95 pb.

Philip Johnson

Philip Johnson: Writings. Preface by Vincent Scully. Introduction by Peter Eisenman. Commentary by Robert Stern. New York: Oxford University Press, 1978. 291 pp., illus.

Philip Johnson/John Burgee: Architecture. Nory Miller. New York: Random House, 1979. 120 pp., illus. $35 hb.

Louis I. Kahn

Louis I. Kahn. Romaldo Giurgola and Jaimini Mehta. Foreword by Jonas A. Salk. Boulder, Colo.: Westview Press, 1976.

Louis I. Kahn. Vincent Scully, Jr. New York: Braziller, 1962.

"Louis Kahn and Paul Zucker, Two Bibliographies," Jack P. Brown and Arnold Markowitz. *American Association of Architectural Bibliographers' Papers*, vol. 12. New York: Garland Publishing, 1978. 153 pp. $23.

Louis I. Kahn: Complete Works. Heinza Ronner, Shard Jhaweri and Allesandro Vasella. Boulder, Colo.: Westview Press, 1977.

Between Silence and Light: Spirit in the Architecture of Louis I. Kahn. John Lobell. Boulder, Colo.: Shambhala Books, 1979. 120 pp. $10.95 pb.

Minard Lafever

Architecture of Minard Lafever. Jacob Landy. New York: Columbia University Press, 1970. 313 pp., illus. $35 hb.

Benjamin Henry Latrobe

"Benjamin Henry Latrobe," Paul F. Norton, ed. *American Association of Architectural Bibliographers' Papers*, vol. 9. Charlottesville: University Press of Virginia, 1972. $10.

The Engineering Drawings of Benjamin Henry Latrobe. Darwin H. Stapleton, ed. New Haven: Yale University Press, 1980. 256 pp., illus. $90 hb.

Benjamin Henry Latrobe. Talbot F. Hamlin. New York: Oxford University Press, 1955. 633 pp., illus.

Bernard Maybeck

Bernard Maybeck: Artisan, Architect, Artist. Kenneth Cardwell. Salt Lake City: Peregrine Smith, 1977. 260 pp., illus. $19.95 pb.

Bernard Ralph Maybeck (1862–1957), the Extraordinary California Architect. James Carlton Starbuck. Monticello, Ill.: Vance Bibliographies, 1978. A-8. $1.50 pb.

Maybeck, The Family View. Jacomena Maybeck. Berkeley, Calif.: Berkeley Architectural Heritage Association, 1980. 39 pp.

McKim, Mead and White

McKim, Mead and White, Architects. Leland M. Roth. New York: Harper and Row, 1983. 463 pp., illus., biblio., append., index. $40 hb.

McKim, Mead and White: Architects. Richard Guy Wilson. New York: Rizzoli, 1983. 240 pp., illus., biblio., appends., index. $35 hb.

The Architecture of McKim, Mead and White, 1870–1920: A Building List. Leland M. Roth. New York: Garland Publishing, 1978. 555 pp., illus. $59.

Ludwig Mies van der Rohe

Mies van der Rohe. Philip C. Johnson. A Museum of Modern Art Book. 1947. Rev. ed. Boston: New York Graphic Society, 1979. 207 pp., illus. $9.95 pb.

Mies van der Rohe. David Spaeth. New York: Rizzoli, 1985. 192 pp., illus. $25 pb.

Mies van der Rohe. Werner Blaser. New York: Praeger, 1972. 203 pp., illus. $8.50 hb, $3.95 pb.

"Ludwig Mies van der Rohe: An Annotated Bibliography and Chronology," David A. Spaeth, ed. *American Association of Architectural Bibliographers' Papers*, vol. 13. New York: Garland Publishing, 1979. 290 pp. $36.

Richard Neutra

Richard J. Neutra and the Blending of House and Nature in American Architecture. Robert B. Harmon. Monticello, Ill.:Vance Bibliographies, 1980. 13 pp.

Richard Neutra. Esther McCoy. New York: Braziller, 1960.

Richard Neutra Building With Nature. Dion Neutra. New York: Universe Books, 1971. 223 pp., illus.

Richard Neutra and the Search for Modern Architecture: A Biography and History. Thomas S. Hines. New York: Oxford University Press, 1982. $49.95 hb, $29.95 pb.

I.M. Pei

The Buildings of I.M. Pei and His Firm. James C. Starbuck. Monticello, Ill.: Vance Bibliographies, 1978. A-21. 14 pp. $1.50 pb.

Purcell and Elmslie

"A Guide to the Architecture of Purcell and Elmslie," David Gebhard. Park Forest, Ill.: *The Prairie School Review,* First Quarter, 1965.

"The Work of Purcell and Elmslie," David Gebhard, ed. In *The Western Architect.* 1913, 1915. Reprint. Park Forest, Ill.: Prairie School Press, 1965. 92 pp., illus.

Henry Hobson Richardson

The Architecture of H.H. Richardson and His Times. Henry-Russell Hitchcock. 1936. 2nd ed., rev. Cambridge: MIT Press, 1966. 343 pp., illus., biblio., index. $9.95 pb.

H.H. Richardson: Complete Architectural Works. Jeffrey Karl Ochsner. Cambridge: MIT Press, 1982. 466 pp., illus., appends., index. $55 hb, $25 pb.

H.H. Richardson and His Office: Selected Drawings. James F. O'Gorman, ed. 1974. Reprint. Cambridge: MIT Press, 1979. 220 pp., color illus., appends., index. $55 hb.

Henry Hobson Richardson and His Works. Mariana Griswold Van Rensselaer. 1888. Reprint. New York: Dover, 1969. 152 pp., illus. $6 pb.

Henry Hobson Richardson, Boston Architect. L. Doumato. Monticello, Ill.: Vance Bibliographies, 1979. 15 pp. $1.50 pb.

John Wellborn Root

The Meaning of Architecture: Buildings and Writings by John Wellborn Root. Donald Hoffmann, ed. New York: Horizon Press, 1967. 238 pp., illus.

Eero Saarinen

Eero Saarinen on His Work: A Selection of Buildings Dating from 1947 to 1964, With Statements by the Architect. Aline R. Saarinen, ed. 1962. Rev. ed. New Haven: Yale University Press, 1968. 115 pp., illus.

William Strickland

William Strickland, Architect and Engineer. Agnes Addison Gilchrist. 1950. Reprint. New York: Da Capo, 1969. 161 pp., illus. $32.50 hb.

Louis H. Sullivan

Autobiography of an Idea. Louis H. Sullivan. 1924. Reprint. New York: Dover, 1956. $6 pb.

The Drawings of Louis Henry Sullivan: A Catalogue of the Frank Lloyd Wright Collection at the Avery Architectural Library. Paul E. Sprague. Princeton: Princeton University Press, 1979. $42.50.

Louis Sullivan: Prophet of Modern Architecture. Hugh Morrison. 1935. Reprint. New York: W.W. Norton, 1962. 391 pp., illus. $5.95.

Louis Sullivan and the Polemics of Modern Architecture. David S. Andrew. Champaign: University of Illinois Press, 1985. $19.95.

William Thornton

William Thornton: A Renaissance Man in the Federal City. Elinor Stearns and David N. Yerkes. Washington, D.C.: American Institute of Architects Foundation, 1976. 58 pp., illus.

Richard M. Upjohn

Richard Upjohn: Architect and Churchman. Everard Upjohn. 1939. Reprint. New York: Da Capo, 1968. 243 pp., illus. $25 hb.

Robert Venturi

Robert Charles Venturi: A Bibliography. Lamia Doumato. Monticello, Ill.: Vance Bibliographies, 1978. A-25. 15 pp. $1.50.

Frederick C. Withers

The Architecture of Frederick Clarke Withers and the Progress of the Gothic Revival in America After 1850. Francis R. Kowsky. Middletown, Conn.: Wesleyan University Press, 1980. 225 pp., illus. $25 hb.

Frank Lloyd Wright

An Autobiography. Frank Lloyd Wright. 1943. Reprint. New York: Horizon Press, 1976. 371 pp., illus. $17.50.

The Architecture of Frank Lloyd Wright: A Complete Catalog. William Allin Storrer. 1974. 2nd ed. Cambridge: MIT Press, 1982. 507 pp., illus. $11.95 pb.

Writings on Wright: Selected Comment on Frank Lloyd Wright. H. Allen Brooks, ed. Cambridge: MIT Press, 1981. 229 pp., illus., index. $7.95 pb.

Frank Lloyd Wright. Vincent Scully, Jr. New York: Braziller, 1960. 128 pp., illus. $7.95 pb.

In the Nature of Materials: The Buildings of Frank Lloyd Wright, 1887–1941. Henry-Russell Hitchcock. 1942. Reprint. New York: Da Capo, 1973. 178 pp., illus. $35 hb, $12.95 pb.

The Architecture of Frank Lloyd Wright: A Guide to Extant Structures. William Allin Storrer. Columbia, S.C.: WAS Productions (3118 Wheat Street, Suite S, 29205), 1979. $6.50 pb.

Frank Lloyd Wright: His Life and His Architecture. Robert C. Twombly. New York: John Wiley and Sons, 1979. 444 pp. $32.50 hb.

Frank Lloyd Wright: His Life, His Work, His Words. Olgivanna L. Wright. New York: Horizon Press, 1966. 224 pp., illus. $10.

Frank Lloyd Wright. Thomas A. Heinz. New York: St. Martin's, 1982. 96 pp., color illus. $12.95 pb.

Man About Town: Frank Lloyd Wright in New York City. Herbert Muschamp. Cambridge: MIT Press, 1983. 224 pp., illus. $15 hb.

Frank Lloyd Wright: Organic Architect and Planner. Cortus T. Koehler. Monticello, Ill.: Vance Bibliographies, 1978. A-19. 17 pp. $1.50 pb.

The Frank Lloyd Wright Book Reviews. Patrick Joseph Meehan. Monticello, Ill.: Vance Bibliographies, 1980. A-254.

"Frank Lloyd Wright in Print 1959–1970," James Muggenberg, ed. *American Association of Architectural Bibliographers' Papers,* vol. 9. Charlottesville: University Press of Virginia, 1972. $10.

Frank Lloyd Wright Archival Sources: A Research Guide to Collections and Manuscripts. Patrick J. Meehan. New York: Garland Publishing, 1983. 500 pp., illus. $100 hb.

Frank Lloyd Wright Newsletter
Frank Lloyd Wright Association
P.O. Box 2100
Oak Park, Ill. 60303

Frank Lloyd Wright
Special Research Collection
Howe Architectural Library
College of Architecture
Arizona State University
Tempe, Ariz. 85281

Frank Lloyd Wright Foundation
Taliesin West
Scottsdale, Ariz. 85261

The master, Frank Lloyd Wright, instructing young Taliesin Fellowship apprentices at Taliesin East, Spring Green, Wis., about 1936. (Hedrich-Blessing)

Drawing of the drafting room at Taliesin East (1911–52), Spring Green, Wis., the studio, school and home established and designed by Frank Lloyd Wright. (© The Frank Lloyd Wright Foundation 1980)

Architects working in the drafting room at Taliesin East, using the specially designed original furniture. (Wollin Studios Ltd.)

H. H. Richardson, c. 1883. From *H. H. Richardson and His Office.*

A Fountainhead of Architects

It is to restore humanity that, at least in part, this book has been written. . . . The collective result is meant to form a bouillabaisse of a book, a great mess of pottage where the carrots, peas and potatoes (words), and dumplings (architects) stand out within a common cookery (architecture). As in cooking, the parts are both bland and spicy, a bite here setting the mouth afire, a bite there bland reality.

Norval White, *The Architecture Book*

Louis H. Sullivan, "saint of the Chicago School of architecture."

Excerpted from *The Architecture Book:*

Bulfinch, Charles (1763–1844)
The State House on Beacon Hill crowns Boston. . . . Bulfinch will always be remembered in official histories for *this* state house at the center of America's early beginnings.

Burnham, Daniel H. (1846–1912)
Grand planning consultant. . . . His greatest influence was through direction and orchestration of the Chicago World's Fair of 1893 (World's Columbian Exposition), which redirected the main route of elite architecture from the recently virile and vigorous Chicago School . . . to a Neoclassical city-sized advertisement for the École des Beaux Arts. . . . Lastly, Burnham was given the Capitol as a toy, and he projected completion of the grand neo-Baroque boulevard system for the District of Columbia. . . .

Davis, Alexander Jackson (1803–92)
Versatile American architect . . . who ranged from Greek to Gothic Revival, all with consummate talent and taste. . . . Davis was one step beyond the copybooks that made individualistic architecture then possible (and he wrote some of his own for others).

Furness, Frank (1839–1912)
Ultimate Victorian. . . . Furness exuberantly combined the bizarre Classical-Gothic vocabulary of the late nineteenth century with its technology of iron, as in the Pennsylvania Academy of Fine Arts. Long ignored, if not forgotten.

Gilbert, Cass (1859–1934)
The Woolworth (5 and 10) Building (1913, New York) was for 17 years the tallest building in the world. . . . Gilbert's gilt pyramidal-towered U.S. Courthouse (New York) and Supreme Court building (Washington) are less radical (or modern) but are careful artifice at the least.

Gill, Irving (1870–1936)
Remembered for his period of cut, sliced, pure-white stuccoed concrete block form. . . . In fact, Gill's work in the semitropical watered desert of Los Angeles was romantic, a foil to verdant nature.

Greene, Charles Sumner (1868–1957) and Greene, Henry Mather (1870–1954)
The saving graces of Los Angeles. . . . The greatest "stick" architects ever, their braced, pegged, interlocked fir-timbered buildings (Gamble House, Pasadena) would bear the respect of a classic Japanese carpenter.

Jefferson, Thomas (1743–1826)
Architect, legislator, and U.S. president. Perhaps the last "renaissance" man . . . admirer and connoisseur of Greek and Roman civilization, "democracy," and archaelogy; architect by self-education but that more so, and more professionally, than his contemporaries; inventor; multiple elitist, ruralist, and antiurbanist; man, father, country gentleman.

Johnson, Philip (1906–)
Midwesterner (Cleveland), he stormed New York (at age 26) with an exhibition and book touting an "International Style" (1932; with Henry-Russell Hitchcock). . . . At 43 he built one of the great touchstones to which historians relate: His own glass-pavilioned house in New Canaan, Connecticut, based on his admiration for Mies van der Rohe. . . . One of the most spontaneous and verbally articulate architects of the century, Johnson is a wonderful anachronism of grace, manners, and versatility. . . .

W. R. Mead, Charles Follen McKim and Stanford White, c. 1905.

Philip Johnson in the 1970s. (Carleton Knight III, NTHP)

Kahn, Louis I. (1901–74)

Kahn's middle-aged self-renaissance searched anew for the reasons for architecture's forms. . . . His success is mixed, his intentions magnificent, and, on occasion, he may have created the greatest buildings of the 1960s and 1970s, as in the new Capitol of Bangladesh at Dacca (formerly East Pakistan) and the Salk Institute at La Jolla, California. . . . He may be remembered as the greatest American architect after Frank Lloyd Wright.

Latrobe, Benjamin (1764–1820)

At the age of 31 he assisted Thomas Jefferson in the exterior detailing and completion of the Capitol at Richmond, Virginia. Later, and on his own, he did the Waterworks of Philadelphia. . . . Most memorable is his participation in the design and construction of *the* Capitol at Washington.

McKim, Charles Follen (1847–1909)

McKim and Stanford White were the two "design" partners of McKim, Mead and White. . . . But McKim is, without question, the designer of the greatest Roman bath away from home, old Pennsylvania Station. . . . The Boston Public Library (now expanded by Philip Johnson) is an austere Renaissance palace, dour in the way that Boston has always unconsciously aped Florence.

Mies van der Rohe, Ludwig (1886–1969)

German American. One of a modern pantheon in architectural literature, with Le Corbusier and Wright, he countered the former's concrete plasticity and the latter's spatial extravaganzas with a serene set of boxes. . . . The Seagram Building is a bronze and bronzed-glass classic lesson in office building construction that has been revived for many clients in many cities, but always less successfully. . . . But with the humor of many great architects, he lived in an ornate Victorian house, painted white for purity, but exotic in detail.

Mills, Robert (1781–1855)

The Washington Monument (1836–84), superobelisk that would have made Imhotep slaver with jealousy, is his apogee. . . . Mills built the quite magnificent U.S. Treasury (1839) in a Roman and Renaissance Revival.

Renwick, James, Jr. (1818–95)

As a youth he competed for the design of Grace Church, won it with a supremely competent English neo-Gothic country church design which sits today as a pivot on bent Broadway at 10th Street, New York City. . . . St. Patrick's Cathedral (1858–79, with later towers) extended Grace. . . . The Smithsonian Institution in Washington is Renwick's too, a brick crenelated palace.

Richardson, Henry Hobson (1838–86)

Richardson was one of a chain of great nineteenth-century American architects, each working for the former and inspiring the further development of his successor: Frank Furness, Richardson, Louis Sullivan and Frank Lloyd Wright. Richardsonian Romanesque is a full-blown American style drawn from Richardson's fascination with utilitarian use of Romanesque arches, with rock-faced (superrock) stonework surrounding. . . . Richardson fancied himself as a medieval monk and had the gall to dress in monkly robes on occasion.

Sullivan, Louis H. (1856–1924)

Saint of the Chicago School of architecture, where the skyscraper was born and where its aesthetics was refined to fulfill a building type (elevator-served steel cage) totally new. . . . The Wainwright Building in St. Louis, the Guaranty Trust Building in Buffalo, the Condict Building in New York City—all remain, . . . ornamented with the quasi-Art Nouveau decoration that Sullivan invented and developed himself. . . . After the World's Columbian Exposition (Chicago World's Fair of 1893), his practice declined, for the corporate clients of America were overtaken by the fair's neo-Renaissance architecture.

White, Stanford (1853–1906)

One of the greatest and most facile architects of all time. He was rich, and of the rich; gourmand, gourmet, lover, and bon vivant: peer architect for peer clients. Most important of his products are the Low House at Bristol, Rhode Island, demolished by a nouveau riche dwarf, and the Newport Casino, happily still there, and worth as much as a score of modern "monuments." White worked for H.H. Richardson, savored his shingle style, seriously contributed to its elegant advancement (Low House), and then wandered into Queene Anne eclecticism.

Wright, Frank Lloyd (1869–1959)

It is hard to separate reality from wishful fantasy, but Wright was, and is, the greatest American architect, even though he said he was! Victorian-born and -bred, Celtic romantic by inheritance, he was steeped in architecture by his mother, who hung etchings of medieval cathedrals over his crib! . . . He lived so long and worked so productively that he should have been a series of men.

THE ARCHITRAVE

JULY 1938

Magazine of the Women's Architectural Club, Chicago. Designed by Ruth H. Perkins.

THE FAIR WOMEN
Jeanne Madeline Weimann

The Story of The Woman's Building
World's Columbian Exposition
Chicago 1893

Sophia Hayden, architect of the Woman's Building (1893), World's Columbian Exposition, Chicago. (MIT Historical Collections)

Women's Work

Even male architects tend to have low public profiles. . . . But women architects are superanonymous.

Paul Gapp, "Superanonymous in Chicago . . . Until Now." *Chicago Tribune,* January 8, 1978.

Anonymity seemed a condition for women, given the prevailing role-models of the past: the white-gloved gentleman-architect of Stanford White's era, or the cape-wearing rugged individualist of Frank Lloyd Wright's.

Suzanne Stephens, "The Women Behind the T Square." Introduction to "Women in Architecture." *Progressive Architecture,* March 1977.

"Women have always been active in planning domestic environments. Countless, anonymous women designed or built houses for their own families. In the 19th century, the writings of Catharine Beecher epitomized the movement that considered house-keeping a science and designed for that purpose. . . . Nineteenth- and early twentieth-century women architects are obscure. Seldom mentioned in histories of American architecture or even local guides, their achievements are more nearly unknown than forgotten. Prejudice nourished anonymity. Denied advancement and frequently employment by established architectural firms, women usually practiced alone or in small offices. . . . Those who departed from the Victorian code of babies, blushes, and bustles risked being labeled improper, peculiar, or both. . . . Today most of their names are faded as the facades they designed. Yet their accomplishments are remarkable."

Judith Paine, "Pioneer Women Architects." In *Women in American Architecture*

First Ladies

Irwin, Harriet (1828–97)
Without architectural training, Irwin patented in 1869 the first dwelling plan by an American woman.

Hicks, Margaret (1858–83)
The first woman architecture graduate—from Cornell, 1880—and the first woman architect to publish her work.

Riddle, Theodate Pope (1868–1946)
When she was refused admission to Princeton's architecture classes in the 1890s, Riddle hired its faculty to tutor her privately.

Hayden, Sophia (1869–1953)
Hayden's first distinction was to become the first woman to graduate from MIT's full four-year program in 1890. Then, in 1893, at age 22, she won the coveted competition to design the Woman's Building at the World's Columbian Exposition.

Bethune, Louise (1856–1913)
This first woman fellow of the AIA opened her own office at age 25 and disdained domestic designs in favor of apartment buildings, schools, stores and industrial structures.

Morgan, Julia (1872–1957)
The first woman in the world to study at the Ecole des Beaux-Arts in Paris, Morgan was among America's most prolific women architects—designing more than 800 buildings. Her most well known: the fantasy castle of San Simeon (1919).

Griffin, Marion Mahony (1871–1961)
The first woman licensed to practice architecture in Illinois, where she worked for Frank Lloyd Wright in his Oak Park studio. Her drawings announced Wright to the world in 1910 and helped her husband, Walter Burley Griffin, win the competition to design the new capital of Australia in 1912.

Women in American Architecture: A Historic and Contemporary Perspective. Susanna Torre, ed. New York: Whitney Library of Design, 1977. 224 pp., illus., chart, notes, biblio., index. $26.50 hb.
"This book is aimed at altering and renovating perceptions of women in a field of master builders." (Ricky Rosenthal, *Christian Science Monitor,* May 17, 1977) It is also the first in-depth survey summarizing and evaluating women's role in American architecture. The book is divided into five parts with chapters by 13 authors: Woman's Place: The Design of Domestic Space; Women in the Architectural Profession: A Historic Perspective; Women as Critics; Women in the Architectural Profession: A Contemporary Perspective; and Women's Spatial Symbolism.

From Tipi to Skyscraper: A History of Women in Architecture. Doris Cole. Boston: i press, 1973. Distributed by MIT Press. 136 pp., illus. $5.95 pb.

"On the Fringe of the Profession," Gwendolyn Wright. In *The Architect: Chapters in the History of the Profession.* Spiro Kostof, ed. New York: Oxford University Press, 1976. $35 hb.

Women as Architects: A Historical View. Lamia Doumato. Monticello, Ill.: Vance Bibliographies, 1978. A-6. 12 pp. $1.50 pb.

Women in American Architecture Historic Chart. Architectural League of New York. $2.50.

Exterior of the Woman's Building (1893, Sophia Hayden), World's Columbian Exposition, Chicago. From *The Fair Women.* (Chicago Historical Society)

San Simeon (1919–37, Julia Morgan), the California castle designed for William Randolph Hearst. (California Department of Natural Resources)

The Fair Women: The Story of The Woman's Building, World's Columbian Exposition, Chicago 1893. Jeanne Madeline Weimann. Chicago: Academy Chicago, 1981. 500 pp., illus. $29.95 hb, $14.95 pb.

Julia Morgan: Architect. Richard W. Longstreth. Berkeley: Berkeley Architectural Heritage Association, 1977. 33 pp.

Architectural Drawings by Julia Morgan: Beaux-Arts Assignments and Other Buildings. Exhibit catalog. Therese Heyman and John Beach. Oakland: Oakland Museum (1000 Oak Street, 94607), 1976. 14 pp., illus. $2 pb.

"The Early Work of Marion Mahony Griffin," David T. Van Zanten. *The Prairie School Review,* Second Quarter 1966.

Mary Colter: Builder Upon the Red Earth. Virginia L. Grattan. Flagstaff, Ariz.: Northland Press (P.O. Box N, 86002), 1980. 131 pp., illus., biblio, index.

"Early K.C. Architect: A Liberated Woman (Nelle E. Peters)," Sherry Piland. *Historic Kansas City News,* April 1978.

The Feminine Influence

The Grand Domestic Revolution: A History of Feminist Designs for American Homes, Neighborhoods, and Cities. Dolores Hayden. Cambridge: MIT Press, 1981. 384 pp., illus. $9.95 pb.

New Space for Women. Gerda R. Wekerle, Rebecca Peterson and David Morley, eds. Boulder, Colo.: Westview Press, 1980. 332 pp., illus., biblio. $15 pb.

The Feminine Influence in Architecture: A Selected Bibliography. Robert B. Harmon. Monticello, Ill.: Vance Bibliographies, 1980. A-243. 10 pp. $2 pb.

"Women in Architecture." *Heresies,* Issue 11. New York: Heresies Collective (P.O. Box 766, Canal Street Station, 10013), 1980.

Women in Landscape Architecture

Women, Design, and the Cambridge School. Dorothy May Anderson. West Lafayette, Ind.: PDA Publishers, 1980. 241 pp. $15.95 hb.

"History of Women in Landscape Architecture," George Arthur Yarwood. *ASLA Bulletin,* July 1973.

"Women in Design." *Design and Environment,* Spring 1974.

Contacts
Women in Architecture Committee
American Institute of Architects
1735 New York Avenue, N.W.
Washington, D.C. 20006

Archive of Women in Architecture
Architectural League of New York
457 Madison Avenue
New York, N.Y. 10022

Women's School of Planning and Architecture
Box 102, Palomar Arcade
Santa Cruz, Calif. 95060

See also: Houses, Women's Sites

Black Architects

A view of Black architects (or any architects) or their work would have to consider time and social forces before aesthetic value could be given to their work. . . . Identification of Black architects or architecture by Blacks, and its relationship to the total Black community of the time, will tell us more about the development of [Black] people over time.

> Richard K. Dozier, "Black Architects and Craftsmen." *Black World*, May 1974.

Drafting room of the Tuskegee Institute in 1893, the first black college to offer a certificate in architecture.

A recent Tuskegee Institute architectural student and Professor Richard K. Dozier examine a high-rise model.

"The African slave brought only the products of his mind to the new world, including the skills of ironworking, woodcarving and proficiency in the use of earth and stone. His innovations in the application of these skills qualified him as an architect alongside many other early American craftsmen.

The colonial plantation system relied upon its slave craftsmen to produce all furniture and tools, and often buildings. . . .

After traveling through the 19th century South, Frederick Law Olmsted wrote that the best houses and the most beautiful grounds that he had visited in Louisiana belonged to a nearly full-blooded Negro.

It is quite possible that the house Olmsted was referring to belonged to a son of Marie Therese, an ex-slave who gained her freedom in 1778, received two land grants from the Spanish government and by 1803 had acquired at least 4,000 acres. Here she established Melrose plantation, which became the center of the Metoyer land holdings of 13,000 acres, which in turn became known as Isle Brevelle, a settlement of 'free people of color'.

Louis Metoyer, one of Marie's 14 children, studied architecture in Paris and is responsible for the design of the Melrose mansion and many of the later buildings in Isle Brevelle. The main buildings of Melrose and its church, also built by Louis Metoyer, remain standing today. The most unusual of these buildings is the African house, built around 1800. Of purely African design, it is the only structure of its type now standing in the U.S. and recently was designated a national landmark."

> Richard Dozier, "The Black Architectural Experience in America." *AIA Journal*, July 1976.

"Blacks have only a small representation in architecture nationally. According to an estimate by the American Institute of Architects, less than one per cent of the nation's 36,000 licensed architects are black. The total black and Hispanic representation is about one per cent, or 360 architects."

> Robert E. Tomasson, "Blacks' Role in Architecture Widens Slowly." *New York Times*, August 27, 1972.

"Black Craftsmen and Architects in History," Richard K. Dozier. *Journal of the Society of Architectural Historians*, October 1974.

"Tuskegee Institute: From Humble Beginnings to National Shrine," Richard K. Dozier. *Historic Preservation*, January–February 1981.

"Afro-American Architecture and the Spirit of Thomas Day," Steven L. Jones. Paper prepared for Howard University School of Architecture. 1973. 92 pp., biblio. unp.

A Directory of Minority and Women-Owned Engineering and Architectural Firms. 1983. 60 pp. Available from the AIA. $15.

Contacts

National Organization of Minority Architects
c/o Marshall Purnell
1730 M Street, N.W.
Suite 401
Washington, D.C. 20036

Richard K. Dozier, AIA
308 Gregory Street
Tuskegee Institute, Ala. 36088

See also: Black Sites

Novel Architects

It may be just as well that the architect does not appear more often in current fiction.

> Cecil D. Elliott

"Another View: The Architect as He Is Pictured in Fiction," Cecil D. Elliott. *AIA Journal*, September 1974.

An examination of the architect's treatment at the hands of fiction writers, which, contends the author, has kept alive a stereotype "throughout the recent decades in which the profession has struggled to redefine itself." Elliott surveys such classics as Charles Dicken's *The Life and Adventures of Martin Chuzzlewit,* Henrik Ibsen's *The Master Builder,* John Galsworthy's *The Man of Property* and television's "The Brady Bunch."

The Fountainhead. Ayn Rand. New York: New American Library. $3.95 pb.

The Architect. Meyer Levin. New York: Simon and Schuster, 1981.

Monticello Fault. Archibald C. Rogers. Durham, N.C.: Moore Publishing Company (P.O. Box 3036, West Durham Station, 27705), 1979. $12.95.

Union Trust Company (Clinton Day), San Francisco, under construction in 1910. (Wells Fargo Bank)

Now restored by Wells Fargo Bank, the 1910 landmark was a banking showcase when it opened. (Wells Fargo Bank)

Building Technology

How very little since things were made,
Things have altered in the building trade.

Rudyard Kipling, "A Truthful Song." *Rewards and Fairies.* 1949.

Bibliography of the History of Technology. Eugene S. Ferguson. Society for the History of Technology. Cambridge: MIT Press, 1968. 347 pp.

Includes general bibliographies and library lists, directories of technical, academic and business organizations, contemporary descriptions of engineering works and government publications and records.

American Building: Materials and Techniques from the Beginning of the Colonial Settlements to the Present. Carl W. Condit. 1968. 2nd ed. Chicago: University of Chicago Press, 1982. 342 pp., illus., biblio. $9.95 pb.

Four chronological periods and materials such as timber, masonry, iron, steel and reinforced concrete are explored.

Technology and Society Series. Daniel J. Boorstin, advisory ed. New York: Arno Press. Titles and prices available on request.

Books in the series survey the variety of technologies that have shaped the American experience.

The Master Builders: A History of Structural and Environmental Design from Ancient Egypt to the Nineteenth Century. Henry J. Cowan. New York: Wiley Interscience, 1977. 299 pp., illus., index, biblio. $37.50.

Science and Building: Structural and Environmental Design in the Nineteenth and Twentieth Centuries. Henry J. Cowan. New York: Wiley Interscience, 1978. 374 pp., illus., index, biblio. $49.95 hb.

It was in the 19th and 20th centuries that "science and technology transformed the traditional craft-based practice of architecture and building."

America's Wooden Age: Aspects of Its Early Technology. Brooke Hindle, ed. Tarrytown, N.Y.: Sleepy Hollow Restorations, 1975. 218 pp., illus., biblio., index. $15 hb.

Covers the earliest settlements through the mid-19th century, including the forests of New England, early lumbering and colonial watermills and waterpower.

Material Culture of the Wooden Age. Brooke Hindle, ed. Tarrytown, N.Y.: Sleepy Hollow Press, 1981. 394 pp., illus., biblio., index. $22.50 hb.

Ten essays examine the influence of wood technology on construction—farms, timber framing, ships, roads, bridges, railroads, factories—in the 18th and 19th centuries.

Why Buildings Stand Up: The Strength of Architecture. Mario Salvadori. New York: W.W. Norton, 1980. 311 pp., illus., index. $6.95 pb.

Covers basic materials, beams and columns, loads, houses, skyscrapers and bridges, plus unusual structures such as domes, tents and balloons.

The Parts of a House. Graham Blackburn. New York: Richard Marek Publishers, 1980. 192 pp., illus. $15 hb.

An alphabetically arranged exploration of how a house is put together, from anchor bolt to yoke. Descriptions of 308 elements are provided in easily understood language on the function, location, derivation and historical development of each.

Encyclopedia of How It's Built. Donald Clarke, ed. New York: A&W Publishers, 1979. 184 pp., color illus. $16.95 hb.

Explains ancient and modern technology, from bridges to underwater tunnels.

The Architecture of the Well-Tempered Environment. Reyner Banham. 1969. 2nd ed. Chicago: University of Chicago Press, 1984. 319 pp., illus., index. $12.50 pb.

An assessment of the impact of environmental technology on building design.

Structures: Or Why Things Don't Fall Down. J.E. Gordon. 1978. New York: Plenum, 1981. 395 pp., illus., appends., biblio., index. $18.95 hb, $8.95 pb.

An explanation of the forces that hold together the ordinary and essential things of the world, such as buildings and bridges.

How Buildings Work: The Natural Order of Architecture. Edward Allen. New York: Oxford University Press, 1980. 256 pp., illus. $27.50 hb.

Tools

The Tools That Built America. Alex Bealer. New York: Clarkson Potter, 1976. 212 pp., illus.

Old Ways of Working Wood: The Techniques and Tools of a Time-Honored Craft. Rev. ed. Alex W. Bealer. New York: Crown, 1980. 225 pp., illus., appends., biblio., index. $12.50 hb.

Tools That Started the Twentieth Century. Jene Lyon. Santa Fe: Lightning Tree, 1976. 112 pp. $6.95 pb.

Tools of the Woodworker. Technical Leaflet Series, nos. 24, 28, 119. Nashville: American Association for State and Local History, 1965-79. 12 pp. $2 pb each.

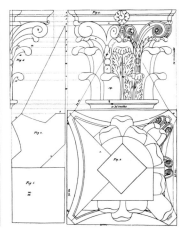

Pattern Books

*Miracles are not wholly gigantic: The Gothic
cottage, with wooden tendrils echoing life
came from a planbook, though it might have grown
by enchantment from an early novel.*

> George Zabriskie, "Window to
> the Past." In *With Heritage So
> Rich.* 1966. Rev. reprint. Wash-
> ington, D.C.: Preservation
> Press, 1983.

*Throughout the eighteenth, the nineteenth and much of
the twentieth centuries architectural pattern books have
provided the designs for a majority of America's
domestic buildings. While some of these pattern books
were essentially carpenter manuals addressed directly
to the artisan, most were general plan books which
were purchased as much by potential clients and literati
as by carpenters and builders. . . . These pattern
books were all pervasive throughout the United States,
with the result that towns and villages as well as the
residential suburban areas of the larger cities were
filled with houses derived from them.*

> David Gebhard, Introduction.
> *Picturesque California Homes*

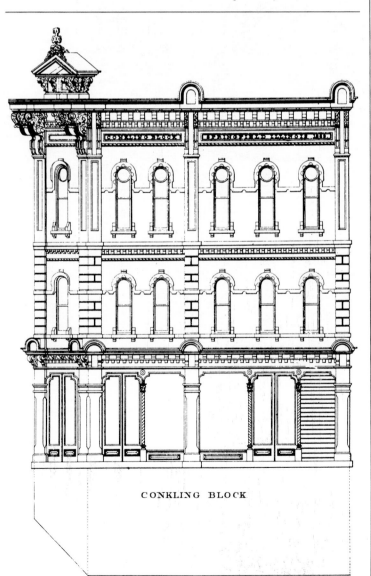

CONKLING BLOCK

Springfield, Ill., commercial building. From *Bicknell's Victorian Buildings.*

*A List of Architectural Books
Available in America Before the
Revolution.* Helen Park. Foreword by Adolf K. Placzek.
1961. Rev. ed. Los Angeles:
Hennessey and Ingalls, 1973. 95
pp. $12.95.

*American Architectural Books:
A List of Books, Portfolios and
Related Subjects* (pre-1895).
Henry-Russell Hitchcock. Intro-
duction by Adolf Placzek. 1946,
1962. Rev. ed. New York: Da
Capo, 1975. 142 pp. $21.50 hb.

Introduction, *200 Years of
American Architectural Drawings.* David Gebhard and Deborah Nevins. New York: Whitney
Library of Design, 1977. 306
pp., illus., biblio., index.

Introduction, David Gebhard.
Picturesque California Homes.
Samuel and Joseph C. Newsom.
1884. Reprint. Los Angeles:
Hennessey and Ingalls, 1978. 48
pp., illus. $18.95 pb.

Reprints: A Sampler

*The American Vignola: A Guide
to the Making of Classical Architecture.* William R. Ware.
1906. New York: W.W. Norton,
1977. 145 pp. $6.95 pb.

*American Domestic Architec-
ture.* John Calvin Stevens and
Albert Winslow Cobb. 1889.
Introduction by Earle Shut-
tleworth, Jr., and William Barry.
Watkins Glen, N.Y.: American
Life Foundation, 1978. 140 pp.
$9 pb.

The Architect. William H.
Ranlett. 1849, 1851. New York:
Da Capo, 1976. 2 vols. 169 pp.
$85 set.

*The Architecture of Country
Houses.* Andrew Jackson Downing. 1850. New York: Da Capo,
1968. 501 pp. $45 hb. New
York: Dover, 1969. $6.50 pb.

*The Beauties of Modern Archi-
tecture.* Minard Lafever. 1835.
2nd ed. Introduction by Denys
Peter Myers. New York: Da
Capo, 1968. 146 pp. $29.50 hb.

*Bicknell's Victorian Buildings:
Floor Plans and Elevations for
45 Houses and Other Structures.* A.J. Bicknell and Company. 1878. 5th ed. New York:
Dover, 1979. 128 pp. $5 pb.

City and Suburban Architect.
Samuel Sloan. 1859. New York:
Da Capo, 1975. 104 pp. $65.

The Model Architect. Samuel
Sloan. 1852. New York: Da
Capo, 1975. 2 vols. 202 pp. $95
set.

National Architect. George E.
Woodward. 1869. Watkins Glen,
N.Y.: American Life Founda-
tion, 1977. 180 pp. $25 hb. New
York: Da Capo, 1975. 48 pp.
$32.50.

*Palliser's Late Victorian Archi-
tecture.* Palliser, Palliser and
Company. 1878. 1887. Introduc-
tion by Michael A. Tomlan.
Watkins Glen, N.Y.: American
Life Foundation, 1980. 312 pp.
$20 pb.

Rural Essays. Andrew Jackson
Downing. 1854. 2nd ed. Introduction by George B. Tatum.
New York: Da Capo, 1975. 640
pp. $45 hb.

Rural Residences. Alexander J.
Davis. 1838. 2nd ed. Introduction by Jane B. Davies. New
York: Da Capo, 1979. 48 pp.,
color illus. $95 hb.

Sloan's Victorian Buildings.
Samuel Sloan. 1853. New York:
Dover, 1981. 400 pp., illus.
$13.95 pb.

Upjohn's Rural Architecture.
Richard Upjohn. 1852. New
York: Da Capo, 1975. 14 pp.
$39.50.

*Victorian Architectural Details:
Two Volumes in One.* Marcus
Fayette Cummings and Charles
Crosby Miller. 1868, 1873. Intro-
duction by Diana S. Waite.
Watkins Glen, N.Y.: American
Life Foundation, 1978. 256 pp.
$15 pb.

*Victorian Architecture: Two Pat-
tern Books.* A.J. Bicknell and
W.T. Comstock. 1873, 1881. In-
troduction by John Maass.
Watkins Glen, N.Y.: American
Life Foundation, 1978. 192 pp.
$15 pb.

Victorian Cottage Residences.
Andrew Jackson Downing. 1842.
New York: Dover. 352 pp., illus.
$6 pb.

*Victorian Country Seats and
Modern Dwellings: Two Vol-
umes in One.* Henry Hudson
Holly. 1865, 1873. Introduction
by Michael A. Tomlan. Watkins
Glen, N.Y.: American Life
Foundation, 1977. 424 pp. $12
pb.

*Villas and Cottages: A Series of
Designs Prepared for Execution
in the United States.* Calvert
Vaux. 1857. 2nd ed. New York:
Dover, 1970. $5.95 pb. New
York: Da Capo, 1968. 318 pp.
$29.50.

The Works of Asher Benjamin. Vol. I: *The Country Builder's Assistant.* 1797. 91 pp. Vol. II: *The American Builder's Companion.* 1806. 157 pp. Vol. III: *The Rudiments of Architecture.* 1814. 162 pp. Vol. IV: *The Practical House Carpenter.* 1830. 248 pp. Vol. V: *The Practice of Architecture.* 1833. 234 pp. Vol. VI: *The Builder's Guide.* 1839. 174 pp. Vol. VII: *Elements of Architecture.* 1843. 290 pp. New York: Da Capo, 1973–74. $42.50 each, $265 set.

Compilations

American Victoriana. Floor Plans and Renderings from the Gilded Age. Eugene Mitchell. Introduction by William J. Murtagh. 1980. New York: Van Nostrand Reinhold, 1983. 103 pp., color illus. $15.50 pb.

Modern American Dwellings—1897. Donald J. Berg, ed. Rockville Centre, N.Y.: Antiquity Reprints, 1981. 80 pp. $7.50 pb.

Classic Old House Plans: Three Centuries of American Domestic Architecture. Lawrence Grow. Pittstown, N.J.: Main Street Press, 1984. 128 pp., illus. $8.95 pb.

Country Patterns: A Sampler of Nineteenth Century Pattern Book Architecture. Donald J. Berg, ed. Rockville Centre, N.Y.: Antiquity Reprints, 1982. 80 pp., illus. $8 pb.

Shoppell's Modern Houses. Robert W. Shoppell. 1887. Rockville Centre, N.Y.: Antiquity Reprints, 1978. 32 pp. $5 pb.

Reprint Publishers

American Life Foundation
P.O. Box 349
Watkins Glen, N.Y. 14891

Dover Publications
180 Varick Street
New York, N.Y. 10014

Da Capo Press
227 West 17th Street
New York, N.Y. 10011

Antiquity Reprints
Box 370
Rockville Centre, N.Y. 11571

Peter Smith
6 Lexington Avenue
Magnolia, Mass. 01930

Hennessey and Ingalls
8321 Campion Drive
Los Angeles, Calif. 90045

Peregrine Smith
Box 667
Layton, Utah 84041

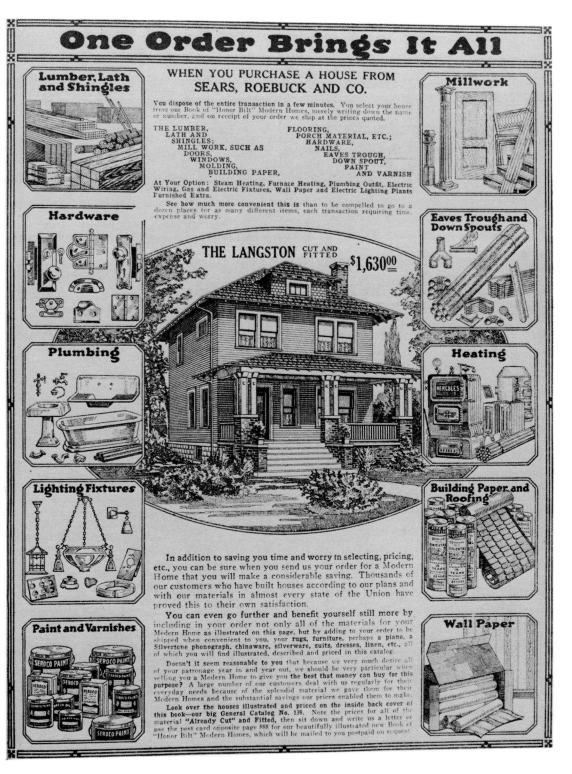

Page from Sears' "Honor Bilt" Modern Homes catalog, through which 20th-century homeowners could order not only houses but also everything to put in them.

Mail-Order Houses

"If your house dates from the late 19th or early 20th century, it could also belong to a whole different class of architecture . . . built from the mail-order plans of a faraway architect-publisher. . . . From the 1890's through about 1930, mail-order houses—entire unassembled buildings sent by rail—were a popular option in the burgeoning residential market."

> Patricia Poore, "Pattern Book Architecture: Is Yours a Mail-Order House?" *Old-House Journal,* December 1980.

"Sears, Roebuck's Best-kept Secret," Kay Halpin. *Historic Preservation,* September–October 1981.

Houses by Mail: A Field Guide to Mail-Order Houses from Sears, Roebuck and Company. Katherine H. Cole and H. Ward Jandl. Washington, D.C.: Preservation Press, 1986. 400 pp., illus.

A guide to identifying more than 450 styles offered by Sears from 1909 to 1937 for houses and other buildings. Invaluable for restoring lost features and details.

A vernacular tin-roof Mississippi Valley-type house showing French and Caribbean influences. (Lloyd Kahn. ©1978 Shelter Publications)

Vernacular Architecture

The true basis for any serious study of the art of architecture still lies in those indigenous, more humble buildings everywhere that are to architecture what folklore is to literature or folk song to music and with which academic architects were seldom concerned. . . . These many folk structures are of the soil, natural. Though often slight, their virtue is intimately related to environment and to the heart-life of the people.

> Frank Lloyd Wright, "The Sovereignty of the Individual." *Metron* (Rome), May–August 1951.

Vernacular can best be understood . . . as the place-related inflection of culture.

> Doug Swaim, Introduction. *Carolina Dwelling*

"A search for patterns in folk material yields regions, where a search for patterns in popular material yields periods."

> Henry Glassie, *Pattern in the Material Folk Culture of the Eastern United States*

"The basic form of the typical eighteenth and nineteenth century vernacular house—its plan and height—was determined by local folk tradition. Its proportions and decorative features, however, generally depended upon the latest popular architectural style to arrive in the countryside. Thus we can today read in these houses inflections towards both time and location."

> Michael Southern, *Carolina Dwelling*

Perspectives in Vernacular Architecture. Camille Wells, ed. Annapolis, Md.: Vernacular Architecture Forum, 1982. 237 pp., illus. $10 pb.

Common Places: Readings in American Vernacular Architecture. Dell Upton and John Michael Vlach, eds. Athens: University of Georgia Press, 1985. 448 pp., illus., biblio. $35 hb, $14.95 pb.

Vernacular Architecture in America: A Selective Bibliography. John Cuthbert, Barry Ward and Maggie Keeler. Boston: G. K. Hall, 1985. 145 pp., illus., index. $39.95 hb.

House Form and Culture. Amos Rapoport. Englewood Cliffs, N.J.: Prentice-Hall, 1969. 146 pp. $14.95 pb.

Discovering the Vernacular Landscape. J. B. Jackson. New Haven: Yale University Press, 1984. 179 pp., illus., index. $16.50 hb.

Wood, Brick and Stone: The North American Settlement Landscape. Allen G. Noble. Vol. 1: *Houses.* 166 pp., illus., index. $27.50 hb. Vol. 2: *Barns and Farm Structures.* $30 hb. Amherst: University of Massachusetts Press, 1984.

Home Sweet Home: American Domestic Vernacular Architecture. Charles W. Moore, Kathryn Smith and Peter Becker, eds. Craft and Folk Art Museum. New York: Rizzoli, 1983. 150 pp., illus. $17.50 pb.

Native Genius in Anonymous Architecture in North America. Sibyl Moholy-Nagy. New York: Schocken Books, 1976. 192 pp., illus.

Architecture Without Architects: A Short Introduction to Non-Pedigreed Architecture. Bernard Rudofsky. 1965. Reprint. Garden City, N.Y.: Doubleday, 1969. 157 pp. $9.95 pb.

American Folk Architecture: A Selected Bibliography. Howard Wight Marshall. Washington, D.C.: American Folklife Center, Library of Congress, 1981. 79 pp.

Common Landscape of America, 1580 to 1845. John R. Stilgoe. New Haven: Yale University Press, 1982. 429 pp., illus., biblio., index. $12.95 pb.

Regional Vernacular

Pattern in the Material Folk Culture of the Eastern United States. Henry Glassie. Philadelphia: University of Pennsylvania Press, 1968. 316 pp., illus., biblio. $7.50 pb.

Hearth and Home: Preserving a People's Culture. George W. McDaniel. Philadelphia: Temple University Press, 1982. 321 pp., illus., biblio., index. $29.95 hb.

Folk Housing in Middle Virginia: A Structural Analysis of Historic Artifacts. Henry Glassie. Knoxville: University of Tennessee Press, 1975. 246 pp., illus. $19.95 hb, $9.50 pb.

Carolina Dwelling. Towards Preservation of Place: In Celebration of the North Carolina Vernacular Landscape. Doug Swaim, ed. Student Publication, vol. 26. Raleigh: School of Design, North Carolina State University, 1978. 258 pp., illus. $10 pb.

Kentucky's Age of Wood. Kenneth W. Clarke and Ira Kohn. Lexington: University of Kentucky Press, 1976. 80 pp., illus. $6.95 hb.

Kentucky Folk Architecture. William Lynwood Montell and Michael L. Morse. Lexington: University of Kentucky Press, 1976. 120 pp., illus., biblio. $6.95 hb.

Alabama Folk Houses. Eugene M. Wilson. Montgomery: Alabama Historical Commission, 1975. 115 pp., illus., biblio. $5 pb.

Shotgun houses, brought first to Louisiana by free Haitian blacks in the early 19th century. From *Shotgun Houses*. (Preservation Alliance)

Arts, Crafts, and Architecture in Early Illinois. Betty I. Madden. Urbana: University of Illinois Press, 1974. 297 pp., illus., maps, index. $10.

Folk Architecture in Little Dixie: A Regional Culture in Missouri. Howard Wight Marshall. Columbia: University of Missouri Press, 1981. 146 pp., illus., biblio., index. $22 hb.

The Arts and Architecture of German Settlements in Missouri: A Survey of a Vanishing Culture. Charles van Ravenswaay. Columbia: University of Missouri Press, 1977. 560 pp., illus. $50 hb.

Built in Texas. Francis Edward Abernethy, ed. Texas Folklore Society. Dallas: E-Heart Press, 1979. 276 pp., illus., maps. $24.50 hb.

Pioneer Texas Buildings. Clovis Heimsath. Austin: University of Texas Press, 1968. 158 pp., illus. $19.95 hb.

Utah Folk Art: A Catalog of Material Culture. Hal Cannon, ed. Provo, Utah: Brigham Young University Press, 1980. 168 pp., illus. $10.95 pb.

The Pure Experience of Order: Essays on the Symbolic in the Folk Material Culture of Western America. Richard C. Poulsen. Albuquerque: University of New Mexico Press, 1982. 182 pp., illus., biblio., index. $21.95 hb.

Shotgun Houses

"The origin of the shotgun house lies in the history of New Orleans's black community. . . . One supposed reason for their name is that pellets from a shotgun fired through one of the outside doorways could allegedly pass through the entire building without doing any damage. . . . Although there may be two shotgun traditions—one black and one white (in the latter, the buildings are wider)—both are clearly derived from a single house form. . . . It is a house in which there is a focus on communal activity; it is an architecture of intimacy."

John Vlach, "Shotgun Houses." *Natural History,* February 1977.

A simple one-room house in rural Virginia about 1899, reflecting old Chesapeake-area building traditions. (Frances B. Johnston, Library of Congress)

Shotgun Houses: Urban Housing Opportunities. Don Weber et al. Louisville: Preservation Alliance of Louisville and Jefferson County, 1980. 36 pp., illus. $3.50 pb.

"The Shotgun Shack as Oil Boomtown Housing," Sylvia Ann Grider. Bloomington, Ind.: Folklore Publications Group (504 North Fess Street, 47401). $.55.

Contacts

Vernacular Architecture Forum
c/o Maryland Historical Trust
21 State Circle
Annapolis, Md. 21401

Pioneer America Society
Pioneer America
Department of Geography
University of Akron
Akron, Ohio 44325

Popular Culture Center
Journal of American Culture
Bowling Green State University
Bowling Green, Ohio 43403

American Folklife Center
Library of Congress
Washington, D.C. 20540

Folklore Institute
Folklore Forum
504 North Fess Street
Bloomington, Ind. 47401

American Folklore Society
Journal of American Folklore
1703 New Hampshire Avenue, N.W.
Washington, D.C. 20009

American Folklife Society
American Folklife
R.D. #2
Oley, Pa. 19547

Association of American Geographers
Annals
1710 16th Street, N.W.
Washington, D.C. 20009

American Geographical Society
Geographical Review
Broadway and 156th Street
New York, N.Y. 10032

Come-All-Ye
Legacy Books
Box 494
Hatboro, Pa. 19040

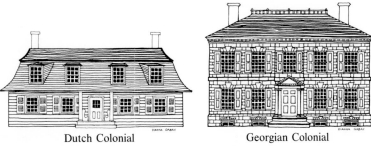

Dutch Colonial   Georgian Colonial   Federal   Greek Revival

Architectural Styles

Architecture depends on development through time in order to be clearly related to society and culture. All that is really meant by a building's "style" is that [it is] more or less understandable in terms of time.

Nathan Silver, *Lost New York.*
Boston: Houghton Mifflin, 1967.

Style is one of the most used—and abused—words in the English language, particularly when pressed into service in the study of architectural history. . . . Stylistic designations aid in describing architecture and in relating buildings—perhaps of different chronological periods—to one another. But more than that, stylistic classification acknowledges that building is not just a craft but an art form that reflects the philosophy, intellectual currents, hopes and aspirations of its time.

John Poppeliers et al., *What Style Is It?*

"If, for the word, 'style' we substitute the word, civilization, we make at once a pronounced stride in advance toward an intelligent understanding of the 'values' of the historical monuments of architecture."

Louis H. Sullivan, *Kindergarten Chats.* 1918, 1947. Rev. reprint. New York: Dover, 1979.

"We want no new style of architecture. Who wants a new style of painting or of sculpture? But we want *some* style."

John Ruskin

"All styles are good except the boring kind."
Voltaire, "L'Enfant Prodigue." 1736.

"We are used to applauding works which are pure, which have a clear paternity. . . . When confronted with a building which has two or more bloodlines we tend to regard it as uncertain or mixed up. . . . This point is, however, that hybrid building often seeks to be hybrid and we misjudge it by applying the canons of stylistic purity. . . . Basically it says with so much other romantic art, 'I'd rather be interesting than good, I prefer character to beauty.' We may disagree with the goal, but at least should try not to misunderstand it."

Charles Jencks, *Bizarre Architecture.* New York: Rizzoli, 1979.

American Architecture Since 1780: A Guide to the Styles. Marcus Whiffen. Cambridge: MIT Press, 1969. 328 pp., illus., gloss., index. $25 hb, $7.95 pb.

The classic treatise on the subject.

What Style Is It? A Guide to American Architecture. John Poppeliers, S. Allen Chambers and Nancy B. Schwartz, Historic American Buildings Survey. 1977. Rev. ed. Washington, D.C.: Preservation Press, 1984. 112 pp., illus., gloss., biblio. $7.95 pb.

A concise survey highlighted by HABS photos, this covers 22 styles in a handy, *Michelin* format.

Identifying American Architecture: A Pictorial Guide to Styles and Terms, 1600–1945. John J.G. Blumenson. Foreword by Nikolaus Pevsner. Nashville: American Association for State and Local History, 1977. Rev. hb. ed. New York: W.W. Norton, 1981. 120 pp., illus., gloss., biblio. $12.95 hb, $7.95 pb.

Notable for its identification of building parts and stylistic details.

Architecture in the United States: A Survey of Architectural Styles Since 1776. Ralph W. Hammett. New York: John Wiley, 1976. 408 pp., illus., biblio. $44.95 hb.

A primer of stylistic periods and outstanding examples.

Architectural styles drawn by Dianna Gabay. From *A Study of a Community: Staten Island Architecture and Environment.* (Work of the Visual Arts. ©1980 Dianna Gabay, George Szekely)

A Field Guide to American Architecture. Carole Rifkind. New York: New American Library, 1980. 336 pp., illus., biblio, index. $19.95 hb, $9.95 pb.

A handbook on building types—residential, ecclesiastical, civic, commercial and utilitarian—rather than pure styles.

American Shelter: An Illustrated Encyclopedia of the American Home. Lester Walker. Preface by Charles Moore. New York: Overlook Press, Viking, 1981. 320 pp., illus., biblio., gloss., index. $27.95 hb.

While restricted to residential styles, this is one of the most understandable and comprehensive guides—a chronological picture and text account of 100 styles, from the tipi to the solar house, from every region.

A Field Guide to American Houses. Virginia and Lee McAlester. New York: Knopf, 1984. 542 pp., illus., index. $19.95 pb.

A uniquely comprehensive handbook on nearly every conceivable style and form, providing a definitive guide to styles.

The American House. Mary Mix Foley. Foreword by James Marston Fitch. New York: Harper and Row, 1981. 300 pp., illus., index. $14.95 pb.

Another guide to styles as much as it is to houses, the book is organized into chronological and stylistic periods (including pioneer and vernacular building traditions).

Gothic Revival

Victorian Italianate

Second Empire

Queen Anne

Indigenous (to 1600)

"The native American architectural styles range from the wigwams and longhouses of the Indians in forested areas, raised shelters of the southeastern Indians, and tepees of the Plains Indians to the igloos of the Eskimos and the sophisticated communal pueblo cities carved out of mountainsides or built of stone or adobe in what is now New Mexico. Some of these briefly served as models for the European colonists before they began to build permanent structures in styles adapted to the climate but derived from their own native traditions."

National Trust et al., *America's Forgotten Architecture*

Native American Architecture. Bob Easton and Peter Nabokov. New York: Oxford University Press, 1986.

Indigenous Architecture Worldwide: A Guide to Information Sources. Lawrence Wodehouse, ed. Detroit: Gale Research, 1980. 392 pp. $44 hb.

Prehistoric American Architecture in the Eastern United States. William Morgan. Cambridge: MIT Press, 1980. 197 pp., illus., biblio., index. $32.50 hb.

Handbook of North American Indians. 20 vols. planned. William C. Sturtevant, ed. Washington, D.C.: Smithsonian Institution Press. Vol. 6: *Subarctic.* $22. Vol. 8: *California.* $21. Vol. 9: *Southwest.* $19. Vol. 15: *Northeast.* $23. Vol. 16, *Technology and Visual Arts,* will cover Native American architecture. Other volumes will deal with housing, dwellings, etc., by specific geographic area and tribe.

"What Is America's Heritage: Historic Preservation and American Indian Culture," Paul E. Wilson and Elaine O. Zingg. *University of Kansas Law Review,* 1974.

The Indian Tipi: Its History, Construction, and Use. Reginald and Gladys Laubin. 1957. Norman: University of Oklahoma Press, 1977. 270 pp., illus. $18.95 hb.

America's Ancient Treasures: A Guide to Archeological Sites and Museums. Franklin and Mary Folsom. 3rd rev. ed. Albuquerque: University of New Mexico Press, 1983. 448 pp. $35 hb, $16.95 pb.

"Housing and Architecture." In *Indians of North America.* Harold E. Driver. Rev. ed. Chicago: University of Chicago Press, 1969. Illus. $7.95 pb.

The World of the American Indian. Jules B. Billard, ed. Washington, D.C.: National Geographic Society, 1974. 400 pp., color illus. $9.95 hb.

A Guide to America's Indians, Ceremonials, Reservations, and Museums. Arnold Marquis. Norman: University of Oklahoma Press, 1974. 267 pp., illus., maps, appends., biblio., index. $21.95 hb, $12.95 pb.

Houses and House-Life of the American Aborigines. Lewis H. Morgan. Chicago: University of Chicago Press, 1966. 319 pp. $6.95.

Ethnographic Bibliography of North America. 5 vols. 4th ed. George P. Murdock and Timothy J. O'Leary. New Haven: Human Relations Area Files Press, 1975. $35 hb.

Early Architecture in New Mexico. Bainbridge Bunting. Albuquerque: University of New Mexico Press, 1976. 122 pp., illus., biblio., index. $12.95 pb.

The Architecture of the Southwest: Indian, Spanish, American. Trent E. Sanford. 1950. Reprint. Westport, Conn.: Greenwood Press, 1971. 312 pp., illus., append., index. $28.25 hb.

Navajo Architecture: Forms, History, Distribution. Stephen Jett and Virginia E. Spencer. Tucson: University of Arizona Press, 1981. 312 pp., illus., biblio., index. $37.50 hb, $14.95 pb.

Hogans: Navajo Houses and House Songs. Poems translated and arranged by David P. McAllester. Middletown, Conn.: Wesleyan University Press, 1980. 113 pp., illus., biblio. $19.50 hb.

Pueblo—Mountain, Village, Dance. Vincent Scully. New York: Viking, 1975. 398 pp., illus., biblio., index.

New Perspectives on the Pueblos. Alfonso Ortiz, ed. School of American Research Advanced Seminar Series. Albuquerque: University of New Mexico Press, 1972. 340 pp., maps.

Acoma: Pueblo in the Sky. Ward Alan Minge. Albuquerque: University of New Mexico Press, 1976. 180 pp., illus.

Tepees on the plains of South Dakota. (Library of Congress)

Acoma Pueblo (1200), N.M. (Joshua Freiwald)

Cliff Palace at Mesa Verde (13th century), Colo. (Jack E. Boucher, NPS)

House of Three Turkeys: Anasazi Redoubt. Stephen Jett. Photos by Dave Bohn. Santa Barbara: Capra Press, 1977. 64 pp., illus., biblio. $10 hb, $3.95 pb.

Pueblo Architecture in the Southwest: A Photographic Essay. Vincent Scully. Photos by William Current. Austin: University of Texas Press, 1971. 97 pp.

Anasazi: Ancient People of the Rock. Donald G. Pike. Photos by David Muench. 1974. New York: Crown, 1981. 192 pp., color illus.

Contacts

Bureau of Indian Affairs
U.S. Department of the Interior
1951 Constitution Avenue, N.W.
Washington, D.C. 20245

National Park Service
U.S. Department of the Interior
P.O. Box 37127
Washington, D.C. 20013-7127

Adam Thoroughgood House (1636), Virginia Beach, Va. (H. J. Sheely, HABS)

Colonial (1607–1700)

"By some strange elision of historical and geographic fact, "Colonial" architecture has become a rosy legend of neatly bricked physical comfort, stretched to cover the entire period from the days of the Pilgrim Fathers down to those of *Gone With the Wind* and extending from sea to shining sea. The actual picture is more complex, for the extent of this style was much smaller in time, space, and class. The term, if it means anything, refers to the relatively standardized system of structure, plan, and ornament in use from about 1700 up to the founding of the Republic. It was largely confined to the English colonies along the eastern seaboard. It was preceded in time by the earlier Spanish building in the Southwest; by the early Dutch settlements in New Amsterdam and upper New York; and—most importantly—by almost a century of experimentation with, and adaptation of, late medieval building theories along the eastern seaboard itself. It coexisted in time with the thriving colonies of the French along the Mississippi and with the Spanish in the Southwest. It was followed by a whole series of Classic idioms. And under it everywhere and all the time, like bedrock, the common people continued the while to erect their own buildings, following inherited structural concepts of their own and using materials which were nearest to hand."

James Marston Fitch, *American Building 1: The Historical Forces That Shaped It*

American Buildings and Their Architects. Vol. 1: *The Colonial and Neoclassical Styles.* William H. Pierson, Jr. Garden City, N.Y.: Doubleday, 1970. 503 pp., illus., gloss., index. $10.95 pb.

The Architectural Treasures of Early America. Russell F. Whitehead and Frank Chouteau Brown, eds. White Pine Series of Architectural Monographs. Reprint. Early American Society. Robert G. Miner, ed. New York: Arno Press, 1978. 1,792 pp., illus., index. 8 vols.

Early American Architecture: From the First Colonial Settlements to the National Period. Hugh Morrison. New York: Oxford University Press, 1952. 619 pp., illus., biblio.

Domestic Architecture of the American Colonies and of the Early Republic. Fiske Kimball. 1922. Reprint. New York: Dover, 1966. 330 pp., illus., index. $6 pb.

The Dwellings of Colonial America. Thomas T. Waterman. 1950. Reprint. New York: W.W. Norton, 1979.

The Log Cabin Myth: A Study of the Early Dwellings of the English Colonists. Harold R. Shurtleff. 1939. Reprint. Magnolia, Mass.: Peter Smith, 1967. Illus. $11.50 hb.

Sticks and Stones: A Study of American Architecture and Civilization. Lewis Mumford. 1924. Reprint. New York: Dover, 1955. 238 pp., illus. $3.50 pb.

The Carpenters' Company of the City and County of Philadelphia. Charles E. Peterson, ed. Radnor, Pa.: Chilton Book Company, 1976. 407 pp., illus.

Architecture of Colonial America. Harold D. Eberlein. 1915. Reprint. New York: Johnson Reprints, 1968. 288 pp., illus., index. $33 hb.

Early American Houses: The Seventeenth Century. Norman M. Isham. 1939. Reprint. New York: Da Capo, 1967. 61 pp., illus., biblio., index. $19.50 hb.

The Cape Cod House: America's Most Popular Home. Stanley Schuler. Exton, Pa.: Schiffer Publishing (Box E, 19341), 1982. 144 pp., illus., index. $25 hb.

The Framed Houses of Massachusetts Bay, 1625–1725. Abbott Lowell Cummings. Cambridge: Belknap Press, Harvard University Press, 1979. 261 pp., illus., appends., index. $40 hb, $12.95 pb.

Architecture in Colonial Massachusetts: A Conference Held by the Colonial Society of Massachusetts. Charlottesville: University Press of Virginia, 1979. 234 pp., illus., index. $25 pb.

Early Domestic Architecture of Connecticut. J. Frederick Kelly. 1924. Reprint. 210 pp., illus. New York: Dover, 1963. $6.95 pb. Magnolia, Mass.: Peter Smith. $16.25 hb.

Colonial and Historic Homes of Maryland. Don Swann, Jr. 1975. Cockeysville, Md.: Liberty Publishing, 1983. 211 pp., illus., index. $14.95 pb.

Domestic Colonial Architecture of Tidewater Virginia. Thomas T. Waterman and John A. Barrows. 1932. Reprint. New York: Da Capo, 1968. 191 pp., illus., index. $35 hb.

The Eighteenth-Century Houses of Williamsburg. Marcus Whiffen. 1960. Rev. ed. Williamsburg: Colonial Williamsburg Foundation, 1984. 298 pp., illus., append., index. $19.95 hb.

The Architecture of the Old South: The Medieval Style, 1585–1850. Henry C. Foreman. 1948. Reprint. New York: Russell, 1967.

Contacts

Early American Society
P.O. Box 1831
Harrisburg, Pa. 17105

Colonial Williamsburg
Foundation
P.O. Box C
Williamsburg, Va. 23185

Institute of Early American
History and Culture
Box 220
Williamsburg, Va. 23185

Spanish Colonial (1600–1840)

"The history of Spanish Colonial architecture, over a period of nearly 300 years, embraces a span of time nearly as long as the whole history of American architecture in other regions. The Spanish also differs from all other Colonial styles in its complete departure from the medieval."

Hugh Morrison, *Early American Architecture*

Santa Barbara Mission (1786), Santa Barbara, Calif.

Spanish Colonial Architecture in the United States. Rexford Newcomb. Locust Valley, N.Y.: J.J. Augustin, 1938. 44 pp., illus. $12 pb.

Early Architecture in New Mexico. Bainbridge Bunting. Albuquerque: University of New Mexico Press, 1976. 122 pp., illus., biblio., index. $12.95 pb.

The Architecture and Art of Early Hispanic Colorado. Robert H. Adams. Boulder: Colorado Associated University Press, 1974. 240 pp., illus., biblio., append.

Ranchos de Taos. Wolfgang Pogzeba. Kansas City, Mo.: Lowell Press, 1981. 68 pp., illus. $7.95 pb.

Art and Architecture in Spain and Portugal and Their Dominions, 1500 to 1800. George Kubler and Martin Soria. Baltimore: Penguin Books, 1959.

Spanish City Planning in North America. Dora P. Crouch, Daniel J. Garr and Axel I. Mundigo. Cambridge: MIT Press, 1982. 304 pp., illus. $40 hb.

Mizner's Florida: American Resort Architecture. Donald Curl. Cambridge: MIT Press, 1984. 256 pp., illus. $30 hb.

Dutch colonial Verplanck House, Fishkill-on-the-Hudson, N.Y.

Dutch Colonial (1625–1750)

"The Dutch were in undisputed control of the Hudson River area for only forty years, but their influence on building in the Middle Colonies lasted from 1625 to 1820. Especially noteworthy were their skills in the manufacture and laying of brick and in the structural framing that made possible characteristic Dutch or gambrel roofs and parapeted gable ends that projected above the roof level. Parapets were frequently stepped or treated with decorative stone or tile cresting."

National Trust et al., *America's Forgotten Architecture*

Dutch Houses in the Hudson Valley Before 1776. Helen W. Reynolds. 1929. Reprint. 1965. 467 pp., illus. New York: Dover, $6.95 pb. Magnolia, Mass.: Peter Smith. $15 hb.

Pre-Revolutionary Dutch Houses and Families in Northern New Jersey and Southern New York. Rosalie Fellows Bailey. 1936. Reprint. New York: Dover, 1968. 612 pp., illus., biblio.

French Colonial (1655–1830)

"That the French is the least known of the Colonial styles may seem strange in view of the immense size of the French colonial empire in North America. Time has dealt harshly with the few remains of French Colonial building: pioneer relics have long since been obliterated in big cities such as Detroit and St. Louis; small towns in the Mississippi bottoms have been destroyed by floods; and French New Orleans was largely wiped out by the disastrous fires of 1788 and 1794."

Hugh Morrison, *Early American Architecture*

"French Colonial Architecture of the Mississippi Valley." In *Early American Architecture: From the First Colonial Settlements to the National Period.* Hugh Morrison. New York: Oxford University Press, 1952. 619 pp., illus., biblio.

"French Colonial Period 1718–1769." In *The Vieux Carre New Orleans—Its Plan, Its Growth, Its Architecture.* Samuel Wilson, Jr. Vieux Carre Historic District Demonstration Study. New Orleans: Bureau of Governmental Research, 1968.

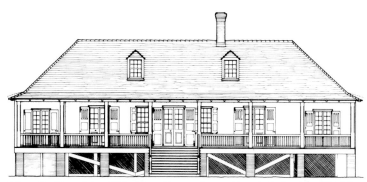

Magnolia Mound (c. 1790), Baton Rouge, La., a French derivation. (HABS)

Bienville's New Orleans—A French Colonial Capital 1718–1768. Samuel Wilson, Jr. New Orleans: Friends of the Cabildo, 1968. 46 pp., illus.

New Orleans Architecture. Friends of the Cabildo. Vol. I: *The Lower Garden District* (1971). 172 pp. $25. Vol. II: *The American Sector* (1972). 244 pp. $27.50. Vol. III: *The Cemeteries* (1974). 198 pp. $27.50. Vol. IV: *The Creole Faubourgs* (1974). 184 pp. $27.50. Vol. V: *The Esplanade Ridge* (1977). 172 pp. $27.50. Vol. VI: *Faubourg Treme and the Bayou Road* (1980). 222 pp. $34.95. Illus., biblio., index. Gretna, La.: Pelican Publishing.

"Creole Architecture 1718–1860," James Marston Fitch. In *The Past as Prelude.* Hodding Carter, ed. Gretna, La.: Pelican Publishing, 1968.

Frenchmen and French Ways in the Mississippi Valley. John Frances McDermott. Champaign: University of Illinois Press, 1969. $60.80.

Georgian (1700–80)

"It is easy to understand that when the colonists came to settle in the wilderness, they not only lacked the time, the skill, the architectural knowl-

edge, the materials, and the money to duplicate the great Renaissance mansions of the aristocracy, they lacked even the desire to do so. It took nearly a century to evolve the economic means, the building skills, and the social ambitions for an aristocratic architecture, and when these arrived, the Georgian style was born."

Hugh Morrison, *Early American Architecture*

American Georgian Architecture. Harold Donaldson Eberlein and Cortlandt Van Dyke Hubbard. Reprint. New York: Da Capo. 64 pp., illus. $32.50 hb.

Great Georgian Houses of America. Architects' Emergency Committee. 1933. Reprint. New York: Dover, 1970. 264 pp., illus. 2 vols. $8.95.

American Buildings and Their Architects. Vol. 1: *The Colonial and Neoclassical Styles.* William H. Pierson, Jr. Garden City, N.Y.: Doubleday, 1970. 503 pp., illus., gloss., index. $10.95 pb.

The Four Books of Architecture. Andrea Palladio. 1738. Reprint. Magnolia, Mass.: Peter Smith. $21 hb. New York: Dover, 1965. 110 pp., illus. $10 pb.

Palladian Studies in America I: Building by the Book 1. Mario di Valmarana, ed. Charlottesville: University Press of Virginia, 1984. 128 pp., illus. $20.

Palladio: A Western Progress. Desmond Guinness and Julius Trousdale Sadler, Jr. New York: Viking, 1976. 184 pp., color illus., biblio., index.

Palladio in America. Walter Muir Whitehill and Frederic D. Nichols. New York: Rizzoli, 1976. 120 pp., illus. $7.95 pb.

Contact
Center for Palladian Studies in America
P.O. Box 5643
Charlottesville, Va. 22905

Cliveden (1763–67), a Georgian mansion in Philadelphia. (NTHP)

Federal/Adamesque (1780–1820)

"In [the] early years of nationhood the sense of American identity demanded an American architecture for the common man as well as the privileged. Though closely derived from contemporary English handbooks, Asher Benjamin's influential builder's guide . . . published in Boston in 1806, declared American cultural independence and social egalitarianism. Architecture in America must be different from architecture in Europe, the author asserted. Americans had different materials to work with, less use for decoration, and a need to economize on labor and materials."

> Carole Rifkind, *A Field Guide to American Architecture*

American Buildings and Their Architects. Vol. 1: *The Colonial and Neoclassical Styles*. William H. Pierson, Jr. Garden City, N.Y.: Doubleday, 1970. 503 pp., illus., gloss., index. $10.95 pb.

"The Adam Style in America, 1770–1820." Sterling M. Boyd. *American Association of Architectural Bibliographers' Papers*, vol. 5. William B. O'Neal, ed. Charlottesville: University Press of Virginia, 1968. $10.

Colonial Interiors: Federal and Greek Revival. Harold D. Eberlein and Cortlandt Van Dyke Hubbard. New York: William Helburn, 1938.

Federal townhouses (1800–26), Washington, D.C. (Norman McGrath)

Jefferson's Monticello (1770–89), Charlottesville, Va. (John Blumenson)

Georgetown Houses of the Federal Period, 1780–1830. Deering Davis, Stephen P. Dorsey and Ralph Cole Hall. 1944. Reprint. New York: Crown, 1982. 130 pp., illus., biblio. $7.95 pb.

The Works in Architecture of Robert and James Adam. Robert Adam and James Adam. 1773–1822. Reprint. New York: Dover, 1980. 144 pp., illus. $50 hb.

Jeffersonian or Roman Revival (1770–1820)

"Jefferson's work should be seen, metaphorically speaking, as a struggle between the fixed European past and the mobile American future, between Palladio and Frank Lloyd Wright, between a desire for contained, classical geometry and an instinct to spread out horizontally along the surface of the land."

> Vincent Scully, *American Architecture and Urbanism*

"Many red brick houses and courthouses that derive from Jefferson's architectural theories are found in Virginia and states where Virginians settled. They could be termed Roman Revival but it is perhaps more fitting to call them Jeffersonian."

> John Poppeliers et al., *What Style Is It?*

Classica Americana: The Greek and Roman Heritage in the United States. Meyer Reinhold. Detroit: Wayne State University Press, 1984. 370 pp., biblio., index. $27.50 hb.

Andalusia (c. 1797, 1834) near Philadelphia. (HABS)

Greek Revival (1820–60)

"Many Greek Revival structures were built in Europe and its colonies, but in the United States during the 1830s and 1840s the style flourished as nowhere else. One reason for its appeal here undoubtedly was the often expressed sentiment that America, with its democratic ideals, was the spiritual successor of ancient Greece. . . ."

> John Poppeliers et al., *What Style Is It?*

"The public sentiment just now runs almost exclusively and popularly into the Grecian school. We build little besides temples for our churches, our banks, our taverns, our court houses and our dwellings. A friend of mine has just built a brewery on the model of the Temple of the Winds in Athens."

> Aristabulus Bragg. In *Home as Found*, James Fenimore Cooper. 1828.

Greek Revival Architecture in America. Talbot Hamlin. 1944. Reprint. New York: Dover, 1969. 439 pp., illus., append., biblio. $7.50 pb.

The Beauties of Modern Architecture. Minard Lafever. 1835. Reprint. New York: Da Capo, 1968. 139 pp., illus., gloss. $29.50 hb.

The Domestic Architecture of the Early American Republic. The Greek Revival. Howard Major. Philadelphia: Lippincott, 1926. 237 pp., illus., index.

Sources of Greek Revival Architecture. Dora Wiebenson. London: A. Zwemmer Ltd., 1969. 136 pp., illus., append., index.

Gothic Revival (1830–60)

"The leading idea of Gothic architecture is found in its upward lines . . . upward, higher and higher, it soars . . . in spires, and steeples, and towers . . . in the vaulted aisles, and the high, open, pointed roofs in the interior of a fine and Gothic church."

> Andrew Jackson Downing

St. Patrick's (1858, James Renwick), New York City.

American Buildings and Their Architects. Vol. 2A: *Technology and the Picturesque. The Corporate and the Early Gothic Styles*. William H. Pierson, Jr. Garden City, N.Y.: Doubleday, 1978. 500 pp., illus., gloss., index. $10.95 pb.

The Only Proper Style: Gothic Architecture in America. Calder Loth and Julius T. Sadler, Jr. Boston: New York Graphic Society, 1976. 184 pp., illus., biblio.

American Gothic: Its Origins, Its Trials, Its Triumphs. Wayne Andrews. New York: Random House, 1975. 150 pp., illus., biblio.

A History of Gothic Revival. Charles Locke Eastlake. 1872. Reprint. New York: Humanities Press, 1970. 581 pp., illus., appends., biblio.

Carpenter Gothic: Nineteenth-Century Ornamented Houses of New England. Alma deC. McArdle and Deirdre B. McArdle. Foreword by Charles Moore. New York: Whitney Library of Design, 1978. 160 pp., illus., appends., biblio., index. $14.95 pb.

"Carpenter Gothic and Nineteenth Century Ornamented Houses in America: A Selected Bibliography." Robert B. Harmon. Monticello, Ill.: Vance Bibliographies, 1979. 10 pp.

The Architecture of Country Houses. Andrew Jackson Downing. 1850. Reprint. New York: Dover, 1969. 484 pp., illus., biblio. $6.50 pb. New York: Da Capo, 1968. $45 hb.

Cottage Residences, Rural Architecture and Landscape Gardening. Andrew Jackson Downing. 1842. Reprint. Watkins Glen, N.Y.: American Life Foundation, 1967. 200 pp., illus., biblio., index. $15 hb. Also available as *Victorian Cottage Residences.* New York: Dover, 1981. 352 pp., illus. $6 pb.

The Gothic Revival and American Church Architecture: An Episode in Taste, 1840–1856. Phoebe B. Stanton. Baltimore: Johns Hopkins University Press, 1968. 350 pp., illus., index, biblio. $27.50 hb.

The Gothic Revival Style in America, 1830–1870. Katherine S. Howe and David B. Warren. Seattle: University of Washington Press, 1976. 102 pp., color illus., biblio., index. $14.95 pb.

Egyptian Revival (1830–50, 1920–30)

"Bonaparte's Egyptian expedition was a military and political fiasco but it brought the mysterious art of ancient Egypt to the attention of a fascinated West. . . . Because of the ancient Egyptians' preoccupation with the afterlife, their style was deemed particularly suitable for cemetery architecture."

John Maass, *The Gingerbread Age*

"For a period of 50 years, from Latrobe's design for the Library of Congress in 1808 to Rague's Dubuque City Jail in 1858, the work of nearly every major architect was influenced by Egyptian themes."

Richard G. Carrott, *The Egyptian Revival*

The Egyptian Revival: Its Sources, Monuments and Meaning, 1808–1858. Richard G. Carrott. Berkeley: University of California Press, 1978. 221 pp., illus., biblio. $37.50 hb.

First Presbyterian Church (1849, Wm. Strickland), Nashville. (HABS)

Victorian Period (1840–1900)

"Antiquarians taught us that this period's wooden gingerbread, its cast-iron tracery, its patterned shingling, and its intricate brickwork were awkward and vulgar substitutes for the hand craftsmanship of colonial days. Modernists explained away Victorian fancywork as a betrayal of the machine aesthetic, a copying of inappropriate handcraft models by a means which should be devoted to its own ends. Social critics also added to the general censure. They deplored these large, lavish, and comfortable dwellings as tokens of a robber baron age, behind which could be glimpsed the sweatshop and the slum. Amateur psychologists even professed to see the unconscious release of Freudian inhibition in every curve and spire. Whatever anyone disliked about the Victorians was gathered up and projected onto the Victorian house. . . . In retrospect, the Victorian Age would seem to have been America's most versatile and creative period, exuberant and uninhibited in its expression and the originator of ideas which we are still exploring today."

Mary Mix Foley, *The American House*

The Gingerbread Age. John Maass. 1957. Reprint. New York: Greenwich House, Crown, 1983. 212 pp., illus., biblio., index. $7.98 hb.

The Victorian Home in America. John Maass. New York: Hawthorn Books, 1972. 235 pp., color illus., appends., biblio., index.

Architectural Polychromy of the 1830's. David Van Zanten. 1970. Reprint. Garland Publishing, 1977. 500 pp., illus. $69.

American Victorian Architecture: A Survey of the 70's and 80's in Contemporary Photographs. Arnold Lewis and Keith Morgan. New York: Dover, 1975. 160 pp., illus. $7.95 pb.

America's Gilded Age. Frederick Platt. San Diego: A.S. Barnes, 1976. 296 pp., illus., index.

Victorian Houses: A Treasury of Lesser-known Examples. Edmund V. Gillon, Jr. and Clay Lancaster. New York: Dover, 1973. 117 pp., illus. $6.95 pb.

A Gift to the Street. Carol Olwell and Judith Lynch Waldhorn. 1976. Reprint. New York: St. Martin's, 1983. 195 pp., illus. $17.95 pb.

Carson House (1884–86), Eureka, Calif. (Library of Congress)

Victorian Sketchbook. Ranulph Bye and Margaret Bye Richie. Wayne, Pa.: Haverford House (34 West Avenue, Box 408, 19087), 1980. 136 pp., color illus., gloss., biblio., index. $35 hb.

Victorian West. Lambert Florin. Seattle: Superior Publishing, 1978. 190 pp., illus., index. $15.95 hb.

American Victorian: A Style and Source Book. Lawrence Grow and Dina Von Zweck. New York: Harper and Row, 1984. 224 pp., illus., index. $35 hb.

The World of Antiques, Art, and Architecture in Victorian America. Robert Bishop and Patricia Coblentz. New York: E.P. Dutton, 1979. 495 pp., illus., biblio., index.

The Antiques Book of Victorian Interiors. Elisabeth Donaghy Garrett, ed. New York: Crown, 1981. 160 pp., color illus., index. $19.95 hb.

Nineteenth-Century America: Furniture and Other Decorative Arts. Berry Tracy et al. New York: Metropolitan Museum of Art, 1973. 272 pp., illus.

Victorian Traveler's Companion: A Pocket Guide to 19th-Century House Museums, Inns, Restaurants, Tours, and Historic Sites in the United States and Canada. Eva Marie Utne, ed. Philadelphia: Victorian Society in America. 1980. 127 pp., illus. $4.95 pb.

Contacts

The Victorian Society in America
The Athenaeum
South Washington Square
Philadelphia, Pa. 19106

Victorian Homes
P.O. Box 61
Millers Falls, Mass. 01349

American Life Foundation
P.O. Box 349
Watkins Glen, N.Y. 14891

The Victorian Vintage
6 Bensonhurst Avenue
Saratoga Springs, N.Y. 12866

See also: Pattern Books; Rehabilitation and Restoration

Villa design (1861) by architect John Riddell.

Italianate (1840–60)

"There is a strong and growing partiality among us for the Italian style. . . . Its broad roofs, ample verandas and arcades, are especially agreeable in our summers of dazzling sunshine. . . . It is remarkable for expressing the elegant culture and variety of accomplishment of the retired citizen or man of the world. . . . The Italian style is one that expresses not wholly the spirit of country life nor of town life, but something between both. . . ."

Andrew Jackson Downing, *The Architecture of Country Houses*

Victorian Cottage Residences. Andrew Jackson Downing. 1842. Reprint. New York: Dover, 1981. 352 pp., illus. $6 pb.

The Architecture of Country Houses. Andrew Jackson Downing. 1850. Reprint. New York: Da Capo, 1968. 501 pp., illus. $45 hb.

"The Italianate Image." In *The Victorian Home in America.* John Maass. New York: Hawthorn Books, 1972. 235 pp., color illus., biblio., index.

John Notman, Architect, 1810–1865. Constance M. Greiff. Philadelphia: The Athenaeum, 1979. 253 pp., illus., biblio., index. $20 pb.

"Italianate Interlude." In *The Gingerbread Age.* John Maass. 1957. Reprint. New York: Greenwich House, Crown, 1983. 212 pp., illus., biblio., index. $7.98 hb.

Second Empire (1860–90)

"The French Second Empire Style ushered in a new era in Victorian architecture, offering Americans cosmopolitan elegance from the reign of Louis XIV. . . . [The style] was immensely appealing to the mid-nineteenth-century mind, a trifle weary of Republican Greek and rural Gothic. It became the favorite of the newly rich and powerful . . . its derisive nickname, the "General Grant Style," [implied] a heavy-handed and overly ornate attempt at elegance. Today, tastes have changed again, and this American echo of a royal palace is admired as a richly worked classic of unique Gallic charm."

Mary Mix Foley, *The American House*

"The Mansardic and Stick Styles." In *The American House.* May Mix Foley. New York: Harper and Row, 1981. 300 pp., illus., index. $14.95 pb.

"General Grant Architecture in Jeopardy!" Lawrence Wodehouse. *Historic Preservation*, January–March 1970.

"Alfred B. Mullett and His French Style Government Buildings," Lawrence Wodehouse. *Journal of the Society of Architectural Historians*, March 1972.

Francois Mansart and the Origins of French Classical Architecture. Reprint. Anthony Blunt. St. Clair Shores, Mich.: Somerset Publications, 1941. $39 hb.

Second Empire Goyer-Lee House (1843–73, Jones and Baldwin), Memphis, Tenn. (HABS)

Chateauesque (1860–90)

"The Chateauesque, whose special piquancy resulted from the adroit mixing of Renaissance and Late Gothic details, was rather tricky for any but the *cordon bleus* of the profession. . . . [Richard Morris Hunt] remained the leader of the movement, and Vanderbilts were its most munificent patrons."

Marcus Whiffen, *American Architecture Since 1780*

Richard Morris Hunt. Paul R. Baker. Cambridge: MIT Press, 1980. 588 pp., illus. $49.95 hb.

"The Age of Elegance, 1872–1913." In *Architecture, Ambition, and Americans: A Social History of American Architecture.* Wayne Andrews. New York: The Free Press, 1979. 332 pp., illus., biblio., index. $24.95.

The American Spirit in Architecture. Talbot F. Hamlin. 1926. Reprint. *Pageant of America*, vol. XIII. R.H. Gabriel, ed. New Rochelle, N.Y.: U.S. Publishers Association, 1968. 353 pp., illus., index. $22.95 hb.

Richardsonian Romanesque (1870–1900)

"In only a few instances has an American architectural style been so influenced by one figure as to bear that person's name. But so it was with Henry Hobson Richardson (1838–86) and the late-19th-century Romanesque Revival."

John Poppeliers et al., *What Style Is It?*

"Monumental and stately, grave, yet not without its lighter side, this mode depends on the heaviness, solidity, and ruggedness of brick and stone masonry, massive low arches, and imaginative towers, turrets, and dormers."

Carole Rifkind, *A Field Guide to American Architecture*

The Architecture of H.H. Richardson and His Times. Henry-Russell Hitchcock. 1936. 2nd ed., rev. Cambridge: MIT Press, 1966. 343 pp., illus., biblio., index. $9.95 pb.

H.H. Richardson: Complete Architectural Works. Jeffrey Karl Ochsner. Cambridge: MIT Press, 1982. 466 pp., illus., appends., index. $50 hb.

H.H. Richardson and His Office: Selected Drawings. James F. O'Gorman, ed. 1974. Reprint. Cambridge: MIT Press, 1979. 220 pp., color illus., appends., index. $50 hb.

Henry Hobson Richardson and His Works. Mariana Griswold Van Rensselaer. 1888. Reprint. New York: Dover, 1969. 152 pp., illus. $6 pb.

The Brown Decades: A Study of the Arts in America, 1865–1895. Lewis Mumford. New York: Dover, 1955. 266 pp., illus., biblio. $3 pb.

The Chateauesque Biltmore (1895, William Morris Hunt), Asheville, N.C.

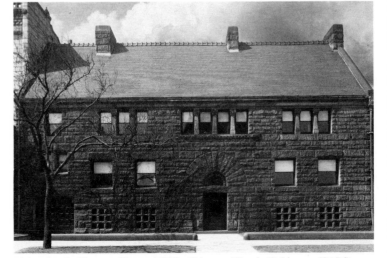

Richardson's Glessner House (1885), Chicago. (Cervin Robinson, HABS)

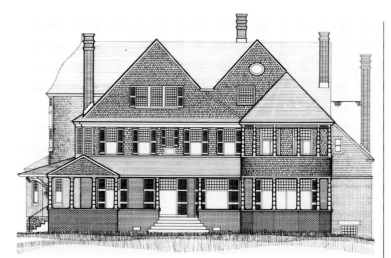

Isaac Bell House (1882, McKim, Mead and White), Newport, R.I. (HABS)

Queen Anne Long-Waterman House (1889), San Diego. (HABS)

Queen Anne (1875–90)

"If the Italianate house is like a svelte, prim dandy standing at attention, his frilled cravat spilling over velvet lapels, then the Queen Anne house is like a buxom gypsy, her ruffled skirts, billowing blouse and patterned kerchiefs infinitely artful, but always in disarray and never quite matching."

City of Oakland Planning Department, *Rehab Right.* Oakland, Calif.: Author, 1978.

Sweetness and Light: The Queen Anne Movement, 1860–1900. Mark Girouard. 1977. New Haven: Yale University Press, 1984. 250 pp., illus., appends., index. $16.95 pb.

California's Architectural Frontier: Style and Tradition in the Nineteenth Century. Harold Kirker. 1960. Reprint. New York: Russell and Russell, 1970. 224 pp., illus., index. $13.

Shingle Style (1880–95)

"It was born in New England, where the fondness for natural wood shingles reflected post-Centennial interest in American colonial architecture, especially the shingle architecture of the coastal towns that were being rediscovered as fashionable watering places. . . . The emphasis . . . was on the surface—the shingle covering that unified all parts of the building. The interior plan continued the Queen Anne trend toward openness and informality."

John Poppeliers et al., *What Style Is It?*

The Shingle Style and the Stick Style: Architectural Theory and Design from Richardson to the Origins of Wright. Vincent Scully, Jr. 1955. Rev. ed. New Haven: Yale University Press, 1971. 184 pp., illus., biblio., index. $13.95 pb.

The Shingle Style Today, or The Historian's Revenge. Vincent Scully, Jr. New York: Braziller, 1974. 118 pp., illus., index. $7.95 pb.

Chicago School (1880–1915)

"Chicago is the site associated with development of the tall commercial building. Although Chicago commercial architecture built on advances made elsewhere—most notably in Philadelphia and New York City—it was in that midwestern city in the last quarter of the 19th century that new technology and materials were exploited by innovative architects and engineers to produce the skeleton-framed 'skyscraper' that would transform cities around the world."

John Poppeliers et al., *What Style Is It?*

The Chicago School of Architecture: A History of Commercial and Public Buildings in the Chicago Area, 1875–1925. Carl W. Condit. Chicago: University of Chicago Press, 1964. 238 pp., illus., biblio., index. $9.95 pb.

Contact

Chicago Architecture Foundation
330 South Dearborn Street
Chicago, Ill. 60604

See also: Skyscrapers

Art Nouveau (1885–1910)

"A group of avant-garde architects in Europe, beginning about 1885, were trying to intro-

duce a new style principally in opposition to the Eclecticists. Their stated aim was to create a new art, *Art Nouveau*. . . . However, Art Nouveau had little effect architecturally in the United States. The style was an attempt to be novel and new, and it glorified the willowy curve above all. It was based on nature, particularly flowers, which were imitated in wrought iron, colored glass, stucco, plaster, paint, and enamel."

Ralph W. Hammett, *Architecture in the United States*

American Art Nouveau. Diane Chalmers Johnson. New York: Abrams, 1979. Color illus., biblio., appends. $45 hb.

Art Nouveau Architecture. Frank Russell, ed. New York: Rizzoli, 1979. 304 pp., color illus. $29.95 pb.

Artistic America, Tiffany Glass, and Art Nouveau. Samuel Bing. Introduction by Robert Koch. Cambridge: MIT Press, 1970. 276 pp., illus., index. $9.95 pb.

New Free Style: Arts and Crafts, Art Nouveau, Secession. Ian Latham, ed. New York: Rizzoli, 1980. 96 pp., color illus. $12.50 pb.

Hector Guimard. David Dunster, ed. New York: Rizzoli, 1978. 104 pp., illus.

The Art Nouveau Style in Jewelry, Metalwork, Glass, Ceramics, Textiles, Architecture and Furniture. Roberta Waddell. New York: Dover, 1977. 288 pp., illus. $8.95 pb.

The Anti-Rationalists: Art Nouveau Architecture and Design. Nikolaus Pevsner and James M. Richards, eds. 1973. New York: Harper and Row, 1976.

Reliance Building (1890, Burnham and Root), Chicago. (Richard Nickel)

City of Paris store (1896, 1906), San Francisco, Calif. (Robert Freed, HABS)

Beaux-Arts (1890–1920)

"Any American architect growing up after World War I has probably felt two great architectural presences around him. First, that of the frontier, with vast spaces, constant growth into those spaces and things made quickly, flimsily, and soon abandoned. Second, that of the Ecole des Beaux-Arts which—when brought to the United States around 1900—caused us to create monumental buildings, boulevards and even whole city centers like monadnocks among the chaos of American ticky-tacky. . . ."

> David Van Zanten, "The Architecture of the Beaux-Arts." *Journal of Architectural Education,* November 1975.

The Beaux-Arts. David Dunster, ed. AD Profiles. New York: Rizzoli, 1979. 88 pp., illus.

The Architecture of the Ecole des Beaux-Arts. Arthur Drexler, ed. New York: Museum of Modern Art, 1977. 525 pp., illus. $55 hb.

The Influence of the Ecole des Beaux-Arts on the Architects of the United States. James P. Noffsinger. Cleveland: J.T. Zubal, 1955. 123 pp., biblio.

"Architecture Without Architecture: Reflections on the Beaux-Arts 'Revival.'" *Art in America,* March–April 1976.

See also: Fair Buildings

Second Renaissance Revival (1890–1920)

"Much as Neo-Classicism began as a movement of discipline after the general classical tradition after the 'licentious' and 'capricious' Baroque age, the Second Renaissance Revival was in the first place the result of a felt need for simplicity and order in reaction to the very different qualities admired in the High Victorian period. The revival opened with the Villard Houses in New York, whose design came from the office of McKim, Mead and White in 1883."

> Marcus Whiffen, *American Architecture Since 1870*

The American Renaissance: 1876–1917. Richard Guy Wilson, Dianne Pilgrim and Richard N. Murray. New York: Brooklyn Museum, 1979. 232 pp., illus. $14.95 pb.

The Villard Houses: Life Story of a Landmark. William C. Shopsin and Mosette Glaser Broderick. Municipal Art Society. New York: Viking, 1980. 144 pp., illus.

Neoclassical Revival (1900–20)

"The peak of Classicism in America was reached during the American Renaissance—the 1880's and 1890's—in many ways the last splurge of the Italian Renaissance of the 15th century. The World's Columbian Exhibition of 1893, held in Chicago, was an unequalled display of American genius . . . peculiarly American for there was nothing in Europe to serve as a model. The generous and consistent aim to adorn America's cities was generated there in 1893, and today's monumental Washington is an example of the Fair's extraordinary influence. . . . The originality considered so important today is not a requirement of the Classical artist, for originality is an intellectual concept, not a visual one. Anyone can be original—ugliness often is."

> Henry Hope Reed, "Classical America." *Historic Preservation,* January–March 1970.

Classical America IV. William A. Coles, ed. New York: W.W. Norton, 1978. 232 pp., illus. $19.95 hb.

The American Renaissance: 1876–1917. Richard Guy Wilson, Dianne Pilgrim and Richard N. Murray. New York: Brooklyn Museum, 1979. 232 pp., illus. $14.95 pb.

The American Vignola: A Guide to the Making of Classical Architecture. William R. Ware. 1906. Reprint. New York: W.W. Norton, 1977. 145 pp. $6.95 pb.

The Golden City. Henry Hope Reed. New York: W.W. Norton, 1971. 160 pp., illus., biblio. $4.95 pb.

The Colonial Revival. William B. Rhoads. 1974. Reprint. New York: Garland Publishing. 1,178 pp., illus. 2 vols. $146 hb.

Contact

Classical America
227 East 50th Street
New York, N.Y. 10022

See also: Fair Buildings

Bungalows (1890–1940)

"[Bungalows] have rarely been the best architecture, but almost always they have provided a comfortable abode *in style* for the average person. In that sense, they are revolutionary in the history of architecture."

> Robert Winter, *The California Bungalow*

Beaux-Arts Library of Congress (1889–97, Smithmeyer and Pelz), Washington, D.C. (Jack E. Boucher, HABS)

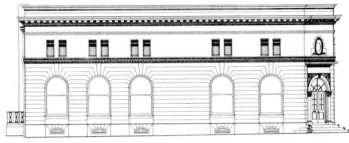

Renaissance Revival-style New Jersey Trust and Safe Deposit Company (1895, Thomas Stevens), Cape May, N.J. (Longnecker, HABS)

Neoclassical Jefferson Memorial (1943, John Russell Pope), Washington, D.C. (Washington Convention and Visitors Bureau)

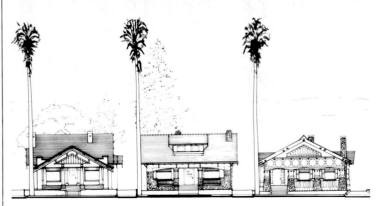

Bungalows in the Hanchett Residence Park, San Jose, Calif. (Barbara Friedman and John Murphy, HABS)

Gamble House (1900, Greene and Greene), Pasadena, Calif. (© Marvin Rand)

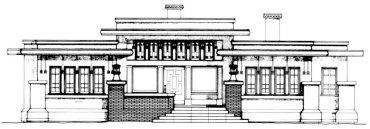

Prairie Style Peter Col House, San Jose, Calif. (Julia Miner, HABS)

The American Bungalow, 1880s–1920s. Clay Lancaster. New York: Abbeville Press, 1985. 256 pp., illus. $29.95 hb.

The Bungalow: The Production of a Global Culture. Anthony D. King. Boston: Routledge and Kegan Paul, 1984. 300 pp., illus. $50 hb.

The California Bungalow, Robert Winter. Foreword by David Gebhard. Los Angeles: Hennessey and Ingalls, 1980. 95 pp., illus., biblio., index. $14.95 pb.

Craftsman (1895–1940)

"The Arts and Crafts movement was inspired by a crisis of confidence. Its motivations were social and moral, and its aesthetic values derived from the conviction that society produces the art and architecture it deserves . . . the realization that technical progress does not necessarily coincide with the improvement of man's lot brought with it the long campaign for social, industrial, and aesthetic reform that is still unresolved today. The Arts and Crafts movement represents one facet of that campaign. . . ."

Gillian Naylor, *The Arts and Crafts Movement*

The Arts and Crafts Movement in America 1876–1916. Robert Judson Clark, ed. Princeton: Princeton University Press, 1972. 190 pp., illus., biblio. $44 hb, $14.50 pb.

The Arts and Crafts Movement: A Study of Its Sources, Ideals, and Influence on Design Theory. Gillian Naylor. Cambridge: MIT Press, 1971. 208 pp., illus., biblio., index. $10.95 pb.

Arts and Crafts in Britain and America. Isabelle Anscombe and Charlotte Gere. 1978. New York: Van Nostrand Reinhold, 1983. 232 pp., color illus. $13.50 pb.

Utopian Craftsmen: The Arts and Crafts Movement from the Cotswolds to Chicago. Lionel Lambourne. 1980. New York: Van Nostrand Reinhold, 1982. 240 pp., illus. $14.95 pb.

Architecture of the Arts and Crafts Movement. Peter Davey. New York: Rizzoli, 1980. 224 pp., illus., biblio., index.

Gustav Stickley: The Craftsman Movement in America. Barry Sanders. Salt Lake City: Peregrine Smith, 1979. 240 pp., illus. $24.95 hb.

Gustav Stickley: The Craftsman. Mary Ann Smith. Syracuse, N.Y.: Syracuse University Press, 1983. 204 pp., illus., index. $22 hb.

The Craftsman: An Anthology. Barry Sanders, ed. Reprint. Salt Lake City: Peregrine Smith, 1978. 328 pp., illus. $9.95 pb.

Craftsman Homes: Architecture and Furnishings of the American Arts and Crafts Movement. Gustav Stickley. 1909. Reprint. New York: Dover, 1979. 224 pp., illus. $6.50 pb.

Craftsman Homes. Gustav Stickley. Reprint. Salt Lake City: Peregrine Smith, 1979. 224 pp., illus. $9.95 pb.

The Simple Home. Charles Keeler. Reprint. Salt Lake City: Peregrine Smith, 1979. 120 pp., illus. $9.95 pb.

Greene and Greene: Architecture as a Fine Art. Randell L. Makinson. Salt Lake City: Peregrine Smith, 1979. 288 pp., illus. $19.95 pb.

Bernard Maybeck: Artisan, Architect, Artist. Kenneth Cardwell. Salt Lake City: Peregrine Smith, 1977. 260 pp., illus. $19.95 pb.

California's Mission Revival: Transition to the Twentieth Century. Karen Weitze. Los Angeles: Hennessey and Ingalls, 1984. 160 pp., illus. $22.50 pb.

California Design 1910. Timothy J. Andersen, Eudorah M. Moore, Robert W. Winter, eds. Salt Lake City: Peregrine Smith, 1980. 144 pp., illus., index. $11.95 pb.

The Arts and Crafts Movement in New York State, 1890s–1920s. Coy L. Ludwig. Salt Lake City: Peregrine Smith, 1984. 128 pp., illus. $15 pb.

Furniture of the American Arts and Crafts Movement: Stickley and Roycroft Mission Oak. David M. Cathers. New York: New American Library, 1981. $9.95 pb.

The Furniture of Gustav Stickley: History, Techniques, and Projects. Joseph J. Bavaro and Thomas L. Mossman. New York: Van Nostrand Reinhold, 1982. 175 pp., illus., biblio., index. $18.95 hb.

Stickley Craftsman Furniture Catalogs. Reprint. Introduction by David M. Cathers. New York: Dover, 1979. 192 pp., illus. $5 pb.

The Arts and Crafts Furniture, Metal Work, Textiles, and Needlework of Gustav Stickley. 1909. Reprint. Watkins Glen, N.Y.: American Life Foundation, 1978. 128 pp., illus. $5 pb.

Greene and Greene: Furniture and Related Designs. Randell L. Makinson. Salt Lake City: Peregrine Smith, 1978. 190 pp., illus., biblio., index. $19.95 pb.

Mission Furniture: How to Make It. Popular Mechanics Company. 1909, 1912. Reprint. New York: Dover, 1980. 342 pp., illus. $5 pb.

Prairie Style (1900–20)

"No house should ever be *on* any hill or on anything. It should be *of* the hill, belonging to it, so hill and house could live together each the happier for the other."

Frank Lloyd Wright, *An Autobiography*

"These architects of the Prairie School consciously rejected currently popular academic revival styles and sought to create buildings that reflected the rolling midwestern prairie terrain. . . ."

John Poppeliers et al., *What Style Is It?*

The Prairie School: Frank Lloyd Wright and His Midwest Contemporaries. H. Allen Brooks. Toronto: University of Toronto Press, 1972. 373 pp., illus., biblio., index. $35 hb. New York: W. W. Norton, 1976. $12.95 pb.

Frank Lloyd Wright and the Prairie School. H. Allen Brooks. New York: Braziller, 1983. 120 pp., illus. $11.95 pb.

The Prairie School Tradition: Sullivan, Adler, Wright and Their Heirs. Brian A. Spencer, ed. New York: Whitney Library of Design, 1979. 304 pp., illus., biblio., index. $30 hb.

Prairie School Architecture: Studies from 'The Western Architect.' H. Allen Brooks, ed. New York: Van Nostrand Reinhold, 1975. 352 pp., illus., index. $19.95 pb.

The Prairie School in Iowa. Richard Guy Wilson and Sidney K. Robinson. Ames, Iowa: Iowa State University Press, 1977. 127 pp., illus., biblio. $7.50 pb.

The Robie House of Frank Lloyd Wright. Joseph Connors. Chicago: University of Chicago Press, 1984. 86 pp., illus., biblio., index. $25 hb, $8.95 pb.

Lloyd Wright: A Prairie School Architect. Patrick Joseph Meehan. Monticello, Ill.: Vance Bibliographies, 1978. 15 pp. $1.50 pb.

Contacts

Prairie School Society
c/o Philip Tompkins
3603 West Roanoke Drive
Kansas City, Mo. 64111

Prairie Archives
Milwaukee Art Center
750 North Lincoln Memorial Drive
Milwaukee, Wis. 53202

Prairie School Review and Prairie Avenue Bookshop
711 South Dearborn Street
Chicago, Ill. 60605

Frank Lloyd Wright Home and Studio
951 Chicago Avenue
Oak Park, Ill. 60302

Building on Michigan Avenue in the Miami Beach Art Deco District. (Walter Smalling, Jr., HABS)

Art Deco (1925–40)

"No style has been more neglected, undervalued, misunderstood, or camped up. No style has been more vulnerable to the bulldozer, egregious remodeling or the disdain of contemporary scholars. . . . It is as easy to be entranced by [Art Deco] as it is to miss its genuine substance. There is immense visual pleasure in its fantasy world of ziggurats, sunbursts, zigzags, waves, stepped triangles, stylized machines, abstract suggestions of energy and speed, and the exotic natural wonders of waterfalls, tortoises, condors, and doves. One marvels at the superb craftsmanship in marble, bronze, glass, bakelite, monel metal, plastics, and rare woods. . . . Art Deco, or Style Moderne, is primarily the art of the skyscraper age."

Ada Louise Huxtable, *Kicked a Building Lately?*

Tulsa Art Deco: An Architectural Era, 1925–1942. Junior League of Tulsa. Introduction by David Gebhard. Tulsa, Okla.: Author (187 London Square, 74105), 1980. 204 pp., illus., biblio., index. $15.95 pb.

Tropical Deco: The Architecture and Design of Old Miami Beach. Laura Cerwinske. New York: Rizzoli, 1981. 96 pp., illus. $14.95 hb.

Portfolio, Miami Beach. Art Deco Historic District. Barbara Baer Capitman, ed. Miami Beach: Miami Design Preservation League, 1979. 40 pp., illus. $3 pb.

Art Deco, Los Angeles. Ave Pildas. New York: Harper and Row, 1977. 64 pp., illus. $4.95 pb.

L.A. in the Thirties. David Gebhard and Harriette Von Breton. Salt Lake City: Peregrine Smith, 1975. 165 pp., illus., biblio.

Skyscraper Style: Art Deco New York. Cervin Robinson and Rosemarie Haag Bletter. New York: Oxford University Press, 1975. 198 pp., illus., map, notes. $16.95 pb.

Art Deco Architecture in New York, 1920 to 1940. Don Vlack. New York: Icon Publishers, Harper and Row, 1975. 177 pp., illus., biblio.

Bronx Art Deco Architecture: An Exposition. Donald Sullivan and Brian Danforth. Hunter College Graduate Program in Urban Planning. New York: Publishing Center for Cultural Resources, 1976. 26 pp., illus. $3.50 pb.

Pueblo Deco: The Art Deco Architecture of the Southwest. Marcus Whiffin and Carla Breeze. Albuquerque: University of New Mexico Press, 1984. 136 pp. $19.95.

The Mayan Revival Style. Marjorie Ingle. Salt Lake City: Peregrine Smith, 1984. 92 pp., illus., biblio., index. $15.95 pb.

Washington Deco: Art Deco Design in the Nation's Capital. Hans Wirz and Richard Striner. Washington, D.C.: Smithsonian Institution Press, 1984. 112 pp., illus. $19.95 hb.

The World of Art Deco. Bevis Hillier, Minneapolis Institute of Arts. New York: E.P. Dutton, 1981. 224 pp., illus., biblio. $14.50 pb.

Art Deco. Victor Arwas. 1977. New York: Abrams, 1980. 316 pp., illus., biblio., index. $49.50 hb.

The Art Deco Style in Household Objects, Architecture, Sculpture, Graphics, Jewelry. Theodore Menten, ed. New York: Dover, 1972. 183 pp., illus., index. $6 pb.

Twentieth Century Limited: Industrial Design in America, 1925–1939. Jeffrey L. Meikle. Philadelphia: Temple University Press, 1979. 249 pp., illus., index. $12.95 pb.

The Streamlined Decade. Donald J. Bush. New York: Braziller, 1975. 214 pp., illus. $10.95 pb.

Contact
Art Deco Societies of America
1300 Ocean Drive
Miami Beach, Fla. 33139

Modern (1927–65)
"Less is more."

Ludwig Mies van der Rohe

"Less is a bore."

Robert Venturi

"Less is less."

Ada Louise Huxtable

"No architect of our time, whatever his opinion of the International Style, could design as if it had never been."

Marcus Whiffen, *American Architecture Since 1780*

The International Style. Henry-Russell Hitchcock and Philip Johnson. 1932. Reprint. New foreword and appendix by Hitchcock. New York: W.W. Norton, 1966. 260 pp., illus. $6.95 pb.

Modern Architecture: A Critical History. Kenneth Frampton. New York: Oxford University Press, 1980. 324 pp., illus., biblio., index. $19.95 hb, $14.95 pb.

Modern Architecture. Manfredo Tafuri and Francesco Dal Co. Translated by Robert E. Wolf. History of World Architecture Series. Pier Luigi Nervi, ed. 1976. New York: Abrams, 1979. 448 pp., illus., biblio., index. $50 hb.

American Buildings and Their Architects. Vol. 4: *The Impact of European Modernism in the Mid-Twentieth Century.* William H. Jordy. Garden City, N.Y.: Doubleday, 1972. 469 pp., illus., gloss., index. $10.95 pb.

Architecture: Nineteenth and Twentieth Centuries. Henry-Russell Hitchcock. 1958. 1963. 2nd ed. Reprint. New York: Viking, Penguin, 1977. 510 pp., illus., biblio. $16.95 pb.

Nineteenth and Twentieth Century Architecture. Garland Library of the History of Art. New York: Garland Publishing, 1976. $55 hb.

Architects on Architecture: New Directions in America. Paul Heyer. 1966. Rev. ed. New York: Walker, 1978. 416 pp., illus., biblio., index. $14.95 pb.

American Building Art: The Twentieth Century. Carl W. Condit. New York: Oxford University Press, 1961. 427 pp., illus., biblio., index.

Mind and Image: An Essay on Art and Architecture. Herb Greene. Lexington: University Press of Kentucky, 1976. 210 pp., illus., biblio., index. $24 hb.

A Visual History of Twentieth Century Architecture. Dennis Sharp. Greenwich, Conn.: New York Graphic Society, 1972. 304 pp., illus., biblio. $34.95 hb.

Space, Time and Architecture: The Growth of a New Tradition. Sigfried Giedion. Cambridge: Harvard University Press, 1967. 897 pp., illus., biblio., notes. $35 hb.

Encyclopedia of 20th-Century Architecture. Rev. ed. New York: Abrams, 1985. $24.95.

Bauhaus 1919–1928. Herbert Bayer, Ise Gropius and Walter Gropius, ed. 1938. Reprint. New York: Museum of Modern Art, 1972. 224 pp., illus. $8.95 pb.

Bauhaus: Weimar, Dessau, Berlin, Chicago. Hans M. Wingler. Cambridge: MIT Press, 1969. 698 pp., illus., biblio. $125 hb, $25 pb.

The Aftermath of the Bauhaus in America: Gropius, Mies and Breuer. William H. Jordy. Cambridge: Harvard University Press, 1968. 485 pp.

The Master Builders: Le Corbusier, Mies van der Rohe, Frank Lloyd Wright. Peter Blake. Rev. ed. New York: W.W. Norton, 1976. 432 pp. $6.95 pb.

Farnsworth House (1950, Ludwig Mies van der Rohe), Plano, Ill., one of the architect's most noted small-scale International Style landmarks. (Bill Hedrich, Hedrich-Blessing)

Public Office Building (1982, Michael Graves), Portland, Ore.

Modern Architecture. Vincent Scully, Jr. 1962. Rev. ed. New York: Braziller, 1974. 128 pp. $9.95 pb.

Age of the Masters: A Personal View of Modern Architecture. Reyner Banham. New York: Harper and Row, 1975. 176 pp. $17.50 hb, $8.95 pb.

Masters of Modern Architecture. John Peter. New York: Braziller, 1958. 230 pp., illus.

The Shingle Style Today, or The Historian's Revenge. Vincent Scully, Jr. New York: Braziller, 1974. 118 pp., illus. $12.50 hb, $5.95 pb.

Form Follows Fiasco: Why Modern Architecture Hasn't Worked. Peter Blake. Boston: Little, Brown, 1974. 169 pp., illus.

The Failure of Modern Architecture. Brent C. Brolin. New York: Van Nostrand Reinhold, 1976. 128 pp., illus., biblio. $7.95 pb.

From Bauhaus to Our House: Why Modern Architects Can't Get Out of the Box. Tom Wolfe. New York: Farrar, Straus and Giroux, 1981. $10.95 hb. New York: Pocket Books, 1982. $2.95 pb.

Global Architecture Series: Modern Masters ($15 pb each), *Houses* ($22.50 each), *Details* ($15 each), *Documents* ($16 each), *Interiors* ($22.50 each) and *Special Issues* ($30 each). Yukio Futagawa, ed. Tokyo, Japan: ADA Edita Tokyo Company, Ltd. (3-12-14 Sendagaya, Shibuya), 1970–.

File Under Architecture. Herbert Muschamp. Cambridge: MIT Press, 1979. 117 pp. $4.95 pb.

Modern Architecture and Design: An Alternative History. Bill Risebero. Cambridge: MIT Press, 1982. 256 pp., illus., biblio., index. $17.50 hb.

Post-Modern and Late Modern (1965–)

"We are moving into a period that some critics have labeled 'postmodern'; others have spoken of it as a time of eclecticism or of the absence of dogma. . . . The best architecture today incorporates elements from a number of styles. It is eclectic in the sense of that word's derivation, 'to select' . . . unbound by the modernists' belief that it is necessary to break off entirely from history and reinvent the wheel with every modern building. . . . The directions in which architecture is now moving are influenced a great deal by the preservation attitude. The preservation movement in the last decade or so has helped reduce our culture's obsession with newness for its own sake, an obsession that, obviously, all too many architects shared."

> Paul Goldberger, "New Directions: Architecture and Preservation." In *Preservation: Toward an Ethic in the 1980s.* Washington, D.C.: Preservation Press, 1980.

"You cannot *not* know history."
> Philip Johnson

The Language of Post-Modern Architecture. Charles Jencks. 1977. 3rd ed. New York: Rizzoli, 1981. 152 pp., illus. $13.50 pb.

New Directions in American Architecture. Robert A.M. Stern. 1969. Rev. ed. New York: Braziller, 1977. 128 pp. $7.95 pb.

Supermannerism: New Attitudes in Post-Modern Architecture. Ray C. Smith. New York: E.P. Dutton, 1977. 354 pp., illus., biblio., index.

"The Search for a Postmodern Architecture." *CRIT 4: The Architectural Student Journal.* Fall 1978. Association of Student Chapters of AIA, 1735 New York Avenue, N.W., Washington, D.C. 20006.

Late-Modern Architecture and Other Essays. Charles Jencks. New York: Rizzoli, 1980. 200 pp., illus., biblio., index. $32.50 hb.

Transformations in Modern Architecture. Arthur Drexler. New York: Museum of Modern Art, 1979. 168 pp., illus. $18.95 pb.

American Architecture Now. Barbaralee Diamonstein. New York: Rizzoli, 1981. 253 pp., illus.

Architecture 1970–1980: A Decade of Change. Jeanne Davern and Editors of Architectural Record. New York: McGraw-Hill, Architectural Record Books, 1980. 265 pp., illus., index. $39.95 hb.

International Handbook of Contemporary Developments in Architecture. Westport, Conn.: Greenwood Press, 1981. 637 pp., illus., appends., index. $75 hb.

Post-Modern Classicism: The New Synthesis. Charles Jencks, ed. AD Profiles. New York: Rizzoli, 1981. 144 pp., color illus. $19.95 pb.

After Modern Architecture. Paolo Portoghesi. New York: Rizzoli, 1981. 160 pp., color illus. $19.95 pb.

Complexity and Contradiction in Architecture. Robert Venturi. 1966. Rev. ed. New York: Museum of Modern Art, 1977. 136 pp., illus., index. $9.95 pb.

Architecture Today. Charles Jencks with William Chaitkin. New York: Abrams, 1982. 359 pp., color illus., biblio., index. $65 hb.

Ornamentalism: The New Decorativeness in Architecture and Design. Robert Jensen and Patricia Conway. New York: Clarkson Potter, 1982. 312 pp., illus., index. $40 hb.

Michael Graves, 1966–1980. Karen Wheeler and Peter Arnell, eds. Introduction by Michael Graves. Essay by Vincent Scully. New York: Rizzoli, 1982. 304 pp., color illus. $45 hb, $29.95 pb.

Robert A.M. Stern, 1965–1980: Towards a Modern Architecture After Modernism. Robert A.M. Stern. Peter Arnell, ed. New York: Rizzoli, 1981. 256 pp., color illus. $29.95 pb.

Five Architects: Eisenman, Graves, Gwathmey, Hejduk, Meier. Foreword by Philip Johnson. Introduction by Colin Rowe. Essay by Kenneth Frampton. 2nd ed. New York: Oxford University Press, 1975. 144 pp., illus. $18.95 pb.

Guide to U.S. Architecture: 1940–1980. Esther McCoy and Barbara Goldstein, eds. Santa Monica, Calif.: Arts and Architecture Press (1119 Colorado Avenue, 90401), 1982. 167 pp., illus., index. $9.95 pb.

Salem Five Cents Savings Bank (c. 1893), with addition (1974, Oscar Padjen Architects), Salem, Mass. (Joseph Borysthen-Tkacz)

Old and New Architecture

A long time ago, when styles of architecture took 500 years on the average to rise and descend, the fabric of buildings and of cities seemed to hold together better; the problems of old and new seemed less difficult. Design relationships evolved gradually; architectural materials and methods were more limited. . . . Today technology allows diverse and confusing choices of materials and methods; styles and trends overlap within short periods; freedom of expression and individual choice conflict with community needs and images. . . .

> Robert Burley, "Introduction: Redirecting the Theater of the Built Environment." In *Old and New Architecture: Design Relationship*

Adding a new building to an existing group of buildings is a commonplace design problem. Yet our cities are proof that the compatible solution is uncommon.

> Keith Ray, ed., *Contextual Architecture*

Trentman House (1968, Hugh Jacobsen), Washington, D.C. (Robert Lautman)

"New construction that mocks its earlier and honest neighbors only dilutes the historical view. The integrity of historic buildings is respected and the historic buildings of the future are created when new architecture not only harmonizes with the old in sensibility, scale and proportion, but also expresses its own time, solves its own needs and relates to the place in which it sits. Slavish reproduction of the past will deprive us of the landmarks of the future."

> John P. Conron, "A Three-Dimensional Approach." In *Old and New Architecture: Design Relationship*

"Anti-historicism today is the most destructive force in the urban landscape. Until now the modernist's fear of borrowing from history has kept the crite-ria for fitting new buildings into old contexts quite lax. The typical list . . . rarely includes evoking the 'style' of the older buildings in detail and ornament, one of the most important factors for a successful fit in. . . . I do believe in evolution and change in architecture, but without the past as a source, creativity and originality will ultimately exhaust themselves."

> Brent Brolin, *Architecture in Context*

"What is needed is not the easy route of imitation, nor the unforgivable arrogance of must-be-new modernism, but the difficult achievement of the in-between."

> Paul Goldberger, "To Preserve the Visibility of Time." In *Old and New Architecture: Design Relationship*

Old and New Architecture: Design Relationship. National Trust for Historic Preservation. Washington, D.C.: Preservation Press, 1980. 280 pp., illus., biblio., index. $25 hb, $15.95 pb.

The first comprehensive look at the subject, drawing together divergent views of 20 noted architects, planners and preservationists. Topics addressed include the history and theory of design relationships, the legality of architectural controls, historic districts, design guidelines, adaptive use and public and professional education. A special photo commentary is provided by architect and critic Peter Blake. Other contributors include Michael Graves, Paul Goldberger, Louis Sauer, Jean Paul Carlhian, Giorgio Cavaglieri and Weiming Lu.

Architecture in Context: Fitting New Buildings with Old. Brent Brolin. New York: Van Nostrand Reinhold, 1979. 144 pp., illus. $16.95 hb, $7.95 pb.

A statement of this architect's philosophy of compatibility, which stresses the fit-ability of detail and ornament.

Contextual Architecture: Responding to Existing Style. Keith Ray and Editors of Architectural Record Magazine. New York: McGraw-Hill, 1980. 189 pp., illus., index. $36.50 hb.

Reprints from the pages of *Architectural Record*, with brief prefaces to the four chapters: interiors, alterations, additions and infill.

"Contemporary Building in Historic Districts." *Historic Preservation*, January–March 1971.

Articles in the special feature: "A Charleston Critique," Philip Johnson; "The Marriage of New Buildings with Old," Harmon H. Goldstone; "Contemporary Design in a Historic Context," John W. Lawrence; "Criteria of Urban Design Relatedness," Paul Muldawer.

"True or False: Architecture Old and New," Carl Feiss and Terry B. Morton. *Historic Preservation*, April–June 1968.

"Old Sites and New Buildings: The Architect's Point of View," Hugh Casson. *The Future of the Past*. Jane Fawcett, ed. New York: Watson-Guptill, 1976. 160 pp., illus., biblio., index.

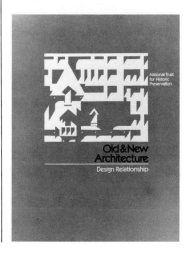

Plans and Dreams: Architectural Design Competitions

The primary purpose of design competitions is to find new possibilities for architectural form, to embody a mood toward which society is tending, and on occasion, to advance new possibilities for living hitherto not clearly disclosed. Competitions operate as well as society operates. They operate at their best, as do other human enterprises, when they are free to concentrate on the main purpose of design—which is design.

Paul D. Spreiregen, *Design Competitions*

Clothespin by Claes Oldenburg submitted in 1967 as a "late entry" in the Tribune Tower competition (later built in Philadelphia). From *Unbuilt America*.

"Design competitions have been used to solve many challenging architectural problems. . . . The East Facade of the Louvre, Paris, 1665. . . . The U.S. Capitol, the White House and the Washington Monument, Washington, D.C., 1792. . . . Central Park, New York City, 1858. . . . The Eiffel Tower, Paris, 1889. . . . The Jefferson Memorial Arch, St. Louis, 1950. . . . It is the nature of buildings, indeed of all habitats, to be offspring of competitions."

"Design Competitions," Paul D. Spreiregen. *Historic Preservation*, October–December 1974.

Design Competitions. Paul D. Spreiregen. New York: McGraw-Hill, 1979. 310 pp., illus., index. $24.95 hb.

A graphic history of design competitions, with a retrospective on competitions from the Spanish Steps to today, plus a working manual for designers and sponsors on competitions.

Handbook of Architectural Design Competitions. American Institute of Architects. Washington, D.C.: AIA Design and Environment Programs Office, 1981. 33 pp., biblio. Free.

Provides an overview of selecting an architect and describes the roles of competition sponsors, jurors and competitors. Includes time planning and cost estimating guides plus conditions when competitions are appropriate and inappropriate.

Winning Designs: The Competitions Renaissance. George G. Wynne, ed. New Brunswick, N.J.: Transaction Books, 1981. 60 pp., illus., append. $5 pb. Available from Council for International Urban Liaison (818 18th Street, N.W., Room 840, Washington, D.C. 20006).

Focuses on the use of design competitions to improve public buildings and spaces in Western Europe, Australia and Japan. Explores the success of competitions abroad in fostering innovative and creative designs for development.

Design Competition Manual. National Endowment for the Arts Design Arts Program and Vision. Cambridge: Vision (678 Massachusetts Avenue, 02139), 1980. 24 pp. $2 pb.

Outlines types of competitions and step-by-step ways to run one.

Competition 1792: Designing a Nation's Capitol. Catalog from an exhibition on the U.S. Capitol. Washington, D.C.: The Octagon (1799 New York Avenue, N.W., 20006). $3.75 pb.

Competitive Designs for the Cathedral of St. John the Divine in New York City. 1891. Reprint. Introduction by Rev. James Parks Morton. New York: Da Capo, 1981. 57 plates. $85.

The Chicago Tribune Competition, Vol. 1. 1923. Reprint. New York: Rizzoli, 1980. 189 pp., illus., index. 2 vols. $30 pb.

"Volume 1 covers the 1922 event, which drew 281 entries seeking the $50,000 first prize. The conservative jury, which included Tribune publisher Col. Robert R. McCormick, of course chose Raymond Hood's and John Mead Howells' Gothic tower—now standing as part of the famous 'gateway' on Lake Michigan. . . . All 281 entries from 55 nations are reproduced in this book, which includes the original program and rules, the jury's report, and biographies of the winners." (Michael Leccese, review in *Preservation News*, October 1980)

Chicago Tribune Tower Competition and Late Entries. Stanley Tigerman. Rev. ed. New York: Rizzoli, 1982. 160 pp., illus. $27.50 pb.

Extended Use

During the 1970s the design competition process was extended to the selection of architects for restoration projects. Among the competitive objects: The Wainwright Building and the Old Post Office in St. Louis and the Old Post Office in Washington, D.C.

Robert Mills's winning Washington Monument design (c. 1837).

Tribune Tower (1925, Howells and Hood). *(Chicago Tribune)*

Contacts

Competitions Advisory Service
Department of Practice and Design
American Institute of Architects
1735 New York Avenue, N.W.
Washington, D.C. 20006

Provides assistance to any individual or organization contemplating the selection of an architect by design competition.

Association of Student Chapters
American Institute of Architects
1735 New York Avenue, N.W.
Washington, D.C. 20006

Cosponsors competitions twice yearly—spring and fall—for students in architectural schools. Some recent competitions have included ones with the Tile Council of America and McDonald's Corporation.

Galleria proposed by Robert Zion to prevent the demolition of New York's Penn Station (1906, McKim, Mead and White). From *Unbuilt America*.

The Science Center by Hugh Ferriss (1889–1962), showing a waterway, wide traffic plane and high central mass. From *Architectural Visions*.

A visionary urban center by Hugh Ferriss, an architect who was one of the most popular renderers of Art Deco buildings.

Forgotten Architecture: The Unbuilt and Visionary

Unbuilt structures can be compared to destroyed buildings. They once did exist, if not in brick and stone then at least in the minds of the designers. They still have a form of existence, if not in photographs, then in drawings or models or words. If the chance to build them has been lost, the chance to remember what might have been has not been lost.

Perhaps most important of all, these designs can teach us a great deal about the way the world was viewed at different points in history, about the way creative individuals chose to relate to their surroundings.

The unbuilt is clearly another form of forgotten architecture.

Ashton Nichols, review of *Unbuilt America*. *Preservation News*, May 1977.

Unbuilt America. Alison Sky and Michelle Stone. 1976. New York: Abbeville Press, 1983. 308 pp., illus. $24.95 hb.

Architectural Visions: The Drawings of Hugh Ferriss. Jean Ferriss Leich. New York: Whitney Library of Design, 1980. 143 pp., illus., biblio. $19.95 hb.

Chicago Tribune Tower Competition and Late Entries. Stanley Tigerman. Rev. ed. New York: Rizzoli, 1982. 160 pp., illus. $27.50 pb.

Visionary Drawings of Architecture and Planning, 20th Century Through the 1960s. George R. Collins. Cambridge: MIT Press, 1979. $15 pb.

Fantastic Architecture: Personal and Eccentric Visions. Michael Schuyt and Joost Elffers. Text by George R. Collins. New York: Abrams, 1980. 247 pp., illus.

The Architecture of Fantasy: Utopian Building and Planning in Modern Times. Ulrich Conrads and Hans G. Sperlich. New York: Praeger, 1962. 187 pp., illus. biblio., index.

Architectural Drawing: The Art and the Process. Gerald Allen and Richard Oliver. New York: Whitney Library of Design, 1981. 200 pp., color illus. $35 hb.

Architectural Fantasies: Creative Alternatives. Washington, D.C.: The Octagon (1799 New York Avenue, N.W., 20006). 13 pp., illus. $2.50 pb.

See also: Architectural Drawings (Building Roots)

The Clay Emerging Into Practical Form. (Hugh Ferriss)

"Ada Louise Huxtable already doesn't like it!" Alan Dunn. (© 1968 The New Yorker Magazine, Inc.)

The Critics: Architecture Observed

For the most part architecture critics have been effective only when talking about specific buildings after the fact of design or construction. . . . Criticism will always be more useful when it informs the future than when it scores the past.

> Wayne Attoe, *Architecture and Critical Imagination*

I seem born to conceive what I cannot execute, recommend what I cannot obtain, and mourn over what I cannot save.

> John Ruskin, 1848

" 'Commodity, firmness and delight' [Vitruvius], between these three values the criticism of architecture has wavered, not always distinguishing very clearly between them, seldom attempting any statement of the relation they bear to one another, never pursuing to their conclusion the consequences which they involved."

> Geoffrey Scott, *The Architecture of Humanism*

"In practice, editors find architecture one large headache. Their problems are: how to find the Renaissance man or woman who can not only grasp the aesthetic, economic, political, and social aspects of urban design but can also write readable prose, and how to label and where to put his or her product. Is urban design an art? a commercial trade or business? Does it belong under environment? real estate? style? . . . Is architecture hard or soft news? criticism or feature? . . . Meanwhile, our built world, hard as stone, both literally and metaphorically, remains all but invisible in the press."

> Jane Holtz Kay, "Architecture and Design—Who Cares?" *Columbia Journalism Review,* July–August 1975.

Architecture and Critical Imagination. Wayne Attoe. New York: John Wiley, 1978. 188 pp., illus., biblio. $39.95 hb.

"The only major effort at a taxonomy of critical methods in architecture. With the premise that all forms of response to the built environment can be described as criticism, and the assumption that both architects and the lay public are something less than methodical in understanding or extrapolating the essence of critical efforts, Attoe offers numerous examples by professional critics, architects and users." (Review by Roger L. Schluntz, AIA. *AIA Journal,* December 1978)

The History, Theory and Criticism of Architecture. Marcus Whiffen, ed. Cambridge: MIT Press, 1966.

Architecture and Morality: The Development of a Theme in Architectural History and Theory from the Gothic Revival to the Modern Movement. David Watkin. New York: Oxford University Press, 1977. 136 pp., biblio.

The Nature of Architectural Criticism. Jayant J. Maharaj. School of Architecture Report Series, no. 36. Halifax, Nova Scotia: Nova Scotia Technical College, 1977. 140 pp., biblio. $5 pb.

"Architectural Comment in American Magazines, 1783–1815," J. Meredith Neil. *American Association of Architectural Bibliographers' Papers,* vol. 5. William B. O'Neal, ed. Charlottesville: University Press of Virginia, 1968. $10 pb.

"Architecture, Criticism and Evaluation." Special issue. Ellen Perry Berkeley, ed. *Journal of Architectural Education,* April 1976.

"Preservation Theory Comes of Age." In *Preservation Comes of Age: From Williamsburg to the National Trust, 1926–1949.* Charles B. Hosmer, Jr. Charlottesville: University Press of Virginia, 1981. 1,291 pp., illus., biblio., chron., index. 2 vols. $37.50 hb.

Traces the role played during the period by architects, architectural historians and critics in developing preservation awareness as a part of their architectural criticism.

Critical Awards
Pulitzer Prize

1970	Ada Louise Huxtable
1979	Paul Gapp
1984	Paul Goldberger

American Institute of Architects

1968	Lewis Mumford
1969	Ada Louise Huxtable
1970	Henry-Russell Hitchcock
1971	Sibyl Moholy-Nagy
1972	Wolf Von Eckardt
1975	Peter Blake

National Trust for Historic Preservation

1971	Ada Louise Huxtable
1974	James Marston Fitch
1977	William Marlin

Contemporary Critics

"Twentieth-century America has seen a steady, persistent decline in the visual and emotional power of its public buildings, and this had been accompanied by a not less persistent decline in the authority of public order. . . . The standard liberal mind has been curiously indifferent or oblivious to this process. This is doubtless in part due to the fact that, as [Huxtable] comments, the institutions that teach American elites to *think* about the modern world are altogether unconcerned with teaching them to *look* at it."

> Daniel P. Moynihan, Preface. *Will They Ever Finish Bruckner Boulevard?*

"With America's enthusiastic embrace of modern architectural and planning principles from the 1930s to the 1960s, four architectural critics emerged as important forces in an ongoing appraisal of its consequences . . . Catherine Bauer, Jane Jacobs, Sibyl Moholy-Nagy, and Ada Louise Huxtable. . . . It took courage, an ability to communicate to public and professionals, and a belief in the power of written language to alter the built environment."

> Suzanne Stephens, "Voices of Consequence: Four Architectural Critics." With a Bibliography of Their Writings. In *Women in American Architecture*

"I couldn't have gotten my job if Ada hadn't won her Pulitzer Prize. She made the whole profession respectable."

> Robert Cuscaden *(Chicago Sun-Times).* Quoted in *Wall Street Journal,* November 7, 1972.

Several score writers now have jobs on the major dailies writing about architecture, preservation and the urban environment, with the most regular coverage appearing in such newspapers as the *New York Times* (Paul Goldberger), *Chicago Tribune* (Paul Gapp), *Boston Globe* (Robert Campbell), *Christian Science Monitor* (Jane Holtz Kay) and *Washington Post* (Benjamin Forgey), as well as in the *Philadelphia Inquirer, Denver Post, Los Angeles Times* and *St. Louis Post-Dispatch.* Thoughtful criticism is harder to find among the commercial magazines but is prevalent in the major architectural magazines.

Ada Louise Huxtable
Will They Ever Finish Bruckner Boulevard? Ada Louise Huxtable. A New York Times Book. New York: Macmillan, 1970. 255 pp., illus.

Kicked a Building Lately? Ada Louise Huxtable. New York: Times Books, 1976. 304 pp., illus.

Ada Louise Huxtable: An Annotated Bibliography. Lawrence Wodehouse. Foreword by Ada Louise Huxtable. New York: Garland Publishing, 1981. 303 pp., illus. $33 hb.

Appendix on Writings by Ada Louise Huxtable. In *American Architects 2: From the First World War to the Present.* Lawrence Wodehouse, ed. Detroit: Gale Research, 1977. 305 pp. $44 hb.

Lewis Mumford. (Alfred Bendiner)

Lewis Mumford
Sketches from Life: The Autobiography of Lewis Mumford— The Early Years. Lewis Mumford. New York: Dial Press, 1982. 500 pp., illus. $19.95 hb. Boston: Beacon Press, 1983. $12.45 pb.

Architecture as a Home for Man: Essays for Architectural Record. Lewis Mumford. New York: Architectural Record Books, 1975. 214 pp., illus., index.

My Work and Days: A Personal Chronicle. Lewis Mumford. New York: Harcourt Brace Jovanovich, 1979. $13.95.

Sticks and Stones: A Study of American Architecture and Civilization. Lewis Mumford. 1924. Reprint. New York: Dover, 1955. 238 pp., illus. $3.50 pb.

Other Critics
The Writings of Architectural Historian Henry-Russell Hitchcock. Lamia Doumato. Monticello, Ill.: Vance Bibliographies, 1980. 12 pp. $2 pb.

In Search of Modern Architecture: A Tribute to Henry-Russell Hitchcock. Helen Searing, ed. Cambridge: MIT Press, 1983. 375 pp., illus., index. $45 hb.

"Sir Nikolaus Pevsner," John R. Barr. *American Association of Architectural Bibliographers' Papers,* vol. 7. William B. O'Neal, ed. Charlottesville: University Press of Virginia, 1970. $10 pb.

On the Rise: Architecture and Design in a Postmodern Age. Paul Goldberger. New York: Times Books, 1983. 340 pp., illus. $23.50 hb.

Paul Gapp's Chicago: Selected Writings of the Chicago Tribune's Architecture Critic. Paul Gapp. Chicago: Chicago Tribune, 1980. 60 pp., illus. $3.50 pb.

Louisville: Architecture and the Urban Environment. William Morgan. Introduction by Noel Perrin. Dublin, N.H.: William L. Bauhan (Dublin 03444), 1979. 100 pp., illus. $6.95 pb.

Critics of the Past
"Men's ideas of how buildings should look change radically as do their methods of building them: the words they use to justify their revolutionary ideas change not at all."
> Russell Lynes, *The Tastemakers.* 1949. Reprint. New York: Grosset and Dunlap, 1980.

Vitruvius (1st cent. B.C.–1st cent. A.D.)
The Ten Books on Architecture. Vitruvius. Reprint. New York: Dover, 1960. 330 pp., illus. $5 pb.
The oldest and most influential book on architecture, addressing the classical principles of symmetry, harmony and proportion. For hundreds of years Vitruvius's specific instructions were faithfully followed.

Andrew Jackson Downing (1815–52)
"Internationally known as a landscape gardener, horticulturist, and critic . . . it was in the latter capacity, as a prolific and persuasive author, that [Downing's] impact on American architecture was to be felt."
> William H. Pierson, Jr., "Andrew Jackson Downing: American Architectural Critic." In *American Buildings and Their Architects.* Vol. 2A: *Technology and the Picturesque. The Corporate and the Early Gothic Styles*

John Ruskin (1819–1900)
"Ruskin . . . wrote more passionately on architecture than any writer in the English language."
> Wayne Andrews, "The Gothic Menace." *Historic Preservation,* January–March 1970.

The Seven Lamps of Architecture. John Ruskin. 1848. Reprint. New York: Farrar, Straus and Giroux, 1961. 210 pp. $5.95 pb.

Ruskin on Architecture: His Thought and Influence. Kristine Ottesen Garrigan. Madison: University of Wisconsin Press, 1973. 220 pp. $27.50.

Looking at Architecture with Ruskin. John Unrau. Toronto: University of Toronto Press, 1978. $20 hb.

Savage Ruskin. Patrick Conner. Detroit: Wayne State University Press, 1979. 189 pp., illus., biblio., index. $14.95 hb.

William Morris (1834–96)
"Alas for those who are to come after us, whom we shall have robbed of works of art which it was our duty to hand down to them uninjured and unimpaired; alas for ourselves, who will be looked upon by foreign nations and by our own posterity as the only people who have ever lived, who, possessing no architecture of their own, have made themselves remarkable for the destruction of the buildings of their forefathers."
> William Morris, letter to *The Times* (London), April 17, 1878.

"Scrape and Anti-Scrape," Nikolaus Pevsner. In *The Future of the Past.* Jane Fawcett, ed. New York: Whitney Library of Design, 1976. 160 pp., illus., index.

Arts and Crafts Essays. William Morris et al. 1893. Reprint. Arts and Crafts Movement Series, vol. 34. New York: Garland Publishing, 1977. $48 hb.

William Morris: His Life and Work. Jack Lindsay. New York: Taplinger, 1979. 432 pp., illus., notes, index. $14.95 hb.

The Works of William Morris. R.C. Briggs, ed. 1962. Reprint. Folcroft, Pa.: Folcroft Library Editions, 1977. 75 pp., biblio. $10.

Charles Eastlake (1833–1906)
"[For Eastlake] the whole idea of architecture projecting an image of social or religious or

political conviction . . . has simply vanished. . . . In its place has come the idea of architecture as a Work of Art, to be appreciated by persons of Cultivated Taste who understand its Principles—principles derived from the art itself, independent of social context."
> Alan Gowans, Introduction. *History of the Gothic Revival*

History of the Gothic Revival. Charles L. Eastlake. 1872. Reprint. New York: Humanities Press, Leicester University Press, 1970. 581 pp., illus., appends., biblio. $44.25 hb. Watkins Glen, N.Y.: American Life Foundation, 1975. $12 pb.

Sir Charles Eastlake and the Victorian Art World. David Robertson. Princeton: Princeton University Press, 1978. $72.50.

Henry Van Brunt (1832–1903)
"Van Brunt's heightened sensitivity to architecture derived from his double perspective as a critic. He looked upon a building as an integrated aesthetic object and as the 'exponent' of a phase of culture. Hence his strict judgment of the way a particular building to a greater or lesser degree realized the potentialities of its style was modulated by his interest in its expressive and, in a broad sense, its 'historical' qualities."
> William A. Coles, *Architecture and Society*

Architecture and Society: Selected Essays of Henry Van Brunt. William A. Coles, ed. Cambridge: Belknap Press, Harvard University Press, 1969.

Montgomery Schuyler (1843–1914)
"In the beginning there was Schuyler . . . the pure aesthete . . . he praised with reason the Brooklyn Bridge, late Sullivan, and early Wright, raising, for two decades, architectural criticism to a height it had never before reached."
> Norval White, *The Architecture Book*

American Architecture and Other Writings by Montgomery Schuyler. William H. Jordy and Ralph Coe, eds. Cambridge: Harvard University Press, 1961. 2 vols. $40 set.
The first volume is a reprint of an 1892 edition of Schuyler's *American Architecture: Studies.* The second concentrates on bridges, skyscrapers, Beaux-Arts reaction and the works of Sullivan and Wright. It also contains a complete bibliography of Schuyler's periodical articles.

"Another monstrosity." Donald Reilly. (© 1969 Look Magazine)

"I *like* it. I really do. It combines a masculine feel of medieval strength with a delightful sense of play in the portcullis treatment." Donald Reilly.(© 1978 The New Yorker Magazine, Inc.)

Humoresque: An Irreverent Look

While architecture might well be, as Goethe so succinctly put it, frozen music, it has, nevertheless, an unfortunate tendency to melt.

> Osbert Lancaster, *A Cartoon History of Architecture*

Today's architect . . . is less concerned with frozen music than with liquid assets.

> Charles Abrams, *The Language of Cities: A Glossary of Terms.* New York: Viking, 1971.

"Cartoons are similar to . . . verbal gags in that they focus on a particular feature of the building and then exaggerate it. They are perhaps more potent than their verbal counterparts in that they make an explicit, visual reference to physical features of the building. Graphic depictions are closer to the original than are verbal comments. Some cartoons depend upon previous experiences or knowledge for their effects, and in fact their content is about something you must already know."

> Wayne Attoe, *Architecture and Critical Imagination*

Architecture Observed. Alan Dunn. New York: Architectural Record Books, 1971. 144 pp., illus.

"Impudent, even fantastic, burlesques on the absurdities of modern American architecture, its inept practitioners and its avid if sometimes baffled public." (Wendell D. Garrett. Review in *Historic Preservation,* January–March 1972)

A Cartoon History of Architecture: A Skeleton Key for the Irreverent, to Architecture, Decoration and Dress. Osbert Lancaster. 1964. Reprint. Ipswich, Mass.: Gambit, 1976. 199 pp., illus. $11.95 hb.

"Around none of the arts, with the possible exception of dry-fly fishing and twelve-tone music, has so formidable a mystique been woven as that which befogs architecture. . . . [The confusion is] wholly deplorable; for with none of the arts is the layman so inescapably involved as with architecture." In Lancaster's hands, the mystique is deftly and entertainingly unraveled.

Great Moments in Architecture. David Macaulay. Boston: Houghton Mifflin, 1978. 128 pp., illus. $5.95 pb.

"Unauthorized by both the Metropolitan Museum of Art and the British Museum, [it] casts a new light and with it the inevitable new shadow, on the perennial inquiry into the spiritual and philosophical meanings of a barely comprehensible yet expressible and often extraordinarily improvisatory pioneering. . . ." (K. Greenland Barry, preface)

"*I feel I should warn you . . .*"

HISTORIC PRESERVATION CARTOONS

"I Feel I Should Warn You . . ." Historic Preservation Cartoons. Terry B. Morton, ed. Essay by Draper Hill. Washington, D.C.: Preservation Press, 1975. 112 pp., illus. $6.95 pb.

In his introduction, cartoonist Draper Hill calls these cartoons "by turns angry and sad, activist and passive, realistic and metaphorical, hard sell and soft." This selection, covering nearly 150 years, represents the work of humorists who have nipped and nudged to keep the wreckers away from architecture worth saving.

Saul Steinberg. Harold Rosenberg. Whitney Museum of American Art. New York: Knopf, 1978. 256 pp., illus., append., biblio. $25 hb, $12.95 pb.

While in Milan, Italy (1933–41) Steinberg studied architecture, which he later claimed "is a marvelous training for anything but architecture. The frightening thought that what you draw may become a building makes for reasoned lines."

And on the Eighth Day. . . . The Last Word on City Planning and Planners. Richard Hedman and Frederick Bair, Jr. Chicago: ASPO Press (American Planning Association), 1976. 68 pp., illus. $8.95 pb.

Stop Me Before I Plan Again. Richard Hedman. Chicago: ASPO Press (American Planning Association), 1977. 112 pp., illus. $8.95 pb.

Irreverent looks at how modern cities are really planned.

San Agustin, Isleta Pueblo, N.M. (pre-1629), showing a prerestoration "Gothicization" blended with the native Southwest and Spanish colonial building techniques. (Dick Kemp)

Region by Region: Architectural Surveys

One place comprehended can make us understand other places better. Sense of place gives equilibrium; extended, it is sense of direction too.

Eudora Welty, *The Eye of the Story: Selected Essays and Reviews.* New York: Random House, 1978.

"Architecture, because of the natural tenacity of its fabric, the immobility and complexity of its examples, and the practical conservatism of its builders and users, has maintained its regional integrity and is of greatest use in the drawing of regions."

Henry Glassie, *Pattern in the Material Folk Culture of the Eastern United States*

"Like climatic ones, architectural borders blur into bands. . . . More often they reveal fascinating mixtures and blends."

Hugh Morrison, *Early American Architecture*

Cultural Regions of the United States. Raymond D. Gastil. Seattle: University of Washington Press, 1975. 366 pp., illus., biblio., index. $21 hb, $7.95 pb.

"Drawing on a wealth of studies of dialect, house styles and architecture settlement patterns, regional history, and many other matters, and combining them with statistical analyses of . . . other elements of social life, Gastil demonstrates that there is still much more life in American regionalism than many of us believed." (Nathan Glazer, foreword)

Regional Series

Records and Catalogs
Historic American Buildings Survey

Records of all states—measured architectural drawings, photographs and architectural and historical documentation—available from the Library of Congress and in printed catalogs and books, including illustrated catalogs of records for various states and cities. A microfiche edition is available from Chadwyck-Healey.

Historic America: Buildings, Structures, and Sites. Alicia Stamm and C. Ford Peatross, eds., HABS/HAER. With a Checklist of the HABS/HAER Collections. Washington, D.C.: Library of Congress, 1983. 708 pp., illus. $29 hb. GPO stock no. 030-000-00149-4.

Historic American Buildings Series. David G. DeLong, ed. New York: Garland Publishing. *California.* 4 vols. *New York.* 8 vols. *Texas.* 2 vols. $109 each.

Historic American Buildings Survey
National Park Service
U.S. Department of the Interior
P.O. Box 37127
Washington, D.C. 20013-7127

Prints and Photographs Division
Library of Congress
Washington, D.C. 20540

Chadwyck-Healey
417 Maitland Avenue
Teaneck, N.J. 07666

The States and the Nation
American Association for State and Local History

A series published for the Bicentennial surveying the historical development of each state. Various authors.

American Association for State and Local History
708 Berry Road
Nashville, Tenn. 37204

W.W. Norton
500 Fifth Avenue
New York, N.Y. 10036

Historical Society Architectural Publications
Mary Vance, ed.

Bibliographies in the Architectural Series listing books and brochures published by historical societies and preservation groups, organized alphabetically in groups of states.

Vance Bibliographies
P.O. Box 229
Monticello, Ill. 61856

Contacts
Journal of Regional Cultures
Popular Culture Center
Bowling Green State University
Bowling Green, Ohio 43405

Regional American Studies
Information Clearinghouse
American Studies Program
The American University
Washington, D.C. 20016

Local Chapters
American Institute of Architects
1735 New York Avenue, N.W.
Washington, D.C. 20006

New England Historical
Association
c/o Jonathan Liebowitz
18 Park Street
Pepperell, Mass. 01463

The Appalachian Center
University of Kentucky
641 South Limestone Avenue
Lexington, Ky. 40506

Center for the Study
of Southern Culture
University of Mississippi
University, Miss. 38677

Southern Historical Association
Tulane University
New Orleans, La. 70118

Center for Great Plains Studies
University of Nebraska
338 Andrews Hall
Lincoln, Neb. 36588

Southwest Studies Program
Scottsdale Community College
9000 East Chaparral
Scottsdale, Ariz. 85253

Western History Association
Department of History
University of Nevada
Reno, Nev. 89507

See also: Architecture on Tour;
Building Roots

Howe Farms, Tunbridge, Vt. (Vermont Travel Division)

New England
Architecture in Early New England. Abbott Lowell Cummings. Sturbridge, Mass.: Old Sturbridge Village, 1974. 38 pp., illus. $2.

Architecture in New England. Wayne Andrews. 1973. New York: Harper and Row, 1980. 202 pp., illus., biblio., index. $9.95 pb.

Revelations of New England Architecture: People and Their Buildings. Curt Brace and Jill Grossman. New York: Viking, 1975. 179 pp., illus., biblio., index.

Connecticut
Heritage Houses: The American Tradition in Connecticut 1660–1900. Sara E. Rolleston. Introduction by David W. Dangremond. New York: Viking, 1979. 176 pp., illus.

Early Connecticut Houses. Norman Isham and Albert Brown. 1900. Reprint. New York: Dover, 1965. 303 pp., illus., biblio., index. $6 pb.

Some Notes on Early Connecticut Architecture. Elmer D. Keith. Arthur W. Leibundguth, ed. 1938. Rev. ed. Hartford: Antiquarian and Landmark Society of Connecticut (394 Main Street, 06103), 1976. 48 pp., illus. $3.50 pb.

Historic Houses and Interiors in Southern Connecticut. Sara E. Rolleston. New York: Hastings House, 1976. 208 pp., illus., index. $16.95 hb.

Maine
Maine Catalog: Historic American Buildings Survey. Denys Peter Myers. Augusta: Maine State Museum (State House, 04330), 1974. 254 pp., illus., index. $8.95 pb.

Maine Forms of American Architecture. Deborah Thompson, ed. Camden, Maine: Down East Magazine, 1976. 362 pp., illus., biblio., index. $19 hb.

200 Years of Maine Housing: A Guide for the House Watcher. Frank A. Beard. Augusta: Maine Historic Preservation Commission (242 State Street, 04333), 1976. 15 pp., illus. Free.

Portland. Martin Dibner, ed. Portland: Greater Portland Landmarks (P.O. Box 4197, Station A, 04101), 1972. 326 pp., illus., gloss., index. $15 hb, $6.95 pb.

Maine's Historic Places. Frank A. Beard and Bette A. Smith, Maine Historic Preservation Commission. Camden, Maine: Down East Books, 1982. 416 pp., illus., maps, index. $9.95 pb.

Massachusetts
Historic Buildings of Massachusetts: Photographs from the Historic American Buildings Survey. New York: Scribner's, 1976. 392 pp., illus. $14.95.

Architecture Boston. Joseph L. Eldredge, Boston Society of Architects. Introduction by Walter Muir Whitehill. New York: Clarkson Potter, 1976. 182 pp., illus., maps, biblio., index. $7.95 pb.

Houses of Boston's Back Bay. Bainbridge Bunting. Cambridge: Harvard University Press, 1967. 494 pp., illus., append., index. $12.50 pb.

Built in Boston: City and Suburb, 1800–1950. D.S. Tucci. Boston: New York Graphic Society, 1978. 269 pp., illus., biblio., index. $23.95 hb.

Survey of Architectural History in Cambridge. Cambridge Historical Commission. Report 1: *East Cambridge.* Report 2: *Mid-Cambridge.* 1967. 118 pp. $8.95 pb. Report 3: *Cambridgeport.* 1971. 159 pp. $8.95 pb. Report 4: *Old Cambridge.* 1973. 208 pp. $8.95 pb. Report 5: *Northwest Cambridge.* 1977. 207 pp. $9.95 pb. Cambridge: MIT Press. illus., maps, biblio.

Rhode Island
Rhode Island Architecture. Henry-Russell Hitchcock. 1939. Rev. ed. New York: Da Capo, 1968. 238 pp., illus. $35 hb.

The Architectural Heritage of Newport, Rhode Island, 1640–1915. Antoinette Downing and Vincent Scully. 1952. Reprint. New York: Crown, 1967. 526 pp., illus., appends., index. $15 pb.

Newport Preserv'd: Architecture of the 18th Century. Desmond Guinness and Julius Trousdale Sadler, Jr. New York: Viking, 1982. 152 pp., illus., index. $20 hb.

1850 courthouse, Guildhall, Vt. (Douglas Baz, Seagram County Court House Archives)

Vermont
Old Vermont Houses: 1763–1850. Herbert Wheaton Congdon. 1940. Reprint. Peterborough, N.H.: Noone House, 1968. 192 pp., illus., gloss. $4.95 pb.

The Burlington Book: Architecture, History, Future. Historic Preservation Program, Department of History, University of Vermont. Chester H. Liebs, Project Director. Burlington: University of Vermont Historic Preservation Program, 1980. 111 pp., illus. $8.95 pb.

Haughwout Building (1857), New York City. (© Cervin Robinson 1983)

Mid-Atlantic

Delaware
"Bibliography of Historic Buildings and Site Surveys." Gretchen Fitting, William J. Cohen and Associates. Wilmington: Greater Wilmington Development Council, 1979. 27 pp.

District of Columbia
The Architecture of Washington, D.C. Bates Lowry, ed. Essex, N.Y.: Dunlap Society (Lake Champlain Road, 12936), 1976, 1979. 2 vols. microfiche and slides. $300 boxed set.

District of Columbia Catalog: Historic American Buildings Survey. Nancy B. Schwartz, comp. Charlottesville: University Press of Virginia, 1974. For Columbia Historical Society. 193 pp., illus., append., index. $9.75 hb, $4.95 pb.

Historic Buildings of Washington, D.C.: A Selection from the Records of the Historic American Buildings Survey. Diane Maddex. Foreword by Arthur Cotton Moore. Pittsburgh: Ober Park Associates (One Station Square, 15219), 1973. 192 pp., illus., append., biblio., index. $7.95 pb.

Washington Architecture, 1791–1861: Problems in Development. Daniel D. Reiff. Washington, D.C.: U.S. Commission of Fine Arts, 1971. 161 pp., illus., biblio., index. GPO stock no. 010-000-00004-1.

Washington: Design of the Federal City. National Archives and Records Service. Washington, D.C.: Acropolis Books, 1981. 96 pp., illus. $11.95 pb.

Maryland
Three Centuries of Maryland Architecture. Maryland Historical Trust and Society for the Preservation of Maryland Antiquities. Annapolis: Maryland Historical Trust (21 State Circle, 21401), 1982. 91 pp. $5.

Architecture and Preservation in Maryland: A Guide to Historic Homes, Churches, and Historic Sites. Coppa and Avery Consultants. Monticello, Ill.: Vance Bibliographies, 1981. 10 pp. A-525. $2 pb.

Historic Sites Inventory. Vol. I: *Southern Maryland.* 87 pp., illus., index. Vol. II: *Lower Eastern Shore.* 75 pp., illus., index. Annapolis: Maryland Historical Trust. $4.50 pb.

Colonial and Historic Homes of Maryland. Don Swann. Cockeysville, Md.: Liberty Publishing, 1983. 1975. 211 pp., illus. $14.95 pb.

Baltimore: The Building of an American City. Sherry H. Olson. Baltimore: Johns Hopkins University Press, 1980. 432 pp., illus., index. $26.50 hb.

"Antiques in Annapolis." *Antiques,* January and February 1977.

Bel Air: The Town Through Its Buildings. Marilyn M. Larew, Town of Bel Air and Maryland Historical Trust. Edgewood, Md.: Northfield Press (2301 Willoughby Beach Road, 21040), 1981. 151 pp., illus. index. $13.95 pb.

New Jersey
Architecture and Preservation in the State of New Jersey: A Guide to Municipalities, Regions, Historic Homes, Church Architecture and Architectural Styles. Coppa and Avery Consultants. Monticello, Ill.: Vance Bibliographies, 1979. 10 pp. $2.

New Jersey Catalog Historic American Buildings Survey. William B. Bassett, comp. Newark: New Jersey Historical Society (230 Broadway, 07104), 1977. 208 pp., illus., index. $13.95 hb, $9.95 pb.

The New Jersey House. Helen Schwartz. New Brunswick, N.J.: Rutgers University Press, 1983. 181 pp., illus. $25 hb, $14.95 pb.

Erie Canal aqueduct (1839), Fort Hunter, N.Y. (HAER)

New York
A Fair Land to Build In: The Architecture of the Empire State. Brendan Gill. Albany: Preservation League of New York State, 1984. 60 pp., illus., index. $7.95 pb.

Architecture in New York. A Photographic History. Wayne Andrews. New York: Harper and Row, 1973. 190 pp., illus., biblio., index. $8.95 pb.

The Architecture of New York City: Histories and Views of Important Structures, Settings, and Symbols. Donald M. Reynolds. New York: Macmillan, 1984. 352 pp., illus. $29.95 hb.

American Architecture: Westchester County, New York: Colonial to Contemporary. Frank E. Sanchis. Westchester: Historic Preservation Committee, Bicentennial Committee of Westchester, 1977. 564 pp., illus., index. $30 hb.

Architecture in Fredonia: 1811–1972. Daniel D. Reiff. Fredonia: Michael C. Rockefeller Arts Center Gallery and Lakeshore Association for the Arts (State University Bookstore, Room 716, 14062), 1972. 124 pp., illus., biblio. $3 pb.

Wayne County: Aesthetic Heritage of a Rural Area. Stephen W. Jacobs, Wayne County Historical Society. New York: Publishing Center for Cultural Resources, 1979. 287 pp., illus., biblio. $42 hb, $20 pb.

The Nineteenth-Century Architecture of Saratoga Springs: Architecture Worth Saving in New York State. Stephen S. Prokopoff and Joan C. Siegfried. New York: New York State Council on the Arts, 1970. 104 pp., illus., gloss. $3.50 pb.

Onondaga Landmarks: A Survey of Historic and Architectural Sites in Syracuse and Onondaga County. Carol T. Jeschke, with Syracuse-Onondaga County Planning Agency. Syracuse: Cultural Resources Council of Syracuse and Onondaga County (Civic Center, 411 Montgomery Street, 13202), 1975. 109 pp., illus., maps. $5.95 pb.

Architecture Worth Saving in Rensselaer County, N.Y. Bernd Foerster. Troy: Rensselaer Polytechnic Institute, 1965. 207 pp., illus. $2.75 pb.

New York State Architectural Guides and Surveys: A Catalogue of Printed Materials. Frederick D. Cawley. Albany, N.Y.: Preservation League of New York State, 1977. 14 pp. $1.50 pb.

Landmarks of Rochester and Monroe County: A Guide to Neighborhoods and Villages. Paul Malo. Syracuse: Syracuse University Press, 1974. 278 pp., illus., appends., gloss., biblio. $6.95 pb.

Landmarks of Otsego County. Diantha Dow Schull. Syracuse: Syracuse University Press, 1980. 288 pp., illus. $18.95 hb, $9.95 pb.

New York Landmarks: A Study and Index of Architecturally Notable Structures in Greater New York. Alan Burnham, ed. Middletown, Conn.: Wesleyan University Press, 1963. 432 pp., illus., index, biblio. $40 hb, $16.95 pb.

Long Island Domestic Architecture of the Colonial and Federal Periods. Barbara Ferris Van Liew. Setauket, N.Y.: Society for the Preservation of Long Island Antiquities (P.O. Box 206, 11733), 1974. 36 pp., illus., index. $2.50 pb.

A Study of a Community: Staten Island Architecture and Environment. George Szekely and Dianna Gabay. Staten Island: Staten Island Continuum of Education, 1980. 174 pp., illus., biblio. $14 pb.

Pennsylvania
Philadelphia Preserved. Historic American Buildings Survey. Richard J. Webster, comp. Philadelphia: Temple University Press, 1976. 512 pp., illus., index. $29.95 hb, $12.95 pb.

Historic Buildings of Centre County, Pennsylvania. Historic Registration Project, Centre County Library. Gregory Ramsey, coordinator. University Park: Pennsylvania State University Press, 1980. 232 pp., illus., appends., biblio., gloss., index. $17.50 hb.

Puerto Rico
Architecture in Puerto Rico. Jose A. Fernandez. New York: Architectural Book Publishing Company, 1965. 267 pp., illus. $16.95 hb.

Virgin Islands
Historic Architecture of the Virgin Islands. Historic American Buildings Survey. 1966. Reprint. Springfield, Va.: National Technical Information Services. $7.25 pb. No. PB 182464.

Historic Architecture of the U.S. Virgin Islands. Pamela W. Gosner. Durham, N.C.: Moore Publishing, 1971.

18th-century house in Charleston, S.C. (Robert Lautman)

South

Southern Architecture: 350 Years of Distinctive American Building. Kenneth Severens. New York: Elsevier-Dutton, 1981. 208 pp., illus., biblio., index. $19.75 hb.

Architecture of the Old South. Henry C. Forman. 1948. Reprint. New York: Russell and Russell, 1967. $15.

Pride of the South: A Social History of Southern Architecture. Wayne Andrews. New York: Atheneum, 1979. 182 pp., illus., biblio., index. $20 hb, $10.95 pb.

The South in Architecture. Lewis Mumford. 1941. Reprint. New York: Da Capo, 1967. 147 pp. $21.50.

The City in Southern History: The Growth of Urban Civilization in the South. Blaine A. Brownell and David R. Goldfield, eds. Port Washington, N.Y.: Kennikat Press, 1976. 228 pp. $14.

Great Southern Mansions. Jozefa Stuart and Wilson Gathings. New York: Walker, 1977. 72 pp., color illus. $6.95 pb.

Historic Houses of the South. Southern Accents. New York: Simon and Schuster, 1984. 196 pp., color illus. $35 hb.

Alabama
The Architectural Legacy of the Lower Chattahoochee Valley in Alabama and Georgia. D. Gregory Jeane and Douglas Clare Purcell, eds. University, Ala.: University of Alabama Press, 1978. 280 pp., illus., biblio., gloss., map. $45 hb.

Alabama Ante Bellum Architecture. E. Walter and Varian Burkhardt. Montgomery: Alabama Historical Commission, 1976. 80 pp., illus. $5 pb.

Historic Eufaula: A Treasury of Southern Architecture. Eufaula: Eufaula Heritage Association (P.O. Box 486, 36027), 1972. 128 pp., illus. $5.

Florida
The Cultural Legacy of the Gulf Coast, 1870–1940. Lucius F. and Linda V. Ellsworth. Pensacola: Gulf Coast History and Humanities Conference, 1976. 139 pp., illus. $10.95 hb, $6.95 pb.

Gulf Coast Architecture. Samuel Wilson, Jr. Pensacola: Historic Pensacola Preservation Board, 1977. 48 pp., illus., biblio. $1.50 pb.

The Houses of St. Augustine, 1565–1821. Albert C. Manucy. 1962. Rev. ed. St. Augustine: St. Augustine Historical Society (271 Charlotte Street, 32084), 1978. 179 pp., illus., gloss., index. $2.75 pb.

Balustrades and Gingerbread: Key West's Handcrafted Homes and Buildings. Marion Bentley Wall, Roland James Dack and James R. Warnke. Miami: Banyan Books, 1978. 93 pp., color illus. $6.95 pb.

Portraits: Wooden Houses of Key West. Sharon Wells and Lawson Little. Key West: Historic Key West Preservation Board (Department of State, Monroe County Courthouse, 33040), 1979. 64 pp., illus., appends. $8 pb.

From Wilderness to Metropolis: The History and Architecture of Dade County (1825–1940). Historic Preservation Division, Metropolitan Dade County Office of Community and Economic Development. Miami: Banyan Books, 1982. 233 pp., illus., gloss., biblio., index. $10.95 pb.

Georgia
The Architecture of Georgia. Frederick D. Nichols and Van Jones Martin. Savannah: Beehive Press, 1976. 436 pp., illus. $36 hb.

Architecture of Middle Georgia: The Oconee Area. John Linley. Athens: University of Georgia Press, 1972. 194 pp., illus., biblio., index. $17.50.

Landmark Homes of Georgia, 1733–1983. Van Jones Martin and William Robert Mitchell, Jr. Savannah: Golden Coast Publishing, 1982. 277 pp., color illus. $45 hb.

Historic Savannah: Survey of Significant Buildings in the Historic and Victorian Districts of Savannah, Georgia. Mary L. Morrison, ed. Savannah: Historic Savannah Foundation, 1979. 299 pp., illus. $30 hb, $15 pb.

Atlanta Architecture: The Victorian Heritage. Elizabeth Mack Lyon. Atlanta: Atlanta Historical Society, 1976. 112 pp., illus., index. $5 pb.

The Buildings of Atlanta. James Carlton Starbuck. Monticello, Ill.: Vance Bibliographies, 1978. A-26. 28 pp. $3 pb.

Atlanta Historic Resources Workbook. Atlanta Urban Design Commission. Atlanta: Urban Atlanta (10 Pryor Street, S.W., 30303), 1981. 244 pp., illus., index. $18 pb.

Kentucky

Architecture and Preservation in Kentucky: A Guide to Historic Homes and Sites. Coppa and Avery Consultants. Monticello, Ill.: Vance Bibliographies, 1981. A-524. 7 pp. $2 pb.

Two Hundred Years at the Falls of the Ohio: A History of Louisville and Jefferson County. George H. Yater. Louisville: Heritage Corporation of Louisville and Jefferson County, 1979. 250 pp., illus. $15.95.

Old Louisville: The Victorian Era. Samuel W. Thomas and William Morgan. Louisville: Data Courier, 1975. 152 pp., illus. $4.95.

Vestiges of the Venerable City: A Chronicle of Lexington, Kentucky—Its Architectural Development and Survey of Its Early Streets and Antiquities. Clay Lancaster. Lexington: Lexington-Fayette County Historic Commission, 1978. 282 pp. $15.70.

The Kentucky Bluegrass: A Regional Profile and Guide. Karl B. Raitz. Chapel Hill: Department of Geography, University of North Carolina, 1980. 151 pp. $5.

Louisiana

Preservation and the Human Scale in New Orleans and Louisiana. Christine Moe. Monticello, Ill.: Vance Bibliographies, 1979. A-94. 78 pp. $8 pb.

New Orleans Architecture. Friends of the Cabildo. Vol. I: *The Lower Garden District* (1971). 172 pp. $25. Vol. II: *The American Sector* (1972). 244 pp. $27.50. Vol. III: *The Cemeteries* (1974). 198 pp. $27.50. Vol. IV: *The Creole Faubourgs* (1974). 184 pp. $27.50. Vol. V: *The Esplanade Ridge* (1977). 172 pp. $27.50. Vol. VI: *Faubourg Treme and the Bayou Road* (1980). 222 pp. $34.95. illus., biblio., index. Gretna, La.: Pelican Publishing.

New Orleans: The Making of an Urban Landscape. Peirce F. Lewis. Cambridge: Ballinger, 1976. 115 pp., illus. $8.95 pb.

Plantation Homes of Louisiana and the Natchez Area. David King Gleason. Baton Rouge: Louisiana State University Press, 1982. 135 color illus. $29.95 hb.

Mississippi

Historic Architecture in Mississippi. Mary Wallace Crocker. Jackson: University Press of Mississippi, 1973. 194 pp., illus., appends., index. $17.50.

The Buildings of Biloxi: An Architectural Survey. Julia Cook Guice, Anthony O. James, James D. Looney and Diane Stanley Woodward. Biloxi: City of Biloxi, Historic Preservation Office (Box W, 39533). 172 pp., illus., gloss., index. $5.

North Carolina

Asheville: Places of Discovery. Lou Harshaw. Lakemont, Ga.: Copple House Books (Road's Ends, 30552), 1980. 197 pp., illus., biblio. $10.95 pb.

Oakleigh (1831–32), Mobile, Ala. (Walter Smalling, Jr.)

South Carolina

Architecture and Preservation in South Carolina. Coppa and Avery Consultants. Monticello, Ill.: Vance Bibliographies, 1981. A-526. 9 pp. $2 pb.

South Carolina Architecture, 1670–1970. Harlan McClure and Vernon Hodges. Columbia, S.C.: South Carolina Tricentennial Commission, 1970. 221 pp., illus., biblio.

This Is Charleston. Samuel Gaillard Stoney. 1944. Rev. ed. Charleston, S.C.: Carolina Art Association, 1970. 139 pp., illus. $3.50 pb.

"Charleston." *Antiques,* April 1970.

Tennessee

Architecture in Tennessee: 1768 to 1897. James A. Patrick. Knoxville: University of Tennessee Press, 1980. 280 pp., illus., biblio., index. $24.95 hb.

Architecture of Middle Tennessee: The Historic American Buildings Survey. Thomas B. Brumbaugh, ed. Nashville: Vanderbilt University Press, 1974. 170 pp., illus. $17.95 hb.

"Tennessee." *Antiques,* September 1971.

Knoxville: Fifty Landmarks. A Sampling of Historically and Architecturally Interesting Buildings in the Greater Knoxville Area. Knoxville: Junior League, 1976. 32 pp., illus. $3.50.

Virginia

Virginia: A Guide to Its Architecture. Coppa and Avery Consultants. Monticello, Ill.: Vance Bibliographies, 1980. A-270. 9 pp. $2 pb.

Virginia Catalogue. Virginia Historic Landmarks Commission and Historic American Buildings Survey, comps. Charlottesville: University Press of Virginia, 1976. 461 pp., illus. $14.95.

The Architecture of Historic Richmond. Paul S. Dulaney. Charlottesville: University Press of Virginia, 1976. 218 pp., illus., appends., index. $4.95 pb.

Architecture in Downtown Richmond. Robert P. Winthrop. Virginius Dabney, ed. Richmond: Junior Board, Historic Richmond Foundation, 1982. 272 pp., illus., index. $27.95 hb.

Winchester: Limestone, Sycamores and Architecture. Walter C. Kidney. Winchester: Preservation of Historic Winchester (8 East Cork Street, 22601), 1977. 121 pp., illus. $17.50 hb.

The Architecture of Historic Lexington. Royster Lyle, Jr., and Pamela H. Simpson. Charlottesville: University Press of Virginia, 1977. 314 pp., illus., appends., biblio., index. $19.50.

Lynchburg: An Architectural History. S. Allen Chambers, Jr. Sarah Winston Henry Branch, Association for the Preservation of Virginia Antiquities. Charlottesville: University Press of Virginia, 1982. 576 pp., illus., biblio., index. $27.50 hb.

The Architectural Heritage of the Roanoke Valley. W.L. Whitwell and Lee W. Winborne. Charlottesville: University Press of Virginia, 1982. 240 pp., illus., index. $14.95 hb.

Alexandria Houses: 1750–1830. Deering Davis, Stephen P. Dorsey and Ralph Cole Hall. Reprint. New York: Crown, 1982. $7.98.

Christ Church (1736), Irvington, Va. (Foundation for Historic Christ Church)

Midwest

Architecture of the Old Northwest Territory: A Study of Early Architecture in Ohio, Indiana, Illinois, Michigan, Wisconsin and Part of Minnesota. Rexford Newcomb. Chicago: University of Chicago Press, 1950. 173 pp., illus., biblio.

Historic Midwest Houses. John Drury. 1947. Reprint. Chicago: University of Chicago Press. 256 pp., illus. $6.95 pb.

Illinois

Illinois Architecture: From Territorial Times to the Present. Frederick Koeper. Chicago: University of Chicago Press, 1968. 320 pp., illus. $11 hb, $3.25 pb.

Old Illinois Houses. John Drury. Chicago: University of Chicago Press, 1948. 240 pp., illus. $3.95 pb.

Chicago Architecture: A Selected Bibliography. Sandra K. Rollheiser. Monticello, Ill.: Vance Bibliographies, 1979. A-153. 11 pp. $2 pb.

Architecture in Chicago and Mid-America. Wayne Andrews. New York: Harper and Row, 1973. 206 pp., illus.

Old Chicago Houses. John Drury. Chicago: University of Chicago Press, 1941. 536 pp., illus. $6.95 pb.

100 Years of Architecture in Chicago: Continuity of Structure and Form. Oswald Grube, Peter Pran, Franz Schulze et al. Chicago: Museum of Contemporary Art, 1976. 192 pp., illus., biblio., index. $17.50 pb.

Chicago Houses. Janet Bailey. New York: St. Martin's, 1981. 256 pp., color illus. $40.

Chicago. A Historical Guide to the Neighborhoods: The Loop and South Side. Glen E. Holt and Dominic A. Pacyga. Chicago: Chicago Historical Society, 1979. 176 pp., illus., biblio., index. $8.95 pb.

Auditorium Building (1887, Adler and Sullivan), Chicago. (Hedrich-Blessing)

Indiana

Indiana Houses of the Nineteenth Century. Wilbur D. Peat. Indianapolis: Indiana Historical Society, 1962. 195 pp., illus., index. $12.50 hb.

Indianapolis Architecture. Wayne S. Schmidt. Indiana Architectural Foundation. Indianapolis: Author, 1975. 261 pp., illus. $6.95 pb.

Iowa

Iowa Catalog: Historic American Buildings Survey. Wesley I. Shank, ed. Iowa City: University of Iowa Press, 1979. 199 pp., illus. $12.50 hb, $8.95 pb.

The Victorian Architecture of Iowa. William Plymat, Jr. Des Moines: Elephant's Eye, 1976. 98 pp., illus., biblio.

American Classic. Laurence Lafore. 1975. Rev. ed. Iowa City: State Historical Society of Iowa, 1979. 95 pp., illus. $10 hb.

Nineteenth Century Home Architecture of Iowa City. Margaret N. Keyes. Iowa City: University of Iowa Press, 1968. 126 pp., illus. $3.95 pb.

Michigan

Architecture in Michigan: A Photographic Survey. Wayne Andrews. 1967. Rev. ed. Detroit: Wayne State University Press, 1982. 182 pp., illus., biblio., index. $22 hb, $13.95 pb.

The Buildings of Detroit: A History. W. Hawkins Ferry. 1968. Rev. ed. Detroit: Wayne State University Press, 1980. 498 pp., illus., chron., maps, index. $40 hb.

Kalamazoo: Nineteenth-Century Homes in a Midwestern Village. Peter Schmitt and Balthazar Korab. Kalamazoo: Kalamazoo City Historical Commission, 1976. 240 pp., illus., biblio., index. $14.95 hb, $9.95 pb.

Legacy of the River Raisin: Historic Buildings of Monroe County. Victor Hogg, Monroe County Historical Society. Monroe: Monroe County Historical Commission (126 South Monroe Street, 48161), 1976. 128 pp., illus. $16.

Minnesota

Minnesota Architecture: Building in Style. Mary Ann Nord. St. Paul: Minnesota Historical Society, 1983. 40 pp., illus., biblio., gloss. $2 pb.

Architecture and Preservation in the State of Minnesota: A Guide to Municipalities, Regions, Historic Homes, and Architectural Styles. Coppa and Avery Consultants. Monticello, Ill.: Vance Bibliographies, 1980. A-268. 9 pp. $2 pb.

Architecture Minnesota: Minneapolis and St. Paul. Minneapolis: Architecture Minnesota (314 Clifton Avenue, 55403), April–May, 1981. 155 pp., illus. $2.50 pb.

The Lake District of Minneapolis: A History of the Calhoun-Isles Community. David A. Lanegran and Ernest R. Sandeen. St. Paul: Living Historical Museum (826 Goodrich Avenue, 55105), 1979. 112 pp., illus., index.

Saint Paul Omnibus: Image of the Changing City. Patricia Kane. St. Paul: Old Town Restorations (411 Selby Avenue, 55102), 1979. 144 pp.

Duluth's Legacy. Vol. I: Architecture. James Allen Scott. Duluth: Department of Research and Planning, 1974. 165 pp., illus., index. $3.50 pb.

Early Homes of Ohio. I.T. Frary. 1936. Reprint. New York: Dover, 1970. 334 pp., illus., biblio., index. $6 pb.

Historic Buildings of Ohio: A Selection from the Records of the Historic American Buildings Survey. Walter C. Kidney. Pittsburgh: Ober Park Associates, 1972. 130 pp., illus., index. $20 hb, $7.95 pb.

Architecture: Columbus. American Institute of Architects, Columbus Chapter. Columbus: Foundation of the Columbus Chapter, AIA, 1976. 305 pp., index, biblio. $30 hb. Available from Readmor, 131 North High Street, Columbus, Ohio 43215.

Cleveland Architecture, 1876–1976. Eric Johannesen. Cleveland: Western Reserve Historical Society, 1979. 268 pp., illus., index. $17.50 hb.

Fascinating, Spirited Cincinnati. Laurence Zink and Dick Perry. Cincinnati: Cincinnati Chapter, American Institute of Architects, 1979. 176 pp., illus. $25 hb, $15 pb.

St. Louis County Courthouse (1839-64). (Richard Pare, Seagram Archives)

Missouri

Kansas City, Missouri: An Architectural History, 1826–1976. George Ehrlich. Kansas City: Historic Kansas City Foundation, 1979. 185 pp., illus., biblio., index. $19.95 hb.

Ohio

Architecture of the Western Reserve, 1800–1900. Richard N. Campen. Cleveland: Case Western Reserve University Press, 1971. 259 pp., illus., biblio., gloss., index. $15.

Wisconsin

Historic Wisconsin Buildings: A Survey of Pioneer Architecture, 1835–1870. Richard W.E. Perrin. Milwaukee: Milwaukee Public Museum, 1981. 2nd ed, rev. 129 pp., illus. $7.95 pb.

Milwaukee Landmarks. Richard W.E. Perrin. 1968. Rev. ed. Milwaukee: Milwaukee Public Museum, 1979. 142 pp., illus., index. $7.95 pb.

Built in Milwaukee: An Architectural View of the City. Randy Garber, ed., Landscape Research. Milwaukee: Department of City Development, 1982. 218 pp., illus., biblio.

I. Cordova Store, Las Truches, N.M. (John Collier, Office of War Information, Library of Congress)

Mission San Francisco de la Espada (1761), San Antonio, Tex. (Robert Lautman)

Southwest

The Architecture of the Southwest: Indian, Spanish, American. Trent E. Sanford. 1950. Reprint. Westport, Conn.: Greenwood Press, 1971. 312 pp., illus., appends., index. $28.25 hb.

Colorado

The Architecture and Art of Early Hispanic Colorado. Robert H. Adams. Boulder: Colorado Associated University Press, 1974. 240 pp., illus., biblio., append.

Historic Sites and Structures: El Paso County, Colorado. Elaine Freed and David Barber. El Paso County, Colo.: El Paso County Land Use Department, 1977. 56 pp., illus., biblio. $3.50 pb. Available from Penrose Public Library, 20 Cascade, Colorado Springs, Colo. 80902.

Cherry Creek Gothic: Victorian Architecture in Denver. Sandra Dallas. Norman: University of Oklahoma Press, 1971. 292 pp., illus. $14.95.

Historic Denver: The Architects, the Architecture, 1858–1893. Richard R. Brettell. Denver: Historic Denver, 1973. 240 pp., illus. $16.95 hb.

Rediscovering Northwest Denver: Its History, Its People, Its Landmarks. Ruth Wiberg. Boulder: Pruett, 1976. 212 pp., biblio., index. $25 hb.

Kansas

Roots: The Historic and Architectural Heritage of Kansas City, Kansas. Larry K. Hancks and Meredith Roberts. Kansas City: Kansas City Community Development Program, 1976. 180 pp., illus., biblio., $2.50 pb.

Nebraska

Omaha City/Architecture. Landmarks, Inc., and Junior League of Omaha. Omaha: Author, 1977. 202 pp., gloss. $10 pb.

New Mexico

Of Earth and Timbers Made: New Mexico Architecture. Bainbridge Bunting. Albuquerque: University of New Mexico Press, 1974. 85 pp., illus., gloss. $12.95 pb.

Design and Preservation in Santa Fe: A Pluralistic Approach. Planning Department, City of Santa Fe. Santa Fe: Author, 1977. 46 pp., illus. $4.

Old Santa Fe Today. Historic Santa Fe Foundation. Preface by John Gaw Meem. 1966. 3rd ed. Albuquerque: University of New Mexico Press, 1982. 108 pp., gloss. $11.95 pb.

Oklahoma

Of the Earth: Oklahoma Architectural History. Howard L. Meredith and Mary Ellen Meredith, eds. Oklahoma City: Oklahoma Historical Society, 1980. 134 pp., illus. $12.75 hb, $8.50 pb.

Oklahoma Homes Past and Present. Charles R. Goins. Norman: University of Oklahoma Press, 1980. 269 pp., illus. $32.50 hb.

Oklahoma Architecture: Landmark and Vernacular. Arn Henderson, Frank Parman and Dortha Henderson. Norman: Point Riders Press (P.O. Box 371, 73030), 1978. 216 pp., illus. $11.95 pb.

Texas

Texas Catalog: Historic American Buildings Survey. Paul Goeldner, comp. San Antonio: Trinity University Press, 1974. 247 pp., illus., index. $5 pb.

Texas Public Buildings of the 19th Century. Willard B. Robinson and Todd Webb. Austin: University of Texas Press. 290 pp., illus., gloss., biblio., index. $29.95 hb.

Texas Homes of the Nineteenth Century. D.B. Alexander. Austin: University of Texas Press, 1966. 276 pp., illus., biblio. $29.95.

The Grand Homes of Texas. Ann Richardson and Editors of Texas Homes. Austin: Texas Monthly Press, 1982. 220 pp., color illus. $45 hb.

Austin: The Past Still Present. Brandt McBee and Virginia Erickson. Austin: Austin Heritage Society, 1975. 130 pp., illus. $8.95 hb.

Dallas Rediscovered: A Photographic Chronicle of Urban Expansion, 1870–1925. William L. McDonald. Introduction by A.C. Greene. Dallas: Dallas Historical Society, 1978. 266 pp., illus., biblio., index. $21.95.

The Galveston That Was. Howard Barnstone. New York: Macmillan, 1966. 224 pp., illus., plans. $14.95.

San Francisco Victorian. (Carol Olwell)

Casa Tierra (1941), Saratoga, Calif. (Jane Lidz, HABS)

Board sidewalk in the Jacksonville Historic District, Jacksonville, Ore. (Jack E. Boucher, HABS)

West

Historic Preservation in the Pacific Northwest: A Bibliography of Sources 1947–1978. Lawrence N. Crumb. Chicago: Council of Planning Librarians. No. 11. 63 pp., index. $7.

Space, Style and Structure: Building in Northwest America. Thomas Vaughan and Virginia Guest Ferriday. Portland, Ore.: Western Imprints, 1974. For Oregon Historical Society. 2 vols. 372 pp., illus.

California

California's Architectural Frontier: Style and Tradition in the Nineteenth Century. Harold Kirker. 1960. Reprint. New York: Russell and Russell, 1970. 224 pp., illus., index. $13.

Building with Nature: Roots of the San Francisco Bay Region Tradition. Leslie M. Freudenheim and Elisabeth S. Sussman. Salt Lake City: Peregrine Smith, 1974. 112 pp., illus.

Here Today: San Francisco's Architectural Heritage. Roger Olmsted. Junior League of San Francisco. San Francisco: Chronicle Books, 1978. 337 pp., illus., append., gloss., index. $14.95 pb.

An Enduring Heritage: Historic Buildings of the San Francisco Peninsula. Dorothy F. Regnery. Palo Alto: Stanford University Press, 1976. 124 pp., illus., biblio., index. $18.95 hb.

A Gift to the Street. Carol Olwell and Judith Lynch Waldhorn. 1976. Reprint. New York: St. Martin's, 1983. 195 pp., illus. $17.95 pb.

Architecture and Preservation in the City of Los Angeles: A Guide to Architectural Styles, Buildings and Homes. Coppa and Avery Consultants. Monticello, Ill.: Vance Bibliographies, 1980. A-269. 10 pp. $2 pb.

Los Angeles: The Architecture of Four Ecologies. Reyner Banham. New York: Harper and Row, 1971. 256 pp., illus., biblio., index. $5.95 pb.

The Architecture of Los Angeles. Paul Gleye, with Los Angeles Conservancy. San Diego: Howell-North, 1981. 236 pp., illus. $35 hb.

L.A. in the Thirties. David Gebhard and Harriette Von Breton. Salt Lake City: Peregrine Smith, 1975. 165 pp., illus., biblio., index.

Santa Barbara Architecture: From Spanish Colonial to Modern. Herb Andree and Noel Young. 1975. 2nd ed. Santa Barbara: Capra Press, 1980. 297 pp., illus., gloss., index. $70 hb.

Houses of Gold. John Carden Campbell. Photographs by Craig Buchanan. San Diego: Howell-North, 1980. 174 pp., illus. $15 pb.

Hawaii

Palaces and Forts of the Hawaiian Kingdom: From Thatch to American Florentine. Walter F. Judd. Palo Alto, Calif.: Pacific Books, 1975. 176 pp., illus., biblio. $14.95.

The Architecture of Honolulu. Geoffrey W. Fairfax. Honolulu: Island Heritage (1020 Auahi Street, Building 3, 96814), 1971. 120 pp., illus., biblio. $6.95.

Idaho

Saints and Oddfellows: A Bicentennial Sampler of Idaho Architecture. J. Meredith Neil. Boise: Boise Gallery of Art Association, 1976. 192 pp., illus., index. $3.95 pb.

Twin Falls Country: A Look at Idaho Architecture. Patricia Wright. Boise: Idaho State Historical Society Preservation Office, 1979. 84 pp., illus. $3.50 pb.

Montana

Historic Uptown Butte. John N. DeHaas, Jr. Bozeman, Mont.: Author, 1977.

Unusual Places in Helena: Remarks on Some Remarkable Buildings. Dennis H. McCahon. Helena, Mont.: Author, 1976. 72 pp., illus.

Oregon

Architecture Oregon Style. Rosalind Clark, City of Albany, Ore. Portland: Professional Book Center, 1983. 231 pp., illus., gloss., biblio., index. $29.95 hb, $19.95 pb.

A Century of Portland Architecture. Thomas Vaughn and George A. McMath. 1967. Rev. ed. Portland: Oregon Historical Society, 1980. 250 pp., illus.

The Grand Era of Cast Iron Architecture in Portland. William J. Hawkins III. Portland: Binford and Mort, 1976. 211 pp., illus., appends., biblio., gloss., index. $25 hb, $18.95 pb.

Utah

"The Architectural History of Utah," Peter L. Goss. *Utah Historical Quarterly,* Summer 1975.

Washington

Seattle Cityscape. Victor Steinbrueck. Seattle: University of Washington Press, 1973. 192 pp., illus., index. $4.75 hb, $12.50 pb.

The House Next Door: Seattle's Neighborhood Architecture. Lila Gault. Seattle: Pacific Search Press (222 Dexter Avenue North, 98109), 1981. $10.95 pb.

Victorian Architecture of Port Townsend, Washington. Allen T. Denison and Wallace Kay Huntington. Seattle: Hancock House Publishers, 1978. Distributed by Books America, 12008 1st Avenue, South, Seattle, Wash. 98168. 176 pp., illus., biblio., gloss., index. $17.95.

Californians toured historic sites in the 1920s and 1930s in buses such as this. (California Historical Society)

Architecture on Tour: American Guidebooks

I have come to think of three generations of guidebooks. The first-generation guidebook is a building-by-building description, generally focusing on landmark structures. The emphasis is on the most important, biggest and most famous buildings.

The second-generation guidebook is more concerned with the overall environment, how buildings relate to each other and form complexes, neighborhoods and cities, and how the urban fabric is used and evolves. Vernacular architecture becomes important.

The third-generation guidebook is a refinement of the second type. It goes beyond description of the urban environment and discusses issues of development and design policy. Additionally, its purpose is to become an instrument of civic education, helping the user deal with policy issues. This type is the most difficult to prepare and is most subject to outdating.

John Fondersmith,
"Architectural Guidebooks:
Proliferating and Maturing."
AIA Journal, December 1976.

Modern Baedekers
"The 'Baedeker Handbook(s) for Travellers' series began in 1839, and the term 'Baedeker' became synonymous with guidebooks. Generations of travellers used 'Baedekers' and they became popular with guidebook collectors."

John Fondersmith. *American Urban Guidenotes*, Summer 1979.

The Architecture of the United States: An Illustrated Guide to Notable Buildings, Open to the Public. G.E. Kidder Smith. With Museum of Modern Art. New York: Anchor Books, Doubleday, 1981. Illus., maps, gloss., index. 3 vols. $29.95 hb, $14.95 pb each.
Vol. I. *New England and the Mid-Atlantic States.* Introduction by Albert Bush-Brown. 756 pp.
Vol. II. *The South and the Midwest.* Introductions by Frederick D. Nichols (South) and Frederick Koeper (Midwest). 784 pp.
Vol. III. *The Plains States and Far West.* Introduction by David Gebhard. 848 pp.

American Architecture: A Field Guide to the Most Important Examples. William Dudley Hunt, Jr. New York: Harper and Row, 1984. 351 pp., illus., index. $19.95 hb, $9.95 pb.

Discovering Historic America. Vol. I: *New England.* Vol. II: *California and the West.* Vol. III: *The Mid-Atlantic States.* Vol. IV: *The Southeast.* S. Allen Chambers, ed. Main Street Press. New York: Dutton, 1982. 288 pp., illus., index. $8.95 pb each.

Historic Houses of America: Open to the Public. Editors of American Heritage. Beverley Hilowitz and Susan Eikov Green, eds. 1971. Rev. ed. New York: Fireside Books, Simon and Schuster, 1980. 350 pp., illus. $6.95 pb.

Great Historic Places. Editors of American Heritage. Beverley Hilowitz and Susan Eikov Green, eds. 1973. Rev. ed. New York: Fireside Books, Simon and Schuster, 1980. 320 pp., illus. $6.95.

American Travelers' Treasury: A Guide to the Nation's Heirlooms. Suzanne Lord. New York: Morrow, 1977. 588 pp. $5.95 pb.

Treasures of America and Where to Find Them. Reader's Digest. Pleasantville, N.Y.: Reader's Digest, 1974. 624 pp., illus. Distributed by W.W. Norton. $15.99.

National Register of Historic Places. Ronald M. Greenberg and Sarah A. Marusin, eds., National Park Service, U.S. Department of the Interior. Washington, D.C.: GPO, 1976. 961 pp., illus., index. $22 hb. GPO stock no. 024-005-00645-1. Vol. II: 638 pp., illus., index. 1979. $19 hb. GPO stock no. 024-005-00747-4.

The Rand McNally Historic America Guide. Chicago: Rand McNally Company, 1978. 281 pp., illus.

"American Architectural Guidebooks—Past, Present and Future: An Introductory Overview," John Fondersmith. Paper presented at annual meeting of Architectural Librarians Association, 1980. $1.50.

Baedeker's Handbook(s) for Travellers. Bibliography of Pre-WW II English Editions. Reprint. Westport, Conn.: Greenwood Press, 1975. 36 pp. $7.50.

The Travel Book: Guide to the Travel Guides. Jon O. Heise, with Dennis O'Reilly. New York: R.R. Bowker Company, 1981. 319 pp., append., index. $26.95 hb.

WPA Guides
"America's most comprehensive guidebook effort was the series of guidebooks compiled and written by the Federal Writers Project of the Works Progress Administration during the Depression. In a seven year period (1935–41), guidebooks were prepared for all the states, the District of Columbia, territories, and many cities. The original guidebooks are often collected today, and many are useful as basic reference sources despite the changes which have occurred over the past forty years. Original copies of guidebooks for many of the states can still be found in secondhand book stores. Many of the guidebooks have been reprinted by various firms and institutions. Some have been updated in the original format."

John Fondersmith, *American Urban Guidenotes*, Fall–Winter 1979.

"One looks back with awe at the great series of WPA guidebooks which covered every state in the Union and many of the cities. We are now a nation without guidebooks or at least without guidebooks of the scope and interest that were evident in the WPA series."

Nathan Glazer, Foreword. *Cultural Regions of the United States*

Remembering America: A Sampler of the WPA American Guide Series. Archie Hobson, ed. New York: Columbia University Press, 1985. 388 pp., illus. $29.95.

WPA Guide Reprint Publishers

Pantheon Books
201 East 50th Street
New York, N.Y. 10022

Hastings House
10 East 40th Street
New York, N.Y. 10016

Somerset Publications
Division of Scholarly Press
19722 East Nine Mile Road
St. Clair Shores, Mich. 48080

AMS Press
56 East 13th Street
New York, N.Y. 10002

Some Specialties

Train Trips: Exploring America by Rail. William G. Scheller. Charlotte, N.C.: East Woods Press, 1981. 263 pp., illus., appends., biblio., index. $7.95 pb.

America's Heritage Trail: A Tour Guide to Historical Sites of the Colonial and Revolutionary War Period (South Carolina, North Carolina and Virginia). M. Victor Alper. New York: Macmillan, 1976.

America's Freedom Trail: A Tour Guide to Historical Sites of the Colonial and Revolutionary War Period. (Massachusetts, New York, New Jersey and Pennsylvania). M. Victor Alper. New York: Macmillan, 1976. 562 pp., illus., index.

Victorian Travelers Companion. Eve Marie Utne, ed. Philadelphia: Victorian Society in America, 1979. 127 pp., illus. $4.95.

Rollin On: A Wheelchair Guide to U.S. Cities. Maxine H. Atwater. New York: Dodd Mead, 1978. 290 pp.

Pocket Guide to the Location of Art in the United States. Emma Lila Fundaburk. Luverne, Ala.: Author (P.O. Box 231, 36049), 1977. 314 pp. $10 hb, $5 pb.

Heritage of Canada. Reader's Digest, Canada. New York: W.W. Norton, 1979. illus.

See also: Form and Function

Contact

American Urban Guidenotes: The Newsletter of Guidebooks c/o John Fondersmith P.O. Box 186 Washington, D.C. 20044

Kitchen hearth in the Richard Jackson House (1664), Portsmouth, N.H. (J. David Bohl, SPNEA)

City, State and Regional Guidebooks

New England

How New England Happened: The Modern Traveller's Guide to New England's Historic Past. Christina Tree. Boston: Little, Brown, 1976. 269 pp. $7.95 pb.

Abandoned New England: Its Hidden Ruins and Where to Find Them. William F. Robinson. Boston: New York Graphic Society, 1976. 240 pp., illus., appends., biblio., index. $12.95 pb.

Exploring Coastal New England: Gloucester to Kennebunkport. Barbara Clayton and Kathleen Whitley. New York: Dodd, Mead, 1979. Illus., maps. $9.95 pb.

Country New England Historical and Sightseeing Guide. Anthony Hitchcock and Jean Lindgren. New York: Burt Franklin, 1981. 228 pp. $4.95 pb.

Houses of New England Open to the Public. Nicholas Zook. Barre, Mass.: Barre Publishing, 1968. 126 pp., illus.

Back Roads of New England. Earl Thollander. 1974. Rev. ed. New York: Clarkson Potter, 1982. 224 pp., illus. $10.95 pb.

Connecticut

New Haven: A Guide to Architecture and Urban Design. Elizabeth Mills Brown. New Haven: Yale University Press, 1976. 228 pp., illus., maps, index. $8.95 pb.

Massachusetts

The WPA Guide to Massachusetts. New introduction by Jane Holtz Kay. 1937. Reprint. New York: Pantheon, 1983. 800 pp., illus. $9.95 pb.

The City Observed. Boston: A Guide to the Architecture of the Hub. Donlyn Lyndon. New York: Random House, 1982. 318 pp., illus., index. $18.50 hb, $7.95 pb.

AIA Guide to Boston Architecture. Susan and Michael Southworth. Boston Society of Architects. Chester, Conn.: Globe Pequot Press, 1984. 512 pp., illus., gloss., index. $24.95 hb, $14.95 pb.

New Hampshire

New Hampshire Architecture: An Illustrated Guide. Bryant F. Tolles, Jr., with Carolyn K. Tolles. Hanover, N.H.: University Press of New England, 1980. For New Hampshire Historical Society. 395 pp., illus., biblio., append., gloss., index. $25 hb, $9.95 pb.

Rhode Island

Rhode Island: An Historical Guide. Sheila Steinberg and Cathleen McGuigan. Providence: Rhode Island Bicentennial Foundation (Old State House, 150 Benefit Street, 02903), 1976. 284 pp., illus., biblio., index. $2.95.

Newport: A Tour Guide. Anne Randall and Robert P. Foley. Rev. ed. Old Saybrook, Conn.: Peregrine Press, 1983. 144 pp., illus., maps. $6.95 pb.

Vermont

Vermont: A Guide to the Green Mountain State. Federal Writers Project. 1937. Reprint. St. Clair Shores, Mich.: Somerset. 450 pp., illus. $49 hb.

Providence row houses. (Rhode Island Historical Commission)

Lafayette's headquarters (c. 1763), Chadd's Ford, Pa., near the Brandywine Battlefield. (Ned Goode, HABS)

Mother's bedroom at Stratford Hall (c. 1725), Westmoreland County, Va., the birthplace of Robert E. Lee. (Jack E. Boucher, HABS)

Mid-Atlantic

District of Columbia

AIA Guide to the Architecture of Washington, D.C. Washington Metropolitan Chapter, AIA. Warren J. Cox, Hugh Newell Jacobsen, Francis D. Lethbridge and David R. Rosenthal, eds. Rev. ed. New York: McGraw-Hill, 1974. 246 pp., illus. $6.95 pb.

The WPA Guide to Washington, D.C. New introduction by Roger G. Kennedy. 1942. Reprint. New York: Pantheon, 1983. 672 pp., illus. $8.95 pb.

Mr. Lincoln's City: An Illustrated Guide to the Civil War Sites of Washington. Richard M. Lee. McLean, Va.: EPM Publications, 1981. 175 pp., illus., biblio., append. $12.95 pb.

Maryland

Maryland: A New Guide to the Old Line State. Edward C. Papenfuse, Gregory A. Stiverson, Susan A. Collins and Lois Green Carr, eds. Baltimore: Johns Hopkins University Press, 1976. 463 pp., illus., maps, index. $5.95 pb.

New Jersey

Tours of Historic New Jersey. Adeline Pepper. 1965. New Brunswick, N.J.: Rutgers University Press, 1973. 286 pp., illus., index. $5.95.

New York

AIA Guide to New York City. New York Chapter, AIA. Norval White and Elliot Willensky, eds. 1967. Rev. ed. New York: Macmillan, 1978. 653 pp. $13.95 pb.

The WPA Guide to New York City: The Federal Writers' Project Guide to 1930s New York. New introduction by William H. White. New York: Pantheon, 1982. 816 pp., illus., biblio., index. $20 hb, $8.95 pb.

The City Observed. New York: A Guide to the Architecture of Manhattan. Paul Goldberger. New York: Random House, 1979. 366 pp., illus. $15 hb, $8.95 pb.

History Preserved: A Guide to New York City Landmarks and Historic Districts. Harmon H. Goldstone and Martha Dalrymple. New York: Schocken Books, 1976. 576 pp., illus., biblio., index. $9.95 pb.

Essential New York: A Guide to the History and Architecture of Manhattan's Important Buildings, Parks, and Bridges. John Tauranac. New York: Holt, Rinehart and Winston, 1979. 273 pp., illus., gloss., biblio., index. $14.95 hb, $8.95 pb.

The Hudson: A Guidebook to the River. Arthur G. Adams. Albany: State University of New York Press, 1981. 424 pp., maps, index. $19.95 hb.

The Hudson River Valley. A History and Guide: From Saratoga Springs to New York City. Tim Mulligan, ed. New York: Random House, 1985. $8.95 pb.

Buffalo Architecture: A Guide. Introductions by Buffalo Architectural Guidebook Corporation, Reyner Banham, Charles Beveridge and Henry-Russell Hitchcock. Cambridge: MIT Press, 1981. 336 pp., illus., biblio., index. $9.95 pb.

Landmarks of Rochester and Monroe County: A Guide to Neighborhoods and Villages. Paul Malo. Landmark Society of Western New York. Syracuse: Syracuse University Press, 1974. 276 pp., illus., biblio. $6.95 pb.

Pennsylvania

Philadelphia Architecture: A Guide to the City. Group for Environmental Education. John Andrew Gallery, ed. Cambridge: MIT Press, 1984. 176 pp., illus. $12.95 pb.

Architecture in Philadelphia: A Guide. Edward Teitelman and Richard W. Longstreth. 1974. Reprint. Cambridge: MIT Press, 1981. 284 pp., illus., maps, biblio., index. $9.95 pb.

Man-Made Philadelphia: A Guide to Its Physical and Cultural Environment. Richard Saul Wurman and John Andrew Gallery. Cambridge: MIT Press, 1972. 104 pp., illus. $1.95 pb.

A Guidebook to Historic Western Pennsylvania. George Swelnam and Helene Smith. Pittsburgh: University of Pittsburgh Press, 1976. 306 pp., illus., index. $6.95 pb.

Lancaster Architecture 1719–1927: A Guide to Publicly Accessible Buildings in Lancaster County. John J. Snyder, Jr. Lancaster, Pa.: Historic Preservation Trust of Lancaster County (13 North Duke Street, 17602), 1979. 36 pp., illus., maps.

South

Great Southern Mansions. With a Traveler's Guide to Houses Open to the Public. Jozefa Stuart and Wilson Gathings. New York: Walker, 1977. 72 pp., illus. $6.95 pb.

Alabama

19th Century Architecture of Mobile, Alabama. Mobile City Planning Commission. Mobile: Author, 1974. 76 pp., illus. $4 pb.

Arkansas

Quapaw Quarter: A Guide to Little Rock's 19th-Century Neighborhoods. Quapaw Quarter Association. Little Rock: Author, 1976. 108 pp., illus. $5 pb.

Florida

The WPA Guide to Florida. New introduction by John I. McCollum. Reprint. New York: Pantheon, 1984. 704 pp., illus. $12.95 pb.

Tallahassee: Downtown Transitions. Lee H. Warner and Mary B. Eastland. Tallahassee: Historic Tallahassee Preservation Board (329 North Meridan Street, 32301), 1976. 94 pp., illus., biblio., index.

Georgia

Guide to Atlanta. Atlanta Chapter, AIA. Atlanta: Author (Architectural Book Center, 1197 Peachtree Street, N.E., 30361), 1975. illus., maps. $5 pb.

The Old in New Atlanta. Elizabeth M. Sawyer and Jane Foster Mathews. Atlanta: JEMS Publications, 1976. 134 pp., illus. $4.95 pb.

Louisiana

A Guide to New Orleans Architecture. New Orleans Chapter, AIA. New Orleans: Author, 1974. 177 pp., illus. $5.95 pb.

The WPA Guide to New Orleans. New introduction by the Historic New Orleans Collection. 1938. Reprint. New York: Pantheon, 1983. 567 pp., illus. $8.95 pb.

New Orleans, Yesterday and Today: A Guide to the City. Walter G. Cowan et al. Baton Rouge: Louisiana State University Press, 1983. 272 pp., illus., index. $14.95 hb, $6.95 pb.

Frenchmen, Desire, Good Children, and Other Streets of New Orleans. John Churchill Chase. 3rd ed. New York: Collier Books, Macmillan, 1979. 272 pp. $5.95 pb.

North Carolina

Exploring the Villages of North Carolina. Faris Jane Corey. Chapel Hill: Provincial Press (P.O. Box 2311, 27514), 1978. 177 pp. $5.95 pb.

Architectural Guide. Winston-Salem—Forsyth County. Winston-Salem Section, North Carolina Chapter, AIA. Winston-Salem: Author, 1978. 199 pp., illus., maps, index. $4.95 pb.

South Carolina

Historic Charleston Guidebook. Junior League of Charleston. Rev. ed. Charleston: Author, 1965. $1.25 pb.

Tennessee

Nashville: A Short History and Selected Buildings. Eleanor Gram, ed. Nashville: Historical Commission of Metropolitan Nashville-Davidson County, 1974. 285 pp., illus., biblio., index. $10 hb, $5 pb.

Virginia

Architecture in Virginia: An Official Guide to Four Centuries of Building in the Old Dominion. William B. O'Neal, ed., Virginia Museum. New York: Walker, 1968. 192 pp., illus., maps, biblio.

Jefferson's Country: Charlottesville and Albemarle Counties. Whit Morse and Linda Firestone. Richmond: Good Life Publishers (713 North Courthouse Road, 23235), 1977. 151 pp. $3.95 pb.

Midwest

Midwest Travel Guides: A Catalog. Chicago: Scudder and Hall Books (P.O. Box 5116, 60680).

"Focus on the Heartland," John Fondersmith, ed. *American Urban Guidenotes,* Summer 1980.

The Great Lakes Guidebook. I: *Lakes Ontario and Erie.* 1978. 192 pp. II: *Lake Huron and Eastern Lake Michigan.* 1979. 192 pp. III: *Lake Superior and Western Lake Michigan.* 1980. 226 pp. George Cantor. Ann Arbor: University of Michigan Press. $6.95 pb each.

Around Lake Michigan. Jean R. Komaiko, Beverly H. Barsy and Ruth S. Mackelmann. Boston: Houghton Mifflin, 1980. 448 pp. $7.95.

Around the Shores of Lake Superior: A Guide to Historic Sites. Margaret Beattie Bogue and Virginia A. Palmer. Madison: University of Wisconsin Press, 1979. 179 pp., illus., biblio., index. $7.95 pb.

Around the Shores of Lake Michigan. Margaret Beattie Bogue. Madison: University of Wisconsin Press, 1985. $35 hb, $19.95 pb.

Illinois

The WPA Guide to Illinois. New introduction by Neil Harris and Michael Conzen. Reprint. New York: Pantheon, 1983. 800 pp., illus. $9.95 pb.

Illinois Architecture: From Territorial Times to the Present. A Selective Guide. Frederick Koeper. Chicago: University of Chicago Press, 1968. 304 pp. $11 hb, $3.25 pb.

Chicago's Famous Buildings: Photographic Guide to the City's Architectural Landmarks and Other Notable Buildings. Ira J. Bach, ed., with Roy Forrey. Introductions by Carl W. Condit and Hugh D. Duncan. 1965. 3rd ed. Chicago: University of Chicago Press, 1980. 265 pp., illus. $15 hb, $6.95 pb.

A Guide to Chicago's Historic Suburbs on Wheels and On Foot. Ira J. Bach with Susan Wolfson. Athens, Ohio: Swallow Press, Ohio University Press, 1982. 726 pp. $19.95 hb, $9.95 pb.

A Guidebook to the Architecture of River Forest. Jeanette S. Fields, ed. River Forest, Ill.: River Forest Community Center (414 Jackson Avenue, 60305), 1981. 68 pp., illus., append., biblio., index. $3.50 pb.

Das Deutsche Haus or The Athenaeum (1898, Vonnegut and Bohn), Indianapolis, Ind. (Jack E. Boucher, HABS)

Indiana

Indiana: A New Guide to the Hoosier State. Indiana Historical Society. Indianapolis: Author (315 West Ohio Street, 46202), 1985.

Indianapolis Architecture. Wayne S. Schmidt. Indianapolis: Indiana Architectural Foundation (148 North Delaware Street, 46204), 1975. 261 pp., illus., biblio. $6.95 pb.

Columbus, Indiana: A Look at Architecture. Columbus Area Chamber of Commerce. Columbus: Author (Visitors Center, 506 Fifth Street, 47201), 1974. 100 pp. $5.

Michigan

Detroit Architecture: AIA Guide. Katharine Mattingly Meyer, ed. 1971. Rev. ed. Detroit: Wayne State University Press, 1980. 264 pp., illus. $5.95 pb.

Historic Buildings, Ann Arbor, Michigan. Ann Arbor Historic District Commission. Ann Arbor: Author (312 South Division, 48104), 1977. 96 pp.

Minnesota

A Guide to the Architecture of Minnesota. David Gebhard and Tom Martinson. Minneapolis: University of Minnesota Press, 1978. 469 pp., illus., biblio., index. $10.95 pb.

Missouri

Kansas City. Kansas City Chapter, AIA. Kansas City: Author (20 West 9th Street, 64105), 1979. 260 pp., illus., index. $6.95 pb.

The Building Art in St. Louis: Two Centuries. George McCue. St. Louis Chapter, AIA. 1964. 3rd ed. St. Louis: AIA (919 Olive Street, 63101), 1981. 192 pp., illus., index. $8.95 pb.

Ohio

Architecture: Columbus. Columbus Chapter, AIA. Columbus: Foundation of the Columbus Chapter of the American Institute of Architects, 1976. $30 hb.

Landmark Architecture of Cleveland. Mary-Peale Schofield. Pittsburgh: Ober Park Associates, 1976. 220 pp. $12.95 hb, $7.95 pb.

South Dakota

Historic Sites in South Dakota: A Guidebook. Business Research Bureau, Univeristy of South Dakota and Historical Preservation Center. Vermillion: Business Research Bureau (University of South Dakota, 57069), 1980. 126 pp., illus. $2 pb.

Wisconsin

An Invitation to Visit Wisconsin's Historic Homes. Virginia Palmer. Milwaukee: University of Wisconsin Extension (145 Johnson Hall, University of Wisconsin, 53201), 1978. 46 pp., illus. $3 pb.

The Heritage Guidebook: Landmarks and Historical Sites in Southeastern Wisconsin. H. Russell Zimmerman. Milwaukee: Heritage Bank, Inland Heritage Corporation, 1976. 406 pp., illus. $13 hb.

Southwest

Colorado

Denver Landmarks. Langdon E. Morris, Jr. Denver: Charles W. Cleworth Publisher, 1979. 324 pp., illus., index. $9.95 pb.

Nebraska

Nebraska: A Guide to the Cornhusker State. Federal Writers Project, Works Progress Administration. 1939. Reprint. Introduction by Tom Allen. Lincoln: University of Nebraska Press, 1979. 458 pp., illus., appends., biblio., index. $24.50 hb, $5.50 pb.

Omaha City Architecture. Junior League of Omaha. Omaha: Landmarks, Inc. and Junior League of Omaha, 1977. 204 pp., illus., gloss. index. $10 pb.

Oklahoma

Mark of Heritage: Oklahoma's Historic Sites. Muriel H. Wright, George H. Shirk, Kenna A. Franks. Norman: University of Oklahoma Press, 1976. 214 pp., illus., index. $5.95 pb.

Texas

Dallasights. Dallas Chapter, AIA. Dallas: Author (2800 Routh, No. 141, 75201), 1978. 191 pp., illus., biblio., index. $12.95 pb.

Austin and Its Architecture. Allen McCree and Kirby Keaney, with Austin AIA Chapter and Women's Architectural League. Austin: Austin Chapter, AIA (1206 West 38th Street, 78705), 1976. 102 pp., illus., index. $12 hb.

A President's Country: A Guide to the LBJ Country of Texas. Jack Maguire, ed. 2nd ed. Austin: Shoal Creek Publishers (P.O. Box 968, 78767), 1973. 84 pp. $1.95.

San Antonio: A Historical and Pictorial Guide. Charles Ransdell. Rev. ed. Carmen Perry. Austin: University of Texas Press, 1976. 291 pp. $5.95.

The Houston Coloring Book. Gregory J. Cook. Houston: Houston Chapter, AIA (3121 Buffalo Speedway, Suite 404, 77098), 1976.

Mission Concepcion (1731–55), San Antonio, Tex. (William Peoples, HABS)

The Alamo (1718), San Antonio. (Jose Jimenez and James Emmrich, HABS)

Main Street stores, Jacksonville, Ore. (Jack E. Boucher, HABS)

West

California

The WPA Guide to California. New introduction by Gwendolyn Wright. 1939. Reprint. New York: Pantheon, 1984. 848 pp., illus. $11.95 pb.

A Guide to Architecture in San Francisco and Northern California. David Gebhard, Roger Montgomery, Robert Winter, John Woodbridge and Sally Woodbridge. 1973. Rev. ed. Salt Lake City: Peregrine Smith, 1976. 557 pp., illus. $9.95 pb.

Architecture San Francisco: The Guide. Sally B. Woodbridge and John M. Woodbridge. San Francisco Chapter, AIA. San Francisco: 101 Productions, 1982. 208 pp., illus., biblio., gloss., index. $10.95 pb.

Architecture in Los Angeles: A Compleat Guide. David Gebhard and Robert Winter. Salt Lake City: Peregrine Smith, 1984. 528 pp., illus., biblio., gloss., index. $14.95 pb.

The City Observed: Los Angeles. Charles Moore and Peter Becker. New York: Vintage Books, Random House, 1984. $7.95 pb.

Combing the Coast, San Francisco to Santa Cruz: A Lively Guide to Beaches, Backroads, Parks, Historic Sites and Towns. Ruth A. Jackson. San Francisco: Chronicle Books, 1981. 112 pp., illus., index. $5.95 pb.

Roaming the Back Roads. Day Trips by Car Through Northern California. Peter Browning and Carol Holleuffer. San Francisco: Chronicle Books, 1979. 175 pp., illus. $6.95 pb.

East Bay Heritage: A Potpourri of Living History. Mark A. Wilson. San Francisco: California Living Books, 1979. 256 pp., illus., maps. $8.95 pb.

LA/Access. Richard Saul Wurman. Los Angeles 200 Committee. Los Angeles: Access Press (P.O. Box 30706, 90030), 1981. 144 pp., illus., index. $8.95 pb.

A Guide to Historic Places in Los Angeles County. History Team, Los Angeles American Revolution Bicentennial Committee, Judson A. Grenier, ed. Dubuque, Iowa: Kendall/Hunt Publishing Company, 1979. 324 pp., illus., biblio., index.

You See San Diego. James Britton, II. San Diego: San Diego Chapter, AIA, 1977. illus., index. $7.50.

Oregon

Portland: A Historical Sketch and Guide. Terrence O'Donnell and Thomas Vaughn. Portland: Oregon Historical Society, 1976. 161 pp., illus., index. $1.95 pb.

Utah

Utah: A Guide to 11 Tours of Historic Sites. Stephanie D. Churchill. Salt Lake City: Utah Heritage Foundation, 1972. 43 pp. $1.

Washington

Guide to Architecture in Washington State: An Environmental Perspective. Sally B. Woodbridge, Roger Montgomery and David C. Streatfield. Seattle: University of Washington Press, 1980. 500 pp., illus., gloss., biblio., index. $25 hb, $12.95 pb.

Back Roads of Washington. Earl Thollander. New York: Clarkson N. Potter, 1981. 208 pp., illus. $17.95 hb, $9.95 pb.

Walking Tours: Looking at 2 mph.

"Old buildings were meant to be viewed at two miles an hour (walking speed) not twenty."

Stanley Miller, *Heritage Conversation.* Heritage Canada.

"On arriving at a town the first thing is to buy the plan of the town, and the book noting its curiosities. Walk around the ramparts when there are any, go to the top of a steeple and have a view of the town and its environs."

Thomas Jefferson, 1788.

"Only on your feet can you truly appreciate that the skyscraper was born in Chicago's Loop; that San Francisco boasts a Civil War Landmark—Fort Point; that the center of the Brooklyn Bridge is the place to stand for a breathtaking view of Manhattan."

Wayne Barrett, *Walking Tours of America*

Walking Tours of America: Mini-Tours on Foot in Major Cities. Louise Feinsot, ed. Introduction by Wayne Barrett. Kinney Shoe Corporation, with President's Council on Physical Fitness and Sports. New York: Collier Books, Macmillan, 1979. 400 pp., maps.

The American Walk Book: An Illustrated Guide to the Country's Major Historic and Natural Walking Trails from New England to the Pacific Coast. Jean Craighead George. New York: Dutton, 1978. 301 pp., illus., index. $6.95 pb.

Walking: A Guide to Beautiful Walks and Trails in America. Jean Calder. New York: Morrow, 1977. 340 pp. $3.95 pb.

New England

Walking Tours of New England: A Footloose Guide to Historic Mansions and Museums, Village Ghosts and Greens, and Yankee Dreamers and Doers. Kenneth Winchester and David Dunbar. Garden City, N.Y.: Dolphin Books, Doubleday, 1980. 448 pp., illus.

Massachusetts
Paul Hogarth's Walking Tours of Old Boston. Paintings by Paul Hogarth. Forewords by Peter Blake and Sinclair Hitchings. New York: Dutton, 1978. 176 pp.

Victorian Boston Today: Ten Walking Tours. Pauline Chase Harrell and Margaret Supplee Smith. Boston: New England Chapter, Victorian Society in America (137 Beacon Street, 02116), 1975. 142 pp. $3.95 pb.

The Boston Globe's Historic Walks in Old Boston. John Harris. Chester, Conn.: Globe Pequot Press, 1984. 352 pp., illus., index. $9.95 pb.

Guide to Cambridge Architecture: Ten Walking Tours. Robert Bell Rettig. Cambridge Historical Commission. Cambridge: MIT Press, 1969. $6.95 pb.

Brookline Walking Tours. Brookline Planning Department. Brookline: Author (Town Hall, 333 Washington Street, 02146), 1977. $1 pb.

Rhode Island
"Benefit Street: A Mile of History in Providence, R.I." Providence Preservation Society. Providence: Author (24 Meeting Street, 02903). $.75 pb.

Faneuil Hall Market, Boston. From *Paul Hogarth's Walking Tours of Old Boston.*

Mid-Atlantic
Maryland
A Guide to Baltimore Architecture. John Dorsey and James D. Dilts. 1973. Rev. ed. Centreville, Md.: Tidewater Publishers, 1981. 327 pp., illus., maps, gloss., indexes. $4.95 pb.

New York
New York: A Guide to the Metropolis. Walking Tours of Architecture and History. Gerard R. Wolfe. 1975. New York: McGraw-Hill, 1983. 516 pp., illus., index. $12.95 pb.

Nooks and Crannies: An Unusual Walking Tour Guide to New York City. David Yeadon. New York: Scribner's, 1979. 330 pp., illus., index. $8.95 pb.

New York Beaux Arts Tour. Deborah Nevins and Marita O'Hare, eds. New York: Architectural League of New York (41 East 65th Street, 10021). $3.

The Dover New York Walking Guide: Greenwich Village. Mary J. Shapiro. New York: Dover, 1985. $1.95 pb.

A Walking Tour of Clinton Hall. Michael and Olga Heisler. Brooklyn: Society for Clinton Hill (P.O. Box 153 Pratt Station, 11205), 1977. 20 pp., biblio. $3.50 pb.

Two Historic Neighborhoods: A Guided Walk Through Hudson-Park and Center Square. Historic Albany Foundation. Albany: Author (300 Hudson Avenue, 12210), 1976. $1.50.

Historic Third Ward House Tour. Robert Minzesheimer, Libby Stewart and Mark Van Volkinburg. Rochester: Landmark Society of Western New York (130 Spring Street, 14608). $1.50 pb.

Pennsylvania
Paul Hogarth's Walking Tours of Old Philadelphia. Paintings by Paul Hogarth. Barre, Mass.: Barre Publishers, 1976.

Bicentennial City: Walking Tours of Historic Philadelphia. John Francis Marion. Harrisburg, Pa.: Stackpole Books, 1974.

Philadelphia Center City Walking Tour. Philadelphia City Planning Commission. Philadelphia: Author (14th Floor, City Hall Annex, 19101), 1976.

Washington, D.C.
Washington on Foot. John J. Protopappas and Lin Brown. 3rd ed. Washington, D.C.: Smithsonian Institution Press, 1984. 224 pp., illus. $4.95 pb.

A Walking Guide to Historic Georgetown. Foundation for the Preservation of Historic Georgetown. Washington, D.C.: Author, 1971. $1.50 pb.

Society for Industrial Archeology members tour the Brooklyn Bridge (1883). (Smithsonian Institution)

Visitors watching crafts displays along Duke of Gloucester Street, Colonial Williamsburg, Va. (John Blumenson, NTHP)

South

Alabama

Downtown Birmingham: Architectural and Historical Walking Tour Guide. Marjorie L. White, ed. Birmingham: Birmingham Historical Society, 1977. $5 pb.

Florida

Miami Beach: A Guide to the Architecture. Arlene R. Olson. Miami: Dade Heritage Trust (P.O. Box 011251, 33101), 1978. 49 pp. $3.95 pb.

Georgia

AIA Guide to Atlanta. Atlanta Chapter, AIA. Atlanta: Author, 1975. 171 pp. $5 pb.

An-Other Atlanta: The Black Heritage. A Bicentennial Tour. Dan Durett and Dana F. White, Atlanta Bicentennial Commission. Atlanta: History Group (300 West Peachtree Street, N.W., 30308), 1975. 48 pp. $1.50.

Kentucky

Walking Thru Louisville. John Cullinane. Louisville: Data Courier, 1976. 112 pp. $1.95.

The Dainty Guide: A Louisville Handbook. A. William Dakan, Lynn Sitler and Claudia A. Craig. Louisville: Department of Geography, University of Louisville, 1980. 60 pp., illus. $3.50.

Tennessee

"Fort Sanders: A Walking Tour of the Neighborhood." Knoxville Heritage. Knoxville: Author (P.O. Box 11501, 37919), 1977.

Virginia

Historic Alexandria Street by Street. Ethelyn Cox. Alexandria: Historic Alexandria Foundation, 1976. $6.25 pb.

A Walking Tour of Historic Winchester. Preservation of Historic Winchester. Winchester: Author (8 East Cork Street, 22601). 40 pp., illus., map. $1.25 pb.

Midwest

Illinois

Chicago on Foot: Walking Tours of Chicago Architecture. Ira H. Bach. Chicago: Rand McNally, 1977. $7.95 pb.

Guide to Frank Lloyd Wright and Prairie School Architecture in Oak Park. Paul E. Sprague. Oak Park Landmarks Commission. Chicago: Follett Publishing, 1976. $3.50 pb.

Michigan

Walking Through Time: A Pictorial Guide to Historic Kalamazoo. Brendan Henehan. Kalamazoo: Kalamazoo Historical Commission (241 West South Street, 49007), 1981. 168 pp., illus., biblio., gloss., index.

Footloose in Washtenaw: A Walkers' Guide to Ann Arbor and Washtenaw. Joyce Bader and Donald N. Gray. Ann Arbor: Ecology Center of Ann Arbor (417 Detroit Street, 48104), 1976. $3 pb.

Missouri

Kansas City: A Place in Time. Landmarks Commission of Kansas City. Kansas City: Author, 1977. 288 pp., illus., biblio., index. $6.95 pb.

Laclede's Landing: A History and Architectural Guide. Carolyn H. Toft and Osmund Overby. St. Louis: Landmarks Association of St. Louis, 1977. $3 pb.

"Walking Map of Downtown St. Louis." St. Louis Chapter, AIA (919 Olive Street, 63101).

Wisconsin

"A Guide to Historic Walker's Point." Historic Walker's Point. Milwaukee: Author (734 South Fifth Street, 53204), 1978. $1.50 pb.

West

California

San Francisco: Walks and Tours in the Golden Gate City. Randolph Delehanty. New York: Dial Press, 1980. 340 pp., illus. $11.95 pb.

The Bay Area at Your Feet: Walks with San Francisco's Margot Patterson Doss. 1970. Rev. ed. San Francisco: Presidio Press, 1981. 269 pp., illus. $7.95 pb.

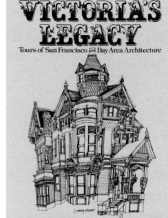

Drawing © 1978 Wendy Wheeler

Victoria's Legacy: Tours of San Francisco Bay Area Architecture. Judith Lynch Waldhorn and Sally B. Woodbridge. San Francisco: 101 Productions, 1978. $5.95 pb.

The Sidewalk Companion to Santa Cruz Architecture. John Chase. Santa Cruz: Santa Cruz Historical Society (P.O. Box 246, 95061), 1974. $6.45 pb.

The Walk Around Santa Cruz Book. A Look at the City's Architectural Treasures. Margaret Koch. Fresno: Valley Publishers, 1978. $4.95 pb.

"Welcome to Los Angeles: An Architectural Discovery Map." *L.A. Architect* (Southern California Chapter, AIA, 304 South Broadway, 90013), June 1977. $1.

Hawaii

A Walk Through Old Honolulu: An Illustrated Guide. O.A. Bushnell. Honolulu: Kapa Associates. $4.50 pb.

Washington

"Seeing Seattle . . . On Foot." A Series of Walking Tours. City of Seattle Office of Urban Conservation. Seattle: Department of Community Development (400 Yesler Way, 98104), 1978.

Seattle's Historic Waterfront: The Walker's Guide to the History of Elliott Bay. Marc J. Hershman, Susan Heikkala and Caroline Tobin. Institute for Marine Studies, University of Washington. Seattle: University of Washington Press, 1981. 98 pp., illus. $5.95 pb.

Bicyclist in Marin County, north of San Francisco. From *Family Bike Rides*. (© Lee Foster)

Bikeology: A Ten-Speed Look at History

"Nothing can be hidden from the bicycle in a city."

Daniel Behman, *The Man Who Loved Bicycles: The Memoirs of an Autophobe*. New York: Harper's Magazine Press, with Harper and Row, 1973.

"A growing number of people consider the bicycle an ideal vehicle—fast enough for efficient transportation, slow enough to enjoy the surroundings and invigorating enough for recreation. Many of these cyclists use their non-polluting vehicle to improve their personal health and to preserve the health of our natural environment."

Chris Miller, "How to Plan a Bicycle Tour of a Historic District." Washington, D.C.: National Trust for Historic Preservation, 1976.

New England

New England Over the Handlebars: A Cyclist's Guide. Michael H. Farny. Boston: Little, Brown, 1975. $6.95 pb.

Short Bike Rides in Connecticut. Jane Griffith and Edwin Mullen. Chester, Conn.: Globe Pequot Press, 1976. 72 pp. $3.95 pb.

Short Bike Rides on Cape Cod, Nantucket and The Vineyard. Jane Griffith and Edwin Mullen. Chester, Conn.: Globe Pequot Press, 1977. 128 pp. $4.95 pb.

20 Bicycle Tours in New Hampshire. Tom Heavey and Susan Heavey. Woodstock, Vt.: Backcountry, 1979. 128 pp. $5.95 pb.

25 Bicycle Tours in Vermont. John S. Freidin. Woodstock, Vt.: Backcountry, 1984. 176 pp. $7.95 pb.

Boston Basin Bicycle Book. Edward Goldfrank et al. Boston: David R. Godine, 1982. 232 pp., illus., index. $3.95 pb.

Mid-Atlantic

Center to Centre: A Bicycle Tour of Historical Brighton (N.Y.). Max Kenemore and Margaret MacNab. Brighton Bicycle Task Force, 1976. $.75. Available from Landmark Society of Western New York, 130 Spring Street, Rochester, N.Y. 14608.

Short Bike Rides on Long Island. Phil Angelilo. Chester, Conn.: Globe Pequot Press, 1977. 136 pp. $4.95 pb.

Circling Historic Landscapes: Bicycling, Canoeing and Walking Trails Near Sugarloaf Mountain, Md. Gail Rothrock, ed. Sugarloaf Regional Trails, Maryland-National Capital Park and Planning Commission. Silver Spring, Md.: Montgomery County Planning Board (8787 Georgia Avenue, 20907), 1980. 109 pp., illus. $2 pb.

Midwest

"Cycle Chicago: Beverly-Morgan Park Bike Tour." City of Chicago and Chicago Tribune. Chicago: Mayor's Office of Inquiry and Information (City Hall, 60602). Other tours available.

Detroit Bike Trips. Tom Holeman. Rochester, Mich.: Author (Harrington Road, 48063), 1975. $1.50 pb.

West

Bicycle Touring in the Western United States. Karen and Gary Hawkins. New York: Pantheon, 1982. 366 pp. $9.95 pb.

Discovering Santa Barbara . . . Without a Car. Ken Kolsbun and Bob Burgess. Santa Barbara: Friends for Bikecology (P.O. Box 863, 93102), 1974. 67 pp. $2.50.

Family Bike Rides: A Guide to Over 40 Specially Selected Bicycle Routes in Northern California. Milton A. Grossberg. San Francisco: Chronicle Books, 1981. 112 pp., illus., index. $5.95 pb.

A Cyclist's Guide to Oakland History. Camille Olmsted. Oakland: Oakland Museum History Department, 1976. $1.50 ring-bound (to fit over the handle bar).

Contacts

Bikecentennial
P.O. Box 8308
Missoula, Mont. 59807

League of American Wheelmen
19 South Bothwell
Palatine, Ill. 60067

Bicycle Federation
1101 15th Street, N.W.
Washington, D.C. 20005

American Youth Hostels
1332 I Street, N.W.
Suite 800
Washington, D.C. 20005

Running Away from Home

"For architecture/running enthusiasts, there is already the 'Frank Lloyd Wright Distance Run,' held annually in Oak Park, Illinois. Along the route are 37 historic and architecturally important buildings designed by Frank Lloyd Wright and his contemporaries from the Prairie School of Architecture."

John Fondersmith, *American Urban Guidenotes*, Summer 1979.

The Runner's Guide to the USA. Martina D'Alton. New York: Summit Books, 1978. 410 pp.

The Great American Runner's Guide. Western States Edition. Edward L. Moore. New York: Beaufort Books, 1985. 160 pp., illus. $6.95 pb.

Traveler's Guide to Running in Major American Cities. Mary-Jo Carroll and Randy Sloan. Harrisburg, Pa.: Stackpole Books, 1980. 219 pp., illus.

Running Away from Home: A Guide to Running Trails in 36 Cities Across the Country. David Colker. New York: Harcourt, Brace Jovanovich, 1980.

Running in Connecticut. Elaine B. Hills. Waterford, Conn.: Waterford Publishing, 1981. $7.95 pb.

Runner's Guide to Chicago and the Suburbs. Tem Horwitz. Chicago: Chicago Review Press, 1978. $6.95 pb.

Running the Twin Cities. Gretchen Kreuter. Minneapolis: Nodin Press, Bookmen, 1980. 95 pp., illus. $1 pb.

Bus Tours: Looking Beyond the Dirty Window

"You miss a lot, the booklet tells you, by keeping your eyes at shopwindow level. Instead, you are advised to crane your neck and look up—at the elaborate green-white-and-gold terra cotta decoration and urns on the top of the Landmark Building at 14th and H, and at the carved lion's heads on the nearby Southern Building."

Anne H. Oman, "Touring Exotic, Exciting S-2/S-4 Land." *Washington Post*, April 7, 1978.

Contacts

D.C. Preservation League
930 F Street, N.W.
Suite 612
Washington, D.C. 20004

Minnesota Society
American Institute of Architects
314 Clifton Avenue
Minneapolis, Minn. 55403

Form and Function

4

F *orm ever follows function.*

Louis Henri Sullivan, "The Tall Office Building Artistically Considered." *Lippincott's Magazine*, March 1896.

N *ot until we raise the dictum, now a dogma, to the realm of thought, and say:* Form and function are one, *have we stated the case for architecture.*

Frank Lloyd Wright, "Some Aspects of the Future of Architecture." 1937.

"The history of building types has fascinated me for many years, because this treatment of buildings allows for a demonstration of development both by style and by function, style being a matter of architectural history, function of social history."

Nikolaus Pevsner, *A History of Building Types*

"Buildings are not so neatly categorized as birds."

Carole Rifkind, *A Field Guide to American Architecture*

"Changing economic and social conditions have endangered a wide variety of building types. Old inner-city churches and synagogues, for instance, face abandonment or demolition as their congregations move to the suburbs; movie theaters of the 1930s and 1940s are disappearing from our cities, victims of the same shift to the suburbs and the lure of television; older school buildings are the first to be closed in response to the continuing decline in the school-age population. Obsolete facili-

ties, high maintenance costs and pressures for development, among other factors, have helped add breweries and banks, mansions and factories, railroad stations and barns to the endangered list."

"Endangered Building Types." In *Preservation: Toward an Ethic in the 1980s*. National Trust for Historic Preservation. Washington, D.C.: Preservation Press, 1980.

Built in the U.S.A.: American Buildings from Airports to Zoos. Diane Maddex, ed., National Trust for Historic Preservation. Washington, D.C.: Preservation Press, 1985. 192 pp., illus., biblio. $8.95 pb.

From airports to zoos, this compact little book covers 42 of the most important and interesting American building types. Included are amusement parks and fairs, apartments, banks, barns, black settlements, breweries, bridges, capitols, city halls, colleges, courthouses, diners, ducks, farms, firehouses, forts, gas stations, hotels, houses, Indian settlements, industrial sites, Main Streets, prisons, railroad stations, religious structures, schoolhouses, skyscrapers, suburbs, theaters and vernacular buildings. Each illustrated essay is written by a noted authority, among them Charles Moore, Ada Louise Huxtable, David Gebhard, Gwendolyn Wright, Richard Gutman and Steven Izenour.

A History of Building Types. Nikolaus Pevsner. Princeton: Princeton University Press, 1976. 352 pp., illus., biblio., index $60 hb, $17.50 pb.

In this worldwide chronology of 20 building types, three stories are interwoven: function, materials and styles. Types covered include national monuments and "monuments to genius," government buildings from the 12th to the late 17th century, town halls and law courts, theaters, libraries, museums, hospitals, prisons, hotels, exchanges and banks, warehouses and office buildings, railroad stations, markets, conservatories and exhibition buildings, shops, stores, department stores and factories.

Buildings and Society: Essays on the Social Development of the Built Environment. Anthony D. King. London and Boston: Routledge and Kegan Paul, 1980. 328 pp., illus., index. $19.95 pb.

Essays explore the rise of several building types: Victorian lunatic asylums, modern hospitals in England and France, 19th-century English prisons, Hindu temples in south India, apartment houses in urban America, vacation houses, restaurants in 19th-century England, office buildings and vernacular architecture.

The Federal Presence: Architecture, Politics, and National Design. Lois Craig and Federal Architecture Project Staff. Cambridge: MIT Press, 1978. 581 pp., illus., biblio., index. $49.50 hb, $17.50 pb.

In surveying the architecture of one of the world's largest builders and landlords, this comprehensive book chronologically covers many building types in which the federal government has had a special role as builder and model. Among them are federal offices, military sites, banks, lighthouses, memorials, prisons, custom houses, bridges, cemeteries, utilities, embassies, educational facilities, hospitals, housing, parks, post offices, railroads, roads, space and atomic sites, WPA constructions, artwork and fairs.

A Field Guide to American Architecture. Carole Rifkind. New York: New American Library, 1980. 336 pp., illus., biblio, index. $9.95 pb.

The book is organized into four main building types: residential, ecclesiastical, civic and commerical, and "utilitarian" (agriculture, transportation and industry), each of which is divided into architectural periods.

Pitkin County Courthouse (1890, William Quay), Aspen, Colo. (William Clift, Seagram County Court House Archives)

Community members reapplying adobe on the wall of a house in Chamisal, N.M., in 1940. (Russell Lee, Library of Congress)

Los Angeles Municipal Airport (Mines Field), c. 1930. (Whittington Collection, Henry E. Huntington Library and Art Gallery)

Adobes

"Adobe and related materials are among the oldest building materials on earth, with rammed earth construction dating back to Neolithic times (3,000 to 10,000 B.C.). The 'Tower of Babel' was apparently constructed with adobe brick. Under favorable conditions, earth structures of this type can be extremely durable."

James R. Clifton, *Preservation of Historic Adobe Structures: A Status Report*

"How can one describe our church? It needs to breathe; it gets old, wrinkles and cracks; it needs to be cared for; it loves to be washed by the rain and to feel the touch of women's hands applying the mud plaster to conceal and heal the cracks of weather and time. Our church is almost human."

Father Michael O'Brien, Foreword. *Ranchos de Taos*

Down to Earth. Jean Dethier. New York: Facts on File, 1983. 192 pp., illus., biblio., index. $21.95 hb.

Adobe: A Comprehensive Bibliography. Rex C. Hopson. Santa Fe: Lightning Tree, 1979. 127 pp. $15 hb, $9.95 pb.

Adobe Past and Present. William Lumpkins. Santa Fe: Museum of New Mexico (P.O. Box 2087, 87501), 1972. 39 pp., illus., biblio. $2.50 pb.

Preservation of Historic Adobe Buildings. Preservation Brief no. 5. Technical Preservation Services. Washington, D.C.: National Park Service, U.S. Department of the Interior, 1978. 8 pp., illus., biblio. $1 pb. GPO stock no. 024-005-00881-1.

Preservation of Historic Adobe Structures: A Status Report. James R. Clifton. U.S. Department of the Interior and National Bureau of Standards. Washington, D.C.: National Technical Information Service, 1977. 36 pp. $8.50 pb. NBS Technical Note 934.

Early Architecture in New Mexico. Bainbridge Bunting. Albuquerque: University of New Mexico Press, 1976. 122 pp., illus., biblio., index. $12.95 pb.

Taos Adobes: Spanish Colonial and Territorial Architecture of the Taos Valley. Bainbridge Bunting et al. Santa Fe: Museum of New Mexico Press, 1975. 80 pp., illus., plans, biblio. $7.95 pb.

Of Earth and Timbers Made: New Mexico Architecture. Bainbridge Bunting. Albuquerque: University of New Mexico Press, 1974. 85 pp., illus. $12.95 pb.

Adobes in the Sun. Morley Baer et al. 1972. San Francisco: Chronicle Books, 1980. 144 pp., illus. $8.95 pb.

The Religious Architecture of New Mexico. George Kubler. 1940. Reprint. Albuquerque: University of New Mexico Press, 1973. 232 pp., illus., index.

Adobe: Pueblo and Hispanic Folk Traditions of the Southwest. Peter Nabokov. Washington, D.C.: Office of Folklife Programs, Smithsonian Institution, 1981. 32 pp., illus., biblio. $.50 pb.

Ranchos de Taos: San Francisco de Asis Church. Wolfgang Pogzeba and Joy Overbeck. Kansas City, Mo.: Lowell Press, 1981. 68 pp., illus. $7.95 pb.

Adobe: Build It Yourself. Paul G. McHenry, Jr. Tucson: University of Arizona Press, 1973. $12.50 pb.

Contacts

Western Archeological Center
Division of Adobe/Stone
Conservation
National Park Service
U.S. Department of the Interior
P.O. Box 41058
Tucson, Ariz. 85717

Institute for Applied Technology
National Bureau of Standards
U.S. Department of Commerce
Washington, D.C. 20234

Southwest Adobe Association
Star Route, Box 268
Placitas, N.M. 87043

Adobe Today
Box 1178
Belen, N.M. 87002

Airports

"Aviation has come so far in so short a time that we take for granted that airports have always been with us and that they have always been larger than life colossal structures, mazes of modern buildings filled with people so numbed by the familiarity of air travel that they no longer discern differences between one airport and another. . . .The earliest structures on early flying fields were undoubtedly buildings acquired with the propery to be used as an air station. A barn or shed was sometimes turned into a hangar and a cottage became an administration building."

Martin Greif, *The Airport Book*

"Beautiful Dulles Airport; one in the entire country! Why can't we have three hundred Dulles Airports?"

Philip Johnson, April 3, 1963. *Historic Preservation*, July–September 1963.

The Airport Book: From Landing Field to Modern Terminal. Martin Greif. New York: Mayflower Books, 1979. 192 pp., illus., index. $12.95 hb.

Some Historic Airports

Douglas Municipal Airport (1928), Douglas, Ariz.

Pan American Sea Plane Base and Terminal Building (1930–38), Miami, Fla.

Lighter-than-Air Ship Hangars (1943), Santa Ana, Calif.

Quinset Point Naval Air Station (1939–40), North Kingston, R.I.

Dulles International Airport (1962), Chantilly, Va.

Contacts

National Air and Space Museum
Smithsonian Institution
Washington, D.C. 20560

Federal Aviation Administration
U.S. Department of Transportation
Washington, D.C. 20590

American Aviation Historical Society
P.O. Box 99
Garden Grove, Calif. 92642

Society of Airway Pioneers
P.O. Box 17020
San Diego, Calif. 92117

National Association of State Aviation Officials
1300 G Street, N.W.
Washington, D.C. 20005

Office of Air Force History
U.S. Air Force
Bolling Air Force Base
Washington, D.C. 20332

Lighter-than-Air Society
1800 Triplett Boulevard
Akron, Ohio 44306

Amusement Parks

"There are hardly any amusement parks in America today where the architecture of the turn of the century still remains. . . .The fantasy of fun is as ephemeral as its architecture. . . . The Astroturf of the sports arena has replaced the family park and its grassy knolls at the end of the trolley line. . . ."

Frederick and Mary Fried,
America's Forgotten Folk Arts

The Great American Amusement Parks. Gary Kyriazi. Secaucus, N.J.: Citadel, 1976. 240 pp., illus., index. $14.95.

Fairground Architecture: The World of Amusement Parks, Carnivals and Fairs. David Braithwaite. New York: Praeger, 1968. 195 pp., illus., biblio., gloss., index.

Fairground Art. Geoff Weedon and Richard Ward. New York: Abbeville, 1982. 312 pp., color illus. $39.98 hb.

America's Forgotten Folk Arts. Frederick and Mary Fried. New York: Pantheon, 1978. 204 pp., color illus., biblio., appends., index.

Art of the Carousel. Charlotte Dinger. Green Village, N.J.: Carousel Art (P.O. Box 150, 07935), 1984. 400 illus. $40 hb.

The Carousel Animal. Tobin Fraley. Berkeley: Zephyr Press, 1983. 127 pp., illus., gloss., biblio. $19.95 hb.

A Pictorial History of the Carousel. Frederick Fried. South Brunswick, N.J.: A. S. Barnes, 1964. 232 pp., color illus., appends., index. $25 hb.

Amusement Parks of America: A Comprehensive Guide. Jeff Ulmer. New York: Dial, 1980. 339 pp., illus., index. $7.95 pb.

Coney Island: A Postcard Journey to the City of Fire. Richard Snow. New York: Brightwaters Press, 1984. 120 pp., color illus. $24.95 hb.

Amusing the Million: Coney Island at the Turn of the Century. John F. Kasson. New York: Hill and Wang, 1978. 120 pp., illus., biblio. $6.95 pb.

Dime-Store Dream Parade: Popular Culture 1923–1955. Robert Heide and John Gilman. New York: Dutton, 1979. 128 pp., illus., index.

American Popular Entertainment: Papers and Proceedings of the Conference on the History of American Popular Entertainment. Myron Matlaw, ed. Westport, Conn.: Greenwood, 1979. 360 pp., biblio. $29.95.

"Eight Ways of Looking at an Amusement Park," Russel B. Nye (and other articles). *Journal of Popular Culture,* Summer 1981.

Contacts

National Amusement Parks
Historical Association
P.O. Box 83
Mt. Prospect, Ill. 60056

Amusement Park Journal
Amusement Park Club
International
P.O. Box 157
Natrona Heights, Pa. 15065

National Carousel Association
P.O. Box 307
Frankfort, Ind. 46041

American Carousel Society
c/o Rosalyn Taylor
55 Sutter Street
Suite 830
San Francisco, Calif. 94104

American Coaster Enthusiasts
34–26 57th Street
Woodside, N.Y. 11377

Outdoor Amusement Business
Association
4600 West 77th Street
Suite 188
Edina, Minn. 55435

International Association of
Amusement Parks and
Attractions
7222 West Cermak Road
Suite 303
North Riverside, Ill. 60546

See also: Circuses, Fair Buildings

The Dakota Apartment House (1884, Henry J. Hardenbergh), New York City. (HABS)

Apartment Buildings

"Poor Americans are apt to be over-sensitive, and, having associated apartment-houses with tenement-houses, were afraid that the former might be confounded with the latter. But when the well-to-do and the rich consented to occupy flats, and really liked them, the . . . not rich felt that they could afford to occupy and like them also. Hence, flats became popular."

New York Times, June 3, 1878.

"The Apartment House in Urban America," John Hancock. In *Buildings and Society: Essays on the Social Development of the Built Environment.* Anthony D. King. London and Boston: Routledge and Kegan Paul, 1980. 328 pp., illus., index. $19.95 pb.

Apartments for the Affluent: A Historical Survey of Buildings in New York City. Andrew Alpern. New York: McGraw-Hill, 1975. 159 pp., illus., biblio., index.

Living It Up: A Guide to the Named Apartment Houses of New York. Thomas E. Norton and Jerry E. Patterson. New York: Atheneum, 1984. 451 pp., illus., index. $25 hb.

Life at the Dakota: New York's Most Unusual Address. Stephen Birmingham. New York: Random House, 1979. 244 pp., illus., index. $12.50 hb.

A Place Called Home: A History of Low-Cost Housing in Manhattan. Anthony Jackson. Cambridge: MIT Press, 1976. 359 pp., illus. $25 hb.

Working Class Housing: A Study of Triple-Deckers in Boston. Joseph Slavet, Project Director. Boston: Boston Redevelopment Agency and Boston Urban Observatory (Harbor Campus, Dorchester, Mass. 02125), 1975. 436 pp., illus.

See also: Houses

The "Helter Skelter," Luna Park, Coney Island, N.Y., in 1905. (Detroit Photographic Collection, Library of Congress)

Architects' Houses

"Architects spend most of their careers building for clients. . . . But the great day usually comes when an architect has the perfect client: himself."

Joseph J. Thorndike, Jr., *The Magnificent Builders and Their Dream Houses*

"Architects, unlike most of us, are willing to risk trying out experimental design concepts in the laboratories of their own houses. If these concepts work, practically and aesthetically, they eventually find their way, in one form or another, into the houses of the rest of us."

Barbara Plumb, *Houses Architects Live In*

"I consider my own house not so much as a home (though it is that to me) as a *clearing house of ideas* which can filter down later, through my own work or that of others."

Philip Johnson. In *Conversations with Artists*, 1957.

"Architects for Themselves." In *The Magnificent Builders and Their Dream Houses*. Jospeh J. Thorndike, Jr. New York: American Heritage Publishing Company, 1978. 352 pp., color illus., index.

Houses Architects Live In. Barbara Plumb. 1977. New York: Penguin, 1978. 168 pp., color illus. $25.

Houses Architects Design for Themselves. Walter F. Wagner, Jr., and Karin Schlegel, eds. New York: McGraw-Hill, 1974. 240 pp., illus. $36.50 hb.

More Houses Architects Design for Themselves. Walter F. Wagner, Jr. New York: McGraw-Hill, 1983. $29.95 hb.

Monticello: A Guide Book. Frederick D. Nichols and James A. Bear, Jr. Thomas Jefferson Memorial Foundation. Charlottesville: University Press of Virginia, 1967. 77 pp., illus. $2.95 pb.

Mr. Jefferson's Monticello. Photographs by Robert Llewelyn. Charlottesville: Upland (Thomasson-Grant), 1982. 80 pp., color illus. $22.50 hb.

Plan for the Restoration and Adaptive Use of the Frank Lloyd Wright Home and Studio. Restoration Committee, Frank Lloyd Wright Home and Studio Foundation. Chicago: University of Chicago Press, 1977. 76 pp., illus. $25 pb.

The Glass House (1949), architect Philip Johnson's International Style residence in New Canaan, Conn. (Carleton Knight III, NTHP)

Artist Georgia O'Keeffe's restored adobe house, Abiquiu, N.M., between Taos and Santa Fe. (Balthazar Korab)

Taliesin East and West. Masami Tanigawa. Global Architecture Series. Yukio Futagawa, ed. Tokyo, Japan: A.D.A. Edita Tokyo, Ltd., 1972. Color illus. $15 pb.

Philip Johnson House. Bryan Robertson. Global Architecture Series. Yukio Futagawa, ed. Tokyo, Japan: A.D.A. Edita Tokyo, Ltd., 1972. 56 pp., illus. $15 pb.

Furniture Designed by Architects. Marian Page. New York: Whitney Library of Design, Watson-Guptill, 1980. 224 pp., illus. $14.95 pb.

Some Historic Architects' Houses

Monticello (1770–89), Charlottesville, Va. Thomas Jefferson.

Poplar Forest (early 19th century), Lynchburg, Va. Thomas Jefferson.

Frank Lloyd Wright Home and Studio (1889–98), Oak Park, Ill.

Taliesin East (1902–38), Spring Green, Wis. F. L. Wright.

Taliesin West, (1938–59), Scottsdale, Ariz. F. L. Wright.

Rudolph M. Schindler House (1921–22), West Hollywood, Calif.

Walter Gropius House (1937), Lincoln, Mass.

Glass House (1949), New Canaan, Conn. Philip Johnson.

Charles and Ray Eames House (1950), Santa Monica, Calif.

Contacts

Thomas Jefferson Memorial Foundation
P.O. Box 316
Charlottesville, Va. 22902

Frank Lloyd Wright Home and Studio Foundation
National Trust for Historic Preservation
951 Chicago Avenue
Oak Park, Ill. 60302

Frank Lloyd Wright Foundation
Taliesin West
Scottsdale, Ariz. 85258

Friends of the Schindler House
835 North Kings Road
Los Angeles, Calif. 90069

Walter Gropius House
Society for the Preservation of New England Antiquities
141 Cambridge Street
Boston, Mass. 02114

See also: The Master Builders (Looking at the Built Environment)

Artists' Places

"When I first saw the Abiquiu house it was a ruin with an adobe wall around the garden broken in a couple of places by falling trees. As I climbed and walked about in the ruin I found a patio with a very pretty well house and bucket to draw up water. It was a good-sized patio with a long wall with a door on one side.

That wall with a door in it was something I had to have. It took me ten years to get it—three more years to fix the house so I could live in it—and after that the wall with the door was painted many times."

Georgia O'Keeffe, *Georgia O'Keeffe.* New York: Viking, 1976.

The Artist and the Built Environment. Donald Stoltenberg. Worcester, Mass.: Davis Publications, 1980. 158 pp., color illus., biblio., index. $18.95.

Imagination's Chamber: A History of the Artist's Studio. Alice Bellony-Rewald and Michael Peppiatt. Boston: New York Graphic Society, 1982. 240 pp., illus. $35 hb.

"The Studio." In *The Professional Artist's Manual.* Richard Hyman. New York: Van Nostrand Reinhold, 1980. 240 pp., illus., biblio., index. $16.95 hb.

"Artists as Builders." In *The Magnificent Builders and Their Dream Houses.* Joseph J. Thorndike, Jr. New York: American Heritage Publishing Company, 1978. 352 pp., color illus., index.

The Hudson River and Its Painters. John K. Howat. 1972. New York: Penguin, 1978. 207 pp., color illus. $14.95 pb.

Alfred R. Ward: Special Artist on Assignment. Profiles of American Towns and Cities, 1850–1880. Exhibition catalog. New Orleans: Historic New Orleans Collection (533 Royal Street, 70130), 1979. 21 pp.

Georgia O'Keeffe: The Artist's Landscape. Todd Webb. Pasadena, Calif.: Twelvetrees Press (Box 188, 91102), 1984. $45.

Artist Colonies. New York: Center for Arts Information (625 Broadway, 10012), 1982. 5 pp. $1.50.

SoHo: The Artist in the City. Charles R. Simpson. Chicago: University of Chicago Press, 1981. 276 pp., illus., appends., biblio., index. $20 hb.

Seattle Artists' Housing Handbook: Creating and Controlling Living/Working Space Through Building Conversion. Larry Mortimer and Dan Carlson. Seattle: Department of Community Development and Arts Commission (400 Municipal Building, 98104), 1980. 38 pp.

Artists Live/Work Space: Changing Public Policy. San Francisco: Artists Equity Association (Northern California Chapter, 81 Leavenworth Street, 94102), 1981. 143 pp. $6 pb.

American Painting: A Guide to Information Sources. Sydney Starr Keaveney. Detroit: Gale Research Company, 1974. 296 pp. $44 hb.

Some Historic Artists' Places
Olana (1874), Church Hill, N.Y. Frederic E. Church.

Chesterwood (1898), Stockbridge, Mass. Daniel Chester French.

Winslow Homer's Studio (c. 1870), Prout's Neck, Maine.

Thomas Eakins House (1854), Philadelphia.

Belfield (1750), Philadelphia, Charles Willson Peale.

Thomas Sully House (1796), Philadelphia.

Mill Grove Farm (1762), Audubon, Pa. John James Audubon.

Charles M. Russell House and Studio (1900), Great Falls, Mont.

Saint-Gaudens National Historic Site (c. 1800), Cornish, N.H. Augustus Saint-Gaudens.

Georgia O'Keeffe House, Abiquiu, N.M.

Contacts
Chesterwood
P.O. Box 248
Stockbridge, Mass. 01262

Saint-Gaudens National
Historic Site
R.D. 2
Windsor, Vt. 05089

The MacDowell Colony
Peterborough, N.H. 03458

Yaddo
Saratoga Springs, N.Y. 12866

Atomic and Nuclear Sites
"There rose as if from the bowels of the earth a light not of this world, the light of many suns in one. It was a sunrise such as the world had never seen, a great green supersun climbing in a fraction of a second to a height of more than eight thousand feet. . . .
Up it went, a great ball of fire

about a mile in diameter, changing colors as it kept shooting upward, from deep purple to orange . . . an elemental force freed from its bonds after being chained for billions of years. . . .
Then out of the great silence came a mighty thunder . . . the first cry of a newborn world."
> William Laurence. In *The History of the Atom Bomb*. New York: American Heritage, 1968.

The Day the Sun Rose Twice: The Story of the Trinity Site Nuclear Explosion, July 16, 1945. Ferenc Morton Szasz. Albuquerque: University of New Mexico Press, 1985. $15.95.

City of Fire: Los Alamos and the Atomic Age, 1943–1945. James W. Kunetka. Rev. ed. Albuquerque: University of New Mexico Press, 1980. 264 pp., illus. $9.95 pb.

City Behind a Fence: Oak Ridge, Tennessee, 1942–1946. Charles W. Johnson and Charles O. Jackson. Knoxville: University of Tennessee Press, 1981. 224 pp., illus. $18.50 hb, $9.50 pb.

"An Historical View of Oak Ridge: The Pre-Oak Ridge Communities and Katy's Kitchen," James A. Young and Ruby A. Miller. Oak Ridge, Tenn.: Union Carbide Corporation, 1976. 9 pp., illus.

Some Atomic and Nuclear Sites
Chicago Pile-1, Stagg Field, University of Chicago (1942)

Pupin Physics Laboratory, Columbia University (1942)

Oak Ridge National Laboratory, Tenn. (1943)

Atomic cloud released during the Baker Day blast at Bikini Atoll, Marshall Islands, July 25, 1946. (National Archives)

Los Alamos Scientific Laboratory, N.M. (1943)

Hanford National Laboratory, Wash. (1943)

Trinity Test Site, Alamogordo, N.M. (1945)

Tinian, Northern Mariana Islands (1945)

Bikini Atoll, Marshall Islands (1946)

Eniwetak Atoll, Marshall Islands (1952)

Yucca Flat, Nev. (1953)

Experimental nuclear reactor Number 1, Arco, Idaho (1949)

Three-Mile Island, Middletown, Pa. (1980)

Contacts
U.S. Department of Energy
Washington, D.C. 20585

Nuclear Regulatory Commission
1717 H Street, N.W.
Washington, D.C. 20555

National Atomic Museum
U.S. Department of Energy
P.O. Box 5400
Albuquerque, N.M. 87115

American Museum of Science and Energy
P.O. Box 117
Oak Ridge, Tenn. 37830

Oak Ridge National Laboratory
P.O. Box X
Oak Ridge, Tenn. 37830

Banks
"There has been a rash of robberies of New York's banks . . . and most of the trouble seems to be that the banks are just too friendly. The low, open counters are easily vaulted; lack of glass or grilles encourages the quick heist. The kind of monumental architecture

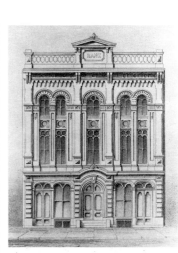
Design by Samuel Sloan for an Italianate bank (1859). From *City and Suburban Architecture*. (Library of Congress)

that used to suggest security, solidity and style has given way to 'people' banks that are as chummy as the laundromat and about as distinguished in design. . . . Who would dare hold up the Parthenon?"
> Ada Louise Huxtable, "Art for Money's Sake." *New York Times*, March 3, 1978.

"The Banking Story," Martin Mayer. *American Heritage*, April–May 1984.

Architectural Record, January 1909. Special issue.

Architectural Forum, June 1923. Special issue.

Forms and Functions of Twentieth-Century Architecture. Talbot Hamlin, ed. New York: Columbia University Press, 1952.

The Fundamentals of Good Bank Building. Alfred Hopkins. New York: Bankers Publishing, 1928.

Buildings for Commerce and Industry. Charles King Hoyt, ed. New York: McGraw-Hill, 1978. 228 pp.

Preservation and Recycling of Buildings for Bank Use. Barbara Ann Cleary, Northeast Regional Office. Information Series, National Trust for Historic Preservation. Washington, D.C.: Preservation Press, 1978. 28 pp., illus. $2 pb.

Contacts
Comptroller of the Currency
U.S. Department of the Treasury
490 L'Enfant Plaza East, S.W.
Washington, D.C. 20219

American Bankers Association
1120 Connecticut Avenue, N.W.
Washington, D.C. 20036

Barn complex near Clare, Mich., with silos, outbuildings and a rainbow-roof barn. (Balthazar Korab)

Barns

"[The] transformation of American agriculture has left an important structure in its wake—the barn. From the traditional general-use barn of New England to the specialized hop-curing warehouse of California, barns are testimony to a disappearing way of life. . . . The American barn . . . shows a variety and yet a simple unity of form which has no direct precedent. . . . For this reason it has always been admired by architects as a forthright expression of form developing out of a utilitarian function."

   Ernest Burden, *Living Barns*

The Barn: A Vanishing Landmark in North America. Eric Arthur and Dudley Witney. 1972. New York: A&W Publishers, 1975. 256 pp., color illus., biblio., index. $29.95 hb, $12.95 pb.

An Age of Barns. Eric Sloane. 1966. New York: Ballantine, 1984. 95 pp., illus., biblio. $9.95 pb.

The New World Dutch Barn: A Study of Its Characteristics, Its Structural System, and Its Probable Erectional Procedures. John Fitchen. Syracuse: Syracuse University Press, 1968. 178 pp., illus., biblio. $15.

Big House, Little House, Back House, Barn: The Connected Farm Buildings of New England. Thomas C. Hubka. Hanover, N.H.:University Press of New England, 1984. 240 pp., illus., biblio., index. $35 hb.

Wood, Brick, and Stone: The North American Settlement Landscape. Vol. 2: *Barns and Farm Structures.* Allen G. Noble. Amherst: University of Massachusetts Press, 1984. 186 pp., illus., index. $30 hb.

American Barns: In a Class by Themselves. Stanley Schuler. Exton, Pa.: Schiffer Publishing, 1984. 224 pp., illus. $29.95 hb.

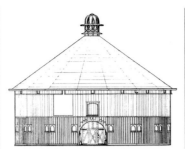

Fountain Grove Barn, Santa Rosa, Calif., with a lantern perched atop a conical roof. (Robert G. Higginbothan, HABS)

Barns, Sheds and Outbuildings. Byron D. Halsted, ed. 1881. Reprint. Brattleboro, Vt.: Stephen Greene Press, 1977. 240 pp., illus.

Practical Plans for Barns, Carriage Houses, Stables and Other Country Buildings. David and Joan Loveless, eds. Stockbridge, Mass.: Berkshire Traveller Press, 1978.

The Barn as an Element in the Cultural Landscape of North America: A Bibliography. Charles F. Calkins. Monticello, Ill.: Vance Bibliographies, 1979. A-84. 20 pp. $2 pb.

Living Barns: How to Find and Restore a Barn of Your Own. Ernest Burden. Boston: New York Graphic Society, 1977. 186 pp., color illus., biblio., index. $24.95 hb, $13.95 pb.

Contacts

Farmers Home Administration
U.S. Department of Agriculture
Washington, D.C. 20250

Babcock Barn Museum
Route 43
Hancock, Mass. 01237

Bizarre and Eccentric Architecture

"Bizarre architecture, if it is being properly bizarre, defies the well-carved pigeonhole."

   Charles Jencks, *Bizarre Architecture*

"Humor in architecture is certainly rarer and more difficult to achieve than in literature."

   Nicholas Pyle, "Views." *Progressive Architecture* April 1979.

Architectural Follies in America: Or, Hammer, Sawtooth and Nail. Clay Lancaster. Rutland, Vt.: Charles E. Tuttle, 1960. 243 pp., color illus., plans, index.

In Celebration of Ourselves. Seymour Rosen. With San Francisco Museum of Modern Art. San Francisco: California Living Books, 1979. 176 pp., illus. $25 hb, $12.50 pb.

All Their Own: People and the Places They Build. Jan Wampler. New York: Oxford University Press, 1978. $12.95 pb.

Handmade Homes: The Natural Way to Build Houses. Arthur Boericke and Barry Shapiro. New York: Delacorte Press, Dell, 1981.

The Craftsman Builder. Art Boericke and Barry Shapiro. New York: Simon and Schuster, 1979. $6.95 pb.

The Wedding Cake House: The World of George W. Bourne. Thomas W. Murphy, Jr. Kennebunkport, Maine: Durrell, 1978. $6.95 pb.

Rolling Homes: Handmade Houses on Wheels. Jane Lidz. New York: A&W, 1979.

The Passionate Collector. Ellen Land-Weber. New York: Simon and Schuster, 1980. 127 pp., illus. $9.95 pb.

Bizarre Architecture. Charles Jencks. New York: Rizzoli, 1979. Academy Editions, London. 80 pp., color illus. $12.50 pb.

Watts Towers (1921–54), Los Angeles, built by Italian immigrant Simon Rodia "to do something big." (Vanguard Photography)

Daydream Houses of Los Angeles. Charles Jencks. New York: Rizzoli, 1978. 80 pp., color illus.

The Dream Come True: Great Houses of Los Angeles. Brendan Gill. New York: Harper and Row, 1980. 216 pp., color illus. $40.

Dream Palaces: Hollywood "At Home." Charles Lockwood. New York: Viking, 1981. 320 pp., illus. $19.95.

Sunset Boulevard: America's Dream Street. Joe Kennelley and Roy Hankey. Burbank, Calif.: Darwin Publications (850 North Hollywood Way, 91505), 1982. 247 pp., illus. $34.95 hb.

Delirious New York: A Retrospective Manifesto for Manhattan. Rem Koolhaas. New York: Oxford University Press, 1978. $18.95 pb.

Dime-Store Dream Parade: Popular Culture 1925–1955. Robert Heide and John Gilman. New York: Dutton, 1979. 128 pp., illus., index.

Amazing America. Jane and Michael Stern. New York: Random House, 1978. 463 pp., illus.

An Eccentric Guide to the United States. James Dale Davison. New York: Berkley, 1977. 500 pp.

Directory of Unique Museums. Bill Truesdell. Kalamazoo, Mich.: Creative Communications, 1979. 100 pp., illus., index. $3.50 pb.

Weird America: A Guide to Places of Mystery in the United States. Jim Brandon. New York: Dutton, 1978. 257 pp., illus.

National Directory of Low-Cost Tourist Attractions. Raymond Carlson, ed. New York: Pilot Books, 1979. 72 pp. $3.50 pb.

Contacts

Saving and Preserving Arts and Cultural Environments
1804 North Van Ness Avenue
Los Angeles, Calif. 90023

Committee for Simon Rodia's Towers in Watts
P.O. Box 1461
Los Angeles, Calif. 90028

See also: Roadside Architecture; Vernacular Architecture (Looking at the Built Environment)

African House (c. 1820), constructed by free blacks at Melrose Plantation, Nachitoches, La. (Paul Thebideaux)

Black Sites

"During the days of slavery and the long, hard years afterward, black men and women had neither the wealth nor the leisure to look back upon their heritage and try to preserve what they could for their children and their children's children. In recent years, however, a small but growing number of museums have been formed—or already established landmarks have been refurbished—honoring black Americans and the role they played in the shaping of this nation."

Marcella Thum, *Exploring Black America*

Exploring Black America: A History and Guide. Marcella Thum. New York: Atheneum, 1975. 402 pp., illus., index. $10.95 hb.

"Archaeology of Black American Culture: An Annotated Bibliography," Geoffrey M. Gyrisco and Bert Salwen. In *Archaeological Perspectives on Ethnicity in America: Afro-American and Asian American Cultural History.* Robert L. Schuyler, ed. Farmingdale, N.Y.: Baywood Publishing, 1980. 147 pp. $7.95 pb.

"Preservation Resources." In *Southeastern Center for Afro-American Architecture: First Annual Research Report.* Richard K. Dozier. Tuskegee, Ala.: Author, 1980. 38 pp., illus. $4 pb.

The Black Towns. Norman L. Crockett. Lawrence, Kans.: Regents Press, 1979. 244 pp., illus., biblio. index. $19.95 hb.

"Black Settlements in America, 1870–1920," Everett L. Fly. *Harvard Graduate School of Design News*, May 1977.

This Was Harlem: A Cultural Portrait, 1900–1950. Jervis Anderson. New York: Farrar, Straus and Giroux, 1982. 390 pp., illus., index. $17.95 hb.

Hearth and Home: Preserving a People's Culture. George W. McDaniel. Philadelphia: Temple University Press, 1982. 375 pp., illus. $34.95 hb, $12.95 pb.

Promiseland: A Century of Life in a Negro Community. Elizabeth Rauh Bethel. Philadelphia: Temple University Press, 1981. 318 pp., illus., index. $9.95 pb.

The Black West. William Loren Katz. 1971. New York: Doubleday, 1973. 349 pp., illus. $10.95.

California's Ethnic Minorities Cultural Resources Survey: Afro-Americans, Chicanos/Latinos, Native Americans, Chinese-Americans, Japanese-Americans. California Department of Parks and Recreation. Sacramento: Author (P.O. Box 2390, 95811), 1982. 400 pp., illus., biblios. $5 pb.

Pioneer Urbanites: A Social and Cultural History of Black San Francisco. Douglas Henry Daniels. Philadelphia: Temple University Press, 1980. 260 pp., illus. $32.95 hb.

The Slave Community: Plantation Life in the Antebellum South. John Blassingame. Rev. ed. New York: Oxford University Press, 1979. $22.50 hb, $8.95 pb.

A Picture Guide to Black America in Washington, D.C. Dolphin G. Thompson. Washington, D.C.: Brownson House Publishers (1101 Pennsylvania Avenue, S.E., 20003), 1976. 48 pp., illus. $4.95.

"Parting Ways." In *In Small Things Forgotten: The Archeology of Early American Life.* James Deetz. Garden City, N.Y.: Doubleday, 1977. 184 pp., biblio., index. $4.95 pb.

Historic Preservation in Kansas: Black Historic Sites. Topeka: Kansas State Historical Society (120 West 10th Street, 66612), 1977. 45 pp., illus., index.

The Afro-American Community in Kansas City, Kansas: A History. Susan D. Greenbaum. Kansas City, Kans.: Department of Community Development (701 North 7th, 66101), 1982. 134 pp., illus., biblio. $5.

Contacts

Entourage, Inc.
209 Wellesley
San Antonio, Tex. 78201

Richard K. Dozier, AIA
308 Gregory Street
Tuskegee, Ala. 36088

Lone Star Brewing Company (1895–1904, E. Jungerfeld and Company), San Antonio, now the home of the San Antonio Museum of Art.

African American Museums Association
420 7th Street, N.W.
Washington, D.C. 20004

Association for the Study of Afro-American Life and History
1407 14th Street, N.W.
Washington, D.C. 20005

Breweries and Distilleries

"Today there are few of the handsome breweries once so prevalent in the 19th century. Many were shut down because of Prohibition and eventually were demolished. Still others were razed and proudly replaced by more modern plants. And, during the past several decades, a great many family concerns have been bought up by large corporations that have abandoned the old brewery buildings and concentrated on large, new factories."

Dianne Newell, "With Respect to Breweries." *Historic Preservation*, January–March 1975.

One Hundred Years of Brewing: A Complete History of the Progress Made in the Art, Science, and Industry of Brewing in the World. The Western Brewer. 1903. Reprint. New York: Arno Press, 1974.

An Index to American Brewers and Breweries. In "One Hundred Years of Brewing." 1975. Will D. Ross (P.O. Box 361, Morristown, Tenn. 37814). $7.50.

Brewed in America: A History of Beer and Ale in the United States. Stanley Wade Baron. 1962. Reprint. New York: Arno Press, 1972. 424 pp. $25 hb.

The Breweries of Brooklyn. Will Anderson. Brooklyn, N.Y.: Author (291 Garfield Place, 11215), 1976. 160 pp., illus. $12.95 pb.

The Cincinnati Brewing Industry: A Social and Economic History. William Downard. Athens, Ohio: Ohio University Press, 1973.

Breweries of Wisconsin: The History of the Beer Industry 1840–1980. Jerry Apps. Madison, Wis.: Stanton and Lee (44 East Mifflin Street, 53703), 1984. $14.95 pb.

"All the Right Ingredients," Marcia Axtmann Smith. *Museum News*, September 1980.

Jack Daniel's Legacy. Ben A. Green. Lynchburg, Tenn.: Lynchburg Hardware and General Store, 1967. 210 pp., illus. $2 pb.

Contacts

National Association of Breweriana Advertising
c/o Gordon Dean
Willson Memorial Drive
Chassel, Mich. 49916

The Brewery-Ana Gazette
Howard P. Strohn
Box 54
San Ardo, Calif. 93450

United States Brewers Association
1750 K Street, N.W.
Washington, D.C. 20006

Michter's Distillery
P.O. Box 387
Schaefferstown, Pa. 17088

Jack Daniel Distillery
Lynchburg, Tenn. 37352

Barton Museum of Whiskey History
Barton Distilling Company
Bardstown, Ky. 40004

Brooklyn Bridge (1869–83, John and Washington Roebling), New York City, the longest suspension bridge in the world when built. (Jet Lowe, HAER)

Bridges

"Since a bridge does not define space, but cuts through it, it is free of all the intricate psychological considerations that must be taken into account when space is moulded or enclosed. Thus, paradoxically, a bridge is at once the most tangible and most abstract of architectural problems. As such, it is capable of extraordinary purity. . . ."

Elizabeth B. Mock, *The Architecture of Bridges*

"Tens of thousands of bridges of all ages will be replaced during the next 10 to 15 years, and bridges built in the 1920s and 1930s will soon be among the oldest examples surviving in many regions."

Donald C. Jackson, *Saving Historic Bridges*

Bridges. Fritz Leonhardt. Cambridge: MIT Press, 1984. 308 pp., illus. $50 hb.

Bridges: The Spans of North America. David Plowden. 1974. New York: W. W. Norton, 1984. 322 pp., illus., biblio., index. $29.95.

A Span of Bridges: An Illustrated History. H. J. Hopkins. New York: Praeger, 1970.

The Architecture of Bridges. Elizabeth B. Mock. 1949. Reprint. New York: Arno Press, 1972. 127 pp., illus. $22 hb.

Bridge Architecture. A Series of Bibliographies. Anthony G. White. Monticello, Ill.: Vance Bibliographies, 1981. $2 pb each.

Bridge Truss Types: A Guide to Dating and Identifying. T. Allan Comp and Donald Jackson. Nashville: American Association for State and Local History, 1977. Technical Leaflet 95. 12 pp., illus., biblio. $2 pb.

Saving Historic Bridges. Donald C. Jackson. Information Series, National Trust for Historic Preservation. Washington, D.C.: Preservation Press, 1984. 15 pp., illus., biblio., append. $2 pb.

Methods of Modifying Historic Bridges for Contemporary Use. William Zuk et al. Charlottesville: Virginia Highway and Transportation Research Council, 1980. 105 pp., illus.

The Great Bridge: The Epic Story of the Building of the Brooklyn Bridge. David McCullough. 1972. New York: Simon and Schuster, 1983. 636 pp., illus. $9.95 pb.

A Picture History of the Brooklyn Bridge. Mary J. Shapiro. New York: Dover, 1983. 128 pp., illus. $7.95 pb.

Brooklyn Bridge: Fact and Symbol. Alan Trachtenberg. 1965. 2nd ed. Chicago: University of Chicago Press, 1979. 216 pp., illus., index. $7.95 pb.

The Great East River Bridge, 1883–1983. Brooklyn Museum. New York: Abrams, 1983. 180 pp., color illus., chron., biblio. $35 hb.

Bridge to the Future: A Centennial Celebration of the Brooklyn Bridge. Margaret Latimer, Brooke Hindle and Melvin Kranzberg. New York: New York Academy of Sciences, 1984. 355 pp., illus., index. $75 pb.

The Bridges of New York. Sharon Reier. New York: Quadrant Press, 1977. 160 pp., illus., append. $14.95 hb, $8.95 pb.

High Steel: Building the Bridges Across San Francisco Bay. Richard Dillon. Millbrae, Calif.: Celestial Arts, 1979. 167 pp., illus.

Spanning the Gate. Stephen Cassady. Mill Valley, Calif.: Squarebooks, 1979. 132 pp., illus. $20 hb.

The Eads Bridge. Howard S. Miller and Quinta Scott. Columbia: University of Missouri Press, 1979. 142 pp., illus., index. $22 hb.

Bridges and the City of Washington. Donald B. Myer. Washington, D.C.: U.S. Commission of Fine Arts, 1974. 96 pp., illus., biblio.

Historic Bridges of Pennsylvania. William H. Shank. Rev. ed. York, Pa.: American Canal and Transportation Center (809 Rathton Road, 17403), 1980. 70 pp., illus., biblio. $3 pb.

Covered Bridges

American Wooden Bridges. Committee on History and Heritage of American Civil Engineering. New York: American Society of Civil Engineering, 1976. Historical Publication no. 4. 176 pp.

Covered Bridges: A List of Books. Mary Vance. Monticello, Ill.: Vance Bibliographies, 1979. A-79. 3 pp. $1.50 pb.

World Guide to Covered Bridges. Richard T. Donovan, ed. Rev. ed. Worcester, Mass.: National Society for the Preservation of Covered Bridges, 1980. 193 pp. $5 pb.

Covered Bridges of the Northeast. Richard Sanders Allen. Brattleboro, Vt.: Stephen Greene Press, 1983. 128 pp., illus. $9.95 pb.

Sentinels of Time: Vermont's Covered Bridges. Phil Ziegler. Camden, Maine: Down East Books, 1983. 144 pp., illus. $8.95 pb.

Vermont Covered Bridges. Ray Bearse. Woodstock, Vt.: Countryman Press, 1982. $8.95 pb.

Covered Bridges in Illinois, Iowa and Wisconsin. Leslie C. Swanson. Rev. ed. Moline, Ill.: Swanson Publishing (P.O. Box 334, 61625), 1970. 48 pp., illus. $5.95 pb.

Covered Bridges of the West: A History and Illustrated Guide—Washington, Oregon, California. Kramer Adams. Berkeley, Calif.: Howell-North, 1963. 146 pp., illus., biblio.

Roofs Over Rivers: A Guide to Oregon's Covered Bridges. Nick and Bill Cockrell. Beaverton, Ore.: Touchstone Press (P.O. Box 81, 97005), 1978. 112 pp., illus., gloss., biblio. $6.95 pb.

Contacts

Federal Highway Administration
U.S. Department of Transportation
400 7th Street, S.W.
Washington, D.C. 20590

Historic American Engineering Record
National Park Service
U.S. Department of the Interior
Washington, D.C. 20013-7127

Committee on History and Heritage of American Civil Engineering
American Society of Civil Engineers
345 East 47th Street
New York, N.Y. 10017

Transportation Research Board
National Academy of Sciences
2101 Constitution Avenue, N.W.
Washington, D.C. 20418

American Association of State Highway and Transportation Officials
444 North Capitol Street, N.W.
Washington, D.C. 20001

National Society for the Preservation of Covered Bridges
c/o Mrs. Arnold L. Ellsworth
44 Cleveland Avenue
Worcester, Mass. 01603

The Brooklyn Bridge Bulletin
c/o Ed Schildders
Kwendelhof 113
Tiburg, Holland

Brothels

"Traditionally, Americans have chosen to preserve buildings with positive historical connotations. Only recently has this practice been challenged by a new breed of preservationists, who feel it's worthwhile preserving structures that may symbolize aspects of history we might like to forget."

Patricia Leigh Brown, "The Problem with Miss Laura's House." *Historic Preservation,* September–October 1980.

Storyville, New Orleans: Being an Authentic Illustrated Account of the Notorious Red-Light District. Al Rose. University: University of Alabama Press, 1974. 256 pp., illus., biblio., appends., index. $12.50 pb.

"The Rise and Fall of the Reno Stockade," Eric N. Moody and Guy L. Rocha. *Nevada* Magazine, April–June 1979.

The American Woman's Gazetteer. Lynn Sherr and Jurate Kazickas. New York: Bantam, 1976. 271 pp., illus.

Wooden "cribs" in the old red-light district of Telluride, Colo., that have been rehabilitated with a National Trust loan.

Lockport on the Erie Canal (1832) by Mary Keys, a watercolor capturing this important New York canal town. (Munson-Williams-Proctor Institute)

"Sexual Commerce on the Comstock Lode," Marion Goldman. *Nevada Historical Society Quarterly,* Summer 1978.

Prostitution: An Illustrated Social History. Vern L. and Bonnie L. Bullough. New York: Crown, 1978. $14.95.

Contacts

Mazzulla Collection
Photo Archives
Amon Carter Museum
Box 2365
Fort Worth, Tex. 76101

Bancroft Library
Berkeley, Calif. 94720

Western America Collection
Denver Public Library
Denver, Colo. 80203

California State Library
Sacramento, Calif. 95809

Special Collections
University of Wyoming Library
Laramie, Wyo. 82071

Special Collections
Dickenson Library
University of Nevada
Las Vegas, Nev. 89154

Nevada Historical Society
1650 North Virginia Street
Reno, Nev. 89503

Canals

"Canals like the Erie, Pennsylvania Main Line, and Chesapeake and Ohio helped end the isolation of great sections of the nation, and not only opened the market place for the farmer, but provided employment for thousands of men who built, maintained, and operated the canal packets. Overnight, cities mushroomed into thriving ports, and emigrants streamed into the towns to continue their way west by schooner or lake transport."

Donald Duke, Introduction. *Water Trails West*

The Best from American Canals. Thomas F. Hahn, ed. York, Pa.: American Canal Society, 1980. 88 pp., illus., index. $6 pb.

Water Trails West. Western Writers of America. 1978. New York: Avon, 1979. 271 pp., illus., index. $3.50 pb.

Canal Days in America: The History and Romance of Old Towpaths and Waterways. Harry Sinclair Drago. New York: Clarkson N. Potter, 1972. 352 pp., illus., biblio., index.

Passage Between Rivers: A Portfolio of Photographs with a History of the Delaware and Raritan Canal. Elizabeth G. Menzies. New Brunswick, N.J.: Rutgers University Press, 1976. $12.50 hb, $7.95 pb.

Juniper Waterway: A History of the Albemarle and Chesapeake Canal. Alexander Crosby Brown. Mariners Museum. Charlottesville: University Press of Virginia, 1981. 277 pp., illus., index. $22.50.

Champlain to Chesapeake: A Canal Era Pictorial Cruise. William J. McKelvey, Jr. Berkeley Heights, N.J.: Author (103 Dogwood Lane), 1978. 224 pp., illus. $25 hb.

American Canal Guide Series. York, Pa.: American Canal Society.

Lehigh Canal. Washington, D.C.: Historic American Engineering Record, U.S. Department of the Interior, 1981. 89 pp., illus., appends. $4.25. GPO stock no. 024-016-00155-9.

Lockport, Illinois. Washington, D.C.: Historic American Engineering Record, U.S. Department of the Interior, 1980. 74 pp., illus. $4.25. GPO stock no. 024-016-00154-1.

Contacts

American Canal Society
809 Rathton Road
York, Pa. 17403

American Canal and
Transportation Center
Box 842
Shepherdstown, W.Va. 25443

The Canal Museum
Weighlock Building
Erie Boulevard East
Syracuse, N.Y. 13202

National Park Service
U.S. Department of the Interior
Washington, D.C. 20013-7127

Chesapeake and Ohio Canal
National Historical Park
P.O. Box 4
Sharpsburg, Md. 21782

Lowell National Historical Park
National Park Service
Lowell, Mass. 08152

Kanawha Canal Library
Reynolds Metals Company
10th and Byrd Streets
Richmond, Va. 23219

See also: Industrial Structures

U.S. Capitol (Michael David Brown)

Capitols

"The state capitols in the United States, almost always centered on a high dome, flanked more or less symmetrically by the two houses of the legislature [present an] explicit image of the body politic."

Kent C. Bloomer and Charles W. Moore, *Body, Memory and Architecture.* New Haven: Yale University Press, 1977.

Temples of Democracy. Henry-Russell Hitchcock and William Seale. New York: Harcourt, Brace, Jovanovich, 1976. 333pp., illus., biblio., index. $29.95 hb.

Landmarks of the U.S.A.: Our 51 Capitols. Waukesha, Wis.: Country Beautiful, 1978. 96 pp., color illus. $3.98 hb.

History of the United States Capitol. Glenn Brown. 1900, 1903. Reprint. New York: Da Capo, 1970. 704 pp., illus. $85.

The United States Capitol: An Annotated Bibliography. John R. Kerwood. Norman: University of Oklahoma Press, 1973. 412 pp. $29.50 hb, $15 pb.

The United States Capitol: An Architectural Overview. Coppa and Avery Consultants. Monticello, Ill.: Vance Bibliographies, 1980. A-338. 9 pp. $2 pb.

Latrobe, Jefferson and the National Capitol. Paul F. Norton. 1952. Reprint. New York: Garland Publishing, 1977. 430 pp, illus. $62 hb.

Contacts

The Architect of the Capitol
Washington, D.C. 20515

Capitol Historical Society of the United States
200 Maryland Avenue, N.E.
Washington, D.C. 20515

Dennis McFadden
Temporary State Commission on the Restoration of the Capitol Building
P.O. Box 7016
Alfred E. Smith Building
Albany, N.Y. 12225

Cast-Iron Architecture

"Many people have been walking past cast-iron buildings all their lives without realizing it. This is not surprising, since the original owners and builders of iron structures intended their buildings to look like stone. Especially in the early days of iron architecture during the pre–Civil War period, builders faithfully copied popular Renaissance stone designs, and then painted the buildings in typical light stone colors. Every effort was made to deceive the beholder into thinking the iron fronts were made of stone."

Margot Gayle, *Cast-Iron Architecture in New York*

"Cast-Iron Architecture, U.S.A.," Margot Gayle. *Historic Preservation,* January–March 1975.

Metals in America's Historic Buildings: Use and Preservation Treatments. Margot Gayle, David W. Look and John G. Waite. Washington, D.C.: Technical Preservation Services, National Park Service, 1980. 170 pp., illus., biblio. $5.50 pb. GPO stock no. 024–016–00143–5.

Badger's Illustrated Catalogue of Cast-Iron Architecture. Daniel D. Badger. 1865. Reprint. New introduction by Margot Gayle. New York: Dover, 1981. 157 pp., illus. $8.95 pb.

The Origins of Cast Iron Architecture in America. James Bogardus and Daniel Badger. 1856, 1865. Reprint. Introduction by W. Knight Sturges. New York: Da Capo, 1970. 257 pp., $55 hb.

Cast-Iron Architecture in New York: A Photographic Survey. Margot Gayle and Edmund V. Gillon, Jr. New York: Dover, 1974. 190 pp., illus., index. $6.95 pb.

The Grand Era of Cast-Iron Architecture in Portland. William J. Hawkins III. Portland, Ore.: Binford and Mort, 1976. 210 pp., illus., biblio., appends., index. $25 hb, $18.95 pb.

Charleston Blacksmith: The Work of Philip Simmons. John Michael Vlach. Athens: University of Georgia Press, 1981. 170 pp., illus., biblio., append., gloss. $19.95 hb, $12.50 pb.

Southwestern Colonial Ironwork: The Spanish Blacksmithing Tradition from Texas to California. Marc Simmons and Frank Turley. Santa Fe: Museum of New Mexico Press, 1980. 215 pp., illus., gloss., biblio., index. $25.95 hb, $14.95 pb.

Cast and Wrought: The Architectural Metalwork of Richmond, Virginia. Robert P. Winthrop. Richmond, Va.: Valentine Museum (1015 Clay Street, 23219), 1981. $17.50.

Architectural Ironwork: A Short List of Books. Mary Vance. Monticello, Ill.: Vance Bibliographies, 1979. A-77. 4 pp. $1.50 pb.

Victorian Iron Work. Wickersham Foundry Catalog. 1857. Reprint. Introduction by Margot Gayle. Philadelphia: The Athenaeum, 1977. 112 pp., illus.

Ornamental Ironwork: An Illustrated Guide to Its Design, History and Use in American Architecture. Susan and Michael Southworth. Boston: David R. Godine, 1978. 202 pp., illus., biblio., index. $32.50 hb, $12.50 pb.

Cast-Iron Decoration: A World Survey. E. Graeme and Joan Robertson. New York: Whitney Library of Design, 1977. 336 pp., illus., biblio., index.

Wrought Iron in Architecture: An Illustrated Survey. Gerald K. Geerlings. 1929. Reprint. New York: Dover, 1983. 214 pp., illus., biblio., index. $9.95 pb.

Iron: Cast and Wrought Iron in Canada from the Seventeenth Century to the Present. Eric Arthur and Thomas Ritchie. Toronto: University of Toronto Press, 1982. 256 pp., illus., biblio., index. $35 hb.

Some Cities with Cast-Iron Buildings

New York City (SoHo)

Louisville, Ky.

Portland, Ore.

Richmond, Va.

Seattle, Wash.

Providence, R.I.

Contacts

Friends of Cast-Iron Architecture
c/o Margot Gayle, Chairman
235 East 87th Street
Room 6C
New York, N.Y. 10028

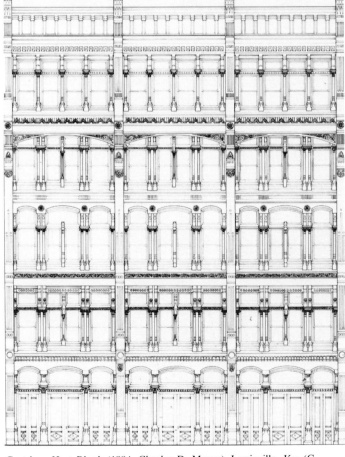

Cast-iron Hart Block (1884, Charles D. Meyer), Louisville, Ky. (C. Alexander, HABS)

Congressional Cemetery (1807), Washington, D.C., during a ceremony marking the 200th anniversary of the birth of architect Robert Mills, whose grave had remained unmarked until 1936. (Carleton Knight III, NTHP)

Cemeteries

"In the old cemetery indifference borders on desecration, and desecration contributes mightily to the regression of the human spirit, robbing us of spiritual values, much as a child is robbed of respect for his elders."

Herschel Miller, "Requiem for a Cemetery." *New Orleans Magazine,* April 1969.

A Celebration of Death: An Introduction to Some of the Buildings, Monuments, and Settings of Funerary Architecture in the Western Tradition. James S. Curl. New York: Scribner's, 1980. 404 pp. $35.

Famous and Curious Cemeteries. John Francis Marion. New York: Crown, 1977. 276 pp., illus., biblio., index.

Here Lies America: A Collection of Memorable Graves. Nancy B. Ellis and E. Parker Hayden, Jr. New York: Hawthorn Books, 1978. 179 pp., illus.

"American Attitudes Toward Death." *Journal of Popular Culture,* Spring 1981. Bowling Green State University, Bowling Green, Ohio 43403.

Masks of Orthodoxy: Folk Gravestone Carving in Plymouth County, Massachusetts, 1689–1805. Peter Benes. Amherst: University of Massachusetts Press, 1977. 288 pp., illus., index, biblio. $20 hb.

Early American Gravestone Art in Photographs. Francis Y. Duval and Ivan B. Rigby. New York: Dover, 1978. 133 pp., biblio., illus. $6 pb.

New England Cemeteries. A Collector's Guide. Andrew Kull. Brattleboro, Vt.: Stephen Greene, 1975. 270 pp., maps, illus., appends., index. $5.95 pb.

The Victorian Celebration of Death: The Architecture and Planning of the 19th-Century Necropolis. James S. Curl. Detroit: Gale Research, 1972. $31.

Victorian Cemetery Art. Edmund V. Gillon, Jr. New York: Dover, 1972. 173 pp., illus., index.

New Orleans Architecture. Vol. III: *The Cemeteries.* Leonard V. Huber et al. Mary Christovich, ed. Gretna, La.: Pelican Publishing, 1974. 197 pp., illus. $27.50 hb.

A Walk Through Graceland Cemetery. Barbara Lanctot. Chicago: Chicago Architecture Foundation, 1977. 61 pp., illus., biblio. $4.50 pb.

Texas Graveyards: A Cultural Legacy. Terry G. Jordan. Austin: University of Texas, 1982. 147 pp., illus., biblio., index. $19.95 hb.

"The Care of Old Cemeteries and Gravestones," Lance R. Mayer. *Markers,* vol. I, 1979–80. Association for Gravestone Studies.

Cemetery Transcribing: Preparations and Procedures. John J. Newman. Nashville: American Association for State and Local History, 1971. Technical Leaflet 9. 12 pp., illus., biblio. $2 pb.

Photographing Tombstones: Equipment and Techniques. Mary-Ellen Jones. Nashville: American Association for State and Local History, 1977. Technical Leaflet 92. 8 pp., illus., biblio. $2 pb.

The Cemetery: An Outdoor Education Resource. David Loggins. New York: Council on the Environment of New York City (51 Chambers Street, Room 228, 10007), 1977. 11 pp. $2.

Contacts

American Cemetery Association 50 East Broad Street Columbus, Ohio 43215

Association for Gravestone Studies c/o American Antiquarian Society Worcester, Mass. 01609

AGS Photo Archive c/o New England Historic Genealogical Society Library 101 Newbury Street Boston, Mass. 02116

U. S. Veterans Administration Department of Memorial Affairs Washington, D.C. 20420

Chautauquas

"The bond between summer places and religion continued to strengthen through most of the nineteenth century. God provided the occasion for the founding of summer colonies, and Mammon turned the colonies into an occasion for profitable real-estate development. . . . Gradually, the religious groups mingled their purposes with those of the nonsectarian Chautauqua movement, which was founded in a grove on the shores of Lake Chautauqua, in western New York State . . . and quickly spread throughout the country. Chautauquas placed strong emphasis upon plain living and high thinking."

Brendan Gill. *The New Yorker,* August 28, 1978.

Chautauqua: Its Architecture and Its People. Pauline Fancher. Miami: Banyan Books (P.O. Box 431160, 33143), 1978. 120 pp., illus., biblio., gloss., index. $9.95 hb, $5.95 pb.

Chautauqua: A Center for Education, Religion and the Arts in America. Theodore Morrison. Chicago: University of Chicago Press, 1974. $6.95 pb.

Three Taps of the Gavel: The Chautauqua Story. Alfreda L. Irwin. 2nd ed. Chautauqua, N.Y.: Chautauqua Institution, 1977. 86 pp., illus., biblio., index. $4.95 pb.

Contacts

Chautauqua Institution Chautauqua, N.Y. 14722

Glen Echo Park National Park Service Glen Echo, Md. 20768

Colorado Chautauqua Association Chautauqua Park Boulder, Colo. 80302

Chapel of the Good Shepherd (1894), Chautauqua, N.Y.

Storefronts lining the Main Street of Locke, Calif., whose Chinese heritage is reflected in its shops. (William F. Hand, Clemson Lam and Gregory Tung, HABS)

Chinese Sites

"The Chinese left little or no written records, only many miles of unmarked stone fences and wild flowers and trees from a distant land. . . ."

Phillip P. Choy, "Veneers of the Orient." *Historic Preservation,* April–June 1972.

"Chinatowns became cities within cities as early-day anti-Chinese agitation forced the Chinese into Chinatowns, their last bastions."

Thomas W. Chinn, "Argonauts Become Americans: The Chinese." *Historic Preservation,* April–June 1976.

An Illustrated History of the Chinese in America. Ruthanne Lum McCunn. San Francisco: Design Enterprises of San Francisco (P.O. Box 27677, 94127), 1979. 133 pp., illus. $6.95 pb.

A History of the Chinese in California: A Syllabus. Thomas W. Chinn, ed. San Francisco: Chinese Historical Society of America, 1969. 81 pp., maps, biblio.

The Chinese in California: A Brief Bibliographic History. Gladys C. Hansen and William F. Heintz. Portland, Ore.: Richard Abel, 1970. 140 pp.

The Chinese in San Francisco: A Pictorial History. Laverne Mau Dicker. New York: Dover, 1980. 144 pp., illus., biblio. $6 pb.

"Chinatown." In *Here Today: San Francisco's Architectural Heritage.* Roger Olmsted and T. H. Watkins. Junior League of San Francisco. San Francisco: Chronicle Books, 1968. 334 pp., illus., gloss., index. $14.95 pb.

"Locke: A Chinese Chinatown," Allen Castle. *Pacific Historian,* Spring 1980.

Portland's Chinatown: The History of an Urban District. Nelson Chia-Chi Ho. Portland, Ore.: Bureau of Planning, 1978. 52 pp., illus., biblio., append.

China Doctor of John Day. Jeffrey Barlow and Christine Richardson. Portland, Ore.: Binford and Mort, 1979. 118 pp., illus., append. $5.95 pb.

Chinatown Street Revitalization. Department of City Planning. New York: Author, 1976. 56 pp., illus., maps, charts.

Contacts

Chinese Historical Society of America
17 Adler Place
San Francisco, Calif. 94133

Chinese Historical Society of Southern California
1648 Redcliff Street
Los Angeles, Calif. 90026

See also: Ethnic Heritages

Churches

"Religious buildings and property pose problems when it comes to preservation and adaptive use, not only in terms of economic concerns but because of the human emotions involved. Foremost among the problems facing many religious institutions today is the question of unused buildings. There are simply more religious edifices than are needed to accommodate present numbers of worshippers, with smaller congregations facing continuing financial burdens. This problem is particularly acute in large cities, where former urban dwellers have moved to the suburbs, leaving inner-city parishes unable to maintain past levels of financial support. At the same time, shifting patterns of residential growth have resulted in other congregations expanding beyond the size limits of an older building or complex. When large new congregations move into large new buildings, the result has often been the demolition of an older structure."

"Born Again." Editorial, *Preservation News,* August 1977.

American Churches. Roger G. Kennedy. New York: Stewart, Tabori and Chang, 1982. 296 pp., color illus., biblio., index. $50 hb.

"Religious Expression in American Architecture," Donald Drew Egbert. In *Religious Perspectives in American Culture.* Vol. 2: *Religion in American Life.* James Ward Smith and A. Leland Jamison, eds. Princeton: Princeton University Press, 1961.

The Gothic Revival and American Church Architecture: An Episode in Taste, 1840–1856. Phoebe B. Stanton. Baltimore: Johns Hopkins University Press, 1968. 350 pp., illus., index. $27.50.

Tradition Becomes Innovation: Modern Religious Architecture in America. Bartlett Hayes. New York: Pilgrim Press, 1983. 176 pp., illus. $27.50 hb, $12.95 pb.

Temples, Churches and Mosques: A Guide to the Appreciation of Religious Architecture. J. G. Davies. New York: Pilgrim Press, 1982. 256 pp., illus. $27.50 hb.

Exploring Churches. Paul and Tessa Clowney. Grand Rapids, Mich.: Eerdmans, 1982. 93 pp., color illus., gloss. $12.95 hb.

Cathedral: The Story of Its Construction. David Macaulay. Boston: Houghton Mifflin, 1973. 80 pp., illus., gloss. $5.95 pb.

White frame church near Greensboro, Vt., with an unusual tiered and shingled tower. (© Steve Rosenthal)

The Preservation of Churches, Synagogues and Other Religious Structures. Rev. Richard Armstrong, Cheswick Center. Information Series, National Trust for Historic Preservation. Washington, D.C.: Preservation Press, 1978. 27 pp., illus., biblio., append. $2 pb.

How to Care for Religious Properties. Michael F. Lynch. Albany: Preservation League of New York State, 1982. 40 pp., illus. $1.50 pb.

Religious Archives: An Introduction. August R. Suelflow. Chicago: Society of American Archivists (330 South Wells Street, Suite 810, 60606), 1981. $7 nonmembers.

Church Architecture: A Bibliographic Guide to Church Architecture in Selected Municipalities and Regions in the United States. Coppa and Avery Consultants. Monticello, Ill.: Vance Bibliographies, 1980. A-388. 10 pp. $2 pb.

The Religious Architecture of New Mexico: In the Colonial Record and Since the American Occupation. George Kubler, School of American Research. Albuquerque: University of New Mexico Press, 1972. 232 pp., illus., biblio., append., index.

The Missions of New Mexico Since 1776. John L. Kessell. Albuquerque: University of New Mexico Press, 1979. 320 pp., illus. $45 hb.

The Franciscan Mission Architecture of Alta California. Rexford Newcomb. 1916. Reprint. New York: Dover, 1973. 74 pp., illus. plans.

The Tree at the Center of the World: A Story of the California Missions. Bruce Walter Barton. Santa Barbara: Ross-Erikson (629 State Street, Suite 222, 93101), 1980. 321 pp., illus., append., biblio., index. $19.95 hb, $12.95 pb.

The Structure of Praise: Architecture for Religion in New England from the 17th Century to the Present. Arthur B. Mazmanian. 1970. Reprint. Barre, Mass.: Barre Publishers, 1973. 151 pp., illus.

Great New England Churches: 65 Houses of Worship that Changed Our Lives. Robert Mutrux. Chester, Conn.: Globe Pequot Press, 1981. 288 pp., illus., gloss., biblio., index. $14.95 pb.

The New England Meeting Houses of the Seventeenth Century. Marian C. Donnelly. Middletown, Conn.: Wesleyan University Press, 1968. 165 pp., illus., biblio. $18.50.

Virginia's Colonial Churches: An Architectural Guide. James S. Rawlings. Charlottesville: University Press of Virginia, 1963.

Chicago Churches and Synagogues: An Architectural Pilgrimage. George Lane. Chicago: Loyola University Press, 1981. 255 pp., illus., appends., gloss., index. $25 hb.

Pioneer Churches. Harold Kalman and John de Visser. New York: W. W. Norton, 1976. 192 pp., color illus., biblio., index.

Early Churches of Washington State. Esther Pearson. Seattle: University of Washington Press, 1980. 182 pp., illus., biblio., index. $25 hb.

White Churches of the Plains: Examples from Colorado. Robert Hickman Adams. Boulder: Colorado Associated University Press, 1970. 88 pp., illus.

St. Patrick's Cathedral. Leland Cook. Introduction by Brendan Gill. New York: Quick Fox, 1981. 160 pp., color illus. $24.95 hb, $9.95 pb.

The Last Cathedral. (National Cathedral, Washington, D.C.) Ty Harrington. Englewood Cliffs, N.J.: Prentice-Hall, 1979. 156 pp., color illus., append., gloss.

Contacts

The Cheswick Center
11 Newberry Street
Boston, Mass. 02116

Interfaith Forum on Religion, Art and Architecture
1777 Church Street, N.W.
Washington, D.C. 20036

Religious Committee for the Arts
287 Park Avenue South
New York, N.Y. 10010

Preservation League of New York State
307 Hamilton Street
Albany, N.Y. 12210

See also: Jewish Landmarks, Mormon Sites, Shakers

The show goes on inside the big top at the circus in 1934. (Circus World Museum, Baraboo, Wis.)

Circuses

"The Circus served as a medium of communication as well as an instrument for presenting wonders from all over the globe."

> Ringling Brothers and Barnum and Bailey Combined Shows, *Circus!*

"Heaven lay before me as a youth and it took the form of a circus."

> William Lyon Phelps, Yale University

Circus in America. Charles P. Fox and Tom Parkinson. Waukesha, Wis.: Country Beautiful, 1969.

A History of the Circus in America. George A. Chindahl. Caldwell, Idaho: Caxton Printers, 1959. 279 pp.

The Circus Moves by Rail. Tom Parkinson and Charles Philip Fox. Boulder, Colo.: Pruett, 1970. 391 pp., illus., index, append. $39.95 hb.

The Old Time Circus. Larry Freeman. Watkins Glen, N.Y.: Century House (Old Irelandville, 14891), 1974, 132 pp. $20 hb.

Circus: From Rome to Ringling. Marian Murray. Westport, Conn.: Greenwood Press, 1956. $29.75 hb.

Menageries, Circuses and Theaters. E. H. Bostock. 1927. Reprint. New York: Arno Press. $15.

Pictorial History of the American Circus. John and Alice Durant. New York: A. S. Barnes, 1957.

Circus Days. Jill Freedman. New York: Harmony Books, 1975. 126 pp., illus.

"The Circus in Ohio." Columbus: Ohio Historic Preservation Office (Ohio Historical Center, I-71 and 17th Avenue, 43211).

American Circus Posters in Full Color. Charles P. Fox. New York: Dover, 1978. 48 pp. $6.95 pb.

The Great Circus Street Parade in Pictures. Charles P. Fox and F. Beverly Kelly. Magnolia, Mass.: Peter Smith, 1978. 127 pp., illus. $15.

The Big Apple Circus. Peter A. Simon. New York: Penguin, 1978.

Contacts

Circus World Museum
436 Water Street
Baraboo, Wis. 53913

Ringling Museum of the Circus
P.O. Box 1838
Sarasota, Fla. 33578

Harry Hertzberg Circus Collection
San Antonio Public Library
210 West Market Street
San Antonio, Tex. 78205

Bandwagon
Circus Historical Society
2515 Dorset Road
Columbus, Ohio 43221

Department of Educational Services
Ringling Brothers and Barnum and Bailey Circus
3201 New Mexico Avenue, N.W.
Washington, D.C. 20016

P. T. Barnum Museum
820 Main Street
Bridgeport, Conn. 06604

The lights of the city: New York at night, with the Chrysler Building (1930, William Van Alen) in the foreground. (Andy Freeberg, *Village Voice*)

Cities

"Like a piece of architecture, the city is a construction in space, but one of vast scale, a thing perceived only in the course of long spans of time. . . . Only partial control can be exercised over its growth and form. There is no final result, only a continuous succession of phases."

Kevin Lynch, *The Image of the City*

"Cities are an immense laboratory of trial and error, failure and success, in city building and city design. This is the laboratory in which city planning should have been learning and forming and testing its theories. Instead the practitioners and teachers of this discipline (if such it can be called) have ignored the study of success and failure in real life, have been incurious about the reasons for unexpected success, and are guided instead by principles derived from the behavior and appearance of towns, suburbs, tuberculosis sanatoria, fairs, and imaginary dream cities—from anything but cities themselves. . . .

There is nothing economically or socially inevitable about either the decay of old cities or the fresh-minted decadence of the new unurban urbanization."

Jane Jacobs, *The Death and Life of Great American Cities*

History

Urban History: A Guide to Information Sources. John D. Buenker, Gerald Michael Greenfield and William J. Murin, eds. American Government and History Information Guide Series, vol. 9. Detroit: Gale Research Company, 1981. 400 pp. $44.

The Urban Wilderness: A History of the American City. Sam Bass Warner, Jr. New York: Harper and Row, 1973. 384 pp., illus., biblio. $14.50 pb.

The City in History: Its Origins, Its Transformations, and Its Prospects. Lewis Mumford. 1961. New York: Harcourt Brace Jovanovich, 1968. 657 pp., illus., biblio., index. $7.95 pb.

The Making of Urban America: A History of City Planning in the United States. John W. Reps. Princeton: Princeton University Press, 1965. 574 pp., illus., biblio., index. $85.

The American City: From the Civil War to the New Deal. Giorgio Ciucci et al. Cambridge: MIT Press, 1979. 580 pp., illus., index. $17.50 pb.

The History of the City. Leonardo Benevolo. Cambridge: MIT Press, 1980. 1,008 pp., illus., index. $125 hb.

American Architecture and Urbanism. Vincent Scully. New York: Praeger, 1969. 275 pp., illus.

American Skyline: The Growth and Form of Our Cities and Towns. Christopher Tunnard and Henry Hope Reed. 1955. New York: New American Library.

The Rise of Urban America. Constance McLaughlin Green. New York: Harper and Row, 1965. 208 pp., biblio., index.

Cities: The Forces That Shape Them. Lisa Taylor, ed. New York: Rizzoli, 1981. 168 pp., illus. $12.50 pb.

The Economy of Cities. Jane Jacobs. New York: Random House, 1969. 268 pp. $3.95 pb.

The Historian and the City. Oscar Handlin and John Burchard, eds. 1963. Cambridge: MIT Press, 1966. 320 pp., biblio., index. $6.95 pb.

The Modern Metropolis: Its Origins, Growth, Characteristics, and Planning. Selected Essays of Hans Blumenfeld. Paul D. Spreiregen, ed. Cambridge: MIT Press, 1967. $4.95.

Urban Legacy: The Story of America's Cities. Diana Klebanow. New York: New American Library, 1977. 491 pp. $2.95 pb.

"Urban USA." In *History of Urban Form: Before the Industrial Revolutions*. A. E. J. Morris. 2nd ed. New York: Wiley, 1979. 317 pp., illus., appends., biblio., index. $51.95 hb, $27.95 pb.

Urban America: From Downtown to No Town. David R. Goldfield and Blaine A. Brownell. Boston: Houghton Mifflin, 1979. 435 pp., illus., biblio., index. $15.50 pb.

The Urban Idea in Colonial America. Sylvia Doughty Fries. Philadelphia: Temple University Press, 1977. 236 pp., illus., biblio., index. $29.95.

Cities of the American West: A History of Frontier Urban Planning. John W. Reps. Princeton: Princeton University Press, 1979. 827 pp., illus., biblio., index. $85 hb.

Town Planning in Frontier America. John W. Reps. 1969. Reprint. Columbia: University of Missouri Press, 1981. 320 pp., illus., biblio., index. $9.95 pb.

The Forgotten Frontier: Urban Planning in the American West Before 1890. John W. Reps. Columbia: University of Missouri Press, 1981. 184 pp., illus., biblio., index. $25 hb, $12.95 pb.

Spanish City Planning in North America. Dora P. Crouch, Daniel J. Garr and Axel I. Mundigo. Cambridge: MIT Press, 1982. 304 pp., illus. $40 hb.

Washington: Design for the Federal City. National Archives and Records Service. Washington, D.C.: Acropolis Books, 1981. $11.95 hb, $6.95 pb.

Urban Design Planning

The Death and Life of Great American Cities. Jane Jacobs. New York: Random House, 1961. 458 pp. $4.95 pb.

The Image of the City. Kevin Lynch. Cambridge: MIT Press, 1960. 194 pp., illus. $20 hb, $5.95 pb.

What Time Is This Place? Kevin Lynch. Cambridge: MIT Press, 1972. 277 pp., illus., append., biblio., index. $8.95 pb.

A Theory of Good City Form. Kevin Lynch. Cambridge: MIT Press, 1981. 514 pp., illus., appends., biblio., index. $25 hb.

Managing the Sense of a Region. Kevin Lynch. Cambridge: MIT Press, 1976. 152 pp., illus. $22.50 hb, $5.95 pb.

Man-Made America: Chaos or Control? Christopher Tunnard and Boris Pushkarev. Harriet Bell, ed. 1963. Reprint. New York: Harmony Books, 1981. 496 pp. $3.98 pb.

The Concise Townscape. Gordon Cullen. New York: Van Nostrand Reinhold, 1961. 199 pp., illus. $7.95 pb.

Close-Up: How to Read the American City. Grady Clay. 1973. Reprint. Chicago: University of Chicago Press, 1980. 192 pp., illus. $7.95 pb.

God's Own Junkyard: The Planned Deterioration of America's Landscape. Peter Blake. 1964. Rev. ed. New York: Holt, Rinehart and Winston, 1979. 160 pp., illus.

Form Follows Fiasco: Why Modern Architecture Hasn't Worked. Peter Blake. Boston: Little, Brown, 1974. 169 pp., illus.

Back to the Drawing Board: Planning for Livable Cities. Wolf Von Eckhardt. Washington, D.C.: New Republic Books, 1978. 245 pp., illus., biblio., index.

American City Planning Since 1890. Mel Scott, American Institute of Planners. Berkeley: University of California Press, 1969. 745 pp., illus., biblio., index. $57.50 hb, $14.95 pb.

The History of Urban and Regional Planning: An Annotated Bibliography. Anthony Sutcliffe. New York: Facts on File (460 Park Avenue South, 10016), 1980, 300 pp., index. $35 hb.

Making City Planning Work. Allan B. Jacobs. Chicago: American Society of Planning Officials (American Planning Association), 1978. 323 pp., illus., index. $15.95 pb.

Introduction to Planning History in the United States. Donald A. Krueckeberg, ed. Rutgers, N.J.: Center for Urban Policy Research, 1983. 275 pp. $12.95.

The American Planner: Biographies and Recollections. Donald A. Krueckeberg, ed. New York: Methuen, 1983. 433 pp., illus., index. $29.95 hb.

The Design of Cities. Edmund Bacon. 1967. Rev. ed. New York: Penguin Books, 1976. 336 pp., illus. $18.95 pb.

Cities. Lawrence Halprin. 1963. Rev. ed. Cambridge: MIT Press, 1973. 224 pp., illus. $9.95.

Urban Design: The Architecture of Towns and Cities. Paul D. Spreiregen. American Institute of Architects. New York: McGraw-Hill, 1965. 252 pp., illus. $29.50 hb.

Townscape as a Philosophy of Urban Design. William M. Whistler and David Reed. Chicago: Council of Planning Librarians, 1977. No. 1342. $2.40 pb.

Interpreting the City: An Urban Geography. Truman Asa Hartshorn. New York: Wiley, 1980. 498 pp., illus., append., index. $28.50.

The Geography of American Cities. Risa Palm. New York: Oxford University Press, 1981. 356 pp., illus. $19.95.

Planning for a Nation of Cities. Sam Bass Warner, Jr., ed. Cambridge: MIT Press, 1966. $4.95 pb.

Cities: Comparisons of Form and Scale. Richard Saul Wurman and School of Design Students, North Carolina State University. Cambridge: MIT Press, 1976. $3.95 pb.

An Introduction to Urban Design. Jonathan Barnett. New York: Harper and Row, 1982. 260 pp., illus., index. $20.95 hb.

The Architecture of the City. Aldo Rossi. Reprint. Introduction by Peter Eisenman. Cambridge: MIT Press, 1981. 252 pp., illus. $30 hb.

Urban Geography. David Clark. Baltimore: Johns Hopkins University Press, 1983. 233 pp., illus., biblio., index. $22.50 hb, $8.95 pb.

Dreaming the Rational City: The Myth of American City Planning. M. Christine Boyer. Cambridge: MIT Press, 1983. 331 pp., biblio., index. $27.50 hb.

Architecture and the Urban Experience. Raymond J. Curran. New York: Van Nostrand Reinhold, 1983. 221 pp., illus., index. $32.95 hb.

Cities and City Planning. Lloyd Rodwin. New York: Plenum, 1981. 317 pp., illus., biblio., index. $29.50 hb.

Recycling Cities for People: The Urban Design Process. Laurence S. Cutler and Sherrie Cutler. 1976. 2nd ed. New York: Van Nostrand Reinhold, 1983. 296 pp., illus., gloss., biblio., index. $16.50 pb.

Cities for People: Practical Measures for Improving Urban Environments. Ronald Wiedenhoeft. New York: Van Nostrand Reinhold, 1981. 224 pp., illus., index. $22.95 hb.

The Urban Pattern. Arthur B. Gallion and Simon Eisner. 1950. 4th ed. New York: Van Nostrand Reinhold, 1983. 464 pp., illus. $14.95 pb.

The American City: An Urban Odyssey to 11 U. S. Cities. Paul Gapp, John McCarron and Stanley Ziemba. New York: New York News Syndicate/Chicago Tribune, 1981. 191 pp., illus. $10.95 pb.

The City: A Dictionary of Quotable Thought on Cities and Urban Life. James A. Clapp. New Brunswick, N.J.: Center for Urban Policy Research, 1984. 288 pp. $30 hb.

Contacts

American Planning Association
1313 East 60th Street
Chicago, Ill. 60637

Regional/Urban Design
Assistance Teams
American Institute of Architects
1735 New York Avenue, N.W.
Washington, D.C. 20006

Partners for Livable Places
1429 21st Street, N.W.
Washington, D.C. 20036

Project for Public Spaces
875 Avenue of the Americas
Room 201
New York, N.Y. 10001

Institute for Urban Design
Main P.O. Box 105
Purchase, N.Y. 10577

See also: Plazas and Urban Open Spaces, Small Towns; Looking at the Built Environment, Main Streets

Cobblestone Buildings

"Cobblestone masonry has its origin in the geology of upstate New York and in traditions of rubble wall techniques imported from Europe, particularly from England. It served the demands of the pioneer farmers especially well, as the gathering of stones cleared their fields. . . . Cobblestone masonry, which originally served as a mere convenience, gradually developed its own canons of beauty."

Gerda Peterich, "Cobblestone Architecture of Upstate New York." *Journal of the Society of Architectural Historians,* May 1956.

Cobblestone Landmarks of New York State. Olaf William Shelgren, Jr., et al. Syracuse, N.Y.: Syracuse University Press, 1978. 176 pp., illus., maps. $12.95 hb, $9.95 pb.

Cobblestone Masonry. Carl F. Schmidt. Scottsville, N.Y.: Author, 1966. 330 pp., illus. $10.50 hb. Available from Milne Library, SUNY, Geneseo, N.Y. 14454.

Ontario County Cobblestones. Barbara C. Swartout. Canandaigua, N.Y.: Ontario County Historical Society (55 North Main Street, 14424), 1981. 48 pp., illus., biblio. $3 pb.

"Wayne County Cobblestone Architecture: Bounty of the Field and Shore." Lyons, N.Y.: Wayne County Historical Society (21 Butternut Street, 14489). 6 pp., map. $2.50 pb.

Contact

Cobblestone Society
Childs, N.Y. 14411

Saunders-Law House (1844), Orleans County, N.Y., a Greek Revival cobblestone landmark. (Cobblestone Society)

Colleges and Universities

"In the last two decades it seems that universities and colleges have been intent on corroding in the name of Modern Architecture any kind of quality their traditional campuses offered. Results ranged from overcooked extravaganzas that have little to do with context, to underdone derivatives that have little to do with design. None of this is over. It is exhilarating, however, to see some different attempts being made—attempts to recognize the special characteristics of the setting, to build upon them, and with them— where design doesn't mean destruction."

> Suzanne Stephens, "The New College Try." *Progressive Architecture*, March 1978.

Campus: An American Planning Tradition. Paul Venable Turner. Cambridge: MIT Press, 1984. 329 pp., illus., index. $35 hb.

Alma Mater: Design and Experience in the Women's Colleges from Their 19th-Century Beginnings to the 1930s. Helen Lefkowitz Horowitz. New York: Knopf, 1984. $25.

The Academical Village: Thomas Jefferson's University. Robert Llewellyn and Douglas Day. Charlottesville: Thomasson-Grant, 1982. 80 pp., color illus., append. $22.50 hb.

Thomas Jefferson's Rotunda Restored, 1973–1976: A Pictorial Review with Commentary. Joseph L. Vaughn and Omer A. Gianniny, Jr. Charlottesville: University Press of Virginia, 1981. 192 pp., illus., index. $27.50 hb.

Thomas Jefferson's Architectural Drawings . . . for the University of Virginia. Frederick D. Nichols. 1961. 4th ed. Charlottesville: University Press of Virginia, 1978. 49 pp., illus., index. $2.95 pb.

The First State University: A Pictorial History of the University of North Carolina. William S. Powell. Rev. ed. Chapel Hill: University of North Carolina Press, 1979. 360 pp., illus. $25 boxed.

The Vanderbilt Campus: A Pictorial History. Robert A. McGaw. Nashville: Vanderbilt University Press, 1978. 160 pp., illus., index. $12 hb.

Everybody Works But John Paul Jones: A Portrait of the U.S. Naval Academy, 1845–1915. Mame Warren and Marion E. Warren, eds. Annapolis, Md.: Naval Institute Press, 1981. 120 pp., illus. $19.95 hb.

Officers and Gentlemen: Historic West Point in Photographs. Jeffrey Simpson. Tarrytown, N.Y.: Sleepy Hollow Restorations, 1982. 222 pp., illus., chron., biblio., index. $12.95 pb.

The Uses of Gothic: Planning and Building the Campus of the University of Chicago, 1892–1932. Jean F. Block. Chicago: University of Chicago Library, 1983. 282 pp., illus., appends., index. $25 hb.

The University of Notre Dame: A Portrait of Its History and Campus. Thomas J. Schlereth. Notre Dame, Ind.: University of Notre Dame Press, 1976. 262 pp., illus., append., biblio., index. $9.95 pb.

Perspectives of a University: University of Wisconsin— Madison. A Survey of the Campus Architectural, Historical, Archeological and Memorial Resources and Recommendations for Preservation. Gordon D. Orr, Jr. Madison: University of Wisconsin (Department of Planning and Construction, 610 West Walnut Street, 53706), 1978. 134 pp., illus., appends.

The University of Texas: A Pictorial Account of Its First Century. Margaret C. Berry. Austin: University of Texas Press, 1981. 452 pp., illus. $25 hb.

Stanford: From the Foothills to the Bay. Peter C. Allen. Palo Alto, Calif.: Stanford Alumni Association and Stanford Historical Society, 1980. 228 pp., color illus., chron., biblio., append. $40 hb.

John Galen Howard and the Berkeley Campus: Beaux-Arts Architecture in the "Athens of the West." Loren Partridge. Berkeley, Calif.: Berkeley Architectural Heritage Association (P.O. Box 7066, Landscape Station, 94707), 1978. 65 pp., illus., biblio.

Denny's Knoll: A History of the Metropolitan Tract of the University of Washington. Neal O. Hines. Seattle: University of Washington Press, 1980. 480 pp., illus., appends., index. $14.95 hb.

"Gallaudet College: A High Victorian Campus," Francis R. Kowsky. *Records of the Columbia Historical Society, 1971–72.* Francis R. Rosenberger, ed. Washington, D.C.: Columbia Historical Society (1307 New Hampshire Avenue, N.W., 20036), 1972.

Conference on Conservation of Campus Resources: A Report of the Proceedings. Kenneth Cardwell, ed. Berkeley: University of California, Center for Planning and Development Research, College of Environmental Design (Berkeley, Calif. 94720), 1981. 115 pp.

Campus and Community. James Peters et al. New York: Educational Facilities Laboratories, 1980. 52 pp. $5 pb.

The University and the Inner City: A Redefinition of Relationships. W. Franklin Spikes, ed. Lexington, Mass.: Lexington Books, 1980. 191 pp. $23.95.

Contacts

Educational Facilities Laboratories
Academy for Educational Development
680 Fifth Avenue
New York, N.Y. 10019

American Council on Education
One Dupont Circle
Washington, D.C. 20036

Association of Physical Plant Administrators of Universities and Colleges
1446 Duke Street
Alexandria, Va. 22314–3492

American Association of State Colleges and Universities
One Dupont Circle
Washington, D.C. 20036

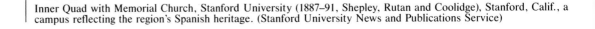

Inner Quad with Memorial Church, Stanford University (1887–91, Shepley, Rutan and Coolidge), Stanford, Calif., a campus reflecting the region's Spanish heritage. (Stanford University News and Publications Service)

Dormitory (1822), New Harmony, Ind. (Indiana State Museum)

Coal mining town in McDowell County, W.Va., with frame houses overlooking the railroad tracks. (Russell Lee, National Archives)

Communal Societies

"The American landscape still bears many traces of the work of nineteenth century communards, who tried to create collective paradise through communal agriculture, horticulture, and symbolic landscape design."

> Dolores Hayden, "Communal Idealism and the American Landscape." *Landscape,* Winter 1976.

Seven American Utopias: The Architecture of Communitarian Socialism, 1790–1975. Dolores Hayden. Cambridge: MIT Press, 1976. 401 pp., illus., biblio., index. $30 hb, $12.50 pb.

Dictionary of American Communal and Utopian History. Robert S. Fogarty. Westport, Conn.: Greenwood, 1980. 297 pp. $35 hb.

New Towns and Utopias. Christine E. Moe. Monticello, Ill.: Vance Bibliographies, 1980. 31 pp. $3.50 pb.

Utopia: An Illustrated History. Ian Tod and Michael Wheeler. New York: Harmony Books, 1978. 160 pp., color illus., biblio., index. $14.95 hb.

Urban Utopias in the Twentieth Century: Ebenezer Howard, Frank Lloyd Wright, Le Corbusier. Robert Fishman. Cambridge: MIT Press, 1982. $8.95 pb.

Heavens on Earth: Utopian Communities in America, 1680–1880. Mark Holloway. 1951. Rev. ed. New York: Dover, 1966. 246 pp., illus., biblio., index. $4 pb.

The Communal Experience: Anarchist and Mystical Communities in Twentieth Century America. Lawrence Veysey. 1973. Reprint. Chicago: University of Chicago Press, 1978. $7.95 pb.

Utopias on Puget Sound, 1885–1915. Charles Pierce LeWarne. Seattle: University of Washington Press, 1978. 340 pp., illus., map, biblio., index. $8.95 pb.

Visions of Utopias: Nashoba, Rugby, Ruskin and the "New Communities" in Tennessee's Past. John Egerton. Knoxville: University of Tennessee Press and the Tennessee Historical Commission, 1977. 95 pp., illus., biblio., index. $3.50 pb.

Moravian Architecture and Town Planning. William J. Murtagh. Chapel Hill: University of North Carolina Press, 1967. 145 pp., illus., biblio., index. $14.95.

The Communistic Societies of the United States, From Personal Visit and Observation. Charles Nordoff. 1875. Reprint. New York: Dover, 1966. 439 pp. $6.95 pb.

Amana: From Pietist Sect to American Community. Diane L. Barthel. Lincoln: University of Nebraska Press, 1984. $19.95.

Amish Society. John Hostetler. 1968. Rev. ed. Baltimore: Johns Hopkins University Press, 1980. 416 pp., illus., biblio., index. $22.50 hb, $6.95 pb.

Hutterite Society. John Hostetler. Baltimore: Johns Hopkins University Press, 1974. 420 pp., illus., biblio., index. $25 hb.

Oneida Community: An Autobiography, 1851–1876. Constance Noyes Robertson, ed. Syracuse: Syracuse University Press, 1970. 416 pp., illus. $9.95 pb.

California's Utopian Colonies. Robert V. Hine. 1973. New York: W. W. Norton, 1983. 216 pp. $6.95 pb.

Contacts

National Historic Communal Societies Association and the Center for Communal Studies Indiana State University Evansville, Ind. 47712

Communal Studies Center c/o Dr. John Hostetler Department of Anthropology Temple University Philadelphia, Pa. 19122

See also: Mormon Sites, Shakers

Company Towns

"Company towns in the mining areas of the United States were unavoidable because great cities seldom were located over rich mineral deposits. . . . Benevolent paternalism . . . dated back to Robert Owen's New Lanark in early Nineteenth-Century Scotland. George Pullman set up the company town of Pullman south of Chicago in the 1880s and provided homes, recreational halls, churches, a hospital and stores for his workers."

> James Allen Scott, *Duluth's Legacy.* Vol. I: *Architecture.* Duluth, Minn.: Department of Research and Planning, 1974.

The Model Company Town: Urban Design Through Private Enterprise in Nineteenth-Century New England. John S. Garner. Amherst: University of Massachusetts Press, 1985. 240 pp., illus., biblio., index. $22.50 hb.

Company Towns: A Bibliography of American and Foreign Sources. Council of Planning Librarians. Monticello, Ill.: Author, 1977. No. 1428. 25 pp.

An Enclave of Elegance: The General Electric Realty Plot Historic District. Bruce Maston. Schenectady, N.Y.: GERPA Publications and Schenectady Museum, 1983. 259 pp., illus., biblio., index. $16.95 pb.

Pullman, Illinois: A Bibliography. Mary Vance. Monticello, Ill.: Vance Bibliographies, 1980. 4 pp. $2.

Factory Under the Elms: A History of Harrisville, New Hampshire, 1774–1969. John B. Armstrong. Cambridge: MIT Press, 1969. 320 pp., illus., appends., biblio., index.

Anthropology Toward History: Culture and Work in a 19th Century Maine Town. Richard Horwitz. Middletown, Conn.: Wesleyan University Press, 1978. 210 pp., illus. $18.50.

Rockdale: The Growth of an American Village in the Early Industrial Revolution. Anthony F. C. Wallace. New York: W. W. Norton, 1978. 553 pp., illus., biblio., append., index. $8.95

Mill Town: A Social History of Everett, Washington. Norman H. Clark. Seattle: University of Washington Press, 1970. 277 pp. $7.95 pb.

Gritty Cities: A Second Look at Allentown, Bethlehem, Bridgeport, Hoboken, Lancaster, Norwich, Paterson, Reading, Trenton, Troy, Waterbury, Wilmington. Mary Procter and Bill Matuszeski. Philadelphia: Temple University Press, 1978. 276 pp., illus., biblio. $17.50 hb.

R. A. Long's Planned City: The Story of Longview. John M. McClelland, Jr. Longview, Wash.: Longview Publishing, 1976. 288 pp., illus., append., index. $9.50.

Company Towns of the Minnesota Iron Ranges: A Bibliography of Historical and Current Sources. Rosalina Levenson. Monticello, Ill.: Vance Bibliographies, 1980. P-412. 25 pp.

Contacts

Society for Industrial Archeology National Museum of American History Room 5020 Washington, D.C. 20560

Historic Pullman Foundation Hotel Florence 1111 South Forrestville Avenue Chicago, Ill. 60628

Institute on Man and Science Rensselaerville, N.Y. 12147

Pope and Talbot Company Museum and National Historic Site Port Gamble, Wash. 98362

See also: Industrial Structures

Courthouses

"Because there was no town until there was a court house; and no court house until . . . the floorless lean-to rabbit-hutch housing the iron chest was reft from the log flank of the jail and transmogrified into a by-neo-Greek-out-of-Georgian-England edifice set in the center of what in time would be the town square. . . ."

> William Faulkner, *Requiem for a Nun.* New York: Random House, 1951.

"Its very bulk often acts as a 'paperweight,' to keep the smaller surrounding buildings from visually blowing away."

> Paul Goeldner, *A Courthouse Conservation Handbook*

Court House: A Photographic Document. Richard Pare, ed. Essay by Henry-Russell Hitchcock and William Seale. New York: Horizon Press, 1978. 256 pp., color illus. $35 hb.

A Courthouse Conservation Handbook. National Trust for Historic Preservation, with National Clearinghouse for Criminal Justice Planning and Architecture. Washington, D.C.: Preservation Press, 1976. 76 pp., illus., append., biblio. $4.95 pb.

The County Court Houses of America. Isabel B. Lowry, ed. The Dunlap Society. Princeton: Princeton University Press. 180 microfiche. 2 vols. $275 each.

On the Courthouse Square in Arkansas. John Purifoy Gill and Marjem Jackson Gill. Little Rock: MJG Publications (5100 Crestwood Drive, 72207), 1980. 138 pp., illus. $21.50 hb.

Indiana County Courthouses of the Nineteenth Century. David R. Hermansen. Muncie: Ball State University, 1968. 25 pp.

Iowa's Magnificent County Courthouses. Edward and Jacqueline Stanek. Des Moines, Iowa: Wallace-Homestead (Box BI, 50304), 1976. 213 pp., illus., biblio. $7.95 pb.

Legacies: Kansas' Older County Courthouses. Julie Wortman and David P. Johnson. Topeka: Kansas State Historical Society, 1981. 70 pp., illus. $3.85 pb.

The History of Kentucky Courthouses. Elisabeth Headley Garr. National Society of Colonial Dames of America in the State of Kentucky, 1972. 166 pp., illus.

Courthouses of the Commonwealth. George Peet and Gabrielle Keller. Robert J. Brink, ed. Amherst: University of Massachusetts Press, 1984. $30 hb, $14.95 pb.

New Mexico Courthouses. Donald W. Whisenhunt. Southwestern Studies, no. 57. El Paso: University of Texas, Texas Western Press, 1979. 46 pp., illus. $3 pb.

Historic Courthouses of New York State: 18th and 19th Century Halls of Justice Across the Empire State. Herbert Alan Johnson and Ralph K. Andrist. New York: Columbia University Press, 1977. 175 pp., illus. $22.50 hb.

Carson, Pirie, Scott Department Store (1899, Louis Sullivan), Chicago.

100 Courthouses: A Report on North Carolina Justice Facilities. 645 pp., illus., biblio. Raleigh: North Carolina State University School of Design, 1978. 2 vols.

Temples of Justice: 19th Century Courthouses in the Midwest and Texas. Paul Goeldner. Doctoral dissertation, 1971. Ann Arbor, Mich.: University Microfilms (300 North Zeeb Road, 48106). 540 pp. $12.50 hb, $10 pb, $4 microfilm.

The Courthouse and the Law Court: Their Design and Construction. Carole Cable. Monticello, Ill.: Vance Bibliographies, 1978. A-20. 31 pp. $3 pb.

Contacts

National Center for State Courts
300 Newport Avenue
Williamsburg, Va. 23185

American Bar Association
Joint Committee on Design of Courtrooms and Court Facilities
1155 East 60th Street
Chicago, Ill. 60637

American Judicature Society
1155 East 60th Street
Chicago, Ill. 60637

U.S. County Court House (Seagram) Archives
Prints and Photographs Division
Library of Congress
Washington, D.C. 20540

Department Stores

"Housed in what are often America's most beautiful buildings and characterized by elegant open vistas [department stores] set their customers free in fantasy land, offering them *everything.*"

> Robert Hendrickson, *The Grand Emporiums*

The Grand Emporiums: The Illustrated History of America's Great Department Stores. Robert Hendrickson. New York: Stein and Day, 1980. 616 pp., illus. $9.95 pb.

Store: A Memoir of America's Great Department Stores. Nan Tillson Birmingham. New York: Putnam, 1979.

Shopfronts. Bill Evans and Andrew Lawson. New York: Van Nostrand Reinhold, 1981. 128 pp. $16.95.

The American Store Window. Leonard S. Marcus. New York: Watson-Guptill, 1978. 192 pp., illus., biblio., index. $25 hb.

"Like No Other Store in the World": The Inside Story of Bloomingdale's. Mark Stevens. New York: T. Y. Crowell, 1979. 256 pp. $2.75 pb.

Bloomies. Maxine Brady. New York: Harcourt Brace Jovanovich, 1979.

Minding the Store. Stanley Marcus. Boston: Little, Brown, 1974. $14.45 hb.

Jury seats, Grady County Courthouse (1908–09, Alexander Blair), Cairo, Ga. (Jim Dow, Seagram County Court House Archives)

Diners

"We can thank our luck that human life and art constantly escape from the models we construct for them. My generation excluded the vulgar Pop world, emphatically including that of the Diner, from our consideration and, by precept, from that of our children—who then grew up and took it and made it art."

Vincent Scully, Introduction. *Diners*

American Diner. Richard J. S. Gutman and Elliott Kaufman. New York: Harper and Row, 1979. 192 pp., color illus. $8.95 pb.

Diners. John Baeder. New York: Abrams, 1978. 145 pp., color illus. $12.50 pb.

Diners of the Northeast. Ronald Kaplan and Alan Bellink. New York: Lippincott and Crowell, 1980. 162 pp., illus., maps.

All Night, All-Night Diner Tour. Douglas A. Yorke, Jr. Boston: Society for Commercial Archeology, 1980. 16 pp.

Contact

Society for Commercial Archeology
National Museum of American History
Room 5010
Washington, D.C. 20560

See also: Roadside Architecture

Estates

"The large estates built throughout America during the 19th and early 20th centuries are an important part of the cultural legacy of their communities. . . . Many properties cover large areas of land, which have an environmental and economic importance to their communities.

Increasingly, however, many estates are threatened. In urban, suburban and rural areas, estate owners are subject to rising taxes, the high costs of maintenance and fuel and development pressures. Because these properties represent an investment opportunity for public conservation and recreation as well as other forms of private and commercial development, community organizations and local governments are becoming increasingly involved in the preservation of endangered estates."

Christopher W. Closs, *Preserving Large Estates*

Saving Large Estates: Conservation, Historic Preservation, Adaptive Reuse. William C. Shopsin and Grania Bolton Marcus. Setauket, N.Y.: Society for the Preservation of Long Island Antiquities, 1977. 199 pp., illus., biblio. $8 pb.

Preserving Large Estates. Christopher W. Closs. Information Series, National Trust for Historic Preservation. Washington, D.C.: Preservation Press, 1982. 24 pp., illus., biblio. $2 pb.

Great American Mansions and Their Stories. 1963. Merrill Folsom. New York: Hastings House, 1976. 310 pp., illus., index. $12.95 pb.

American Castles. Julien Cavalier. Cranbury, N.J.: A. S. Barnes, 1973. 243 pp., illus., gloss., index.

The Berkshire Cottages: A Vanishing Era. Carole Owens. Englewood Cliffs, N.J.: Cottage Press, 1984. $27.95 pb.

A Pride of Palaces: Lenox Summer Cottages 1883–1933. Photographs by Edwin Hale Lincoln. Donald T. Oakes, ed. Lenox, Mass.: Lenox Library Association, 1981. 84 pp., illus., append. $15 pb.

Boston's Gold Coast: The North Shore, 1890–1929. Joseph E. Garland. Little, Brown, 1981. $19.95.

Great Camps of the Adirondacks. Harvey H. Kaiser. Boston: Godine, 1982. 256 pp., color illus., biblio., index. $60 hb.

Durant: The Fortunes and Woodland Camps of a Family in the Adirondacks. Craig Gilborn, Adirondack Museum. Sylvan Beach, N.Y.: North Country Books, 1981. 176 pp., illus., appends., index. $19.95 hb.

Long Island Country Houses and Their Architects 1860–1940. Society for the Preservation of Long Island Antiquities. New York: W. W. Norton, 1986.

Beaux-Arts Estates: A Guide to the Architecture of Long Island. Lisa and Donald Sclare. New York: Viking, 1980. 274 pp., illus., appends., biblio., index.

The Mansions of Long Island's Gold Coast. Monica Randall. New York: Hastings House, 1979. 240 pp., color illus., biblio., index. $27.50 hb.

Empire Diner (1976) by John Baeder. (Dennis McWaters, Frances and Sydney Lewis Collection)

Vizcaya (1916, Hoffman and Chalfin), Miami, a Renaissance palace on Biscayne Bay. (Miami-Metro Department of Publicity and Tourism)

Mansions and Millionaires. Arlene Travis and Carole Aronson. New York: Designers' Showcase, 1983. 119 pp., illus., gloss.

Mizner's Florida: American Resort Architecture. Donald W. Curl. Cambridge: MIT Press, 1984. 256 pp., illus. $30 hb.

Plantation Homes of Louisiana and the Natchez Area. David King Gleason. Baton Rouge: Louisiana State University Press, 1982. 134 pp., color illus., index. $29.95 hb.

The Estates of Beverly Hills. Charles Lockwood and Jeff Hyland. Beverly Hills, Calif.: Margrant Publishing, 1984. 164 pp., color illus. $95 hb.

Hearst Castle: San Simeon. Thomas R. Aidala. Introduction by David Niven. Foreword by William Randolph Hearst, Jr. New York: Hudson Hills Press, 1981. 240 pp., color illus., append., biblio., index. $45 hb.

Guernsey Hall: Economic Analysis of Adaptive Use Projects. Information Series, National Trust for Historic Preservation. Washington, D.C.: Preservation Press, 1976. 12 pp., illus. $2 pb.

Contacts

Society for the Preservation of Long Island Antiquities
93 North Country Road
Setauket, N.Y. 11733

Preservation Society of Newport County
118 Mill Street
Newport, R.I. 02840

Society for the Preservation of New England Antiquities
141 Cambridge Street
Boston, Mass. 02114

Trustees of Reservations
224 Adams Street
Milton, Mass. 02186

See also: Houses, Resorts and Spas

Ethnic Heritages

"E Pluribus Unum." (Out of Many, One.)

Motto of the United States of America

"There is an Irish Boston, a Polish Chicago, a German Cincinnati, a Slavic Pittsburgh, a Portuguese Gloucester, and a Scandinavian Minneapolis. There are Chinatowns, Little Tokyos, and Little Italies in many cities, and centres of Native American life like Taos, Four Corners and Wounded Knee. . . .

When independence was proclaimed in 1776, this was already a land of many peoples. It had been explored, visited and occasionally settled by Spanish, French, Italians, Africans, Portuguese, Greeks, Scandinavians, Germans and Jews. . . .

The nation [has] discovered that it is no melting pot and never has been."

Yen Lu Wong and Herbert Chivambo Shore, "A Living Heritage of Many Cultures and Peoples." *UNESCO Courier,* July 1976.

Ethnic America: A History. Thomas Sowell. New York: Basic Books, 1981. 353 pp., index. $16.95 hb.

Ethnic American Minorities: A Guide to Media and Materials. Harry A. Johnson, ed. New York: R. R. Bowker, 1976. 304 pp., index. $21.50 hb.

Guide to Ethnic Museums, Libraries and Archives in the United States. Lubomyr R. Wynar and Lois Buttlar. Kent, Ohio: Center for Ethnic Publications, Kent State University (School of Library Science, 44242), 1978. 378 pp.

Ethnic Groups: Part One, Research for the Local Historical Society. Dorothy Weyer Creigh. Nashville: American Association for State and Local History, 1978. Technical Leaflet 108. 8 pp., illus., biblio. $2 pb.

Explorers and Settlers: Historic Places Commemorating the Early Exploration and Settlement of the United States. Robert G. Ferris, ed., Historic Sites Survey. Washington, D.C.: National Park Service, U.S. Department of the Interior, 1968. 506 pp., illus., maps, biblio., index. $17 hb. GPO stock no. 024–005–00006–2.

In Search of Liberty: The Story of the Statue of Liberty and Ellis Island. James B. Bell and Richard I. Abrams. New York: Doubleday, 1984. 128 pp., color illus. $10.95 pb.

Right hand of the Statue of Liberty, displayed at the 1876 Centennial. From *In Search of Liberty.*

Strangers at the Door: Ellis Island, Castle Garden and the Great Migration. Ann Novotny. New York: Dodd, Mead, 1984. 249 pp., illus. $24.95.

California's Ethnic Minorities Cultural Resources Survey: Afro-Americans, Chicanos/Latinos, Native Americans, Chinese-Americans, Japanese-Americans. California Department of Parks and Recreation. Sacramento: Author (P.O. Box 2390, 95811), 1982. 400 pp., illus., biblios. $5 pb.

La Comunidad: Design, Development, and Self-Determination in Hispanic Communities. Evagene H. Bond, ed. Washington, D.C.: Partners for Livable Places, 1982. 64 pp., illus. $7.50 pb.

The Complete Guide to Ethnic New York. Zelda Stern. New York: St. Martin's Press, 1980. 312 pp., index. $6.95 pb.

Museums, Sites and Collections of Germanic Culture in North America: An Annotated Directory of German Immigrant Culture in the United States and Canada. Margaret Hobbie, comp. Westport, Conn.: Greenwood, 1980. 184 pp. $27.50 hb.

The Arts and Architecture of German Settlements in Missouri: A Survey of a Vanishing Culture. Charles Van Ravenswaay. Columbia: University of Missouri Press, 1977. 536 pp., biblio., index. $50 hb.

The Volga Germans: Pioneers of the Northwest. Richard D. Scheuerman and Clifford E. Trafzer. Moscow: University Press of Idaho, 1980. 245 pp., illus., biblio., index.

The Pennsylvania German Family Farm: A Regional Architecture and Folk Cultural Study of an American Agricultural Community. Amos Long, Jr. Breinigsville, Pa.: Pennsylvania German Historical Society (R.D. 1, Box 469, 18031), 1972. 518 pp., illus., biblio., index.

A Pictorial History of Asian America. Franklin Shoichiro Odo. Los Angeles: Visual Communications, Asian American Studies Central (1601 Griffith Park Boulevard, 90026), 1977. 157 pp., illus., index.

Years of Infamy: The Untold Story of America's Concentration Camps. Michi Weglyn. New York: Morrow, 1976. $7.95 pb.

The Cajuns: From Acadia to Louisiana. William Faulkner Rushton. New York: Farrar, Straus and Giroux, 1979. 342 pp., illus., maps, appends., biblio. $19.95 hb, $8.95 pb.

The Ethnic Heritage of an Urban Neighborhood. Series: Carondelet, The Ville and Soulard. St. Louis: Washington University, Social Science Institute (Box 1202, 63130), 1975. 40 pp. $2 each.

Guide to Chicago Neighborhoods. Ron Grossman. Piscataway, N.J.: New Century Publishers (275 Old New Brunswick Road, 08854), 1981. 212 pp., illus., index. $7.95 pb.

"Early Architecture and Settlements of Russian America," Anatole Senkevitch, Jr. *Proceedings of Conference on Russian America.* Washington, D.C.: Kennan Institute for Advanced Russian Studies (Smithsonian Institution, 20560), 1981.

"Hungarian Settlement and Building Practices in Pennsylvania and Hungary: A Brief Comparison," Laszlo Kurti. *Pioneer America,* February 1980.

The Italians of San Francisco, 1850–1930. Deanna Paoli Gumina. Staten Island, N.Y.: Center for Migration Studies, 1978. 230 pp., illus., biblio., index. $9.95 hb.

Some National Register Listings

Alaska: Sitka National Historical Park (Russian and Tlingit Indians)

Arizona: Canyon de Chelly National Monument (Native American)

California: Monterey Old Town Historic District (Hispanic)

Colorado: Curtis-Champa Streets District, Denver (Oriental, Mexican, Black)

Connecticut: Wooster Square Historic District, New Haven (Italian)

District of Columbia: Le Droit Park (Black)

Florida: Ybor City Historic District, Tampa (Cuban, Italian, Black)

Georgia: Martin Luther King, Jr., Historic District, Atlanta (Black)

Hawaii: Chinatown Historic District, Honolulu (Chinese, Filipino, Japanese, Korean, Puerto Rican, Black, Hawaiian)

Illinois: Bishop Hill Historic District (Swedish); French Colonial Historic District, Prairie du Rocher (French)

Micronesia: Nan Madol, Ponape (Ponapean)

Missouri: Hermann Historic District (German)

New Mexico: Acoma Pueblo (Native American)

Puerto Rico: San Juan National Historic Site (Hispanic)

Tennessee: Beale Street Historic District, Memphis (Black)

Contacts

The Balch Institute
18 South Seventh Street
Philadelphia, Pa. 19106

National Center for Urban Ethnic Affairs
P.O. Box 33279
Washington, D.C. 20033

Center for Migration Studies
American Italian Historical Association
209 Flagg Place
Staten Island, N.Y. 10304

Pioneer America Society
Department of Geography
University of Akron
Akron, Ohio 44325

National Council of La Raza
1725 I Street, N.W.
Washington, D.C. 20006

Japanese-American Citizens League
1765 Sutter Street
San Francisco, Calif. 94115

American Swedish Institute
2600 Park Avenue
Minneapolis, Minn. 55407

Polish American Historical Association
984 North Milwaukee Avenue
Chicago, Ill. 60622

See also: Black Sites, Chinese Sites, Jewish Landmarks; Indigenous Architecture (Looking at the Built Environment)

Executive Mansions

"For the President's house, I would design a building which should also look forward but execute no more of it at present than might suit the circumstances of this country, when it shall be first wanted. A plan comprehending more may be executed at a future period when the wealth, population and importance of it shall stand upon much higher ground than they do at present."

George Washington, March 8, 1792.

The White House: An Architectural History. William Ryan and Desmond Guinness. New York: McGraw-Hill, 1980. 196 pp., color illus., biblio., index. $29.95 hb.

The White House: An Historic Guide. Washington, D.C.: White House Historical Association, 1979. 160 pp., color illus. $3 pb.

White House History. Washington, D.C.: White House Historical Association, 1984. 64 pp., illus., biblio. $6 pb.

Executive Mansions and Capitols of America. Jean Houston Daniel and Price Daniel. Waukesha, Wis.: Country Beautiful (24198 West Bluemound Road, 53186), 1974. 258 pp., color illus., append., biblio. $9.98.

An Illustrated Guide to the Mississippi Governor's Mansion. Helen Cain and Anne D. Czarniecki. Jackson: University Press of Mississippi, 1984. 92 pp., color illus. $14.95 hb.

New York City's Gracie Mansion: A History of the Mayor's House. Mary Black. New York: J. M. Kaplan Fund, for Gracie Mansion Conservancy, 1984. 93 pp. $17.95 hb, $10.95 pb.

Contact

White House Historical Association
740 Jackson Place, N.W.
Washington, D.C. 20506

The White House (1792). (*National Geographic,* WHHA)

Court of Honor (1893, C. B. Atwood, Daniel H. Burnham, Frederick Law Olmsted), World's Columbian Exposition, Chicago, which helped usher in an era of classical revival architecture. (Library of Congress)

Fair Buildings

"Like the movies and baseball, fair-going became a recognized American pastime. . . . Fairs offered an escapism similar to but more tangible than Hollywood. . . . Great, white, magical, temporary cities thrilled millions of awed visitors."

Arnold L. Lehman, "1930s Expositions." New York Cultural Center, 1973.

The Great Exhibitions. John Allwood. London: Cassell and Collier Macmillan, 1978. 192 pp., illus., biblio., index, append.

Fairground Architecture: The World of Amusement Parks, Carnivals, and Fairs. David Braithwaite. New York: Praeger, 1968. 195 pp., illus., biblio., gloss., append., index.

"International Expositions 1851–1900," Julia F. Davis. *American Association of Architectural Bibliographers' Papers,* vol. 4. William B. O'Neal, ed. Charlottesville: University Press of Virginia, 1967. $10 pb.

Here Today and Gone Tomorrow: The Story of World's Fairs and Expositions. Suzanne Hilton. Philadelphia: Westminster Press, 1978. 192 pp., illus., biblio., index. $8.95 hb.

Centennial Philadelphia. Richard R. Nocolai. Bryn Mawr, Pa.: Bryn Mawr Press, 1976. 96 pp., illus.

The Glorious Enterprise: The Centennial Exhibition of 1876 and H. J. Schwarzmann, Architect-in-Chief. John Maass. Watkins Glen, N.Y.: American Life Foundation, 1973. 196 pp., illus. $25.

The Great American Fair: The World's Columbian Exposition and American Culture. Reid Badger. Chicago: Nelson-Hall, 1979. 228 pp., illus. $32.95 hb.

The Chicago World's Fair of 1893: A Photographic Record. Stanley Applebaum. New York: Dover, 1980. 127 pp., illus., biblio., index. $6 pb.

The Fair Women: The Woman's Building, Chicago, 1893. Jeanne Madeline Weimann. Chicago: Academy Chicago, 1981. 600 pp., illus. $29.95 hb, $14.95 pb.

Treasure Island: San Francisco's Exposition Years. Richard Reinhardt. Mill Valley, Calif.: Squarebooks, 1979. 175 pp., illus., index. $6.95 pb.

San Francisco: Creation of a City. Tom Moulin and Don DeNevi. Millbrae, Calif.: Celestial Arts, 1978. 177 pp., illus., index.

The Dawn of a New Day: The New York World's Fair, 1939–1940. Helen Harrison, ed. New York: Columbia University Press, 1980. 128 pp., illus. $30 hb, $15.95 pb.

The New York World's Fair, 1939–1940. Stanley Applebaum. New York: Dover, 1977. 152 pp., illus. $5 pb.

Contacts

World's Fair Collectors Society
148 Poplar Street
Garden City, N.Y. 11530

World's Fair Newsletter
P.O. Box 339
Corte Madera, Calif. 94925

1876 Centennial Records
Philadelphia Department of Records
Room 523
City Hall Annex
Philadelphia, Pa. 19107

Chicago Public Library
Special Collections Division
78 East Washington
Chicago, Ill. 60602

Chicago Historical Society
Clark Street at North Avenue
Chicago, Ill. 60614

Committee of 100
Box 6541
San Diego, Calif. 92106

See also: Amusement Parks

The Cornell Farm (1849) by Edward Hicks, showing buildings and stock on the farm of James C. Cornell. (Garbisch Collection, National Gallery of Art)

Farms

"Farm life was never easy, but the well planned and well built farmstead nourished a pleasant and secure way of life, even in the earlier days. The farm was practically a self-contained, self-supported economic unit. . . . The barn, house and outbuildings, with the adjoining yards, garden, and roadway comprised the center of farm life. . . . The many outbuildings and appendages needed in the performance of domestic and farm-related chores were conveniently arranged about or attached to the house and barn."

Amos Long, *Farmsteads and Their Buildings*

The American Farm: A Photographic History. Maisie and Richard Conrat. Boston: Houghton Mifflin, 1977. 256 pp., illus. $17.50 hb, $9.95 pb.

The American Farmhouse. Henry J. Kauffman. New York: Hawthorn, 1975. 280 pp., color illus., biblio., index.

Big House, Little House, Back House, Barn: The Connected Farm Buildings of New England. Thomas C. Hubka. Hanover, N.H.: University Press of New England, 1984. 240 pp., illus., biblio., index. $35 hb.

"The Site Arrangement of Rural Farmsteads," William H. Tishler. *Bulletin,* Association for Preservation Technology, February 1978.

Farmsteads and Their Buildings. Amos Long. Lebanon, Pa.: Applied Arts Publishers, 1972. 40 pp., illus.

Farmsteads and Market Towns. Albany: Preservation League of New York State, 1982. 50 pp., illus., biblio. $4 pb.

The Fruited Plain: The Story of American Agriculture. Walter Ebeling. Berkeley: University of California Press, 1980. 433 pp., illus., biblio., index. $30 hb.

Whereby We Thrive: A History of American Farming, 1607–1972. John T. Schlebecker. Ames: Iowa State University Press, 1975. 342 pp., illus. $16.50.

A Long, Deep Furrow: Three Centuries of Farming in New England. Howard S. Russell. Abr. ed. Hanover, N.H.: University Press of New England, 1981. 432 pp. $12.95 pb.

Minnesota Farmscape: Looking at Change. St. Paul: Minnesota Historical Society (240 Summit Avenue, 55102), 1980. 25 pp., illus., biblio.

Midwestern Vernacular: Farm Structures in Kane County, Illinois. Jean Hervert and Elizabeth Allen. Geneva, Ill.: Kane County Urban Development (719 South Batavia Avenue, 60134), 1980. 160 pp., illus., maps, appends., biblio.

The Life and Death of a Family Farm: Archeology, History and Landscape Change in Brighton, New York. David Howard Day. Rochester, N.Y.: Monroe Community College (1000 East Henrietta Road, 14623) and Monroe County Historian's Office, 1980. 31 pp.

Farm Town: A Memoir of the 1930's. J. W. McManigal and Grant Heilman. Brattleboro, Vt.: Stephen Greene Press, 1974. 100 pp., illus. $9.95 pb.

"Restoring the American Farmhouse." *Old-House Journal,* July 1978.

Arrowhead Farm: 300 Years of New England Husbandry and Cooking. Pauline Chase Harrell, Charlotte Moulton Chase and Richard Chase. Woodstock, Vt.: Countryman Press, 1983. 234 pp., illus., index. $12.95 pb.

The 1870 Agriculturist for the Farm, Garden, and Household. American Agriculturist. 1870. Reprint. Steven J. Rakeman and Donald Berg, eds. Rockville Centre, N.Y.: Antiquity Reprints (Box 370, 11571), 1980. 124 pp., illus. $8.50 pb.

Living Historical Farms Handbook. John T. Schlebecker and Gale E. Petersen. Smithsonian Studies in History and Technology, vol. 16. Washington, D.C.: Smithsonian Institution Press, 1972. 91 pp.

Living Historical Farms: The Working Museums. David O. Percy. Accokeek, Md.: National Colonial Farm (3400 Bryan Point Road, 20607), 1981. 121 pp., illus., appends.

Passing Farms: Enduring Values. California's Santa Clara Valley. Yvonne Jacobson. Los Altos, Calif.: William Kaufmann, 1985. 240 pp., illus. $39.50 hb.

Travel Historic Rural America: A Guide to Agricultural Museums and Events in the U.S. and Canada. Sam Rosenberg, ed. St. Joseph, Mich.: American Society of Agricultural Engineers (Box 10, 49085), 1982. 108 pp., illus., maps. $6.95 pb.

Contacts

Association for Living Historical Farms and Agricultural Museums National Museum of American History Room 5035 Washington, D.C. 20560

American Farmland Trust 1717 Massachusetts Avenue, N.W. Washington, D.C. 20036

U.S. Department of Agriculture Farmers Home Administration Washington, D.C. 20250

Agricultural History Branch U.S. Department of Agriculture 500 12th Street, S.W. Washington, D.C. 20250

Luther Burbank Experimental Farm Sebastopol, Calif. 95472

Connecticut Agricultural Experiment Station 123 Huntington Street New Haven, Conn. 06511

Midwest Coast R.R. #1 Clinton, Wis. 53525

See also: Barns, Rural Areas and Landscapes

Fences

"Farmers knew that good fences make good neighbors long before Robert Frost immortalized this particular bit of folk wisdom in 'Mending Wall.' "

John Fraser Hart, "Fences." In *Built in the U.S.A.*

Fences, Gates and Bridges: A Practical Manual. George A. Martin, ed. 1887. Reprint. Brattleboro, Vt.: Stephen Greene Press, 1974. 196 pp., illus., index. $6.95 hb.

"Walls and Fences," Wilbur Zelinsky. In *Changing Rural Landscapes.* Ervin H. Zube and Margaret J. Zube, eds. Amherst: University of Massachusetts Press, 1977. 151 pp., illus. $12 hb, $6 pb.

"Fences and Walls." In *Our Vanishing Landscape.* Eric Sloane. New York: Ballantine, 1975. 110 pp., illus. $4.95 pb.

Victorian Ironwork: The Wickersham Catalogue of 1857. Reprint. Preface by Margot Gayle. Philadelphia: The Athenaeum, 1977. 78 pp., illus. $20 hb.

"Barbed Wire and the Art of Stringing It." In *From the High Plains.* John Fischer. New York: Harper and Row, 1978. 181 pp., illus. $12.45 hb.

Contact

Fence Industry Communication Channels 6285 Barfield Road Atlanta, Ga. 30328

See also: Cast-Iron Buildings

Picket fence, Camden, Maine. (Cervin Robinson, HABS)

Firehouses

"Since the days of the volunteers, the design of fire stations has been characterized by an unusual combination of features: their role as public buildings, their program that calls for both a garage and living quarters, their peculiar size and shape, and the fact that they are associated with the fire service and whatever it stands for. Because fire stations have been linked with the popular image of firemen and fire engines, they often have had an extra element of humor or fantasy—you might even call it affection—that sets them apart from other buildings."

> Rebecca Zurier, *The American Firehouse*

The American Firehouse: An Architectural and Social History. Rebecca Zurier. Photographs by A. Pierce Bounds. New York: Abbeville, 1982. 288 pp., illus., index. $29.95 hb.

Heritage of Flames: The Illustrated History of Early American Firefighting. Harold S. Walker et al. New York: Doubleday, 1977. 372 pp., illus., biblio., index.

Fire Engines, Firefighters: The Men, Equipment, and Machines from Colonial Days to the Present. Paul C. Ditzel. New York: Crown, 1976. 256 pp., illus.

Contacts

Hall of Flame Museum
National Historical Fire Foundation
6101 East Van Buren
Phoenix, Ariz. 85008

National Fire Protection Association
Batterymarch Park
Quincy, Mass. 02269

INA Museum
Insurance Company of North America
1600 Arch Street
Philadelphia, Pa. 19101

The Fire Museum
7 Duane Avenue
New York, N.Y. 14305

Fire Museum of Maryland
1301 York Road
Lutherville, Md. 21093

Philadelphia Fire Department Museum
149 North 2nd Street
Philadelphia, Pa. 19106

Boston Fire Museum
20 Eustis Street
Roxbury, Mass. 02119

Vigilant Fire Company certificate, Philadelphia, 1827. (INA Museum)

Forts

"War is as old as humanity, and the construction of fortresses almost as old as war. The first buildings erected by man seem, indeed, to have been protecting walls."

> Henri Pirenne, *Medieval Cities: Their Origins and the Revival of Trade.* Princeton: Princeton University Press, 1925.

American Forts: Architectural Form and Function. Willard B. Robinson. 1977. Ann Arbor, Mich.: University Microfilms. 256 pp., illus., gloss., biblio., index. $61 hb.

Stronghold: A History of Military Architecture. Martin Brice. New York: Schocken, 1984. $24.50 hb.

Exploring Military America. Marcella and Gladys Thum. New York: Atheneum, 1982. 336 pp., illus., index. $11.95 pb.

A Pictorial Guide to the Military Museums, Forts, and Historic Sites of the United States. James Sweeney. New York: Crown, 1981. 320 pp. $19.95.

A Guide to the Sources of United States Military History. Robin Higham, ed. 1975. $27.50. *Supplement I.* Robin Higham and Donald J. Mrozek, eds. Hamden, Conn.: Shoe String Press, 1981. 312 pp. $37.50.

Seacoast Fortifications of the United States: An Introductory History. Emanuel Raymond Lewis. 1970. Reprint. San Francisco: Presidio Books, 1981. 160 pp., illus. $7.95 pb.

Fort Jefferson (1846), Dry Tortugas, Fla., a large garrison guarding the southeastern coast. (Jack E. Boucher, HABS)

Soldier and Brave: Historic Places Associated with Indian Affairs and the Indian Wars in the Trans-Mississippi West. Robert G. Ferris, ed., Historic Sites Survey. Washington, D.C.: U.S. Department of the Interior, National Park Service, 1971. 453 pp., illus., maps, biblio., index. $13 hb. GPO stock no. 024–005–00236–7.

Guide to U.S. Army Museums and Historic Sites. Norman M. Cary, Jr., ed. Washington, D.C.: U.S. Army Center of Military History, 1975. 116 pp., illus. $5.50 pb. GPO stock no. 008–020–00561–4.

Tour Guide to Old Western Forts: The Posts and Camps of the Army, Navy and Marines, 1804–1916. Herbert M. Hart. Boulder, Colo.: Pruett, 1980. 212 pp., illus., biblio. $24.95 hb.

Tour Guide to Old Forts of Montana, Wyoming, North and South Dakota. Herbert M. Hart. Boulder, Colo.: Pruett, 1980. 150 pp., illus. $3.95 pb.

The Black Military Experience in the American West. John M. Carroll, ed. New York: W. W. Norton, 1974. $17.50 hb, $3.95 pb.

The Presidio: Bastion of the Spanish Borderlands. Max L. Moorhead. Norman: University of Oklahoma Press, 1975. 288 pp., illus., append., biblio., index. $18.95 hb.

New York Forts in the Revolution. Robert B. Roberts. Rutherford, N.J.: Fairleigh Dickenson University Press, 1980. 521 pp., illus.

Fort McHenry: Home of the Brave. Norman G. Ruckert. Baltimore: Bodine and Associates, 1983. 120 pp., illus., biblio., index. $8.95 pb.

Fort Johnson, Amsterdam, New York: A Historic Structure Report, 1974–1975. Mendel-Mesick-Cohen. Washington, D.C.: U.S. Department of the Interior, 1978. 54 pp., illus., appends. $5 pb. GPO stock no. 024–005–00706–7.

Contacts

Council on America's Military Past
P.O. Box 171
Arlington, Va. 22210

U.S. Army Center of Military History
Washington, D.C. 20314

Naval Historical Center
Washington, D.C. 20374

Marine Corps Historical Center
Washington, D.C. 20380

U.S. Army Military History Institute
Carlisle Barracks, Pa. 17013

Navy and Old Army
National Archives and Records Service
Washington, D.C. 20408

National Park Service
U.S. Department of the Interior
Washington, D.C. 20013-7127

Gardens and Parks

"A study of a garden in a particular area becomes a complete study of a way of life in a particular time and place."

Mary Mackay Harvey. In *Bulletin*, Association for Preservation Technology, no. 2, 1975.

History

The Landscape of Man: Shaping the Environment from Prehistory to the Present Day. Geoffrey and Susan Jellicoe. 1975. New York: Van Nostrand Reinhold, 1983. 382 pp., illus., biblio., index. $19.95 pb.

Design on the Land: The Development of Landscape Architecture. Norman T. Newton. Cambridge: Harvard University Press, 1971. 714 pp., illus., biblio., index. $32.50 hb.

The Politics of Park Design: A History of Urban Parks in America. Galen Cranz. Cambridge: MIT Press, 1982. 361 pp., illus., biblio., index. $29.95 hb.

A History of Gardens. Christopher Thacker. Berkeley: University of California Press, 1979. 228 pp., illus., biblio., index. $35 hb.

A History of Gardens and Gardening. Edward Hyams. New York: Praeger, 1971. 345 pp., color illus., biblio., index.

History of Landscape Architecture from Western Traditions Since 1800. John A. Nelson. Chicago: Council of Planning Librarians, 1977. No. 1355. 15 pp. $1.50 pb.

History of Landscape Architecture: The Relationship of People to Environment. G. B. Tobey. New York: American Elsevier, 1973. 300 pp., illus., biblio., appends., index. $35.

Civilizing American Cities: A Selection of Frederick Law Olmsted's Writings on City Landscape. S. B. Sutton, ed. Cambridge: MIT Press, 1971. 310 pp., illus., index. $7.95 pb.

Early American Gardens: "For Meate and Medicine." Ann Leighton. Boston: Houghton Mifflin, 1970. 411 pp., illus. $14.95 hb.

American Gardens in the Eighteenth Century: "For Use or for Delight." Ann Leighton. Boston: Houghton Mifflin, 1976. 514 pp., illus., biblio., index. $17.50 hb.

Falmouth (Mass.) Historical Society garden summerhouse and boxwood. From *New England Gardens Open to the Public.* (© 1979 Cymie R. Payne)

Colonial Gardens. Rudy J. Favretti and Gordon P. DeWolf. Barre, Mass.: Barre Publishers, 1972. 163 pp., illus.

Colonial Kitchens: Their Furnishings and Their Gardens. Frances Phipps. New York: Hawthorn, 1972.

A Treatise on the Theory and Practice of Landscape Gardening Adapted to North America. Andrew Jackson Downing. 1875. Reprint. Little Compton, R.I.: Theophrastus (P.O. Box 458, 02837), 1981. 608 pp., illus. $20.

Victorian Gardens: The Art of Beautifying Suburban Home Grounds. Frank J. Scott. 1870. Reprint. Watkins Glen, N.Y.: American Life Foundation, 1977. 304 pp. $12 pb.

A Nineteenth Century Garden. Charles Van Ravenswaay. New York: Universe, 1977. 75 pp., color illus. $5.95 pb.

"Art Out-Of-Doors." American Gardens 1890–1930: A Selected Bibliography. Pittsburgh: Hunt Institute for Botanical Documentation and Winterthur Museum and Gardens, 1979. 16 pp. $3.

Biographies

FLO: A Biography of Frederick Law Olmsted. Laura Wood Roper. Baltimore: Johns Hopkins University Press, 1974. 573 pp., illus. $28.50 hb, $9.95 pb.

The Papers of Frederick Law Olmsted. Charles C. McLaughlin, ed. Baltimore: Johns Hopkins University Press. Vol. I: *The Formative Years, 1822–1852.* 1977. 423 pp. Vol. II: *Slavery and the South, 1852–1857.* Charles E. Beveridge and Charles C. McLaughlin, eds. 1981. 528 pp. $28.50 hb. Vol. III: *Creating Central Park, 1857–1861.* Charles E. Beveridge and David Schuyler, eds. 1983. 498 pp., illus. $28.50 hb.

Park Maker: A Life of Frederick Law Olmsted. Elizabeth Stevenson. New York: Macmillan, 1977. 484 pp., illus.

Frederick Law Olmsted and the American Environmental Tradition. Albert Fein. New York: Braziller, 1972. 180 pp., illus., appends., biblio., index. $7.95 pb.

Frederick Law Olmsted. John Emerson Todd. Boston: Twayne Publishers, 1982. 212 pp., biblio., index. $13.95 hb.

Frederick Law Olmsted and the Boston Park System. Cynthia Zaitzevsky. Cambridge: Harvard University Press, 1982. 272 pp., illus., index. $30 hb.

Frederick Law Olmsted's New York. Elizabeth Barlow, Whitney Museum. New York: Praeger, 1972. 173 pp., illus.

Thomas Jefferson, Landscape Architect. Frederick D. Nichols and Ralph E. Griswold. Charlottesville: University Press of Virginia, 1977. 196 pp., illus., biblio., index. $4.95 pb.

E. I. duPont, Botaniste: The Beginning of a Tradition. Norman B. Wilkinson. Charlottesville: University Press of Virginia, 1972. 139 pp., color illus., append. $7.50 hb, $3.95 pb.

Guides

A Guide to Significant and Historic Gardens of America. Mary Helen Ray and Robert P. Nichols, eds. Athens, Ga.: Garden Club of Georgia, 1983. $8.98 pb.

The Great Public Gardens of the Eastern United States: A Guide to Their Beauty and Botany. Doris M. Stone. New York: Pantheon, 1982. 300 pp., illus., gloss., biblio. $12.95 pb.

An Illustrated and Annotated Guide to New England Gardens Open to the Public. Rolce Redard Payne. Boston: Godine, 1979. 240 pp., illus., gloss., biblio., index.

Historic Virginia Gardens: Preservations by the Garden Club of Virginia. Dorothy H. Williams. Charlottesville: University Press of Virginia, 1975. 350 pp., color illus., biblio., append., index. $20 hb.

The Gardens and Grounds at Mount Vernon: How George Washington Planned and Planted Them. Elizabeth Kellam de Forest, Mount Vernon Ladies' Association of the Union. Charlottesville: University Press of Virginia, 1983. 116 pp., color illus. $17.95 hb, $8.95 pb.

Central Park: A Photographic Guide. Victor Laredo and Henry Hope Reed. New York: Dover, 1979. 78 pp., illus. $4.50 pb.

The Making of Golden Gate Park: The Early Years, 1865–1906. Raymond H. Clary. San Francisco: California Living Books, 1979. 208 pp., illus., maps. $25 hb, $10.95 pb.

Garden Structures
The Glass House. John Hix. Cambridge: MIT Press, 1974. 208 pp., illus., biblio., index. $9.95 pb.

The Greenhouse at Lyndhurst: Construction and Development of the Gould Greenhouse, 1881. Billie Sherrill Britz. Washington, D.C.: Preservation Press, 1977. 48 pp., illus. $5.50 pb.

Glasshouses and Wintergardens of the Nineteenth Century. Stefan Koppelkamm. New York: Rizzoli, 1981. 112 pp., illus.

Summerhouses of Virginia. Gwynn C. Prideaux. Richmond, Va.: Mary Wingfield Scott Fund, 1976. 143 pp., illus., biblio. $16.95 hb. Available from Valentine Museum Shop, 1015 East Clay Street, Richmond, Va. 23219.

Gazebos and Other Garden Structures. Janet A. and Richard H. Strombeck. Delafield, Wis.: Sun Designs (P.O. Box 157, 53018), 1983. 96 pp., illus. $7.95 pb.

Contacts
Alliance for Historic Landscape Preservation University of Oregon 216 Lawrence Hall Eugene, Ore. 97403

National Association for Olmsted Parks 175 Fifth Avenue New York, N.Y. 10010

American Society of Landscape Architects Historic Preservation Committee 1733 Connecticut Avenue, N.W. Washington, D.C. 20009

Society of Architectural Historians American Landscape and Garden History Society 1700 Walnut Street Suite 716 Philadelphia, Pa. 19103

Garden Clubs of America Conservation Committee 598 Madison Avenue New York, N.Y. 10022

National Council of State Garden Clubs Historic Preservation Committee 4401 Magnolia Avenue St. Louis, Mo. 63110

The Plaza (1907, Henry J. Hardenbergh), New York City, overlooking Central Park (1858–78, Olmsted and Vaux). (William J. McNamara)

Shell Station (1930–33, J. H. Glenn, Jr., and Bert L. Bennett), Winston-Salem, N.C. (Joann Sieburg, N.C. Division of Archives and History)

Association for Preservation Technology Chairman of Landscapes and Gardens P.O. Box 2487, Station D Ottawa, Ontario K1P 5W6, Canada

Landscape Architecture 1733 Connecticut Avenue, N.W. Washington, D.C. 20009

Central Park Conservancy 830 Fifth Avenue New York, N.Y. 10021

Dumbarton Oaks Center for Studies in the History of Landscape Architecture 1703 32nd Street, N.W. Washington, D.C. 20007

American Horticultural Society Mount Vernon, Va. 22121

Longwood Program Seminars University of Delaware Newark, Del. 19711

See also: Gardens and Landscaping: Restoring the Green (Rehabilitation and Restoration)

Gas Stations
"The gas station, the first structure built in response to the automobile, is undoubtedly the most widespread type of commercial building in America, and yet it is the most ignored. Its very ubiquity allows the motorist to screen out its image. . . . Echoing larger movements in architecture, gas stations are often the only examples of current design trends in areas isolated from the architectural mainstream."
Daniel Vieyra, *"Fill 'Er Up"*

"Fill 'Er Up": An Architectural History of America's Gas Stations. Daniel Vieyra. New York: Collier Books, Macmillan, 1979. 126 pp., color illus., biblio., index. $7.95 pb.

A New Life for the Abandoned Service Station. Albert L. Kerth. Massapequa Park, N.Y.: Author, 1974. 83 pp., illus. $15.

Successful Business Uses for Abandoned Service Stations. Albert L. Kerth. Washington Crossing, Pa.: Author (P.O. Box 321, 18977), 1982. 213 pp., illus. $35 hb.

Contact
Society for Commercial Archeology National Museum of American History Room 5010 Washington, D.C. 20560

See also: Roadside Architecture

Abandoned and deteriorated storefronts in the ghost town of Tombstone, Ariz., in 1940. (Russell Lee, Farm Security Administration)

Ghost Towns

"All the appointments and the appurtenances of a thriving and prosperous and promising young city—and now nothing is left of it but a lifeless, homeless solitude. The men are gone, the houses have vanished, even the name of the place is forgotten. In no other land, in modern times, have towns so absolutely died and disappeared."

Mark Twain, *Roughing It.* 1875.

Taken by the Wind: Vanishing Architecture of the West. Ronald Woodall and T. H. Watkins. Boston: New York Graphic Society, 1977. 256 pp., color illus.

Magnificent Derelicts: A Celebration of Older Buildings. Ronald Woodall. 1975. Seattle: University of Washington Press. 152 pp., color illus., index. $29.95 hb.

Ghost Towns: A Selected Bibliography. Mary Vance. Monticello, Ill.: Vance Bibliographies, 1979. A-63. 4 pp. $1.50 pb.

A Guide to Western Ghost Towns. Lambert Florin. Seattle: Superior, 1978. 96 pp., illus., maps. $4.95 pb.

Ghost Towns of the West: A Pictorial Guide to Towns and Mining Camps that Opened the West. William G. Carter. 1971. 2nd ed. Menlo Park, Calif.: Lane, 1978. 255 pp., color illus., biblio., index.

Ghost Towns Series: California. $18.95. *Idaho.* $13.95. *Montana.* $9.95. *Nevada.* $18.95. *Wyoming.* $7.50 pb. *Washington and Oregon.* Donald C. Miller. Boulder, Colo.: Pruett, 1974–79.

Helldorados, Ghosts and Camps of the Old Southwest. Norman D. Weis. Caldwell, Idaho: Caxton, 1977. 361 pp., illus., biblio., index. $9.95 hb.

Ghost Towns of the Northwest. Norman D. Weis. Caldwell, Idaho: Caxton, 1971. $11.95.

Abandoned New England: Its Hidden Ruins and Where to Find Them. William F. Robinson. Boston: New York Graphic Society, 1976. 240 pp., illus., appends., biblio., index. $12.95 pb.

Dead Towns of Alabama. W. Stuart Harris. University, Ala.: University of Alabama Press, 1977. 176 pp., illus., biblio. $9.95 hb.

Ghost Towns of Alaska. Mary Balcom. 1965. 6th ed. Chicago: Adams, 1982. 90 pp., illus. $3.75.

Arizona's Best Ghost Towns: A Practical Guide. Philip Varney. Flagstaff, Ariz.: Northland Press, 1980. 231 pp., illus., appends., biblio., index. $19.95 hb.

Ghost Towns of Arizona. James E. and Barbara H. Sherman. Norman: University of Oklahoma Press, 1977. $18.95 hb, $9.95 pb.

Ghosts of the Adobe Walls. Nell Murbarger. Tucson, Ariz.: Treasure Chest Publications (P.O. Box 5250, 85703), 1963. 398 pp., illus., append., index. $9.95 hb.

California Gold Towns. Lambert Florin. Seattle: Superior, 1971.

Stampede to Timberline: The Ghost Towns and Mining Camps of Colorado. Muriel Sibell Wolle. 2nd rev. ed. Athens, Ohio: Swallow Press, 1974. 583 pp., illus., gloss., index. $24.95 hb.

Colorado Ghost Towns and Mining Camps. Sandra Dallas. Norman: University of Oklahoma Press, 1985. 264 pp., illus. $24.95 hb.

Ghosts of the Colorado Plains. Perry Eberhart. Athens, Ohio: Swallow Press, 1984. $25.95 hb.

The Dead Towns of Georgia. Charles C. Jones, Jr. 1878. Reprint. Covington, Ga.: Cherokee Publishing Company, 1974. 263 pp. $10.

Mining Town: The Photographic Record of T. N. Barnard and Nellie Stockbridge from the Coeur d'Alenes. Patricia Hart and Ivar Nelson. Seattle: University of Washington Press, 1984. 192 pp., illus. $24.95.

Ghost Towns of Idaho. Idaho Chapter, AIA. Boise: Author (842 La Lassia Drive, 83705) 1979. $5.50.

Montana Pay Dirt: A Guide to the Mining Camps of the Treasure State. Muriel Sibell Wolle. Athens, Ohio: Swallow Press, 1963. 410 pp., illus., biblio., index. $19.95 hb.

A Guide to the Ghost Towns and Mining Camps of Nye County, Nevada. Shawn Hall. New York: Dodd, Mead, 1981. 256 pp., illus., biblio., index. $12.95 pb.

Gold Cities: Grass Valley and Nevada City. A History and Guide. Jim Morley and Doris Foley. 1965. 2nd ed. San Diego: Howell-North, 1980. 96 pp., illus. $9.95 hb, $3.50 pb.

Haunted Highways: The Ghost Towns of New Mexico. Ralph Looney. Albuquerque: University of New Mexico Press, 1979. 220 pp., illus., biblio., index. $9.95 pb.

New Mexico's Best Ghost Towns: A Practical Guide. Philip Varney. Flagstaff: Northland Press, 1981. 204 pp., color illus., gloss., biblio., append. $19.95 hb, $12.95 pb.

Ghost Towns and Mining Camps of New Mexico. James E. and Barbara H. Sherman. Norman: University of Oklahoma Press, 1975. 270 pp., illus. $19.95 hb, $10.95 pb.

Ghost Towns of Oklahoma. John W. Morris. Norman: University of Oklahoma Press, 1978. 229 pp., illus., biblio., index. $18.95 hb, $11.95 pb.

Deadwood: The Golden Years. Watson Parker. Lincoln: University of Nebraska Press, 1981. 334 pp., illus. $24 hb, $10.95 pb.

Black Hills Ghost Towns. Watson Parker and Hugh K. Lambert. Athens, Ohio: Swallow Press, 1974. 216 pp., illus., maps, biblio. $21.95 hb, $11.95 pb.

Ghost Towns and Mining Camps: Selected Papers. Washington, D.C.: Preservation Press, 1977. 38 pp., illus.

Contacts

Montana Ghost Town Preservation Society
P.O. Box 1861
Bozeman, Mont. 59715

Western Montana Ghost Town Preservation Society
P.O. Box 2245
Missoula, Mont. 59801

National Park Service
U.S. Department of the Interior
Washington, D.C. 20013-7127

An early 20th-century traveler following the old Natchez Trace Parkway. (National Archives)

Highways and Roads

"If Americans agreed in any opinion, they were united in wishing for roads."

Henry Adams

Americans on the Road: From Autocamp to Motel, 1910–1945. Warren James Belasco. Cambridge: MIT Press, 1979. 212 pp., illus., biblio., index. $25 hb, $6.95 pb.

Route 1: The First Super Highway. Mark McGarrity. Chester, Conn.: Globe Pequot Press, 1980. 280 pp., illus.

U.S. One: Maine to Florida. Federal Writers' Project. 1938. Reprint. St. Claire Shores, Mich.: Somerset Publishers (22929 Industrial Drive East, 48080), 1972. 344 pp., $39.

U.S. 40 Today: Thirty Years of Landscape Change in America. Thomas R. and Geraldine R. Vale. Madison: University of Wisconsin Press, 1983. 208 pp., illus. $27.50 hb, $14.95 pb.

Historic American Roads. Albert C. Rose. New York: Crown, 1976. $12.95 hb.

Historic Highways of America. Archer Hulbert. 1905. Reprint. New York: AMS Press, 1971. 16 vols. $27.50 each, $440 set.

Our Vanishing Landscape. Eric Sloane. New York: Ballantine, 1975. 110 pp., illus. $4.95 pb.

A Nation in Motion: Historic American Transportation Sites. Washington, D.C.: U.S. Department of Transportation (Office of Environmental Affairs, Department of Transportation, Washington, D.C. 20590), 1976. 133 pp., illus.

Pictorial Americana: The National Road. Harry G. Black. Hammond, Ind.: HMB Publications (7406 Monroe Avenue, 46324), 1984. $4.95 pb.

A History of Roads. Geoffrey Hindley. Seacaucus, N.J.: Citadel Press, 1972. $4.95 pb.

America Adopts the Automobile, 1895–1910. James J. Flink. Cambridge: MIT Press, 1970. $22.50 hb.

Adventures Along Interstate 80: A Guide to Nature and History Along the Pioneer and Gold Rush Corridor from San Francisco to Nevada. John Olmsted and Eleanor Huggins. Palo Alto, Calif.: Tioga Publishing (Box 98, 94302), 1984.

U.S. 40: A Roadscape of the American Experience. Thomas J. Schlereth. Indianapolis: Indiana Historical Society, 1985. 150 pp. $13.95 pb.

Contacts

Society for Commercial Archeology
National Museum of American History
Room 2010
Washington, D.C. 20560

Park Superintendent
Natchez Trace Parkway
Rural Route 1, NT-143
Tupelo, Miss. 38801

Park Superintendent
Blue Ridge Parkway
700 Northwestern Bank Building
Asheville, N.C. 28801

Federal Highway Administration
U.S. Department of Transportation
Washington, D.C. 20591

The National Road/Zane Grey Museum
8850 East Pike
Norwich, Ohio 43767

See also: Roadside Architecture, Trails; Taking Action

Hospitals

"The physical stature of man was basic. From it could be determined the proper size of a hospital bed. . . . The sick man's gait determined the design and construction of staircases. The variety of human ailment governed the location of wards within the hospitals."

Louis S. Greenbaum, "'Measure of Civilization.'" *Bulletin of the History of Medicine,* Spring 1975.

The Hospital: A Social and Architectural History. John D. Thompson and Grace Goldin. New Haven: Yale University Press, 1975. 349 pp., illus., append., biblio., index.

The Nation Builds for Those Who Served: An Introduction to the Architectural Heritage of the Veterans Administration. Washington, D.C.: Veterans Administration and the National Building Museum, 1980. 31 pp., illus.

The Discovery of the Asylum: Social Order and Disorder in the New Republic. David J. Rothman. Boston: Little Brown, 1971.

Contacts

Historic Preservation Office
Veterans Administration
Washington, D.C. 20420

American Hospital Association
840 North Lake Shore Drive
Chicago, Ill. 60611

Old Johns Hopkins Hospital (1877–85, John Niernsee and Cabot and Chandler), Baltimore, a Gothic Revival complex, in 1903. (M. E. Warren)

The Chalfonte (1876), Cape May, N.J., a rambling Italianate hotel in this seaside resort.

Hotels and Inns

"The history of the American inn and tavern runs parallel to the history of American transportation. The early inns on the postroads derived much of their trade from horsemen and stagecoaches. Inns lined the canals for the patronage of the bargemen and their passengers. Wagon trains to the West made regular stops at taverns along the trail. Later steamers, railroads, and the automobile created the inns and taverns along ports, railroads, and highways to accommodate the weary traveller."

Irvin Haas, *America's Historic Inns and Taverns*

History

America's Grand Resort Hotels. Jeffrey W. Limerick, Nancy Ferguson and Richard Oliver. New York: Pantheon, 1979. 303 pp., illus. $20 hb.

The Last of the Grand Hotels. Jack J. Kramer. New York: Van Nostrand Reinhold, 1978. 156 pp., color illus., index. $24.95 hb.

The Palace Inns: A Connoisseur's Guide to Historic American Hotels. Brian McGinty. Harrisburg, Pa.: Stackpole Books, 1978. 192 pp., illus., biblio., index. $9.95 pb.

America's Historic Inns and Taverns. Irvin Haas. Rev. ed. New York: Arco, 1977. 192 pp.

The Greatest of Them All: The Waldorf-Astoria. Frank Farrell. Introduction by Lowell Thomas. New York: Frederick Fell, 1982. 176 pp., illus. $8.95.

America's Grand Hotels. Rod Fensom. Charlotte, N.C.: East Woods Press, 1985. 250 pp., illus. $10.95 pb.

The City at the End of the Rainbow: San Francisco and Its Grand Hotels. David Siefkin. New York: Putnam, 1976. 256 pp., illus.

Historic Alabama Hotels and Resorts. James F. Sulzby, Jr. University, Ala.: University of Alabama Press, 1960. 294 pp., illus., biblio., index. $14.95 hb.

Rehabilitating Historic Hotels: Peabody Hotel, Memphis, Tennessee. Floy A. Brown. Washington, D.C.: U.S. Department of the Interior, 1980. 43 pp., illus., biblio. $3.50 pb. GPO stock no. 024–016–00142–7.

A Different World: Stories of Great Hotels. Christopher Matthew. New York: Bookthrift, 1976. 352 pp., illus. $9.98.

Guidebooks

Country Inns Series: California, Pacific Northwest, New England, New York State, Mid-Atlantic, Old South, Great Lakes. San Franciso: 101 Productions. $7.95 pb.

Country Inns of America Series: Southeast, Great Lakes, South, Southwest, California, Pacific Northwest. New York: Holt, Rinehart and Winston, 1981–83. $8.95–12.95 pb.

The Morrow Book of Havens and Hideaways: A Guide to America's Unique Lodgings. Thomas Tracy and James O. Ward. New York: William Morrow, 1980. 448 pp., illus., maps, index. $12.95 hb, $6.95 pb.

Country Inns of America: Upper New England and *Lower New England.* Roberta Gardner et al. New York: Holt, Rinehart and Winston, 1985. $10.95 pb each.

Country Inns and Back Roads, North America. Norman T. Simpson. Stockbridge, Mass.: Berkshire Traveller Press, 1984. 480 pp., illus., index. $9.95 pb.

America's Wonderful Little Hotels and Inns. Barbara Crosette, ed. 3rd ed. New York: Congdon and Weed, 1982. 496 pp., illus., maps. $12.95.

The New England Guest House Book. Corinne Madden Ross. 1979. 3rd ed. Charlotte, N.C.: East Woods Press, 1984. 207 pp., illus. $7.95 pb.

The Southern Guest House Book. Corinne Madden Ross. 1981. 2nd rev. ed. Charlotte, N.C.: East Woods Press, 1984. 185 pp., illus. $7.95 pb.

Inns of the Southern Mountains. McLean, Va.: EPM Publications, 1985. $9.95.

Historic Country Inns of California. Jim Crain. 1977. Rev. ed. San Francisco: Chronicle Books, 1984. 167 pp., illus., index. $8.95 pb.

Small Hotels of California. Bill Gleeson. San Francisco: Chronicle Books, 1984. 134 pp., illus., index. $7.95 pb.

Bed and Breakfast U.S.A.: A Guide to Tourist Homes and Guest Houses. Betty Rundback and Nancy Ackerman. New York: Dutton, 1983. 297 pp. $5.95 pb.

Bed and Breakfast, American Style. Norman T. Simpson. Stockbridge, Mass.: Berkshire Traveller Press, 1984. 402 pp., illus. $10.95 pb.

The California Bed and Breakfast Book. Kathy Strong. Charlotte, N.C.: East Woods Press, 1984. 182 pp., illus. $7.95 pb.

Bed and Breakfast: The Pacific Northwest. Myrna Oakley. San Francisco: Chronicle Books, 1984. 132 pp., illus. $7.95 pb.

Contacts

Hotel-Motel Association
888 Seventh Avenue
New York, N.Y. 10019

Hotel and Motel Management Magazine
757 Third Avenue
New York, N.Y. 10017

American Historic Homes
Bed and Breakfast
P.O. Box 388
San Juan Capistrano, Calif. 92693

See also: Resorts and Spas, Taverns and Saloons

Lobby, Old Faithful Inn (1903, Robert C. Reamer), Yellowstone National Park, Wyo., in 1905. (Detroit Photographic Collection, Library of Congress)

Houseboats in the cove between Belvedere and Corinthian islands near San Francisco in 1892. (San Francisco Maritime Museum)

Houseboats

"It is not known who first conceived the idea of the California ark but the shape it took was much the same as the one Noah built in obedience to the Lord's commandment, little thinking he was starting a fashion that would come sailing down the rivers of the world to the present time."

The Strand, 1899.

Houseboats: Living on the Water Around the World. Mark Gabor. New York: Ballantine, 1979. 128 pp., color illus. $17.95 hb, $8.95 pb.

Houseboat: Reflections of North America's Floating Homes . . . History, Architecture, and Lifestyles. Ben Dennis and Betsy Case. Seattle: Smuggler's Cove Publishing (107 West John Street, 98119), 1977. 122 pp., color illus. $14.95 hb, $9.95 pb.

"Neighborhood Preservation as an Ecology Issue," Stewart Brand. *Co-Evolution Quarterly*, Fall 1977. $3 pb. Box 428, Sausalito, Calif. 94965.

"Venerable Arks Ride the Tides," Phil Frank. *Historic Preservation*, July–September 1978.

Houseboats. Daniel L. Schodek. Cambridge, Mass.: Harvard Graduate School of Design (Department of Architecture, Gund Hall, 48 Quincy Street, 02138), 1980. A-7902. 22 pp., illus., biblio. $3 pb.

The Complete Guide to Houseboating. John W. Malo. New York: Macmillan, 1974.

Water Squatters. E. Beverly Dubin. Santa Barbara, Calif.: Capra Press, 1975.

Houses

"Our house was not unsentient matter—it had a heart, and a soul, and eyes to see us with. . . . We never came home from an absence that its face did not light up and speak out its eloquent welcome—and we could not enter it unmoved."

Mark Twain

Architecture, Ambition, and Americans: A Social History of American Architecture. Wayne Andrews. 1955. Rev. ed. New York: Free Press, Macmillan, 1978. 334 pp., illus., biblio., index. $24.95 hb, $12.95 pb.

A Field Guide to American Houses. Virginia and Lee McAlester. New York: Knopf, 1984. 542 pp., illus., index. $19.95 pb.

American Shelter: An Illustrated Encyclopedia of the American Home. Lester Walker. Preface by Charles Moore. New York: Overlook Press, Viking, 1981. 320 pp., illus. $27.95 hb.

The American House. Mary Mix Foley. New York: Harper and Row, 1981. 300 pp., illus., index. $14.95 pb.

Traditional house pattern for quilts. (Kathy Fidler)

The Place of Houses. Charles W. Moore, Donlyn Lyndon and Gerald Allen. 1974. Rev. ed. New York: Holt, Rinehart and Winston, 1979. 288 pp., illus., index. $8.95 pb.

The Form of Housing. Sam Davis, ed. New York: Van Nostrand Reinhold, 1977. 299 pp., illus., biblio. $24.50 hb.

Evolution of the House. Stephen Gardiner. 1974. Reprint. Chicago: Academy Chicago, 1980. 302 pp., illus., append., index. $5.95 pb.

The Palace or the Poorhouse: The American House as Cultural Symbol. Jan Cohn. East Lansing: Michigan State University Press, 1979. 300 pp., illus., biblio., index. $15 hb.

The House and the Art of Its Design. Robert Woods Kennedy. 1953. Reprint. Huntington, N.Y.: Robert E. Krieger Publishing, 1975. 550 pp., illus., biblio., index. $22.50 pb.

Home Sweet Home: American Domestic Vernacular Architecture. Charles W. Moore, Kathryn Smith and Peter Becker, eds. Craft and Folk Art Museum. New York: Rizzoli, 1983. 150 pp., illus. $17.50 pb.

Wood, Brick and Stone: The North American Settlement Landscape. Allen G. Noble. Vol. I: *Houses.* Amherst: University of Massachusetts Press, 1984. 166 pp., illus., index. $27.50 hb.

The American Home: Architecture and Society, 1815–1915. David P. Handlin. Boston: Little, Brown, 1979. 545 pp., illus., biblio., index. $20 hb.

The Architecture of Country Houses. Andrew Jackson Downing. 1850. Reprint, New York: Dover, 1969. 501 pp., illus. $6.50 pb.

The Natural House. Frank Lloyd Wright. New York: Horizon, 1954. 221 pp., illus. $11.95 hb.

The Grand Domestic Revolution: A History of Feminist Designs for American Homes, Neighborhoods, and Cities. Dolores Hayden. Cambridge: MIT Press, 1981. 384 pp., illus. $19.95 hb, $9.95 pb.

The Home: Its Work and Influence. Charlotte Perkins Gilman. 1903. Reprint. Urbana: University of Illinois Press, 1978. 347 pp.

New Space for Women. Gerda R. Wekerle, Rebecca Peterson and David Morley, eds. Boulder, Colo.: Westview Press, 1980. 352 pp., illus., biblio. $32 hb, $15 pb.

Moralism and the Model Home: Domestic Architecture and Cultural Conflict in Chicago, 1873–1913. Gwendolyn Wright. Chicago: University of Chicago Press, 1980. 384 pp., illus., biblio., index. $17.50 hb.

Building the Dream: A Social History of Housing in America. Gwendolyn Wright. New York: Pantheon, 1981. $18.50 hb.

The Fall of a Doll's House: Three Generations of American Women and the Houses They Lived In. Jane Davison. New York: Avon, 1981. 256 pp., biblio., index. $3.50 pb.

See also: Apartment Buildings, Estates, Row Houses

Industrial Structures

"No single building type exists in a greater profusion of scales, styles, shapes, materials and other variables than industrial structures. This nearly limitless variation is due to the equally limitless nature of industry itself, which ranges from the infinitely delicate—plants no larger than houses—to massive, amorphously styled mills (not to mention 'public' industrial buildings such as railroad stations and others, which process mainly people.)"

Robert M. Vogel, "Industrial Structures." In *Built in the U.S.A.*

Industrial Archeology: A New Look at the American Heritage. Theodore Anton Sande. 1976. New York: Penguin Books, 1978. 152 pp., illus., append.

Traces of the Past: A Field Guide to Industrial Archeology. David Weitzman. New York: Scribner's, 1980. 229 pp., illus., index.

An Introductory Bibliography in Industrial Archeology. David R. Starbuck, ed. Washington, D.C.: Society for Industrial Archeology, 1983. 15 pp.

The Archaeology of Industry. Kenneth Hudson. New York: Scribner's, 1976. 128 pp., illus., biblio., index.

World Industrial Archaeology. Kenneth Hudson. Cambridge, England: Cambridge University Press, 1979. 247 pp., illus., biblio., index. $49.50 hb, $15.50 pb.

Working Places: The Adaptive Use of Industrial Buildings. Walter Kidney. Pittsburgh: Ober Park Associates (One Station Square, 15219), 1976. 169 pp., illus., index. $8 pb.

Historic Preservation of Engineering Works. Emory L. Kemp and Theodore Anton Sande, eds. New York: American Society of Civil Engineers, 1981. 321 pp., illus. $29 pb.

The Mill Works Handbook. Northeast Regional Office, National Trust for Historic Preservation. Washington, D.C.: Preservation Press, 1983. 250 pp., illus., appends. $24.95 binder.

The Techniques of Industrial Archaeology. J. P. M. Pannell. 2nd ed. J. Kenneth Major, ed. North Pomfret, Vt.: David and Charles, 1974. 200 pp., illus., biblio.

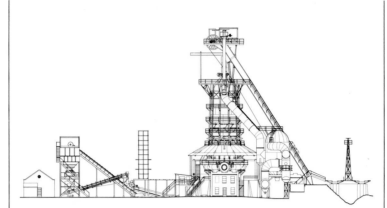

Sloss-Sheffield Steel and Iron Company Furnaces (1902–64), Birmingham, Ala. (James Hunt, HAER)

Rehabilitation: An Alternative for Historic Industrial Buildings. Selma Thomas, ed. Washington, D.C.: Historic American Engineering Record, U.S. Department of the Interior, 1978. 182 pp., illus., appends.

Bibliography of the History of Technology. Eugene S. Ferguson. Society for the History of Technology Series, no. 5. Cambridge: MIT Press, 1968. 347 pp. Updated annually in *Technology and Culture* (University of Chicago Press).

Technology and Society Series. New York: Arno Press.

The American Civil Engineer 1852–1974. William H. Wisely. New York: American Society of Civil Engineers, 1974. 464 pp., index. $20.

A Biographical Dictionary of American Civil Engineers. American Society of Civil Engineers, Committee on History and Heritage of American Civil Engineering. Historical Publication no. 2. New York: ASCE, 1972. 163 pp., illus., biblio., notes, index.

History of Public Works in the United States, 1776–1976. Ellis L. Armstrong, ed. Chicago: American Public Works Association, 1976. 736 pp., illus., biblio., index. $20 hb.

Public Works History in the United States: A Guide to the Literature. Suellen M. Hoy and Michael C. Robinson, eds. Nashville: American Association for State and Local History, 1982. 512 pp., index. $50 hb.

America in Ruins: The Decaying Infrastructure. Pat Choate and Susan Walter, Council of State Planning Agencies. Durham, N.C.: Duke University Press, 1981. 116 pp., biblio., index. $9.75 pb.

Designing for Industry: The Architecture of Albert Kahn. Grant Hildebrand. Cambridge: MIT Press, 1974. 232 pp., illus., biblio., index.

Industry and the Photographic Image: 153 Great Prints from 1850 to the Present. F. Jack Hurley, ed., George Eastman House. New York: Dover, 1980. 150 pp., illus. $7.95 pb.

Detroit: An Industrial History Guide. Charles K. Hyde, Detroit Historical Society. Detroit: Wayne State University Press, 1981. 72 pp., illus. $5 pb.

Connecticut: An Inventory of Historic Engineering and Industrial Sites. Matthew Roth. Washington, D.C.: Society for Industrial Archeology, 1981. 279 pp.

Rehabilitation: Fairmount Waterworks 1978, Conservation and Recreation in a National Historic Landmark. Washington, D.C.: Historic American Engineering Record, U.S. Department of the Interior, 1979. 35 pp., illus., append.

Industrial Landscape. David Plowden. New York: W. W. Norton, 1985. $39.95 hb.

Pig iron kiln near Escanaba, Mich., constructed of stone and brick with towers creating the effect of a fortress. (Balthazar Korab)

Inventories of Historic Engineering and Industrial Sites Series. Historic American Engineering Record.

Contacts

Society for Industrial
Archeology
National Museum of
American History
Room 5020
Washington, D.C. 20560

Historic American Engineering
Record
National Park Service
U.S. Department of the Interior
Washington, D.C. 20013-7127

Northeast Regional Office
National Trust for Historic
Preservation
45 School Street
Boston, Mass. 02108

Public Works Historical Society
1313 East 60th Street
Chicago, Ill. 60637

American Society of Civil
Engineers
345 East 47th Street
New York, N.Y. 10017

Society for the History of
Technology
c/o Department of History
University of California
Santa Barbara, Calif. 93106

Early American Industries
Association
P.O. Box 2128
Empire State Plaza Station
Albany, N.Y. 12220

See also: Bridges, Company
Towns, Mills, Windmills

Jazz Sites

"Jazz has very few landmarks. It simply 'happened' at parades, funerals, and parties, on the decks of riverboats, and in forgotten social halls, bars, churches, backyards, and bordellos."

> Mary Cable, *Lost New Orleans.*
> 1980. New York: Crown, 1984.

"The Gift of Song." In *Exploring Black America: A History and Guide.* Marcella Thum. New York: Atheneum, 1975. 402 pp., illus., index. $10.95 hb.

Story of Jazz. Marshall W. Stearns. New York: Oxford University Press, 1970. $19.95 hb.

The Encyclopedia of Jazz. Leonard Feather. New York: Horizon. $20 hb.

Jazz Text. Charles Nanry. 1979. Reprint. New Brunswick, N.J.: Transaction Books, 1982. $9.95 pb.

Jazz City: The Impact of Our Cities on the Development of Jazz. Leroy Ostransky. Englewood Cliffs, N.J.: Prentice-Hall, 1978. $11.95 hb, $5.95 pb.

New Orleans Jazz: A Family Album. Al Rose and Edmund Souchon. 1978. 3rd ed. Baton Rouge: Louisiana State University Press, 1984. 416 pp., illus. $35 hb, $19.95 pb.

Storyville, New Orleans: Being an Authentic Illustrated Account of the Notorious Red Light District. Al Rose. University: University of Alabama Press, 1974. 256 pp., illus., biblio., appends., index. $12.50 pb.

Jazz Style in Kansas City and the Southwest. Ross Russell. Berkeley: University of California Press, 1971. $22.50 hb, $8.95 pb.

Beale Black and Blue: Life and Music on Black America's Main Street. Margaret McKee and Fred Chisenhall. Baton Rouge: Louisiana State University Press, 1981. 274 pp., illus. $17.95 hb.

"Black Men in a White World: The Development of the Black Jazz Community in Detroit, 1917–1940," Lars Bjorn. *Detroit in Perspective: A Journal of Regional History,* Fall 1980.

Mr. Jellyroll: The Fortunes of Jellyroll Morton, New Orleans Creole and 'Inventor.' Alan Lomax. Berkeley: University of California Press, 1973.

Contacts

William Ransom Hogan Jazz
Archive
c/o Howard-Tilton Memorial
Library
Tulane University
New Orleans, La. 70118

Institute of Jazz Studies
Rutgers University
Newark, N.J. 07102

New Orleans Jazz Club
4635 Dryades Street
New Orleans, La. 70117

Archives of Traditional Music
Indiana University
Maxwell Hall 057
Bloomington, Ind. 47405

National Music Council
250 West 54th Street
Room 300
New York, N.Y. 10019

The Schomburg Center for
Research in Black Culture
103 West 135th Street
New York, N.Y. 10030

Radial roof trussing, Gasholder House (1873, Frederick A. Sabbaton), Gas Light Company, Troy, N.Y. (Jack E. Boucher, HAER)

Members of the Olympia Brass Band serenading listeners in New Orleans. (Carleton Knight III, NTHP)

Door of Chasam Sopher Synagogue (1853), the second oldest in New York City. From *The Synagogues of New York's Lower East Side.* (Jo Renee Fine)

Jewish Landmarks

"There has never been an accepted form of architecture identified exclusively with the synagogue. It has always tended to reflect the community, the era and society in which it developed."

Oscar Israelowitz, *Synagogues of New York City*

American Jewish Landmarks: A Travel Guide and History. Bernard Postal and Lionel Koppman. New York: Fleet Press. Vol. I: *The Northeast.* 672 pp., index. $18.50 hb, $11.50 pb. Vol. II: *The South and the Southwest.* 334 pp., index. $14.95 hb, $7.50 pb. Vol. III: *The Middlewest.* 287 pp., index. $20.95 hb, $12.50 pb. Vol. IV: *The West.* 416 pp., index. $20 hb, $12.50 pb.

How We Lived: A Documentary History of Immigrant Jews in America, 1880–1930. Irving Howe and Kenneth Libo. New York: Richard Marek, Putnam, 1979. $22.50.

We Lived There Too: A Documentary History of Pioneer Jews and the Westward Movement of America, 1630–1930. Kenneth Libo and Irving Howe. New York: St. Martin's, 1984. $24.95.

The Synagogue. Brian de-Breffny. Photographs by George Mott. New York: Macmillan, 1978. 215 pp., illus., gloss., biblio., index.

Two Hundred Years of American Synagogue Architecture. Carl I. Belz, Bernard Wax, Gerald Bernstein, Gary Tinterow et al. Waltham, Mass.: American Jewish Historical Society, 1976.

The Synagogues of New York's Lower East Side. Gerald R. Wolfe and Jo Renee Fine. Introduction by Harry Golden. New York: New York University Press, 1978. 172 pp., illus. $19.95 hb, $10.95 pb.

Synagogues of New York City: A Pictorial Survey in 123 Photographs. Oscar Israelowitz. New York: Dover, 1982. 94 pp., illus. $6 pb.

The Preservation of Churches, Synagogues and Other Religious Structures. Richard S. Armstrong. Information Series, National Trust for Historic Preservation. Washington, D.C.: Preservation Press, 1978. 27 pp., illus., biblio. $2 pb.

Jewish Agricultural Utopias in America, 1880–1910. Uri D. Herscher. Detroit: Wayne State University Press, 1981. 198 pp., illus., append., biblio., index. $15.95 hb.

The Lower East Side: A Guide to Its Jewish Past in 99 New Photographs. Ronald Sanders and Edmund V. Gillon, Jr. New York: Dover, 1979. 96 pp., illus. $4.50 pb.

Jewish Landmarks in New York. Bernard Postal and Lionel Koppman. New York: Fleet Press, 1978. 288 pp. $13.95 hb. (Taken from *American Jewish Landmarks,* vol. I.)

"Preservation of Jewish Landmarks in California," Seymour Fromer, Judah Magnes Museum. Paper presented to College Art Association, 1981. Abstract available from CAA, 16 East 52nd Street, New York, N.Y. 10022.

Contacts

American Jewish Historical Society
2 Thornton Road
Waltham, Mass. 02154

American Jewish Archives
3101 Clifton Avenue
Cincinnati, Ohio 45220

Libraries

"Libraries have been in existence since around 2000 B.C. and were evident in the United States from the early colonial period. . . . However, it was not until about 100 years ago that libraries began to be built in great numbers in separate buildings. Andrew Carnegie stimulated library development through his funding of 1,679 public library buildings in 1,412 communities as well as 108 academic library buildings, primarily during the period 1897–1917. Of the approximately 15,000 library buildings in the United States, half have been built since World War II."

George S. Bobinski, "Libraries."
In *Built in the U.S.A.*

The Great Libraries of America: A Pictorial History. Alan F. Pater and Jason R. Pater, eds. Beverly Hills, Calif.: Monitor Book Company (195 South Beverly Drive, 90212), 1981. $35.

Carnegie Libraries: Their History and Impact on American Public Library Development. George S. Bobinski. Chicago: American Library Association, 1969. 257 pp. $10.

The Best Gift: A Record of Carnegie Libraries in Ontario. Margaret Beckman, Stephen Langmead and John Black. Toronto: Dundurn Press, 1984. 192 pp., illus. $29.95 hb.

The Library of Congress: Its Architecture and Decoration. Herbert Small. Henry Hope Reed, ed. Foreword by Daniel J. Boorstin. 1901. Rev. ed. New York: W. W. Norton, 1982. Classical America Series. 215 pp., color illus., gloss., append., index. $19.95 hb, $6.50 pb.

Ten First Street, Southeast: Congress Builds a Library, 1886–1897. Helen-Anne Hilker. Library of Congress. Washington, D.C.: U.S. Government Printing Office, 1980. 102 pp., illus., biblio. $4.75 pb. Stock no. LC 12: C76/9.

Treasures of the Library of Congress. Charles A. Goodrum. New York: Harry N. Abrams, 1980. 318 pp., illus.

A Handbook to the Art and Architecture of the Boston Public Library. Peter A. Wick. Boston: Boston Public Library (P.O. Box 286, 02117), 1978. 62 pp., illus. $2.

Guidelines for the Preservation, Restoration and Alterations to the Central Library of Los Angeles. Los Angeles: Southern California Chapter/AIA Library Study Team, 1978. 126 pp., illus.

Contact

American Library Association
Architecture for Public Libraries Committee
50 East Huron Street
Chicago, Ill. 60611

Carnegie Library (1901), Guthrie, Okla., one of 1,679 supported by Andrew Carnegie. (Julian Smith, HABS)

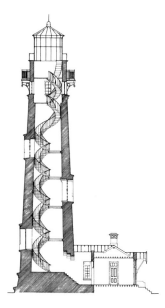

Pigeon Point Lighthouse (1872), San Mateo, Calif. (HABS)

Lighthouses

"Nothing indicates the liberality, prosperity or intelligence of a nation more clearly than the facilities which it affords for the safe approach of the mariner to its shores."

Report of the Lighthouse Board, 1868.

America's Lighthouses: Their Illustrated History Since 1716. Francis Ross Holland, Jr. 1972. Rev. ed. Brattleboro, Vt.: Stephen Greene Press, 1981. 226 pp., illus., append., biblio., index. $19.95 pb.

The Lighthouse. Dudley Witney. Boston: New York Graphic Society, 1975. 256 pp., illus., biblio.

Lighthouses and Lightships. Christine E. Moe. Monticello, Ill.: Vance Bibliographies, 1979. A-145. 11 pp. $2 pb.

The Lighthouses of New England. Edward Rowe Snow. New York: Dodd, Mead, 1984. $9.95 pb.

The Lighthouses of the Chesapeake. Robert de Gast. Baltimore: Johns Hopkins University Press, 1973. 170 pp., illus., biblio. $15 hb.

Reef Lights: Seaswept Lighthouses of the Florida Keys. Love Dean. Key West, Fla.: Historic Key West Preservation Board (Monroe County Courthouse, 33040), 1982. 134 pp., illus. $9.95 pb.

Lighthouses of San Francisco Bay. Ralph C. Shanks, Jr., and Janetta Thompson Shanks. San Anselmo, Calif.: Costano Books (Box 791, 94960), 1976. 126 pp., illus., biblio.

Lighthouses and Lifeboats on the Redwood Coast. Ralph C. Shanks, Jr., and Janetta Thompson Shanks. San Anselmo, Calif.: Costano Books, 1978. 255 pp., illus., biblio., gloss. $19.95 hb, $8.95 pb.

"Historically Famous Lighthouses." Washington, D.C.: U.S. Coast Guard Public Information Division. 88 pp., illus.

Contacts

United States
Lighthouse Society
130 St. Elmo Way
San Francisco, Calif. 94127

U.S. Coast Guard
Public Information Division
Washington, D.C. 20590

Chesapeake Bay Maritime Museum
Box 636
St. Michaels, Md. 21663

See also: Maritime Sites, Waterfronts

Log Buildings

"In the generations from the beginning of the westward movement until the beginning of Republican/Democratic government, the log cabin became a symbol of the self-reliance, the courage, and the ingenuity of the American people."

Alex W. Bealer and John O. Ellis, *The Log Cabin*

American Log Buildings: An Old World Heritage. Terry G. Jordan. Chapel Hill: University of North Carolina Press, 1985. 240 pp., illus. $26.

The Log Cabin Myth: A Study of the Early Dwellings of the English Colonists in North America. Harold R. Shurtleff. Introduction by Samuel Eliot Morison, ed. 1939. Reprint. Magnolia, Mass.: Peter Smith, 1967. 243 pp., illus. $11.50.

Log Structures: Preservation and Problem-Solving. Harrison Goodall and Renee Friedman. Nashville: American Association for State and Local History, 1980. 120 pp., illus., append., biblio., index. $10.95 pb.

The Log Cabin: Homes of the North American Wilderness. Alex W. Bealer and John O. Ellis. Barre, Mass.: Barre Publishing, 1978. 193 pp., illus., biblio., index.

The Log Cabin in America: From Pioneer Days to the Present. Clinton A. Weslager. New Brunswick, N.J.: Rutgers University Press, 1969. 382 pp., illus., biblio. $30.

Pattern in the Material Folk Culture of the Eastern United States. Henry Glassie. Philadelphia: University of Pennsylvania Press, 1968. 316 pp., illus. $7.50 pb.

The Architecture of Migration: Log Construction in the Ohio Country, 1750–1850. Donald Hutslar. Athens: Ohio University Press, 1985. $50 hb.

Texas Log Buildings: A Folk Architecture. Terry G. Jordan. Austin: University of Texas Press, 1982. $9.95 pb.

The Foxfire Book, No. 1. Eliot Wigginton, ed. Garden City, N.Y.: Doubleday, 1972. 320 pp., illus. $15.95 hb, $7.95 pb.

The Complete Log House Book. Dale Mann and Richard Skinulis. New York: McGraw-Hill, 1979. 175 pp., illus., biblio., gloss., index. $12.95 pb.

Contacts

National Park Service
U.S. Department of the Interior
Washington, D.C. 20013-7127

Forest Products Laboratory
Forest Service
U.S. Department of Agriculture
P.O. Box 1521
Madison, Wis. 53705

American Wood Preservers Institute
1615 Old Meadow Road
McLean, Va. 22101

B. Allan Mackie School
of Log Building
P.O. Box 1205
Prince George, B.C. V2L 4V3, Canada

Log Cabin Village Historical Complex
2100 Log Cabin Village Lane
Forth Worth, Tex. 76107

See also: Vernacular Architecture (Looking at the Built Environment)

Illustration for sheet music of "General Harrison's Log Cabin March and Quick Step" (1840), published by Samuel Carusi, Baltimore. (Library of Congress)

Maritime Sites

"We are all joined by a common interest, a common devotion and love for the sea."

John F. Kennedy

America's Maritime Heritage. Eloise Engle and Arnold S. Lott. Annapolis, Md.: Naval Institute Press, 1975. 371 pp., illus., appends., biblio.

American Ships of the Colonial and Revolutionary Periods. John Fitzhugh Millar. New York: W. W. Norton, 1978. 356 pp., illus., biblio., index. $24.95.

Shipbuilding in Colonial America. Joseph A. Goldenberg, Mariners Museum. Charlottesville: University Press of Virginia, 1976. 319 pp., biblio., index. $15.

New England and the Sea. R. G. Albion, W. A. Baker and Benjamin Labaree. Middletown, Conn.: Wesleyan University Press, 1972. $15.95 hb, $9 pb.

The Maritime History of Massachusetts, 1783–1860. Samuel Eliot Morison. Boston: Northeastern University Press, 1979. 431 pp. $24.95 hb, $9.95 pb.

Water Trails West. Western Writers of America. 1978. New York: Avon, 1979. 271 pp., illus., index. $3.50 pb.

Steamboats on the Colorado River, 1852–1916. Richard E. Lingenfelter. Tucson: University of Arizona Press, 1978. 195 pp., illus., appends., biblio., index. $17.50 hb, $9.50 pb.

A History of Steamboating on the Upper Missouri River. William E. Lass. Lincoln: University of Nebraska Press, 1977. 218 pp., illus., biblio., index. $16.95 hb.

Stern-Wheelers Up Columbia: A Century of Steamboating in the Oregon Country. Randall V. Mills. Lincoln: University of Nebraska Press, 1977. 212 pp., illus., biblio., appends., index. $15.95 hb, $3.95 pb.

Tall Ships on Puget Sound: The Maritime Photographs of Wilhelm Hester. Robert A. Weinstein. Seattle: University of Washington Press, 1978. 144 pp., illus.

Maritime New York in Nineteenth-Century Photographs. Harry Johnson and Frederick S. Lightfoot. New York: Dover, 1980. 160 pp., illus., index. $7.95 pb.

Re-created 19th-century waterfront at Mystic Seaport, Conn., with the whaler *Charles W. Morgan.* (Mary Ann Stets, Mystic Seaport)

Paddle Steamers: An Illustrated History of Steamboats on the Mississippi and Its Tributaries. Ken Watson. New York: W. W. Norton, 1985. $18.95 hb.

First National Maritime Preservation Conference: Proceedings. National Trust for Historic Preservation. Washington, D.C.: Preservation Press, 1977. 66 pp., illus. $3.50 pb.

Wooden Shipbuilding and Small Craft Preservation. National Trust for Historic Preservation. Washington, D.C.: Preservation Press, 1976. 104 pp., illus., appends., biblio. $5.50 pb.

U.S. Naval History Sources in the United States. Dean C. Allard et al. Washington, D.C.: Department of the Navy, Naval History Division, 1979. 235 pp., illus.

Maritime Folklife Resources: A Directory and Index. Peter Bartis. Washington, D.C.: American Folklife Center, Library of Congress, 1980. 129 pp., illus., gloss.

Florida Maritime Heritage. Barbara A. Purdy, ed. Gainesville: Florida State Museum (University of Florida, 32611), 1980. 79 pp., illus. $5 pb.

The Monitor: Its Meaning and Future. National Trust for Historic Preservation. Washington, D.C.: Preservation Press, 1978. 132 pp. $6.50 pb.

Contacts

Maritime Preservation Office National Trust for Historic Preservation 1785 Massachusetts Avenue, N.W. Washington, D.C. 20036

Council of American Maritime Museums c/o The Mariners Museum Newport News, Va. 23606

Mystic Seaport Mystic, Conn. 06355

Maine Maritime Museum 375 Front Street Bath, Maine 04530

Maritime Museum Association of San Diego 1306 North Harbor Drive San Diego, Calif. 92101

Northwest Seaport P.O. Box 395 Kirkland, Wash. 98033

Advisory Council for Underwater Archaeology c/o Reynold J. Ruppe, President Department of Anthropology Arizona State University Tempe, Ariz. 85281

Steamboat Historical Society 139 Kenyon Street Hartford, Conn. 06105

Book and Chart Store 25 Fulton Street New York, N.Y. 10038

National Fisherman 21 Elm Street Camden, Maine 04843

The Woodenboat P.O. Box 268 Brooksville, Maine 04843

The Waterways Journal Weekly 319 North Fourth Street 666 Security Building St. Louis, Mo. 63102

The American Neptune Peabody Musuem East India Marine Hall Salem, Mass. 01970

See also: Canals, Lighthouses, Waterfronts

Markets

"The market reached the height of its importance and vitality in the late 19th and early 20th century. Most older American cities had a flourishing centrally located market, and many also had smaller, neighborhood-oriented markets that catered directly to the needs of individual communities. . . .

While the market can transform an economic activity into a social one, it can do this only if it is economically viable. The heart and soul of the market is that it is an egalitarian setting in which people come to buy real and essential things."

Padraic Burke. "Reviving the Urban Market: 'Don't Fix It Up Too Much.' " *Nation's Business,* February 1978.

Farmers Markets of America: A Renaissance. Robert Sommer. Santa Barbara, Calif.: Capra Press, 1980. 96 pp., illus., append. $6.95 pb.

"To Market, To Market," Padraic Burke. *Historic Preservation,* January–March 1977.

Market Book, Containing a Historical Account of the Public Markets in the Cities of New York, Boston, Philadelphia and Brooklyn. Thomas F. De Voe. 1862. Reprint. New York: Burt Franklin, 1969. $27.50.

Market Sketchbook. Victor Steinbrueck. Seattle: University of Washington Press, 1978. 212 pp., illus., map. $8.95 pb.

The Pike Place Market: People, Politics, and Produce. Alice Shorett and Murray Morgan. Seattle: Pacific Search Press, 1982. 160 pp., illus., biblio. $12.95 pb.

The World of a Market. Mark Tobey. 1964. Reprint. Seattle: University of Washington Press, 1982. $9.95.

South Water Street Market, Chicago, c. 1900, with farmers selling their produce from wagons and carts in the street between wholesale grocers. (Chicago Historical Society)

Contacts

Pike Place Market Historical Commission
Office of Urban Conservation
400 Yesler Way
Seattle, Wash. 98104

Faneuil Hall Marketplace
1 Faneuil Hall Marketplace
Boston, Mass. 02109

Bureau of Markets
Pier 4, Pratt Street
Baltimore, Md. 21202

The French Market
Vieux Carre Commission
630 Chartres Street
New Orleans, La. 70130

Market Hall
Preservation Society of
Charleston
130 Meeting Street
Charleston, S.C. 29401

Reading Terminal Market
Philadelphia Historical
Commission
1313 City Hall Annex
Philadelphia, Pa. 19107

Farmers Home Administration
U.S. Department of Agriculture
Washington, D.C. 20250

Mills

"The evolution of industry in America has left the country with a great legacy of mills, ranging from small flour-grinding gristmills or village-scaled New England textile companies, to vast midwestern grain milling operations. Although the diversity in age, size, and function makes generalizations difficult,

many of the mill buildings still standing today are characterized by structural strength and by large open interiors which make them highly adaptable for new uses. This potential for reuse is fortunately joined by a growing awareness of the mill's value as a physical record of America's historical, technological, and social development."

> Urban Land Institute, *Adaptive Use: Development Economics, Process, and Profiles.* Washington, D.C.: ULI, 1978.

The Mill. William Fox et al. Boston: New York Graphic Society, 1977. 224 pp., color illus., biblio., index. $29.50.

Early American Mills. Martha and Murray Zimiles. New York: Bramhall House, 1973. 304 pp., color illus., gloss., biblio., index.

Mill. David Macaulay. Boston: Houghton Mifflin, 1983. 128 pp., illus., gloss. $14.95 hb.

The New England Mill Village, 1790–1860. Gary Kulik, Roger Parks and Theodore Z. Penn, eds. Documents in American Industrial History. Cambridge: MIT Press, 1982. 520 pp., illus. $45 hb.

The Young Mill Wright and Miller's Guide. Oliver Evans. 1795, 1850. Reprint. New York: Arno Press, 1972. $24 hb.

A Future from the Past: The Case for Conservation and Reuse of Old Buildings in Industrial Communities. Randolph Langenbach. Gene Bunnell, ed. Washington, D.C.: U.S. Department of Housing and Urban Development and Massachusetts Department of Community Affairs, 1978. 119 pp., illus.

Amoskeag: Life and Work in an American Factory City. Tamara K. Hareven and Randolph Langenbach. New York: Pantheon, 1978. 395 pp., illus. $6.95 pb.

The Run of the Mill: A Pictorial Narrative of the Expansion, Dominion, Decline and Enduring Impact of the New England Textile Industry. Steve Dunwell. Boston: Godine, 1978. 312 pp., illus., biblio., index. $14.95 hb.

The New England Textile Mill Survey: Selections from the Historic American Buildings Survey. Washington, D.C.: U.S. Department of the Interior, 1971. 176 pp., illus.

Lowell Preservation Plan. 83 pp., illus. *Details of the Preservation Plan.* 176 pp., illus. Lowell, Mass.: Lowell Historic Preservation Commission (204 Middle Street, 01852), 1980.

Rehabilitation: Claremont (N.H.) 1978. Planning for Adaptive Use and Energy Conservation in an Historic Mill Village. Historic American Engineering Record. Washington, D.C.: U.S. Department of the Interior, 1979. 89 pp., illus.

Grist Mills of Early America and Today. Lebanon, Pa.: Applied Arts Publishers (Box 479, 17042), 1978. 32 pp., illus. $2 pb.

Waterwheels and Millstones: A History of Ohio Gristmills and Milling. D. W. Garber. Columbus: Ohio Historical Society (1-71 and 17th Avenue, 43211), 1970. 146 pp., illus., gloss. $4.50 pb.

Mills of the Midwest. Jerry Apps. Madison, Wis.: Tamarack Press (P.O. Box 5650, 53705), 1980. 128 pp., illus., biblio., index. $12.50 pb.

Contacts

Society for the Preservation of Old Mills
P.O. Box 435
Wiscasset, Maine 04578

Society for Industrial Archeology
National Museum of American History
Room 5020
Washington, D.C. 20560

Eleutherian Mills-Hagley Foundation
P.O. Box 3630
Wilmington, Del. 19807

Lowell National Historical Park
National Park Service
Lowell, Mass. 01852

Great Falls Development Corporation
176 Naples Street
Paterson, N.J. 07522

Slater Mill Historic Site
P.O. Box 727
Pawtucket, R.I. 02862

See also: Company Towns, Industrial Structures, Windmills

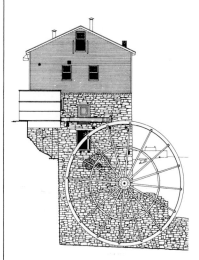

Shepherd's Mill (c. 1739), Shepherdstown, W.Va., a gristmill with a 40-foot overshot waterwheel. (Belmont Freeman, HAER)

Mormon Sites

"Learn how to apply your labor. Build good houses, make fine farms . . . and build up and adorn a beautiful city. . . ."

Brigham Young

"Coming by the thousands, [Mormon] pioneers migrated as an organized community bringing instant urbanism. . . . Cooperation, essential for the construction and administration of necessary irrigation systems, was inherent in the organization of the Church. . . ."

Paul Goeldner, *Utah Catalog: Historic American Buildings Survey.* Salt Lake City: Utah Heritage Foundation, 1969.

The Early Temples of the Mormons: The Architecture of the Millennial Kingdom in the American West. Laurel B. Andrew. Albany: State University of New York Press, 1978. 218 pp., illus., biblio. $21.50 hb.

The Mormon Landscape. Richard V. Francaviglia. New York: AMS Press, 1979. 176 pp., illus., biblio., index. $14.95 hb.

Building the City of God. Leonard J. Arrington et al. Salt Lake City: Deseret Book Company, 1976.

The Mormon Village: A Pattern and Technique of Land Settlement. Lowry Nelson. Salt Lake City: University of Utah Press, 1952.

"The Architecture of Equal Comfort," Paul Goeldner. *Historic Preservation,* January–March 1972.

"The Architecture of Zion," Jan H. Brunvand. *The American West,* March–April 1976.

Mormon Country. Wallace E. Stegner. 1942. Reprint. Lincoln: University of Nebraska Press, 1981. 372 pp., index. $23.50 hb, $6.95 pb.

Utah Folk Art: A Catalog of Material Culture. Hal Cannon, ed. Provo, Utah: Brigham Young University Press, 1980. 168 pp., illus. $10.95 pb.

The Grand Beehive. Hal Cannon, ed. Salt Lake City: University of Utah Press, 1980. 88 pp., illus., biblio. $9.50 pb.

"A Bibliography of Studies in Mormon Folklore," William A. Wilson. *Utah Historical Quarterly,* Fall 1976.

The Mormon Experience: A History of the Latter-Day Saints. Leonard J. Arrington. New York: Knopf, 1979.

A Mormon Bibliography, 1830–1930. Dale Morgan. Salt Lake City: University of Utah Press, 1978. $80.

Contacts

Genealogical Department
Church of Jesus Christ of
Latter-day Saints
50 East North Temple
Salt Lake City, Utah 84150

Mormon Historical Association
P.O. Box 7010
University Station
Provo, Utah 84602

Peaks and valleys created by the Colorado River in Grand Canyon National Park, Ariz., established in 1919. (Ansel Adams, National Archives)

National Parks and Forests

"The importance of reserving space for what we have come to call recreation has long been understood. The first American settlers provided their towns with commons or village greens, and as communities grew larger they included parks in their civic planning. . . . They scored a remarkable early success with the establishment of a state park in the Yosemite Valley of California in 1864, and with that the movement got well under way."

Conrad L. Wirth, *Parks, Politics and the People*

General

National Parks: The American Experience. Alfred Runte. Lincoln: University of Nebraska Press, 1979. 240 pp., illus. $16.50 hb.

America's National Parks and Their Keepers. Ronald A. Foresta, ed. Resources for the Future. Baltimore: Johns Hopkins University Press, 1984. 400 pp. $45 hb, $11.95 pb.

Parks, Politics and the People. Conrad L. Wirth. Norman: University of Oklahoma Press, 1980. 450 pp., illus., index. $24.95 hb.

Mountains Without Handrails: Reflections on the National Parks. Joseph L. Sax. Ann Arbor: University of Michigan Press, 1980. 152 pp., append., biblio., index. $12.50 hb, $5.95 pb.

Presence of the Past: A History of the Preservation Movement in the United States Before Williamsburg. Charles B. Hosmer, Jr. 1965. Washington, D.C.: Preservation Press, 1970. 386 pp., illus., index. $12.95 hb.

Preservation Comes of Age: From Williamsburg to the National Trust, 1926–1949. Charles B. Hosmer, Jr. For Preservation Press. Charlottesville: University Press of Virginia, 1981. 1,291 pp., illus., biblio., chron., index. 2 vols. $37.50 hb.

National Parks of the U.S.A. James V. Murfin. New York: Mayflower Books, 1981. 288 pp., color illus. $24.95 hb.

National Parks. Michael Frome and David Muench. 1977. Rev. ed. Chicago: Rand McNally, 1981. 160 pp., color illus. $9.95 pb.

American Photographers and the National Parks. Robert Cahn and Robert Ketchum, National Park Foundation. New York: Viking, 1981. 180 pp., illus. $75.

The National Parks. Freeman Tilden. 1968. Rev. ed. New York: Knopf, 1970. $10.95 pb.

Our National Parks. John Muir. Foreword by Richard F. Fleck. 1901. Reprint. Madison: University of Wisconsin Press, 1981. 394 pp., index. $25 hb, $7.95 pb.

Mormon family outside their commodious brick house, built to accommodate the polygamist lifestyle in equal comfort. (Utah State Historical Society)

Redwoods in Redwood National Park, Crescent City, Calif., created in 1968. (Carleton Knight III, NTHP)

The octagonal house (1853) in Fishkill, N.Y., of Orson Squire Fowler, the leading 19th-century promoter of octagonal houses. From *A Home for All.*

Trains of Discovery: Western Railroads and the National Parks. Alfred Runte. Flagstaff, Ariz.: Northland Press, 1984. $14.95 hb, $9.95 pb.

America's Parks and Recreation Heritage: A Chronology. Carlton S. Van Doren and Louis Hodges. Washington, D.C.: U.S. Department of the Interior, Bureau of Outdoor Recreation, 1975. 37 pp.

Citizens Action Guide to the National Park System. Washington, D.C.: National Parks and Conservation Association, 1979. 23 pp.

Guidebooks
The Pocket Books Guide to National Parks. William Wallace Rhodes. New York: Pocket Books, 1984. 384 pp. $3.95 pb.

Exploring Our National Parks and Monuments. Devereux Butcher. 1947. 8th ed. Harvard, Mass.: Gambit, 1985. 373 pp., illus. $19.95 hb, $11.95 pb.

Your National Parks: A State-by-State Guide to Visiting and Enjoying Over 300 Units of the National Park System. George Hornby, ed. New York: Crown, 1980. 320 pp., illus., maps, append., index.

The Complete Guide to America's National Parks: The Official Visitor's Guide of the National Park Foundation. National Park Foundation. Rev. ed. New York: Penguin Books, 1982. 360 pp., maps, biblio., index. $7.95 pb.

Old Lodges and Hotels of Our National Parks. Bill McMillon. South Bend, Ind.: Icarus Press, 1984. 130 pp., illus. $24.95 hb.

The Complete Guide to Cabins and Lodges in America's State and National Parks. George Zimmermann. Boston: Little, Brown, 1984. $9.95 pb.

The Blue Ridge Parkway. Harley E. Jolley. Knoxville: University of Tennessee Press, 1969. $12.50 hb, $4.95 pb.

National Parks of the West. Editors of Sunset Books. Rev. ed. Menlo Park, Calif.: Author, 1980. 256 pp., color illus., index. $8.95 pb.

Nature's Yellowstone. Richard A. Bartlett. Albuquerque: University of New Mexico Press, 1974. 250 pp., illus. $10 hb.

Forests
Whose Woods These Are: The Story of the National Forests. Michael Frome. Garden City, N.Y.: Doubleday, 1962. 360 pp., color illus., biblio., index.

North American Forest History: A Guide to Archives and Manuscripts in the United States and Canada. Richard C. Davis. Santa Barbara: American Bibliographic Center and Clio Press (P.O. Box 4397, 93103), 1977.

North American Forest and Conservation History: A Bibliography. Ronald J. Fahl. Santa Barbara. American Bibliographical Center and Clio Press, 1977.

The Forest Service. Michael Frome. Boulder, Colo.: Westview Press, 1983. 300 pp. $25.

Contacts
National Park Service
U.S. Department of the Interior
Washington, D.C. 20013-7127

National Parks and
Conservation Association
1701 18th Street, N.W.
Washington, D.C. 20009

Sierra Club
530 Bush Street
San Francisco, Calif. 94108

Wilderness Society
729 15th Street, N.W.
Washington, D.C. 20005

National Wildlife Federation
1412 16th Street, N.W.
Washington, D.C. 20036

National Audubon Society
Audubon House
1130 Fifth Avenue
New York, N.Y. 10028

Forest History Society
109 Coral Street
Santa Cruz, Calif. 95060

Forest Service
U.S. Department of Agriculture
P.O. Box 2417
Washington, D.C. 20013

See also: Trees

Octagons

"Nature's forms are mostly spherical. . . . Since, then, the octagon is more beautiful as well as capacious, and more consonant with the predominant or governing form of Nature—the spherical—it deserves consideration."
    Orson Squire Fowler, *The Octagon House: A Home for All*

The Octagon House: A Home for All. Orson S. Fowler. 1853. Reprint. New York: Dover, 1973. 192 pp., illus., biblio. $4 pb.

The Octagon Fad. Carl F. Schmidt. Scottsville, N.Y.: Author, 1958. 207 pp., illus., append., biblio. $6. Available from Milne Library, SUNY, Geneseo, N.Y. 14454.

More About Octagons. Carl F. Schmidt and Philip Parr. Caledonia, N.Y.: Authors, 1978. 214 pp., illus.

"'A Home for All'—The Octagon in American Architecture," John J. G. Blumenson. *Historic Preservation,* July–September 1973.

"Octagon Houses," Leonard Todd. *Americana,* November 1976.

"Age of the Octagon," Alexander Ormond Boulton. *American Heritage,* August–September 1983.

"Portal" (1976) by Isamu Noguchi, Cuyahoga County Courthouse (1913, Lehman and Schmitt), Cleveland. From *Outdoor Sculpture in Ohio*. (© Richard N. Campen)

Outdoor Sculpture

"Public sculpture is an outdoor mirror in which a society looks to see what it is: heroic, boastful, managerial, sentimental, or perhaps just in love with aluminum rivets."

> George Nelson, *How to See: Visual Adventures in a World God Never Made*. Boston: Little, Brown, 1977.

"Sculpture should be seen outside; there it becomes an architectonic element more than decoration. It can symbolize all of man's aspirations; in fact, it can become so identified with a city that its image *is* the city. . . . Great sculptures are focal points which are vital elements in the hearts of cities; they are pivots in great plazas; spaces eddy around them, are pinned down by them, focus on them."

> Lawrence Halprin, *Cities*. 1963. Rev. ed. Cambridge: MIT Press, 1973.

Outdoor Sculpture: Object and Environment. Margaret A. Robinette. New York: Whitney Library of Design, 1976. 191 pp., illus., biblio., append., index.

The Place of Art in the World of Architecture. Donald W. Thalacker. New York: Chelsea House, R. R. Bowker, 1980. 238 pp., color illus., appends. $35 hb.

Place Makers: Public Art That Tells You Where You Are. Ronald Lee Fleming and Renata von Tscharner. New York: Hastings House, 1981. 128 pp., illus. $9.95 pb.

Art in Public Places. John Beardsley. Washington, D.C.: Partners for Livable Places, 1981. 149 pp. $5.

Public Art: New Directions. Louis G. Redstone, ed. New York: McGraw-Hill, 1980. 256 pp., illus. $34.50.

Daniel Chester French: An American Sculptor. Michael Richman. 1976. Washington, D.C.: Preservation Press, 1983. 222 pp., illus. $14.95 pb.

The Work of Augustus Saint-Gaudens. John H. Dryfhout. Hanover, N.H.: University Press of New England, 1982. 370 pp., illus., appends., index. $60 hb.

Lincoln. George Tice. New Brunswick, N.J.: Rutgers University Press, 1984. 72 pp., illus. $37.95 hb.

New York Civic Sculpture: A Pictorial Guide. Frederick Fried and Edmund V. Gillion, Jr. New York: Dover, 1976. 180 pp., illus. $5 pb.

Architectural Sculpture in New York City. Stephen M. Jacoby. Introduction by Clay Lancaster. New York: Dover, 1975. 115 pp., illus. $9 pb.

A Century of American Sculpture: Treasures from Brookgreen Gardens. A. Hyatt Mayor et al. New York: Abbeville, 1981. 128 pp., color illus., biblio. $35 hb, $18.95 pb.

The Statue of Liberty. Michael George. New York: Abrams, 1985. 30 color illus. $14.95 pb.

Statue of Liberty. Charles Mercer. New York: Putnam, 1985. $12.95 hb, $7.95 pb.

The Statue of Liberty: Enlightening the World. Frederic Auguste Bartholdi. New York: New York Bound, Publishers, 1985. 66 pp., illus. $7.95 pb.

Sculpture and the Federal Triangle. George Gurney. Washington, D.C.: Smithsonian Institution Press, 1985. 380 pp., illus.$35.

The Outdoor Sculpture of Washington, D.C.: A Comprehensive Historical Guide. James M. Goode. Washington, D.C.: Smithsonian Institution Press, 1974. 528 pp., illus., biblio. $12.50 pb.

Sculpture of a City: Philadelphia's Treasures in Stone and Bronze. Fairmount Park Art Association. New York: Walker, 1974.

The Sculptures at Gettysburg. Wayne Craven. Philadelphia: Eastern Acorn Press, Eastern National Park and Monument Association, 1982. 96 pp., illus., biblio. $4.95 pb.

Hidden Treasure: Public Sculpture in Providence. Robert Freeman and Vivienne Lasky. Providence: Rhode Island Bicentennial Foundation, 1980. 72 pp., illus., biblio. $4.95 pb.

A Guide to Chicago's Public Sculpture. Ira J. Bach and Mary Lackritz Gray. Chicago: University of Chicago Press, 1983. 403 pp., illus., biblio., index. $20 hb, $8.95 pb.

Chicago Sculpture. James L. Riedy. Champaign: University of Illinois Press, 1981. 352 pp., illus., appends., biblio., index. $24.95 hb.

Outdoor Sculpture in Ohio. Richard N. Campen. Chagrin Falls, Ohio: West Summit Press, 1980. 175 pp., illus., biblio., index. $20 hb.

The Public Monument and Its Audience. Marianne Doezema and June Hargrove. Cleveland: Cleveland Museum of Art, 1977. Distributed by Indiana University Press. 72 pp., illus. $4.95 pb.

Art in Detroit Public Places. Dennis Alan Nawrocki. Detroit: Wayne State University Press, 1980. 160 pp., biblio., index, maps. $9.95 hb, $4.95 pb.

Outdoor Sculpture in Michigan Series: Lansing, Grand Rapids and *Kalamazoo*. Fay L. Hendry. Photographs by Balthazar Korab. Okemos, Mich.: Iota Press (2749 Mt. Hope Road, 48864), 1980. $3.50 pb each.

The Carving of Mount Rushmore. Rex Alan Smith. New York: Abbeville, 1985. $19.95 hb.

A Carrot for a Nose: The Form of Folk Sculpture on America's City Streets and Country Roads. M. J. Gladstone. New York: Scribner's, 1974. 70 pp., illus. $1.99 pb.

American Folk Sculpture. Robert Charles Bishop. New York: Dutton, 1983. 392 pp., illus., biblio., index. $19.95.

Scarecrows. Avon Neal. Photos by Ann Parker. New York: Clarkson Potter, 1978.

Contacts

Anonymous Arts Recovery Society
380 West Broadway
New York, N.Y. 10012

American Battle Monuments Commission
20 Massachusetts Avenue, N.W.
Washington, D.C. 20314

Public Art Preservation Committee
John Jay College of Criminal Justice
444 West 56th Street
Room 1309
New York, N.Y. 10019

Outhouses

"The flush toilet is causing increasing concern among environmentalists . . . because of the damage it has done and is doing by polluting the water. . . . [One solution] may well signal a return of the small building in the backyard."

> Arthur C. Downs, Jr., "Andrew Jackson Downing and the American Bathroom." *Historic Preservation*, October–December 1971.

The Specialist. Charles ("Chic") Sale. 1929. Reprint. Burlingame, Calif.: Specialist Publishing Company (109 La Mesa Drive, 94010), 1974. 27 pp., illus. $5 hb.

I'll Tell You Why. Charles ("Chic") Sale. Reprint. St. Louis: Specialist Publishing Company, 1980. 44 pp., illus. $5 hb.

Backyard Classic: An Adventure in Nostalgia. Lambert Florin. Seattle: Superior Publishing, 1975. 160 pp., illus.

Privy: The Classic Outhouse Book. Janet and Richard Strombeck. Delafield, Wis.: Sun Designs (P.O. Box 206, 53018), 1980. 92 pp., illus. $7.95 pb.

Ornate outhouse, Georgetown, Colo. (Carleton Knight III, NTHP)

"On Recognizing a WPA Rose Garden or a CCC Privy," Phoebe Cutler. *Landscape,* Winter 1976.

Contact

Rural Life Museum
Louisiana State University
Baton Rouge, La. 70803

Plazas and Urban Open Spaces

"What is expressed in open spaces is the essential quality of urban life—its casualness and variety, its ability to crystallize community feeling. People find in outdoor meeting places the chance to sense what is going on, to test the mood of the community, to mingle and communicate."

August Heckscher, *Open Spaces: The Life of American Cities*

Justin Herman Park and Plaza (1971, Ciampi, Halprin, Bolles), San Francisco, near the Ferry Building (1895, A. Page Brown). (Joshua Freiwald)

Open Spaces: The Life of American Cities. August Heckscher. New York: Harper and Row, 1977. 386 pp., illus., index.

Urban Open Spaces. Lisa Taylor, ed. Cooper-Hewitt Museum. New York: Rizzoli, 1980. 128 pp., illus., biblio. $9.95 pb.

On Common Ground: Caring for Shared Land from Town Common to Urban Park. Ronald Lee Fleming and Lauri A. Halderman. Preface by John Updike. Harvard, Mass.: Harvard Common Press, 1982. 194 pp., illus., biblio., append., index. $25 hb, $12.95 pb.

The Social Life of Small Urban Spaces. William H. Whyte, Jr. Washington, D.C.: Conservation Foundation, 1980. 125 pp., illus., appends. $9.50 pb.

Town and Square: From the Agora to the Village Green. Paul Zucker. Cambridge: MIT Press, 1970. 287 pp., illus., biblio., index.

Urban Space: A Brief History of the City Square. Jere Stuart French. Dubuque, Iowa: Kendall/Hunt Publishing, 1978. 187 pp., illus., biblio. $11.95 pb.

Nature in Cities: The Natural Environment in the Design and Development of Urban Green Space. Ian C. Laurie, ed. New York: Wiley, 1979. 428 pp. $71.95 hb.

Economic, Planning, and Political Processes Altering Urban Open Space: Selected References with a Case Study. Marilyn Myers. Chicago: Council of Planning Librarians (1313 East 60th Street, 60637), 1981. 78 pp. No. 56. $11 pb.

Times Square: A Pictorial History. Jill Stone. New York: Macmillan, 1982. 176 pp., illus., index. $19.95 hb, $9.95 pb.

Times Square: Forty-five Years of Photography. Lou Stoumen. New York: Aperture, 1985. 160 pp., illus. $25 hb, $15 pb.

Contacts

Project for Public Spaces
875 Avenue of the Americas
Room 201
New York, N.Y. 10001

American Planning Association
1313 East 60th Street
Chicago, Ill. 60637

Townscape Institute
2 Hubbard Park
Cambridge, Mass. 02138

See also: Cities, Gardens and Parks; Looking at the Built Environment

Presidential Sites

"Our Presidents are commemorated by scores of sites, ranging from the humble to the palatial: birthplaces, residences, other buildings, inaugural places, monuments, and tombs. Visits to them enhance understanding of the distinguished group of men who have led the Nation; their ways of life; family backgrounds; locales and regions in which they were born or resided; eras in which they have lived; and the social, economic, and intellectual influences that molded them."

Robert G. Ferris, *The Presidents*

The Presidents: From the Inauguration of George Washington to the Inauguration of Jimmy Carter. Historic Places Commemorating the Chief Executives of the United States. Robert G. Ferris, ed., Historic Sites Survey. Rev. ed. Washington, D.C.: National Park Service, U.S. Department of the Interior, 1977. 666 pp., illus., biblio.

Where the American Presidents Lived. Ellyn R. Kern. Indianapolis: Cottontail Publications (P.O. Box B44761, 46204), 1982. 120 pp., illus., biblio. $10.95.

Historic Homes of American Presidents. Irvin Haas. New York: McKay, 1976. $10.95 hb.

Plains, Ga., railroad station. (Columbus *Ledger-Enquirer*)

Homes of the American Presidents. Cranston Jones and William H. Schleisner. New York: Crown, 1962. 232 pp., illus., index, biblio.

Pictorial History of American Presidents. John and Alice Durant. Cranbury, N.J.: A. S. Barnes, 1978.

"Inaugural Stands." In *Capital Losses: A Cultural History of Washington's Destroyed Buildings.* James M. Goode. Washington, D.C.: Smithsonian Institution Press, 1979. 517 pp., index, biblio. $37.50 hb, $19.95 pb.

Contacts

National Park Service
U.S. Department of the Interior
Washington, D.C. 20013-7127

Association for Presidential Houses and Museums (Va.)
c/o Berkley Plantation
Route 5
Charles City, Va. 23030

Office of Presidential Libraries
National Archives and Records Administration
8th Street and Pennsylvania Avenue, N.W.
Washington, D.C. 20408

Presidential Papers Program
National Historical Publications and Records Commission
8th Street and Pennsylvania Avenue, N.W.
Washington, D.C. 20408

Woodrow Wilson House
National Trust for Historic Preservation
2340 S Street, N.W.
Washington, D.C. 20008

Mount Vernon Ladies' Association of the Union
Mount Vernon, Va. 22121

See also: Executive Mansions

Prisons

"The programmes of hospital and prison accommodations have much in common. In both cases a number of people are confined in one particular place, although they would prefer not to be, and in both cases constant supervision is necessary."

Nikolaus Pevsner, *A History of Building Types*

"The young American republic's first great contribution to world architectural thought was . . . the novel design of our jails and prisons. . . ."

Robert B. MacKay, "Prisons." In *Built in the U.S.A.*

The Human Cage: A Brief History of Prison Architecture. Norman Johnston. New York: Walker, 1973. 68 pp., illus. $5.95.

American Prisons: A History of Good Intentions. Blake McKelvey. 1936. 2nd rev. ed. Montclair, N.J.: Patterson Smith, 1977. $18 hb, $9 pb.

A Selected Bibliography on the American Jail with Special Emphasis on Illinois Jails. Hans W. Mattick. Chicago: Council of Planning Librarians, 1975. No. 821. $8.50.

The Architecture of Correctional Institutions: A Checklist of Sources. M. Lynne Struthers Swanick. Monticello, Ill.: Vance Bibliographies, 1980. A-211. 4 pp. $2 pb.

Development of American Prisons and Prison Customs, 1776–1845. Orlando F. Lewis. 1922. Reprint. Montclair, N.J.: Patterson Smith, 1967. 350 pp. $15 hb.

Prison Architecture. U.N. Social Defense Research Institute. New York: Nichols, 1975. 239 pp., illus. $100.

A Just Measure of Pain: The Penitentiary in the Industrial Revolution, 1750–1850. Michael Ignatieff. New York: Pantheon, 1978. 258 pp., illus.

The Discovery of the Asylum: Social Order and Disorder in the New Republic. David J. Rothman. Boston: Little, Brown, 1971. 376 pp., illus., index.

"The Rotary Jail, or Human Squirrel Cage," Walter A. Lunden. *Journal of the Society of Architectural Historians,* December 1959.

Newgate Prison (c. 1650), Hartford, Conn., a community including a guard room, workshop and bake house. (Connecticut Historical Society)

Contacts

Robert MacKay
Society for the Preservation of Long Island Antiquities
93 North Country Road
Setauket, N.Y. 11733

National Criminal Justice Reference Service
National Institute of Justice
U.S. Department of Justice
Box 6000
Rockville, Md. 20850

Bureau of Prisons
U.S. Department of Justice
Washington, D.C. 20534

Old Newgate Prison and Copper Mine
c/o Connecticut Historical Commission
59 South Prospect Street
Hartford, Conn. 06106

Public Buildings

"In acting like a great nation, the United States became one. The first federal buildings, the Capitol and the White House, the Treasury and the Patent Office, set a standard of excellence for the entire country. Under the decentralized system of government, Americans lived under four authorities: the town or city, the county, the state and the United States. Each had its own architectural symbols: the town hall or city hall, the county courthouse, the state capitol, the custom house and post office. Their quality was remarkable, with handsome public buildings in many a raw settlement. There is something moving about the efforts of so many little-known builders and craftsmen to embody the ideal of a community."

John Maass et al., "Historic Preservation and the National Mythology." *Monumentum.* Terry B. Morton, ed. Washington, D.C: US/ICOMOS, 1976.

The Federal Presence: Architecture, Politics, and National Design. Lois Craig and Federal Architecture Project Staff. Cambridge: MIT Press, 1978. 581 pp., illus., biblio., index. $49.50 hb, $17.50 pb.

Hints on Public Architecture. Robert Dale Owen. 1849. Reprint. Introduction by Cynthia R. Field. Washington, D.C.: Smithsonian Institution Press, 1978. 119 pp., illus. $49.50 hb.

Duluth City Hall (1928, Thomas Shefchik). (Wade Lawrence)

America's City Halls. William L. Lebovich, Historic American Buildings Survey. Washington, D.C.: Preservation Press, 1984. 224 pp., illus., biblio., append. $18.95 pb.

Wall-to-Wall America: A Cultural History of Post Office Murals in the Great Depression. Karal Ann Marling. Minneapolis: University of Minnesota Press, 1982. 344 pp., illus. $35 hb, $14.95 pb.

Democratic Vistas: Post Offices and Public Art in the New Deal. Marlene Park and Gerald Markowitz. Philadelphia: Temple University Press, 1984. 260 pp., illus., append., index. $37.95 hb.

A Short History of the Mail Service. Carl H. Scheele. Washington, D.C.: Smithsonian Institution Press, 1970. 250 pp., illus., biblio., index. Available from University Microfilms, 300 North Zeeb Road, Ann Arbor, Mich. 48106.

Three Centuries of Custom Houses. Washington, D.C.: National Society of the Colonial Dames of America, 1972. 356 pp.

Recycling Public Buildings. Judith N. Getzels. Chicago: American Society of Planning Officials, 1976. PAS no. 319. 34 pp., illus., appends., biblio. $6 pb.

Some Post Offices with New Deal Artwork

Anchorage, Alaska, Post Office and Courthouse, 1946

Benton, Ark., Federal Building, 1942

San Francisco, Mint, 1937

Rifle, Colo., Post Office, 1942

Rehoboth Beach, Del., Post Office, 1940

Honolulu, Schofield Barracks Post Office, 1943

Alamagordo, N.M., Federal Building, 1940

Mayaguez, P.R., Post Office, 1940

Weirton, W.Va., Cove Station Post Office, 1940

Yellowstone Park, Wyo., Post Office, 1941

From *Democratic Vistas: Post Offices and Public Art in the New Deal*

Contacts

Historic Preservation Officer
Public Buildings Service
U.S. General Services Administration
Washington, D.C. 20405

Treasury Historical Association
Main Treasury Building
Washington, D.C. 20220

Research Historian
Office of the Postmaster
General
U.S. Postal Service
Washington, D.C. 20260

Customs Service
Bureau of the Mint
U.S. Department of the
Treasury
Washington, D.C. 20220

See also: Capitols, Courthouses, Firehouses, Libraries

Railroad Stations

"The supply of railroad stations
is not to be underestimated. Of
the approximately 40,000 stations which served the nation
during the height of the railroad
era, an estimated 20,000 still
remain, of which most await
rehabilitation. . . . The railroad
station was usually built as the
gateway into the city to impress
arriving passengers with its
wealth or economic stature. The
size of a station, the style of its
architecture and the lavishness
of its interior were reflections of
the community's economic and
social character, its tastes and
self-image. . . . Consequently,
the station is often one of the
finest and most prominent
buildings in the community and
a superb expression of the community's individuality and local
character."

   Anderson Notter Finegold, *Recy-*
   cling Historic Railroad Stations

The Railroad Station: An Archi-
tectural History. Carroll L. V.
Meeks. New Haven: Yale University Press, 1956. 203 pp.,
illus., append., index.

Down At the Depot: American
Railroad Stations from 1831 to
1920. Edwin P. Alexander. New
York: Clarkson Potter, 1970. 320
pp., illus., index.

Recycling Historic Railroad Sta-
tions: A Citizens' Manual. Anderson Notter Finegold.
Washington, D.C.: U.S. Department of Transportation (Office
of the Secretary, Room 10223,
20590), 1978. 83 pp., illus. $3
pb.

Reusing Railroad Stations,
Book Two. Educational Facilities
Laboratories. New York: EFL
(680 Fifth Avenue, 10019), 1975.
79 pp., illus. $4 pb.

Historic Railroad Stations: A
Selected Inventory. National
Register of Historic Places.
Washington, D.C.: National
Park Service, U.S. Department
of the Interior, 1974.

Baltimore and Ohio Railroad Station (1870, attributed to E. Francis Baldwin), Point of Rocks, Md., a picturesque High Victorian Gothic suburban station. (Wm. Edmund Barrett, HAER)

The Vanishing Depot. Ranulph
Bye. Wynnewood, Pa.:
Livingston, 1973. 113 pp., color
illus.

Classic American Railroad Sta-
tions. Julian Cavalier. San Diego: A. S. Barnes, 1980. 212
pp., color illus., index $25.

North American Railway Sta-
tions. Julian Cavalier. Cranbury,
N.J.: A. S. Barnes, 1979. 215
pp., illus., index.

The Country Railroad Station in
America. H. Roger Grand and
Charles W. Bohi. Boulder,
Colo.: Pruett, 1978. 183 pp.,
illus., biblio., index. $24.95 hb.

Metropolitan Corridor: Rail-
roads and the American Scene.
John R. Stilgoe. New Haven:
Yale University Press, 1983. 397
pp., biblio., illus., index. $29.95
hb.

Railroad Stations in the United
States. Jack W. Seto. Chicago:
Council of Planning Librarians,
1978. No. 1450. 37 pp. $3.50.

Waiting for the 5:05: Terminal,
Station, and Depot in America.
Lawrence Grow. Main Street
Press. New York: Universe
Books, 1977. 128 pp., illus.,
append., index.

Grand Central Terminal: City
Within the City. Deborah Nevins, ed. Foreword by Jacqueline
K. Onassis. New York: Municipal Art Society (457 Madison
Avenue, 10022), 1982. 145 pp.,
illus. $25.

Grand Central: The World's
Greatest Railway Terminal. William D. Middleton. San Marino,
Calif.: Golden West Books,
1977. 216 pp., illus., append.,
biblio., index. $22.95 hb.

Penn Station: Its Tunnels and
Side Rodders. Fred Westing.
1912. Reprint. Seattle: Superior,
1978. 192 pp., illus. $19.95.

Rail City: Chicago U.S.A.
George H. Douglas. San Diego,
Calif.: Howell-North, 1981.
$27.50 hb.

The Railroad and the City: A
Technological and Urbanistic
History of Cincinnati. Carl W.
Condit. Columbus: Ohio State
University Press, 1977. 335 pp.,
illus., append., biblio., index.
$15 hb.

Speaking of Union Station: An
Oral History of a Nashville
Landmark. Nashville: Union
Station Trust Fund, 1977. 122
pp., illus.

The Last of the Great Stations:
Los Angeles Union Passenger
Terminal. Bill Bradley. Glendale, Calif.: Interurbans, 1979.
110 pp., illus. $9.95 pb.

"The Short-Lived Phenomenon
of Railroad Station-Hotels," Dianne Newell. *Historic Preserva-*
tion, July–September 1974.

Contacts

Railroad Station Historical
Society
430 Ivy Avenue
Crete, Neb. 68333

Federal Railroad Administration
U.S. Department of
Transportation
Washington, D.C. 20590

Society for Industrial
Archeology
National Museum of
American History
Room 5020
Washington, D.C. 20560

Association of Railway
Museums
P.O. Box 3454
Portland, Maine 04104

Railroadians of America
c/o Joseph Hittle
P.O. Box 134
Iselin, N.J. 08830

National Railway Historical
Society
P.O. Box 2051
Philadelphia, Pa. 19103

Railway and Locomotive
Historical Society
P.O. Box 1194
Boston, Mass. 02103

Boswell Ranch (c. 1875), near Cheyenne, Wyo. (Fred McCabe)

Ranches

"At first ranch life was hard and lonely. . . . For some hands it was a 100-mile ride from the bunkhouse to the front gate. Later a ranchhouse and scattered buildings would replace the wickiup, and other evidences of civilization would follow."

Robert G. Ferris, ed., *Prospector, Cowhand, and Sodbuster*

Prospector, Cowhand, and Sodbuster: Historic Places Associated with the Mining, Ranching, and Farming Frontiers in the Trans-Mississippi West. Robert G. Ferris, ed., Historic Sites Survey. Washington, D.C.: National Park Service, U.S. Department of the Interior, 1967. 320 pp., illus., maps, biblio., index. $11 hb. GPO stock no. 024–005–00005–4.

Ranch: Portrait of a Surviving Dream. Dudley Witney and Moira Johnston. Garden City, N.Y.: Doubleday, 1983. 240 pp., color illus. $35 hb.

The LS Brand: The Story of a Texas Panhandle Ranch. Dulcie Sullivan. 1968. Austin: University of Texas Press, 1982. 178 pp., illus., index. $6.45 pb.

6,000 Miles of Fence: Life on the XIT Ranch of Texas. Cordia Sloan Duke and Joe B. Frantz. Austin: University of Texas Press, 1983. 231 pp., illus., index. $6.95 pb.

The American Cowboy. Lonn Taylor and Ingrid Maar. Library of Congress. New York: Harper and Row, 1983. 228 pp., illus. $18.95 pb.

Buckaroos in Paradise: Cowboy Life in Northern Nevada. Howard W. Marshall and Richard E. Ahlborn. Lincoln, University of Nebraska Press, 1981. 112 pp., illus., biblio. $15.95 pb.

The Ranchers: A Book of Generations. Stan Steiner. New York: Knopf, 1980. 241 pp. $13.95 hb.

The Modern Cowboy, John R. Erickson. Lincoln: University of Nebraska Press, 1981. 247 pp., illus., biblio. $15.95 hb.

Contacts

Ranching Heritage Center and Association
Texas Tech University
P.O. Box 4499
Lubbock, Tex. 79409

Grant-Kohrs Ranch
National Historic Site
Deer Lodge, Mont. 59722

Grove Farm Homestead
P.O. Box 1631
Lihue, Kauai, Hawaii 96766

Nevada Ranch Inventory
Historic Preservation Program
University of Nevada
Mack Social Science Building
Reno, Nev. 89557

Resorts and Spas

"The idea is escape—from everything that ordinarily dominates and binds, from all things onerous and demanding. Escape laced with enchantment and ease. It takes a conscious act to create such a place—and the shrewd understanding that it should be no place like home, and a home away from home, as well."

Ada Louise Huxtable. *New York Times,* August 13, 1980.

Great Resorts of America. Chuck Lawliss. New York: Holt, Rinehart and Winston, 1983. 160 pp., color illus. $25.

America's Grand Resort Hotels. Jeffrey W. Limerick, Nancy Ferguson and Richard Oliver. New York: Pantheon, 1979. 303 pp., illus. $20 hb.

Dream Resorts. Andrea Chambers. New York: Clarkson Potter, 1983. 215 pp., illus., biblio. $21.95 hb.

Summer Places. Brendan Gill and Dudley Witney. New York: Methuen, 1978. 224 pp., color illus.

Summertime: Photographs of Americans at Play, 1850–1900. Floyd and Marion Rinhart. New York: Clarkson Potter, 1978. 191 pp., illus.

Victorian Resorts and Hotels: Essays from a Victorian Society Symposium. Richard Guy Wilson, ed. Watkins Glen, N.Y.: American Life Foundation, 1982. 127 pp., illus. $10 pb.

The Architecture of Resorts, Clubhouses and Spas in the United States. Coppa and Avery Consultants. Monticello, Ill.: Vance Bibliographies, 1984. 8 pp. $2 pb.

The Palace Inns: A Connoisseur's Guide to Historic America. Brian McGinty. Harrisburg, Pa.: Stackpole Books, 1978. 192 pp., illus. $9.95 pb.

Resorts of the Catskills. Architectural League of New York and Gallery League of New York State. Photos by John Margolies. New York: St. Martin's, 1979. 113 pp., color illus., biblio., index. $14.95 hb, $7.95 pb.

The Catskill Mountain House. Roland Van Zandt. New Brunswick, N.J.: Rutgers University Press, 1966. 415 pp., illus., biblio., append.

The Nineteenth-Century Architecture of Saratoga Springs. Stephen S. Prokopoff and Joan C. Siegfried. New York: New York State Council on the Arts, 1970. 104 pp., illus., map, gloss.

The Short Season of Sharon Springs: Portrait of an American Village. Stuart M. Blumin and Deborah Adelman Blumin. Ithaca: Cornell University Press, 1980. 128 pp., illus. $22.50 hb.

Amusing the Million: Coney Island at the Turn of the Century. John F. Kasson. New York: Hill and Wang, 1978. 120 pp., illus., biblio. $12.50 hb, $6.95 pb.

Atlantic City: 125 Years of Ocean Madness. Vicki Gold Levi and Lee Eisenberg. New York: Clarkson Potter, 1979. 224 pp., illus. $15.95 hb, $8.95 pb.

Cape May, Queen of the Seaside Resorts: Its History and Architecture. George E. Thomas and Carl Doebley. Philadelphia: Art Alliance Press, 1976. 202 pp., illus. $40 hb.

The Cape May Handbook. Carolyn Pitts, ed. Philadelphia: The Athenaeum, 1977. 77 pp., illus., append., gloss., biblio. $5 pb.

Hot Springs and Pools of the Southwest: California, Nevada, Arizona, New Mexico. Jayson Loam. Santa Barbara, Calif.: Capra Press, 1979. 160 pp., illus., index. $8.95 pb.

Hot Springs and Spas of California: A Guide to Taking the Water. Patricia Cooper and Laurel Cook. San Francisco: 101 Productions, 1978. 156 pp., illus., index. $8.95 pb.

Hot Springs and Pools of the Northwest: Colorado, Oregon, Washington, Idaho, Utah, Montana, Wyoming. Jayson Loam. Santa Barbara, Calif.: Capra Press, 1980. 160 pp., illus., index. $8.95 pb.

The Lost World of the Great Spas. Joseph Wechsberg. New York: Harper and Row, 1979. 208 pp., color illus., index. $24.95 hb.

Contacts

Resort Management
Box 4169
Memphis, Tenn. 38104

Adirondack Park Agency
Ray Brook, N.Y. 12977

Catskill Center for Conservation and Development
Hobart, N.Y. 13788

Saratoga Springs Preservation Foundation
432 Broadway
Saratoga Springs, N.Y. 12866

Cape May Planning Board
635 Columbia Avenue
Cape May, N.J. 08204

Miami Design Preservation League
1630 Euclid Avenue
Miami Beach, Fla. 33139

See also: Estates, Chautauquas, Hotels and Inns

Cyclists outside the Hotel Del Monte (1887, A. Page Brown), Monterey, Calif. From *America's Grand Resort Hotels.* (California State Library)

Hat 'n' Boots (1947), Seattle, built to house a discount store and now adapted as a gas station; the boots are the restrooms. (Carleton Knight III)

Row houses on Fulton Avenue, Baltimore, c. 1885, a city famed for this compact house type. (Maryland Historical Society)

Roadside Architecture

"It is easy to like a gas station from the 1930s or a resort hotel from the 1880s because they are both relics, like fish out of water. It is far harder—and it is also far more important—to take due notice of mansarded, shingle-sided fast-food restaurants of the 1970s, to distinguish the superior version from the ordinary, and thus to complete the historical picture."

> Richard Oliver and Nancy Ferguson, "Place, Product, Packaging." *Architectural Record,* February 1978.

Main Street to Miracle Mile: American Roadside Architecture. Chester Liebs. Boston: New York Graphic Society, 1985. $40 hb, $19.95 pb.

The Well-Built Elephant and Other Roadside Attractions: A Tribute to American Eccentricity. J. J. C. Andrews. New York: Congdon and Weed, 1984. 146 pp., illus., biblio. $16.95 pb.

The Colossus of Roads: Myth and Symbol Along the American Highway. Karal Ann Marling. Minneapolis: University of Minnesota Press, 1984. $27.50 hb, $12.95 pb.

Gas, Food, and Lodging. John Baeder. New York: Abbeville, 1982. 132 pp., color illus., index. $29.95 hb.

Learning from Las Vegas: The Forgotten Symbolism of Architectural Form. Robert Venturi, Denise S. Brown, Steven Izenour. 1971. Rev. ed. Cambridge: MIT Press, 1977. 192 pp., illus., append., biblio. $25 hb, $9.95 pb.

The End of the Road: Vanishing Highway Architecture in America. John Margolies. New York: Viking, 1981. 96 pp., color illus. $12.95 pb.

California Crazy: Roadside Vernacular Architecture. Jim Heimann and Rip George. Introduction by David Gebhard. San Francisco: Chronicle Books, 1981. 139 pp., color illus., biblio., index. $8.95 pb.

Americans on the Road: From Autocamp to Motel, 1910–1945. Warren James Belasco. Cambridge: MIT Press, 1979. 212 pp., illus., biblio., index. $25 hb, $6.95 pb.

Souvenirs from the Roadside West: A Personal Collection. Richard Ansaldi. New York: Harmony, 1978. 72 pp., color illus.

White Towers. Paul Hirshorn and Steven Izenour. Cambridge: MIT Press, 1979. 189 pp., illus. $22.50 hb, $9.95 pb.

"Commercial Archeology in Print: A Guide to the Guides of the Roadside," Peter H. Smith. *American Urban Guidenotes* (P.O. Box 186, Washington, D.C. 20044), Spring 1980.

Let There Be Neon. Rudi Stern. New York: Abrams, 1979. 160 pp., illus., gloss., biblio. $19.95 hb, $12.50 pb.

Vanishing Roadside America. Warren H. Anderson. Tucson: University of Arizona Press, 1981. 144 pp., color illus. $14.95 pb.

Lost America Postcards. John Margolies. New York: Dial, 1982. 16 pp., color illus. $3.95 pb.

Roadside Empires: How the Chains Franchised America. Stan Luxenberg. New York: Viking, 1985. 313 pp., index. $17.95 hb.

The Strip: An American Place. Richard P. Horwitz. Lincoln: University of Nebraska Press, 1985. $24.95 hb, $14.95 pb.

Automobile and Culture. Gerald Silk, Angelo Tito Anselmi, Strother MacMinn and Henry Flood Robert, Jr. 319 pp., color illus. New York: Abrams, 1984. $45.

Contact

Society for Commercial Archeology
National Museum of American History
Room 2010
Washington, D.C. 20560

See also: Bizarre and Eccentric Architecture, Diners, Gas Stations, Highways and Roads

Row Houses

"The first row houses in America were built of brick, much of it brought in as ballast on Dutch and English ships. . . . Around 1840 . . . stone replaced brick in many of the nation's public buildings and row houses. The most popular was brownstone. . . . It became so popular that today the world 'brownstone' is often used to mean any nineteenth-century row house, even those with brick or limestone facades."

> H. Dickson McKenna, *A House in the City.* New York: Van Nostrand Reinhold, 1971.

"The revival of suburban row houses between 1960 and 1975 came about almost in spite of the existence of an earlier row house tradition. The centers of origin and early adoption of townhouses were California and Florida, not the Mid-Atlantic states. The great bulk of new townhouses exists in the suburbs, rather than in the inner city. . . . The architectural style of the new townhouses usually ignores the nineteenth century Georgian precedents, imitating instead detached house models."

> Dennis J. Dingemans, "The Urbanization of Suburbia: The Renaissance of the Row House." *Landscape,* October 1975.

Bricks and Brownstone: The New York Row House 1783–1929. An Architectural and Social History. Charles Lockwood. 1972. New York: Abbeville, 1983. 288 pp., illus., biblio. $16.95 pb.

Houses of Boston's Back Bay: An Architectural History, 1840–1917. Bainbridge Bunting. Cambridge: Harvard University Press, 1967. 494 pp., illus., maps, plans, biblio. $25 hb, $12.50 pb.

"The Philadelphia Row House: Is It Peculiarly American, or Even Uniquely Philadelphia?" T. Kaori Kitao. *Swarthmore Alumni Magazine,* April 1977.

The Form of Housing. Sam Davis, ed. New York: Van Nostrand Reinhold, 1977. 320 pp., illus., biblio. $16.95 pb.

Contact

Brownstone Revival Committee
200 Madison Avenue
3rd Floor
New York, N.Y. 10016

See also: Houses, Suburbs; Neighborhoods

Tree Hill Farm, separated from Richmond, Va., by the James River—a dramatic illustration of urban encroachments on rural areas. (Tim McCabe, Soil Conservation Service, USDA)

Rural Areas and Landscapes

"Woe unto them that join house to house,
That lay field to field,
Till there be no place,
That they may be placed alone in the midst of the earth."

Isaiah 5:7–8

"Every rural community is heir to a unique identity formed in part by people, in part by geography. . . .
The functional and harmonious relationship between early rural structures and their surroundings evolved over decades. To preserve this relationship, rural conservationists must concern themselves with the protection of farmland, forests, wetlands and wildlife habitat as well as cultural resources. The interdisciplinary nature of rural conservation also requires careful attention to local economic, political and social factors."

A. Elizabeth Watson, Samuel N. Stokes et al., *Rural Conservation*

Saving America's Countryside: The Rural Conservation Handbook. Genevieve P. Keller, J. Timothy Keller, Samuel N. Stokes and A. Elizabeth Watson. Washington, D.C.: Preservation Press, 1986. 320 pp., illus., biblio., append., index.

Rural Environmental Planning. Frederick O. Sargent. South Burlington, Vt.: Author (330 Spear Street, 05401), 1976. 199 pp., illus., appends. $10.

Changing Rural Landscapes. Ervin H. Zube and Margaret J. Zube, eds. Amherst: University of Massachusetts Press, 1977. 151 pp. $12 hb, $6 pb.

A Sand County Almanac: With Other Essays on Conservation from Round River. Aldo Leopold. New York: Oxford University Press, 1966. $17.95.

First Majority—Last Minority: The Transforming of Rural Life in America. John L. Shover. De Kalb, Ill.: Northern Illinois University Press, 1976. 338 pp., illus., append., index. $15 hb, $6 pb.

Historic Preservation in Rural North Carolina: Problems and Potentials. Kathleen Pepi Southern. Ernest Wood, ed. Raleigh: Historic Preservation Society of North Carolina (109 East Jones Street, 27601), 1982. 188 pp., appends. $5 pb.

The Development of Rural Conservation Programs: A Case Study of Loudoun County, Virginia. A. Elizabeth Watson. Information Series, National Trust for Historic Preservation. Washington, D.C.: Preservation Press, 1981. 32 pp., illus., biblio. $2 pb.

Rural and Small Town Planning. Judith Getzels and Charles Thurow, eds. Old West Regional Commission. Chicago: American Planning Association, 1980. 326 pp. $14.95 pb.

Planning in Rural Environments. William R. Lassey. New York: McGraw-Hill, 1977. 257 pp., illus., biblio., index. $29.95.

New Directions in Rural Preservation. Washington, D.C.: U.S. Department of the Interior, 1980. Preservation Planning Series. 114 pp., illus.

Rural Conservation. A. Elizabeth Watson, Samuel N. Stokes et al. 1979. Rev. ed. Information Series, National Trust for Historic Preservation. Washington, D.C.: Preservation Press, 1984. 16 pp., biblio. $2 pb.

Land Use Planning

"The preservation of historic landscapes is a complex and many-faceted problem because it is embroiled in issues relating to land use, urban sprawl, preservation of agricultural land and natural resource conservation. Yet in the words of the eminent British historian W. G. Hoskins (in *The Making of the English Landscape*), 'the man-made . . . landscape itself, to those who know how to read it aright, is the richest historical record we possess.' Historic preservationists have always accepted the concept of preserving buildings as the essence of our heritage. Now we must work to bring the land itself to this same level of recognition."

William H. Tishler, *Bulletin*, Association for Preservation Technology, vol. XI, no. 4, 1979.

The Last Landscape. William H. Whyte. Garden City, N.Y.: Doubleday, 1968. 428 pp.

Design with Nature. Ian McHarg. New York: Natural History Press, Doubleday, 1969. 200 pp., illus. $11.95 pb.

World with a View: An Inquiry into the Nature of Scenic Values. Christopher Tunnard. New Haven, Conn.: Yale University Press, 1978. 196 pp., illus., index. $25 hb.

Managing the Sense of a Region. Kevin Lynch. Cambridge: MIT Press, 1976. 221 pp., illus., biblio., index. $22.50 hb, $5.95 pb.

The Nature of Landscape Design: As an Art Form, a Craft, a Social Necessity. Nan Fairbrother. New York: Knopf, 1974. 752 pp., illus.

Caring for the Land: Environmental Principles for Site Design and Review. Bruce Hendler. Chicago: American Planning Association, 1977. PAS no. 328. 94 pp., illus. append. $12 pb.

The Community Land Trust Handbook. Institute for Community Economics. Emmaus, Pa.: Rodale Press, 1982. 240 pp., illus., biblio., index. $14.95 hb, $9.95 pb.

Private Options: Tools and Concepts for Land Conservation. Montana Land Reliance and Land Trust Exchange. Covelo, Calif.: Island Press (Box 38, Star Route 1, 95428), 1982. 306 pp., appends., biblio., index. $25 pb.

Land-Saving Action. Russell L. Brenneman and Sarah M. Bates, eds. Covelo, Calif.: Island Press, 1984. 480 pp. $64.95.

Creative Land Development: Bridge to the Future. Robert A. Lemire. Boston: Houghton Mifflin, 1979. 153 pp., biblio., index. $8.95.

Building an Ark: Tools for the Preservation of Natural Diversity Through Land Protection. Phillip M. Hoose. Covelo, Calif.: Island Press, 1981. 221 pp., append., index. $12 pb.

Getting It All Together: The Application of Environmental Information to Land Use Planning. Elisabeth A. Fraser and Anne F. Morris. Mendham, N.J.: Association of New Jersey Environmental Commissions (Box 157, 07945), 1980. 323 pp., illus., biblio. $15.

Land Use Issues of the 1980s. Robert W. Burchell and Edward E. Duensing, eds. Rutgers, N.J.: Center for Urban Policy Research, 1982. 220 pp. $9.95 pb.

Planning the Total Landscape: A Guide to Intelligent Land Use. Julius G. Fabos. Boulder, Colo.: Westview Press, 1979. 181 pp., illus., index. $22 hb.

Toward a New Land Use Ethic: Essays and Comments. Warrenton, Va.: Piedmont Environmental Council (28-C Main Street, 22186), 1981. 166 pp., biblio. $15.

Visual Resource Management. Edward H. Stone. Washington, D.C.: American Society of Landscape Architects, 1978. 32 pp., biblio. $5.

Landscape Assessment: Value, Perceptions and Resources. Ervin H. Zube, Robert O. Brush and Julius G. Fabos, eds. Stroudsburg, Pa.: Dowden, Hutchinson, Ross, 1975. 367 pp.

The Language of Open Space: A Glossary to Help You Say Exactly What You Mean. Duluth Department of Research and Planning. Duluth, Minn.: Author, 1975. 275 pp. $5 pb.

Cultural Landscapes
"Places in nature that have acquired significant associations with human activities and human events become historic and cultural landscapes. . . . While these landscapes seem to retain their natural forms and features, they are, in fact, transformed in the minds of those

Citrus estate near Weslaco, Tex., 1948. (Russell Lee, Standard Oil of New Jersey Collection, University of Louisville)

The Old Oaken Bucket (1943) by Grandma Moses, capturing a variety of rural activities. (New York State Historical Association, Cooperstown)

Bodie, Calif., a boom-and-bust mining town of the mid-1870s whose fragile remains represent a cultural landscape preservation problem. (National Register)

who associate historic events with them. These landscapes are no longer strictly a product of nature, valued for their inherent characteristics, but also become a product of the human mind."
> Carol J. Galbreath, "Criteria for Defining the Historic and Cultural Landscape." In *Conserving the Historic and Cultural Landscape*

Common Landscape of America, 1580 to 1845. John R. Stilgoe. New Haven: Yale University Press, 1982. 429 pp., illus., biblio., index. $29.95 hb.

Past Landscapes: A Bibliography for Historic Preservationists from the Literature of Historical Geography. John A. Jakle, comp. Rev. ed. Monticello, Ill.: Vance Bibliographies, 1980. 68 pp. A-314. $7.50 pb.

Geographic Perspectives on America's Past: Readings on the Historical Geography of the United States. David Ware, ed. New York: Oxford University Press, 1979. 364 pp. $10.95 pb.

The Interpretation of Ordinary Landscapes: Geographical Essays. D. W. Meining, ed. New York: Oxford University Press, 1979. 255 pp. $8.95 pb.

The Landscape of Man: Shaping the Environment from Prehistory to the Present Day. Geoffrey and Susan Jellicoe. 1975. New York: Van Nostrand Reinhold, 1982. 382 pp., illus., biblio., index. $19.95 pb.

Conserving the Historic and Cultural Landscape: Selected Papers. National Trust for Historic Preservation. Washington, D.C.: Preservation Press, 1976. 41 pp., illus. $2.75 pb.

Cultural Landscapes: Rural Historic Districts in the National Park System. Robert Z. Melnick, with Daniel Sponn and Emma Jane Saxe. Washington, D.C.: Park Historic Architecture Division, National Park Service, 1984. 80 pp., illus., biblio., index.

"Capturing the Cultural Landscape," Robert Z. Melnick; "Landscape Preservation Deserves a Broader Meaning," Lisa A. Kunst and Patricia M. O'Donnell. *Landscape Architecture*, January 1981. $4.

Farmlands
"Every day in the United States, 12 square miles of prime farmland are lost forever. . . . In the course of a year, that adds up to more than three million acres of productive soils that are paved over to make room for urban sprawl."

American Farmland Trust, 1981

"While in the East the rural conservation problem is that buildings are engulfing farmland, in the Midwest, the problem—at least as far as historic preservationists are concerned—is that farmland is engulfing buildings of cultural significance."

Samuel N. Stokes, 1981

The Unsettling of America: Culture and Agriculture. Wendell Berry, with Sierra Club. New York: Avon, 1978. 228 pp. $5.95 pb.

National Agricultural Lands Study: Final Report. U.S. Department of Agriculture and Council on Environmental Quality. Washington, D.C.: National Agricultural Lands Study, 1981. 94 pp., biblio. $4.75. GPO stock no. 0–411–011–00062–9.

The Protection of Farmland: A Reference Guidebook for State and Local Governments. Robert E. Coughlin and John C. Keene, eds. A Report to the National Agricultural Lands Study. Washington, D.C.: GPO, 1981. 284 pp. $7.50. GPO stock no. 0–411–011–00067–0.

Agricultural Land Retention and Availability: A Bibliographic Source Book. Washington, D.C.: National Agricultural Lands Study, 1981. $2.50. GPO stock no. 0–411–011–00059–9.

Executive Summary of Protecting Farm Land. Washington, D.C.: National Agricultural Lands Study, 1981. $2.50. GPO stock no. 0–411–011–00055–6.

Protecting Farmlands. Frederick R. Steiner and John E. Theilacker, eds. Westport, Conn.: AVI Publishing, 1984. 312 pp. $32.50 hb.

Disappearing Farmlands: A Citizen's Guide to Agricultural Land Preservation. National Association of Counties Research Foundatin. 2nd ed. Washington, D.C.: Author, 1980. 18 pp., biblio.

Saving Farms and Farmland: A Community Guide. William Toner. Chicago: American Planning Association, 1978. 45 pp. $10.

New Directions in Farm, Land, and Food Policies: A Time for State and Local Action. Joe Belden et al., eds. 2d ed. Washington, D.C.: Conference on Alternative State and Local Policies (2000 Florida Avenue, N.W., 20009), 1981. 320 pp., biblio. $9.95.

Land Banking: European Reality, American Prospect. Ann L. Strong. Baltimore: Johns Hopkins University Press, 1979. 312 pp., illus., biblio., index. $25 hb.

Ecological Planning for Farmlands Preservation. Frederick Steiner. Chicago: Planners Press, American Planning Association, 1981. 122 pp., illus., gloss., biblio. $15.95 pb.

Farmland or Wasteland: A Time to Choose. R. Neil Sampson. Emmaus, Pa.: Rodale Press, 1981. 422 pp., illus., biblio., index. $16.95 hb.

Contacts

National Trust for Historic Preservation
1785 Massachusetts Avenue, N.W.
Washington, D.C. 20036

American Farmland Trust
1717 Massachusetts Avenue, N.W.
Washington, D.C. 20036

Farmers Home Administration
Office of Rural Development Policy
U.S. Department of Agriculture
Washington, D.C. 20250

American Planning Association
1313 East 60th Street
Chicago, Ill. 60637

The Conservation Foundation
1717 Massachusetts Avenue, N.W.
Washington, D.C. 20036

Agricultural Lands Project
National Association of Counties Research Foundation
1735 New York Avenue, N.W.
Washington, D.C. 20006

National Association of Conservation Districts
1025 Vermont Avenue, N.W.
Room 1105
Washington, D.C. 20005

American Land Resource Association
5410 Grosvenor Lane
Bethesda, Md. 20814

Trust for Public Land
82 Second Street
San Francisco, Calif. 94105
245 West 31st Street
New York, N.Y. 10001

Land Trust Exchange
Box 364
Bar Harbor, Maine 04609

National Community Land Trust Center
639 Massachusetts Avenue
Suite 316
Cambridge, Mass. 02139

Alliance for Historic Landscape Preservation
University of Oregon
216 Lawrence Hall
Eugene, Ore. 97403

American Society of Landscape Architects
1733 Connecticut Avenue, N.W.
Washington, D.C. 20009

Landscape Journal: Design Planning and Management of the Land
University of Wisconsin Press
114 North Murray Street
Madison, Wis. 53715

Nature Conservancy
1800 North Kent Street
Suite 800
Arlington, Va. 22209

Rural America
1302 18th Street, N.W.
Suite 302
Washington, D.C. 20036

Soil Conservation Society of America
7515 North Ankeny Road
Ankeny, Iowa 50021

National Association of State Departments of Agriculture
Farmland Project
1616 H Street, N.W.
Washington, D.C. 20006

How to Save the Countryside
1. Develop comprehensive programs covering the whole range of a community's resources—natural, scenic, historic and agricultural.
2. Creatively combine several techniques to achieve more protection than a single approach.
3. Involve both private non-profit organizations and local governments working in tandem.
4. Develop public education programs and involve as many citizens as possible to ensure community acceptance.
5. Take into account social and economic problems in developing and implementing programs.
6. Plan for the long term by having laws and organizations in place to meet new problems and challenges as they arise.

From *Rural Conservation*

See also: Farms, Small Towns; Protecting the Past

Aerial view of a farm in Carroll County, Md., stripcropped to help protect against erosion. (Tim McCabe, Soil Conservation Service, USDA)

Little red schoolhouse (1813) by the side of the road, Prescott, Mass. While many country schools were frame, most were not red. (HABS)

Schools

"An important social institution, the school also is often a significant visual element in a neighborhood. The abandonment or deterioration of an old school—a symbol of continuity and stability from one generation to another—can have a negative effect both physically and psychologically on an entire community."

Urban Land Institute, *Adaptive Use: Development Economics, Process, and Profiles*. Washington, D.C.: ULI, 1978.

America's Country Schools. Andrew Gulliford. Washington, D.C.: Preservation Press, 1984. 296 pp., illus., biblio., append., index. $18.95 pb.

Victorian School-House Architecture. Samuel F. Eveleth. 1870. Reprint. Watkins Glen, N.Y.: American Life Foundation, 1978. 128 pp. $7 pb.

"The Little Red Schoolhouse," Fred E. H. Schroeder. In *Icons of America*. Ray B. Browne and Marshall Fishwick, eds. Bowling Green, Ohio: Popular Press, 1978. 301 pp., illus. $14.95 hb, $6.95 pb.

"Schoolhouse Reading: What You Can Learn from Your Rural School," Fred E. H. Schroeder. *History News*, April 1981.

The Little White Schoolhouse. Ellis Ford Hartford. Lexington: University Press of Kentucky, 1977. 128 pp., illus., biblio. $6.95 hb.

The Little Red Schoolhouse. Eric Sloane. Garden City, N.Y.: Doubleday, 1972. 47 pp., illus.

Rural One-Room Schools of Mid-America. Leslie C. Swanson. Moline, Ill.: Author (P.O. Box 334-RS, 61265), 1976. $5.95.

The Old Country School: The Story of Rural Education in the Middle West. Wayne E. Fuller. Chicago: University of Chicago Press, 1982. $22.50 hb.

Surplus Schools. Holly Harrison Fiala. Information Series, National Trust for Historic Preservation. Washington, D.C.: Preservation Press, 1982. 36 pp., illus., biblio., append. $2 pb.

Surplus Schools: Adaptive Reuse. Paul Abramson, ed. New York: Educational Facilities Laboratories, 1985. 100 pp. $5 pb.

A Guide for the Adaptive Use of Surplus Schools. Jack W. Giljahn and Thomas R. Matheny. Columbus, Ohio: Columbus Landmarks Foundation, 1981. 124 pp., illus., biblio., appends.

Surplus School Space: Options and Opportunities. New York: Educational Facilities Laboratories, 1976. 72 pp., illus., biblio. $4 pb.

The Secondary School: Reduction, Renewal, and Real Estate. New York: Educational Facilities Laboratories, 1976. 64 pp., illus., biblio. $4 pb.

Surplus School Space: The Problem and the Possibilities. Columbus, Ohio: Council of Educational Facilities Planners, 1978. 47 pp., illus., biblio. $3.50 pb.

To Recreate a School Building: "Surplus" Space, Energy and Other Challenges. Arlington, Va.: American Association of School Administrators, 1976. 123 pp., illus. $10 pb.

Solutions for Surplus Schools. Technical Series, no. 6. Albany: Preservation League of New York State, 1978. 6 pp., illus., biblio.

The Arts in Surplus Schools. New York: Educational Facilities Laboratories, 1981. 32 pp., illus. $5 pb.

Contacts

Educational Facilities Laboratories
Academy for Educational Development
680 Fifth Avenue
New York, N.Y. 10019

Council of Educational Facilities Planners
29 West Woodruff Avenue
Columbus, Ohio 43210

American Association of School Administrators
1801 North Moore Street
Arlington, Va. 22209

Midwest Regional Office
National Trust for Historic Preservation
407 South Dearborn Street
Suite 710
Chicago, Ill. 60605

Preservation League of New York State
307 Hamilton Street
Albany, N.Y. 12210

Community Education Program
U.S. Department of Education
400 Maryland Avenue, S.W.
Washington, D.C. 20202

See also: Colleges and Universities

Black school (1917) Nicodemus, Kans. (Everett L. Fly, HABS)

Interior of the Centre Family Dwelling House (c. 1820), Shakertown at Pleasant Hill, Ky. (Jack E. Boucher, HABS)

Shakers

"The streets are quiet; for here you have no grog shop, no beer house, no lock up, no pound; . . . and every building, whatever may be its use, has something of the air of a chapel. The paint is all fresh; the planks are clean bright; the windows are all clean. A sheen is on everything; a happy quiet reigns."

William Hepworth Dixon, 19th-century writer

Shaker Built: Catalog of Shaker Architectural Records from the Historic American Buildings Survey. John Poppeliers, ed. Washington, D.C.: Historic American Buildings Survey, U.S. Department of the Interior, 1974. 87 pp., illus., biblio.

Shaker Architecture. Herbert Schiffer. Exton, Pa.: Schiffer Publishing, 1979. 190 pp., illus., map, biblio., index. $20 hb.

Shaker Architecture. William L. Lassiter. New York: Bonanza Books, 1966. 127 pp., illus., plans, maps, biblio.

Shaker Literature: A Bibliography. Mary L. Richmond, Shaker Community, Inc. Hanover, N.H.: University Press of New England, 1977. 656 pp. $60.

The People Called Shakers: A Search for the Perfect Society. Edward D. Andrews. 1953. Reprint. New York: Dover, 1963. $5.50 pb.

The Shaker Image. Elmer R. Pearson and Julia Neal. Boston: New York Graphic Society and Shaker Community, Inc., 1974. 190 pp., illus., biblio.

A Shaker Reader: Milton C. and Emily Mason Rose, eds. New York: Universe Books, 1977. 128 pp., illus., index.

The Shakers and the World's People. Flo Morse. New York: Dodd, Mead, 1980. 378 pp., illus., biblio., index. $17.95 hb.

The Shaker Way. Charles Muller. Worthington, Ohio: Ohio Antique Review, 1979. 143 pp., illus. $9.50 pb.

The Kentucky Shakers. Julia Neal. 1977. Reprint. Lexington: University Press of Kentucky, 1982. 120 pp., illus., index. $10 hb.

Recapturing Wisdom's Valley: The Watervliet Shaker Heritage 1775–1975. Dorothy M. Filley. Mary L. Richmond, ed. Albany: Albany Institute of History and Art, 1975. 128 pp., illus., maps, biblio. $10 hb, $5 pb.

The Shaker Holy Land: A Community Portrait (Harvard, Mass.). Edward R. Morgan. Harvard, Mass.: Harvard Common Press, 1982. 224 pp., illus., biblio., index. $15.95 hb.

Contacts

Shakertown at Pleasant Hill
Route 4
Harrodsburg, Ky. 40330

Hancock Shaker Village
Shaker Community, Inc.
P.O. Box 898
Pittsfield, Mass. 01202

Shaker Collection
Western Reserve Historical Society
c/o Microfilming Corporation of America
200 Park Avenue
New York, N.Y. 10166

See also: Communal Societies

Skyscrapers

"The first tall building that 'scraped' the sky was not built in New York in 1868, and a more accurate history will take us back much further in time— to the first obelisks, ziggurats and pyramids built 3,000 years ago, or to heaven-aspiring structures built before that. Man has been constructing skybuildings for a long time."

Charles Jencks, *Skyscrapers-Skycities*

"A New View of Skyscraper History," Winston Weisman. In *The Rise of an American Architecture.* Henry-Russell Hitchcock et al. Edgar Kaufmann, Jr., ed. New York: Praeger, 1970. 241 pp., illus., append., biblio., index.

The Skyscraper. Paul Goldberger. New York: Knopf, 1981. 224 pp., illus., index. $12.95 pb.

The Tall Building Artistically Reconsidered: The Search for a Skyscraper Style. Ada Louise Huxtable. New York: Pantheon, 1985. 144 pp., illus. $21.95 hb.

Skyscrapers-Skycities. Charles Jencks. New York: Rizzoli, 1980. 80 pp., color illus., biblio.

History of the Skyscraper. Francisco Mujica. 1929. Reprint. New York: Da Capo, 1977. $95 hb.

Skeleton Construction in Buildings: With Numerous Practical Illustrations of High Buildings. William H. Birkmire. 1894. Reprint. Salem, N.H.: Ayer Company, 1972. $19 hb.

Skyscraper Odyssey: An Informal History of Tall Buildings in America. George H. Douglas. New York: Hastings House, 1984. $29.95.

Human Response to Tall Buildings. Donald J. Conway, ed. New York: Van Nostrand Reinhold, 1977. 362 pp., illus., index. $44.50 hb.

The Center: A History and Guide to Rockefeller Center. Walter Karp. New York: Van Nostrand Reinhold, 1983. 128 pp., illus. $19.50 hb.

The Ultimate Highrise: San Francisco's Mad Rush Toward the Sky. Bruce B. Brugmann et al., eds. San Francisco: San Francisco Bay Guardian, 1971. 255 pp., illus.

Contacts

Commission on Chicago Historical and Architectural Landmarks
320 North Clark Street
Room 800
Chicago, Ill. 60610

New York City Landmarks Preservation Commission
20 Vesey Street
New York, N.Y. 10007

See also: Chicago School (Looking at the Built Environment)

Chicago Board of Trade (1930, Holabird and Root). (Hedrich-Blessing)

Small town patchwork quilt. (Beverly Bancroft Davis, NTHP)

Small Towns

"The country town is one of the great American institutions; perhaps the greatest, in the sense that it has had . . . a greater part than any other in shaping public sentiment and giving character to American culture."

Thorstein Veblen, "The Country Town." 1923.

"A Gallup Poll reported that the happiest Americans live in towns with populations of 2,500 to 50,000. The largest proportion of sad people live in big cities. . . ."

"Playing the Averages: Our Thoughts and Moods." *Washington Star*, August 7, 1980.

Small Town America: A Narrative History, 1620 to the Present. Richard Lingeman. New York: Putnam, 1980. 547 pp., biblio., index. $8.95 pb.

Change and Tradition in the American Small Town. Robert Craycroft and Michael Fazio. Jackson: University Press of Mississippi, 1983. 133 pp. $7.50 pb.

The American Small Town: Twentieth-Century Place Images. John A. Jakle. Hamden, Conn.: Shoe String Press, 1981. 195 pp., illus., biblio., index. $25 hb.

Order and Image in the American Small Town. Michael W. Fazio and Peggy Whitman Prenshaw, eds. Jackson: University Press of Mississippi, 1981. 200 pp., illus. $12.50 hb.

The Small Town in American Literature. 2nd ed. David M. Cook and Craig G. Swauger, eds. New York: Harper and Row, 1977. $13.95 pb.

Historic Preservation Resourcebook for Small Communities. Kenneth Munsell and Anne Smith Denman. Ellensburg, Wash.: Small Towns Institute, 1983. 100 pp., illus., biblios. $10 pb.

Historic Preservation in Small Towns: A Manual of Practice. Arthur P. Ziegler, Jr., and Walter C. Kidney. Nashville. American Association for State and Local History, 1980. 146 pp., illus., biblio., append. $11.95 pb.

From Main Street to State Street: Town, City and Community in America. Park Dixon Goist. Port Washington, N.Y.: Kennikat Press (90 South Bayles Avenue, 11050), 1977. 180 pp., biblio., index. $17.95 hb.

As a City Upon a Hill: The Town in American History. Page Smith. 1966. Reprint. Cambridge: MIT Press, 1973.

Small Towns and Small Towners: A Framework for Survival and Growth. Bert B. Swanson and Richard A. Cohen. Beverly Hills, Calif.: Sage Publications, 1979. 280 pp., illus., biblio., index.

Special Places: In Search of Small Town America. William Shawn. Boston: Little, Brown, 1982. $12.95.

Rural and Small Town Planning. Judith Getzels and Charles Thurow, eds. Old West Regional Commission. Chicago: American Planning Association, 1980. 326 pp. $14.95 pb.

Planning Smaller Cities. Herrington J. Bryce. Lexington, Mass.: Lexington Books, D.C. Heath, 1979. 214 pp.

The Small Towns Book: Show Me the Way to Go Home. James and Carolyn Robertson. Garden City, N.Y.: Anchor Books, Doubleday, 1978. 208 pp., illus., biblio.

Middletown. Robert S. Lynd and Helen M. Lynd. 1929. Reprint. New York: Harcourt, Brace, Jovanovich, 1959. $7.95 pb.

Middletown in Transition: A Study in Cultural Conflicts. 1937. Reprint. New York: Harcourt, Brace, Jovanovich, 1963. $9.95 pb.

Middletown Families: Fifty Years of Change and Continuity. Theodore Caplow et al. Minneapolis: University of Minnesota Press, 1982. 400 pp. $18.95.

Small Town in Mass Society: Class, Power and Religion in a Rural Community. Arthur I. Vidich and Joseph Bensman. Rev. ed. Princeton: Princeton University Press, 1968. $29 hb, $11.50 pb.

Sod dugout, Norton County, Kans. (Kansas State Historical Society)

New Burlington: The Life and Death of an American Village. John Baskin. 1976. Reprint. New York: New American Library, 1977. $2.95 pb.

A Vanishing America: The Life and Times of the Small Town. Thomas C. Wheeler, ed. New York: Holt, Rinehart and Winston, 1964. 191 pp.

Plains Country Towns. John C. Hudson. Minneapolis: University of Minnesota Press, 1985. $25 hb, $13.95 pb.

Biography of a Small Town. Elvin Hatch. New York: Columbia University Press, 1979. 312 pp., biblio., index. $27.50.

Old Burnside. Harriette Simpson Arnow. Lexington: University Press of Kentucky, 1977. 142 pp., illus. $6.95.

Hidden Country Villages of California. Frances Coleberd. San Francisco: Chronicle Books, 1977. 180 pp., illus. $7.95 pb.

Contacts

Small Towns Institute
P.O. Box 517
Ellensburg, Wash. 98926

Institute on Man and Science
Rensselaerville, N.Y. 12147

Center for Small Town Research and Design
Mississippi State University
P.O. Drawer A.Q.
Mississippi State, Miss. 39762

National Association of Smaller Communities
888 17th Street, N.W.
Suite 800
Washington, D.C. 20006

Office of Rural Development Policy
Farmers Home Administration
U.S. Department of Agriculture
Washington, D.C. 20250

See also: Cities, Company Towns, Rural Areas and Landscapes; Main Streets

Sod Houses

"When the wagon halted, the head of the family took out a spade and began to construct the dwelling. . . . The whole thing, as one pioneer said, was 'made without mortar, square, plumb, or greenbacks.' "

Everett Dick, *The Sod-House Frontier*

The Sod-House Frontier: A Social History of the Northern Plains from the Creation of Kansas and Nebraska to the Admission of the Dakotas. Everett Dick. 1937. Reprint. Lincoln: University of Nebraska Press, 1979. 550 pp., illus. $12.95 pb.

The Sod House. Cass G. Barns. 1930. Reprint. Lincoln: University of Nebraska Press, 1978. 301 pp., illus. $21.50 hb, $7.95 pb.

Sod Walls: The Story of the Nebraska Sod House. Roger L. Welsch. Lincoln: Author. $10.

Sod and Stubble: The Story of a Kansas Homestead. John Ise. Lincoln: University of Nebraska Press, 1967. 340 pp., illus. $23.50 hb, $6.95 pb.

"Sod Houses and Similar Structures: A Brief Evaluation of the Literature," Allen C. Noble. *Pioneer America*, vol. 13, no. 2, 1981.

"Soddies," Terry B. Morton. *Historic Preservation*, vol. 12, no. 4, 1960.

Contacts

Pioneer America Society
c/o Allen G. Noble
Department of Geography
University of Akron
Akron, Ohio 44325

Sod Town Pioneer Museum
Sod House Society of America
P.O. Box 393
Colby, Kans. 67701

Solomon Butcher Photograph Collection
Nebraska State Historical Society
1500 R Street
Lincoln, Neb. 68508

Kansas State Historical Society
120 West 10th Street
Topeka, Kans. 66612

Sod House
Panhandle-Plains Historical Museum
P.O. Box 967, W.T. Station
Canyon, Tex. 79016

Apollo Launch Complex 39 (1965), Kennedy Space Center, Cape Canaveral, Fla., a new landmark spared from demolition.

San Francisco cable cars in 1934. (S. Bloom)

Space Age Sites

"Since the 1960s the space age, with its missile sites and launch facilities, has created or inflated such towns as Huntsville, Ala., Cape Canaveral, Fla., and Houston, Tex., just as the first travel systems did in the colonies. In 1969, with the first lunar landing, a bit of built environment was transplanted even to the moon."

National Trust et al., *America's Forgotten Architecture.* New York: Pantheon, 1976.

"It is a breathtaking sight: a 100,000-acre set for a Fellini movie. Dead flat, with red steel gantries lined up like giant robots on the horizon. There is no scale: the huge new Vehicle Assembly Building (VAB) is first seen from 14 miles away, looking no larger than an electric toaster. VAB is, in fact, by far the biggest building in the world—130 million cubic feet of space, more than the Empire State and the Chicago Merchandise Mart combined!"

Peter Blake, "Cape Kennedy." *Architectural Forum,* January–February 1967.

Reconnaissance: Man in Space. Report to Congress on NASA Sites to Be Preserved. Harry Butowsky et al. Washington, D.C.: National Park Service, 1981. 175 pp., illus., appends.

The History of Manned Space Flight. David Baker. New York: Crown, 1982. 512 pp., color illus., index. $35 hb.

Chariots for Apollo: A History of Manned Lunar Spacecraft. Courtney G. Brooks et al. Washington, D.C.: National Aeronautics and Space Administration, 1979. 539 pp., illus., index.

Orders of Magnitude: A History of NACA and NASA, 1915–1980. Frank W. Anderson. Washington, D.C.: National Aeronautics and Space Administration, 1981. 100 pp., illus., index.

Beyond the Atmosphere: Early Years of Space Science. Homer E. Newell. Washington, D.C.: National Aeronautics and Space Administration, 1980. 501 pp., illus., index.

Some Historic Space Sites
Launch Complex 39, Kennedy Space Center, Fla.

Redstone Test Stand, Marshall Space Flight Center, Huntsville, Ala.

Launch Complexes 13, 19, 37, Kennedy Space Center

Johnson Manned Space Center, Houston

Goddard Rocket Launching Site (1926), Pakachoag Golf Course, near Auburn, Mass.

Contacts

National Aeronautics and Space Administration
400 Maryland Avenue, S.W.
Washington, D.C. 20546

National Air and Space Museum
Smithsonian Institution
Washington, D.C. 20560

History Office
National Aeronautics and Space Administration
300 7th Street, S.W.
Room 706
Washington, D.C. 20546

American Society for Aerospace Education
806 15th Street, N.W.
Washington, D.C. 20005

Streetcars and Trolleys

"The trolley car for well over three decades . . . was the most outstanding feature of the American urban scene. People saw them, heard them and, if they went anywhere at all rode them; for the trolley . . . went virtually everywhere."

William M. Moedinger, *The Trolley: Triumph of Transport.* Lebanon, Pa.: Applied Arts Publishers, 1971.

Trolley to the Past: A Companion to and History of the Operating Trolley Museums of North America. Andrew D. Young. Glendale, Calif.: Interurban Press, 1983. 158 pp., illus., index. $19.95 pb.

From Streetcar to Superhighway: American City Planners and Urban Transportation, 1900–1940. Mark S. Foster. Philadelphia: Temple University Press, 1981. 263 pp., illus. $34.95 hb.

Streetcar Suburbs: The Process of Growth in Boston, 1870–1900. Sam Bass Warner, Jr. Cambridge: Harvard University Press, 1962. $14 hb, $7.95 pb.

Trolleys and Streetcars on American Picture Postcards. Ray D. Appelgate. New York: Dover, 1979. 87 pp., color illus. $5 pb.

Horsecars, Cable Cars and Omnibuses. John White, Jr. New York: Dover, 1974. 107 pp. $6.50 pb.

The Great Cable Car Adventure Book. Gene Anthony and Jill Losson. Novato, Calif.: Presidio Press, 1981. 144 pp., illus., index.

The Cable Car in America. George W. Hilton. Rev. ed. San Diego: Howell-North, 1982. 484 pp., illus., biblio., index. $30 hb.

Cable Car. Christopher Swan. Berkeley, Calif: Ten Speed Press, 1978. 127 pp., illus., biblio. $8.95 hb, $4.95 pb.

The New York Elevated. Robert C. Reed. New York: A. S. Barnes, 1978. 176 pp., illus., index. $17.50 hb.

Destination Loop: The Story of Rapid Transit Railroading in and Around Chicago. Brian J. Cudahy. Brattleboro, Vt.: Stephen Greene, 1982. $16.95.

From Horsecars to Streamliners: An Illustrated History of the St. Louis Car Company. Park Forest, Ill.: Transport History Press (Box 201, 60466), 1978. $22.50 hb.

Streetcar Man: Tom Lowry and the Twin City Rapid Transit Company. Goodrich Lowry. Minneapolis: Lerner Publications, 1979. 178 pp., illus., biblio., appends., index. $7.95 hb.

Street Railways of Louisiana. Louis C. Hennick and E. Harper Charlton. Gretna, La.: Pelican, 1979. 152 pp., illus., index. $19.95 hb.

The Streetcars of New Orleans. Louis C. Hennick and E. Harper Charlton. 1962. Rev. ed. Gretna, La.: Pelican, 1975. 240 pp., illus. $19.95 hb.

The Last Line: A Streetcar Named St. Charles. August Perez and Associates. Gretna, La.: Pelican, 1973. 96 pp., illus. $8.95 pb.

The Streetcar Guide to Uptown New Orleans. Louis Costa et al. New Orleans: Transitour, 1980. 136 pp., illus., biblio. $5 pb.

100 Years of Capital Traction: The Story of Streetcars in the Nation's Capital. LeRoy O. King, Jr. Dallas: Taylor Publishing Co. 328 pp., illus., biblio., index.

Contacts

Committee to Save the Cable Cars
San Francisco Chamber of Commerce
465 California Street
San Francisco, Calif. 94104

National Museum of Transport
3015 Barrett Station Road
St. Louis, Mo. 63122

Baltimore Streetcar Museum
P.O. Box 7184
Baltimore, Md. 21218

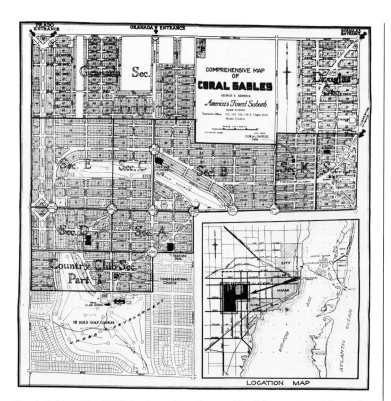

Coral Gables, Fla. (1920s), planned by George Merrick as a city of Spanish-style buildings. (Historical Museum of Southeast Florida and the Caribbean)

Suburbs

"A series of neighborhoods of a peculiar character is already growing up in close relation with all large towns, and though many of these are as yet little better than rude over-dressed villages, or fragmentary half-made towns, it can hardly be questioned that, already, there are to be found among them the most attractive, the most refined and the most soundly wholesome forms of domestic life, and the best application of the arts of civilization to which mankind has yet attained."

Frederick Law Olmsted, 1868.

"The truth is that the suburbs we are building now, based as they are on the automobile, are not the ones we idealize. It is the earlier suburb that represents the desirable paradigm, not only from the point of view of the design of the individual buildings, but also from the standpoints of convenience and of economic value. That is why Garden City and not Levittown, Shaker Heights and not Columbia continue to ring the bell of status."

Robert A. M. Stern, "The Suburban Alternative for the 'Middle City.' " *Architectural Record*, August 1978.

Suburbia: A Guide to Information Sources. Joseph Zikmund and Deborah E. Dennis, eds. Detroit: Gale, 1979. 142 pp. $55.

The Design of Suburbia: A Critical Study in Environmental History. Arthur M. Edwards. Hamden, Conn.: Shoe String Press, 1981. 281 pp., $32.50.

The Anglo-American Suburb. Robert A. M. Stern, ed. New York: St. Martin's, 1981. 96 pp., illus. $9.95.

Civilizing American Cities: A Selection of Frederick Law Olmsted's Writings on City Landscapes. S. B. Sutton, ed. Cambridge: MIT Press, 1971. $7.95 pb.

Streetcar Suburbs: The Process of Growth in Boston, 1870–1900. Sam Bass Warner, Jr. Cambridge: Harvard University Press, 1962. $14 hb, $7.95 pb.

"The Suburban Ideal: 19th-Century Planned Communities," Michael Robinson. *Historic Preservation*, April–June 1978.

" 'A Village in a Park': Riverside, Illinois," Robert W. Heidrich. *Historic Preservation*, April–June 1973.

"The Crabgrass Frontier: 150 Years of Suburban Growth in America," Kenneth T. Jackson. In *The Urban Experience: Themes in American History.* Raymond A. Mohl and James F. Richardson, eds. Belmont, Calif.: Wadsworth, 1973. 276 pp., biblio.

New Towns and the Suburban Dream: Ideology and Utopia in Planning and Development. Irving Lewis Allen, ed. Port Washington, N.Y.: Kennikat Press, 1976. 285 pp., illus., biblio., index. $24.

Suburbia: The American Dream and Dilemma. Philip Dolce, ed. Garden City, N.Y.: Doubleday, 1976. 238 pp., biblio., index.

Urban America: From Downtown to No Town. David R. Goldfield and Blaine A. Brownell. Boston: Houghton Mifflin, 1979. 435 pp., illus., biblio., index. $17.50 pb.

The Levittowners: Ways of Life and Politics in a New Suburban Community. Herbert J. Gans. 1967. Reprint. New York: Columbia University Press, 1982. 512 pp. $39 hb, $14.50 pb.

The Form of Housing. Sam Davis, ed. New York: Van Nostrand Reinhold, 1977. 320 pp., illus., index. $16.95 pb.

Suburb: Neighborhood and Community in Forest Park, Ohio, 1935–1976. Zane L. Miller. Knoxville: University of Tennessee Press, 1981. 296 pp. $19.95.

See also: Gardens and Parks, Houses

Subways

" 'Preposterous!' scoffed American tycoon Russell Sage to the first proposal for an underground transit system in New York City. 'The people of New York will never go into a hole in the ground to ride.' "

James Meyers, *Eggplants, Elevators, Etc.: An Uncommon History of Common Things.* New York: Hart, 1978.

Labyrinths of Iron: A History of the World's Subways. Benson Bobrick. New York: Newsweek Books, 1981. 352 pp., illus., biblio., index.

Under the Sidewalks of New York: The Story of the Greatest Subway System in the World. Brian J. Cudahy. Brattleboro, Vt.: Stephen Greene, 1979. 176 pp., illus., appends., index. $16.95 hb.

Subway kiosk on Broadway. (New York City Transit Authority)

"Tunnels, Tracks, and Trippers." In *Under the City Streets.* Pamela Jones. New York: Holt, Rinehart and Winston, 1978. 275 pp., illus., index, biblio.

Uptown, Downtown: A Trip Through Time on New York's Subways. Stan Fischler. New York: Hawthorn Books, 1976. 271 pp., illus., index, appends.

"Art and the IRT: First Subway Art," John Touranac. *Historic Preservation*, October–December 1973.

Moving the Masses: Urban Public Transit in New York, Boston, and Philadelphia, 1880–1912. Charles W. Cheape. Cambridge: Harvard University Press, 1980. 285 pp., illus., index. $18.50.

Moving Millions: An Inside Look at Mass Transit. Stanley I. Fischler. New York: Harper and Row, 1979. 262 pp., illus., index.

Contacts

Electric Railroaders Association
89 East 42nd Street
New York, N.Y. 10017

American Public Transit Association
1225 Connecticut Avenue, N.W.
Washington, D.C. 20036

Adopt-a-Station Program
Culture Station Program
Metropolitan Transit Authority
347 Madison Avenue
New York, N.Y. 10017

Everybody's Saloon, Hazen, Nev., c. 1905, featuring a board-and-batten storefront. (Bureau of Reclamation, National Archives)

Taverns and Saloons

"There is nothing which has yet been contrived by man by which so much happiness is produced as by a good tavern or inn."

Samuel Johnson

America's Historic Inns and Taverns. Irvin Haas. Rev. ed. New York: Arco, 1977. 182 pp., illus.

Stage-Coach and Tavern Days. Alice Morse Earle. 1900. Reprint. Williamstown, Mass.: Corner House, 1977. 449 pp., illus., index. $18.50.

Appendix on Inns and Taverns. In *American Interiors: From Colonial Times to the Late Victorians.* Harold L. Peterson. New York: Scribner's, 1979. 206 pp., illus., index.

The Saloon on the Rocky Mountain Mining Frontier. Elliott West. Lincoln: University of Nebraska Press, 1979. 197 pp., illus., appends., biblio., index. $14.50 hb.

The City and the Saloon: Denver, 1858–1916. Thomas J. Noel. Lincoln: University of Nebraska Press, 1982. 148 pp., illus., biblio., index. $16.50 hb.

Saloons of the Old West. Richard Erdoes. New York: Knopf, 1979. 227 pp., illus., biblio., index.

Taverns and Travelers: Inns of the Early Midwest. Paton Yoder. Bloomington: Indiana University Press, 1969. 237 pp., illus., biblio., index.

Early American Inns and Taverns. Elise L. Lathrop. 1935. Reprint. New York: Arno Press, 1968. $17.50 hb.

The Old-Time Saloon: Not Wet—Not Dry, Just History. George Ade. 1931. Reprint. Detroit: Gale, 1975.

The 'Twenty-One' Club: The Life and Times of America's Most Famous Saloon. Marilyn Kaytor. New York: Viking, 1975. 176 pp., illus. $19.95.

Early American Taverns: For the Entertainment of Friends and Strangers. Kym S. Rice. Chicago: Regnery Gateway, 1983. 168 pp. $12.95.

See also: Hotels and Inns

Theaters and Cinemas

"Since the mid-1960s, there has been a significant slowing of the trend toward the extinction of historic theaters as interest in their preservation and reuse for the performing arts has grown. . . . They are proving to be of great interest because almost all are architecturally and historically significant and are readily adaptable for contemporary performing arts usage.

Most historic theaters were built to be the focal point of a community's cultural life and their architectural significance stems from this fact. The theater builders did not want ordinary structures for the representation of cultural events, but buildings that would reflect the cultural level of their community."

> Robert Stoddard, *Preservation of Concert Halls, Opera Houses and Movie Palaces*

Theatre and Cinema Architecture: A Guide to Information Sources. Richard Stoddard. Performing Arts Information Guide Series, vol. 5. Detroit: Gale, 1978. 368 pp., indexes. $55 hb.

Preservation of Concert Halls, Opera Houses and Movie Palaces. Robert Stoddard. Information Series, National Trust for Historic Preservation. Washington, D.C.: Preservation Press, 1978. 28 pp., illus., biblio. $2 pb.

Theaters

Theater Design. George Izenour. New York: McGraw-Hill, 1977. 631 pp., color illus., append., index. $195.

Theatres: An Architectural and Cultural History. Simon Tidworth. New York: Praeger, 1973. 224 pp., illus., biblio., index.

The Development of the Playhouse: A Survey of Theatre Architecture from the Renaissance to the Present. Donald C. Mullin. Berkeley: University of California Press, 1970. $41 hb.

Documents of American Theater History: Famous American Playhouses. Vol. I: *1716–1899.* Vol. II: *1899–1971.* William C. Young. Chicago: American Library Association, 1973.

Times Square: A Pictorial History. Jill Stone. New York: Macmillan, 1982. 192 pp., illus. $9.95 pb.

Radio City Music Hall: An Affectionate History of the World's Greatest Theatre. Charles Francisco. New York: Dutton, 1979. 136 pp., color illus.

At This Theatre: Playbill Magazine's Informal History of Broadway Theatres. Botto. New York: Dodd, Mead, 1984. $25.95.

The Auditorium Building: Its History and Architectural Significance. Chicago: Roosevelt University (430 South Michigan Avenue, 60605), 1976.

The Central City Opera House: A 100 Year History. Charlie H. Johnson, Jr. Colorado Springs: Little London Press (716 East Washington Street, 80907), 1980. 78 pp., illus., append., biblio. $4.95 pb.

A Grand Strategy: The Scenario for Saving the Grand Opera House, Wilmington, Del. Robert Stoddard. Washington, D.C.: Preservation Press, 1978. 44 pp., illus., appends. $4.50 pb.

Cinemas

The Best Remaining Seats: The Golden Age of the Movie Palace. Ben M. Hall. New York: Clarkson Potter, 1961. 266 pp., illus.

American Picture Palaces: The Architecture of Fantasy. David Naylor. New York: Van Nostrand Reinhold, 1981. 224 pp., color illus., append., biblio., index. $29.95 hb.

Movie Palaces. Ave Pildas. New York: Crown, 1980.

The Picture Palace and Other Buildings for the Movies. Dennis Sharp. New York: Praeger, 1969. 224 pp., illus., biblio., index.

Nickelodeon to Movie Palace: Ten Twentieth Century Theatres, 1910–1931. A. Craig Morrison and Lucy Pope Wheeler, eds. Washington, D.C.: Historic American Buildings Survey, U.S. Department of the Interior, 1978.

Indiana Theatre (1927, Rubush and Hunter), Indianapolis, now home of the Indiana Repertory Theatre. (Brandt, Indiana Repertory Theatre)

The Mormon Trail (1853). From *Exploration and Survey of the Valley of the Great Salt Lake of Utah* by Howard Stansbury. (National Archives)

Movie Palaces: Renaissance and Reuse. Joseph M. Valerio and Daniel Friedman. New York: Educational Facilities Laboratories, 1982. 120 pp., illus., biblio., append. $11 pb.

Scene II: Re-Using Old Movie Theaters. Robert E. Freeman. Providence, R.I: Author (18 Savoy Street, 02906), 1977. 135 pp., illus., biblio. $10.

A Pictorial Survey of Marquees. Notre Dame, Ind.: Theatre Historical Society, 1980. 38 pp., illus.

The Oakland Paramount. Susannah Harris Stone. Berkeley, Calif.: Lancaster Miller, 1981. 94 pp., illus. $11.95 hb.

The Ohio Theatre: 1928–1978. Mary Bishop, ed. Columbus: Columbus Association for the Performing Arts, 1978. 144 pp.

The Front Row: Missouri's Grand Theatres. Mary Bagley. St. Louis: Gateway Publishing, 1984. $26.95.

Contacts

League of Historic American Theaters
1600 H Street, N.W.
Washington, D.C. 20006

Theatre Historical Society
2215 West North Avenue
Chicago Ill. 60642

Marquee
Theatre Historical Society
P.O. Box 101
Notre Dame, Ind. 46556

American Theater Organ Society
Box 1002
Middleburg, Va. 22117

Trails

"This type of cultural landscape may be the most ephemeral and the most difficult to document and to protect; for example, today over half the length of the Oregon Trail is paved or otherwise beyond documentation."

> Carol J. Galbreath, "Criteria for Defining the Historic and Cultural Landscape." In *Conserving the Historic and Cultural Landscape.* Washington, D.C.: Preservation Press, 1975.

"And yet, there are still trails and vistas where the skyline is not laced by power lines or fences nor punctuated by grain elevators. There are still white water rapids and magnificent stands of timber. There is still time."

> Mary and Paul Macopia, *Lewis and Clark's America*

The Plains Across: The Overland Emigrants and the Trans-Mississippi West, 1840–60. John D. Unruh, Jr. Urbana: University of Illinois Press, 1979. 568 pp., illus., biblio., index. $7.95 pb.

"National Trails: The Unexplored Potential," Craig Evans. *National Parks and Conservation Magazine,* October 1980.

Wagon Roads West: A Study of Federal Surveys and Construction in the Trans-Mississippi West, 1848–1869. W. Turrentine Jackson. 1964. Reprint. Lincoln: University of Nebraska Press, 1979. 422 pp., maps, biblio., index. $28.50 hb, $6.50 pb.

Explorers and Settlers: Historic Places Commemorating the Early Exploration and Settlement of the United States. Robert G. Ferris, ed., Historic Sites Survey. Washington, D.C.: National Park Service, U.S. Department of the Interior, 1968. 506 pp., illus. $17 hb. GPO stock no. 024-005-00006-2.

Water Trails West. Western Writers of America. 1978. New York: Avon, 1979. 271 pp., illus., index. $3.50 pb.

Lewis and Clark: Historic Places Associated with Their Transcontinental Exploration (1804–06). Robert G. Ferris, ed., Historic Sites Survey. Washington, D.C.: National Park Service, U.S. Department of the Interior, 1975. 429 pp., illus. $14 hb. GPO stock no. 024-005-00559-5.

American Odyssey: The Journey of Lewis and Clark. Ingvard Henry Eide. Chicago: Rand McNally, 1979. 272 pp., illus.

Lewis and Clark's America. Part I: *A Voyage of Discovery.* Part II: *A Contemporary Photo Essay.* Paul and Mary E. Macopia. Seattle: Seattle Art Museum, 1976. 192 pp., illus. $12.50 pb.

Lewis and Clark Country. Archie Satterfield and David Muench. Portland, Ore.: Beautiful America Publishing Company, 1978.

The Oregon Trail. Francis Parkman. New York: New American Library. $2.25 pb.

The Oregon Trail Revisted. Gregory M. Franzwa. 3rd ed. Gerald, Mo.: Patrice Press (Box 42, 63037), 1983. 417 pp., illus., biblio., index. $5.95 pb.

The Oregon Trail: The Missouri River to the Pacific Ocean. Federal Writers' Project, WPA. 1939. St. Clair Shores, Mich.: Scholarly Press, 1972. 256 pp., illus., biblio.

Historic Sites Along the Oregon Trail. Aubrey L. Haines. 2nd ed. Gerald, Mo.: Patrice Press, 1981. 453 pp., illus., biblio., index. $24.95 hb, $12.95 pb.

Maps of the Oregon Trail. Gregory M. Franzwa. 2nd ed. Gerald, Mo.: Patrice Press, 1982. 296 pp., illus. $14.95 pb.

The Wake of the Prairie Schooner. Irene D. Paden. Gerald, Mo.: Patrice Press, 1969. 514 pp., illus. $5.95 pb.

The Chisholm Trail. Wayne Gard. 1954. Reprint. Norman: University of Oklahoma Press, 1984. 308 pp., illus., biblio., index. $8.95 pb.

The Chisholm Trail: High Road of the Cattle Kingdom. Don Worchester. Lincoln: University of Nebraska Press, 1980. 207 pp., illus., biblio., index. $14.50 hb.

The Road West: Saga of the 35th Parallel. Bertha S. Dodge. Albuquerque: University of New Mexico Press, 1980. 222 pp., illus., biblio., append., index. $15.95 hb.

The California Trail: An Epic with Many Heroes. George R. Stewart. 1962. Reprint. Lincoln: University of Nebraska Press, 1983. 339 pp. $8.95 pb.

Over the Chihuahua and Santa Fe Trails, 1847–1848: George Rutledge Gibson's Journal. Robert W. Frazer, ed. Historical Society of New Mexico. Albuquerque: University of New Mexico Press, 1981. 96 pp., illus. $7.95 pb.

The Santa Fe Trail to California, 1849–1852: The Journal and Drawings of H. M. T. Powell. 1931. Reprint. New York: AMS Press, 1979. $125 hb.

Following the Santa Fe Trail: A Guide for Modern Travelers. Marc Simmons. Santa Fe, N.M.: Ancient City Press, 1984. 233 pp., illus., append. $8.50 pb.

The Outlaw Trail: A Journey Through Time. Robert Redford. New York: Grosset and Dunlap, 1978. 225 pp., illus. $25 hb, $14.95 pb.

The Overland Migrations. David Lavender. Gerald, Mo.: Patrice Press, 1982. 112 pp., illus. $8.95 pb.

The Latter-day Saints' Emigrants Guide. William Clayton. 1848. Reprint. Gerald, Mo.: Patrice Press, 1983. Stanley B. Kimball, ed. 117 pp., illus. $9.95 hb.

Contacts

National Historic and Scenic Trails
National Trails System
National Park Service
U.S. Department of the Interior
Washington, D.C. 20013-7127

Appalachian Trail Conference
P.O. Box 236
Harpers Ferry, W.Va. 25425

National Trails Council
Box 493
Brookings, S.D. 57006

National Recreation and Park Association
3101 Park Center Drive
Alexandria, Va. 22302

American Hiking Society
1701 18th Street, N.W.
Washington, D.C. 20009

National Parks and Conservation Association
1701 18th Street, N.W.
Washington, D.C. 20009

Trees

"Asked to name some physical symbol of America, the first thing coming to mind might be the skyscraper. But the tree, which once imaged the New World, still symbolizes it more than anything else."

Eric Sloane, *Our Vanishing Landscape.* New York: Ballantine, 1975.

Famous and Historic Trees. Charles Randall and Henry Clepper. Washington, D.C.: American Forestry Association, 1976. 90 pp., illus., index. $4.50 pb.

Historic Glimpses of Trees of the West. Lambert Florin. Seattle: Superior Publishing, 1977. 192 pp., illus., index, biblio.

Trees. Andreas Feininger. New York: Penguin, 1978. 116 pp., illus., index.

Should Trees Have Standing? Toward Legal Rights for Natural Objects. Christopher D. Stone. Los Altos, Calif.: William Kaufman, 1974. 102 pp. $5.50 pb.

Trees of Our National Forests. Forest Service. Washington, D.C.: U.S. Department of Agriculture, 1980. 32 pp., illus. Free.

City of Trees: 300 Species of Asian, African, European and American Trees Found in the Nation's Capital. Melanie Choukas-Bradley and Polly Alexander. Washington, D.C.: Acropolis Books, 1981. 280 pp., color illus. $24.95 hb.

Some Historic Tree Ordinances
Hawaii (all counties)
Mobile, Ala.
Atlanta, Ga.
Palm Beach, Fla.
Oakland, Calif.
Carmel, Calif.

Contacts

Natural Landmarks Program
National Park Service
U.S. Department of the Interior
Washington, D.C. 20013-7127

National Register of Big Trees
American Forestry Association
1319 18th Street, N.W.
Washington, D.C. 20036

Save-the-Redwoods League
114 Sansome Street
Room 605
San Francisco, Calif. 94104

Forest Service
U.S. Department of Agriculture
P.O. Box 2417
Washington, D.C. 20013

American Society of Consulting Arborists
315 Franklin Road
North Brunswick, N.J. 08902

International Society of Arboriculture
P.O. Box 71
Urbana, Ill. 61801

See also: National Parks and Forests

The Wye Oak (c. 1540), Wye Mills, Md., in 1914. (National Archives)

Trompe l'oeil painting (1977) by Richard Haas on the west wall of the Boston Architectural Center, designed to relate to the Back Bay. (Michael Miller)

Wall Murals

"The wall is the sleeper of the environment. There is nothing more infinitely expressive than its receptive expanse: It establishes style and setting, creates mood as well as enclosure, defines time and place. The wall is an environmental event."

Ada Louise Huxtable, *Kicked a Building Lately?* New York: Times Books, 1976.

"A people without murals are a demuralized people."

Sign on a wall in Adams-Morgan, Washington, D.C.

Community Murals: The People's Art. Alan W. Barnett. Art Alliance Press. Cranbury, N.J.: Associated University Presses, 1984. 516 pp., illus., biblio., index. $60 hb.

Mural Manual: How to Paint Murals for the Classroom, Community Center, and Street Corner. Mark Rogovin et al. Boston: Beacon, 1975. 116 pp., illus., biblio. $5.95 pb.

Toward a People's Art. Eva Cockcroft et al. New York: Dutton, 1976. 320 pp., color illus., index.

Big Art: Megamurals and Supergraphics. David Greenberg et al. Philadelphia: Running Press, 1977. 84 pp., color illus. $19.80 hb, $7.95 pb.

Nuts and Bolts: Case Studies in Public Design. Al Gowan. Cambridge, Mass.: Public Design Press, 1980. 96 pp., illus.

California Murals. Berkeley, Calif.: Lancaster Miller, 1980. 64 pp., color illus. $8.95 hb.

The Lost Years: Mural Painting in New York City Under the WPA Federal Art Project, 1935–1943. Greta Berman. New York: Garland, 1978. 255 pp., illus., appends., biblio.

Walls. Deidi von Schaewen. New York: Pantheon, 1977. 142 pp., illus.

Richard Haas: An Architecture of Illusion. Richard Haas. Introduction by Paul Goldberger. New York: Rizzoli, 1981. 160 pp., color illus. $35 hb.

Street Murals. Volker Barthelmeh. New York: Knopf, 1982. $20 hb, $11.95 pb.

Billboard Art. Sally Henderson and Robert Landau. San Francisco: Chronicle Books, 1980. 112 pp., color illus., biblio. $9.95 pb.

Contacts

National Society of Mural Painters
c/o American Federation of Arts
41 East 65th Street
New York, N.Y. 10021

Public Art Workshop
5623 West Madison Street
Chicago, Ill. 60644

City Walls
Public Art Fund, Inc.
25 Central Park West
Suite 25R
New York, N.Y. 10023

Cambridge Arts Council
57 Inman Street
Cambridge, Mass. 02139

See also: Outdoor Sculpture, Public Buildings

Waterfronts

"Travel America today and you will discover a degree of waterfront revival that would have seemed like a pipe dream in 1970. . . . The wonder of waterfront development, if it's done right, is the new heart and soul it can bring to a city. Oceans and lakes and rivers offer to a city what concrete streets so often lack: serenity, mysterious reflection, a sense of light and wind and seasons."

Neal R. Peirce. Syndicated column, August 1981.

Improving Your Waterfront: A Practical Guide. Washington, D.C.: Office of Coastal Zone Management, U.S. Department of Commerce, 1980. 108 pp., illus., appends., biblio.

Urban Waterfront Development. Douglas M. Wrenn and John A. Casazza. Washington, D.C.: Urban Land Institute, 1983. 224 pp. $37.75 pb.

Urban Waterfront Lands. Committee on Urban Waterfront Lands. Washington, D.C.: National Academy Press, 1980. 243 pp., illus., biblio. $12.95 pb.

Reviving the Urban Waterfront. Andy Leon Harney, ed. Washington, D.C.: Partners for Livable Places, 1979. 48 pp., illus., index.

Small Seaports: Revitalization Through Conserving Heritage Resources. John Clark et al. Washington, D.C.: Conservation Foundation, 1979. 67 pp., illus., biblio. $6.50 pb.

Urban Waterfront Revitalization: The Role of Recreation and Heritage. Washington, D.C.: U.S. Department of the Interior, 1980.

Waterfront Development: A Bibliography. Charles W. Barr. Monticello, Ill.: Vance Bibliographies, 1980. P-462. 51 pp. $11.40 pb.

Urban Waterfront Revitalization: A Review of the Literature. Seattle: University of Washington, Institute for Marine Studies, Coastal Resources Program (3731 University Way, N.E., 98195), 1980. 34 pp.

Urban Waterfront Redevelopment in North America: An Annotated Bibliography. Research Report no. 66. Downsview, Ontario: University of Toronto, York University, 1980. 104 pp.

Harborplace (1980, Benjamin Thompson Associates), a key addition to Baltimore's waterfront. (Rouse Company)

"Is South Street Seaport on the Right Tack?" Patricia Leigh Brown. *Historic Preservation,* July–August 1981.

"Methods of Planning for Protection and Enhancement of Historic Waterfronts," Ann Satterthwaite. In *Conserving the Historic and Cultural Landscape: Selected Papers.* National Trust for Historic Preservation. Washington, D.C.: Preservation Press, 1976. 41 pp., illus. $2.75 pb.

"Seaport Chic: Parks, Condominiums and Boutiques Are Transforming Urban Waterfronts," Gail Robinson. *Environmental Action,* September 1979.

Changing New York City's Waterfront: A Citizen's Guide. Stephen Lopez. Ithaca, N.Y.: New York Sea Grant Extension Program, 1979. 9 pp., illus. $.60 pb.

Waterfront Festivals: Potential for Developing Events on Public Lands and Availability of Technical Services. Jon A. Lucy. Gloucester Point, Va.: Sea Grant Marine Advisory Services, Virginia Institute of Marine Science, College of William and Mary, 1980. 10 pp. Free.

Rivers in the City. Roy Mann. New York: Praeger, 1973.

Ports Around the World. Yehuda Karmon. New York: Crown, 1979. 320 pp., illus.

Contacts

Maritime Preservation Office
National Trust for
Historic Preservation
1785 Massachusetts Avenue, N.W.
Washington, D.C. 20036

Waterfront Center
1536 44th Street, N.W.
Washington, D.C. 20007

Office of Coastal Zone
Management
3300 Whitehaven Street, N.W.
Washington, D.C. 20235

California Coastal Zone
Commission
631 Howard Street, 4th floor
San Francisco, Calif. 94105

Coastal Conservancy
1212 Broadway, Room 514
Oakland, Calif. 94612

New York State Sea Grant
Extension Program
Cornell University
Cooperative Extension
111 Broadway, Suite 1700
New York, N.Y. 10006

Sierra Club National Coastal
Committee
P.O. Box 2692
Tallahassee, Fla. 32304

South Street Seaport Museum
16 Fulton Street
New York, N.Y. 10038

Waterfront Historic Area of
New Bedford League
(WHALE)
19 Irving Street
New Bedford, Mass. 02740

See also: Canals, Maritime Sites

Windmills

"But look, your Grace, those are not giants but windmills, and what appear to be arms are their wings which, when whirled in the breeze, cause the millstone to go."

Miguel de Cervantes Saavedra, *Don Quixote*

A Field Guide to American Windmills. T. Lindsay Baker. Norman: University of Oklahoma Press, 1985. 528 pp., illus. $65 hb.

Wind-catchers: American Windmills of Yesterday and Tomorrow. Volta Torrey. Brattleboro, Vt.: Stephen Greene, 1976. 226 pp., illus., biblio., index. $9.95 pb.

Windmills. Suzanne M. Beedell. 1975. 2nd ed. North Pomfret, Vt.: David and Charles, 1982. 222 pp., illus., append., gloss., biblio., index. $21.50 hb, $9.95 pb.

Windmills, Bridges, and Old Machines: Discovering Our Industrial Past. David Weitzman. New York: Scribner's, 1982. 128 pp., illus. $13.95.

The Wind Power Book. Jack Park. Palo Alto, Calif.: Cheshire Books, 1981. 253 pp., illus., append., gloss., biblio., index. $21.95 hb, $12.95 pb.

Energy from the Wind: Annotated Bibliography. Barbara L. Burke and Robert Meroney. Fort Collins, Colo.: Colorado State University Engineering Research Center, 1975.

Windmills of Long Island. Robert J. Hefner, Society for the Preservation of Long Island Antiquities. Introduction by T. Allan Comp. New York: W. W. Norton, 1984. 112 pp., illus. $19.95 hb.

Contacts

Society for the Preservation of
Old Mills
P.O. Box 435
Wiscasset, Maine 04578

Society for Industrial
Archeology
National Museum of
American History
Room 5020
Washington, D.C. 20560

American Wind Energy
Association
1516 King Street
Alexandria, Va. 22314

Windmill Manufacturers Trade
Literature Collection
Panhandle-Plains Historical
Museum
Historical Research Center
P.O. Box 967, W.T. Station
Canyon, Tex. 79016

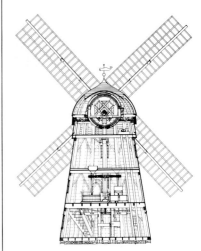

Beebe Windmill (1820), Bridgehampton, N.Y., with a mechanism to drive four millstones. (Chalmers G. Long, Jr., HAER)

Fountain Grove Winery, Santa Rosa, Calif. (Jack E. Boucher, HABS)

Elizabeth Cady Stanton House (c. 1836), Seneca Falls, N.Y. (NPS)

Wineries

"Many early wineries were modest frame structures that perished long ago, but the greats of the wine trade built more enduring memorials of their success. By the 1880s and 1890s handsome stone wineries and their prosperous owners' ornate homes abounded throughout the wine districts."

> Roy Brady, "Vintage Wineries." *Historic Preservation,* September–October 1979.

Vintage Places: A Connoisseur's Guide to North American Wineries and Vineyards. Suzanne Goldenson. Pittstown, N.J.: Main Street Press, 1985. $14.95 hb, $8.95 pb.

Vineyards and Wineries of America: A Traveler's Guide. Patrick W. Fegan. Brattleboro, Vt.: Stephen Greene, 1982. $9.95 pb.

Wine Country: California. Sunset Magazine Editors. Menlo Park, Calif.: Sunset Books, 1982. 160 pp., illus. $7.95 pb.

Napa Wine Country. Earl Roberge. Portland, Ore.: Graphic Arts Center Publishing Company (2000 N.W. Wilson, 97209), 1975. 207 pp., color illus., gloss. $12.95 pb.

Of Vines and Missions. Alvin Gordon. Flagstaff, Ariz.: Northland Press, 1971.

Pocket Encyclopedia of American Wineries East of the Rockies. William I. Kaufman. San Francisco: Wine Appreciation Guild (155 Connecticut Street, 94107), 1984. 128 pp. $4.95 pb.

The California Wine Industry: A Study of the Formative Years, 1830–1895. Vincent P. Carosso. 1951. California Library Reprint Series. Berkeley: University of California Press, 1976. 250 pp., biblio., index. $29.75 hb.

Contacts

Association of American Vintners
Box 84
Watkins Glen, N.Y. 14891

Wine Institute
165 Post Street
San Francisco, Calif. 94108

Wine Museum of San Francisco
633 Beach Street
San Francisco, Calif. 94109

Women's Sites

"Where are the markers commemorating the achievements of women? Among the hundreds of historic places designated as National Historic Landmarks or listed in the National Register of Historic Places, those associated with famous women are few in proportion to those commemorating great men. The women who are honored by state historical markers are apt to be relatives of famous men, or women whose fame rests on slim historical evidence. . . . Others are nameless women—the Pioneer Mother, the Madonna of the Trail, the Indian Maiden."

> Marion Tinling and Linda Ruffner-Russell, "Famous and Forgotten Women." *Historic Preservation,* July–September 1976.

The American Woman's Gazetteer. Lynn Sherr and Jurate Kazickas. New York: Bantam, 1976. 271 pp., illus.

Women's History Sources: A Guide to Archives and Manuscript Collections in the United States. Andrea Hinding, ed. Ann Arbor, Mich.: R. R. Bowker, 1980. 1,505 pp. 2 vols. $175 hb.

"Feminine Marks on the Landscape: An Atlanta Inventory," Darlene Roth. *Journal of American Culture,* Winter 1980.

Contacts

Women's Rights National Historical Park
National Park Service
Seneca Falls, N.Y. 13148

National Register of Historic Places
National Park Service
U.S. Department of the Interior
Washington, D.C. 20013-7127

National Archives for Negro Women
Mary Bethune House
1318 Vermont Avenue, N.W.
Washington, D.C. 20005

Upstate New York Women's History Conference
1202 East State Street
Ithaca, N.Y. 14850

See also: Houses, Writers' Worlds; Women's Work (Looking at the Built Environment)

Writers' Worlds

"A new country has to be domesticated in the imagination as well as in concrete reality. Emerson's Concord, Owen Wister's Wyoming, Sinclair Lewis's Main Street: These are territories of the intangible United States that exist in our consciousness. Their existence is one reason for the importance of landmarks connected with American writers."

> Stephanie Kraft, "The Nonfiction World of Writers." *Historic Preservation,* April–June 1977.

The Oxford Illustrated Literary Guide to the United States. Eugene Ehrlich and Gorton Carruth. New York: Oxford University Press, 1982. $35 hb.

Writers in Residence: American Authors at Home. Glynne Robinson Betts. Introduction by Christopher Lehmann-Haupt. New York: Viking, 1981. 240 pp., illus. $16.95 hb.

Who Lived Where: A Biographical Guide to Homes and Museums. John Eastman. New York: Facts on File, 1983. 513 pp., illus., index. $29.95.

Literary Houses. Rosalind Ashe. New York: Facts on File, 1982. 144 pp., illus. $17.95 hb.

More Literary Houses. Rosalind Ashe. New York: Facts on File, 1983. 141 pp., illus. $17.95 hb.

A Literary Guide to the United States: A Tour of Literary Landmarks in Fact and Fiction. Steward Benedict, ed. New York: Facts on File, 1981. 256 pp., illus. $15.95 hb.

No Castles on Main Street: American Authors and Their Homes. Stephanie Kraft. Chicago: Rand McNally, 1979. 239 pp., illus., append., biblio.

A Literary Tour Guide to the United States. Northeast. Emilie C. Harting. 1978. *South and Southwest* and *West and Midwest.* Rita Stein. 1979. New York: William Morrow.

Exploring Literary America: A Biography and Travel Guide. Marcella Thum. New York: Atheneum, 1973. 342 pp., illus., indexes.

"What Good Is a Poet's House?" Terry B. Morton. *Historic Preservation,* no. 2, 1960.

Regional Guides

A Guide to Writers' Homes in New England. Miriam Levine. Cambridge: Apple-wood Books, 1984. 186 pp., illus. $10.95 pb.

Literary Places: A Guided Pilgrimage—New York and New England. John Deedy. Mission, Kans.: Andrews and McMeel, 1978. 290 pp., illus., biblio., index.

Literary New York: A History and Guide. Susan Edmiston and Linda D. Cirino. Boston: Houghton Mifflin, 1976. 409 pp., illus., index.

"Maps and Tours of the Town of Concord," Junior League of Boston. Concord: Concord Historical Commission, 1975.

On Common Ground: A Selection of Hartford Writers. Alice DeLana and Cynthia Reik, eds. Hartford: Stowe-Day Foundation, 1975. 156 pp., chron., biblio. $5.95 pb.

Literary San Francisco: A Pictorial History from Its Beginning to the Present Day. Lawrence Ferlinghetti and Nancy J. Peters. New York: Harper and Row, 1980. 256 pp., illus., biblio., index. $9.75 pb.

A Booklover's Guide to Los Angeles. Ryan Garcia. San Francisco: California Living Books, 1979. 36 pp., color illus.

Writers' Places

The World of Willa Cather. Mildred R. Bennett. 1961. Rev. ed. Lincoln: University of Nebraska Press, 1978. 302 pp., illus., index. $22.50 hb, $8.25 pb.

Mark Twain Memorial (1874, Edward T. Potter and Alfred H. Thorp), Hartford, Conn. (Mark Twain Memorial)

Willa Cather: A Pictorial Memoir. Bernice Slote. Lincoln: University of Nebraska Press, 1973. 134 pp., color illus.

The Emily Dickinson Homestead: A Historical Study of Its Setting with Recommendations for Preservation and Restoration. Amherst: Department of Landscape Architecture and Regional Planning, University of Massachusetts, 1978.

F. Scott Fitzgerald in Minnesota: His Homes and Haunts. John J. Koblas. Minnesota Historic Sites Pamphlet no. 18. St. Paul: Minnesota Historical Society Press, 1978. 58 pp., illus., append., biblio. $3.75 pb.

Robert Frost: A Tribute to the Source. Robert Frost and Dewitt Jones. David Bradley, ed. New York: Holt, Rinehart and Winston, 1979. 165 pp., color illus. $22.95 hb.

Robert Frost Country. Betsy and Tom Melvin. Garden City, N.Y.: Doubleday, 1977.

The Knickerbocker Tradition: Washington Irving's New York. Andrew B. Myers, ed. Tarrytown, N.Y.: Sleepy Hollow Restorations, 1974. 160 pp., illus., biblio., index. $8 hb.

Washington Irving's Sunnyside. Joseph T. Butler. Tarrytown, N.Y.: Sleepy Hollow Restorations, 1974. 80 pp., illus., biblio., chron. $3.95 hb, $1.95 pb.

Jeffers Country: The Seed Plots of Robinson Jeffers' Poetry. Robinson Jeffers and Horace Lyon. 1971. 2nd ed. San Francisco: Scrimshaw Press, 1974. 80 pp., illus.

Not Man Apart: Photographs of the Big Sur Coast. Robinson Jeffers. David Brower, ed. San Francisco: Sierra Club Books, 1965. 160 pp., color illus.

Jack London Sketchbook. William R. Johnston. San Rafael, Calif.: Publishers' Services, 1980.

Steinbeck Country. Steve Crouch. American West Books. New York: Crown, 1973. 192 pp., color illus. $9.95 pb.

Steinbeck's Street: Cannery Row. Maxine Knox and Mary Rodriguez. San Rafael, Calif.: Presidio Press, 1980. 104 pp., illus.

John Steinbeck's Cannery Row: A Time to Remember. Tom Weber. Mill Valley, Calif: Orenda Publishing/Unity Press, 1983. 64 pp., illus. $7.95.

Harriet Beecher Stowe's House in Nook Farm, Hartford: A Guidebook. Hartford, Conn.: Stowe-Day Foundation, 1970. 20 pp., illus., chron. $1.25 pb.

Dylan Thomas' New York. Tryntje Van Ness Seymour. 1977. Reprint. Owings Mills, Md.: Stemmer House (2627 Cavers Road, 21117), 1978. 128 pp. $7.95 pb.

The Illustrated World of Thoreau. Henry David Thoreau and Ivan Messar. Afterword by Loren Eiseley. New York: Grosset and Dunlap, 1976. 174 pp., illus.

Thoreau Country. Henry David Thoreau and Herbert W. Gleason. Mark Silber, ed. San Francisco: Sierra Club Books, 1975. 160 pp., illus.

Thoreau's Cape Cod with the Early Photographs of H. W. Gleason. Thea Wheelwright. Barre, Mass.: Barre Publishers, 1974. 102 pp., illus. $3.95 pb.

Mark Twain in Hartford. Hartford, Conn.: Mark Twain Memorial. 40 pp., illus. $1.75 pb.

The Renaissance of Mark Twain's House: Handbook for Restoration. Wilson H. Faude. Larchmont, N.Y.: Queens House, 1978. 106 pp., illus., index. $20 hb.

Mark Twain's Hannibal. John A. Winkler, ed. Hannibal, Mo.: Becky Thatcher Book Shop, 1971.

Contacts
The Millay Colony for the Arts
Steepletop
Austerlitz, N.Y. 12017

The MacDowell Colony
Peterborough, N.H. 03458

Yaddo
Saratoga Springs, N.Y. 12866

Curry Hill
P.O. Box 514
Bainbridge, Ga. 31717

Cahill and Company
145 Palisade Street
Dobbs Ferry, N.Y. 10522

Stowe-Day Foundation
77 Forest Street
Hartford, Conn. 06105

Mark Twain Memorial
351 Farmington Avenue
Hartford, Conn. 06105

Zoos
"In our cultural history the buildings provided for keeping wild animals in captivity have often been of splendid and elaborate design. They boasted of the might and wealth of their owners and echoed not only the magnificence of these brute beasts, but also man's eventual conquest of these bizarre creatures. Today the housing of wild animals still needs splendid and elaborate architecture, though with a different interpretation, and for different reasons."

David Hancocks, *Animals and Architecture*

Animals and Architecture: The Story of Buildings for Animals. David Hancocks. New York: Beekman Publishers, 1971. 200 pp., illus., biblio., index.

Bronx Zoo (c. 1870). (© New York Zoological Society)

Great Zoos of the World: Their Origin and Significance. Lord Zuckerman, ed. Boulder, Colo: Westview Press, 1980. 230 pp., illus. $42 hb.

"Zoos: The Physical Plant." In *The Animals Next Door: A Guide to Zoos and Aquariums of the Americas.* Harry Gersh. New York: Fleet Academic, 1971. 170 pp., illus., appends. $5 pb.

Zoo and Aquarium Design. David Walker Lupton. Chicago: Council of Planning Librarians, 1978. No. 1484. 52 pp. $5.

Animal Gardens. Emily Hahn. Garden City, N.Y.: Doubleday, 1967.

Zoos of the World. James Fisher. Garden City, N.Y.: Natural History Press, Doubleday, 1967.

The World of Zoos. Rosl Kirchshofer, ed. New York: Viking, 1968.

A Zoo for All Seasons: The Smithsonian Animal World. Alfred Mayer. Washington, D.C.: Smithsonian Books, 1979. 192 pp. $16.95 hb.

Some Noteworthy Zoos
Milwaukee Zoo
Bronx Zoo
Lincoln Park Zoo, Chicago
St. Louis Zoo
Boston Zoo
Philadelphia Zoo
Los Angeles Zoo
National Zoo, Washington, D.C.
Dallas Zoo

Contact
American Association of Zoological Parks and Aquariums
Oglebay Park
Wheeling, W.Va. 26003

Preservationists

W*hy," I asked myself, "do we do it?" . . . We are un-American. Preservationists oppose the conventional American idea of consuming ever more. We are actually the new wave of pioneers. We are struggling to reverse the "use it up and move on" mentality. . . . We are taking individual buildings and whole neighborhoods that have been discarded and trying to make them live again. . . . Preservationists are citizens of the future, not the past.*

Clem Labine, "Preservationists Are Un-American!"
Historic Preservation, March–April 1979.

"What is very good . . . is the sophistication of today's preservation in terms of urban design and environmental excellence. And what is better yet is the power base from which preservation now operates—a true public coalition from grass roots to *grandes dames*, recognized from Congress to City Hall. And what is best of all—the results are seen not only in that litany of worthy old structures saved from the bulldozer by little old ladies in tennis shoes chaining themselves to fences but in the technical achievements of zoning lawyers and Congressional tax reforms that direct the larger goals and results of the planning and development process. . . .

We've turned in our tennis shoes for running shoes now."

Ada Louise Huxtable. *Vogue,* March 1977.

Staff of the Chinatown Neighborhood Improvement Resource Center, San Francisco. (Blumensaadt, © MATRIX 1984)

The campaign to save the Grand Rapids (Mich.) City Hall (1884–88, Elijah E. Myers), a spur to creation of the Heritage Hill Foundation. (Colorama)

"In a nation traditionally epitomizing free enterprise, individual initiative and limited government, it is not surprising that the impulse for historic preservation comes in large measure from the private or nongovernmental sector. The roots of this private initiative are historically grounded, and George Washington's home, Mount Vernon, is the classic illustration. Despite its unquestioned importance, neither the federal government nor the state of Virginia would step in to save it from imminent ruin in the mid-19th century, and it fell to the Mount Vernon Ladies' Association of the Union to raise the $200,000 necessary to acquire Washington's estate. The same organization preserves and operates it today. . . .

Without diluting private participation, the federal government has assumed a progressively larger role in historic preservation. . . .

The preservation partnership between and among the private and public sectors is sometimes marked by tension, for there is not always agreement on the direction and speed of the preservation movement in its many manifestations. Yet the relationship is less often one of adversaries than of parties challenging one another to advance by various means toward a common goal."

Robert M. Utley and Barry Mackintosh et al., "Historic Preservation in a Democracy: The Partnership Between Government and the Private Sector in the United States." *Monumentum,* vol. XIII. Washington, D.C.: US/ICOMOS, 1976.

Mrs. Joe Graves and Curtis Harrison protesting a demolition in Lexington, Ky. *(Louisville Courier-Journal)*

The People

Behind nearly every preservation project, public or private, can be found a small number of dedicated individuals (sometimes just one or two) who have worked long and hard to realize a personal dream. The contribution of individual citizens to preservation, so often hidden behind agency or organizational titles, must not go unrecognized. In addition to the essential support provided by private citizens as members of preservation organizations, individuals can and do function most effectively as lobbyists, letter-writers, spokesmen, and defenders of the preservation cause. Even where there is an effective network of public agencies and private organizations devoted to preservation, there is still room for the individual citizen to keep his eyes and ears open and to speak out where necessary.

Perhaps the most essential role of the private citizen in preservation is that of property owner—the base on which all other public and private preservation efforts rest. . . .

Almost never recognized, but just as important, are those citizens who conserve and maintain unheralded properties—ordinary buildings on ordinary streets that, if kept from deterioriating, can become the historic districts of the future without having to go through the agonizing process of economic and social upheaval that accompanies rescuing a neighborhood from decline. . . . the unrecognized conservers of everyday houses and neighborhoods are the unsung heroes of the preservation movement in the United States.

Robert B. Rettig, *Conserving the Man-made Environment: Planning for the Protection of Historic and Cultural Resources in the United States.* Washington, D.C.: National Park Service, 1975.

Avocation and Vocation

"In the beginning, the American preservation movement was largely the domain of individuals whose preservation-related activities were avocational in nature. They formed the backbone of the preservation community. The success of these preservationists in awakening public interest in conservation of the built environment, in serving as stewards of significant properties and in lobbying for the passage of significant preservation legislation stimulated an increased demand for technical and managerial skills to meet increasingly complex problems. This situation has highlighted the interdependence of activist volunteers and career professionals. Preservation requires coordinated efforts of both the trained professional and the committed volunteer to resolve complex issues and to further the cause."

"Preservation: Avocation and Vocation." In *Preservation: Toward an Ethic in the 1980s.* National Trust for Historic Preservation. Washington, D.C.: Preservation Press, 1980.

"In the original meaning of the term . . . amateurs were . . . people who did their jobs for love, not for money. That certainly describes the great mass of people in America who are engaged in preservation today."

James Marston Fitch, "Standards." In *Preservation: Toward an Ethic in the 1980s*

"There is a high price to be paid for professionalization. The preservation movement needs engineers, lawyers, economists and other technicians of contemporary society but not to the exclusion of generalists, those whom we might call the 'professional amateurs.' Preservationism is a humanistic movement, inspired by basic human motives. Its core constituency and leadership must remain people who can speak to one another and to all parties—and not merely in the language of numbers and dollars."

Roderick S. French, "On Preserving America: Some Philosophical Observations." In *Preservation: Toward an Ethic in the 1980s*

"I've been thinking of joining the historical society, but I don't want to be that sort of person." (Saxon. © 1978 The New Yorker Magazine, Inc.)

That Sort of Person

"'I've been thinking of joining the historical society, but I don't want to be that sort of person.'

There is, of course, not one sort of person, but there has been a nebulous stigma of social and intellectual elitism associated with being actively absorbed in history's trappings. The emergence of such a cartoon [as Saxon's], however, is a positive and hopeful sign of change. It is an indication that the absurdity has come to light, and that it is being scrutinized. The pursuit of history is becoming democratic. . . .

The most earnest historical organizations have never looked upon themselves as custodians of the 'good old days,' but as recorders of our total civilized experience . . . rescuing business records as well as Chinese export ceramics and handsome edifices."

Editorial. *Rhode Island Historical Society Newsletter,* September 1978.

Alan Dunn. From *Architecture Observed.* (© 1971 Architectural Record Books)

Preservation for the People

"Five years ago, in most cities, minority community leaders and historic preservationists stared at each other across a tense communications gap.

Preservation—like ecology— was perceived by blacks as a white issue that could do them harm. Upper middle-class professionals ran local 'societies.' Historical people were white people. Preservationists spoke in a relatively exclusive architectural jargon and showed too little concern for the people in the buildings they admired. . . .

Some of these perceptions and attitudes have changed. . . . preservationists have shown that it is possible to preserve buildings *and* people. Together, we have shown that there's more to a historic district than rising property values and Sunday supplement features. Preservationists are beginning to speak the language of social need."

Michael L. Ainslie, former National Trust president. Speech to Historic Preservation and the Minority Community Conference, Cincinnati, 1980.

"I like it when people—all kinds and types of people—get involved in historic preservation. Our past—a past that includes the pain of a dumbbell tenement, a railroad shack or a mill town as well as the glory or elegance of a country manse— belongs to all of us, rich, poor, young, old, black, white and everything in between."

Michael deH. Newsom, "Preserving American Cultures." *Historic Preservation,* January–March 1973.

The Trimbles in their converted warehouse near downtown Atlanta. (Tom Hill)

Women in Preservation

Q: "The preservation movement is largely one headed by women. Is that a coincidence?"

A: "No. Houses belong to women, they always have. They're symbols of the female body in many parts of the world. People dream of houses and dream of female bodies. They are things that contain other things. Houses contain people the way a woman's body contains a baby.

And women, in most of the world, rule inside the house."

"An Interview with Margaret Mead." *American Preservation,* February–March 1978.

"When women wore hoop skirts, were generally
flattered and despised as the weaker sex,
they showed their strength: Washington's house
is ours, because they made it theirs."

George Zabriskie, "Images of Tradition." In *With Heritage So Rich.* Special Committee on Historic Preservation, U.S. Conference of Mayors. Albert Rains and Laurence G. Henderson, eds. 1966. Rev. reprint. Washington, D.C.: Preservation Press, 1983.

"The women of San Antonio, Tex., were years ahead of the men because they viewed their city as a total environment; they wanted to save the things that went into making the community lively and beautiful."

Charles B. Hosmer, Jr., "Historic Communities Awaken." *Preservation Comes of Age*

"It's old ladies in tennis shoes that we owe more to than anybody else I can think of."

Edmund N. Bacon. In "Bacon Issues Challenge to Preservation Movement." *Preservation News,* December 1976.

Presence of the Past: A History of the Preservation Movement in the United States Before Williamsburg. Charles B. Hosmer, Jr. 1965. Washington, D.C.: Preservation Press, 1974. 386 pp., illus., biblio., index. $12.95 hb.

History of the people and the events that shaped the early years of the movement, including classic campaigns such as Ann Pamela Cunningham's struggle to save Mount Vernon.

Preservation Comes of Age: From Williamsburg to the National Trust, 1926–1949. Charles B. Hosmer, Jr. Charlottesville: University Press of Virginia, 1981. Published for the National Trust. 1,291 pp., illus., biblio., chron., index. 2 vols. $37.50 hb.

Documents key years and accomplishments as well as the people who created new climates for preservation in places such as Williamsburg, Charleston, San Antonio, Richmond, Annapolis, Natchez, Newport and Monterey. Also highlights the people who developed the National Park Service programs and founded the National Trust.

The History of the National Trust for Historic Preservation, 1963–1973. Elizabeth D. Mulloy. Washington, D.C.: Preservation Press, 1976. 315 pp., color illus., appends., index. $9.95 hb.

Provides an overview of the creation of the Trust in addition to an account of the leaders and programs during the active years before and after passage of the 1966 preservation act.

"What I see . . . as the most difficult challenge facing the preservation movement is to transform ourselves mentally from the underdogs we were to the leaders we are."

Chester Liebs, "Developing a Preservation Philosophy." In *Preservation: Toward an Ethic in the 1980s*

Designer working on rehabilitation drawings for a Chinatown neighborhood, San Francisco. (Blumensaadt, © MATRIX 1984)

Artist Pat Vecchione, Providence, R.I., at work restoring a masonry frieze. (*Providence Journal-Bulletin*)

Preservation educator guiding Cornell University students during a field trip. (Cornell University)

The Preservation Professions

Preservationists need no longer talk only to themselves. They have a broad range of new allies, tools and programs dedicated to improvement of the environment or the quality of American life.

Goals and Programs: A Summary of the Study Committee Report to the Board of Trustees. Washington, D.C.: National Trust for Historic Preservation, 1973.

Administrators

Oversee public agencies and private organizations, often concentrating on fund raising.

Anthropologists

Use archeological data and artifacts to search for and reconstruct cultural patterns.

Antiques Dealers, Appraisers and Restorers

Help illuminate past lifestyles through period furnishings and objects, books and documents.

Appraisers

Assess property for tax purposes—making preservation feasible or difficult.

Archeologists

Unearth, protect and interpret architectural sites, including prehistoric villages, earthen mounds, ancient ruins and historic sites with foundations and artifacts of successive periods.

Architects

Design the buildings worth preserving and restore the ones that can be recycled.

Architectural Historians

Use their knowledge of early design, construction materials and craftsmanship as consultants to preservation projects, as well as being the movement's writers, critics, teachers, researchers and scholars.

Archivists

Preserve records and drawings used in historical research and restoration.

Artists

May leave the only records of a building as painters, and are often muralists and creators of art in buildings.

Bankers

Lend money to developers and make rehabilitation loans to homeowners, increasingly viewing preservation as a sound investment.

Conservators

Provide solutions to problems of deterioration, combining the chemistry of building materials with architectural history.

Construction Workers

Assemble a building on site and rehabilitate it when needed.

Craftspeople

Use skills in early building crafts to restore intrinsic qualities of historic buildings.

Critics

Mold public opinion and chronicle trends, as journalists, historians, cartoonists, architects and planners.

Developers

Reuse old buildings because preservation pays.

Economists

Advise preservationists how—or if—to proceed in the marketplace, including contributing to feasibility studies.

Educators

Initiate or further preservation education on every level: elementary school awareness, secondary school studies, undergraduate courses, graduate school programs and continuing education for the community and professionals.

Engineers

Help ensure that buildings are built to last and that they are rehabilitated to last even longer.

Environmentalists

Increasingly view the built environment—as well as the natural—as worthy of conservation.

Geographers

Bring a holistic view to preservation, looking at past cultural landscapes and their changes through time.

Historians

Assess the value of architectural remains to the overall study of American history and culture.

Former Rep. Barber Conable (R-N.Y.), a key preservation supporter, in his Capitol Hill office. (Paul Kennedy)

Interior Designers
Study past interior design trends and furnishings as a prelude to restoration.

Landscape Architects
Tend the gardens and cultural landscapes already created and develop plans for saving them and larger areas of cultural landscapes.

Lawyers
Litigate, regulate and draft statutes in the cause of preservation.

Librarians
Make preservation information accessible to professionals, volunteers and the public.

Manufacturers and Suppliers
Make and sell the things we thought they didn't make anymore—authentic hardware, lighting fixtures, wallpapers, fabrics and close facsimiles of the originals.

Merchants
Turn around old commercial areas and Main Streets, especially when joined together in an association of store owners.

Museum Professionals
Serve as curators of house museums, outdoor museums, historic villages and history museums, conserving and interpreting artifacts and architecture for the future.

Photographers
Freeze the essence and the emotion of architecture and preservation controversies in frames to be consulted again and again.

Planners
Prepare comprehensive plans and preservation components for cities, states, regions and neighborhoods; document sites and buildings; address land use and environmental policies; and monitor urban and community development, neighborhood conservation and housing.

Public Officials
Are elected or appointed architects of public policy who can make or break preservation efforts, through legislation, setting priorities, budget appropriations, staff appointments and the establishment of preservation agencies.

Publishers
Control communication within the field and to the public, possessing the power to propagandize through the printed word.

Realtors
Sell historic properties, creating a climate toward old buildings that affects whole neighborhoods as well as resale values.

Sociologists and Psychologists
Address the personal and societal effects of preservation—from the sense of nostalgia to that of displacement.

"Occupations and Organizations." In *Preservation and Conservation: Principles and Practices.* International Centre for Conservation and National Trust. Washington, D.C.: Preservation Press, 1976. 547 pp., illus., biblio. $17.95 pb.

Addresses the preservation roles of major professions—architect, historian, architectural historian, curator, educator, conservator, archeologist, planner, administrator, lawyer.

Locators
The Americans of all ages, all conditions and all dispositions constantly form associations. . . . The Americans make associations to give entertainments, to found establishments for education, to send missionaries to the antipodes. Wherever at the head of some new undertaking you see the government of France or a man of rank in England, in the United States you will be sure to find an association.

Alexis de Tocqueville, 1840.

Directory of Historical Societies and Agencies in the United States and Canada. 12th ed. Donna MacDonald, comp. Nashville: American Association for State and Local History, 1982. 474 pp. $36 pb.

Contains the names, addresses, telephone numbers, founding dates and other pertinent information for 5,865 state and local historical societies and agencies, indexed alphabetically and by special-interest categories. An expanded edition is to be released in 1985.

THE BROWN BOOK

A DIRECTORY OF PRESERVATION INFORMATION
NATIONAL TRUST FOR HISTORIC PRESERVATION

The Brown Book: A Directory of Preservation Information. Diane Maddex, ed., with Ellen R. Marsh. Washington, D.C.: Preservation Press, 1983. 160 pp., illus., index. $17.95 spiral bound.

A guide to more than 1,000 preservation individuals, associations and agencies, including contacts and telephone numbers, plus recommended reading.

Directory of Private, Nonprofit Preservation Organizations: State and Local Levels. National Trust for Historic Preservation. Washington, D.C.: Preservation Press, 1980. 136 pp. $6.95 pb.

A state-by-state, city-by-city listing of more than 4,000 preservation organizations at the state, regional and local levels—community groups, neighborhood associations, statewide organizations, historical societies and allied preservationists.

National Directory of Landscape Architecture Firms. Washington, D.C.: American Society of Landscape Architects Professional Practice Institute, 1984. 145 pp. $10 hb.

A two-part directory, with profiles of firms arranged first alphabetically and then by state and area of expertise, including preservation.

The Official Museum Directory. American Association of Museums. Wilmette, Ill.: National Register Publishing Company, 1985. 1,164 pp. $85 pb.

Lists institutions by states and territories, describing personnel, collections, research fields, facilities, activities and publications. Includes a directory of museum product and service suppliers.

Directory of Historical Consultants. Washington, D.C.: National Coordinating Committee for the Promotion of History (400 A Street, S.E., 20003), 1981. 97 pp. $5 pb.

Gives qualifications, experience and specialties for 30 firms and 73 individuals.

Directory of American Preservation Commissions. Stephen N. Dennis, ed. Washington, D.C.: Preservation Press, 1981. 132 pp. $6.95 pb.

Guide to more than 850 historic district and landmarks commissions, arranged by state and city and giving address, telephone number, chairman and staff contact.

Conservation Directory. Jeannette Bryant, ed. 30th ed. Washington, D.C.: National Wildlife Federation, 1985. 300 pp. $15. Annual.

Lists public and private organizations, agencies and officials concerned with natural resource use and management, state groups and related information such as national parks and periodicals.

The American Institute of Architects Membership Directory. Washington, D.C.: American Institute of Architects, 1981. 307 pp., appends.

Guide to more than 30,000 corporate and 5,000 associate AIA members, plus information on the association, officers, chapters and awards.

Sen. Daniel P. Moynihan (D-N.Y.) at a rally to save the U.S. Capitol's West Front, cosponsored by the AIA and the National Trust. (Lisa Berg, NTHP)

Nellie Longsworth of Preservation Action. (Max Hirshfeld)

National Preservation Organizations

Since 1966 there has been rapid growth in the number of national, private, nonprofit preservation organizations. Older organizations such as the American Association for State and Local History, American Association of Museums and the National Trust have seen their memberships grow in number and have, in some instances, structured their governing and advisory bodies toward a regionalized system. Professional organizations have moved toward creation of new, or expansion of existing, organizational networks to better serve regions and states.

"Patterns in Organizing for Preservation: National." In *Preservation: Toward an Ethic in the 1980s*

"Private [preservation] organizations can and do perform an invaluable service in educating the public, in political lobbying, in training technicians and in building a constituency. They are, in fact, the most effective of all voices in attempting to reverse the forces of ignorance, indifference and inertia. They are much freer in what they can do and say than any public body, supported by public funds, can afford to be."

Harmon H. Goldstone, "Administrative, Legal and City Planning Aspects of Historic Preservation Programs." In *Preservation and Conservation: Principles and Practices*

"Because governments respond most readily to organized constituencies, preservationists working in concert and in alliance with other groups are far more influential than individuals working autonomously."

Robert M. Utley and Barry Mackintosh et al., "Historic Preservation in a Democracy: The Partnership Between Government and the Private Sector in the United States." *Monumentum*, vol. XIII, 1976.

Key Organizations

American Association for State and Local History
708 Berry Road
Nashville, Tenn. 37204

Serves state and local historical societies in the United States and Canada, house and history museums, professional and amateur historians and educators. Services include extensive publications (the monthly *History News*, Technical Leaflets and books), an annual awards program, training programs, consulting, job placement and a clearinghouse for inquiries and research.

American Institute of Architects
1735 New York Avenue, N.W.
Washington, D.C. 20006

Founded in 1857 as the national professional society of American architects. Sponsors a Committee on Historic Resources with State Preservation Coordinators and coordinates state and local AIA chapters. Promotes public awareness of architectural and environmental issues, supports educational programs from the elementary level to graduate schools of architecture, publishes two magazines, sponsors Regional/Urban Design Assistance Teams, gives honor awards for achievement in architectural design, maintains a library and sells publications.

Association for Preservation Technology
P.O. Box 2487, Station D
Ottawa, Ontario K1P 5W6,
Canada

A Canadian-American association of professional preservationists, architects, museum curators, architectural educators and archeologists devoted to promoting preservation research and disseminating technical information. Maintains a list of specialists in various phases of preservation; produces technical publications, a newsletter, journal, books and monographs; and holds conferences and workshops.

Partners for Livable Places
1429 21st Street, N.W.
Washington, D.C. 20036

A coalition of organizations, municipalities and individuals dedicated to improving the built environment through public and private efforts. Emphasizes the importance of design consciousness and amenities to the well-being of cities. Serves as a clearinghouse for information on urban amenities and preservation, holds conferences and symposia, provides technical assistance teams, conducts research and development projects and publishes regular and special publications.

Preservation Action
1700 Connecticut Avenue, N.W.
Suite 401
Washington, D.C. 20009

A national grass-roots citizens' lobby for preservation with lobbying coordinators in each state. Assists in drafting legislation, monitors proposed legislation, provides expert testimony and works with federal agencies that administer preservation programs and with the National Trust's public policy office.

Society for Commercial Archeology
National Museum of American History
Room 5010
Washington, D.C. 20560

Promotes public awareness and preservation of the structures, artifacts, signs and symbols of the historic commercial landscape: transportation facilities, roadside architecture, resorts and amusement parks. Its focus is on rapidly disappearing resources often considered too recent to be evaluated or preserved. Publications, conferences and field trips are available to members.

Society for Industrial Archeology
National Museum of American History
Room 5020
Washington, D.C. 20560

A preservation-oriented scholarly society dedicated to the study of the physical survival of America's technological, engineering and industrial past. Sponsors field investigations, research and educational programs; publishes a newsletter, a journal and special reports; coordinates local chapters; and has produced a book and film, *Working Places*.

Society of Architectural Historians
1700 Walnut Street
Suite 716
Philadelphia, Pa. 19103

A scholarly organization of architectural historians, architects, educators and others interested in architectural history. Sponsors a Historic Preservation Committee and a Decorative Arts Trust; promotes preservation of significant architectural landmarks; coordinates local chapters; serves as an international forum on architecture and related arts; encourages scholarly research; gives awards; conducts tours; and publishes a newsletter and quarterly journal.

The Victorian Society in America
219 South Sixth Street
Philadelphia, Pa. 19106

Promotes the study and preservation of Victorian-era culture and architecture through lectures, conferences, publications, tours, awards, a speaker's bureau and research.

See also: The National Trust

Preservation-Related Organizations

Alliance for Historic
Landscape Preservation
c/o Robert Melnick
University of Oregon
School of Architecture and
Allied Arts
216 Lawrence Hall
Eugene, Ore. 97403

American Association of
Museums
1055 Thomas Jefferson Street, N.W.
Suite 428
Washington, D.C. 20007

American Council for the Arts
570 Seventh Avenue
New York, N.Y. 10018

American Historical Association
400 A Street, S.E.
Washington, D.C. 20003

American Institute for
Conservation of Historic
and Artistic Works
3545 Williamsburg Lane, N.W.
Washington, D.C. 20008

American Planning Association
1313 East 60th Street
Chicago, Ill. 60637
Historic Preservation Division
1776 Massachusetts Avenue, N.W.
Washington, D.C. 20036

American Society of
Civil Engineers
Committee on History and
Heritage of American
Civil Engineering
345 East 47th Street
New York, N.Y. 10017

American Society of
Interior Designers
Historic Preservation Committee
1430 Broadway
New York, N.Y. 10018

American Society of
Landscape Architects
Historic Preservation Committee
1733 Connecticut Avenue, N.W.
Washington, D.C. 20009

Association for Living
Historical Farms and
Agricultural Museums
National Museum of
American History
Room 5035
Washington, D.C. 20560

Association of American
Geographers
1710 16th Street, N.W.
Washington, D.C. 20009

Association of Junior Leagues
825 Third Avenue
New York, N.Y. 10022

Classical America
227 East 50th Street
New York, N.Y. 10022

Council of American
Maritime Museums
Mariners Museum
Museum Drive
Newport News, Va. 23606

Council of Preservation
Executives
1785 Massachusetts Avenue, N.W.
Washington, D.C. 20036

Council on America's
Military Past—U.S.A.
P.O. Box 1151
Fort Myer, Va. 22211

Decorative Arts Trust
106 Bainbridge Street
Philadelphia, Pa. 19147

Early American Society
P. O. Box 8200
Harrisburg, Pa. 17105

Educational Facilities
Laboratories
Academy for Educational
Development
680 Fifth Avenue
New York, N.Y. 10019

Friends of Cast-Iron
Architecture
235 East 87th Street
Room 6C
New York, N.Y. 10028

Friends of Terra Cotta
P.O. Box 421393
Main Post Office
San Francisco, Calif. 94142

Institute for Urban Design
Main P.O. Box 105
Purchase, N.Y. 10577

Institute of Early American
History and Culture
P.O. Box 220
Williamsburg, Va. 23187

International Downtown
Executives Association
915 15th Street, N.W.
Suite 900
Washington, D.C. 20005

League of Historic American
Theatres
1600 H Street, N.W.
Washington, D.C. 20006

National Alliance of
Preservation Commissions
Hall of the States
444 North Capitol Street, N.W.
Suite 332
Washington, D.C. 20001

National Association for
Olmsted Parks
175 Fifth Avenue
New York, N.Y. 10010

National Association of
Historic Preservation Attorneys
P.O. Box 45, Century Station
Raleigh, N.C. 27602

Court of the Pension Building (1885, Montgomery C. Meigs), Washington, D.C., now the National Building Museum. (Walter Smalling, Jr.)

National Association of
Housing and Redevelopment
Officials
2600 Virginia Avenue, N.W.
Washington, D.C. 20037

National Building Museum
440 G Street, N.W.
Washington, D.C. 20001

National Center for
Preservation Law
2101 L Street, N.W.
Washington, D.C. 20037

National Conference of State
Historic Preservation Officers
Hall of the States
444 North Capitol Street, N.W.
Suite 332
Washington, D.C. 20001

National Council for
Preservation Education
P.O. Box 23
Middle Tennessee State
University
Murfreesboro, Tenn. 37132

National Institute for the
Conservation of Cultural
Property
Smithsonian Institution
Arts and Industries Building
Room 2225
Washington, D.C. 20560

National Main Street Center
1785 Massachusetts Avenue, N.W.
Washington, D.C. 20036

Organization of American
Historians
112 North Bryan Street
Bloomington, Ind. 47401

National Council for
Public History
Department of History
West Virginia University
Morgantown, W.Va. 26506

Pioneer America Society
Department of Geography
University of Akron
Akron, Ohio 44325

Popular Culture Association
Popular Culture Center
Bowling Green University
Bowling Green, Ohio 43403

Project for Public Spaces
875 Avenue of the Americas
Room 201
New York, N.Y. 10001

Public Works Historical Society
1313 East 60th Street
Chicago, Ill. 60637

Railroad Station Historical
Society
430 Ivy Avenue
Crete, Neb. 68333

Small Towns Institute
P.O. Box 517
Ellensburg, Wash. 98926

Smithsonian Institution
Washington D.C. 20560

Society for Historical
Archaeology
P.O. Box 241
Glassboro, N.J. 08028

Society of American Historians
610 Fayerweather Hall
Columbia University
New York, N.Y. 10027

Urban Land Institute
1090 Vermont Avenue, N.W.
Suite 300
Washington, D.C. 20005

See also: Form and Function

Former Great Western Power Company (1916), San Francisco, adapted to house the Sierra Club. (Storek and Storek)

The Conservationists

"The urban environment must be high on the environmental movement's agenda for the 1980s if the movement is to survive."

William Futrell. *Sierra,* February–March 1978.

"The only national environmental organization that has focused concern on protecting natural rural as well as urban areas is the Conservation Foundation. Most others have limited their concerns to wilderness areas. The Sierra Club recently has shown an interest in urban conservation in addition to its traditional concern for wilderness but evidences less interest in the rural areas that fall between the wilderness and the city. . . .

At the state and local levels there are few organizations that show a combined concern for historic preservation and open space protection. Examples of those that do are the French and Pickering Creeks Conservation Trust, Pa.; the Piedmont Environmental Council, Va.; the Catskill Center, N.Y.; Massachusetts Trustees of Reservations; and the Maine Coast Heritage Trust.

It is interesting to note that in England, in sharp contrast to the United States, both government and private organizations traditionally have shown a combined interest in preservation and open space protection."

"Preservation and Conservation: A Convergence of Interests?" In *Preservation: Toward an Ethic in the 1980s*

The Conservation Foundation
1717 Massachusetts Avenue, N.W.
Washington, D.C. 20036

Environmental Action
Foundation
1346 Connecticut Avenue, N.W.
Suite 724
Washington, D.C. 20036

Environmental Defense Fund
444 Park Avenue, South
New York, N.Y. 10016

Environmental Law Institute
1346 Connecticut Avenue, N.W.
Suite 600
Washington, D.C. 20036

Friends of the Earth
1045 Sansome Street
San Francisco, Calif. 94111

Land Trust Exchange
P. O. Box 364
Bar Harbor, Maine 04609

League of Conservation Voters
320 4th Street, N.E.
Washington, D.C. 20002

National Parks and
Conservation Association
1701 18th Street, N.W.
Washington, D.C. 20009

National Recreation and Park
Association
3101 Park Center Drive
Alexandria, Va. 22302

National Wildlife Federation
1412 16th Street, N.W.
Washington, D.C. 20036

Natural Resources Defense
Council
122 East 42nd Street
New York, N.Y. 10168

The Nature Conservancy
1800 North Kent Street
Suite 800
Arlington, Va. 22209

Sierra Club
530 Bush Street
San Francisco, Calif. 94108

Trust for Public Land
82 Second Street
San Francisco, Calif. 94105

254 West 31st Street
12th Floor
New York, N.Y. 10001

The Wilderness Society
1901 Pennsylvania Avenue, N.W.
Washington, D.C. 20006

See also: Rural Areas and Landscapes (Form and Function)

The National Trust

A National Trust, properly supported and financed to act, could meet emergencies which no existing organization in this country is now prepared to meet. . . . Beyond [this], there remains the great intangible value of the sentiments, ideas, and public opinion brought together, mobilized, and embodied in the National Trust. The preservation of the physical body of our historic sites and buildings is only a part of the task. . . . The National Trust will not only preserve property, but it will also contribute to the perpetuation of the historical fabric of our national life in a way that only the mobilized participation of all interested societies and individual citizens can do.

Report of the Committee on Organization of the National Trust, 1948.

National Trust for
Historic Preservation
1785 Massachusetts Avenue, N.W.
Washington, D.C. 20036
(202) 673-4000

The National Trust is the leading national private preservation organization. Chartered by Congress in 1949, its programs are designed to increase public awareness and encourage public participation in the preservation of buildings, districts, sites and objects significant in American history and culture. The National Trust acts as a clearinghouse for information on all aspects of preservation, assists in coordinating efforts of preservation groups, provides professional advice on preservation, conducts conferences and seminars, maintains historic properties, administers grant and loan programs and issues a variety of publications. A board of trustees directs the organization's policies, and a board of advisors in the states helps implement programs.

Membership is open to all interested individuals, organizations, public agencies, libraries and businesses. All members receive benefits including the monthly newspaper, *Preservation News,* the bimonthly magazine, *Historic Preservation,* free admission to all National Trust properties, a 10 percent discount on books and items from the Preservation Shops, special study tours and invitations to National Trust–sponsored local and national conferences.

National Trust headquarters in the former McCormick Apartments (1917, Jules H. de Sibour), once home to Andrew Mellon. (Robert C. Lautman)

Programs

Preservation services. Advice on all preservation issues and problems, from organizing to fund raising.

Regional offices. Services to state and local organizations and individuals in six regions, including field visits, advisory assistance, aid to preservation commissions, conferences and special projects on issues of particular concern to each region.

Grants and loans. Financial support through the National Preservation Loan Fund, Preservation Services Fund, Inner-City Ventures Fund and Critical Issues Fund.

Publications. The monthly newspaper, *Preservation News;* bimonthly magazine, *Historic Preservation;* books; an annual report; booklets, newsletters and brochures on preservation topics.

Public policy and legislation. Advocacy on preservation issues, coordination of a national lobbying network and testimony on pending federal legislation.

Legal services. Monitoring of preservation litigation and state and local legislation, filing of suits and *amicus curiae* briefs and advice on tax incentives and easements.

Properties. Maintenance and interpretation of Trust house museums, advice to other historic sites, ownership of easements and real estate development.

Education. Sponsorship of conferences and workshops, coordination of internships, liaison on preservation education programs and administration of a restoration workshop.

Information services. Maintenance of a library, audiovisual collection and research facilities.

National Main Street Center. Guidance in the economic and architectural revitalization of downtowns, including advisory aid, workshops, films and publications.

Special projects. Assistance in preservation issues such as neighborhood conservation, maritime preservation and rural environmental planning.

Member organization program. Services to member preservation and related organizations and libraries, including publications, special networks, advisory services, insurance and publications discounts.

Public awareness. Media and public communications programs, an annual National Historic Preservation Week, public service advertising, study tours and an awards program.

Book and merchandise sales. Books and gift items for sale by mail and from shops in Washington, D.C., and at several Trust properties.

Board of Advisors. A network of preservationists in all states who advise on and help disseminate information about preservation and the Trust.

Program Council. Obtains views of preservationists nationwide to guide the Trust in ongoing strategic planning and development of program emphases.

Departments

Executive Office
J. Jackson Walter, President

Department of Preservation Programs
Dwight Young, Vice President

Department of Development and Communications
Robert H. Angle, Vice President

Department of the General Counsel
Harrison B. Wetherill, Jr., Vice President and General Counsel

Department of Finance and Administration
Bonnie Cohen, Vice President

Board of Trustees
Alan S. Boyd, Chairman

Regional Offices

The National Trust maintains six regional offices and one field office that serve preservation groups and individuals in their areas. In addition to offering a wide range of information and advice, each office has responded to particular regional needs by specializing in various aspects of preservation.

Northeast Regional Office
Old City Hall
45 School Street
Boston, Mass. 02108
(617) 223-7754

Connecticut
Maine
Masssachusetts
New Hampshire
New York
Rhode Island
Vermont

Special interests: reuse of industrial sites, old and new architectural design relationships, preservation of campus buildings.

Mid-Atlantic Regional Office
Cliveden
6401 Germantown Avenue
Philadelphia, Pa. 19144
(215) 438-2886

Delaware
District of Columbia
Maryland
New Jersey
Pennsylvania
Virginia
West Virginia
Puerto Rico
Virgin Islands

Special interests: urban neighborhood conservation, historic property management and development, downtown revitalization.

Southern Regional Office
456 King Street
Charleston, S.C. 29403
(803) 724-4711

Alabama
Arkansas
Florida
Georgia
Kentucky
Louisiana
Mississippi

North Carolina
South Carolina
Tennessee

Special interests: stragetic planning development for local preservation groups, design review in local historic districts.

Midwest Regional Office
407 South Dearborn Street
Suite 710
Chicago, Ill. 60605
(312) 353-3419

Illinois
Indiana
Iowa
Michigan
Minnesota
Missouri
Ohio
Wisconsin

Special interests: rural conservation, corporate financial support for preservation.

Mountains/Plains Regional Office
1407 Larimer Street
Suite 200
Denver, Colo. 80202
(303) 844-2245

Colorado
Kansas
Montana
Nebraska
North Dakota
Oklahoma
South Dakota
Wyoming

Special interests: rural preservation, Main Street revitalization, local economic development in urban areas and rural communities, organization of local preservation efforts.

Texas/New Mexico Field Office
500 Main Street
Suite 606
Forth Worth, Tex. 76102
(817) 334-2061

Texas
New Mexico

Special interests: Main Street revitalization, organization of local preservation efforts.

Western Regional Office
One Sutter Street
Suite 900
San Francisco, Calif. 94104
(415) 974-8420

Alaska
Arizona
California
Hawaii
Idaho
Nevada
Oregon
Utah
Washington
American Samoa
Guam
Micronesia

Special interests: Main Street revitalization, development and administration of local preservation ordinances, rural preservation, design review in local historic districts.

Farm Craft Days at Belle Grove (1794), Middletown, Va., a working farm that was designed with input from Thomas Jefferson. (NTHP)

National Trust Properties

"The breadth and diversity of American life are reflected in the historic properties of the National Trust. While each property represents a different aspect of the nation's architectural and historical development, each is also symbolic of the wide-ranging preservation efforts of the National Trust. . . .

As community preservation centers, National Trust properties provide a link between the individuals and groups in their locales and the National Trust headquarters and its six regional offices across the nation. Because of their unique characters and diversity, the properties are used by the National Trust to supplement its services and to serve as laboratories for developing new preservation programs and techniques useful to preservationists nationwide."

Theodore A. Sande, Foreword. *American Landmarks*

Belle Grove (1794)*
P.O. Box 137
Middletown, Va. 22645
(703) 869-2028

Brucemore (1885, Joselyn and Taylor)*
2160 Linden Drive, S.E.
Cedar Rapids, Iowa 52403
(319) 362-7375

Casa Amesti (c. 1834, 1846)*
516 Polk Street
Monterey, Calif. 93940
(408) 372-2311

Chesterwood (1898, 1900–01, Henry Bacon)
P.O. Box 827
Stockbridge, Mass. 01262
(413) 298-3579

Cliveden (1763–67, Benjamin Chew)*
6401 Germantown Avenue
Philadelphia, Pa. 19144
(215) 848-1777

Cooper-Molera Adobe (c. 1832)*
Monterey, Calif. 93940
(408) 649-2980

Decatur House (1818–19, Benjamin H. Latrobe)
748 Jackson Place, N.W.
Washington, D.C. 20006
(202) 673-4030

Drayton Hall (1738–42)
Route 4, Box 276
Charleston, S.C. 29407
(803) 766-0188

Filoli (1916–17, Willis Polk)*
Canada Road
Woodside, Calif. 94062
(415) 364-8300

Frank Lloyd Wright Home and Studio (1889–1911, Frank Lloyd Wright)*
951 Chicago Avenue
Oak Park, Ill. 60302
(312) 848-1976

Lyndhurst (1838, 1864–65, Alexander J. Davis)
635 South Broadway
Tarrytown, N.Y. 10591
(914) 631-0046

Montpelier (1750s, 1798–1811)
P.O. Box 67
Montpelier Station, Va. 22957
(703) 672-2728

Detail of a Corinthian capital at Oatlands (c. 1800), Leesburg, Va., a portion of the house's extensive decoration. (NTHP)

Oatlands (c. 1800)*
Route 2, Box 352
Leesburg, Va. 22075
(703) 777-3174

Pope-Leighey House (1940, Frank Lloyd Wright)
Mount Vernon, Va. 22121
(703) 557-7880

The Shadows-on-the-Teche (1831–34, David Weeks)
P.O. Box 254
New Iberia, La. 70560
(318) 369-6446

Woodlawn Plantation (1800–05, William Thornton)
Mount Vernon, Va. 22121
(703) 557-7880

Woodrow Wilson House (1915, Waddy B. Wood)
2340 S Street, N.W.
Washington, D.C. 20008
(202) 673-4034

*Costewardship properties (owned but not operated by the National Trust)

American Landmarks: Historic Properties of the National Trust for Historic Preservation. Washington, D.C.: Preservation Press, 1980. 72 pp., illus. $5.95 pb.

Belle Grove. Washington, D.C.: Preservation Press, 1968. 84 pp., illus. $3.95 pb.

Decatur House. Washington, D.C.: Preservation Press, 1967. 104 pp., illus., appends. $3.95 pb.

Lyndhurst. Washington, D.C.: Preservation Press, 1965. 44 pp., color illus. $2.50 pb.

The Pope-Leighey House. Washington, D.C.: Preservation Press, 1969. 120 pp., illus. $5.95 pb.

The Shadows-on-the-Teche. Marian Page. Washington, D.C.: Preservation Press, 1979. 16 pp., color illus. $2 pb.

Daniel Chester French: An American Sculptor. Michael Richman. 1976. Washington, D.C.: Preservation Press, 1983. 224 pp., illus., chron. $14.95 pb.

Measured Drawings of Trust Properties. Historic American Buildings Survey. Washington, D.C.: Preservation Press. $3.95 pb each.
Belle Grove, Casa Amesti, Decatur House, Drayton Hall, Lyndhurst, Pope-Leighey House, The Shadows, Woodlawn.

The History of the National Trust for Historic Preservation, 1963–1973. Elizabeth D. Mulloy. Washington, D.C.: Preservation Press, 1976. 315 pp., illus., biblio., appends., index. $9.95 hb.

History of the National Trust for Historic Preservation, 1947–1963. David E. Finley. Washington, D.C.: National Trust for Historic Preservation, 1965. 115 pp., appends., index. Available in microfilm, hardbound and paperbound editions only from University Microfilms, 300 North Zeeb Road, Ann Arbor, Mich. 48106.

"The Formation of the National Trust for Historic Preservation." In *Preservation Comes of Age: From Williamsburg to the National Trust, 1926–1949.* Charles B. Hosmer, Jr. Charlottesville: University Press of Virginia, 1981. Published for the National Trust. 1,291 pp., illus., biblio., chron., index. 2 vols. $37.50 hb.

Preservation Press Book Catalog. Washington, D.C.: Preservation Press (1785 Massachusetts Avenue, N.W., 20036). Free.

U.S. Capitol (1793–1865, Thornton, Latrobe, Bulfinch, Mills, Walter). (Carleton Knight III, NTHP)

Federal Programs

Although the major burdens of historic preservation have been borne and major efforts initiated by private agencies and individuals, and both should continue to play a vital role, it is nevertheless necessary and appropriate for the Federal Government to accelerate its historic preservation programs and activities, to give maximum encouragement to agencies and individuals undertaking preservation by private means, and to assist State and local governments and the National Trust for Historic Preservation in the United States to expand and accelerate their historic preservation programs and activities.

Section 1(b)(7), National Historic Preservation Act of 1966, as amended.

"Federal leadership, as expressed by public laws and executive orders, does establish the priority of the national preservation goal in relation to other national goals, particularly those affecting the built environment. In addition, the activities of the federal government influence every historic preservation project in the United States. . . .

Recent federal policy has brought preservation to almost every part of the federal bureaucracy, both through review procedures and the increasing number of programs for which preservation is an eligible expenditure."

Constance Werner Ramirez, "Historic Preservation as a National Goal." *Monumentum,* vol. XIII, 1976.

The New Trim Look

When the National Trust cataloged federal preservation and related programs in the mid-1970s, it found some 230 programs in 49 permanent departments, agencies, boards and commissions. This number did not include the preservation responsibilities required of federal agencies by law. Federal programs aiding preservation increased in number and scope until 1981, when the Reagan administration's government-wide cuts took effect. Preservation programs were among the social and cultural services targeted for reduction or elimination. The outline of federal programs here is only a shadow of the network of aid once available, and the programs change annually with each new budget. Readers should consult the agencies or federal regional offices for the current status.

"The myopic viewpoint that sometimes comes with Washington supposes that federal government is the centerpiece of historic preservation. It can be the catalyst. It need not be the program. . . . The federal government cannot be the perpetual overseer and provider. The parent of a movement that has now reached maturity must turn over this movement to the people that make it successful."

James G. Watt, "Preservation Will Survive." *Preservation News,* June 1981.

Executive Branch

U.S. Department of Agriculture

Provides aid for the rehabilitation of historic structures in rural areas; manages and interprets historic areas in national forests.

Farmers Home Administration
Office of Rural Development Policy
14th Street and Independence Avenue, S.W.
Washington, D.C. 20250

National Forest System
Forest Service
P.O. Box 2417
Washington, D.C. 20013

Soil Conservation Service
P.O. Box 2890
Washington, D.C. 20013

U.S. Department of Commerce

Administers economic development and small business programs that can be used for the renovation, reuse and management of historic buildings and commercial revitalization programs; conducts research in materials and standards; distributes government-sponsored research and reports.

Economic Development Administration
Washington, D.C. 20230

National Bureau of Standards
Center for Building Technology
National Engineering Laboratory
Washington, D.C. 20234

Coastal Zone Management Program
National Oceanic and Atmospheric Administration
2001 Wisconsin Avenue, N.W.
Washington, D.C. 20235

National Technical Information Service
5285 Port Royal Road
Springfield, Va. 22161

U.S. Department of Defense

Component services administer historical records, maintain museums and issue publications; the Corps of Engineers recovers archeological data from project sites.

U.S. Air Force
Office of Air Force History
Bolling Air Force Base
Washington, D.C. 20332

U.S. Army
Center of Military History
Washington, D.C. 20314

U.S. Army
Corps of Engineers
20th Street and Massachusetts Avenue, N.W.
Washington, D.C. 20314

U.S. Navy
Library
Naval Historical Center
Washington Navy Yard
Washington, D.C. 20374–0571

U.S. Marine Corps
History and Museums Division
Washington, D.C. 20380

U.S. Department of Education

Establishes policy, administers and coordinates federal assistance to education.

400 Maryland Avenue, S.W.
Washington, D.C. 20202

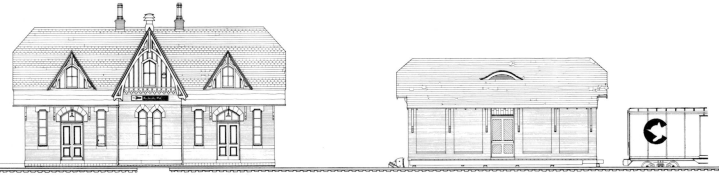

B&O Railroad Station and Freight House (c. 1875), Rockville, Md., a Gothic depot in continuous operation. (Ken Payson and Jonathan Fine, HABS)

U.S. Department of Energy

Responsible for research, development and demonstration of energy and technology; energy conservation, including solar technology; energy production, regulation and use; and central energy data and analysis.

1000 Independence Avenue, S.W.
Washington, D.C. 20585

U.S. Department of Housing and Urban Development

Administers housing, community development and neighborhood programs, including aid to rehabilitate historic residential structures; home ownership and rental assistance for low- and moderate-income families, the elderly and handicapped; an urban homesteading program; Community Development Block Grants allocated to local governments for community development projects; and Urban Development Action Grants for revitalization of distressed cities and urban counties.

451 7th Street, S.W.
Washington, D.C. 20410

U.S. Department of the Interior

The principal federal preservation and conservation agency. Administers national parks, national historic sites and other public lands as well as the major federal preservation programs.

National Park Service
P.O. Box 37127
Washington, D.C. 20013-7127

Administers all National Historic Sites and national parks.

Interagency Resources Division
National Park Service
Washington, D.C. 20013-7127

Maintains the National Register of Historic Places—districts, buildings, sites, structures and objects significant in American history, architecture, archeology and culture.
Reviews nominations from state historic preservation offices and others, approves state preservation plans and establishes guidelines and procedures used by federal agencies, states and others in preservation planning.

Preservation Assistance Division
National Park Service
Washington, D.C. 20013-7127

Serves as a clearinghouse for technical information on the repair and maintenance of historic buildings; develops policy and oversees project review for acquisition and development grants under the Historic Preservation Fund; develops preservation standards and policies; monitors reviews of rehabilitation projects undertaken with federal tax incentives for their conformance to the Secretary of the Interior's Standards for Historic Preservation Projects; administers a Federal Surplus Property Program in conjunction with the regional offices; monitors endangered National Historic Landmarks.

Historic American Buildings Survey
Historic American Engineering Record
National Park Service
Washington, D.C. 20013-7127

Records historic buildings and engineering landmarks through photographs, measured architectural drawings and written documentation, often in cooperation with other preservation and professional organizations.

National Historic Landmark Program
History Division
National Park Service
Washington, D.C. 20013-7127

Identifies National Historic Landmarks, based on studies to determine their national significance.

Street in Harpers Ferry National Historical Park, W.Va., before restoration by the National Park Service. (National Park Service)

Archeological Assistance Division
National Park Service
Washington, D.C. 20013-7127

Issues permits for surveys and excavation of archeological sites on federal land; assists in protecting antiquities on these lands; provides technical assistance and funding to recover archeological data endangered by federal projects; offers technical aid to federal, state and local governments and the public on the preservation of archeological sites.

National Park Service Regional Offices (for federal tax incentives)
Mid-Atlantic Regional Office
Office of Cultural Programs
143 South Third Street
Philadelphia, Pa. 19106

Southeast Regional Office
Preservation Services Division
75 Spring Street, N.W.
Atlanta, Ga. 30303

Rocky Mountain Regional Office
Division of Cultural Resources
655 Parfet Street
P.O. Box 25287
Denver, Colo. 80225

Western Regional Office
National Historic Preservation Programs
450 Golden Gate Avenue
San Francisco, Calif. 94102-3491

Alaska Regional Office
Cultural Resources Division
540 West 5th Avenue, Suite 220
Anchorage, Alaska 99501

Other Regional Offices
National Capital Regional Office
18th and C Streets, N.W.
Washington, D.C. 20240

North Atlantic Regional Office
15 State Street
Boston, Mass. 02109

Midwest Regional Office
1709 Jackson Street
Omaha, Neb. 68102

Southwest Regional Office
Box 728
Santa Fe, N.M. 87501

Pacific Northwest Regional
Office
601 4th and Pike Building
Seattle, Wash. 98101

Harpers Ferry Center
National Park Service
Harpers Ferry, W.Va. 25425

Denver Service Center
National Park Service
755 Parfet Street
Denver, Colo. 80225

U.S. Department of Labor

Administers ongoing and special
public employment programs
that may aid rehabilitation of
historic properties.

Employment and Training
Administration
200 Constitution Avenue, N.W.
Washington, D.C. 20210

U.S. Department of Transportation

Establishes national transportation policy, including highway
planning; supervises programs
for urban mass transit, railroads, aviation and safety of
waterways, ports, highways and
pipelines. Administers the
Transportation Act of 1966,
which protects historic sites
from transportation projects.

Office of the Secretary
Washington, D.C. 20590

Urban Mass Transportation
Administration
400 7th Street, S.W.
Washington, D.C. 20590

Federal Highway Administration
400 7th Street, S.W.
Washington, D.C. 20590

Federal Railroad Administration
400 7th Street, S.W.
Washington, D.C. 20590

U.S. Department of the Treasury

Develops and administers regulations affecting the tax aspects of federal preservation tax
incentives and other tax issues
affecting cultural property; supervises bank actions; manufac-
tures coins and maintains
historic mint museums.

Internal Revenue Service
1111 Constitution Avenue, N.W.
Washington, D.C. 20224

Bureau of the Mint
501 13th Street, N.W.
Washington, D.C. 20220

Comptroller of the Currency
490 L'Enfant Plaza East, S.W.
Washington, D.C. 20219

Independent Agencies

Advisory Council on Historic Preservation

Reviews proposed federal projects affecting properties listed
in the National Register of Historic Places or determined eligible for listing and provides
suggestions for ensuring their
preservation. Advises the president and Congress on preservation matters; suggests changes
in laws and procedures pertaining to historic properties; recommends new regulations and
legislation; and initiates studies
of special preservation
problems.

1100 Pennsylvania Avenue, N.W.
Suite 809
Washington, D.C. 20004

National Foundation on the Arts and Humanities

Provides grants for design, historical and public programs and
museum operations.

National Endowment for
the Arts
1100 Pennsylvania Avenue, N.W.
Washington, D.C. 20506

National Endowment for
the Humanities
1100 Pennsylvania Avenue, N.W.
Washington, D.C. 20506

Institute of Museum Services
1100 Pennsylvania Avenue, N.W.
Washington, D.C. 20506

Monumental cortile of the Old Post Office (1892–99, Willoughby J. Edbrooke), Washington, D.C., c. 1930, before its conversion to offices including the Advisory Council and National Endowments.

U.S. Treasury Department (1836–69, Mills, Walter, Young, Rogers, Mullett), Washington, D.C., an influential Greek Revival design using fireproof construction. (GSA)

Smithsonian Institution

Maintains major collections of historic and culturally significant objects in various history and art museums; preserves its own historic public buildings; administers document collections useful in historical research; and provides grants to museums.

Curator
Smithsonian Institution Building
1000 Jefferson Drive, S.W.
Washington, D.C. 20560

Archives of American Art
National Museum of
American Art
Smithsonian Institution
8th and G Streets, N.W.
Washington, D.C. 20560

Cooper-Hewitt Museum of
Decorative Arts and Design
2 East 91st Street
New York, N.Y. 10028

National Museum Act Program
Smithsonian Institution
Arts and Industries Building
Room 3465
Washington, D.C. 20560

General Services Administration

Owns or manages most federal buildings except those of the military, Veterans Administration and Postal Service; transfers surplus historic public buildings to state and local governments for reuse; is required under the Public Buildings Cooperative Use Act of 1976 to locate federal offices in buildings of historical, architectural or cultural significance when possible; and commissions works of art for federal buildings under its Art-in-Architecture Program.

Public Buildings Service
18th and F Streets, N.W.
Washington, D.C. 20405

Surplus Property Program
Historic Preservation Staff
Officer
18th and F Streets, N.W.
Washington, D.C. 20405

National Archives and Records Administration

Administers the National Archives and its collections; and provides grants for historical papers publication and preservation projects through the National Historical Publications and Records Commission.

8th Street and Pennsylvania
Avenue, N.W.
Washington, D.C. 20408

The Smithsonian "Castle" (1847–55, James Renwick), Washington, D.C., a Norman Revival landmark on the Mall that was the first of the institution's buildings. (Jack E. Boucher, HABS)

Council on Environmental Quality

Reviews environmental impact statements and oversees federal efforts to achieve the goals of the National Environmental Policy Act of 1969.

722 Jackson Place, N.W.
Washington, D.C. 20006

Small Business Administration

Provides financial assistance, management counseling and training to small businesses, including owners of historic properties.

1441 L Street, N.W.
Washington, D.C. 20416

Other Independent Agencies

American Battle Monuments
Commission
20 Massachusetts Avenue, N.W.
Room 5127
Washington, D.C. 20314

Amtrak
National Railroad Passenger
Corporation
400 North Capitol Street, N.W.
Washington, D.C. 20001

Commission of Fine Arts
708 Jackson Place, N.W.
Washington, D.C. 20006

U.S. Fire Administration
Federal Emergency
Management Agency
500 C Street, N.W.
Washington, D.C. 20472

Pennsylvania Avenue
Development Corporation
425 13th Street, N.W.
Suite 1148
Washington, D.C. 20004

Legislative Branch

Architect of the Capitol

Maintains and develops the U.S. Capitol, grounds and congressional office buildings; and provides a reference library on the Capitol, Library of Congress, U.S. Supreme Court and House and Senate offices.

U.S. Capitol Building
Washington, D.C. 20515

Library of Congress

Serves as the national library of the United States; maintains collections of manuscripts, photographs, maps and related historical documents; preserves its own building; and produces publications and exhibits.

First Street, N.E.
Washington, D.C. 20540

See also: Paying for Preservation

Locators

Cultural Directory II: Federal Funds and Services for the Arts and Humanities. Federal Council on the Arts and the Humanities. Washington, D.C.: Smithsonian Institution Press, 1980. 256 pp. $8.95 pb.

Issued before the 1981 cutbacks and reorganizations. Covers the range of federal assistance including information services, technical assistance, counseling, employment, financial aid, reference collections, etc.

United States Government Manual. Office of the Federal Register, U.S. General Services Administration. Washington, D.C.: GPO, 1984. 918 pp. $12 pb. GPO stock no. 022–033–01109–9. Annual.

Gives names, addresses, phone numbers of federal offices, agencies, councils, commissions, etc.

Washington Information Directory. Washington, D.C.: Congressional Quarterly, Inc. (1414 22nd Street, N.W., 20037), 1985. 1,000 pp. $39.95. Annual.

Provides more than 5,000 information sources in Congress, the Executive Branch and private associations, organized by topic: economics and business; energy; health and consumer protection; education and culture; employment; etc.

Federal Staff Directory. Charles B. Brownson, ed. Mount Vernon, Va.: Congressional Staff Directory, Ltd., 1985. 1,346 pp. $40 hb.

A guide to key employees and helpful contacts in federal agencies.

Federal Regulatory Directory. Washington, D.C.: Congressional Quarterly, Inc., 1983. 893 pp. $35.95 hb. Annual.

Resource tool that discusses regulation and current trends and presents extensive profiles of 13 of the largest agencies plus other regulatory agencies.

Federal Agency Area Offices
Listed in local telephone directories by agency under "U.S. Government."

Federal Information Centers
More than 30 centers (listed under "Federal Information Center, U.S. Government") are listed locally and connected to more by toll-free lines.

Federal Preservation Officers
"The head of each Federal agency shall, unless exempted under section 214, designate a qualified official to be known as the agency's 'preservation officer' who shall be responsible for coordinating that agency's activities under this Act. Each Preservation Officer may, in order to be considered qualified, satisfactorily complete an appropriate training program established by the Secretary under section 101(g)."

> Section 110(c), National Historic Preservation Act of 1966, as amended.

Federal preservation officers have been designated for the agencies listed earlier in this section as well as for the following additional agencies. Contacts may be made by addressing the federal preservation officer at a particular agency. The Advisory Council on Historic Preservation maintains a current comprehensive list.

Executive Branch
Deputy Assistant Secretary for Natural Resources and Environment
U.S. Department of Agriculture
14th Street and Independence Avenue, S.W.
Washington, D.C. 20250

Rural Electrification Administration
Engineering Standards Division
U.S. Department of Agriculture
14th Street and Independence Avenue, S.W.
Washington, D.C. 20250

Agricultural Stabilization and Conservation Service
Conservation and Environmental Protection Division
U.S. Department of Agriculture
P.O. Box 415
Washington, D.C. 20013

Office of Buildings Management
Energy Conservation Office
U.S. Department of Commerce
14th Street and Constitution Avenue, N.W.
Washington, D.C. 20230

National Oceanic and Atmospheric Administration
Sanctuary Programs Office
U.S. Department of Commerce
Washington, D.C. 20235

Office of the Assistant Secretary
Environmental Policy Office
U.S. Department of Defense
The Pentagon
Washington, D.C. 20301

Office of Environmental Compliance
U.S. Department of Energy
1000 Independence Avenue, S.W.
Washington, D.C. 20585

Institutional Conservation Program
U.S. Department of Energy
1000 Independence Avenue, S.W.
Washington, D.C. 20585

Federal Energy Regulatory Commission
U.S. Department of Energy
825 North Capitol Street, N.E.
Washington, D.C. 20426

Historic Preservation Officer
U.S. Department of Health and Human Services
200 Independence Avenue, S.W.
Washington, D.C. 20201

Office of Environment and Energy
U.S. Department of Housing and Urban Development
451 7th Street, S.W.
Washington, D.C. 20410

Deputy Assistant Secretary for Community Planning and Development
U.S. Department of Housing and Urban Development
451 7th Street, S.W.
Washington, D.C. 20410

Fish and Wildlife Service
National Wildlife Refuge System
U.S. Department of the Interior
Washington, D.C. 20240

Bureau of Indian Affairs
Environmental Services Office
U.S. Department of the Interior
1951 Constitution Avenue, N.W.
Washington, D.C. 20240

Bureau of Land Management
Senior Archeologist
U.S. Department of the Interior
18th and C Streets, N.W.
Washington, D.C. 20240

Bureau of Reclamation
U.S. Department of the Interior
P.O. Box 25007
Denver, Colo. 80225

Office of Surface Mining
Division of Permit and Environmental Analysis
U.S. Department of the Interior
Washington, D.C. 20240

Office of Surface Mining
Western Technical Center
U.S. Department of the Interior
1020 15th Street
Denver, Colo. 80202

Office of Territorial Affairs
U.S. Department of the Interior
Washington, D.C. 20240

U.S. Geological Survey
Environmental Affairs Office
U.S. Department of the Interior
12201 Sunrise Valley Drive
Reston, Va. 22092

Justice Management Division
Facilities and Property Management Staff
U.S. Department of Justice
10th Street and Pennsylvania Avenue, N.W.
Washington, D.C. 20530

Design and Special Projects Unit
U.S. Department of Justice
10th Street and Pennsylvania Avenue, N.W.
Washington, D.C. 20530

Division of Program Review and Fiscal Services
U.S. Department of Labor
601 D Street, N.W.
Washington, D.C. 20004

Assistant Secretary for Administration
U.S. Department of State
Washington, D.C. 20520

International Center Project
U.S. Department of State
Washington, D.C. 20520

Office of Economics
U.S. Department of Transportation
Washington, D.C. 20590

Deputy Assistant Secretary for Policy and International Affairs
U.S. Department of Transportation
Washington, D.C. 20590

Federal Aviation Administration
Environmental Policy Division
U.S. Department of Transportation
Washington, D.C. 20590

Office of Budget and Finance
U.S. Department of the Treasury
Washington, D.C. 20220

Independent Agencies
Environmental Protection Agency
Environmental Protection Specialist
Waterside Mall, S.W.
Washington, D.C. 20460

Federal Communications Commission
Washington, D.C. 20554

Federal Deposit Insurance Corporation
Division of Accounting and Corporate Services
550 17th Street, N.W.
Washington, D.C. 20429

Federal Home Loan Bank Board
Office of Community Investments
1700 G Street, N.W.
Washington, D.C. 20552

National Aeronautics and Space Administration
Real Estate Management
Washington, D.C. 20546

National Capital Planning Commission
Office of Historic Preservation
1325 G Street, N.W.
Washington, D.C. 20005

Nuclear Regulatory Commission
Regional Impact Analysis Section
1717 H Street, N.W.
Washington, D.C. 20555

National Science Foundation
Office of International Programs
1800 G Street, N.W.
Washington, D.C. 20550

U.S. Postal Service
Office of Real Estate
Real Estate and Buildings Department
275 L'Enfant Plaza, S.W.
Washington, D.C. 20260

Tennessee Valley Authority
Cultural Resources Program
Division of Land and Economic Resources
Norris, Tenn. 37828

Tennessee Valley Authority
Office of Natural Resources and Economic Development
1E61 Old City Hall
Knoxville, Tenn. 37902

Veterans Administration
Office of Construction
810 Vermont Avenue, N.W.
Washington, D.C. 20420

Judge Randall T. Shepard, chairman of the National Trust Board of Advisors, at the Vanderburgh County Courthouse (1888), Evansville, Ind. (John Blair)

State Preservationists

The National Historic Preservation Act [of 1966] established a partnership between the States and the Federal Government. . . . To nurture this partnership, the Secretary of the Interior was empowered to grant funds to the States for historic surveys and plans and to establish grants-in-aid for preservation projects. Under regulations issued by the Secretary for implementing the Act, the Governor of each State participating in the national program is required to name a State Historic Preservation Officer who is responsible for administering the various aspects of the program.

> Advisory Council on Historic Preservation, *Report to the President and the Congress of the United States, 1978.*

A major reason why every state needs a private statewide preservation organization is to have a private group to work with, support, reinforce, and sometimes prod the state historic preservation office. . . . A combination of public and private effort is generally better than either alone.

> Robert B. Rettig, *Conserving the Man-made Environment*

"State government involvement in preservation dates back as far as 1850, when New York State appropriated funds to preserve the Hasbrouck House in Newburgh, N.Y., George Washington's headquarters during the final two years of the American Revolution. . . . By the 1960s most states had established agencies to protect their cultural resources.

But the emphasis was on state ownership of important landmarks, often supplemented with a program to place historical markers in front of other sites. Few states had broad programs to identify significant buildings, aid local preservation efforts or inform the public of preservation strategies and techniques.

It was not until 1966 that the federal government became extensively involved with—and provided assistance and standards for—preservation at the state level."

> Tom E. Donia, "1966 Preservation Act—10 Years Later." *Preservation News*, November 1976.

"The impetus for founding statewide preservation organizations has changed radically since their inception as antiquity societies organized primarily to protect structures and historical artifacts associated with prominent state and national figures. . . . The preservation organization at the state level now has a more diverse set of goals and delves into a greater number of legal, economic and social issues in supporting the work of local, activist and, usually, autonomous preservation organizations than did the early associations.

The fundamental purpose of most statewides is to provide a state-level presence for preservation. As such, statewides coordinate information and assistance to local organizations, provide a central networking resource, represent preservation interests in state legislation, provide spokesmanship on preservation goals, values and needs, and in several notable instances, operate revolving funds or raise funds in order to make grants and loans to local organizations.

Statewides have proved to be an essential, complementary force in state preservation. In many cases, statewides have been formed in support of the state historic preservation offices, providing public education and outreach activities and assisting in the development and passage of legislation supporting preservation protections and funding. Where such a partnership between private organiza-

Fred C. Williamson, Rhode Island state preservation officer, receiving a theatrical Washington, D.C., welcome. (Carleton Knight III)

tions and public agencies exists, we have seen significant advances in preservation's role in community development policy, cultural affairs and economic development issues, resulting in a significantly enhanced environment for the private property owner, investors in historic property, and for local preservation activities."

Kathryn Welch, National Trust for Historic Preservation

State Historic Preservation Offices

As the key state and territorial government preservation officials, the SHPOs conduct cultural resources surveys, prepare statewide preservation plans, nominate properties to the National Register of Historic Places, review federal undertakings for effects on landmarks, administer grants-in-aid, help certify projects for federal tax incentives, provide public education, cooperate with related state agencies, administer historic properties and supervise archeological activities. For a list, see Preservationists State by State.

Statewide Preservation Organizations

Private statewide preservation groups serve as the network centers and representatives of local preservation activities within their states. They work with the SHPOs, assist local groups, intervene in preservation issues, advocate state legislative support, provide membership and educational programs, issue publications, engage in real estate and revolving fund programs and serve as preservation clearinghouses. For a list, see Preservationists State by State.

National Trust Regional Offices

The six regional and one field office of the National Trust represent all Trust programs and services and provide leadership to preservationists within their regions. They work to strengthen local and state preservation organizations, provide on-site technical assistance, advocate preservation positions, respond to inquiries, advise on Trust financial aid programs, hold conferences and develop special projects to address key regional preservation issues. Preservationists are encouraged to refer inquiries to their National Trust regional office before contacting Trust headquarters. For a list, see The National Trust.

National Trust Advisors

A Board of Advisors composed of one or two members in each state and territory assists the National Trust by advising on preservation concerns in the states and serving as a channel for the expression of local opinions and interests. For a list, contact your National Trust regional office or Trust headquarters.

AIA State Preservation Coordinators

As members of the Committee on Historic Resources of the American Institute of Architects, the preservation coordinators serve as state-level contacts dealing with preservation issues of concern to the AIA, working with preservation organizations and SHPOs and speaking out on various issues. For a list, contact the AIA.

Other State Preservation Activities

"While the state historic preservation office is (or should be) the fulcrum of state concern for conserving the man-made environment, it is by no means the only place in state government where such concern may be expressed. . . . The state government may involve itself with historic sites, museums and artifact collections, historical and archeological research, publications, archives and records conservation, natural and recreational resource conservation, land-use and other comprehensive planning, and (through the state university) education of archeologists, architects, historians, planners, and preservationists. . . . In addition, the state government's role as a property owner is a valuable area for conservation activity in terms both of preserving valuable older buildings owned by the state and of seeking adaptive-use possibilities in lieu of new construction."

Robert B. Rettig, *Conserving the Man-made Environment*

State Agencies Involved in Preservation

Planning departments
Community development offices
Forest and parks departments
Natural resources and conservation agencies
Highway and transportation departments
Education agencies
State universities and libraries
Travel bureaus and tourism departments
State arts councils
State legislatures

Cast-iron facade of the Wilking Building (1872), Indianapolis, rescued by the Historic Landmarks Foundation of Indiana. (Tina Connor, HLFI)

Contacts

National Conference of State Historic Preservation Officers
Hall of the States
444 North Capitol Street, N.W.
Suite 322
Washington, D.C. 20001

Nonprofit organization founded in 1969 to represent the 57 state historic preservation officers and deputies. Exchanges information among its members, maintains liaison with federal, state and private preservation agencies, prepares legislative proposals and develops educational programs for state staffs.

National Trust for Historic Preservation
Office of Regional Services
1785 Massachusetts Avenue, N.W.
Washington, D.C. 20036

In addition to administering the regional offices, which work with private statewide organizations in their regions, the Trust provides services designed to help strengthen state groups. It has provided challenge grants to develop financial stability, publishes a newsletter, initiates joint programs in membership, fund raising and legislation, and generally serves as an information clearinghouse on statewide activities.

State Legislation Clearinghouse
National Trust for Historic Preservation
1785 Massachusetts Avenue, N.W.
Washington, D.C. 20036

Conducts research into state legislation affecting preservation and answers inquiries. A projected series of publications includes *State Enabling Legislation for Local Preservation Commissions* ($12) and *Preservation Easements: The Legislative Framework* ($8).

American Institute of Architects
Professional Interest Programs
1735 New York Avenue, N.W.
Washington, D.C. 20006

Administers the Committee on Historic Resources, which appoints architect members to serve as state preservation coordinators.

American Society of Landscape Architects
Historic Preservation Committee
1733 Connecticut Avenue, N.W.
Washington, D.C. 20009

Committee members in many of the states serve as liaisons for landscape preservation issues; an annual list is available.

National Society of Interior Designers
Historic Preservation Committee
1430 Broadway
New York, N.Y. 10018

Provides contacts in many states for issues regarding interior preservation and restoration.

Council of State Community Affairs Agencies
Hall of the States
444 North Capitol Street, N.W.
Suite 251
Washington, D.C. 20001

A national organization representing the state executive agencies responsible for a variety of local assistance functions in community development, housing, economic development, planning, training and technical aid. A monthly newsletter chronicles its activities.

American Council for the Arts
570 Seventh Avenue
New York, N.Y. 10018

An umbrella organization representing state, regional and local arts agencies, many of which support preservation activities. Distributes information and publishes books and a magazine. Provides mailing lists for state and community arts councils, regional arts alliances and related groups.

Preservationists State by State

State	State Historic Preservation Office	Statewide Preservation Organization	National Trust Regional Office
Alabama	Alabama Historical Commission 725 Monroe Street Montgomery, Ala. 36130	Live-in-a-Landmark Council c/o Alabama Historical Commission 725 Monroe Street Montgomery, Ala. 36130	Southern
Alaska	Office of History and Archaeology Division of Parks 225A Cordova Street Anchorage, Alaska 99501	Alaska Association for Historic Preservation 524 West Fourth Avenue Suite 203 Anchorage, Alaska 99501	Western
American Samoa	Department of Parks and Recreation Government of American Samoa Pago Pago, American Samoa 96799		Western
Arizona	Arizona State Parks 1688 West Adams Phoenix, Ariz. 85007	Heritage Foundation of Arizona P.O. Box 25616 Tempe, Ariz. 85282	Western
Arkansas	Arkansas Historic Preservation Program The Heritage Center 225 East Markham Street Suite 200 Little Rock, Ark. 72201	Historic Preservation Alliance of Arkansas P.O. Box 305 Little Rock, Ark. 72203	Southern
California	Department of Parks and Recreation P.O. Box 2390 Sacramento, Calif. 95811	California Preservation Foundation 55 Sutter Street Suite 593 San Francisco, Calif. 94104	Western
Colorado	Colorado Historical Society 1300 Broadway Denver, Colo. 80203	Colorado Preservation 1501 West Cucharras Colorado Springs, Colo. 80904	Mountains/Plains
Connecticut	Connecticut Historical Commission 59 South Prospect Street Hartford, Conn. 06106	Connecticut Trust for Historic Preservation 152 Temple Street New Haven, Conn. 06510	Northeast
Delaware	Bureau of Archeology and Historic Preservation Old State House The Green Dover, Del. 19901	Historical Society of Delaware 505 Market Street Mall Wilmington, Del. 19801	Mid-Atlantic
District of Columbia	Department of Consumer and Regulatory Affairs 614 H Street, N.W. Washington, D.C. 20001	D.C. Preservation League 930 F Street, N.W. Suite 612 Washington, D.C. 20004	Mid-Atlantic
Florida	Division of Archives, History and Records Management Department of State The Capitol Tallahassee, Fla. 32301-8020	Florida Trust for Historic Preservation P.O. Box 11206 Tallahassee, Fla. 32302	Southern
Georgia	Historic Preservation Section Department of Natural Resources 270 Washington Street, S.W. Room 704 Atlanta, Ga. 30334	Georgia Trust for Historic Preservation 1516 Peachtree Street, N.W. Atlanta, Ga. 30309	Southern
Guam	Department of Parks and Recreation Government of Guam P.O. Box 2950 Agana, Guam 96910		Western
Hawaii	Department of Land and Natural Resources P.O. Box 621 Honolulu, Hawaii 96809	Historic Hawaii Foundation P.O. Box 1658 Honolulu, Hawaii 96806	Western

State	State Historic Preservation Office	Statewide Preservation Organization	National Trust Regional Office
Idaho	Idaho Historical Society 610 North Julia Davis Drive Boise, Idaho 83702	Idaho Historic Preservation Council P.O. Box 1495 Boise, Idaho 83701	Western
Illinois	Department of Conservation Division of Historic Sites 405 East Washington Street Springfield, Ill. 62706	Landmarks Preservation Council of Illinois 407 South Dearborn Street Suite 970 Chicago, Ill. 60605	Midwest
Indiana	Department of Natural Resources Division of Historic Preservation 202 North Alabama Street Indianapolis, Ind. 46204	Historic Landmarks Foundation of Indiana 3402 Boulevard Place Indianapolis, Ind. 46208	Midwest
Iowa	State Historical Department Historic Preservation Office East 12th and Grand Avenue Des Moines, Iowa 50319		Midwest
Kansas	Kansas State Historical Society Historic Preservation Department 120 West 10th Street Topeka, Kans. 66612	Kansas Preservation Alliance c/o Wichita—Sedgwick County Historical Museum Association 204 South Main Wichita, Kans. 67202	Mountains/Plains
Kentucky	Kentucky Heritage Council Capitol Plaza Tower Ninth Floor Frankfort, Ky. 40601	Commonwealth Preservation Council of Kentucky P.O. Box 1122 Campbellsville, Ky. 42718	Southern
Louisiana	Office of Cultural Development Division of Historic Preservation P.O. Box 44247 Baton Rouge, La. 70804	Louisiana Preservation Alliance P.O. Box 1587 Baton Rouge, La. 70821	Southern
Maine	Maine Historic Preservation Commission 242 State Street Augusta, Maine 04333	Citizens for Historic Preservation 597 Main Street South Portland, Maine 04106	Northeast
Maryland	Maryland Historical Trust 21 State Circle Annapolis, Md. 21401	Maryland Preservation 2335 Marriottsville Road Marriottsville, Md. 21104	Mid-Atlantic
Massachusetts	Massachusetts Historical Commission 294 Washington Street Boston, Mass. 02108	Architectural Conservation Trust 45 School Street Boston, Mass. 02108	Northeast
Michigan	Michigan History Division Department of State 208 North Capitol Lansing, Mich. 48918		Midwest
Micronesia	Department of Resources and Development Land Resources Branch Federated States of Micronesia Ponape, W.C.I. 96941		Western
Minnesota	Minnesota Historical Society 690 Cedar Street St. Paul, Minn. 55101	Minnesota Preservation Alliance c/o Kensington Properties 730 Hennepin Suite 200 Minneapolis, Minn. 55403	Midwest
Mississippi	Mississippi Department of Archives and History P.O. Box 571 Jackson, Miss. 39205		Southern
Missouri	State Department of Natural Resources P.O. Box 176 Jefferson City, Mo. 65102	Missouri Heritage Trust P.O. Box 895 Jefferson City, Mo. 65102	Midwest

State	State Historic Preservation Office	Statewide Preservation Organization	National Trust Regional Office
Montana	Montana Historical Society Historic Preservation Office 225 North Roberts Street Helena, Mont. 59620		Western
Nebraska	Nebraska State Historical Society 1500 R Street Lincoln, Neb. 68501	Nebraska Historical Network Route 3 Seward, Neb. 68434	Mountains/Plains
Nevada	Department of Conservation and Natural Resources Division of Historic Preservation and Archeology Nye Building, Room 106 201 South Fall Street Carson City, Nev. 89710		Western
New Hampshire	Division of Parks and Recreation Historic Preservation Office P.O. Box 856 Concord, N.H. 03301	Inherit New Hampshire 4 Bicentennial Square Concord, N.H. 03301	Northeast
New Jersey	Department of Environmental Protection Office of New Jersey Heritage P.O. Box 1390 Trenton, N.J. 08625	Preservation New Jersey R.D. 4, Box 864 Mapleton Road Princeton, N.J. 08540	Mid-Atlantic
New Mexico	Office of Cultural Affairs Historic Preservation Division 228 East Palace Avenue Santa Fe, N.M. 87503		Mountains/Plains (Texas/N.M.)
New York	Office of Parks, Recreation and Historic Preservation Agency Building No. 1 Empire State Plaza Albany, N.Y. 12238	Preservation League of New York State 307 Hamilton Street Albany, N.Y. 12210	Northeast
North Carolina	Department of Cultural Resources Division of Archives and History 109 East Jones Street Raleigh, N.C. 27611	Historic Preservation Foundation of North Carolina P.O. Box 27632 Raleigh, N.C. 27611	Southern
North Dakota	State Historical Society of North Dakota Liberty Memorial Building Bismarck, N.D. 58501		Mountains/Plains
Northern Mariana Islands	Department of Community and Cultural Affairs Commonwealth of the Northern Mariana Islands Saipan, M.R. 96950		Western
Ohio	The Ohio Historical Society Interstate 71 at 17th Avenue Columbus, Ohio 43211	Ohio Preservation Alliance 22 North Front Street Columbus, Ohio 43215	Midwest
Oklahoma	Oklahoma Historical Society Historical Building 2100 North Lincoln Boulevard Oklahoma City, Okla. 73105		Mountains/Plains
Oregon	State Parks Administrator 525 Trade Street, S.E. Salem, Ore. 97310	Historic Preservation League of Oregon P.O. Box 40053 Portland, Ore. 97240	Western
Pennsylvania	Pennsylvania Historical and Museum Commission P.O. Box 1026 Harrisburg, Pa. 17120	Pennsylvania Trust for Historic Preservation Chester County Courthouse Annex 17 North Church Street Westchester, Pa. 19380 Preservation Fund of Pennsylvania 2470 Kissell Hill Road Lancaster, Pa. 17601	Mid-Atlantic

State	State Historic Preservation Office	Statewide Preservation Organization	National Trust Regional Office
Puerto Rico	Office of Cultural Affairs Box 82 La Fortaleza San Juan, P.R. 00901		Mid-Atlantic
Rhode Island	Department of Community Affairs Rhode Island Historical Commission Old State House 150 Benefit Street Providence, R.I. 02903	Heritage Foundation of Rhode Island One Hospital Trust Plaza Providence, R.I. 02903	Northeast
South Carolina	Archives and History Department 1430 Senate Street Columbia, S.C. 29211	Confederation of South Carolina Local Historical Societies Box 11669 Columbia, S.C. 29211	Southern
South Dakota	Office of Cultural Preservation Historic Preservation Center 216 East Clark Street Vermillion, S.D. 57069	Historic South Dakota Foundation P.O. Box 2998 Rapid City, S.D. 57709	Mountains/Plains
Tennessee	Department of Conservation Tennessee Historical Commission 701 Broadway Nashville, Tenn. 37203	Association for the Preservation of Tennessee Antiquities 110 Leake Avenue Nashville, Tenn. 37205 Tennessee Heritage Alliance c/o Historic Nashville 100 Second Avenue North Nashville, Tenn. 37201	Southern
Texas	Texas Historical Commission P.O. Box 12276, Capitol Station Austin, Tex. 78711	Texas Historical Foundation P.O. Box 12243 Austin, Tex 78711	Mountains/Plains (Texas/N.M.)
Utah	Utah State Historical Society 300 Rio Grande Salt Lake City, Utah 84101	Utah Heritage Foundation 355 Quince Street Salt Lake City, Utah 84103	Western
Vermont	Agency of Development and Community Affairs Pavilion Building Montpelier, Vt. 05602	Preservation Trust of Vermont 104 Church Street Burlington, Vt. 05401	Northeast
Virginia	Virginia Historic Landmarks Commission 221 Governor Street Richmond, Va. 23219	Preservation Alliance of Virginia P.O. Box 142 Waterford, Va. 22190 Association for the Preservation of Virginia Antiquities 2705 Park Avenue Richmond, Va. 23220	Mid-Atlantic
Virgin Islands	Virgin Islands Planning Office Division for Archeology and Historic Preservation P.O. Box 2606 Charlotte Amalie, St. Thomas, V.I. 00801	St. Thomas Historical Trust 9-33 Estate Nazareth St. Thomas, V.I. 00801	Mid-Atlantic
Washington	Office of Archeology and Historic Preservation 111 West 21st Avenue, KL-11 Olympia, Wash. 98504	Washington Trust for Historic Preservation 111 West 21st Avenue Olympia, Wash. 98501	Western
West Virginia	Department of Culture and History Capitol Complex Charleston, W.Va. 25305	Preservation Alliance of West Virginia P.O. Box 1135 Clarksburg, W.Va. 26302-1135	Mid-Atlantic
Wisconsin	State Historical Society of Wisconsin Historic Preservation Division 816 State Street Madison, Wis. 53706	Wisconsin Heritages 2000 West Wisconsin Avenue Milwaukee, Wis. 53223	Midwest
Wyoming	Wyoming Recreation Commission Historic Preservation Office 122 West 25th Street Cheyenne, Wyo. 82002	Wyoming Historic Preservation Association P.O. Box 1041 Cheyenne, Wyo. 82003	Mountains/Plains

Local Preservationists

Much of the structure of today's preservation movement has come down from the top—federal government, the National Trust and national organizations— but preservation always has advanced from the bottom up. Many of the most exciting preservation advances have percolated from the grass roots.

Louise McAllister Merritt, "A Local Organization's View." In *Preservation: Toward an Ethic in the 1980s*

"The past decade has witnessed a proliferation of organized preservation activities at the local level. Sometimes the impetus for action comes from a long-established historical society that expands its perceived mandate. More often, however, the preservation organization is a spin-off or entirely new group, formed in response to an immediate threat, then broadened in purpose. . . .

Depending on the level of sophistication and availability of resources, local preservation groups have conducted surveys, drafted preservation ordinances, supported commissions, performed feasibility studies, developed educational programs and even entered the real estate market through revolving funds."

"Patterns in Organizing for Preservation: Local." In *Preservation: Toward an Ethic in the 1980s*

"It is at the local level that private preservation organizations exist in the largest numbers and have accomplished the greatest amount. . . . [They] are usually better equipped to carry out brick-and-mortar preservation projects, easement and revolving fund programs, and other action-oriented projects, especially those involving real estate. . . . There is a whole new breed. . . . Concerned with commercial and industrial architecture as much as with residential, and with neighborhood character as much as with individual buildings, these new preservation groups are engaging in sophisticated legal, financial, and public relations techniques. . . . They encourage, support, and occasionally prod the local preservation agency; they keep track of what other local agencies are doing and speak up for preservation where necessary; and they engage in a variety of activities . . . that the private sector can accomplish more flexibly and economically. . . . Private preservation organizations often have to fulfill some of the functions of the public agency,

such as inventorying properties, preparing documentation for National Register nominations, and participating in environmental reviews."

Robert B. Rettig, *Conserving the Man-made Environment*

Local Umbrellas

In some cities with a proliferation of preservation organizations, historical societies and neighborhood associations, umbrella groups have been formed to unify local preservation activities under one name and place. The umbrella organization typically coordinates the varied efforts of its participating groups, serves as a municipal preservation information center and acts as the local voice of preservation for the general public. Some examples:

Boston Preservation Alliance
45 School Street
Boston, Mass. 02108

The Urban Center
457 Madison Avenue
New York, N.Y. 10011

Preservation Alliance of
Louisville and Jefferson County
716 West Main Street
Louisville, Ky. 40202

Atlanta Preservation Center
84 Peachtree Street, N.W.
Suite 401
Atlanta, Ga. 30303

Preservation Resource Center of
New Orleans
604 Julia Street
New Orleans, La. 70130

Preservation Coalition of
Greater Philadelphia
1629 Locust Street
Philadelphia, Pa. 19103

Historic Preservation Council
for Tarrant County
1110 Penn Street
Fort Worth, Tex. 76102

Victorian Alliance
4143 23rd Street
San Francisco, Calif. 94132

Headquarters of the Miami Design Preservation League in the Miami Beach Art Deco District. (Walter Smalling, Jr., HABS)

Private Preservation Groups

A recent count of local preservation activities turned up some 4,000 groups involved in preservation in cities across the United States. Hardly a large city or small town is without one. Here is a sampler:

Birmingham Historical Society
1425 22nd Street South
Birmingham, Ala. 35205

Quapaw Quarter Association
P.O. Box 1104
Little Rock, Ark. 72203

Los Angeles Conservancy
849 South Broadway
Los Angeles, Calif. 90014

Pasadena Heritage
54 West Colorado Boulevard
Pasadena, Calif. 91105

Foundation for San Francisco's
Architectural Heritage
2007 Franklin Street
San Francisco, Calif. 94109

Historic Boulder
1733 Canyon Boulevard
Boulder, Colo. 80302

Historic Denver
770 Pennsylvania Avenue
Denver, Colo. 80203

Hartford Architecture
Conservancy
130 Washington Street
Hartford, Conn. 06106

Greater Middletown
Preservation Trust
27 Washington Street
Middletown, Conn. 06457

Wilmington Alliance to Conserve Our Heritage (WATCH)
c/o Roy Smith
304 West Street
Wilmington, Del. 19801

D.C. Preservation League
930 F Street, N.W.
Suite 612
Washington, D.C. 20004

Dade Heritage Trust
66 East Flagler Street
Miami, Fla. 33130

Historic Savannah Foundation
Box 1733
Savannah, Ga. 31402

Lahaina Restoration Foundation
Box 338
Lahaina, Maui, Hawaii 96761

South Bend Heritage
Foundation
1016 West Washington Street
South Bend, Ind. 46601

Sherman Hill Association
705 19th Street
Des Moines, Iowa 50314

Preservation and Conservation
Association of Champaign
County
P.O. Box 2555
Station A
Champaign, Ill. 61820

Blue Grass Trust for
Historic Preservation
201 North Mill Street
Lexington, Ky. 40508

Greater Portland Landmarks
165 State Street
Portland, Maine 04101

Historic Annapolis
194 Prince George Street
Annapolis, Md. 21401

Historic Boston
3 School Street
Boston, Mass. 02108

Waterfront Historic Area
League (WHALE)
13 Centre Street
New Bedford, Mass. 02740

Heritage Hill Foundation
120 Madison Avenue, S.E.
Grand Rapids, Mich. 49503

Old Town Restorations
411 Selby Avenue
St. Paul, Minn. 55102

Historic Natchez Foundation
P.O. Box 1761
Natchez, Miss. 39120

Historic Kansas City
Foundation
20 West Ninth Street
Suite 450
Kansas City, Mo. 64105

Landmarks Association of
St. Louis
611 Olive Street
Room 2187
St. Louis, Mo. 63101

Billings Preservation Society
c/o Montana Institute of Arts
Foundation
P.O. Box 1456
Billings, Mont. 59103

Landmarks
1058 Howard Street
Omaha, Neb. 68102

Washoe Heritage Council
Box 10271
Reno, Nev. 89510

Old Santa Fe Association
Sena Plaza, No. 61
Santa Fe, N.M. 87501

Historic Albany Foundation
300 Hudson Avenue
Albany, N.Y. 12210

New York Landmarks
Conservancy
330 West 42nd Street
New York, N.Y. 10036

The Municipal Art Society
457 Madison Avenue
New York, N.Y. 10011

Historic Salisbury
P.O. Box 4221
Salisbury, N.C. 28144

Miami Purchase Association
812 Dayton Street
Cincinnati, Ohio 45245

Preservation Tulsa
P.O. Box 4768
Tulsa, Okla. 74159

Pittsburgh History and
Landmarks Foundation
One Station Square
Pittsburgh, Pa. 15219

Providence Preservation Society
24 Meeting Street
Providence, R.I. 02903

Historic Charleston Foundation
51 Meeting Street
Charleston, S.C. 29401

Historic Nashville
100 Second Avenue North
Nashville, Tenn. 37201

Historic Preservation League
2902 Swiss Avenue
Dallas, Tex. 75204

Galveston Historical Foundation
P.O. Drawer 539
Galveston, Tex. 77553

San Antonio Conservation
Society
107 King William Street
San Antonio, Tex. 78204

Historic Windsor
P.O. Box 1777
Windsor, Vt. 05089

Historic Richmond Foundation
2407 East Grace Street
Richmond, Va. 23223

Historic Staunton Foundation
P.O. Box 2534
Staunton, Va. 24401

Preservation of Historic
Winchester
8 East Cork Street
Winchester, Va. 22601

Friends of Wheeling
c/o Jeanne Doughty
105 Carmel Road
Wheeling, W. Va. 26003

Historic Milwaukee
P.O. Box 2132
Milwaukee, Wis. 53201

House rehabilitated through a Historic Boulder workshop. (Jerry Stowall)

The Local Public Sector

"It is at the local level that most actual preservation activities take place. Without a commitment on the part of local government, however small or unsophisticated the jurisdiction, Federal and State preservation programs will be able to do little to ensure the protection of locally significant resources."

Robert B. Rettig, *Conserving the Man-made Environment*

"The traditional link between government and preservation has been the designation of landmarks and the related work of historical commissions or landmark and historic district commissions. In fact, the areas of mutual interest are much broader, extending into many government departments and reflecting the many aspects of preservation. . . .

[A] factor to be aware of is the limitation on government authority. The powers of local governments are authorized and defined by the state constitution and state enabling legislation. The state government may retain oversight power in such areas as environment, highways, establishment of parks and distribution of federal monies. Municipalities may lack state authorization to do certain things, such as change zoning laws and taxes or even charge admission fees in park areas."

Leila Smith, *Working with Local Government.* Information Series, National Trust for Historic Preservation. Washington, D.C.: Preservation Press, 1977. 9 pp., biblio. $2 pb.

Preservation functions of local government include:

Direct preservation responsibilities: municipal preservation office, preservation coordinators, property ownership, historic site designation through a related agency.

Landmarks, historic district and historical commissions and architectural review boards: staffing, administration, coordination.

Parks and recreation facilities: development, maintenance.

Planning: land use, budget preparation, reuse of public buildings, housing.

Zoning: allowable uses, density, adjustments.

Revenue: taxation, bond issuance, fund raising, grants.

Permits and licenses: demolition, construction, occupancy.

Building codes: condemnation, repair, safety, adaptive use.

Human resources assistance: housing, neighborhoods, education, welfare, health aid and facilities.

Public services: trash removal, street and light maintenance.

Public works: bridges, civic centers, public utilities, office buildings.

Promotion: tourism, public activities.

Contacts

League of Women Voters
1730 M Street, N.W.
Washington, D.C. 20036

Each of the 1,500 local chapters of the league publishes a *Know Your Town* study of the town or towns in its area outlining the organization, activities, policies and public services of the government.

National League of Cities
1301 Pennsylvania Avenue, N.W.
Washington, D.C. 20004

Coordinator for state leagues of cities, which serve as information sources for municipal governments within their states. The municipalities communicate urban concerns—including neighborhood conservation and urban revitalization—to state leagues.

United States Conference of
Mayors
1620 I Street, N.W.
Washington, D.C. 20006

Represents the urban interests of larger cities and has participated in several preservation undertakings, including a study committee whose work led to passage of the 1966 act and a nationwide survey of historic city halls.

Regional Preservationists

Regional preservation organizations are desirable for sections of the country with a common cultural and economic heritage, so that problems may be identified and solutions worked out on a larger than statewide basis.

Robert B. Rettig, *Conserving the Man-made Environment*

"Today it is generally recognized that many problems and opportunities facing [the] city and county . . . cut across traditional . . . boundaries, and that in an increasing number of areas the action of one community can and often does have a major impact on the development of the surrounding areas. The resulting interdependency . . . has led to an increasing need for multicounty planning."

W. Wayne Gray, "Regional Planning Office," *11593*.

Some Interstate Regionalists

Society for the Preservation of New England Antiquities
141 Cambridge Street
Boston, Mass. 02114

The largest regional preservation organization in the country, SPNEA owns more than 50 properties, sponsors a consulting team of architectural conservation specialists to advise historic property owners, maintains a research collection and provides publications and other services for its membership.

Appalachian Regional Commission
1666 Connecticut Avenue, N.W.
Washington, D.C. 20235

An independent federal agency concerned with the cultural, economic, social and physical development of 13 states. The region includes 397 counties in parts of Alabama, Georgia, Kentucky, Maryland, Mississippi, New York, North Carolina, Ohio, Pennsylvania, Tennessee, South Carolina and Virginia, and all of West Virginia.

Tennessee Valley Authority
400 Commerce Avenue
Knoxville, Tenn. 37902

A Cultural Awareness Program and Operation Townlift are two preservation-related activities of TVA's Office of Community Development. These programs function in Tennessee and portions of Alabama, Georgia, Kentucky, Mississippi, North Carolina and Virginia.

National Association of Regional Councils
1700 K Street, N.W.
Washington, D.C. 20006

A membership association for public organizations tied to local governments through local and state actions. Their basic responsibility: to serve as an umbrella agency for comprehensive areawide policy planning, functional planning and implementation of regional policies.

Some Intrastate Regionalists

Regional Conference of Historical Agencies
1509 Park Street
Syracuse, N.Y. 13208–1620

Landmark Society of Western New York
130 Spring Street
Rochester, N.Y. 14608

Brandywine Conservancy
P.O. Box 141
Chadds Ford, Pa. 19317

Regional Historic Preservation Planners
Historic Preservation Division
South Carolina Department of Archives and History
P.O. Box 11669
Columbia, S.C. 29211

Plains Architectural Heritage
P.O. Box 5412
State University Station
Fargo, N.D. 58102

Preserving America: The Regions Series. Published in cooperation with the National Trust for Historic Preservation. New York: Pantheon, 1985–.

Preservationists in the regions analyzed in this projected six-book series—covering New England, the Mid-Atlantic, South, Midwest, Rocky Mountains/Plains and West—are facing preservation issues often common throughout their regions and are developing techniques that can be applied beyond their own cities and states. Each volume, written by a noted preservation writer in the region, introduces the region's historic buildings and examines key preservation issues and pressures for change. As they show, regional solutions to saving cultural resources endangered by region-based threats are beginning to take hold.

Officials of Rochester, N.Y., and the Landmark Society of Western New York marching from the old city hall to the new city hall in the converted Federal Building (1887, Harvey Ellis), saved at the society's urging.

Libby Barker of the Trust's Texas/New Mexico Field Office flanked by Marty Craddock and Linda Guminski of the Historic Preservation Council for Tarrant County, with one of 494 Fort Worth streetlights they saved. (Byrd Williams)

Warning to watch for flying angels at the crumbling Basilica of Santa Maria della Salute (1631), Venice, since restored. The photograph was part of an international exhibit. (Lotti, Italian Art and Landscape Foundation)

The International and Foreign Network

The conservation of our architectural heritage can no longer be seen as a marginal exercise to be undertaken by rich countries only. It is a matter of concern to every nation of the world, however limited its means may be. This heritage includes not only great monuments but also those often humble buildings that provided the background to the daily lives of our forebears and to our own lives as well.

Raymond M. Lemaire, Introduction. *Monumentum,* vol. XIII, 1976.

International Organizations

Council of Europe
Directorate for Environment
and Local Authorities
BP 431 R6
67006 Strasbourg Cedex, France

Europa Nostra
International Federation of
Associations for the Protection
of Europe's Cultural,
Architectural and
Natural Heritage
86 Vincent Square
London SW1P 2PG, England

International Centre for the
Study of the Preservation and
the Restoration of Cultural
Property (ICCROM)
13 Via di San Michele
00153 Rome, Italy

International Centre U.S.
Committee
c/o Advisory Council on
Historic Preservation
1100 Pennsylvania Avenue, N.W.
Suite 809
Washington, D.C. 20004

International Congress for the
Conservation of the Industrial
Heritage (TICCIH)
Department of Economic and
Social History
University of Birmingham
P.O. Box 363
Birmingham B15 2TT, England

International Council of
Museums (ICOM)
Maison de l'Unesco
1, rue Miollis
F75732 Paris Cedex 15, France

U.S. National Committee for
ICOM (AAM/ICOM)
c/o American Association of
Museums
1055 Thomas Jefferson Street, N.W.
Suite 428
Washington, D.C. 20007

International Council on Monuments and Sites (ICOMOS)
Hotel Saint Aignan
75, rue du Temple
F75003 Paris, France

U.S. Committee (US/ICOMOS)
1600 H Street, N.W.
Washington, D.C. 20006

International Fund for
Monuments
3624 Legation Street, N.W.
Washington, D.C. 20015

International Institute for
Conservation of Historic and
Artistic Works (IIC)
6 Buckingham Street
London WC2N 6BA, England

International Union of
Architects
51, rue Raynouard
75016 Paris, France

Committee on International
Relations
c/o American Institute of
Architects
1735 New York Avenue, N.W.
Washington, D.C. 20006

Organization of American States
Department of Cultural Affairs
Cultural Patrimony Division
1889 F Street, N.W.
Washington, D.C. 20006

Royal Oak Foundation
41 East 72nd Street
New York, N.Y. 10021

United Nations Educational,
Scientific and Cultural
Organization
Division of Cultural Heritage
Culture Sector
1, place de Fontenoy
75700 Paris, France

World Heritage Committee
c/o Unesco
Division of Cultural Heritage
7, place de Fontenoy
75700 Paris, France

U.S. Coordinator
Federal Interagency Panel
for World Heritage
National Park Service
U.S. Department of the Interior
Washington, D.C. 20240

Foreign Organizations

Association for Industrial
Archeology
Church Hill, Ironbridge
Telford, Salop TF8 7RE,
England

Australian Council of
National Trusts
14 Martin Place
11th Floor
Sydney 20(a), New South Wales

Canadian Department of Indian
and Northern Affairs
Treaties and Historical Research
Centre
Les Terrasses de la Chaudiere
Ottawa, Ontario K1A OH4,
Canada

Civic Trust
17 Carlton House Terrace
London SW1Y 5AW, England

Heritage Canada Foundation
P.O. Box 1358, Station B
Ottawa, Ontario K1P 5R4,
Canada

Irish Georgian Society
Castletown House
Celbridge, County Kildare,
Ireland

L'Association des Vieilles
Maisons Francaises
93, rue de l'Universite
75005 Paris, France

L'Inspection Generale des
Monuments Historiques
Direction du Patrimonie
Ministere de la Culture
3, rue de Valois
75042 Paris Cedex 01, France

National Monuments Record
Fortress House
23 Savile Row
London W1X 1AB, England

National Trust for Places of
Historic Interest or Natural
Beauty
42 Queen Anne's Gate
London SW1H 9AS, England

Northern Ireland Region
Rowallance House
Saintfield, Ballynahinch
County Down BT24 7L4,
Northern Ireland

National Trust for Scotland for
Places of Historic Interest or
Natural Beauty
5 Charlotte Square
Edinburgh EH2 4DU, Scotland

Royal Institute of British
Architects
British Architectural Library
66 Portland Place
London W1N 4AD, England

Scottish Civic Trust
24 George Square
Glasgow G2 1EF, Scotland

Scottish Georgian Society
39 Castle Street
Edinburgh EH2 3BH, Scotland

Society for the Protection of
Ancient Buildings
37 Spital Square
London E1 6DY, England

Victorian Society
1 Priory Gardens
Bedford Park
London W4 1TT, England

Protecting the Past

6

Developing strategies for historic preservation hinges on three fundamental issues: whether and how to search for historic properties (identification), how to recognize important properties among all those identified (evaluation), and how to determine the best action to be taken (protection).

U.S. Department of the Interior, *Resource Protection Planning Process*. Washington, D.C.: Survey and Planning Branch, National Park Service, 1980.

"The survey or inventory is . . . the sine qua non of preservation planning. . . .

Before any country can develop a comprehensive policy for the care of its artistic and historic heritage, it must be able to quantify, identify, and classify the artifacts in question. Although this might seem a perfectly obvious precondition, it is a remarkable fact that the process has not been completed in any country on earth."

James Marston Fitch, *Historic Preservation: Curatorial Management of the Built World*. New York: McGraw-Hill, 1982.

"Over the past 50 years, all 50 States and over [1,000] municipalities have enacted laws to encourage or require the preservation of buildings and areas with historic or aesthetic importance. These nationwide legislative efforts have been precipitated by two concerns. The first is recognition that, in recent years, large numbers of

St. Bartholomew's Church (1919, Bertram Goodhue), New York City. Both a national and a local landmark, the site became the center of controversy over designation of churches when a plan to build an adjacent tower was denied by New York City's landmarks commission. (© Walter Smalling, Jr.)

historic structures, landmarks, and areas have been destroyed without adequate consideration of either the values represented therein or the possibility of preserving the destroyed properties for use in economically productive ways. The second is a widely shared belief that structures with special historic, cultural, or architectural significance enhance the quality of life for all."

United States Supreme Court, *Penn Central Transportation Company v. City of New York*

"As the preservation ethic in America turns increasingly to one favoring conservation and rehabilitation of older structures over preservation and period restoration . . . there is increasing recognition that legal approaches to preservation must become an integral part of normal land use planning and control procedures and programs. Increasingly it is believed that while historic district zoning and landmark protection ordinances do play an important part in preservation, taken alone they are mere stopgap measures."

Robert E. Stipe et al., "The Impact of Law on Preservation Activities in the United States." *Monumentum*, vol. XIII, 1976.

Group surveying a New Orleans cemetery under guard after members were robbed while photographing vaults. (G. Arnold, Save Our Cemeteries)

Landmarks Reconnaissance: Surveying Cultural Resources

As soon as you can, have a survey made of what you are trying to save, property by property. This serves two purposes. First, it gets all the important information about any given property in one place. Second, it gives you moral support in any appeal to preserve or restore a property.

Arthur P. Ziegler, Jr., and Walter C. Kidney, *Historic Preservation in Small Towns: A Manual of Practice.* Nashville: American Association for State and Local History, 1980.

"There is the question of whether needed inventories and surveys of cultural resources throughout the state can be speeded up and completed. This is a slow and difficult task because it is not very visible politically, funds for the work are hard to come by, and the supply of adequately trained individuals to conduct such surveys is limited. Yet the entire structure of preservation law, including every aspect from public expenditure and environmental review procedures to the use of the police power, rests upon the credibility, accuracy, and thoroughness with which the process of identification, evaluation, and documentation is carried out."

Robert E. Stipe, "A Decade of Preservation and Preservation Law." *North Carolina Central Law Journal,* vol. 11, no. 2, April 1980.

"The inventory, in addition to identifying . . . landmarks, invites the public to value them. . . .

A comprehensive inventory, professionally done with broad public support, can identify an area's architectural heritage and unify support for it. It can trigger such direct action as protective sign ordinances, design and redevelopment projects and programs for rehabilitation. The published material of such a survey, if aimed at the public and not just planners, can provide fuel for historical societies and preservationists to kindle enthusiasm for saving and using old buildings. Though only a first step, an identification study can open eyes and turn them appreciatively toward irreplaceable landmarks of the past."

Elaine Freed, "What an Inventory Finds—and Causes." *Historic Preservation,* January–March 1978.

Surveys, Inventories and Plans: Preservation's First Step

Q: What is a survey?

A: A comprehensive gathering of detailed data on the historical and physical character of a community or region through fieldwork and historical research.

Q: What is an inventory?

A: A selective list of properties chosen from a survey based on professional evaluation against set criteria, such as those used for the National Register of Historic Places.

Q: Why undertake a historic resource survey?

A: The information obtained can be used to define public preservation policies. The resulting inventory can become the basis for making sound judgments in community planning and protecting the resources identified.

Q: What are the major values of a historic resource survey and inventory?

A: They identify buildings, sites, districts, structures and objects that should be nominated to the National Register and receive its protection; locate properties that deserve consideration in the local planning process; provide planners with a data base to monitor new development; establish priorities for conservation and restoration in a community; determine potential local historic districts; provide the basis for legal and financial tools to protect historic resources; increase awareness of the built environment; and enable participation in federal programs and planning. A survey should be flexible enough to integrate properties discovered through later research.

Q: How do surveys and inventories relate to preservation planning?

A: An official preservation plan, prepared and adopted by the community planning agency, provides a basis for integrating survey information with other planning data and serves as a tool for comprehensive master planning.

Q: Who should sponsor a survey?

A: Surveys should have the local government's official endorsement, although historical societies, professional groups and interested individuals can help in the documentation, research and fieldwork.

Q: How can surveys help fulfill preservation responsibilities of communities that receive federal funding?

A: Communities participating in various federal programs may be required to assume federal agency environmental and preservation review responsibilities by identifying resources to be safeguarded early in project planning, including those listed in or eligible for the National Register.

Q: What kinds of resources may be included in a survey?

A: Broad categories include buildings, sites, objects, structures and districts. *Buildings* are notable representatives of styles, periods, construction methods, industries, institutions and ethnic groups as well as curiosities, rare survivors and places where significant advances occurred. *Sites* are archeological findings that contain information useful in scientific research or shed light on local, state or national history. *Objects* are important cultural items such as outdoor sculpture, fountains, ships and petroglyphs. *Structures* are industrial, engineering and transportation landmarks such as mills, utilities, railroads, canals and bridges. *Districts* are groups of buildings such as cohesive streetscapes, neighborhoods and agricultural areas.

Q: What types of information do surveys seek out?

A: Basic data include a physical description of the property, a statement of significance, and

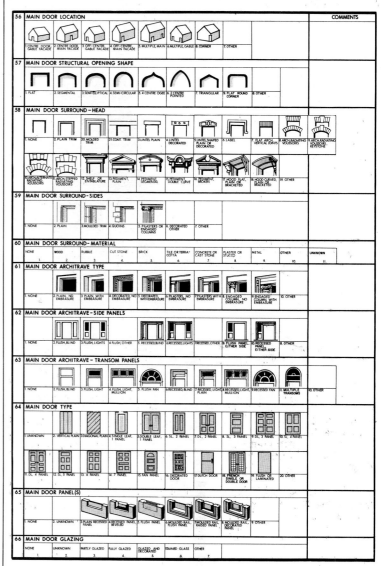

Survey form with detailed graphics and codes to facilitate identification and computerization. (Canadian Inventory of Historic Buildings)

photographs and maps. Specific details include the property's historic and common names, location, resource classification, owner, inclusion in existing surveys, detailed description, significance, a bibliography, geographical data and photographs.

Q: How large an area should be included in the survey?

A: This can be city or county limits, potential development areas or significant neighborhoods previously identified. More specialized surveys may identify certain themes, such as commercial development in a region or the work of a particular architect.

Q: How detailed must a survey be to meet community planning needs and federal regulations?

A: A comprehensive survey is necessary to determine the significance of all resources and their eligibility for the National Register, although a less thorough "windshield" survey may be a first step, for example, where a large development may threaten resources of obvious significance.

Q: What sources of information should be consulted?

A: Primary sources include tax rolls, deeds and wills, census reports, local directories, public construction records, family papers, local newspapers, school records and oral history. Secondary resources include the ongoing statewide survey, published histories, WPA guides and federal surveys (HABS, HAER, National Register, etc.).

Q: What type of training is necessary for a high-quality survey?

A: Training should stress the interrelatedness of historical research and field survey work, historical development of the area, location of source material, visual analysis, architectural and environmental elements, recording and mapping techniques, and the goals and objectives of the survey.

Q: Where can qualified professionals be located?

A: Helpful organizations include the SHPO, the state archeologist and archeological societies, local colleges, professional organizations of architects, historians, architectural historians, planners and landscape architects, and regional offices of the National Trust (see Preservationists).

Q: How are survey data recorded?

A: Most states have developed standardized survey forms. Photographs are an essential part of the survey data (black and white, with supplemental

Surveyors from the Indianapolis Historic Preservation Commission recording the White Castle (1927). (IHPC)

slides). Field maps also are used.

Q: Are due process considerations involved in evaluating properties?

A: Not if listing in an inventory carries no legal protection or restrictions. However, communities may notify property owners (and in some cases their consent is required), hold public hearings and provide opportunities for appeal.

Q: Are numerical ratings appropriate in historic resource inventories?

A: Systems that assign "scores" are not the most effective way of setting preservation priorities because they give a false sense of certainty by quantifying intangibles such as significance.

Q: How can communities generate public interest in survey work?

A: Use neighborhood meetings, public displays, walking tours, films, publications, newspaper series, campaigns to collect historical data and coordination with local civic and historical groups.

Q: In what other ways are surveys disseminated?

A: Publications can communicate the survey and preservation recommendations to planners, decision makers and residents alike. General publications derived from surveys range from leaflets and posters to guidebooks and book-length illustrated local histories.

Q: What survey assistance can SHPOs provide?

A: Information on what resources have already been surveyed by the state, advice on the development of a local survey, integration of local and federally sponsored surveys into the state survey, nomination of properties to the National Register, provision of grants and funding information for survey work and participation in review of federal projects.

From *Guidelines for Local Surveys: A Basis for Preservation Planning.* Anne Derry, H. Ward Jandl, Carol D. Shull and Jan Thorman. Washington, D.C.: National Register of Historic Places, U.S. Department of the Interior, 1977. 83 pp., illus., appends., biblio., index.

Reflections of a Streetwalker

"We arrive at the neighborhood we have been assigned to survey, to describe the individual houses and neighborhood groupings and to express our opinions of their value. 'The Streetwalkers Guide' and 'Historic Resources Inventory' in one hand, sewer connection maps and propaganda in the other, we approach the area.

'The Streetwalkers Guide' tells us what to look for and the 'Historic Resources Inventory' tells us how to describe it in terms which will not offend the professionals who will eventually read our comments. . . . 'Curlyques under the roof seem to support it' becomes 'Overhanging eaves have indented rafters and decorated brackets.'

The sewer maps help in our detective work. When was the

house built? How much of the house is original? Was the house moved onto the present site?

The propaganda, 'The Treasures on Your Block,' helps us allay the fears of residents who view us suspiciously. . . . During this process we find we have become part of the neighborhood. . . . We are hoping to preserve whole neighborhoods, not only individual dwellings."

Bunny Gould and Carol Robillard. *Pasadena Heritage* Newsletter, Summer 1977.

Treasures on Your Block Series: Walking Tours of Pasadena Neighborhoods. Pasadena, Calif.: Pasadena Urban Conservation Program (100 North Garfield Avenue, 91109), 1977–. $1 each.

See also: Building Roots

Contacts

Survey and Planning Branch
Interagency Resources Division
National Park Service
U.S. Department of the Interior
P.O. Box 37127
Washington, D.C. 20013-7127

Reviews and approves the preservation survey and planning efforts of SHPOs and provides technical assistance.

National Register of
Historic Places
National Park Service
U.S. Department of the Interior
P.O. Box 37127
Washington, D.C. 20013-7127

Maintains the National Register, compiled from nominations approved by state review boards and SHPOs, often on the basis of state and local surveys and inventories.

State Historic Preservation
Offices (SHPOs)

Responsible for preparation of the state preservation plan and annual programs. Many SHPOs have issued instruction manuals for preservation surveys in their states. For a list, see Preservationists.

Historic American
Buildings Survey
Historic American
Engineering Record
National Park Service
U.S. Department of the Interior
P.O. Box 37127
Washington, D.C. 20013-7127

Specialized national surveys designed to develop a national archive on American architecture and engineering landmarks, they record individual structures and districts through measured drawings, photographs and written data. Their decision to document sites may help localities recognize their significance; the information also may be used in National Register nominations.

Preservation Plans: Protecting the Sense of Place

The planner, charged with the management of community resources and shaping options for the future, should recognize that preservation planning offers both short term opportunities and long range advantages. . . .

Knowledge of the community's past helps in understanding emerging patterns and future expectations. In fully built communities, preservation planning may be, in fact, the most realistic approach to reviving or maintaining the viability of the city. A greater knowledge of the community's cultural resources provides a stronger base for better planning and more informed decision-making.

In the end everyone benefits. Historic preservation planning makes for a better community by stressing positive community attributes. By providing assurance that the special sense of place will survive, the people are given reason to commit their own futures to the community.

California Office of Planning and Research, *Historic Preservation Element Guidelines.* 1976.

Preservation Plan Components

Historical overview
Treatment of architectural styles, construction and other distinguishing features
Description of the setting of the community
Inventory of significant cultural resources

Notation of areas that may be eligible for local historic districts or the National Register
Evaluation of the impact of public policy affecting cultural resources (zoning, building codes, municipal plans, transportation, housing, etc.)
Review of private policy and growth plans

Indication of special problem areas (parking, traffic flow, utilities, etc.)
Establishment of preservation planning goals and specific objectives
Suggestion of a cultural resources management program
Potential funding sources

Resource Protection Planning Process. Washington, D.C.: Survey and Planning Branch, National Park Service, 1980. 37 pp., illus. Free.

Outlines a system for helping the states integrate preservation surveys into their planning process by determining preservation priorities. The basis for the surveys is a series of study units chosen for geographic, thematic and temporal reasons.

Historic Preservation Plans: An Annotated Bibliography. National Trust for Historic Preservation. Washington, D.C.: Preservation Press, 1976. 42 pp., append. $3.95 pb.

Listings of 91 preservation plans for districts, cities, regions, states, ethnic areas, highway sites, open spaces and waterfronts, organized by population.

Legacy of Minneapolis: Preservation Amid Change. John R. Borchert, David Gebhard, David Lanegran and Judith A. Martin. Bloomington, Minn.: Voyager Press, 1983. 205 pp., illus., append. $14.95 pb.

Something to Preserve. Ipswich, Mass.: Ipswich Historical Commission, 1975. 111 pp., illus.

New Life for Maryland's Old Towns. Land Design/Research. Annapolis: Maryland Historical Trust and Department of Economic and Community Development, 1979. 52 pp., illus. $5 pb.

Waterford: The Challenge. Constance K. Chamberlin. Waterford, Va.: Waterford Foundation (P.O. Box 142, 22190), 1980. 24 pp., illus. $3 pb.

The Small Town as an Art Object: Holly Springs, Ocean Springs and Starkville, Miss. James F. Barker, Michael W. Fazio and Hank Hildebrandt, Mississippi State University School of Architecture. New York: Wittenborn, 1976. 189 pp., illus.

Marshall: A Plan for Preservation. Johnson, Johnson and Roy. Marshall, Mich.: Marshall Historical Society, 1973. 96 pp., illus., appends.

A Plan for Ephraim. Land Plans, Inc. Madison: Department of Landscape Architecture, University of Wisconsin, 1973. 60 pp. $10.

Maintaining the Spirit of Place: A Guidebook for Citizen Professional Participation in the Preservation and Enhancement of Texas Towns. Harry Launce Garnham. College Station, Tex.: Texas A&M University, 1976. 84 pp., illus., biblio.

Willard: A Plan for Its Historic Preservation. Gerald Brown and Teddy Griffith. Logan, Utah: Institute for Study of Outdoor Recreation and Tourism, Utah State University, 1973. 79 pp.

The Way It Was: A Program for Historic Preservation. Fairfield, Calif.: Department of Environmental Affairs (City Hall, 94533), 1975. 99 pp., illus., append.

See also: Looking at the Built Environment; Cities (Form and Function)

Contacts

American Planning Association
1313 East 60th Street
Chicago, Ill. 60637

The national organization of professional urban, regional and state planners. It serves as a planning information clearinghouse, lobbies for better planning, provides professional services such as accreditation, maintains a library, issues a variety of publications such as *Planning,* PAS Reports and *Land Use Law and Zoning Digest,* and sells a variety of planning books.

Street in the Frederick, Md., historic district. (Jet Lowe, National Register of Historic Places)

Honolulu House (1860), Marshall, Mich., built by a former U.S. consul to the Sandwich Islands. (George Vallillee)

Regional/Urban Design
Assistance Teams
American Institute of Architects
1735 New York Avenue, N.W.
Washington, D.C. 20006

Ad-hoc teams of professionals who volunteer to resolve sometimes conflicting public and private community design priorities. Teams visit towns, meet with community groups, establish strategies and develop courses of action, whose implementation is the local community's responsibility.

Partners for Livable Places
1429 21st Street, N.W.
Washington, D.C. 20036

A national alliance of organizations and individuals working to improve communities with an emphasis on the human factors in city planning. It administers special projects such as the Economics of Amenity program, issues publications and maintains a library and a computerized Livability Clearinghouse for information on the built environment.

Urban Land Institute
1090 Vermont Avenue, N.W.
Suite 300
Washington, D.C. 20005

A nonprofit research and educational organization serving as a source of information on land use trends, development, growth management and planning. Membership is drawn from the land use professions—developers, architects, public officials, planners, real estate brokers and others. Research issues addressed include housing costs, rural growth, land prices, energy, joint development and adaptive use. Major publications include books and periodicals such as *Urban Land* and *Land Use Digest;* seminars and conferences also are held.

Project for Public Spaces
875 Avenue of the Americas
Room 201
New York, N.Y. 10001

Encourages improved quality in streets, plazas, parks and other public areas using research on the behavior of people in public places. Sponsors seminars, publications, a library and training programs.

American Society of
Landscape Architects
1733 Connecticut Avenue, N.W.
Washington, D.C. 20009

Addresses increasingly broad land use and planning concerns, maintains a preservation committee and provides registration, accreditation, publications, liaison and related services for members and affiliates.

Council of Planning Librarians
1313 East 60th Street
Chicago, Ill. 60637

Prepares bibliographies on planning topics, a directory of planning libraries and a newsletter.

Institute for Urban Design
Main P.O. Box 105
Purchase, N.Y. 10577

Dedicated to improving urban design and the quality of life as influenced by physical planning and construction. Sponsors seminars, workshops and the magazine *Urban Design International.*

Preservation Law: Protecting Scarce Resources

There remains a strong and vocal division of opinion among Americans as to how far government at any level should be permitted to go in regulating the use of private property. What has been described as a "frontier mentality" that regards land and buildings, whether of cultural importance or not, as commodities to be freely traded to produce income or capital gains for the current owner—rather than as scarce resources to be treated with respect and consideration—is still a disappointingly widespread phenomenon among the vast majority of American citizens and, hence, their governments.

Robert E. Stipe et al., "The Impact of Law on Preservation Activities in the United States." *Monumentum,* vol. XIII, 1976.

"Historic preservation by force of law is well rooted in antiquity and is replete with interesting and enlightening precedents."

Jacob H. Morrison, *Historic Preservation Law.* 1957. Rev. ed. Washington, D.C.: Preservation Press, 1974.

"The monuments of consular or Imperial greatness were no longer revered as the immortal glory of the capital: They were only esteemed as an inexhaustible mine of materials, cheaper, and more convenient, than the distant quarry. . . . Majorian, who had often sighed over the desolation of the City, applied a severe remedy to the growing evil. He . . . imposed a fine of fifty pounds of gold . . . and threatened . . . a severe whipping and the amputation of both their hands."

Edward Gibbon, *Decline and Fall of the Roman Empire.* 1776–87.

"Basically, land use controls may be divided into two general areas: those that anyone with the right to purchase land may use, and those that only the government may exercise. The first of these, those legal mechanisms that anyone can use, are called private land use controls. . . .

Private land use controls . . . all have one basic aspect in common: They involve acquiring property. This means that a right must be purchased from the owner of the property over which some control is sought. . . . The most obvious private land use control is the outright purchase of property. . . . The common law has also established a set of procedures enabling one party to purchase some lesser right in a piece of property owned by another. These rights can mean that it is possible to buy a restriction on an owner's use of historic property. Similarly, one could acquire a restriction on the owner's right to alter any specific aspect of its design. . . .

The government can act just as any other legal person in acquiring rights in property. It may bargain for and ultimately purchase these rights. But, in addition, the government has unique powers which can be brought to bear to preserve historic buildings and sites . . . eminent domain, police power, and the power to tax."

Grady Gammage, Jr., Philip N. Jones and Stephen L. Jones, *Historic Preservation in California: A Legal Handbook*

"Certain types of laws—not necessarily designed for preservation purposes—have made a material contribution to the maintenance of historic landmarks. Zoning laws, which are of comparatively recent origin, have done much for preservation though tailored to the comfort and convenience of the modern urban citizen."

Jacob H. Morrison, *Historic Preservation Law*

Statue of Justice, Old State House (1796, Bulfinch), Hartford, Conn.

Preservation Law Primers

"Until the [1970s] there was nothing that could be called a body of historic preservation law. Even today many laypersons and lawyers are unaware that there is a cluster of statutes, ordinances, court decisions and procedures that constitutes an interrelated body of law on the subject."

Russell V. Keune, Introduction. *Historic Preservation Law: An Annotated Bibliography*

A Handbook on Preservation Law. Christopher J. Duerksen, ed. Washington, D.C.: Conservation Foundation, 1983. 523 pp., biblio., append., index. $50 hb, $30 pb.

Presents articles by experts in local, state and federal preservation law on environmental protection laws useful in preservation, constitutional questions, litigation techniques, drafting and administering local ordinances, formulating a preservation plan and the relationship of preservation and economics. The appendix reprints the National Trust's "Recommended Model Provisions for a Preservation Ordinance, with Annotations." Cosponsored by the National Trust and the National Center for Preservation Law.

"The Impact of Law on Preservation Activities in the United States," Robert E. Stipe et al. *Monumentum,* vol. XIII. Terry B. Morton, ed. Washington, D.C.: US/ICOMOS, 1976. 128 pp., illus., biblio. $10 pb.

An introduction to the bases, history, techniques, successes and problems of preservation law.

The Historic Preservation Yearbook. Russell V. Keune, ed. Bethesda, Md.: Adler and Adler (4550 Montgomery Avenue, 20814), 1984. Published in cooperation with the National Trust for Historic Preservation. 590 pp., appends. $78 hb.

A detailed reference book giving significant coverage to the legal foundations of preservation: major federal laws, innovative state and local legislation, historic districts, the Advisory Council on Historic Preservation, taxation, financing, real estate, building codes, plus policy analyses of recent developments.

Directory of Preservation Lawyers. Stephen Dennis, ed. Washington, D.C.: National Trust for Historic Preservation, 1984. 53 pp. $3.50 pb.

A list by state of 212 attorneys with descriptions of their expertise in preservation law.

Reusing Old Buildings: Preservation Law and the Development Process. Conservation Foundation, National Trust for Historic Preservation and American Bar Association. Washington, D.C.: National Trust, 1984. 450 pp. $30 pb.

Study materials and papers prepared for a conference.

Practising Law Institute Handbooks: Historic Preservation Law. 1981 and 1982. *Rehabilitating Historic Buildings.* 1983. 862 pp. *Rehabilitating Historic Properties.* 1984. 427 pp. New York: Practising Law Institute (810 Seventh Avenue, 10019). $35 each.

A series of lecture outlines and papers for annual PLI preservation law courses, together with significant state and federal preservation statutes and court decisions.

"A Symposium on Historic Preservation Law." *Pace Law Review,* vol. 1, no. 3, 1981. 280 pp. $4.50 pb. Pace University School of Law, 78 North Broadway, White Plains, N.Y. 10603.

Topics addressed include the reach of landmark regulation to include aesthetic values, perspectives of the real estate community on preservation and transfer of development rights.

"Historic Preservation Symposium: In Honor of Robert E. Stipe." *North Carolina Central Law Journal,* vol. 11, no. 2, Spring 1980. 200 pp., biblio. $20. Available from William W. Gaunt and Sons, 3011 Gulf Drive, Holmes Beach, Fla. 33510.

Articles surveying a decade of preservation law, adaptive use, revolving funds, annotated court decisions, bibliography of legal periodicals and North Carolina's innovative 1979 legislation.

Environmental Regulation of Real Property. Nicholas A. Robinson. New York: Law Journal Seminars Press (111 8th Avenue, 10011), 1982. $70.

Includes a chapter on historic and archeological sites, as well as discussions of constitutional environmental law, environmental impact assessment, roadside aesthetic controls, solar access and land use controls.

"Symposium: Perspectives on Historic Preservation." *Connecticut Law Review,* Winter 1975–76. $8.50. Available from Fred B. Rothman.

Contents include historic district ordinances, state statutes, rehabilitation of neighborhoods, tax incentives, public attitudes and involvement and a survey of conservation restrictions.

"Historic Preservation Symposium." *Wake Forest Law Review,* vol. 12, Spring 1976. $10. Available from Fred B. Rothman and Company, 10368 West Centennial Road, Littleton, Colo. 80127.

A compendium encompassing developments in and suggested directions for federal legislation, preservation cases, preservation in North Carolina and a bibliography.

"Historic Preservation." *Law and Contemporary Problems,* vol. 36, no. 3, Summer 1971. Duke University School of Law. 136 pp., biblio. $13.75 pb. Available from William S. Hein and Company, 1285 Main Street, Buffalo, N.Y. 14209.

Papers from the first national conference on preservation law commenting on a broad range of early preservation law issues.

"Annotated Bibliography of Law-Related Journal Citations on Historic Preservation," Thomas R. French. *Northern Kentucky Law Review,* vol. 9, 1982. 26 pp. Salmon P. Chase College of Law, Northern Kentucky University, Highland Heights, Ky. 41076.

Listing of works published during 1976–81, with an appendix of relevant articles in legal publications.

Historic Preservation Law: An Annotated Bibliography, Ellen L. Kettler and Bernard D. Reams, Jr. Washington, D.C.: Preservation Press, 1976. 115 pp., appends., index.

A compilation of articles and cases in preservation law. Chapters include general materials, legislation, historic districts, easements, aesthetic zoning, case studies, urban renewal, archeology and standing.

"Bibliography to Legal Periodicals Dealing with Historic Preservation and Aesthetic Regulation." *North Carolina Central Law Journal,* vol. 11, no. 2, Spring 1980. $20. Available from William H. Gaunt and Sons.

"Bibliography to Legal Periodicals Dealing with Historic Preservation and Aesthetic Regulation." *Wake Forest Law Review,* vol. 12, Spring 1976.

Historic Preservation in California: A Legal Handbook. Grady Gammage, Jr., Philip N. Jones and Stephen L. Jones. 1975. Rev. ed. Stanford, Calif.: Stanford Environmental Law Society (Stanford Law School, 94305), 1982. 146 pp. $10 pb.

Presents basic preservation legal concepts—private property and land use controls, historic district zoning and alternatives, impact analysis, planning tools, transfer of development rights, with thorough coverage of California preservation law.

Decorative porch railing of the Delsea in Cape May, N.J., a National Register historic district. (Jack E. Boucher, HABS)

Portland Head Light (1787) and keeper's house, Cape Elizabeth, Maine, a National Register property. (Jack E. Boucher, HABS)

Dome, City of Paris Department Store (1909, James R. Miller), San Francisco, all that was saved after a long legal battle. (Carleton Knight III)

A Primer on Preservation Law in the State of New York. Berle, Butzel, Kass and Case. Washington, D.C.: National Center for Preservation Law, 1981. 58 pp. $5 pb.

Designed to assist public agencies, community groups and citizens in using the legal tools available in the state, including building codes.

A Handbook of Historic Preservation Laws for Connecticut. New Haven, Conn.: Connecticut Trust for Historic Preservation (152 Temple Street, 06510), 1984. 30 pp. $8 pb.

An overview of federal, state and local laws affecting the preservation of historic resources in Connecticut.

Urban Law: A Guide to Information Sources. Thomas P. Murphy and Robert D. Kline, eds. Detroit: Gale, 1980. 320 pp. $55.

An annotated bibliography covering legal aspects of administering urban areas: land use planning law, urban finance, housing, transportation and public works. Includes relevant court cases and urban law textbooks.

The Environmental Decade in Court. Lettie M. Wenner. Bloomington, Ind.: Indiana University Press, 1982. 224 pp., appends., index. $22.50 hb.

Examines the role of the federal judiciary in implementing environmental laws in the 10 years after passage of NEPA. Analyzes 1,900 federal cases and focuses on policy patterns emerging from court decisions, demonstrating the role of the courts as public policy makers.

Architectural Preservation and Urban Renovation: An Annotated Bibliography of U.S. Congressional Documents. Richard Tubesing. New York: Garland, 1982. 500 pp., index. $83.

Includes all relevant bills, resolutions and public laws considered during the preceding decade by the House and Senate, with abstracts and legislative history.

Periodicals

Preservation Law Reporter
National Trust for Historic Preservation
1785 Massachusetts Avenue, N.W.
Washington, D.C. 20036

A looseleaf reporting service providing up-to-date coverage of new developments in preservation law and litigation. Contents include news of federal legislation and regulations; agency actions; state and local laws; court decisions and related activities; in-depth discussions of practical and theoretical issues, often with sample forms; summaries of important cases; bibliographies and a cumulative index. A permanent reference volume includes federal, state and local preservation laws and regulations, interpretive material and a case digest. Subjects regularly covered include real estate, tax incentives, ordinances, easements, estate planning, zoning and land use law, and nonprofit organizations.

Housing and Development Reporter
Bureau of National Affairs, Inc.
2300 M Street, N.W.
Washington, D.C. 20037

Weekly reporting service on federal and state housing programs, land use controls and environmental actions. Preservation is covered in the environmental-land use and community development categories.

Environmental Law Reporter
Environmental Law Institute
1346 Connecticut Avenue, N.W.
Suite 600
Washington, D.C. 20036

Service supplying information on environmental issues—litigation, administrative proceedings, regulations, legislation, articles and bibliographies, in a looseleaf format.

Land Use Law and Zoning Digest
American Planning Association
1313 East 60th Street
Chicago, Ill. 60637

Features digests of cases and legislation on land use and zoning as well as other land use management issues.

Index to Legal Periodicals. Stephen Rosen, ed. Bronx, N.Y.: H.W. Wilson Company (950 University Avenue, 10452).

Includes a historic preservation category.

Contacts

National Trust for Historic Preservation
Office of the General Counsel
1785 Massachusetts Avenue, N.W.
Washington, D.C. 20036

Assists state and local preservation organizations and agencies with legal and related preservation issues such as taxation and easements. Maintains liaison with lawyers, legislators and law schools; coordinates information collection on preservation litigation and legislation, including a State Legislation Clearinghouse; intervenes in significant preservation cases. The office prepares the *Preservation Law Reporter* and related publications, and maintains files of documents such as ordinances, complaints and briefs. Through its Office of Regional Services, the Trust also provides advisory services to preservation commissions on local preservation ordinances.

National Center for Preservation Law
2101 L Street, N.W.
Suite 906
Washington, D.C. 20037

A public-interest center staffed on a part-time basis to provide free legal assistance, particularly in litigation, to local nonprofit preservation organizations and public officials.

Natural Resources Defense Council
122 East 42nd Street
New York, N.Y. 10168

1350 New York Avenue, N.W.
Suite 300
Washington, D.C. 20005

Membership organization dedicated to protecting endangered natural resources, including land use and resource management. The council was a plaintiff in the 1981–82 litigation to stop demolition of the Helen Hayes and Morosco theaters in New York City.

Environmental Law Institute
1346 Connecticut Avenue, N.W.
Suite 600
Washington, D.C. 20036

National nonprofit research center devoted to the analysis of environmental and natural resource protection law.

Conservation Foundation
1717 Massachusetts Avenue, N.W.
Washington, D.C. 20036

Maintains an interest in preservation law, cosponsors legal conferences with the National Trust and has published a leading law handbook.

Historic Preservation Collection
School of Law Library
University of Virginia
Charlottesville, Va. 22901

New special collection of preservation law cases and materials.

Historic district of Nantucket, Mass., showing the island's unique "tout ensemble." (Jack E. Boucher, HABS)

The Language of Preservation Law

amicus curiae. Friend of the court (Latin). A party that may be allowed to present a brief on an issue before the court, frequently one with relevant special expertise.

antineglect ordinance. A local regulation that provides penalties for owners who allow historic property to deteriorate as a means of undermining preservation efforts.

certificate of appropriateness. A document awarded by a preservation commission or architectural review board allowing an applicant to proceed with a proposed alteration or new construction, following a determination of the proposal's suitability according to applicable criteria; may also permit demolition.

demolition delay. A temporary halt or stay in the planned razing of a property, sometimes resulting from a court injunction obtained by preservationists to allow a period of negotiation.

design guidelines. Criteria developed by preservation commissions to identify design concerns in an area and help property owners ensure that rehabilitation and new construction respect the character of designated buildings or districts.

design review. The process of ascertaining whether modifications to historic structures or settings meet standards of appropriateness established by a review board.

easement. A less-than-fee interest in real property acquired through donation or purchase and carried as a deed restriction to protect the appearance of open spaces, building exteriors and interiors.

eminent domain. The power of a government to acquire private property for public benefit after payment of just compensation to the owner.

enabling legislation. Federal or state laws that authorize a governing body within their jurisdiction to enact particular measures or delegate powers such as enactment of local landmarks and historic district ordinances, zoning and taxation.

historical commission. A municipal entity usually with no regulatory authority; its responsibilities are often limited to identification of landmarks and districts, research and public education.

historic district ordinance. A municipal law designating certain areas to be preserved or authorizing the general establishment of historic districts, typically establishing a review commission, procedures seeking review of changes in the area and an appeals process.

landmarks register. A listing of buildings and districts designated for historical, architectural or other special significance that may carry a variety of forms of protection for listed properties; local registers often are maintained by a preservation commission and may be modeled after the National Register of Historic Places.

police power. The inherent right of a government to restrict individual conduct or use of property to protect the public health, safety and welfare; it must follow due processes of the law but unlike eminent domain does not carry the requirement of compensation for any alleged losses. Police power is the basis for such regulations as zoning, building codes and preservation ordinances.

preservation commission. A generic term for a municipal agency that designates and regulates historic districts and landmarks; it may be called a historic district review board or commission, landmarks commission or architectural or design review board.

standing to sue. The doctrine that cases presented to a court must be concrete controversies between parties with a real stake in the dispute, such as a financial injury. In environmental matters, others may gain the right to sue.

taking. The appropriation by government of private property, e.g., condemnation through eminent domain for a public use or purpose with just compensation. The taking issue arises also when the use of the police power appears to diminish the value of affected property, such as a decision under a preservation ordinance.

tout ensemble. All together (French). Used to connote the cohesive ambience of an entire area, derived from *City of New Orleans v. Pergament,* 5 So. 2d 129 (La. 1941): "The purpose of the ordinance is not only to preserve the old buildings themselves, but to preserve the antiquity of the whole French and Spanish quarter, the tout ensemble, so to speak, by defending this relic against iconoclasm or vandalism."

Adapted from *Landmark Words: A Glossary for Preserving the Built Environment.* National Trust for Historic Preservation. Forthcoming.

Rainbow Lake in Overton Park, Memphis, Tenn., spared under the Department of Transportation Act. (Bill Williams, Citizens to Preserve Overton Park)

Significant Federal Preservation Legislation

1906
Antiquities Act. Authorized the president to designate national monuments and established regulations to protect archeological sites on public lands.

1935
National Historic Sites Act. Authorized the secretary of the interior to acquire national historic sites and designate National Historic Landmarks.

1966
National Historic Preservation Act. Expanded the National Register of Historic Places to include listings of local, state and regional significance; authorized grants to the states and National Trust; established protections for Register properties from federal projects; and created the Advisory Council on Historic Preservation.

Department of Transportation Act. Extended protection to historic sites affected by federal transportation projects.

Demonstration Cities and Metropolitan Development Act. Authorized funding for preservation projects under HUD urban renewal and housing programs.

1969
National Environmental Policy Act. Established the Council on Environmental Quality and included preservation among considerations requiring environmental impact statements.

1971
Executive Order 11593: "Protection and Enhancement of the Cultural Environment." Required federal agencies to develop procedures for protecting federal historic properties.

1972
Surplus Real Property Act. Amended the Federal Property and Administrative Services Act of 1949 to allow the U.S. General Services Administration to transfer surplus federal property to states and municipalities for public or revenue-producing uses.

1974
Archeological and Historic Preservation Act. Authorized the secretary of the interior and other federal agencies to preserve or salvage sites affected by federal projects, including use of project funds.

Housing and Community Development Act. Consolidated urban grant programs under a single Community Development Block Grant Program.

1976
Tax Reform Act. Created tax incentives for the rehabilitation of income-producing historic structures, penalized demolition and codified deductions for charitable transfers of preservation easements.

Public Buildings Cooperative Use Act. Directed GSA to acquire historic structures for federal office use and to promote mixed public uses of such buildings.

1977
Housing and Community Development Act. Established the Urban Development Action Grant Program.

1978
Revenue Act. Provided an investment tax credit for the rehabilitation of old buildings used for commercial and industrial purposes.

1980
Amendments to the National Historic Preservation Act. Required consent of owners before listing a property in the National Register; changed the membership of the Advisory Council; directed federal agencies to nominate and protect federal properties; and provided for a National Museum of the Building Arts.

1981
Economic Recovery Tax Act. Created a three-tiered tax credit for investment in old and historic buildings favoring certified historic structures.

Draper Hill. (*The Commercial Appeal,* February 1, 1975)

National Register of Historic Places

The quality of significance in American history, architecture, archeology, and culture is present in districts, sites, buildings, structures, and objects that possess integrity of location, design, setting, materials, workmanship, feeling and association, and:

1. That are associated with historical events;

2. That are associated with significant people;

3. That embody distinctive characteristics of a type, period or method of construction, represent the work of a master, possess high artistic values or are otherwise distinguished; or

4. That may yield information important in prehistory or history.

Ordinarily not eligible (unless they are integral parts of historic districts or meet special criteria) are cemeteries, birthplaces and graves of historical figures; religious and commemorative properties; structures that have been moved; reconstructed buildings; and properties that have achieved significance within the last 50 years.

National Register of Historic Places

Mount Vernon Place Historic District, Baltimore, a National Historic Landmark. (A. Aubrey Bodine Collection, Peale Museum)

Touro Synagogue National Historic Site (1763, Peter Harrison), Newport, R.I., the oldest U.S. synagogue. (Jack E. Boucher, HABS)

The National Register of Historic Places is the official list of the nation's cultural resources worthy of preservation. In addition to recognition of significance, listing in the Register provides some protection, through review by the Advisory Council on Historic Preservation, against federally financed, assisted or licensed undertakings and makes owners of listed properties eligible for tax benefits and funding programs. Authorized in 1935, the Register was expanded under the National Historic Preservation Act of 1966 to become a planning device to guide federal, state, local and private actions. Register listing is not an absolute bar to destruction of listed properties by private owners or federal projects, although properties affected by federal undertakings may be the recipients of funds authorized for recovery of important historical or archeological data.

Properties gain National Register listing primarily through nominations by the state historic preservation offices, which work with state review boards. Certified communities with local preservation ordinances also review and vote on new nominations before they reach the state level. Federal agencies nominate their own properties. Properties within the National Park System and National Historic Landmarks are automatically included—but the White House, U.S. Capitol, Supreme Court and Library of Congress have been exempted.

Potential entries are reviewed against set criteria and are classified as districts, sites, buildings, structures or objects. Multiple resource nominations based on city or areawide surveys and thematic group nominations also may be made.

Some 37,500 listings were in the National Register as of April 1985, 10 percent of which were historic districts—representing more than a quarter million buildings—and the task is far from complete. Additions are published in the *Federal Register* each month.

The National Register Does

1. Identify historically significant buildings, structures, sites, objects, and districts, according to the National Register Criteria for Evaluation.

2. Encourage the preservation of historic properties by documenting the significance of historic properties and by lending support to local preservation activities.

3. Enable federal, state, and local agencies to consider historic properties in the early stages of planning projects.

4. Provide for review of federally funded, licensed, or sponsored projects which may affect historic properties.

5. Make owners of historic properties eligible to apply for federal grants-in-aid for preservation activities.

6. Encourage the rehabilitation of income-producing historic properties which meet preservation standards through tax incentives; discourage the demolition of income-producing properties through tax disincentives.

The National Register Does Not

1. Restrict the rights of private property owners in the use, development, or sale of private historic property.

2. Lead automatically to historic district zoning.

3. Force federal, state, local or private projects to be stopped.

4. Provide for review of state, local, or privately funded projects which may affect historic properties.

5. Guarantee that grant funds will be available for all significant historic properties.

6. Provide tax benefits to owners of residential historic properties, unless those properties are rental and treated as income-producing by IRS.

Georgia Department of Natural Resources

Sample National Register plaque.

National Register of Historic Places. Ronald M. Greenberg and Sarah A. Marusin, eds., National Park Service, U.S. Department of the Interior. Washington, D.C.: GPO, 1976. 961 pp., illus., index. $22 hb. GPO stock no. 024–005–00645–1. *Vol. II*. 1979. 638 pp., illus., index. $19 hb. GPO stock no. 024–005–00747–4.

Descriptive entries, organized by state, for properties added to the Register through 1974 (vol. I) and 1975–76 (vol. II). An annual cumulative listing is published in the *Federal Register* on the first Tuesday in February, with additions published on the first Tuesday of each month.

How to Complete National Register Forms. National Register of Historic Places. Washington, D.C.: U.S. Department of the Interior, 1979. 74 pp., illus., appends., index. Free.

A guide to types of information necessary for making Register nominations, with examples and texts of pertinent regulations.

A Profile of the National Register of Historic Places. Betsy Chittenden. Preservation Policy Research Series. Washington, D.C.: National Trust for Historic Preservation, 1984. 80 pp., appends. $7 pb.

A detailed analysis of factors such as ownership, geographic areas, ages, subject types, occupancy, accessibility and uses.

Contacts

National Register of
Historic Places
Interagency Resources Division
National Park Service
U.S. Department of the Interior
P.O. Box 37127
Washington, D.C. 20013-7127

State Historic Preservation Offices (see Preservationists)

National Historic Landmarks
Begun in 1960 after authorization in 1935, this program identifies sites and buildings of clearly national significance. Potential additions are surveyed under specific themes, evaluated by a National Park Service advisory board and recommended to the secretary of the interior; all are included in the National Register. Once an owner agrees to adhere to accepted preservation practices, the designation is recognized by the award of a plaque and certificate. Studies leading to selection of these national landmarks have been published in a series of books. The survey themes include:
1. Original Inhabitants
2. European Exploration and Settlements
3. Development of the English Colonies, 1700–75
4. Major American Wars
5. Political and Military Affairs
6. Westward Expansion, 1763–1898
7. America at Work
8. The Contemplating Society
9. Society and Social Conscience

Contact
National Historic Landmarks
Program
History Division
National Park Service
U.S. Department of the Interior
P.O. Box 37127
Washington, D.C. 20013-7127

Advisory Council on Historic Preservation

In instances where there are conflicts, the Council attempts to weigh the public interest rather than blindly support development at any cost or preservation at any price.

Advisory Council on Historic
Preservation, 1980.

The council is an independent federal agency established by the National Historic Preservation Act of 1966 to protect historic properties from federal activities. With a membership drawn from private citizens, professionals, state and local officials and ex-officio representatives of federal agencies involved with preservation issues, the council reviews and comments on federal, federally assisted and federally licensed undertakings that may affect properties listed in or eligible for the National Register of Historic Places. Its work is carried out under sec. 106 of the 1966 preservation act and 1980 amendments codifying responsibilities specified in Executive Order 11593 of 1971; its procedures are published at 36 C.F.R. Part 800.

Federal agencies are required in the earliest stages of project planning to determine whether a National Register (or eligible) property is involved, evaluate the potential effect of the project and find ways to remove or minimize any adverse impact, through consultation with the council and the SHPO. Agencies must afford the council an opportunity to comment on pertinent projects ranging from dams, highways and urban renewal to grants, construction of

federally insured banks and federally guaranteed loans. Possible outcomes reach from visual intrusions in historic districts to severe alteration and demolition. The council either negotiates a memorandum of agreement (in 99 percent of the cases) or provides written recommendations from the full council to the agency head after consideration at a formal meeting and often on-site review. The agency makes the ultimate decision about how or whether to proceed with the project.

During its first 10 years, the council reviewed some 4,000 federal undertakings, the majority of which were settled through negotiation; the remainder went before the full council—and some reached the courts. In 1984, 3,700 federal undertakings were considered, of which 2,250 required review, 1,025 required consultation and 225 were subjects of memorandums of agreement. In three cases, agreements were not reached, requiring full council review.

To fulfill its other responsibilities—to advise the president and Congress on preservation and to make recommendations on programs, policies and legislation—the council issues an annual report and other periodic publications.

Digest of Cases, 1967–1977. Washington, D.C.: Advisory Council on Historic Preservation, 1977. 50 pp.

A report on 33 projects to reach the full council for formal hearing and comment during its first decade, giving a synopsis of the undertaking, the council's findings, the agency response and the outcome.

Preservation Litigation: A Sourcebook. Washington, D.C.: Advisory Council on Historic Preservation, 1978. 42 pp.

A compilation of litigation involving federal agencies' compliance with federal preservation requirements, with citations and brief descriptions of the issues litigated.

Contact
Advisory Council on
Historic Preservation
1100 Pennsylvania Avenue, N.W.
Suite 809
Washington, D.C. 20005

Swearing in of the first citizen members of the Advisory Council on Historic Preservation in 1967. (Advisory Council on Historic Preservation)

State Preservation Statutes

Twenty years ago, state preservation law was virtually nonexistent except in Louisiana, Massachusetts, and South Carolina, where such laws resulted from an interest in the patrimony of New Orleans, Boston, and Charleston. For the most part, however, preservation law . . . was confined to state maintenance of historic sites and some tax exemptions for historic properties. . . .

In the past decade, however, there has been a rapid acceleration in both the scope and quality of preservation regulation, with by far the greatest increase in the designation of local historic districts and individual landmarks under the police power. In addition, in some states the common law governing the transfer of property rights has been modified to insure the preservation of properties remaining under private control through such devices as facade and scenic easements or covenants. Besides significant new federal tax incentives for historic preservation, various incentives for preservation have been created under state tax law in the form of exemptions, abatements, differential assessments, deferrals and credits. Preservation administrative agencies also have grown in tandem with these developments.

James P. Beckwith, Jr., *Significant State Historic Preservation Statutes*

Charleston, S.C., whose historic areas have been protected since 1931 because of state enabling legislation. (Dewey A. Swain)

Types of State Legislation Affecting Preservation

Environmental Laws

Archeology
Underwater archeology and maritime preservation
Mining
Environmental review
Coastal zone management
Open space
Easements
Historic trails
Highways and transportation
Energy

Land Use Regulation

Local preservation commissions
Zoning and planning
Conservation commissions
Enterprise zones

Tax Incentives

Funding

Appropriations for preservation purposes; grants
Revolving funds
Use of government funds (limits)
Public contracts
Community development
Housing
Bonds

Regulation

Building and fire codes
Disaster control
Cornice protection

State Preservation Program

State historic preservation officer
State register of historic places
State project review
State historical commission or society
Historical societies within the state
State archives
State parks
State historic sites
State capitols
Acquisition of historic properties
Disposition of historic properties

Miscellaneous

Crimes and penalties
Cemeteries
Handicapped access
Tourism
Nonprofit corporations
Tort liability

Significant State Historic Preservation Statutes. James P. Beckwith, Jr. Information Series, National Trust for Historic Preservation. Washington, D.C.: Preservation Press, 1979. 34 pp., append., biblio. $2 pb.

An overview covering state preservation enabling legislation, historic district and landmarks laws, constitutionality of state legislation, review of public and private actions, easements, tax policy, opinions of state attorneys general and related statutes. The appendix lists enabling statutes for each state (through 1979), organized by topic.

"Preservation Law 1976–1980: Faction, Property Rights, and Ideology," James P. Beckwith, Jr. *North Carolina Central Law Journal,* vol. 11, no. 2, Spring 1980. Available from William W. Gaunt and Sons.

Surveys developments in state preservation law since 1976 and includes an appendix of all preservation statutes and uncodified session laws.

Contact

National Trust for Historic Preservation
State Legislation Clearinghouse
1785 Massachusetts Avenue, N.W.
Washington, D.C. 20036

A national clearinghouse designed to collect and study existing state preservation laws and assist in developing improved state legislation. Cosponsored with the National Conference of State Historic Preservation Officers, the project provides information and publishes reports on key legislative areas such as enabling legislation for local preservation commissions and easements (listed elsewhere in this chapter).

Examples of Charleston's typical single houses (one room wide) on Chalmers Street. (Charleston Chamber of Commerce)

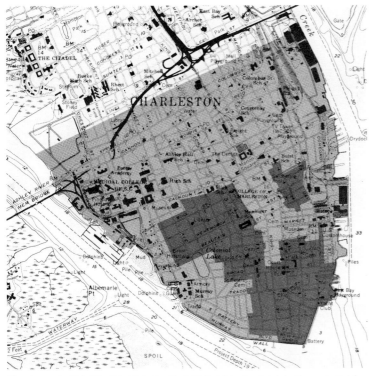

Charleston's Old City District, the first U.S. historic district. From *A Guide to Delineating Edges of Historic Districts.*

Local Preservation Ordinances

Local historic preservation ordinances are like old buildings. No two of them are alike. Nor should they be. It took skilled craftsmen to hew the grey stone in the fine old mansions of Chicago's Astor Street, to carve the Italianate bracketing in the river mansions of Galena, and to assemble the marble mosaics of the State Capitol. It takes some old fashioned craftsmanship and 20th century ingenuity to create a local preservation ordinance that fits the needs and aspirations of a particular . . . community.

Richard J. Roddewig, "Components of a Good Historic Preservation Ordinance." Historic Preservation Commissions Conference, Springfield, Ill., April 28, 1979.

"In 1931 Charleston, S.C., enacted the first American historic preservation ordinance and led the way for the development across the country of strong municipal preservation programs."

Stephen N. Dennis, *Directory of American Preservation Commissions*

Purposes of a Preservation Ordinance

Preserve properties of architectural, historical, cultural, archeological, engineering, scenic and other special value
Encourage restoration and adaptive use
Foster civic pride
Promote economic development
Promote the general welfare
Enhance attraction to visitors

Basic Provisions

Creation of a Preservation Commission

Members, powers, records, etc.

Designation of Districts and Landmarks

Surveys of local historic resources
Designation of historic districts (criteria, boundaries, evaluation of properties, existing zoning, etc.)
Designation of landmarks (criteria, consent of owners, boundary, etc.)
General matters (public hearings, notification, amendment of decisions, moratoriums, etc.)

Applications for Certificates of Appropriateness

Approval of alterations and new construction
Guidelines
Public hearings
Hardship
Notification

Demolition Applications

Municipal Properties

Maintenance of Historic Properties

Enforcement

Penalties

Appeal Provisions

Preparing a Historic Preservation Ordinance. Richard J. Roddewig. Chicago: American Planning Association, 1983. PAS Report 374. 46 pp., illus., appends. $16 pb.

Surveys the historical background, legal bases, ordinance components, commissions, designation criteria for landmarks and historic districts, and related issues. Includes sample ordinances.

"Recommended Model Provisions for a Preservation Ordinance, with Annotations," Stephen N. Dennis, ed. National Trust for Historic Preservation. In *A Handbook on Preservation Law* and *Preservation Law Reporter* at 14,001 (Ref.).

Organized according to the major provisions of preservation ordinances, presents annotated sample sections from local laws throughout the country as a guide to drafting or amending landmarks and historic district laws.

Preservation Commissions

It is obvious that American preservation commissions now have, because of their growth in number and precedents such as the Penn Central *opinion, a sense of their potential that would have been impossible only 10 years ago. . . . Preservation commissions have become a permanent and even routine part of local governments in America. But their full potential is undoubtedly only beginning to be felt in many communities that have recently enacted ordinances and created commissions.*

Stephen N. Dennis, *Directory of American Preservation Commissions*

"Once a district is established, application of the ordinance criteria by the volunteer historic district commission is what counts."

Pringle Hart Symonds, "The Architect in the Historic District." In *Old and New Architecture: Design Relationship*

"Review board effectiveness depends ultimately on the support of two constituencies: the public, particularly district property owners, and the local government, particularly elected officials and the planning and building inspection departments."

Alice Meriwether Bowsher, *Design Review in Historic Districts*

State Enabling Legislation for Local Preservation Commissions. Pamela Thurber and Robert Moyer. Preservation Policy Research Series. Washington, D.C.: National Trust for Historic Preservation, 1984. 87 pp. $12 pb.

An analysis of typical provisions and issues, covering the preservation commission, designation of districts and landmarks and the certificate of appropriateness process.

Directory of American Preservation Commissions. Stephen N. Dennis, ed. Washington, D.C.: Preservation Press, 1981. 132 pp. $6.95 pb.

A guide by state and city to more than 850 commissions in 48 states, giving addresses, telephone numbers and contacts.

Design Review in Historic Districts: A Handbook for Virginia Review Boards. Alice Meriwether Bowsher. 1978. Reprint. Washington, D.C.: Preservation Press, 1980. 128 pp., appends., biblio. $6.95 pb.

A guide to legal and design issues that preservation commissions and boards encounter: preservation ordinances, making good decisions, developing and using guidelines for rehabilitation, new construction,

signs and demolition, adhering to procedures and working with the public. Includes many sample documents and is useful to commissions everywhere.

A Manual for North Carolina Historic District Commissions. Robert M. Leary and Associates, Ltd. Raleigh: Keep North Carolina Beautiful (401 Oberlin Road, Suite 106, 27605), 1979. 72 pp., illus. $5 spiral bound.

A Manual for North Carolina Historic Properties Commissions. Robert M. Leary and Associates, Ltd. Raleigh: Keep North Carolina Beautiful, 1980. 60 pp., illus. $5.

Designed to guide preservationists in establishing historic districts and landmarks commissions, outlining preservation plans, inventories, ordinances, procedures, guidelines for new construction, rehabilitation, landscaping, signage and staff support.

Contacts

National Alliance of Preservation Commissions
Hall of the States
444 North Capitol Street, N.W.
Suite 332
Washington, D.C. 20001

Formed in 1981 to aid the 1,000 preservation commissions operating under state and local ordinances in the United States, it serves as a resource center for all preservation commissions.

Statewide Associations

A number of states—Florida, Georgia, Illinois, Kentucky, Maryland, Michigan, New Hampshire, Ohio, Oregon and Wisconsin—have formed statewide associations of preservation commissions, designed to provide a clearinghouse on the state level similar to the National Alliance.

National Trust for Historic Preservation
Office of Regional Services
1785 Massachusetts Avenue, N.W.
Washington, D.C. 20036

Provides advisory services to aid in establishing commissions and evaluating procedures.

Art Deco Historic District, Miami Beach, the first 20th-century district in the National Register. (Robert Chisholm, Anderson Notter Finegold)

Historic Districts

Increasingly historic districts are collections of buildings, few of which may be individually of outstanding significance but the group of which have a distinctive ambience that is worth maintaining. The phrase "tout ensemble" has often been used to describe the totality of an architecturally or historically unique neighborhood.

Stephen N. Dennis, "Recommended Model Provisions for a Preservation Ordinance, with Annotations." In *A Handbook on Preservation Law*

"Historic districts are not outdoor museums, but rather places where people live, and business, industry, and government function."

John Murphy, "The Special Nature of Historic Area Zoning." *Urban Land,* July–August 1975. Urban Land Institute.

"Throughout the 1930s and 1940s historical groups began to unite for the first time to save whole districts in a number of cities and small towns. Few people before World War I had appreciated enough the signs of continuous growth that formed the urban landscape to try to save them. . . . The urban preservation movement seemed to center in the seaport and riverport communities of the South. . . . The emphasis was nostalgic and centered on beautiful homes. This was distinctly different from the current emphasis on buildings of all types."

Charles B. Hosmer, Jr., *Preservation Comes of Age: From Williamsburg to the National Trust, 1926–1949.* Charlottesville: University Press of Virginia, 1981.

"There are two types of historic districts, federal and local. One involves a listing in the National Register of Historic Places; the other is a district created and controlled by a city or town.

National Register listing enables the owners of commercial and income-producing properties in the area to claim tax write-offs for certified rehabilitation and also offers protection to buildings slated for demolition or alteration due to federally funded projects.

But listing in the Register does not put design controls on a district's development. Only local historic districts authorized by state statute and enacted by local ordinance can control changes to exterior architectural features that are visible from the street."

Editor's Note. "The Saga of a Historic District," Les Stanwood. *Historic Preservation,* November–December 1981.

Farmhouse in the Goose Creek Historic District, Loudoun County, Va., a locally protected rural area. (Ashton Nichols)

Small cottages in the Ordeman-Shaw Historic District, Montgomery, Ala., a National Register district. (National Register of Historic Places)

"The primary purpose of the preservation of districts should be the maintenance of the environmental amenity, or the sense of time and place, of culturally significant living parts of communities. . . . The creation of districts is a means rather than an end. As such, districts are not something that the government or some other entity *does* for an area or community. On the contrary, districting is a tool for residents and other citizens who are already concerned about conserving or revitalizing certain areas."

A Guide to Delineating Edges of Historic Districts

"If a community is interested in establishing a historic district, it should follow the sequence of (1) conducting a survey, (2) preparing a plan that treats the defined district area or areas specifically and generally, (3) writing the ordinance and (4) appointing a review board or commission. If a community already is administering a historic district without a survey and plan, efforts should be initiated immediately to remedy the situation.

Communities beginning their first survey need not only to examine closely the survey system but also to anticipate its application. The distinction must be made between a city-wide survey to identify individual buildings and areas of interest and a building-by-building survey that will be used to administer a historic district."

Ellen Beasley, "New Construction in Residential Historic Districts." In *Old and New Architecture: Design Relationship*

Defining the "Tout Ensemble"

Location
Buildings, structures, sites, objects and spaces existing in their traditional relationships

Design
A sense of cohesiveness in scale, materials, colors, textures, etc.

Setting
Definable by natural or created boundaries with a major focal point

Materials
Similarity or dissimilarity in materials

Workmanship
Homogeneity through high-quality workmanship

Feeling
Impact on human consciousness with a sense of time and place

Association
Relationships to lives, events or visual qualities

From "Aesthetic and Social Dimensions of Historic Districts," William J. Murtagh. *Historic Districts*. Washington, D.C.: Preservation Press, 1975.

A Guide to Delineating Edges of Historic Districts. Russell Wright, principal consultant. National Trust for Historic Preservation. Washington, D.C.: Preservation Press, 1976. 96 pp., illus., gloss., biblio. $7.50 pb.

A handbook on how to determine the locations and value of potential historic districts, with an examination of the factors—historic, visual, physical, political, economic and social—that create districts; with case studies of how 20 local historic districts were formed.

Lake Anne Village Center (1965, Whittlesey and Conklin), Reston, Va., a Fairfax County historic district. (Robert Lautman)

The Contribution of Historic Preservation to Urban Revitalization. Advisory Council on Historic Preservation. Washington, D.C.: GPO, 1979. 215 pp.

Quantifies the social and economic effects of preservation in four major historic districts: Old Town, Alexandria, Va.; The Strand, Galveston, Tex.; Pioneer Square, Seattle; and Savannah, Ga.

The Impacts of Historic District Designation: Summary Report. Raymond, Parish, Pine and Weiner. New York: New York Landmarks Conservancy (330 West 42nd Street, 10036), 1977. 11 pp. $3.

An analysis of the Park Slope Historic District in Brooklyn, with comparative data for the West 76th Street and Mount Morris historic districts in Manhattan.

Boston preservationists sought landmark designation for this 1960s-era Citgo sign, but settled for restoration and temporary preservation.

Landmark Designation

For maximum protection, a building should be both locally designated and listed in the National Register and the state register.

> Stephen N. Dennis, "Recommended Model Provisions for a Preservation Ordinance, with Annotations"

"[Landmark protection ordinances] typically deal with the protection of isolated landmarks located outside the confines of a historic district and provide essentially for a stay of demolition for periods varying from 90 days to one year. . . . A major advantage of these ordinances is that they buy time for a threatened building and afford local governments and private groups an opportunity to marshall support and money for the preservation of the landmark building."

> Robert E. Stipe et al., "The Impact of Law on Preservation Activities in the United States." *Monumentum,* vol. XIII, 1976.

"Landmark designation employs the police power in the same way as historic district designation does, and state landmark statutes are as diverse as those authorizing historic districts. Some statutes allow the local designation of a landmark without any specific guidance on procedure, as typified by the New York statute. . . . Some states specify detailed procedures. North Carolina, for example, authorizes city or county governments to establish a historic properties commission with regulatory power over individual structures. The procedures for designation are specific and include the requirement of a hearing."

> James P. Beckwith, Jr., *Significant State Historic Preservation Statutes*

Typical Selection Criteria

New York City

Landmark: Any improvement 30 years or older that has a special character, historical interest or aesthetic value as part of the development, heritage or cultural characteristics of the city, state or nation

Interior landmark: Any interior or portion more than 30 years old with special historical or aesthetic value that is customarily accessible to the public

Landmark site: A parcel on which a designated landmark is situated

Scenic landmark: A landscape feature or aggregate 30 years or older and located on city-owned property

Boston

National Register property: Any property included in the National Register of Historic Places

Events: Structures, sites, objects, built or natural, at which events occurred that have made an outstanding contribution to the commonwealth, region or nation

Persons: Properties and sites associated significantly with the lives of outstanding historic personages

Architecture: Structures, sites and objects embodying distinctive characteristics of period, style or construction method and work of notable designers whose work has influenced the commonwealth, region or nation

Interior Landmarks

"We really have not been paying attention to preservation of interiors the way we have done with exteriors, and this is wrong. The story of our lives is written in interiors, how we lived, how we worked, how we played, how we worshipped. Interiors are much more fragile than exteriors."

> R. Michael Brown. In "Volunteers Tracking Down New York's Significant Interiors," Bryan Miller. *New York Times,* February 18, 1982.

"The whole notion of interior preservation is particularly important today in light of recent trends towards the adaptive reuse of older buildings, as often the refurbishing of the old buildings directly conflicts with the protecting of historic interior spaces."

> Elizabeth G. Miller, "Interior Preservation: Issues and (Some) Answers." *Progressive Architecture,* November 1976.

Facades are often just that: An apparently mundane exterior may hide a gem of an interior within its plain walls. But few local ordinances provide for the designation of interior landmarks. New York City became a notable exception in 1973 when it extended protection to significant interiors. The idea is still considered radical by many cities and public agencies partly because of problems inherent in policing the insides of privately owned buildings and in defining interior features worth preserving.

New York City's ordinance defines an interior feature as "the architectural style, design, general arrangement, and components of an interior, including but not limited to, the kind, color, and texture of the building material and the type and style of all windows, doors, lights, signs, and other features appurtenant to such interior." Interior landmarks may be associated with historical figures, have unique design features, be rare or remaining examples of a style or reveal excellent craftsmanship. By 1985 the city had designated 45 interiors as landmarks—although by one estimate 10 percent of New York's 850,000 buildings may contain interiors worth preserving.

The American Society of Interior Designers has undertaken surveys of interiors in New York and other cities to collect the data necessary to increase the number of interior landmark nominations.

Contacts

New York City Landmarks Preservation Commission
20 Vesey Street
New York, N.Y. 10007

Significant Interiors Survey
American Society of Interior Designers
1430 Broadway
New York, N.Y. 10018

Lobby of the Rookery (1886, Burnham and Root), Chicago, redesigned by Frank Lloyd Wright in 1905. (Hedrich-Blessing)

Design Review

No owner or person in charge of a landmark, landmark site or structure within an Historic District shall reconstruct or alter all or any part of the exterior of such property or construct any improvement upon such designated property or properties within an Historic District or cause or permit any such work to be performed upon such property unless a Certificate of Appropriateness has been granted by the Landmarks Commission.

Madison, Wis., Landmarks Ordinance, sec. 33.01(5)(6)(2)

"The preservation commission should have the authority to review and approve *all* changes affecting the exterior of a landmark or a structure within a historic district. Some ordinances will restrict a commission's authority to alterations affecting only those exterior facades that may be viewed from public streets, but a few preservation ordinances give commissions the authority to review changes to all exterior facades."

Stephen N. Dennis, "Recommended Model Provisions for a Preservation Ordinance, with Annotations"

Typical Design Review Process

Property owner, architect or contractor files application with preservation commission

Staff reviews application

Commission considers application at public meeting

Certificate of appropriateness granted

Work proceeds or compliance checked with other regulations (building permits, etc.)

Certificate of appropriateness denied

Accepted or appealed to higher authority

Denial upheld or reversed

Construction inspected by building officials

Remedial procedures

Work done violates provisions of certificate and must be corrected

Work is done without applying for a certificate and must be stopped or redone

Design Guidelines

"If buildings within a historic district are relatively homogeneous in age and style, guidelines need not be complicated. But if the buildings within the district represent a number of different periods and styles, then a much more complicated set of guidelines may have to be

"Regulating Relationships Through Design Review." In *Old and New Architecture: Design Relationship.* National Trust for Historic Preservation. Washington, D.C.: Preservation Press, 1980. 280 pp., illus., biblio., index. $25 hb, $15.95 pb.

An overview covering legal aspects, developing review criteria, the architect's role and how the process has worked in urban areas (Boston and Dallas) and in nine residential historic districts.

Design Review Boards: A Handbook for Communities. Washington, D.C.: American Institute of Architects, Committee on Design, 1974. 54 pp. $8.50.

A resume of the law on design review and an annotated model ordinance to guide communities with review boards.

Urban Design Review: A Guide for Planners. Hamid Shirvani. Chicago: Planners Press, American Planning Association, 1981. 230 pp., illus. $21.95 pb.

Analysis of how projects go through the public negotiating and permitting process, with comparison of procedures in Boston, Minneapolis, New York and San Francisco.

Residential Solar Design Review: A Manual on Community Architectural Controls and Solar Energy Use. Martin Jaffe and Duncan Erley, American Planning Association. For HUD, with U.S. Department of Energy. Washington, D.C.: GPO, 1980.

Examines solar energy design issues and suggests methods of review for solar installations in keeping with the aesthetic goals of historic and newer communities.

Infill house in a historic New York row. (© Cervin Robinson 1980)

developed for the use of property owners wishing to gain commission approval for alterations to their properties.

No community should copy the guidelines developed for another community without checking to determine whether the two communities are similar enough for the same guidelines to work in both communities."

Stephen N. Dennis, "Recommended Model Provisions for a Preservation Ordinance, with Annotations"

Design Guidelines: An Annotated Bibliography. Merrill Ware Carrington. Washington, D.C.: National Endowment for the Arts, 1977. 30 pp. Distributed by Preservation Press.

A list of 60 local guidelines prepared both for historic district review purposes and for general use among area residents in caring for their historic properties.

Good Neighbors: Building Next to History. Denver: Colorado Historical Society (1300 Broadway, 80203), 1980. 44 pp. $3.

Building with Nantucket in Mind: Guidelines for Protecting the Historic Architecture and Landscape of Nantucket Island. Christopher J. Lang. Nantucket, Mass.: Nantucket Historic District Commission (Town and County Building, 02554), 1978. 128 pp., illus., append., biblio. $8.50 pb.

Annapolis Historic District Design Guidelines for New Construction. Annapolis, Md.: Annapolis Historic District Commission (P.O. Box 1688, 21401), 1979. $5.

Architect Hugh Hardy seeking design approval. (Carleton Knight III)

Chapel Hill Historic District Guidelines Handbook. Elizabeth Staples. Chapel Hill, N.C.: Historic District Commission (Planning Department, 27514), 1979. 62 pp., illus.

Design Guidelines for the Historic Districts in Galveston. Ellen Beasley. Galveston, Tex.: Galveston Department of Urban Planning and Transportation and Historic District Board (P.O. Box 779, 77553), 1981. 64 pp.

Guidelines for Construction, Alteration, Demolition Within Historic Huning Highland. Architectural Research Consultants. Albuquerque, N.M.: Municipal Development Department and New Mexico Historic Preservation Program, 1979. 108 pp., illus., appends., biblio.

The Beaufort Preservation Manual. John Milner Associates. Beaufort, S.C.: Community Development Office (P.O. Drawer 1167, 29901), 1979. 159 pp., illus., biblio. $10 pb.

Design Guidelines for Old Pasadena. Charles Hall Page and Associates. Pasadena, Calif.: Urban Conservation Program (100 North Garfield Avenue, 91109), 1979. $6.

Beacon Hill Architectural Handbook: Guidelines for Preservation and Modification. Boston: Beacon Hill Civic Association (74 Joy Street, 02114), 1975. 36 pp.

The Salem Handbook: A Renovation Guide for Homeowners. Anderson Notter Associates. Salem, Mass.: Historic Salem (15 Summer Street, 01970), 1977. 113 pp.

See also: Old and New Architecture (Looking at the Built Environment); Neighborhoods

Landmark Decisions: Preservation in Court

Although government regulation is invalid if it denies a property owner all reasonable return, there is no constitutional imperative that the return embrace all attributes, incidental influences, or contributing external factors derived from the social complex in which the property rests. . . . It is enough . . . that the privately created ingredient of property receive a reasonable return. . . . All else is society's contribution by the sweat of its brow and the expenditure of its funds. To that extent society is also entitled to its due.

> New York State Court of Appeals, *Penn Central Transportation Company v. City of New York*

"The Eagle is preserved, not for its use, but for its beauty."

> *Barret v. State,* 116 N.E. 99, 101 (1917)

"Nearly three times as many cases involving historic preservation issues have been decided in the last ten years as in the seventy-four years between the United States Supreme Court's 1896 opinion in *United States v. Gettysburg Electric Railway Company* and 1970. . . .

States in which there has been a significant amount of historic preservation litigation are likely to be states in which knowledgeable preservationists are aware of the protections available to important buildings under federal statutes and local ordinances. . . . Certain topics are litigated more frequently than others. By far the largest number of listed cases involved local preservation ordinances or the actions of local preservation commissions. . . .

From almost any viewpoint a major period of preservation litigation came to its conclusion in *Penn Central Transportation Company v. City of New York,* the United States Supreme Court's 1978 decision upholding against 'taking' claims the validity of a landmark designation of a large commercial building located in the heart of a major American metropolis. In the future there should be fewer attacks than there have been in the past on the validity of local preservation ordinances under state law or the designation of landmarks and historic districts under such ordinances."

> Stephen N. Dennis, "An Annotated List of Major Historic Preservation Court Decisions." *North Carolina Central Law Journal,* Spring 1980.

Contact

National Trust for
Historic Preservation
Office of the General Counsel
1785 Massachusetts Avenue, N.W.
Washington, D.C. 20036

Maintains information on preservation litigation, including lists and copies of opinions, complaints and briefs on major cases as well as pending, dropped and other cases. Its *Preservation Law Reporter* regularly publishes new developments in preservation case law and contains a comprehensive digest of leading cases in its permanent reference volume.

Negotiation vs. Litigation

"Environmental negotiation . . . has been successful in resolving conflicts ranging from siting controversial public facilities to locating highway corridors to managing water and other resources. Because many of the elements present in environmental disputes are present in historic preservation disagreements, the technique warrants closer attention and use by preservationists. . . .

Given the possibilities of redesign, adaptive use and transfer of development rights, historic preservation offers many varied options for a process that depends upon developing creative alternatives and trade-offs. . . .

Until recently, preservationists may not have had sufficient leverage to get their opponents to the bargaining table. But as legal precedents build, as developers tire of delays and as preservationists broaden their political base, negotiation becomes not only feasible but a very attractive alternative."

> Elizabeth B. Waters, "Talking Things Over: The Subtle Art of Environmental Negotiation Can Solve Preservation Disputes." *Historic Preservation,* March–April 1982.

Contacts

Institute for Environmental
Negotiation
School of Architecture
University of Virginia
Campbell Hall
Charlottesville, Va. 22903

Environmental Mediation
Institute
605 First Avenue
Suite 525
Seattle, Wash. 98104

Some Major Preservation Cases

United States v. Gettysburg Electric Railway Company. 160 U.S. 668 (1896). Upheld use of eminent domain by federal government to take historic properties.

Roe v. Kansas ex rel. Smith, 278 U.S. 191 (1929). Upheld use of eminent domain by state government to take historic properties.

City of New Orleans v. Impastato, 3 So. 2d 559 (La. 1941). Upheld power of the Vieux Carre Commission to regulate all exterior changes to buildings.

Flaccomio v. Mayor and City Council of Baltimore, 71 A. 2d 12 (Md. 1950). Upheld use of eminent domain by city government to take historic properties.

City of New Orleans v. Levy, 64 So. 2d 798 (La. 1953). Upheld constitutionality of the Vieux Carre ordinance against allegations of vague standards, denial of equal protection and use of police power for aesthetic purposes.

City of Santa Fe v. Gamble-Skogmo, Inc., 389 P. 2d 13 (N.M. 1964). Upheld historic district ordinance under general grant of zoning power to city from state.

Manhattan Club v. Landmarks Preservation Commission of City of New York, 273 N.Y.S. 2d 848 (N.Y. 1966). Landmark designation of a building held not confiscatory when the owner is guaranteed a reasonable return with an option to demolish.

Trustees of Sailors' Snug Harbor v. Platt. 288 N.Y.S. 2d 314 (N.Y. 1968). Designation of landmark owned by charitable organization held to depend on interference with use, adaptability to a useful purpose and cost of maintenance; constitutionality of municipal landmarks ordinance upheld.

Bohannan v. City of San Diego, 106 Cal. Rep. 333 (Cal. 1973). Ordinance detailing "pre-1871" criteria for alterations and new construction held valid exercise of police power.

City of Dallas v. Crownrich, 506 S.W. 2d 654 (Tex. 1974). Upheld authority of municipality to use police power to impose moratorium on issuance of building permits pending historic district designation.

Save the Courthouse Committee v. Lynn, 408 F. Supp. 1323 (S.D.N.Y. 1975). Injunction upheld against HUD and local renewal agency for failure to comply with federal environmental regulations.

Eyerman v. Mercantile Trust Company, 524 S.W. 2d 210 (Mo. 1975). Testamentary provision that a house on a designated street be demolished held void as a violation of public policy.

Forg v. Jaquith, No. 35391, Middlesex Sup. Ct., Mass. (1975). Upheld denial of permission to install vinyl siding on house fronting on Lexington Battle Green.

Grand Central Terminal (1903–13, Reed and Stem; Warren and Wetmore), New York City, saved through a landmark Supreme Court decision. (Ed Nowak)

One proposal for a tower defacing Grand Central Terminal. (Marcel Breuer and Associates)

Maher v. City of New Orleans, 516 F. 2d 1051 (5th Cir., 1975), *cert. denied*, 426 U.S. 905 (1976). Upheld constitutionality of Vieux Carre ordinance creating historic district, adequacy of standards, denial of demolition and minimum maintenance requirements.

Stop H-3 Association v. Coleman, 533 F. 2d 434 (9th Cir., 1976), *cert. denied*, 429 U.S. 999 (1976). Held that determination of possible National Register eligibility triggers protections under Department of Transportation Act.

Sleeper v. Old King's Highway Regional Historic District Commission, No. 22799, Mass. Second District Ct. (1978), *Sleeper v. Bourne*, No. 216, Mass. App. Div., 1980. Denial of 68-foot radio antenna in historic district held not to infringe on First Amendment rights.

Crownrich v. City of Dallas, No. CA-3-76-1080-G, U.S. District Ct., N.D. Tex. (1978). Prohibition against high-rise construction in a historic district held a risk of investment not requiring compensation.

Penn Central Transportation Company v. City of New York, 438 U.S. 104 (1978). Designation of Grand Central Terminal and denial of permission to construct a 55-story office tower on its site held not a taking because the "restrictions imposed are substantially related to the promotion of the general welfare. . . ."

Society for Ethical Culture in City of New York v. Spatt, 415 N.E. 2d 922 (N.Y. 1980). Upheld landmark designation against claims of taking without due compensation and interference with charitable and religious activities.

WATCH (Waterbury Action to Conserve Our Heritage, Inc.) v. Harris, 603 F. 2d 310 (2d Cir.), *cert. denied*, 62 L.Ed. 2d 426 (1979). HUD held to have continuing responsibilities under National Historic Preservation Act for federally funded urban renewal projects and to protect National Register–eligible buildings after contract signing.

Agins v. City of Tiburon, 447 U.S. 255 (1980). Held that rezoning of land into category designed to encourage some open-space retention did not "take" property.

Faulkner v. Town of Chestertown, 428 A.2d 879 (Md. Ct. App. 1981). Upheld regulation by Maryland historic district commissions of nonhistoric properties in local historic districts.

Historic Green Springs, Inc. v. Bergland, 497 F. Supp. 839 (E.D. Va. 1980), *vacated sub nom.*, *Historic Green Springs, Inc. v. Block*, No. 77-0230-R (July 20, 1981) 3049. Reinstated Historic Green Springs District in National Register following earlier ruling invalidating listing because of alleged vagueness in criteria for selecting National Historic Landmarks.

The view from Little Oatlands, Leesburg, Va., encompassing rolling land, fencing and farm structures typical of rural areas. (John J. G. Blumenson, NTHP)

Land Use and Zoning

Land, like a magnet, attracts two specific forces in our culture, and always has. One is the personal objective of some to achieve prosperity, indeed to accumulate wealth. The other is the visible, much debated movement toward increased government regulation. When these two powerful forces collide over land-related issues, links are created between public regulatory power and private wealth which reveal our national priorities, which indeed express where power and control reside in our so-called free enterprise system.

Peter Wolf, *Land in America*

Land in America: Its Value, Use and Control. Peter Wolf. New York: Pantheon, 1981. 591 pp., illus., append., biblio., index. $20 hb.

Examines land as investment—past, present and future—from many points of view, including a chapter on "Preservation and Profit."

This Land Is Your Land: The Struggle to Save America's Public Lands. Bernard Shanks. San Francisco: Sierra Club Books, 1984. 320 pp., illus., biblio., index. $19.95 hb.

A chronicle of the history of public lands, from the birth of the national parks and the emergence of the conservation movement to current threats.

American Land Planning Law: Cases and Materials. Norman Williams, Jr., ed. New Brunswick, N.J.: Center for Urban Policy Research, 1978. 1,792 pp. 2 vols. $35 hb.

Presents some 170 cases plus questions, notes and cross references to other major resources in the field.

The Federal Lands Revisited. Marion Clawson. Washington, D.C.: Resources for the Future, 1983. Distributed by Johns Hopkins University Press. 320 pp., biblio., appends., index. $8.95 pb.

An overview of the federally owned lands, including historic and present uses, current policy issues and major alternatives for future use and management. Considers the commodity, environmental and amenity values of federal lands.

Legal Foundations of Land Use Planning: A Textbook/Casebook and Materials on Planning Law. Jerome G. Rose. New Brunswick, N.J.: Center for Urban Policy Research, 1979. 480 pp., index. $17.95 hb.

An encyclopedia of land use law that explains legal concepts with case studies of major legal issues, judicial decisions and statutes.

The Illustrated Book of Development Definitions. Harvey S. Moskowitz and Carl G. Lindbloom. New Brunswick, N.J.: Center for Urban Policy Research, 1981. 263 pp., illus., appends., index. $15 pb.

Defines planning, zoning and related terms used in preparing, interpreting, administering and litigating environmental and land use ordinances.

Regulating Sensitive Lands: A Guide Book. Jon A. Kusler. Cambridge: Ballinger, 1980. 256 pp., illus., biblio., appends., gloss., index. $30 hb.

Examines state and local policies for resource conservation, including defining sensitive lands (e.g., wetlands, coastal areas), performance standards and regulatory programs. Reviews 800 ordinances and discusses legal considerations, with precedent court cases.

Land Use and the States. Robert G. Healy and John L. Rosenberg, Resources for the Future. 2nd ed. Baltimore: Johns Hopkins University Press, 1979. 284 pp., index. $24 hb, $8 pb.

An analysis of the role of the states in controlling privately owned land, with an examination of programs in California, Florida and Vermont.

Land Use Controls in the United States: A Handbook on the Legal Rights of Citizens. Natural Resources Defense Council. New York: Dial Press, 1977. 362 pp.

Explains laws and programs affecting land use established at the national, state and local levels, and discusses means for citizen involvement in influencing land use.

The Taking Issue. Fred Bosselman, David Callies and John Banta, Council on Environmental Quality. Washington, D.C.: GPO, 1971. 329 pp.

A study of the constitutional limits of government to regulate the use of privately owned land without compensation to the owners.

The Use of Land: A Citizens Guide to Urban Growth. William Reilly et al. New York: Crowell, 1974.

Recommendations on more responsible land use covering policy legislation, state land use and growth policies, urban growth management and citizen concern for the quality of life.

Land-Use Planning and the Law. Alexandra D. Dawson. New York: Garland, 1982. 252 pp., biblio., index. $36 hb.

A layperson's overview of the "rules of the game"—zoning, comprehensive planning, environmental laws, taxation, aesthetic and development controls and urban renewal.

The Land Use Awakening: Zoning Law in the Seventies. Robert H. Freilich and Eric O. Stuhler, eds. Chicago: American Bar Association (1155 East 60th Street, 60637), 1981. 301 pp., case table. $25.

Papers summarizing key zoning law developments in the 1970s—growth management, the state role in land use planning, the ALI model land development code, the transfer of development rights.

A Model Land Development Code. Philadelphia: American Law Institute (4025 Chestnut Street, 19104), 1976. 524 pp., case tables, index. $35 hb.

A code designed for use by local governments in drafting land use legislation, with commentary on land use controls and techniques, including preservation districts, rural areas and land banking.

Land Saving Action. Russell L. Brenneman and Sarah Bates. Covelo, Calif.: Island Press, 1984. 272 pp., biblio., index. $64.95 hb, $34.95 pb.

Covers all aspects of private land conservation from tax questions involving easements to establishing land trusts.

Toward Eden. Arthur E. Palmer. Winterville, N.C.: Creative Resource Systems, 1981. 417 pp. $33.20 pb. Available from Environmental Book Distributing Company, 2105 Lakeland Avenue, Ronkonkoma, N.Y. 11779.

Chronicles the creation of an environmental land development regulatory system and new master plan and zoning law in Medford, N.J., with documents from the process.

A Bibliography of Open Space Control Literature Including Regulatory, Compensatory, and Taxation Devices. Robert A. Johnston and Seymour I. Schwartz et al. Monticello, Ill.: Vance Bibliographies, 1980. P-404. 105 pp. $21.20 photocopy.

The Citizen's Guide to Planning. Herbert H. Smith. 2nd ed. Chicago: Planners Press, American Planning Association, 1979. 208 pp. $9.95 pb.

The Citizen's Guide to Zoning. Herbert H. Smith. Chicago: Planners Press, American Planning Association, 1983. 242 pp. $14.95 pb.

Overviews of the basic principles of planning and zoning explained in layman's terms.

Zoning and Historic Preservation: A Survey of Current Zoning Techniques in U.S. Cities to Encourage Historic Preservation. Ellen Kettler Paseltiner and Deborah Tyler. Rev. ed. Chicago: Landmarks Preservation Council of Illinois, 1984. 33 pp. $5.

A summary of key tools being used for preservation purposes across the country.

Zoning and Property Rights. Robert H. Nelson. Cambridge: MIT Press, 1977. 259 pp. $17.95 pb.

Analyzes the development of zoning and its objectives, successes and failures, proposing a radical revision of existing zoning practices.

Winning at Zoning. Dudley S. Hinds et al. New York: McGraw-Hill, 1979. 247 pp., illus., index. $21.95 hb.

Provides a step-by-step explanation of the zoning process, with hypothetical cases to clarify the concepts discussed.

Performance Zoning. Lane H. Kendig et al. Chicago: Planners Press, American Planning Association, 1980. 358 pp., illus., gloss. $39.95 hb.

Proposes an alternative approach to regulating development through zoning, taking into account constraints of the site and design considerations that promote creative solutions.

Constitutional Issues of Growth Management. David R. Godschalk et al. 2d ed. Chicago: Planners Press, American Planning Association, 1979. 476 pp., biblio., gloss. $20.95.

A comparative analysis of growth management practices within the context of constitutional law.

See also: Cities, Rural Areas and Landscapes (Form and Function)

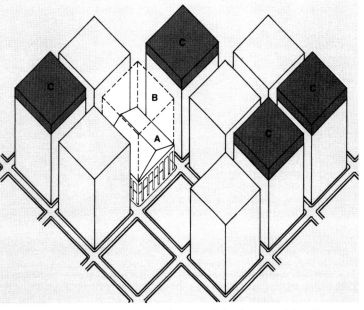

TDR allows a landmark (A) to transfer unused development rights (B) to neighboring sites (C). From *Space Adrift*.

Transfer of Development Rights

Landmarks are often located in the center of cities where zoning resolutions would permit much larger buildings should they be replaced. . . . In New York City the owner of a landmark may now transfer unused development rights from his lot to an adjacent site where a new building is to be constructed. This transaction, allowing the new building to be larger, enables the landmark owner to realize some of the present-day value of his land without destroying the historic building.

Frank B. Gilbert, "Saving Landmarks: The Transfer of Development Rights." *Historic Preservation*, July–September 1970.

"The legal concept underlying TDR is that title to real estate is not a unitary or monolithic right, but rather it may be compared to a 'bundle of individual rights,' each one of which may be separated from the rest and transferred to someone else, leaving the original owner with all other rights of ownership. . . . One of the components of this 'bundle of rights' is the right to develop the land."

Jerome G. Rose, *Transfer of Development Rights*

"The major advantage claimed for TDR in contrast to other land-use planning tools is that it can provide the desired control over land use without major outlays of public funds, and yet simultaneously avoid imposing windfall losses ('wipeouts') on landowners."

Leslie E. Small et al., *Transfer of Development Rights Marketability*

Space Adrift: Saving Urban Landmarks Through the Chicago Plan. John J. Costonis. Champaign: University of Illinois Press, 1974. 228 pp., illus., appends., biblio., index.

An innovative proposal detailing the economic, legal and design considerations of TDR, developed particularly for Chicago following the demolition of the Old Chicago Stock Exchange. "The scheme is a brilliant, practical, progressive extension of existing zoning tools." (Ada Louise Huxtable, *New York Times*)

Transfer of Development Rights. Jerome G. Rose, ed. New Brunswick, N.J.: Center for Urban Policy Research (4051 Kilmer Campus, 08903), 1975. 341 pp. $12.95 hb.

A comprehensive roundup of articles covering many aspects of this technique, including landmark preservation.

"Transfer of Development Rights." *Urban Land,* January 1975. $3.50. Urban Land Institute.

Provides a general description of the technique, planning for a local ordinance, a bibliography, a synopsis of *Space Adrift*, a proposal to integrate TDR into a total growth management program and use of the technique as an alternative to zoning.

Transferable Development Rights. Frank S. Bangs, Jr., and Conrad Bagne, eds. Chicago: American Planning Association, 1975. PAS Report 304. 64 pp. $7 pb.

Presents critical analyses of the theory and practice of TDR.

Zoning for Sale: A Critical Analysis of Transferable Development Rights Programs. Franklin J. James and Dennis E. Gale. Washington, D.C.: Urban Institute, 1977. URI 16600. 39 pp.

Evaluates the potential and problems of TDR, such as its limited scope and the creation of private markets in development rights. The authors are skeptical about the practicality of "large-scale programs that promise to draw together many of the tools of land-use control."

Transfer of Development Rights Marketability. Leslie E. Small, Victor Kasper, Jr., and Donn A. Derr. New Brunswick, N.J.: New Jersey Agricultural Experiment Station (Cook College, Rutgers University, 08903), 1978. Bulletin 848. 77 pp., biblio. $1 pb.

A plan to create an agricultural preservation zone by transferring development rights to other areas, using South Brunswick, N.J., as a case study.

A Bibliography on the Transfer of Development Rights. Dwight H. Merriam and Ann Hayes Merriam. Monticello, Ill.: Vance Bibliographies (P.O. Box 229, 61856), August 1977. No. 1338. 35 pp. $3.50 pb.

Transfer of Development Rights. Janet Bloom and Emily Regnier. Monticello, Ill.: Vance Bibliographies, September 1977. No. 1344. 9 pp. $1.50 pb.

Easements: Less-than-Fee Restrictions

Increasing use has been made in recent years of what are now referred to as "preservation restrictions" . . . easements, restrictive covenants, deed restrictions, defeasible estates, leasing and similar devices. Through the use of these "less-than-fee" private law approaches, a preservation organization . . . may be able to exercise continuing control over the architectural character of a property or protect its surroundings without the necessity of purchasing the full bundle of ownership rights.

Robert E. Stipe et al., "The Impact of Law on Preservation Activities in the United States." *Monumentum*, vol. XIII, 1976.

Haas-Lilienthal House (c. 1886), San Francisco, protected by a facade easement conveyed to the National Trust. (Morley Baer)

Bowen House (c. 1845), Woodstock, Conn., on which SPNEA holds an easement. (J. David Bohl, SPNEA)

"A preservation easement gives the organization to which it is conveyed the legal authority to enforce its terms. These terms usually create negative covenants, prohibiting the owner from making alterations to the property without prior review, consultation and approval by the holder. Some easements also impose positive covenants that require the owner to make certain improvements to the property or maintain it in a certain physical condition."

Charles E. Fisher et al., *Directory of Historic Preservation Easement Organizations*

Establishing an Easement Program to Protect Historic, Scenic and Natural Resources. A. Elizabeth Watson. Information Series, National Trust for Historic Preservation. 1980. Rev. ed. Washington, D.C.: Preservation Press, 1982. 40 pp., biblio., appends. $2 pb.

Covers basics on easements, legal and tax aspects and how to organize and enforce an easement program; includes a sample easement document.

Appraising Easements: Guidelines for Valuation of Historic Preservation and Land Conservation Easements. National Trust for Historic Preservation and Land Trust Exchange. Washington, D.C.: National Trust, 1984. 68 pp., appends., biblio. $7.95 pb.

A guide to the appraisal process, a significant factor in substantiating the value of charitable contributions of easements for tax purposes.

Preservation Easements: The Legislative Framework. Steven J. Zick. Preservation Policy Research Series. Washington, D.C.: National Trust for Historic Preservation, 1984. 51 pp. $8 pb.

Report on state easement statutes with analysis of the history of easements and the Uniform Conservation Easement Act.

Easements and Other Legal Techniques to Protect Historic Houses in Private Ownership. Thomas Coughlin III. Washington, D.C.: Historic House Program (1785 Massachusetts Avenue, N.W., 20036), 1981. 28 pp., appends., biblio. $3 pb.

A guide for property owners focusing on the contents of deeds of easement and computation of an easement's value, with sample deeds and tax calculations.

Directory of Historic Preservation Easement Organizations. Charles E. Fisher, William G. MacRostie and Christopher A. Sowick. Washington, D.C.: Technical Preservation Services, U.S. Department of the Interior, 1981. 23 pp.

State-by-state listing of groups that have active easement programs or can provide information on preservation and open-space easements.

"Does a Historic Easement Have Value? IRS May Be Targeting Easements." *Urban Conservation Report*, July 20, 1984.

A discussion of recent developments questioning the deductibility of easements.

Charles Street Meetinghouse (1807, Asher Benjamin), Boston, whose facade easement is held by SPNEA. (J. David Bohl, SPNEA)

Another SPNEA easement property, the Short House (1733), Newbury, Mass. (J. David Bohl, SPNEA)

Cathedral of Chartres, France, a World Heritage Site noted for its two different Gothic towers. (French Tourist Office)

Preservation Easements: A Legal Mechanism for Protecting Cultural Resources. Marilyn Meder-Montgomery. Denver: Colorado Historical Society, 1984. 165 pp. $27.50.

The Conservation Easement in California. Thomas S. Barrett and Putnam Livermore. Covelo, Calif.: Island Press, 1983. 173 pp., biblio., index. $44.95 hb, $24.95 pb.

Preservation Easements. Annapolis: Maryland Historical Trust, 1977. 29 pp.

Conservation and Historic Preservation Easements to Preserve North Carolina's Heritage. Raleigh: North Carolina Division of Archives and History, 1980.

The Landowner's Options: A Guide to the Voluntary Protection of Land in Maine. Janet E. Milne. Rev. ed. Augusta: Maine Coast Heritage Trust (335 Water Street, 04330) and Maine State Planning Office, 1978. 43 pp., illus.

Preservation Easements in Illinois. Landmarks Preservation Council and Nature Conservancy. Chicago: Landmarks Preservation Council, 1980. 98 pp.

Contacts
U.S. Department of the Interior
Technical Preservation Services
Branch and
Land Resources Division
National Park Service
P.O. Box 37127
Washington, D.C. 20013-7127

National Trust for
Historic Preservation
Office of the General Counsel
1785 Massachusetts Avenue, N.W.
Washington, D.C. 20036

Land Trust Exchange
Box 364
Bar Harbor, Maine 04609

The Nature Conservancy
1800 North Kent Street
Arlington, Va. 22209

Trust for Public Land
82 Second Street
San Francisco, Calif. 94105

National Conference of
Commissioners on Uniform
State Laws
645 North Michigan Avenue
Suite 510
Chicago, Ill. 60611

Society for the Preservation
of New England Antiquities
141 Cambridge Street
Boston, Mass. 02114

The L'Enfant Trust
1425 21st Street, N.W.
Washington, D.C. 20036

Virginia Historic Landmarks
Commission
221 Governor Street
Richmond, Va. 23219

Waterford Foundation
P.O. Box 142
Waterford, Va. 22190

French and Pickering Creeks
Conservation Trust
Box 360, R.D. 2
Pottstown, Pa. 19464

Brandywine Conservancy
P.O. Box 141
Chadds Ford, Pa. 19317

Protecting the World's Landmarks
Previously the world's conscience had been awakened from time to time to rescue sites that were threatened by dramatic destruction or decay, Abu Simbel, Borobudur or Aldabra. But now men and women everywhere have come to appreciate that this is one earth and the people on it one people; that the properties in any one country are part of a universal heritage of inestimable value not only to those now alive but to generations yet unborn.

Unesco

To meet the dangers "threatening the cultural and natural monuments and sites that make up the common heritage of us all," Unesco in 1972 adopted the Convention for the Protection of the World Cultural and Natural Heritage. This established a system of international cooperation to complement preservation efforts in the Unesco member nations by:
1. Identifying, on the basis of nominations from member countries to the World Heritage Committee, properties of "outstanding universal value."
2. Supporting countries in safeguarding properties within their borders using resources of the World Heritage Fund.
3. Undertaking educational programs to strengthen appreciation for this heritage and dangers to properties.

The World Heritage Fund, financed by contributions from participating countries, supports training programs, services of specialists and equipment supplies. By the early 1980s, more than 100 universal landmarks had been designated. U.S. properties, previously determined to be of national significance, include Independence Hall; Yellowstone, Grand Canyon, Mesa Verde, Redwood, Olympic and Everglades national parks; and Mammoth Cave.

Participation by the United States is directed by the National Park Service with the cooperation of the Advisory Council on Historic Preservation. Initial review of nominations is provided by the International Council on Monuments and Sites.

Contacts
U.S. Coordinator
Federal Interagency Panel for
World Heritage
National Park Service
U.S. Department of the Interior
P.O. Box 37127
Washington, D.C. 20013-7127

World Heritage Committee
Division of Cultural Heritage
Unesco
7, place de Fontenoy
75700 Paris, France

US/ICOMOS
1600 H Street, N.W.
Washington, D.C. 20006

Taking Action

*I*t *is not accidental that many preservation words derive from the field of military experience because, in effect, what people in the preservation movement are doing is defending their habitats. These habitats are under ferocious assault by all kinds of agencies. Often citizens and amateurs have only their own strength to defend them.*

James Marston Fitch, "Standards." In *Preservation: Toward an Ethic in the 1980s.* National Trust for Historic Preservation. Washington, D.C.: Preservation Press, 1980.

"Preservationists have heretofore lacked the gumption to exert the sort of influence in behalf of cultural resources that one sees from groups like the Sierra Club and the Wilderness Society in behalf of things natural. The cultural resources of this country desperately need defenders—principled, unselfish and, if necessary, litigious groups whose sole concern is the protection of the resource, without regard to any program or vested interest or hope for a grant. Without such a counter-weight to government, the future of our cultural heritage appears bleak."

David A. Cleary, "Historic Preservation and Environmental Protection: The Role of the Historian." *The Public Historian,* Fall 1978.

Some famous faces—Lucie Arnaz, Laurence Luckinbill, Martin Balsam and Tony Roberts—on the picket line for an Actors Equity Association rally in 1980 to save several Times Square theaters. Despite the star billing, the Helen Hayes, Morosco and Bijou theaters were demolished to make way for a hotel designed by John Portman and funded by an Urban Development Action Grant (UDAG) from HUD. (Camera 1)

"In dealing with the broad fabric of a community, efforts to protect the historic and cultural environment must have a different nature than in the past. No longer can they be solely desperate battles, but must take the form of continuous, on-the-scene negotiations. The crisis orientation of the past, the race to beat the wrecking ball, should give way to a positive approach to the decisions that shape the environment."

"Goals and Programs: A Summary of the Study Committee Report to the Board of Trustees, the National Trust for Historic Preservation," 1973.

"Change is a continuing process that is going to take place whether we like it or not. Prudent preservation can accommodate change and at the same time insure quality and continuity. The question for preservationists is how to deal with this flow of everyday life. . . .

We must offer realistic solutions to preservation problems to succeed. These solutions may mean slight or extensive interior adaptation in order to preserve the exterior . . . or they may mean not restoring a community when that effort would drastically alter its character. . . .

It has often been said that there is no way to stop progress. However, preservationists can slow down and help improve development by finding ways that can fit a community's contemporary needs into an old setting. If we stop time for the sake of stopping it, we gain nothing and the community is the loser. We must be wary of becoming our own worst enemies."

"The Enemy Within." Editorial, *Preservation News,* October 1976.

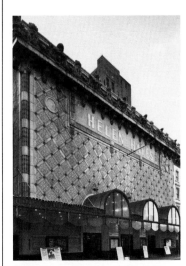

Helen Hayes Theatre (1910), once a 46th Street landmark. (HABS)

"The image of the preservation advocate as an adversary of government is outdated. As constructive associations develop between preservationists and local government decision makers, preservation is being accepted as a public concern and responsibility. The time to stop an adverse action, or to develop a commitment to preservation, is not at the final city council reading of a resolution or law or when the bulldozer arrives on the site, but at the early budget discussion and the agenda meetings, long before issues hit the news pages. Preservation will become a more integral part of the government process when its advocates become part of that process."

Leila Smith, *Working with Local Government*

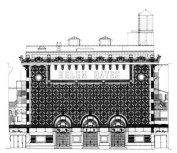

Facade view showing terra-cotta blocks. (Robert Hartman, HABS)

"To arms! To arms! The bulldozers are coming!" (Robt. Day. © 1966 The New Yorker Magazine, Inc.)

Citizen Participation

American democracy was founded on principles of limited governmental authority and formal public accountability. These principles, so deeply embedded in American political culture, also furnish the intellectual roots of the contemporary movement for greater citizen involvement in governmental decision making.

The demand for expanded citizen involvement represents the latest chapter in the continuing evolution of popular control over government in the United States.

Nelson M. Rosenbaum, *Citizen Involvement in Land Use Governance*

The Backyard Revolution: Understanding the New Citizen Movement. Harry C. Boyte. Philadelphia: Temple University Press, 1980. 287 pp., appends., biblio., index. $9.95 pb.

A study of the origins, development and themes of grass-roots political activism.

Lobbying for the People: The Political Behavior of Public Interest Groups. Jeffrey M. Berry. Princeton: Princeton University Press, 1977. 336 pp., append., biblio., index. $35 hb, $8.95 pb.

Considers the work of Common Cause, the Sierra Club and similar groups in terms of their development, resources, recruitment and lobbying tactics.

The Citizen's Guide to Planning. Herbert H. Smith. 1961. Rev. ed. Chicago: Planners Press, 1979. 198 pp., gloss., append., biblio., index. $8.95 pb.

"We need civic leaders, neighborhood organizers, educators, and young people who are aware that the future, their future, is too important to leave to the work of others or to chance. This book is intended to provide some thought and encouragement to any concerned person who is resolved to be more a part of the future."

Citizen Involvement in Land Use Governance: Issues and Methods. Nelson M. Rosenbaum. Washington, D.C.: Urban Institute, 1976. 82 pp., biblio. $3.50 pb.

History of citizen participation, techniques for designing and implementing citizen participation programs and the benefits and costs of such participation in land use planning.

The Environmental Impact Statement Process: A Guide to Citizen Action. Neil Orloff. Arlington, Va.: Information Resources Press (1700 North Moore Street, 22209), 1978. 242 pp., illus., appends. $12.95.

Discussion of the National Environmental Policy Act and procedures for citizens to take part in the process. Appendixes reprint legislation and list other sources of information on NEPA.

Citizen Participation Technology. Barry Checkoway et al. Chicago: Council of Planning Librarians (1313 East 60th Street, 60637), 1977. No. 1329. 36 pp. $2.80 pb.

Public Participation in Environmental Policy: An Annotated Bibliography. Joseph Chisholm. Chicago: Council of Planning Librarians, 1976. 17 pp. $1.20.

A Handbook for Citizen Participation in Community Planning and Change. Allen Stoval et al. Washington, D.C.: Appalachian Regional Commission (Communications Division, 1666 Connecticut Avenue, N.W., 20235). 15 pp.

The Unfinished Agenda: The Citizen's Policy Guide to Environmental Issues. Gerald O. Barney, ed. New York: Thomas Y. Crowell, 1977. 184 pp. $3.95 pb.

Working With Groups, Committees, and Communities. Harleigh B. Trecker and Audrey R. Trecker. New York: Cambridge, 1979. 192 pp., index. $9.95 hb.

How to Make Citizen Involvement Work: Strategies for Developing Clout. Duane Dale. Amherst, Mass.: Citizen Involvement Training Project (138 Hasbrouck, University of Massachusetts, 01003), 1978. 92 pp. $5 pb.

Planning, for a Change: A Citizen's Guide to Creative Planning and Program Development. Duane Dale and Nancy Mitiguy. Amherst, Mass.: Citizen Involvement Training Project, 1978. 88 pp. $5 pb.

Citizen Committees: A Guide to Their Use in Local Government. Joseph Lee Rodgers, Jr. Cambridge: Ballinger, 1977. 103 pp., appends., biblio. $15 hb.

The Job of the Planning Commissioner: A Guide to Citizen Participation in Local Planning. Albert Solnit. 1974. Rev. ed. Berkeley: University of California (University Extension Publications, 2223 Fulton Street, 94720), 1977. 107 pp. $4.50 pb.

Private Planning for the Public Interest: A Study of Approaches to Urban Problem Solving by Nonprofit Organizations. American Society of Planning Officials. Chicago: American Planning Association, 1975. 152 pp., appends., biblio. $10 pb.

"Public Hearing Pointers (and Pitfalls)," Leslie E. This. *Historic Preservation*, October–December 1975.

A San Francisco policeman stopping a bulldozer at gunpoint to halt demolition of a hotel near Chinatown. (Musura, *San Francisco Examiner*)

Getting Started: Public Advocacy

Getting other people to work actively for a cause is perhaps the best way to win broad public support.

John Huenefeld, *The Community Activist's Handbook*

Campaigns for Community Change

1. *Organization:* Organize a private citizens association to undertake the project, usually without official input or aid.
2. *Education:* Mount an educational campaign to pressure public agencies through public opinion to bring about the goal.
3. *Election:* Support candidates who will carry out the desired activity.

John Huenefeld, *The Community Activist's Handbook*

Organizing: A Guide for Grassroots Leaders. Si Kahn. New York: McGraw-Hill, 1982. 396 pp., index. $12.95 hb, $7.95 pb.

A comprehensive guidebook on how ordinary people can band together to achieve extraordinary results. Covered are organizing, leaders, constituencies, members, strategy, tactics, training, communication, money, coalitions, politics and culture.

Basic Preservation Procedures. Information Series. National Trust for Historic Preservation. 1979. Rev. ed. Washington, D.C.: Preservation Press, 1983. 20 pp., biblio. $2 pb.

Outlines key steps to a successful preservation program, including taking action, communications, conducting surveys, recording and documenting, financial and technical resources, National Trust assistance and legal tools.

Working with Local Government. Leila Smith. Information Series. National Trust for Historic Preservation. Washington, D.C.: Preservation Press, 1977. 9 pp. $2 pb.

Provides an overview of the functions and the faces in government agencies affecting preservation.

The Community Activist's Handbook: A Guide to Organizing, Financing, and Publicizing Community Campaigns. John Huenefeld. Boston: Beacon Press, 1970. 160 pp., appends.

If you can find a copy in your library, this will provide an overview of community action including developing campaigns and "managing the showdown," with sample documents.

Action Now! A Citizen's Guide to Better Communities. Richard W. Poston. Carbondale, Ill.: Southern Illinois University Press, 1976. 257 pp., index. $7.95 pb.

"One of the hard facts of life is that no community or area can achieve real improvements beyond the willingness and determination of its own citizens." This book offers principles, recommendations and organizing suggestions for effective action.

Community Action Tool Catalogue: Techniques and Strategies for Successful Action Programs. American Association of University Women. Washington, D.C.: AAUW (Sales Office, 2401 Virginia Avenue, N.W., 20037), 1978. 252 pp., index. $7 pb.

Describes tactics for conducting a campaign or project: dealing with institutions, demonstrations of support and opposition, fact finding, information and publicity techniques, organization and planning.

Techniques for Organizational Effectiveness. Claire Fulcher and Mary Grefe. Washington, D.C.: American Association of University Women, 1973. 89 pp., biblio. $3 pb.

Based on the experience of two AAUW members, designed to aid in developing leadership and membership skills.

"Neighborhood Organizing Guide: Ideas for Bringing Your Neighborhood Together." *Conserve Neighborhoods,* September–October 1981. National Trust for Historic Preservation.

Why neighborhoods must organize and how to accomplish this effectively and efficiently, including how to get started and create a formal organization. Also available: *CN Organizing Kit.*

Arts Advocacy: A Citizen Action Manual. Robert Porter, ed. New York: American Council for the Arts (570 Seventh Avenue, 10018), 1980. 70 pp. $6.95 pb.

Directed at strategies for encouraging arts activities and programs, the guide addresses how to develop a campaign and examples of selected advocacy programs.

Vietor. © 1971 The New Yorker Magazine, Inc.

Don't Tear It Down members protesting the demolition of Red Lion Row, Washington, D.C. The facades were later saved. (Carleton Knight III, NTHP)

Joseph Grano outside Rhodes Tavern (1799), Washington, D.C., which he struggled for four years to spare from demolition for an office complex.

One of the rooms in Rhodes Tavern, considered Washington's first town hall, overlooking the U.S. Treasury Department. (Arnold Kramer, HABS)

Basic Preservation Procedures

Strong, continuous, well-organized local action is the key to successful preservation efforts.

1. *Organize.* Define local preservation issues and goals, determine if a preservation group exists, seek the aid of concerned individuals and groups.

2. *Communicate.* Publicize preservation efforts, approach news media, write letters to the editor, give out bumper stickers, publish flyers, hold meetings.

3. *Act quickly.* Meet with all parties, explore all options, seek fast solutions, mount petition drives, secure public endorsements, retain consultants, prepare statements.

4. *Conduct a survey.* Survey historic, architectural and cultural resources as the basis for preservation planning.

5. *Seek landmark designation.* Obtain listing in local, county, state and national landmarks registers.

6. *Document historic sites.* Prepare historical information, obtain photographs, make drawings of important and endangered sites.

7. *Locate technical and financial aid sources.* Seek out the network of preservation, professional and funding assistance.

8. *Use legal tools.* Learn about local, state and federal laws affecting preservation, protective easements, rehabilitation tax benefits.

9. *Learn from others.* Find models for future preservation efforts, learn lessons from the past.

10. *Stay involved and keep informed.* Join preservation organizations, read publications, attend meetings and conferences.

From *Basic Preservation Procedures*

The corner spot once occupied by Rhodes Tavern. (Arnold Kramer, HABS)

Lessons from the Past: A Compendium of Preservation in Action

Almost any building has historical associations for somebody; almost any building manifests some style; almost any building is a delight in somebody's eyes. The result is that, generally speaking, whenever any old building is threatened with destruction, for whatever reason, there is always somebody ready to defend it.

Alan Gowans, "Preservation." *Journal of the Society of Architectural Historians,* October 1965.

I have drawn examples of hope from architectural preservation. . . . These people express a strong discontent with the deliberate destruction of buildings that, in their opinion, still have useful lives and, in many cases, striking beauty. This discontent is expressed in a variety of ways—anger, frustration, sadness and calculation among them. All hope for something better for themselves, their contemporaries and their descendants. . . . The stories of these preservationists show their absolute refusal to accept defeat and their determination to go further, even when victory has been painstakingly won. In defeat they have seen visions, and in victory they have seen possibilities.

Harlan H. Griswold, "Six Preservationists Beat the Odds." *Historic Preservation,* November–December 1979.

St. Louis Cathedral (1849–51, J. N. B. de Pouilly), one of the Vieux Carre's landmarks. (New Orleans Convention and Visitors Bureau)

Hallowell, Maine, residents stopping traffic as well as a highway from taking over their Water Street. *(Maine Times)*

Highways

Hallowell, Maine

"Don't Pave Me" buttons and T-shirts began appearing in Hallowell, Maine, in 1975 when the Save Hallowell committee rallied to keep the town's quiet Main Street from being turned into a four-lane highway. The tiny 19th-century riverport and antiques center happened to be the site of a major rush-hour slowdown, so the Maine Department of Transportation's solution was to widen Main Street. The preservationists' solution was to bring public attention to their contention that "places like Hallowell are more important than traffic flow." Today, brick sidewalks and old gas-light lamp posts—not more asphalt—enhance Hallowell's townscape.

"Maine Residents Rally to Stall Highway," Geoffrey C. Upward. *Preservation News,* November 1975.

Vieux Carre Expressway

When plans for a six-lane interstate expressway along the Mississippi River, announced in 1967, threatened the integrity of the Vieux Carre Historic District in New Orleans, the citizen protests began. Because the district is a National Historic Landmark and the Interstate Highway System is federally funded, the proposal came under review by the Advisory Council on Historic Preservation. The council recommended relocation of the roadway, and Transportation Secretary John A. Volpe barred use of federal funds for the project—the first such veto.

The Second Battle of New Orleans: A History of the Vieux Carre Riverfront-Expressway Controversy. Richard O. Baumbach, Jr., and Willia E. Borah. For the Preservation Press. University, Ala.: University of Alabama Press, 1981.

Overton Park

One of the longest preservation battles ever waged got under way in 1955 when a six-lane federally funded expressway bisecting this historic mid-city park in Memphis was first proposed. Citizens to Preserve Overton Park formed and, with aid from the National Trust, fought the highway from local courts to the U.S. Supreme Court—which held that the state's plans did not meet federal environmental standards. But plans to find other routes for the highway were laid to rest only in 1977 when Transportation Secretary Brock Adams rejected the highway.

"DOT Says No." *Preservation News,* November 1977.

Citizens to Preserve Overton Park
192 Williford Street
Memphis, Tenn. 38112

Interior of Wesley Chapel (1831), Cincinnati, demolished in the dark of night. (Jerry Morgenroth)

Some of the preservationists who rallied to save the West Front of the U.S. Capitol. (Lisa Berg, NTHP)

Commercial Expansion

Wesley Chapel

"Who would send a wrecking crew out into 6 below zero weather, at night, with instructions to level an 1831 church before dawn? Procter & Gamble did. The company obtained a permit to demolish Cincinnati's Wesley Chapel on Friday afternoon, February 4. Without further notice and unbeknownst to preservationists who had been trying to negotiate with the corporation, the crew was dispatched Friday night . . . . the building was gone when citizens awoke on Saturday. The chapel had been in jeopardy since 1968 when P & G bought it for $700,000 [but] the Methodist congregation continued to meet in the church . . . giving preservationists hope that there was still time to save it." The church occupied a small portion of the two-block area earmarked for the company's expansion. A reflecting pool now occupies the site.

"Wesley Chapel Caught in Company Expansion." *Preservation News*, June 1970. "Midnight Crew Levels Chapel in Cincinnati." *Preservation News*, March 1972.

Windsor House Hotel

"On Monday before Labor Day 1971, we learned that Windsor House Hotel [Windsor, Vt.], built in 1840 in Greek Revival style, would be bulldozed to make way for a one-story 'colonial' drive-in bank . . . within a week. It was the final blow in a continuing loss of assets on Main Street. . . . A seemingly hopeless situation was reversed when four people within 48 hours secured 400 names on a petition, found promise of a $5,000 challenge grant . . . and

rallied unprecedented attendance at a Selectman's meeting. . . . Letters from depositors persuaded the bank to extend the deadline until January 1. . . . It was necessary to persuade the voters before the March Town Meeting that Windsor House should be given to the town. . . . Hundreds of phone calls to voters prior to the Town Meeting resulted in a unanimous affirmative vote."

Georgianna Brush. In "Six Preservationists Beat the Odds," Harland H. Griswold. *Historic Preservation*, November–December 1979.

Mapleside, Madison, Wis.

"See the 116-year-old historic house. See it being knocked down. See the hamburger stand in its place. Pow. America, of thee I sing; sweet land of Burger King.

The house was Mapleside, built solidly of sandstone with the classical graces characteristic of the mid-nineteenth century. . . . it was bought and demolished by the hamburger chain, which professed to be ignorant of the building's esthetic and historical worth. Last-minute attempts by preservationists to raise $100,000 to save it failed. Good-bye history, hello hamburger. From historic home to 'home of the whopper' with a swing of the wrecker's ball.

This hamburger stand got an extra onion. It was given as part of the 'orchids and onions' awards program of the Capital Community Citizens, a lively environmental action group in Dade County, Wisconsin."

Kicked a Building Lately? Ada Louise Huxtable. New York: Quadrangle, New York Times Books, 1976.

First National Bank Building

Bank officials decided to discontinue use of this structurally sound 1873 Italianate building in Ashland, Ohio, and build a modern bank and a 13-space parking lot on the site. Preservationists fought the move; city officials resisted. The chairman of the parent corporation, National City Corporation of Cleveland, stated that "this is one instance where an understandable concern for historical value has to give way to some intractable economics." The 1978 destruction of the bank was immortalized on film in the National Trust production, *Main Street*.

"Ohio Bank Hopes to Build Bicentennial Parking Lot," Geoffrey C. Upward. *Preservation News*, August 1976.

Institutional Expansion

Robie House

"The destruction of a thing like this could happen only in America." The speaker was the 87-year-old Frank Lloyd Wright. The "thing" was the Robie House (1909) in Chicago, the acclaimed Prairie School landmark—designed by Wright. An internationally distinguished Committee to Preserve the Robie House was assembled hastily when the Chicago Theological Seminary decided to replace the Wright masterpiece with a new dormitory. The University of Chicago stepped in and took title to the house in 1963, agreeing to restore and preserve it in perpetuity for educational use.

Preservation News, February 1963.

Capitol Hill

"Westward, no!" cried preservationists, led by the American Institute of Architects and the National Trust, each time Congress, through the Architect of the Capitol, suggested that the Capitol's West Front be extended—which would have destroyed the last remaining original exterior portion and a Frederick Law Olmsted terrace. Galvanized by a rally on the steps of the Capitol in 1983, victory came soon afterward when the House and Senate voted for restoration rather than extension. Constant vigilance by Capitol Hill citizens groups also helped bring about the first master plan for the Capitol in 1981, designed to make room for a growing Congress as well as the small-scale buildings that form its neighborhood. The plan tempered expansion—but formally proposed that the Supreme Court move to a new location.

1983 Annual Report, National Trust for Historic Preservation.

Stevens Castle

In 1954 Stevens Institute of Technology restored Stevens Castle in Hoboken, N.J. In 1959 college trustees called the Italianate mansion "an architectural monstrosity" and decided to raze it. The plan drew outcries from the National Trust, chamber of commerce, AIA, local newspapers and the Stevens family; the state legislature passed a resolution. "We must remember Stevens is not a historical society," said the college president. The building was soon replaced by a modern student-faculty center.

Historic Preservation, 1959–62.

Galveston's Ufford Building (1860), after it burned in a 1978 fire. (Van Edwards)

Abandonment and Arson

Glessner House

Its marble sinks smashed, windows cracked, imported fittings and William Morris wall lights stolen, Glessner House (1886), H. H. Richardson's last remaining Chicago work, lay abandoned until the Chicago School of Architecture Inc. was formed to purchase and preserve it in 1966. Because neighboring Prairie Avenue had become an area of tenements and deteriorating factories, it was difficult to find an organization willing to undertake continued operation of the structure after Glessner's death. Today, with revenue from renting part of the building to other organizations and with donations of furniture from the Glessner family, the Chicago School (now the Chicago Architecture Foundation) has restored the house as a museum.

Chicago Architecture
Foundation
330 South Dearborn Street
Chicago, Ill. 60604

Gable and chimney, Glessner House, Chicago. (J. J. Glessner)

Ellis Island

"Pilfered by vandals, polluted by pigeons, falling plaster and stagnant pools of water, weed choked with rampant vegetation and reduced by a crumbling seawall gradually sliding into the bay, Ellis Island had reached the nadir of its existence." This is part of the picture that led to a search for restoration funds and creation of the Statue of Liberty/Ellis Island Foundation. Stabilization and restoration of the New York landmark are under way, and the island is now open to visitors. "Ellis Island, in essence the Plymouth Rock to some 16 million people, is rising from its abyss."

"Doorway to America," Lee Dennis. *Historic Preservation,* April–June 1978.

Statue of Liberty/
Ellis Island Foundation
101 Park Avenue
New York, N.Y. 10017

Ufford Building

A six-month campaign to save one of Galveston's cast-iron buildings ended when the 1860 structure burned in February 1978. It was the third historic building in The Strand historic district to be destroyed within five days. The Galveston Historical Foundation had been negotiating with bank officials, whose parking lot plans had been halted by a temporary restraining order and preliminary court injunction to prevent demolition. Preservationists only months before had occupied the building to prevent demolition.

"Galveston Group Works to Save Ufford Building." *Preservation News,* November 1977.

Galveston Historical Foundation
P. O. Drawer 539
Galveston, Tex. 77553

Endangered Houses

Ainsley Hall Mansion

"The bulldozers were at work on the grounds and demolition crews were working in the cellar of Ainsley Hall Mansion [Charleston, S.C.], one of the last two remaining masonry houses by Robert Mills when a visiting architect noticed them, just before quitting time. He spread notice of the impending destruction to local civic leaders, who formed the Historic Columbia Foundation overnight, and found funds before morning to stop the destruction. The house was purchased from the ecclesiastical institution which had owned it and was preparing to sell it for a parking lot."

George Zabriskie, "Window to the Past." *With Heritage So Rich.* Special Committee on Preservation, U.S. Conference of Mayors. Albert Rains and Laurence Henderson, eds. 1966. Rev. reprint. Washington, D.C.: Preservation Press, 1983.

McCormick Seminary Townhouses

Renters who refused to let their homes fall into the hands of real estate developers mobilized in 1974 to rescue 58 historic townhouses threatened when the Mc-Cormick Theological Seminary announced its plan to vacate its Chicago campus. Eight families formed a nonprofit association that bid to purchase the buildings from the seminary. Units were offered to potential buyers by lottery, and half the former renters became owners, with the remainder of the purchasers found in the nearby area. Their success was attributed to a "very, very strong" feeling of community among the residents.

"Chicago Group Saves 58 Townhouses," Geoffrey C. Upward. *Preservation News,* March 1976.

Dodge House

Designed by Irving Gill, the 1916 house in Los Angeles was "a classic building, destroyed in a classic case of official bungling, malplanning and highhandedness." Preservationists' seven-year efforts to raise the funds to save it were dashed when the city's decision to rezone the property resulted in inflating the price of the land. The developer who purchased the property considered the house "expendable."

Lost America: From the Mississippi to the Pacific. Constance M. Greiff. Princeton: Pyne Press, 1972.

Lockefield Gardens

Representatives of the Indianapolis black community and preservationists, including the Advisory Council on Historic Preservation, tried valiantly over several years to preserve one of the country's first large-scale housing projects (1936). In the end, the city housing agency refused to consider rehabilitating all but a portion of the mammoth complex, and three-quarters was torn down in 1983—with HUD funds once intended for renovation. The remaining section, added to the National Register, was to be rehabilitated and receive some historical protection. New apartments, and a lot of parking for an adjacent university hospital, will take the place of the lost buildings.

"Saving Lockefield Gardens," Birch Bayh. *Preservation News,* June 1977, August 1977.

Historic Landmarks
Foundation of Indiana
3402 Boulevard Place
Indianapolis, Ind. 46208

Aerial view of Lockefield Gardens (1936), Indianapolis, most of which was demolished in 1983. (Robert Lavelle)

Start of demolition on the roof of the National Presbyterian Church (1887–89, J. C. Cady), Washington, D.C. *(Washington Post)*

Entrance of the Pioneer Courthouse (1875), Portland, Ore., which was saved through judicial intervention. (Carleton Knight III, NTHP)

Endangered Churches

Old Brick Church

The tale ended happily for this 1856 Romanesque Revival church in Iowa City, but not without 12 years of controversy that saw hunger strikes and the excommunication of two church members. In 1974 the Presbyterian congregation tried to sell the building to the University of Iowa with a stipulation that it would be demolished to create green space for the campus. An injunction obtained by the Old Brick Defense Committee bought time to raise $154,000 to purchase the building. After a preservation campaign and out-of-court negotiations, the preservationists purchased the church in 1977. One occupant is now the Iowa state historic preservation office.

"Preserving Churches," Ashton Nichols. *Preservation News,* August 1977.

National Presbyterian Church

The church (1887–89) was one of the few important Washington, D.C., buildings bearing a clear debt to H. H. Richardson. When affordable adjacent property to construct a larger church center could not be obtained, many members disapproved of the plan to sell it to a developer. Although the church had been declared a city landmark, the land was rezoned for a high-rise office building. Preservationists' offers to raise funds to re-purchase the property were to no avail by the time the city ruled that it could not stay the demolition in 1966. Some salvaged details were incorporated into the new National Presbyterian Church and Center in northwest Washington, and the congregation placed a bronze plaque on the undistinguished office building that replaced the church.

Historic Preservation, January–February 1964, July–August 1966.

Historic Buildings of Washington, D.C. Diane Maddex. Pittsburgh: Ober Park Associates, 1973.

Mt. Moriah A.M.E. Church

Historic Annapolis spent $5,000 in legal fees to assist preservationists opposing the church's demolition by Anne Arundel County. Located two blocks from the statehouse, the soon-to-be vacant church (1874) was eyed for a parking lot. The Annapolis historic district commission denied the request for a demolition permit—and won a series of court battles that included a unanimous ruling in its favor from the state's highest court. The Maryland Commission on Negro History and Culture, the Maryland Historical Trust and the state of Maryland all joined in the fight.

"Annapolis Wins Church Preservation Suit." *Preservation News,* March 1974.

Endangered Public Buildings

Pioneer Courthouse

In 1967 Judge Richard H. Chambers and other judges on the U.S. Court of Appeals for the Ninth Circuit made a landmark decision: to convince the U.S. General Services Administration to spare the life of the 1875 courthouse in Portland, Ore., designed by Alfred B. Mullett. GSA undertook a feasibility study and found that providing the same amount of space in a new building would cost substantially more than renovating the old. The restoration was completed in 1976. The National Trust later honored Judge Chambers for this act and similar work in San Francisco.

Preservation News, September 1973, February 1976.

St. Clair County Courthouse

When the Belleville, Ill., city council declared this 1861 building to be historic, requiring its approval for alterations, preservationists breathed a sigh of relief and scheduled an appreciation dinner—only to watch the council recant a few weeks later. Wrecking company workers finished what the council began, by pulling down a section of a wall and then speeding away. A $10 million lawsuit against the wreckers, the contractor for the new courthouse and the public buildings commission; a temporary restraining order; an offer of $350,000 from HUD; and a 200-person human chain failed to stay the June 1, 1972, demolition.

"Illinois County Loses Courthouse in Sneak Attack." *Preservation News,* July 1972.

Old Post Office

"Does Postage Go Up Because Buildings Go Down?" asked a picketer's sign in a 1971 march to gain public attention for this downtown landmark in the nation's capital. Often described as a Victorian thumb in a neoclassical body, the post office was targeted by the U.S. General Services Administration for replacement to complete the Federal Triangle as originally planned. Don't Tear It Down, formed to fight this battle and taking its rallying cry for a name (recently changed), twisted GSA's arm when a feasibility study revealed the building's potential for office and commercial use. Reopened in 1983 with shops and offices, the post office has become the figurehead in the revitalization of Pennsylvania Avenue instead of a dead letter.

"Rally Held Round the Old D.C. Post Office," Diane Maddex. *Preservation News,* June 1971.

D.C. Preservation League
930 F Street, N.W.
Suite 612
Washington, D.C. 20004

Endangered Schools

Stephen Palmer School

When the old elementary school in the center of Needham, Mass., became vacant, the members of the town meeting decided to postpone a proposed $40,000 demolition and study the matter. The Stephen Palmer School Study Committee began investigating alternative uses for the 1914 school and made recommendations to the next town meeting. Massachusetts Department of Community Affairs planners joined the committee members and debated several plans, finally settling on an apartment conversion scheme. Committee members still remained skeptical that it would work. The turning point came when the committee left town to visit a newly converted school in Gloucester. Seeing was believing, and the Palmer School adaptation to badly needed housing and community space was soon on its way.

Built to Last: A Handbook on Recycling Old Buildings. Gene Bunnell, Massachusetts Department of Community Affairs. Washington, D.C.: Preservation Press, 1977.

Central High School

When the 1925 Jacobean Revival school in Jackson, Miss., closed its doors in 1977, the Mississippi Department of Archives and History recommended that the state purchase the school and recycle it into a temporary state capitol. It was pointed out that purchase and modification would be one-half the cost of new construction and that eventually the building

could be used for office space for the growing legislative complex. The governor and the state legislature were so pleased with their temporary quarters that they planned to keep the building for office space even after the state capitol was renovated.

"Mississippi Schoolhouse to Statehouse?" *Preservation News,* June 1977.

Mississippi Department of Archives and History P. O. Box 471 Jackson, Miss. 39205

Endangered Commercial Buildings

Wainwright Building

Despite the fact that this 1892 building in St. Louis, designed by Adler and Sullivan, is considered a landmark in the development of modern American architecture, in the early 1970s it was slated for replacement by a parking lot. The National Trust stepped in to help save it in 1973 by purchasing an option, which it turned over to the state of Missouri. Gov. Christopher S. Bond wanted the Wainwright to become state offices. The legislature argued over funding; the governor lost the next election. But during years of delay, renovation and an annex went forward, and Bond was reelected. The effort, says architecture critic Paul Goldberger, "serves as a reminder that governments can find it in their interest to preserve important parts of older cities."

"Wainwright Rededicated as State Office Complex," Carleton Knight III. *Preservation News,* August 1981.

Cornice detail of the Wainwright Building (1892), St. Louis, showing its typical Sullivanesque detail. (Piaget, HABS)

Chicago Stock Exchange

"The 1893 Chicago Stock Exchange, considered one of the most important achievements of Chicago School architects Adler and Sullivan, was relinquished to the wrecking ball in October 1971. The Chicago City Council had refused to award the historic structure protective designation as a city landmark, and court battles, economic development proposals, new legislation, fund-raising drives and editorial appeals failed to rescue the building. Pleas came from the Commission on Chicago Historical and Architectural Landmarks and support from many individuals and organizations. . . . The efforts were to no avail, except that some architectural details were saved by various preservation and museum groups."

"I Feel I Should Warn You . . ." Historic Preservation Cartoons. Terry B. Morton, ed. Washington, D.C.: Preservation Press, 1975.

Prudential Building

A 1977 threat to demolish the Prudential Building (1894–95, Adler and Sullivan), Buffalo, N.Y., called "the first formal skyscraper in the world," prompted an outcry from local preservationists; the mayor declared Buffalo's first preservation week. Studies by the National Trust and New York preservation groups confirmed that office use was the most economical for the building.

Shortly thereafter, the owners decided to sell the building. In 1978 the new owners announced demolition plans. By the end of 1978, however, new developers decided to spend more than $6 million of their own funds and government grants to renovate the building for office use. Exterior cleaning and interior renovation began in 1981 when UDAG funding was approved.

Buffalo Landmark and Preservation Board 641 Delaware Avenue Buffalo, N.Y. 14202

First and Merchants Bank

In 1971 the First and Merchants Bank of Richmond, Va., decided to replace a street-long row of antebellum cast-iron buildings with an office tower, parking facility and plaza. Preservation groups promptly took up the case. One, SAVE (Committee to Save a Vanishing Environment), took out a full-page ad in a Richmond newspaper, organized picketing and started a massive mailing campaign. The bank first offered only to pay for the removal of ornamental iron from the facades, but later agreed to save the entire front of two structures and the first floor of another. Flood damage and storage problems eventually caused most of the 28 tons of cast iron to wind up on the scrap heap. Cast-iron architecture now is regaining popularity in Richmond.

Preservation News, January, March, July 1971.

Central High School (1925), Jackson, Miss., saved through conversion to offices. (Eleana Turner, Mississippi Department of Archives and History)

Union Station (1885), New London, Conn., before it was preserved and converted to a transportation center. (Randolph Langenbach)

Endangered Railroad Stations

New London Union Station

An economic feasibility study, the reversal of negative press coverage and Claire Dale changed the minds of the citizens of New London, Conn., who thought that Union Station (1885) obstructed their view of the Thames River and wanted to demolish the H. H. Richardson-designed structure. The fight took 13 years. In 1975 the station was sold to an architectural firm that planned office, restaurant and shopping space—as well as use as a railroad station.

"Six Preservationists Beat the Odds," Harlan H. Griswold. *Historic Preservation,* November–December 1979.

Cincinnati Union Terminal

Unable to raise the funds to save the concourse from demolition to enlarge Southern Railway's freight area, Save the Terminal did manage to preserve the WPA-era concourse murals and have them moved to the airport. The remainder of the 1933 Art Moderne building survived in limbo for many years in the 1970s as plans for its use were debated—ranging from a roller rink to a disco. Finally the city leased the station to a commercial developer who converted it into an impressive salesroom for discount apparel.

Cincinnati Historic
Conservation Board
Urban Conservator's Office
801 Plum Street
Cincinnati, Ohio 45202

Pennsylvania Station

Philip Johnson, Aline Saarinen, Peter Blake, MOMA, Lewis Mumford, Alfred Knopf, Columbia University School of Architecture, Pratt Institute, the National Trust, *The New Yorker,* *Life* and the *New York Times*—these were a few of the preservationists allied against a plan to demolish McKim, Mead and White's 1906 New York landmark in order to construct a new Madison Square Garden. The protests did not sway the city council, and the station ended up in a landfill in a New Jersey meadow. Yet, it was the loss of this building that led to enactment of New York City's landmarks law, one of the strongest and most active in the nation.

"I Feel I Should Warn You . . ." *Historic Preservation Cartoons.* Terry B. Morton, ed. Washington, D.C.: Preservation Press, 1975.

Lost America: From the Atlantic to the Mississippi. Constance M. Greiff, ed. Princeton: Pyne Press, 1971.

Endangered Hotels

General Worth Hotel

Hudson, N.Y., claimed that the hotel was a fire, health and safety hazard, so it was razed under a spot urban renewal program in 1969—with a HUD demolition grant. Local, state and national preservationists all tried to save it, and even HUD tried to back out because the rare Greek Revival hotel was in the National Register, but the city threatened to sue. Hudson today is more preservation minded—sponsoring a model renewal program using facade easements.

Lost America: From the Atlantic to the Mississippi. Constance M. Greiff, ed. Princeton: Pyne Press, 1971.

Preservation News, February 1970.

Willard Hotel

In the first plans developed in the 1960s to revitalize Pennsylvania Avenue in Washington, D.C., the "Hotel of Presidents" (1901, Henry J. Hardenburgh) was slated to succumb to a new National Square. Not until the late 1970s were local preservationists able to convince a new Pennsylvania Avenue Development Corporation to spare the Willard and rescue it from the pigeons, its careless tenants during more than a decade of abandonment.

"Sprucing Up America's Main Street." *Preservation News,* February 1979.

Pennsylvania Avenue
Development Corporation
425 13th Street, N.W.
Washington, D.C. 20004

General Worth Hotel (1836–37), Hudson, N.Y., constructed in this river port during an era of urban competition to build the most luxurious downtown hotels but torn down under an urban renewal program. (Jack E. Boucher, HABS)

Endangered Theaters
Radio City Music Hall
Would New York City be the same without Radio City Music Hall? When the owners of the nation's largest theater (6,200 seats) announced in 1978 that because of a $2 million-plus operating deficit, the hall would close, concerned citizens organized to keep it going. The interior—an Art Deco masterpiece—was refurbished to the tune of $5 million in 1979, and the theater reopened as the Radio City Entertainment Center. Although the owners sued the New York City Landmarks Preservation Commission to protest the landmark designation of the interior (later approved), the return of the Rockettes and stage shows have since given attendance and budget figures a kick.

Preservation News, February 1978, April 1978.

New York City Landmarks Preservation Commission
20 Vesey Street
New York, N.Y. 10007

5th Avenue Theatre
Seattle needed a theater, and the 5th Avenue Theatre, built in 1926 as a vaudeville and movie house but empty since 1978, needed a reason to continue its existence. The owner, the University of Washington, considered uses for the building that would have destroyed its sumptuous oriental interior. Seattle business people formed the 5th Avenue Theatre Association and raised enough private money to remodel the interior for live theatrical performances. No federal or other government funding was used.

"Safe on 5th," Michael Leccese. *Preservation News,* October 1980.

Orchestra Hall
A last-ditch effort by a bassoonist to save the former home of the Detroit Symphony was turned into a preservation success *con brio.* The Renaissance-style city landmark (1919) was spared in 1972 after Save Orchestra Hall purchased it from Gino's, Inc. A National Trust grant helped local preservationists determine the feasibility of the theater's restoration and continued use. Proof of the hall's superb acoustics was confirmed in 1976 when Orchestra Hall was partially restored and performances of the symphony began there *da capo.*

"Detroit and the Bulldozer," Carleton Knight III. *Preservation News,* March 1973.

"Haven't we met someplace before? Penn Station? The Metropolitan Opera House? The Villard Houses?" (Dana Fradon. © 1978 The New Yorker Magazine, Inc.)

Endangered Historic Areas
Gettysburg Battlefield Tower
"In spite of a preservation effort led by Pennsylvania Gov. Milton J. Shapp and Attorney General J. Shane Creamer, the Pennsylvania Supreme Court ruled on October 5, 1973, in favor of Maryland businessman Thomas R. Ottenstein's plan to build an observation tower at the site of the pivotal battle of the Civil War. As planned, the tower was to loom high above the ground where the Battle of Gettysburg was fought in 1863 and where Abraham Lincoln delivered his eloquent 'Gettysburg Address.'

Joining the state leaders and other Pennsylvania preservationists in opposition to the tower was the Advisory Council on Historic Preservation. . . . The strip of commercial development—motels, souvenir stands and fast-food marts—that proliferated in the area before the tower was built and the lack of protective zoning ordinances that made this sort of commercial enterprise possible also meant that there was little environmental basis on which to fight the tower proposition.

The tower, completed in 1974, now offers tourists a view of the battleground from a height of 307 feet."

"I Feel I Should Warn You . . ." Historic Preservation Cartoons. Terry B. Morton, ed. Washington, D.C.: Preservation Press, 1975.

San Antonio Riverfront
The movement to save San Antonio's riverfront began in 1924 when a dedicated group of women artists concerned about the appearance of the city and its parks learned of plans to drain the last great bend in the San Antonio River and cover it with concrete for parking. "The society called a mass meeting and got a respected judge to speak to the multitude on the value of the river bend." The river was saved and, with it, a long list of successful campaigns by the San Antonio Conservation Society was begun.

Preservation Comes of Age: From Williamsburg to the National Trust, 1926–1949. Charles B. Hosmer, Jr. For the National Trust. Charlottesville: University Press of Virginia, 1981.

The Mount Vernon Overlook
George Washington asserted about his home that "no estate . . . is more pleasantly situated than this, on one of the finest Rivers in the world." The view of the Maryland bank of the Potomac from Mount Vernon, Va., has remained much as it was in 1750 only through several decades of action by the Accokeek Foundation, the late Rep. Frances P. Bolton and the National Park Service. Through fund raising to purchase land and scenic easements, they have kept out a sewage treatment plant and an amusement park, among others.

Accokeek Foundation
600 Maryland Avenue, S.W.
Suite 205, West Wing
Washington, D.C. 20024

George Washington's view from Mount Vernon, as sketched in 1796 by architect Benjamin H. Latrobe "from under one of the Locust trees extending from the House to the North." (Maryland Historical Society)

Endangered Small Towns

Locke, Calif.

The residents and wooden structures of one of the last U.S. rural communities still inhabited by Chinese face the constant threat of fire, despite efforts by the Sacramento Housing and Development Agency. The agency received a U.S. Department of the Interior grant to rehabilitate the town's hydrant system and saw to it that the entire town was placed in the National Register of Historic Places. The California legislature appropriated funds to purchase the town land from its Hong Kong developer owner. (The residents will own the buildings.) A special ordinance discourages development, but the future of Locke remains inscrutable.

Californians for Preservation Action Newsletter, November 1977.

Harrisville, N.H.

When the mill that had provided the town's livelihood closed in October 1970, the future looked dim for Harrisville, N.H. Local citizens formed Historic Harrisville and became the means through which funds were channelled and possible solutions were developed. The old mill found a new owner; local investors purchased the land of the vacant private school; the school buildings were purchased by a college; protective covenants went into effect and the process of raising funds to restore and rehabilitate core buildings of the village began. "As a resident . . . said, we are struggling to work things out 'not because it is old, but because it is good.'"

"Why Save Harrisville?" John J. Colony III. *Historic Preservation,* April–June 1972.

Gruene, Tex.

Once a small farming town and commercial empire, Gruene, Tex., was about to be razed by developers. Then Chip Kaufman, doing some photographic survey work for the Texas Historical Commission, found Gruene and convinced the developers that it was economically feasible to let Gruene be restored. In nine months all the old buildings were sold to people committed to restoring them, and the entire town is now in the National Register. An abandoned cotton gin was converted into a winery, an old tin warehouse into an ice cream parlor and antiques showroom. A ghost town became a thriving community.

"Texas Town Saved," Chip Kaufman. *Preservation News,* March 1976.

Litigation

Louisville Woman's Club

The battle began in 1974 when the Louisville Landmarks Commission tabled the Woman's Club's application for demolition of two 1887 Victorian residences it owned. The club wanted to use the space for a parking lot. The Preservation Alliance, neighborhood residents and the landmarks commission persuaded the mayor to use eminent domain to condemn the houses so that they could be preserved. The club fought the condemnation up to the Kentucky Supreme Court, which upheld the city's power to condemn the property. Meanwhile, preservationists raised $140,000 for the city to use to buy the houses. A private owner then purchased them from the city.

Preservation Alliance of Louisville and Jefferson County 712 West Main Street Louisville, Ky. 40202

Philip Johnson, Jacqueline Onassis, Bess Myerson and Edward Koch marching in support of Grand Central Terminal. (Jack Manning, NYT Pictures)

Grand Central Terminal

When New York's landmarks commission designated the 1913 terminal a landmark in 1967 and later rejected designs for a cantilevered office tower submitted by its owner, Penn Central, a legal contest of landmark dimensions was enjoined. The railroad claimed that the commission's action amounted to the taking of private property without compensation. The trial court ruled in the owner's favor, but the appeals court reversed the decision. Following a nationwide preservation effort that attracted public luminaries, the case finally reached the U.S. Supreme Court, which in 1978 ruled in favor of the terminal and the legality of landmarks commissions nationwide.

New York City Landmarks Preservation Commission 20 Vesey Street New York, N.Y. 10007

Green Springs, Va.

In one of the longest-running and most complex legal fights waged in preservation, this historic rural area (the first rural district added to the National Register) has battled a proposed state penal facility, strip-mining for vermiculite, legal interpretations of its National Historic Landmark status—and itself. Some residents favored the potential economic development the new activity would bring; some did not, and formed Historic Green Springs. In its litigation, the association added new chapters to the emerging field of preservation law. For the present, only one thing is assured: that Green Springs's status as a historic district and eligibility for some measure of protection have been affirmed.

Historic Green Springs Box 270 Gordonsville, Va. 22942

Harrisville, N.H., showing the Harris Mill Storehouse and Harris Mill. (Jack E. Boucher, HABS)

The rambling Pike Place Market, Seattle, saved through public support, petition drives and voter turnout to approve an ordinance creating a historic district. (Nick Jahn)

Petitions

Pike Place Market

To save Seattle's beloved downtown market, a Pike Place Market Historic Site was proposed. But as soon as the city attempted to reduce the protected area to one-tenth the hoped-for size, the Friends of the Market drew up a proposed ordinance for a seven-acre district providing for city ownership, a supervisory commission and design review. They gathered 25,478 signatures (only 5,560 were needed) to validate the initiative motion. Rather than pass the Friends' ordinance, the council drafted one of its own, then dropped it and placed the group's ordinance on the ballot. On November 2, 1971, Seattle voters approved the controversial measure to protect the market.

Pike Place Market Historical Commission
215 Columbia
Seattle, Wash. 98104

Rialto Theater

When residents of South Pasadena, Calif., discovered that the Rialto Theater was to be razed to make room for a shopping center under a city redevelopment plan, they formed a group called Rescue the Rialto and drew up a petition. They held some small fund raisers, produced some publicity and in three weeks collected more than 3,600 signatures. The petition was presented to the city council and redevelopment commission, which were persuaded to ask the developer to alter his plans for the shopping center so that the Rialto could stay.

Pasadena Heritage
54 West Colorado Boulevard
Pasadena, Calif. 91105

Weber House

"Demolition of the Weber House," said the director of an environmental consulting firm, "would be one step toward Miamisburg's loss of image." Friends of Weber House (1840) in Miamisburg, Ohio, agreed. When the city decided to raze the building for a parking lot and playground across from the new civic center, they collected enough signatures to persuade the county preservation group to seek a restraining order. A study was undertaken, but city council had its way. The demolition was carried out as soon as the order expired. Now, the city has an architectural review board and has granted local historic district status to the Market Square District.

Preservation News, November 1974.

Boycotts

Austin Shot Tower

Preservationists in Austin made their money talk. When Capital National Bank began demolition of the Shot Tower (1866), a registered Texas landmark, the Austin Heritage Society removed nearly $150,000 in deposits in October 1974. Their actions came too late. By the time the restraining order preventing further demolition was obtained, the building had been so heavily damaged that all hopes for saving it were lost. Since then, however, no further bank properties have been destroyed and preservationists report that they are on much better terms with local bankers.

"Preservationists Withdraw Without Firing a Shot." *Preservation News*, November 1974.

City of Paris Store

In the spring of 1974, Nieman-Marcus announced that it intended to build a new store on the site of San Francisco's City of Paris store (1896, 1906). More than 100,000 persons signed petitions against the demolition, citizens committees were formed, and a letter-writing campaign began. Many long-time store credit card holders returned their cards and cancelled their accounts in disapproval of the store's actions.

Despite the public reaction and legal and political actions, the building was doomed to the wrecking ball in 1980. Only its famed glass dome was spared, for insertion into a new Philip Johnson-designed store.

"San Francisco Store Threatened," Carleton Knight III. *Preservation News*, September 1977. "The Eiffel Tower Is Coming Down." *Preservation News*, October 1980.

Union Station Arcade

When Columbus, Ohio, allowed the demolition of this 1897 National Register property it lost more than an ornate railroad entryway designed by Daniel H. Burnham. It lost some $6 million in capital grants previously approved by the Urban Mass Transportation Administration of the U.S. Department of Transportation. The city's violation of the National Historic Preservation Act of 1966, in using federal funds for demolition, DOT concluded, would "prejudice . . . future DOT applications on this site." The federal agency's funding boycott—a first—stalled a convention and transportation center planned for the site.

"Columbus Loses $6 Million Grant." *Preservation News*, May 1977.

The Eiffel Tower atop the City of Paris, San Francisco, a detail lost when the store was replaced by Neiman-Marcus. (Carleton Knight III, NTHP)

Lobbying

Historic Sites Act of 1935

In 1935 the United States was the only major Western nation with no national preservation policy. "A number of private preservation organizations had begun to realize that the time had come to expand the historical program of the Park Service, especially when the haphazard work of the federal government was compared to the massive preservation efforts in most European countries." Leading preservationists of the day, including staff and officials of Colonial Williamsburg Foundation, became prominent lobbyists for a strong national policy. A Historic Sites Act was drafted and presented to Secretary of the Interior Harold Ickes. The bill was introduced in the Senate by Sen. Harry F. Byrd on February 29, 1935, in the House by Rep. Maury Maverick (Tex.) on March 13 and signed into law on August 21, 1935, declaring, for the first time, "a national policy to preserve for public use historic sites, buildings and objects of national significance for the inspiration and benefit of the people of the United States."

Preservation Comes of Age: From Williamsburg to the National Trust, 1926–1949. Charles B. Hosmer, Jr. For the National Trust. Charlottesville: University Press of Virginia, 1981.

The Delta Queen

"In 1970 the Trust was presented with an opportunity to expand its tour program and at the same time pursue its mission. This expansion grew out of Trust attempts to save the *Delta Queen*, the last steam-powered riverboat still making overnight trips in the continental United States." The wooden paddlewheeler had been condemned

Old North Side Post Office (1894–97), Pittsburgh, saved by the Pittsburgh History and Landmarks Foundation and local citizens who contributed funds to turn it into a museum. (PHLF)

under the fire provisions of the 1966 Safety at Sea Law. Trust members and preservationists sent letters and telegrams to the president and congressional leaders urging them to grant a permanent exemption from the regulations. The exemption was granted, but only temporarily. Congress has since extended the *Delta Queen's* life at least until 1987.

The History of the National Trust for Historic Preservation, 1963–1973. Elizabeth D. Mulloy. Washington, D.C.: Preservation Press, 1976.

Californians for Preservation Action

Formed in 1975 to lobby for preservation causes, the group scored a significant victory before it was a year old. It successfully mounted opposition to California SB 1514, a bill that would have required that the permission of a property owner be obtained before the property

could be nominated for state or national landmark designation. Legislative alerts, letter writing and telephone campaigns, participation in meetings and hearings, and discussions with individuals whose opinions might influence the bill's fate defeated the legislation. (The owner-consent proposal later was enacted on the national level.)

"California Lobby Group Wins 1st Victory," Geoffrey C. Upward. *Preservation News*, October 1976.

California Preservation Foundation
55 Sutter Street, Suite 593
San Francisco, Calif. 94109

Fund Raising

Andrew Mellon Building

When the National Trust for Historic Preservation purchased this 1917–18 apartment building as its Washington, D.C., headquarters in 1976, it was determined to restore the landmark to its former grandeur. The building had originally been six luxury apartments—with such tenants as Andrew Mellon and Perle Mesta. In November 1977 a $1.9 million fund-raising effort began. Contributions were sought from corporations as well as individuals. A matching grant from the U.S. Department of the Interior assisted the Trust in the project. In August 1979, the restoration was completed, the Trust staff moved in and the names of contributors of $10,000 or more were inscribed in the building's foyer.

"1785: A Landmark for the National Trust," Anne Woodward. *Historic Preservation*, July–August 1979.

Old North Side Post Office

Lying in the midst of Pittsburgh's Allegheny Center Redevelopment area, the handsome granite building (1894–97) seemed doomed. It was deemed ineligible for state funds, and special legislation to allow the city to donate it bogged down. But through a four-year effort by the Pittsburgh History and Landmarks Foundation, and the contributions of more than 700 organizations and "just people," the $850,000 needed for acquisition and restoration was raised. The building, now the Allegheny Museum and headquarters for PHLF, was immediately dubbed "the lively landmark."

"A Modern Fable: The Tale of Three Post Offices," Diane Maddex. *Preservation News*, February 1972.

Pittsburgh History and Landmarks Foundation
One Station Square
Pittsburgh, Pa. 15219

Mechanics Hall

In an impressive show of solidarity and enthusiasm, Worcester, Mass., citizens raised $3 million to restore this 1857 landmark. After being condemned as a fire hazard in 1974, its owners decided to raze it. The entire community of Worcester joined in the preservation effort. School children collected $900 in pennies for the project. A National Trust grant paid for a feasibility study. Tours were given to instill civic pride. Even the press gave its support. To professional fund raisers, the effort represented "a remarkable amount of money for a city the size of Worcester (pop. 185,000)."

"Mechanics Hall Rescued," Carleton Knight III. *Preservation News*, February 1978.

Delta Queen crew and passengers celebrating its new lease on life during its first cruise after being rescued in 1970. (Sabin Robbins, NTHP)

Leadership
Historic Denver

Organized in 1970 to save the "unsinkable Molly Brown" house, Historic Denver is one of the largest local private preservation groups. After restoring the Molly Brown House, which it operates as a museum, Historic Denver rehabilitated 14 Victorian houses, conducted a building survey of Denver with almost 200 volunteers, adopted Curtis Park, a declining in-town neighborhood, and moved old buildings there as infill, used its revolving fund to purchase properties and paid for exterior renovation of low-income residents' houses to enable them to stay in the community, and committed itself to improving Denver's downtown, including acquisition of the Paramount Theatre, which it will restore and operate under a 48-year lease as a cinema and performing arts center. In addition to bricks-and-mortar preservation, Historic Denver has an active publications program and educational activities.

Historic Denver
770 Pennsylvania Street
Denver, Colo. 80203

Hartford Architecture Conservancy

To meet its goals of being Hartford's preservation advocate, encouraging neighborhood diversity, working for better urban design and informing residents about the benefits of preservation, HAC has organized its work into three main areas: a revolving fund, preservation services and a community design center. Since 1977 the revolving fund has prompted the purchase of endangered properties. Community design services, including storefront, street, park and related improvements, have been offered since 1978. To service the community, HAC answers requests for information and provides a contractor referral service, library workshops, home repair training, preparation of National Register nominations and publications, including the three-volume *Hartford Architecture.*

Hartford Architecture
Conservancy
130 Washington Street
Hartford, Conn. 06106

Grant Humphreys Mansion (1902), Denver, headquarters of Historic Denver. (Roger Whitacre)

Preservation League of New York State

As a leader among the new breed of active statewide preservation organizations, the league represents the preservationists of the state and provides the tools to spur grass-roots efforts. It is an information clearinghouse and a lobbyist; publishes a newsletter, technical leaflets and books; maintains a library; provides technical assistance; sponsors conferences, organizes tours and conducts research on special topics such as churches and Adirondack camps.

Preservation League of
New York State
307 Hamilton Street
Albany, N.Y. 12210

Eleventh-grade history students helping move the Rock School, New Canaan, Conn., to a new location to spare it from demolition. (Mark Toms)

Youth Brigades
Hammond, La.

Students in a Hammond, La., class for gifted children, sparked by preservationist Laurie Moon Chauvin, each adopted a downtown building in the 19th-century railroad town. The children sketched, photographed and researched their buildings and collected oral histories of older residents' memories of the buildings. Some of the drawings were made into postcards, which local stores and the chamber of commerce sold. The mothers baked cakes in the shapes of buildings, which were then sold at a "cake walk" at Hammond Heritage Day. With the money raised, the children commissioned two redwood signs to designate the boundaries of the downtown historic district.

Conserve Neighborhoods, January–February 1981.

Scio Bridge

When county commissioners in Sublimity, Ore., opposed placing any of Linn County's covered bridges in the National Register or investigating alternatives to their destruction, a group of 6th, 7th and 8th graders led by teacher Mark Wooley began a public relations campaign that influenced the reelection of several commissioners and saved almost all the covered bridges in the county. The students wrote letters to the editor, canvassed door-to-door, testified at meetings, published information and sold Bridge Brigade T-shirts to get their message across.

National Trust Youth Achievement Award, 1979.

Rock School

In November 1972 11th-grade history students in New Canaan, Conn., learned of plans to demolish a 175-year-old one-room school. They launched a campaign to raise $3,500 needed to move the school to a site owned by the New Canaan Historical Society. Their efforts netted enough to begin the needed restoration, much of which was done by the students, who also researched and designed the interior furnishings. The school continues to serve an educational role as a museum.

"New Canaan Students Save, Restore School," Geoffrey C. Upward. *Preservation News,* February 1974.

Action Lessons in a Grand Old Theater

Preservation struggles tend to have a common ground of problems and successes. Actors in preservation dramas often learn by example, taking their lessons in winning, losing and organizing from past preservation scripts. A Grand Strategy: The Scenario for Saving the Grand Opera House, *one in a series of National Trust case studies, provides some clear lessons about essential ingredients of successful projects:*

1. *An appealing project*
2. *Concern about an area's future*
3. *Community involvement*
4. *Leadership*
5. *Team effort*
6. *Credibility of the sponsor*
7. *Political support*
8. *Fund-raising ability*
9. *Expertise from outside consultants*
10. *Press coverage*

House in the Swiss Avenue Historic District, Dallas, created through efforts of the Historic Preservation League of Dallas. (Bob Stump, NTHP)

Grand Opera House (1871), Wilmington, Del.

Saving Graces: How Others Do It

The Failure to Preserve the Queen City Hotel, Cumberland, Maryland. Dianne Newell. Case Studies in Preservation. Washington, D.C.: Preservation Press, 1975. 36 pp., illus., appends. $4.50 pb.

"During the years 1970–71, the B & O Railroad's century-old station-hotel, the Queen City, in Cumberland, Md., was the object of an intensive, two-year preservation campaign for restoration and reuse. The effort can be viewed as a classic case for preservationists, because although the fight to save the Queen City looked like a sure thing, it failed." (Author)

The Making of a Historic District, Swiss Avenue, Dallas, Texas. Case Studies in Preservation. Lyn Dunsavage and Virginia Talkington. Washington, D.C.: Preservation Press, 1975. 40 pp., illus., appends. $4.50 pb.

"The Historic Preservation League in Dallas faced the same problem that groups in many urban areas face. It wanted to save an inner-city neighborhood that was historically significant but had deteriorated over the years into a classic example of urban blight." (Authors)

The Grand Strategy: The Scenario for Saving the Grand Opera House, Wilmington, Delaware. Case Studies in Preservation. Robert Stoddard. Washington, D.C.: Preservation Press, 1978. 44 pp., illus., appends. $4.50 pb.

"This case study documents how a group of determined people went about convincing an entire community of the need to restore and reuse a deteriorating and sadly neglected landmark, and how they went on to raise $5 million and complete most of the project by their Bicentennial deadline." (Author)

The Grass Roots Primer: How to Save Your Piece of the Planet . . . by the People Who Are Already Doing It. James Robertson and John Lewallen, eds. San Francisco: Sierra Club Books, 1975. 287 pp., illus.

An inspiring book to consult for useful ideas and techniques that have been tested in the field. The contents: "Grass Roots Heroes" (18 case studies), steps to power and information sources for environmental activists. It shows "that small is powerful," says a club official.

The Small Towns Book: Show Me the Way to Go Home. James and Carolyn Robertson. Garden City, N.Y.: Anchor Books, Doubleday, 1978. 208 pp., illus., append.

A *Grass Roots Primer* for small towns, describing in case studies how rural communities are coping with "progress," from St. George, Vt., to Mendocino, Calif. "Since most small towns lack the resources or the trained people to effectively cope with large scale pressures from outside, they must either succumb or invent their own defenses."

Heritage Fights Back. Marc C. Denhez. Toronto: Fitzhenry and Whiteside, 1978. 286 pp., illus., index. $9.95 pb. Available from Heritage Canada, P.O. Box 1358, Station B, Otttawa, Ontario K1P 5R4, Canada.

An irreverent book describing the legal, financial and promotional aspects of Canada's efforts to save its historic sites.

Queen City Hotel (1872), Cumberland, Md., before it was razed despite an extended preservation campaign. (B&O Collection, Smithsonian Institution)

Volunteers: Adding Backbone

A volunteer is any individual committed to improving the quality of life through citizen participation in community service.

People Power Conference, Minneapolis, 1974.

The one unique aspect of managing nonprofits as compared with profit-making organizations is the phenomenon of volunteerism.

Lionel Rolfe and Alan Kumamoto, "Managing the Nonprofit." *Grantsmanship Center News,* July–September 1977.

"Throughout its history, the American preservation movement has been largely the domain of individuals whose preservation-related activities have been avocational in nature. These individuals have formed the backbone of the preservation community. Their activities have been and continue to be varied: conducting tours of historic houses, organizing to save endangered landmarks, carrying out do-it-yourself renovation projects and securing the enactment of preservation legislation."

"Preservation as an Avocation." In *Preservation: Toward an Ethic in the 1980s.* National Trust for Historic Preservation. Washington, D.C.: Preservation Press, 1980.

"Volunteering as an option is a basic human right—everyone can help someone. We all need to be needed.

Volunteers can represent a significant program resource, and they can provide a capacity to mobilize community support.

Volunteers can extend and reinforce the work of paid staff—but they should never be used to supplant paid staff.

Volunteers can improve program performance by acting as linkages within the community, interpreters of services, advocates for the inarticulate, as recruiters, trainers, or supervisors, and extend the outreach of the paid staff in delivering services.

Volunteers come from all parts of communities, are all ages and do all sorts of things. Never underestimate the value of youth, older persons, the poor, or minorities to improve the quality of programs."

Harriet H. Naylor, *Leadership for Volunteering*

Helping People Volunteer. Judy Rauner. San Diego: Marlborough Publications, 1980. 95 pp. $9.95 pb.

A workbook with reusable sheets covering program needs, management skills, program planning, recruitment, orientation, interviews, training, supervision, recordkeeping, evaluation and recognition.

The Effective Management of Volunteer Programs. Marlene Wilson. Boulder, Colo.: Volunteer Management Associates (279 South Cedar Brook Road, 80302), 1977. 197 pp., illus., append., biblio. $6.95 pb.

Survival Skills for Managers. Marlene Wilson. Boulder, Colo.: Volunteer Management Associates, 1981. 246 pp., illus., append., biblio. $9.95 pb.

Volunteers Today: Finding, Training and Working with Them. Harriet H. Naylor. Dryden, N.Y.: Dryden Associates (P.O. Box 363, 13053), 1973. 198 pp., appends., biblio. $3.95 pb.

Marshall (Mich.) Historical Society volunteers painting an 1860 school.

Investing in Volunteers: A Guide to Effective Volunteer Management. Kathy Adams. Information Series. National Trust for Historic Preservation. Washington, D.C.: Preservation Press, 1985. 20 pp., illus. $2 pb.

Four-One-One Community Green Sheets: Selected Resources for Program Leaders. Harriet L. Kipps. Annandale, Va.: Four-One-One (7304 Beverly Street, 22003), 1981. 332 pp. $30 looseleaf binder.

By the People: A History of Americans as Volunteers. Susan J. Ellis and Katherine H. Noyes. Philadelphia: Energize (5440 Wissahickon Avenue, No. 534, 19144), 1978. 308 pp., index. $7.25 pb.

Contacts

The Support Center
1709 New Hampshire Avenue, N.W.
Washington, D.C. 20009

Provides consulting services and workshops to nonprofits in financial management and program planning, including fund raising, tax-exempt status counseling and bookkeeping. Fees are based on the client's ability to pay. Offices are maintained in Chicago, Houston, Newark-New York, Oklahoma City, San Francisco and Washington, D.C. Publishes *Management Support Organizations Directory* and *Resources and Strategies for Improving the Management of Non-Profit Organizations.*

American Association for State and Local History
708 Berry Road
Nashville, Tenn. 37204

Publishes extensively on administration and related special programs of historical societies and history museums. Also provides training programs, consulting, job placement, awards and a clearinghouse for information on local history concerns.

Volunteer: The National Center for Citizen Involvement
1111 North 19th Street
Suite 500
Arlington, Va. 22209
P.O. Box 4179
Boulder, Colo. 80306

Created in 1979 through a merger of the National Center for Voluntary Action and the National Information Center on Volunteerism to stimulate and strengthen citizen volunteer involvement. Sponsors conferences, training programs, publications and a library. Publishes an annual catalog of books and manuals on volunteer and nonprofit management that are available through Volunteer. Associates receive the center's regular publications: *Voluntary Action Leadership, Volunteering* and *Exchange Networks.*

Citizen Involvement Training Project
Division of Continuing Education
University of Massachusetts
138 Hasbrouck
Amherst, Mass. 01003

Trains citizen groups to be more effective, beginning as a pilot project in Massachusetts in 1976 and expanding to other states in 1982. In addition to its publications, CITP has a library and is available for consulting and conducting workshops on a fee basis on a variety of organization and management topics.

American Council for the Arts
570 Seventh Avenue
New York, N.Y. 10018

A national service organization founded in 1960 to promote and strengthen cultural activities, principally public and performing arts. Because of its focus on management and advocacy for the arts, the organization provides services and publications of value to preservationists.

The Information Center
208 West 13th Street
New York, N.Y. 10011

Offers a free phone reference service that provides titles of films, videotapes and slide shows on community issues. A newsletter, books and pamphlets on using media also are available.

National Self-Help Clearinghouse
City University of New York Graduate School
33 West 42nd Street
Room 1227
New York, N.Y. 10036

Encourages and coordinates self-help groups nationwide. Publishes a newsletter, books and guides. A "switchboard" provides referrals to specific groups.

Managing Nonprofit Organizations

Many of today's exciting voluntary efforts involve short-term projects to deal with immediate problems. . . . This characterization of "ad-hocracy" is one of voluntarism's best attributes. Unfortunately, though, there are many problems which just are not that amenable to early solution. . . . When a good-sized army is needed, then a conscious effort has to be devoted to building the organization.

Brian O'Connell, *Effective Leadership in Voluntary Organizations*

"It is best to approach the subject of nonprofit management by studying the literature that developed out of the experience of the profit sector. The trick comes in making the 'adaptive fit'—making the principles fit your specific situation. . . ."

Lionel Rolfe and Alan Kumamoto, "Managing the Nonprofit: Can You Learn It From a Book?" *Grantsmanship Center News*, July–September 1977.

Effective Leadership in Voluntary Organizations. Brian O'Connell. New York: Walker, 1981. 216 pp. $5.95 pb.

A personalized guide to management of volunteer organizations by a leader in the field. Among the topics are getting organized, roles of the president, volunteers and staff; recruiting and training staff, meetings, membership, boards and committees, fund raising, communications, budgeting and finances, dealing with controversy and evaluating results.

The Successful Volunteer Organization: Getting Started and Getting Results in Nonprofit, Charitable, Grass Roots and Community Groups. Joan Flanagan. Chicago: Contemporary Books, 1981. 376 pp., biblio., index. $8.95 pb.

A practical handbook that covers a wide range—getting started, tax-exempt status, incorporation, members, committees, program planning, fund raising, publicity, staff, budgets—with a listing of free government services and publications.

How to Set Up and Operate a Non-Profit Organization. Carole C. Upshur. Englewood Cliffs, N.J.: Prentice-Hall, 1982. 256 pp., biblio., appends., index. $18.95 hb, $9.95 pb.

Designed for small and medium-sized groups. Surveys the entire organizational process, including a review of the impact of cutbacks in federal grants and contracts.

The Effective Voluntary Board of Directors: What It Is and How It Works. William R. Conrad, Jr., and William E. Glenn. Institute for Voluntary Organizations. Rev. ed. Athens, Ohio: Swallow Press, Ohio University Press, 1983. 244 pp., append., biblio. $9.95 pb.

Answers questions on policy, board functions, board members, staff, power, why people join boards, meetings, committees, recruitment and evaluation of members and related issues. Includes many charts and sample documents.

Managing Nonprofit Organizations. Diane Borst and Patrick J. Montana, eds. New York: Amacom (American Management Association, 135 West 50th Street, 10020), 1977. 328 pp., index. $6.95 pb.

A survey of a wide variety of approaches, tackling program budgeting, management by objectives and organizational development, as well as the question, "Can nonprofits be managed at all?"

The Nonprofit Organization Handbook. Tracy Daniel Connors, ed. New York: McGraw-Hill, 1980. 734 pp., appends., index. $44.95 hb.

"The essential element of an NPO [nonprofit organization] is voluntary action. Voluntary action is what one is neither paid to do nor made to do. In their broadest sense, NPOs are simply the collective forms of individual voluntary action. That is, NPOs are the vehicles by means of which people pursue together goals that are not primarily remunerative and that they are not forced to pursue."

Making Things Happen: The Guide for Members of Volunteer Organizations. Joan Wolfe. Andover, Mass.: Brick House Publishing, 1981. 139 pp., append., biblio. $7.95 pb.

Down-to-earth advice on how organizations can attract newcomers, have successful publicity and programs, raise money, conduct elections, appoint committees, draft bylaws and manage board meetings. The author offers "Wolfe's Rules of Order" for small organizations.

Hartford Architecture Conservancy members with neighbors and townspeople who helped move this Gothic Revival house. (Roger V. Dollarhide)

Non-Profit Organization Handbook: A Guide to Fund Raising, Grants, Lobbying, Membership Building, Publicity and Public Relations. Patricia V. Gaby and Daniel M. Gaby. Englewood Cliffs, N.J.: Prentice-Hall, 1979. 333 pp., biblio. Looseleaf binder.

In addition to the title's topics, covers communication, training and supervising volunteers, meetings and how to find information.

Non-Profit Corporations, Organizations and Associations. Harold L. Oleck. 1956. 4th ed. Englewood Cliffs, N.J.: Prentice-Hall, 1980. 1,000 pp., index. $49.95 hb.

A technical book on the law and practice of nonprofit organizations, including statutory classification, unincorporated associations, minutes, bylaws, meetings, election procedures, the powers and duties of officers and parliamentary procedure.

Management Control in Nonprofit Organizations. Robert N. Anthony and Regina E. Herzlinger. Homewood, Ill.: Richard W. Irwin Publishing (1818 Ridge Road, 60430). 355 pp. $26.95.

A somewhat theoretical approach detailing management by objectives, budgeting, operating, accounting and boards of trustees.

How to Manage a Non-Profit Organization. John Fisher. Management and Fund Raising Center. Hartsdale, N.Y.: Public Service Materials Center, 1978. $17.50.

Provides more than 200 ways to improve operations in raising funds, enlisting volunteers, dealing with government and publicity.

MBO for Nonprofit Organizations. Dale D. McConkey. New York: Amacom, 1975. 223 pp. $14.95.

Comprehensive and practical guide to management by objectives, a newly popular system under which managers look at their organizations in terms of basic objectives.

"Steering Nonprofits: Advice for Boards and Staff," Management Assistance Group. *Conserve Neighborhoods*, February 1984. 20 pp., illus. $2 pb.

A brief overview highlighting the relationship between managers and boards.

Arts Administration: How to Set Up and Run a Successful Nonprofit Arts Organization. Tem Horwitz. Chicago: Chicago Review Press, 1979. 256 pp., appends., biblio. $8.95 pb.

Although written for the arts, this book is helpful for most nonprofit organizations.

The Arts Management Reader. Alvin Reiss. New York: Marcel Dekker, 1979. 686 pp. $27.50.

Successful methods and case histories exploring fund raising, promotion, management and communications.

Financial and Accounting Guide for Nonprofit Organizations. Malvern J. Gross, Jr., and William Warshauer, Jr. 1972. 3rd ed. New York: Ronald Press, 1983. 568 pp., append., biblio., index. $49.95 hb.

Guide to bookkeeping for small groups, emphasizing good procedures while minimizing bureaucracy.

Financial Management for the Arts: A Guidebook for Arts Organizations. Charles A. Nelson and Frederick J. Turk. New York: American Council for the Arts, 1975. 52 pp., illus. $5.95 pb.

Description of how to manage money, develop budgets and institute financial planning, including accounting principles.

Financial Resource Management for Nonprofit Organizations. Leon Haller. Englewood Cliffs, N.J.: Prentice-Hall, 1982. 191 pp. $17.95 hb, $8.95 pb.

Comprehensive guide to improving financial administration, with step-by-step guidelines for obtaining funding and sample budgets and financial reports.

The Use of Small Computers in Preservation Management. Ralph J. Megna. Information Series. National Trust for Historic Preservation. Washington, D.C.: Preservation Press, 1982. 30 pp., illus., gloss., biblio. $2 pb.

Guidelines for using computers to fill typical tasks of preservation groups, e.g., for mailing lists, financial records, historic sites and related information.

See also: Paying for Preservation

Using Consultants

"Consultants serve many functions. They provide expert and professional advice. They also provide a degree of objectivity. . . . [But] before calling in a consultant, be sure that you really need one."

William T. Alderson, *Using Consultants Effectively*

Using Consultants Effectively. William T. Alderson. Nashville: American Association for State and Local History, 1975. Technical Leaflet 82. 8 pp. $2 pb.

Using Professional Consultants in Preservation. Ellen Beasley. Information Series. National Trust for Historic Preservation. Washington, D.C.: Preservation Press, 1980. 34 pp., appends., biblio. $2 pb.

Using Consultants: A Guide for Administrators. Linda Hartman-Mundel and Jerry Mundel. Los Angeles: Tandem Training Associates (2578 Verbena Drive, 90068), 1978. 22 pp. $2.25.

Administering Preservation Groups

Administration. Vol. 5, *A Bibliography on Historical Organization Practices.* Frederick L. Rath, Jr., and Merrilyn Rogers O'Connell, eds. Rosemary Reese, comp. Nashville: American Association for State and Local History, 1980. 237 pp., append., index. $15.95 hb.

Sources of information on every aspect of administration: governing boards, management, ethics, personnel, fund raising, tax and legal issues, insurance problems, buildings, publishing, public relations, collections management, libraries and archives.

David Moffat Mansion (1911), Denver, which was torn down despite the efforts of Historic Denver. (Howard Brock, *Rocky Mountain News*)

Legal Considerations in Establishing a Historic Preservation Organization. Collette C. Goodman. Information Series. National Trust for Historic Preservation. 1977. Rev. ed. Washington, D.C.: Preservation Press, 1982. 23 pp. $2 pb.

Guidance on forming an organization, organizational structures and qualifying for federal tax exemption; with sample articles of incorporation and bylaws.

"The Impact of Taxes on a Local Historic Preservation Organization," Peter H. Brink. In *Tax Incentives for Historic Preservation.* Gregory E. Andrews, ed. 1980. Rev. ed. Washington, D.C.: Preservation Press, 1981. 240 pp., illus., appends. $12.95 pb.

The legal history of the Galveston Historical Foundation and its 501(c)(3) status.

Organizing a Local Historical Society. Clement M. Silvestro. Rev. ed. Nashville: American Association for State and Local History, 1968. 38 pp. $4.50 pb.

Includes examples of articles of incorporation, a constitution and bylaws.

A Primer for Local Historical Societies. Dorothy Weyer Creigh. Nashville: American Association for State and Local History, 1976. 162 pp., illus., appends., index. $8.95 pb.

How to establish a local historical society, covering financing, tours, publicity, volunteers, libraries and museums.

Recruiting Members for Your Historical Society. Daniel R. Porter. 1966. Rev. ed. Nashville: American Association for State and Local History, 1971. Technical Leaflet 37. 8 pp., illus. $2 pb.

Membership Handbook: A Guide for Membership Chairmen. Fort Worth, Tex.: Sperry and Hutchinson Company (Consumer Services, 2900 West Seminary Drive, 76133), 1977. 24 pp. $.50.

How to plan and run a campaign to obtain new members and how to keep them, with forms and checklists.

Local Preservation Handbooks

Organizing for Preservation: A Resource Guide. Wayne Linker, Jack A. Gold and Caroline P. Adams. New Haven: Connecticut Trust for Historic Preservation (152 Temple Street, 06510), 1982. 48 pp., illus., append., biblio. $8 pb.

Preservation Illinois: A Guide to State and Local Resources. Illinois Department of Conservation. Springfield: Division of Historic Sites (405 East Washington Street, 62706), 1977. 288 pp., illus., index. $2 pb.

Historic Preservation Handbook: A Guide for Volunteers. Department of Planning and Natural Resources. Atlanta: Historic Preservation Section, (270 Washington Street, S.W., 30334), 1974. 101 pp., illus., biblio.

New Jersey: A Heritage for Now and Tomorrow. A Handbook for Historic Preservation. State Council of New Jersey Junior Leagues, 1976. 173 pp., illus., biblio. $6.50 pb. Available from Nancy Reid, Junior League of Monmouth County, 322 Prospect Avenue, Little Silver, N.J. 07739.

Heritage Projects: A Practical Guide for Community Preservation Organizations. Michael J. Smith. Lansing: Michigan Department of State, Michigan History Division (208 North Capitol, 48918), 1975. 58 pp., illus., append., biblio.

Proposed skyscraper behind St. Bartholomew's Church (1919, Bertram Goodhue), New York, which sparked lobbying to save historic churches.

Lobbying: Politic Preservation

Preservation, at least on a large scale, is a matter of both public and private interest: and, therefore, by definition, political. The only question about the relationship of politics and preservation is whether the political system works for you or against you.

Bruce K. Chapman, "Politics and Preservation." *Democratic Review*, February–March 1975.

"Ten years ago, lobbying had a grim connotation. It tended to be associated with men in baggy suits and dark, smoke-filled rooms. During this past decade, the environmental, preservation, consumer and other public-interest advocacy movements raised public consciousness. Now, more people consider lobbying a constitutional right—which has given lobbying popularity and acceptability. Preservationists have joined the ranks of lobbyists pushing for legislation favorable to their cause."

Nellie Longsworth, "The Layman as Lobbyist." *Historic Preservation*, January–February 1980.

"The Tax Reform Act of 1976 liberalized the lobbying provisions applicable to public foundations. . . . [It] provides that up to 20% of an organization's first five hundred thousand dollars of income . . . may be spent on direct lobbying. . . .

Lobbying does not include contacts of an informational nature presented upon the written request of legislators. . . .

Remember that citizens may always give their own point of view as individuals to any legislator and this is not lobbying. . . . Volunteers who spend personal time and dollars representing an organization's point of view are not 'lobbying' because the activity doesn't involve an expenditure of the organization's funds."

Julia Churchman, Preservation Action

Lobbying Techniques

Blueprint for Lobbying: A Citizens Guide to the Politics of Preservation. Washington, D.C.: Preservation Action, 1984. 40 pp., gloss., appends. $10 spiral bound.

Nonprofits' Handbook on Lobbying: The History and Impact of the New 1976 Lobbying Regulations on the Activities of Non-Profit Organizations. John T. Grupenhoff and James T. Murphy. Washington, D.C.: Taft Corporation (5125 MacArthur Boulevard, 20016), 1977. 140 pp., appends. $9.95 pb.

Common Cause Action Manual. Washington, D.C.: Common Cause (2030 M Street, N.W., 20036). 68 pp. Free.

The Sierra Club Political Handbook. Gene Coan, ed. San Francisco: Sierra Club (530 Bush Street, 94108), 1979. 76 pp., illus. $1 pb.

"How to Affect Legislation Before It Affects You," Howard Marlowe. *Grantsmanship Center News* (1031 South Grand Avenue, 90015). February 1978. Reprints. $1.75.

"21 Rules for Successful Legislation," Robert E. Stipe. *Historic Preservation*, October–December 1976.

Nellie Longsworth, president of Preservation Action, left, meeting on Capitol Hill with Rep. Dan Rostenkowski (D-Ill.), right, to discuss tax incentives. Also present were staff members Jayne Boyle and John Salmon. (Max Hirshfeld)

Apollo launch tower, Kennedy Space Center, Fla., which was spared through intensive lobbying efforts and litigation by preservationists. (NASA)

Associations and Lobbying Regulation: A Guide for Non-Profit Organizations. George D. Webster and Frederick J. Krebs. Washington, D.C.: Chamber of Commerce of the United States (1615 H Street, N. W., 20006), 1979. 76 pp. $9 pb.

Lobbying Congress

How You Can Influence Congress: The Complete Handbook for the Citizen Lobbyist. George Alderson and Everett Sentman. New York: E. P. Dutton, 1979. 362 pp., biblio., appends., index. $15.95 hb, $9.95 pb.

Covers how representatives work, correspondence, face-to-face meetings, organizing for influence, using the media, publications, campaign tactics, congressional hearings and building long-term influence. Many of the lessons came from Sierra Club and other environmental experiences.

Capitol Hill Manual. Frank Cummings. Washington, D.C.: Public Affairs Library (Bureau of National Affairs, 1231 25th Street, N.W., 20037), 1976. 331 pp., appends., gloss., index. $17.50 hb.

Explains the rules, customs, procedures and operations of Congress; tells what happens at each stage of the legislative process; discusses power centers in both chambers; and describes how authorizations and appropriations of public funds are made.

How to Lobby Congress: A Guide for the Citizen Lobbyist. Donald E. deKieffer. Forewords by John Glenn and Barry Goldwater. New York: Dodd, Mead, 1981. 241 pp., index. $8.95 pb.

Details how to organize information, letter-writing strategy, using the press, working with congressional staffs and testifying at committee hearings.

Congressional Directory. U.S. Government Printing Office. Washington, D.C.: Superintendent of Documents. Published for each Congress.

Lists information about the current Congress, including biographies of the members, committee memberships, federal agency officials, governors, diplomats and members of the press.

Congressional Staff Directory. Charles Brownson, ed. Mount Vernon, Va.: Congressional Staff Directory (Box 62, 22121). Published annually. 1,176 pp., index. $30.

Includes state delegations, committee assignments, district and staff offices, key personnel in the Executive Branch and staff biographies.

A Common Cause Guide to Money, Power and Politics. Washington, D.C.: Common Cause, 1981. 246 pp., append. $8. Updated for each Congress.

Lists the political action committee contributions to the House and Senate leadership and to committee chairmen.

Contacts

Preservation Action
1700 Connecticut Avenue, N.W.
Suite 401
Washington, D.C. 20009

Founded in 1974 as the national citizens' lobby for preservation because "people were frustrated that preservation decisions were made, and they had no part in the process because of lobbying restrictions," according to President Nellie Longsworth. Because Preservation Action is a full-time lobbyist, contributions to it are not tax exempt. It maintains a list of state lobbying coordinators. "Preservation Action . . . was born to lobby. Not in the cigar-chomping, back-room wining and dining, but in a straight-forward, education-communication system." (Joanne Ditmer, "Raising the Roof." *Denver Post,* December 1, 1976)

National Trust for Historic Preservation
Office of Public Policy
1785 Massachusetts Avenue, N.W.
Washington, D.C. 20036

Established in 1981 to influence public policy decisions and legislation affecting preservation, including obtaining federal financial support for national preservation programs.

Preservation Coordinating Committee
1785 Massachusetts Avenue, N.W.
Washington, D.C. 20036

Represents the National Trust, Preservation Action, National Conference of State Historic Preservation Officers and others, directing a network of preservation organizations and individuals who are informed about legislative matters and asked to participate in lobbying efforts as.issues arise. Publishes regular and special-issue newsletters.

Americans for Historic Preservation
1827 Park Road, N.W.
Washington, D.C. 20010

A political action committee set up to make contributions to pro-preservation candidates.

National Coordinating Committee for Promoting History
400 A Street, S.E.
Washington, D.C. 20003

Represents historians in seeking favorable public policy positions.

Coordinating Council of National Archeological Societies
P.O. Box 1249
Fayetteville, Ark. 72702-1249

Represents archeologists on public policy matters.

Public Relations: The Preservation Message

The preservation communicator must confront our throwaway society with compelling reasons for reassessing the built environment. . . . our preservation story not only has to clarify the facts, but also has to help change attitudes and behavioral patterns.

"The Preservation Message and the Press," G. Donald Adams. In *Preservation: Toward an Ethic in the 1980s.* National Trust for Historic Preservation. Washington, D.C.: Preservation Press, 1980.

Costumed participants in the "Dickens Evening on The Strand," an annual promotional event of the Galveston Historical Foundation. (GHF)

An entry in the Historic Landmarks Foundation of Indiana's "Wear a Building to Lunch" contest during Preservation Week. (Tina Connor, HLFI)

"Unfortunately, one of the most visible public relations events is the worst enemy of preservation: the eleventh-hour attempt to save an endangered property. . . . this last minute 'call to arms,' while it may show widespread support for preservation, cannot alone sustain a long-term commitment and too often does not result even in the preservation of the threatened property. The best public relations program, like the best preservation program, is well planned, includes both short and long-range goals, and may include crisis strategies as part of its overall effort."

Tom Donia, *Public Relations for Local Preservation Organizations*

Public Relations for Local Preservation Organizations: Press Relations, Public Education and Special Events. Tom Donia. Information Series. National Trust for Historic Preservation. Washington, D.C.: Preservation Press, 1980. 31 pp., illus., appends., biblio. $2 pb.

A guide to organizing a publicity program, media contacts, press releases, radio and TV, public service ads and public education, with samples.

A Communications Manual for Nonprofit Organizations. Lucille A. Maddalena. New York: Amacom, 1981. 222 pp. $17.95 hb.

A complete guide filled with specific tips from speakers to annual meetings to newspaper coverage.

The Publicity Handbook. David R. Yale. New York: Bantam Books, 1982. 300 pp., append., index. $3.50 pb.

Billed as a step-by-step guide to reaching the largest audience for the least money, the book covers the role of the publicist, media relations, getting into print and onto the air—and into controversy.

Publicity for Volunteers: A Handbook. Virginia Bortin. New York: Walker, 1981. 159 pp., gloss. $6.95 pb.

Just about all you need to know about publicity in newspapers, magazines, radio and TV; organizational promotion; public relations and publicity campaigns for large and small events.

Publicity: How to Get It. Richard O'Brien. New York: Harper and Row, 1977. 176 pp., index. $12.45.

"If this book has one underlying theme, it is the underlying theme of every good press agent. To publicize well, you must touch all the bases; you must make every effort to reach every possible press outlet available to you."

Effective Public Relations. Robert C. Wheeler. Nashville: American Association for State and Local History, 1973. Technical Leaflet 3. 8 pp., illus., biblio. $2 pb.

"How you deliver your message is often as important as the message itself. For public relations is an essential communication process, and communication implies a receiver as well as a sender."

Managing Your Public Relations: Guidelines for Nonprofit Organizations. Frances A. Koestler, ed. New York: National Communication Council for Human Services, 1977. $14.40 set. Available from Foundation for Public Relations Research and Education, 415 Lexington Avenue, Room 1305, New York, N.Y. 10017.

The six volumes include "Planning and Setting Objectives," "Using Publicity to Best Advantage," "Working with Volunteers," "Making the Most of Special Events," "Measuring Potential and Evaluating Results" and "Using Standards to Strengthen Public Relations."

"Media." In *Common Cause Action Manual.* Washington, D.C.: Common Cause. 11 pp. Free.

A summary of ways to obtain publicity and news coverage.

Guide to Public Relations for Nonprofit Organizations or, How to Avoid the Potential Perils of Relating to the Press and the Public. Los Angeles: Grantsmanship Center (1031 South Grand Avenue, 90015). $1.75.

Reaching Your Public Through the Newspaper. Marguerite Gignilliat. Nashville: American Association for State and Local History, 1968. Technical Leaflet 45. 6 pp., illus. $2 pb.

"The tool most readily available to historical societies wishing to obtain publicity in newspapers is the press release."

Reaching Your Public Through Television. Roy A. Smith. Nashville: American Association for State and Local History, 1965. Technical Leaflet 26. 8 pp., illus. $2 pb.

How to handle public service announcements, new programming and preparing for on-the-air performance.

If You Want Air Time: A Publicity Handbook. National Association of Broadcasters. 1977. Rev. ed. Washington, D.C.: NAB (1771 N Street, N.W., 20036), 1981. 18 pp. $.75.

What the radio and television stations look for.

Bob Vila, whose "This Old House" television show helped convert many to preservation while making over old houses. (Bill Schwob)

There's a lot worth saving in this country.

Today more Americans who value the best of yesterday are saving and using old buildings, waterfront areas and even neighborhoods.

Preservation saves energy, materials and the artistry of these quality structures.

Help preserve what's worth saving in your community. Contact the National Trust, P.O. Box 2800, Washington, D.C. 20013.

National Trust for Historic Preservation

One of many public service ads placed by the National Trust.

Preservation Week
May 8-14, 1983

National Trust for Historic Preservation

Logo for a National Trust Preservation Week celebration. (NTHP)

Preservation is taking care of America.

Preservation Week   May 13-19, 1984
National Trust for Historic Preservation

A well-taken care of old house, the focal point for the 1984 National Preservation Week. (Inlandesign, NTHP)

Handbook of Special Events for Nonprofit Organizations: Tested Ideas for Fund Raising and Public Relations. Edwin R. Leibert and Bernice E. Sheldon. New York: Association Press, 1972. 224 pp., biblio. $12.95.

Guidelines for special projects to dramatize various causes, from a theater party to an open house, debate to building dedication.

101 Ideas from History News. American Association for State and Local History. Nashville: AASLH, 1975. 151 pp., illus.

Useful ideas contributed by the readers of *History News*—money-making projects, exhibits and displays, special and seasonal programs, publications ideas, and volunteer and education activities, among others.

Old Glory: A Pictorial Report on the Grass Roots History Movement and the First Hometown History Primer. James Robertson, ed. For America the Beautiful Fund. New York: Warner, 1973. 192 pp., illus.

Tales of how American communities are preserving their heritage. The Primer section tells how to preserve and record personal history, family history and home-town history.

"Community Events and How to Organize Them." *Conserve Neighborhoods,* July–August 1980.

Step-by-step descriptions of various kinds of neighborhood fun and frolic. A special insert outlines the basic steps in selecting, organizing and conducting a community event.

How to Raise Money: Special Events for Arts Organizations. American Council for the Arts. New York: ACA. 32 pp. $3 pb.

A compilation of fund-raising ideas from the U.S. and Canada.

National Preservation Week

In 1973 the National Trust succeeded in making preservation official for at least one week in the year—during National Preservation Week. Since then the observance has been held annually in May, designed to provide a specific time to recognize preservation efforts and to make more Americans aware of the preservation movement and its accomplishments. The week is celebrated in cities and towns with a variety of activities, often based on the year's theme:

    State and city proclamations
    Posters and exhibits
    Tours and seminars
    Photo contests and film showings
    Awards
    Children's programs
    Ceremonial starts and finishes to preservation
    projects

For more information, write: Office of Public Affairs, National Trust, 1785 Massachusetts Avenue, N.W., Washington, D.C. 20036.

Publish or Perish

Orator Edward Everett, who stumped the nation for funds to rescue Mount Vernon over a century ago, must have been one of the greatest influences of his time, but he seems to have been unique. The idea of historic preservation was generally promulgated through literary channels.

Charles E. Peterson, "Historic Preservation U.S.A.: Some Significant Dates." *Antiques*, February 1966.

"Publications have helped build a strong communications network among preservationists. . . .Preservation publishing is steadily increasing, as evidenced by the several hundred local organizations with active newsletters, more ambitious publishing programs, trade interest in preservation-related books and the number of new government preservation publications. . . .

The concept 'publish or perish' is especially pertinent for preservation. Without creating popular support and general understanding of its purposes and techniques, preservation's future cannot be assured. . . .

Among their attributes, publications share with old buildings a number of special characteristics: They are not readily disposable; they are cost-effective and useful; they provide for greater freedom of expression and diversity; they last, in memory and form."

"Publishing for Preservation." In *Preservation: Toward an Ethic in the 1980s*. National Trust for Historic Preservation. Washington, D.C.: Preservation Press, 1980.

A handbook for rehabilitation and new construction, one of the basic preservation publications. (City of Lowell, Mass., and Anderson Notter Associates)

"Publications are a major program because they enable the [Preservation League of New York State] to provide services to and maintain communication among preservationists statewide. Publications have also helped establish the credibility of the League as a viable organization. They serve as an important membership benefit because they are the main contact many members have with the League."

Diana Waite. In "Publishing for Preservation." *Preservation News*, March 1978.

Printing It: A Guide to Graphic Techniques for the Impecunious. Clifford Burke. Berkeley, Calif.: Wingbow Press, 1972. 128 pp. $4.95 pb.

Slinging Ink: A Practical Guide to Producing Booklets, Newspapers, and Ephemeral Publications. Jan Sutter. Los Altos, Calif.: William Kaufmann (95 First Street, 94022), 1982. 152 pp. $6.95 pb.

Publishing in the Historical Society. John Walklet, Jr. 1966. Rev. ed. Nashville: American Association for State and Local History, 1973. Technical Leaflet 34. 6 pp., illus., biblio. $2 pb.

Researching, Writing, and Publishing Local History. Thomas E. Felt. Nashville: American Association for State and Local History, 1976. 180 pp., biblio., append. $9 pb.

Reaching Your Public: The Historical Society Newsletter. Charlotte S. Derby. 1967. Rev. ed. Nashville: American Association for State and Local History, 1973. 6 pp. Technical Leaflet 39. $2 pb.

How to Do Leaflets, Newsletters and Newspapers. Nancy Bingham. New York: Hastings House, 1982. 144 pp. $7.95 pb.

Publishing Newsletters. Howard Penn Hudson. New York: Scribner's, 1982. 224 pp. $17.95.

How to Produce a Small Newspaper: A Guide for Independent Journalists. Kathleen Cushman and Edward Miller. 1978. 2nd ed. rev. Harvard, Mass.: Harvard Common Press, 1983. 192 pp., illus., gloss., biblio., index. $8.95 pb.

Editing the Small Magazine. Rowena Ferguson. 2nd ed. New York: Columbia University Press, 1976. 221 pp. $9.50 pb.

Editing by Design: A Word-and-Picture Communication for Editors and Designers. Jan V. White. 1974. 2nd ed. New York: R. R. Bowker, 1982. 248 pp. $24.95 pb.

The Self-Publishing Handbook. David M. Brownstone and Irene M. Franck. New York: NAL, 1985. $7.95.

The Self-Publishing Manual: How to Write, Print, and Sell Your Own Book. Dan Poynter. Santa Barbara, Calif.: Parachute Publications (P.O. Box 4232, 93103), 1979. $14.95 hb, $9.95 pb.

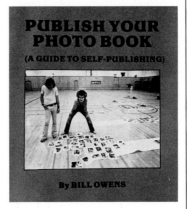

Publish Your Photo Book: A Guide to Self-Publishing. Bill Owens. Livermore, Calif.: Author (P.O. Box 687, 94550), 1979. $13.95 hb, $8.95 pb.

Book Publishing: What It Is, What It Does. John P. Dessauer. 1974. 2nd ed. New York: R. R. Bowker, 1981. 231 pp., gloss., biblio., index. $23.95 hb, $13.95 pb.

Bookmaking: The Illustrated Guide to Design and Production. Marshall Lee. 2nd ed. New York: R. R. Bowker, 1980. $32.50.

Indianapolis Architecture Guidebook: Program Package 8. Indianapolis Chapter, American Institute of Architects. Washington, D.C.: AIA Public Relations Department (1735 New York Avenue, N.W., 20006), 1977. 6 pp., illus.

"Look Homeward Angle: A Guide to Writing the City Guidebook," Martin Fischoff. *Writer's Digest*, December 1978. $2.

Guide to Book Publishing Courses: Academic and Professional Programs. Susan E. Shaffer, ed. Princeton: Peterson's Guides, 1979. 168 pp. $6.95 pb.

A Manual on Bookselling: How to Open and Run Your Own Bookstore. Sanford Cobb, ed. 3rd ed. American Booksellers Association (800 Second Avenue, New York, N.Y. 10017). New York: Crown, 1980. 416 pp. $8.95 pb.

Contacts

The Preservation Press
National Trust for
Historic Preservation
1785 Massachusetts Avenue, N.W.
Washington, D.C. 20036

In addition to publishing periodicals, books and other publications for the National Trust, provides limited advisory services to preservation publishers.

American Association for
State and Local History
708 Berry Road
Nashville, Tenn. 37204

Issues publications and sponsors occasional seminars on publishing for the history and museum profession.

Publishing Center for
Cultural Resources
625 Broadway
New York, N.Y. 10012

A nonprofit organization serving nonprofit cultural institutions by planning, producing and distributing books, pamphlets, posters and color reproductions and arranging cooperative printing projects.

Association of American
Publishers
220 East 23rd Street
New York, N.Y. 10010

The professional organization of book publishers; maintains information on publishing courses.

Plan book for Richmond, Va. (Preservation/Urban Design)

Folly Theater (1898, Louis S. Curtiss), Kansas City, Mo., which was restored through innovative ideas such as candy sales, aided by a UDAG grant.

Making Money: Some Bright Ideas

Auction
The D.C. Preservation League holds an annual Great Preservation Auction, selling such donated items as a carved sandstone lion's head from a demolished bank and the services of preservation consultants.

Bon Apetit
Popcorn from an antique popcorn wagon was sold by the Champaign County (Ill.) Historical Museum, offering a lifetime popcorn credit card for $100.

The Palladian window of the Folly Theater in Kansas City, Mo., was re-created in chocolate by Kron Chocolatier and sold to raise funds.

Camel Walk
Members of the Save Spruce Street Committee in Philadelphia walked a live camel at least a mile in a fund-raising benefit.

Fire Sale
To help finance renovations, St. Michael's Church in Chicago sold jars of ashes shoveled into the basement after the Great Chicago Fire of 1871. The price: $18.71 a jar.

Love Match
Preservationists in Fell's Point and Federal Hill in Baltimore have sponsored a tennis benefit in an old railroad station now recycled as an indoor tennis court.

Music for a Movie Theater
In 1978 Arthur Fiedler conducted the Atlanta Symphony Orchestra in a "Pops for the Fox" concert to obtain funds for Atlanta Landmarks to continue restoration of the Fox Theater.

Recycling
A "recycling for recycling" campaign in Farber, Mo., produced a million aluminum cans and $7,000 to move and restore the Illinois Central Gulf Railroad depot.

Renting History
The Pittsburgh History and Landmarks Foundation rented a two-bedroom log house to its members for weekend getaways. Other house-museum owners, including the National Trust, rent their properties for receptions, meetings and weddings.

A Star Is Born
"Heaven Can Wait," starring Warren Beatty and Julie Christie, is one of several motion pictures filmed at National Trust properties. The 1978 film was shot at Filoli in Woodside, Calif., and brought rent plus repairs and new furnishings for the house.

When "The Duchess and the Dirtwater Fox" was filmed in Georgetown, Colo., 20th Century-Fox provided a donation to the town and the Georgetown Historical Society.

Time Sharing
The Victorian Society in America "sold" the 100 years between 1800 and 1900 for $1,000 apiece. Donors received certificates—one year to a customer.

Toasting Preservation
When the Franklin Pierce Manse in Concord, N.H., was endangered by an urban renewal project and had to be moved, the state awarded $20,000 raised from the sale of bourbon in commemorative bottles depicting the New Hampshire State House.

A cache of rare wine turned up in the Ten Broeck Mansion in Albany County, N.Y., including bottles of Chateau Mouton-Rothschild 1875 and Chateau Lafite 1868. The wine was sold at auction by the Albany County Historical Association, some for $500 and $1,000 a bottle.

Wish Book
Mount Holly, N.J., community leaders published a gift catalog for residents to choose what they wanted to buy for their town—trees, bicycle racks and planters. The nine-page wish book brought in $4,000.

See also: Paying for Preservation

A walking tour of New York conducted during a meeting of the Society for Industrial Archeology. (Smithsonian Institution)

Tours

A primary step in the preservation of landmarks is public awareness of their existence, and understanding of their importance. One of the most effective means of accomplishing this is the walking tour, which can bring large numbers of people in direct contact with a landmark. An opportunity is afforded to look at the landmark and become personally, enthusiastically concerned with the need for its preservation.

The walking tour is an old concept. It can be traced to the ancients; there is no doubt that there were guides to take the pilgrims around Delphi just as they were later to take them around Jerusalem.

Henry Hope Reed

"Tours need not be conducted on a grand scale. They can be three weeks long, or over in a day. They can be in your own locality or overseas. They can involve many people or just a few, jet lines or buses, professional staff members or dedicated volunteers. They can be very complex or quite simple. Set your own pace—but do the job right."

Robert C. Wheeler, *Planning Tours for Your Local Historical Society.* Nashville: American Association for State and Local History, 1965. Technical Leaflet 25. 6 pp., illus. $2 pb.

"History Hikes: How to Put History in Your Walking Tour," Catherine Baker. *History News,* April 1981.

Pointers for tour planners based on the Oak Park, Ill., program in the Frank Lloyd Wright and Prairie School historic district.

"A Primer on Walking Tours," Henry Hope Reed. *Museum News,* November 1974.

Guidance by an eminent tour leader and founder of the Museum of the City of New York Tour Program.

See also: Architecture on Tour (Looking at the Built Environment)

Awards: Orchids and Onions

"Orchids" for the beautiful. "Onions" for the odoriferous. "Shame of the neighborhood" certificates for the unmentionable. Preservation groups are using time-honored—and some unique—ways of publicizing their goals and thanking their supporters: presenting awards to the deserving and the not-so-deserving. Awardees can be people, places, publications, organizations and businesses.

National Trust for
Historic Preservation
Honor Awards Program
1785 Massachusetts Avenue, N.W.
Washington, D.C. 20036

National Trust awards recognize the achievements of individuals and organizations active in the preservation, conservation, restoration or interpretation of the built and maritime environments and cultural landscapes in the United States. Its awards include the Lousie du Pont Crowninshield Award and certificates of commendation for public officials.

American Association for
State and Local History
708 Berry Road
Nashville, Tenn. 37204

Provides a variety of annual awards to history and historic house museums, historical societies and preservation projects.

American Society of Interior
Designers
1430 Broadway
New York, N.Y. 10018

Sponsors the Scalamandre Historic Preservation Excellence of Design Awards, which include all aspects of interior design as applied to old buildings.

American Institute of Architects
1735 New York Avenue, N.W.
Washington, D.C. 20006

Extended-use projects involving restoration, rehabilitation and adaptive use have been capturing nearly as many of the AIA's annual Honor Awards as those given for new buildings. The AIA also recognizes architects and firms, communicators, artisans and leaders in the field.

Progressive Architecture
600 Summer Street
Stamford, Conn. 06904

There is no special category for preservation or renovation, but all categories are acceptable for such designs. Awards are given for designs of buildings scheduled to be under construction the succeeding year.

Housing
1221 Avenue of the Americas
New York, N.Y. 10020

Restoration projects are recognized in the Production Houses category (a joint program with the American Institute of Architects).

Mill Race Village and Northville Historical Society, Detroit, recipients of an orchid from the American Society of Interior Designers.

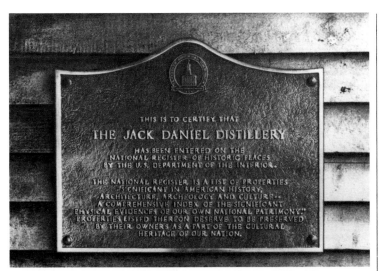

A National Register plaque, proudly displayed by Jack Daniel's (1886), the nation's oldest continuously operating distillery. (Jack Daniel Distillery)

Show and Tell: Plaques and Markers

Some advantages to using well-planned historical markers are that they provide simplified interpretation and furnish essential knowledge in capsule form—they are quickly read and understood; they may be used for both on-site and off-site interpretation; and they require no full-time interpretive personnel.

Raymond F. Pisney, "Historical Markers: Planning Local Programs"

Plaque and Marker Facts

There is no standardized plaque or marker.

Common types include designation plaques or seals, historical tour and trail markers, area map markers, interpretive markers and highway historical markers.

The National Trust does not award plaques.

The National Register of Historic Places does not present plaques, but owners of listed properties may purchase them.

National Historic Landmark owners may receive a bronze plaque from the National Park Service.

Many states and private preservation organizations have plaque programs, and most states administer marker programs.

Historical Markers: A Bibliography. Raymond F. Pisney. Verona, Va.: McClure Press (P.O. Box 936, 24482), 1977. 161 pp., index. $12 pb.

Publications on markers and marking programs are interspersed with general guidebooks in this wide-ranging compendium. The several thousand citations are divided among books (general, regional, state and foreign), pamphlets, brochures and leaflets; articles; public documents; and manuscript collections and administrative documents.

"Historical Markers: Planning Local Programs," Raymond F. Pisney. Nashville: American Association for State and Local History, 1978. Technical Leaflet 104. 8 pp., illus. $2 pb.

Overview of how to develop and manage a marker program, including discussion of subjects, research, design, costs, sizes, materials and placement.

Tombstones on Posts?: A Preview to Historical Marking. Raymond F. Pisney. Verona, Va.: McClure Press, 1976. $3.95 pb.

Criteria, funding, types of markers, research, editing, placement, fabrication, maintenance, published guides and dedications are among the topics.

Contacts

National Register of
Historic Places
National Park Service
U.S. Department of the Interior
P.O. Box 37127
Washington, D.C. 20013-7127

State Historic Preservation
Offices(*See* Preservationists)

"Today, the sponsoring organization of practically every urban conservation district provides some sort of marking system that will provide identification and some visual interpretation. Oftentimes, tour and trail markers are also used in conjunction with the building plaques to point out places of interest on urban walking and driving tours. . . .

Many state historic preservation programs are . . . devising appropriate markers which are affixed to the exteriors of National Register properties.

Another expansion in marking has been caused by the proliferation of leisure time and the automobile. . . .

Highway historical marking began initially with private sponsors. . . . Presently there is scarcely a state which does not have such a program, and several are now imposing new statewide systems of tour and trail markers over the old framework."

Raymond Pisney, *Historical Markers: A Bibliography*

Sightseers reading the historical marker outside St. Stephen's Church (1804, Charles Bulfinch), Boston, the only Bulfinch church left in the city. (Boston 200)

"Can you roller skate on an expressway?" asked these demonstrators who helped stop a Boston freeway. From *The End of the Road*. (Daniel S. Brody)

Concrete spaghetti. From *God's Own Junkyard*.

Holding Up the Highwaymen

During the 1960s a new conflict emerged in urban America—a conflict between environmentalists and developers. It was a conflict of attitudes and values, people and institutions, citizens and their government. The stakes in this new battle were high: the future of the environment, urban and rural, and the life-styles of the American people.

Some of the most dramatic conflicts between environmentalists and developers had to do with segments of the federal Interstate Highway System.

Richard O. Baumbach, Jr., and
William E. Borah, *The Second
Battle of New Orleans*

"As the Interstate system winds down and fewer and fewer new roads are constructed, road *improvements* may damage historic and cultural resources in the long run as much as new interstates. Slow encroachments on the front porches of old homes as streets are widened, increased traffic through older districts as new lanes are added to old highways, and the attendant noise, pollution, and decline in property values as more neighborhoods are misused to make room for more cars present as great a threat to the future as the remaining controversial segments of the Interstate Highway System. Thus, in spite of all the new laws, protection of our cultural heritage is likely to require more vigilant, more sophisticated citizens in the future."

Diane L. Donley, Afterword. *The Second Battle of New Orleans*

Back Routes

Road to Ruin. A. Q. Mowbray. Philadelphia: Lippincott, 1969.

Superhighway—Superhoax. Helen Leavitt. Garden City, N.Y.: Doubleday, 1970.

Highways to Nowhere. Richard Hebert. Indianapolis: Bobbs Merrill, 1972.

The Pavers and the Paved. Ben Kelley. New York: D. W. Brown, 1971.

From Streetcar to Superhighway: American City Planners and Urban Transportation, 1900–1940. Mark S. Foster. Philadelphia: Temple University Press, 1981. 246 pp., illus., index. $34.95 hb.

The evolution of the highway system and suburban sprawl and why the automobile won out over urban mass transit systems in the 1920s and 1930s.

The Second Battle of New Orleans: A History of the Vieux Carre Riverfront-Expressway Controversy. Richard O. Baumbach, Jr., and William E. Borah. University, Ala.: University of Alabama Press, 1981. For the Preservation Press. 359 pp., illus., biblio., chron., index. $27.50 hb, $12.95 pb.

The definitive case study of a highway battle—the long but successful campaign started in the 1960s to keep a highway out of the French Quarter.

Concrete Problem Solving

"The key to citizen effectiveness in influencing transportation projects and policies is public pressure. An important means of expressing concern is participation in the public hearings regarding [highway] plans."

"Highways and Preservation Issues." National Trust for Historic Preservation, 1974.

Federal Highway Laws

National Historic Preservation Act of 1966

Department of Transportation Act of 1966

Federal-Aid Highway Act of 1968

National Environmental Policy Act of 1969

Urban Mass Transportation Act of 1970

Airport-Airways Development Act of 1970

Techniques for Incorporating Historic Preservation Objectives into the Highway Planning Process. Russell Wright for National Trust for Historic Preservation. Washington, D.C.: U.S. Department of Transportation, 1974. 257 pp., appends., biblio.

Discusses cultural resource inventories as a major way to ensure that highway projects do not destroy historic properties, use of the inventory during the public hearing process and guidelines for minimizing environmental impacts of roadways.

The End of the Road: A Citizen's Guide to Transportation Problem-Solving. Dave Burwell and Mary Ann Wilner. Washington, D.C.: National Wildlife Federation and Enviornmental Action Foundation, 1977. 159 pp., illus., biblio., appends.

Explains the basics of transportation planning and how citizens can get involved.

Design, Art and Architecture in Transportation: A Directory of Technical and Financial Resources. Durham, N.H.: New England Municipal Center (P.O. Box L, 03824), 1980. 28 pp. $3 pb.

Although geared to New England, this is useful in locating programs and services of selected national, regional and state-based agencies and organizations. A companion to *Integrating Design, Art and Architecture with Local Transportation Planning: A Concept Paper for New England Municipal Officials.* June 1980. 10 pp. $2 pb.

Small-Scale Control

"Traffic is a major problem in many neighborhoods. These neighborhoods lack the defenses against traffic that now are built into suburban areas: the curved streets, cul de sacs and street patterns that discourage through traffic. Consequently, old neighborhoods frequently become saddled with high levels of through traffic and their straight streets invite speeding."

"Managing Traffic." *Conserve Neighborhoods*, January–February 1980.

Livable Streets. Donald Appleyard. Berkeley: University of California Press, 1981. 364 pp., illus., appends., biblio., index. $27.50 hb, $14.95 pb.

Evaluation of efforts to lessen excessive traffic in residential neighborhoods, including a survey of residents' attitudes towards their streets.

State of the Art Report: Residential Traffic Management. Daniel T. Smith, Jr., Donald Appleyard et al. Washington, D.C.: U.S. Department of Transportation, 1980. 172 pp., illus., appends., biblio. $6 pb. Available from GPO.

Covers control devices, emphasizing techniques for community involvement in neighborhood traffic management.

Thinking Small: Transportation's Role in Neighborhood Revitalization. Phyllis Myers and Gordon Binder. Washington, D.C.: U.S. Department of Transportation, Urban Mass Transportation Administration, 1979. 166 pp., illus., appends., biblio. $14 pb. Available from National Technical Information Service, 5285 Port Royal Road, Springfield, Va. 22161. No. PB 296-979.

Stresses small-scale solutions to transportation planning, the need for citizen involvement and governmental response, with three case studies: Boston, St. Louis and Seattle.

Improving the Residential Street Environment: Final Report. Daniel T. Smith, Jr., and Donald Appleyard. Washington, D.C.: Department of Transportation, 1981. 142 pp., illus., append. $5.50 pb. Available from GPO.

Summarizes research on residential traffic management techniques, resident preferences and legal considerations.

The Restraint of the Automobile in American Residential Neighborhoods. Howard Simkowitz, Lajos Heder and Edward Barber. Washington, D.C.: U.S. Department of Transportation, Urban Mass Tranportation Administration, 1978. 73 pp., appends., biblio. $8 pb. Available from NTIS. No. PB 287-485.

Reviews two techniques: residential parking permits and traffic restraint devices.

See also: Main Streets

Contacts

U.S. Department of Transportation
Office of the Secretary
Washington, D.C. 20590

Federal Highway Administration
U.S. Department of Transportation
Washington, D.C. 20590
(and local division offices)

Advisory Council on Historic Preservation
1100 Pennsylvania Avenue, N.W.
Suite 809
Washington, D.C. 20004

Council on Environnmental Quality
722 Jackson Place, N.W.
Washington, D.C. 20006

National Park Service
Archeological Assistance Division
P.O. Box 37127
Washington, D.C. 20013-7127

State Historic Preservation Offices(*See* Preservationists)

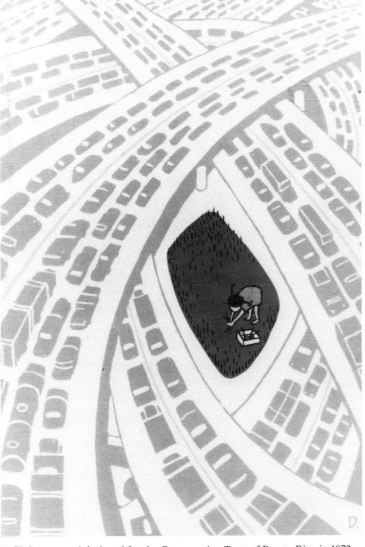

A Christmas card designed for the Conservation Trust of Puerto Rico in 1972. (Jack and Irene Delano)

"I underestimated the power of the highway lobby in this state." (Stevenson. © 1972 The New Yorker Magazine, Inc.)

Arson: Putting Out the Fires

Someone is burning our heritage, building by building.

> Curtis Hartman, "Torching History." *Boston*, February 1980.

Old or abandoned buildings offer an attractive target as do buildings that symbolize authority, such as schools and churches. In areas where arson is a problem to begin with, historic buildings burn with the rest. But in many cases, preservationists fear it may be the historic designation itself that is making the buildings so vulnerable.

> Jonathan Walters, "Arson: A Heritage in Flames." *Historic Preservation*, March–April 1981.

"Arson can take many forms. The U.S. Fire Administration has identified 24 different 'brands' of arson. . . . Some of the more common causes of arson in historic buildings are revenge, vandalism, juvenile fire setting, and arson-for-profit. Arson-for-profit can include burning a historic building to clear the land for new construction, to collect insurance, to move out existing tenants for new ones, and . . . to avoid the restrictions of historic preservation laws. . . ."

> The Conservancy Group

"Citizen organizations in Boston and New York City are now pioneering techniques to enable neighborhoods to fight arson. These organizations realize that arson is a housing and community development problem—not simply a crime to be handled by law enforcement agencies."

> "Fighting Arson." *Conserve Neighborhoods*, November–December 1979.

"Stop Arson." *Conserve Neighborhoods*, January–February 1982. 20 pp., illus. $2 pb.

A special issue outlining steps a community can take to combat arson, illustrated by examples from U.S. cities.

Anti-Arson Resources Kit. The Conservancy Group. Washington, D.C.: National Trust for Historic Preservation, 1981. $5 fireproof box.

Includes "Stop Arson" and numerous helpful and how-to brochures. A slide show and related materials also are available.

Arson Resource Directory. Herman M. Weisman, with Nancy Stone, eds. Washington, D.C.: Arson Resource Center, U.S. Fire Administration, 1982.

Identifies key resources: organizations and individuals active in arson prevention and control.

How to Fight Arson

Support programs to mothball vacant buildings

Conduct a public education program

Get to know law enforcement, fire and arson officials

Join or form a local arson task force

Attend insurance company and police and fire department seminars

Organize community-watch programs in arson-prone areas

> Kim Davis and the Conservancy Group. *Historic Preservation*, March–April 1981.

Contacts

Arson Resource Center
U.S. Fire Administration
Federal Emergency
Management Agency
Washington, D.C. 20472

The key federal agency in the anti-arson effort. Publishes *Arson Resource Exchange Bulletion*, which gives news on arson, management of anti-arson programs, investigations and prosecutions, new publications, etc.; and *Arson Control Guide for Volunteer Fire Departments*, which provides guidance in developing arson task forces and helping firefighters be alert to the symptoms of arson.

National Arson Prevention
and Action Coalition
Urban Educational Systems
153 Milk Street
Boston, Mass. 02109

Publishes *The Arson Action Guide* ($3.50), *Research: A Manual for Arson Analysis and Property Research* ($15) and *Tools: A Handbook for Anti-Arson Programs and Laws* ($10).

National Fire Protection
Association
Batterymarch Park
Quincy, Mass. 02269

Publishes *Fire Journal, Fire Service Today, Fire Service Catalog* (films, tapes and slides for sale and rental, books and phamplets), *Arson Investigation Series* (slides, tapes and manuals) and *Catalog of Firesafety Films and Audiovisuals*.

Aftermath of a 1982 fire in Lynn, Masss., showing buildings being converted to new uses. The fire started in the foreground area and heavily damaged the Vamp Building in the background. *(Lynn Daily Evening Item)*

Lucy the Elephant (1881), Margate, N.J., being moved to a new home after she was saved by her friends. (Jack E. Boucher)

The Rochester (1887), Los Angeles, en route to a new location out of harm's way.

Moving Experiences

One of the sights to stare at in America is that of a house being moved from place to place. . . . The largest house that I saw in motion was one containing two stories of four rooms each; forty oxen were yoked to it. The first few yards brought down the two stacks of chimneys, but afterwards all went well.

Mrs. Frances Trollope, *Domestic Manners of the Americans.* 1832.

"Moving a historic building is sometimes the only way to save it from demolition, but such an action should be undertaken only as a last resort when all other preservation options have been exhausted. When a historic building has been moved, it loses its integrity of setting and its 'sense of place and time'— important aspects of the historic character of a building and its environment."

Lee H. Nelson, Foreword. *Moving Historic Buildings*

Moving Historic Buildings. John O. Curtis. Washington, D.C.: U.S. Department of the Interior, Technical Preservation Services Branch, 1979. 50 pp., illus., biblio. $3.50 pb. GPO stock no. 024-016-00109-5.

The leading handbook on how to relocate a building when there is no other way to save it. Topics covered: selecting a moving contractor, licenses, the best procedure (intact, total disassembly, partial disassembly), planning the route, historical documentation, interim protection, selecting and preparing the new site, preparing the structure for the move. Includes a case study of the moving of the Gruber Wagon Works, Berks County, Pa., plus a wealth of fascinating illustrations.

Housemoving: Old Houses Make Good Neighbors. Rosaria F. Hodgdon and S. Gregory Lipton. Eugene, Ore.: Housing and Community Conservation Department (City Hall, Room 106, 777 Pearl Street, 97401), 1979. 91 pp., illus., append. $3.50 pb.

Details the types of houses that can be moved, compatible neighborhoods, preparing a house for the move, siting, modifying the structure, financing the move and obtaining required permits; with case studies.

"An 1834 Landmark House Finds a New Home," Barbara Schiller. *Old-House Journal,* May 1978.

"House moving companies are easy to come by—just look in the yellow pages under 'House and Building Movers.' They have been at their trade at least since the Revolution, for the British expressed surprise at the colonists' propensity for moving their houses around."

"Moving Experiences," W. Dale Nelson. *Historic Preservation,* July–August 1980.

"Do You Want to Move a House?" Cole Gagne. *Old-House Journal,* October 1981.

Buildings on Parade: New Homes for Old Buildings

Old Sturbridge Village, Sturbridge, Mass.

Village Crossroads, Farmers' Museum, Cooperstown, N.Y.

Greenfield Village, Dearborn, Mich.

Sharon Woods Village, Miami Purchase Association, Cincinnati

Lockerbie Square, Indianapolis, Ind.

Heritage Square, Los Angeles

Mystic Seaport, Mystic, Conn.

Heritage Park, Old Town, San Diego

Lucy the Elephant, Margate, N.J.

Strawbery Banke, Portsmouth, N.H.

Sankey Milk Bottle, Boston (from Taunton, Mass.)

Pope-Leighey House, Mount Vernon, Va.

The Lindens, Washington, D.C. (from Danvers, Mass.)

Building Roots

*R*esearch remains the key to historic preservation efforts. . . . Like the genealogist, the building researcher must use ingenuity and imagination in searching for possible new sources.

Frederick I. Olson, "Documenting American Cities' Physical History." Supplement to *Preservation News,* September 1977.

*T*he many varied resources available to those engaged in historic preservation research often make it difficult for one to know where to begin.

The resources are located in a variety of places in addition to well-known academic and public libraries. Small libraries are maintained in museums, planning offices, national professional organizations, private architectural and legal firms, historical societies and preservation organizations. Most state governments have official archives. . . . Many state universities and public libraries (especially main city libraries) have a room or collection containing information about the history of their region.

Jean Travers, ed., *Guide to Resources Used in Historic Preservation Research*

Plan for Rock Crest-Rock Glen (1912, Walter Burley Griffin), Mason City, Iowa, drawn by Marion Mahony Griffin. (Art Institute of Chicago)

American Gothic (1930) by Grant Wood. Paintings are one of the varied resources that can be used in historic preservation research. This famous depiction of an Iowa farmer and his daughter provides evidence of typical styles for midwestern farmhouses and period clothing. (Art Institute of Chicago)

Tracking the Past: What to Look For

Architectural plans and drawings
Art
Assessment records
Bibliographies
Books
Building inspection records
Cemetery records
Censuses
City directories
Conference proceedings
Deeds
Directories
Dissertations and theses
Film and videotape
Genealogical records
Guidebooks
Household inventories
Insurance records
Legal resources
Magazines
Manuscripts
Maps
Measured drawings
Newspapers
Oral history
Photographs and slides
Postcards
Reports, plans and feasibility studies
Sound recordings
Surveys and inventories
Trade catalogs
Wills

Grand entrance to the Library of Congress (1889–97, Smithmeyer and Pelz). (Library of Congress)

Archives and Libraries: Keepers of the Records

[Public archives] are treasures of so sacred a character, that the public enemy who wantonly devotes them to the flames is, by all civilized people, branded as a barbarian; and of so priceless a value, that no money could purchase them of the poorest state in the union, or replace them when once destroyed.

> Richard Bartlett, *Remarks and Documents Relating to the Preservation and Keeping of the Public Archives.* 1837.

As more organizations become involved in historic preservation the demand for easily accessible information is increasing. Established library collections are adding new subjects to their catalogs to accommodate information generated by preservationists, and many state and local organizations are starting specialized collections and cataloging them specially for the use of preservationists.

> Brigid Rapp, "Information Resources for Historic Preservation." Supplement to *Preservation News*, September 1977.

Cooperative Preservation
of Architectural Records
Prints and Photographs Division
Library of Congress
Washington, D.C. 20540

A new national center for information on architectural records throughout the United States, COPAR directs researchers to repositories in all states and assists in finding a home for materials. Found-ed to improve the problem of locating and making architectural records accessible, COPAR continues to identify repositories to expand and computerize a National Catalog of American Architectural Records. It guides the creation of state and local branches, publishes a newsletter and has issued guides to architectural research materials in New York City and Philadelphia.

Library of Congress
Washington, D.C. 20540

The library's architectural books, manuscripts, bound serials, pamphlets, photographs, drawings and related architectural records constitute perhaps the world's largest grouping of such materials. In addition to the photographic and map collections described elsewhere in this chapter, the library's Manuscript Division contains more than 40 million items of manuscripts, personal papers and organizational records, chiefly American, organized in some 10,000 collections, including the American Society of Landscape Architects holdings and records of individual architects—Olmsted, Gilbert, L'Enfant and McKim among others. Original architectural materials also include early 19th-century drawings by Latrobe, Bulfinch and Thornton and buildings of Washington, D.C.

"Architectural Collections in the Library of Congress," C. Ford Peatross. *Quarterly Journal of the Library of Congress*, July 1977.

Avery Architectural and
Fine Arts Library
Columbia University
New York, N.Y. 10017

The nation's foremost architectural library, its holdings number more than 125,000 volumes, plus 67,000 volumes in the Fine Arts Library. "It is the combination of all the classics of architecture, from 1485 on to the newest, diversified and forward-looking material, which makes the library so unique," says former Avery Librarian Adolf Placzek. The collection includes approximately 35,000 architectural drawings and 10,000 rare books.

Catalog of the Avery Memorial Architectural Library of Columbia University. Avery Architectural Library, Columbia University. 2nd ed. Boston: G. K. Hall, 1968. 19 vols. $1,590 hb. *Supplement,* 1973. 4 vols. 3,166 pp. $440 hb. *Supplement,* 1980. 4 vols. $340 hb.

Avery Architectural and Fine Arts Library (1913, McKim, Mead and White), Columbia University, New York City. (Columbia University)

HABS measured drawing of the U.S. Assay Office (1871, A. B. Mullett), Boise, Idaho. (Mark T. Wellen, HABS)

Historic American Buildings Survey Historic American Engineering Record Prints and Photographs Division Library of Congress Washington, D.C. 20540

These collections record historic architecture and engineering landmarks through historical documentation, drawings and photographs. HABS, created in 1933 as a cooperative effort of the Interior Department, AIA and Library of Congress, was one of the first major federal preservation programs. HAER was established in 1969 by the National Park Service, American Society of Civil Engineers and Library of Congress. Records comprise more than 44,000 architectural measured drawings, 102,000 photographs and 53,000 pages of written historical documentation on 19,000 sites. In addition to the following publications, directories include card catalogs, microfiche and numerous published state catalogs; a publications list is available from HABS/HAER, National Park Service, U.S. Department of the Interior, Washington, D.C. 20240.

Historic America: Buildings, Structures, and Sites. Alicia Stamm and C. Ford Peatross, eds., HABS/HAER. With a Checklist of the HABS/HAER Collections. Washington, D.C.: Library of Congress, 1983. 708 pp., illus. $29 hb. GPO stock no. 030–000–00149–4.

Historic American Buildings Series. David G. DeLong, ed. New York: Garland (136 Madison Avenue, 10016). *California.* 4 vols. *New York.* 8 vols. *Texas.* 2 vols. $109 each.

The Historic American Buildings Survey. Microfiche Edition. Introduction by C. Ford Peatross. Teaneck, N.J.: Somerset House and Chadwyck-Healey (417 Maitland Avenue, 07666), 1983. 1,400 microfiche. $4,950 complete, $20–595 individual states.

Historic American Engineering Record Catalog. Donald E. Sackheim, comp. Washington, D.C.: GPO, 1976. 193 pp., illus.

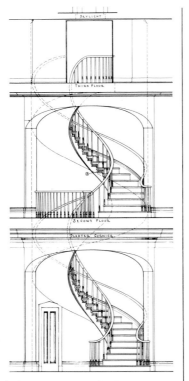

Stairway, James Lanier House (1844), Madison, Ind. (HABS)

American Institute of Architects Foundation Prints and Drawings Collection 1799 New York Avenue, N.W. Washington, D.C. 20006

The collection of more than 25,000 items includes drawings and photographs of the works of prominent architects including Thornton, Walter and Charles Greene. Richard Morris Hunt's drawings and photographs form the nucleus of the collection.

American Institute of Architects Library 1735 New York Avenue, N.W. Washington, D.C. 20006

As a guide for AIA members to its extensive holdings, the library has prepared bibliographies on more than 200 subjects. These include aesthetic and behavioral aspects of architecture, architectural practice, architecture by place, energy, preservation, housing, various building types, technical concerns and urban issues. It also maintains films and slides and provides a list of audiovisual materials for loan and sale.

"Bibliography of Bibliographies." Washington, D.C.: American Institute of Architects, 1981. 4 pp. Free to AIA members.

National Building Museum 440 G Street, N.W. Washington, D.C. 20001

Plans to create a national center to prevent the loss or dispersal of major collections of documents of national significance. It also will encourage and assist regional archives to retain such collections.

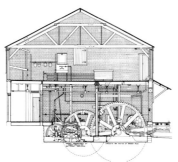

Thames Tow Boat Company Headhouse (1903), New London, Conn. (Patrick Curley and Arnold Jones, HAER)

The Athenaeum 219 South Sixth Street Philadelphia, Pa. 19106

Founded in 1814 as a library to collect materials "connected with the history and antiquities of America," it now maintains a research library specializing in 19th-century social and cultural history (to 1930). Its architecture and building technology collection, one of the country's largest, represents nearly a half million original items: drawings, manuscripts, correspondence and photographs on architects including Strickland, Walter, Notman, Haviland, Furness, Meigs and Howe. These are supplemented by some 1,000 19th-century books on architecture, trade catalogs and periodicals. A broadsheet on the archives is published regularly.

National Trust for Historic Preservation Library 1785 Massachusetts Avenue, N.W. Washington, D.C. 20036

A multimedia collection forming the largest preservation information resource in the country. Included are some 10,000 books plus periodicals, monographs, news clippings, 20,000 photographs, 30,000 slides and other audiovisual materials. Special collections include information on Trust properties, out-of-print books and local preservation publications.

Yale University Manuscripts and Archives Collection Sterling Memorial Library 1603A Yale Station New Haven, Conn. 06520

Includes the papers and drawings of Eero Saarinen plus materials on Yale buildings. The university's Art and Architecture Library maintains photographs and slides for research only, including the Carroll Meeks collection on Connecticut.

American Antiquarian Society 185 Salisbury Street Worcester, Mass. 01609

The first national historical society to be established (1812) in the United States, the society supports the largest collection of printed materials on the history and culture of the first 250 years of the country.

The Athenaeum (1847, John Notman), Philadelphia, noted for its collection on 19th-century architecture. (Jack E. Boucher, HABS)

Regional Archives

Massachusetts COPAR
P.O. Box 129
Cambridge, Mass. 02142

New York COPAR
c/o New York Chapter
American Institute of Architects
457 Madison Avenue
New York, N.Y. 10022

Northern California COPAR
c/o Architectural Foundation of
Northern California
7900 Market Street
San Francisco, Calif. 94102

New York Building Records
Collection Municipal Archives
52 Chambers Street
New York, N.Y. 10007

A comprehensive record of structures in New York's oldest area below 14th Street, including handwritten forms, correspondence, drawings and blueprints dating from the establishment of the country's first department of buildings in 1866.

New Orleans Notarial Archives
421 Loyola Avenue
New Orleans, La. 70112

Watercolor and gouache drawings from 1802 to 1918 of some 2,000 local buildings that were commissioned by the sheriff whenever any building was to be sold at public auction. The notaries' books preserved the building contracts and specifications in addition to the plan books indicating elevations, floor plans and location of the buildings.

Western Reserve
Historical Society
18025 East Boulevard
Cleveland, Ohio 44106

Has published a catalog of architectural drawings in the society collections and the Cuyahoga County Archives, *Make No Little Plans*. Michael G. Lawrence. 1980. 44 pp., illus. $5 pb.

Art Institute of Chicago
Architectural Archive
Burnham Library of
Architecture
Michigan Avenue at Adams
Chicago, Ill. 60603

Special emphasis is on Chicago architecture—the World's Columbian Exposition of 1893 and firms such as Burnham and Root and Adler and Sullivan. Included are more than 40,000 drawings and documents depicting early buildings in the Chicago area and some 18,000 photographs of American architecture. Has published a guide to architectural resources in Chicago and Cook County ($14.95).

Northwest Architectural
Archives
University of Minnesota
Libraries
Manuscripts Division
826 Berry Street
St. Paul, Minn. 55114

Holdings include architectural records from 1867 solicited from architects, engineers, contractors and others from Minnesota, Iowa, North and South Dakota and Wisconsin.

University of California
Architectural Drawing
Collection
University Art Museum
Santa Barbara, Calif. 93106

Represents many western architects such as Irving Gill, Rudolph Schindler, Myron Hunt and others; a catalog is available.

Oregon Historical Society
230 S.W. Park Avenue
Portland, Ore. 97205

Its architectural collection encompasses more than 5,000 architectural renderings drawn for Oregon houses, public buildings, bridges, etc., from the late 1800s.

National Archives (1935, John Russell Pope), facing Pennsylvania Avenue, Washington, D.C. (Abbie Rowe, National Park Service)

Canadian Centre for
Architecture
1440 West rue Sainte-Catherine
Montreal, Quebec H3G 1R8,
Canada

A collection of drawings, books and photographs of world architecture encompassing some of the earliest architectural works. The library emphasizes the history and practice of architecture in North America; the drawings include numerous Canadian buildings.

Other Research Resources

Association of Architectural
Librarians
c/o Librarian
American Institute of Architects
1735 New York Avenue, N.W.
Washington, D.C. 20006

An informal group of individuals from special architectural libraries, AIA chapters, architecture schools and firms.

ARLIS/NA
Art Libraries Society of
North America
3775 Bear Creek Circle
Tucson, Ariz. 85715

Acts as a forum for exchange of materials and information on the visual arts. Members include individuals and institutions interested in art librarianship (in public libraries, museums, galleries, art institutes, art academies, universities, colleges and publishing houses).

Society of American Archivists
330 South Wells Street
Suite 810
Chicago, Ill. 60606

A professional association that promotes the preservation and use of archives, manuscripts, current records, sound recordings, pictures, films and maps. Its publications include the journal *American Archivist* and titles on archival management.

National Historical Publications
and Records Commission
National Archives and
Records Administration
Washington, D.C. 20408

Provides financial aid to public and nonprofit organizations for the preservation and publication of historical records, including microfilming, surveys, records management and publication of records, such as the papers of presidents and other prominent Americans. State historical advisory boards cooperate with the commission.

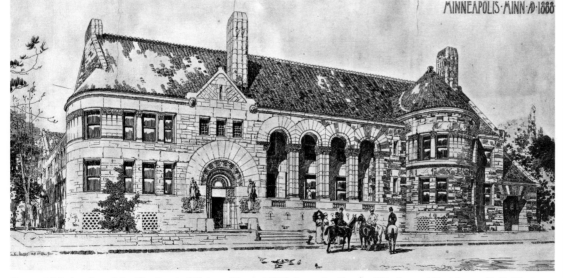

Pen and ink drawing of the Charles A. Pillsbury House (1888) drawn by Harvey Ellis for architect Leroy S. Buffington. (Northwest Architectural Archives, University of Minnesota)

Information Clearinghouses

The Information Exchange
Municipal Art Society
457 Madison Avenue
New York, N.Y. 10022
(212) 935-3960

A telephone referral service and an in-person reference center on all issues concerning the built environment and the arts, with special emphasis on New York City. It maintains files on government agencies, universities, research institutes and professional organizations and collects information about innovations and experience in planning, designing, managing and funding open-space and park improvement projects.

Livability Clearinghouse
Partners for Livable Places
1429 21st Street, N.W.
Washington, D.C. 20036

A computerized data retrieval system and information referral service on the design arts, urban affairs and environmental issues, based on projects funded by the National Endowment for the Arts, programs of the 250 members of Partners and information on related organizations and activities in the design arts.

Center for the Study
of American Architecture
Graduate School of Architecture and Planning
Avery Hall
Columbia University
New York, N.Y. 10027

Southwest Center for the Study
of American Architecture
University of Texas
Austin, Tex. 78712

Plans call for the Center to establish other regional centers to serve as local collection points for architectural records of the region, be research centers and provide seminars, study programs and fellowships.

Locators

Guide to Resources Used in Historic Preservation Research. Jean Travers and Susan Shearer. Washington, D.C.: National Trust for Historic Preservation, 1978. 26 pp.

Explains the various formats of resources used in preservation work and how to find materials from architectural plans to wills.

Library Resources in Washington, D.C., Relating to Historic Preservation. Lelahvon Lugo. Washington, D.C.: National Trust for Historic Preservation, 1977. 55 pp.

An alphabetical guide to 71 organizations, including many national preservation-related ones, describing collections of use to the preservation researcher.

Information Exchange staff. (The Information Exchange)

Architectural Research Materials in the District of Columbia. Sally Hanford, ed. Washington, D.C.: American Institute of Architects Foundation, 1982. 140 pp., index. $6.50 pb.

A guide to more than 80 repositories of source materials including associations, universities, federal agencies, libraries and museums.

Architectural Records in Boston: A Guide to Architectural Research in Boston, Cambridge, and Vicinity. Nancy Carlson Schrock, ed. New York: Garland, 1983. $35.

A directory to aid in locating materials in universities, museums and related depositories.

Directory of Archives and Manuscript Repositories. Washington, D.C.: National Historical Publications and Records Commission, 1978. 905 pp., index. $25 hb.

Contains information on 3,250 institutions, arranged alphabetically by state and town. Entries report on documents, photographs, architectural drawings, oral history collections and other source materials, with lists of institutions by type (corporate archives, religious archives, etc.) and descriptions of local public records programs in each state.

National Union Catalog of Manuscript Collections. Washington, D.C.: Library of Congress (Cataloging Distribution Service, Building 159, Navy Yard Annex, Washington, D.C. 20541), 1959–83. 21 vols. $95–100 each.

The complete series describes more than 40,000 collections in 1,000 repositories, arranged by name of collection within each volume. The listings are indexed by 440,000 references to topical subjects and personal, family, corporate and geographical names.

American Art Directory. Anne McEntire, ed. Jaques Cattell Press. New York: R. R. Bowker, 1984. 721 pp., indexes. $85 hb. Biennial.

Lists nearly 3,000 art museums, associations and schools in the U.S., Canada and abroad, including 100 corportions with art holdings or that support the visual arts. Statistics on 1,500 art libraries are presented. Includes references to state arts councils, art education programs, newspapers, scholarships and fellowhips.

Directory of Art Libraries and Visual Resource Collections in North America. Judith A. Hoffberg and Stanley W. Hess, Art Libraries Society of North America. New York: Neal-Schuman, 1982. 298 pp., indexes. $49.95.

Describes collections and policies of 1,300 libraries, museums, galleries, art schools, colleges and universities.

American Architecture and Art: A Guide to Information Sources. David M. Sokol, ed. Detroit: Gale, 1976. 341 pp., index. $55.

A bibliography on American architecture, architects, aesthetics, painters, sculptors and decorative arts.

Arts in America: A Bibliography. Bernard Karpel, ed., Archives of American Art, Smithsonian Institution. Washington, D.C.: Smithsonian Institution Press, 1979. 4 vols. Vol. 1: Includes architecture, decorative arts, design, sculpture. 2,800 pp. $190 hb set.

An authoritative research tool representing annotated entries selected by experts in these subjects.

Art Books, 1950–1979. New York: R. R. Bowker, 1979. 1,500 pp., index. $75 hb. *Art Books, 1876–1949.* 1981. 780 pp., index. $85. *Arts Books, 1980–1984.* 1984. 650 pp. $65.

Covers 100 years of Library of Congress cataloging of American titles on art, architecture, historic sites, antiquities, city planning and related topics, listing 21,000 books by subject. Also describes 2,000 museum collections worldwide.

Art Index. New York: H. W. Wilson Company. Vols. 1–8: 1929–53. $55 each. Vols. 9–18: 1953–70. $105 each. Vols. 19–31: 1971–83. Set sold as service to subscribers.

A quarterly author and subject index to publications in preservation, archeology, architecture, art history, city planning, interior design, landscape architecture, museology and related design subjects.

Art and Archeology Technical Abstracts. International Institute for Conservation of Historic and Artistic Works.

Technical articles, news items, books and other publications are abstracted, with general books and reviews in archeology, scientific analysis, technology and art included when of value as reference works. Available in conservation libraries.

Avery Index to Architectural Periodicals. Columbia University, ed. 2nd ed. Boston: G. K. Hall, 1973. 15 vols. $1,485. *First Supplement.* 2nd ed. 1975. $145. *Third Supplement.* 1979. $140.

The most comprehensive index for the fields of architecture, planning and decorative arts, arranged alphabetically by subject. Available in major libraries.

The Architectural Index. Boulder, Colo.

Annual index to articles appearing in *Architecture, Architectural Record, Housing, Interior Design, Interiors, Journal of Architectural Education, Journal of Architectural Research, Landscape Architecture, Progressive Architecture, Research and Design* and *Residential Interiors.* Available in major libraries.

Directory of Historical Societies and Agencies in the United States and Canada. Donna McDonald. 12th ed. Nashville: American Association for State and Local History, 1982. 416 pp., illus., index. $36 pb.

Describes 6,000 historical societies' library and research capacity and special emphases; includes federal records centers. To be enlarged in 1985.

Directory of Planning and Urban Affairs Libraries in the United States and Canada 1980. Chicago: Council of Planning Librarians (1313 East 60th Street, 60637), 1980. 112 pp., append., index. $15 pb.

Includes information on library holdings, services, special strengths and publications.

American Library Directory. Jaques Cattell Press, ed. New York: R. R. Bowker, 1984. 2 vols. 2,050 pp., indexes. $110 hb. Biennial.

Lists all libraries in the United States, by city, with brief notes about special collections.

Focus: A Design Arts Film and Video Guide. Mary Burton, ed. Washington, D.C.: Partners for Livable Places (1429 21st Street, N.W., 20036), 1981. 62 pp., index. $5 pb.

A compendium of film and video programs on architecture, architectural history, preservation, adaptive use, urban and regional planning, landscape design, and graphic, industrial, interior and fashion design.

Architectural Records

Q: *What are architectural records?*

A: *They are the graphic and written records of the built environment. They are drawings, renderings, blueprints, and photographs. They are contracts, personal and business correspondence, office records, diaries, change orders, specifications. . . .*

Q. *Where are they?*

A: *In libraries, museums, historical societies, government agencies, building departments, architects' offices, closets, attics, cellars. . . .*

Cooperative Preservation of
Architectural Records

"Architectural records are the unrefined raw material from which architectural history is developed. Preservationists have discovered the value of these records for interpretive studies of historic sites and for architectural planning in restoration and adaptive use."

Michael E. Wilson, "Managing Architectural Records." Supplement to *Preservation News,* March 1977.

"It is as important to save architectural records as it is to save the buildings themselves. These records consist of renderings, image sketches, underlays, tracings, specifications, business correspondence, financial data and reports. They document specific buildings and present evidence on the careers of individual architects that is unavailable anywhere else. Such records all too often do not survive their creators, much less the buildings they depict. Yet they are invaluable for the study of architecture and can be of exceptional aid to preservationists. They frequently are of intrinsic artistic merit and always are historically significant."

Alan K. Lathrop, "Architectural Records: A Heritage on Paper." *Historic Preservation,* October–December 1973.

"The Provenance and Preservation of Architectural Records," Alan K. Lathrop. *American Archivist,* Summer 1980.

Records in Architectural Offices: Suggestions for the Proper Organization, Storage, and Conservation of Architectural Office Archives. Cambridge: Massachusetts COPAR, 1981. $5.

Collecting and Preserving Architectural Records. Enid Thornton Thompson. Nashville: American Association for State and Local History, 1980. Technical Leaflet 132. 8 pp. $2 pb.

"Collecting and Preserving Architectural Drawings: An Archival Crisis." Tape-recorded conference session. $8.80. Available from Liberty Audio, 824 West Broad Street, Richmond, Va. 23220.

Index of American Architectural Drawings Before 1900. Charlottesville, Va.: American Association of Architectural Bibliographers, 1957. 24 pp. *Supplement,* 1958.

American Architectural Drawings: A Catalogue of Original and Measured Drawings of Buildings of the United States of America to December 31, 1917. George S. Koyl, ed., with Moira B. Mathieson. Philadelphia: Philadelphia Chapter, American Institute of Architects, 1969. 5 vols. *Supplement,* 1978. John Harbison, ed.

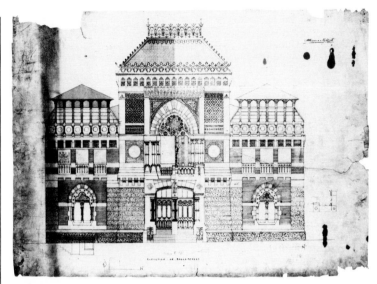

Drawing by Atkinson and Myhlerts of the Pennsylvania Academy of the Fine Arts (1876, Frank H. Furness), Philadelphia. (Academy of the Fine Arts)

Architectural Drawings: Ideas Materialized

Buildings not only change in a more or less natural way; they are often torn down, neglected, renovated, or added on to. In such situations, the architectural drawing offers valuable evidence about what once was. The architect's initial drawings preserve at least a simulacrum of his original intentions and the client's original expectations. . . . Since the first architect, talking to a workman, used a stick to mark on the dirt an idea about a building, the majority of architectural drawings have been regarded pretty much as instrumentalities or tools produced without artistic intentions other than to help effect the realization of architecture in three dimensions. Nonetheless, a great many architectural drawings appeal to us as works of art even though, and perhaps for the very reason, that they are highly technical. While they may confuse us, they also have the capacity to astonish us by their complexity.

Robert A. M. Stern, Introduction. *The Architect's Eye*

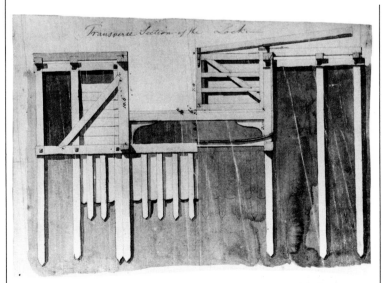

Innovative design for Washington, D.C., canal locks (c.1810, Benjamin H. Latrobe). From *The Engineering Drawings of Benjamin Henry Latrobe.*

"In architectural designs ideas are materialized. Frequently, the realism of a drawing bridges the final communication gap between the architect and his client. Therefore, to the architect, the drawing—be it an elaborate rendering or a quick sketch—is still the most important sales tool. Architect Philip Johnson, F.A.I.A., has said that clients like drawings better than buildings."

Alfred M. Kemper, *Drawings by American Architects*

The Architect's Eye: American Architectural Drawings from 1799–1978. Deborah Nevins and Robert A. M. Stern. New York: Pantheon, 1979. 175 pp., illus. $45 hb.

Two Hundred Years of American Architectural Drawing. David Gebhard and Deborah Nevins. New York: Whitney Library of Design, 1977. 306 pp., illus., biblio., index.

Masterpieces of Architectural Drawing. Helen Powell and David Leatherbarrow, eds. New York: Abbeville, 1983. 192 pp., illus., index. $45 hb.

Chicago Architects Design: A Century of Architectural Drawings from the Art Institute of Chicago. John Zukowsky, Pauline Saliga and Rebecca Rubin. New York: Rizzoli, 1984. 192 pp., illus. $25 pb.

Honor and Intimacy: Drawings of the AIA Gold Medal Winners. Essay by Richard Guy Wilson. Washington, D.C.: American Institute of Architects Foundation, 1984. $6 pb.

Architecture of the 20th Century in Drawings. Vittorio Magnago Lampugnani. New York: Rizzoli, 1982. 192 pp., illus., index. $35 hb.

The Architect as Artist. Jill Lever and Margaret Richardson. New York: Rizzoli, 1984. 144 pp., illus. $25 hb.

Drawings by American Architects. Alfred M. Kemper with Sam Mori and Jacqueline Thompson. New York: Wiley, 1973. 613 pp., illus., index.

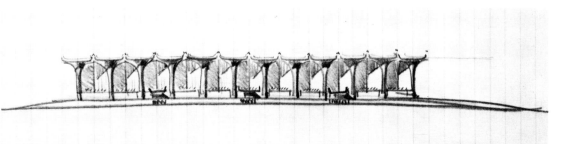

Architect Eero Saarinen's elevation study for Washington Dulles International Airport (1962), Chantilly, Va., a landmark of the modern movement epitomizing the age of flight. (Yale University Library)

The Architectural Drawing: Its Development and History, 1300–1950. Carole Cable. Monticello, Ill.: Vance Bibliographies, 1978. A–16. 18 pp. $3.80 photocopy.

Sources for American Architectural Drawings in Foreign Collections: A Preliminary Survey Carried Out Under a Grant from the Ford Foundation. James C. Massey. Washington, D.C.: Historic American Buildings Survey, U.S. Department of the Interior, 1969. 140 pp., illus., plans.

Architectural Drawing: The Art and the Process. Gerald Allen and Richard Oliver. New York: Whitney Library of Design, 1981. 200 pp., color illus. $35 hb.

How to Read Architectural Drawings. C. P. Atkins and J. P. Graham. 1956. Rev. reprint. Chicago: United States Gypsum (101 South Wacker Drive, 60606), 1983. 62 pp., illus. Free.

Master Drawings

Thomas Jefferson's Architectural Drawings with Commentary and a Check List. Frederick D. Nichols. 3rd ed., rev. Charlottesville: University Press of Virginia, 1961. 46 pp., illus. $3.95 pb.

The Engineering Drawings of Benjamin Henry Latrobe. Darwin H. Stapleton, ed., Maryland Historical Society. New Haven: Yale University Press, 1980. 256 pp., illus., appends., biblio., index. $95 hb.

H. H. Richardson and His Office: Selected Drawings. James F. O'Gorman. 1974. Cambridge: MIT Press, 1979. 220 pp., illus. $55 hb.

The Drawings of Louis Henry Sullivan: A Catalogue of the Frank Lloyd Wright Collection at the Avery Architectural Library. Paul E. Sprague. Foreward by Adolf K. Placzek. Princeton: Princeton University Press, 1979. 214 pp., illus. $50 hb.

Drawings and Plans of Frank Lloyd Wright: The Early Period (1893–1909). Frank Lloyd Wright. 1910. Reprint. New York: Dover, 1983. 112 pp., illus. $7.95 pb.

Frank Lloyd Wright: Three Quarters of a Century of Drawings. Alberto Izzo and Camillo Gubitosi. 1976. New York: Horizon, 1982. 200 pp., color illus., chron., biblio. $30 hb, $18.50 pb.

The Notebooks and Drawings of Louis I. Kahn. Richard S. Wurman and Eugene Feldman, eds. 2nd ed. Cambridge: MIT Press, 1974. 75 pp., illus., index.

Ludwig Mies van der Rohe: Drawings in the Collection of the Museum of Modern Art. Ludwig Glaeser. Cambridge: MIT Press, 1974. 72 pp., illus.

Le Corbusier Sketchbooks. Architectural History Foundation. Vol. 1: *1914–1948.* 456 pp., illus. $165. Vol. 2: *1950–1954.* 444 pp., color illus. $165. Vol. 3: *1954–1957.* 520 pp., illus. $165. Vol. 4: *1954–1964.* 520 pp., illus. $165. Cambridge: MIT Press, 1981–82.

Giovanni Battista Piranesi: Drawings in the Pierpont Morgan Library. Giovanni Battista Piranesi. New York: Dover, 1978. 121 pp., illus. $8.50 pb.

Piranesi. Nicholas Penny. New York: Hippocrene, 1980. 88 pp., illus. $15.95 pb.

See also: The Master Builders, Pattern Books (Looking at the Built Environment)

Brooklyn Mercantile Library (P. B. Wight). (Art Institute of Chicago)

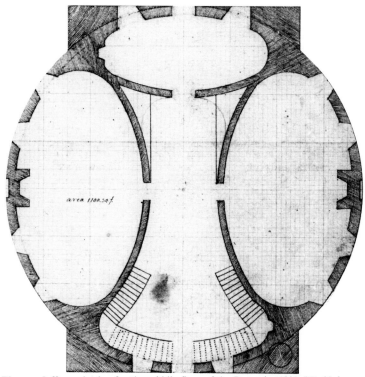

Thomas Jefferson's plan for the middle floor of the Rotunda (1823–26), University of Virginia, Charlottesville. (Library of Congress)

Stereographic view of West Main Street, Mystic, Conn., c. 1869, by one of the town's first photographers, E. A. Scholfield. (Mystic Seaport)

The Camera's Record

The time in which we are living might well be known as the age of photography. It is at least possible to believe that of all the wonderful discoveries or inventions of the nineteenth century that photography is the most important, and that it will prove more far-reaching in its effects than any other since the invention of printing. . . . Printing can only record what man knows or thinks; photography can record many things which man does not know and has not seen, much less understand. . . . Within limits it is an accurate statement of what was. Hence, photography is one of the most valuable of the tools of science, at once a means of research and an invaluable, because impersonal, record. Its applications are infinite, and we are probably only at the beginning of them. . . . It will make history something different in the future from what it has been in the past.

Kenyon Cox. *Scribner's Magazine*, May 1898.

Training dogs in front of photographer E. A. Hegg's photo studio, Skagway, Alaska, c. 1898. (University of Washington Libraries)

"Imagination often romanticizes our sense of the past, whether the memories are our own or those gleaned from tradition or textbooks. For better or worse, photography enables us to remember with a more factual perspective the way life has been since the invention of the camera."

Mame Warren, Introduction. *The Train's Done Been and Gone: An Annapolis Portrait, 1859–1910*

"Photographs present the historian with a visual record of a 'moment in time' stopped indefinitely for his inspection. As such, it provides a direct record of how things and people looked, in a way that endless accounts of written records could never achieve. . . . One of the greatest qualities of the photograph in the long run is the way in which it presents a changing model of a culture over time."

Arthur C. Townsend, "Interpreting the Historical Photograph." In *The Train's Done Been and Gone: An Annapolis Portrait, 1859–1910*

"A frequent lack of appreciation of photographic techniques still lingers. Verbal sources continue to maintain the favor of many historians, even though the information to be derived from thorough exploitation of even a single image often produces startling results. Combined with related sources, the results may be all that much the better."

Richard Rudisill, "The Photograph: A Source Often Overlooked." Supplement to *Preservation News*, July 1978.

Silver Cities: The Photography of American Urbanization, 1839–1915. Peter Bacon Hales. Philadelphia: Temple University Press, 1984. 315 pp., illus., index. $47.95 hb.

Photography and the American Scene: A Social History, 1839–1889. Robert Taft. 1938. Reprint. New York: Dover, 1964. 546 pp., illus., appends., biblio., index. $6 pb.

"Mirrors of the Past: Historical Photography and American History." In *Artifacts and the American Past.* Thomas J. Schlereth. Nashville: American Association for State and Local History, 1980. 294 pp., illus., appends., index. $15.95 hb.

Historic Photographs: Collection and Care

"As yesterday's photographs are secured and their significance more deeply understood, we will come to regard them properly as precious documents, opening new visual windows to our pasts and enlarging our pictorial curiosities. . . . The existence of an increasing resource of photographs must alter the present-day attitude of the archivist, the librarian, the curator, and the historian about them. As these people become more familiar with photographs, adopt critical views about their significance, learn to recognize valuable and pertinent historical images, they must also develop the skills to preserve and restore old and new photographs in their collections."

Robert A. Weinstein and Larry Booth, *Collection, Use and Care of Historical Photographs*

Collection, Use and Care of Historical Photographs. Robert A. Weinstein and Larry Booth. Nashville: American Association for State and Local History, 1977. 236 pp., illus. $20 hb.

An authoritative handbook on the collection, identification, handling, preservation, restoration and storage of photographs, old and recent. It also surveys the use of photographs as primary historical source material.

Shoots: A Guide to Your Family's Photographic Heritage. Thomas L. Davies. Danbury, N.H.: Addison House, 1977. 72 pp., illus., appends., biblio., index.

A useful guide to the restoration and archival preservation of photographs for the beginning photohistorian.

Collecting Old Photographs. Margaret Haller. New York: Arco, 1977. 264 pp., illus.

A reference work covering history, processes, landmark dates, inventors, museum collections, photo types and language of the field.

Collector's Guide to Nineteenth-Century Photographs. William B. Welling. New York: Macmillan, 1976. 224 pp., illus. $7.95 pb.

"Conserving and Restoring Photographic Collections," Eugene Ostroff. *Museum News*, May, September, November, December 1974. American Association of Museums, 1055 Thomas Jefferson Street, N.W., Washington, D.C. 20007. Reprints $1.25.

Photohistories: Places Recaptured

Photographs and drawings and sketches of buildings, just like the pictures of our family and ancestors, allow us glimpses into the past that really are unattainable any other way. The visual depiction of the form and style of old buildings, their character, their setting in or near the city or on a farm, the interplay of textures on old and weathered materials, the intricate architectural details, the many origins of American architecture provide a background for the words of oral and written histories. Pictures of the buildings that served as the backdrop to our ancestors' daily life make our perception of that life just that much clearer.

> David Weitzman, *Underfoot: A Guide to Exploring America's Past*

America's Yesterdays: Images of Our Lost Past. Oliver Jensen. New York: American Heritage Publishing Company, 1978. 352 pp., illus.

New England Past: Photographs 1880–1915. Jane Sugden, ed. Text by Norman Kotker. New York: Abrams, 1981. 298 pp., illus.

Night Train at Wiscasset Station: A Maine Retrospect. Lew Dietz. Foreword by Andrew Wyeth. New York: Doubleday, 1977.

Historic Portsmouth. James L. Garvin. Somersworth, N.H.: New Hampshire Publishing Company, 1974. 158 pp., illus.

A New England Town in Early Photographs: Illustrations of Southbridge, Massachusetts, 1878–1930. Edmund V. Gillon, Jr., ed. New York: Dover, 1976. 176 pp., illus. $6 pb.

A Photographic History of Cambridge. Cambridge Historical Commission. Cambridge: MIT Press, 1984. 188 pp., illus., biblio. $9.95 pb.

Nantucket in the 19th Century. Clay Lancaster. New York: Dover, 1979. 125 pp., illus. $7.95 pb.

This Was Connecticut: Images of a Vanished World. Martin W. Sandler. Boston: Little, Brown, 1977. 224 pp., illus.

The Hudson River, 1850–1918: A Photographic Portrait. Jeffrey Simpson. Tarrytown, N.Y.: Sleepy Hollow Press, 1981. 208 pp., illus., biblio., index. $29.95 hb.

Long Island: People and Places, Past and Present. Bernie Bookbinder. Newsday Books. New York: Abrams, 1983. 256 pp., color illus., biblio., append., index. $30 hb.

Old New York in Early Photographs, 1853–1901. Mary Black. 2nd rev. ed. New York: Dover, 1976. 228 pp., illus. $8.95 pb.

Nineteenth-Century New York in Rare Photographic Views. Frederick S. Lightfoot, ed. New York: Dover, 1981. 151 pp., illus. $6.95 pb.

New York 1900: Metropolitan Architecture and Urbanism 1890–1915. Robert A. M. Stern, Gregory Gilmartin and John Massengale. New York: Rizzoli, 1983. 440 pp., illus., index. $60 hb.

New York in the Thirties. Berenice Abbott. 1939. Reprint. New York: Dover, 1973. 97 pp., illus. $6.50 pb.

New York in the Forties. Andreas Feininger. Text by John von Hartz. New York: Dover, 1978. 181 pp., illus. $6.95 pb.

Old Brooklyn in Early Photographs, 1865–1929. William Lee Younger. New York: Dover, 1978. 174 pp., illus. $7.95 pb.

Nineteenth-Century Photography in Philadelphia: 250 Historic Prints from the Library Company of Philadelphia. Kenneth Finkel. Magnolia, Mass.: Peter Smith, 1980. 226 pp., illus., append., index. $18 pb.

Old Washington, D.C., in Early Photographs. Robert Reed. New York: Dover, 1979. 240 pp., illus. $7.95 pb.

Maryland Time Exposures, 1840–1940. Mame Warren and Marion E. Warren. Baltimore: Johns Hopkins University Press, 1984. 334 pp., illus., biblio. $37.50 hb.

Baltimore: When She Was What She Used to Be. A Pictorial History, 1850–1930. Marion E. Warren and Mame Warren. Baltimore: Johns Hopkins University Press, 1983. 160 pp., illus. $29.95 hb.

The Train's Done Been and Gone: An Annapolis Portrait, 1859–1910. Marion E. Warren and Mary Elizabeth Warren. Boston: Godine and M. E. Warren, 1976. 96 pp., illus. $19.95.

Chesapeake and Ohio Canal Old Picture Album. Thomas F. Hahn. Shepherdstown, W.Va.: American Canal and Transportation Center (P.O. Box 842, 25443), 1976. 104 pp., illus. $4.95 pb.

Vanishing Georgia. Sherry Konter, Georgia Department of Archives and History. Athens: University of Georgia Press, 1982. 239 pp., illus. $24.95 hb.

The Forgotten Frontier: Florida Through the Lens of Ralph Middleton Munroe. Arva Moore Parks. Miami: Banyan Books, 1977. 178 pp., illus., index. $29.95 hb.

Chicago at the Turn of the Century in Photographs. Larry A. Viskochil, Chicago Historical Society. New York: Dover, 1984. 144 pp., illus., index. $8.95 pb.

Second View: The Rephotographic Survey Project. Paul Berger, Mark Klett et al. Albuquerque: University of New Mexico Press, 1984. 224 pp., illus. $75.

Santa Fe Then and Now. Sheila Morand with John Swenson. Santa Fe: Sunstone Press, 1984. 96 pp., illus. $14.95 pb.

Through Camera Eyes. Nelson Wadsworth. Salt Lake City: Brigham Young University Press, 1975. 180 pp., illus., biblio., index.

Frank Matsura: Frontier Photographer. JoAnn Roe. Seattle: Madrona Publishers, 1981. 144 pp., illus. $27.50 hb.

Klondike Lost: A Decade of Photographs by Kinsey and Kinsey. Norm Bolotin. Anchorage: Alaska Northwest Publishing Company, 1980. 128 pp., illus., biblio. $12.95 pb.

Commercial Los Angeles, 1925–1947: Photographs from the "Dick" Whittington Studio. Bill Bradley, ed. Glendale, Calif.: Interurban Press (P.O. Box 6444, 91205), 1981. 144 pp., illus., biblio. $14.95 pb.

In This Proud Land: America 1935–43 as Seen in the FSA Photographs. Roy Emerson Stryker and Nancy Wood. Boston: New York Graphic Society, 1975. 192 pp., illus., biblio. $12.95 pb.

Yesterday's Cities Series. Miami: E. A. Seemann (8766 S.W. 129th Terrace, 33176), 1971 to present. $5.95–14.95. List available.

Pictorial histories of Akron, Atlanta, Augusta, Ga., Birmingham, Ala., California, Chicago, Columbus, Ohio, Connecticut, Florida, Florida Keys, Indiana, Los Angeles, Massachusetts, Memphis, Miami, Milwaukee, Palm Beach, Philadelphia, San Diego, Sarasota, Tampa, Washington, D.C.

Portraits of American Cities Series. Norfolk, Va.: Donning Company (5659 Virginia Beach Boulevard, 23502), 1974 to present. $18.95 hb, $14.95 pb. List available.

Photohistories with introductory essays written by local authors on more than 65 cities, from Anchorage, Alaska, to Spartanburg, S.C.

Fairmount Waterworks (1812–72, Frederick Graff), Philadelphia, photographed in 1876 by James Cremer. (Library Company of Philadelphia)

Postcard of the never-built Ararat Temple, c. 1908, Kansas City, Mo. From *Postcards from Old Kansas City.*

Twilight at Dreamland, Coney Island, N.Y., in 1905. From *Coney Island: A Postcard Journey to the City of Fire.*

The Courthouse on the Public Square, Norwalk, Ohio. From the National Trust postcard collection.

Postcards: History by Mail

The American picture postcard made its debut at the World's Columbian Exposition in Chicago on May 1, 1893. . . . Today old postcards are more than diverting bits of memorabilia—they are an important visual resource that not only document historic architecture but also capture early social habits, clothing and transportation.

Historic Preservation, May–June 1981.

"These cards . . . bearing illustrations of late nineteenth and early twentieth century buildings, furnish a panorama of American architecture and may supply both students of architecture and of local history with hard-to-find views of structures no longer standing."

> Elizabeth K. Freyschlag, "Picture Postcards: Organizing a Collection." *Special Libraries*, May–June 1980.

Picture Postcards in the United States, 1893–1918. Dorothy B. Ryan. 1976. New York: Clarkson Potter, 1982. 288 pp., illus. $24.95 hb, $10.95 pb.

Prairie Fires and Paper Moons: The American Photographic Postcard, 1900–1920. Hal Morgan and Andreas Brown. Boston: Godine, 1981. 208 pp., illus. $25 hb, $15.95 pb.

Collecting Postcards in Colour, 1894–1914. William Duval and Valerie Monahan. Dorset, England: Blandford Press, 1978. Distributed by Sterling Publishing. 176 pp., illus. $10.95 hb.

Collecting Postcards in Colour, 1914–1930. Valerie Monahan. Dorset, England: Blandford Press, 1980. Distributed by Sterling Publishing. 176 pp., illus.

Postcard Collections in the Local Historical Society. Charles J. Semovich and Enid T. Thompson. Nashville: American Association for State and Local History, 1979. Technical Leaflet 116. 8 pp. $2 pb.

Roadside New England, 1900–1955. R. Brewster Harding. Portland, Maine: Old Port Publishing (422 Fore Street, 04101), 1982. 80 pp., illus. $9.95 pb.

A Pennsylvania Album: Picture Postcards, 1900–1930. George Miller. University Park: Pennsylvania State University Press, 1979. 160 pp., illus. $18.75 hb, $12.50 pb.

Coney Island: A Postcard Journey to the City of Fire. Richard Snow. New York: Brightwaters Press, 1984. 120 pp., color illus. $24.95 hb.

Postcards from Old Kansas City. Mrs. Sam Ray. Kansas City, Mo.: Historic Kansas City Foundation (20 West Ninth Street, 64105), 1980. 48 pp. $9.50 pb.

Hooray for Hollywood. Jim Heimann. San Francisco: Chronicle Books, 1984. 96 pp., illus. $7.95 pb.

Greetings from Los Angeles: A Visit to the City of Angels in Postcards. Kerry Tucker. Cambridge: Steam Press, 1982. 112 pp., color illus. $8.95 pb.

Monterey Bay Yesterday: A Nostalgic Era in Postcards. Betty Lewis. Santa Cruz, Calif.: Western Tanager Press, 1977. 124 pp., illus. $3.98.

Trolleys and Streetcars on American Postcards. Ray D. Applegate. New York: Dover, 1979. 87 pp., illus. $5 pb.

Thirty-Two Picture Postcards of Old American Cities Series. New York: Dover. 16 pp., illus. $2.25–2.95 pb each.

Old Knoxville Postcards. William J. MacArthur. Knoxville: University of Tennessee Press, 1982. 16 pp., illus. $3.95 pb.

Wish I Were Here: 19 Vintage Tourist Postcards for the Armchair Traveler. Hal Morgan and Kerry Tucker. Cambridge: Steam Press, 1982. 16 pp., color illus. $4.95 pb.

Lost America Postcards. John Margolies. New York: Dial Press, 1982. 12 pp., color illus.

Contact

Deltiologists of America
10 Felton Avenue
Ridley Park, Pa. 19078

Files begun in 1892 contain 1 million postcards of the world, historical events, world's fairs, expositions and community scenes and are available by mail.

Photographer D. W. Butterfield taking a photograph of Refectory Hill, Franklin Park, Boston, 1892. (Olmsted National Historic Site, NPS)

Architectural Photography: A System for Looking

The nice thing about architectural photography is that it . . . provides an excuse and something of a system for looking at buildings. . . . The finder of the camera helps us to see architecture in a different way; with a telephoto lens, we'll see even more than we saw before. Very likely the excitement you felt when you looked close-up at that old daguerreotype of your great-great-grandfather will happen again as you discover an expressive little stone carving high up on that plain old warehouse down the street.

David Weitzman, "Historical Buildings." In *Underfoot: An Everyday Guide to Exploring America's Past*

"Got it!" (Alan Dunn. © 1972 The New Yorker Magazine, Inc.)

Architectural Photography: Techniques for Architects, Preservationists, Historians, Photographers, and Urban Planners. Jeff Dean. Nashville: American Association for State and Local History, 1982. 144 pp., illus., appends., biblio., index. $20.95 hb.

The first guide to focus on architectural photography for 35mm equipment rather than large-format view cameras. Explained in language for the nonprofessional are perspective control, film, sun and sky, the basics of composition, interiors and also medium- and large-format photography. Includes lists of camera suppliers and photographic organizations.

Recording Historic Buildings. Harley J. McKee. Washington, D.C.: Historic American Buildings Survey, U.S. Department of the Interior, 1976. 176 pp., illus., biblio., index.

The basic handbook to preparing pictorial and historical documentation of historic sites based on HABS procedures. Topics include organizing a survey, measured drawings, photographs and graphic material, documentation and specialized recording techniques.

The Photography of Architecture and Design: Photographing Buildings, Interiors and the Visual Arts. Julius Shulman. New York: Whitney Library of Design, 1977. 238 pp., illus., index. $27.50 hb.

A guide by an architectural photographer covering the tools and the techniques—composition, effects of sunlight and shadows and lighting interiors, with case studies.

Architectural Photography. Eric de Mare. London: B. T. Batsford Ltd. (4 Fitzhardinge Street, W1H OAH), 1975. 96 pp., illus.

Presents a series of photographs illustrating such subjects as townscape, texture, detail, architecture without architects, etc.

"Suggestions for Producing Publishable Photographs," Jack E. Boucher. Washington, D.C.: Preservation Press, 1976. 4 pp.

A checklist on cameras, film, lighting, composition, distortion, lenses and the darkroom.

Architectural Photography. John Veltri. Garden City, N.Y.: Amphoto Books, 1974. 190 pp., illus., biblio.

A general guide focusing on new architecture and covering the photographic approach to architecture, equipment and uses, film, printing processes and photographic communication.

Photographing Historic Buildings. Terry Buchanan. London: Royal Commission on Historical Monuments, 1983. 128 pp., illus., index. $14.95 pb. Available from HMSO, Kraus-Thomson Organization Ltd., Route 100, Millwood, N.Y. 10546.

A heavily illustrated guide covering exteriors and interiors as well as basic techniques. Interior details are discussed detail by detail.

"An Amateur's Guide to Architectural Photography," Daniel D. Reiff. *Historic Preservation*, January–March 1975.

An overview with explanatory photographs.

Planning for Exterior Work on the First Parish Church, Portland, Maine: Using Photographs as Project Documentation. John Hecker and Sylvanus Doughty. Washington, D.C.: U.S. Department of the Interior, 1979. HCRS no. 20. 55 pp., illus., append.

Case study showing how photographs can be used as an important part of the planning process for preservation.

"How to Photograph a Restoration: Advice From a Pro," Gary Walther. *Americana*, January–February 1980.

The Architectural Photography of Hedrich-Blessing. Robert A. Sobieszek, ed. New York: Holt, Rinehart and Winston, 1984. 92 pp., illus., index. $25 hb.

Contact

Architectural Photographers Association
435 North Michigan Avenue
Chicago, Ill. 60611

Photogrammetry

"Photogrammetry is the science of measuring by means of photography . . . concerned always with the geometrical relationships between photographic images and the real objects and space recorded upon these images. . . .

A major application of photogrammetry is the recording of cultural resources. Photogrammetric recording is a two-stage process, involving 1) photography and survey control upon the site, and 2) orientation of the photographs and measurement or plotting in the laboratory.

Because all the data is secured in the first stage of photography on the site, photogrammetry is an efficient and quick method for recording structures. . . ."

Perry E. Borchers, *Photogrammetric Recording of Cultural Resources*

Photogrammetric Recording of Cultural Resources. Perry E. Borchers. Washington, D.C.: Technical Preservation Services, U.S. Department of the Interior, 1977. 38 pp., illus., biblio.

Rectified Photography and Photo Drawings for Historic Preservation. J. Henry Chambers. Washington, D.C.: Technical Preservation Services, U.S. Department of the Interior, 1975.

"Witness for the Preservation." *Progressive Architecture*, September 1975.

Measured Drawings for Architects. Robert Chitham. New York: Nichols Publishing, 1980. 128 pp., illus., biblio., index. $17.50 pb.

Contact
American Society of Photogrammetry 210 Little Falls Street Falls Church, Va. 22046

Publishes a monthly journal that includes the names and addresses of leading photogrammetric concerns.

Tips on Photographing Buildings
1. If possible, use a perspective correction lens on a 35mm camera to eliminate distortion common in architectural photography (such as buildings that appear to lean).
2. A view camera provides the most professional photographs.
3. When shooting color photographs, use transparency rather than color print film.

A Historic American Buildings Survey team taking detailed measurements of a barn to be used in a measured drawing.

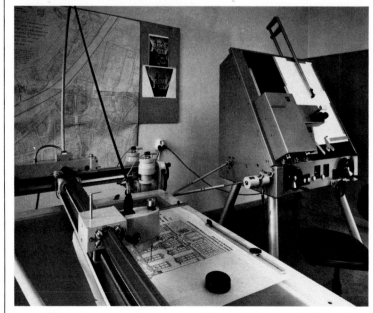

Some of the equipment used to convert architectural photographs through photogrammetry into measured drawings.

4. Avoid mid-day photography, because this tends to produce photographs flat in tone and lacking in shadows necessary for good contrast.
5. To obtain a comprehensive set of views, take an overall view of the structure as well as views of its site and surrounding environment. Also take a full, close-up shot of the facade, plus details such as doors, windows, dormers, hardware, brick bonding. For interiors, take views of full rooms, stairs, mantels, attic construction, fixtures. Include dependent structures such as outbuildings, barns, carriage houses.
6. Don't necessarily exclude present-day distractions such as people, cars and street furniture, because these will have future research value.
7. Spring and fall are the best seasons for photographing buildings; winter snow and summer foliage both conceal architectural details.
8. Have film developed and printed by a professional photographic laboratory rather than the corner drugstore.

From "Suggestions for Producing Publishable Photographs"

Photographic Collections
Library of Congress Prints and Photographs Division Washington, D.C. 20540

The first photographs came to the Library in 1846 under the copyright law. The collection now numbers about 9 million photographic prints, negatives, transparencies and stereographs—a sizable portion of which document American architecture and its environment and may be reproduced through the library's Photoduplication Service. In addition to the HABS and HAER collections described earlier, key collections are the *Pictorial Archives of Early American Architecture*—more than 10,000 prints emphasizing pre-1850 sites in the East but including master photographers' work and other documentation; *Detroit Publishing Company Collection*—more than 22,000 prints and original negatives of towns, buildings, resorts, parks and U.S. scenery from the 1880s through the early 1930s; *Carnegie Survey of the Architecture of the South*—10,000 images photographed by Frances Benjamin Johnston; *Farm Security Administration/Office of War Information Collection*—some 140,000 negatives, 75,000 mounted photographs and transparencies documenting urban and rural life in America during the 1930s and 1940s organized by region and subject; *Master Photographs*—including architectural examples by Johnston, Talbot, Brady, Atget, Stieglitz, Evans and Steichen, plus the Seagram County Court House Archives.

A Century of Photographs, 1846–1946: Selected from the Collections of the Library of Congress. Renata V. Shaw, comp., Prints and Photographs Division. Washington, D.C.: GPO, 1980. 219 pp., illus. $10 hb. GPO stock no. 030–000–00117–6.

More than 200 photographs representing the collection—including master photos and classics—plus interpretive essays on the pioneers, creative photography and documentary photographs.

National Archives
Still Pictures Branch
Audiovisual Archives Division
Washington, D.C. 20408

As the final resting place for inactive federal records, the Archives has amassed some 6 million still pictures since its establishment in 1934. These are organized by agency (135) and document social, economic, cultural and political activities from the colonial period. Special areas covered include the American city, the Revolution, Civil War and the West. Also available is the Documerica project undertaken by the Environmental Protection Agency in the 1970s to document the contemporary landscape of America.

The American Image: Photographs from the National Archives, 1860–1960. National Archives Trust Fund Board. Introduction by Alan Trachtenberg. New York: Pantheon, 1979. 224 pp., illus., index. $20 hb, $10 pb.

Features more than 200 illustrations surveying this large photographic collection.

The National Archives of the United States. Herman J. Viola. Introduction by David Mc-Cullough. New York: Abrams, 1984. 288 pp., color illus., biblio., index. $49.50 hb.

A lavish overview of all the collections, photographic as well as documentary.

Bettmann Archive
136 East 57th Street
New York, N.Y. 10022

A comprehensive collection of 5 million photographs and other illustrations on all aspects of American history.

Bettmann Archive. Picture History of the World: The Story of Western Civilization in 4250 Pictures. Otto L. Bettmann. New York: Random House, 1978.

A graphic history of almost everything from the files of the Bettmann Archive.

Society for the Preservation of New England Antiquities
141 Cambridge Street
Boston, Mass. 02114

Maintains one of the largest collections (1 million) of photographic negatives on New England architecture and social and maritime history.

San Diego Historical Society Photograph Collections
P.O. Box 1150
San Diego, Calif. 92112

Includes the Title Insurance and Trust Company's historical collection.

Eastman Kodak's first factory (1883) in Rochester, N.Y., now demolished and preserved only in this early photograph. (Eastman Kodak Company)

The Dunlap Society
Lake Champlain Road
Essex, N.Y. 12936

Compiles and sells visual material on art and architecture, particularly slides, for scholars and the general public. Among its publications is *The Architecture of Washington, D.C.,* and a microfiche series on *County Court Houses of the United States,* an expansion of the Seagram project that includes historic photographs.

International Museum of Photography
George Eastman House
900 East Avenue
Rochester, N.Y. 14607

Maintains 400,00 19th- and 20th-century photographs, including works of the masters. Also supports photographic research, offers courses and publishes a magazine.

Library Catalog of the International Museum of Photography at George Eastman House. Boston: G. K. Hall, 1982. 4 vols. 47,000 cards. $365 hb.

Historic New Orleans Collection
533 Royal Street
New Orleans, La. 70130

Prints and 15,000 photographs documenting life, history and culture in Louisiana, featuring New Orleans, including the Leonard Huber Collection.

Dover Publications
Pictorial Archive
180 Varick Street
New York, N.Y. 10014

A series of 300 well-produced, inexpensive paperbound books reproducing illustrations collected by the publisher on a range of graphic subjects. The line art is suitable for reproduction and is copyright free. Motifs, emblems, patterns, symbols, engravings, etc., are drawn from historic ornament, architectural renderings, signs, furniture, interior design, stained glass and more. A catalog is available. Dover also publishes an extensive list of reprints, photographic and other books useful in historical research.

Early Illustrations and Views of American Architecture. Edmund V. Gillon, Jr., Pictorial Archive Series. New York: Dover, 1971. 308 pp., illus. $8.95 pb.

Underwood Photo Archives
3109 Fillmore Street
San Francisco, Calif. 94123

A collection of more than one million photographs from the Underwood and Underwood News Photo Services, 1895–1975.

Photo Sources

An Index to American Photographic Collections. James McQuaid, ed., International Museum of Photography. Boston: G. K. Hall, 1982. 407 pp., illus., index. $78 hb.

A comprehensive guide to 450 collections, with an index of 19,000 photographers.

Photography Index: A Guide to Reproductions. Pamela Jeffcott Parry, ed. Westport, Conn.: Greenwood Press, 1979. 372 pp. $35 hb.

Based on illustrations available in more than 80 major books and catalogs published from the 1820s to the 1970s. Includes a chronological listing of works by unknown photographers, an alphabetical index to works by known photographers and firms and a detailed subject and title index.

Picture Sources Four. Ernest H. Robl, ed. 4th ed. New York: Special Libraries Association, 1983. 200 pp. $35 pb.

Includes information on 980 institutions and organizations that have photograph collections, with indexes of collections, geographic location and subject.

Stock Photo and Assignment Source Book: Where to Find Photographs Instantly. Fred W. McDarrah, ed. 2nd ed. New York: Photographic Arts Center, 1984. 320 pp., index. $29.95 pb.

Includes sections on historical sources and historic sites listing major state archives, private collections and libraries with historic photographs. Also indicates contemporary commercial photographers available for assignment, some of whom maintain historical collections.

"Sources of Illustrative Material." Washington, D.C.: Preservation Press, 1976. 4 pp.

Information on reference books, archives, historical and American collections and other sources.

Survey of the Architecture of Completed Projects of the Public Works Administration. 1939. Reprint in microfiche. Teaneck, N.J.: Somerset House and Chadwyck-Healey, 1983. 60 microfiche. $280.

Pictorial Resources in the Washington, D.C., Area. Shirley L. Green. Washington, D.C.: Library of Congress (Information Office, Box A, 20540), 1976. 297 pp., illus., index. $5.75 hb.

A guide to the rich photographic collections of the nation's capital.

Union Guide to Photograph Collections in the Pacific Northwest. Elizabeth Winroth. Portland: Oregon Historical Society (1230 S.W. Park Avenue, 97205), 1978. 419 pp., illus., biblio., index. $15.

Lists by state, city and institution collections in Oregon, Washington, Idaho and Montana.

Mapping the Past: Tracks Through Space

Time and space are related not only in Einstein's theories, but in the everyday work of historians and geographers as well. The historian can make sense of mankind's wanderings over time only if he can also track his subject through space.

Thomas E. Felt, *Researching, Writing, and Publishing Local History*

"Maps are invaluable to the historic preservationist not only in locating towns, streets or landmarks but also for the statistical information they provide such as population data, land-use patterns, and public utilities location. . . . Plat maps contain information needed to research particular structures such as lot numbers and property owners and can also be used to produce a date for when a lot was laid out. . . . Sometimes these maps are called insurance maps or atlases because they were developed for use by local insurance companies in the 19th century. They are also called Baist's or Sanborn Atlases after two companies that publish them."

Guide to Resources Used in Historic Preservation Research

Fire Insurance Maps in the Library of Congress: Plans of North American Cities and Towns Produced by the Sanborn Map Company. Geography and Map Division. Introduction by Walter R. Ristow. Washington, D.C.: Library of Congress, 1981. 773 pp., illus. $32 hb. GPO stock no. 030–004–00018–3.

Alphabetical checklist by state and principal city surveying the 50,000 fire insurance maps (and 700,000 sheets) produced by the Sanborn Map Company since 1867. The maps show the size, shape and construction of buildings as well as interior details, widths and names of streets, boundaries, uses and block numbers.

This Remarkable Continent: An Atlas of United States and Canadian Society and Cultures. John F. Rooney, Jr., Wilbur Zelinsky and Dean R. Louder, eds. Society for the North American Cultural Survey. College Station: Texas A & M University Press, 1982. 324 pp., illus., index. $45 hb.

An exploration through maps, drawings and text of the locational patterns of social and cultural traits. Topics depicted include general cultural and popular regions, land divisions, structures, social behavior, language, place names, ethnicity and place perception.

Early American Maps and Views. Clive E. Driver. Rosenbach Museum and Library. Charlottesville: University Press of Virginia, 1981. 64 pp., illus. $3.95 pb.

Selection of maps and views documenting the early American scene in cartouches, engravings, oils, murals and silver.

"Past Cityscapes: Uses of Cartography in Urban History." In *Artifacts and the American Past.* Thomas J. Schlereth. Nashville: American Association for State and Local History, 1980. 304 pp., illus., appends., index. $15.95 hb.

Maps in the Small Historical Society: Care and Cataloging. James Bartlett and Douglas Marshall. Nashville: American Association for State and Local History, 1979. Technical Leaflet 111. 12 pp. $2 pb.

Contacts

National Cartographic Information Center Geological Survey U.S. Department of the Interior Reston, Va. 22091

The primary public source for cartographic information, NCIC collects data from federal, state and local governments and private companies, sells maps, provides related information and conducts searches. Aerial views, topographic maps and out-of-print editions are available.

Library of Congress Geography and Map Division Washington, D.C. 20540

In addition to its Sanborn map collection, the library maintains some 3,000 19th- and 20th-century atlases of U.S. counties and cities, produced commercially and illustrated with views of buildings.

Historic Urban Plans Box 276 Ithaca, N.Y. 14851

Sells reproductions of old maps and urban views useful in research; a catalog is available.

Urban Views

"[Lithographic city views] provide an incredible amount of reliable detail. Comparisons with photographs of the time can be made to show that even in the tiny buildings on the prints such matters as fenestration, roof types, porches, signs, chimneys, and dozens of similar architectural minutiae are rendered with faithful accuracy."

John W. Reps, *Cities on Stone*

Views and Viewmakers of Urban America: Lithographs of Towns and Cities in the United States and Canada, Notes on the Artists and Publishers, and a Union Catalog of Their Work, 1825–1925. John W. Reps. Columbia: University of Missouri Press, 1984. 586 pp., illus., append., index. $89.50 hb.

Cities on Stone: Nineteenth Century Lithograph Images of the Urban West. John W. Reps. Fort Worth, Tex.: Amon Carter Museum of Western Art (3501 Camp Bowie Boulevard, 76107), 1976. 99 pp., illus. $14.95 hb, $9.95 pb.

Color lithograph of Fort Worth, Tex. (1876, D. D. Morse). (Amon Carter Museum, Fort Worth)

Quiet street in the small town of Collinsville, Conn., founded in the 19th century as a company town. (Ted Ancher)

Researching Local History: The Fundamental Foundation

The sense of the past in our communities—the historical awareness of our people—is the fundamental resource that underlies the preservation of all the others.

> *Historic Resources in Minnesota.* St. Paul: Minnesota Historical Society, 1979.

At a time when the world seems so much involved in global problems and space exploration, some might question the role and importance of local history. But local history is the true beginning of all history.

> Marcia Muth Miller, *How to Collect and Write Local History.* Santa Fe, N.M.: Sunstone Press, 1975.

"An understanding of the physical development of the community will provide researchers with a broad historical, architectural, archeological and cultural context for research undertaken on particular properties. Evidence of the evolving plan and character of a community can be seen in the pattern of streets as laid out and modified, and in the location of transportation systems (canals, trolley lines, railroads, etc.), industries, institutions, commercial and residential areas, and reserved public spaces and parks.

Location of natural resources, soil types, availability of power and fuel, and accessibility to transportation systems were factors that frequently contributed to the siting and development of towns and cities. The development of agriculture, mining or other activities that shaped the form of rural communities or small towns should be considered.

Research should also involve the investigation of sites associated with events, individuals, groups and trends significant in the community's history. In developing their research methodology, researchers may find it helpful to be aware of certain historical themes, such as commerce, ethnic history and education. . . .

Trends reflected in existing cultural properties may include emigration, population shifts, changing economic and labor systems, reform movements, the status of minority groups, the development of industrial and technical processes, and important religious developments. . . . Depending on the intensity of the survey effort, researchers may attempt to consider reasons for the use or introduction of particular styles, materials or methods of construction in specific structures."

> Anne Derry, H. Ward Jandl, Carol D. Shull, Jan Thorman, *Guidelines for Local Surveys: A Basis for Preservation Planning.* Washington, D.C.: U.S. Department of the Interior, 1977.

"The best place to look for old books on local history is in older libraries—the older the better—and in main libraries rather than in branches. It is in the main library that you're most likely to find complete or nearly complete collections of state historical journals, local histories, town records, maps and surveys, business directories, and family documents."

> David Weitzman, "Library Archaeology." In *Underfoot*

Underfoot: An Everyday Guide to Exploring America's Past. David Weitzman. New York: Scribner's, 1976. 192 pp., illus., biblio., index.

A guide to historical research for nonprofessionals: organizing a search, using equipment, interpreting original source material, using libraries, cemetery research and investigating historic buildings. The text is a melange of diary excerpts, newspaper ads, recipes and old photographs.

Families and Communities: A New View of American History. David J. Russo. Nashville: American Association for State and Local History, 1974. 322 pp. $10 pb.

Proposes an approach to American history that begins at the local level and moves outward to the national, emphasizing the small, local social unit: family, neighborhood, community and town.

Nearby History: Exploring the Past Around You. David E. Kyvig and Myron A. Marty. Nashville: American Association for State and Local History, 1982. 313 pp., illus., appends., index. $16.95 hb.

A guide to finding and using local and family history resources. Covered are published, unpublished, visual and material records; interviews; photographs; documents and objects; landscapes and buildings; with techniques for linking "the particular and the universal."

Researching, Writing and Publishing Local History. Thomas E. Felt. 1976. 2nd ed. Nashville: American Association for State and Local History, 1981. 179 pp., illus., biblio., index. $9 pb.

A basic handbook for the inexperienced. Topics include research sources and records, copying documents, manuscripts and archives, illustrations, editing documents and production considerations.

Methods of Research for the Amateur Historian. Richard W. Hale, Jr. Nashville: American Association for State and Local History, 1969. Technical Leaflet 21. 8 pp. $2 pb.

Outlines attitudes toward research and shortcuts to finding and organizing information.

Local Historical Records: Programs for Historical Agencies. Bruce W. Dearstyne. Nashville: American Association for State and Local History, 1979. Technical Leaflet 121. 8 pp. $2 pb.

Gives advice on organizing, determining which records to collect, financial and other help, plus further reading.

Videotaping Local History. Brad Jolly. Nashville: American Association for State and Local History, 1982. 160 pp., illus., gloss., index. $12.95 pb.

Surveys video technology, hardware and equipment, oral history, interpretation, training and video archives.

Local History Collections: A Manual for Librarians. Enid T. Thompson. Nashville: American Association for State and Local History, 1978. 100 pp., illus. $8.95 pb.

A practical manual on assembling and caring for local history materials that addresses components, authentication, legal aspects, cleaning, cataloging, storing and using collections.

"The Use of Federal Records in Writing Local History," Jane F. Smith. *Prologue,* Spring 1969. National Archives.

Directory of Historical Societies and Agencies. Donna McDonald, comp. 12th ed. Nashville: American Association for State and Local History, 1982. 416 pp., illus., index. $36 pb.

Lists nearly 5,000 local and state historical organizations, indicating location, staff, membership, programs, officers. Indexed by special interests.

Contact

American Association for
State and Local History
708 Berry Road
Nashville, Tenn. 37204

A leading source of aid for local history research, AASLH helps individuals, museums and historical societies through books, a Technical Leaflet Series, a magazine, videotapes, seminars and related programs.

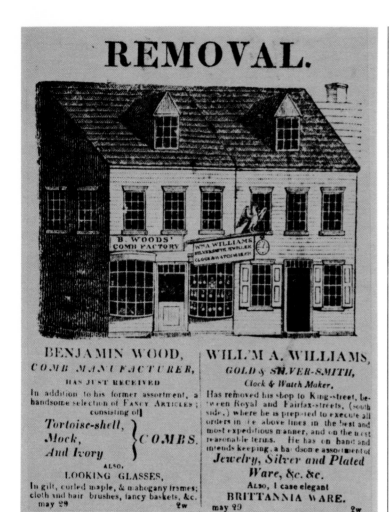

1823 notice that William A. Williams, an Alexandria, Va., gold and silversmith, has moved to new quarters. From *The City of Washington*.

Illustrated Local Histories

The Drawing of America: Eyewitnesses to History. Marshall B. Davidson. New York: Abrams, 1983. 256 pp., illus., biblio., index. $49.50 hb.

The Way We Lived in North Carolina Series. Sydney Nathans, ed., North Carolina Department of Cultural Resources. Chapel Hill: University of North Carolina Press, 1983. 5 vols. 110 pp., illus. $11.95 hb, $6.95 pb each.

Windsor Publications Series on American Cities. Woodland Hills, Calif: Windsor Publications (Box 1500, 91365), 1980 to present. 140 vols. 144–385 pp., illus. $17.95–27.95 each.

The City of Washington: An Illustrated History. Tomas Froncek, ed. Junior League of Washington, D.C. New York: Knopf, 1977. 384 pp., illus., biblio., index. $15.95 pb.

The City of New York: A History Illustrated from the Collections of the Museum of the City of New York. Jerry E. Patterson. Introduction by Joseph Veach Noble. Foreword by Louis Auchincloss. New York: Abrams, 1978. 252 pp., color illus.

New York: A Pictorial History. Marshall B. Davidson. New York: Scribner's, 1977. 370 pp., illus., biblio., index. $9.95 pb.

Massachusetts: A Pictorial History. Walter M. Whitehill and Norman Kotker. New York: Scribner's, 1976. 356 pp., illus., biblio., index. $9.95 pb.

Life and Architecture in Pittsburgh. James D. Van Trump. Pittsburgh: Pittsburgh History and Landmarks Foundation, 1983. 416 pp., illus., biblio., index. $18.95 hb.

Virginia: A Pictorial History. Parke Rouse, Jr. New York: Scribner's, 1975. 368 pp., illus., biblio., index. $14.95 pb.

New Orleans: A Pictorial History. Leonard V. Huber. 1971. New York: Crown, 1982. 384 pp., illus. $12.98.

Two Hundred Years at the Falls of the Ohio: A History of Louisville and Jefferson County. George H. Yater. Louisville, Ky.: Heritage Corporation of Louisville and Jefferson County, 1979. 250 pp., illus., index. $15.95 hb. *Notes.* 118 pp. $3.50 pb. Available from Filson Club, 118 West Breckinridge Street, Louisville, Ky. 40203.

Benicia: Portrait of an Early California Town. An Architectural History. Robert Bruegmann. San Francisco: 101 Productions, 1980. 158 pp., illus., appends., biblio., index. $8.95 pb.

Claremont: A Pictorial History. Judy Wright. Claremont, Calif.: Claremont Historic Resources Center, 1980. 273 pp., illus., biblio., index. $15.

Port Townsend: Years That Are Gone. An Illustrated History. Peter Simpson and James Hermanson. Port Townsend, Wash.: Quimper Press (Port Townsend Publishing Company, 98368), 1979. 192 pp., illus., biblio., index.

State Histories

The States and the Nation Series. James Morton Smith, ed., American Association for State and Local History. New York: W. W. Norton, 1976 to present. 51 vols. 224 pp., illus. $14.95 hb, $7.95 pb each.

Histories of the 50 states and the District of Columbia, written by leading state historians as an AASLH Bicentennial project and "designed to assist the American people in a serious look at the ideals they have espoused and the experiences they have undergone in the history of the nation" (James Morton Smith). Each book contains a photographic essay "in which a skilled photographer presents his own personal perceptions of the state's contemporary flavor."

Engraving of Main Street, Hartford, Conn., with the Old State House at left, c. 1850. From Gleason's Picture Drawing Room Companion.

Histories in Asphalt: Street and Place Names

Aloha, Wash.

In the early 1900's two young men just out of college, W. H. Dole and Ralph Emerson, teamed up and founded this town. They set up a sawmill, later expanding their investment to a flour mill and then a large shingle mill.

Dole, a relative of the famous pineapple Doles, had been raised in Hawaii. He named the town Aloha after a Hawaiian word used for both greetings and good-byes.

Seven Mile, Ohio

Back in the days when the automobile was first developed, drivers used to stop and ask local residents how far the next big town, Hamilton, was. The farmers used to look slowly to the left and say: "Seven mile down the pike."

Allan Wolk, *The Naming of America*

Place Names

Illustrated Dictionary of Place Names: United States and Canada. Kelsie B. Harder, ed. New York: Facts on File, 1985. 632 pp., illus., biblio. $19.95 hb, $12.95 pb.

Names on the Land: The Classic Story of American Place-naming. George R. Stewart. New introduction by Wallace Stegner. 1967. 4th ed. San Francisco: Lexikos, 1982. 560 pp., illus., biblio., index. $10 pb.

The Naming of America: How Continents, Countries, States, Counties, Cities, Towns, Villages, Hamlets and Post Offices Came by Their Names. Allan Wolk. 1977. New York: Simon and Schuster, 1980. 192 pp., index.

Illustrated Dictionary of American Place Names: United States and Canada. Kelsie B. Harder. New York: Van Nostrand Reinhold, 1975.

American Place-Names: A Concise and Selective Dictionary for the Continental United States of America. George R. Stewart. New York: Oxford University Press, 1970. $25.

Origin of Certain Place Names in the United States. Henry Gannett. 1902. Reprint. Williamstown, Mass.: Corner House, 1978. 280 pp. $16.50.

American Place Names. Alfred H. Holt. 1938. Reprint. Detroit: Gale, 1969. $40.

Alaska-Yukon Place Names. James W. Phillips. Seattle: University of Washington Press, 1973.

Arizona Place Names. Byrd H. Granger. 1960. 2nd rev. ed. Tucson: University of Arizona Press, 1982. 419 pp. $14.95 pb.

One Thousand California Place Names: Their Origin and Meaning. Erwin G. Gudde. 3rd rev. ed. Berkeley: University of California Press, 1969. $3.95 pb.

California Place Names: The Origin and Etymology of Current Geographical Names. Erwin G. Gudde. Berkeley: University of California Press, 1969. $32.50.

Florida Place Names. Allen Morris. Miami: University of Miami Press, 1974.

Placenames of Georgia: Essays of John H. Goff. Francis L. Utley and Marion R. Hemperley, eds. Athens: University of Georgia Press, 1975. 534 pp. $20.

Place Names of Hawaii. Mary Kawena Pukui, Samuel H. Pukui and Esther T. Mookini. 2nd ed. Honolulu: University Press of Hawaii, 1974.

Illinois Place Names. James N. Adams and William E. Keller, eds. Springfield: Illinois State Historical Society, 1968.

Indiana Place Names. Ronald L. Baker and Marvin Carmony. Bloomington: Indiana University Press, 1976. 224 pp. $7.95 pb.

Kansas Place-Names. John Rydjord. Norman: University of Oklahoma Press, 1972. 400 pp. $32.50 hb, $14.95 pb.

Maine Place Names and the Peopling of Its Towns. Ava H. Chadbourne. 4 vols.: Cumberland, Hancock, Lincoln, Washington and York counties. Freeport. Maine: Bond Wheelwright Company, Cumberland Press (Box 296, 04032), 1970–83. $1.95–4.95 pb.

Names of the Land: Cape Code, Nantucket, Martha's Vineyard, and the Elizabeth Islands. Eugene Green and William Sachse. Chester, Conn.: Globe Pequot, 1980. 192 pp. $8.95 pb.

Minnesota Geographic Names: Their Origin and Historic Significance. Warren Upham. 1920. Reprint. Minneapolis: Minnesota Historical Society, 1979. 788 pp. $12.50.

Our Storehouse of Missouri Place Names. Robert L. Ramsay. Columbia: University of Missouri Press, 1952. 160 pp. $5.95 pb.

Nebraska Place-Names. Lilian L. Fitzpatrick. Rev. ed. Lincoln: University of Nebraska Press, 1960. 227 pp. $5.95 pb.

Nevada Place Names: A Geographical Dictionary. Helen S. Carlson. Reno: University of Nevada Press, 1974. $15.

New Mexico Place Names: A Geographical Dictionary. Helen S. Carlson. Albuquerque: University of New Mexico Press, 1974. 282 pp. $15 pb.

Pennsylvania Place Names. A. H. Espenshade. 1925. Reprint. Baltimore: Genealogical Publishing, 1970. 375 pp. $20.

1001 Texas Place Names. Fred Tarpley. Austin: University of Texas Press, 1980. 256 pp., illus. $14.95 hb, $6.95 pb.

Vermont Place-Names: Footprints of History. Esther M. Swift. Brattleboro, Vt.: Stephen Greene Press, 1977. $35 hb.

Geographic and Cultural Names in Virginia. T. H. Biggs. Charlottesville: Department of Conservation and Economic Development (Division of Mineral Resources, P.O. Box 3667, 22903), 1974. 374 pp. $5.

Main Street, Sauk Centre, Minn., c. 1951, made famous by Sinclair Lewis in *Main Street*. (Minnesota Historical Society)

Washington State Place Names. James Philips. Rev. ed. Seattle: University of Washington Press, 1971. 186 pp. $16.50 hb, $8.95 pb.

Street Names

Street Names of Philadelphia. Robert I. Alotta. Philadelphia: Temple University Press, 1975. 160 pp., illus., biblio. $10.95.

The Street Book: An Encyclopedia of Manhattan Street Names and Their Origins. Henry Moscow. New York: Hagstrom Company, 1979. 119 pp., illus., appends.

History in Asphalt: The Origin of Bronx Street and Place Names. John McNamara, Bronx County Historical Society. 2nd ed. Bronx., N.Y.: Bronx County Historical Society, 1978. 576 pp., illus. $15 pb.

Streets of San Francisco: The Origins of Street and Place Names. Louis K. Lowenstein. San Francisco: Lexikos, 1984. $5.95 pb.

Contact

United States Board on Geographic Names Geological Survey U.S. Department of the Interior 12201 Sunrise Valley Drive Reston, Va. 22092

Established in 1890 to bring order to the process of changing place names. Maintains the *Geographic Names Information System*, an indexed gazetteer for each state on cultural and physical features, populated areas and geographic coordinates; available in print, printouts or microfiche.

Tracing a Building's Past

Researching an old house is something that many owners put off "until the more important things are done." Unfortunately, this common attitude is exactly the wrong *way to approach a vintage house. It's like setting out to construct a home without building a foundation.*

When restoring or rehabilitating an old house, the goal is to do work that is in keeping with the style and tradition of the structure. . . . But to do a restoration, you have to know what the house was like originally. And that means research at the outset. . . .

Once you've immersed yourself in the history of the house, it acquires a new personality. You feel differently about the house—and what you want to do to it. Usually, the desire to "remodel" decreases and the desire to restore increases. You become less eager to make drastic changes in a house that has meant so much to so many.

"How to Date an Old House."
Old-House Journal, October
1976.

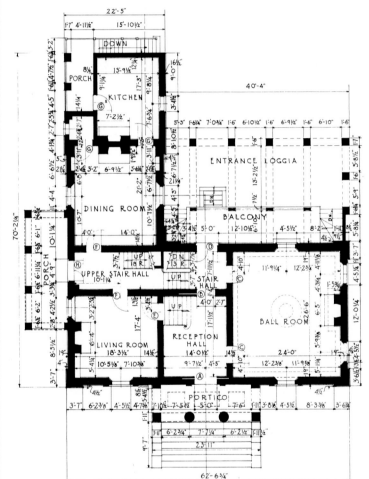

HABS drawings helped rescue Oaks Place (1840, George Steele), Huntsville, Ala., by providing ready-made floor plans for adaptive use. (J. T. Latimer, HABS)

Where to Go, What to Look For

Registry of Deeds
Deeds
Extracts of wills
Maps, plans and atlases

Probate Office
Inventories
Wills

Town or City Hall
Annual reports
Building inspector's files
Cemetery records
Maps, plans and atlases
Tax records
Vital statistics

Library and Historical Society
Annual reports
Architectural drawings
Biographical publications
Cemetery records
Census data
Commemoratives
Directories
Genealogies
Histories
Insurance records and maps
Manuscripts (private papers)
Maps, plans and atlases
Newspapers
Obituary items
Photographs, paintings, prints
  and postcards
Publications
Scrapbooks
Tax records
Vital statistics

Local Newspaper Office
News articles
Obituary items
Photographs

Neighbors
Memories
Photographs
  From *Researching the Old House*

Four Types of Research

1. Study of physical evidence in the structure itself.
2. Investigation of legal records to find names, dates and transactions documenting the building's past.
3. Research of original documents found in libraries and archives to supply facts pertaining to the building or its owners.
4. Comparative research into structures similar in type or style, to put the structure into a historical framework.

Cynthia Durko, "Researching a Building." In *Preservation Illinois: A Guide to State and Local Resources.* Ruth Eckdish Knack, ed. Springfield: Illinois Department of Conservation, 1977.

House Histories. Barbara Howe et al. Nashville: American Association for State and Local History, 1986.

A practical how-to-do-it guide for the amateur historian detailing how to research houses, apartments and dwellings of all kinds.

Researching the Old House. Portland, Maine: Greater Portland Landmarks (165 State Street, 04101), 1981. 72 pp., biblio. $3.95 pb.

A concise, practical guide produced in Maine but written for a national audience.

The History of a House: How to Trace It. Linda Ellsworth. Nashville: American Association for State and Local History, 1976. Technical Leaflet 89. 8 pp., biblio. $2 pb.

An introductory overview of documentary research.

"How to Date a House," David M. Hart. *Yankee Magazine,* July 1976 and November 1976.

Describes methods of ferreting out the physical evidence indicating the age and changes in a structure.

A Guide to Resources for Researching Historic Buildings in Washington, D.C. Kim Hoagland. Washington, D.C.: D.C. Preservation League (930 F Street, N.W., Suite 715, 20004) and Columbia Historical Society, 1981. 30 pp., illus., append. $2.50 pb.

Researching Maryland Buildings. Annapolis: Maryland Historical Trust (21 State Circle, 21401).

How Old Is This Building? A Guide for the Amateur Researcher. Mobile, Ala.: Mobile Historic Development Commission (P.O. Box 1827, 36633).

How to Research Your Own House. Salt Lake City: Utah Heritage Foundation (355 Quince Street, 84103), 1980. 28 pp., illus. $1 pb.

Genealogy: The People Connection

The process of finding out about the people who owned and lived in your house is a long one. You will have to consult many sources and piece together the bits of information you find. In the end, though, you will learn the "social history" of your house, and, in doing so, learn the human dimensions of your neighborhood.

Greater Portland Landmarks,
Researching the Old House

Genealogical Research: A Basic Guide. Carolynne L. Miller. Nashville: American Association for State and Local History, 1969. Technical Leaflet 14. 8 pp., illus., biblio. $2 pb.

The Researcher's Guide to American Genealogy. Val D. Greenwood. 1973. Baltimore: Genealogical Publishing (521–23 St. Paul Place, 21202), 1983. 535 pp., illus., biblio., index. $15.

Know Your Ancestors: A Guide to Genealogical Research. Ethel W. Williams. Rutland, Vt.: Charles E. Tuttle, 1960. 314 pp. $12.50.

How to Find Your Family Roots. Timothy Field Beard with Denise Demong. New York: McGraw-Hill, 1978. 1,007 pp., index., biblio.

Guide to Genealogical Research in the National Archives. 1964. Rev. ed. Washington, D.C.: National Archives, 1983. 320 pp., illus., appends., index. $21 hb, $17 pb.

Tracing Your Ancestry: A Step-by-Step Guide to Researching Your Family History. F. Wilbur Helmbold. Birmingham, Ala.: Oxmoor House, 1978. $5.29 pb.

Searching for Your Ancestors: The How and Why of Genealogy. Gilbert H. Doane and James B. Bell. 5th ed. Minneapolis: University of Minnesota Press, 1980. 270 pp., illus., biblio., index. $12.95.

"Where to Write for Vital Records." Washington, D.C.: GPO. $1.50. GPO stock no. 017–022–00847–5.

Kin and Communities: Families in America. Allan J. Lichtman and Joan R. Challinor. Washington, D.C.: Smithsonian Institution Press, 1979. 335 pp., illus. $22.50 hb, $10.95 pb.

Genealogical Books in Print. Netti Schreiner-Yantis, ed. 4th ed. Springfield, Va.: Author (6818 Lois Drive, 22150), 1985. 1,500 pp. $27.50 pb.

Genealogy: A Selected Bibliography. Milton Rubincam. 5th ed., rev. Birmingham, Ala.: Banner Press, for Institute of Genealogy and Historical Research, Samford University (Box 20180, 35216), 1983. 19 pp. $3 pb.

Genealogies in the Library of Congress: A Bibliography. 1972. Marion J. Kaminkow, ed. Baltimore: Magna Carta Book Company, 1985. 2 vols. 1,865 pp. $175. *Supplement 1972–76.* 1977. 285 pp. $25. *A Complement.* 1981. 1,118 pp. $83.50 hb.

A Survey of American Genealogical Periodicals and Periodical Indexes. Kip Sperry. Detroit: Gale, 1978. 199 pp., biblio., index. $55.

Directory of Genealogical Societies in the U.S.A. and Canada. 3rd ed., rev. Mary K. Meyer, ed. Pasadena, Md.: Author (297 Cove Road, 21122), 1980. 88 pp. $9 pb.

Contacts

National Archives
Correspondence Branch
Washington, D.C. 20408

Issues a free kit describing what is available at the Archives. Regional depositories are in Boston, New York, Philadelphia, Atlanta, Chicago, Fort Worth, Denver, San Francisco, Laguna Niguel, Calif., and Kansas City, Mo.

National Genealogical Society
1921 Sunderland Place, N.W.
Washington, D.C. 20036

Provides a public library and loan-by-mail service to members. Offers publications and correspondence courses.

Church of Jesus Christ
of Latter-day Saints
Genealogical Society
50 East North Temple Street
Salt Lake City, Utah 84105

Maintains an extensive collection (in a hollowed-out mountain) of microfilmed records of interest beyond Mormon descendants. The facilities are available to non-Mormons through 200 branch libraries.

Library of Congress
Genealogical Department
Washington, D.C. 20540

New England Historic
Genealogical Society
101 Newbury Street
Boston, Mass. 02116

New York Genealogical and
Biographical Society
122 East 58th Street
New York, N.Y. 10022

Genealogical Society
of Pennsylvania
1300 Locust Street
Philadelphia, Pa. 19107

National Society of the
Daughters of the
American Revolution
1776 D Street, N.W.
Washington, D.C. 20006

Los Angeles Branch
LDS Genealogical Library
10741 Santa Monica Boulevard
Los Angeles, Calif. 90024

The American Genealogist
1232 39th Street
Des Moines, Iowa 50311

The Genealogical Helper
P.O. Box 368
Logan, Utah 84321

Journal of Family History
National Council on Family
Relations
1219 University Avenue, S.E.
Minneapolis, Minn. 55414

The Genealogist's Bookshelf
P.O. Box 468
New York, N.Y. 10028

Goodspeed's Book Shop
7 Beacon Street
Boston, Mass. 02108

The Rice family on their porch, Sturbridge, Mass. From *Small Town Source Book*, Old Sturbridge Village. (Carol Simpson; Old Sturbridge Village)

Oral History: The Past Recollected

Oral history is primary source material obtained by recording spoken words, generally by means of a planned tape recorded interview of persons with previously unavailable information worth preserving. . . .

The field of oral history is both ancient and modern. Historians since Herodotus . . . have been interviewing individuals about significant historical events. Oral history as an organized activity dates only from 1948, when Professor Allan Nevins launched "The Oral History Project" at Columbia University.

Nancy Whistler, *Oral History Workshop Guide*

Foxfire student Sam Adams tape recording the techniques used by fur trapper Phil Nichols. (Foxfire Fund)

"In this day of hurried contacts, telephone or face-to-face meetings, and multitudinous evening activities, people no longer write the long letters, the routinely kept diaries, the series of letters back and forth to work out agreements, the careful memos that heretofore have always served as the bones of historical research. And, as always, there are many classes of persons who will not set down in writing the description of their way of life although they may have a very rich oral tradition and may be able to talk with much color and accuracy about this life.

These gaps can now be filled by oral history. Through the relatively painless medium of relaxed conversations based upon well-planned questions, it is possible to elicit information that would not ordinarily get into the written record: the descriptions of the appearance and character of leading citizens, the motivations as to why and how and by what 'gentleman's agreement' things came to pass, the life and color of a community or an industry or an ethnic group."

Willa K. Baum, *Oral History for the Local Historical Society*

The Voice of the Past: Oral History. Paul Thompson. New York: Oxford University Press, 1978. 257 pp., biblio., appends., index. $8.95 pb.

An essential guide to the methodology of oral history, with model questions for interviews.

Oral History: An Interdisciplinary Anthology. David K. Dunaway and Willa K. Baum, eds. Nashville: American Association for State and Local History and Oral History Association, 1984. 460 pp., append., index. $29.50 hb., $17.95 pb.

A comprehensive anthology drawing together significant writings on topics such as designing oral history programs; local, ethnic, family and women's history; folklore; anthropology; gerontology; and school projects.

From Memory to History: Using Oral Sources in Local Historical Research. Barbara Allen and Lynwood Montell. Nashville: American Association for State and Local History, 1981. 176 pp. $13.50 hb.

Describes the contributions oral sources can make to local history, including productive topics for seeking oral information, physical artifacts, identifying attitudes about the past and community values and beliefs embodied in nonfactual accounts.

Oral History Workshop Guide. Nancy Whistler. Denver: Colorado Center for Oral History, Denver Public Library, 1979. 55 pp., biblio., appends. $3.50 pb.

A concise handbook for community history projects, including questions to ask, processing and legal forms.

Oral History for the Local Historical Society. Willa K. Baum. 1969. 2nd ed., rev. Nashville: American Association for State and Local History, 1975. 63 pp., illus., biblio. $5 pb.

An overview of oral history techniques—starting a program, equipment, the interview, indexing agreements, depositing tapes and use of materials.

Transcribing and Editing Oral History. Willa K. Baum. Nashville: American Association for State and Local History, 1977. 127 pp., biblio. $9 pb.

A handbook emphasizing the transcription process of transcribing, editing and indexing.

Oral History: From Tape to Type. Cullom Davis, Kathryn Black and Kay MacLean. Chicago: American Library Association (50 East Huron Street, 60611), 1977. 151 pp., biblio., appends., gloss. $10 pb.

Covers oral history interviews and processing the resulting tapes into written form.

Tape-Recording Local History. William G. Tyrrell. Nashville: American Association for State and Local History, 1973. Technical Leaflet 35. 12 pp. $2 pb.

A brief explanation of the "why" and "how" of doing oral history.

Oral History: An Introduction for Students. James Hoopes. Chapel Hill: University of North Carolina Press, 1979. 155 pp., biblio., index. $15 hb, $5.95 pb.

A guide for students who wish to use oral history in classes.

Oral History: A Reference Guide and Annotated Bibliography. Patricia Pate Havlice. Jefferson, N.C.: McFarland and Company (Box 611, 28640), 1985. 180 pp. $18.95.

Describes sources, depositories, methodology, interviewing techniques, periodicals and associations.

"Guidebooks for Oral History Projects," Willa K. Baum, ed. *History News,* December 1980.

A brief bibliography of basic books and some featuring special oral history subjects.

The Tape-Recorded Interview: A Manual for Field Workers in Folklore and Oral History. Edward D. Ives. Knoxville: University of Tennessee Press, 1980. $11.95 hb, $5.50 pb.

Shows how to document the lives of common people and preserve verbatim accounts of folkways.

"Oral History: More Than Tapes Are Spinning," Charles T. Morrissey. *Library Journal,* April 15, 1980.

A brief but comprehensive overview of the state of the art in oral history with names, addresses, publications and programs.

"Oral History and the Mythmakers," Charles T. Morrissey. *Historic Preservation,* November–December 1964.

Describes ways to identify or avoid inaccuracies in the recollections recorded by oral historians and cautions that "the limitations of oral history lie in the fallibility of the human faculty for recall."

How to Tape Instant Oral Biographies. William Zimmerman. 3rd rev. ed. New York: Guarionex Press (201 West 77th Street, 10024), 1982. 112 pp., illus. $4.95.

A guide to preserving one's life stories on tape and how to interview people, designed especially to help youngsters elicit information from their parents and other relatives.

Using Oral History for a Family History Project. Linda Shopes. Nashville: American Association for State and Local History, 1980. Technical Leaflet 123. $2 pb.

Provides how-to information from background research and focus to conducting the interviews, with a bibliography.

Contacts

Oral History Association
North Texas State University
P.O. Box 13734, NT Station
Denton, Tex. 76203

International association of individuals and organizations using oral history. Publishes a newsletter, *Oral History Review;* periodic bibliographies; and proceedings of its annual fall workshops and colloquia.

Oral History Research Office
Butler Library
Columbia University
New York, N.Y. 10027

The first formal sound-recorded oral history program. Transcripts of its collections of prominent people in many fields are available on microfilm.

International Journal of Oral History
P.O. Box 405
Saugatuck Station
Westport, Conn. 06880

Published three times a year, with articles on local efforts, grants, book reviews, conference notes and equipment evaluations.

Prof. Charles B. Hosmer, Jr.
Principia College
Elsah, Ill. 62028

In 1981 initiated an oral history project to record the efforts of contemporary preservationists. His two published histories of the preservation movement, *Presence of the Past* (1965) and *Preservation Comes of Age* (1981), were based heavily on interviews and other oral history sources.

Foxfire: Lighting Up the Past

"Daily our grandparents are moving out of our lives, taking with them, irreparably, the kind of information contained in this book. They are taking it, not because they want to, but because they think we don't care. . . .

If this information is to be saved at all, for whatever reason, it must be saved now; and the logical researchers are the grandchildren, not university researchers from the outside. In the process, these grandchildren (and we) gain an invaluable, unique knowledge about their own roots, heritage and culture."

Eliot Wigginton, Introduction. *The Foxfire Book.* New York: Doubleday, 1972.

The Foxfire industry began in 1966 when Eliot Wigginton, a high school teacher in the Appalachian Mountains of northeast Georgia, helped his students found a quarterly magazine they named *Foxfire* (a lichen that glows in the dark). The magazine articles became books and were followed by records, teaching handbooks, television, furniture and a Foxfire Press. The magazine remains the project's cornerstone. The Foxfire educational concept, based on oral history and recording of local culture and folklore, has spread to schools throughout the country.

Foxfire. Eliot Wigginton, ed., vols. 1–6. Paul Gillespie, ed., vol. 7. Eliot Wigginton and Margie Bennett, eds., vol. 8. New York: Doubleday, 1972–84. $15.95–19.95 hb, $8.95–9.95 pb.

Skills from the past—from log cabin building to blacksmithing, cooking, spinning and weaving—recounted by former practitioners and recaptured by their descendants.

Leonard Webb explaining to Foxfire students Wesley Taylor and Mitch Whitmire how he makes gourd banjos. (Foxfire Fund)

Tony Whitmire and Robert Bleckley taking notes on how an ax handle is made. (Foxfire Fund)

Moments: The Foxfire Experience. B. Eliot Wigginton. Nederland, Colo.: IDEAS, Inc. (Magnolia Star Route, 80466). 146 pp., illus. $7.95.

Presents the philosophy behind Foxfire for teachers.

Hands On: Newsletter for Cultural Journalism. Foxfire Fund. Quarterly. $4 annually.

Network of communication for cultural journalism projects.

Contact

The Foxfire Fund, Inc.
Rabun Gap, Ga. 30568

Rehabilitation and Restoration

9

There is so much activity these days in the improvement of older housing that a new set of verbs has been introduced into common parlance. Most of the words start with the prefix re—*which means to begin anew, and it is not hard to become confused among the definitions. The variations in meaning between* restore, rehabilitation, *and* remodel *may seem subtle, but the words represent powerful attitudes which make all the difference in the way a job turns out.*

City of Oakland (Calif.) Planning Department,
Rehab Right

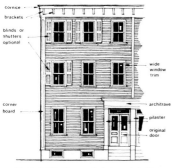

Rehabilitation retaining details

Inappropriate "antiquing"

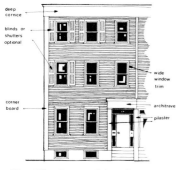

Simplification retaining character

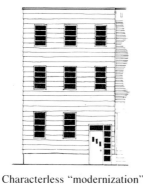

Characterless "modernization".

Appropriate and inappropriate ways to rehabilitate an old house. From *Revitalizing Older Houses in Charlestown*, by George Stephen. (Boston Redevelopment Authority)

Half-rehabilitated house in Washington, D.C. (Carleton Knight III, NTHP)

The 8 Most Common Mistakes

"As more and more people turn to restoring old houses, it is becoming apparent that certain serious mistakes are being made over and over again. This article outlines these most common mistakes and tells you, at least in general terms, how to avoid them."

1. Don't destroy the evidence. Make tracks.
2. Don't overrestore.
3. Don't make a building that never was.
4. Don't scrape.
5. Don't sandblast. Avoid destructive repointing.
6. Don't assume it can't be fixed.
7. Get the design right.
8. Get help. Don't barge ahead.

Morgan Phillips, *The Eight Most Common Mistakes in Restoring Houses and How to Avoid Them.* Nashville: American Association for State and Local History, 1979. 8 pp., illus., biblio. Technical Leaflet 118. $2 pb. Reprinted from *Yankee* Magazine, December 1975.

"Don't rush in where carpenters fear to tread."

Greater Portland Landmarks, *Living With Old Houses*

"Restoring and rehabilitating old buildings is becoming so popular that almost as many crimes are being committed by misguided remodelers as were committed in the 1960's by the 'clear and destroy' bulldozers of the urban renewal forces."

Old-House Journal, 1977.

"It is better to preserve than to repair, better to repair than to restore, better to restore than to reconstruct."

A. N. Didron, 1839.

Recommended	Not Recommended
restore	reconstruct
rehabilitate	reconstitute
renovate	replicate
remodel	re-erect
repair	rebuild
revitalize	re-create
rejuvenate	redesign
revive	rework
reclaim	redevelop
renew	relocate
reuse	revamp
replace	remake
reproduce	remuddle
reinforce	
refurbish	
repaint	
repoint	
retrofit	
remember	
respect	

Original condition	Restored clapboard	Restored windows	Restored entrance

Steps in the restoration of an old frame house from its altered, "as found" condition. From *Remodeling Old Houses Without Destroying Their Character.* (Courtesy Alfred A. Knopf)

The Secretary's Standards

The Secretary of the Interior has developed standards for preservation projects as well as guidelines for applying them to activities ranging from acquisition through rehabilitation and even including reconstruction when necessary. The standards are used as the official criteria by which work on National Register historic properties is evaluated and eligibility for federal tax credits is certified:

1. Every reasonable effort shall be made to provide a compatible use for a property which requires minimal alteration of the building structure, or site and its environment, or to use a property for its originally intended purpose.
2. The distinguishing original qualities or character of a building, structure, or site and its environment shall not be destroyed. The removal or alteration of any historic material or distinctive architectural features should be avoided when possible.
3. All buildings, structures, and sites shall be recognized as products of their own time. Alterations that have no historical basis and which seek to create an earlier appearance shall be discouraged.
4. Changes which may have taken place in the course of time are evidence of the history and development of a building, structure, or site and its environment. These changes may have acquired significance in their own right, and this significance shall be recognized and respected.
5. Distinctive stylistic features or examples of skilled craftsmanship which characterize a building, structure or site shall be treated with sensitivity.
6. Deteriorated architectural features shall be repaired rather than replaced, wherever possible. In the event replacement is necessary, the new material should match the material being replaced in composition, design, color, texture, and other visual qualities. Repair or replacement of missing architectural features should be based on accurate duplications of features, substantiated by historical, physical, or pictorial evidence rather than on conjectural designs or the availability of different architectural elements from other buildings or structures.
7. The surface cleaning of structures shall be undertaken with the gentlest means possible. Sandblasting and other cleaning methods that will damage the historic building materials shall not be undertaken.
8. Every reasonable effort shall be made to protect and preserve archeological resources affected by, or adjacent to any project.

The Secretary of the Interior's Standards for Historic Preservation Projects

Patience

"First step, then, before the professional restorationist arrives, is to hesitate."

> Henry A. Judd, *Before Restoration Begins: Keeping Your Historic House Intact.* Nashville: American Association for State and Local History, 1973. Technical Leaflet 67. 10 pp. $2 pb.

"Irreversible removal of historic building fabric, especially decorative details, should be avoided. In fact, it is often less expensive to repair or make use of the existing material than to tear it out and start anew.

The most important quality in any rehabilitation is patience.

The end product will be only as good as the hours of careful thought that go into the planning and the time taken during reconstruction to repair and protect the important qualities of the building."

> Robert N. Pierpont, "Planning a Preservation Project." In *A Primer: Preservation for the Property Owner*

"Restoration" and Beyond

"Needless to say, if the building is to be lived in, total restoration is impossible, since few of us would care to rely on eighteenth-century plumbing, open fireplaces, and candles for our utilities. In other words, *total restoration is only possible when the building is to be a museum piece.* . . . Restoration, then, is almost always a compromise and ranges from almost total restoration where only the essential services are modernized to restoration of only a part of the building when the exterior, perhaps, or a particular part of the interior, is of historic or architectural interest."

> George Stephen, *Remodeling Old Houses Without Destroying Their Character*

"Preservationists who only recently labored to save a building from demolition and then turned without much inner questioning to its restoration to an earlier point in time are now increasingly searching their consciences, and many are adopting the philosophy of conservators, who seek to maintain the structure of an object as it has evolved, to keep it in good condition and to regard recent changes within the fabric as being of equal significance to the earliest changes. So much has this become the case that one is becoming accustomed to hearing nowadays, as a variation on the familiar alarm 'threatened with demolition,' that a certain building is 'threatened with restoration'."

> Abbott L. Cummings, Commentary on "Procedures and Performance Standards." In *Preservation and Conservation: Principles and Practices*

"The position of the S.P.N.E.A. is that what matters most about an old building is not its design but the old material in it, the fact that the building is a direct physical transference of the past into the present. . . . We reject the concept that old buildings are made all at once and observe that they normally and naturally consist of a continuum. . . . A second reason why the Society no longer restores is that restoration obliterates so much of the human history of a building. Historic architecture is more than architecture, it is also history."

> Morgan W. Phillips, "The Philosophy of Total Preservation." *Bulletin*, Association for Preservation Technology, vol. 3, no. 1, 1971.

Contacts

Technical Preservation Services
National Park Service
U.S. Department of the Interior
P.O. Box 37127
Washington, D.C. 20013-7127

Develops and publishes technical information on appropriate techniques for preserving and maintaining historic properties; administers the Secretary of the Interior's Standards; and certifies rehabilitation work for federal tax credits.

Association for Preservation Technology
P.O. Box 2487, Station D
Ottawa, Ontario K1P 5W6, Canada

A leading disseminator of technical preservation information, APT publishes a quarterly journal, the *Bulletin*, and a monthly newsletter, and sponsors an annual meeting and seminars throughout the year on a variety of restoration topics.

Holler House in Lockerbie Square, Indianapolis, before and after rehabilitation. (Barry Kaplan; Historic Landmarks Foundation of Indiana)

Weekend volunteers helped restore the Chalfonte Hotel (1876), Cape May, N.J. (Walter Smalling, Jr.)

National Trust for
Historic Preservation
Historic House Program
1785 Massachusetts Avenue, N.W.
Washington, D.C. 20036

Provides general information on restoration and publishes books and other publications on the subject. Its periodicals, including the magazine *Historic Preservation*, often feature restoration and rehabilitation-related topics and carry advertisements for services and products.

American Association for
State and Local History
708 Berry Road
Nashville, Tenn. 37204

Publishes the Technical Leaflet Series, a magazine, *History News*, and books on restoration topics. Also holds training seminars and produces slide shows on restoration.

American Institute of Architects
1735 New York Avenue, N.W.
Washington, D.C. 20006

Publishes information on working with architects, such as "How to Find, Evaluate, Select, Negotiate with an Architect" and related subjects. Its Committee on Historic Resources addresses preservation issues and has sponsored *The Preservation Workbook*, a resource guide for architects.

The Victorian Society in
America
219 South Sixth Street
Philadelphia, Pa. 19106

Focuses on 19th-century architecture and decorative arts, publishing a newsletter, a magazine, *19th-Century*, and reference lists. Also sponsors old-house workshops.

Society for the Preservation of
New England Antiquities
141 Cambridge Street
Boston, Mass. 02114

Maintains a building conservation division to care for its properties and also provides advisory services to owners of historic properties through its consulting services group.

The Old-House Journal
69-A Seventh Avenue
Brooklyn, N.Y. 11217

A monthly newsletter that strives to answer most of the questions old-house owners ask. Its back issues (many available in *The Old-House Journal Compendium*) address a wealth of issues.

Technology and Conservation
One Emerson Place
Boston, Mass. 02114

A quarterly magazine treating more technical restoration subjects, with case studies.

Center for Building Technology
National Bureau of Standards
U.S. Department of Commerce
Washington, D.C. 20234

Through research and publications, treats topics including conservation of building materials, energy conservation, color identification, fire retardation and insulation performance.

National Institute for the
Conservation of Cultural
Property
Smithsonian Institution
Arts and Industries Building
Room 2225
Washington, D.C. 20560

Reports on all aspects of object and building conservation through a system of study committees. The membership is institutional but individuals may contact the institute for information and to obtain copies of its reports.

International Centre for the
Study of the Preservation
and the Restoration of Cultural
Property (ICCROM)
13 Via di San Michele
00153 Rome, Italy

Leading center for conducting and coordinating research into technical problems of preserving and restoring all types of cultural resources, objects and structures.

North Atlantic Regional
Preservation Laboratory
National Park Service
15 State Street
Boston, Mass. 02109

Conducts research for application to Park Service buildings under restoration.

American Society for Testing
and Materials
1916 Race Street
Philadelphia, Pa. 19103

Establishes voluntary standards for materials, products and services. Has a subcommittee of its Committee on Performance of Materials dealing with preservation standards.

Decorative Arts Trust
106 Bainbridge Street
Philadelphia, Pa. 19147

Organization of professionals and others interested in furnishings and related historic decorative arts.

American Institute for
Conservation of Historic and
Artistic Works
3545 Williamsburg Lane, N.W.
Washington, D.C. 20008

Organization of professionals and educators dedicated to improving methods of conserving objects and structures and to encouraging research in art conservation.

The Language of Renovation

protection. ". . . to affect the physical condition of a property by defending or guarding it from deterioration, loss or attack, or to cover or shield the property from danger or injury. In the case of buildings and structures, such treatment is generally of a temporary nature and anticipates future historic preservation treatment. . . ."

stabilization. ". . . to reestablish a weather resistant enclosure and the structural stability of an unsafe or deteriorated property while maintaining the essential form as it exists at present."

preservation. " . . . to sustain the existing form, integrity, and material of a building or structure, and the existing form and vegetative cover of a site. . . ."

rehabilitation. " . . . returning a property to a state of utility through repair or alteration which makes possible an efficient contemporary use while preserving those portions or features of the property which are significant to its historical, architectural, and cultural values."

restoration. " . . . accurately recovering the form and details of a property and its setting as it appeared at a particular period of time by means of the removal of later work or by the replacement of missing earlier work."

The Secretary of the Interior's Standards for Historic Preservation Projects

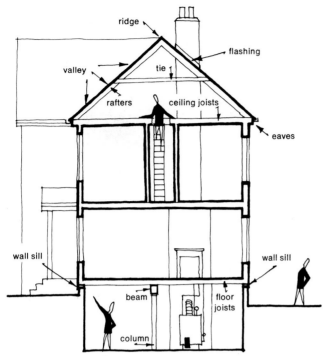

Places to look when inspecting a house. From *Remodeling Old Houses Without Destroying Their Character*. (Courtesy Alfred A. Knopf)

The condition of ceilings, walls, floors, stairways and decorative details should be examined before purchase and restoration. (Library of Congress)

Property and Problem Hunting: Finding and Inspecting Old Buildings

A thorough knowledge of the physical condition of a building should precede its purchase or rehabilitation. . . . When investigating a building, a property owner should consider the services of a building inspector, architect, or engineer experienced in preservation.

Robert N. Pierpont, "Physical Investigation." In *A Primer: Preservation for the Property Owner*

"To diagnose failures of structure and finish, the restoration architect must understand the technology of early American buildings—just as a doctor must understand physiology and anatomy before he practices therapy or performs surgery."

Charles F. Peterson, "The Role of the Architect in Historical Restorations." In *Preservation and Conservation: Principles and Practices*

"The roof may be one of the first items that will have to be repaired or replaced and should be looked at as closely as possible; particularly important are the flashing where it butts against chimneys, dormer windows, parapets, etc., these being the source of most leaks. As it is usually difficult to see these points from the ground, it may be helpful to take along a pair of binoculars."

George Stephen, *Rehabilitating Old Houses*

Clues for "Reading" a Building:

Detailed Examination
Floorboards
Exposed joists
Baseboards
Paneling and trim
Plaster work
Framing members
Nail holes
Old materials
Architectural woodwork
Exterior features

Dating Sections
Brickwork
Exterior wall covering
Roof covering
Species of wood
Framing members
Floor boards
Lath
Architectural trim
Moldings
Painted work
Nails
Hardware
Glass or glazing
Miscellaneous features

Contents, *The Restoration Manual*

Inspection Checklist for Vintage Houses: A Guide for Buyers and Owners. Old-House Journal. Brooklyn, N.Y.: Author, 1977. 4 pp. Free.

How to Inspect a House: Exactly What to Look for Before You Buy. George Hoffman. 1979. Rev. ed. Reading, Mass.: Addison-Wesley, 1985. $8.95 pb.

Rehabilitating Old Houses. George Stephen. Information Series. National Trust for Historic Preservation. Washington, D.C.: Preservation Press, 1976. 13 pp., illus., biblio. $2 pb.

Reading a Building: Colonial. John Obed Curtis. Nashville: American Association for State and Local History. Slide and tape program. $44.50.

Diagnosing and Repairing House Structure Problems. Edgar O. Seaquist. New York: McGraw-Hill, 1980. 265 pp., illus., gloss., index. $14.95 hb.

Inspecting a House: A Guide for Buyers, Owners, and Renovators. Alan Carson and Robert Dunlop. New York: Beaufort Books, 1982. 272 pp., illus., gloss., index. $9.95 pb.

The Complete Book of Home Inspection: For the Buyer or Owner. Norman Becker, P.E. New York: McGraw-Hill, 1970. 172 pp., illus., gloss., append., index. $8.95 pb.

"Getting to Know an Old House," Beverly A. Reece. *Historic Preservation*, September–October 1979.

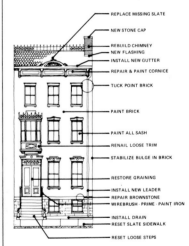

Checklist of items to be rehabilitated. From *A Primer: Preservation for the Property Owner*. (Preservation League of New York State)

Buying and Renovating a House in the City: A Practical Guide. Deirdre Stanforth and Martha Stamm. New York: Knopf, 1972. 428 pp., illus., appends., index.

X-Ray Examination of Historic Structures. David M. Hart. Washington, D.C.: Technical Preservation Services. 24 pp., illus. Available from NTIS.

From "The Agony and Ecstasy of Restoring Your First House." *Historic Preservation*, July–August 1982. (Ed Koren)

X-Rays: Modern Medicine for Old-House Problems

"An answer to the problems [of inspecting old buildings] could be supplied by x-ray radiography. . . . Once the radiographs are obtained, they can be utilized in a variety of ways to analyze an historic building. The data contained within these film records can provide historical and dating information. Or the radiographs can be used to survey the structural elements of the building. Or . . . the film records can reveal signs of internal deterioration and thereby allow the physical condition of the structure to be better assessed."

> David McLaren Hart, "X-Ray Inspection of Historic Structures: An Aid to Dating and Structural Analyses." *Technology and Conservation*, Summer 1977.

Danger: Rehabilitation May Be Hazardous to Your Health

"A European conservator on a recent trip to the U.S. remarked that American restorers are 'chemical crazy.' He was astonished at the number of organic chemicals that are used in such a casual way by old-house owners. . . .

We don't want to scare you into abandoning restoration. Rather, we want to scare you into observing sensible precautions for your own well-being. After reviewing a lot of literature in the field, we sure have succeeded in scaring ourselves. . . . The new information . . . sure is going to change *how* we do some things."

> "Danger: Restoration May Be Hazardous to Your Health." *Old-House Journal*, May 1976.

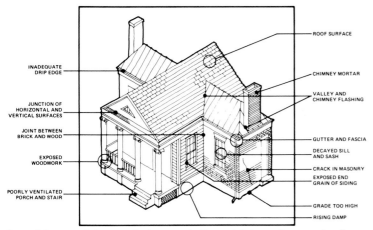

Potential areas of decay to be inspected. From *A Primer: Preservation for the Property Owner.* (Preservation League of New York State)

Hard-hat area: replacing masonry on the Renwick Gallery (1859, James Renwick), Washington, D.C. (Preservation Technology Group, Ltd.)

Local chapter of Women in Construction at work rehabilitating a house in the Lockerbie Square Historic District, Indianapolis. (Carleton Knight III, NTHP)

Rehabilitation Handbooks

Today nearly a million buildings are listed in the National Register of Historic Places, either individually or as part of registered historic districts. These—and countless other old buildings—require not only continuing maintenance and preservation but also the rehabilitation needed to accommodate new uses dictated by changing times. While many owners, architects and contractors are familiar with modern construction technologies and products, relatively few have had extensive experience dealing with historic buildings.

Lee H. Nelson, Foreword.
Respectful Rehabilitation

Respectful Rehabilitation: Answers to Your Questions About Old Buildings. Technical Preservation Services, U.S. Department of the Interior. Washington,D.C.: Preservation Press, 1982. 192 pp., illus., append., biblio., index. $9.95 pb.

Down-to-earth advice based on the Secretary of the Interior's Rehabilitation Standards, compiled as a browsable collection of 150 frequently asked questions for all building types, inside and out. Includes the complete Rehabilitation Standards and detailed guidelines.

The Secretary of the Interior's Standards for Rehabilitation and Guidelines for Rehabilitating Historic Buildings. W. Brown Morton III, Gary L. Hume and Kay D. Weeks. 1979. Rev. ed. Washington, D.C.: Technical Preservation Services, U.S. Department of the Interior, 1983. 61 pp. Free.

Presents the official federal standards for rehabilitation with detailed guidelines in a "recommended" and "not recommended" format.

Remodeling Old Houses Without Destroying Their Character. George Stephen. New York: Knopf, 1972. 244 pp., illus., appends., gloss., index. $5.95 pb.

The grandfather of design-rehabilitation advice directed to the property owner. The book covers why to rehabilitate; general design terms and principles; selecting a house; choosing an architect or builder; the exterior—general considerations, materials and colors, existing details and new additions; the interior—planning the layout, special details and finishes.

The Original Old-House Journal Compendium. Clem Labine and Carolyn Flaherty, eds. Woodstock, N.Y.: Overlook Press, 1980. 400 pp., illus., index. $14.95 pb.

The Old-House Journal New Compendium: A Complete How-to Guide for Sensitive Rehabilitation. Patricia Poore and Clem Labine, eds. New York: Doubleday, 1983. 426 pp., illus., gloss., index. $15.95 pb.

Compilations of *OHJ* articles providing the "whys" and "hows" of rehabilitation advice. Topics included are buying an old house; architectural and decorative styles; roofs and windows; masonry; energy efficiency; wiring; plumbing; plastering; floors; chimneys, fireplaces and stoves; molding, woodwork and shutters; kitchens and bathrooms; painting, graining and stenciling; and exterior design and landscaping.

Renovation: A Complete Guide. Michael Litchfield. New York: John Wiley and Sons, 1982. 586 pp., illus., appends., biblio., index. $34.95 hb.

A detailed, well-organized and well-illustrated handbook covering all facets of rehabilitating old buildings, including a "wealth of practical trade secrets and technical tips learned from master craftsmen."

A Guide to the Maintenance, Repair, and Alteration of Historic Buildings. Frederick A. Stahl. New York: Van Nostrand Reinhold, 1984. 185 pp., illus $24.95 hb.

Shows how to use modern technology to solve deterioration in building materials and systems and adapt historic buildings without affecting their character.

Preserving and Maintaining the Older Home. Shirley Hanson and Nancy Hubby. New York: McGraw-Hill, 1983. 237 pp., illus., biblio., append., index. $29.95 hb.

A practical overview organized by house styles and individual features such as windows, doors, walls, roofs, shutters and porches.

Old Houses: A Rebuilder's Manual. George Nash. Englewood Cliffs, N.J.: Prentice-Hall, 1980. 366 pp., illus., biblio., index. $12.95 pb.

A sensitive, detailed handbook covering all facets of rehabilitation, with an added "Cookbook for Comfortable Living."

The Old House. Home Repair and Improvement Series. Alexandria, Va.: Time-Life Books, 1979. 136 pp., illus., index. $12.95 hb.

An explicitly illustrated manual providing comprehensive guidance in carrying out a variety of tasks, featuring details, utilities and structural problems.

This Old House: Restoring, Rehabilitating and Renovating an Older House. Bob Vila with Jane Davison. Boston: Little, Brown, 1980. 285 pp., illus. $22.95 hb, $14.95 pb.

Chronicles the rescue of a neglected 120-year-old house, based on the WGBH-TV series "This Old House." A photographer who doubled as a carpenter's apprentice recorded the renovation in color and black-and-white photos. The result is a step-by-step story of a renovation.

Bob Vila's This Old House. Bob Vila. New York: Dutton, 1981. 284 pp., illus., biblio., index. $22.50 hb, $17.45 pb.

Camera's-eye view of the conversion of H.H. Richardson's Bigelow House in Newton, Mass., into condominiums. More recycling than restoration takes place.

Restoring Old Houses. Nigel Hutchins. New York: Van Nostrand Reinhold, 1980. 240 pp., illus., append., gloss., biblio., index. $29.95 hb.

A Canadian overview ranging from preservation philosophy and research to structural, exterior, mechanical and finishing guidance.

So You Want to Fix Up an Old House. Peter Hotton. Boston: Little, Brown, 1979. 274 pp., illus., biblio., gloss., index. $11 pb.

An illustrated guide from the ground up, with do's and don'ts.

Renovating the Victorian House: A Guide for Owners and Aficionados of Old Houses. Katherine Rusk. San Francisco: 101 Productions, 1982. 200 pp., illus., biblio., appends., index. $12.95 pb.

A handbook based on the author's experience in renovation and writing a newspaper column.

The New Complete Book of Home Remodeling, Improvement, and Repair. Arthur Martin Watkins. Piermont, N.Y.: Building Institute (855 Piermont Road, 10968), 1979. 363 pp., illus., index. $9.95 pb.

An orderly approach with a strong remodeling focus, based on the engineer-author's experiences.

The Old-House Rescue Book: Buying and Renovating on a Budget. Robert Kangas. Reston, Va.: Reston Publishing, 1982. 253 pp., illus., gloss., index. $12.95 pb.

A guide to low-budget renovation surveying purchasing, repairing and adapting.

Home Renovation. Francis
D. K. Ching and Dale E. Miller.
New York: Van Nostrand Reinhold, 1983. 338 pp., illus., index.
$22.45 hb, $15.45 pb.

A basic, clearly illustrated rehabilitation guide, not necessarily designed
for historic houses.

Technical Leaflet Series.
Nashville: American Association
for State and Local History. $2
pb each.

Brief pamphlets surveying a wide
range of preservation topics, including many on restoration and
rehabilitation.

Slide and Tape Programs.
Nashville: American Association
for State and Local History.
$44.50 each.

A series, each lasting 20 minutes
with 70–80 slides. Topics in addition
to those listed under specific sections in this chapter include bedding,
cleaning masonry buildings, furniture care, housekeeping for museums, restoration planning, log buildings, energy, adobes, wallpaper and
window glass.

*A Primer: Preservation for the
Property Owner*. Albany: Preservation League of New York
State (307 Hamilton Street,
12210), 1978. 40 pp., illus., biblios. $2 pb.

A collection of short articles covering historical research, physical investigation, emergency repairs and
stabilization, exterior rehabilitation,
roofing, painting, floor coverings,
energy efficiency, mechanical systems, grounds and landscapes.

*Our Home Memory and Main-
tenance Album*. Roberta Ritz
Mathews, National Association
of Home Builders. Washington,
D.C.: Acropolis Books, 1982.
127 pp., illus. $12.95 hb,
$6.95 pb.

A handbook-scrapbook in which to
record events, furnishings and dates
related to work and improvements
on one's house.

*Antique Houses: Their Con-
struction and Restoration*. Edward P. Friedland. New York:
Dutton, 1982. 288 pp., illus.
$24.95 hb, $14.95 pb.

*Maintenance, Repairs and Re-
modeling: A List of Books for
the Homeowner*. Mary Vance.
Monticello, Ill.: Vance Bibliographies, 1980. A-201. 12 pp.
$2 pb.

On the Technical Side

Technical Preservation Briefs.
Technical Preservation Services,
U.S. Department of the Interior.
Washington, D.C.: GPO.

A series presenting the department's
recommended procedures for properly caring for historic buildings.
Topics cover cleaning buildings, masonry, roofing, aluminum siding,
windows and energy. See listings
under specific subject headings that
follow.

*Conservation of Historic Build-
ings*. Bernard M. Feilden.
Woburn, Mass.: Butterworths,
1982. 482 pp., illus., appends.,
gloss., biblio., index. $124 hb.

A definitive handbook based on the
author's British experience and
using international examples. Topics
range from structural aspects of
historic buildings to causes of decay,
the work of the conservation architect, repairs and special techniques,
with numerous appendixes.

*Preservation and Conservation:
Principles and Practices*. National Trust for Historic Preservation, ed. For International
Centre for the Study of the
Preservation and the Restoration of Cultural Property. Washington, D.C.: Preservation
Press, 1976. 547 pp., illus.,
biblio. $17.95 pb.

Surveys nearly all materials used in
building construction, presenting
their history, composition, strengths
and weaknesses, life expectancy,
destructive agents and means of
preservation.

*The Restoration Manual: An Il-
lustrated Guide to the Preservation and Restoration of Old
Buildings*. Orin M. Bullock.
1966. Reprint. New York: Van
Nostrand Reinhold, 1983. 192
pp., illus. gloss., biblio., append.
$12.95 hb.

An early contribution that describes
restoration and maintenance procedures. Directed more toward the
architect-in-charge than an individual property owner.

*The Technology of Historic
American Buildings*. H. Ward
Jandl, ed. Washington, D.C.:
Foundation for Preservation
Technology, 1984. 225 pp., illus.,
index. $25 pb.

A reference on the history of building materials and construction methods designed especially for architects and scholars. Presents studies
by authorities on the balloon frame,
hardware, I beam, cast iron, terra
cotta, metal roofing and exterior
19th-century painting.

*The Care of Old Buildings
Today: A Practical Guide*.
Donald Insall. London: Architectural Press, 1972. 197 pp.,
illus., biblio.

A technical guide based on extensive British conservation experience.

Restoring the Belknap Playhouse
(1874), Louisville. (© 1980 *Courier-
Journal* and *Louisville Times*)

**Handyman Manuals: Okay—
With a Caveat**

"How-to-do-it books and manuals can deal only with specifically defined cases or broad
generalities, and may not be
useful for solving unique problems found in the preservation,
repair, and maintenance of historic structures. It is perhaps
for this reason that there is such
a dearth of technical literature
applicable to historic structures
preservation. . . .

Available literature can be
broken down into 'yes,' 'no'
and 'maybe' sources. And,
those categories should have
the underlining caveat of 'just
because it is in print doesn't
mean it's so.' Furthermore, it is
the responsibility of the preservationist to ask, 'If it is so,
does it really apply to my
buildings?' . . .

While it is possible to establish a working library of references, you should remember
that the problem at hand is
probably not discussed in a
manual."

Hugh C. Miller, "Technical Literature for the Repair and Maintenance of Historic Structures."
*Cultural Resources Management
Bulletin*, December 1978. National Park Service, U.S. Department of the Interior, Washington,
D.C. 20240.

Home Improvement Manual.
John Speicher, ed. Pleasantville,
N.Y.: Reader's Digest Associa-
tion, 1982. 384 pp., illus., index.
$21.50 hb.

Exceptionally detailed all-purpose
handbook covering all aspects of
renovation, with specific sections on
rehabilitation.

America's Handyman Book. The
Family Handyman Magazine
Staff. Rev. ed. New York:
Scribner's, 1983. 432 pp., illus.
$16.95 hb.

Basic reference on repairing and
maintaining a house.

Basic Home Repairs Illustrated.
Editors of Sunset Books and
Sunset Magazine. 1971. Menlo
Park, Calif.: Lane Publishing,
1980. 96 pp., illus. $4.95 pb.

Provides practical information and
drawings for solving household repair problems.

Rehabilitation for Profit

"The profitable recycling of a
building—and it must be profitable if the recycling process is
to be continued—requires imagination, know-how, and the
courage to speculate. A great
deal of the speculative risk can
be removed by intelligent forward planning and by following
a step-by-step procedure that
will assure a lending institution
that everything that can be done
has been done by the architect,
the engineer, and the developer
to make the project a success."

Laurence E. Reiner, *How to Recycle Old Buildings*

How to Recycle Old Buildings.
Laurence E. Reiner. New York:
McGraw-Hill, 1979. 256 pp.,
illus., index.

*Building Renovation and Recy-
cling*. Edgar Lion. New York:
Wiley Interscience, 1982. 132
pp., illus., index. $29.95 hb.

Rehabbing for Profit. Jerry C.
Davis. New York: McGraw-Hill,
1981. 224 pp. $24.95 hb.

*How to Renovate Townhouses
and Brownstones*. William H.
Edgerton. New York: Van
Nostrand Reinhold, 1980. 150
pp., appends., index. $18.95 hb.

*How We Made a Million Dollars
Recycling Great Old Houses*.
Sam and Mary Weir. Chicago:
Contemporary Books, 1979. 294
pp., illus., append., biblio., in-
dex. $8.95 pb.

*Restore Your Future: A Profit
Guide to Renovation*. Markley
Lee Jones, Jack B. Curry and
Shirley F. Curry. Englewood
Cliffs, N.J.: Prentice-Hall, 1982.
$5.95 pb.

*Home-Tech Restoration and
Renovation Cost Estimator*. Vol.
II. Henry Reynolds. Bethesda,
Md.: Home-Tech Publications
(7315 Wisconsin Avenue, 20014),
1982. 200 pp. $28.80 pb.

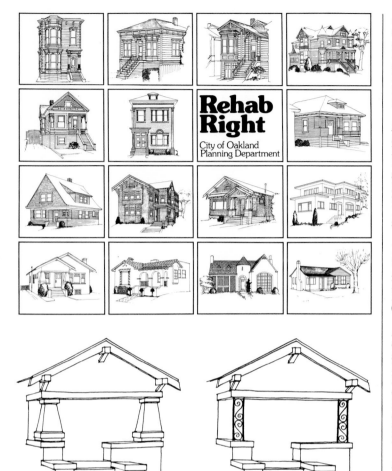

Do's and don'ts for retaining the elephantine columns typical of 20th-century bungalows. From *Rehab Right*. (Courtesy City of Oakland Planning Department)

Local Rehabilitation Guidelines

"This genre is an ever-expanding phenomenon in the United States. Nevertheless, many communities still undertake the preparation of such guidelines with little sense of the quantity and diversity of existing publications. While some localities possess architectural resources requiring specifically adapted guidelines, many others easily could make use of publications which are already available, at least as a starting point for their own efforts."

Merrill Ware Carrington, Introduction. *Design Guidelines: An Annotated Bibliography*. Washington, D.C.: National Endowment for the Arts, 1977. Distributed by Preservation Press. 26 pp., index.

"Nao se deixe levar por um promotor de vendas que lhe fale em processos de limpeza miraculosos."

"Don't be taken in by a salesman promoting miracle cleaning methods."

Fixing Up: A Bilingual Handbook for Older Homes

Rehab Right: How to Rehabilitate Your Oakland House Without Sacrificing Architectural Assets. Helaine Kaplan and Blair Prentice. Oakland, Calif.: City of Oakland Planning Department (1421 Washington Street, 6th Floor, 94612), 1978. 140 pp., illus., append., biblio. $6 pb.

An exemplary, award-winning preservation manual. The book surveys Oakland's architectural styles and describes how to rehabilitate exteriors and interiors. It gets down to details such as how to repair an elephantine column, where to put weatherstripping on a double-hung window, how to remedy loose floorboards and more.

Living With Old Houses. Advisory Service, Greater Portland Landmarks. Portland, Maine: Author (Station A, Box 4197, 04101), 1975. 110 pp., illus., gloss., biblio.

Slates, Shingles and Shakes: A Renovation Guide for Laconia's Historic Homes. David McLaren Hart and Associates and Peter B. Hance. Laconia, N.H.: City of Laconia Planning Department, 1978. 127 pp., illus., append. $1.

Fixing Up: A Bilingual Handbook for Older Homes. Dennis P. Albert, Ancelin V. Lynch, Lombard John Pozzi and Elizabeth S. Warren. Warren, R.I.: Massasoit Historical Association (P.O. Box 203, 02885), 1979. 127 pp., illus., gloss. Portuguese and English. $3.75 pb.

The Salem Handbook: A Renovation Guide for Homeowners. Anderson Notter Associates and Historic Salem. Salem, Mass.: Historic Salem (P.O. Box 865, 01970), 1977. 113 pp. $5.95.

Lowell: The Building Book. City of Lowell Division of Planning and Development and Anderson Notter Associates. Lowell, Mass.: City of Lowell (50 Arcand Drive, JFK Civic Center, Division of Planning and Development, 01852), 1977. 71 pp., illus., biblio., gloss., appends. $3.25 pb.

How to Love and Care for Your Old Building in New Bedford. Maximilian L. Ferro. New Bedford, Mass.: Office of Historic Preservation (Room 13, City Hall, 133 William Street, 02740), 1977. 158 pp., illus. $3 pb.

Beacon Hill Architectural Handbook: Guidelines for Preservation and Modification. Beacon Hill Civic Association. Boston: Author (74 Jay Street, 02114), 1975.

Back Bay Residential District: Guidelines for Exterior Rehabilitation and Restoration. Back Bay Architectural Commission. Boston: Author (One Beacon Street, 02108). 36 pp.

Historic Preservation Guidelines. Marie Kennedy, Mayor's Office of Community Development, Boston Redevelopment Authority and Massachusetts Historical Commission. Boston: City of Boston (Massachusetts Historical Commission, 294 Washington Street, 02108), 1977. 40 pp., illus., biblio.

The House Book: The Better Way to Restore Older Homes In Springfield. Janice Cunningham. Springfield, Mass.: Springfield Community Development Department and Springfield Historical Commission (Planning Department, City Hall, Room 226, 01103). 32 pp.

Fixing Up Older Houses: Handbook of Exterior Renovations. Vision, Inc. Brookline, Mass.: Brookline Planning Department (333 Washington Street, Town Hall, 02146), 1975. 44 pp.

The Cape May Handbook. Carolyn Pitts, Michael Fish, Hugh J. McCauley, Trina Vaux, for the Athenaeum of Philadelphia, City of Cape May and Historic American Buildings Survey. Philadelphia: The Athenaeum (219 South Sixth Street, 19106), 1977. 82 pp., illus., append., gloss., biblio., index.

Historic Rittenhouse: A Philadelphia Neighborhood. Bobbye Burke, Otto Sperr, Hugh J. McCauley and Trina Vaux. Philadelphia: University of Pennsylvania Press, 1985. 144 pp., illus. $22.50 hb, $14.95 pb.

Chapel Hill Historic District Guidelines Handbook. Elizabeth Staples. Chapel Hill, N.C.: Historic District Commission (306 North Columbia Street, 27514), 1979. 62 pp., illus.

The Beaufort Preservation Manual. John Milner Associates. Beaufort, S.C.: City of Beaufort, 1979. 159 pp., illus., biblio., gloss., index. $10 pb.

The Cleveland Old House Handbook: A Guide to Maintaining Your Historic House on the Near West Side. Carol Poh Miller. Cleveland: Neighborhood Housing Services, 1979. 48 pp.

City House: A Guide to Renovating Older Chicago-Area Houses. Linda Legner. Chicago: Commission on Chicago Historical and Architectural Landmarks (320 North Clark Street, Room 800, 60610), 1979. Distributed by Chicago Review Press. 90 pp., illus., gloss., biblio. $4.95 pb.

Tucson Preservation Primer: A Guide for the Property Owner. Robert C. Giebner, ed. Tucson, Ariz.: College of Architecture, University of Arizona, 1979. 44 pp.

Confronting the Older House: A Homeowner's Guide. Kip Harris. Salt Lake City: Utah Heritage Foundation (603 East South Temple Street, 84102), 1979. 75 pp., illus., append., biblio.

Santa Cruz Renovation Manual: A Homeowner's Handbook. Charles Hall Page and Associates. Santa Cruz, Calif.: Department of Planning and Community Development (City Hall, 809 Center Street, 95060), 1976. 106 pp., illus., gloss., biblio. $5 pb.

Lucy the Elephant (1881, William Free), Margate, N.J., received a facelift before being converted into a community center. (Jack E. Boucher)

St. Johns Building Improvement Handbook. City of Portland Development Commission and Goebel McClure Ragland, Architects and Planners, AIA. Portland, Ore.: St. Johns Improvement Association (7302 North Richmond, 97203), 1978. 86 pp., illus., appends., gloss., biblio.

Case Studies

Restored America. Deirdre Stanforth. New York: Praeger, 1975. 246 pp., illus.

A pictorial look at five dozen buildings and neighborhoods. More than half are restored houses; the remainder are adaptive uses.

Historic Houses Restored and Preserved. Marian Page. New York: Whitney Library of Design, 1976. 208 pp., illus., biblio., index.

The stories of 14 structures, including five National Trust properties and Lucy the Margate Elephant (N.J.), accompanied by plans and photographs.

Recycling Buildings: Renovations, Remodelings, Restorations and Reuses. Elizabeth Kendall Thompson, ed. New York: McGraw-Hill, 1977. 213 pp., illus., index.

Taken from the pages of *Architectural Record*, the examples here are a mixture of adaptive use, heavy remodeling, infill and authentic restorations.

New Life for Old Buildings. Mildred F. Schmertz and Editors of Architectural Record. New York: McGraw-Hill, 1982. 189 pp., illus., index. $34.50 hb.

Adaptive use, renovation and restoration case histories of urban marketplaces, civic and cultural buildings, colleges, offices, showrooms, a bank, restaurants, houses and apartments.

New Living in Old Houses. Frank R. Werner. New York: Abrams, 1982. 160 pp., illus. $35 hb.

A look book featuring lavish restorations and adaptive uses around the world.

Fort Johnson, Amsterdam, New York: A Historic Structure Report, 1974–1975. Mendel, Mesick, Cohen, Architects. Technical Preservation Services, U.S. Department of the Interior. Washington, D.C.: GPO, 1978. 54 pp., illus., appends. $5 pb. GPO stock no. 024-005-00706-7.

Fort Stanwick: History, Historic Furnishings and Historic Structures Report. National Park Service, U.S. Department of the Interior. Washington, D.C.: GPO, 1976. 107 pp.

The Morse-Libby Mansion, Portland, Maine: A Report on Restoration Work, 1973–1977. Morgan W. Phillips. Technical Preservation Services, U.S. Department of the Interior. Washington, D.C.: GPO, 1977. 55 pp., illus., appends. Available from NTIS.

Lucky Landmark. A Study of a Design and Its Survival: The Galveston Customhouse, Post Office and Courthouse of 1861. Donald J. Lehman. Washington, D.C.: U.S. General Services Administration, Public Buildings Service, 1973.

The Plan for Restoration and Adaptive Use of the Frank Lloyd Wright Home and Studio. Restoration Committee, Frank Lloyd Wright Home and Studio Foundation. Chicago: University of Chicago Press, 1978. 82 pp., illus.

The Renaissance of Mark Twain's House: Handbook for Restoration. Wilson H. Faude. Larchmont, N.Y.: Queens House, 1978. 106 pp., illus., biblio. $20 hb.

The Calkins Law Office: Its History and Restoration. Gordon L. Olson. Grand Rapids, Mich.: Grand Rapids Public Museum (54 Jefferson Street, S.E., 49503), 1976. 32 pp., illus. $2.50 pb.

Baltimore's salvage depot, operated by the city to sell architectural artifacts for restorations—to city residents only. (Commission for Historical and Architectural Preservation)

Sources of Materials and Services

I needed something they didn't make any more. It was a hinge of the type called a 2½ inch parliament butt.

I suspected they didn't make it any more. Once they find out they are making something you might need one of these days, they immediately call the factory and tell them not to make it any more.

Russell Baker, "They Don't Make That Any More." *New York Times*, 1975. Reprinted in *Preservation News*, November 1975.

The Old-House Journal 1985 Catalog: A Buyer's Guide for the Pre-1939 House. Old-House Journal Editors. Brooklyn: Old-House Journal, 1984. 212 pp., illus., index. $12.95 pb.

Lists more than 1,200 companies that sell more than 9,000 items and services, from millwork to old-style roofing, ironwork to wainscoting, furniture to tools, paints to plumbing.

The Fourth Old House Catalogue. Lawrence Grow. Pittstown, N.J.: Main Street Press, 1985. 224 pp., illus., index. $11.95 pb.

A guide to locating products and services for everything from woodwork and hardware to lighting and paints, from decorative accessories to garden materials.

Salvaged Treasures: Designing and Building with Architectural Salvage. Michael Litchfield and Rosemarie Hausherr. New York: Van Nostrand Reinhold, 1983. 253 pp., illus., append., biblio., index. $35 hb.

Shows how to reclaim discarded elements such as windows, woodwork, plumbing fixtures and whole houses.

Sourcebook of Architectural Ornament: Designers, Craftsmen, Manufacturers, and Distributors of Exterior Architectural Ornament. Brent C. Brolin and Jean Richards. New York: Van Nostrand Reinhold, 1982. 288 pp., illus., index. $7.95 pb.

A catalog from awnings to wood providing suppliers, examples and other information on a wide range of building materials usable as ornamentation, replacement or new. Among the topics: brick, terra cotta, ceramics, glass, iron, murals, fiber art, signs, stucco and sculpture.

Contacts

Renovator's Supply
71 Northfield Road
Millers Falls, Mass. 01349

"The Old House Emporium"
The Old-House Journal
69-A Seventh Avenue
Brooklyn, N.Y. 11217

"Marketplace"
Preservation News
National Trust for
Historic Preservation
1785 Massachusetts Avenue, N.W.
Washington, D.C. 20036

Salvage Depots: Cash and Carry

Cannibalism is what it's called, architecturally speaking: scavenging, stripping, stealing irreplaceable features and fixtures from buildings about to be demolished or "modernized."

Says the Landmarks Preservation Commission of New York City: "If the artifacts thus collected were locally recycled to assist the average homeowner who wishes to renovate his brownstone or similar building, the activity might be viewed as socially useful. Unfortunately, this is often not the case. While some of the material is used in renovation, some of the vanishing ornamentation is sold as art and a sizable portion is sold outside the city to auction and antique dealers."

In an attempt both to serve the growing numbers of rehabilitators and to stop architectural vandalism, cities are creating their own "salvage depots" to regulate the sales of used building parts. In addition to those listed here, depots have been started in Oklahoma City, Detroit, Pittsburgh, St. Charles, Mo., Chicago and Portland, Ore.

A parliament butt like the one Russell Baker wanted. From *Preservation News*. (Tim Evans)

Contacts

Baltimore Salvage Depot
c/o Commission for Historical and Architectural Preservation
601 City Hall
Baltimore, Md. 21202

Parts Warehouse
Saratoga Springs Preservation Foundation
P.O. Box 442
Saratoga Springs, N.Y. 12866

Parts Warehouse
Historic Albany Foundation
300 Hudson Avenue
Albany, N.Y. 12210

Salvage Program
Broome County Historical Society
30 Front Street
Binghamton, N.Y. 13905

SAVE: Salvage of Architecturally Valuable Elements
Landmarks Preservation Commission of New York City
20 Vesey Street
New York, N.Y. 10007

Salvage Program
Newark Housing Development and Rehabilitation Corporation
11 Hill Street
Newark, N.J. 07102

Architectural Antiques and Artifacts Advertiser
P.O. Box 31
Merion, Pa. 19066

Yellow Pages
"Wrecking Contractors"
"Architectural Artifacts"

Old-House Journal Publisher Clem Labine looks over the Bradbury and Bradbury wallpapers at the Trust's ReHabitat. (Richard Lippenholz)

Sandblasting made the brick on the left pitted and rough and removed mortar from the joints. (Laurie Hammel, U.S. Department of the Interior)

Fair News: Old-House Shows

Several cities and preservation groups have launched a new scheme for putting renovators in touch with contractors, craftspeople, supplies and proper rehabilitation techniques: the old-house fair. Chicago's City House fair, held first in 1979, became a model for others. The National Trust now offers a ReHabitat at its annual fall conference to showcase services and materials to a national audience.

Contacts

National Trust for
Historic Preservation
ReHabitat Show
1785 Massachusetts Avenue,
N.W.
Washington, D.C. 20036

Assistant Commissioner
Chicago Department of Housing
320 North Clark Street
Chicago, Ill. 60610

Utah State Historical Society
307 West 200, South
Salt Lake City, Utah 84101

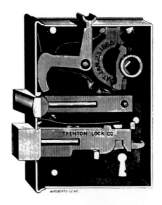

Cleaning Buildings

Abrasive cleaning methods are responsible for causing a great deal of damage to historic building materials. . . . There are alternative, less harsh means of cleaning and removing paint and stains from historic buildings. . . . A historic building is irreplaceable, and should be cleaned using only the "gentlest means possible" to best preserve it.

Anne E. Grimmer, *Dangers of Abrasive Cleaning to Historic Buildings*

Dangers of Abrasive Cleaning to Historic Buildings. Anne E. Grimmer. Preservation Brief no. 6. Technical Preservation Services, U.S. Department of the Interior. Washington, D.C.: GPO, 1979. 8 pp., illus. $1 pb. GPO stock no. 024-005-00882-9.

Tells why not to sandblast wood, metal and other materials, inside and out. "The crux of the problem is that abrasive cleaning is just that—abrasive. An abrasively cleaned historic structure may be physically as well as aesthetically damaged." The "gentlest" cleaning alternatives are detailed.

The Cleaning and Waterproof Coating of Masonry Buildings. Robert C. Mack, AIA. Preservation Brief no. 1. Technical Preservation Services, U.S. Department of the Interior. Washington, D.C.: GPO, 1978. 4 pp., illus. $1 pb. GPO stock no. 024-005-00877-2.

Outlines techniques for cleaning and waterproofing.

Exterior Cleaning of Historic Masonry Buildings. Norman R. Weiss. Technical Report. Technical Preservation Services, U.S. Department of the Interior. Washington, D.C.: GPO, 1977. 18 pp. Available from NTIS.

Discusses methods of cleaning and the factors to consider before selecting a suitable method. Designed for architects and professional administrators.

Peeling paint on a brick wall. (Miami Purchase Association)

Visitors to the City House fair in Chicago watch as a restoration craftsman plies his trade.

Ornamental masonry, including vermiculated stone at bottom, found in Boston's Back Bay Historic District. (Pierce Pearman, courtesy Back Bay Architectural Commission)

Smooth and rock-faced masonry finishes found in Boston's Back Bay. (Pierce Pearman, courtesy Back Bay Architectural Commission)

Masonry

Every kind of stone is more or less porous; it absorbs moisture from a damp atmosphere, from rain, from groundwater and from condensation on the interior of the building. . . . Dirty surfaces attract moisture thus making them particularly vulnerable to disintegration or "stone diseases." If water in the pores of stone freezes, it can cause portions of the surface to break away. . . . The introduction of dampproofing courses can protect a wall against rising damp, but moisture from other sources cannot be completely controlled.

Harley J. McKee, *Introduction to Early American Masonry*

Introduction to Early American Masonry: Stone, Brick, Mortar and Plaster. Harley J. McKee, FAIA. Washington, D.C.: Preservation Press, 1973. 92 pp., illus., biblio., index. $7.95 pb.

Surveys the history, construction (to 1860) and restoration of all masonry types. The book covers how stone is quarried and dressed, how brick is made, how masonry buildings are constructed, how deterioration occurs and how restoration should take place. Also covered: plasterwork, both exterior and ornamental interior; tools; terra cotta and special brickwork. Illustrations and diagrams clearly explain each topic.

Conservation of Historic Stone Buildings and Monuments. Report of the Committee on Conservation of Historic Stone Buildings and Monuments. National Materials Advisory Board. Washington, D.C.: National Academy Press, 1982. 365 pp., append., index. $21.25 pb.

Compilation of technical papers on all aspects of stone conservation, with a report on recommended preservation policies and treatments.

Moisture Problems in Historic Masonry Walls: Diagnosis and Treatment. Baird M. Smith, National Park Service. Washington, D.C.: GPO, 1984. 48 pp., illus. $2.25 pb. GPO stock no. 024-005-00872-1.

Technical report on water damage with a methodology for treatments.

A Glossary of Historic Masonry Deterioration Problems and Preservation Treatments. Anne E. Grimmer, National Park Service. Washington, D.C.: GPO, 1984. 65 pp., illus. $2.50 pb. GPO stock no. 024-005-00870-5.

Covers 22 deterioration problems and known treatments as an aid to maintenance.

Stucco. Brian D. Conway. Illinois Preservation Series, no. 2. Springfield: Illinois Department of Conservation, Division of Historic Sites (405 East Washington Street, 62706), 1980. 6 pp., illus., biblio.

Restoring Houses of Brick and Stone. Nigel Hutchins. New York: Van Nostrand Reinhold, 1982. 192 pp., illus., gloss., biblio., index. $29.95 hb.

A guide to inspecting, repairing and enlarging masonry houses that covers history, construction techniques and related topics.

A Selection of Historic Papers on Concrete: 1876–1926. American Concrete Institute. Detroit: Author, 1976. 334 pp. $28 hb. Order no. SP-52.

Contacts

Building Stone Institute of America
420 Lexington Avenue
New York, N.Y. 10017

American Concrete Institute
P.O. Box 19150, Redford Station
Detroit, Mich. 48219

See also: Adobes, Cobblestone Buildings (Form and Function)

Brick and Mortar

There are three things to watch out for if you want to create new brick-work that is indistinguishable from the original: New bricks must be selected to match the originals with regard to size, color and texture; new mortar must match the old, both in color and texture; new mortar joints must be shaped the same as the old.

"Matching Bricks and Mortar." *Old-House Journal*, December 1973.

Repointing Mortar Joints in Historic Brick Buildings. Robert C. Mack, AIA. Preservation Brief no. 2. Technical Preservation Services, U.S. Department of the Interior. Washington, D.C.: GPO, 1976. 8 pp., illus., biblio. $1 pb. GPO stock no. 024-005-00878-1.

Tells when and how to repoint, how to analyze the mortar and the bricks and what the properties of mortar are, with illustrations of brick bonding patterns and mortar joints.

Restoring Brick and Stone: Some Do's and Don'ts. James Cheston Thomas. Nashville: American Association for State and Local History, 1975. Technical Leaflet 81. $2 pb.

Decorative and Ornamental Brickwork. James Stokoe. New York: Dover, 1982. 94 pp., illus. $6 pb.

A photographic exploration of the possibilities of brick, as used on old buildings, most in St. Louis.

Baring Bricks—a Mistake?

"Painting of masonry is an old and valued technique. . . . The most important reason for painting . . . was to reduce the permeability of such a highly porous material as brick. The paint forms a continuous film that tends to shed water. . . . The simplest and least expensive procedure is to replace or repair the existing paint."

Theodore H.M. Prudon, "The Case Against Removing Paint from Brick Masonry." *Old-House Journal*, February 1975.

"The Bare-Brick Mistake." *Old-House Journal*, November 1973.

Contact

Brick Institute of America
11490 Commerce Park Drive
Reston, Va. 22091

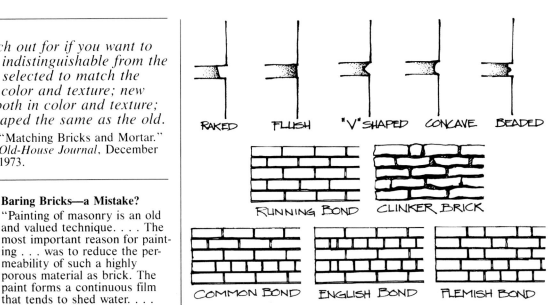

Typical brick bonding patterns and mortar joints found in American buildings. From *Rehab Right*. (Courtesy City of Oakland Planning Department)

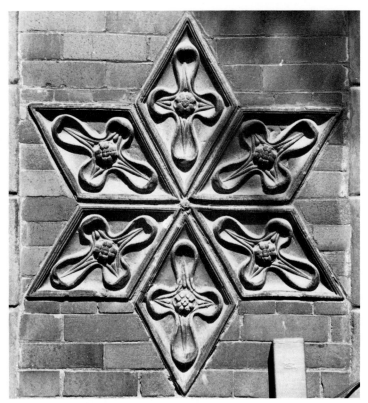

Facade detail from the Terra Cotta (1892), Alfred. N.Y., a cottage built to display the offerings of a local terra-cotta manufacturer.

Terra Cotta

Glazed architectural terra-cotta probably comprises one of the largest if not the largest constituent material in some of our urban environments today. . . . Simply put, terra-cotta is an enriched molded clay brick or block. . . . Historically there are four types or categories of terra-cotta which have enjoyed wide use in the history of the American building arts: 1) brownstone, 2) fireproof construction, 3) ceramic veneer, and 4) glazed architectural. . . . Restoration/rehabilitation work on glazed architectural terra-cotta is demanding and will not tolerate half-way measures.

de Teel Patterson Tiller, *The Preservation of Historic Glazed Architectural Terra-Cotta*

The Preservation of Historic Glazed Architectural Terra-Cotta. de Teel Patterson Tiller. Preservation Brief no 7. Technical Preservation Services, U.S. Department of the Interior. Washington, D.C.: GPO, 1979. 8 pp., illus., biblio. $1 pb. GPO stock no. 024-005-0883-7.

Terra Cotta: Preservation of an Historic Building Material. Nancy D. Berryman and Susan M. Tindall. Chicago: Landmarks Preservation Council of Illinois (407 South Dearborn Street, 60605), 1983. 38 pp., illus. $7.50 pb.

"Terra-Cotta as a Building Material: A Bibliography," Theodore H.M. Prudon. *Communique*, Association for Preservation Technology, vol. 3, June 1976.

Last of the Handmade Buildings: Glazed Terra Cotta in Downtown Portland. Virginia Guest Ferriday. Portland, Ore.: Mark Publishing (Box 40668, 97240), 1984. 150 pp., illus. $22 pb.

American Architectural Terra-Cotta: A Bibliography. Susan M. Tindall. Monticello, Ill.: Vance Bibliographies, 1981. 48 pp.

American Terra Cotta Index. Statler Gilfillen, ed. Palos Park, Ill.: Prairie School Press, 1974. 487 pp. $25.

Contact

Friends of Terra Cotta
P.O. Box 421393
Main Post Office
San Francisco, Calif. 94142

Rotted floorboards at Lyndhurst (1838, 1864–65, Alexander J. Davis), a National Trust property in Tarrytown, N.Y., were numbered for use as patterns in cutting and assembling replacement boards. (NTHP)

Wood

The fungi that gradually reduce a fallen tree into a rich brown humus devour with equal gusto the sills and roofs of privies and palaces. . . . Since the primary factor leading to wood deterioration is moisture, the best control is to dry the wood and keep it dry. . . . Detection is the first step in controlling wood deterioration.

> William Merrill, *Wood Deterioration: Causes, Detection and Prevention.* Nashville: American Association for State and Local History, 1974. Technical Leaflet 77. 8 pp., biblio. $2 pb.

Epoxies for Wood Repairs in Historic Buildings. Morgan W. Phillips and Judith E. Selwyn. Technical Preservation Services, U.S. Department of the Interior. Washington, D.C.: GPO, 1978. 72 pp., illus., append. Available from NTIS.

Old House Woodwork Restoration: How to Restore Doors, Windows, Walls, Stairs, and Decorative Trim to Their Original Beauty. Ed Johnson. Englewood Cliffs, N.J.: Prentice-Hall, 1983. 201 pp., illus., biblio., index. $22.95 hb, $12.95 pb.

Contacts

Forest Products Laboratory
U.S. Department of Agriculture
P.O. Box 5130
Madison, Wis. 53705

American Wood Council
1619 Massachusetts Avenue,
N.W., Suite 500
Washington, D.C. 20036

See also: Log Buildings (Form and Function)

Detail of sawn-wood porch ornamentation, Honolulu House (1860), Marshall, Mich. (Balthazar Korab)

Aluminum and Vinyl Siding

Historic building materials such as wood, brick and stone, when properly maintained, are generally durable and serviceable materials. Their widespread existence on tens of thousands of old buildings after many decades in serviceable condition is proof that they are the original economic and long-lasting alternatives . . . . Because applications of substitute materials such as aluminum and vinyl siding can either destroy or conceal historic building material and features and, in consequence, result in the loss of a building's historic character, they are not recommended by the National Park Service.

John H. Myers and Gary L. Hume, *Aluminum and Vinyl Siding on Historic Buildings*

Aluminum and Vinyl Siding on Historic Buildings: The Appropriateness of Substitute Materials for Resurfacing Historic Wood Frame Buildings. John H. Myers and Gary L. Hume. Preservation Brief no. 8. Technical Preservation Services, U.S. Department of the Interior. 1979. Rev. ed. Washington, D.C.: GPO, 1984. 8 pp., illus. $1 pb. GPO stock no. 024-005-00869-1.

Explains the aesthetic and technical factors involved in use of these replacement materials.

The Hazards of Synthetic Siding. Brian D. Conway. Illinois Preservation Series, no. 1. Springfield: Illinois Department of Conservation, Division of Historic Sites, 1979.

Saving Synthetic Siding

Not all preservationists remove all synthetic siding. In keeping with its philosophy of preserving many of its properties in an "as-found" state, the Society for the Preservation of New England Antiquities has even saved artificial siding. The Pierce House, a 17th-century saltbox in Dorchester, Mass., came to SPNEA with early 20th-century asbestos shingles overlaying wooden clapboarding. Because the shingles were not thought to be a threat to the building's structural integrity, the siding was left intact to illustrate this particular house's historical and architectural evolution.

Permastone veneer on the row house at left hides brickwork detailing still visible on its neighbor at right. (A. Pierce Bounds)

Aluminum siding on this triple decker (1897) in Cambridgeport, Mass., alters its historic character. (Cambridge Historical Commission)

Revitalization of the Grand Opera House (1871, Dixon and Carson), Wilmington, Del., required restoration of its ornamental cast-iron facade. (Lubitsh and Bungarz)

Metals

Like other building materials, metals can deteriorate in time or be damaged and require conservation or replacement to continue to serve their intended functions. The problems of size and weight or the integration of these metals into the structure of a building can complicate conservation attempts.

> John G. Waite, "Preservation of Architectural Metals." In *Metals in America's Historic Buildings*

Missing sections of the opera house's facade were recast and replaced. (Grand Opera House Inc.)

Metals in America's Historic Buildings: Uses and Preservation Treatments. Margot Gayle, David W. Look, AIA, and John G. Waite. Technical Preservation Services, U.S. Department of the Interior. Washington, D.C.: GPO, 1980. 170 pp., illus., biblio. $6 pb. GPO stock no. 024-005-00910-8.

Surveys the historic uses of metals such as lead, tin, zinc, copper, nickel, iron, steel and aluminum. Also provides advice on metal deterioration and suggests preservation techniques for each type.

Conservation of Metals. Harold L. Peterson. Nashville: American Association for State and Local History, 1968. Technical Leaflet 10. 8 pp., illus. $2 pb.

A survey of various metal types focusing on object conservation.

See also: Cast-Iron Buildings (Form and Function)

Hardware

Imported hinges were often used on doors in principal rooms of American houses, yet the same houses may have had locally made surface-mounted hinges on lesser doorways. This 'hierarchy' of hardware is a manifestation of the 'best foot forward' concept, which was so prevalent in early American buildings. . . . It meant that the best rooms got the best hinges, locks, bell pulls, as well as the best glass and perhaps the narrowest floor boards, the most elaborate woodwork and mouldings. Thus, it is quite possible to find the mixture of local and imported hardware in a single building. . . .

> Lee H. Nelson, "Rediscovering American Hardware." *Historic Preservation*, November–December 1980.

Illustrated Catalogue of American Hardware of the Russell and Erwin Manufacturing Company. 1865. Reprint. Introduction by Lee H. Nelson. Ottawa: Association for Preservation Technology, 1980. 469 pp., illus. $15 pb. Available from American Life Foundation, Box 349, Watkins Glen, N.Y. 14891.

A reprint of the most important early American hardware catalog, with 1,000 entries and 3,330 engravings. Contains information on virtually every hardware item made in the U.S. in 1865, including nomenclature, construction, materials, finishes and technology as well as stylistic evolution and technological change.

Hardware Restoration. Frank G. White. Nashville: American Association for State and Local History, 1977. Slide and tape program. $44.50.

Nail Chronology as an Aid to Dating Old Buildings. Lee H. Nelson. Nashville: American Association for State and Local History, 1968. Technical Leaflet 48. 12 pp., illus. $2 pb.

Antique Builders' Hardware: Knobs and Accessories. Maudie L. Eastwood. Tillamook, Ore.: Author (3900 Latimer Road North, 97141), 1982. 224 pp., illus. $18.50 pb.

Contact

Lock Museum of America
P.O. Box 104
Terryville, Conn. 06786

Wrought-bronze knob and escutcheon plate in the "Victoria" design by Corbin Hardware (c. 1910). (Katherine Palmer)

Iron and brass cupboard latches sold in 1865 in acorn and leaf patterns.

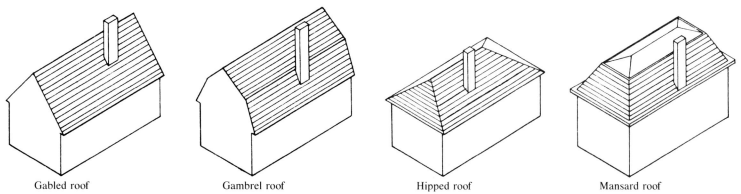

Gabled roof   Gambrel roof   Hipped roof   Mansard roof

Sampler of typical American roof shapes. From *The Cape May Handbook*. (Hugh J. McCauley)

Roofs

A weather-tight roof is basic in the preservation of a structure. . . . During some periods in the history of architecture, the roof impart[ed] much of the architectural character. . . . Before any repair work is performed, the historic value of the materials used on the roof should be understood.

Sarah M. Sweetser, *Roofing for Historic Buildings*

Common Sources of Roof Leaks

Loose flashing around chimneys and valleys
Water backup from plugged gutters or other debris
Loose or missing shingles
Cracks in chimney masonry
Bubbles and cracks on flat roofs
Protruding nailheads
Cracks caused by settling rafters

Old-House Journal, November 1974.

Roofing for Historic Buildings. Sarah M. Sweetser. Preservation Brief no. 4. Technical Preservation Services, U.S. Department of the Interior. Washington, D.C.: GPO, 1978. 8 pp., illus., biblio. $1 pb. GPO stock no. 024-005-00880-2.

Describes the history of roofing materials, failures of materials and support systems, replacing historic roofing material, stabilization and maintenance.

"Early Roofing Materials." *Bulletin*, Association for Preservation Technology, vol. 2, nos. 1-2, 1970.

Nineteenth Century Tin Roofing and Its Use at Hyde Hall. Diana S. Waite. Albany: New York State Historic Trust, 1971. 56 pp., illus., biblio.

Slate Roofs. National Slate Association. 1926. Rev. reprint. Fairhaven, Vt.: Vermont Structural Slate Company (05743), 1977.

Roofing Simplified. Donald R. Brann. Rev. ed. Briarcliff Manor, N.Y.: Directions Simplified, 1977. 98 pp. $2.50 pb.

Olmsted Park System—Jamaica Pond Boathouse, Jamaica Plain, Massachusetts: Planning for Preservation of the Boathouse Roof. Richard White. Preservation Case Studies. Technical Preservation Services, U.S. Department of the Interior. Washington, D.C.: GPO, 1979. 58 pp., illus.

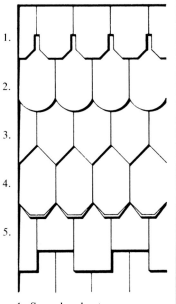

1. Spaced and cut
2. Fishscale
3. Feather cut
4. Imbrecated and beveled
5. Stagger butt

Types of wood shingle cuts. From *The Cape May Handbook*. (Hugh J. McCauley)

The importance of retaining original roofing materials is evidenced by these before-and-after views of the George W. Frank House (1899), Kearney, Neb. (U.S. Department of the Interior)

Bay window in a house in the Swiss Avenue Historic District, Dallas, Tex. (Bob Stump, NTHP)

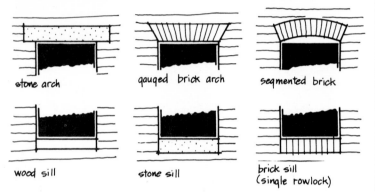

stone arch   gauged brick arch   segmented brick

wood sill   stone sill   brick sill (single rowlock)

Window lintels and sills commonly found on Federal and Greek Revival houses. From *Otterbein Homestead Area.* (Land Design/Research)

Windows

Our windows are our oldest, simplest and most direct medium of communication. . . . They have more to tell you—about your heritage and about your present self— than they have ever shown you.

Val Clery, *Windows.* New York: Penguin, 1978.

Because windows are a very important element of design, any changes made, such as installation of new sash, should be based on research into the date of the[building,] its style and the probable design of the original windows.

George Stephen, *Rehabilitating Old Houses*

The Repair of Historic Wooden Windows. John H. Myers. Preservation Brief no. 9. Technical Preservation Services, U.S. Department of the Interior. Washington, D.C.: GPO, 1981. 8 pp., illus. $1 pb. GPO stock no. 024-005-00884-5.

The Repair and Thermal Upgrading of Historic Steel Windows. Sharon C. Park. Preservation Brief no. 13. Technical Preservation Services, U.S. Department of the Interior. Washington, D.C.: GPO, 1984. 12 pp., illus. $1.25 pb. GPO stock no. 024-005-00868-3.

"Special Window Issue." *Old-House Journal,* April 1982.
Entire issue addresses concerns such as replacing old windows and installing weatherstripping.

"A Restorationist View of Windows." *Old-House Journal,* June 1974.
A good introduction to windows, this includes a glossary of window parts and a review of styles.

Window Glass

Often neglected, carelessly treated and broken, and replaced with inappropriate materials, historic window glass is becoming a rare architectural feature. . . .

Glass is a two way visual experience. Sunlight playing on the exterior facade of a structure with its original glass intact presents a unique and lively visual statement. One also receives a unique impression looking out *through historic glass. The world is softened, distorted and given visual movement as the viewer moves. To needlessly destroy this visual characteristic greatly diminishes the quality of the expression a structure articulates. Unlike paint and other renewable surfaces, glass is often the only 'original' visual element that gives the same view to each viewer from generation to generation.*

Richard O. Byrne, "Conservation of Historic Window Glass." *Bulletin,* APT, vol. 13, no. 3, 1981.

"Architectural Glass: History and Conservation." *Bulletin,* Association for Preservation Technology, vol. 13, no. 3, 1981. 55 pp., illus.

Your Residential Stained Glass: A Practical Guide to Repair and Maintenance. H. Weber Wilson. Chambersburg, Pa.: Architectural Ecology (447 East Catherine Street, 17201), 1979. 46 pp., illus. $5 pb.

Stained Glass: Music for the Eye. Robert and Jill Hill and Hans Halberstadt. Seattle: University of Washington Press, 1979. 108 pp., color illus. $10.95 pb.

Architectural Stained Glass. Brian Clarke, ed. New York: McGraw-Hill, 1979. 234 pp. $39.50.

The Preservation of Historic Pigmented Structural Glass (Vitrolite and Carrara Glass). Rocky Mountain Regional Office. Preservation Brief no. 12. Technical Preservation Services, U.S. Department of the Interior. Washington, D.C.: GPO, 1984. 8 pp., illus. $1 pb. GPO stock no. 024-005-00851-9.

Stained Glass from Medieval Times to the Present: Treasures to Be Seen in New York. James L. Sturm. New York: Dutton, 1982. 152 pp., illus., biblio., index. $29.95 hb, $16.95 pb.

Chicago Ceramics and Glass: An Illustrated History From 1871 to 1933. Sharon S. Darling. Chicago: Chicago Historical Society, 1980. Distributed by University of Chicago Press. 234 pp., illus., append., index. $25 hb.

Tiffany Windows: The Indispensable Book on Louis C. Tiffany's Masterworks. Alastair Duncan. New York: Bookthrift, Simon and Schuster, 1980. 224 pp., color illus., chron., biblio.,

"Field Guide to American Residential Stained Glass," H. Weber Wilson. *Old-House Journal,* November 1979.

"How to Revive the Splendor of Your Stained Glass," H. Weber Wilson. *Historic Preservation,* May–June 1979.

"Stained Glass Preservation: Guidelines for Repair and for Restoration," Richard Millard. *Technology and Conservation,* Spring 1979.

"Some Tips on Old Glass: Leaded Glass, Mirrors," Felicia Elliot. *Old-House Journal,* January 1977.

"Fancy Beveled Glass," H. Weber Wilson. *Old-House Journal,* November 1978.

"Window Glass," H. Weber Wilson. *Old-House Journal,* April 1978.

Contacts
Stained Glass Association of America
Repair and Restoration Committee
Box 376
Fishkill, N.Y. 12424

Census of Stained Glass Windows in America, 1840–1940
c/o Prof. Willene B. Clark
Department of Art History
Marlboro College
Marlboro, Vt. 05344

One of San Francisco's bevy of painted ladies. (Carol Olwell)

Paint

Because one of the main causes of wood deterioration is moisture penetration, a primary purpose for painting wood is to exclude such moisture, thereby slowing deterioration not only of a building's exterior siding and decorative features but, ultimately, its underlying structural members. Another important purpose for painting wood is, of course, to define and accent architectural features and to improve appearance.

> Kay D. Weeks and David W. Look, *Exterior Paint Problems on Historic Woodwork*

Century of Color: Exterior Decoration for American Buildings, 1820–1920. Roger Moss. Watkins Glen, N.Y.: American Life Foundation, 1981. 112 pp., color illus., gloss., append., index. $15 hb.

A guide to authentic exterior colors and combinations, with 100 color plates showing how houses and other buildings were painted. Included are 200 combinations arranged in color affinity charts, some matched to Munsell Color Notations. Examples in the book are keyed to 40 "Heritage Colors" paints by Sherwin-Williams.

Exterior Paint Problems on Historic Woodwork. Kay D. Weeks and David W. Look, AIA. Preservation Brief no. 10. Technical Preservation Services, U.S. Department of the Interior. Washington, D.C.: GPO, 1982. 12 pp., illus. $1 pb. GPO stock no. 024-005-00885-3.

Describes common paint conditions and failures and recommends appropriate treatments. Addresses paint removal and dealing with toxic lead paint.

Paint Color Research and Restoration. Penelope Hartshorne Batcheler. Nashville: American Association for State and Local History, 1968. Technical Leaflet 15. 4 pp. $2 pb.

A brief overview of how to date and match old colors.

Property Owner's Guide to Paint Restoration and Preservation. Frederick D. Cawley. Technical Series, no. 1. Albany: Preservation League of New York State, 1976. 8 pp., biblio. $1 pb.

Introduction to the complex problems encountered when investigating, preserving and reproducing paints in old buildings. Topics include types of historic paints and their uses, colors and special finishes, physical investigation of paint colors, preservation and maintenance of historic paints and choosing the proper paint for an old building.

Paint Color Research and Restoration of Historic Paint. Kevin H. Miller, ed. Ottawa, Ont.: Association for Preservation Technology, 1977. 49 pp. $3 pb.

"How to Assure a Satisfactory Paint Job." Scientific Section, Circular 784. Washington, D.C.: National Paint and Coatings Association (1500 Rhode Island Avenue, N.W., 20005).

Paint Problem Solver. National Decorating Products Association. St. Louis: Author (1050 North Lindbergh Boulevard, 63132), 1980.

"Avoiding Mistakes in Exterior Painting," Edward F. Gola. *Old-House Journal*, June 1976.

"Selecting the Best Exterior Paint," Clem Labine. *Old-House Journal*, July 1976.

"Exterior Painting." *Old-House Journal*, April 1981.

Historic House Paint Analysis. Edward R. Gilbert. Nashville: American Association for State and Local History, 1980. Slide and tape program. $44.50.

Victorian House Colors: Exterior. Samuel J. Dornsife and Roger Moss, Jr. Nashville: American Association for State and Local History. Slide and tape program. $44.50.

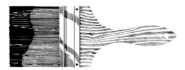

Local Color
"An unpainted town is a bad advertisement."

Member, Amana Society (Iowa)

Painted Ladies: San Francisco's Resplendent Victorians. Elizabeth Pomada and Michael Larsen. Photographs by Morley Baer. New York: Dutton, 1978. 80 pp., color illus., biblio. $11.50 pb.

San Antonio: A History of Color and Graphics. Daniel Withers. San Antonio: San Antonio Conservation Society (107 King William Street, 78204), 1977. 122 pp., illus., biblio.

What Color Should I Paint My House? Bruce E. Lynch. Indianapolis: Historic Landmarks Foundation of Indiana (3402 Boulevard Place, 46208).

Historic Colors: A Guide to Recommended Colors for Buildings Located Within Historic Districts. Mobile Historic Development Commission. Mobile: Author (P.O. Box 1827, 36601).

Paint Colors for Your 19th Century House. Cambridge Historical Commission. Rev. ed. Cambridge: Author (57 Inman Street, 02139).

Range foreman's bedroom (c. 1900), refurnished from contemporary accounts at the U Lazy S Ranch, Ranching Museum, Lubbock, Tex. From *Recreating the Historic House Interior.* (Ranching Museum, Texas Tech University)

Interiors

To the interior of a structure as well as to its exterior and surroundings the same principle might be applied: Change with thought and care. The loss or change of too many original interior details may thin the fabric of the interior so that it no longer has an identifiable historical character. The choice to remove or significantly alter a structural element can only be made once; the action cannot be reversed.

"Threads of a Fabric." *Historic Preservation,* October–December 1975.

The barren "architect-white" interiors imposed upon old houses in the 1960s are giving way . . . to rooms refurbished to reflect, if they do not attempt sometimes actually to duplicate, the past of the house.

William Seale, *Recreating the Historic House Interior*

Inside Tips: What Not to Do

1. Removing original material, architectural features, and hardware, except where essential for safety or efficiency.
2. Installing new decorative material and paneling which destroys significant architectural features or was unavailable when the building was constructed, such as vinyl plastic, or imitation wood wall and floor coverings, except in utility areas such as bathrooms and kitchens.
3. Removing plaster to expose brick to give the wall an appearance it never had.
4. Enclosing important stairways with ordinary fire rated construction which destroys the architectural character of the stair and the space.
5. Altering the basic plan of a building by demolishing principal walls, partitions, and stairways.

The Secretary of the Interior's Guidelines for Rehabilitating Historic Buildings

Recreating the Historic House Interior. William Seale. Nashville: American Association for State and Local History, 1979. 270 pp., illus., biblio., index. $25 hb.

Written "with museum houses in mind," the book also serves as a guide for private owners of houses and other building types. Contents include research, architectural decisions, walls, floors, modernizing mechanical systems, furnishings, objects, lighting and textiles. A separate photo section provides examples of restored and re-created interiors.

Decorating with Americana: How to Know It, Where to Find It, and How to Make It Work for You. Carter Smith. Birmingham, Ala.: Oxmoor House, 1985. 224 pp., color illus., biblio., index. $35 hb.

Uses views of private residences and museum rooms to provide a chronological compendium of decorating ideas using period furnishings and antiques.

American Victorian: A Style and Source Book. Lawrence Grow and Dina Von Zweck. New York: Harper and Row, 1984. 224 pp., illus., index. $15.95 pb.

A popular guide to the many facets of Victorian interiors, showing how to decorate by example.

The Old House Book Series: Living Rooms and Parlors; Bedrooms; Kitchens and Dining Rooms; Outdoor Living Spaces. Lawrence Grow, ed. New York: Warner Books, 1980–81. 96 pp., color illus., biblio., index. $16.95 hb, $7.95 pb each.

A room-by-room series intended to show "how a room may be designed to serve both modern comfort and the desire for traditional pleasure," the books include a historical survey of the room type, discussion of the parts of the room, a color portfolio of restored period rooms and sections on architectural features, paint, papers and fabrics plus ideas on furnishings the period room.

The Antiques Book of American Interiors: Colonial and Federal Styles. Elisabeth Donaghy Garrett, ed. Main Street Press. New York: Crown, 1980. 160 pp., color illus., biblio., index. $9.98 hb.

The Antiques Book of Victorian Interiors. Elisabeth Donaghy Garrett, ed. Main Street Press. New York: Crown, 1981. 160 pp., color illus., index.

A selection of articles from *Antiques* covering the architecture, fabrics, floor coverings, wallpaper, furniture and other furnishings of grand historic houses.

Historic Interiors. Paige Rense, ed. Worlds of Architectural Digest Series. Los Angeles: Knapp Press, 1979. Distributed by Crown. 160 pp., color illus. $14.95 hb.

An opulent peek at 18 restored marvels in the U.S. and abroad, such as a Savannah mansion, Newport houses, Sagamore Hill, the Woodrow Wilson House, Sunnyside, Bayou Bend, Biltmore and the Morris-Jumel House.

New Orleans Interiors. Mary Louise Christovich. New Orleans: Friends of the Cabildo-Louisiana State Museum, 1980. 80 pp., color illus. $12.95 hb, $8.95 pb.

Photos of restored interiors organized by historic neighborhoods, with explanatory text.

Special Rooms: Louisville, Kentucky. Monica Orr, ed. Photographs by John Beckman. Chicago: Chicago Review Press, 1981. 88 pp., color illus. $12.95 pb.

A photo tour of a variety of Louisville houses.

Living-dining room of the Pope-Leighey House (1940, Frank Lloyd Wright), a National Trust property near Mount Vernon, Va., with its architect-designed furniture. (Jack E. Boucher, HABS)

Watercolor of Mrs. William Cooper (c. 1816) shows period furnishings. From *American Interiors.* (New York State Historical Association)

Buttrick Publishing, New York, in 1904 showing its Tiffany interior and Craftsman-style furniture. From *Photographs of New York Interiors at the Turn of the Century.* (Byron Collection, Museum of the City of New York)

A graduate of the Hampton (Va.) Institute, dining with his family in 1899. From *The Tasteful Interlude.* (Frances Benjamin Johnston, Library of Congress)

Interiors in Pictures: Moments Isolated in Time

Despite the imbalance in coverage and the possibility of accidental or deliberate error on the part of the artist, these pictures offer a source for information about the American home that is unparalleled elsewhere. No written document can offer so much data about the treatment of rooms and their contents, the details of interior decoration and taste, the use of rooms, and the exact type and quality of the furnishings found in each situation.

Harold L. Peterson, *American Interiors*

The Tasteful Interlude: American Interiors Through the Camera's Eye, 1860–1917. William Seale. 1975. Rev. ed. Nashville: American Association for State and Local History, 1980. 288 pp., illus., index. $17.50 pb.

A documentation, through more than 200 period photos, of the decorative influences on the living places of Victorian America.

American Interiors: From Colonial Times to the Late Victorians. A Pictorial Source Book of American Domestic Interiors with an Appendix on Inns and Taverns. Harold L. Peterson. 1971. Reprint. New York: Scribner's, 1979. 205 illus., index. $9.95 pb.

Rich and diversified collection of views and types of interiors, taken from paintings, watercolors, drawings and photos of houses from 1659 to 1876.

A Documentary History of American Interiors from the Colonial Era to 1915. Edgar deN. Mayhew and Minor Myers, Jr. New York: Scribner's, 1980. 412 pp., illus., appends., biblio., index. $45 hb.

A record of American room arrangements to WWI. Organized by periods from 1607 to 1915, the book examines details such as furniture, floor coverings, pictures, textiles, wall treatments, architectural details, ceilings, lighting, color schemes and accessories.

American Interiors 1675–1885: A Guide to the American Period Rooms in the Brooklyn Museum. Marvin D. Schwarts. New York: Brooklyn Museum (Eastern Parkway and Washington Avenue, 11238), 1968. 124 pp., color illus., biblio. $4.95 pb.

American Interiors: New England and the South. Period Rooms at the Brooklyn Museum. Donald C. Peirce and Hope Alswang. New York: Universe, 1983. 64 pp., color illus. $7.95 pb.

Photographs of eastern U.S. period rooms and their furnishings in the museum with descriptive text.

Early American Rooms: 1650–1858. Russell H. Kettell. New York: Dover, 1967. 200 pp., illus. $10.95 pb.

Twelve rooms, each furnished, decorated and occupied in the style of its period.

Photographs of New York Interiors at the Turn of the Century. Photographs by Joseph Byron. Introduction by Clay Lancaster. New York: Dover, 1976. 154 pp., illus.

A series of photos taken from 1893 to 1915, the book shows commercial as well as residential views, and a slum dwelling contrasts sharply with the other predominantly opulent Victorian interiors.

The Columbia Historical Portrait of New York: An Essay in Graphic History in Honor of the Tricentennial of New York City and the Bicentennial of Columbia University. John A. Kouwenhoven. 1953. Reprint. New York: Octagon Books, 1983.

A collection of interior views, many of them nondomestic.

Chicago Interiors: Views of a Splendid World. David Lowe. Chicago: Contemporary Books, 1979. 192 pp., illus., biblio., index.

More than 250 old photographs of late 1880s and early 1900s Chicago interiors.

At Home: Domestic Life in the Post-Centennial Era— 1876–1920. George Talbot, ed. Madison: State Historical Society of Wisconsin (816 State Street, 53706), 1977.

A selection of photographs from the historical society's collection.

American Interior Design: The Traditions and Development of Domestic Design from Colonial Times to the Present. Meyrick R. Rogers. 1947. Reprint. New York: Arno, 1976. $31.

Illustrations of whole rooms as well as individual pieces of furniture, furnishings, plus interior designs and floor plans.

Hints on Household Taste: The Originals

There is a class of young ladies who are in the habit of anticipating all differences of opinion in a picture-gallery or concert-room by saying that they "know what they like." Whatever advantage may be derived from this remarkable conviction in regard to music or painting, I fear it would assist no one in furnishing a house—at least, in accordance with any established principles of art.

Charles L. Eastlake, *Hints on Household Taste in Furniture, Upholstery and Other Details*, 1878

Hints on Household Taste in Furniture, Upholstery and Other Details. Charles L. Eastlake. 1872. Reprint. Salem, N.H.: Ayer Company. 334 pp., illus. $18.

Eastlake was the arbiter of "good" and particularly Victorian taste. This became one of the most influential books on 19th-century domestic design, covering all aspects from the movable to the immovable.

The Decoration of Houses. Edith Wharton and Ogden Codman, Jr. 1897. Reprint. Introductions by John Barrington Bayley and William A. Coles. New York: W.W. Norton, 1978. 204 pp., illus., index. $14.95 hb.

A classic often credited with helping to shape modern interior decoration.

The Opulent Eye: Late Victorian and Edwardian Taste in Interior Design. Nicholas Cooper. New York: Watson-Guptill, 1977. 258 pp., illus.

Photographs of British interiors.

Art Deco Interiors in Color. Charles R. Fry, ed. New York: Dover, 1977. 48 pp., color illus. $6 pb.

Sixty-two original watercolors by European designers, showing living, dining and bedrooms, kitchens and a bathroom.

Victorian Country Seats and Modern Dwellings: Two Volumes in One. Henry Hudson Holly. 1865, 1873. Reprint. Introduction and index by Michael A. Tomlan. Watkins Glen, N.Y.: American Life Foundation, 1977. 424 pp., illus. $6.95 pb.

A key 19th-century source for the latest fashions in architecture and interior decoration.

Craftsman Homes: Architecture and Furnishings of the American Arts and Crafts Movement. Gustav Stickely. 1909. Reprint. New York: Dover, 1979. 224 pp., illus. $6.50 pb.

From the pages of *The Craftsman* magazine, essays and illustrations of furniture and house plans and drawings.

American Woman's Home. Catharine E. Beecher and Harriet Beecher Stowe. 1869. Reprint. Introduction and bibliography by Joseph S. Van Why. Watkins Glen, N.Y.: American Life Foundation, 1979. 556 pp., illus. $12.50 pb.

A classic treatise that attempted to set moral and domestic as much as decorative standards.

See also: Pattern Books, Craftsman style (Looking at the Built Environment); Houses (Form and Function)

MOULDINGS AT LARGE

Replacement pressed-tin ceiling being installed. *(Old-House Journal)*

To reproduce plaster ornament from the 1860s, clay is used to make repairs before preparing the mold; plaster is poured into the mold; and the finished reproduction is readied for mounting. (Robert Sweeney)

The New York office of Thomas Cook and Sons, shown in 1906, featured a pressed-tin ceiling. From *Photographs of New York Interiors at the Turn of the Century.* (Byron Collection, Museum of the City of New York)

Walls and Ceilings

Whatever you have in your rooms, think first of the walls, for they are that which makes your house a home.

William Morris

Many inexperienced renovators are enchanted with exposed brick as a charming and rustic touch—whether or not the house was originally designed that way. . . . Bare brick can be a terrible mistake! First, plaster was integral to the original design of the house. . . . Second, plaster is a good thermal insulator. . . . Third, plaster is a good sound insulator. . . . So pause before you take that hammer and cold chisel in your hands.

Old-House Journal, November 1973.

How to Repair, Renovate and Decorate Your Walls, Floors and Ceilings. Jackson Hand. New York: Harper and Row, 1976. 212 pp. $4.95 pb.

Plastering Skill and Practice. Van Den Branden and Thomas L. Hartsell, eds. 2nd ed. Chicago: American Technical Society (5608 Stony Island Avenue, 60637), 1971. 543 pp., illus., appends., index. $10.95 hb.

Presents step-by-step instructions on ornamental plastering.

"Ornamental Plastering," Charles Granquist. *Historic Preservation,* April–June 1970.

"The Art of Getting Plastered." *Old-House Journal,* December 1973–March 1974.

Articles on minor repairs, major repairs and duplicating cornices and castings.

"Preserving an Old-World Heritage," Christopher Weeks. *Historic Preservation,* November–December 1981.

"Recreating the Effect of Colonial Plaster Walls," Jack R. Cunningham. *Old-House Journal,* September 1975.

"Metal Ceilings," Barbara Schiller. *Old-House Journal,* March 1979.

Blue-and-white marble flooring in the entrance hall at Lyndhurst, added for its second owner. (Louis Reens)

Marble-floored rotunda of the National Trust headquarters (1915, Jules H. de Sibour), Washington, D.C. (Robert A. Grove)

Detail of parquet floor in Decatur House (1818–19, Benjamin H. Latrobe), a National Trust property in Washington, D.C. (Jack E. Boucher, HABS)

Floors

The question of floors seems a simple matter. Yet the foul practices of restorationists make it a major one. Those who restore American houses seem to wait in eager anticipation for that moment when the heavy sanding machines roll in to peel the floors to abject nakedness, and utter flatness, whereupon one of any number of tawdry finishes then renders them "beautiful."

William Seale, *Recreating the Historic House Interior*

Finishing Touches. Willoughby House Junior Board. Brooklyn, N.Y.: Author (Willoughby House Settlement, c/o Ritorto, 10 Monroe Place, 11201). $3.25.

A book of "recipes" for finishing wood and other interior objects.

American Rugs and Carpets from the Seventeenth Century to Modern Times. Helene Von Rosenstiel. New York: Morrow, 1978. 192 pp., illus., gloss., biblio.

A survey ranging from dirt floors, painted and sanded floorboards, straw and rush matting to the development of the American carpet industry. Also covered are home-made rugs, floorcloths, oilcloths and linoleum.

Floors and Stairways. Home Repair and Improvement Series. Alexandria, Va.: Time-Life Books, 1978. 128 pp., illus., gloss., index. $17 hb.

An illustrated handbook on how to restore damaged floors—wood, resilient and hard surfaces—and stairways.

America Underfoot: A History of Floor Coverings from Colonial Times to the Present. Anthony N. Landreau. Washington, D.C.: Smithsonian Institution Traveling Exhibition Service, 1976. 76 pp., illus., biblio. $6.60 pb.

Provides background information and technical analyses of floor coverings.

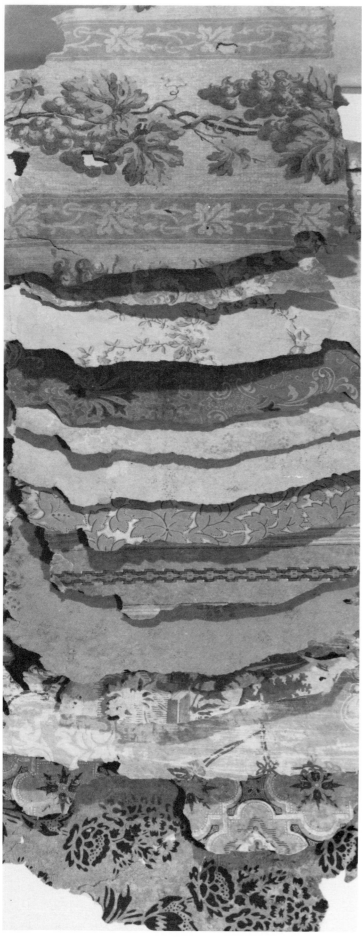

Restoration of the Nathan Beers House, Fairfield, Conn., uncovered 13 layers of wallpaper. (Cooper-Hewitt Museum, Smithsonian Institution)

Wallpaper

Bedraggled walls buried under tattered, stained and overpainted layers of paper are prime targets for would-be restorers of old houses. Scraping, steaming and scrubbing visibly improve their state of sanitation, which duly pleases their owners. However, the cleansing, even when undertaken in a search for original paint colors or paneling, can obliterate evidence eloquent of the decorative history of a house. After the paper has been thrown away, the house restorer may be left staring at blank walls that tell nothing about early decorative schemes. The original paint colors or wood finishes that were the object of the search may never have existed. The bottom most layer of paper thrown out with all its successors may have been the original wall covering, even in a very old house.

Since the 18th century, the walls in many American houses have been finished only to a point suitable for papering. . . . It is not unusual to find paper as old as a house at the bottom of 6, 10 or even 16 layers of paper.

Catherine Lynn Frangiamore,
"The Story Wallpapers Tell."
Historic Preservation, October–
December 1975.

Wallpapers in Historic Preservation. Catherine Lynn Frangiamore. Technical Preservation Services, U.S. Department of the Interior. Washington, D.C.: GPO, 1977. 56 pp., illus., biblio. Available from NTIS.

A guide to wallpaper technology, styles and restoration.

Wallpapers for Historic Buildings. Richard Nylander. Washington, D.C.: Preservation Press, 1983. 128 pp., illus., biblio., gloss., appends. $9.95 pb.

A catalog of reproduction wallpapers currently available from U.S. manufacturers, with an explanation of how to select and use them in historic buildings.

Wallpaper in America: From the Seventeenth Century to World War I. Catherine Lynn. New York: W.W. Norton, 1980. 533 pp., illus., biblio., appends., index. $45 hb.

A definitive historical survey from the earliest wall hangings through 20th-century innovations and changed fashions.

Wallpapers: An International History and Illustrated Survey from the Victoria and Albert Museum. Charles C. Oman and Jean Hamilton. New York: Abrams, 1982. With Victoria and Albert Museum. 464 pp., color illus., biblio., index. $75 hb.

A survey from the early 16th century to the present, organized into anonymous wallpaper design (1509–1978), pattern books and designers from the 18th century.

Rescuing Historic Wallpaper: Identification, Preservation, Restoration. Catherine L. Frangiamore. Nashville: American Association for State and Local History, 1974. Technical Leaflet 76. 8 pp., illus., biblio. $2 pb.

Brief overview of the decisions to be made in restoring or replacing wallpaper.

Wallpaper. Brenda Greysmith. New York: Macmillan, 1976. 208 pp., color illus., append., biblio.

Predominantly British, but with some American references.

Wallpaper: A History. Francoise Teynac, Pierre Nolot and Jean-Denis Vivien. Foreword by David Hicks. New York: Rizzoli, 1982. 250 pp., color illus. $50 hb.

A comprehensive history with details on manufacturing techniques.

Contacts

Cooper-Hewitt Museum
2 East 91st Street
New York, N.Y. 10028

New England Document
Conservation Center
Abbot Hall
24 School Street
Andover, Mass. 01810

The Victorian Society in
America
219 South Sixth Street
Philadelphia, Pa. 19106

Society for the Preservation of
New England Antiquities
141 Cambridge Street
Boston, Mass. 02114

Stencil by architect George Elmslie of a design detail from a Purcell and Elmslie building. (Northwest Architectural Archives)

Decorative Painting and Stenciling

It is not sufficient that an ornament be pleasing when first viewed, it must give lasting satisfaction. . . . Another test of good ornament is this—it powerfully affects the spirits. It can soothe as does sweet music, promote mirth as does the merry air, or hush to reverence as does the solemn anthem.

Christopher Dresser, *The Art of Decorative Design.* 1862.

The Art of Decorative Stenciling. Adele Bishop and Cile Lord. New York: Penguin, 1978. 199 pp., color illus. $16.95 pb.

Early American Wall Stencils in Color. Alice Bancroft Fjelstul and Patricia Brown Schad with Barbara Marhoefer. New York: Dutton, 1982. 138 pp., color illus., biblio., index. $25.75 hb, $15.75 pb.

More Early American Stencils in Color. Alice Fjelstul, Patricia Schad and Barbara Marhoefer. New York: Dutton, 1985. $29.95 hb, $15.95 pb.

Early New England Wall Stencils: A Workbook. Kenneth Jewett. New York: Harmony Books, 1979. 128 pp., illus., biblio. $8.95 pb.

Early American Cut and Use Stencils. JoAnne C. Day. New York: Dover, 1975. 64 pp., color illus. $3.95 pb.

Early American Stencils on Walls and Furniture. Janet Waring. New York: Dover, 1968. 147 pp., illus. $8.95 pb.

Dresser's Victorian Decorative Design. Christopher Dresser. 1862. Reprint. Watkins Glen, N.Y.: American Life Foundation, 1977. 320 pp., illus. $12 pb.

Modern Ornamentation. Christopher Dresser. 1886. Reprint. Watkins Glen, N.Y.: American Life Foundation, 1976. 64 pp., illus. $7 pb.

Victorian Cut and Use Stencils. Carol Belanger Grafton. New York: Dover, 1976. 55 pp., color illus. $3.95 pb.

Graining: Ancient and Modern. William E. Wall. 1955. Rev. ed. by F. N. Vanderwalker. New York: Drake, 1972. 209 pp., illus., index.

"The Art of Graining," Nat Weinstein. *Old-House Journal,* December 1978, January 1979.

"The Art of Painted Graining," Frank Welsh. *Historic Preservation*, July–September 1977.

"Painted Floors." *Old-House Journal,* December 1974.

Fabrics

Because textiles are more perishable and more frequently updated than building materials, modern reproductions are often the most authentic fabrics available. . . . The use of reproduction fabrics . . . allows the preservation of original documents while recreating authentic period effects.

Jane Nylander, *Fabrics for Historic Buildings*

Textiles in America, 1650–1870. Florence M. Montgomery. New York: W. W. Norton, 1984. 430 pp., illus., biblio. $39.95 hb.

A combination history and dictionary, this definitive book traces varied textile furnishings in America and England, such as upholstery, curtains and bed hangings.

Textile Collections of the World: United States and Canada. Cecil Lubell. New York: Van Nostrand Reinhold, 1976. 320 pp. $30.

Fabrics for Historic Buildings. Jane C. Nylander. 3rd ed. Washington, D.C.: Preservation Press, 1983. 160 pp., illus., gloss., biblio. $9.95 pb.

Provides guidance on the use of modern reproductions of fabrics and a catalog of manufacturers' current offerings. An introduction covers why reproductions should be used, documentary research, how to select reproduction fabrics, custom designs and installation of fabric furnishings.

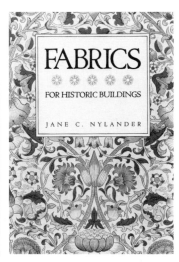

Washington-Franklin Toile (c. 1783–1800), a historic fabric in light red on cream reproduced by Scalamandré. From *Fabrics for Historic Buildings*.

Desk (c. 1910, George Niedecken) designed for Frank Lloyd Wright's Avery Coonley House (1907–09), Riverside, Ill. From *American Furniture*. (Art Institute of Chicago)

Furniture

American furniture rarely can be mistaken for furniture made abroad, but Americans from the seventeenth century to the present have continued the international tradition of style launched by Greeks borrowing from Egyptians and Romans from Greeks. Among many influences, English taste prevailed through the seventeenth and eighteenth centuries, English and French in the nineteenth and French and German in the twentieth. European books and magazines [were] directly pertinent to the evolution of American styles. . . . Their significance is documented, but equally pertinent and rarely known specifically are the influences of immigrant craftsmen, imported furniture and patrons traveling abroad.

Milo M. Naeve, *Identifying American Furniture*

Identifying American Furniture: A Pictorial Guide to Styles and Terms, Colonial to Contemporary. Milo M. Naeve. Nashville: American Association for State and Local History, 1982. 102 pp., illus. $15 hb.

Field Guide to American Antique Furniture. Joseph T. Butler. New York: Facts on File, 1985. 384 pp., illus., index. $24.95 hb.

American Furniture: 1620 to the Present. Jonathan L. Fairbanks and Elizabeth Bidwell Bates. New York: Richard Marek, 1981. 576 pp., illus., gloss., biblio., index. $50 hb.

An inclusive survey including furniture out of the "mainstream"— Native Americans, Pennsylvania Dutch, Shakers, Mission. Furniture is compared with related examples of architecture, painting and sculpture and analyzed as an index of social and technological evolution.

Three Centuries of American Furniture. Oscar P. Fitzgerald. Englewood Cliffs, N.J.: Prentice-Hall, 1982. 323 pp. $34.95 hb, $16.95 pb.

A comprehensive history of the styles and their evolution.

Nineteenth Century Furniture: Innovation, Revival and Reform. Arts and Antiques. Introduction by Mary Jean Madigan. New York: Watson-Guptill, 1982. 160 pp., illus., biblio., index. $25 hb.

Surveys the variety of styles— American empire, Gothic and rococo revivals to Renaissance revival, Arts and Crafts and Art Nouveau—made between 1820 and World War I.

American Decorative Arts: 360 Years of Creative Design. Robert Bishop and Patricia Coblentz. New York: Abrams, 1982. 406 pp., color illus., biblio., index. $65 hb.

Documents the full range of American design, from furniture, sculpture, paintings, interiors to textiles, decorative objects and household items, organized chronologically.

New England Furniture: The Colonial Era. Brock Jobe and Myrna Kaye. Boston: Houghton Mifflin, 1984. 494 pp., illus., biblio., index. $40 hb.

Catalogs the SPNEA collection, with essays on craftsmanship and design.

Furniture for the Victorian Home. A. J. Downing, 1850. J.C. Loudon, 1833. Reprint. Watkins Glen, N.Y.: American Life Foundation, 1982. 224 pp., illus. $15.

Facsimiles of the furniture sections from *Country Houses* and the *Encyclopedia*, useful as a sourcebook on early Victorian styles.

Victorian Gothic and Renaissance Revival Furniture. Henry Carey Baird. 1868. Reprint. Introduction by David Hanks. Philadelphia: The Athenaeum, 1977. 96 pp., illus. $20. Available from American Life Foundation.

Reprint of two early and rare furniture guides.

Innovative Furniture in America: From 1800 to the Present. David A. Hanks, with Russell Lynes, Rodris Roth and Page Talbott. New York: Horizon Press, 1981. 200 pp., illus., biblio., index. $30 hb, $17.50 pb.

A catalog of unique home-grown designs developed for comfort or convenience.

Victorian Chair for All Seasons: A Facsimile of the Brooklyn Chair Company Catalogue of 1887. Reprint. Watkins Glen, N.Y.: American Life Foundation, 1978. 114 pp., illus. $9.

Furniture Made in America, 1875–1905. Eileen and Richard Dubrow. Exton, Pa.: Schiffer Publishing (Box E, 19341), 1982. 320 pp., illus. $17.95 pb.

Facsimile reprint of catalog entries for furniture for the dining room, parlor, library, bedroom and office.

Furniture Designed by Architects. Marian Page. New York: Whitney Library of Design, 1980. 224 pp., illus., biblio., index. $14.95 pb.

Furniture by Architects: 500 International Masterpieces of Twentieth-Century Design and Where to Buy Them. Marc Emery. New York: Abrams, 1983. 276 pp., illus., index. $49.50 hb.

Architects' Designs for Furniture. Jill Lever. New York: Rizzoli, 1982. 160 pp., illus. $25 hb, $15 pb.

The Furniture Doctor. George Grotz. New York: Doubleday, 1983. 366 pp., illus., index. $14.95 hb.

Restoring and Renovating Antique Furniture. Tom Rowland. New York: Van Nostrand Reinhold, 1976. 172 pp., illus., append., index. $5.95 pb.

See also: Craftsman style (Looking at the Built Environment)

Tall case clock (1820, Jacob Hostetter) from Hanover, Pa. (Philadelphia Museum of Art)

Chair used in the U.S. House of Representatives, 1857–59. (Henry Ford Museum and Greenfield Village)

A brass "French bedstead" offered in the 19th century by a mattress company. From *Furniture Made in America, 1875–1905.*

Spectators' benches in the Lincoln County Courthouse (1824), Wiscasset, Maine. (Stuart C. Schwartz)

An ornate dining or "pillar extension" table with a carved rim, veneered base and unusual carving. From *Furniture Made in America, 1875–1905.*

Lighting

Unfortunately, lighting is often one of the most neglected areas in house restoration and often (with ridiculous results) we find Colonial fixtures (because they are readily available) in Victorian houses. In the United States most Victorians used gas, kerosene, and/or electricity in their lighting fixtures—no candles!

Tom H. Gerhardt, "Victorian Lighting Fixtures." *Old-House Journal,* September 1975.

Gaslighting in America: A Guide for Historical Preservation. Denys Peter Myers. Technical Preservation Services, U.S. Department of the Interior. Washington, D.C.: GPO, 1978. 248 pp., illus., append., biblio., index. $8.50 pb.

A standard reference for establishing authentic lighting schemes, providing contemporary views, advertisements and catalog entries for fixtures and paraphernalia.

Lighting in America: From Colonial Rushlights to Victorian Chandeliers. Lawrence S. Cooke, ed. 1975. Rev. ed. Pittstown, N.J.: Main Street Press, 1985. 176 pp., illus., index. $10.95 pb.

An anthology of 50 years of articles on lighting from *Antiques,* focusing on movable devices.

Victorian Lighting: The Dietz Catalogue of 1860. Reprint. Introduction by Ulysses G. Dietz. Watkins Glen, N.Y.: American Life Foundation, 1982. 178 pp., illus., biblio. $30.

Facsimile reprint showing the offerings of the leading U.S. manufacturer of Victorian kerosene lamps, 1840–60.

Picture Book of Authentic Mid-Victorian Gas Lighting Fixtures. Mitchell, Vance and Company. Reprint. New introduction by Denys Peter Myers. New York: Dover, 1985. $6.95 pb.

Reprint of an 1870s catalog with 1,000 illustrations of gas fixtures.

The Electric Light: A Century of Design. Daniele Baroni. New York: Van Nostrand Reinhold, 1983. 168 pp., illus. $25.50 hb.

Traces the electric lamp to the present, presenting the work of well-known designers.

Identification of Nineteenth-Century Domestic Lighting. Roger W. Moss, Jr. Nashville: American Association for State and Local History. Slide and tape program. $44.50.

Identifies styles and tells how to choose correct lighting for restorations.

The Electric-Lamp Industry: Technological Change and Economic Development from 1800 to 1947. Arthur Aaron Bright, Jr. 1949. Reprint. Salem, N.H.: Ayer Company, 1979. 554 pp., illus. $41 hb.

Art Nouveau and Art Deco Lighting. Alastair Duncan. New York: Simon and Schuster, 1978. 208 pp., illus., gloss., index.

Lighting Bibliography. LaVerne Koelsch Jones and Roopinder Kaur Sandhu. Monticello, Ill.: Vance Bibliographies, 1979. A-42. 22 pp. $2 pb.

One in a row of reading room light fixtures in the Cleveland Public Library. (Thomas R. Tucker)

Corridor lights in the Cleveland Public Library (1925, Walker and Weeks). (Thomas R. Tucker)

Mechanical and Utility Systems

It is better to choose well-designed modern units and place them carefully than to destroy historic building fabric in trying to hide or conceal them with inappropriate, anomalous period design.

Robert N. Pierpont, "Mechanical Systems." In *A Primer: Preservation for the Property Owner*

The do-it-yourselfer who finds a plumbing job too tool-ridden to attempt will be happy to learn that electrical equipment can be installed with only a few inexpensive tools. The kicker, however, is that while a plumbing mistake can get you wet, an electrical mistake can get you dead.

Jim Stratton, *Pioneering in the American Wilderness*. New York: Urizen, 1977.

Antiques and Collectibles: A Bibliography of Works in English, 16th Century to 1976. Linda Campbell Franklin. Metuchen, N.J.: Scarecrow Press, 1978. 1,115 pp., biblio., index. $45 hb.

The subject classification "Heating, Lighting, Refrigeration and Electricity: Some Things That Smoke and Burn" provides historical reading.

"Central Heating and Forced Ventilation: Origins and Effects on Architectural Design," Robert Bruegmann. *Journal*, Society of Architectural Historians, October 1978.

A historical overview of hot air, hot water and steam heating systems.

Lectures on Victorian Ventilation. Lewis W. Leeds. 1868. Reprint. Watkins Glen, N.Y.: American Life Foundation, 1976. 64 pp., illus. $5 pb.

Leeds argues against the prevalent Victorian fear of night air: "Man's own breath is his greatest enemy." Testimonial letters came from Calvert Vaux, F. L. Olmsted and A. B. Mullett.

The Forgotten Art of Building a Good Fireplace. Vrest Orton. Dublin, N.H.: Yankee, 1969. 64 pp., illus.

18th-century smokeless fireplace designs of Sir Benjamin Thompson, translated for contemporary use.

"Catalogue Your House's Secret Passages." *Old-House Journal*, January 1974.

How to chart potential spaces for hidden pipes, wiring and ducts.

"Installing a Hot Air Heating System," Susan Burns. *Old-House Journal*, September 1978.

"Sprucing Up Old Radiators." *Old-House Journal*, October 1978.

Contact

American Society of Heating, Refrigerating and Air-Conditioning Engineers
1791 Tullie Circle, N.E.
Atlanta, Ga. 30329

See also: Building Codes (Adaptive Use)

Dick Hesser, NTHP

An ornate fireplace at Mar-a-Lago (1923–27, Marion Sims Wyeth), Palm Beach, Fla. (Jack E. Boucher, HABS)

Steam Heat

"From the standpoint of maximum heat efficiency, a radiator shouldn't have any paint on it. Any paint that is added on top of the iron will reduce heat transfer marginally. However, from the standpoint of preventing rust (a rusty surface also cuts down heat transfer) and from the appearance standpoint, a thin coat of paint is desirable . . . .

The biggest factor in selecting a radiator paint is that it be heat resistant, i.e., it won't flake and discolor as it is heated by the iron.

That's why the aluminum and bronze powder paints have been so popular for radiators over the years. These paints are heat resistant because of their metallic pigments. . . .

Many readers, however, report satisfactory results with ordinary wall paint. So the odds are that if you paint a radiator with the same paint as you are using on the walls (or a contrasting color) the paint will probably adhere all right and won't be adversely affected by heat."

"Sprucing Up Old Radiators." *Old-House Journal*, October 1978.

Painted radiator, c. 1905. From *Respectful Rehabilitation*. (David J. Baker)

Bathrooms

No dwelling can be considered complete which has not a water closet under its roof.

Andrew Jackson Downing, 1842.

While we cannot say that Downing invented the American bathroom, he should receive full credit for helping spread the idea across the country. Even before his untimely death in 1852 it was commonly said that nobody "builds a house or lays out a garden without consulting Downing's works. . . ." After his death his tremendously popular books continued to carry his ideas around the nation.

Arthur Channing Downs, Jr.,
"Andrew Jackson Downing and
the American Bathroom."
Historic Preservation, October–
December 1971.

"Prior to the mid-1890s—and as late as 1920 in rural areas—most houses were originally constructed without the benefit of indoor plumbing. When toilet facilities were finally installed they were usually stuck in any cranny available: a closet, summer kitchen, side porch, or as in the case of my 1894 farmhouse in Ohio, in an area walled off from an existing room."

Dan Diehl, "Coping With a Small Bathroom." *Old-House Journal*, August 1979.

Clean and Decent: The Fascinating History of the Bathroom and the Water Closet. Lawrence Wright. 1967. Boston: Routledge and Kegan Paul, 1984. 224 pp. $9.95 pb.

Temples of Convenience. Lucinda Lambton. New York: St. Martin's, 1978. 60 pp., color illus. $5.95 pb.

Flushed With Pride: The Story of Thomas Crapper. Wallace Reyburn. Englewood Cliffs, N.J.: Prentice-Hall, 1970. $3.95.

"The Plumbing Paradox: American Attitudes Toward Late Nineteenth-Century Domestic Sanitary Arrangements," May N. Stone. *Winterthur Portfolio*, Fall 1979.

Cleanliness and Godliness: or, The Further Metamorphosis. Reginald Reynolds. 1946. New York: Harcourt Brace Jovanovich, 1976. 326 pp. $3.95.

See also: Outhouses

Luxurious 1909 bathroom in the home of Mrs. Helen Terry Potter, New Rochelle, N.Y. From *Photographs of New York Interiors at the Turn of the Century.* (Byron Collection, Museum of the City of New York)

Kitchens

The care of the Kitchen, Cellar, and Store-room is necessarily the foundation of all proper housekeeping.

Catharine E. Beecher and
Harriet Beecher Stowe,
American Woman's Home. 1869.

One thing all types of kitchens had in common was the plainness of their decoration. It was only after the practice of hiding the cooking utensils and food from view became popular in the 20th century that wallpapers and fabrics designed especially for the kitchen became popular.

Carolyn Flaherty, "Kitchens in
the Victorian Home." *Old-
House Journal,* April 1976.

Colonial Kitchens, Their Furnishings and Their Gardens. Frances Phipps. New York: Hawthorne Books, 1972.

"Early American Kitchens," Carolyn Flaherty. *Old-House Journal,* March 1976.

"The Kitchen Compromise," David S. Gillespie. *Old-House Journal,* June 1978.

"Kitchen Cabinets for the Old House," David and Ruth Gillespie. *Old-House Journal,* October 1978.

Re-creation of the Harriet Beecher Stowe House (1871) kitchen, Hartford, Conn., embodying the author's domestic ideas. (Stowe-Day Foundation)

Open chimney dampers in summer; close them in winter. Insulate attic.

Ventilation controls attic heat build-up in summer, releases excess moisture in winter.

Awnings shield windows from sun in summer.

Shades, drapes and shutters keep out sun in summer, insulate in winter.

Deciduous trees provide cooling shade in summer, let in sun during winter.

Caulking around framing woodwork stops air leaks.

Porch roof shades house in summer.

Weatherstripping on doors and windows keeps out cold air in winter, retains cool air in summer.

Simple energy-saving steps to help reduce energy consumption in old buildings. From *A Primer: Preservation for the Property Owner.* (Douglas Bucher; Preservation League of New York State)

Energy Conservation

We now have proof that the buildings with the poorest energy efficiency are those that were built between 1941 and 1970 and that old houses often use less heat and less energy for heating and cooling than do new houses.

Ann Webster Smith, "Introduction: Saving Energy in Old Buildings." In *New Energy from Old Buildings*

If the attributes of historic buildings are considered and allowed to function as they were intended, a great deal of energy may be saved without any retrofitting.

Baird M. Smith, "Making Buildings Work as They Were Intended." In *New Energy from Old Buildings*

"In determining what measures should be considered and which should not, two basic factors must be considered. First, will the improvement threaten the structure either by causing premature deterioration or by causing an unacceptable threat by fire or other trauma. Second, is the cost of the item going to be returned in energy savings within a reasonable length of time. . . .

Energy-related improvements for older structures should be divided into four categories: (1) modifications in the way the homeowner uses the house as an energy consuming unit; (2) mechanical improvements to the house that reduce energy use without affecting the integrity of the structure; (3) improvements that dramatically reduce the heating bill without significantly affecting the appearance or basic construction of the house if properly installed; (4) modifications to the structure that could save energy but also cause aesthetic or structural damage that is not justified by the corresponding savings in energy."

Douglas C. Peterson, "Ways to Save Energy and Stay Warm." *Historic Preservation*, March–April 1979.

Energy-Saving Steps for Old Buildings

Weatherstripping and caulking
Insulation of attic and crawl spaces
Shutters (interior and exterior) and draperies
Well-maintained equipment
Reduced energy usage
Circulating and attic fans
Roof vents
Awnings
Landscaping
Storm windows

New Energy from Old Buildings. National Trust for Historic Preservation. Washington, D.C.: Preservation Press, 1981. 208 pp., illus., gloss., biblio., index. $9.95 pb.

A survey of the major preservation-energy issues. Leading architects and preservationists tell how architecture once was designed to conserve energy naturally, what conservation steps an old-building owner can take and factors involved in retrofitting with passive and active solar systems.

Conserving Energy in Historic Buildings. Baird M. Smith. Preservation Brief no. 3. Technical Preservation Services, U.S. Department of the Interior. Washington, D.C.: GPO, 1978. 8 pp., illus., biblio. $1 pb. GPO stock no. 024-005-00879-9.

Outlines recommended and not recommended procedures for retrofitting old buildings, including insulation, weatherizing and passive solar measures.

"Special Energy Issue." *Old-House Journal*, September 1981.

Includes discussions on solar energy, indoor air quality, energy audits, sunspaces and heating alternatives.

"The Energy-Efficient Old House." *Old-House Journal*, September 1980.

Describes how to insulate, caulk, weatherstrip and weatherize windows.

Retrofit Right: How to Make Your Old House Energy Efficient. Sedway Cooke, with Sol-Arc. Oakland, Calif.: City of Oakland Planning Department, 1983. 180 pp., illus., index. $7.95 spiral bound.

A sequel to *Rehab Right* detailing conservation strategies sensitive to a wide range of historic architectural styles. Also includes a guide to appropriate products and installation problems typical to old houses.

Energy Conservation and Solar Energy for Historic Buildings: Guidelines for Appropriate Designs. Thomas Vonier Associates. For Technical Preservation Services, U.S. Department of the Interior. Washington, D.C.: Thomas Vonier Associates (3741 W Street, N.W., Suite 200, 20007), 1981. 24 pp., illus., biblio. $6.95 pb.

An overview of the design factors involved in using conservation techniques and devices in historic buildings, comparing the energy considerations with the historical and design considerations expressed in the Secretary of the Interior's Preservation Standards.

From the Walls In. Charles Wing. Boston: Atlantic Monthly Press, Little Brown, 1979. 238 pp., illus., biblio., index. $12.95 pb.

A preservation-oriented guide to energy conservation written in a casual style but with technical illustrations and figures.

Insulating the Old House: A Handbook for the Owner. Sally E. Nielson, ed. Portland, Maine: Greater Portland Landmarks (Station A, Box 4197, 04101), 1979. 48 pp., illus. $1.90 pb.

A brief overview of factors to be considered.

Improving Thermal Efficiency: Historic Wooden Windows. The Colcord Building, Oklahoma City, Okla. Sharon C. Park, AIA. Technical Preservation Services, U.S. Department of the Interior. Washington, D.C.: GPO, 1983. 16 pp., illus. $3 pb. GPO stock no. 024-005-00840-3.

Provides cost and retrofitting information for preserving significant wooden window sash while conserving energy.

Assessing the Energy Conservation Benefits of Historic Preservation: Methods and Examples. Booz, Allen and Hamilton. For Advisory Council on Historic Preservation. Washington, D.C.: GPO, 1979. 91 pp., illus.

Statistical study examining three types of energy consumption: embodied energy, demolition energy and operating energy. Includes three case studies of National Register properties indicating that renovation results in impressive energy savings.

Energy and the Cultural Community. Report of the Arts/Energy Study. Washington, D.C.: American Association of Museums, 1979. 18 pp. Available from Energy Information Clearinghouse.

An assessment of the energy needs of all sectors of the cultural community, including museums and historic houses.

Energy Management for Museums and Historical Societies. Robert A. Matthai, ed. New York: Energy Information Clearinghouse, 1982.

A comprehensive manual of energy-related information for museums and the cultural community that includes results of Department of Energy-sponsored workshops.

Landscape Design That Saves Energy. Anne Simon Moffat and Marc Schiler. New York: William Morrow, 1981. 223 pp., illus., index, biblio. $17.95 hb, $9.95 pb.

A guide for using plantings to conserve energy.

House Warming. Charlie Wing. Boston: Atlantic Monthly Press, 1983. 204 pp., illus., index. $24.95 hb.

A step-by-step guide based on the PBS television series examining a "leaky old Maine house" retrofitted with state-of-the-art technology.

The Integral Urban House: Self-Reliant Living in the City. The Farallones Institute. San Francisco: Sierra Club Books, 1979. 504 pp., illus., appends., index. $14.95 pb.

Describes ways to apply an ecosystem concept to the urban dwelling, based on an experiment with an 1896 Victorian house in Berkeley.

How to Insulate Your Home and Save Fuel. U.S. Department of Housing and Urban Development. 1975. New York: Dover, 1977. 80 pp. $2.95 pb.

A basic manual on general energy-conservation techniques.

Weatherizing Your Home. George R. Drake. Reston, Va.: Reston Publishing, 1978. 381 pp., illus., gloss., index. $12.95.

Techniques and charts describing the full range of procedures.

Architecture and Energy: Conserving Energy Through Rational Design. Richard G. Stein. New York: Anchor Press, 1977. 322 pp., illus., index. $12.95 hb.

A statement of choices for rediscovering a rational architecture that conserves energy, with some review of the history of architecture as it relates to natural use of ventilation, light and heat.

Handbook of Energy Use for Building Construction. Richard G. Stein, C. Stein, M. Buckley, M. Green, the Stein Partnership. Washington, D.C.: U.S. Department of Energy, 1981. $11. DOE CE 20220-1. Available from National Technical Information Service, 5285 Port Royal Road, Springfield, Va. 22161.

An authoritative guide detailing how much energy is consumed in construction and rehabilitation.

Energy Conservation Standards. Fred Dubin and Gary Long. New York: McGraw-Hill, 1978. 448 pp., illus. $34.50 hb.

A how-to guide for keeping energy costs down in new buildings through design and construction techniques.

The Energy and Environment Checklist: An Annotated Bibliography of Resources. Betty Warren. San Francisco: Friends of the Earth, 1980. 228 pp. $5.95 pb.

Annotated guide to more than 1,600 sources on subjects such as energy conservation, alternative energy sources, organizations, home energy savings, etc.

Greenhouse restaurant addition, Old City Hall (1893), Tacoma, Wash. (Carleton Knight III, NTHP)

Installation of insulation in a Mobile, Ala., house. (Carleton Knight III, NTHP)

Shaded piazzas, Edmonston House (1828), Charleston. (Louis Schwartz)

Nesmith-Greeley Building (1888), San Diego, sporting an awning popular in the 19th century to save energy. (San Diego Historical Society Collection)

Solar devices have been around longer than many people realize: This Pomona Valley, Calif., family had a solar water heater on the roof of its house in 1911. From *A Golden Thread*. (Courtesy Ken Butti and John Perlin)

Solar Energy

"Active solar systems for old buildings are a difficult design problem, one that for architects and preservationists will become more pressing as the price of fuels goes up and the price of solar equipment comes down. . . . The problem is both a design problem and a preservation problem: how to place the hard-edged equipment of a new technology on an old roof without destroying the appearance of the building and how to integrate a new solar system with radiators, grilles and boilers that are themselves important elements of an old building.

It is critically important that an active solar system, like any other mechanical system, be considered only after reasonable conservation measures have been taken. This cannot be emphasized enough."

Gary Long, "Active Solar Applications in Old Buildings." In *New Energy from Old Buildings*

A Golden Thread: 2500 Years of Solar Architecture and Technology. Ken Butti and John Perlin. Palo Alto, Calif.: Cheshire Books, 1980. Distributed by Van Nostrand Reinhold. 304 pp., illus., index. $19.95 hb, $9.95 pb.

A history that proves there is nothing new under the sun, even solar energy usage. Surveys the passive efforts of the 5th-century Greeks to 20th-century active solar systems.

Residential Solar Design Review: A Manual on Community Architectural Controls and Solar Energy Use. Martin Jaffe and Duncan Erley, American Planning Association. For U.S. Department of Housing and Urban Development, with U.S. Department of Energy. Washington, D.C.: GPO, 1980. 88 pp.

Provides guidance on evaluating solar installations, e.g., in historic districts, and suggests strategies for maintaining aesthetic goals.

Passive Solar Retrofit Handbook. Southern Solar Energy Center. Atlanta: Author (61 Perimeter Park, 30341), 1981. 166 pp., illus. $5.95 pb.

An exploration of designs for retrofitting existing buildings, including methods and project examples.

The Passive Solar Energy Book: A Complete Guide to Passive Solar Home, Greenhouse and Building Design. Edward Mazria. Emmaus, Pa.: Rodale Press, 1979. 435 pp. $14.95 pb.

A complete guide to passive solar building and design; includes rules of thumb for system calculations.

Solar Retrofit: Adding Solar to Your Home. Daniel K. Reif. Andover, Mass.: Brick House Publishing (34 Essex Street, 01810), 1981. 200 pp., illus. $11.95 pb.

Provides practical advice and detailed instructions for using solar methods in existing structures.

Solarizing Your Present Home: Practical Solar Heating Systems You Can Build. Joe Carter, ed. Emmaus, Pa.: Rodale Press, 1982. 671 pp., illus., index. $24.95 hb.

Useful mainly for its technical and theoretical information; many of the recommended alterations should never be undertaken on a historic house.

The Second Passive Solar Catalog. David A. Bainbridge. Bascom, Ohio: Passive Solar Institute (P.O. Box 722, 44809). 115 pp., illus. $12.50 pb.

Emphasizes solar retrofitting of commercial and residential buildings, with a products and services directory.

Passive Solar Retrofit: A Practical Homeowner's Guide to Saving Energy Dollars. Darryl J. Strickler. New York: Van Nostrand Reinhold, 1982. 176 pp., illus. $18.95 hb, $10.95 pb.

Contacts

Conservation and Renewable
Energy Inquiry and Referral
Service
P.O. Box 8900
Silver Spring, Md. 20907
(800) 523-2929

Energy Information
Clearinghouse
c/o New York Hall of Science
2 Columbus Circle
New York, N.Y. 10019

National Center for Appropriate
Technology
P.O. Box 3939
Butte, Mont. 59701

U.S. Department of Energy
Washington, D.C. 20545

*DOE Regional Solar Energy
Centers*
Northeast Solar Energy
Center
470 Atlantic Avenue
Boston, Mass. 02110

Southern Solar Energy Center
61 Perimeter Park
Atlanta, Ga. 30341

Mid-American Solar Energy
Complex
8140 26th Street
Bloomington, Minn. 55420

Western Sun
715 S.W. Morrison
Portland, Ore. 97205

Solar Lobby
1001 Connecticut Avenue, N.W.
Washington, D.C. 20036

Solar Energy Research Institute
1617 Cole Boulevard
Golden, Colo. 80401

Solar Energy Institute of North
America
1110 Sixth Street, N.W.
Washington, D.C. 20001

United States Section of the
International Solar Energy
Society
1230 Grandview Avenue
Boulder, Colo. 80302

Citizens' Energy Project
1110 Sixth Street, N.W.,
Suite 300
Washington, D.C. 20001

Golden Gate Energy Center
Golden Gate National
Recreation Area
Building 1055, Fort Cronkhite
Sausalito, Calif. 94956

Manchester Citizens
Association
1120 Pennsylvania Avenue
Pittsburgh, Pa. 15233

State Energy Offices

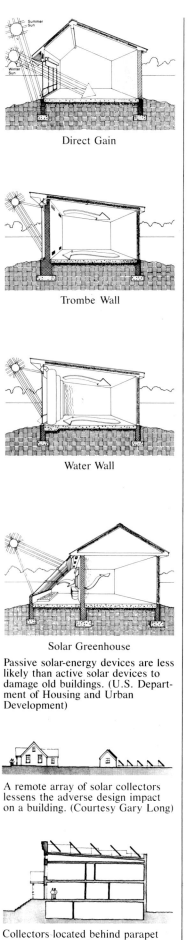

Direct Gain

Trombe Wall

Water Wall

Solar Greenhouse

Passive solar-energy devices are less
likely than active solar devices to
damage old buildings. (U.S. Department of Housing and Urban
Development)

A remote array of solar collectors
lessens the adverse design impact
on a building. (Courtesy Gary Long)

Collectors located behind parapet
roofs provide an alternative means
of preventing a disruptive appearance. (Courtesy Gary Long)

Maintenance

A little neglect may breed mischief. . . .

Ben Franklin, *Poor Richard's
Almanac*

*Maintenance is not a single branch of learning or a
single trade capable of definition. It is a mongrel
science of a varied ancestry: part architecture, part
physical chemistry, part management, and more.*

J. Henry Chambers, *Cyclical
Maintenance for Historic
Buildings*

"Maintenance . . . consists of
all activities carried out to
maintain a building's structural
integrity and appearance after
acquisition or after restoration
has been completed. It ranges
from the installation of fire-
detection devices and other
safety features to the control of
tourism."

> Discussion Summary, "Mainte-
> nance: The Life Expectancy of
> Materials and Problems of In-
> creasing Visitor Use." In *Preser-
> vation and Conservation:
> Principles and Practices*

*Cyclical Maintenance for His-
toric Buildings*. J. Henry Chambers. Technical Preservation
Services, U.S. Department of
the Interior. Washington, D.C.:
GPO, 1976. 125 pp., illus., appends., biblio. $6.50 pb. GPO
stock no. 024-005-00637-1.

A step-by-step handbook for building managers, architects and others
involved in the routine maintenance
of historic properties. Each maintenance technique is discussed in
terms of historic and modern methods—good, bad and why. Appendixes contain maintenance charts and
sample forms.

"Maintenance: The Life Expectancy of Materials and Problems
of Increasing Visitor Use." In
*Preservation and Conservation:
Principles and Practices*. Washington, D.C.: Preservation
Press, 1976. 547 pp., illus.,
biblio. $17.95 pb.

Describes various problems in maintaining monumental historic properties and explores preservation
philosophy on maintenance.

*Protecting Our Heritage: A Dis-
course on Fire Protection and
Prevention in Historical Build-
ings and Landmarks*. Joseph F.
Jenkins, ed. Boston: National
Fire Protection Association
(Batterymarch Park, Quincy,
Mass. 02269) with American
Association for State and Local
History, 1970. 39 pp., illus.,
appends. $2 pb.

Discusses the evaluation of risk and
protection measures, housekeeping,
planning for emergencies and cost
considerations.

*Housekeeping Techniques for
the Historic House*. Joseph M.
Thatcher. Nashville: American
Association for State and Local
History. Slide and tape program.
$44.50.

A guide to safe cleaning methods
and maintenance of floors, woodwork, fireplaces, furniture and other
artifacts, designed for museum staff.

*Historic Preservation Mainte-
nance Procedures*. U.S. Department of the Army. Washington,
D.C.: Headquarters, Department of the Army, 1977. Technical Manual no. 5-801-2. 50 pp.,
biblio. $2.60 pb. Available from
U. S. Army AG Publications
Center, 1655 Woodson Road, St.
Louis, Mo. 63114.

Cyclical Maintenance for Historic Buildings

A San Francisco Victorian being
repainted. (Lee Foster)

In the mid-19th century, pointed trees were considered picturesque and repeated architectural features of Gothic Revival houses. From *For Every House a Garden.* (Andrew Jackson Downing)

Gardens and Landscaping: Restoring the Green

Preservation must not be limited to the saving of a historic structure alone, it must include the landscape around the structure, the total environment.

James Biddle, "Landscapes."
Preservation News, June 1975.

We espouse the philosophy that the grounds are just as important as the structure.

Rudy J. Favretti and Joy Putman Favretti, *Landscapes and Gardens for Historic Buildings*

"A landscape by its very nature is always changing. Unlike architectural remains, which are static, the landscape will have undergone alteration even when it is intact. . . . Any landscape or garden you plan to restore will have already gone through a series of changes. . . .
You must decide what period to choose for your site interpretation. . . . The terminal date can be as late as the time the site was taken over for restoration. Landscape and architectural terminal dates do not need to be identical. . . . The cut-off date is often determined by the character and pattern of the landscape rather than by a fixed form as in architecture. In your planning, consider carefully the historical relationship between the buildings and the nature of the extant landscaping. . . . Usually if the material reflects the character and pattern of the landscape it should be preserved. But make each decision on an individual basis."

John J. Stewart, *Historic Landscapes and Gardens*

Landscapes and Gardens for Historic Buildings: A Handbook for Reproducing and Creating Authentic Landscape Settings. Rudy J. Favretti and Joy Putman Favretti. Nashville: American Association for State and Local History, 1978. 202 pp., illus., append., biblio., index. $13 pb.

Oriented to museum sites, the book is nonetheless general enough for broad use. Topics include a history of American landscape design and landscape types (residences, public buildings, cemeteries); how to research a site and plan a restoration; authentic plants, including a list of historic plants and contemporary sources; and maintaining the restored landscape.

Historic Landscapes and Gardens: Procedures for Restoration. John J. Stewart. Nashville: American Association for State and Local History, 1974. Technical Leaflet 80. 12 pp., illus., biblio. $2 pb.

Reviews procedures for preserving and restoring historic landscape designs from the site survey to maintenance. Includes sample as-found plans.

For Every House a Garden: A Guide for Reproducing Period Gardens. Rudy J. Favretti and Joy P. Favretti. Chester, Conn.: Globe-Pequot Press, 1977. 137 pp., illus., index. $4.95 pb.

A handbook on American landscape architecture, restoration principles and horticultural information for property owners and professionals. Includes a list of authentic plants, 1620–1900.

Victorian Gardens: How to Plan, Plant and Enjoy 19th-Century Beauty Today. Jack Kramer. New York: Harper and Row, 1981. $9.95 pb.

A guide to reviving 19th-century landscape techniques and patterns.

"Landscaping the Pre-1840 House," Donna Jealoz. *Old-House Journal,* February 1977. "Victorian Landscaping," Donna Jealoz. *Old-House Journal,* April 1977.

Popular discussions of the design and plant materials used in 18th- and 19th-century domestic gardens and how these can be re-created.

Maymont Park: The Italian Garden, Richmond, Virginia. Using HCRS Grant-in-Aid Funds for Landscape Restoration. Barry W. Starke. Technical Preservation Services, U.S. Department of the Interior. Washington, D.C.: GPO, 1980. 39 pp., illus., appends.

Case study of the restoration of a public garden.

Archeology and the Colonial Gardener. Audrey Noel-Hume. Williamsburg, Va.: Colonial Williamsburg Foundation, 1974. Colonial Williamsburg Archeological Series no. 7. 96 pp., illus., biblio. $2.95 pb.

Describes the approaches to discovering fences, walls, steps, walks, garden houses, arbors, plantings, flower pots and urns, bell glasses ("portable greenhouses"), watering pots, gardening tools and bird houses.

"Preservation and Restoration of Historic Gardens and Landscapes." *Landscape Architecture,* May 1976.

A technical survey of the philosophy of landscape restoration, archeological work, garden research and interpretation, and case studies of U.S. and other restorations.

"Preservation Leaps the Garden Wall." *Landscape Architecture,* January 1981. Reprint. 52 pp., color illus. $4.50 pb.

A survey of garden and landscape issues, focusing on broad cultural landscape concerns. Projects featured include Mount Vernon and the National Colonial Farm, Accokeek, Md.

"Standards for Historic Garden Preservation and Restoration," David Streatfield. *Landscape Architecture,* April 1969.

Proposes categories of landscapes worth preserving.

"The Case for the Commemoration of Historic Landscapes and Gardens," John Stewart and Susan Buggey. *Bulletin,* Association for Preservation Technology, vol. 7, no. 2, 1975.

Defines types of historic landscaping that should be preserved, using categories established by David Streatfield.

Historic Landscape Preservation and Restoration: An Annotated Bibliography for New York State. Frederick D. Cawley, ed. Albany: Preservation League of New York State, 1977. 6 pp. $1 pb.

As the introduction notes, "New York State has long been recognized as the birthplace of American horticulture and of a peculiar American tradition of design on the land." Many of the sources apply to other areas as well. Five sections are used: historical studies, contemporary sources in print, preservation and restoration reports, plant materials and bibliographies.

Bold-foliage plants were favored in the Victorian era. (*Vick's Illustrated Monthly,* 1878)

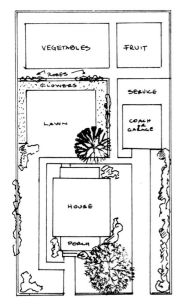

A typical plan for a modest town garden often included grass panel surrounded by a flower bed near the rear of the house. From *For Every House a Garden*. (Rudy and Joy Favretti)

Florida house (1882) shows a common mid-19th-century treatment. From *Landscapes and Gardens for Historic Buildings*. (Frank Leslie's Illustrated Newspaper, 1882)

A maze (1934, Arthur A. Shurcliff) was added during reconstruction of the Governor's Palace, Williamsburg, Va. (Colonial Williamsburg Foundation)

Contacts

American Society of Landscape Architects
Historic Preservation Committee
1733 Connecticut Avenue, N.W.
Washington, D.C. 20009

Has liaison members in each state and has issued publications on the role of landscape architects in preservation and the preservation functions of state and local ASLA chapters.

Society of Architectural Historians
American Landscape and Garden History Society
1700 Walnut Street
Suite 716
Philadelphia, Pa. 19103

Coordinates interests in landscape and horticultural conservation and recording of significant regional landscapes, gardens and documents. It also maintains bibliographic, scholarly and related technical information.

Association for Preservation Technology
Chairman of Landscapes and Gardens
P.O. Box 2487, Station D
Ottawa, Ontario K1P 5W6, Canada

Designates a member of its board to oversee landscape preservation concerns and has published extensively on the subject in its *Bulletin* and *Communique*.

Garden Clubs of America
Conservation Committee
598 Madison Avenue
New York, N.Y. 10022

Addresses preservation issues and makes an annual award to the most preservation active person or chapter. Numerous local garden clubs have sponsored projects to restore historic gardens.

National Council of State Garden Clubs
Historic Preservation Committee
4401 Magnolia Avenue
St. Louis, Mo. 63110

Works in the area of historic horticulture and encourages the restoration of structures for use as garden centers.

Alliance for Historic Landscape Preservation
University of Oregon
216 Lawrence Hall
Eugene, Ore. 97403

Fosters communication and exchange of ideas among professionals.

Landscape Architecture
1733 Connecticut Avenue, N.W.
Washington, D.C. 20009

Monthly magazine of the American Society of Landscape Architects, providing coverage of landscape design, land planning and garden restoration.

Cherokee Garden Library
Atlanta Historical Society
3099 Andrews Drive, N.W.
Atlanta, Ga. 30305

Information center for gardening and horticultural research for the southeastern United States.

See also: Gardens and Parks, Estates, Fences, Rural Areas and Landscapes (Form and Function)

Heavy foundation plantings and ornamental bedding were popular in the late 19th century. From *For Every House a Garden*. (Knox Foundation)

Adaptive Use

10

*Y*ou cannot hang a building on a wall like a painting; you have to find a use for it.

Arthur P. Ziegler, Jr. In *New Life for Old Buildings.* Ontario: Frontenac Historic Foundation, 1977.

*T*he best hope of saving our cities' landmarks is to find new uses for them. . . . We have no patience with simply embalming a building that is dead. The job is only worth doing if it creates a more interesting environment than the one that is there now. We come not to bury these buildings, but to bring them back alive.

Gordon Gray. In "New Life for Landmarks." New York: American Federation of Arts, 1966.

"Use it up,
Wear it out,
Make it do
Or do without."

Old New England proverb

"Although adaptive use is not always cheaper than new construction, the cost of adaptive use falls within the range of new construction costs. It would seem, then, that adaptive use stands as an equally feasible alternative to new construction to meet the space needs of a tenant. . . . The real bonus comes at the conclusion of the project. There is no comparison to a project which creatively re-uses and adapts an old building, rich in decades of character and life, to a new building of only average construction."

Advisory Council on Historic Preservation, *Adaptive Use: A Survey of Construction Costs*

Old Post Office (1892–99, Willoughby J. Edbrooke), Washington, D.C. Under a GSA-sponsored conversion to office and commercial use, the monumental interior court of the building was reclaimed to allow three levels of shops and restaurants. Offices for preservation, arts and humanities agencies now overlook the revived space. (Paul Kennedy)

"Recycling buildings may be as much an expression of the 1980s as disposable clothing and planning obsolescence were of the 1950s and 1960s. We are no more pious than our predecessors; we are responding to a different normalcy. . . . The discovery of preservation is natural to my generation because we live in a time of steadily rising costs and expensive capital. . . .
   Computations produced more preservation, I'll bet, than sentiment did. . . . When it makes economic sense to reuse an existing plant, there is presented an opportunity to do the job well. When among one's choices for reuse there are ugly buildings and handsome buildings, at nearly the same price, one will be likely to use a handsome one. . . . Solving an aesthetic and economic puzzle simultaneously is fun, like Chinese checkers. And there are good reasons for doing so."

Roger G. Kennedy, Preface. *New Profits from Old Buildings*

"There is always the possibility that this generation's Golden Arches will become the next generation's jungle gym."

Judith N. Getzels, *Recycling Public Buildings.* Chicago: American Society of Planning Officials, 1976.

The Richardsonian Romanesque Old Post Office, a long-revered but once threatened landmark on Pennsylvania Avenue. (Paul Kennedy)

"This is a concept so old and so commonplace that it seems new and shocking, especially to twentieth-century Americans who are firmly committed to novelty and to built-in obsolescence. Preservation through adaptive use can therefore ride the crest of novelty today."

Helen Duprey Bullock, "Preservation Features." *Historic Preservation,* May–June 1966.

"An environment that cannot be changed invites its own destruction. We prefer a world that can be modified progressively against a background of valued remains, a world in which one can leave a personal mark alongside the marks of history."

Kevin Lynch, *What Time Is This Place?* Cambridge: MIT Press, 1972.

Reusing Old Buildings: The Savings

Financial. Old buildings can be cheaper—low acquisition costs, no demolition costs, lower materials costs.

Tax. Tax and benefits are provided—to developers and governments for putting buildings back on the tax rolls.

Time. Rehabilitated buildings are finished quickly—through fast-track construction, staged or continued occupancy, early marketing.

Location. The site is often right—available utilities and public services, nearby labor, transportation, retail areas, new amenities such as revived urban centers.

Energy. Saving old buildings saves energy—in fewer natural resources for new building materials, demolition and construction energy, commuting time, energy efficiency gained.

Environmental. Natural resources are conserved—producing less urban sprawl and loss of open space from new construction.

Social. Community disruption is avoided—reducing trauma caused by dilapidation, abandonment and demolition; attracting new residents and workers.

Employment. Reusing buildings saves jobs—businesses do not have to move, rehabilitation is labor intensive.

Image. Old buildings are popular—improve business image, create community goodwill because of preservation, spur neighborhood improvement.

Design. Old buildings can be nicer than new—unique, soundly constructed, spacious, more pleasantly scaled.

Cultural. Saving buildings saves historic resources—local landmarks, irreplaceable buildings.

The Tannery Apartments, Peabody, Mass., created from two 1894 tanneries. Industrial vestiges such as these vats were retained. (Phokion Karas)

Chickering Piano Factory (1853), Boston, transformed into apartment-studios for artists and artisans in the city's South End. (© Greg Heins)

"Can 300 people find happiness living in a piano factory?" asked a National Trust ad promoting adaptive use. The answer was, "Yes!" (NTHP)

REUSING OLD BUILDINGS

IS NOT JUST A NICE IDEA.

Poster focusing on the new Piano Craft Guild to highlight the benefits of adaptive use. (Linda Mancini, Gelardin Bruner Cott)

Drawing of the Tannery complex showing the former industrial buildings connected by bridges to the Federal-style Crowninshield Mansion (1814), which was converted to offices and community space. (Anderson Notter Finegold)

The Language of Adaptive Use

adaptive abuse. Inappropriate conversion of a building to a new use that is detrimental to the structure's architectural character or undesirable in relation to its neighborhood.

adaptive use. The process of converting a building to a use other than that for which it was designed, e.g., changing a factory into housing. This is accomplished with varying alterations to the building.

bootleg conversion. An illegal change in a structure contrary to zoning regulations, as in the partitioning of a single-family dwelling into two or more units.

boutique-and-drippy-candle syndrome. A trend in historic areas by which old buildings are converted into small shops offering specialized merchandise, often replacing service-oriented businesses and increasing tourism.

building codes. Local regulations that control design, procedures and materials used in construction and renovation. Based on public safety and health standards, codes are usually designed for new construction but are applied to old buildings when substantial adaptive use is undertaken; this necessitates flexible enforcement for the differing requirements of historic buildings.

double-decking. Insertion of a mezzanine or extra floor in a building with a high ceiling or a two-story space to increase the usable area.

exposed brick-and-hanging-fern syndrome. The stripping of plaster from interior walls to expose the brick to make a building appear old coupled with the use of plants as decoration, both prevalent in the adaptive use of old buildings as restaurants or boutiques. In addition to changing a building's original character, the process results in a homogeneity that has been criticized as a negative outgrowth of the adaptive use process.

extended use. Any process that increases the useful life of an old building, e.g., adaptive use or continued use.

false-face preservation. The retention of only the facade of a historic building during conversion while the remainder is severely altered or demolished to accept the new use; also called "facadism."

fast tracking. A method of construction or rehabilitation in which plans are drawn, bids are obtained and contracts are made for each stage of the project as it progresses instead of before all work begins.

feasibility study. An analysis made to evaluate appropriate uses, physical condition, anticipated costs, work time, procedures and revenues of a proposed project. Adaptive use feasibility studies generally analyze several possible courses of action.

found space. Old buildings or spaces within them that have been retrieved from near oblivion for rehabilitation or adaptive use after having been abandoned or "lost."

handicapped access. Efforts to ensure that facilities and programs in buildings are made available to those with limited mobility, the blind and other handicapped persons. Accommodation of the handicapped in converted historic buildings and museums is planned for consistency with the buildings' historical and architectural integrity and may not require that existing facilities be completely barrier free.

mixed-use development. A relatively large-scale real estate project that may incorporate old buildings and is characterized by three or more significant revenue-producing uses (retail, office, residential, hotel, recreation, etc.), functional and physical integration of project components and development under a coherent plan.

nonconforming use. A building or use that is inconsonant with an area's zoning regulations. Nonconforming uses may be "grandfathered" in following zoning changes, but upon conversion to a new or adaptive use, the exemption may be forfeited and the new use required to adhere to the applicable regulations unless an exception is granted.

seismic reinforcement laws. Building regulations that seek to minimize dangers to human safety should an earthquake occur, often requiring stabilization of outer walls, reinforcement of overhangs and the tying of floors to outer walls.

surplus property. A building or site no longer in demand for its current use. Unused property owned by federal, state or local governments may be transferred with minimal or no charge to another owner for rehabilitation and new use.

Adapted from *Landmark Words: A Glossary for Preserving the Built Environment.* National Trust for Historic Preservation. Forthcoming.

Buildings Reborn poster and cover by Richard Haas. (SITES)

Actors Theatre took over the Bank of Louisville (1836, James Dakin). (Steve Grubman)

Floor plan for the new Actors Theatre. (Harry Weese and Associates)

Basic Books for Recycling

Probably the single most important aspect of the preservation movement is the recycling of old buildings—adapting them to uses different from the ones for which they were originally intended. . . . Successful revitalization demonstrates that the forms and materials devised in the past are still valid when properly adapted to the functions of today's life. . . . The approach, moreover, may involve the conversion of a girdle factory into an early education center, as has been done in Pittsburgh; a Federal-period house into an Off-Track Betting parlor, as in New York City; a torpedo factory into an arts center, as in Alexandria, Virginia; a tannery into a 284-unit apartment complex, as in Peabody, Massachusetts; a grammar school into senior citizens' housing, as in Boston.

Barbaralee Diamonstein, *Buildings Reborn*

Adaptive Use: Development Economics, Process, and Profiles. Washington, D.C.: Urban Land Institute, 1978. 246 pp., illus., biblio., index. $37 hb.

Detailing both the economics and the process, this book provides step-by-step considerations and suggestions for adapting an old building to a new use, with emphasis on private development projects. Case studies provide data on projects, including the redevelopment process, feasibility studies, planning, design and engineering features, statistics, experience gained and illustrations. A descriptive catalog of project profiles is arranged by building type.

Adaptive Use: A Survey of Construction Costs. Washington, D.C.: Advisory Council on Historic Preservation (1100 Pennsylvania Avenue, N.W., 20005), 1976. 28 pp., biblio.

An early comparison of a selected group of adaptive use projects with new construction of the same type. Project expenses were compared for land and building acquisition, hard costs (building construction) and soft costs (fees and financing costs). Conclusions: (1) The cost of adaptive use falls within the range of new construction costs, and (2) the key to successful adaptive use is an inventive matching up of the new plan to the existing building.

Recycling Buildings: Renovations, Remodeling, Restorations, and Reuses. Elizabeth Kendall Thompson, ed. New York: Architectural Record Books, McGraw-Hill, 1977. 213 pp., illus.

Reprints from *Architectural Record* featuring photographs and drawings, with accompanying text. The brief case histories (not all are adaptive uses) are divided into chapters on residential, business, retail, community use, continued use, restoration and additions to historic buildings and neighborhoods.

Buildings Reborn: New Uses, Old Places. Barbaralee Diamonstein. New York: Harper and Row, 1978. 255 pp., illus., biblio., index. $10 pb.

Provides 95 examples of adaptive use, with the projects arranged alphabetically by city and more emphasis on the excitement of recycling than on the economics.

New Life for Old Buildings. Mildred F. Schmertz and Editors of Architectural Record. New York: McGraw-Hill, 1982. 189 pp., illus., index. $32.50 hb.

Many conversions are included among the case histories of recycling and renovation of urban marketplaces, civic and cultural buildings, campus structures, offices, showrooms, restaurants and houses and apartments.

New Profits from Old Buildings: Private Enterprise Approaches to Making Preservation Pay. Raynor M. Warner, Sibyl M. Groff and Ranne P. Warner. New York: INFORM (381 Park Avenue, South, 10016), 1978. $14 pb. New York: McGraw-Hill, 1979. 307 pp., illus., gloss., index. $29.95 hb.

A business-oriented guide to preservation, originally published as *Business and Preservation.* By means of case studies, 71 examples of corporate interest in preservation are examined: background, costs, problems and benefits to the corporation. The first section is on adaptive use and covers recycling of 17 historic buildings.

Restored America. Deirdre Stanforth. New York: Praeger Publishers, 1975. 243 pp., illus.

An early sampler of preservation success stories, divided into two sections: examples of buildings restored by individuals and nonprofit organizations and examples of a variety of adaptive uses. The photographs span the country's towns and cities.

New Uses for Old Buildings. Sherban Cantacuzino. New York: Whitney Library of Design, 1975. 264 pp., illus.

Intended for individuals and organizations "with redundant buildings on their hands," the author uses 73 examples from around the world. Many are conversions of industrial buildings, although 10 building types are discussed. The emphasis is on the original character of the building, with the onus on the architect to preserve that character in the conversion.

Saving Old Buildings. Sherban Cantacuzino and Susan Brandt. 1980. New York: Nichols Publishing, 1981. 230 pp., illus., append. $65 hb.

In contrast to Cantacuzino's earlier *New Uses for Old Buildings,* the focus here is on the new use, pointing up the important strategic issues of urban and rural development. The book is organized around major case studies of Bologna's regeneration and of English village renewal, with nearly 100 illustrations from Europe and the United States. The appendix, "Found Space," emphasizes the need to find short-life uses at minimal cost.

Built to Last: A Handbook on Recycling Old Buildings. Gene Bunnell, Massachusetts Department of Community Affairs. Washington, D.C.: Preservation Press, 1977. 126 pp., illus., append., index.

Shows how one state (Massachusetts) has combined private investment, public money, tax incentives and professional guidance to recycle historic buildings. Describes financial strategies, design solutions and community cooperation. Case histories (many adaptive use) of public, commercial, residential, industrial, religious and educational buildings.

Community Harmony: The Reuse of Ordinary Structures. Robert E. Mendelson et al. Edwardsville, Ill.: Center for Urban and Environmental Research and Services, Southern Illinois University (Box 32, 62026), 1980. 126 pp., illus., append. $7.50 pb.

Twenty-three commonplace structures in the St. Louis metropolitan area were selected to show how ordinary structures can be recycled at the neighborhood level. Also includes analytical tables and conclusions.

Recycled Buildings: A Bibliography of Adaptive Use Literature Since 1970. Margaret Thomas Will. Monticello, Ill.: Vance Bibliographies, 1979. A-154. 71 pp. $7.50 pb.

Includes books, journal and magazine articles, conference proceedings, special reports and monographs.

Quaker Oats Company grain silos (1932) reborn as a hotel (1980, Curtis and Rasmussen) at Quaker Square, Akron, Ohio. (Akron Planning Department)

Case Studies

Older buildings, especially those that have been used for warehousing and/or manufacturing, often have hidden assets that make reuse attractive for developers. These hidden assets can be either tangible, such as increased height, space and volume, or intangible, such as increased character and amenities, all of which add to the value of a property.

Urban Land Institute, *Economic Analyses of Adaptive Use Projects: Long Wharf*

Economic Analyses of Adaptive Use Projects. Urban Land Institute. Information Series. National Trust for Historic Preservation. Washington, D.C.: Preservation Press, 1976. $2 pb each.

An illustrated series presenting detailed project data for:
Butler Square, Minneapolis, a 1906 warehouse converted into retail, office and hotel use. 15 pp.
Guernsey Hall, Princeton, N.J., an 1852 mansion adapted as luxury condominiums. 12 pp.
Long Wharf, Boston, two waterfront commercial buildings transformed into apartments, retail and office space and a restaurant. 14 pp.
Stanford Court, San Francisco, a 1912 apartment building changed to a hotel. 12 pp.
Trolley Square, Salt Lake City, Mission-style streetcar barns adapted as a shopping and entertainment center. 16 pp.

Project Reference File. Washington, D.C.: Urban Land Institute (1090 Vermont Avenue, N.W., 20005). 4 pp., illus. Quarterly. $3.50 each, $60 annual subscription.

Profiles of five development projects are issued each quarter, many on adaptive use. Sample titles include:
Grand Central Arcade, Seattle, Wash., an opera house-office building converted to shopping and office space. (vol. 3, no. 19)
Cast Iron Building, New York City, an 1868 industrial building changed to residential use. (vol. 5, no. 7)
Court House Square, Columbus, Ohio, a 19th-century residential-commercial area converted to commercial and office space. (vol. 5, no. 15)
Mercantile Wharf Building, Boston, a large commercial building adapted as apartments and commercial space. (vol. 8, no. 3)
Quaker Square, Akron, Ohio, factory buildings and grain silos converted to specialty shops, restaurants and offices. (vol. 8, no. 8)
Fowler Square, Little Rock, Ark., an 1840 mansion adapted as apartments, with new units. (vol. 9, no. 19)
Station Square, Pittsburgh, an urban railroad station converted to a complex of restaurants, offices and specialty shops. (vol. 9, no. 14)

Chateau Clare, Woonsocket, Rhode Island; Rodman Candleworks, New Bedford, Massachusetts: Rehabilitation Through Federal Assistance. Floy A. Brown. Preservation Case Study Series. Washington, D.C.: Technical Preservation Services, National Park Service (U.S. Department of the Interior, 20240), 1979. 32 pp., illus.

Highlights Chateau Clare (1889–1920), a school and convent converted into 88 apartment units for the elderly and handicapped; and Rodman Candleworks (1810), a maritime industry building adapted for a bank, offices and restaurant. Includes detailed project history, economics and benefits, tax implications and rehabilitation work.

Carr Mill, Carrboro, North Carolina: A Rehabilitation Project Under the Tax Reform Act of 1976. Margaret A. Thomas. Preservation Case Study Series. Washington, D.C.: Technical Preservation Services, National Park Service, 1979. 32 pp., illus.

Details the conversion of the first floor of the mill into a shopping mall, reuse of the second floor as office space and construction of additional shopping facilities on the property.

Recycled Boston. Boston Redevelopment Authority. Boston: Author (Public Information Department, City Hall, 02201), 1978. 32 pp., illus. $2 pb.

A pictorial look at a broad spectrum of conversions from old to new uses, both downtown and in the neighborhoods, including the well-known examples and some lesser-known ones.

A Handbook for Building Re-Use. Ken Wong. Boston: Metropolitan Area Planning Council (110 Tremont Street, 02108), 1979. 123 pp., illus. $9.50.

Case studies of four Boston MAPL projects that outline steps taken to implement a building reuse program for different purposes.

Renovating and Utilizing Chicago's Older Buildings. Robert J. Piper. Chicago: Chicago Association of Commerce and Industry (130 South Michigan Avenue, 60603), 1980. 12 pp.

An overview of Chicago's experience with adaptive use.

Adaptive Use: Alleys to Zoos. National Endowment for the Arts. Washington, D.C.: Design Arts Program (1100 Pennsylvania Avenue, N.W., 20506), 1977.

Listing of projects by building type funded by the NEA, 1966–77.

Case Studies in Adaptive Use: A Selected Bibliography. Gregory Longhini. *PAS Memo* (American Planning Association), 1980.

Adaptive Use on Film
Adaptive Reuse. Alan Karchmer, Tulane University. 15 min., 16 mm., color. 1976. Louisiana Architects Association, 521 America Street, Baton Rouge, La. 70802.

Examples of commercial and residential projects in New Orleans; National Trust film competition winner.

Built to Last: Reusing Old Buildings. Gelardin Bruner Cott for Massachusetts Department of Community Affairs. 20 min., slide-tape. 1977. Center for Information Sharing, 77 North Washington Street, Boston, Mass. 02114.

Based on *Built to Last* with the addition of some examples not in the book.

Here Today. Roger Hagan. 26 min., 16 mm., color. 1978. Heritage Conservation Branch, Resource Information Center, Parliament Building, Victoria V8V 1X4, B.C.

The case for adaptive use in old commercial structures and houses in Canada.

Stations. Roger Hagan. 63 and 28 min., 16 mm., color. 1974. Roger Hagan Associates, 1019 Belmont Place East, Seattle, Wash. 98102.

Presents various adaptive uses for old and abandoned railroad stations.

Working Places. John Karol, Society for Industrial Archeology. 22 min., 16 mm., color. 1975. SIA, c/o Robert Vogel, National Museum of History and Technology, Room 5020, Washington, D.C. 20560.

Surveys industrial reuse projects in the U.S. and Canada through interviews with planners, local officials, construction workers and others.

Reborn to Travel
Buildings Reborn: New Uses, Old Places. Traveling exhibit sponsored by the Smithsonian Institution Traveling Exhibition Service (Washington, D.C. 20560). 40 panels. 1978; updated 1979. On exhibit in the U.S. through 1985.

Based on the book *Buildings Reborn* by Barbaralee Diamonstein, the exhibit presents photographs and text illustrating 53 adaptive use projects.

The Car Barn (1910), New Bedford, Mass., once home to trolleys and buses but now 114 units of housing for the elderly developed by the Clairmont Company (1980, Philip Hresko, Boston Architectural Team). (© Nick Wheeler)

Take a Building Type

The key to. . .preservation successes is imagination. Asking the question, "What could this building become?" may reveal more possibilities than, "What has this building been?"

James Biddle, Foreword. *Built to Last*

Railroad Stations

"Finding new lives for old railroad stations is no longer a 'good cause' that is waiting around the corner. There are enough successful completed conversions to convince the most skeptical that it's not the latest advocacy fad but a business venture that can at least be self-supporting.

Stations are being conserved, not preserved, so that the splendors of their architecture can be put to use while being enjoyed. . . . Examples of small-station conservation projects abound. Many are now privately owned antique stores, gift shops, homes, or studios. Not as many middle size stations have been conserved because their location is far more critical. . .and because they require more money to buy (or lease) and convert to a new purpose—difficulties that usually require concerted action and inventiveness to overcome. . . . Then there are the big stations, terminals that require a big business approach before anything can be done for them. A few have been conserved, and they provide exemplary directions for what can be done for those large stations whose fate is now in abeyance."

Educational Facilities Laboratories, Introduction. *Reusing Railroad Stations: Book Two*

Recycling Historic Railroad Stations: A Citizens' Manual. Anderson Notter Finegold. Washington, D.C.: U.S. Department of Transportation (Office of the Secretary, Room 10223, 20590), 1978. 83 pp., illus. $3 pb.

Reusing Railroad Stations: Book Two. Educational Facilities Laboratories. New York: EFL (680 Fifth Avenue, 10019), 1975. 79 pp., illus. $4 pb.

Industrial Buildings

"Few eyebrows are raised when shoe and textile companies locate in historic mills in the Northeast, for these products are part of the region's industrial tradition. The surprise is that many of the current tenants are engaged in sophisticated research and technology and other nontraditional industrial processes. A carefully rehabilitated mill can be the ideal answer to a progressive new company's site selection requirements. . . .

Economy of time and money is the compelling reason that many companies locate in historic mill buildings. Many mill towns have a readily available labor pool and mill space that is easily adapted for industrial or office use. The time saved by rehabilitating a vacant mill rather than constructing a new building translates into dollars for a company that has outgrown its present location. A potential savings in construction costs for rehabilitation compared to new construction frees money for research and development or production. An urban facility, renovated at a reasonable cost and accented by a clock tower, spiral stairs, a marble fireplace, abundant natural lighting or a river view, will attract high-quality labor to a growing company in a competitive field."

National Trust Northeast Regional Office, Introduction. *The Mill Works Handbook*

Working Places: The Adaptive Use of Industrial Buildings. Walter C. Kidney, Society for Industrial Archeology. Pittsburgh: Ober Park Associates (One Station Square, 15219), 1976. 169 pp., illus., index. $8 pb.

A Future from the Past: The Case for Conservation and Reuse of Old Buildings in Industrial Communities. Randolph Langenbach. Gene Bunnell, ed. Washington, D.C.: U.S. Department of Housing and Urban Development and Massachusetts Department of Community Affairs, 1978. 119 pp., illus.

The Mill Works Handbook. Northeast Regional Office, National Trust for Historic Preservation. Leslie E. Donovan, project director. Washington, D.C.: Preservation Press, 1983. 250 pp., illus., appends. $24.95 binder.

Union Depot (1892), Duluth, Minn., a Chateauesque railroad station converted to the St. Louis County Heritage and Arts Center. (© Bruce Ojarro)

Pittsburgh and Lake Erie Terminal (1901) restaurant. (PHLF)

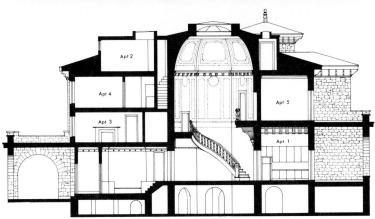

Stairway and section of Guernsey Hall (1849, John Notman), Princeton, N.J., adapted as condominiums. (Oto Baitz; Short and Ford Architects)

Central Grammar Apartments, Gloucester, Mass., created from an 1889 high school to house elderly residents. (SITES)

Mansions and Estates

"Sophisticated urban city-planning concepts and complex design-control mechanisms are often anathema to suburban and rural communities. . . . If we are to achieve any success in saving large estates, much of the traditional antipathy of small communities to planning and controls will have to be modified. . . .

The concept of appropriate use, however, is nebulous. For example, a proposed institutional adaptation may require no major structural changes and may best preserve the architectural character of the property and its landscaped surroundings. Yet the neighbors may find it totally unacceptable. . . . Thus what is appropriate in preservation terms may not be so in a social sense.

Perhaps the dominant concern in converting a residence to a new use is the preservation of the original intent of the owner, designers and builders. . . . The nature of the planned intervention, modification or addition can then be evaluated:

1. How visible will the changes be?
2. Is the new design compatible with the old?
3. Will the new materials blend sympathetically with the old?
4. Will the modifications be reversible at some future date?"

William C. Shopsin, "Design Considerations in Transforming Large Estates to New Uses." In *Saving Large Estates*

"In many cases, a number of solutions are necessary to make the estate financially secure as well as to meet the needs of the community. For example, a portion of the property could be sold to a private developer for a new housing development, providing the funds necessary to establish an endowment to support the main house, outbuildings and grounds. The main building might become a house museum and the grounds marked as jogging or cross-country ski trails for the enjoyment of the community; supplementary funds might be raised by using other parts of the house for a conference center and renting outbuildings to retail establishments such as a garden nursery or art gallery."

Christopher W. Closs, *Preserving Large Estates*

Saving Large Estates: Conservation, Historic Preservation, Adaptive Reuse. William C. Shopsin and Grania Bolton Marcus. Setauket, N.Y.: Society for the Preservation of Long Island Antiquities (93 North Country Road, 11733), 1977. 199 pp., illus., biblio. $8 pb.

Preserving Large Estates. Christopher W. Closs. Information Series. National Trust for Historic Preservation. Washington, D.C.: Preservation Press, 1982. 24 pp., illus., biblio., append. $2 pb.

Schools

"Once school buildings no longer serve an educational purpose, taxpayers should have the opportunity to assist in determining how that cumulative investment should be used. . . .

The citizens' task force should first determine what statutory limitations are placed on school properties that are not functioning as educational facilities. . . . In some cases, state law . . . restricts the types of tenants that are eligible to lease space in a school as well as the length of the lease. Other states or communities restrict who may purchase school property. . . . Local zoning and building ordinances must be taken into account, and the task force should determine whether zoning variances or special-use permits need to be sought to expand the property's market or lease potential. All reuse options should be completely explored so that they can be given full consideration for their compatibility with a particular community and neighborhood."

Holly Harrison Fiala, *Surplus Schools*

Surplus Schools. Holly Harrison Fiala. Information Series. National Trust for Historic Preservation. Washington, D.C.: Preservation Press, 1982. 36 pp., illus., biblio., append. $2 pb.

Surplus School Space: Options and Opportunities. Educational Facilities Laboratories. New York: EFL, 1976. 72 pp., illus., biblio. $4 pb.

Spiritualist temple (1884), Boston, rehabilitated as a multiuse facility including the Exeter Street Theatre and a restaurant. (CBT Architects)

Living-dining area of a home created from the former Providence Church (1889), Glenelg, Md. From *Buildings Reborn*. (Louis Reens)

Ohio Theatre (1928, Thomas W. Lamb), Columbus, Ohio, an ornate movie palace designed by a master architect. (D. R. Goff, Quicksilver Photography)

Opening night for the restored Loew's Ohio Theatre, new home for the Columbus Association for the Performing Arts. (CAPA)

Religious Buildings

"Theology determined the architecture of churches. Use for other than church activities was not a consideration. A building that was perfectly executed for worship and church school may be especially hard to adapt to new uses. . . .

Location can be a problem to a church seeking income through new use of its building. Certain uses . . . may be unacceptable to the surrounding area or uneconomical in the particular setting. For example, use as a restaurant might be unacceptable in one community while there might already be too many dance studios in another area for that type of use. Large public or cultural spaces may not be in demand for the very reasons a church finds it difficult to survive: shifting population, commercial deterioration, and so on."

Rev. Richard Armstrong, *The Preservation of Churches, Synagogues and Other Religious Structures*

The Preservation of Churches, Synagogues and Other Religious Structures. Rev. Richard Armstrong, Cheswick Center. Information Series. National Trust for Historic Preservation. Washington, D.C.: Preservation Press, 1978. 27 pp., illus., biblio., append. $2 pb.

Theaters

"It is best to put old theaters to the use for which they were intended, the performing arts. If that cannot be done, an adaptive use may be considered. . . . Such adaptive uses might be storage or workshop space, although the sheer volume of theater structures often means they are inefficient and expensive to operate for these purposes. It is possible to convert the buildings to retail, office, residential or community center use, but doing so usually requires a major capital investment to make such necessary structural changes as gutting the interior, building new floors and reorganizing the space. If possible it is preferable for the building to be used in its 'as is' condition. Not only is it less expensive but it preserves the integrity of the structure in the event that a need for a theater evolves."

Robert Stoddard, *Preservation of Concert Halls, Opera Houses and Movie Palaces*

Preservation of Concert Halls, Opera Houses and Movie Palaces. Robert Stoddard. Information Series. National Trust for Historic Preservation. Washington, D.C.: Preservation Press, 1978. 28 pp., illus., biblio. $2 pb.

Movie Palaces: Renaissance and Reuse. Educational Facilities Laboratories. New York: Academy for Educational Development, 1982. 120 pp., illus., biblio., append. $11 pb.

National Museum of American Art-National Portrait Gallery Library, Old Patent Office (1836–67), Washington, D.C. (Smithsonian Institution)

"We live a few miles from here in an architecturally significant former gas station." (Koren. © 1978 The New Yorker Magazine, Inc.)

Old City Hall (1865), Boston, now offices. (Anderson Notter Finegold)

Astor Library, New York, now host to Shakespeare. (George Cserna)

Public Buildings

"In some cases, a jurisdiction finds after careful study that it cannot continue to use an existing building or that it would like to preserve a good courthouse or city hall that has already been vacated. . . . New uses present some pitfalls. An architectural review board and an experienced, sensitive developer can help to avoid the excesses of self-conscious boutiques or pseudo-Victorian amusement complexes. Community meeting rooms, offices of nonprofit organizations, shops, and restaurants can, however, be sympathetically designed to enhance the quality of the old building."

Judith N. Getzels, *Recycling Public Buildings*

Recycling Public Buildings. Judith N. Getzels. Chicago: American Society of Planning Officials (American Planning Association), 1976. PAS Report 319. 34 pp., illus., appends., biblio. $6 pb.

Barns

"Barn frames and barn spaces are very different from other structures. Except for the few uprights and supporting beams, there are no interior bearing partitions. This tremendous, flexible space can give rise to many imaginative solutions. . . .

Many potentially valuable barns that are in the path of suburban development may not be suitable for residences due to their large size or to encroaching commercial zoning. It is also usually impractical to move them. But we can no longer afford to tear down irreplaceable structures such as [these]."

Ernest Burden, *Living Barns*

Adaptive Reuse: Barns. Monticello, Ill.: Vance Bibliographies, 1979. A-134. 6 pp. $2 pb.

Living Barns: How to Find and Restore a Barn of Your Own. Ernest Burden. Boston: New York Graphic Society, 1977. 186 pp., color illus., biblio., index. $24.95 hb, $13.95 pb.

Gas Stations

"Before putting the bulldozer to the abandoned station that might have been erected only five or ten years ago, an examination should be made of ways in which part of the initial investment can be recovered. . . .

A remodeling of these buildings in most cases can be accomplished for less than half the cost of a new structure. . . .

There are more than ninety . . . uses for these stations on the 'For Sale' list of many oil companies and independents."

Albert L. Kerth, *A New Life for the Abandoned Service Station*

A New Life for the Abandoned Service Station. Albert L. Kerth. Massapequa Park, N.Y.: Author (P.O. Box 142, 11262), 1974. 83 pp., illus. $15 hb.

See also: Form and Function

A wooden barn, transformed into a residence with the addition of an ell at right, new windows and doors, an entranceway, a new roof and a restored cupola. From *Living Barns: How to Find and Restore a Barn of Your Own.*

New Uses from Old Buildings

Every reasonable effort shall be made to provide a compatible use for a property that requires minimal alteration of the building structure, or site and its environment, or to use a property for its originally intended purpose.

The Secretary of the Interior's Standards for Historic Preservation Projects

The principal triumph of these adaptive use projects has been to demonstrate that form does not follow function but rather that function gets its life from all the varied ways the forms of architecture can be used.

Arthur P. Ziegler, Jr., "Large-Scale Commercial Adaptive Use." *North Carolina Central Law Journal*, Spring 1980.

Housing

"A perhaps bizarre example: . . . The Colosseum built by the Romans at Arles [was] converted into housing during the Middle Ages. It sums up the two main goals of the whole reuse and recycling game, and both goals are extremely obvious. The first is purely practical: if you have a useless colosseum on your hands and you need some housing, it makes perfect sense to try to make the latter out of the former. The second goal is equally simple: it would be a gas to live in a converted colosseum—just as it would be fun to live in a cunningly converted Vermont barn, or a factory loft in SoHo, or in a found attic turret on Beacon Hill."

Gerald Allen, "A Conservative Approach: Housing the Past as We House Ourselves." In *The Form of Housing*. Sam Davis, ed. New York: Van Nostrand Reinhold, 1977.

1893 firehouse, San Francisco, now a home. (Fred Lyon)

"Whether the delight is in the patina of age, in the whimsy of entering a room through an oversized freezer door, or in the enjoyment of the warmth of old-brick walls, the person who transforms an environment once utilized as a factory, barn, water tower, or whatever other non-dwelling use into a home is opting for an unusual living experience: a flight from the increasing conformity, artificiality, anonymous construction, and shoddy craftsmanship that afflict modern society."

Charles A. Fracchia and Jeremiah O. Bragstad, *Converted Into Houses*. New York: Viking Penguin, 1976.

Rescued Buildings: The Art of Living in Former Schoolhouses, Skating Rinks, Fire Stations, Churches, Barns, Summer Camps and Cabooses. Roland Jacopetti et al. Santa Barbara, Calif.: Capra Press, 1977. 96 pp., illus. $8.95 pb.

Presents efforts to convert abandoned buildings into unusual dwellings.

The former domitory on the second floor of the firehouse, made into living quarters and an office furnished with an Art Nouveau table. (Fred Lyon)

47 Creative Homes That Started as Bargain Buildings. Jean and Cle Kinney. New York: Funk and Wagnalls, 1974. 228 pp., illus.

Suggestions for finding bargain buildings and ways of looking into their conversion possibilities.

The Wizard's Eye: Visions of American Resourcefulness. Charles Milligan and Jim Higgs. San Francisco: Chronicle Books, 1978. 103 pp., illus., index.

A sourcebook of "imaginative money-making, energy-producing, house-building and fixing ideas that all use recycled materials, and the ability to see the gold in the scrapheap."

Recycling for Housing. Los Angeles Community Design Center. Los Angeles: LACDC (849 South Broadway, Suite 310, 90014), 1977. 89 pp., illus., append. $7.50 pb.

Concentrates on the conversion of central-city high-rise office buildings as an answer to the housing needs of L.A.'s elderly.

Lofts

"What is a loft conversion?. . . . It is any conversion of a commercial, industrial, manufacturing, or warehouse building to residential use. A structural engineer or an architectural historian may define a loft building more narrowly. It is that type of industrial architecture prevalent from the mid-nineteenth century to about 1920, characterized by masonry external walls and heavy timber post-and-beam construction on the interior. But, in some cities, even early twentieth-century industrial buildings with concrete floors and columns are being converted to residential use."

Richard J. Roddewig, *Loft Conversions*

Westbeth Artists Housing, New York, an old factory. (Ezra Stoller)

Loft Conversions: Planning Issues, Problems, and Prospects. Richard J. Roddewig, Chicago: American Planning Association, 1981. PAS Report 362. 38 pp., illus., append. $12 pb.

Loft Living: Recycling Warehouse Space for Residential Use. Kingsley Fairbridge and Harvey-Jane Kowal. New York: Saturday Review Press, Dutton, 1976. 156 pp., illus.

Manual discussing techniques for finding, assessing and remodeling lofts.

Pioneering in the Urban Wilderness: All About Lofts. Jim Stratton. New York: Urizen Books, 1977. 208 pp. $7.95 pb.

Thorough discussion of real estate potential, code regulations and basic renovation, with personal experience as a guide.

The Loft Book. Jim Wilson. Philadelphia: Running Press, 1975. 95 pp., illus., biblio.

Addresses "the creative use of any limited space by the amateur."

Lofts. Jeffrey Weiss. New York: W. W. Norton, 1979. $7.95 pb.

Full-color exploration of the many faces of the loft, using examples from coast to coast.

Special Space: A Guide to Artists' Housing and Loft Living. Wilkie Farr and Gallagher. New York: Volunteer Lawyers for the Arts (1560 Broadway, Room 711, 10036), 1981. 157 pp.

Includes material on artists' certification, building and zoning regulations, duties of tenants and landlords, lease provisions and litigation involving artists and lofts.

Loft Living. Sharon Zukin. Baltimore: Johns Hopkins University Press, 1982. 212 pp., illus., biblio., index. $16.95.

An analysis of the rise of loft conversions, including the social benefits and real estate investment. Examines the struggles among business people, bankers, developers, politicians, arts patrons and residents.

Arts Centers and Museums
"Once a firehouse always a firehouse? By no means. A surplus or outmoded firehouse can make a fine dance studio or community arts center or museum. Increasingly, all over the United States, buildings originally designed for quite different purposes are being transformed into theaters, galleries, concert halls, and all kinds of places for making or performing or displaying the arts."

The Arts in Found Places

"In recent years museum collections have found new homes in rehabilitated warehouses, firehouses, office buildings, jails, post offices and railroad depots, to name only a few. In fact, museum professionals were arguably the forerunners of the adaptive use movement, for many early residences important for their associative history have been 'adaptively used' as house museums for years."

Marcia Axtmann Smith, "Renewed Museums: Ten Case Studies." *Museum News,* September 1980.

Lone Star Brewing Company (1895–1904, E. Jungerfeld), San Antonio, Tex., whose crenellated towers now house the San Antonio Museum of Art. (Cambridge Seven Associates, Inc.)

The Arts in Found Places. Educational Facilities Laboratories and the National Endowment for the Arts. New York: EFL, 1976. 138 pp., illus., append. $7 pb.

A review of where and how the arts are finding homes in recycled buildings, with 200 examples and some do's and don'ts.

New Places for the Arts, Book Two. Educational Facilities Laboratories. New York: EFL, 1978. $3 pb.

Provides brief descriptions, plans and consultants for 60 museums, arts centers and multiuse facilities.

Museums and Adaptive Use. Marcia Axtmann Smith, ed. *Museum News,* September 1980. 104 pp., illus., biblio. Reprints $3.25 pb. Available from American Association of Museums, 1055 Thomas Jefferson Street, N.W., Washington, D.C. 20007.

A special issue featuring examples of buildings that have been transformed into museum space. Includes a planning checklist and sources of technical and financial assistance.

The Arts in Surplus Schools and *Putting the Arts in Surplus Schools: A Planning Workbook.* Educational Facilities Laboratories. New York: EFL, 1981. 170 pp., illus. 2 vols. $3 and $5 or $8 set.

Ideas for reusing schools, selecting arts programs, space and program alternatives, affordability and space evaluation.

Will It Make a Theatre: A Guide to Finding, Renovating, Financing, Bringing Up-to-Code, the Non-Traditional Performance Space. Eldon Elder et al. New York: Off Off Broadway Alliance (162 West 56th Street, Room 206, 10019), 1979. 215 pp., illus. $8 pb.

Information for theaters involved in acquiring and preparing new performing facilities. Includes a special code section in lay terms.

SoHo: The Artist in the City. Charles R. Simpson. Chicago: University of Chicago Press, 1981. 276 pp., illus. $20 hb.

The story of how abandoned and underused factories and commercial buildings in Lower Manhattan have been converted into artists' studios and living space and galleries.

American Architecture for the Arts. Vol. I. H. Michael Stewart, ed. Dallas: Handel and Sons (Ambit Publications, 4227 Herschel, Suite 107, 75219), 1978. 239 pp., illus., index. $22.95 hb.

Covers primarily new theaters and art centers, but includes some restored ones.

Buildings for the Arts. Editors of Architectural Record. New York: McGraw-Hill, 1978. 247 pp.

Examples of museums, performing arts centers and libraries, only a few of which are adaptive uses.

Hook and Ladder Company 13 (1854), New York, an early adaptation to museum use. *(New York Times)*

Detroit Cornice and Slate Company (1897, Henry J. Rill), Detroit, renovated for architectural offices and a restaurant. (Balthazar Korab)

Before-and-after views of the Tips Building (1876), Austin, Tex., restored as offices for the Franklin Savings Association. (Austin Heritage Society)

Row of 19th-century brownstones, Albany, N.Y., hiding a new addition built at the rear. (George Cserna)

Addition to the brownstones housing the New York State Bar Center (1971, James Stewart Polshek and Partners). (George Cserna)

Commercial and Business Centers

"Perhaps by sensing the ubiquitous love people had for old houses, a few visionaries turned their attention to other kinds of buildings; old warehouses, factories, transportation terminals, dock buildings, and trolley barns came back to life as new kinds of commercial centers.

The pacesetter was Ghirardelli Square in San Francisco. . . . This project, more than any other, spawned large-scale commercial revitalization across the country."

Arthur P. Ziegler, Jr., "Large-Scale Commercial Adaptive Use"

Adaptive Reuse: Shopping Malls from Old Buildings. Carol J. Gray. Chicago: Council of Planning Librarians, 1977. No. 1314. 6 pp. $1.50.

"Large-Scale Commercial Adaptive Use: Preservation Revitalizes Old Buildings—And New Ones Too." Arthur P. Ziegler, Jr. *North Carolina Central Law Journal,* Spring 1980. Available from North Carolina Central School of Law, Durham, N.C. 27707.

A brief survey of some notable projects, such as Chattanooga Choo-Choo, Trolley Square, Faneuil Hall Marketplace and Station Square.

"Planning the Urban Marketplace." Charles Hoyt, ed. *Architectural Record,* October 1980.

Features adaptive use for new mixed commercial uses, including Cleveland Arcade; Salem, Mass.; Pittsburgh Bank Center; Chicopee, Mass.; Georgetown Marketplace, Washington, D.C.; Harborplace, Baltimore.

So This Is Where You Work! A Guide to Unconventional Working Environments. Charles A. Fracchia and Mark Kauffman. New York: Viking, 1979. 110 pp.

Views of the insides and outsides of 32 buildings transformed into unusual working places: a bordello into law offices, a lighthouse into a restaurant, a power station into a woodworking studio, a spice factory into dental offices.

Preservation and Recycling of Buildings for Bank Use. National Trust Northeast Regional Office. Information Series. National Trust for Historic Preservation. Washington, D.C.: Preservation Press, 1978. 28 pp., illus. $2 pb.

A review of the issues, with descriptions of banks now in some unusual quarters.

Faneuil Hall (1805–06, Charles Bulfinch) and Quincy Market (1826, Alexander Parris) seen from Boston Harbor in 1827. (Bostonian Society)

Ghirardelli Square, San Francisco, created from a candy factory complex to become a precursor of many waterfront revitalizations. (Joshua Freiwald)

Pre-restoration plan for the revitalization of the market complex (1976, F. A. Stahl and Associates, Benjamin Thompson and Associates).

The Ghirardelli sign, an old harbor landmark relighted at Ghirardelli Square. (Ghirardelli Square)

Opening day of the new Faneuil Hall Marketplace, a model for commercial rehabilitation projects in other cities. (Carleton Knight III, NTHP)

Drawing showing the varied buildings recycled to form Ghirardelli Square, a two and one-half acre complex. (George Albertus, Ghirardelli Square)

Old Federal Courts Building (1892–1902, Willoughby J. Edbrooke), St. Paul, Minn. (Landmark Center; Perry, Dean, Stahl and Rogers)

The Federal Example

Adaptive use provides a unique opportunity for the federal government to contribute to the economic vitality and architectural diversity of communities that host its buildings. As an integral part of the public buildings program, it would signify a national government of human dimensions, sensitive to the past and concerned for the future.

Merrill Ware, *Federal Architecture: Adaptive-Use Facilities.* 1975

"Federal agencies should give priority consideration to adapting existing buildings for federal use, particularly structures of architectural or historic significance. The Government should consider both leasing and purchasing such structures as an alternative to a new structure, considering relative cost and adaptability of the existing building. This alternative should include consideration of satisfying space needs by adapting a cluster of smaller buildings as well as adapting single large buildings.

Federal agencies . . . should be required . . . to give priority consideration to the use of existing buildings to meet current or projected space needs at the earliest possible stage of the planning process. Commonplace as well as historically and architecturally significant structures should be considered for reuse."

Federal Architecture Task Force, 1974.

Federal Architecture: A Framework for Debate, Federal Architecture: Adaptive-Use Facilities and *Federal Architecture: Multiple-Use Facilities.* Federal Architecture Project. Washington, D.C.: National Endowment for the Arts, 1974–75.

A report and supplementary papers prepared under a White House directive to review the guiding principles of federal architecture. Their recommendations were followed by the Public Buildings Cooperative Use Act of 1976, which encourages GSA to acquire historic buildings for federal use and to foster mixed use of such buildings.

Turning Over Surplus Property

Since 1949 the U.S. General Services Administration has been authorized to transfer its unneeded buildings to state and local governments for "historic monument purposes." More flexibility was provided in 1972 with permission to allow use of these buildings for compatible revenue-producing purposes. Private purchasers may acquire these surplus properties under certain circumstances. Transfers are made variously without cost, at discounts of up to 100 percent, through negotiated sale or by competitive sale. During the Reagan administration, the focus was placed on obtaining fair market value for all surplus federal properties. In the past decade, more than 30 surplus federal properties have been reclaimed, among them the Baltimore Courthouse, Frankfort Arsenal in Philadelphia, Fenwick Island, Del., Lighthouse and:

Federal Building, St. Paul, Minn.
Vacated in 1965 when court, post office and other federal offices moved to a new building, the 1902 landmark was the target of a lengthy preservation effort. When the Surplus Property Act was amended to allow revenue-producing purposes, the building was conveyed to the city. An arts council raised money and supervised the transformation into The Landmark Center.

A Landmark Reclaimed. Eileen Michels with Nate Bomberg. St. Paul: Minnesota Landmarks (404 Landmark Center, 75 West Fifth Street, 55102), 1977. 111 pp., illus. $5 hb.

Piney Point Lighthouse, St. Marys, Md.
Once a Coast Guard station, the 1836 lighthouse is now open for tours by the local recreation department; the keeper's house is leased to a caretaker in return for renovation; outbuildings are used for water quality studies; and the beach is a bird sanctuary under guidance of the Audubon Society.

Contacts

Historic Preservation
Staff Officer
Public Buildings Service
U.S. General Services
Administration
Washington, D.C. 20405

Federal Property Resource
Management Service
U.S. General Services
Administration
Washington, D.C. 20405

U.S. Mint (1838, William Strickland), New Orleans, a surplus federal building transferred to the state for conversion by the Louisiana State Museum. It now includes the archives, exhibits, shops and restaurants. (Andrew J. Pickett IV)

Planning Adaptive Use Projects

While many of the same basic factors involved in any successful real estate development project apply to adaptive use investments, there are variations that can be highly important in successfully adapting an old structure to a new use. Differences relate to the development process itself and the need for substantial front-end technical evaluation of the project.

Thomas J. Martin and Melvin A. Gamzon, "Economics and Process." Part I, *Adaptive Use: Development Economics, Process, and Profiles*

"The profitable recycling of a building—and it must be profitable if the recycling process is to be continued—requires imagination, know-how, and the courage to speculate. A great deal of the speculative risk can be removed by intelligent forward planning and by following a step-by-step procedure that will assure a lending institution that everything that can be done has been done by the architect, the engineer, and the developer to make the project a success."

Laurence E. Reiner, *How to Recycle Buildings*

"Economics and Process." Thomas J. Martin and Melvin A. Gamzon. Part I, *Adaptive Use: Development Economics, Process, and Profiles*. Washington, D.C.: Urban Land Institute, 1978. 246 pp., illus. biblio., index. $37 hb.

A detailed statement of the adaptive use development process: project initiation, initial analysis, market, site, structural and architectural feasibility; project planning and financing and implementation through rehabilitation, management and marketing.

An unlikely adaptive use. (R. O. Blechman. *Architecture Plus*, March–April 1974)

How to Recycle Buildings. Laurence Reiner, New York: McGraw-Hill, 1979. 244 pp., illus., index. $29.95 hb.

Describes how to achieve "a profitable and commercially sound recycling," including feasibility surveys, code requirements, financing, contracts, bidding, maintenance, marketing and management. Four case studies detail adaptive use projects from start to finish.

Adaptive Reuse Handbook: Opportunities for Housing in Old Buildings. Buckhurst Fish Hutton Katz. New Haven: Tri-State Regional Planning Commission et al., 1981. 98 pp., illus., biblio. $12.50 pb. Available from Buckhurst Fish Hutton Katz, 72 Fifth Avenue, New York, N.Y. 10011.

Designed to inform local officials about the recycling process, the book outlines project identification, neighborhood context, market analysis, building evaluation, financial feasibility and implementation. Developer's kits documenting three demonstration projects also are available ($3 each)

The Adaptive Reuse Handbook: Procedures to Inventory, Control, Manage, and Reemploy Surplus Municipal Properties. Robert W. Burchell and David Listokin. New Brunswick, N.J.: Center for Urban Policy Research (Rutgers University, P.O. Box 489, Piscataway, N.J. 08854), 1981. 575 pp., illus., append., biblio., index. $28.50 hb.

Written primarily for municipalities as a guide to recycling abandoned neighborhood property, this is a technical and thorough explanation of procedures for surveying, controlling, managing and reusing surplus buildings.

Second Empire house (1865), Southbridge, Mass., converted to a bank. (© Steve Rosenthal)

The Feasibility Study

The preservation process requires an honest appraisal by all participants. . . . Snap decisions by the public sector to "save" a landmark can unduly burden a community. Conversely, a declaration that a landmark is too costly to reuse without a genuine cost appraisal and feasibility study could allow an irreplaceable historic asset to be destroyed.

> Roger S. Webb, "Overcoming Preservation Problems." In *Economic Benefits of Preserving Old Buildings*. Washington, D.C.: Preservation Press, 1976. 168 pp., illus. $7.95 pb.

"Following [an] initial overview of a project's potential, a detailed feasibility evaluation is often required. This more detailed evaluation should encompass four key areas: market support and economic evaluation; site and lcoational characteristics; structural considerations; and architectural and historical aspects."

> Thomas J. Martin and Melvin A. Gamzon, "Economics and Process." Part I, *Adaptive Use: Development Economics, Process, and Profiles*

The New York Federal Archives Building: A Proposal for a Mixed Re-Use. New York: Columbia University, Center for Advanced Research in Urban and Environmental Affairs, 1976. 96 pp., illus. $7.95. Available from Jaap Rietman, Inc., 157 Spring Street, New York, N.Y. 11012.

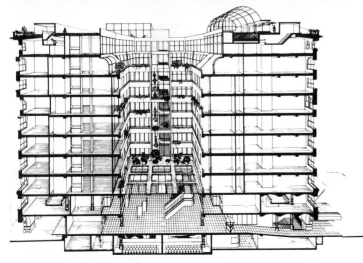

Federal Archives Building (1899, Willoughby J. Edbrooke), New York, adapted for residential and retail use. (Warner Burns Toan Lunde Architects)

Reuse plan for Jessie Street utility station (1905, Willis Polk), San Francisco. (Werner and Sullivan)

Adaptive Reuse Feasibility Study and Proposal: Jessie Street Substation. John Weese, Foundation for San Francisco's Architectural Heritage. San Francisco: Author (2007 Franklin Street, 94109), 1977. $5 pb.

Economic Reuse Potentials: The Fox Theater. Hammer, Siler, George Associates. Atlanta: Georgia Department of Natural Resources, 1974. 129 pp. $10. Available from Hammer, Siler, George, 230 Peachtree Street, N.W., Suite 2607, Atlanta, Ga. 30303.

Economic Feasibility Study of the Prudential Building, Buffalo, New York. American Institute of Architects, Buffalo-Western New York Chapter. Buffalo: Landmark Society of the Niagara Frontier (25 Nottingham Court, 14216), 1976. 80 pp., illus.

Cleveland Warehouse District Plan 1977. William A. Gould and Associates. Cleveland, Ohio: City of Cleveland, 1977. 40 pp., illus., biblio. Available from Cleveland Landmarks Commission, Room 28, City Hall, Cleveland, Ohio 44114. $5.

Rehabilitation: Claremont 1978. Planning for Adaptive Use and Energy Conservation in an Historic Mill Village. Historic American Engineering Record, National Park Service. Washington, D.C.: U.S. Department of the Interior, 1979. 89 pp., illus. $3.75 pb. GPO stock no. 024-016-00118-4.

Study of the Alternative Uses for the Old Nueces County Courthouse. Associated Planners and Wukasch and Associates. Corpus Christi: Texas Historic Preservation Office and the Friends of the Courthouse, 1978. 79 pp., illus.

Feasibility Factors

Market Evaluation

Community market dynamics
Social and demographic characteristics
Recent development trends
Specific markets for each reuse alternative
The competition (successful and unsuccessful)
Locational factors

Site and Location Evaluation

Planned and existing uses of adjoining property
Public services, transportation, jobs
Hidden assets of the area
Entertainment offerings, social and environmental quality
Real estate sales and rental market

Structural and Physical Analysis

Structural stability
Mechanical systems
Feasibility and cost of code compliance

Architectural and Historical Evaluation

Space utilization and circulation
Elements to be preserved
Needed repairs or restoration
Historical designation benefits
Design review or special permits

> Adapted from *Adaptive Use: Development Economics, Process, and Profiles*

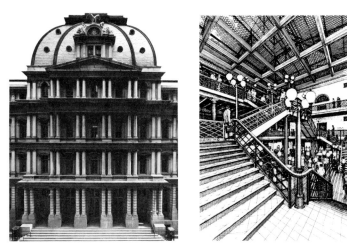

St. Louis Post Office and Customs House (1884, Alfred B. Mullett) with suggested renovations maintaining interior features such as cast-iron stairs.

Proposal for creation of an enclosed interior atrium with a restored skylight in the post office. (Patty Berkebile Nelson Associates)

The Design Challenge

Once an appropriate use has been selected, the building itself is examined in depth to identify its unique characteristics. If it is an elegant place, it should remain elegant; if it is dignified, the response should be dignified. Awkward mistakes occur when an adaptive use design is approached with a preconceived notion of "style." Egocentric architectural intellectualization provides few or no adequate solutions for adapting old buildings.

Charles N. Tseckares, "Design Considerations in Adaptive Use Projects." In *Old and New Architecture: Design Relationship.* Washington, D.C.: Preservation Press, 1980. 280 pp., illus., biblio., index. $25 hb, $15.95 pb.

"Adapting buildings for extended use challenges architects in new and exciting ways. They must use existing space with maximum efficiency for modern needs, yet they must re-create an environment of grace and beauty. Discreet ways to introduce modern heating, cooling, electrical and fire prevention systems must be found. They must choose new materials that harmonize with the old ones. Above all, the original spirit of the building must be carefully preserved."

American Institute of Architects. "Adaptive Re-use: Extending the Life of Old Buildings," 1979.

"An important consideration in developing schematic designs is to work with the fabric of the building rather than to fight it. By understanding a structure's physical constraints and eccentricities, the creative architect can take advantage of features such as large windows or cast-iron columns which give the building its own identity.

The unusual forms and patterns which older buildings typically provide can be a marketing asset, while minimizing construction and operating costs for the sponsor. . . .

Because the net to gross square-footage ratio is a key determinant in the revenue capability of a building, imaginative design must be used to maximize the useable space within a structure. High ceilings, when not used for their spacious effect, can contain mechnaical equipment which would reduce rentable square footage if installed elsewhere."

Thomas J. Martin and Melvin A. Gamzon, "Economics and Process." Part I, *Adaptive Use: Development Economics, Process, and Profiles*

Exposing Adaptive Abuse

"When old warehouses and abandoned factories all over the country started being scrubbed up into boutiques several years ago, we travelling people accepted them more or less the way we had accepted the advent of Holiday Inns—at first marvelling at their presence, and then grumbling that they all looked alike. The brick exposed in Ghirardelli Square in San Francisco tended to look like the brick exposed in Pioneer Square in Seattle, which had some similarity to the brick exposed in Old Town, Chicago, or Underground Atlanta or the River Quay in Kansas City or Larimer Square in Denver or Gas Light Square in St. Louis. . . . Some of the historic renovations are chic and some of them are tacky. . . . I walk through all of them—the ones whose buildings do evoke the history of a city and the ones whose buildings seem a comment only on the history of American brick. . . . Sometimes, I am fearful that my commitment to civil liberties will someday collapse in the face of a proposal that all producers of macrame be jailed without trial."

Calvin Trillin, "U.S. Journal: New England. Thoughts Brought On by Prolonged Exposure to Exposed Brick." *The New Yorker,* May 16, 1977.

"Experts warn that alterations for adaptive use and energy retrofitting are robbing old buildings of their historic identities. . . . As buildings are freshly outfitted with new materials, updated to meet modern energy-saving standards and codes, gutted or expanded in the process of adapting to new uses, tough questions are being asked, questions that reflect the growing willingness of preservationists to be self-critical: Does the face-lift destroy the characer of the face? Has the building lost what was most worth saving?. . . .

Federal tax incentives have helped push marginally profitable properties into the mainstream and commercial recycling into high profile. . . . What troubles many are the damaging liberties taken in the process of adapting buildings for current use. . . . In both technical and design alterations, changes seem most disturbing when they separate a building's future irretrievably from its past."

Tina Laver, "In the Name of Preservation." *Historic Preservation*, September–October 1981.

"[There is] an unfortunate tendency to concentrate only on the building's exterior. . . . When you mutilate the interior, you end up creating a fake, Disneyland world inside. The facade no longer reflects what's behind it. . . . Buildings were conceived with a certain degree of integrity as a unit; we must be very careful about retaining that integrity."

Jean Paul Carlhian. In "In the Name of Preservation." *Historic Preservation,* September–October, 1981.

"It is a failure not to realize that there is a form of demolition short of the wrecker's ball."

Arthur Cotton Moore, "Adaptive Abuse: Examining Some Perils of (and to) the Preservation Movement." *AIA Journal,* August 1979.

See also: Rehabilitation and Restoration

Building Codes: Preserving Safety and History

The rehabilitation of existing buildings is not, in general, addressed directly by building codes and by the building regulatory system. Few communities have a building rehabilitation code, or a special chapter on building rehabilitation as part of their building code. Rehabilitation is usually addressed indirectly, in two categories: alterations and repairs, and change of occupancy. In the former category, varying degrees of compliance with the building code's provisions for new construction are often required, as a function of the value of the repairs in proportion to the value of the building (25–50% Rule). In the latter category, full compliance with the code's provisions for new construction is usually required (change of occupancy regulation).

David B. Hattis. In "Regulating Existing Buildings"

"The lack of effective regulations for building rehabilitation forces the use of codes created for new construction. This frequently impedes those who attempt rehabilitation, and increases costs. . . . These codes tend to be less effective, or even inappropriate, when applied to the process required to determine rehabilitation needs of existing structures."

James H. Pielert, *Removing Regulatory Restraints to Building Rehabilitation: The Massachusetts Experience*

"Too often interpretation, or perhaps misapplication, of code requirements, dictates the destruction or modification of the very elements which the restoration or rehabilitation process is intended to preserve. . . .

Occasionally architects, engineers, code enforcement officers and owners, working together have been able to develop creative solutions which meet the intent, if not always the letter, of codes. This is the exception rather than the rule."

Tomas H. Spiers, Jr. In "Regulating Existing Buidings"

"A building official must perform in an atmosphere of conflict: charged by legislation and conscience to preserve that which is irreplaceable and also charged by legislation, knowledge and experience to enforce all safety standards. Fortunately, these conditions do not exclude each other. . . ."

W. I. Kelley. In *Preservation and Building Codes*. National Trust for Historic Preservation. Washington, D.C.: Preservation Press, 1975.

"There are two ways to deal with an unsatisfactory building code regulation. Either change the regulation or seek some kind of waiver through an appeals board such as the one in New Orleans. Construction materials businesses do not hesitate to try to change requirements, but designers and preservationists seem willing to take the less creative route by seeking individual waivers, which means that subsequent appeals must go through the same route."

Discussion, *Preservation and Building Codes*

Rehabilitation Guidelines. National Institute of Building Sciences. For U.S. Department of Housing and Urban Development. Washington, D.C.: GPO, 1980–82. Available from HUD User, P.O. Box 280, Germantown, Md. 20874.

A series of congressionally mandated guidelines designed for voluntary adoption and use with building codes. The most recent are *Guidelines for Structural Assessment* and *Guidelines on Rehabilitation of Walls, Windows and Roofs* ($5 for both). Out-of-print titles include *Setting and Adopting Standards, Municipal Approval, Statutory Guideline, Managing Official Liability, Egress Guideline, Electrical Guideline, Plumbing DWV Guideline* and *Fire Ratings.*

"Regulating Existing Buildings." *Bulletin,* Association for Preservation Technology, vol. XIII, no. 2, 1981. 39 pp. $5 pb. Available from APT, P.O. Box 2487, Station D, Ottawa, Ontario K1P 5W6, Canada.

A special issue with articles analyzing the *Rehabilitation Guidelines* and related code topics.

Removing Regulatory Restraints to Building Rehabilitation: The Massachusetts Experience. James H. Pielert. Washington, D.C.: National Bureau of Standards, 1981. 53 pp., illus., append. $10 pb. Available from National Technical Information Service, 5285 Port Royal Road, Springfield, Va. 22151. NTIS no. PB 82121047.

Details the state's experience in formulating and working with a new regulatory concept encouraging the reuse of existing buildings, with four case studies.

Impact of Building Regulations on Rehabilitation—Status and Technical Needs. James G. Gross et al. Washington, D.C.: U.S. Department of Commerce, 1979. 43 pp. append. $10 pb. NTIS no. PB 295708.

Reports on the impact of regulations on building rehabilitation. Includes an explanation of activities of the Center for Building Technology's Building Rehabilitation Technology Group.

Proceedings of the National Conference on Regulatory Aspects of Building Rehabilitation. Sandra A. Berry, ed. Washington, D.C.: National Bureau of Standards, 1979. $19 pb. NTIS no. PB 300329.

Provides an overview of the impact of regulations on the rehabilitation of existing buildings and the Massachusetts regulations.

Survey of Building Code Provisions for Historic Structures. Melvyn Green and Patrick Cooke. Washington, D.C.: National Bureau of Standards, 1976. $8.50 pb. NTIS no. PB 256830.

Analysis of what states, territories and cities are doing to resolve building code and preservation conflicts.

An Investigation of Regulatory Barriers to the Re-Use of Existing Buildings. N. John Habraken et al. For Center for Building Technology. Washington, D.C.: National Bureau of Standards, 1978. 122 pp., append., biblio. $13 pb. NTIS no. PB 287801.

Makes recommendations for resolving specific code problems and future study.

Building Rehabilitation Research and Technology for the 1980s. National Conference of States on Building Codes and Standards. Herndon, Va.: Author, 1980. 324 pp. $11.75 pb.

Papers reporting on innovative technical aspects of rehabilitation, including code development and enforcement and seismic considerations.

Assessment of Current Building Regulatory Methods as Applied to the Needs of Historic Preservation Projects. National Trust for Historic Preservation. Washington, D.C.: National Bureau of Standards, 1978. 87 pp., illus., biblio., append. $11.50 pb. NTIS no. PB 287413.

Prescribes performance standards for various levels of preservation and rehabilitation, discusses methods to mitigate adverse impacts of regulatory systems and presents case studies.

Flexible Code Enforcement: A Key Ingredient in Neighborhood Preservation Programming. Roger S. Ahlbrandt, Jr. Washington, D.C.: National Association of Housing and Redevelopment Officials (2600 Virginia Avenue, N.W., 20037), 1976. 93 pp. $9.

A study of innovative code enforcement programs developed to promote neighborhood preservation.

Alternative Life Safety Systems for Historic Structures. Melvyn Green and Harriet Watson. For National Endowment for the Arts. El Segundo, Calif.: Melvyn Green (690 North Sepulveda Boulevard, No. 120, 90245), 1976. $25.

A lay explanation of fire protection engineering, the action of fire and the effects of fire protection features.

Selected Papers Dealing with Regulatory Concerns of Building Rehabilitation. Patrick W. Cooke. Washington, D.C.: National Bureau of Standards, 1979. 90 pp. $11.50 pb. NTIS no. PB 293240.

Model Codes

"The first model code. . . .appeared in 1905. . . . Primary users were smaller political subdivisions that had neither the resources nor the capability of independently developing and maintaining a building code, while collectively they could and did maintain a code."

Robert E. O'Bannon. In *Preservation and Building Codes*

Developed by national associations of building officials, model codes serve as minimum standards for the local jurisdictions that adopt them. They evolved on a regional basis and may be modified by and for the locality to meet its needs. The three major codes have many similarities but were drafted to reflect regional building differences. The model codes undergo periodic revision, and in recent years a number have been amended to provide greater flexibility and sensitivity for older buildings and districts.

Bradbury Building (1893, George C. Wyman), Los Angeles, a landmark repeatedly endangered because of difficulties in meeting local building codes while maintaining its historical integrity. (Carleton Knight III, NTHP)

Code Organizations
Building Officials and Code Administrators, International
17929 South Halstead Street
Homewood, Ill. 60430

Maintains the Basic Building Code. Section 516.1 pertaining to historic buildings and districts allows flexibility in rehabilitation on a case-by-case basis.

International Conference of Building Officials
5360 South Workman Mill Road
Whittier, Calif. 90601

Maintains the Uniform Building Code. Section 104f provides flexibility for designated historic buildings.

Southern Building Code Congress, International
900 Montclair Road
Birmingham, Ala. 35213

Maintains the Standard Building Code and also sponsors the *Standard Housing Code* ($12) for older residential dwellings from apartments to single-family homes. Its *Rehabilitation Inspector's Manual* ($55) provides suggestions on bringing older homes up to code.

National Fire Protection Association
Batterymarch Park
Quincy, Mass. 02269

Maintains the Life Safety Code 101, a limited model code that focuses on egress and survival during a fire; approximately 25 states, in addition to government agencies, have adopted it.

American Insurance Association
85 John Street
New York, N.Y. 10038

Sponsors the National Building Code, which parallels portions of the three major model codes with more on fire issues. No revisions have been made since 1976, and it is maintained only for the benefit of current members.

Contacts
National Conference of States on Building Codes and Standards
481 Carlisle Drive
Herndon, Va. 22101

Represents all states and territories in seeking uniform building codes and annually publishes the *State Building Code Directory* ($52.50), which provides information on all types of codes within each state and territory including rehabilitation variances and amendments.

Center for Building Technology
National Bureau of Standards
U.S. Department of Commerce
Washington, D.C. 20234

The major federal agency conducting research into code-related technical problems, including materials durability, fire and seismic standards and rehabilitation concerns. Has published numerous reports on codes (many are available from National Technical Information Service).

Occupational Safety and Health Administration
U.S. Department of Labor
200 Constitution Avenue, N.W.
Washington, D.C. 20210

Develops and enforces standards affecting employees and work places. Variances may be granted to historic buildings and sites presenting comparable alternatives.

American Institute of Architects
Division of Codes and Standards
1735 New York Avenue, N.W.
Washington, D.C. 20006

Together with the AIA Committee on Historic Resources, works to ensure that model codes provide preservation alternatives.

National Institute of Building Sciences
1015 15th Street, N.W.
Suite 700
Washington, D.C. 20005

Nonprofit organization created by Congress to encourage a better building regulatory environment and to facilitate the introduction of new technologies into the building process.

Council of American Building Officials
5205 Leesburg Pike
Falls Church, Va. 22041

An association of building officials and building code organizations that has developed the Model One and Two Family Dwelling Code as a cooperative project of its members.

National Science Foundation
1800 G Street, N.W.
Washington, D.C. 20226

Conducts research into materials-related problems, including seismic protection.

American National Standards Institute
1430 Broadway
New York, N.Y. 10018

Promulgates voluntary standards for materials by affected industries.

Seismic Reinforcement

One of the most difficult problems of pre-1933 structures is the fact that many are constructed of under-reinforced masonry brick. As a class, they perform worst under earthquake loading conditions. Yet, even these buildings will not always fail when an earthquake occurs. As Robert Olsen states, "Past earthquakes have also proven that we have lots of older buildings that have survived well, yet are legally unsafe. They won't meet the code today but they have performed."

Richard E. Reed. In *Living with Seismic Risk*

Living with Seismic Risk: Strategies for Urban Conservation. Richard E. Reed, ed. Washington, D.C.: American Association for the Advancement of Science (Office of Public Sector Programs (1333 H Street, N.W., 20005), 1977. 143 pp., illus.

Seminar proceedings surveying problems and solutions—structural, seismological, legal, financial and historical—to perserving buildings and safety.

Reducing Earthquake Risks: A Planner's Guide. Martin Jaffe, JoAnn Butler and Charles Thurow. Chicago: American Planning Association, 1981. PAS no. 364. 88 pp., illus., appends. $20 pb.

Shows how to map and evaluate local hazards and examines seismic safety programs that can be adopted, including means to upgrade building codes to deal with substandard buildings likely to fail during an earthquake.

"Seismic Rehabilitation of Historic Buildings: A Damage Analysis Approach," Melvyn Green. In "Regulating Existing Buildings." *Bulletin*, Association for Preservation Technology, vol. XIII, no. 2, 1981. 39 pp. $5 pb.

Presents new research on seismic reinforcement of old buildings, with two case studies.

San Francisco Mint (1874, Alfred B. Mullett), with its cornice removed because of earthquake threats.

Earthquake Resistant Design: A Manual for Engineers and Architects. D. J. Dowrick. Somerset, N.J.: Wiley, 1978. 374 pp. $67.95 hb.

New construction is the focus, including information on risk analysis, building materials, mechanical systems and the resistance of specific structures.

Repair, Strengthening and Rehabilitation of Buildings: Recommendations for Needed Research. Robert D. Hanson. Ann Arbor: University of Michigan, Department of Civil Engineering, 1977. 70 pp.

Proceedings from a National Science Foundation-sponsored workshop, with information on earthquake-damaged buildings.

San Francisco's Parapet Ordinance. Paul Newman and Jay Turnbull. San Francisco: Foundation for San Francisco's Architectural Heritage, 1977. 50 pp.

A response to new seismic requirements affecting decorative parapets, with analysis of reinforcement details and cost estimates.

"Seismic Rehabilitation of the California State Capitol West Wing." Lloyd A. Lee, Henry H. Lee, J. P. Nicoletti. 30 pp. Available from URS/John A. Blume and Associates, Engineers, 130 Jessie Street, San Francisco, Calif. 94105.

Feasibility Study on Rehabilitation of the Old Administration Building at Fresno City College as an Agricultural Museum. Fresno, Calif.: Fresno City and County Historical Society (7160 West Kearny, 93706), 1977. Available also at Fresno County Library, 2420 Mariposa, Fresno, Calif. 93721.

Earthquakes and Cities: A Selected Bibliography. Anthony G. White. Chicago: Council of Planning Librarians, 1976. No. 1109. 99 pp. $1.50 pb.

Ramp for the handicapped in a lightwell at National Trust headquarters (1915–17, Jules Henri de Sibour), Washington, D.C. (Walter Smalling, Jr.)

Accessibility for the Handicapped

Historically, most buildings were designed to be readily accessible only to the able bodied. Barriers to access seemingly evolved from functional or ceremonial needs into traditional building practices, such as the long flight of steps often separating the principal floor from grade level. Architectural barriers have served to perpetuate a general exclusionary attitude toward disabled people, keeping them from participating fully in the activities that take place within many buildings. Since the 1960s, however, this nation has become increasingly conscious of the need to make our buildings and the activities within them more accessible to our disabled citizens.

Charles Parrott, *Access to Historic Buildings for the Disabled*

"No otherwise qualified handicapped individual in the United States. . .shall, solely by reason of. . .handicap, be excluded from the participation in, be denied the benefits of, or be subject to discrimination under any program or activity receiving federal financial assistance."

Rehabilitation Act of 1973

"The guidelines require accessibility of *programs,* rather than facilities. . . . The requirement is, further, that facilities be 'accessible,' rather than 'barrier-free.' 'Barrier-free' means that a handicapped person can enter by the doorway, reach all floors, and use all public amenities such as rest rooms, telephones, and water fountains. 'Accessible' means that a disabled person can enter by at least one doorway, reach important areas, and use some public amenities."

Alice P. Kenney, *Access to the Past*

"In the case of historic properties, program accessibility shall mean that, when viewed in their entirety, programs are accessible to and usable by handicapped persons. After all other methods of providing access have been examined and found unsatisfactory in achieving access, recipients of Federal assistance may find it necessary to make alterations to historic properties. Certain alterations may cause substantial impairment of significant historic features. . . .

Where access cannot be achieved without causing a substantial impairment of significant historic features, the recipient may seek a modification or waiver of access standards from the responsible Federal agency."

Advisory Council on Historic Preservation. "Supplementary Guidance: Handicapped Access to Historic Properties," 1980.

Proposal to make the entrance of LaFortune Student Center (1883, Willoughby J. Edbrooke), University of Notre Dame, Ind., accessible through slopes and ramps. From *Adapting Historic Campus Structures for Accessibility*. (APPA)

Access to Historic Buildings for the Disabled: Suggestions for Planning and Implementation. Charles Parrott. Washington, D.C.: Technical Preservation Services, U.S. Department of the Interior, 1980. TPS Reports. 92 pp., illus., biblio., appends. $5.50 pb. GPO stock no. 024-016-00149-4.

A guide to providing barrier-free access to historic buildings through methods that conform to the Secretary of the Interior's Standards for Historic Preservation Projects. Covered are key federal laws, state and local building codes, evaluating barriers, the compliance process and a variety of architectural changes.

Access to the Past: Museum Programs and Handicapped Visitors. Alice P. Kenney. Nashville: American Association for State and Local History, 1980. 131 pp., index, biblio. $8.95 pb.

Explains potential adaptations that museums and historical agencies can make to accommodate more handicapped visitors. Contents include defining disability, Sec. 504 of the Rehabilitation Act of 1973, implementation guidelines and representative programs.

Design for Accessibility. Robert James Sorenson. New York: McGraw-Hill, 1979. 256 pp., illus. $28.95 hb.

A practical book that explains graphically currently developed standards and recommendations for handicapped access design—site development, parking, building access and circulation, building areas, details, accessories, codes, standards and regulations.

"The Accessible Path in Historic Properties." Theodore Prudon and Stephen Dalton. In "Regulating Existing Buildings." *Bulletin,* Association for Preservation Technology, vol. XIII, no. 2, 1981.

Following a general discussion of evaluating a historic building for accessibility, two New York State examples are presented in detail.

Adapting Historic Campus Structures for Accessibility. Margaret Milner. Alexandria, Va.: Association of Physical Plant Administrators of Universities and Colleges (1446 Duke Street, 22314-3492) and National Center for a Barrier Free Environment, 1980. 90 pp., illus., biblio., append., index. $5.50 pb.

Surveys the historical, architectural and legal considerations of making college buildings accessible. Six design solutions proposed by architecture schools are presented as models.

"Open Door for the Handicapped." Alice P. Kenney. *Historic Preservation,* July–September 1978.

An overview of efforts to make house museums accessible, with examples from National Trust and other property programs.

A Guidebook to the Minimum Federal Guidelines and Requirements for Accessible Design. Architectural and Transportation Barriers Compliance Board. Washington, D.C.: National Conference of States on Building Codes and Standards, 1981. 76 pp., illus., append. Free.

Provides explanations of such problem areas as elevators, restrooms, alterations and additions to existing buildings.

Specifications for Making Buildings and Facilities Accessible to and Usable by Physically Handicapped People. New York: American National Standards Institute, 1980. 68 pp., append. $5 pb.

A comprehensive standard, organized into site and building elements and listing specific dimensions and criteria.

Access for the Handicapped: The Barrier-Free Regulations for Design and Construction in All 50 States. Peter S. Hopf and John A. Raeber. New York: Van Nostrand Reinhold, 1984. 712 pp., illus. $56.50 hb.

A comprehensive reference presenting the applicable laws through diagrams and charts.

Accessibility: Designing Buildings for the Needs of Handicapped Persons. National Library Service for the Blind and Physically Handicapped. Washington, D.C.: Library of Congress. Free.

Selected and annotated bibliography on barrier-free design for disabled persons.

Resource Guide to Literature on Barrier-Free Environments, with Selected Annotations. Architectural and Transportation Barriers Compliance Board. 1977. 2nd ed. Washington, D.C.: Author, 1980. 279 pp., appends., index. $7.50 pb. GPO stock no. 017-090-00049-6.

Includes a large section on architecture in general by building type, as well as sections on parts, monuments and historic sites and travel guides for handicapped travelers (by state and country).

Arts and the Handicapped: An Issue of Access. Larry Malloy. New York: Educational Facilities Laboratories, 1975. 80 pp. Available from Interbook, 611 Broadway, Room 227, New York, N.Y. 10012. $4 hb.

Describes efforts to make cultural facilities and programs accessible to the handicapped.

Rollin' On: A Wheelchair Guide to American Cities. Maxine H. Atwater. New York: Dodd, Mead, 1978. 290 pp.

Details how the wheelchair-bound can travel independently and see the sights—historic sites, museums, restaurants and other major attractions in eight major cities, with itineraries.

Access to the World: A Travel Guide for the Handicapped. Louise Weiss. New York: Chatham Square Press, 1977. 178 pp., index. $8.95.

A comprehensive guide to all aspects of travel for the handicapped in cities around the world including detailed transportation information, advice and travel tips.

Access National Parks: A Guide for Handicapped Visitors. Washington, D.C.: National Park Service, 1978. 197 pp., maps. $4. GPO stock no. 024-005-00691-5. Also available in braille and talking book editions.

A guidebook to national parks and historic sites, listed by state, with detailed information describing special facilities and programs for the disabled.

International Directory of Access Guides. New York: Rehabilitation International U.S.A. (20 West 40th Street, 10018), 1981. 61 pp. Free. Biannual.

Lists 458 guides to cities and sites around the world.

Contacts

Architectural and Transportation Barriers Compliance Board 330 C Street, S.W. Washington, D.C. 20201

Established by the Rehabilitation Act of 1973 as an independent federal agency to ensure compliance with accessibility standards. A publications list is available.

National Center for a Barrier Free Environment 1015 15th Street, N.W. Suite 700 Washington, D.C. 20005

Works to eliminate architectural barriers for the handicapped and publishes a bimonthly *Report* and other publications.

Historic Sites

11

How can historical buildings, furnishings, settings, and isolated objects—frozen bits of history, as it were—convey understanding of a dynamic, continuous flow of human experience? This is the basic problem to which history museums should address themselves. . . .

Edward P. Alexander, *Museums in Motion*

The Truth About the Past

"There are, it seems to me, four broad areas of concern under which to consider the fundamental purpose of historic site preservation. They are: 1) continuity, 2) integrity, 3) plausibility, and 4) meaning. Not mutually exclusive categories by any means, they represent four different ways of approaching the same important issue of historic preservation.

By *continuity,* I mean the will and the ability of a society to assure that it retains its memory. We do so in many ways [including] the way we maintain the continuity of our civilization's history through the conservation and preservation of its physical evidence.

In practical terms there are two things to keep in mind. The first is the extent to which we choose to reflect the different periods of occupancy at a historic property. Should each prior or resident receive equal treatment? If not, why? . . .

Costumed docent in a window, Shakertown at Pleasant Hill, Ky. (1805). Shakertown, one of the most complete Shaker villages, is restoring 27 original buildings and reconstructing others to interpret the Shaker way of life. (Martha K. Janzen, Shakertown at Pleasant Hill)

The second consideration is more difficult to come to grips with. To what extent does the organization or agency that controls a historic property at any particular time become a part of the texture of continuity? . . . To what extent do we in the present have an obligation to future generations to remain detached from the historical evidence to retain its validity?

For historic sites, in general, we may . . . [ask] two questions that have to do with *integrity:*

1) How much of a site's history are we able to tell?
2) How much of a site's history do we choose to tell? . . .

What is the historical 'truth' and can that 'truth' ever be detached from the historian's platform, one's own ear and its preconceptions and prejudices about the past? . . .

Plausibility brings the professional into a closer relationship to the house museum and historic site visitor. Where continuity and integrity involve intellectual considerations, plausibility introduces the emotional side of the historic site experience. . . .

Whatever the reason, historic sites and houses have been set aside to remind us of some clearly, or not so clearly, articu-

Sleigh near the East Family Dwelling, Shakertown at Pleasant Hill.

lated aspect of the past and, further, that by so treating these places, an educational benefit may emerge for those who visit them. . . .

Is it possible to take a once active farm or a once lived-in house, make it into a historic site or museum, and retain its earlier vitality? . . . the placement of objects from a historical period in rooms of that time or the setting aside of a parcel of land with older buildings on it, no matter how well preserved, does not guarantee the recreation of a true feeling of an earlier time. . . . It may be a

fundamental limitation of our human existence that we can only simulate the surface of the past and that we are forever prevented from reaching a deeper understanding through the presentation of its artifacts and places.

For the visitor to historic property, *meaning* is the sum total experience gained from the physical evidence of a site or museum, measured against the mythos of contemporary civilization. . . .

How much does a visitor fantasize about . . . relationships when strolling a historic village lane, leaning on a fence watching the sheep graze or standing beside a blacksmith as he hammers out an iron implement? What are the hopes, dreams, the satisfactions that such sites nurture in those who are embraced by its presence? And, how well do we understand these motivations and desires? . . .

Meaning goes beyond the fact, truth, and experience of a site to place these components into a cultural unity locked into the deepest forces that shape a civilization."

Theodore Anton Sande, "Presenting the Truth About the Past." *Cultural Resources Management Bulletin,* December 1984.

The Village Crossroads at the Farmers' Museum, Cooperstown, N.Y. Begun in the 1940s, the museum village has been created from buildings moved to the site, all designed to simulate New York farm life in the early 19th century. (New York State Historical Association)

The Language of Historic Sites

curator. A professional charged with the care, custodianship, study and interpretation of artifacts in a museum, house museum or related context.

docent. A guide at a historic building or site whose function is to educate visitors about the property during tours.

historical museum. A museum, which may or may not be housed in a historic building, whose primary purpose is the interpretation of history. Its collections may include objects, sites and structures related to persons and events significant in history.

house museum. A museum whose structure itself is of historical or architectural significance and whose interpretation relates primarily to the building's architecture, furnishings and history.

interpretation. All the educational activities designed to explain the history and meanings inherent in historic sites, including tours, furnishings, displays, exhibits and related programs.

living historical farm. A working farm on which visitors can observe animals, plants, tools, methods and structures common to some specific past place and time being used in unstaged agricultural activities.

living history. Interpretive programs, generally in conjunction with historic sites, that emphasize participatory activities involving visitors and re-creations of historical events and techniques.

material culture. Tangible objects used by people to cope with the physical world, "that sector of our physical environment that we modify through culturally determined behavior." *(In Small Things Forgotten)*

museum. A public or private nonprofit institution organized on a permanent basis for essentially educational or aesthetic purposes that, using a professional staff: (1) owns or uses tangible objects, animate or inanimate; (2) cares for these objects; and (3) exhibits them to the public on a regular basis (through its own or other facilities). (Institute of Museum Services)

museum village. A site in which several or many structures have been restored, rebuilt or moved and whose purpose is to interpret a historical or cultural setting, often within the context of daily trades and activities of a past time. Often also called an "outdoor museum."

national park. A federally owned area administered by the National Park Service, often extensive in size, individually designated by Congress for purposes of recreation, culture or scenic or historic preservation.

period room. A collection of original furniture and furnishings, usually re-created in a historical or art museum, illustrating a lifestyle or historical era or presenting an aesthetically pleasing combination that never existed in that form in a particular building.

shrine. A building or place that is held sacred. More frequently used in the early history of preservation than it is today, the term often is applied to sites such as Mount Vernon that have intense patriotic associations.

Adapted from *Landmark Words: A Glossary for Preserving the Built Environment.* National Trust for Historic Preservation. Forthcoming.

Re-created 19th-century lawyer's office at the Farmers' Museum. (New York State Historical Association)

Thomas Filer Schoolhouse (c. 1820), now located at the Farmers' Museum. (New York State Historical Association)

Contacts

American Association of Museums
1055 Thomas Jefferson Street, N.W.
Suite 428
Washington, D.C. 20007

A nonprofit service organization that represents the interests of the museum profession and promotes museums as major cultural resources. Its accreditation program sets standards for all types of museums and includes new criteria for historic sites. AAM publishes a bimonthly magazine, *Museum News;* a monthly newsletter, *Aviso;* and a variety of books and reprints on museum and curatorial concerns (a list is available).

American Association for State and Local History
708 Berry Road
Nashville, Tenn. 37204

The best single source of information and assistance for the small history museum, historic site and local historical society. Services include workshops, seminars, training programs, independent study courses, the monthly magazine *History News* and an extensive series of books and reprints (a list is available).

National Park Service
U.S. Department of the Interior
P.O. Box 37127
Washington, D.C. 20013-7127

The National Park System includes some 300 historical, natural and recreational parks, including National Historic Sites, National Historical Parks, National Monuments, National Battlefields and Parks, National Parks and Historic Areas. Historic properties in these parks are generally open to the public and are the subjects of a variety of archeological, research and interpretive programs. Conservation management and education techniques developed within the system may serve as prototypes for the field.

National Trust for Historic Preservation
Office of Museum Services
1785 Massachusetts Avenue, N.W.
Washington, D.C. 20036

Receives donations of sites, buildings and objects significant in American history and culture, "to preserve and administer them for the public benefit." Owns 16 historic properties that are open as museums, half of which are operated by local costeward organizations. Using the expertise of its staff and its Historic House Program, the Trust also provides assistance to related historic sites and organizations. For a list of properties, see Preservationists.

Smithsonian Institution
Office of Museum Programs
Arts and Industries Building
Room 2235
Washington, D.C. 20560

Administers the Museum Reference Center, which maintains a comprehensive collection of technical literature on museum operations and provides reference assistance in many areas of museum activities; audiovisual programs in conservation, education and folklife for loan or sale; and workshops held at the Smithsonian for individuals employed in museums.

Society for the Preservation of New England Antiquities
141 Cambridge Street
Boston, Mass. 02114

Operates 40 house museums and other properties not open to the public. It administers its house museums as interpretive centers where the public can study and enjoy examples of New England living patterns from the 17th through the 20th centuries and encourages the use of historic sites as community cultural resources. The Consulting Services Department provides expertise on the analysis and conservation of historic structures.

Arts and Industries Building (1879–81, Adolph Cluss and Paul Schulze), Smithsonian Institution, Washington, D.C., built to house 1876 Centennial exhibits donated to the United States. (Smithsonian Institution)

Museums

A museum is an institution for the preservation of those objects which best illustrate the phenomena of nature and the works of man, and the utilization of those for the increase of knowledge and for the culture and enlightenment of the people.

> George Brown Goode, *The Principles of Museum Administration.* 1895.

The world is a museum. Andre Malraux said as much in the title of his classic book Museum Without Walls. *Historic preservationists are perhaps more receptive to this idea than the generality of those working in museums.*

> Craig Gilborn, "Museums and Historic Preservation." In *Saving Large Estates.* Setauket, N.Y.: Society for the Preservation of Long Island Antiquities, 1977.

America's Museums: The Belmont Report. A Report to the Federal Council on the Arts and Humanities by a Special Committee of the American Association of Museums. Washington, D.C.: American Association of Museums, 1969. 99 pp., append.

The guiding document detailing the need for federal support of museums that led to funding and implementation of the National Museum Act. Surveys the functions of museums, demands for education and research, unmet needs and general problems.

Museums: Their New Audience. A Report to the U.S. Department of Housing and Urban Development by a Special Committee of the American Association of Museums. Washington, D.C.: American Association of Museums, 1972. 116 pp., illus., biblio., appends.

Recommendations covering communities, neighborhoods, minorities, urban problems and budgets, with case studies of museums focusing on new audiences.

The Museum in America: A Critical Study. Laurence Vail Coleman. Washington, D.C.: American Association of Museums, 1939. 730 pp., illus., appends., index. 3 vols.

A classic study designed "to see museums as a whole . . . all in the matrix of society" and provide a commentary on the condition, strengths, weaknesses, limitations and opportunities of museums. Covers museums as a social movement, museum types, financing, buildings, museum work, staff, with a listing of house museums (644 in 1939).

The Sacred Grove: Essays on Museums. S. Dillon Ripley. 1969. Washington, D.C.: Smithsonian Institution Press, 1979. 159 pp. $4.50 pb.

An account of the growth of museums from "sacred groves" and "cabinets of curiosities" to community centers, raising questions about the development of museums in present society.

A Cabinet of Curiosities: Five Episodes in the Evolution of American Museums. Walter Muir Whitehill, Whitfield J. Bell et al. Charlottesville: University Press of Virginia, 1967. 168 pp., illus.

A history of U.S. museums looking at the Smithsonian Institution, American Antiquarian Society, American Philosophical Society, William Clark Indian Museum and Western Museum of Cincinnati.

Museums for a New Century. Commission on Museums for a New Century. Washington, D.C.: American Association of Museums, 1985. 144 pp., illus., append., index. $17.95 pb.

A look at the new role of museums in society designed to be a blueprint for the future, highlighting innovative and successful museum programs.

Museums: In Search of a Usable Future. Alma S. Wittlin. Foreword by S. Dillon Ripley. Cambridge: MIT Press, 1970. 317 pp., illus., append., index.

Covers roles of museums, preludes to public museums, early U.S. and European collections and public museums, and efforts at reform, with a program for museum renewal.

A Culture at Risk: Who Cares for America's Heritage? Charles Phillips and Patricia Hogan. Nashville: American Association for State and Local History, 1985. 100 pp. $10.

An analysis of the current state of historical agencies and local museums beginning with a historical overview of their development and proliferation in the mid-20th century. Covers income sources, membership, major programs, collections, budgets and visitors.

Museum Masters: Their Museums and Their Influence. Edward P. Alexander. Nashville: American Association for State and Local History, 1983. 438 pp., illus., biblios., index. $22.95 hb.

A study of 12 museum innovators in the United States, Europe, Great Britain and Scandinavia who have helped shape modern museums. Included are art, science, botanical, decorative arts and zoological museums. One chapter illustrates the rise of house museums through the founding of the Mount Vernon Ladies' Association by Ann Pamela Cunningham.

America's Castle: The Evolution of the Smithsonian Building and Its Institution, 1840–1878. Kenneth Hafertepe. Washington, D.C.: Smithsonian Institution Press, 1984. 180 pp., illus., index. $19.95 hb.

The story of the famous "castle" designed to reflect the vision of the Smithsonian as a multifaceted cultural institution.

The Official Museum Directory. American Association of Museums. Wilmette, Ill.: National Register Publishing Company (3004 Glenview Road, 60091), 1985. 1,164 pp. $85 pb.

Lists geographically 6,000 museums in the U.S. and Canada, with program data and museum products and services.

Catalog of Museum Publications and Media: A Directory and Index of Publications and Audiovisuals Available from United States and Canadian Institutions. Paul Wasserman, ed. 2nd ed. Detroit: Gale, 1980. 1,053 pp., index. $235 hb.

Some 900 museums and sites listed alphabetically, indicating their books, periodicals, catalogs, films and other audiovisual resources, with ordering information.

Historic House Museums

A great difference exists between the historic house experience and the one offered the visitor by the great urban museums or even regional historic villages and historical societies. The function of the historic house museum as a tangible piece of history can with skillful interpretation evoke for visitors of all ages and diverse backgrounds and interests the presence of the past, and bring to life the original mood and events which are identified with a particular . . . house.

William Shopsin, *Saving Large Estates*

"Americans developed their own distinctive version of historic preservation while Europeans were restoring their churches and castles or gathering vernacular architecture and folk objects into outdoor museums. The historic house museum, in the opinion of its founders, was a way to teach love of country. . . .

Today there are about two thousand historic house museums in the United States, and new ones open every year. One reason for this expansion has been the increased interest Americans are taking in their early history. In an era of rapid technological change, threatening atomic annihilation, and deteriorating economic prosperity, thoughtful citizens seek reassurance that the American system of government is well conceived and sturdy enough to survive. Emphasis on a common national background has important psychological values. Then, practical sociological/economic developments—the automobile and increased leisure—are other reasons for historic house museum proliferation. At the same time, leaders of the historic preservation movement agree that its great future growth lies not in the museum field, but in historic districts—areas of residential and adaptive uses in our cities."

Edward P. Alexander, *Museums in Motion*

Museums in Motion: An Introduction to the History and Functions of Museums. Edward P. Alexander. Nashville: American Association for State and Local History, 1979. 322 pp., illus., biblio., index. $13.50 pb.

Documents the changing social roles of all museums, tracing their rise since the 1800s and exploring philosophies and practices of collection, conservation, research, exhibitions, interpretation and social responsibility. "The History Museum" chapter is a brief survey of the history of preservation and history museums, including outdoor villages and house museums.

Historic House Museums. Laurence Vail Coleman. 1933. Reprint. Detroit: Gale, 1973. 199 pp., illus., biblio., append., index. $45.

A pioneer work addressing in full the problems of the house museum, many of which continue to exist a half century later. Different solutions for some (notably, interpretation) have since been developed and documented in other publications.

Historic House Museums: A Selected Bibliography. Mary Vance. Monticello, Ill.: Vance Bibliographies, 1983. 36 pp., biblio. A–880. $5.25 pb.

Includes general references plus a list of museums and places referred to in the citations.

Ancestral Voices: 1942–1943. James Lees-Milne. London: Faber and Faber, 1975. 312 pp., index. $8.95 pb.

Prophesying Peace: 1944–1945. James Lees-Milne. London: Faber and Faber, 1977. 261 pp., index. $8.95 pb.

Caves of Ice: 1946–1947. James Lees-Milne. London: Faber and Faber, 1983. 286 pp., index. $8.95 pb.

Diaries kept from 1942 to 1947, when the author was employed to inspect historic buildings offered to the National Trust of England. Provides entertaining insights into the owners as well as their houses.

Directory of Historical Societies and Agencies. Donna McDonald, comp. 12th ed. Nashville: American Association for State and Local History, 1982. 416 pp., illus., index. $36 pb.

Lists 6,000 historical groups and related organizations, with properties owned, plus national historic sites. To be enlarged in 1985.

American Landmarks: Properties of the National Trust for Historic Preservation. Washington, D.C.: Preservation Press, 1980. 72 pp., illus. $5.95 pb.

Philipsburg Manor: A Guidebook. Tarrytown, N.Y.,: Sleepy Hollow Restorations, 1969. 56 pp., illus. $.85 pb.

Van Cortlandt Manor. Joseph T. Butler. Tarrytown, N.Y.: Sleepy Hollow Restorations, 1978. 96 pp., illus., biblio. $1.95 pb.

Washington Irving's Sunnyside. Joseph T. Butler. Tarrytown, N.Y.: Sleepy Hollow Restorations, 1974. 80 pp., illus., biblio. $3.95 hb, $1.95 pb.

Historic and Memorial Buildings of the Daughters of the American Revolution. Washington, D.C.: National Society, Daughters of the American Revolution (1776 D Street, N.W., 20006), 1979. 339 pp., illus., index. $8.

Images of Connecticut Life: A Self-Guided Tour to the Properties and Collections of the Antiquarian and Landmarks Society of Connecticut. Ronna L. Reynolds. Hartford: Antiquarian and Landmarks Society of Connecticut (394 Main Street, 06103), 1978. 155 pp., illus. $7.50 pb.

Houses of the Essex Institute. Anne Farnam and Bryant F. Tolles, Jr., eds. Salem, Mass.: Essex Institute (132 Essex Street, 01970), 1978. *John Ward House.* 40 pp. *Crowninshield-Bentley House.* 54 pp. *Assembly House.* 35 pp. *Peirce-Nichols House.* 49 pp. *Gardner-Pingree House.* 35 pp. *Andrew-Stafford House.* 42 pp. *John Tucker Daland House.* 36 pp. $2 each, $15 boxed set.

Stair hall relocated from Montmorenci, a North Carolina house, in the 1930s by Henry Francis du Pont to Winterthur, his museum of decorative arts in Winterthur, Del. (© Winterthur Museum)

Henry Ford at his own Scotch Settlement School, c. 1928, moved to Greenfield Village, Dearborn, Mich. (Ford Archives, Henry Ford Museum)

Duke of Gloucester Street, Williamsburg, restored beginning in 1927 with aid from John D. Rockefeller. (Colonial Williamsburg Foundation)

Outdoor Museums

We're going to start something. I'm going to start up a museum and give people a true picture of the development of the country. That's the only history that is worth observing, that you can preserve in itself. We're going to build a museum that's going to show industrial history, and it won't be bunk!

Henry Ford, 1919.

"In the narrowest and perhaps most accurate sense of the word the typical 'outdoor museum' or 'museum village' is a carefully selected and situated collection of original buildings, grouped compatibly and designed to illustrate in three dimensional form, as totally as possible, not only the architecture and building forms of a given geographical area and period of time in history, but also to recreate as nearly as possible the atmosphere and life-style of a segment of human development in its entire context."

Richard W. E. Perrin, *Outdoor Museums.* Milwaukee: Milwaukee Public Museum, 1975.

"Colonial Williamsburg, the preserved and restored capital of eighteenth-century Virginia, is probably the best-known outdoor museum in the United States. As a history museum, it is an expansion of the historic-house concept to include the major part of a colonial city, some 175 acres and about 30 buildings with carefully furnished interiors open to the visiting public. As a living historic district, it also has about 100 properties occupied by residents of Williamsburg or rented to tourists."

Edward P. Alexander, *Museums in Motion*

"Although the large outdoor museums that opened to the public in the 1930s and 1940s are closely linked to the popularization of history, it is difficult today to view these exhibition areas as historic preservation activity. . . .

The people who founded the outdoor museums . . . were a sensitive group who saw that continuity in history might be better objectified through the use of machines and buildings than in the classroom. The idea of preservation for its own sake was secondary to them. The didactic role assigned to most of these projects was more important than any need to keep buildings on their original sites. They believed that the greatest good for the largest number of Americans could only be achieved by creating a setting."

Charles B. Hosmer, Jr., "The Outdoor Museums." In *Preservation Comes of Age*

"We shall need enclaves of the past—communities in which turnover, novelty and choice are deliberately limited. These may be communities in which history is partially frozen. . . . Unlike Williamsburg or Mystic, however, through which visitors stream at a steady and rapid clip, tomorrow's enclaves of the past must be places where people faced with future shock can escape the pressures of overstimulation for weeks, months, even years, if they choose."

Alvin Toffler, *Future Shock.* New York: Random House, 1970.

Preservation Comes of Age: From Williamsburg to the National Trust, 1926–1949. Charles B. Hosmer, Jr. Charlottesville: University Press of Virginia, 1981. Published for the National Trust. 1,291 pp., illus., biblio., chron., index. 2 vols. $37.50 hb.

Describes the establishment of the early outdoor museums—Williamsburg, Greenfield Village, Old Sturbridge Village, Cooperstown, Deerfield and National Park Service sites—plus the differing restoration philosophies behind each.

Museum Studies Reader: An Anthology of Journal Articles on Open Air Museums in America. Ormond Loomis and Willard B. Moore, comps. Noblesville, Ind.: Conner Prairie Pioneer Settlement (30 Conner Lane, 46060), 1978.

Restored Towns and Historic Districts of America: A Tour Guide. Alice Cromie. New York: Dutton, 1979. 385 pp., illus.

Brief descriptions, arranged geographically, of museum villages in addition to historic sites, buildings and districts.

A Guide to Museum Villages: The American Heritage Brought to Life. Mitchell R. Alegre. New York: Drake, 1978. 160 pp., illus., index.

Lists and describes 102 museum villages, indexed by name and historical emphasis.

Museum Villages U.S.A. Nicholas Zook. Barre, Mass.: Barre Publishers, 1971. 136 pp., illus.

Arranged thematically (the American Heritage, Indian Villages, First Settlements and Colonial Towns, That Old-Time Religion, etc.) this early guidebook also contains a brief section on walking tours.

America's Historic Villages and Restorations. Irvin Haas. New York: Arco, 1974. 150 pp., illus.

A picture book of 50 better-known museum villages—restored, re-created and relocated—arranged by geographic region.

Selected Living Historical Farms, Villages and Agricultural Museums in the United States and Canada. Washington, D.C.: Association for Living Historical Farms and Agricultural Museums, 1975. 64 pp., illus.

Colonial Williamsburg: Its Buildings and Gardens. A. L. Kocher and Howard Dearstyne. 1949. Williamsburg, Va.: Colonial Williamsburg Foundation, 1976. 112 pp. $5.95.

A Home for Our Heritage: The Building and Growth of Greenfield Village and Henry Ford Museum, 1929–1979. Geoffrey C. Upward. Dearborn, Mich.: Henry Ford Museum Press, 1979. 192 pp., illus., appends., index. $16.95 hb, $9.95 pb.

American Ingenuity: Henry Ford Museum and Greenfield Village. James S. Wamsley. New York: Abrams, 1985. $37.50.

Hancock Shaker Village: An Effort to Restore a Vision. Amy Bess Miller. Hancock, Mass.: Hancock Shaker Village, 1984. 170 pp. $10.95 pb.

Old Sturbridge Village, Mass., opened in 1946 as a re-created New England community of about 1800. (Old Sturbridge Village)

Plimoth Plantation, Mass., a reconstruction of the 1626 Pilgrim Colony where mud and flies are tolerated for verisimilitude. (Plimoth Plantation)

A Tour of Old Sturbridge Village. Samuel Chamberlain. 1955. Rev. ed. New York: Hastings House, 1972. 72 pp., illus. $1.50 pb.

Plimoth Plantation: Then and Now. Jean Poindexter Colby. New York: Hastings House, 1979. 128 pp., illus.

Cliff Palace, Mesa Verde National Park, Colo., one of the dwellings of the Anasazi Indians. (Fred Mang, National Park Service)

Some Outdoor Museums

Native Americans
Mesa Verde National Park, Colo.
Oconaluftee Indian Village, Cherokee, N.C.

Colonial Settlements
Jamestown Festival Park, Va.
Plimoth Plantation, Plymouth, Mass.
Colonial Williamsburg, Va.

Early American Villages
Shelburne Museum, Vt.
Old Sturbridge Village, Mass.
Mystic Seaport, Mystic, Conn.
Farmers' Museum, Cooperstown, N.Y.
Henry Ford Museum and Greenfield Village, Dearborn, Mich.

Westward Migration
Arkansas Territorial Restoration, Little Rock
Stuhr Museum of the Prairie Pioneer, Grand Island, Neb.
Kern County Pioneer Village, Bakersfield, Calif.

Gold and Silver Rush
Bodie State Historic Park, Calif.
Columbia State Historic Park, Calif.
South Pass City, Wyo.

Civil War Era
Harpers Ferry, W.Va.
New Salem State Park, Ill.

Communal Societies
New Harmony, Ind.
Old Economy Village, Ambridge, Pa.
Hancock Shaker Village, Mass.
Old Salem, Winston-Salem, N.C.
Shakerstown at Pleasant Hill, Harrodsburg, Ky.
Nauvoo, Ill.
Bishop Hill, Ill.

Industrial and Farm Villages
Hopewell National Historic Site, Pa.
Paul Bunyan Camp, Eau Claire, Wis.
National Colonial Farm, Accokeek, Md.

Contacts
Association for Living Historical Farms and Agricultural Museums
National Museum of American History
Room 5035
Washington, D.C. 20560

Colonial Williamsburg Foundation
P.O. Box C
Williamsburg, Va. 23187

Eleutherian Mills–Hagley Foundation
Greenville, Del. 19807

Ephrata Cloister
632 West Main Street
Ephrata, Pa. 17522

The Farmers' Museum
P.O. Box 800
Cooperstown, N.Y. 13326

Hancock Shaker Village
P.O. Box 898
Pittsfield, Mass. 01202

Henry Ford Museum and Greenfield Village
P.O. Box 1970
Dearborn, Mich. 48121

Historic Deerfield
P.O. Box 321
Deerfield, Mass. 01342

Historic New Harmony
P.O. Box 579
New Harmony, Ind. 47631

Mystic Seaport Museum
Route 27
Mystic, Conn. 06355

National Park Service
U.S. Department of the Interior
P.O. Box 37127
Washington, D.C. 20013-7127

Old Economy Village
Harmonie Associates
14th and Church Streets
Ambridge, Pa. 15003

Old Salem
Drawer F, Salem Station
Winston-Salem, N.C. 27108

Old Sturbridge Village
Route 20
Sturbridge, Mass. 01566

Old World Wisconsin
Route 2, Box 18
Eagle, Wis. 53119

Plimoth Plantation
P.O. Box 1620
Plymouth, Mass. 02061

Ranching Heritage Center
Texas Tech University
P.O. Box 4040
Lubbock, Tex. 79409

Shakertown at Pleasant Hill
Route 4
Harrodsburg, Ky. 40330

Shaker Village
Shaker Road
Canterbury, N.H. 03224

The Shelburne Museum
Route 7
Shelburne, Vt. 05482

Strawbery Banke
P.O. Box 300
Portsmouth, N.H. 03801

Waioli Mission House Museum
Grove Farm Homestead Museum
Box 1631
Lihue, Hawaii 96766

Interpretation: Lowering the Velvet Rope

Interpretation is regarded as an educational process, imparted in an interesting fashion through exhibits, slides, films, tours and talks . . . [and] is predicated on the assumption that a visit is (and should be) an educational experience. . . . The changes that have been made to improve interpretation over the years have often been imitative . . . from living history (craft demonstrations and period costumes) to push-button audio equipment to an environmental thrust in programs.

Carole T. Scanlon, "Interpretation: The Language of the Visitor." *Historic Preservation,* October–December 1974.

"[Interpretation] seeks to teach certain truths . . . [and] has a serious educational purpose.

It is based on original objects . . . [with] innate powers to . . . inform.

It is supported by sound research.

It makes use, wherever possible, of sensory perception—sight, hearing, smell, taste, touch and the kinetic muscle sense.

It is informal education . . . voluntary and dependent only upon the interest of the viewer . . . often enjoyable."

Edward P. Alexander, "What Is Interpretation?" In *The Longwood Program Seminars, 1977.* Debbie Clayton, ed. Vol. 9. Newark, Del.: University of Delaware, 1977.

"It will help to clarify planning if all historic sites are thought of as fitting into three broad categories based upon their primary purpose.
1. *The documentary site.* Documents an important historical event or the life or lives of a person or family. "This usually—but not always—means that we should do our utmost to restore the structure or place to its precise condition at a specific point in time."
2. *The representative site.* Intended to help the visitor understand a period of history or a way of life.
3. *The aesthetic site.* A display in period room settings of outstanding examples of furniture and furnishings. "One goes to the aesthetic site as to an art museum, to appreciate good taste and to please the visual sense."

From *Interpretation of Historic Sites*

"Planners and administrators . . . seem driven by certain pressures, or 'urges,' to do things that depart from the ideal. . . .

First is the urge not to fool with Mother Nature. This is the naturalist syndrome and it is most prevalent in agencies that manage both natural and historical parks. . . .

Next is the urge to beautify. The cosmetic syndrome is the opposite of the Mother Nature syndrome. . . .

Third is the urge to develop. This is the self-glorification syndrome. . . .

The final urge, to tell a story, is another dimension of the self-glorification syndrome. It is characterized by dramatic presentations in which flashy gimmickry takes precedence over substance. . . .

The urge to tell a story has spawned two secondary, closely related urges. One is the urge to re-create history. This results in what is popularly known as living history. . . .

The other secondary and related urge is the urge to reconstruct. As if preservation of the real thing were not difficult enough, we try to re-create that which has vanished and even (if such is possible) that which never existed at all."

Robert M. Utley, "A Preservation Ideal." *Historic Preservation,* April–June 1976.

"The Society for the Preservation of New England Antiquities has abandoned its former policy of restoring old buildings. Instead it seeks to preserve its . . . historic properties just as they were at the date when it acquired them, and when their active and natural life ended. . . . We have not forgotten the value of restorations in educating the public in the various periods of historic architecture. We would suggest, however, that there are now enough period restorations to which the public may resort for this basic education, and that it is now time to teach the public the more sophisticated lesson that change is part of the natural life of buildings and only increases their interest as antiquities."

Morgan W. Phillips, "The Philosophy of Total Preservation." *Bulletin,* Association for Preservation Technology, vol. III, no. 1, 1971.

Interpretation of Historic Sites. William T. Alderson and Shirley Payne Low. Nashville: American Association for State and Local History, 1976. 199 pp., illus. $9.50 pb.

Handbook on the development of interpretive programs for house museums and historic sites. Topics covered include planning the interpretation, presenting the site, interpreting for school tours, selection and training of interpreters, security and evaluation.

Material Culture Studies in America. Thomas J. Schlereth, ed. Nashville: American Association for State and Local History, 1982. 435 pp., illus., biblio., index. $16 pb.

An anthology on the history, theory, methodology and practice of material culture. Essays cover artifacts, manuscripts, folk art, furnishings, funerary elements, household technology, archeology, photography and service stations.

Re-creating a day at a one-room school for a television show, Old Sturbridge Village, Mass. (Robert S. Arnold, Old Sturbridge Village)

A daily cooking demonstration at Old Sturbridge Village, based on authentic period "receipts" for open-hearth cooking. (Old Sturbridge Village)

Artifacts and the American Past. Thomas J. Schlereth. Nashville: American Association for State and Local History, 1981. 294 pp., illus., appends., biblio., index. $15.95 hb.

A sampler of research and teaching techniques useful in developing interpretive programs for museum villages and house museums. Also covered are photography, mail-order catalogs, cartography, the 1876 Centennial, vegetation as historical data, regional studies and above-ground archeology.

In Small Things Forgotten: The Archeology of Early American Life. James Deetz. Garden City, N.Y.: Anchor Press, Doubleday, 1977. 184 pp., illus. $4.95 pb.

A basic resource for understanding the role of material culture in interpreting history and historic sites. "We must remember these bits and pieces, and we must use them in new and imaginative ways so that a different appreciation for what life is today, and was in the past, can be achieved," says Deetz.

Historic Houses as Learning Laboratories: Seven Teaching Strategies. Thomas Schlereth. Nashville: American Association for State and Local History, 1978. Technical Leaflet 105. 12 pp. $2 pb.

Suggests seven imaginative approaches for using the historic house as a "cross-disciplinary learning laboratory," involving cultural anthropology and folklife (house forms and types), environmental and social psychology (interior spaces), decorative arts (furnishings), cultural and historical geography, American studies and literary history, architectural history and museum studies. Extensive readings are suggested.

Interpreting Our Heritage. Freeman Tilden. 1957. Rev. ed. Chapel Hill: University of North Carolina Press, 1977. 138 pp., illus., index. $5.95 pb.

Personal account covering the philosophy and psychology of interpretation based on experience with sites in the National Park System.

"It Wasn't That Simple," Thomas J. Schlereth. *Museum News,* January–February 1978. 8 pp., illus. Reprints $1. American Association of Museums.

A critical analysis of interpretation programs and approaches at historic sites with suggestions (including reading matter) to compensate for shortcomings.

Basic Interpretation of Historic Sites. Norman L. Wilson. Independent Study Program. Nashville: American Association for State and Local History, 1984. $160.

A study kit showing how to develop a sound interpretive program for a historic site.

Fife and drum corps performing in Revolutionary dress outside Woodlawn Plantation (1800–05, William Thornton), a National Trust property near Mount Vernon, Va. (NTHP)

Interpretation. Rosemary Reese, comp. Vol. 3, *A Bibliography on Historical Organization Practices.* Frederick L. Rath, Jr., and Merrilyn Rogers O'Connell, eds. Nashville: American Association for State and Local History, 1978. 102 pp., index. $11 hb.

A bibliography of resources on educational activities listing works on interpretation, museum programs, exhibits, audiovisuals, museums and schools plus a suggested basic reference shelf.

"The Changing Historic House Museum": "Can It Live?" James Deetz. "What Is a Historic House Museum?" George L. Wrenn III. "Will It Be There Tomorrow?" Margaret B. Klapthor. *Historic Preservation,* January–March 1971.

A series of brief articles describing the interpretation philosophies at Plimoth Plantation and the Society for the Preservation of New England Antiquities and curatorial considerations.

Interpreting for Park Visitors. William J. Lewis. Philadelphia: Eastern Acorn Press, Eastern National Park and Monument Association (339 Walnut Street, 19106), 1981. 160 pp., illus. $1.95 pb.

A handbook of principles and methods of interpretation for park interpreters that is applicable to historic sites.

Living History: "About Time"

"Living history is a medium of historical research, interpretation, and celebration that is absolutely right for our times. The medium has three characteristics that will, I believe, insure its historical significance as an effective way of 'doing' history.

Living history strives for what T. S. Eliot called 'felt-truth.' It challenges us to think *and* feel. To living historians, empathy is as important as understanding. . . . People today are not content to know just the bones of history; they want to sense its flesh and blood. . . .

The medium is also very presbyterian. Living history lies outside the boundary of established academic and public history. It thrives on independence. Each museum, each project, and each unit makes its own covenant with historical truth and determines the way it will carry on its dialogue with the past. This form of populist democracy breeds a tough-mindedness. . . .

Finally, living history rejects a linear view of the past. . . . Living historians point out that the history establishment has often failed to study, interpret, and experience the everyday reality of ordinary people in the past. . . . When asked why they are attempting to communicate with their counterparts in the past the living historians' quiet answer is: It's about time."

Jay Anderson, *Time Machines*

Time Machines: The World of Living History. Jay Anderson. Nashville: American Association for State and Local History, 1984. 217 pp., illus., append., index. $19.95 hb.

A three-part survey of living-history programs—at museums, as research and in reenactments. The book seeks to answer why people choose to "slip away from the modern world" and take up "time traveling." Among the programs and sites covered are Greenfield Village, Colonial Williamsburg, Stockholm's Skansen, Canada's Fortress of Louisbourg, the *Kon-Tiki, Mayflower II* and reenactments of various wars.

"Viewpoint: Living History, Clio or Cliopatra," Frank Barnes. *History News,* September 1974. American Association for State and Local History.

Urges historic sites to interpret the past honestly, rather than cater to tourists' nostalgia or present the past as an artificially happy world without pain, death, hard work, discrimination and disappointment.

"Living Museums of Everyman's History," Cary Carson. *Harvard Magazine,* July–August 1981.

Explores the "democratized" interpretation of the past through artifacts of ordinary people.

Contact

Living History Magazine
P.O. Box 2309
Reston, Va. 22090

Walter Gropius House (1937), Lincoln, Mass., a modern landmark left to the Society for the Preservation of New England Antiquities and recently opened as one of its historic houses. (Damora, SPNEA)

Stewardship: Museum Management

Ideally, custodians of historic resources should operate primarily as stewards, charged with passing on unimpaired to future generations the irreplaceable evidences of past generations that temporarily have been entrusted to their care. All planning for development, interpretation and public use and all management activities should be founded on the concept of stewardship, should scrupulously respect the integrity of historic resources and place their preservation above all other purposes.

Robert M. Utley, "A Preservation Ideal." *Historic Preservation*, April–June 1976.

"Stewardship means, literally, taking care of someone else's property. For SPNEA that translates into something almost poetic. The concept is that historic houses are really the property of the public and of posterity, regardless of who happens to own them legally. This means that the legal owners join hands with SPNEA in a contract of perpetual care, so that both parties act as stewards on behalf of the future—the ultimate owner."

Robert Campbell, "Making Properties Pay Their Way." *Historic Preservation*, January–February 1982.

An Annotated Bibliography for the Development and Operation of Historic Sites. Historic Sites Committee. Washington, D.C.: American Association of Museums, 1982. 48 pp. $3 pb.

Listings compiled to promote the use of professional standards in operating historic sites, history museums and historical agencies. Topics covered are site development and planning, structures and objects, interpretation, visitor and support services, professional standards and practices, management, bibliographies, organizations and legislation.

Introduction to Museum Work. G. Ellis Burcaw. Nashville: American Association for State and Local History, 1975. 209 pp., illus., biblio., index. $10.75 pb.

A textbook covering basic theory and practice of collections, interpretation and the role of museums in society—including definitions, exhibitions, education programs, building design, security, maintenance, professional attitudes and standards.

The Management of Small History Museums. Carl E. Guthe. 1959. 2nd ed. Nashville: American Association for State and Local History, 1964. 80 pp. $5.50 pb.

Provides advice on museum definition and purpose, organizational patterns, policy structure, governing bodies, physical facilities and funding.

Manual for Museums. Ralph H. Lewis. Washington, D.C.: National Park Service, U.S. Department of the Interior, 1976. 425 pp., illus., biblio., appends., index.

A basic reference based on museums in national parks, it covers furnished historic sites, acquisition principles, caring for collections, exhibits, research, accessioning, cataloging and related techniques.

Professional Standards for Museum Accreditation. H. J. Swinney, ed. Washington, D.C.: American Association of Museums, 1978. 79 pp. $6.50 pb.

A handbook on AAM accreditation and a guide to the standards of the museum profession.

Administration. Frederick L. Rath, Jr., and Merrilyn Rogers O'Connell, eds. Vol. 5, *A Bibliography on Historical Organization Practices.* Nashville: American Association for State and Local History, 1980. 237 pp., index. $15.95 hb.

Readings for staff and board members of museums and related cultural institutions on management, governing boards, standards and ethics, personnel and employment practices, volunteers, guides, membership development, fund raising, tax, law, insurance, maintenance, security, printing and publishing, public relations, collections policies and library and archives management.

Museum Accounting Handbook. William H. Daughtrey, Jr., and Malvern J. Gross, Jr. Washington, D.C.: American Association of Museums, 1978. 158 pp., illus., biblio., index. $16 pb.

Suggested approaches for nonaccountants to budgeting, accounting policies and reporting procedures, with sample forms and financial statements.

Museums and the Law. Marilyn Phelan. Nashville: American Association for State and Local History, 1982. 298 pp., biblio., appends., index. $22 hb.

A handbook for museum directors on a range of management issues: organizational structure, IRS regulations, legal liability of museums, rights of artists, museum acquisitions, employee relations and duties of museum officials. With numerous sample documents.

Personnel Policies for Museums: A Handbook for Management. Ronald L. Miller. Washington, D.C.: American Association of Museums, 1980. 164 pp., biblio. $11.50 pb.

Describes how to establish, implement and revise personnel policies for all sizes and types of museums.

Documentation of Collections. Rosemary S. Reese, comp. Vol. 4, *A Bibliography on Historical Organization Practices.* Frederick L. Rath, Jr., and Merrilyn Rogers O'Connell, eds. Nashville: American Association for State and Local History, 1979. 233 pp., index. $13.50 hb.

Listings on artifacts, decorative arts, fine arts and folk arts to aid curators and registrars in accessioning and cataloging.

Care and Conservation of Collections. Rosemary S. Reese, comp. Vol. 2, *A Bibliography on Historical Organization Practices.* Frederick L. Rath, Jr., and Merrilyn Rogers O'Connell, eds. Nashville: American Association for State and Local History, 1977. 115 pp., index. $11 hb.

Covers care of museum collections—paintings, documents, books, photographs and other artifacts, plus background information on conservation laboratories, principles of conservation and training.

Museum Registration Methods. Dorothy H. Dudley, Irma Bezold Wilkinson et al. 3rd ed. rev. Washington, D.C.: American Association of Museums, 1979. 437 pp., illus., gloss., biblio. $26.50 hb, $21 pb.

Handbook for all museums on registration procedures, storage and care of objects, packing, shipping, loans, insurance and computerization of records, with sample forms.

Registration Methods for the Small Museum. Daniel B. Reibel. Nashville: American Association for State and Local History, 1978. 160 pp., illus. $9.95 pb.

Outlines registration and record-keeping systems conforming to professional standards, with detailed instructions accompanying sample registrars' manuals and other necessary forms that can be copied or adapted.

Museum Cataloging in the Computer Age. Robert G. Chenhall. Nashville: American Association for State and Local History, 1975. 269 pp., illus.

Covers computer use in collection management and documentation, data processing principles, record forms, computer input and some systems in use.

The Care of Antiques and Historical Collections. A. Bruce MacLeish. 1972. Rev. ed. Nashville: American Association for State and Local History, 1985. 246 pp., illus., index. $14.95 pb.

Covering antiques in private collections as well as museums, emphasizes preventive maintenance and conservation, with chapters dealing with specific objects.

Exhibits for the Small Museum: A Handbook. Arminta Neal. Nashville: American Association for State and Local History, 1976. 181 pp., illus. $11 pb.

Gives practical advice on effective design, lighting, labeling, arrangement of exhibits.

Good Show! A Practical Guide for Temporary Exhibitions. Lothar P. Witteborg. Washington, D.C.: Smithsonian Traveling Exhibition Service (P.O. Box 1949, 20013), 1981. 172 pp., illus., biblio., append., index. $18.95 spiral bound.

A new practical guide "for the people behind the scenes of exhibit installation," designed to be carried along to the hardware store and lumberyard.

Planning Exhibits: From Concept to Opening. Charles L. Baker. Nashville: American Association for State and Local History, 1981. Technical Leaflet 137. 8 pp., biblio. $2 pb.

A primer on planning, scheduling, development and production, with checklists.

Technical Leaflet Series. Nashville: American Association for State and Local History. 8 pp. (average). $2 pb each.

More than 100 brief how-to-do-it guides on topics such as museum exhibits, interpretation, administration and conservation of collections and related programs. A list is available.

Regional Conservation Centers
Regional centers have been established as alliances of member museums to examine, care for and treat objects in the members' collections—paintings, works of art on paper, furniture and other decorative objects—and to conduct research into new conservation techniques. Their outreach services to nonmembers vary but may include inspection and referrals.

Balboa Art Conservation Center
P.O. Box 3755
San Diego, Calif. 92103

Center for Conservation
and Technical Studies
Fogg Art Museum
Harvard University
32 Quincy Street
Cambridge, Mass. 02138

Conservation Laboratory
University Museum
33rd and Spruce Streets
Philadelphia, Pa. 19104

Division for Historic
Preservation
New York State Parks,
Recreation and Historic
Preservation
Peebles Island
Waterford, N.Y. 12188

Intermuseum Laboratory
Allen Art Building
Oberlin, Ohio 44074

Northeast Document
Conservation Center
24 School Street
Andover, Mass. 01810

Pacific Regional Conservation
Center
Bishop Museum
P.O. Box 19000-A
1525 Bernice Street
Honolulu, Hawaii 96817

Rocky Mountain Regional
Conservation Center
University of Denver
2420 South University
Boulevard
Denver, Colo. 80208

Williamstown Regional Art
Conservation Center
Clark Art Institute
225 South Street
Williamstown, Mass. 01267

Upper Midwest Conservation
Association
c/o Minneapolis Institute of Arts
2400 Third Avenue South
Minneapolis, Minn. 55404

Contacts
National Institute for the Conservation of Cultural Property
c/o Smithsonian Institution
Arts and Industries Building
Room 2225
Washington, D.C. 20560

Serves as a national forum for conservation interests, gathers information, develops conservation policies and has published a list of treatment facilities. It represents 60 preservation, museum and art conservation groups and is preparing proposals for a national institute for conservation.

American Institute for
Conservation of Historic and
Artistic Works
3545 Williamsburg Lane, N.W.
Washington, D.C. 20008

Professional organization for persons engaged in the preservation and restoration of historic and artistic works. Facilitates an exchange of information and improved methods.

Museum Funding
Funding Sources and Technical Assistance for Museums and Historical Agencies: A Guide to Public Programs. Hedy A. Hartman, comp. Nashville: American Association for State and Local History, 1979. 144 pp. $11 pb.

A guide for history, art and science museums and other historical organizations describing 103 programs of federal and regional agencies and national organizations.

Institute of Museum Services
1100 Pennsylvania Avenue, N.W.
Room 510
Washington, D.C. 20506

One of the few sources providing funds for general operating expenses, IMS awarded $15.5 million in 530 grants in 1984. Of this, 24.9 percent of the general operating support funds went to history museums and 7 percent to historic house museums. General operating support funds are used for basic services such as salaries, utilities, maintenance, education and outreach programs.

National Museum Act Program
Smithsonian Institution
Arts and Industries Building
Room 3465
Washington, D.C. 20560

Supports studies of critical museum problems and professional museum training. Recipient projects "must be of substantial value to the museum profession as a whole; they must contribute to the improvement of museum methods and practices, or to the professional growth of individuals entering or working in the museum field." Museum conservation is given major attention.

National Endowment for
the Arts
Museum Program
1100 Pennsylvania Avenue, N.W.
Washington, D.C. 20506

Among its categories that apply to historic sites are Wider Availability of Museums, Cooperative Programs, Special Exhibitions, Utilization of Museum Collections, Catalogues, Conservation, Collection Maintenance, Fellowships for Museum Professionals and Museum Purchase Plan.

National Endowment for
the Humanities
Division of Public Programs
Museums and Historical
Organizations Program
1100 Pennsylvania Avenue, N.W.
Washington, D.C. 20506

Supports a variety of museum-related activities under the Historic Sites category, which makes grants to plan interpretive projects, interpretive catalogs and interpretive exhibitions for the general public.

Consultant Service
American Association for
State and Local History
708 Berry Road
Nashville, Tenn. 37204

Provided under the National Museum Act to assist museums needing long-range planning and specific advice on a broad range of topics, such as exhibit planning, care and conservation of collections, public relations and marketing. Grants cover consultant fees and partial expenses.

Digging Deeper: Archeology for Historic Sites

It is important not to consider archeology as only prehistory, and not to think that archeological data exist only under the ground.

Anne Derry et al., *Guidelines for Local Surveys: A Basis for Preservation Planning.* Washington, D.C.: National Register of Historic Places, 1977.

The great majority of the historical sites that have been archaeologically explored in any depth have received attention not for the purpose of studying the past through its artifacts but as a prelude for restoration or reconstruction into a shrine, an exhibit, a tourist attraction. But . . . the time has come to think of American historical sites as being worthy of excavation simply to obtain information. . . .

There is no denying that the fruits of archaeology can be very bitter. . . . in some cases supposed mansions were found to have been mere cottages. . . . In short, archaeology is no respecter of persons, conventions, or traditions.

Ivor Noël-Hume, *Historical Archaeology*

"In recent years there has been a growing realization . . . that documentary information alone is sometimes inadequate. Often it is scanty and non-specific. And this lack of hard evidence can raise some very basic and important questions about the use and occupancy of a site. . . . When was a house built? Where were the outbuildings located? How did the inhabitants live?

With available written records not revealing the complete answer to these types of inquiries, a logical next step would be to seek visual evidence which might fill in the gaps. Archeological investigations at the site can yield just such artifacts."

Beth Anne Bower, "Historical Archeology Investigations: A Methodology for Developing Insights into Colonial/Early American Life." *Technology and Conservation,* Fall 1977.

"Culture is highly perishable, and therefore cannot be excavated. No one has ever dug up a political system, a language, a set of religious beliefs, or a people's attitude toward their ancestors. Yet such things . . . affect what the archaeologist does recover. The patterning which the archaeologist perceives in his material is a reflection of the patterning of the culture which produced it. Pots, arrowheads, house floors and axes are the products of culture, not culture in themselves, but they are linked to culture in a systematic manner. It is the archaeologist's task to discover how cultural behavior is shown in its products."

James Deetz, *Invitation to Archaeology*

Archeological work to uncover the foundations of William Penn's Pennsbury Manor, Pa., c. 1932. (Pennsylvania Historical and Museum Commission)

Excavations of the site of Raleigh Tavern, Williamsburg, 1929, a prelude to its reconstruction in 1932. (Colonial Williamsburg Foundation)

Site of the Governor's Palace, Williamsburg, c. 1931, excavated to guide the reconstruction in 1934. (Colonial Williamsburg Foundation)

The Language of Archeology

above-ground archeology. The study of a building or other visible artifact by careful scrutiny, as distinct from conventional archeology's focus beneath the surface of the ground.

archeology. The study of past human lifeways through evidence found in the ground.

artifact. An object made in whole or modified in part by human activity, constituting one form of archeological data.

conservation archeology. A field of archeology concerned with limiting excavations to an absolute minimum consistent with research objectives and with the preservation of archeological sites for future scientific investigation.

historical archeology. The study of the cultural remains of literate societies, as distinct from prehistoric archeology. American historical archeology deals with excavated material as well as with above-ground resources such as buildings, pottery, weapons, tools, glassware, cutlery and textiles.

Humpty Dumpty archeology. Archeology conducted with the primary purpose of reconstruction, so named because it tries to find the pieces of the past and put them back together again.

landscape archeology. A branch of archeology that concentrates on vegetative evidence and other signs of human occupancy (such as boundary lines, earth mounding, changes in ground contours, buildings and their siting and the outlines of paths and roads) as indicators of buried features and clues to original land use.

prehistoric archeology. The scientific study of human lifeways and cultures that existed before recorded history.

public archeology. Archeological programs and projects funded by governments.

salvage archeology. Rescue of archeological materials and data threatened by damage or destruction; also called "rescue archeology."

underwater archeology. The scientific investigation of submerged or inundated cultural properties such as drowned prehistoric or historic sites or historic shipwrecks.

Adapted from *Landmark Words: A Glossary for Preserving the Built Environment.* National Trust for Historic Preservation. Forthcoming.

Visitors viewing archeological work at Jamestown, Va., in the 1930s. (NPS)

Archeology and Preservation. Rex Wilson. Information Series, National Trust for Historic Preservation. Washington, D.C.: Preservation Press, 1980. 20 pp., biblio. $2 pb.

An overview of archeology's relationship to preservation, presenting basic archeological concepts and practices, planning considerations, organizations, legislation and publications.

Beginner's Guide to Archaeology. Louis A. Brennan. New York: Dell, 1979. 379 pp., illus.

Introduces basic techniques such as site location, exposing features, dating, report writing, with a listing of key sites and museums.

The Amateur Archaeologist's Handbook. Maurice Robbins and Mary B. Irving. 1965. 3rd ed. New York: Harper and Row, 1981. 304 pp., illus., appends., biblio., index. $13.95 hb.

A reference on techniques and methods for the amateur, with a new brief chapter on historical archeology.

Fundamentals of Archaeology. Robert J. Sharer and Wendy Ashmore. Menlo Park, Calif.: Benjamin/Cummings, 1979. 636 pp., illus., gloss., biblio., index. $24.95 hb.

A textbook surveying the techniques, methods and theoretical frameworks of contemporary prehistoric archeology.

Field Methods in Archaeology. Thomas R. Hester, Robert F. Heizer and John A. Graham. 6th ed. Palo Alto, Calif.: Mayfield Publishing (285 Hamilton Avenue, 94301), 1975. 408 pp., illus., biblio., index.

Provides a worldwide review of methods used in archeological field research and describes up-to-date procedures.

Prehistoric Archeology: A Brief Introduction. Frank Hole and Robert F. Heizer. 1977. 2nd ed. New York: Holt, Rinehart and Winston, 1982. 477 pp., illus., biblio., gloss., index. $19.95 hb.

A textbook presenting the basis for and history of archeology, basic concepts in prehistory that apply to most American archeology regardless of the time period, techniques and analysis, dating reconstruction, settlement patterns and social and cultural systems.

Prehistory of North America. Jesse D. Jennings. 2nd ed. New York: McGraw-Hill, 1974. 436 pp., illus.

Surveys archeological and cultural developments region by region from the earliest times to the present and incorporates recent discoveries and theoretical advances.

An Introduction to American Archeology. Vol. I: *North and Middle America.* Gordon R. Willey. Englewood Cliffs, N.J.: Prentice-Hall, 1966. 530 pp., illus. $37.95 hb.

Interprets the beginnings of native cultures and the rise of complex civilizations in the New World based on the findings of archeologists.

Elusive Treasure: The Story of Early Archaeologists in the Americas. Brian Fagan. New York: Scribner's, 1977. 369 pp., illus., biblio.

Traces the development of archeology in North and Central America, concentrating on specific discoveries while highlighting the social forces that related exploration to evolving European attitudes toward American Indians.

Introducing Archeology

Invitation to Archaeology. James Deetz. Garden City, N.Y.: Natural History Press, 1967. 150 pp., illus., append., biblio., index. $3.95 pb.

A brief and readable introduction for the layperson to present-day archeology, explaining the field in broad terms—dating, analysis of form, space and time, context, function, structure and behavior—as well as its place among the social sciences.

Discover Archaeology: An Introduction to the Tools and Techniques of Archaeological Fieldwork. George Sullivan, ed. 1980. Reprint. New York: Penguin, 1981. 288 pp., append., gloss., index. $5.95 pb.

Includes a chapter on historical archeology with lengthy listings of sources of information, including organizations.

Historical Archeology

Sponsors of archaeological research . . . are usually interested in:

1. The validation of a historic site in relation to documents

2. The discovery of architectural features

3. The determination of the occupation sequence of the site

4. The determination of the temporal occupation of the site

5. The recovery and preservation of artifacts associated with the occupation of the site

6. The development of the site as a historical exhibit.

The total excavation of a site is not always necessary to obtain important information. Architectural details, such as walkways, doorways, outbuildings and drainage systems, and landscaping can be determined by excavating around standing structures, as well as by examining subsurface remains of ruins.

Stanley South, "The Role of the Archeologist in the Conservation-Preservation Process." In *Preservation and Conservation: Principles and Practices.* Washington, D.C.: Preservation Press, 1976.

"Ghost" of Ben Franklin's Philadelphia house based on available archeological evidence (1976, Venturi and Rauch). (Carleton Knight III)

Historical Archaeology: A Comprehensive Guide for Both Amateurs and Professionals to the Techniques and Methods of Excavating Historical Sites. Ivor Noël-Hume. New York: Knopf, 1969. 355 pp., illus., biblio. $16.95 hb.

An introduction to historical archeology, with extensive descriptions of excavations the author has directed as resident archeologist of Colonial Williamsburg. The bibliography gives sources to assist in the identification of various types of artifacts.

Historical Archaeology: A Guide to Substantive and Theoretical Contributions. Robert L. Schuyler, ed. Farmingdale, N.Y.: Baywood Publishing (120 Marine Street, 11735), 1978. 286 pp., illus., biblio. $18 pb.

A series of essays by eminent historical archeologists exploring the emergence of the field as a new discipline and highlighting numerous projects as well as theoretical positions and future trends, with case studies.

Archaeological Perspectives on Ethnicity in America: Afro-American and Asian American Culture History. Robert L. Schuyler, ed. Farmingdale, N.Y.: Baywood Publishing, 1980. 160 pp., illus. $7.95 pb.

A compilation of papers on projects in black and Asian American archeology, with annotated bibliographies on black and Asian American culture.

Archaeology of Urban America: The Search for Pattern and Process. Roy S. Dickens, Jr., ed. New York: Academic Press, 1982. Studies in Historical Archaeology. 485 pp., illus., index. $39.50 hb.

Essays on topics such as methods, bioarcheology and artifact analysis, with examples from Paterson, N.J., Atlanta, Middletown, Conn., and other sites.

"Urban Archaeology in America," Robert L. Schuyler, ed. *North American Archaeologist,* vol. 3, no. 2, 1982. 92 pp., biblio. Baywood Publishing.

A special issue with essays on archeology in cities spanning the entire range of American history. Areas covered include St. Augustine, Detroit, Sacramento and Harvard Yard.

Above-ground Archeology

"Buildings are no more than large artifacts—things constructed by our predecessors as a part of their way of life. If . . . we are to understand and conserve the essence of those past lifeways so that present and future generations may experience and benefit from them, more must be preserved than empty shells. Life must be put into those buildings by gaining appreciation of how they came to be, what influences determined their form, how they were used and what other artifacts complemented them, making them into living viable entities."

Charles R. McGimsey III, "Why Archeology?" *Preservation News,* August 1979.

"Material culture may be the most objective source of information we have concerning America's past. It certainly is the most immediate. When an archaeologist carefully removes the earth from the jumbled artifacts at the bottom of a trash pit, he or she is the first person to confront those objects since they were placed there centuries before. . . .

It is terribly important that the 'small things forgotten' be remembered. . . . The written document has its proper and important place, but there is also a time when we should set aside our perusal of diaries, court records, and inventories, and listen to another voice.

Don't read what we have written; look at what we have done."

James Deetz, *In Small Things Forgotten*

In Small Things Forgotten: The Archeology of Early American Life. James Deetz. Garden City, N.Y.: Anchor Press, Doubleday, 1977. 184 pp., illus. $4.95 pb.

An eloquent statement of the value of the artifacts left behind by early Americans. Deetz presents his case for digging into such things as old houses, ceramics, furniture, refuse dumps, gravestones and other artifacts for discerning cultural patterns. The book also provides a look at Parting Ways, a settlement of freed slaves near Plymouth, Mass.

Artifacts and the American Past. Thomas J. Schlereth. Nashville: American Association for State and Local History, 1981. 294 pp., illus., appends., biblio., index. $15.95 hb.

Essays supporting the author's view that "artifacts are cultural statements, whether the artifact is a steriography view, a historical house interior, an Osage orange hedge-row, a mail-order catalog, or a White Tower restaurant."

Material Culture Studies in America. Thomas J. Schlereth, ed. Nashville: American Association for State and Local History, 1982. 435 pp., illus., biblio., index. $16 pb.

A related compilation of essays examining various artifacts and their places in the methodology of material culture.

A Guide to Artifacts of Colonial America. Ivor Noël-Hume. New York: Knopf, 1970. 348 pp., illus., index. $20.

An alphabetical guide from armor to wig curlers, based on Noël-Hume's work conducted at Colonial Williamsburg to interpret the life and activities of the early town.

Underwater Archeology

"Wrecks can provide archeological data unparalleled on any terrestrial site. They are, in effect, time capsules torn from the pages of history. Unlike the trash that the archeologist must make the most from on land, wrecked ships contain cargoes of complete objects, all irrefutably associated and possessing an unimpeachable *terminus ante quem.*"

Ivor Noël-Hume, *Historical Archeology*

A History of Seafaring Based on Underwater Archaeology. George F. Bass, ed. New York: Walker, 1972. 320 pp., illus., biblio., gloss.

A significant contribution to the history of underwater archaeology.

Underwater Archaeology: Guidelines for the Amateur Explorer. Paul J. Scudiere. Nashville: American Association for State and Local History, 1972. Technical Leaflet 61. 8 pp., illus., biblio. $2 pb.

Overview on preparation, surveying the area, retrieval, preservation and identification procedures.

The Monitor: Its Meaning and Future. Washington, D.C.: Preservation Press, 1978. 132 pp. $6.50 pb.

Experts on the U.S.S. *Monitor* debate what should be done with this underwater landmark.

Well at Kingsmill Plantation exposed by river erosion.

Remains of the 18th-century Kingsmill Plantation mansion house near Williamsburg, excavated by the Virginia Research Center for Archaeology. (Virginia Historic Landmarks Commission)

Conservation Archeology

Conservation archaeology, contract archaeology, cultural resource management, emergency, *and* salvage *are all terms to designate the archaeology, or the philosophy of archaeology, that pertains to work necessary because of planned modification of the earth's surface by construction activity.*

Preface, *Conservation Archaeology*

"A conservation approach to archaeology is very different from the exploitation of archaeological sites that has traditionally been archaeology's stock in trade. Conservation by no means forbids archaeologists from investigating and learning from the remnants of the past, but it does require thinking before digging—about whether digging is necessary, whether there is not some other, less destructive or more productive way to learn."

Thomas F. King, Introduction. *A Field Guide to Conservation Archaeology in North America*

A Field Guide to Conservation Archeology in North America. Georgess McHargue and Michael Roberts. Philadelphia: Lippincott, 1977. 319 pp., illus., appends., gloss., biblio., index. $9.95 hb, $4.95 pb.

An important book for the avocational archeologist based on the basic premise that "archeological sites must be regarded as a resource that, like oil, uranium or redwood trees, must be used prudently lest the supply run out forever." The book is designed to teach amateurs everything they need to know to assist in the process of locating, recording, cataloging and preserving sites.

Conservation Archaeology: A Guide for Cultural Resource Management Studies. Michael B. Schiffer and George J. Gumerman, eds. New York: Academic Press, 1977. 516 pp., index. $43 hb.

Contributions by leading archeologists present an ethic for professionals engaged in contract conservation work. Topics include cultural resource management, preparing environmental impact statements, research strategies, survey data, forecasting and mitigating adverse impacts, with project examples.

Rescue Archeology: Papers from the First New World Conference on Rescue Archeology. Rex L. Wilson and Gloria Loyola, eds. Government of Ecuador, Organization of American States and National Trust for Historic Preservation. Washington, D.C.: Preservation Press, 1982. 272 pp. $14.95 pb. Spanish edition available from OAS.

Provides an overview of key issues such as principles of rescue archeology, economics and legislation affecting the field, professional practices and research advances. Identifies activities affecting archeological resources (public works construction, highways, development, etc.) and recommends public and private actions.

Remote Sensing: A Handbook for Archeologists and Cultural Resource Managers. Thomas Lyons and Thomas Eugene Avery. Washington, D.C.: Cultural Resources Management Division, National Park Service, U.S. Department of the Interior, 1977. 117 pp., illus., biblio., gloss., index. $6 pb. GPO stock no. 024–005–00688–5.

A guide to using aerial photography and related remote surveying methods, based on research at Chaco Canyon. Supplements also have been published.

Locally made 17th-century clay pipe with a ship motif found at Kingsmill Plantation.

Archeological dig in downtown Baltimore near the Inner Harbor area. (Baltimore Center for Urban Archaeology)

Public Archeology

There is no such thing as "private archeology." We are none of us born in a vacuum. We all are products and recipients of thousands of years of biological and cultural history. . . . Knowledge of this past, just as knowledge about our environment, is essential to our survival, and the right to that knowledge is and must be considered a human birthright. Archeology, the recovery and study of the past, thus is a proper concern of everyone. It follows that no individual may act in a manner such that the public right to knowledge of the past is unduly endangered or destroyed.

Charles R. McGimsey III, *Public Archeology*

"It must be acknowledged that archeological sites have not received as much attention in National Register programs as other kinds of cultural property. Several reasons for this are apparent. The most obvious is money. It costs more to record a site that you have to look for than it does one that stands up and looks back at you."

Robert M. Utley. Address to Society for Historical Archaeology, 1973.

Federal Legislation and Policies Affecting Archeology

Antiquities Act of 1906

Historic Sites Act of 1935

Reservoir Salvage Act of 1960

National Historic Preservation Act of 1966

National Environmental Policy Act of 1969

Executive Order 11593, "Protection and Enhancement of Cultural Property" (1971)

Archeological and Historic Preservation Act of 1974

Archeological Resources Protection Act of 1979

Archeological sites, if they have "yielded, or may be likely to yield, information important in prehistory or history," may be afforded the same protection from federal or federally funded or licensed undertakings as historic properties. If such a site is listed in the National Register of Historic Places or is eligible for inclusion, the Advisory Council on Historic Preservation must determine if any such undertaking will have an adverse effect on that site. For more information, contact your state historic preservation office or the National Park Service.

Anthropology in Historic Preservation: Caring for Culture's Clutter. Thomas F. King, Patricia Parker Hickman and Gary Berg. New York: Academic Press, 1977. 344 pp., biblio., appends., index. $37.50 hb.

Suggests ways in which archeologists can work more effectively in preservation, defining the relationships of the professions and summarizing preservation in America, protective regulations and preservation surveys as a means of safeguarding archeological sites.

Treatment of Archeological Properties: A Handbook. Thomas F. King. Washington, D.C.: Advisory Council on Historic Preservation, 1982. 39 pp. Free.

Designed to assist federal agencies, state historic preservation offices and others affected by the council's regulations in conducting archeological programs and implementing its archeological recommendations.

The Archeological Survey: Methods and Uses. Thomas F. King. Washington, D.C.: National Park Service, U.S. Department of the Interior, 1978. Cultural Resources Management Series. 134 pp., illus., append. $13. PB 276775/AS. Available from National Technical Information Service, 5285 Port Royal Road, Springfield, Va. 22161.

Manual addressed to nonarcheologists as well as professionals whose management responsibilities include archeological properties. Presents the development of an archeological record in a hypothetical locality and survey efforts to document it.

Public Archaeology. Charles R. McGimsey III. New York: Academic Press, 1972. 282 pp., append. $39.50 hb.

Describes state support and programs and summarizes federal support for archeology. An appendix gives state-by-state statutes relating to archeology.

Are Agencies Doing Enough or Too Much for Archeological Preservation? Report to the Chairman, Committee on Interior and Insular Affairs, House of Representatives. Comptroller General of the United States. Washington, D.C.: U.S. General Accounting Office (Document Handling and Information Services Facility, P.O. Box 6015, Gaithersburg, Md. 20877), 1981. 102 pp. No. CED 81–61. Free.

"The National Archeology Program, which costs about $100 million a year, is not working well," charges this study of federal programs to identify, protect and recover archeological resources. It urges stronger leadership from the Interior Department in establishing criteria for site significance, a more active role for state historic preservation offices and more critical review of data recovery plans by the Advisory Council on Historic Preservation.

The Management of Archeological Resources: The Airlie House Report. Charles R. McGimsey III and Hester A. Davis, eds. Washington, D.C.: Society for American Archaeology, 1977. 124 pp., gloss., appends. $3 pb.

A survey of key issues including law in archeology, cultural resource management, preparation of archeological reports, communicating with the public and project participants, Native Americans and certification of professionals.

Case Studies

Preservation Comes of Age: From Williamsburg to the National Trust, 1926–1949. Charles B. Hosmer, Jr. Charlottesville: University Press of Virginia, 1981. Published for the National Trust. 1,291 pp., illus., biblio., chron., index. 2 vols. $37.50 hb.

Describes the birth of historic sites archeology efforts during this period, with coverage of projects at Williamsburg, National Park Service sites, Wakefield (Washington's birthplace), Hopewell Village, Jamestown, La Purisima Mission and Stratford Hall.

Martin's Hundred: The Discovery of a Lost Colonial Virginia Settlement. Ivor Noël-Hume. 1979. New York: Dell, 1983. 366 pp., illus., append., biblio., index. $9.95 pb.

The story of the discovery and excavation of the lost English settlement of Martin's Hundred on the James River in Virginia, occupied 1618–21. This account of "sleuthing, suspense and feats of deduction" tells how the settlement's history was reconstructed through its archeology.

Williamsburg Archeological Series. Ivor Noël-Hume. Williamsburg, Va.: Colonial Williamsburg Foundation. $2.95 pb each.

An illustrated series detailing excavations and research at Williamsburg. Titles include *Archaeology and Wetherburn's Tavern.* 1969. 48 pp. *Digging for Carter's Grove.* 1974. 64 pp. *Discoveries in Martin's Hundred.* 1983.

Dublin Seminar for New England Folklife: Annual Proceedings 1977, New England Historical Archeology. Peter Benes, ed. Boston: Boston University, 1977. 159 pp., illus., biblio.

Archeological site reports and essays on historical archeology and the community, with a bibliography of New England historical archeology.

Historical Archaeology at Black Lucy's Garden, Andover, Massachusetts: Ceramics from the Site of a Nineteenth Century Afro-American. Vernon G. Baker. Andover, Mass.: Robert S. Peabody Foundation for Archaeology, 1978. 122 pp., illus. $8 pb.

One of the first attempts (in the 1940s) to devise cultural hypotheses about the late 18th- and early 19th-century American social system from the study of pottery.

Belle Grove Excavations. Tim O. Rockwell. Washington, D.C.: Preservation Press, 1973. 102 pp., appends., biblio. $2.75 pb.

Archeological report for the National Trust property near Middletown, Va. Includes an example of a contemporary inventory used to check both artifacts and the reconstruction of interiors.

Preliminary Excavations at Oatlands, Loudoun County, Va. Lynne G. Lewis. Washington, D.C.: Preservation Press, 1978. 80 pp., illus. $7 pb.

A report on investigations at the National Trust property near Leesburg, Va.

Drayton Hall: Preliminary Archeological Investigation at a Low Country Plantation. Lynne G. Lewis. Charlottesville: University Press of Virginia, 1978. Published for the National Trust. 217 pp., illus., gloss., biblio. $12.95 hb.

Excavations conducted at the National Trust's 18th-century property near Charleston, S.C., to aid in the interpretation and development of the property.

The Life and Death of a Family Farm: Archaeology, History and Landscape Change in Brighton, New York. David Howard Day. Rochester, N.Y.: Monroe Community College (1000 East Henrietta Road, 14623) and Monroe County Historian's Office, 1980. 32 pp., illus., biblio.

Report on the investigation of the recent past, a 19th-century family farm studied through archeology, history and ethnology.

Koster: Americans in Search of Their Prehistoric Past. Stuart Struever and Felicia Antonelli Holton. New York: New American Library, 1979. 282 pp., illus., append., biblio., index. $2.95 pb.

Story of the discovery and excavation of a significant find, an Illinois site first settled by Amerindians some 10,000 years ago, with detailed descriptions of the process.

Ancient Ruins of the Southwest: An Archaeological Guide. David Grant Noble. Flagstaff, Ariz.: Northland Press, 1981. 128 pp., illus., maps. $8.95 pb.

A guide presenting history and information on the sites' archeological investigations, arranged by tribe.

Ancient Cities of the Southwest. Buddy Mays. San Francisco: Chronicle Books, 1982. 120 pp., illus. $7.95.

A guide to more than 30 prehistoric ruins in Arizona, New Mexico, Utah and Colorado.

Those Who Came Before: Southwestern Archeology in the National Park System. Robert H. Lister and Florence C. Lister. Tucson: University of Arizona Press, 1984. 184 pp., illus., index. $32.50 hb.

Describes the archeological remains in 28 national parks and monuments, explaining the significance of the major ruins and the history of the research.

Contacts

Archeological Assistance Division
National Park Service
U.S. Department of the Interior
P.O. Box 37127
Washington, D.C. 20013-7127

Directs and coordinates a nationwide effort to protect significant prehistoric and historic remains threatened by federal construction projects, programs or activities. Activities include assisting federal agencies in meeting their preservation and data recovery responsibilities, developing national goals, providing permits for projects on federal lands and publishing archeological reports.

State Historic Preservation Offices

SHPOs have staff archeologists to aid in fulfilling their responsibilities to inventory state cultural resources, implement a state plan for cultural resource preservation and ensure compliance with state and federal preservation laws. SHPOs without professional archeologists often rely on the state archeologist, other state or federal agencies, independent contract archeologists or universities and museums. For a list, see Preservationists.

Society for American Archaeology
1511 K Street, N.W.
Suite 716
Washington, D.C. 20005

Oldest and largest of the American archeological organizations, it welcomes amateur and professional members.

Society for Historical Archaeology
P.O. Box 241
Glassboro, N.J. 08028

Addresses interests of members who limit their research and activities to sites of the historic period in North America.

American Society for Conservation Archeology
c/o Curtis F. Schaafsma
Museum of New Mexico
Box 2087
Santa Fe, N.M. 87504

Provides a forum for specialized archeological interests in conservation and cultural resource management.

Archaeological Conservancy
415 Orchard Drive
Santa Fe, N.M. 87501

National nonprofit organization established to protect endangered archeological sites on private lands through acquisition of properties or purchase of easements.

Society of Professional Archeologists
c/o Dena Dincauze
Department of Anthropology
University of Massachusetts
Amherst, Mass. 01003

Limits membership to professionals and is a source of professional aid in archeological projects.

Association for Field Archeology
Department of Archaeology
Boston University
745 Commonwealth Avenue
Boston, Mass. 02215

Promotes the interests of archeologists who conduct field work.

Archaeological Institute of America
53 Park Place
New York, N.Y. 10007

Emphasizes classical archeology of the Old and New Worlds.

National Trust for Historic Preservation
Office of Museum Services
1785 Massachusetts Avenue, N.W.
Washington, D.C. 20036

Administers archeological investigations at Trust properties.

Victim of a 1622 Indian uprising found in a grave at Carter's Grove, Va., the site of the 1619 Wolstenholme Towne. (Colonial Williamsburg Foundation)

Some of the throngs of people who crowd Baltimore's Harborplace on a summer weekend, enjoying the revitalized Inner Harbor area, adjacent historic sites, shops and restaurants. (The Rouse Company)

The Impact of Tourism

The revolutionary element in the preservation picture [of the early 20th century] was the arrival of the automobile. By 1926 the effects of this new mode of transportation were obvious. In 1914 the National Park System had recorded 240,000 visitors, but twelve years later that figure swelled to 2,315,000. . . . One other factor helped to intensify the effects of the automotive invasion—many families had more spare time than ever before.

> Charles B. Hosmer, Jr., Introduction. *Preservation Comes of Age*

"Modern man has been condemned to look elsewhere, everywhere, for his authenticity, to see if he can catch a glimpse of it reflected in the simplicity, poverty, chastity or purity of others."

> Dean MacCannell, *The Tourist: A New Theory of the Leisure Class.* New York: Schocken Books, 1976. 224 pp. $6.95 pb.

"Tourism for many is an attempt to re-establish cultural roots, for others a search for frontiers and new horizons. . . . Yet tourism is also a rather frivolous activity. As an escape from everyday life, it demands more entertainment and relaxation than education. And, since contacts are fleeting and limited, tourist perceptions and attitudes are often superficial and romantic, colored by nostalgia.

Tourists do not leave a city untouched by their presence. A classic instance of the observer affecting the observed, the tourist, through his demands, subtly and sometimes drastically changes the character of a place. Residents in most cities want tourists for economic reasons and will change their cities and lives to serve them. A tourist-oriented veneer begins to cover the old city like a film."

> Donald Appleyard, ed. *The Conservation of European Cities.* Cambridge: MIT Press, 1979.

"Using the cost-benefit model, an analogy can be made between heavy industry and the tourist industry. At first the more industry a community has the more benefits it will reap. After a certain point, however, the cost of industry, in terms of pollution, social problems, etc., becomes greater than the benefits derived from the industry. We contend that this formula inevitably applies to tourism."

> Frances Edmunds, "Controlling Tourism Impact." *Livability Digest,* Fall 1981.

"In the flush of youthful success, arts advocates and preservationists may sometimes have looked at tourists as sugar daddies and at tourism as a panacea for solving the ever-present problem of justifying public and philanthropic expenditures on the arts and design. But this rosy glow has faded. . . . Indeed, in many cases the impact of tourism has been perceived as so serious a threat that communities are getting ready to close the door on it altogether."

> Carole Rifkind, "The Difficult Issues." *Livability Digest,* Fall 1981.

"Tourism and Communities: Process, Problems and Solutions," Carole Rifkind, ed. *Livability Digest,* Fall 1981. 48 pp. $5. Partners for Livable Places, 1429 21st Street, N.W., Washington, D.C. 20036.

A special issue compiling case studies, essays and papers that outline the tourism dilemma and approaches to its resolution.

"Historic Preservation, Tourism and Leisure," Charles B. Hosmer, Jr., et al. *Monumentum,* vol. XIII. Terry B. Morton, ed. Washington, D.C.: US/ICOMOS, 1976. 128 pp., illus. $10 pb.

A chronology of the linked development of preservation and tourism, with an evaluation of their impact on American society.

Measuring Historic Preservation's Impact on Tourism: A Study of California and Other States. Paula Huntley and Hisashi B. Sugaya. Washington, D.C.: National Trust for Historic Preservation, 1984. 57 pp., biblio., appends. $5 pb.

Demonstrates a direct link between the state's lucrative tourism industry and its heritage resources plus the future potential to be realized. An appendix includes heritage tourism information from other states.

"Tourism: An Asset . . . or a Liability?" Anthony C. Wood. *Historic Preservation,* May–June 1979.

Do we preserve sites to promote tourism—or use tourism to support the preservation of important sites? A brief consideration of the problem of inviting nonresidents to share historic places—congestion, parking, displacement of existing businesses, commercialization, homogenization.

"Tourism and Conservation: A Bibliography." Carole Rifkind. Washington, D.C.: Partners for Livable Places, 1981. 11 pp.

A comprehensive listing of publications that relate tourism development to issues of historic preservation and cultural conservation.

Tourism: The Good, the Bad, and the Ugly. John E. Rosenow and Gerreld L. Pulsipher. Lincoln, Neb.: Century Three Press (304 South 13th Street, 68508), 1980. 264 pp., illus., index. $17.95 hb.

A preservation-oriented guide to a new attitude toward tourism planning that would seek to preserve the sense of place of communities, cities and special sites such as parks. Explores the limits of tourism, marketing, energy considerations and the future, and includes a case study of St. George, Utah.

"Cultural Tourism and Industrial Cities," Carole Rifkind, Jeanne V. Beekhuis and James Rovelstad. *Environmental Comment,* January 1981.

Essays contend that "gritty cities" can succeed as tourist destinations with careful planning that includes the restoration and promotion of historical and cultural amenities as the core of a comprehensive approach to economic development, preservation and adaptive use.

"Tourism: Managing Regional Assets," Carole Rifkind, Thomas Martin and Clare Gunn. *Environmental Comment,* December 1981. Urban Land Institute, 1090 Vermont Avenue, N.W., Washington, D.C. 20005.

Articles highlight planning, design issues and economic considerations needed to guide sensitive development in historic communities such as seaports.

Tourism Planning. Clare A. Gunn. New York: Crane, Russak, 1979. 378 pp., maps, charts, index. $19.50 hb.

A textbook by a landscape architect that highlights opportunities to engage in regional strategic planning to minimize the negative and enhance the positive environmental aspects of pleasure travel.

Tourism and Urban Regeneration: Some Lessons From American Cities. Steve Beioley. London: English Tourist Board (4 Grosvenor Gardens, SW1 0DU), 1981. 28 pp., illus.

From Portland, Maine, to Alexandria, Va., 10 case studies illuminate how tourism development relates to overall economic development in current American planning.

Tourist Traffic in Small Historic Cities: Analysis, Strategies and Recommendations. Roger F. Teal, Edward W. Wood, Jr., and William Loudoun. Washington, D.C.: U.S. Department of Transportation, 1976. Final Report (PB 269492/AS). 317 pp., illus. $25 pb. Executive Summary (PB 261931/AS). 23 pp., illus. $7 pb. Available from National Technical Information Service, 5285 Port Royal Road, Springfield, Va. 22161.

Five small cities provide case study material that suggests methods to deal with the impact of tourist automobile traffic. The authors emphasize the importance of local initiative in controlling tourism and suggest the need for more attention to tourism's state, regional and national significance.

The Economic Impacts of Recreation and Tourism: A Selective Bibliography. William D. Cahill and Charles A. Neale. Monticello, Ill.: Vance Bibliographies, 1979. 16 pp. P–356. $2 pb.

Listings of reports, papers, scholarly journals and books on the subject, featuring many case studies.

Preservation Pays: Tourism and the Economic Benefits of Conserving Historic Buildings. Marcus Binney and Max Hanna. London: SAVE Britain's Heritage (6A Bedford Square, WC1B 3RA), 1978. 152 pb., illus., appends.

An account of how Britain's historic buildings are recognized and understood as a major economic resource and an irreplaceable capital asset.

In the Wake of the Tourist: Managing Special Places in Eight Countries. Fred P. Bosselman. Washington, D.C.: Conservation Foundation, 1978. 278 pp., illus., biblio. $15 hb.

Provides an overview and useful insights into tourism development issues in places such as Jerusalem, Cancun, the Cote d'Azur, English and Dutch countrysides and seaside communities, and Australia.

Tourism and Heritage Conservation Conference, Bangkok, Thailand, November, 1979. Michael Tratner, ed. San Francisco: Pacific Area Travel Association, 1980. 70 pp., illus.

Includes an essay on tourism and preservation in the United States.

The Impact of Tourism on the Environment. Paris: Organization for Economic Co-operation and Development, 1980. 150 pp., biblio. Available from OECD Publications and Information Center, 1750 Pennsylvania Avenue, N.W., Suite 1207, Washington, D.C. 20006.

A report with recommendations on the economic and environmental effects of tourism, principally abroad.

Hosts and Guests: The Anthropology of Tourism. Valene L. Smith, ed. Philadelphia: University of Pennsylvania Press, 1977. 254 pp., biblio., index. $17.50 hb.

A study of tourism as a medium for cultural, rather than economic, exchange. Case studies examine five types of tourism—historical, cultural, ethnic, environmental and recreational—and their impact on a range of cultures, including North Carolina towns and southwestern Indians.

A Plan to Preserve the Historic Resources of the Gettysburg Area of the Commonwealth of Pennsylvania. Washington, D.C.: Advisory Council on Historic Preservation, 1977. 40 pp.

Recommendations on better management of a special historic resource surrounded by tourist attractions in a town that needs the profits but not the problems of runaway tourist trade.

Visitors bureau in an old shop in the 19th-century mining town of Virginia City, Nev. (Martin Stupich, Comstock Project)

Travelers: The American Tourist from Stagecoach to Space Shuttle. Horace Sutton. New York: William Morrow, 1980. 320 pp., illus., index.

A lively look at the history of tourism by Americans at home and abroad.

Travels in America. Garold L. Cole. Tulsa: University of Oklahoma Press, 1984. 344 pp., biblio., index. $48.50 hb.

An annotated bibliography to periodical articles focusing on travel accounts from the earliest voyages of discovery to the present.

The Tourist: Travel in Early Twentieth Century America. John A. Jakle. Lincoln: University of Nebraska Press, 1985. 396 pp. $24.95 hb, $12.95 pb.

Summary and Recommendations: International Symposium on Tourism and the Next Decade. Donald E. Hawkins, Elwood L. Shafer and James M. Rovelstad, eds. Washington, D.C.: George Washington University, 1980.

Contacts

Travel and Tourism Research Association
P.O. Box 8066
Foothill Station
Salt Lake City, Utah 84108

United States Travel and Tourism Administration
U.S. Department of Commerce
Washington, D.C. 20230

Pacific Area Travel Association
228 Grant Avenue
San Francisco, Calif. 94108

U.S. Travel Data Center
1899 L Street, N.W.
Washington, D.C. 20036

THE ROAD LESS TRAVELED BY... (FOR OBVIOUS REASONS)

Neighborhoods

12

N*early all of us live in a neighborhood. It could be a few square blocks of a city that have resisted the hustle of urban life and remained a residential enclave. Or it could be an old residential area of a smaller city where the trees have survived the traffic engineers and the houses have aged with dignity. It could be a piece of the suburbs that has somehow established an identity that separates it from surrounding subdivisions. Or it could be the west end of a small town on the prairie. There are almost as many categories of neighborhoods as there are neighborhoods; each seems to be at least a little different from any other. And that is one of the most important reasons for preserving them.*

Russell W. Peterson. In *Neighborhood Conservation*

"A sense of neighborhood haunts our history and our fondest memories."

David Morris and Karl Hess, *Neighborhood Power*

What Is a Neighborhood?

"Just what is a neighborhood? It is not defined only by population and geographical shape and size. It can be as small as a single tenement building in Manhattan or as large as a U.S. state, as illustrated by Alaska's North Slope. A neighborhood can contain as few as 71 residents (in the Spring Creek Colony) or as many as a million people (the number of Chicanos in the East Los Angeles area). . . . A neighborhood is the social fabric—the people and how they feel about one another. It is difficult to define, perhaps because it is self-defining. Community is an insider's commodity; it belongs to those who belong."

Stewart Dill McBride, "A Nation of Neighborhoods." *Christian Science Monitor*, 1977.

Rehabilitated house in the Logan Circle neighborhood, Washington, D.C., a historic district whose large Victorian row houses (built 1875–1900) are undergoing revitalization. (Arnold Kramer)

Children in Chicago's Pullman neighborhood lending a hand wth fall raking. (© 1982 Fred Leavitt and the City of Chicago)

"Neighborhoods are composed of people who enter by the very fact of birth or chosen residence into a common life."

Lewis Mumford, *The Urban Prospect*. New York: Harcourt Brace Jovanovich, 1968.

"In real terms, people live in neighborhoods, not cities."

Geno Baroni, "Looking at America." *Preservation News*, December 1976.

1. Does the area have a variety of facilities and opportunities for residence, employment, shopping, recreation, and education?
2. Is the area associated with groups of existing or former residents who because of their common employment or heritage have contributed significantly to the city's development?
3. Is there a special activity associated with the area—a central market, an educational or transportation facility, wharves, warehousing?
4. What is the overall effect of structures and spaces in the area on its utility as well as its attractiveness?
5. Is the sense of place enhanced significantly by some important natural or man-made feature such as a canal or river, a hillside, vistas, a park or public square?
6. Do the people who live, work, and shop there have a clear and consistent sense of the area as an identifiable urban place with definable boundaries?
7. Can it house people of various incomes? Will restoration permit those who have made it a home to stay there if they wish? Are there distinctive social as well as economic characteristics?

Lawrence O. Houston, Jr. In *Neighborhood Conservation*

"Beyond the family, the neighborhood is the most universal base of social life to be found in any society. It requires no membership and pays no wages, and yet we belong actively or passively to a neighborhood."

Rachelle B. Warren and Donald I. Warren, *The Neighborhood Organizer's Handbook*

Apartment building in the South Bronx, N.Y., converted from an abandoned tenement into 28 units through sweat equity. (Mark Haven)

The Language of Neighborhoods

back-to-the-city movement. A growing awareness of the merits of living in an urban environment, manifested in the increasing numbers of people moving into and revitalizing old neighborhoods.

blockbusting. The actions of speculators to depreciate an area's property values in order to purchase properties at below-market prices and resell them at often inflated prices.

CDBG. The Community Development Block Grant Program, a revenue-sharing program administered by the U.S. Department of Housing and Urban Development to provide grants for approved community development projects.

code enforcement. Local regulation of building practices and enforcement of safety and housing code provisions, a principal tool to ensure neighborhood upkeep.

community development corporation. Community-owned venture capital funds set up by local groups in low-income areas for economic revitalization and rehabilitation.

disinvestment. The withdrawal of private and public investment from high-risk areas or the tendency to avoid such neighborhoods; the opposite of reinvestment.

displacement. The movement of individuals, businesses or industries from property or neighborhoods because of real estate activities.

flipping. Speculative property acquisition whereby a property is purchased and quickly placed back on the market at a substantial profit with no or little improvement.

gentrification. English term for the process by which young professionals or "gentry" buy into inner-city areas as part of a neighborhood preservation trend.

greenlining. Activities and investments designed to combat redlining, or discriminatory lending practices.

historic district ordinance. A local law designating and protecting an area of significant historical, architectural, cultural or other special character.

homesteading. Programs under which abandoned buildings are made available at little or no cost to persons who agree to rehabilitate and occupy them for a specified period of time. Similar programs to recycle commercial structures may be called "shopsteading."

mixed use. A variety of authorized activities in an area or a building, as distinguished from the isolated uses and planned separatism prescribed by many zoning ordinances.

neighborhood. A relatively small area in a town with sufficient binding character, such as architectural or social unity or clear boundaries, so that it is recognized as an entity by residents and outsiders alike. Usually an area in which all parts are within easy walking distance from one another.

NHS. Neighborhood Housing Services, a program of technical assistance and grants administered by the Neighborhood Reinvestment Corporation for low- and moderate-income neighborhoods.

redlining. A practice among financial institutions and insurance companies of refusing to provide services to certain supposedly high-risk geographical areas, regardless of the merits of individual applicants. The term is derived from the red line that may be drawn around the area on a map by the institutions.

rehabilitation guidelines. Standards or recommendations to assist property owners in improving structures while preserving their special historical character.

reinvestment. The channelling of public and private resources into declining neighborhoods in a coordinated manner to combat disinvestment.

relocation. Settling households or businesses in new locations, necessitated by urban renewal or other government actions.

sweat equity. The investment of property owners' or occupants' own labor in rehabilitation work as a form of payment.

Adapted from *Landmark Words: A Glossary for Preserving the Built Environment.* National Trust for Historic Preservation. Forthcoming.

The Neighborhood Network

Networking is essential to the survival of the neighborhood movement and helps conserve a resource neighborhoods don't have much of—time.

Stewart Dill McBride, *A Nation of Neighborhoods*

National Trust for Historic Preservation
1785 Massachusetts Avenue, N.W.
Washington, D.C. 20036

Publishes *Conserve Neighborhoods* newsletter, conducts training programs on neighborhood conservation techniques and, through the Inner-City Ventures Fund, provides grants and loans to neighborhood organizations for rehabilitation projects for low- and moderate-income people in historic neighborhoods.

National Association of Neighborhoods
1651 Fuller Street, N.W.
Washington, D.C. 20009

A membership coalition that provides referrals and information-sharing services for its 450 multiracial and ethnic neighborhood groups.

National Neighbors
815 15th Street, N.W.
Suite 525-A
Washington, D.C. 20005

An affiliation of multiethnic neighborhood groups dedicated to integration and involved in education, fair housing and antidisplacement programs.

ACORN (Association of Community Organizations for Reform Now)
401 Howard Avenue
New Orleans, La. 70130

A network of neighborhood-based community associations in 26 states and the District of Columbia that organizes neighborhoods and uses direct-action tactics to influence local, state and national policy on issues such as redlining, housing rehabilitation and utility reform.

Center for Community Change
1000 Wisconsin Avenue, N.W.
Washington, D.C. 20007

Offers assistance in housing rehabilitation, reinvestment, redlining and a CDBG monitoring program.

National Urban Coalition
1120 G Street, N.W.
Suite 900
Washington, D.C. 20005

An urban action and advocacy organization working to revitalize cities through housing, economic and business development with a national information service on neighborhoods.

National Training and Information Center
954 West Washington Boulevard
Chicago, Ill. 60607

Provides organizing assistance and information on a variety of housing issues, including workshops, training sessions and publications.

National Center for Urban Ethnic Affairs
P.O. Box 33279
Washington, D.C. 20033

Promotes neighborhood development in urban ethnic and minority neighborhoods.

Community Design Center Directors Association
c/o Bruce Kriviskey
Staff Liaison
American Institute of Architects
1735 New York Avenue, N.W.
Washington, D.C. 20006

A national network of nonprofit centers in more than 30 cities established to provide free design assistance in planning, architecture and community development to low-income communities.

Civic Information and Techniques Exchange (CIVITEX)
Citizens Forum on Self-Government
(800) 223-6004
(212) 730-7930 (N.Y. State, Alaska, Hawaii)

A computer database of citizen-initiated community service and development projects available free of charge. Topics covered include community economic development, housing, human services and adaptive use.

National Self-Help Clearinghouse
Graduate School
City University of New York
33 West 42nd Street
Room 1222
New York, N.Y. 10036

Encourages and coordinates self-help groups nationwide. Publishes a newsletter, books and guides. A "switchboard" provides referrals to specific groups.

Trust for Public Land
82 Second Street
San Francisco, Calif. 94105

A national land conservation organization whose Urban Land Program helps inner-city groups locate, acquire and improve urban property by forming land trusts that the community manages in common.

See also: Reinvestment and Finance section

Periodicals

Urban Conservation Report
Preservation Reports, Inc.
1620 I Street, N.W.
Washington, D.C. 20006

Newsletter reporting on government programs, neighborhood financing and neighborhood-related events and projects.

Stone Soup: The Neighborhood Partnership Report
Neighborhood Reinvestment Corporation
1850 K Street, N.W.
Suite 400
Washington, D.C. 20006

Quarterly newsletter dealing with Neighborhood Housing Services and related local partnership efforts.

Home Again
P.O. Box 421, Village Station
New York, N.Y. 10014

A magazine for professionals who develop, finance and manage housing and community preservation projects, covering projects, resources, products and reviews.

Wall mural capturing community activities in the Pilsen neighborhood, Chicago, where the National Trust's Inner-City Ventures Fund has helped teach construction trades through rehabilitation. (Rosemary Kaul)

Neighborhood Conservation

We are beginning to see that it is only through the healthy functioning of the neighborhoods that cities function at all.

Ada Louise Huxtable. National Conference on Neighborhood Conservation, 1975.

Urban neighborhood conservation is as simple in concept—yet as complex in implementation—as any approach to urban planning or improving environmental quality. It not only encompasses the preservation of a neighborhood's existing qualities—be they architecturally significant buildings, street vitality, scenic vistas, neighborhood business, parks, or ethnic solidarity—but it also seeks to improve neighborhood conditions. In short, it is a concept that attempts to protect what people value about the place they live, while at the same time accommodating change—new people, new buildings, new commerce—in a manner and form harmonious with what's already there.

Gordon Binder, "Neighborhoods Are Back in Urban Style." *Conservation Foundation Letter,* January 1976.

Carpenters at work on a rehabilitation project in Chicago's Pilsen neighborhood. (Rosemary Kaul)

Announcing a metamorphosis through restoration, this house in Atlanta's Inman Park flies a butterfly banner designed by Ken Thompson. (Robert Griggs)

"There has been a long history of interest in preserving neighborhoods in this country. As far back as 1938 the National Association of Real Estate Boards called for the passage of a federal 'Neighborhood Improvement Act.' . . .

Most of these early neighborhood programs had serious defects. In those days, neighborhood conservation was really a poor cousin of the more grandiose federal slum clearance and urban renewal programs.

The intellectual watershed in these matters came in 1961, with the publication of *The Death and Life of Great American Cities.* The author, a New York City housewife, mother, and sometime architecture critic named Jane Jacobs, was at the time the guiding force behind the effort to prevent the construction of a highway through her West Village neighborhood. It is hard to exaggerate the importance of Jacobs's book. In many respects, it turned city planning on its ear."

Robert Cassidy, *Livable Cities*

"The ethnic revival that has engulfed the United States . . . has proved to be a powerful force in the revitalization process that is transforming the American city.

In Chicago, Pittsburgh, Boston, Baltimore and many other cities, predominantly ethnic residents of inner-city working-class neighborhoods have refused to give ground. They have risen up in dramatic displays of grass-roots political power to fight highways, high-rises, and other renewal efforts which have threatened their communities."

Ward W. Smith, "Is the Melting Pot Curdling?" *The Christian Science Monitor,* April 21, 1978.

"The chief ingredients [of urban renovation] are accelerating middle-class return to the cities, the energy crisis, the explosion of the post–World War II baby boom into the household market, changing lifestyles and mounting dissatisfaction with suburban life—especially among young people.

All this is complemented by out-of-sight single family home costs, the economics of restoration over new construction, shifts in federal policy away from the pro-suburban bias of the last three decades, the strong and growing national neighborhood movement and a prominent decline in urban crime. The net result: a new psychology of hope in the city that breeds fresh investment and confidence."

Neal R. Peirce, "Nation's Cities Poised for Stunning Comeback." *Nation's Cities,* March 1978.

"Landmarks provide ballast in a neighborhood. They steady it and bring out its character. A designation alone is sometimes enough to check a certain kind of deterioration in the quality of life. If you know a building, a street, a neighborhood will stay, *you* are more likely to stay. The result has been psychological, social, physical, and fiscal reinvestment."

Beverly Moss Spatt. In *Neighborhood Conservation*

"Neighborhood conservation offers the preservation community a major opportunity to save countless numbers of older buildings. . . .

Preservationists and neighborhood leaders rely on similar tactics: development of effective citizen organizations, dependence on small self-help projects, involvement with local government and use of a variety of public and private resources. . . .

By working together, I believe preservation and neighborhood conservation organizations can achieve the highly ambitious but attainable goal of creating healthy, thriving neighborhoods that retain the architecture of the past, allow for the new and provide decent, affordable housing for all."

Michael L. Ainslie. In "Neighborhood Conservation." Supplement to *Preservation News,* January 1981.

Neighborhood Conservation: A Handbook of Methods and Techniques. Robert H. McNulty and Stephen A. Kliment, eds. 1976. Reprint. New York: Whitney Library of Design, 1979. 288 pp., illus., appends., index. $9.95 pb.

A guide to the administrative, legal, financial, social and physical design issues of neighborhood conservation. Case studies of 45 American cities with a record of activity in neighborhood conservation are presented, along with a compendium of printed resources arranged by issue and subject matter.

Livable Cities: A Grass-Roots Guide to Rebuilding Urban America. Robert Cassidy. New York: Holt, Rinehart and Winston, 1980. 340 pp., biblio., append., index.

This is a down-to-earth overview of neighborhood conservation, including an explanation of why neighborhoods decline, how to organize a community, neighborhood planning, reinvestment strategies, overcoming displacement, historic preservation and neighborhood commercial revitalization.

The Death and Life of Great American Cities. Jane Jacobs. New York: Random House, 1961. 458 pp., index. $4.95 pb.

In the author's words, "This book is an attack on current city planning and rebuilding. It is also, and mostly, an attempt to introduce new principles of city planning and rebuilding. . . . In setting forth different principles, I shall mainly be writing about common, ordinary things: for instance . . . why some slums stay slums and other slums regenerate themselves even against financial and official opposition; what makes downtowns shift their centers; what, if anything, is a city neighborhood, and what jobs, if any, neighborhoods in great cities do. In short, I shall be writing about how cities work in real life."

Conserve Neighborhoods Notebook. Washington, D.C.: National Trust for Historic Preservation. 424 pp., illus., biblios., index. $20 binder.

Complete set of more than 40 issues of *Conserve Neighborhoods* newsletter covering a spectrum of topics—organizing, rehabilitation, fund raising, reinvestment, special events, public relations and related issues.

Remember the Neighborhoods: Conserving Neighborhoods Through Historic Preservation Techniques. Washington, D.C.: Urban Policy Group, Advisory Council on Historic Preservation, 1981. 20 pp., illus.

According to the council, "To analyze the potential of preservation techniques in meeting neighborhood conservation objectives, one should first identify ends that preservation can achieve. Almost by definition, preservation promotes the creation of a sense of neighborhood and special characteristics that are worth keeping. Beyond that, preservation can help build residents' ability to control forces of physical change in their neighborhood."

Historic Preservation in Inner City Areas: A Manual of Practice. Arthur P. Ziegler, Jr. 1971. Rev. ed. Pittsburgh: Ober Park Associates (One Station Square, 450 Landmarks Building, 15219), 1974. 85 pp., illus. $3.95 pb.

A classic on how preservation can instill pride in inner-city neighborhoods, written by a pioneer in the movement. Details the early work of the Pittsburgh History and Landmarks Foundation in that city's neighborhoods.

Neighborhood Conservation: Lessons from Three Cities. Phyllis Myers and Gordon Binder. Washington, D.C.: Conservation Foundation (1717 Massachusetts Avenue, N.W., 20036), 1977. 111 pp., illus., biblio.

Examines the dynamics of change in six older neighborhoods: three in Cincinnati, two in Seattle and one in Annapolis, Md.

How to Save Your Own Street. Raquel Ramati, with Urban Design Group, New York Department of City Planning. Garden City, N.Y.: Dolphin Books, Doubleday, 1981. 159 pp., illus.

"This book is about saving the kinds of streets that thread through thousands of retail and residential neighborhoods across the country. They tie together the physical characteristics, social activities, and cultural resources of our immediate surroundings. Saving your own street, turning neglect around and beating back blight, is a way of taking part in some very practical pioneering." Three New York neighborhoods are featured: Little Italy, Newkirk Plaza in Brooklyn and Beach 20th Street in Queens.

"A Nation of Neighborhoods," Stewart Dill McBride. *Christian Science Monitor,* 1977.

A series of 10 profiles covering community building, technology, economics, arts, saving small towns, preservation and organizers' schools. The articles highlight five urban communities: New York's Lower East Side, Southeast Baltimore, Chicago's West Side, East Los Angeles and Little Rock. Others cited range from the San Francisco suburb of Mill Valley and Alaska's North Slope to two small towns, Granbury, Tex., and North Bonneville, Wash.

Private-Market Housing Renovation in Older Urban Areas. J. Thomas Black, Allan Borut and Robert Dubinsky. Washington, D.C.: Urban Land Institute, 1977. 41 pp., illus. ULI Research Report 26. $11.50 pb.

Analysis concluding that of the 260 cities with populations over 50,000, almost half are experiencing some private-market, nonsubsidized housing rehabilitation in their older core areas. Of those over 250,000, the rate goes up to 70 percent.

Return to the City: How to Restore Old Buildings and Ourselves in America's Historic Urban Neighborhoods. Richard Ernie Reed. Garden City, N.Y.: Doubleday, 1979. 206 pp., illus.

Surveys a number of highly publicized urban neighborhoods in the process of revitalization.

Back-to-the-City. Annual Conference Proceedings. New York: Back to the Cities (12 East 41st Street, 10017), 1974, 1975, 1978. $5 pb each.

Amalgams of neighborhood perspectives, experiences, techniques and case studies of St. Paul's Historic Hill District, Chicago's Historic Pullman Foundation, St. Louis's Lafayette Square, Brooklyn's Bedford-Stuyvesant and Milwaukee's Historic Walker's Point.

Optimism About the Future

"More than half of the nation's city dwellers are relatively optimistic about the future of their neighborhoods. . . .

1. More than eight in ten (85 percent) take pride in their neighborhood and city.
2. A majority (53 percent) do not want to leave their neighborhood and nearly seven in ten (69 percent) are certain they will be living in the same neighborhood five years from now.
3. A surprisingly small portion (8 percent) said they would like to move from their neighborhood to the suburbs.
4. More than four in ten (42 percent) belong, or would like to belong, to a neighborhood group or organization.
5. One-third have already participated in a neighborhood improvement effort and feel their involvement contributed to solving a problem.
6. A majority are willing to take direct action in defense of their neighborhood when it is threatened: 60 percent would sign a petition, 54 percent would attend meetings, 49 percent would participate in face-to-face discussions."

Stewart Dill McBride, "A Nation of Neighborhoods." *Christian Science Monitor,* 1977.

"Our data strongly suggest that the so-called Back-to-the-City movement is really a 'Stay-in-the-City' phenomenon."

Dennis E. Gayle, *The Back-to-the-City Movement . . . Or Is It?* Washington, D.C.: Department of Urban and Regional Planning, George Washington University, 1976.

"Back-to-the-city is the demographic misnomer of the decade. Back-to-selected-neighborhoods would be a much more accurate label."

John Goodman, Jr., "People of the City." *American Demographics,* September 1980.

Displacement

Change is part of life, and neighborhoods change their populations over time. . . . The filtering of neighborhoods from one social or economic class to another is a historically recognized urban process.

Why is there now such concern with this change? One reason is that this process has accelerated. . . .

Furthermore, much of the demographic change in the past reflected a transition from wealthy residents to less affluent residents. The filtering down of neighborhoods is now being reversed with a filtering up from low-income to affluent.

> Anthony C. Wood, "The Perils of Preservation: A Study of the Criticisms of Historic Preservation." Master's degree thesis, Graduate College, University of Illinois, Urbana-Champaign, 1978.

Victorian District residents working through the Savannah Landmark Rehabilitation Project to recycle buildngs without displacement. (SLRP)

"Displacement is distinguished from normal turnover in principle by several factors: first, displacement is not caused by a change in the lifestyle or circumstances of the individual household in a displacement area, but rather by external changes in the neighborhood such as rapidly rising rents or property taxes, or a loss of supporting institutions, services, friends or relatives. Second, the persons moving into the neighborhood and precipitating these changes are of generally higher income and often of substantially higher income than the persons residing there first. Third, the external changes in the neighborhood make it economically and socially infeasible or undesirable for some or all of the residents to remain. Fourth, the movement of the original residents from the neighborhood may be partially voluntary in that the pressures to move merely help them to make a move they wished to make anyway. But often the move is largely involuntary and undesired."

Conrad Weiler, *NAN Handbook on Reinvestment Displacement*

"The poor are frequent movers, but only a fraction of their moves are caused by displacement. And the great bulk of displacement is caused by the abandonment of housing, by disinvestment, planned arson, and the almost total lack in our cities of housing affordable for the poor—or, for that matter, affordable for the middle class. This problem is going to get worse, but let us not bewail gentrification as the cause. Gentrification is something we should welcome, and liberals' feeling guilt about it is one of the reasons we've been unable to get decent legislation to spur the gentrification movement. As small as it may be numerically, it is absolutely vital to cities."

William H. Whyte, "Aging Cities: Damn the Demographics, Full Speed Ahead." *Livability,* Summer 1981. Partners for Livable Places (1429 21st Street, N.W., Washington, D.C. 20036).

"There is little that preservationists can do to address [displacement] in the absence of meaningful federal or state housing programs for the poor. With the subsidies which such programs could provide, preservation can serve the poor as well as, in fact better than, programs for new construction. Ironically, our poorest city neighborhoods are often those with the most preservation potential. They are often the oldest, architecturally the richest, and the most conveniently located.

In the long run, of course, no housing policy will address the root problem. The root problem is not that the poor cannot afford housing, it is that they are poor. If the poor had adequate income to pay for private market housing like the rest of us, we would not need housing programs. Until that immense issue is faced up to by our society and resolved satisfactorily, however, we have no choice but to work with the tools at hand. And the best tool at hand is historic preservation."

Editorial, *Hartford Architecture Conservancy News,* Winter 1977.

"A handful of groups working in a variety of historic neighborhoods are preserving without displacing. . . . The trick is to bring these to neighborhood people, not to bring people with these to the neighborhood."

Bruce M. Kriviskey, "Neighborhoods." *Journal of Architectural Education,* November 1977. Association of Collegiate Schools of Architecture (1735 New York Avenue, N.W., Washington, D.C. 20006).

Tools to Fight Displacement

Encouragements to home ownership
City-guided reinvestment
Education of realtors, bankers, developers, residents
Property tax abatements
Low-cost loans
Rehabilitation aid
Antispeculation tax
Active community organizations
Freeze on tax assessments

Displacement: How to Fight It. Chester Hartman, Dennis Keating and Richard LeGates. Berkeley, Calif.: National Housing Law Project, 1982. 232 pp., illus., index. $10 pb.

Neighborhood Transition Without Displacement: A Citizens' Handbook. Sandra Solomon. Washington, D.C.: National Urban Coalition, 1979. 60 pp., illus., append., biblio. $6 pb.

Displacement: Where Things Stand. George Grier and Eunice Grier. Bethesda, Md.: Grier Partnership (6532 East Halbert Road, 20817), 1981. 70 pp., biblio. $8.

Neighborhood Renewal: Trends and Strategies. Philip L. Clay. Lexington, Mass.: Lexington Books, 1979. 128 pp., biblio., index. $19 hb.

NAN Handbook on Reinvestment Displacement: HUD's Role in a New Housing Issue. Conrad Weiler. Washington, D.C.: National Association of Neighborhoods, 1978. 104 pp. $6 pb.

Private Reinvestment, Gentrification, and Displacement: Selected References with Annotations. Susan J. Vaughn. Chicago: Council of Planning Librarians, 1980. No. 33. 21 pp. $6 pb.

Displacement: A Selected Bibliography. Allen C. Goodman and Richard Shain, Center for Metropolitan Planning and Research, Johns Hopkins University. Monticello, Ill.: Vance Bibliographies, 1980. P-490. 33 pp. $7.80 photocopy.

Back to the City: Issues in Neighborhood Renovation. Shirley Bradway Laska and Daphne Spain, eds. Elmsford, N.Y.: Pergamon Press, 1980. 374 pp., gloss., biblio., index. $50 hb, $9.95 pb.

Quaker Hill: Reinvestment Displacement in an Historic District. Timothy K. Barnekov and John E. Caron. Newark, Del.: College of Urban Affairs and Public Policy, 1980. 106 pp., maps, biblio.

Neighborhood Conservation and the Elderly. Phyllis Myers. Washington, D.C.: Conservation Foundation, 1978. 72 pp.

Rehabilitating Residential Hotels. Bradford Paul. Information Series, National Trust for Historic Preservation. Washington, D.C.: Preservation Press, 1981. 46 pp., illus., append., biblio. $2 pb.

Neighborhood Reinvestment and Displacement: A Working Paper. Michael H. Schill. Princeton, N.J.: Princeton Urban and Regional Research Center (Transaction Books), 1981. 60 pp. $2.50 pb.

The Back to the City Movement Revisited: A Survey of Recent Home Buyers in the Capitol Hill Neighborhood of Washington, D.C. Occasional Paper Series. Washington, D.C.: Department of Urban and Regional Planning, George Washington University, 1977.

"Middle Class Resettlement in Older Urban Neighborhoods," Dennis Gale. *Journal of the American Planning Association*, vol. 45, 1979.

The City-Suburb Income Gap: Is It Being Narrowed by a Back-to-the-City Movement? Larry H. Long and Donald C. Dahmann. Washington, D.C.: Bureau of the Census (Data User Services Division, Customer Services-Microfiche, 20233), 1980. Special Demographic Analysis, CDS-80-1. 22 pp., biblio. $5 microfiche.

Housing Successions Among Blacks and Whites in Cities and Suburbs. Daphne Spain, John Reid and Larry Long. Washington, D.C.: Bureau of the Census, 1980. Current Population Reports, Special Studies Series P-23, no. 101. $5 microfiche.

Contacts
National Housing Law Project
1950 Addison Street
Berkeley, Calif. 94704

509 C Street, N.E.
Washington, D.C. 20002

National Neighbors
815 15th Street, N.W.
Suite 525-A
Washington, D.C. 20005

Savannah Landmark
Rehabilitation Project
P.O. Box 8801
Savannah, Ga. 31412

Pittsburgh History and
Landmarks Foundation
One Station Square
450 Landmarks Building
Pittsburgh, Pa. 15219

SWAP (Stop Wasting
Abandoned Properties)
439 Pine Street
Providence, R.I. 02907

Mount Auburn Good Housing
Foundation
P.O. Box 19334
Cincinnati, Ohio 45219

St. Ambrose Housing
Aid Center
321 East 25th Street
Baltimore, Md. 21218

Bureau of the Census
Center for Demographic Studies
Washington, D.C. 20233

Glencoe Place in Cincinnati's Mount Auburn, whose Good Housing Foundation is striving to revive housing while keeping residents. (Carleton Knight III)

Renovation in progress in Pittsburgh, a pioneering city in neighborhood anti-displacement efforts. (Deborah Powell)

A last gasp in Detroit's Poletown, whose residents organized to stop General Motors from demolishing their neighborhood. (Rick Hodas)

Part of the 465 acres in Poletown cleared of 1,000 houses, 150 businesses and 16 churches for a GM assembly plant. (Rick Hodas)

Community Organizing

A community organization is essential to any neighborhood that hopes to win the battle against decline. Too many forces and institutions stand poised to destroy your neighborhood—greedy slumlords, insensitive government bureaucrats, uncompromising financial institutions, power-hungry legislators. A neighborhood without an organization to fight for itself will surely be overrun by one or more of these forces.

Robert Cassidy, *Livable Cities*

Neighborhoods: A Self-Help Sampler. U.S. Department of Housing and Urban Development. Washington, D.C.: GPO, 1980. 161 pp., illus., appends.

Some "first steps" in organizing, presenting a range of projects accomplished by people "who started from scratch."

"Neighborhood Organizing Guide: Ideas for Bringing Your Neighborhood Together." *Conserve Neighborhoods*, September–October 1981. 20 pp., illus. $2 pb.

An outline of why and how groups should organize.

Neighborhood Power: The New Localism. David Morris and Karl Hess. Boston: Beacon Press, 1975. 180 pp., biblio.

"The importance of the neighborhood begins with the importance of citizenship. To be a citizen is to participate in civic affairs. 'Participate' is the key concept. To simply live in a place, and not participate in its civic affairs, is to be merely a resident, not a citizen."

Strengthening Volunteer Initiative: A Neighborhood Self-Help Curriculum. Libby Leonard, ed. Washington, D.C.: National Center for Urban Ethnic Affairs, 1981. 270 pp., appends., index, biblio. $12 pb.

A training curriculum for community organizers with 28 exercises to teach new staff and leaders the various elements of effective community organizing, such as identifying issues, developing strategies, planning meetings and coordinating fund-raising events.

Yerba Buena: Land Grab and Community Resistance in San Francisco. Chester Hartman. San Francisco: Glide Publications (Volcano Press), 1974. 233 pp., illus., index.

The story of how "powerless and obscure people" managed to stall construction of a massive downtown redevelopment project.

The Neighborhood Organizer's Handbook. Rachelle B. Warren and Donald I. Warren. Notre Dame, Ind.: University of Notre Dame Press, 1977. 237 pp., index. $5.95 pb.

A sociological approach to starting the organization process and identifying a neighborhood's strengths and weaknesses.

Building Neighborhood Organizations. James R. Cunningham and Milton Kotler. Notre Dame, Ind.: University of Notre Dame Press, 1983. 224 pp. $15.95 hb, $7.95 pb.

Provides profiles of 15 neighborhood development organizations, advocacy organizations and neighborhood government agencies followed over a five-year period.

The Rape of Our Neighborhoods: And How Communities Are Resisting Take-Overs by Colleges, Hospitals, Churches, Businesses, and Public Agencies. William Worthy. New York: Morrow, 1976. 276 pp., index.

A manifesto of urban political warfare. Its targets: institutional take-overs of neighborhoods, for example, hospitals, churches, universities, airports, the Kennedy Library-Museum, highways, McDonalds and proposed development in Beacon Hill.

The Backyard Revolution: Understanding the New Citizen Movement. Harry C. Boyte. Philadelphia: Temple University Press, 1980. 287 pp., appends., biblio., index. $29.95 hb.

A study of the origins, development and themes of grass-roots political activism, including a community group's protest of bank redlining and changes in a city charter that threaten a neighborhood.

Uplift: What People Themselves Can Do. Washington Consulting Group, Inc. Salt Lake City: Olympus Publishing (1670 East 13th South, 84105), 1974. 465 pp., illus. $8 hb, $5 pb.

Gives 114 case studies of self-help projects accomplished by low-income people.

New York Self-Help Handbook. Karin Carlson. New York: Citizens Committee for New York City (630 Fifth Avenue, Room 306, 10020), 1977. 135 pp., illus.

How New Yorkers can help themselves in organizing, safety, open spaces, park projects, housing, consumer affairs, monitoring city services, publicity, fund raising and more.

Baltimore Neighborhood Self-Help Handbook. Baltimore: Citizens Planning and Housing Association (340 North Charles Street, 21201), 1984. 165 pp. $11.50.

A step-by-step guide to 100 programs and activities for solving neighborhood problems that is a model for other groups.

See also: Taking Action

Public Planning

A sympathetic political climate and administrative scheme lays fertile ground for conservation; when local officials—from the mayor on down through agency staff—set out to nurture neighborhoods, the atmosphere is ripe for businesspeople, lenders, citizen groups and private owners to do the same. . . .

The actual and potential impact of local government on conservation is very large. It resides chiefly in its application of land-use controls, its discretion as to choice of districts for attention, its direct financial support through use of tax revenues and as a conduit for state and federal funds, its powers of code enforcement and use of the property tax, its ability to expand or reduce the power of local subdepartments such as community boards, and its power to shape the quality of program planning and execution via its staff appointments. . . .

Prospective conservation neighborhoods must be integrated into an overall city planning process, including traffic planning, zoning policy, and official attitudes in general. Conservation areas cannot stand alone, grafted onto a general planning process as an extra.

Robert H. McNulty and Stephen A. Kliment, eds., *Neighborhood Conservation*

A Guide to Neighborhood Planning. Joel T. Werth and David Bryant. Chicago: American Planning Association, 1979. PAS Report 342. 46 pp., append., biblio. $10.

A guide for planners examining the role of the neighborhood, how to involve citizens, elements in a neighborhood plan and the impact of planning on residents.

A New Public Policy for Neighborhood Preservation. Roger S. Ahlbrandt, Jr., and James V. Cunningham. Foreword by Geno C. Baroni. New York: Holt, Rinehart and Winston, 1979. 304 pp., append., biblio., index. $39.95 hb.

Recommendations of ways to strengthen neighborhood-based institutions and the social fabric of the neighborhood.

Planning with Neighborhoods. William M. Rohe and Lauren B. Gates. Chapel Hill: University of North Carolina Press, 1985. 260 pp. $35 hb, $12.95 pb.

A comprehensive description of 51 neighborhood planning programs and evaluation of their effectiveness, with recommendations for designing a successful program. Includes in-depth case studies of Atlanta, Cincinnati, Houston, St. Paul, Wilmington and Raleigh.

Neighborhood Revitalization: Theory and Practice. Roger S. Ahlbrandt, Jr., and Paul C. Brophy. Lexington, Mass.: Lexington Books, 1975. 188 pp., append., biblio., index.

Describes a variety of public investment used to renew a Pittsburgh neighborhood: code enforcement, street paving, tree planting, streetlights, demolition of deteriorated buildings, recreational facilities, and school construction and renovation.

Neighborhoods That Work: Sources for Viability in the Inner City. Sandra P. Schoenberg and Patricia P. Rosenbaum. New Brunswick, N.J.: Rutgers University Press, 1980. 195 pp., appends, biblio., index. $16 hb.

A study of five St. Louis neighborhoods with lessons that can be applied to other neighborhoods.

Neighborhoods and Urban Development. Anthony Downs. Washington, D.C.: Brookings Institution (1775 Massachusetts Avenue, N.W., 20036), 1981. 250 pp., index. $26.95 hb, $9.95 pb.

Analyzes population shifts within cities, revitalization programs, and public and private policies to determine the future of neighborhoods and older cities.

Understanding Neighborhood Change: Role of Expectations in Urban Revitalization. Rolf Goetze. Cambridge: Ballinger, 1979. 192 pp., biblio., index. $22.50.

Building Neighborhood Confidence: A Humanistic Strategy for Urban Housing. Rolf Goetze. Cambridge: Ballinger, 1976. 176 pp., tables, append., index.

Companion volumes that develop an approach to understanding housing dynamics and neighborhood revitalization.

The Adaptive Reuse Handbook: Procedures to Inventory, Control, Manage, and Reemploy Surplus Municipal Properties. Robert W. Burchell and David Listokin. New Brunswick, N.J.: Center for Urban Policy Research, 1981. 575 pp., illus., gloss., appends., biblio., index. $28.50 hb.

Provides an exceptionally detailed guide for municipal officials and other planners who want to recycle abandoned buildings.

Housing Rehabilitation: Economic, Social, and Policy Perspectives. David Listokin, ed. New Brunswick, N.J.: Center for Urban Policy Research, 1983. 380 pp., index. $12.95 pb.

Examines rehabilitation as a strategy for providing low-cost, conveniently located housing, including the private-public record, gentrification and financing proposals.

Planning Neighborhood Space with People. Randolph T. Hester, Jr. 1975. 2nd ed. New York: Van Nostrand Reinhold, 1984. 205 pp., illus., index. $32.50 hb.

A guide to environmental design covering social factors in site planning, user needs and planning by archetypes, with numerous case studies.

Neighborhood Planning Primer. Urban Systems Research and Engineering, Inc. Washington, D.C.: U.S. Department of Housing and Urban Development, 1980. 100 pp., illus., maps, charts, biblio., append., index.

Identifying Urban Neighborhoods: An Annotated Bibliography. Thomas Broden, Ronn Kirkwood, Susan Roberts, John Roos and Thomas Swartz. Chicago: Council of Planning Librarians, 1980. No. 28. 40 pp. $8.50 pb.

The Neighborhood: A Viable Unit for Planning? Steve Manning. Monticello, Ill.: Vance Bibliographies, 1978. P-73. 25 pp. $2.50 pb.

Cincinnati's Findlay Market (1855), the center of a city historic district. (Miami Purchase Association)

Typical houses in the Historic Hill District, St. Paul. (Tom Lutz, Old Town Restorations)

A Model in St. Paul

"The Historic Hill District Planning Program is . . . intended to be a model for other community programs. Can residents work more effectively with government agencies and city departments? Can a more efficient system of citizen participation be developed? Can the 'restoration' movement be used not only to ease urban blight but also to help the victims of that blight enjoy some of the benefits of urban preservation?"

Building the Future from Our Past

Building the Future from Our Past: A Report on the Saint Paul Historic Hill District Planning Program. Old Town Restorations. St. Paul, Minn.: Old Town Restorations, 1975. 136 pp., illus., append., gloss.

Urban Dynamics in Saint Paul: A Study of Neighborhood and Center City Interaction. David Lanegran. St. Paul: Old Town Restorations, 1977. 79 pp., illus.

Selby Avenue: Status of the Street. St. Paul: Old Town Restorations, 1978. 49 pp., illus.

Selby Avenue: Future of the Street. St. Paul: Old Town Restorations, 1978. 77 pp., illus.

Physical Design Planning

"The physical design or visual aspects of a neighborhood are in many ways the hardest to control because they are so largely the outcome of the social, political, economic, and legal forces operating in the city's neighborhoods.

Seven mechanisms to consider in the management of a neighborhood's appearance . . . are:
1. Architectural review commissions. These mostly operate only in special districts.
2. Sign ordinances. These control the environmental impact of signs on neighborhoods.
3. Special design districts. These allow neighborhoods to control their appearance to conform to a theme each considers appropriate.
4. Historic district regulations.
5. City performance standards.
6. The building code, its provisions and enforcement.
7. Tax incentives. These are an effective means of eliminating or discouraging negative visual elements."

Robert H. McNulty and Stephen A. Kliments, eds., *Neighborhood Conservation*

"A variety of controls are available to communities for the protection and enhancement of their old neighborhoods:
1. Historic districts to preserve areas of historical, architectural and cultural value.
2. Special-purpose districts to protect neighborhoods of social and cultural merit threatened by development pressures.
3. Rezoning to allow uses consistent with a neighborhood's character and uses.
4. Purchase of buildings to prevent demolition.

5. Facade easements and other legal techniques permitting retention of building character without full ownership."

National Trust for Historic Preservation

Design Guidelines
Edgefield: A Neighborhood Design Study. Preservation/Urban Design/Incorporated. Nashville: Metropolitan Historical Commission (Second and Broadway, 37201), 1977. 81 pp., illus.

Neighborhood Design Book: A Guide to Styles, Renovation, and New Construction in Nashville's Neighborhoods. Ann Reynolds and David Paine. Nashville: Metropolitan Historical Commission, 1978. 28 pp., illus., biblio.

How to Make Cities Liveable: Design Guidelines for Urban Homesteading. Gary O. Robinette, ed. New York: Van Nostrand Reinhold, 1984. 153 pp., illus., index. $27.50 hb.

Fixing Up: A Bilingual Handbook for Older Homes (Manual de Consertos em Casas Antigas). Dennis P. Albert et al. Warren, R.I.: Massasoit Historical Association (Box 203, 02885), 1979. English and Portuguese. 127 pp.

Back Bay Residential District: Guidelines for Exterior Rehabilitation and Restoration. Boston: Back Bay Architectural Commission (One Beacon Street, 02108), 1977. 36 pp., illus.

Old Allentown Houses: Design Guidelines for an Historic District. Allentown, Pa.: Old Allentown Preservation Association (P.O. Box 1584), 1979. 39 pp., illus., biblio.

The Logan Circle Historic Preservation Area. P. C. Turner Associates and Nicholas Saterlee and Associates. Washington, D.C.: District of Columbia Redevelopment Land Agency, 1973. 113 pp., illus.

Recommended Architectural Design Guidelines for the Exterior of Buildings in Rockville's Historic Districts. Rockville, Md.: Rockville Planning Commission, 1977. 75 pp., illus.

A General Development Plan for Park Place. Norfolk, Va.: Norfolk Department of City Planning (508 City Hall, 23510), 1978. 116 pp.

Historic Preservation Plan for the Central Area General Neighborhood Renewal Area: Savannah, Georgia. Eric Hill Associates and Muldawer and Patterson. Savannah: Housing Authority of Savannah, 1973. 32 pp., illus.

Guidelines for Preservation of Houses in Historic Districts. Commission on Chicago Historical and Architectural Landmarks (320 North Clark Street, Suite 800, 60610), 1974. 12 pp.

Old West Side: Ann Arbor, Michigan. Richard G. Wilson, Edward J. Vaughn and Antoinette Downing. Ann Arbor: Old West Side Association (P.O. Box 405, 48107), 1971. 93 pp., illus.

The Cleveland Old House Handbook. Carol Poh Miller. Cleveland: Neighborhood Housing Services of Cleveland, 1980. 48 pp., illus.

See also: Protecting the Past

Original   Simplified   Inappropriate and Expensive

Design guidelines showing an appropriate way (center) and an inappropriate way (right) to rehabilitate the old house at left. From *Old Allentown Houses.*

Reinvestment and Finance

It seems clear, from a point of view based on practice in the field and an understanding of urban economics, that neighborhood revitalization must give preeminence to economic factors. The causes of urban neighborhood decay have historically and demonstrably been economic, and it follows therefore that the suggested remedies must be mainly economic if they are to have a chance of succeeding in restoring the viability of neighborhoods.

Benjamin Goldstein and Ross Davis, eds., *Neighborhoods in the Urban Economy.* Lexington, Mass.: Lexington Books, 1977.

Neighborhood Reinvestment: A Citizen's Compendium of Programs and Strategies. Karen Kollias with Arthur Naparstek and Chester Haskell. Washington, D.C.: National Center for Urban Ethnic Affairs, 1977. 151 pp. $4 pb.

The Community Reinvestment Act: A Citizens Action Guide. Neighborhood Revitalization Project. Washington, D.C.: Center for Community Change, 1981. 48 pp., illus. $2.50 pb.

Insurance Redlining: Organizing to Win. Robert Schachter. 1979. Rev. ed. Chicago: National Training and Information Center, 1981. 130 pp., illus. $7.50 pb nonprofits, $25 others.

Redlining Update: A Supplement to Exchange Bibliography No. 1486. Francis R. Doyle. Chicago: Council of Planning Librarians, 1981. No. 58. 27 pp. $6 pb.

Creating Neighborhood Enterprise: A Primer for Nonprofits. Washington, D.C.: National Center for Neighborhood Enterprise (1376 Connecticut Avenue, N.W., 20036), 1984. 48 pp. $2 pb.

Grants for Community and Urban Development. New York: Foundation Center (79 Fifth Avenue, 10003), 1984. $30.

State Aid to Neighborhoods. Germantown, Md.: HUD User, 1984. 86 pp. HUD-PDR-913. $5.

Revolving Funds for Neighborhood Preservation: Lafayette Square, St. Louis. Information Series, National Trust for Historic Preservation. Washington, D.C.: Preservation Press, 1977. 20 pp., illus., appends., biblio. $2 pb.

"Revolving Funds: Recycling Resources for Neighborhoods. *Conserve Neighborhoods,* May–June 1981. 22 pp., illus. $2 pb.

Contacts

U.S. Department of Housing and Urban Development Program Information Center Washington, D.C. 20410

In addition to its homesteading program, offers a variety of housing, rehabilitation and related neighborhood programs. Information on programs is available also from HUD User, P.O. Box 280, Germantown, Md. 20874.

Neighborhood Reinvestment Corporation 1850 K Street, N.W. Suite 400 Washington, D.C. 20006

A public nonprofit corporation that, among other activities, establishes Neighborhood Housing Services. These autonomous private nonprofit corporations develop coordinated reinvestment strategies to improve housing and public amenities with the help of local officials, financial institutions and residents.

Local Initiatives Support Corporation Ford Foundation 666 Third Avenue New York, N.Y. 10017

A national nonprofit enterprise designed to help local organizations draw new private and public resources toward neighborhood revitalization and managing housing and commercial developments.

Inner-City Ventures Fund National Trust for Historic Preservation 1785 Massachusetts Avenue, N.W. Washington, D.C. 20036

Provides grants and low-interest loans to help neighborhood organizations leverage additional financing to undertake rehabilitation projects that preserve buildings while helping low- and moderate-income residents.

The Enterprise Foundation 505 American City Building Columbia, Md. 21044

A foundation established by developer James Rouse to help house the very poor, it works with community organizations to achieve "holistic" housing and social-service regeneration.

The National Housing Partnership 1133 15th Street, N.W. Washington, D.C. 20005

The largest private developer of low- and moderate-income housing, it was created through the Housing Act of 1968 to stimulate such housing by the private sector, using partnerships of developers, builders and local community organizations. Some of its projects are rehabilitations and reuses of historic buildings.

Center for Community Change Neighborhood Revitalization Project 1000 Wisconsin Avenue, N.W. Washington, D.C. 20007

Advises community groups on reinvestment strategies, including an effort to link expanded banking powers with investment in low-income communities.

U.S. Department of Health and Human Services Office of Community Services Washington, D.C. 20506

National Congress for Community Economic Development 2025 I Street, N.W. Suite 901 Washington, D.C. 20006

Administer programs to aid community development corporations, which are controlled by local residents to develop the economy of their community.

National Credit Union Administration 1776 G Street, N.W. Washington, D.C. 20456

Regulates and insures federally chartered credit unions, including community development credit unions, which are created as alternative financial institutions capable of supporting neighborhood reinvestment efforts.

National Development Council 1025 Connecticut Avenue, N.W. Suite 517 Washington, D.C. 20036

Provides assistance for local commercial revitalization and industrial job development.

Federal National Mortgage Association Public Finance Division 3900 Wisconsin Avenue, N.W. Washington, D.C. 20016

Fannie Mae, a privately owned corporation chartered by Congress, operates in the secondary mortgage market by purchasing mortgages originated by other lenders, issues and guarantees mortgage-based securities and has developed urban programs useful in neighborhood reinvestment.

Center for Corporate Public Involvement 1850 K Street, N.W. Washington, D.C. 20006

Acts as a clearinghouse for neighborhood activities of insurance companies and as a catalyst for community revitalization and development programs.

Lenders Community Investment Report 1120 G Street, N.W. Suite 300 Washington, D.C. 20005

Covers lender participation in public and private partnerships for housing, small business, community and economic development.

Community Investment Institute 100 West Cold Spring Lane Room T-6W Baltimore, Md. 21210

Community Lending Institute 173 West Madison Street Suite 612 Chicago, Ill. 60602

Designed for community development organizations, bank staff and public agencies, the programs provide training in techniques and procedures for community reinvestment financing.

Community Investment Corporation Printer's Square 600 South Federal Street Suite 306 Chicago, Ill. 60605

A leader in urban lending for a decade, this mortgage banking firm represents a consortium of Chicago banks.

South Shore Bank 7054 South Jeffery Boulevard Chicago, Ill. 60649

The first neighborhood development bank in the country, it provides an example of how a bank can work for community betterment.

Woodstock Institute 417 South Dearborn Street Chicago, Ill. 60605

Has extensive experience in discussing community credit needs with local leaders and provides several publications on reinvestment.

Council of State Community Affairs Agencies Hall of the States 444 North Capitol Street, N.W. Suite 251 Washington, D.C. 20001

Serves as a clearinghouse on redevelopment programs administered by state community affairs agencies and advises on housing and community and economic development in state programs. Also contact the agency in your state or the city or county department of community affairs, housing department and related agencies.

See also: Paying for Preservation

Homesteading

"The potent metaphor of the self-reliant pioneer wresting a home from a hostile environment is an important factor in the wide public and political interest in urban homesteading. . . . There are many differences in methods and outcomes, but . . . any homesteading program must face the common problems of granting real property to settlers to achieve social goals."

U.S. Department of Housing and Urban Development, *The Urban Homesteading Catalogue*, vol. III.

"Increasingly, cities are using urban homesteading as a solution to such problems as displacement and abandonment. . . . Housing abandonment . . . refers to vacant, deteriorated properties that have been vandalized and whose owners have seemingly walked away from their investment. Abandonment, however, is more than an empty house. It is a complex process of social, political and economic forces. . . . One of the main reasons for concern over abandoned housing is the devastating impact it has on individual neighborhoods. Abandoned structures act as a focus of neighborhood decay and constitute a physical and psychological hazard to neighborhood residents."

Ron Doyle and Hugh Allen, "New Frontiers in Urban Homesteading." HUD *Challenge,* May 1979.

"Until 1973, no city had formally recognized the peril posed by abandonment. Then, little Wilmington, Delaware, poxed at the time by 1,200 abandoned one- and two-story homes, passed its 'Urban Homesteading Ordinance.' The new law made it possible to deal with abandonment by giving away the homes acquired in tax foreclosures."

William G. Conway, "'People Fire' in the Ghetto Ashes." *Saturday Review,* July 23, 1977.

Homesteading programs:
1. Prevent abandoned properties from infecting a community.
2. Fix up houses as a tonic for the area.
3. Provide decent housing for low- and moderate-income people.
4. Preserve old and interesting houses.
5. Return tax-delinquent property to the tax rolls.
6. Make home ownership realistic.

Before-and-after views of brick row houses that were rescued and brought back to life in Baltimore's Oldtown homesteading neighborhood. (Baltimore Department of Housing and Community Development)

The Urban Homesteading Catalogue. Urban Systems Research and Engineering. Washington, D.C.: HUD, 1977. 169 pp. 3 vols.

Urban Homesteading: A Guide for Local Officials. Urban Systems Research and Engineering. Washington, D.C.: HUD, 1979. 53 pp., illus., append., index.

Evaluation of the Urban Homesteading Demonstration Program: Final Report. Vol. 1: *A Summary Assessment.* Urban Systems Research and Engineering. Washington, D.C.: HUD, 1981. 107 pp. $5. HUD–PDR–719. Available from HUD User, P.O. Box 280, Germantown, Md. 20874.

Urban Homesteading. James W. Hughes and Kenneth D. Bleakly, Jr. New Brunswick, N.J.: Center for Urban Policy Research, 1975. 276 pp.

Homesteading in Urban U.S.A. Anne Clark and Zelma Riven. New York: Praeger, 1977. 179 pp., append., biblio.

Urban Homesteading: An Annotated Bibliography. Mary Vance. Chicago: Council of Planning Librarians, 1976. No. 963. 22 pp. $2 pb.

Contact
Director of Urban Homesteading
U.S. Department of Housing and Urban Development
Office of Urban Rehabilitation
451 7th Street, S.W.
Room 7168
Washington, D.C. 20410

The Housing and Community Development Act of 1974 authorized HUD to implement a federal urban homesteading program. As of 1984, 132 localities were participating in the program and another 52 were using other sources (including CDBG funds) to sponsor homesteading programs. Contact your city or county housing or community development agency to determine if it is a participant.

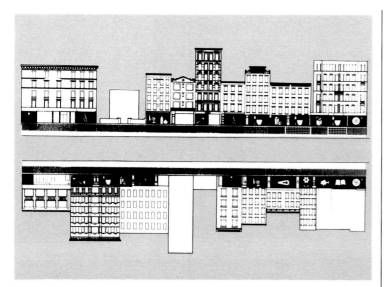

Analysis of storefront activities on Mulberry Street in New York's Little Italy, showing the variety of commercial businesses that provide vitality for neighborhoods. From *How to Save Your Own Street.*

Abandoned building in Washington Hill offered through Baltimore's shopsteading program, before and after rehabilitation. (Doug Barber)

The Neighborhood's Business

"Just as neighborhoods have traditionally played an important role in the vitality of cities, so have commercial centers played a key role in the viability of neighborhoods. It was at the corner grocery store . . . that early neighborhood residents bought their staples. At the local dressmaker's christening and wedding dresses were carefully made. Local bakeries and pubs, beauty parlors, and barber shops provided not only services but a place where neighborly conversation abounded. Clearly, neighborhood commercial centers served important social as well as economic functions. As America became more and more a melting pot; as population shifted to the suburbs . . . and as public transportation and the personal auto increased mobility, neighborhood commercial centers became less important. In some urban areas, only skeletons remain to remind residents what the neighborhood commercial center once was."

> Adrienne M. Levatino, *Neighborhood Commercial Rehabilitation.* Washington, D.C.: National Association of Housing and Redevelopment Officials (2600 Virginia Avenue, N.W., 20037), 1978.

"In magazine spreads on the latest 'recycled' neighborhoods, the ghosts don't show. What about the little Greek grocer with the penny candy who has been replaced with yet another plant boutique? How about the window signs that once called out Hardware, Shoe Repair and Panaderia? Now they all say Antiques in three different, clever ways. Where did the shot-and-a-beer crowd go when Mike's Good Luck Tap became the Serendipity Scene?"

> Bruce M. Kriviskey, "Neighborhoods." *Journal of Architectural Education,* November 1977.

"Before the designation to a special zoning district, the Little Italy zoning permitted high-rise tower development, as well as encouraging manufacturing and parking uses. Such development would certainly conflict with the community efforts of maintaining the unique neighborhood quality of Little Italy, and disrupt the continuity of the street at ground level. The result would defeat the major objectives of the revitalization efforts. . . . The Little Italy Preservation District has become a prototype for other communities to create guidelines for the preservation of neighborhoods."

> Raquel Ramati, *How to Save Your Own Street*

Analyzing Neighborhood Retail Opportunities: A Guide for Carrying Out a Preliminary Market Study. Wim Wiewel and Robert Mier. PAS Report 358. Chicago: American Planning Association, 1981. 22 pp., appends. $10 pb.

Neighborhood Commercial Revitalization Conference. Washington, D.C.: National Center for Urban Ethnic Affairs, 1980. 40 pp. $2.50.

"Revitalization of Commercial Areas in Urban Neighborhoods," Benjamin Goldstein. *Practicing Planner,* June 1976. American Planning Association (1313 East 60th Street, Chicago, Ill. 60637).

"Commercial Revitalization: A Conservation Approach." *Conserve Neighborhoods,* Summer 1979.

Neighborhood Commercial Revitalization. Helen Rosenberg and Dottie Stephenson. Monticello, Ill.: Vance Bibliographies, 1980. P-406. 6 pp. $1.40 photocopy.

Little Italy Special District. Urban Design Group. New York: City Planning Commission, 1976. 68 pp., illus.

Montague Street Revitalization. Mayor's Office of Downtown Brooklyn Development. New York: Department of City Planning (185 Montague Street, Brooklyn, N.Y. 11201), 1976. 80 pp., illus., append.

Atlantic Avenue: Special Zoning District. Office of Downtown Brooklyn Development, 1974. 47 pp.

Back Bay Architectural District: Business Sector Guidelines. Back Bay Architectural Commission. Boston: Boston Redevelopment Authority (City Hall, 02201), 1977.

Haverhill Streetscape: Washington Street Shoe District, Haverhill, Massachusetts. Guidelines for Architectural Preservation. Society for the Preservation of New England Antiquities Consulting Services Group. Haverhill: City of Haverhill and Haverhill Public Library, 1977.

See also: Main Streets

Shopsteading: New Business Frontiers

"Baltimore has a unique shopsteading program, begun in 1977, that is modeled on the city's successful homesteading program. . . . With shopsteading, the city sells unused commercial buildings for $100 to merchants who will renovate the property and operate a business there for two or more years. Most of the shopsteading activity is concentrated in neighborhoods where the commercial area is a key factor in stabilizing and upgrading the surrounding residential communities. The city helps the shopsteader finance the rehabilitation, which must comply with certain architectural guidelines agreed upon in each neighborhood."

> *Conserve Neighborhoods,* November–December 1980.

Contacts

Shopsteading Coordinator
Commercial Revitalization Division
Department of Housing and Community Development
222 East Saratoga Street
Room 705
Baltimore, Md. 21202

Office of Special Housing
Department of Housing, Preservation and Development
100 Gold Street
Room 8043
New York, N.Y. 10038

Poster developed by HUD illustrating a kaleidoscope of neighborhood activities. (U.S. Department of Housing and Urban Development)

Grant Avenue in Chinatown, one of San Francisco's most famous neighborhoods, home to 70,000. (San Francisco Convention and Visitors Bureau)

A Nation of Neighborhoods

The people most important for the neighborhood's future are the people who live and work there. By working as a team, homeowners, tenants and business people can reinforce each other's confidence in the neighborhood. Even a small neighborhood group can have a strong impact as its presence often spurs residents to initiate individual improvement efforts in their homes and on their streets.

> "Organizing Guide: Ideas for Bringing Your Neighborhood Together." *Conserve Neighborhoods*, September–October 1981.

Jogging Neighborhood Spirit

Trails through historic neighborhoods have been blazed by community group sponsorship of preservation races. In Baltimore, 7-Eleven food stores cosponsored a race through eight neighborhoods. Three Reading, Pa., neighborhoods welcomed racers in a contest sponsored by the runners club, citizens association and city government, with prizes awarded by local retailers. Runners in Kansas City retraced the historic trail of early settlers in the Pioneer Run, cosponsored with a local hospital as a finale to the neighborhood's 150th anniversary celebration.

Callowhill Citizens' Association
P.O. Box 717
Reading, Pa. 19603

Westport Tomorrow
4000 Baltimore Street
Kansas City, Mo. 64111

Organized to the Core

Using a grant from Apple Computer, Inc., neighborhood organizations in Kansas tied their main technical activities into a single network. In return for a computer, printer, software and telephone hookups, each organization volunteered to develop one or more of 10 programs or data pools for rehabilitation contractor specifications and financial pro formas as well as marketing programs for old houses and weatherization loans.

Kansas City Neighborhood Alliance
1627 Main Street
Suite 1200
Kansas City, Mo. 64108

Painting the Neighborhood

For low-income people who could buy paint but could not do the work of painting their houses, this program hired young people aged 16–21 to pick up the paint brushes. Other "Operation Paint Brushes" supply the paint rather than the labor.

Eight-CAP
121 Franklin Street, S.E.
Grand Rapids, Mich. 49503

The People Who Care Enough

When hard times hit Hallmark Cards, the company made available teams of surplus workers for a weatherization program in low-income neighborhoods. Employee groups weatherized the houses of needy people at no cost.

Westport Tomorrow
4000 Baltimore Street
Kansas City, Mo. 64111

Worth Another Look

To launch an aggressive marketing program for older neighborhoods, city officials, realtors and neighborhood associations joined together to sponsor "Worth Another Look." Beginning with a Sunday open house, the program proceeded to workshops on investing in an older home, structural and safety improvements and developing an old home's character.

Citizens Information Center
129 North 10th Street
Lincoln, Neb. 68508

Bettering by Bartering

Recent economic hard times have brought a resurgence of resource exchange networks, otherwise known as bartering. A home repair in exchange for a hand-painted sign is just one of many barters beautifying neighborhoods. Some organizations allow a credit for hours worked by a barter network member or a team. Training workshops often are provided to strengthen the available skills.

Germantown Residents Acting to Conserve Energy (GRACE)
5002 Wayne Avenue
Philadelphia, Pa. 19144

Resident repairing his porch in Anacostia, Washington, D.C., where a NHS program is active. (Neighborhood Housing Services)

Grand Rapids, Mich., house acquired by the Heritage Hill Foundation with National Trust aid and revitalized by students. (Grand Rapids Press)

Miller's River Self-Help
Network
New Boston Road
South Royalston, Mass. 01331

Hello Pages Barter Network
Neighborhood Economic
Development Corporation
357 Van Buren
Eugene, Ore. 97402

On Common Ground
An association of neighborhood groups in low-income areas of Dallas has gotten into the house-moving business in order to save several dozen old houses while also providing needed housing. The Southland Corporation donated the houses and moving costs to spare them from a large inner-city develop-ment. Moved to vacant lots in five neighborhoods, the houses were rehabilitated and then sold or leased.

Common Ground Community
Economic Development
Corporation
5405 East Grand
Dallas, Tex. 75223

Dallas Historic Preservation
League
2902 Swiss Avenue
Dallas, Tex. 75204

Hands-on History
Based on the assumption that all of the city's neighborhoods had a history worth researching and publicizing, Rochester's ses-quicentennial proved to be a catalyst for a citywide effort to research the history of its neigh-borhoods. A tremendous amount of volunteer effort culminated in Neighborhood History Week, when 17 pam-phlets, 18 exhibits and walking tours were unveiled for the entire city.

Daniel Karin, Director
Neighborhood History Project
251 Sherwood Avenue
Rochester, N.Y. 14619

A Model Block
Historical streetlights were only one of the improvements achieved under a city Model Block Program that also spurred tree planting, new curbs, gutters and sidewalks and demolition of an unsafe property. Residents helped by hanging banners and planting flowers.

Gifford Park Association
71 Park Row
Elgin, Ill. 60120

A Tree Grows in Manhattan
Proving that you don't have to be a Rockefeller to own a piece of New York, friends of an endangered city garden sold "deeds" to single square-inch parcels of this neighborhoood oasis in return for $5 contribu-tions when the city made plans to sell the land at auction. The mayor bought the first inch. The city then sold the land to the Trust for Public Land, the Green Guerillas hold title and the urban gardeners maintain the site.

Trust for Public Land
254 West 31st Street
New York, N.Y. 10001

Green Guerillas
417 Lafayette Street
New York, N.Y. 10003

Something to Celebrate
Among many cities celebrating their neighborhoods, Oklahoma City sponsored a citywide event with 200 organizations taking part in weeklong festivities—block parties, flower and tree planting in parks, an awards ceremony and a car rally through historic neighborhoods. Louisville highlighted its neigh-borhood celebration with a slide show series in which local groups depicted their history, architecture and neighborhood activities.

Old Louisville Information
Center
1340 South Fourth Street
Louisville, Ky. 40208

One-Way Turnaround
By documenting such hazards as speeding, traffic volume, pol-lution and reluctance of some people to live on one-way streets, Denver residents have worked to return a number of one-way neighborhood streets to two ways.

West Washington Park
Neighborhood Association
Washington Park Community
Center
809 South Washington
Denver, Colo. 80209

More Than a Home
Two local Neighborhood Hous-ing Services found out that a historic house can be more than just a home. In Clearwater, Fla., the cooperation of a physician, the city government, historical society and board of realtors helped put the NHS into its new home, which also serves as a museum. A Philadelphia land-mark that received the nation's first mortgage from a savings and loan association was re-stored for another NHS.

Clearwater NHS
P.O. Box 11726
Clearwater, Fla. 33516

Philadelphia NHS
1705 Unity Street
Philadelphia, Pa. 19124

Main Streets

13

Main Street was and is more than just bricks and mortar, more than just another shopping center. It is the traditional center of a community, a center not defined so much geographically or architecturally as it is socially. It is a place where people doing a quick errand run into people they know and end up spending several hours. It is a place for strolling and window shopping, and watching other people go by. It is a place where most merchants know customers by face if not by name. It is a place where parades and other public celebrations are held. It is, in short, a place for activities of all kinds, for all kinds of people.

Project for Public Spaces, *What Do People Do Downtown? How to Look at Main Street Activity*

"It was called Town Street when it was a single wilderness road in New England, High Street in a southern New Jersey town, Broad Street in Pennsylvania or South Carolina, Market Street in Ohio, Grand Street in a brash Wyoming city, Broadway in California. But as Main Street, it was uniquely American, a powerful symbol of shared experience, of common memory, of the challenge and the struggle of building a civilization. . . . Main Street was always familiar, always recognizable as the heart and soul of village, town or city. Main Street is one moment, and many, in the flow of time."

Carole Rifkind, *Main Street: The Face of Urban America*

"The principal street of a small town, in the United States, used to be Main Street, but since the appearance of Sinclair Lewis's novel of that name, in 1920, the designation has taken on a derogatory implication, and is going out."

H. L. Mencken, *The American Language*. New York: Knopf, 1938.

Main Street, Minot, N.D., c. 1910, a broad avenue lined with Italianate brick buildings. (State Historical Society of Wisconsin)

Sinclair Lewis's Main Street: Sauk Centre, Minn., c. 1925. (*St. Paul Dispatch*, Minnesota Historical Society)

"This is America—a town of a few thousand, in a region of wheat and corn and dairies and little groves.

The town is, in our tale, called 'Gopher Prairie, Minnesota.' But its Main Street is the continuation of Main Streets everywhere. The story would be the same in Ohio or Montana, in Kansas or Kentucky or Illinois, and not very differently would it be told Up New York State or in the Carolina Hills."

Sinclair Lewis, Foreword. *Main Street*. 1920. New York: New American Library, 1974.

"In most countries, the great streets have memorable names. London, for instance, has a lot of them—Bond Street, Fleet Street, Carnaby Street, Piccadilly. Paris has the Champs Elysees. What do we have? . . . Of the 25 most common street names, seven are former Presidents, nine of them are named after trees. If you thought Broadway or Main were in there—Main is 32nd. . . ."

"A Few Minutes with Andy Rooney," *60 Minutes*. CBS News, September 17, 1978.

"As with any real street, there are two sides to the idea of Main Street. The idea of Main Street can be as uncomplicated as the shortest distance between two points, or as complex as the entire subject of human society. . . . Main streets are commercial streets. . . . On the other side, main streets are historic streets, religious streets, important streets, cultural streets, dignified streets. There is more to main street than buying and selling and the jingle of trade."

Main Streets. Champion Papers Imagination XXII. New York: Champion Papers International (Marketing Services, 245 Park Avenue, 10017), 1978.

Washington Street, Junction City, Kans., in 1921. From *Main Street: The Face of Urban America*. (Joseph J. Pennell, Kansas Collection, University of Kansas Libraries)

Roots in the American Memory

During the first quarter of the nineteenth century, seaport cities such as Boston, New York, Philadelphia, Baltimore and Charleston experienced remarkable growth, while many inland towns and villages developed as a result of improved land transportation. Main Street stretched many times its original mile or two-mile length, to link one town with the next, to join with the growing network of stage routes, post roads and turnpikes. By the 1820s, there were more than 100,000 miles of roads lacing the East and connecting it to the trans-Appalachian West. . . . Towns sprang up as if "by the power of enchantment." The through route passed by Main Street; along its length the colonnaded temple fronts of hotels, churches and public buildings grandly embellished the street facade with the optimism of a young nation. . . .

It was principally from New England that Main Street traced its origins, in the century and a half between the first colonial settlement and the nation's independence. As an expression of that time, and that place, Main Street has deep roots in the American memory.

Carole Rifkind, *Main Street: The Face of Urban America*

Main Street: The Face of Urban America. Carole Rifkind. New York: Harper and Row, 1977. 267 pp., illus., appends., biblio., index. $20 hb, $8.95 pb.

The best pictorial record of Main Street past—its origins, its form, the experience of Main Street and its downfalls and rebirths.

Small Town America: A Narrative History, 1620—The Present. Richard Lingeman. New York: Putnam, 1980. 547 pp., biblio., notes, index. $15.95 hb, $8.95 pb.

A sensitive analysis of American towns that includes extensive looks at their most important street and the role it has played in community life.

"The Fall and Rise of Main Street." Ada Louise Huxtable. Reprint from *New York Times,* May 30, 1976. Albany: Preservation League of New York State (307 Hamilton Street, 12210). 4 pp. $1 pb.

A brief but classic analysis of the beginnings and the decline of American downtowns.

MAIN STREET
The Face of Urban America

Main Street, Salt Lake City, c. 1925. (Shipler, Utah State Historical Society)

"Main Street is more than a fond image of the past; it is a vision of the future as well."

Frank W. Naylor, Under Secretary of Agriculture

See also: Roadside Architecture, Small Towns (Form and Function)

Deadwood, S.D., c. 1880, the main trade center in the Black Hills during the gold rush years. (Nebraska State Historical Society)

Main Street, Wabasha, Minn., c. 1863, with its substantial brick storefronts. (Minnesota Historical Society)

Abandoned buildings on Main Street, Eureka, Colo., in 1949. (Russell Lee, Farm Security Administration)

Street fair in the 1940s in Galesburg, Ill., one of three towns originally selected for the National Trust Main Street Project.

Commercial building (c. 1883) in Galesburg, Ill., seen in an old view before the three bay windows were replaced with an aluminum false front.

Nebraska City, Neb., in the 1920s. (Nebraska State Historical Society)

Pendleton, Ore., c. 1902. (Bowman, University of Oregon Library)

Main Street, Sauk Centre, Minn., in 1957, with the Main Street cinema at left. (Minnesota Historical Society)

The Look of Main Street

Main Street U.S.A. is essentially a 19th-century phenomenon; its prosperity and vitality were intensified as towns and cities grew. False-front, wood-framed frontier streets developed into solid brick and stone mercantile avenues. The street was pedestrian in scale, geared to the horse and buggy and the family enterprise. Its style was solidly Victorian. There were those Jones Blocks and Brown Blocks and Smith Buildings of pressed red brick with General Grant trim, their dates proudly centered in bracketed and pedimented cornices. Ornate cast-iron-fronted structures borrowed Roman and Venetian references from elaborate and handsome "palaces of trade." A common commercial vernacular tied together anything from Georgian and Greek Revival to High Victorian Gothic. A sequence of fashionable facades became the unified 19th-century blockfront. . . .

It was, in the American tradition, largely speculative construction. But this was sound building that served its purpose with character, humanity and style.

Ada Louise Huxtable, "The Fall and Rise of Main Street"

"The ever-expanding scope and complexity of commercial endeavors resulted in buildings that were increasingly specialized in their function and diversified in their use. Mass manufacture of building products, including ornament, and the creation of new materials enabled thousands of buildings to possess a distinctive appearance heretofore reserved for only the costliest edifices. Facades served as advertisements for the businesses within. Small and large buildings alike were often conceived as monuments to the industriousness of the men who commissioned them. Main Street rapidly grew to be a collage, offering a great spectrum of images."

Richard Longstreth, "Compositional Types in American Commercial Architecture: 1800–1950." In *The Main Street Book*

The Arcade (1904, Frank Andrews), Dayton, Ohio. (Craig MacIntosh, Landfall Press)

"Main Street was generally left to grow anarchically—a proliferation of stores and buildings of varying shapes, sizes, and materials with relationship to one another. . . .

Must of the ugliness Carol Kennicott [in *Main Street*] saw was attributable to new technology—the automobile and its noise, the telephone and electric wires. In towns that had, unlike Gopher Prairie, some manufacturing, the soot and pollution of soft-coal smoke could be added to the indictment. All these developments came in the 1890s and 1900s, further contributing to the chaotic look of many towns. Citizens of real-life Main Streets, who were less disaffected than Carol, may not have noticed the clutter, or perhaps they regarded it as tangible evidence of Growth and Prosperity."

Richard Lingeman, *Small Town America: A Narrative History, 1620—The Present*

O Modernization

"O modernization, what crimes are committed in thy name. The 1950's was a period of wholesale destruction. The debacle was aided, abetted and accelerated by building-products manufacturers who promoted the use of plastic and metal panels for the total resurfacing of old buildings for a 'new look.' This had the curious advantage of deliberately reproducing the worst feature of the new shopping centers with which they were trying to compete: their total lack of architectural distinction."

Ada Louise Huxtable, "The Fall and Rise of Main Street"

"What hurts are not the bygone buildings but the mutilated ones, the proud old houses that are publicly humiliated with 'modernistic' formica fronts, aluminum siding, glazed Bauhaus Box additions or neon signs sadistically stuck on ornate facades. . . . Crude architectural huckstering never helped the economy of a town. It helped kill it."

Wolf Von Eckardt, "Main Street, U.S.A.: Encouraging a Grassroots Revival." *Washington Post,* November 26, 1977.

Lithograph of Chestnut Street, Philadelphia, c. 1879, showing commercial buildings on the south side between Seventh and Eighth streets.

Commercial block (1890s), Galesburg, Ill., with distinctive gable ends over altered storefronts. (B. Clarkson Schoettle, NTHP)

A "modernized" downtown building, Mount Vernon, Ohio, in 1949. (U.S. Information Agency Collection, National Archives)

Remodeled storefronts on Seminary Street, Galesburg, Ill., before the start of the National Trust Main Street Project. (B. Clarkson Schoettle, NTHP)

The progressive loss of a Main Street building's architectural character through alteration and disuse. From *Worcester: A New England Cityscape.* (Vision, Inc.)

Hardship on Main Street

Give wily old Walt the credit. If he and his army of architects hadn't seen fit to immortalize it in his vision of the past and future that is Disneyland, few of us would have noticed the eclipse of that venerable American institution, Main Street.

That the corpse was still warm when Disney decided to embalm it in his Magic Kingdom is not important. That Main Street somehow deserved a better fate is. To be miniaturized, sanitized, and put on display with the Country Bears' Jamboree, the Enchanted Tiki Room and Mr. Toad's Wild Ride is not the way an American tradition ought to be enshrined.

Jim Wright, "Final Tribute." *New Times,* November 26, 1976.

"Main Street U.S.A." at Disneyland, Anaheim, Calif., designed to reflect the "serenity and charm of the nation's small towns c. 1900." (Disneyland)

"As Main Street loses its vitality, the community loses its special character and becomes an indistinguishable part of an endless stretch of shopping centers, car dealerships and fast food chains. If villages are not to become suburbs, if suburbs are not to become cities and if cities are not to become wastelands, then their Main Streets must survive."

Franke Keefe, review of *Main Street: The Face of Urban America. Historic Preservation,* April–June 1978.

"If one should ask the average citizen why he avoids downtown, why he goes there for one purpose only, namely, to make money, but stays away when it comes to spending it, he would probably give the following reasons:
1. He can't get into it.
2. He can't get out of it.
3. He can't get around it.
4. He finds public transportation uncomfortable and distasteful, and he can't use his car because he can't find parking space.
5. The values he receives downtown, as compared with those he can get in suburbia, become less attractive as far as shopping, movies, conveniences, amenities and beauty are concerned.
6. The sacrifices he has to make in time and nervous energy become constantly greater. And finally,
7. The city is a downright dangerous place to live in or to move around in."

Victor Gruen, *The Heart of Our Cities.* New York: Simon and Schuster, 1964.

A Downtown Research and Development Center survey asked merchants, property owners, elected officials, city staff and others connected with central business districts to identify the five most serious problems facing their downtowns. The results:

Most Serious Problems	Percent Mentions
Poor image	47
Poor cooperation	47
Parking shortage	45
Increasing competition	44
Need more downtown housing	43
Weak promotion	43
Lack retail stores	42
Ugliness/blight	31
Traffic congestion	29
Lack malls/amenities	27
Need government funds	22
Poor planning	18
Poor transit	12
Safety/crime	11
Dirtiness	10
Racial problems	10

"What is impressive is that a number of 'soft issues' rate very high. In fact, in combination, they are the leading 'problem.' "

Downtown Research and Development Center. *Downtown Idea Exchange: Downtown Recycling Bulletin,* December 1, 1977.

Country Club Plaza (1922), Kansas City, Mo., one of the oldest U.S. shopping centers. Shown are the 1923 open-air parking lot, replaced in 1958 by a parking garage, and an offstreet parking lot from 1934, replaced in 1965 by the Halls Store. (Bill Mott, Pic Studio, for J. C. Nichols Company)

Quincy Market (1826, Alexander Parris), Boston, before it was converted into Faneuil Hall Marketplace in 1976 by F. A. Stahl and Associates, with Benjamin Thompson and Associates. (© Randolph Langenbach)

"The deficiencies and problems of the typical central business district may be summarized as follows:
Physical and functional obsolescence of buildings and their environment, and unattractive, poorly maintained stores and shops.
Incompatible land uses that interrupt and interfere with the core retailing function.
Cluttered streets and sidewalks with a maze of poles, standards, trash baskets, parking meters, signs, hydrants, and overhead wires.
Poorly maintained streets, sidewalks, steps and building entrances, including alleys and rear entrances.
Lack of sign controls to avoid ugly, garish, oversize and excessive numbers of signs.
Poor accessibility over routes marked by rail conflicts, angle parked cars backing into traffic, double parked cars, and trucks loading and unloading on the streets.
Inadequate, unattractive parking at inconvenient locations.
Inadequate attention to the pedestrian and shopper, failing to offer him the safety, comfort, convenience, courtesy, and pleasant surroundings he deserves.
Failure to adhere to any total design concept tying buildings and open spaces together.
Failure to take positive, effective action, or taking trivial, futile, or detrimental action when problems are recognized."

> Chamber of Commerce of the United States of America, *Downtown Redevelopment.* Washington, D.C.: Urban Strategy Center, Chamber of Commerce, 1974.

The Faneuilization of Downtown: A Debate

" 'We really have become the downtown of Boston,' said James B. McLean Jr., general manager of the [Faneuil Hall] marketplace. 'We get 15 million visitors a year on 6½ acres of land while Disney World gets 14 million on 43 square miles.' "

> Fred Bayles, "Faneuil Hall Market Outdraws Disney World." *Washington Post* (Associated Press), August 28, 1981.

"At Quincy Market, the genius of Cambridge's most notable architect [Benjamin Thompson] was to remember a distant past and enact a familiar present—the superimposition of the safe suburbs on the risky city."

> Andrew Kopkind, "Kitsch for the Rich." *The Real Paper* (Boston), February 19, 1977.

"The truly sophisticated in Boston, of course, now treat Quincy Market the way they might treat a large and overcrowded cocktail party—explaining to anyone they happen to meet there that they just dropped in for a minute and really despise large gatherings and just wanted to show a friend from out of town what all the talk is about."

> Calvin Trillin, "U.S. Journal: New England. Thoughts Brought On by Prolonged Exposure to Exposed Brick." *The New Yorker,* May 16, 1977.

The Malling of America

They have replaced the movies, baseball and football games, eating out, Sunday driving, and lovers lanes as the favorite haunts of most people. Americans of all ages spend more time in them than anywhere else except at home or work. . . . Rather than replacing the old neighborhood drugstores or candy stores as hangouts for kids, they are replacing villages and towns themselves.

Robert Hendrickson, "The Malling of Main Street: Suburban and City Shopping Centers." *The Grand Emporiums: The Illustrated History of America's Great Department Stores.* New York: Stein and Day, 1979.

Henry Martin. (©1981 New York Times Company)

"On low-clouded nights in Greensburg, Pennsylvania, there are two immense glowing spots in the sky: The one to the west, which is always orange, hovers over Greengate Mall; the one to the east, which for some reason is always white, is the aureole of Westmoreland Mall. These are the signatures written across the night deciding Greensburg's future. They are the culmination of the Highway Comfort Culture's sacking of the city, the drawing-out of its middle-class traffic, the abandonment of downtown to those who work in the county courthouse and to motorless old people and students. The city has been slow to adapt to the changes, immersed in the lethargy and squabbling that is sometimes known as the political process. Town governments and merchant associations simply can't function or respond as efficiently as the mall's single management. The town isn't a controllable unit; a lot of people are too independent to be controlled anyway. So a large part of what has happened to the culture in the last decade has happened out on the highway: The circus is no longer in town."

William Severini Kowinski, "The Malling of America." *New Times,* May 1, 1978.

Main Street vs. the Malls

"Till now, most small cities have supinely succumbed to the pressures of developers and the big chains: Sears, J.C. Penney, Gimbels and similar retailers. They find it easier (and usually cheaper) to plunk a mall into the middle of a cornfield and surround it with asphalt than undergo the delicate negotiations necessary to insert major development into a downtown setting.

Now—belatedly, yet in increasing numbers—smaller cities are starting to fight back."

Neal R. Peirce, "America's S(mall) Cities." *Washington Post,* June 12, 1978.

Stopping Shopping Centers

1. Making downtowns more competitive to preempt the suburban shopping center market
2. Creating incentives for downtown development (tax abatements, eminent domain, zoning bonuses, parking, transit)
3. New zoning controls and review procedures
4. Instituting impact review requirements for new suburban development
5. Targeting public investment to cities and away from suburbs
6. Using political pressure for downtown revitalization

From *Strategies for Stopping Shopping Centers*

The Malling of America: An Inside Look at the Great Consumer Paradise. William Severini Kowinski. New York: Morrow, 1985. 415 pp., illus. $17.95 hb.

A description of the "mallaise" and "mal de mall" in "our united states of shopping" by a vocal critic. Kowinski looks at some of the 5,000 "capitals of suburbia" and their successful principles of enclosure, protection and control.

Shopping Centers: U.S.A. George Sternlieb and James W. Hughes. New Brunswick, N.J.: Center for Urban Policy Research, Rutgers University (P.O. Box 489, 08854), 1981. 256 pp. $17.95 hb.

A comprehensive analysis of the impact of shopping centers, with contributions from 27 retail experts. Subjects include community conservation guidelines, economic impact of regional malls and appraising central city options.

Strategies for Stopping Shopping Centers: A Guidebook on Minimizing Excessive Suburban Shopping Center Growth. Laurence A. Alexander, ed. New York: Downtown Research and Development Center, 1980. 100 pp. $35.

"How to Win Mall Wars," Jay Neugeboren. In "Mall Mania," *Mother Jones,* May 1979.

"Methods of Stopping Shopping Centers." *Downtown Idea Exchange,* 1979.

Robert MacNeil, "Main Street vs. the Malls." The MacNeil/ Lehrer Report, January 26, 1979. Transcripts available from MacNeil/Lehrer Report, WNET/13, Box 345, New York, N.Y. 10101. $2.

"Two Sides of a Pyramid: The Case Against the Burlington Mall (John G. Simon); The Case for It (Fred Blair, Jr.)." *Planning,* May 1980.

"What Is the Future for Downtown Retailing in Middle America: A Middle Market Mallaise," Rodney E. Engelen. *Urban Land,* October 1979.

Suburban Shopping Centers vs. The Central Business Districts: A Bibliography. Edward Duensing, ed. Monticello, Ill.: Vance Bibliographies, 1980. 9 pp. $2 pb.

Central Business District Planning and Control of Outlying Shopping Centers. Clifford L. Weaver and Christopher J. Duerksen. *Urban Law Annual,* vol. 14, 1977.

"The Impact of Regional Malls: Legal Questions," Michael Fix. *Center City Report,* March 1980.

"What is thrown up in a field overnight cannot compete with a century of style."

Ada Louise Huxtable, "The Fall and Rise of Main Street"

Learning From the Other Side

"Main Street must learn from the mall and adopt its strategies. . . . In many ways, Main Street areas can't compete on the mall's terms because Main Street can never provide the conveniences of totally enclosed, climate-controlled shopping, unlimited free parking with easy visual access to the stores, and a carefully managed store mix. However, Main Street *can* provide a much-needed alternative shopping experience, and it *can* adopt some of the same marketing and managerial actions that make the malls so effective."

"Main Street: Some Commonly Asked Questions." Supplement to *Preservation News,* May 1978.

Dollars and Cents of Shopping Centers. 1981. 2nd ed. Washington, D.C.: Urban Land Institute, 1984. 325 pp., illus. $115.

A statistical analysis of 950 shopping centers in the United States and Canada.

New Dimensions in Shopping Centers and Stores. Louis G. Redstone. New York: McGraw-Hill, 1976. 344 pp. $32.50.

A primer for architects and developers on development of regional shopping centers, with examples.

Shopping Center Development Handbook. J. Ross McKeever, Nathaniel M. Griffin, Frank H. Spink, Jr., with Commercial and Office Development Council, Urban Land Institute. 1977. 2nd ed. Washington, D.C.: Urban Land Institute, 1985. 290 pp., illus., appends., index. $50 hb.

Covers renovation of old commercial centers as well as planning and design of new ones.

Downtown mall created in Salem, Mass. (Laurence Lowry)

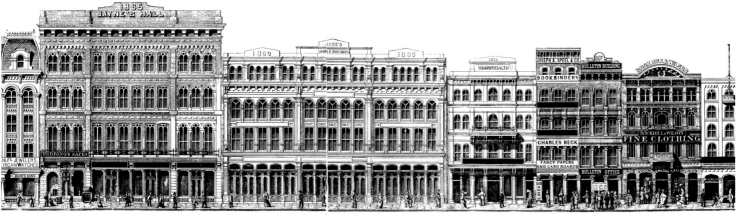

North side of Chestnut Street, Philadelphia, c. 1879, showing Italianate-style commercial buildings favored in the 19th century.

Bringing Back Main Street

A revived Main Street preserves history—and also offers aesthetic satisfaction, sociability, comfort, convenience and economy.

Carole Rifkind, *Main Street: The Face of Urban America*

There are two major arguments for preserving downtowns. One is "because it is there" and represents too large an investment in property development and government services to be written off. A second reason is that a city's official boundaries seldom conform to the size and scope of today's metropolitan area. With business and upper-income families migrating beyond the city's boundaries, the municipality must do what it can to preserve its tax base.

Johnathan Barnett, "What's New in Downtown Planning?" *Urban Design,* Spring 1977.

"If Main Street cannot recapture its former position as a town's main or sole shopping district, it can at least recapture its position as a clearly identifiable and attractive place by uncovering, improving, restoring and maintaining its older commercial structures."

National Main Street Center

"The results [of some restoration efforts] were sometimes false gingerbread, endless candle shops, anemically stocked boutiques, saloons with sawdust on the floor, and ersatz ice cream parlors. But, when the restoration was done with integrity and there was something there to restore in towns such as Corning, New York, Medina, Ohio, Madison, Indiana, and Jacksonville, Oregon, when the patina of neon and aluminum siding was scraped away, a considerable beauty was often revealed. Towns that restored found that they also succeeded in revitalizing their downtowns."

Richard Lingeman, *Small Town America: A Narrative History, 1620—The Present*

Contacts

National Main Street Center
National Trust for
Historic Preservation
1785 Massachusetts Avenue, N.W.
Washington, D.C. 20036

International Downtown
Executives Association
915 15th Street, N.W.
Suite 900
Washington, D.C. 20005

Downtown Research and
Development Center
1143 Broadway
Suite 1407
New York, N.Y. 10010

National Development Council
1421 29th Street, N.W.
Washington, D.C. 20007

City Economic Development
Program
National League of Cities
1301 Pennsylvania Avenue, N.W.
Washington, D.C. 20004

U.S. Department of Agriculture
Office of Rural Development
Policy
Washington, D.C. 20250

Institute for Environmental
Action
530 West 25th Street
New York, N.Y. 10001

Urban Land Institute
1090 Vermont Avenue, N.W.
Suite 300
Washington, D.C. 20005

Project for Public Spaces
875 Avenue of the Americas
Room 201
New York, N.Y. 10001

Small Business Administration
1441 L Street, N.W.
Washington, D.C. 20416

National Council for Urban
Economic Development
1730 K Street, N.W.
Washington, D.C. 20036

Partners for Livable Places
1429 21st Street, N.W.
Washington, D.C. 20036

Chamber of Commerce of the
United States
1615 H Street, N.W.
Washington, D.C. 20062

National Retail Merchants
Association
100 West 31st Street
New York, N.Y. 10001

1000 Connecticut Avenue, N.W.
Suite 700
Washington, D.C. 20036

Institutional and Municipal
Parking Congress
915 15th Street, N.W.
Washington, D.C. 20006

International Council of
Shopping Centers
665 Fifth Avenue
New York, N.Y. 10022

Periodicals

Main Street News
National Main Street Center
1785 Massachusetts Avenue, N.W.
Washington, D.C. 20036

Center City Report
International Downtown
Executives Association
915 15th Street, N.W.
Suite 900
Washington, D.C. 20005

Downtown Idea Exchange
Downtown Promotion Reporter
Downtown Planning and
Development Annual
Downtown Research and
Development Center
1143 Broadway
Suite 1407
New York, N.Y. 10010

City Economic Development
Nation's Cities Weekly
National League of Cities
1301 Pennsylvania Avenue, N.W.
Washington, D.C. 20004

National Mall Monitor
Arbor Office Center
1321 U.S. 19 South
Suite 500
Clearwater, Fla. 33516

Shopping Center World
Communication Channels, Inc.
6285 Barfield Road
Atlanta, Ga. 30328

Shopping Centers Today
International Council of
Shopping Centers
665 Fifth Avenue
New York, N.Y. 10022

Sign Craft Magazine
P.O. Box 06031
Fort Myers, Fla. 33906

Signs of the Times
Signs of the Times Publishing
Company
407 Gilbert Avenue
Cincinnati, Ohio 45202

Logo of the National Trust Main Street program, based on a Madison, Ind., paving brick.

The National Main Street Center

"What we're trying to enrich and preserve on Main Street is more than just the quality of the buildings. It's the quality of life on Main Street—its traditional role as a place where people meet each other, argue with their newspaper editor, and so on. But Main Street must be economically thriving in order to keep the buildings going. So, as preservationists, we must look at what the business people and civic officials are doing or not doing that's causing the place to die. Look at how—without radical surgery—we can incrementally upgrade Main Street and bring it back to life."

Mary C. Means. In "Main Streets Get Street-wise," *Historic Preservation*, March–April 1979.

"What is the Main Street methodology? The foundation of the program is preservation: using those elements of quality that have survived as assets upon which we can build a lasting, positive physical and emotional image for everyone who uses downtown. We have adopted many of the strategies of modern shopping mall management, although on a voluntary basis. Three components—*organization, promotion* and *design*—are carefully orchestrated to create a positive, identifiable image of downtown. As the program evolves and confidence in downtown improves, a fourth component is brought into play: *economic restructuring*. Careful economic and market analysis usually confirms that while most small city downtowns will never regain their dominance as primary retail centers, they can maintain economic strength by attracting new nonretail functions, including office, recreational and residential uses."

National Main Street Center

National Main Street Center
National Trust for
Historic Preservation
1785 Massachusetts Avenue, N.W.
Washington, D.C. 20036

The National Main Street Center, a special demonstration program of the National Trust, is an expansion of the Trust's nationally recognized Main Street Project, whose goal was to encourage economic revitalization within the context of historic preservation in downtowns of small cities.

Can small-town Main Streets compete with malls? Should towns attempt to halt the flight of larger stores to the malls? How can downtown be marketed as "historic" without resorting to fake history and period pieces?

These and other questions were explored from 1977 to 1980 in three pilot communities: Hot Springs, S.C. (pop. 5,000); Madison, Ind. (pop. 13,600); and Galesburg, Ill. (pop. 38,000). In each, significant improvements in the downtown's economy and general appearance were achieved over a three-year period under the guidance of a full-time National Trust project manager.

The program has since been expanded to more than a dozen states and 130 towns. In communities of 50,000 and under in each state, model strategies are created to support local downtown revitalization efforts. The center brings together existing private and public resources in towns whose older central business districts retain some vestige of their visual character yet whose economic position is slipping. Its goal is a return to community self-reliance and vigorous Main Streets. During the first three years, 80 towns achieved 600 rehabilitations totaling $64 million, 650 facade renovations and 69 new projects bringing in $84 million.

In 1985 the center launched a new program to help revive business districts in eight larger cities. It also has started a membership network, provides technical assistance and training programs, and issues publications and audiovisual materials. A videotape series was supported by the National Endowment for the Arts and the U.S. Department of Agriculture. The center also works with numerous other public and private agencies to coordinate the use of financial and technical aid for Main Street activities. The success of the center has spread to other states and nations that are now adopting the Main Street approach.

State Coordinators

Main Street Arkansas
One State Capitol Mall
Little Rock, Ark. 72201

Office of Main Street
Revitalization
1313 Sherman Street
Denver, Colo. 80203

Bureau of Historic Preservation
Division of Archives, History
and Records Management
The Capitol
Tallahassee, Fla. 32301

Main Street Program
Department of Community
Affairs
40 Marietta Street, N.W.
Atlanta, Ga. 30303

Main Street Center
Office of Communities
and Development
100 Cambridge Street
Boston, Mass. 02202

Michigan Main Street
Department of Commerce
P.O. Box 30004
Lansing, Mich. 48909

Main Street Project
State Planning Agency
101 Capitol Square Building
St. Paul, Minn. 55101

State Main Street Coordinator
Department of Natural
Resources and Community
Development
P.O. Box 27687
Raleigh, N.C. 27611

Main Street Program
P.O. Box 172
Salem, Ore. 97308

Community Development
Division
513 Forum Building
Harrisburg, Pa. 17120

State Main Street Coordinator
Downtown Development
Association
P.O. Box 11637
Columbia, S.C. 29211

Main Street Project
Department of Conservation
701 Broadway
Nashville, Tenn. 37203

Main Street Project
Texas Historical Commission
P.O. Box 12276
Austin, Tex. 78711

Main Street Project
9th and Columbia Building
Olympia, Wash. 98501

Main Street: Open for Business.
Linda S. Glisson. Washington,
D.C.: National Main Street
Center, 1984. 112 pp., color
illus. $10 pb.

A special three-year report on the demonstration program in six states and 30 towns.

Removal of a sign on a Madison, Ind., store was suggested and filmed by the National Trust. (John Beckman)

Tom Moriarity of the Trust and businessman Paul Steinhardt review design plans in Madison, Ind. (James L. Ballard, NTHP)

Downtown Hot Springs, S.D., an original National Trust Main Street town, is noted for its rustic sandstone buildings. (James L. Ballard, NTHP)

The Main Street Book

Drawing on the National Trust's experience in the field of downtown revitalization, *The Main Street Book* is the first handbook to describe how to use preservation as a strategy for commercial revitalization. *The Main Street Book* chronicles the legacy and rebirth of Main Street America from the initial visions of town boosters and village improvement associations; through the more recent vicissitudes of "Modernize Main Street" campaigns, postwar sprawl and urban renewal; to the emergence of the self-help Main Street ethic embodied in the preservation movement. The book documents revitalization techniques employed by the National Trust's National Main Street Center on topics such as:

The Place of Main Street in American Life
The case for Main Street's survival: Its continuing role as a multifunctional center. The impact of the nonmetropolitan population shift on towns of under 50,000. Economic revitalization within the context of preservation.

The Image of Main Street
Its traditional role: From the early civic improvement efforts of the mid-19th century through the modernization movement of the 1930s. The impact of postwar sprawl in towns such as Columbus, Ind.; Medina, Ohio; Portsmouth, N.H.; and Corning, N.Y.

Learning From the Grassroots: The National Trust Main Street Project
The National Trust Main Street Project: Precedents for the concern for the economic and architectural integrity of downtowns. The project's inception to more recent efforts to monitor the economic impact of revitalization in the demonstration communities. Accomplishments in the Trust's original Main Street towns: Hot Springs, S.C.; Madison, Ind.; and Galesburg, Ill.

Managing Main Street Revitalization
Initial organizing: Hiring a local project manager. Assessing local needs. Working with consultants.

Doing Business on Main Street
The importance of organization, image, people and economic restructuring for downtown revitalization: Learning management lessons from the mall—consistent image, advertising, group promotions, special events, uniform hours and other cooperative techniques. Improving parking and circulation problems. Bringing business and tourism to Main Street.

Design in the Downtown
Assessing the uniqueness of each Main Street: How to analyze its design character (historical development, street patterns, building types and styles, storefront designs, signs, public amenities). Imaginative reuse of older buildings. Storefront evolution and cost-effective design techniques. Signs. Conserving and maintaining building materials. Public improvements—landscaping, pavements, street lighting, benches and other amenities.

Financing Revitalization
Public and private-sector funding sources for a Main Street project: Local sources (special assessment districts, tax increment financing, tax abatements and other mechanisms). Contributions from local organizations, foundations and corporations. State and federal funding mechanisms. Tax incentives for building rehabilitation.

Legal and Planning Considerations
Integrating Main Street concerns into private and public land-use decisions: Private land-use controls (leases, easements, covenants). Public controls (zoning, tax assessment policies, building codes, historic district ordinances, actions by local school, hospital and public works boards). Enabling legislation for local ordinances. Federally mandated review procedures for historic buildings and districts.

Typology of Commercial Building Forms
Richard Longstreth

Bibliography

Sources of Assistance

The Main Street Book: A Guide to Downtown Revitalization. Peter Hawley. National Main Street Center, National Trust for Historic Preservation. Washington, D.C.: Preservation Press, 1986. 324 pp., illus., biblio., append., index. $45 hb.

Main Street on Film

Main Street. John Karol, National Trust for Historic Preservation. 29 min., 16 mm., color. $15 rental. National Main Street Center.

Depicts towns where Main Street is coming back to life, featuring merchants and civic leaders who cope with the problems of revitalizing older commercial areas.

Main Street at Work. National Main Street Center. 20 min. Videocassette.

Series detailing revitalization in successful Main Street towns. Accompanied by a booklet with discussion questions and workshop exercises. $300 set, $80 each purchase.

The Four Point Approach, highlighting Tarboro, N.C., and Bloomsburg, Pa.

Getting Organized, profiling McKinney, Tex.; Fergus Falls, Minn.; and Shelby, N.C.

Investing in Your Image, featuring Jim Thorpe, Pa.; Hillsboro, Tex.; and Thomasville, Ga.

Bringing in Business, focusing on Statesville, N.C., and Bloomsburg, Pa.

Revitalizing Downtown. National Main Street Center. 120 min. Set of two videocassettes. $250 purchase.

Best presentations from a national videoconference addressing economic restructuring, design, organization and promotion.

The Main Street Approach. National Main Street Center. 80 slides with speech outline. $50 purchase.

Illustrates the four elements of the Main Street approach: organization, design, promotion and economic restructuring, with before-and-after views.

Keeping Up Appearances. National Main Street Center. 20 min. Slide-tape. $50 purchase.

Provides a brief nontechnical history of Main Street architecture and explores a variety of appropriate maintenance, rehabilitation and restoration techniques. With a booklet.

Signs for Main Street: Messages and Images. Norman Mintz, National Main Street Center. 11 min. Slide-tape. $50 purchase. National Main Street Center.

Offers nontechnical examples of effective sign placement and creative sign designs.

Main Street's Looking Up! National Main Street Center. 20 min. Slide-tape. $50 purchase.

Presents ideas for converting upper stories of buildings as well as large downtown buildings to new uses such as apartments, restaurants and offices. With a booklet.

Survival of a Small City. Frasconi-Salzer Films. 28 min., 16mm., color. $75 rental ($55 nonprofits); $750 purchase ($550 nonprofits). Frasconi-Salzer Films, 825 West End Avenue, 9D, New York, N.Y. 10025.

Documents South Norwalk, Conn., efforts to revitalize its run-down commercial district.

Downtowns for People. Roger Hagan, American Institute of Architects. 26 min., 16 mm., color. $40 rental; $295 purchase. Roger Hagan, 1019 Belmont Place East, Seattle, Wash. 98102. Free loan to AIA members: Audiovisual Department, American Institute of Architects, 1735 New York Avenue, N.W., Washington, D.C. 20006.

Depicts European and American downtowns from the pedestrian's viewpoint.

Nine by Nine for Downtown: How Nine Top Designers Revitalized Nine American Downtowns. Downtown Research and Development Center. Slides with script. $69 purchase.

Features projects in Muskegon and Battle Creek, Mich.; Oshkosh and Madison, Wis.; Augusta, Ga.; Cincinnati; Niagara Falls, Rome and Troy, N.Y.

Street Graphics. Landscape Architecture Foundation and U.S. Department of Housing and Urban Development. 23 min., 16 mm., color. $25 rental; $125 purchase. Landscape Architecture Foundation, 1717 N Street, N.W., Washington, D.C. 20036.

A companion to *Street Graphics: A Concept and a System.*

Modern Malls on Main Streets: 14 New Case Studies. Downtown Research and Development Center. 80 slides with script. $42 purchase. Downtown Research and Development Center.

Features new downtown malls in such cities as Baltimore, Ithaca, N.Y.; Winchester, Va.; Winona, Minn.; and Tacoma, Wash.

Converting unused upper stories of Main Street buildings such as these in Franklin, Tenn., which were renovated for apartment use, is a revitalization strategy designed to bring 24-hour activity to Main Streets.

Strategies for Revitalization

Only public-private cooperation can make downtown revitalization work, whoever starts it. And you need to get all the major downtown interests into the act— including major retailers, local bankers, the newspaper, and key citizens' groups. They should all be part of the planning process right from the start if it is to be effective.

> Anthony Downs, "The Future of Downtowns." *Small Town,* July–December 1979.

Downtown Columbus, Ind., where restoration of historic buildings has taken place along with an innovative program to retain well-known contemporary architects to design new buildings. (Balthazar Korab)

Ten Essential Elements

"1. Vision. The community must have either a strong identity of its own or a vision of what it would like to become. . . .
2. Dissatisfaction. Without a strong sense of concern or dissatisfaction with problems of the community, any effort to revitalize will be met by apathy, resistance, and complacency.
3. Cultural Activity. Cultural events such as ethnic festivals and architectural sites play a significant role in building the image of the community and creating an exciting and inspiring environment that attracts customers, investors, and new residents.
4. Market Potential. Retail businesses along a commercial corridor are critical to sustain most urban communities. . . .
5. Entrepreneurs. Risk-taking businessmen must be available. . . .
6. Leadership. Local residents and businessmen must provide the direction, organization and commitment for any effort. . . .
7. Support. Broad-based political support is necessary in order to bring both funding resources and government agency staffing assistance. . . .
8. Money. Venture capital and public money must be available. . . .
9. Time. Revitalization is not an overnight process. . . .
10. Plan. An effective plan should not copy another community's plan but should be designed to meet your unique needs, problems, and goals."

> Robert Lynch, "Things to Know Before Beginning Main Street Revitalization: Essential Elements, Obstacles, Leveraging Points." New England Neighborhood Revitalization Center, 1977. Available from The Warren Company, 43 Miller Street, Warren, R.I. 02885. 9 pp. $1.

"To develop a workable plan in a community, a broad-based group of committed persons representing all sections must first establish goals, including economic and design aspects. The group should look carefully at its Main Street to determine visual strengths and weaknesses and conduct a complete survey of the area's buildings, streets, sidewalks, parking lots, alleys, parks. The other major analysis necessary concerns the economic health of the area. Are there vacancies on Main Street? What is the effect of any nearby shopping malls or other commercial centers? Have new businesses opened lately? How many buildings are owned by absentee landlords? Are any customer groups being ignored? Are the businesses open late or on Sunday so working people and families can shop there? Is parking a real problem or an issue diverting attention from more complex problems? Is a broad range of merchandise available?

When these questions have been answered by the group, the task force can begin to formulate specific, achievable objectives for the revitalization effort."

> "Main Street: Some Commonly Asked Questions." Supplement to *Preservation News,* May 1978.

Van Buren's 11-Point Strategy

"Our first consultants had pie-in-the-sky ideas of escalators descending from the rear of the buildings and fancy modern faces. . . . But from the start, the urban-renewal commission recognized the architectural integrity of Main Street. We decided Van Buren has as much history as any place."

> Susan Guthrie. In "Arkansas Butt of 'Hillbilly' Humor May Have Last Laugh," Patricia Leigh Brown. *Christian Science Monitor,* August 1, 1980.

1. Nominate the Main Street corridor to the National Register of Historic Places.
2. Establish a local historic district.
3. Improve traffic patterns within the Central Business District.
4. Rehabilitate/restore facades on Main Street.
5. Acquire/restore the King Opera House.
6. Improve the streetscape of Main Street.
7. Acquire and rehabilitate/restore the Frisco Railroad Depot.
8. Facilitate development of the downtown area.
9. Provide off-street parking.
10. Improve adjacent residential neighborhoods.
11. Redevelop the Arkansas Riverfront Area.

Main Street Historic District, Van Buren, Arkansas: Using Grant-in-Aid Funds for Storefront Rehabilitation/Restoration Within a Districtwide Plan. Susan Guthrie. Preservation Case Studies. Washington, D.C.: U.S. Department of the Interior, 1980. 31 pp., illus., appends.

Downtown Improvement Manual. Emanuel Berk, Illinois Department of Local Government Affairs. Chicago: APA Planners Press, 1976. 780 pp., illus., biblio., append. $26.95 pb.

An early handbook that covers areas of downtown planning such as land use, preservation, parking, traffic and circulation, financing, malls, legal aspects, attitude surveys, with sample forms.

Thoughts on the Revival of Downtown, U.S.A. Larry Bramblett. Athens, Ga.: Institute of Community and Area Development (307 Old College, University of Georgia, 30601), 1976. $3 pb.

Surveys the economic, design and promotional considerations of reviving downtowns.

A Guide for the Revitalization of Retail Districts. Ted Silberberg et al. Toronto: Saving Small Business Project, Ministry of Industry and Tourism, 1976. 120 pp., illus., biblio., appends. $5. Available from Ted Silberberg, Deliotte, Haskins and Sells, P.O. Box 159, First Canadian Place, Toronto, Ontario M5X 1H4, Canada.

A concise handbook identifying problems affecting urban and strip commercial areas and providing examples of districts that have transformed their downtowns.

Downtown Development Handbook. Ralph J. Basile, J. Thomas Black, Douglas R. Porter and Lynda Lowy, with Urban Development/Mixed Use Council, Urban Land Institute. Washington, D.C.: Urban Land Institute, 1980. 264 pp. $48 hb.

A guide for developers covering a variety of aspects of CBD renewal—stages of development, the real estate market, the capital market, catalysts for downtown revitalization, downtown development plans and the economic potential of central cities.

What Do People Do Downtown? How to Look at Main Street Activity. Project for Public Spaces. Washington, D.C.: National Main Street Center, National Trust for Historic Preservation, 1981. 106 pp., illus., appends. $8 pb.

Based on the work of William H. Whyte, describes surveys to determine what people think about downtown and presents techniques to find out how people actually use downtown.

Reviving Main Street. Deryck Holdsworth, ed., Heritage Canada Foundation. Buffalo: University of Toronto Press, 1985. $25 hb, $12.95 pb.

Describes how seven Canadian towns revived their Main Streets, with practical advice from restoration to organizing merchants and signage.

Managing Downtown Public Spaces. Project for Public Spaces. Chicago: Planners Press, 1984. 76 pp., illus. $18.95 pb.

Stresses management aspects to supplement city services, create a downtown marketplace, improve the design of public spaces and start a management program.

Revitalizing Main Street: Small Town Public Policy. Robert Craycroft. Mississippi State, Miss.: School of Architecture, Mississippi State University (P.O. Drawer AQ, 39762), 1982. 35 pp. $3 pb.

A primer for small towns considering a Main Street project addressing appropriate steps to take and how public policy relates to revitalization.

National Trust Main Street Center Training Manual. Washington, D.C.: National Main Street Center, 1981. 115 pp. $35 binder.

Presents the comprehensive Main Street methodology utilizing the four-point approach.

Rehabilitation and Pro Forma Analysis. Donovan D. Rypkema. Washington, D.C.: National Main Street Center, 1983. 12 pp. $3 pb.

Worksheets allowing property owners to assess the economic feasibility of rehabilitation projects.

Forming State Downtown Associations. International Downtown Executives Association. Washington, D.C.: Author, 1981. 76 pp. $8.

ADDS: The Annual Downtown Data System. International Downtown Executives Association. Washington, D.C.: Author.

Downtown Promotion Handbook. International Downtown Executives Association. Washington, D.C.: Author, 1980. 110 pp., illus. $10 pb.

How to Promote to Bring People Back Downtown: 17 Successful Downtown Promotional Case Studies. Downtown Research and Development Center. New York: Author, 1980. $25.

Downtown District Action Guide. Laurence A. Alexander, ed. New York: Downtown Research and Development Center, 1979. 48 pp. $14 pb.

Old Reliable Citizens Bank, Van Buren, Ark.

Old Reliable Citizens Bank, Van Buren, Ark., before and after federally assisted efforts to rehabilitate the historic downtown. The early photograph was used to guide restoration after the building had been altered, including loss of its stained-glass windows. The replacement doors and windows were based on the evidence found in the photograph. From *Main Street Historic District, Van Buren, Arkansas.*

Logo used by the Market Street Restoration Agency, Corning, N.Y., an early Main Street revitalization program assisted by Corning Glass Works and others.

State and Local Manuals

Georgia Downtown Development Association Downtown Development Manual. Robert Hughes, R. Bruce MacGregor and J. Steven Storey. Atlanta: Georgia Downtown Development Association, with Georgia Power Company and Georgia Department of Community Affairs (32 Peachtree Street, Room 220, 30383), 1979. 250 pp., biblio. $17.50 binder.

Downtown Revitalization Guide. Anne Marie Beal. Annapolis: Maryland Department of Economic and Community Development (2525 Riva Road, 21401), 1979. 358 pp., appends., biblio., index.

Downtown Revitalization in North Carolina: A Guidebook for Community Action. Patricia J. Jenny et al. Center for Urban and Regional Studies, University of North Carolina at Chapel Hill. Raleigh: Division of Community Assistance, North Carolina Department of Natural Resources and Development (P.O. Box 27687, 27611), 1978. 54 pp.

Downtown Revitalization Handbook: A Primer. Technical Assistance Guide for Maine Communities. Maine State Development Office. Augusta: Author (Community and Economic Development Division, 193 State Street, 04333), 1979. 97 pp.

Downtown Revitalization: A State Resource Guide. Agency of Development and Community Affairs, Vermont Department of Housing and Community Affairs. Montpelier: Author (Pavilion Office Building, 05602), 1980. 116 pp.

Main Street Texas. Texas Historical Commission. Austin: Author (P.O. Box 12276, Capitol Station, 78711), 1980.

Your Town—Past and Future: Downtown Revitalization Through Historic Preservation. Historic Landmarks Foundation of Indiana. Indianapolis: Author (3402 Boulevard Place, 46208), 1977. 106 pp.

Revitalization of Downtown: Self-Help Guidelines for the Smaller City. Private Revitalization of Downtown. Santa Cruz, Calif.: Author (410 Chestnut Street, 95060), 1975. 120 pp.

It's TIME for Springfield: Rebirth of Downtown. Anderson Notter Finegold. Springfield, Mass.: City of Springfield and Springfield Central, Inc., 1978. 96 pp., color illus.

Abbeville, South Carolina: Using Grant-in-Aid Funds for Rehabilitation Planning and Project Work in the Commercial Town Square. Triad Architectural Associates. For City of Abbeville. Preservation Case Studies. Washington, D.C.: U.S. Department of the Interior, 1979. 54 pp., illus., appends., biblio.

A variety of promotional activities are held in The Strand, Galveston, Tex. (Suzanne D. King, Galveston Historical Foundation)

Uptown, Downtown: Revitalizing by Example

"Corning [N.Y.] did what many other downtowns are trying and they did it well. In a small town with a large industry it is essential to get cooperation, and they did. The restoration also links up with an older urban renewal project at the other end of downtown creating a nice balance. They also solved a difficult problem—getting many small firms and many people to participate. This is necessary in harnessing support. The sidewalk work and tree plantings represent good decisions, too. While strong business gains are not reported, vacancies are down, and downtown is now a far more appealing place."

Winning Downtown Projects

"Market Street Rehabilitation." *Project Reference File,* no. 15. Washington, D.C.: Urban Land Institute, 1979. 4 pp., illus. $3 pb.

Downtown Revitalization: A Compendium of State Activities. Carole Carlin, ed., State Community Affairs Agencies. Washington, D.C.: International Downtown Executives Association, 1980. 227 pp. $20 pb.

A directory of programs, policies and legislation supporting downtown revitalization efforts in 45 states.

Downtown USA: Design in Nine American Cities. Kenneth Halpern. New York: Whitney Library of Design, 1978. 256 pp., illus., biblio., index. $27.50 hb.

Surveys New York, Chicago, Philadelphia, Houston, Washington, D.C., San Francisco, Boston, Atlanta and Minneapolis. The author urges cities to exert more control over downtown land and to establish coherent urban design policies to avoid "a continued exodus of jobs and a continually deteriorating, demeaning, and unhealthy environment."

Winning Downtown Projects: A Photographic Case Study Report of Outstanding Downtown Developments. Downtown Research and Development Center. New York: Author, 1981. $25.

Award-winning examples of riverfronts, downtown shopping centers, restorations, pedestrian areas, multiuse developments, adaptive use and other downtown projects in small, medium and large cities.

Learning From Seattle. Roberto Brambilla and Gianni Longo. New York: Institute for Environmental Action, with Partners for Livable Places, 1979. 119 pp., illus. $6.95 pb.

Learning From Baltimore. Roberto Brambilla and Gianni Longo. New York: Institute for Environmental Action, with Partners for Livable Places. 1979. 151 pp., illus. $6.95 pb.

Learning From Galveston. Roberto Brambilla and Gianni Longo. Institute for Environmental Action, with Partners for Livable Places. New Brunswick, N.J.: Transaction Books, 1982. $6.95 pb.

Learning From Atlanta. Roberto Brambilla and Gianni Longo. Institute for Environmental Action, with Partners for Livable Places. New Brunswick, N.J.; Transaction Books, 1981. $6.95 pb.

Titles in an extensive planned series, *Learning From the USA,* that combines books, short films and traveling exhibits focusing on actions and programs that have significantly improved the livability of American cities. This project on American urbanism, designed to help cities learn from each other, addresses decision makers in the private sector—business people, community leaders and individuals—as well as architects, planners and city officials.

See also: Tourism (Historic Sites)

Before-and-after views of the restored facade of Ecker Drug Store (1885, E. B. Gregory), Corning, N.Y. (Kellogg Studio; Norman Mintz, Market Street Restoration Agency)

Rehabilitated storefronts in Crested Butte, Colo., a small town spared from proposed new mining development. (Walter Smalling, Jr., National Park Service)

Surveys of Downtown Resources

Splendid Survivors: San Francisco's Downtown Architectural Heritage. Michael R. Corbett, Charles Hall Page and Associates. For Foundation for San Francisco's Architectural Heritage. San Francisco: California Living Books, 1979. 288 pp., illus., maps. $32.50 hb, $19.95 pb.

Downtown Providence: Statewide Historical Preservation Report P-P-5. W.M. MacKenzie Woodward, Rhode Island Historical Preservation Commission. Providence, R.I.: State Historical Preservation Commission, with City of Providence, 1981. 80 pp., illus. $3.95 pb. Available from Providence Preservation Society (24 Meeting Street, 02903).

Central Business District Preservation Study Part II: Draft Summary of Findings. Pamela W. Fox and Mickail Kock. Boston: Boston Landmarks Commission, with Boston Redevelopment Authority and Massachusetts Historical Commission, 1980. 68 pp., illus.

The Feasibility of Incorporating Landmark Buildings in the Redevelopment of Chicago's North Loop. Landmarks Preservation Council of Illinois. For National Trust for Historic Preservation. Chicago: Landmarks Preservation Council of Illinois, 1981. 65 pp., illus., appends.

Historic Architectural Resources of Downtown Asheville, North Carolina. David R. Black, ed. Asheville, N.C.: City of Asheville, 1979. 60 pp., illus., appends., gloss.

Historic Uptown Butte: An Architectural and Historical Analysis of the Central Business District of Butte, Mont. John N. DeHaas, Jr. Bozeman, Mont: Author (1021 South Tracy, 59715), 1977. 154 pp., illus.

Denver's Larimer Street: Main Street, Skid Row and Urban Renaissance. Thomas J. Noel. Denver: Historic Denver, 1981. 196 pp., illus., index. $14.95 pb.

This landscaped Lancaster, Pa., parking lot was designed to fit into the historic area. (Mary Means)

Design Guidelines

Downstreet Building Book. Lewiston City Planning Department. Lewiston, Maine: Author, 1978. 32 pp.

The Montpelier Cityscape Workbook: A Guide for Development in the Design Control District. Robert Burley Associates. Montpelier, Vt.: Cityscape Work Committee, 1976. 75 pp., illus., gloss.

Rutland Townscape: An Opportunity for the Revitalization of Downtown Rutland. Crandell Associates Architects. For Rutland Historic Preservation Project. Rutland, Vt.: Downtown Development Corporation (c/o Paul A. Bienvenu and Associates, 56½ Merchants Row, 05701), 1977. 142 pp., illus., appends.

Good Neighbors: Building Next to History. Nore Winter, Barbara A. Cole and Joslyn Green. Denver: State Historical Society of Colorado, 1980. 44 pp., illus. $3 pb.

Lowell: The Building Book. Anderson Notter Associates. Lowell, Mass.: City of Lowell, Division of Planning and Development, 1977. 71 pp., illus., biblio., gloss.

Worcester: A New England Cityscape. Vision, Inc. Worcester, Mass.: Worcester Heritage Preservation Society (321 Main Street, 01608), 1978. 56 pp., illus.

Brookline 2: Guide to Environmental Design Review for Commercial Facade Renovation. Brian Mitchenere, Vision, Inc. Brookline, Mass.: Planning Department, 1977. 22 pp., illus.

Historic Jim Thorpe: Historic Preservation and Commercial Revitalization. Venturi, Rauch and Scott Brown. Jim Thorpe, Pa.: Carbon County Planning Commission, 1979. 130 pp., illus.

Main Street Manual. Jinna M. Anderson et al. Warrenton, Va.: Piedmont Environmental Council, 1978. 115 pp., illus., append.

A Notebook for Storefront Renovation. Edith S. Overton. Goldsboro, N.C.: Downtown Goldsboro Association and City of Goldsboro (Department of Planning and Redevelopment, P.O. Drawer A, 37530), 1979.

Steam cleaning a storefront, Jim Thorpe, Pa. (Thomas J. Lutz)

Design for the Business District. Robert R. Hartmann. Racine, Wis.: Racine Urban Aesthetics, Inc. (936 South Main Street, 53403), 1979. 36 pp., illus.

The Action Plan for The Strand. Venturi and Rauch. Galveston: Galveston Historical Foundation, 1975. 81 pp., illus.

Townlift: Building Improvement Manual. Tennessee Valley Authority. Knoxville: TVA Architectural Design Branch, Regional Planning Staff, Townlift Planning Section (280 Liberty Building, 37902), 1978. 64 pp., illus.

Lockport, Illinois: A Historic District Preservation Plan. Preservation/Urban Design/Inc. Lockport: Historic Preservation Council (P.O. Box 294, 60441), 1978. 126 pp., illus., append.

Victorian Commercial Architecture in Indiana. Indianapolis: Historic Landmarks Foundation of Indiana (3402 Boulevard Place, 46208), 1978. 16 pp., illus. $1.

The Terre Haute Downtown Manual: Guidelines for Design in Downtown. Jim Burns and Stephen Levine. For City of Terre Haute. Terre Haute, Ind.: Housing Authority (P.O. Box 3086, 47803), 1980. 74 pp., illus., appends.

Ann Arbor Downtown Facade Study. Preservation/Urban Design/Inc. Ann Arbor, Mich.: Ann Arbor Tomorrow, 1976. 48 pp., illus.

Design for Downtown. Roger L. Schluntz, Nebraska State Department of Economic Development. Lincoln, Neb.: Urban Research and Development Center, University of Nebraska College of Architecture, 1973. 109 pp., illus.

See also: Rehabilitation and Restoration

clean, restore and paint facade   restore existing window frames, install new window shades   clean building facade   restore pilasters at the ground level

restore existing eave detail

restore window frames, install coordinated window shades

clean, patch and paint building facade

install uniform sign band   do not obscure building pilasters

Rehabilitation guidelines prepared for commercial storefronts on Main Street, Worcester, Mass. From *Worcester: A New England Cityscape*. (Vision, Inc.)

Storefronts: Putting on a Good Face

There are many advantages to storefront rehabilitation over other types of improvements. One important advantage is economic: rehabilitation is relatively inexpensive compared to other current facade treatments. . . . The public relations benefits to the community are important too; rehabilitated commercial buildings contribute to local pride by enhancing the visual environment and by helping to preserve the community's character and history.

Norman Mintz, *A Practical Guide to Storefront Rehabilitation*

Facade Stories: Changing Faces of Main Street Storefronts and How to Care for Them. Ronald Lee Fleming. New York: Hastings House, 1982. 128 pp., illus., biblio., append., gloss., index. $13.50 pb.

A photo montage of good, bad and in-between storefronts—originals, restored, adapted, "reinterpreted," "freestanding" and lost. The book explains how and sometimes why the historic facades shown have come to look the way they do, as well as what should be done to maintain a good facade.

Rehabilitating Historic Storefronts. H. Ward Jandl. Preservation Brief no. 11. Technical Preservation Services, U.S. Department of the Interior. Washington, D.C.: GPO, 1982. 12 pp., illus. $1 pb. GPO stock no. 024-005-00886-1.

Provides guidelines for repairing wooden, masonry and metal components of historic storefronts and, when necessary, designing compatible replacements for deteriorated storefronts. Includes historical background on storefronts.

"Old Storefronts: 1870–1920," Mara Gelbloom. *Old-House Journal*, March 1978. $1.50.

Keeping Up Appearances: Storefront Guidelines. B. Clarkson Schoettle. Washington, D.C.: National Main Street Center, 1983. 16 pp., illus. $4 pb.

A Practical Guide to Storefront Rehabilitation. Norman Mintz. Technical Series no. 2. 1977. 3rd ed. Albany: Preservation League of New York State (307 Hamilton Street, 12210), 1982. 8 pp., illus. $1.50 pb.

The Preservation of Historic Pigmented Structural Glass (Vitrolite and Carrara Glass). Rocky Mountain Regional Office. Preservation Brief no. 12. Technical Preservation Services, U.S. Department of the Interior. Washington, D.C.: GPO, 1984. 8 pp., illus. $1 pb. GPO stock no. 024-005-00851-9.

Storefront Rehabilitation: A 19th Century Commercial Building. The Harding Building, Jackson, Mississippi. Sharon C. Park, AIA. Preservation Studies. Washington, D.C.: Technical Preservation Services, National Park Service, U.S. Department of the Interior, 1980. 12 pp., illus.

A plethora of commercial signs in Cincinnati, Ohio, in 1887 not only advertised a variety of wares and services—including the signmaker's art—but also created its own vibrant streetscape. (Cincinnati Historical Society)

Signs ready to be picked up in 1889 at a Guthrie, Okla., sign painter's shop, which had already supplied the adjacent marshall's office and Elite Bakery. (Swearingen Collection, University of Oklahoma)

Signs of the Times

Main Street advertising—as American as the hot dog— has always been as aggressive as technology permitted.

Carole Rifkind, *Main Street: The Face of Urban America*

"The basic function of all street graphics is to communicate a message to the observer, either for the purpose of *indexing* the environment in such a way that suppliers of goods and services and their prospective customers can locate one another, or for *selling* (the use of the environment for the latter purpose is to be considered a special privilege, not a right).

William R. Ewald, Jr., *Street Graphics*

Street Graphics: A Concept and a System. William R. Ewald, Jr. and Daniel R. Mandelker. 1971. 2nd ed. Washington, D.C.: Landscape Architecture Foundation, 1977. 176 pp., illus., appends., biblio. $15 pb.

Proposes a system of ordered street graphics that "index the environment—i.e., tell people where they can find what."

The Mechanics of Sign Control. Carolyn Browne. Chicago: American Planning Association, 1980. PAS Report 354. 26 pp. $10 pb.

Sign Sense: Arlington, Massachusetts. Vision, Inc. For Arlington Department of Planning and Community Development and Arlington Redevelopment Board. Arlington, Mass.: City of Arlington, 1977. 40 pp., illus.

Sign Design Review. Brookline Planning Department. Brookline, Mass.: Author, 1977. 18 pp.

Sign Language: A Guide for Salem Merchants. Baldwin Design. Salem, Mass.: Salem Redevelopment Authority, 1979. 36 pp., illus.

Sign Up: A Survey of Signs in Older Commercial Areas of Rockford, Illinois. Restoration Education, Inc. Rockford, Ill.: Author (2127 Broadway, 61108), 1979. $1.

Proceedings of the Urban Signage Forum, April 22 and 23, 1976. U.S. Department of Housing and Urban Development. Washington, D.C.: GPO, 1977. 587 pp., biblio. GPO stock no. 023-000-00383-0. $6.40 pb.

Transcripts, supplemental statements and extensive bibliography on sign regulation, design, history and impact.

Lettering on Architecture. Alan Bartram. New York: Whitney Library of Design, 1975. 176 pp., gloss., biblio., index.

An illustrated history of styles on lettering on buildings, using examples from England and Italy.

Words and Buildings: The Art and Practice of Public Lettering. Jock Kinneir. New York: Whitney Library of Design, 1980. 191 pp., illus., biblio., index.

Surveys the development of the alphabet and the history of public signage, presenting criteria of legibility and design and types of lettering found throughout the built environment.

Downtown mall created on Market Street in Wilmington, Del., unified the shopping area and provided a setting for the restored Grand Opera House (1871, Dixon and Carson) at center left. (Lubitsh and Bungarz)

The Mall Goes Downtown

Automobiles made the suburbs possible. Now, banning them downtown may help cities survive.

Roberto Brambilla and Gianni Longo, *Banning the Car Downtown*

American Urban Malls: A Compendium. Roberto Brambilla, Gianni Longo and Virginia Dzurinko, Institute for Environmental Action. With Columbia University Center for Advanced Research in Urban and Environmental Affairs. Footnotes no. 4. Washington, D.C.: U.S. Department of Housing and Urban Development, 1976. 143 pp., illus. GPO stock no. 023-000-00376-7.

Banning the Car Downtown: Selected American Cities. Roberto Brambilla and Gianni Longo, Institute for Environmental Action. With Columbia University Center for Advanced Research in Urban and Environmental Affairs. Footnotes no. 3. Washington, D.C.: U.S. Department of Housing and Urban Development, 1976. 149 pp., illus. GPO stock no. 023-000-00375-9.

For Pedestrians Only: Planning Design and Management of Parking Free Zones. Roberto Brambilla and Gianni Longo. New York: Whitney Library of Design, 1977. 208 pp., illus., appends., biblio. $24.95 hb.

Downtown Mall Annual and Urban Design Report. Downtown Design Series. Laurence A. Alexander, ed. New York: Downtown Research and Development Center, 1978. $11 pb.

Malls, Pedestrian Malls and Shopping Centers: A Selected Bibliography. James F. Orr. Monticello, Ill.: Vance Bibliographies, 1979. 48 pp. $5 pb.

Pedestrian Areas: From Malls to Complete Networks. Klaus Uhlig. New York: Architectural Book Publishing Company, 1979. 152 pp., illus., index. $40 hb.

Planning and Construction of Municipal Malls. American Public Works Association. Chicago: Author (1313 East 60th Street, 60637), 1979. Special report 46. 52 pp., illus., append., biblio. $5.

Public Attitudes Toward Downtown Malls. Downtown Research and Development Center. New York: Author, 1975. $25.

Paying for Preservation

14

T oday there is little wisdom in waiting to bump into angels or calculating the cost of preservation in bake-sale receipts. Even the most eloquent of eleventh-hour laments is drowned out by the noise of the marketplace.

Economic pressures are a constant fact of life in preservation. Little has been achieved through rhetoric alone, no matter how brilliant. What saves old buildings and rejuvenates them is money. Historic preservation was once viewed as a charity that must be subsidized. As it has moved out of the realm of the historic house museum and into the reuse of existing built resources, preservationists have found that reliance on private charity and, recently, government grants is not enough. The surest means to save a structure is to buy it. This is not always possible. Therefore, preservationists have been developing a variety of financial and economic tools and methods that can be used to save buildings.

National Trust et al., *America's Forgotten Architecture.* New York: Pantheon, 1976.

Economic Benefits of Preservation

In addition to giving people a sense of time, place, and meaning in terms of where they live, historic preservation has been successful for purely business reasons—it costs less to rehabilitate a building than to construct a new one, and these preserved buildings compete successfully in the marketplace. Some of the most important benefits to society from preserving and adapting our built environment are economic: providing jobs, stimulating business activity, revitalizing downtown areas.

Thomas D. Bever, *The Economic Benefits of Historic Preservation.* Washington, D.C.: U.S. Department of the Interior, 1978.

"When we preserve an older building we are preserving not only a cultural and visual asset but an economic asset as well. America has a large investment in its older and historic buildings, and these buildings should be as prudently and wisely managed as any other scarce resource. . . .

Older and historic buildings make up more than one-fourth of America's total stock of existing buildings. Furthermore, these buildings are being used as intensively as their newer neighbors; they pull their weight in providing both work space and housing. . . . Adapting older buildings for modern uses often costs less than constructing new ones and . . . operating costs are usually less than those for new buildings. . . .

Preservation is an increasingly important part of our national economy—total investment in older and historic buildings is currently approximately $21 billion annually. The tourist industry also benefits greatly from the appeal of our older and historic buildings. Furthermore, policymakers are discovering that, for a given investment, rehabilitation work often creates more jobs than new construction. . . .

In a historical sense, older and historic buildings are our memory—a repository for history and a record of our evolving culture. In a social sense, they provide the setting in which we live and work. Economically, they are an enormous storehouse of materials, human effort and wealth."

Betsy Chittenden, with Jacques Gordon, *Older and Historic Buildings and the Preservation Industry*

"How much are amenities worth? . . .

How much is a museum worth? An open air market? A theater? A waterfront? A sports center? A historic district? . . .

The economic vitality of a community is closely linked to the quality of local amenities. More and more, economic planners are realizing that the physical, cultural, social, and natural environments in which Americans live and work exert a complex influence on their prosperity."

Economics of Amenity News, December 1, 1980.

Everyone profits when we find adaptive uses for our fine historic buildings which are sound and usable. Unique business quarters can be found at bargain prices. Restoration and rejuvenation provide employment for the construction industry. And historic landmarks are retained in their communities. Historic preservation makes good business sense.

For more information on historic preservation, write Membership Department, Office of Public Affairs, The National Trust for Historic Preservation, 740 Jackson Place, NW, Washington, DC 20006.

Historic Preservation makes cents.

Public service advertisement by the National Trust for Historic Preservation promoting the economic benefits of preservation. (NTHP)

Building on Chicago's Printers Row, a Tax Act project. (Ron Gordon)

Lit Brothers Store (1859–1918), Philadelphia, saved for mixed use development after a cliffhanging campaign. (Christopher Ransom, John Milner Associates)

The Preservation Industry

Reinvestment in Older Buildings

$10 billion is invested annually in nonresidential private buildings more than 50 years old

$11 billion annually goes toward rehabilitating residential buildings more than 50 years old

$4.5 billion annually is spent on rehabilitation of single-unit, owner-occupied homes built before 1940

Rehabilitation vs. New Construction

Rehabilitation costs about half that of new construction

Energy is saved by reuse over demolition and new construction

Materials can be reused

Less time is required

Existing infrastructure such as streets and sewers can be used

Chicago Stock Exchange (1893, Adler and Sullivan), lost because the development economics were not right in 1971. (Richard Nickel)

Operating Costs

Older buildings cost the same or less than new buildings for heating, cooling, maintenance, insurance, etc.

Pre-1940 houses cost less to heat annually than most newer (pre-1970) houses

Employment

Rehabilitation is labor intensive, requiring fewer materials but more skilled labor and creating more jobs for an investment than new construction

More than 96% of architects are involved in rehabilitation, which represents one-fifth of an average firm's business

Small construction firms and residential builders are increasingly dependent on rehabilitation work

Tourism

Visiting historic sites is the fourth most popular recreational activity

26 million households visit historic sites each year

Historical visits support 200,000 to 550,000 travel industry jobs and generate expenditures of $5 to $14 billion

One tourist dollar generates $7 of economic activity compared to $4 for industrial payrolls

> From *Older and Historic Buildings and the Preservation Industry*

Older and Historic Buildings and the Preservation Industry. Betsy Chittenden, with Jacques Gordon. Preservation Policy Research Series. Washington, D.C.: National Trust for Historic Preservation, 1984. 19 pp., biblio. $5 pb.

Measuring Historic Preservation's Impact on States: A Study of California's Historic and Cultural Resources. J. Laurence Mintier, California Heritage Task Force. Preservation Policy Research Series. Washington, D.C.: National Trust for Historic Preservation, 1984. 26 pp., biblio. $5 pb.

Economic Benefits of Preserving Old Buildings. National Trust for Historic Preservation. Washington, D.C.: Preservation Press, 1976. 168 pp., illus. $7.95 pb.

Values of Residential Properties in Urban Historic Districts: Georgetown, Washington, D.C., and Other Selected Districts. John B. Rackham. Information Series, National Trust for Historic Preservation. Washington, D.C.: Preservation Press, 1977. 28 pp. $2 pb.

Economic Impact of Landmark Designation on the Auditorium Building. Shlaes and Company. Chicago: Commission on Chicago Historical and Architectural Landmarks, 1976. 56 pp., illus.

The Economics of Historic Houses: The Impact of Property Location on Economic Performance. Akron, Ohio: Tourism and Leisure Development Program, Department of Urban Studies, University of Akron, 1983. 44 pp.

The Contribution of Historic Preservation to Urban Revitalization. Advisory Council on Historic Preservation. Washington, D.C.: GPO, 1979. 215 pp.

The Impacts of Historic District Designation: Summary Report. Raymond, Parish, Pine and Weiner. New York: New York Landmarks Conservancy (330 West 42nd Street, 10036), 1977. 11 pp. $3.

"Economic Impact of a Historic District." In *A Guide to Delineating Edges of Historic Districts.* Russell Wright, principal consultant. Washington, D.C.: Preservation Press, 1976. 96 pp., illus., gloss., biblio. $8.95 pb.

The Economics of Urban Amenities. Douglas Diamond, Jr., and George S. Tolley, eds. New York: Academy Press, 1982. $29.50.

See also: The Impact of Tourism (Historic Sites); Energy Conservation (Rehabilitation and Restoration)

Contacts

National Trust for Historic Preservation
Office of Public Policy
1785 Massachusetts Avenue, N.W.
Washington, D.C. 20036

Conducts and sponsors research on preservation issues that affect policy decisions such as economic benefits.

Partners for Livable Places
1429 21st Street, N.W.
Washington, D.C. 20036

Sponsors an Economics of Amenity Program to study economic development issues such as tourism, design, open space management, cultural planning and scenic resources.

Pennsylvania Hospital (1755–1805), Philadelphia, built through matching grants dreamed up by its founder, Ben Franklin.

Fund Raising: The Great Treasure Hunt

There are obviously only a limited number of "charitable" dollars available from individuals, corporations and foundations for the support of private, nonprofit groups. . . . It is also obvious that there is, and probably always will be, intense competition for these dollars, with cultural organizations competing both with each other and with other types of "nonprofits" for available funds. . . . This simply means that preservation organizations must be prepared to make a strong case for their share of the charitable dollars and must understand the basic principles of successful fund raising before undertaking any fund-raising program.

Lawrence J. Biddle, *Private Funds for Historic Preservation*

"For active preservationists struggling to finance a preservation, restoration or renovation project, playing the foundation game has all the elements of a great treasure hunt. It involves research and analysis (Where's the money?), identification of clues (Which foundations might be responsive?), phrasing the appeal and waiting. Searching for the pot of gold are many players: mostly losers and a few winners. To the winners, a grant can mean a completed preservation project and community support rather than skepticism."

Carol U. Sisler and Marion G. Phillips, "The Foundation Game and How Historic Ithaca Won." *Historic Preservation*, January–March 1975.

"Wily old Ben Franklin was the first person in America to use the matching grant. In 1750, he lobbied the Pennsylvania Assembly to create the first government matching grant—for his favorite project, the Pennsylvania Hospital. The assemblymen agreed to appropriate £2,000 if Franklin's volunteers could raise £2,000. As Franklin wrote in his autobiography:

'. . . the members [of the Assembly] now conceiv'd they might have the credit of being charitable without the expense . . . ; and then, in soliciting subscriptions among the people, we urg'd the conditional promise of the law as an additional motive to give, since every man's donation would be doubled; thus the clause work'd both ways.' "

Joan Flanagan, *The Grass Roots Fundraising Book*

Private Funds for Historic Preservation. Lawrence J. Biddle. Information Series, National Trust for Historic Preservation. Washington, D.C.: Preservation Press, 1979. 38 pp., append., biblio. $2 pb.

Basic information on preservation fund raising: approaches, sources, techniques, proposals, budgets and planning for a benefit.

The Grass Roots Fundraising Book: How to Raise Money in Your Community. Joan Flanagan, for the Youth Project. 1977. Rev. ed. Chicago: Contemporary Books, 1982. 344 pp., biblio., index. $8.95 pb.

Features practical, upbeat advice and detailed ideas for planning and carrying out single-handedly any kind of campaign.

Grants: How to Find Out About Them and What to Do Next. Virginia P. White. New York: Plenum, 1975. 354 pp., append., index. $19.50 hb.

"No book has succeeded quite so well. . . . Its section on private foundations is more concise, thoughtful and carefully researched than most books devoted exclusively to the subject. . . . Best of all, *Grants* is beautifully written." (Jack Shakely, "Best and the Worst Fund Raising Books." *Grantsmanship Center News,* May–June 1976)

The Grantsmanship Center Whole Nonprofit Catalog, vol. 1, no. 1, Winter 1984–85. Special issue.

Includes a compendium of sources and resources for managers and staff of nonprofit organizations.

Organizing for Local Fundraising: Self-Sufficiency for the 80s. Boulder, Colo.: Volunteer Readership (P.O. Box 1807, 80306), 1984. $7.95 pb.

A practical guide for community-based nonprofits on how to raise support in their communities, with examples of planning and implementation strategies.

The 13 Most Common Fund-Raising Mistakes and How to Avoid Them. Paul H. Schneiter and Donald T. Nelson. Washington, D.C.: Taft Corporation, 1983. 95 pp. $14.95 pb.

A concise booklet intended especially for nonprofit executives and board members.

Prospecting: Searching Out the Philanthropic Dollar. Washington, D.C.: Taft Corporation, 1983. $19.95 kit.

Kit includes a handbook on the basics of identifying and analyzing potential donors plus forms for donor records and prospect information.

The Complete Fund Raising Guide. Howard R. Mirkin. Hartsdale, N.Y.: Public Service Materials Center, 1975. 159 pp., biblio., index. $16.75 pb.

Tells how to raise money from business, labor, foundations, government and bequests through mail appeals, special events, large donations and house-to-house solicitations.

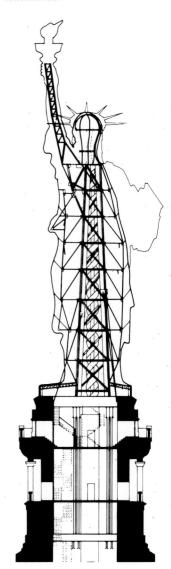

Restoration goal: $230 million. (French-American Committee)

Restoration of the Clinton House (1830), Ithaca, N.Y., made possible by Historic Ithaca's fund-raising ability. (Constance Saltonstall)

Completed Clinton House, now used for offices and the DeWitt Historical Society museum. (John Reis)

Fund Raising: The Guide to Raising Money from Private Sources. Thomas E. Broce. Norman: University of Oklahoma Press, 1979. 254 pp., illus., appends., index. $17.50 hb.

A basic reference for beginners and professionals covering fund-raising principles, preparing proposals, capital and annual campaigns, deferred giving, foundation and corporate support, wtih sample documents.

Getting a Grant in the 1980s: How to Write Successful Grant Proposals. Robert Lefferts. 1978. 2nd ed. Englewood Cliffs, N.J.: Prentice-Hall, 1982. 168 pp., appends., gloss., index. $14.95 hb, $6.95 pb.

A practical handbook on basic skills and principles for seeking human services grants.

Getting Grants. Craig W. Smith and Eric W. Skjei. New York: Harper and Row, 1979. 286 pp., append., index. $14.95 hb.

Topics include government and private funding, how to find the right source and how to write a successful proposal.

Program Planning and Proposal Writing. Norton J. Kiritz. Los Angeles: Grantsmanship Center, 1980. 48 pp. $3.25.

Based on the center's training course, it includes examples and covers each step from cover letter to the budget.

The KRC Fund Raiser's Manual: A Guide to Personalized Fund Raising. Paul Blanshard, Jr. New Canaan, Conn.: KRC Development Council, 1974. 248 pp., appends. $38.95 hb.

Highlights campaign leadership, preparing case statements, cost cutting, using volunteers, securing gifts from businesses, clubs and civil organizations, with sample letters and materials.

The KRC Desk Book for Fund Raisers: With Model Forms and Records. Lisa Pulling. New Canaan, Conn.: KRC Development Council, 1979. $38.50.

Specific detailed guidance for all types of fund-raising campaigns, including annual giving, special events, deferred and corporate gifts, foundation and government grants, capital campaigns and direct mail. Staffing, planning, budgeting, writing, public relations and record-keeping are covered, with model documents.

What Volunteers Should Know for Successful Fund Raising. Maurice C. Gurin. Briarcliff Manor, N.Y.: Stein and Day, 1981. 151 pp., index. $14.95 hb.

Explains how to plan direct-mail and personal solicitations, phonathons, telethons, annual giving and capital fund campaigns.

Designs for Fund-Raising: Principles-Patterns-Techniques. Harold J. Seymour. New York: McGraw-Hill, 1966. 210 pp., index. $33.95.

A primer for big-money fund raisers, written for established groups with leadership, influence and affluence.

Annual Fund Ideas. Virginia L. Carter, ed. Washington, D.C.: Council for Advancement and Support of Education, 1979. 48 pp. $10.50.

Spiral-bound collection of 40 ideas from *CASE Currents,* developed for colleges, on how to plan, organize and carry out a successful annual fund.

The Capital Campaign. Editors, *CASE Currents.* Washington, D.C.: Council for Advancement and Support of Education, 1979. 64 pp. $5.

Covers capital, annual and deferred giving: planning, rating prospects, volunteers, public relations support.

A Guide to Successful Phonathons. Nelson Cover, comp. Washington, D.C.: Council for Advancement and Support of Education, 1980. 89 pp., append. $14.50.

Raising money through phone campaigns: timetables, training volunteers and follow-through, with sample letters, forms and instructions.

Grants for the Arts. Virginia P. White. New York: Plenum, 1980. 378 pp., appends., index. $19.50 hb.

Directions for finding out about grants for artistic activities available from local, state and federal agencies, foundations and corporations.

United Arts Fundraising Policybook. Robert Porter, ed. New York: American Council for the Arts, 1984. 270 pp. $125 binder.

Examples of 13 united arts funds, their bylaws, policies and procedures.

America's Most Successful Fund Raising Letters. Joseph Dermer, ed. Hartsdale, N.Y.: Public Service Materials Center, 1976. $19.95.

Successful appeal letters from a nationwide contest sponsored by PSMC, with commentary by the authors.

The KRC Collection of Direct Mail Fund Raising Letters. Mitchell Keller, ed. New Canaan, Conn.: KRC Development Council. 125 pp. $34.95 hb.

A collection of model fund-raising letters and supporting materials with commentary.

The KRC Guide to Direct Mail Fund Raising. Richard J. Crohn and Mitchell Keller, eds. New Canaan, Conn.: KRC Development Council, 1977. $39.50 hb.

Ideas on successful methods for fund raising and increasing income through mail, including sample forms.

Enterprise in the Nonprofit Sector. James C. Crimmins and Mary Keil, Partners for Livable Places. New York: Publishing Center for Cultural Resources (625 Broadway, 10012), 1983. 144 pp. $7 pb.

Profiles the experiences of 11 non-profit organizations in developing income-producing ventures to supplement traditional fund-raising drives.

Securing Grant Support: Effective Planning and Preparation. William T. Alderson, Jr. Nashville: American Association for State and Local History, 1972. Technical Leaflet 62. 12 pp. $2 pb.

Generalities of grantsmanship for local historical societies.

Financing Your History Organization: Setting Goals. Laurence R. Pizer. Nashville: American Association for State and Local History, 1978. Technical Leaflet 105. 8 pp. $2 pb.

Ways to finance an organization, including donations, membership dues, corporate gifts and governmental assistance.

Cases and Readings on Marketing for Non-Profit Organizations. Philip Kotler, O. C. Ferrell and Charles Lamb. Englewood Cliffs, N.J.: Prentice-Hall, 1983. 380 pp. $21.95 pb.

See also: Taking Action

Contacts

The Foundation Center
79 Fifth Avenue
New York, N.Y. 10003

Supported by foundations to provide a single authoritative source on foundation giving, it collects and disseminates information on more than 20,000 active donors and maintains major libraries in New York and Washington, field offices in San Francisco and Cleveland and collections in cooperating libraries in 139 cities, all open to the public. Also offers research aid, orientations,

The fund raiser's motto (as well as the U.S. Flagship *Niagara*'s), displayed at a maritime conference supported by the National Trust. (Harley Seeley)

copying facilities and an Associate program. In addition to *The Foundation Directory,* it publishes a *Foundation Center Sourcebook, National Data Book* and *Foundation Grants Index,* all providing profiles of foundations. Comsearch Printouts provide computerized reports on grants by category such as a recent one on "Architecture, Historical Preservation and Historical Societies."

The Grantsmanship Center
1031 South Grand Avenue
Los Angeles, Calif. 90015

Provides services for nonprofit public and private groups that have not yet developed professional grant-seeking skills and that cannot afford to use an outside research service. Publishes the bimonthly *Grantsmanship Center News,* which gives information on government and private funding programs, how-to articles and reviews of new publications. Conducts workshops, provides proposal critiques and staff consultation and maintains a reference library.

Public Service Materials Center
111 North Central Avenue
Hartsdale, N.Y. 10530

Publishes books on fund raising and sells a wide variety of related books. Also conducts seminars for nonprofessional fund raisers. Ask for "The Complete Fund Raising Catalogue," published three times a year.

KRC Development Council
431 Valley Road
New Canaan, Conn. 06840

Publisher of reference books on fund-raising techniques and the *KRC Letter,* a newsletter about fund raising.

Washington International Arts Letter
P.O. Box 15240
Washington, D.C. 20003

Issues a monthly newsletter and other publications with information on grants and other financial aid in the fields of art, the humanities and education.

American Council for the Arts
570 Seventh Avenue
New York, N.Y. 10018

National service organization for the arts providing advocacy, information and publications.

Council for Advancement and Support of Education
11 Dupont Circle
Suite 400
Washington, D.C. 20036

Nonprofit membership organization assisting in fund raising and public relations for educational institutions through publications and workshops.

Taft Corporation
5125 MacArthur Boulevard, N.W.
Washington, D.C. 20016

Provides consulting services as well as publications on fund raising.

Independent Sector
1828 L Street, N.W.
Washington, D.C. 20036

Representing corporations, foundations and national voluntary organizations, its purpose is to preserve voluntary giving and personal support of health and welfare programs.

American Association of Fund Raising Counsel
500 Fifth Avenue
New York, N.Y. 10036

Represents professional fund raisers. Publishes the annual *Giving USA,* a statistical report on trends in American philanthropy, and the *Giving USA Bulletin,* a newsletter updating current donor and recipient activities.

Old State House (1796, Charles Bulfinch), Hartford, Conn., restored by reviving an 18th-century window tax idea: Owners of 2,753 windows overlooking the building were asked to pay a $5 annual viewing fee.

Council on Foundations
1828 L Street, N.W.
Washington, D.C. 20036

Membership consists of grant-making organizations. Sponsors workshops and seminars on current trends in giving and the administration of philanthropic funds. Publishes *Foundation News: The Journal of Philanthropy* (bimonthly), *The Council Newsletter* (bimonthly), an annual report and monographs and handbooks, including *The Handbook for Community Foundations* ($40), a guide to starting a community foundation.

National Society of Fund Raising Executives
1511 K Street, N.W.
Suite 831
Washington, D.C. 20005

Membership consists of individuals charged wtih fund raising for nonprofit organizations, agencies, churches, counseling firms, education, health and welfare organizations and institutions.

Trust rural programs have been supported by foundations such as the Richard King Mellon Foundation and Cecil Howard Charitable Trust.

Gracie Mansion (1799), New York City, restored with support from the J. M. Kaplan Fund, Vincent Astor Foundation, city and corporations.

Foundations

Nearly half of all foundation giving comes from what are considered to be small foundations—those with assets of less than $25 million. In the most recent analysis, this group gave a total of 185,951 grants averaging between $3,000 and $11,000 each.

Giving USA

Types of Foundations

General Purpose
Independent, usually large ones such as Ford, Rockefeller and Carnegie Corporation, they award half of all foundation grants.

Company Sponsored
Legally independent of their companies, but often supportive of allied interests.

Community
Recipients of funding from local sources that distribute aid to a variety of local causes.

Family
Founded by wealthy donors often to support narrow interests, they form the largest category.

Special Purpose
Established often by will or trust to aid a specific cause or locality.

From *The Art of Winning Foundation Grants*

The Foundation Directory. 9th ed. New York: Foundation Center, 1983. 672 pp., appends., gloss., index. $60. Supplement, $30. Set, $75.

A key guide to more than 4,000 corporate, private and community foundations describing their purposes, activities, financial data, officers and application procedures, with analyses of foundation giving and indexes by subject and locality.

About Foundations: How to Find the Facts You Need to Get a Grant. Judith B. Margolin. New York: Foundation Center, 1977. 48 pp., biblio., append. Free.

A step-by-step guide that concentrates on the Foundation Center's resources. Suggestions are arranged according to ways of selecting a foundation: name, subject and region.

National Directory of Arts Support by Private Foundations. Daniel Millsap and Editors of WIAL. 1972. 5th ed. Washington, D.C.: Washington International Arts Letter, 1983. 340 pp., index. $79.95 pb.

Where America's Large Foundations Make Their Grants. Joseph Dermer, ed. 1973. 5th ed. Hartsdale, N.Y.: Public Service Materials Center, 1983. 253 pp. $44.50 pb.

Information on 600 large foundations—who receives their grants, amounts and purposes.

The 1983–84 Survey of Grant-Making Foundations with Assets of Over $1,000,000 or Grants of Over $100,000. Hartsdale, N.Y.: Public Service Materials Center, 1982. 94 pp. $15.95 pb.

Information on 1,000 and how they make their grants, including what the grant seeker needs to know before approaching these foundations—the best time to apply, geographic area of interest, whether they will give you an appointment, etc.

The Art of Winning Foundation Grants. Howard Hillman and Karin Abarbanel. New York: Vanguard Press, 1975. 188 pp., biblio., append. $12.

A primer for 10 "steps to success": defining goals, assessing chances, organizing resources, identifying and researching prospects, making initial contacts, meeting with a foundation, writing a formal proposal and follow up.

Foundation Fundamentals: A Guide for Grantseekers. Carol M. Kurzig. 1980. Rev. ed. New York: Foundation Center, 1981. 148 pp., illus., append. $6.50 pb.

A basic sourcebook from the provider of primary working tools for grant seekers.

The New How to Raise Funds from the Foundations. Joseph Dermer. 1968. Rev. ed. Hartsdale, N.Y.: Public Service Materials Center, 1979. 96 pp. $11.50.

Basic manual outlining how to approach foundations, tools, presentation writing, etc., with examples.

The Bread Game: The Realities of Foundation Fund Raising. Herb Allen, ed. 1975. 4th ed. San Francisco: Volcano Press (330 Ellis Street, 94102), 1981. 150 pp., illus., biblio. $9.95 pb.

Advice on how to write a proposal and how to form a tax-exempt organization.

Corporate Foundation Profiles. New York: Foundation Center, 1983. 593 pp. $50 pb.

Detailed analysis of more than 230 of the largest company-sponsored foundations with summary financial data for more than 400 additional corporate foundations.

Businesses and Corporations

There is no end to what you can get American business to do, if it is in their interest and if you don't care who gets the credit.

Robertson E. Collins. In "Business and Preservation." Supplement to *Preservation News*, April 1976.

Types of Corporate Support
Outright gifts and grants
Matching gifts by employees
United Campaign contributions
Gifts in kind
Program-related investments
Restoration of headquarters and other properties

The Art of Winning Corporate Grants. Howard Hillman. New York: Vanguard Press, 1980. 180 pp. $10.95 hb.

Provides sources for corporate grants, tips on how to write a proposal, how to meet grants officials, etc.

National Directory of Corporate Charity. San Francisco: Regional Young Adult Project (330 Ellis Street, Suite 518, 94102), 1984. 613 pp. $80.

Contains profiles of 1,600 corporate giving programs, providing contacts, area of interest, previous recipients, assets, grant ranges and policies.

How To Get Corporate Grants. San Francisco: Public Management Institute (333 Hayes Street, 94102), 1981. 350 pp. $49 binder.

Forms, charts, tables and checklists interspersed with instructions and discussions on successful corporate grant seeking.

CASE Currents, November 1981. $5. Council for Advancement and Support of Education.

Special issue on obtaining corporate support.

The Corporate Fund Raising Directory. Hartsdale, N.Y.: Public Service Materials Center, 1984. 400 pp., index. $79.50 pb.

Information on the charitable giving activities of more than 350 U.S. corporations, with a special listing of oil companies and an index of corporations by state.

Corporate 500: The Directory of Corporate Philanthropy. 3rd ed. San Francisco: Public Management Institute, 1984. 730 pp. $245 pb.

Entries include name, address and phone; contact person; corporate contributions committee members; corporate giving policy; areas of interest; a financial profile and a list of sample grants and nonprofit recipients.

National Directory of Arts and Education Support by Business Corporations. Daniel Millsap and Editors of WIAL. 1980. 5th ed. Washington, D.C.: Washington International Arts Letter, 1983. 340 pp., index. $79.95 pb.

Lists corporations, their products, services and cultural budgets. Updated every two or three years and monthly in the newsletter.

Guide to Corporate Giving in the Arts 3. Robert Porter, ed. New York: American Council for the Arts, 1983. 592 pp., index. $39.95 hb.

Profiles of more than 500 large corporations, their giving policies and practices.

The New Corporate Philanthropy: How Society and Business Can Profit. Frank Koch. New York: Plenum Press, 1979. 315 pp., illus. $22.50 hb.

New Profits from Old Buildings: Private Enterprise Approaches to Making Preservation Pay. Raynor M. Warner, Sibyl M. Groff and Ranne P. Warner, Inform, Inc. 1978. Reprint. New York: McGraw-Hill, 1979. 307 pp., illus., gloss., index. $29.95 hb.

Case studies of adaptive use, continued use and new additions by banks, business firms and corporations; residential and commercial revitalization by businesses and banks; and general preservation support by corporations.

A New Frontier for Business Opportunities: A Handbook for Private Initiative in Community Revitalization. Washington, D.C.: Industry Task Force in Community Revitalization, 1980. 102 pp., biblio. $3 pb. Available from U.S. League of Savings Institutions, 111 East Wacker Drive, Chicago, Ill. 60601.

A handbook on how business people, bankers and realtors can organize as community activists. Includes sources of government funding, case histories, dealing with news media and how to work with city officials.

Preservation for Profit: Ten Case Studies in Commercial Rehabilitation. Cornelia Brooke Gilder. Albany: Preservation League of New York State (307 Hamilton Street, 12210), 1980. 28 pp., illus., biblio. $3 pb.

Presents examples of commercial rehabilitation in New York State.

Contacts
Business Committee for the Arts
1775 Broadway
Suite 510
New York, N.Y. 10019

Stimulates support of the arts by the business community.

Center for Corporate Public Involvement
1850 K Street, N.W.
Washington, D.C. 20006

Sponsored by the American Council of Life Insurance and the Health Insurance Association of America to encourage insurance companies to participate in socially helpful activities—urban and civic affairs, education, culture, etc.

National Association of Realtors
Community Programs Division
430 North Michigan Avenue
Chicago, Ill. 60611

Sponsors efforts such as a community revitalization program to encourage realtors to save existing housing stock.

National Trust for Historic Preservation
Office of Resources Development
1785 Massachusetts Avenue, N.W.
Washington, D.C. 20036

Businesses that contribute more than $1,000 annually to the National Trust are recognized as Corporate Associates. By 1985 some 220 preservation-minded corporations had joined, from Aetna Life Insurance Company to the Xerox Corporation.

Council for Advancement and Support of Education
11 Dupont Circle
Suite 400
Washington, D.C. 20036

Maintains a Clearinghouse for Corporate Matching Gift Programs, through which business corporations match donations made by employees to nonprofit organizations.

Promotion for a Jack Daniel's–National Trust program to support preservation projects and groups throughout the country. (Jack Daniel's)

Individual Giving

It is a difficult task to harness financial commitment for preservation from individuals, particularly for general operating purposes. However, if a potential donor is well educated by the organization and called upon for specific participation in a project, a major gift commitment could be forthcoming.

"Private Philanthropy and Preservation." In *Preservation: Toward an Ethic in the 1980s.* National Trust for Historic Preservation. Washington, D.C.: Preservation Press, 1980.

When bequests and individual giving are lumped together, they constitute 89.7 percent of all gifts to charitable organizations.

Giving USA

Planned Giving Ideas. Virginia L. Carter and Catherine S. Garigan, eds. Washington, D.C.: Council for Advancement and Support of Education, 1980. 48 pp. $9.50 pb.

Encouraging various types of gifts—bequests, unitrusts, annuity trusts, charitable income trusts, pooled income funds, gifts of land, etc.; hiring and training planned giving officers; relationships with prospects, volunteers and estate planning professionals.

The Art of Asking: A Handbook for Raising Money Successfully. Paul H. Schneiter. New York: Walker, 1978. $8.95 pb.

Chapter 5 is entitled "Model Approaches to Individuals."

The Complete Estate Planning Guide. Robert Brosterman. 1966. Rev. ed. New York: New American Library, 1981. 346 pp., appends., index. $4.95 pb.

Explains in terms understandable to the general reader all aspects of modern estate planning.

Taxwise Giving. Monthly. 13 Arcadia Road, Old Greenwich, Conn. 06870. $115 a year.

Tells development officers of philanthropic institutions how to use the tax law to increase their institution's resources.

The National Trust

The following types of gifts made to the National Trust are similar to those made to other nonprofit preservation and historical organizations, all of which may provide tax savings to the donors as well as benefit the recipients.

Gifts of Life Insurance
Policies may be transferred or purchased and donated to the Trust as an irrevocable beneficiary.

Bequests
Bequests from a donor's estate

Batchelor's Hope, St. Marys, Md., a gift to the National Trust.

may take a variety of forms, such as property, cash or securities.

Income-producing Gifts
A donor may make a contribution while retaining an income for life or a term of years in a fixed dollar amount or a percentage of the fund assets.

Gifts of Real Estate
Under a Gifts of Heritage program, historic property that is not appropriate for retention as a museum is sold with protective covenants. Through a Surplus Real Estate program, other gifts of real estate are accepted.

Gifts of Other Appreciated Property
Donations of art objects, jewelry or furniture may be used to augment house museum collections or sold to provide income for the museums.

Gifts That Provide Continuing Income
Charitable lead trusts may be used to provide income for a specified number of years, after which the principal is returned to the donor.

National Trust for Historic Preservation Office of Resources Development 1785 Massachusetts Avenue, N.W. Washington, D.C. 20036

Real Estate Development

Historic preservation is in many ways a sophisticated type of real estate development.

John Sower, "Financing and Developing Large Commercial Preservation Projects." In *Economic Benefits of Preserving Older Buildings*

"Personal motivation, civic awareness and social desirability are not sufficient by themselves to launch a recycling project. . . . It takes money. Ordinarily the largest portion of that money must be borrowed from a bank, an insurance company, a savings and loan association or some other institutional lender. Although the picture is changing rapidly . . . it is still the availability of borrowed money that triggers most real estate investment and development."

Jared Shlaes and Michael S. Young, *Financing Preservation in the Private Market*

Financing Preservation in the Private Market. Jared Shlaes and Michael S. Young. Information Series, National Trust for Historic Preservation. Washington, D.C.: Preservation Press, 1981. 40 pp., gloss., biblio. $2 pb.

Describes ways of financing rehabilitation and adaptive use, with explanations about money and real estate values, selecting the right financing device, major lenders, government financing sources, income tax factors and types of ownership and tax implications. Lists essential steps to follow for a successful project.

Historic building on Royal Street, New Orleans, when it was available for development. (Franck Collection, Historic New Orleans Collection)

Mayan Theater (1930), Denver, subject of a Trust grant to Historic Denver to study reuse alternatives. (Morgan-Gerard)

Economic Benefits of Preserving Old Buildings. National Trust for Historic Preservation. Washington, D.C.: Preservation Press, 1976. 164 pp., illus. $7.95 pb.

A comprehensive look at preservation's profit potential through papers by leading developers and architects. Topics include municipal action to encourage private investment, adaptive use, the costs of preservation, private financing and large- and small-scale commercial renovation projects, with many case studies.

Investing in Old Buildings. Sally E. Nielsen. Portland, Maine: Greater Portland Landmarks (165 State Street, 04101), 1980. 73 pp., illus., append., biblio. $4.70 pb.

This handbook for small-scale, owner-occupied projects as well as commercial ventures covers the physical analysis of an old building, planning for reuse, the feasibility study and financing.

"Preservation/Development Conflicts." *Urban Land,* October 1980. Urban Land Institute, 1090 Vermont Avenue, N.W., Washington, D.C. 20005.

A special issue covering means of resolving conflicts, examples of successful cooperation, preservationists as developers, the federal review process and UDAG's record.

An Introduction to the Economic Development Planning Process. Washington, D.C.: National Council for Urban Economic Development, 1980. 112 pp., biblio. $12 photocopy.

A summary of how to plan and evaluate economic development.

Fundamentals of Real Estate Development. James A. Graaskamp. Washington, D.C.: Urban Land Institute, 1981. 31 pp., biblio. $10.

An Introduction to Risk Management in Property Development. James D. Vernor. Washington, D.C.: Urban Land Institute, 1981. 20 pp., biblio. $10.

Monographs on the basic principles, practices and case studies of real estate development.

Real Estate Desk Book. IBP Research and Editorial Staff. 1964. 6th ed. Englewood Cliffs, N.J.: Institute for Business Planning, 1979. 498 pp., gloss., append., index. $39.50 hb.

Discusses tax planning with real estate, depreciation and mortgage amortization, real estate acquisition methods, financing opportunities and various methods of ownership.

The VNR Real Estate Dictionary. David M. Brownstone and Irene M. Franck. New York: Van Nostrand Reinhold, 1981. 344 pp. $21.95 hb.

More than 2,000 key terms from financing, law, accounting, construction, architecture, government regulation, financial planning, taxation and investment.

The Language of Real Estate. John Reilly. Rev. 2nd ed. Aurora, Ill.: Caroline House (920 West Industrial Drive, 60506), 1982. 570 pp. $28.95 hb, $21.95 pb.

The Illustrated Book of Development Definitions. Harvey S. Moskowitz. New Brunswick, N.J.: Center for Urban Policy Research, 1981. 263 pp., append. $15 pb.

Dictionary of Development Terminology. Robert J. Dumouchel. New York: McGraw-Hill, 1975. 278 pp.

See also: Adaptive Use; Rehabilitation and Restoration

The Language of Finance and Development

accelerated depreciation. A depreciation method resulting in larger deductions from income in the early years than the straight-line method.

amortization. The periodic repayment of debt under a loan agreement or deduction of an equal portion of the cost of a capital asset on a periodic basis.

certified historic structure. For the purposes of the federal preservation tax incentives, any structure subject to depreciation as defined by the Internal Revenue Code that is listed individually in the National Register of Historic Places or located in a registered historic district and certified by the secretary of the interior as being of historical significance to the district.

certified rehabilitation. Any rehabilitation of a certified historic structure that the secretary of the interior has determined is consistent with the historic character of the property or the district in which the property is located.

construction loan. An interim loan used to finance the construction of buildings and other improvements on a site.

historic preservation certification application. The form required for certified historic structure designation if the property is not itself listed individually in the National Register.

joint venture. A legal arrangement in which two or more parties undertake to share the risks and rewards of a project on an agreed basis.

leverage. The use of fixed-cost funds to acquire property that is expected to produce a higher rate of return either by way of income or through appreciation.

limited partnership. A form of ownership in which partners are divided into two classes: the general partner or partners who actively manage the operations of the group and bear full responsibility for its affairs, and the limited partners, whose exposure is normally limited to the amounts for which they are obligated under the terms of the partnership agreement and who have no control over the affairs of the partnership.

loan-to-value ratio. The ratio between the original principal amount of a mortgage loan and the actual or appraised value of the property.

soft costs. Development expenses other than those devoted to land and actual construction, such as interest on borrowed funds, architectural and other fees, marketing costs and incidental expenses.

straight-line depreciation. A depreciation deduction calculated by subtracting from the initial cost or value of the improvements any anticipated salvage value and then dividing the estimated economic life of the improvements into that figure.

takeout. A loan commitment issued by a permanent lender intended to repay an interim loan or funds advanced by the developer.

wrap-around mortgage. A form of mortgage in which the mortgage holder provides secondary financing and collects from the borrower periodic payments large enough to cover debt requirements of both primary and secondary financing, using them to make any payments due to the primary lender under the first mortgage.

Adapted from *Financing Preservation in the Private Market*

Union Commerce Bank (1924), Cleveland, an award-winning bank restoration. (Score Photographers)

Banks and Other Financial Institutions

Private financial institutions, principally insurance companies, banks, savings and loans and real estate developers, are playing an increasing role in the preservation movement. Interest . . . results in part from federal and state antiredlining laws, corporate image building concerns and demonstrated interest and accomplishments of real estate developers. To some extent, both developers and institutions from which they seek financing have grown to view preservation as a profitable form of real estate development as a result of special tax incentives, increased costs of new construction and consumer demand for space in old buildings.

"Private Financial Institutions and Real Estate Developers." In *Preservation: Toward an Ethic in the 1980s.* National Trust for Historic Preservation. Washington, D.C.: Preservation Press, 1980.

"The [Community Reinvestment Act] provides an important new tool for community organizations, whether their purpose is fighting redlining or establishing community development programs which require private investment. By itself CRA, passed by Congress in 1977, establishes that some 19,000 lending institutions in the United States have an affirmative responsibility to provide credit to their communities. The Act ties this responsibility into bank examinations and more significantly into federal approval of new charters, branch offices, mergers, relocations, and many other banking activities. . . . CRA makes it easier for community organizations to influence directly the lending policies of banks, savings and loan associations and other lenders."

Allen J. Fishbein and Jeffrey Zinsmeyer, *Neighborhood-Based Investment Strategies: A CRA Guidebook.* Washington, D.C.: HUD, 1980.

Investing in the Future of America's Cities: The Banker's Role. National Council for Urban Economic Development, for Comptroller of the Currency. Washington, D.C.: NCUED, 1981. 83 pp. $12.50 pb.

Six case studies of innovative ways in which banks have contributed to economic development through profit-making ventures—neighborhood, commercial and industrial revitalization projects and loan pools for downtowns.

Bankers and Community Involvement: Profiles of Selected Bank Programs in Community and Economic Development. Washington, D.C. American Bankers Association, 1978. 181 pp. $22.50 pb.

Eighty-three case studies designed to help bankers compare their community development approaches with others. Includes neighborhood redevelopment and rehabilitation policies of various banks.

"Selective Bibliography on Commercial Lending." Washington, D.C.: American Bankers Association. Annual.

Among the topics covered are the Community Reinvestment Act and community involvement.

Reaching Out: A Community Investment Initiative. Washington, D.C.: Office of Community Investment, Federal Home Loan Bank Board, 1981. Free.

150 ways in which savings and loans are using community investment funds.

Taking the Mystery Out of Banks and Community-Based Organizations. Boston: Council for Northeast Economic Action, 1981. 52 pp. Available from First National Bank of Boston, 100 Federal Street, 17th Floor, Boston, Mass. 02110.

Outlines the business opportunities CBOs present to banks and offers practical advice on how to approach banks.

Community Development Credit Unions. Washington, D.C.: National Center for Urban Ethnic Affairs (P.O. Box 33279, 20033), 1977. 12 pp. $3 pb.

A handbook intended for neighborhood organizations interested in forming a community development credit union.

1984 Savings and Loan Sourcebook. Chicago: United States League of Savings Associations. 64 pp., gloss., index. Annual. Free.

A source of information on the savings and loan industry, federal agencies that affect it and data on savings, mortgage lending and housing.

Mortgage Banking Terms: A Working Glossary. 1975. 4th ed. Washington, D.C.: Mortgage Bankers Association of America, 1981. 115 pp. $6.

Defines some 750 terms used in mortgage banking.

See also: Neighborhoods

Contacts

Federal Home Loan Bank Board
1700 G Street, N.W.
Washington, D.C. 20552

An independent federal agency established to encourage thrift and economical home ownership and to supervise and regulate federal savings and loan associations. Its Office of Community Investment stimulates efforts to revitalize communities.

United States League of Savings Associations
111 East Wacker Drive
Chicago, Ill. 60601

Represents savings and loan associations, cooperative banks and state and local savings and loan association leagues.

National Association of Mutual Savings Banks
200 Park Avenue
New York, N.Y. 10166

Maintains an interest in neighborhood revitalization programs and has an Urban and Consumer Affairs Committee.

National Consumer Cooperative Bank
2001 S Street, N.W.
Washington, D.C. 20009

Established in 1978 to provide loans and technical assistance to cooperatives in such areas as housing and energy.

Federal National Mortgage Association
Community Development Division
3900 Wisconsin Avenue, N.W.
Washington, D.C. 20016

A privately owned, federally chartered corporation, Fannie Mae supports the housing market by buying commercial mortgages. Its policies aid older neighborhoods and increase home buying in small towns and rural areas.

Government National Mortgage Association
U.S. Department of Housing and Urban Development
Washington, D.C. 20410

A wholly owned corporate instrumentality of the federal government operating within HUD, Ginnie Mae was created in 1968 to assume certain functions formerly belonging to FNMA and to guarantee securities backed by government insured or guaranteed mortgages.

Federal Home Loan Mortgage Corporation
1776 G Street, N.W.
Washington, D.C. 20006

A subsidiary of the Federal Home Loan Bank Board chartered by Congress in 1970 to help mortgage lenders make mortgage financing readily available. Develops and supports an active secondary mortgage market in conventional residential mortgages.

Mortgage Bankers Association of America
1125 15th Street, N.W.
Washington, D.C. 20005

Association of mortgage banking firms, savings and commercial banks, life insurance, fire and casualty insurance and title companies, savings and loan associations.

American Bankers Association
1120 Connecticut Avenue, N.W.
Washington, D.C. 20036

Trade association representing most American banks and trust companies.

State Bank Building (c. 1813), Raleigh, N.C., moved and reopened as a bank in 1969 after serving temporarily as a rectory. (Lewis P. Watson)

National Credit Union Administration
1776 G Street, N.W.
Washington, D.C. 20456

Regulates and insures all federally chartered credit unions.

Credit Union National Association
P.O. Box 431
Madison, Wis. 53701

An association serving more than 90 percent of the local U.S. credit unions.

Frank Lloyd Wright Home and Studio (1889–98, Frank Lloyd Wright), Oak Park, Ill., whose purchase and resale by a preservation group to the National Trust was underwritten by four local banks. (NTHP)

Revolving Funds: Recycling Dollars and Buildings

Preservationists need power. Without it, legislation cannot be effected, bulldozers cannot be stopped. The quickest way for an organization to gain political stature is to contribute to real estate by buying and restoring, selling and renting property.

Arthur P. Ziegler, Jr., "Revolving Funds." *Historic Preservation,* April–June 1971.

"A revolving fund is a pool of capital created and reserved for a specific activity with the condition that money will be returned to the fund for additional activities. Revolving funds have proven to be an effective tool to stimulate preservation of historic properties both through acquisition and resale of properties and through loans to individuals for restoration or rehabilitation. Funds are replenished through proceeds from sales, rentals, loan repayments and interest, and revolved to new projects."

National Trust for Historic Preservation

"The purpose of a revolving fund is to conserve buildings. If the market conditions require that money be lost on a transaction, lose it. Results in restoration and revitalization are what count. Only with such results will additional people and funds be drawn to the effort."

Leopold Adler. In *Commercial Area Revolving Funds for Preservation.*

The Revolving Fund Handbook: A Practical Guide to Establishing a Revolving Fund and the Development Through Adaptive Reuse of Historic Properties. Architectural Conservation Trust for Massachusetts and Architectural Heritage Foundation. Boston: Architectural Conservation Trust, 1979. 112 pp., illus., biblio.

Gives information on different kinds of revolving funds, how to establish one, financing a fund, hiring staff, formulating a project, the real estate development process and project completion, including easements and covenants. Uses a preservation development project in New Bedford, Mass., as a case study.

Revolving Funds for Neighborhood Preservation: Lafayette Square, St. Louis. Steven J. Coffey. Information Series, National Trust for Historic Preservation. Washington, D.C.: Preservation Press, 1977. 20 pp., biblio., appends. $2 pb.

Includes discussions of administration, loans and funds, the restoration subcommittee and its decisions, survey of properties, purchases, marketing, house sales and cooperation of local government.

Revolving Funds for Historic Preservation: A Manual of Practice. Arthur P. Ziegler, Jr., Leopold Adler II and Walter C. Kidney. Pittsburgh: Ober Park Associates (One Station Square, 15219), 1975. 111 pp., illus., gloss. $4.95 pb.

A practical guide to the workings of and reasons for revolving funds in preservation, as well as the basics of real estate and finance. Includes six studies: Charleston, Savannah, Annapolis, Pittsburgh, Neighborhood Housing Services and Action Housing Development funds.

Second Empire-style row houses in Lafayette Square, St. Louis, where a revolving fund is preserving neighborhood houses. (Barbara Elliott Martin)

Commercial Area Revolving Funds for Preservation. Peter H. Brink. Information Series, National Trust for Historic Preservation. Washington, D.C.: Preservation Press, 1976. 15 pp., biblio. $2 pb.

Focuses on The Strand, a downtown commercial area in Galveston, Tex. Discusses selection of an area, sources of funding, advantages of local historic district designation, financing, marketing, facade easements and long-term preservation possibilities.

"Revolving Funds: In the Vanguard of the Preservation Movement," J. Myrick Howard. *North Carolina Central Law Journal,* Spring 1980. $20 pb. Available from William W. Gaunt and Sons, 3011 Gulf Drive, Holmes Beach, Fla. 33510.

Covers setting up a fund, raising money and dealing with properties. Includes information on protective covenants and restoration agreements with samples.

"Revolving Funds: Recycling Resources for Neighborhoods." *Conserve Neighborhoods,* May–June 1981. National Trust for Historic Preservation.

A primer on neighborhood funds with profiles of leading local revolving funds.

Contacts

Architectural Conservation Trust
45 School Street
Boston, Mass. 02108

Historic Preservation Fund of North Carolina
P.O. Box 27632
Raleigh, N.C. 27611

Historic Landmarks Foundation of Indiana
3402 Boulevard Place
Indianapolis, Ind. 46208

Utah Heritage Foundation
603 East South Temple Street
Salt Lake City, Utah 84102

Preservation of Historic Winchester
8 East Cork Street
Winchester, Va. 22601

Historic Kansas City Foundation
20 West 9th Street
Kansas City, Mo. 64105

Historic Charleston Foundation
51 Meeting Street
Charleston, S.C. 29401

Historic Savannah Foundation
Box 1733
Savannah, Ga. 31402

Historic Albany Foundation
300 Hudson Avenue
Albany, N.Y. 12210

Providence Preservation Society
P.O. Box 1386
Providence, R.I. 02901

Preservation Fund of Pennsylvania
R.D. 1, Box 315
Mount Joy, Pa. 17550

Portland Development Commission
1120 S.W. 5th Avenue
Portland, Ore. 97204

Renovated 1882 building in Galveston's Strand. (Richard Tichich)

Galveston Historical Foundation
P.O. Drawer 539
Galveston, Tex. 77553

Pittsburgh History and Landmarks Foundation
One Station Square
Pittsburgh, Pa. 15219

Federal Programs

Historic preservation is an area the federal government has not had to substantially subsidize, like urban renewal. Instead, federal funds have been used for their most effective purpose—as seed money to get a project started, later allowing the private sector to take its place.

> Thomas D. Bever, *Economic Benefits of Historic Preservation.* Washington, D.C.: U.S. Department of the Interior, 1978.

Local, state and federal appropriations of public monies for preservation are typically on the order of less than one one-hundredth of 1 percent of the total governmental budget. . . .

> Robert E. Stipe, "The Impact of Law on Preservation Activities in the United States." *Monumentum*, vol. XIII. Washington, D.C.: US/ICOMOS, 1976.

Newbury House Inn (1880), Rugby, Tenn., restored and reopened as a hotel with CDBG and National Trust financial aid. (Historic Rugby)

During the 1960s and 1970s an array of several hundred federal programs could be tapped for preservation purposes. Beginning in 1981, this growth slowed and in some departments came to a halt. The federal funding programs to which preservationists can turn now are fewer in number, less money is available, and continued existence for many remains in doubt, dependent on annual budget requests and legislative action. Each funding agency or division should be contacted for the latest program information.

Cabinet Departments

U.S. Department of Agriculture
Channels credit to farmers, rural residents and rural communities to purchase or rehabilitate property. Programs include farm ownership loans, community facility loans, business and industrial loans, the Rural Housing Program and support for Main Street revitalization.
Farmers Home Administration
Washington, D.C. 20250

U.S. Department of Commerce
Provides grants to state and local governments to develop and implement land management programs to protect coastal land and water resources and revitalize waterfronts.
National Oceanic and Atmospheric Administration
Coastal Zone Management Program
Washington, D.C. 20230

U.S. Department of Education
Many programs have been incorporated into block grants to the states, which determine the allocations. Other programs support elementary and secondary education as well as postsecondary education efforts such as cooperative education, college work-study and general activities designed to enhance postsecondary education.
Office of the Assistant Secretary for Postsecondary Education
Washington, D.C. 20202

U.S. Department of Energy
Funds are apportioned to the states and are channeled through community action agencies to assist low-income residents in weatherizing their homes. Aid is also provided to state energy conservation programs.
Office of Weatherization Assistance
Washington, D.C. 20545

U.S. Department of Health and Human Services
Has administered programs to spur urban and rural economic development and encourage self-help, employment and ownership opportunities for low-income persons.
Office of Community Services
Washington, D.C. 20506

U.S. Department of Housing and Urban Development
Community Development Block Grants
Grants and guaranteed loans to cities, urban counties, public agencies and neighborhood organizations to improve housing and community development and revitalize deteriorating neighborhoods.

Section 312 Rehabilitation Loans
Loans to property owners for property rehabilitation made available through a city government, local public agency, housing authority or other local departments.

Historic Preservation Loans
FHA-insured loans to community residents and organizations, public and private institutions and state and local governments for historic residential properties and properties in historic districts.

Urban Development Action Grants
Grants to cities, urban counties and small communities to encourage private funding and revitalize localities by stimulating their economies and reclaiming neighborhoods.

Section 8—Housing Assistance Payments
Rental subsidies for low-income families, including housing in rehabilitated structures.

Section 202—Housing for the Elderly and Handicapped
Long-term, low-interest loans to private nonprofit sponsors to provide rental or cooperative housing for the elderly or handicapped through new construction or rehabilitation of properties.

Title I—Property Improvement Loan Program
FHA insurance for loans made by private financial institutions for property improvements.

Urban Homesteading Program
Low-cost, conditional conveyance of unoccupied HUD-owned residential properties to individuals in communities participating with HUD in the program.

Section 221—Public Housing Program
FHA mortgages for low- and moderate-income families.

Policy Development and Research
Supports research and demonstration projects by states, localities and academic, public and private institutions to improve HUD programs.

Monitoring Community Development: Citizens' Evaluation of the Community Development Block Grant Program. Washington, D.C.: Center for Community Change (1000 Wisconsin Avenue, N.W., 20007), 1980. 72 pp., appends. $4.50 pb. *Summary.* 16 pp. $2.50 pb.

"Conserving Our Cities: Assessing UDAG's Record." In *Urban Conservation and Federally Assisted Economic Development in Cities: Putting It Together.* Phyllis Myers, ed. Washington, D.C.: Conservation Foundation (1717 Massachusetts Avenue, N.W., 20036), 1980. 63 pp. $6.95 pb.

"UDAG." Supplement to *Preservation News,* September 1980.

The Urban Development Action Grant Program. Richard P. Nathan and Jerry A. Webman, eds. Princeton, N.J.: Princeton Urban and Regional Research Center, Woodrow Wilson School of Public and International Affairs, 1980. 125 pp. $5 pb.

Office of Community Planning and Development
Washington, D.C. 20410

U.S. Department of the Interior

National Park Service
Grants-in-aid to the states to conduct preservation surveys, prepare preservation plans and, when appropriations are available, provide matching grants to owners of properties in the National Register of Historic Places. The program helps support operations of the state historic preservation offices and the National Trust.

Archeological Services
Funding and technical assistance to recover archeological resources endangered by federal projects.

Urban Park and Recreational Recovery Program
Matching grants to state and local governments, which support local agencies, nonprofit organizations and park authorities in developing innovative urban park and recreation projects.

P.O. Box 37127
Washington, D.C. 20013–7127

U.S. Department of Labor

Supports youth employment and senior community services programs that may be used for rehabilitation or revitalization efforts.

Employment and Training Administration
Washington, D.C. 20213

U.S. Department of Transportation

Highway Planning and Construction
Programs include grants for planning, constructing and improving highways and roads; inventorying, moving or rehabilitating historic bridges under the Highway Bridge Replacement and Rehabilitation Program; and support for research on archeological, historic and architectural sites that may be affected by a federally funded highway.

Urban Mass Transportation
Grants and loans to local and state public transportation agencies for renovation of bus, rapid transit and railroad terminals of historical significance if used for mass transit.

Railroad Rehabilitation and Improvement
Guaranteed loans used to rehabilitate structures and operate railroad facilities.

Airport Improvement
Grants and advisory services to improve or repair airport facilities.

Federal Highway Administration
Federal Railroad Administration
Urban Mass Transportation Administration
Federal Aviation Administration
Washington, D.C. 20590

U.S. Department of the Treasury

Internal Revenue Service
Investment tax credits allowed for rehabilitation of income-producing properties 30 years or older based on a sliding scale. Certified historic structures are eligible for a 25 percent credit on rehabilitation of income-producing residential (rental) or nonresidential buildings.

Revenue Sharing
Federal tax revenues allocated to local governments quarterly, based on population, general tax effort, per capita income of residents and intergovernmental transfers. Localities may spend the funds for any legal purpose, including matching other federal grants and transferring them to other groups, such as preservation or neighborhood groups.

2401 E Street, N.W.
Washington, D.C. 20226

Independent Agencies
Economic Development Administration

Programs to create jobs in low-income, high-unemployment areas through public works programs and funding to leverage private investment.

14th Street and Constitution Avenue, N.W.
Washington, D.C. 20230

U.S. General Services Administration

Surplus Property Donations and Sales
Nonprofit, tax-exempt public or private educational organizations, museums, libraries and public agencies may obtain property no longer needed by the federal agencies.

Art-in-Architecture Program
Commissions artists to produce works of art to be incorporated into new buildings and those undergoing renovation.

Cooperative Use of Public Buildings
GSA is directed to acquire new federal space in historic buildings where feasible as a spur to preservation.

18th and F Streets, N.W.
Washington, D.C. 20405

Institute of Museum Services

Aids museum operating and program expenses through grants and support services.
1100 Pennsylvania Avenue, N.W.
Washington, D.C. 20506

National Archives and Records Administration

Supports projects to collect, preserve and describe documents and records of American history such as papers of presidents, statesmen and artists.
National Historical Publications and Records Commission
Washington, D.C. 20408

National Endowment for the Arts

Design Arts Program
Grants for projects that promote excellence in architecture, landscape architecture, urban design and planning, interior design, industrial design, graphic design and fashion design.

Museum Program
Matching grants to museums, organizations providing museum services, state arts agencies and regional groups; nonmatching grants to individual professionals.

Artists in Education Program
Funded through state arts agencies or nonprofit organizations to provide artists' or architects' residencies in an educational setting.

State Programs
Matching grants to state arts councils or regional arts agencies, which make grants and provide services to nonprofit public and private organizations.

Challenge Grant Program
Grants to cultural organizations requiring a 3:1 match to open new funding sources.

1100 Pennsylvania Avenue, N.W.
Washington, D.C. 20506

Renovation in progress in Oakland, Calif., documented by a storefront museum created with NEA funding. (Joffre Clark, Oakland Museum)

National Endowment for the Humanities

Division of General Programs
Grants for humanities projects providing information and insight on the history and culture of American societies for an adult audience, including museum and historical organization exhibits and programs, library activities and media productions. Special projects include out-of-school youth projects, grants to young individuals and groups, program development in research and dissemination for adults.

Division of Research Programs
Supports basic research, conferences, state, local and regional studies, reference works and publications by educational publishers.

State Programs
Grants to state humanities councils for projects on topics of concern to citizens of the state.

Education Programs
Grants to improve teaching and education programs in the humanities for elementary, secondary and higher education, including teacher institutes, consultant grants and development of curriculum materials.

Challenge Grants
Aid to develop a permanent capital base for institutions, to be matched on a 3:1 basis.

Fellowships and Seminars
Aid for independent study and research awarded to scholars, teachers and journalists.

1100 Pennsylvania Avenue, N.W.
Washington, D.C. 20506

Small Business Administration

Loan programs include Section 502—Local Development Company Loans and Loan Guarantees; 7A Loans—short-term loans with an SBA guarantee, made directly to small businesses with no LDC involvement; and the formerly separate Economic Opportunity Loan Program for low-income and disadvantaged persons.

1441 L Street, N.W.
Washington, D.C. 20416

Smithsonian Institution

Supports studies of critical museum problems and professional museum training that contribute to the improvement of museum methods.

National Museum Act Program
Arts and Industries Building
Room 3465
Washington, D.C. 20560

See also: Neighborhoods; Preservationists

Directories and Guides

Catalog of Federal Domestic Assistance. Office of Management and Budget. 17th ed. Washington, D.C.: GPO, 1984. Annual. 1,230 pp. $36. GPO stock no. 941–001–00000–9.

An annual listing of some 1,000 federal programs based on input by the agencies. It is not totally comprehensive, but is an essential guide to types of aid available, uses, eligibility and application procedures. Computer access to the *Catalog* is available from the Foundation Center as part of its Associate program ($275 annual fee).

"How to Use the Catalog of Federal Domestic Assistance." Los Angeles, Calif.: Grantsmanship Center, 1979. $2.

1985 Federal Funding Guide. Arlington, Va.: Government Information Services (1611 North Kent Street, Suite 508, 22209), 1985. 622 pp. $122.95 pb. Annual.

Annually updated information on major programs, complete with names, addresses and phone numbers.

Federal Information Centers
Listed in local telephone directories under "Federal Information Center, United States Government."

Federal Agency Area Offices
Listed in local telephone directories by agency under "United States Government."

Cultural Directory II: Federal Funds and Services for the Arts and Humanities. Federal Council on the Arts and the Humanities. Washington, D.C.: Smithsonian Institution Press, 1980. 267 pp., appends., index. $8.95 pb.

A good sourcebook (although outdated) on federal programs that can benefit the arts and humanities in the form of financial aid, employment and technical services.

Funding Sources and Technical Assistance for Museums and Historical Agencies: A Guide to Public Programs. Hedy A. Hartman. Nashville: American Association for State and Local History, 1979. 138 pp. $11 pb.

Still useful but somewhat out of date. Gives funding and technical assistance sources, exhibition services, miscellaneous government services and programs, national museum assistance agencies, and state and regional museum coordinators.

Federal Assistance Programs Retrieval System
A computerized system for identifying federal programs that can be used to meet community development needs, keyed to the *Catalog of Federal Domestic Assistance.* Information available from FAPRS, Rural Development Service, U.S. Department of Agriculture, Washington, D.C. 20250.

Guide to Federal Housing Programs. Barry G. Jacobs et al. Washington, D.C.: Bureau of National Affairs, Inc., 1982. 297 pp., append., index. $24 pb.

Surveys the federal role in housing and surveys major programs such as UDAG, CDBG and rehabilitation funding.

Working Partners. Washington, D.C.: Office of Community Planning and Development, HUD, 1984. 39 pp. Free.

Profiles 90 award-winning public-private partnerships that used CDBGs to revive housing, downtowns and neighborhoods.

Housing and Community Development Guide: Housing and Community Development Programs for Small Towns and Rural Areas. Washington, D.C.: Housing Assistance Council (1025 Vermont Avenue, N.W., 20005), 1985.

Lists federal programs that aid low-income housing in rural areas. Updated as government regulations change.

CUED's Guide to Federal Economic Development Programs. Washington, D.C.: National Council for Urban Economic Development, 1981. 138 pp., index. $50 looseleaf binder.

Describes the eligible applicants and activities, application and review processes and what the agency is looking for. Some of the agencies no longer exist or have been severely limited in scope.

The Art of Winning Government Grants. Howard Hillman. New York: Vanguard Press, 1977. 256 pp. $10.95 hb.

Outlines step-by-step methods for grant applicants to avoid rejection.

How Small Grants Make a Difference: Examples from the Design Arts Program. Pamela Baldwin, Design Arts Program. Washington, D.C.: National Endowment for the Arts, 1977. 67 pp., illus. $3.50 pb. Available from Partners for Livable Places, 1429 21st Street, N.W., Washington, D.C. 20036.

Periodicals

The Federal Register
Superintendent of Documents
U.S. Government Printing Office
Washington, D.C. 20402

Published every weekday; gives the most up-to-date information about new federal programs, program changes and new regulations. $300 a year.

The Commerce Business Daily
Superintendent of Documents
U.S. Government Printing Office
Washington, D.C. 20402

A daily record of all potential federal contracts, contract awards that exceed $25,000 and upcoming sales of government surplus property. $160 a year.

Housing and Development Reporter
Bureau of National Affairs, Inc.
2300 M Street, N.W.
Washington, D.C. 20037

A reporting service on federal and state legislation and programs, the private response and major court cases. Deals with housing, community development, energy conservation, neighborhood preservation and development. A three-volume looseleaf reference file is updated when necessary, and a newsletter on current developments is published weekly. $556 a year.

Urban Conservation Report
Preservation Reports
1620 I Street, N.W.
Washington, D.C. 20006

A current source of information, published twice a month, on federal programs, legislation and legal matters dealing with rehabilitation, reinvestment and neighborhood preservation. $105 a year.

Commentary
National Council for Urban Economic Development
1730 K Street, N.W.
Washington, D.C. 20006

Quarterly newsletter on federal urban policy. $18 a year. NCUED also publishes *Legislative Report* (monthly) and *Urban Economic Developments* (monthly) for members.

Community Development Digest
8555 16th Street
Suite 100
Silver Spring, Md. 20910

Up-to-date information on federal, state and local programs affecting community development. Published twice a month. $199 a year.

Federal Programs Monitor
Center for Community Change
1000 Wisconsin Avenue, N.W.
Washington, D.C. 20007

Information on programs that affect community development organizations in low-income areas. Published 4–6 times a year. $5–25 a year.

Restoration of the California Assembly Chamber (1874), Sacramento, during the state's capitol restoration. (Welton Becket Associates)

State Programs

There are essentially two methods by which state and local governments provide aid for preservation through the use of their taxing and spending powers. The first is what might be termed the direct approach, dealing with the means by which state governments raise and spend dollars for preservation activities—whether in the form of direct expenditures for public projects or in the form of loans, grants or other subsidies to public, quasi-public or private agencies or individuals. Also included in any consideration of the direct approach would be the means by which local units of government, deriving their authority from the state, tax and spend specifically for these purposes. . . .

The second method might be termed the indirect approach and would include all of the varied means by which the states, directly and through their local units of government, aid preservation efforts indirectly through authorized manipulations of the state and local taxing systems. . . .

The major point to be made is that there is no state in which appropriations for historic preservation, from whatever source derived, even begin to approach one-half of one percent of the total state budget.

Robert E. Stipe, "State and Local Tax Incentives for Historic Preservation." In *Tax Incentives for Historic Preservation*

State Historic Preservation Offices

The key preservation agency in each state and territory, established following the National Historic Preservation Act of 1966. With funding from the National Park Service, U.S. Department of the Interior, SHPOs carry out programs such as surveys and planning, National Register nominations, ownership of state historic sites, publications, research, training and historical markers. Some provide grants-in-aid to private organizations and individuals for restoration of designated properties. For a list, see Preservationists.

State Arts Agencies

Provide grants and related programs for a variety of arts activities, including preservation. Regional arts groups also have been formed to administer multistate programs. The National Endowment for the Arts assists these agencies in carrying out Endowment-approved plans for support of the arts.

American Council for the Arts
570 Seventh Avenue
New York, N.Y. 10018

National Assembly of
State Arts Agencies
1010 Vermont Avenue, N.W.
Suite 920
Washington, D.C. 20005

National Assembly of
Local Arts Agencies
1785 Massachusetts Avenue, N.W.
Washington, D.C. 20036

National Endowment for
the Arts
State Programs
Office for Public Partnership
1100 Pennsylvania Avenue, N.W.
Washington, D.C. 20506

State Humanities Councils

Award aid to statewide and local humanities projects (including history, archeology, history and theory of the arts and the application of the humanities to the human environment) sponsored by organizations, civic associations and groups. Funding is provided by the National Endowment for the Humanities to eligible state councils.

Division of State Programs
National Endowment for
the Humanities
1100 Pennsylvania Avenue, N.W.
Washington, D.C. 20506

State Housing Finance Agencies

Independent agencies that draw together private development, mortgage resources and public funds to help create low-income housing. They offer low-interest loans to homeowners and developers, second mortgage financing, loans to lenders, start-up money and technical aid. Of the states that provide rehabilitation loans and grants for rehabilitation projects, the Massachusetts Housing Finance Agency has been especially active.

Council of State Housing Agencies
444 North Capitol Street, N.W.
Suite 118
Washington, D.C. 20001

State Historical Commissions and Societies

May give grants and awards for local history projects and preservation activities.

State Community Development and Planning Agencies

Provide planning and aid for community projects such as neighborhood and housing revitalization, local parks and public facilities.

State Tourism and Commerce Agencies

Guide efforts to develop and manage travel and tourism, including programs involving historic sites and districts.

State Highway and Transportation Agencies

Fund preservation-related projects such as archeological salvage in the path of highways and inventories of historic bridges, often with federal assistance.

State Environmental and Natural Resources Agencies

May provide loans or other financial aid for preservation activities including protection of historic rural resources.

State Park Agencies

Preserve and restore historic sites in park areas in states where this function is not administered by the state historic preservation office.

State Education Departments and Universities

Provide research grants, teach preservation courses and administer historic properties on state college campuses.

State Economic and Industrial Development Authorities

Assist small businesses and other corporations with loans and financial aid, often using public funds obtained through bond issues or tax revenue.

National Congress for
Community Economic
Development
2025 I Street, N.W.
Suite 901
Washington, D.C. 20006

Many of the programs listed in the Federal Programs section are administered through the states.

Local Programs

Inevitably, the ultimate success of a national historic preservation program is contingent upon the effectiveness of local preservation efforts. . . . It is the local agencies that determine the use of community development block grant (CDBG) funds, develop and administer housing improvement and rehabilitation programs, and formulate the local zoning machinery that constitutes the essential historic district ordinances.

Lisa Soderberg, "Community Preservation Synopsis." *11593,* October 1977. National Park Service.

Local Economic Development Tools and Techniques: A Guidebook for Local Government. 83 pp., biblio. $5. *The Private Economic Development Process: A Guidebook for Local Government.* 33 pp. U.S. Conference of Mayors, National Community Development Association and Urban Land Institute. Washington, D.C.: HUD and U.S. Department of Commerce, 1980. $8 photocopy. Available from HUD User, P.O. Box 280, Germantown, Md. 20874.

Industrial Revenue Bond Report: State-by-State Summary. National Association of Historic Preservation Attorneys. Raleigh, N.C.: Author (P.O. Box 45, Century Station, 27602), 1981. 3 pp. Free.

Report based on a questionnaire sent to each state industrial revenue bond authority. It recommends that preservationists investigate the permitted uses of IRBs within their states and urge their use by potential renovators.

See also: Neighborhoods

"In spite of legal and financial constraints, municipalities can take a number of actions to help encourage private investment in old buildings. For example, they can:

1. Survey landmarks and educate the public to their value
2. Initiate both local and state legislation to support preservation
3. Fund capital improvements
4. Establish nonprofit corporations or preservation foundations
5. Lease or acquire landmarks, and in some cases participate in ventures with private developers
6. Use incentive zoning and tax relief to promote preservation
7. Develop design guidelines and preservation criteria
8. Prepare comprehensive preservation plans."

Weiming Lu, "Public Commitment and Private Investment in Preservation." In *Economic Benefits of Preserving Old Buildings*

More Local Funding Techniques

Rehabilitation loan and grant programs
Loan guarantees to lenders
Allocation of federal programs
Subsidies for private development
Neighborhood Housing Services
Tax relief
Public revolving funds for preservation
Municipal preservation offices and landmarks commissions
Tax increment financing
City services and urban amenities
Downtown revitalization programs
Urban homesteading programs
Tax-exempt revenue bonds
Waterfront redevelopment
Adaptive use development
Net leasing of public properties
Transfer of development rights zoning
Facade easement acceptance

Camron-Stanford House (1876), Oakland, Calif., saved by the Junior League and the city. (Carleton Knight III)

The local private preservation organization or SHPO is one of the best sources of information on what programs are available in each city. For a list, see Preservationists.

"Municipal Action to Encourage Private Investment in Preservation." In *Economic Benefits of Preserving Old Buildings*. National Trust for Historic Preservation. Washington, D.C.: Preservation Press, 1976. 164 pp., illus. $7.95 pb.

Details a variety of programs used to support preservation in cities such as Dallas, New York and Sacramento. The book also presents case studies of Seattle's innovative efforts.

Coordinated Urban Economic Development: A Case Study Analysis. Washington, D.C.: National Council for Urban Economic Development, 1978. 269 pp., gloss. $10 pb.

Analyzes the coordination of public and private development resources, plans and programs in cities, with 21 case studies.

Abandoned 1906 gas company structures in Seattle, converted by the city into a waterfront Gas Works Park. (Carleton Knight III, NTHP)

Enterprise Zones

"Since the inception of the federal public housing program in the 1930s, American policy toward distressed inner-city areas has focused on public intervention and direct financial aid.

The Reagan administration hopes to alter this policy by cutting back or eliminating many urban programs, and relying instead on the resources of private investment. One approach that has received a great deal of publicity is enterprise zones—special districts that would be created in urban areas of high unemployment and poverty. In these zones . . . tax breaks and other incentives would stimulate the creation of new businesses and new jobs."

Gregory Longhini, "Enterprise Zones." *PAS Memo,* May 1981.

"The idea is to provide an irresistible array of federal tax exemptions and credits to employers who locate plants in the blighted urban neighborhoods that are to be the designated zones. . . .

Cities have also had a lot of experience with renewal. It's possible, as hundreds of projects have demonstrated, but it's extremely expensive and, in all but the rarest of circumstances, requires direct federal subsidies. The tax breaks offered by the enterprise zones are very modest in comparison with the real costs of urban redevelopment."

Editorial. *Washington Post,* January 7, 1982.

"Preservationists should make no mistake about the implications of streamlining and defederalization. Should there be a dispute over National Register–quality buildings in a zone, there is likely to be limited recourse to federal appeal. . . .

Preservationists learned, in the UDAG program, that after a complex financial package has been worked out between the developer, the lenders and the city, it is difficult to modify the plan or even to find listeners. In enterprise zones, as in UDAG projects, preservationists will need to emphasize up-front planning and to be involved early, at the transaction state."

Phyllis Myers, "Urban Enterprise Zones: UDAG Revisited?" *Historic Preservation,* November–December 1981.

Enterprise Zone Activity in the States. Richard Cowden and Gerald Bonetto. Washington, D.C.: Sabre Foundation, 1983. 34 pp. $15 pb.

Lafayette Square row houses, St. Louis, rehabilitated with a Trust revolving fund loan. (Ken J. MacSwan)

Enterprise Zones: Greenlining the Inner Cities. Stuart M. Butler. New York: Universe Books, 1981. 175 pp., biblio., index. $12.95 hb, $7.95 pb.

An explanation and defense of the concept, emphasizing its role in potential job creation, providing a history of enterprise zones in Britain, offering a model for federal legislation and examining some of the objections to the idea.

New Tools for Economic Development: The Enterprise Zone, Development Bank, and RFC. George Sternlieb and David Listokin. New Brunswick, N.J.: Center for Urban Policy Research, 1981. 238 pp. $12.50 pb.

An analysis of enterprise zones as well as possible alternative and supplementary economic programs.

"Enterprise Zones," Gregory Longhini. *PAS Memo,* May 1981. 4 pp. American Planning Association, 1313 East 60th Street, Chicago, Ill. 60637.

A review of the concept, federal and state legislation and potential effects.

Sourcebook on Enterprise Zones: Executive Summary. Mark Frazier, ed. Washington, D.C.: Sabre Foundation (317 C Street, N.E., 20002), 1981. 92 pp. $15 pb.

"Enterprise Zones—Would They Mean the Loss of Other Federal Help?" Neal R. Peirce and Carol Steinbach. *National Journal,* February 14, 1981.

Some Thoughts on Enterprise Zones. William R. Barnes. Washington, D.C.: National League of Cities (1301 Pennsylvania Avenue, N.W., 20004), 1982. 31 pp. $8.

National Trust Programs

Preservation Services Fund
Provides small matching grants to National Trust member organizations for consultant services on preservation projects, education programs and cosponsored conferences. Information is available from Trust regional offices; for a list, see Preservationists.

National Preservation Loan Fund
Awards loans to forestall immediate threats to National Historic Landmarks as well as to spur the creation of local revolving funds.

Critical Issues Fund
Supports studies of major current preservation issues to achieve early resolution and negotiation to save historic properties.

Inner-City Ventures Fund
Awards grants and low-interest loans to urban community groups to revitalize historic neighborhoods while minimizing displacement and leveraging additional project funds.

National Trust for Historic Preservation Office of Financial Services and Regional Offices 1785 Massachusetts Avenue, N.W. Washington, D.C. 20036

Engine No. 6 of the Waialua Agricultural Company on Kauai, Hawaii, a rare sugar plantation locomotive, saved with the help of a National Trust grant to Historic Hawaii Foundation. (Hawaii Railway Society)

Taxation of Historic Properties

Tax incentives have the ability to reach far more buildings worthy of preservation, and to do so more efficiently and effectively, than grants and other forms of direct government assistance.

Michael L. Ainslie, Preface.
Tax Incentives for Historic Preservation

"The power to tax involves the power to destroy."

Chief Justice John Marshall, 1819.

"In preservation terms, the question is whether the potentially destructive power of taxation of which Justice Marshall spoke can be reversed to become a positive power for the protection of historic buildings."

Robert E. Stipe, "State and Local Tax Incentives for Preservation." In *Tax Incentives for Historic Preservation*

Types of Preservation Tax Relief

Property Tax (Local)

Tax exemption: Historic properties may be exempted from general property taxes.

Tax reduction or deferral: Property may be assessed at lower than market value, deferred or frozen for a period of time following rehabilitation. The granting of an easement, life estate or development rights also may reduce the market value of a property.

Tax abatement or credit: Taxes are temporarily reduced in return for rehabilitation or restoration.

Tax-increment financing: Assessed values in a designated area are frozen for a time, with the accrued value allocated to a special fund used to finance public improvements in the area.

Non-exclusive programs: Miscellaneous tax incentives not instituted specifically for preservation, e.g., farmland retention and rehabilitation of structures for low-income housing.

Open space: Credit or abatement is provided for leaving land undeveloped.

Income Tax (Federal)

Investment tax credit: Substantial rehabilitation expenses may be deducted from taxes owed for qualified rehabilitation of income-producing properties more than 30 years old.

Accelerated cost recovery: Depreciation may be elected over predetermined periods on an accelerated or straight-line (mandatory with ITC for rehabilitation expenditures) basis.

Charitable contributions: Deductions may be taken for gifts to nonprofit organizations including real estate or appreciated property.

Inheritance Tax

Charitable contributions: Deductions are allowed for bequests of property to qualified organizations.

Assessments: Present use rather than fair market value may be assigned where authorized (e.g., by a state).

Capital Gains

Donations: Avoidance of tax for contributions for charitable purposes and establishment of trusts.

Tax Incentives for Historic Preservation. Gregory E. Andrews, ed. 1980. Rev. ed. Washington, D.C.: Preservation Press, 1981. 236 pp., illus., appends. $12.95 pb.

An overview with analyses, examples and figures from attorneys and other tax experts. Topics include state and local tax law, easements and taxation of preservation groups.

Taxation and Valuation of Historic Buildings. Margaret Thomas Will. Monticello, Ill.: Vance Bibliographies, 1979. P-383. 14 pp. $2 pb.

Covers general literature, federal, state and local tax policies and valuation of historic buildings.

Fairmont (Bellevue-Stratford) Hotel (1904, Hewitt Brothers), Philadelphia, restored by Day and Zimmermann Associates using federal tax credits and an EDA loan. (Hyman Myers Collection)

Federal Tax Incentives

The Economic Recovery Tax Act of 1981 . . . made dramatic and sweeping changes in the federal tax treatment of investment in real estate. . . . The 25 percent investment tax credit now allowed for rehabilitating certified historic structures has been a significant stimulus to identifying, designating and sensitively rehabilitating individual historic buildings as well as historic commercial districts and residential neighborhoods.

Federal Tax Incentives for the Rehabilitation of Historic Buildings

Despite the documented success of the federal tax incentives for rehabilitation as one of the most effective preservation tools, efforts to simplify federal income taxes have targeted them for elimination. Proposed changes in the tax code would repeal the 15, 20 and 25 percent investment tax credit for rehabilitation. The National Trust, Preservation Action and other preservationists are working to retain the current incentives available since 1981.

Tax Facts and Figures, 1977–83

Approved projects: 7,510
Investment in approved projects: $4.82 billion
Average project cost: $642,000
Mid-Atlantic: 54%
Midwest: 21%
Southeast: 18%
West: 5%
Housing: 48%
Mixed use: 22%
Office use: 16%
Commercial use: 8%
Hotels: 3%
Other: 3%
New housing units created: 26,500
New low- and moderate-income housing units: 13,617

From *Facts and Figures from Certification Applications for the Investment Tax Credit, 1977–83*

Investment Tax Credit Provisions

Allowable Credit
25%: certified historic structures
20%: 40 years and older
15%: 30 years and older

Certified Historic Structures
Individual property or district in the National Register or in certified state or local historic districts

Rehabilitation Categories
Income-producing purposes
Nonresidential and residential buildings (for 25% credit)
Nonresidential industrial and commercial buildings (for 15% and 20% credits)

Rehabilitation Expenditures
Substantial rehabilitation exceeding $5,000 or adjusted basis of the property

Certified Rehabilitation
Conforming to the Secretary of the Interior's Standards

Depreciation
Accelerated cost recovery system over 18, 35 or 45 years
Straight-line (with ITC) and accelerated methods

Demolition
Deduction of demolition costs and losses for certified historic structures is prohibited

Federal Tax Incentives for the Rehabilitation of Historic Buildings. Information Series, National Trust for Historic Preservation. Washington, D.C.: Preservation Press, 1984. 7 pp., illus. $2 pb.

A concise overview of the basic provisions of federal tax incentives contained in ERTA.

Decisions Confronting Owners of Older Buildings: An Economic Choice Model. Russell Holden. Preservation Policy Research Series. Washington, D.C.: National Trust for Historic Preservation, 1984. 36 pp. $5 pb.

Proposed model for estimating the effect of tax provisions on the demand for preservation of older buildings.

Rehabilitating Historic Office Buildings: Two Projects Using Federal Tax Incentives. William MacRostie. Technical Preservation Services, National Park Service. Washington, D.C.: GPO, 1983. 33 pp., illus. $4.50 pb. GPO stock no. 024–005–00841–1.

Provides financial figures as well as the rehabilitation processes used for the Physicians Building, Fresno, Calif., and the Wyandotte Building, Columbus, Ohio.

Facts and Figures from Certification Applications for the Investment Tax Credit, 1977–83. Christopher A. Sowick, Preservation Assistance Division, National Park Service. Preservation Policy Research Series. Washington, D.C.: National Trust for Historic Preservation, 1984. 54 pp. $6 pb.

Covers certifications and approvals of rehabilitation projects, National Park Service involvement, denials and appeals, with an analysis of the effectiveness of the tax incentives in promoting rehabilitation activity.

Contacts

Technical Preservation Services
Preservation Assistance Division
National Park Service
U.S. Department of the Interior
P.O. Box 37127
Washington, D.C. 20013-7127

Responsible for making historical and architectural determinations of which properties and districts qualify as certified historic structures and which proposals qualify as certified rehabilitations, using the Secretary of the Interior's Standards for Rehabilitation. Complete information on the preservation provisions of ERTA is available from this office.

State Historic Preservation Offices

Provide preservation certification application forms, review them following submission by applicants and forward them to the National Park Service. Also provide information on National Register listings for determining historical certification.

Internal Revenue Service
U.S. Department of
the Treasury
Washington, D.C. 20224

Responsible for developing and administering the tax aspects of the ERTA preservation provisions, including issuance of regulations.

National Trust for
Historic Preservation
1785 Massachusetts Avenue, N.W.
Washington, D.C. 20036

Active in efforts to achieve passage and retention of ERTA, cosponsors instructional conferences with the National Park Service and National Conference of State Historic Preservation Officers, conducts research, issues publications and maintains an involvement in a variety of related tax issues. A special project, Preservation and Rehabilitation Impact Estimation or PRIME, predicts the impact of tax incentives on the amount of income-producing property preserved.

State and Local Taxes

A number of states and municipalities now offer relief from real property or income taxation for privately owned historically or architecturally significant properties, in addition to the more traditional property tax exemption granted historic properties owned by nonprofit organizations such as historical societies. These measures encompass relief ranging from complete or partial exemption from property taxes to state income tax deductions similar to those found in [federal legislation].

"State and Local Statutes Providing Tax Relief for Historic Preservation." In *Tax Incentives for Historic Preservation*

The tax policy of most United States cities and other local governmental entities is centered on the ad valorem taxation of private property. . . . [Thus] the only significant effect local tax policy can have on the conservation of the environment is through the administration of the real property tax.

Joseph H. McGee, "Local Taxation: Current Practices, Procedures and Effects." In *Tax Incentives for Historic Preservation*

"Property tax exemptions are comparatively weak preservation tools because to be eligible for exemption, explicit actions by owners to help preserve their historic property are generally not required. Measures containing an incentive to engage in a preservation activity, therefore, are preferred to those that merely provide property tax relief."

Richard R. Almy, "Considerations in Creating Property Tax Relief for Historic Preservation." In *Tax Incentives for Historic Preservation*

State and Local Tax Relief
The following types of tax incentives for preservation are authorized by various states and municipalities (although all may not have been implemented or used widely).

Property Tax Exemption
Alaska
New York State
Puerto Rico
Texas
Oyster Bay, N.Y.
New York City

Property Tax Credits
Maryland
New Mexico

Property Tax Abatement
Arizona
Connecticut
North Carolina
Oregon
Tennessee
Austin, Tex.
Brookhaven, N.Y.
Petersburg, Va.

Actual-Use Assessment
California
District of Columbia
Louisiana
Nevada
Oregon
Virginia
Washington

Assessment Increase Deferral
Maryland

East Main Street, Oyster Bay, N.Y., one of the U.S. cities offering preservation property tax exemptions. (Nore Winter, Vision, Inc.)

*Assessments Reflecting
Easements and Landmark
Designation*
California
Colorado
Connecticut
Georgia
Illinois
North Carolina
Oregon
South Carolina
Tennessee
Texas
Virginia
West Virginia

Income Tax Relief
Maryland
Puerto Rico

*Property Tax Relief for
Rehabilitation*
Colorado
Illinois
Rhode Island
Virginia
Utica, N.Y.

"State and Local Tax Law." In
*Tax Incentives for Historic Pres-
ervation.* Gregory E. Andrews,
ed. 1980. Rev. ed. Washington,
D.C.: Preservation Press, 1981.
236 pp., illus., appends. $12.95 pb.

Papers survey the subject, including
practices, procedures and effects,
case studies and innovations in the
conservation field.

*Significant State Historic Pres-
ervation Statutes.* James P.
Beckwith, Jr.. Information Series, National Trust for Historic
Preservation. Washington, D.C.:
Preservation Press, 1979. 34 pp.,
biblio. $2 pb.

Includes citations for preservation-
oriented state tax statutes.

*Landmarks Preservation and the
Property Tax: Assessing Landmark Buildings for Real Taxation Purposes.* David Listokin.
New Brunswick, N.J.: Center
for Urban Policy Research,
1982. 248 pp., biblio., illus. $20.

A study of the effects of historical
status on property values, with a
detailed examination of New York
City's experiences conducted with
the New York Landmarks Conservancy. Includes recommendations of
specific property tax incentives to
promote preservation and shows
how the deterrent to maintenance
stemming from higher taxation can
be removed.

*Reviving Cities with Tax Abate-
ment.* Daniel R. Mandelker,
Gary Feder and Margaret R.
Collins. New Brunswick, N.J.:
Center for Urban Policy Research, 1980. 160 pp., biblio.,
append. $12.95 pb.

Presents the legal and equity issues,
a cost analysis and the effectiveness
of the Missouri Urban Redevelopment Corporations Law, which enables private developers to organize
redevelopment corporations to rehabilitate designated blighted areas in
St. Louis.

*Federal Policy Toward Property
Tax Exemptions and Abatement
for Housing Rehabilitation.*
Harold A. Hovey with Susan
Mick. Washington, D.C.: Urban
Institute (2100 M Street, N.W.,
20037), 1980. 88 pp., append.,
biblio. $8.40.

Based on a HUD study, provides
insights into 28 cities whose abatement programs are used to encourage the rehabilitation of rental units.

"Urban Property Tax Incentives: State Laws." Chicago:
International Association of Assessing Officers, 1978. Research
and Information Series, no. 246.
21 pp. $8.50.

Compilation of state laws offering
exemptions or abatements of property taxes to nonpublic bodies for
constructing or renovating property
or locating commercial or industrial
property in certain areas.

Tax Incremental Financing.
Debra L. Allen and Jack R.
Huddleston. Chicago: Council
of Planning Librarians, 1979.
No. 9. 13 pp. $3.50 pb.

Annotated bibliography of articles,
papers, books and research tools.

Property Appraisal

"Basic economic principles
govern the appraisal of all real
property. Four of the most
important principles—all interrelated—are: economic use,
contribution, supply and demand and substitution. These
economic principles apply to
the appraisal of properties with
historical significance just as
they apply to the valuation of
other real property."

Judith Reynolds and Anthony
Reynolds, *Factors Affecting Valuation of Historic Property*

"The majority of state laws
direct the tax assessors to ap-
praise real property at its fair
market value, and this in turn is
interpreted to mean at its 'highest and best' use, a rule that
probably causes most of the
resentment against tax
appraisals."

Joseph H. McGee, "State and
Local Taxation: Current Prac-
tices, Procedures and Effects." In
*Tax Incentives for Historic
Preservation*

"Present-use assessment is the
most frequently used technique
that employs the property tax to
alter land use decisions. Since
the basic problem is that landmarks and open spaces often
cannot return sufficient revenue
to offset taxes which are based
on a higher and better use of
the land, present-use assessment mitigates the problem by
taxing the property only on its
value for present uses, not on
the basis of any speculative or
future uses."

Grady Gammage, Jr., et al., *His-
toric Preservation in California: A
Legal Handbook.* 1975. Rev. ed.
Stanford: Stanford Environmental
Law Society, 1982.

*Historic Properties: Preserva-
tion and the Valuation Process.*
Judith Reynolds. Chicago:
American Institute of Real Estate Appraisers, 1982. 115 pp.,
illus., biblio., appends., index.
$15 hb.

Outlines appraisal methods and analyzes economic considerations affecting appraisals. Topics include
recognizing significant properties,
public policy and the appraisal process, the effect of tax provisions,
adaptive use, easements and sales
comparison, cost and income
approaches.

*Improving Real Property As-
sessment.* Chicago: International Association of Assessing
Officers, 1978. 444 pp. $25 pb.

Comprehensive manual includes discussion of assessment techniques
(data collection, analysis and computerization) and approaches (comparison, cost and income),
evaluation of effectiveness and cost
of these techniques, appeals systems and economic administration
of an assessment program.

*Factors Affecting Valuation of
Historic Property.* Judith Rey-
nolds and Anthony Reynolds.
Information Series, National
Trust for Historic Preservation.
Washington, D.C.: Preservation
Press, 1976. 9 pp., biblio. $2 pb.

A basic overview of the special
assessment needs of historic
properties.

"Historical Significance. . . .
How Much Is It Worth?" An-
thony Reynolds and William D.
Waldron. *Appraisal Journal,*
July 1969.

An introduction to the valuation of
historic buildings and standard appraisal techniques.

"Incremental Elements of Mar-
ket Value Due to Historical
Significance," John P. Dolman.
Appraisal Journal, July 1980.

A case study of Val-Kill, Eleanor
Roosevelt's home, with guidelines
for determining "highest and best
use" and market value of the home.

See also: Easements (Protecting
the Past)

Contacts

American Institute of
Real Estate Appraisers
National Association of Realtors
430 North Michigan Avenue
Chicago, Ill. 60611

Among other activities, publishes
the quarterly *Appraisal Journal.*

International Association of
Assessing Officers
1313 East 60th Street
Chicago, Ill. 60637

Publishes numerous materials, including a Research and Information
Series and Bibliographic Series, and
has a property tax information
service.

American Society of Appraisers
P.O. Box 17265
Washington, D.C. 20041

Multidisciplinary testing and certify-
ing appraisal organization dealing
with personal property, insurance,
business enterprise, machinery and
equipment, public utilities, real
property, technical valuation and
appraisal education.

Education

15

> To be deeply rooted in a place may be the best gift a child can receive because it remains with him in adulthood and may suggest to him unawares that sense of identity with the external world that serves as a compass to guide him through life.
>
> Rene Dubos, *The American Scholar*

> In response to the renewed interest in saving old buildings nationwide, many historic preservationists have come to realize that educating children about the built environment is an essential part of protecting America's heritage for future generations. . . . students are becoming highly conscious participants in urban life by learning to understand and appreciate the buildings around them.
>
> Patricia Leigh Brown, "Young Students Meeting Old Buildings, with Appreciation." *Christian Science Monitor,* May 23, 1980.

Architecture: The Fourth R

"The built environment is architecture in its broadest interpretation. Comprised of the cities, streets, houses, and parks that man builds and the spaces that connect them, it is the physical framework of our activities and interactions and thus an important determinant of the shape of our lives. . . . We all need to be trained to be aware of what is around us, to sense the qualities and interrelationships of the colors, textures, noises, objects, and spaces that are part of our everyday life. . . .

Sensory awareness must be accompanied by understanding. Children must begin to think about the functions of the built environment, how it works, and how it influences attitudes and activities."

Aase Eriksen and Valerie Smith, "Art Education and the Built Environment." *Art Education,* September 1978.

Teacher Sarah Parsons of the Massie Heritage Interpretation Center, Savannah, encouraging elementary school students to enjoy the architecture around them. The Massie program is part of the Savannah-Chatham County social studies curriculum for grades 1–12. (Grant Compton)

From Awareness to Careers

"There are two goals of formal education in preservation. One goal is general awareness, appreciation and commitment to preservation among individuals who will support preservation efforts but who are not involved as full-time professionals. This objective is most commonly associated with the primary and secondary school population and, to a lesser extent, with those colleges and universities that now sponsor individual courses in preservation. The second goal of formal education is career-oriented. This objective is embraced by the degree programs in preservation currently sponsored by colleges and universities. Professional development also is the objective of the many shorter and nondegree training programs and educational opportunities available to practicing professionals involved in . . . work related to preservation."

"Preservation Education: Student Perspectives." In *Preservation: Toward an Ethic in the 1980s.* National Trust for Historic Preservation. Washington, D.C.: Preservation Press, 1980.

Students building an arch with their fingers. (Grant Compton)

Preservation Education Is . . .

Elementary and Secondary School Programs
The integration of preservation-related material and activities into the required curriculum for history, math, science, English, etc.

Higher Education Programs
Courses and degree programs sponsored by schools or departments of architecture, law, planning, history, business, anthropology, landscape architecture, etc.

Continuing Education and Training Programs
Short courses and seminars offered by colleges, universities and organizations for professionals, paraprofessionals, active volunteers and the public.

Internships
Short-term, practical work experience sponsored by colleges independently or in cooperation with other organizations.

Program Enrichment
Community education programs, field trips, publications, specialized libraries and research opportunities offered by colleges and organizations to reinforce commitment to community service and maintain knowledge of work in the field.

Personal Enjoyment
Books, games, tours and similar activities for young and old that instill a lifelong appreciation for our architectural environment.

Children's Nonfiction

Good environmental and preservation books for children are so few and far between that when a new one comes along we seize it with great expectation. Under the circumstances, it is small wonder that they have difficulty measuring up. We adults have contributed to a climate of disregard for our physical environment— man-made and natural. . . . Yet the flood of environmental problems is slowly bringing the realization that life for our children just might be more difficult, as they will have to deal with deterioration of the environment and depletion of resources. In our children's books we sometimes place a heavy hand on the young to make up for our shortcomings. As our environmental concerns mature and become less frantic, perhaps our children's books will follow suit.

Janet N. Frank, Book Review.
Historic Preservation, October–
December 1974.

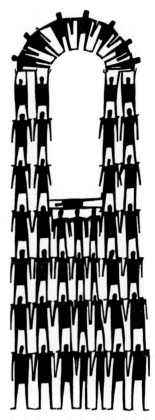

How an arched window feels. From *What It Feels Like to Be a Building.*

Architecture and Construction

People and Spaces: A View of History Through Architecture. Anita Abramovitz. New York: Viking, 1979. 207 pp., illus., biblio., index. $14.95 hb. Ages 12 up.

"This book about spaces and people is also a book with a view of history, the European heritage; a book that attempts to understand the huge hieroglyphics that different people of the Western world have left behind."

Building: From Caves to Skyscrapers. Mario Salvadori. Illustrated by Saralinda Hooker and Christopher Ragus. Reprint. New York: Atheneum, Margaret K. McElderry Books, 1985. $3.95 pb. Ages 12 up.

A child's introduction to how buildings are built.

Understanding Architecture. George Sullivan. New York: Frederick Warne, 1971. Ages 12 up.

Easy-to-understand descriptions of the structural and aesthetic aspects of architecture.

Archabet: An Architectural Alphabet. Photographs by Balthazar Korab. Washington, D.C.: Preservation Press, 1985. 64 pp., illus. $12.95 hb.

Makes a game of looking for alphabets in architecture for all ages. Includes quotations from architectural observers such as Frank Lloyd Wright and Mies van der Rohe.

Building: The Fight Against Gravity. Mario Salvadori. New York: Atheneum, 1979. 192 pp., illus. $10.95 hb. Ages 12 up.

Introduction to the basic principles of architectural structures.

Structure: The Essence of Architecture. Forrest Wilson. New York: Van Nostrand Reinhold, 1971. 96 pp., illus. Ages 14 up.

A simple look at the art of building, which the author says humans have mastered, and the art of understanding our built environment, which he says they have not.

What It Feels Like to Be a Building. Forrest Wilson. Garden City, N.Y.: Doubleday, 1969. 64 pp., illus. Ages 7–14.

A translation of the basic laws of building into physical feelings, based on the fact that buildings experience similar stresses and strains of gravity as humans.

Faces on Places: About Gargoyles and Other Stone Creatures. Suzanne Haldane. New York: Viking, 1980. 40 pp., illus. $11.50 hb. Ages 8–12.

A look at creatures and faces carved on stone buildings throughout the United States.

How to Wreck a Building. Elinor Lander Horwitz. New York: Pantheon, 1982. 56 pp., illus. $9.95 hb. Ages 8–14.

The demolition of a 70-year-old school in Baltimore told as if through a student's eyes.

The Skyscraper Book. James Giblin. New York: Crowell Junior Books, 1981. 96 pp., illus., append., biblio., gloss., index. $9.95 hb. Ages 8–12.

Describes how skyscrapers are built, their advantages and the problems they create.

Skyscrapers. Anne and Scott MacGregor. New York: Morrow, 1981. 56 pp., illus. $5.95 pb. Ages 9 up.

Simple instructions for building your own skyscraper while learning engineering principles and the history of this building type.

Bridges. Scott Corbett. Illustrated by Richard Rosenblum. New York: Four Winds, 1978. 122 pp., illus. $9.95 hb. Ages 8–12.

Explores the history of bridges and the techniques used to build them.

The Brooklyn Bridge: They Said It Couldn't Be Built. Judith St. George. New York: Putnam, 1982. 128 pp., illus. $10.95 hb. Ages 10 up.

The story of the bridge built by John and Washington Roebling, told through anecdotes and period illustrations.

Joseph Stella: The Brooklyn Bridge. Robert Saunders and Ernest Goldstein. New York: New American Library, 1984. 52 pp. $9.95 hb.

A look at the 100-year-old landmark as part of the Let's Get Lost in a Painting Series.

Tunnels. Samuel and Beryl Epstein. Boston: Little, Brown, 1985. $13.95. Ages 9 up.

Stories of the world's most famous tunnels, from Jerusalem to Japan, explaining how they are planned and built.

The Merry-Go-Round. Oretta Leigh. Illustrated by Kathryn E. Shoemaker. New York: Holiday House, 1985. $12.95. Ages 3–7.

Presents a vicarious trip on a carousel.

How They Built Our National Monuments. Paul C. Ditzel. New York: Bobbs-Merrill, 1976. 198 pp., illus., biblio. Ages 9 up.

The story of 10 famous landmarks, including the Liberty Bell, the White House, Old Ironsides, Hoover Dam and the Golden Gate Bridge.

The Factories. Leonard Everett Fisher. Nineteenth Century America Series. New York: Holiday House, 1979. 62 pp., illus., index. $9.95 hb. Ages 9–12.

The history of factories in America from the late 18th century to 1900.

Architects

Significant American Artists and Architects: A Picture and Text Reference. Janet Tegland, ed. Chicago: Children's Press, 1975. 78 pp., illus., index.

Capsule biographies of architects (and many artists) arranged alphabetically in six chronological periods.

Famous American Architects. Sigmund A. Lavine. New York: Dodd, Mead, 1967. Ages 12 up.

A survey of leading master builders.

What Can She Be? An Architect. Gloria and Esther Goldreich. New York: Lothrop, Lee and Shepard, 1974. 48 pp., illus. $11 hb. Ages 4–11.

Designed to whet the child's interest with an account of a building's planning and construction.

Styles

To Grandfather's House We Go: A Roadside Tour of American Homes. Harry Devlin. 1967. Englewood Cliffs, N.J.: Four Winds Press, 1980. 48 pp., color illus. $9.95 hb. Ages 9–13.

Popular architectural styles, simply discussed and colorfully illustrated.

What Kind of a House Is That? Harry Devlin. New York: Parents' Magazine Press, 1969. 48 pp., color illus. Ages 10–13.

Brief discussions of unusual and now uncommon American buildings from fun house to outhouse.

A Building on Your Street. Seymour Simon. New York: Holiday House, 1973. 44 pp., illus. Ages 4–8.

An introduction to various building styles and materials.

Houses

Houses. Irving and Ruth Adler. New York: John Day, 1965. $10.89 hb. Ages 8–12.

How the form of houses from caves to apartment buildings is determined by tools on hand, location and vocation.

American Houses: Colonial, Classic, Contemporary. Edwin Hoag. New York: Lippincott, 1964. Ages 12–14.

An illustrated history emphasizing how architectural style is determined by lifestyle.

Homes, Shelter, and Living Space. Joanna Foster. New York: Parents' Magazine Press, 1972. Ages 8–10.

A history of types and styles.

Have You Seen Houses? Joanne Oppenheim. Reading, Mass.: Young Scott Books, 1973. 48 pp., illus. Ages 6–9.

Free verse and photographs explain the many forms houses take.

Simple Shelters. Lee Huntington. New York: Coward, McCann and Geoghegan, 1979. Ages 9–12.

A survey of basic dwelling types from around the world.

Building a House. Byron Barton. New York: Greenwillow Books, Morrow, 1981. 32 pp., illus. $10.25 hb. Ages 4–6.

A first book of house building for the very young.

Children's Literary Houses. Rosalind Ashe and Lisa Tuttle. New York: Facts on File, 1984. 112 pp., color illus. $17.95 hb. Ages 12 up.

Explores in words and pictures eight popular dwellings in children's literature.

The Houses We Build. Lisl Weil. New York: Atheneum, 1985. $13.95 hb. Ages 7–11.

An overview of Western architecture from caves to high-rises.

The Tipi: A Center of Native American Life. David and Charlotte Yue. New York: Knopf, 1985. $10.95. Ages 9–12.

Outlines Plains Indian dwellings, with diagrams of tipi types.

History

Old Names and New Places. Robert I. Alotta. Illustrated by Lee DeGroot. Philadelphia: Westminster, 1979. 112 pp., illus. $8.95.

Offers local history about America's towns and cities and shows the reader how to find the stories behind the names.

Exploring Literary America. Marcella Thum. New York: Atheneum, 1979. 340 pp., illus., indexes. Ages 10 up.

Short biographies of more than 50 American authors and descriptions of memorials that can be visited.

Who Put the Cannon in the Courthouse Square? A Guide to Uncovering the Past. Kay Cooper. Illustrated by Anthony Accardo. New York: Walker, 1985. $11.85. Ages 10 up.

First volume in Walker's American History Series.

The Mount Rushmore Story. Judith St. George. New York: Putnam, 1985. $12.95. Ages 10 up.

Details the famous monument and its sculptor, Gutzon Borglum.

Digging the Past. Bruce Porell. Illustrated by Bruce Elliott. Reading, Mass.: Addison-Wesley, 1979. 150 pp., illus., append., gloss., biblio., index. $8.95 hb. Ages 11 up.

Archeology is revealed in stories, activities and games to be enjoyed at any backyard site.

Waves Across the Past: Adventures in Underwater Archeology. Richard B. Lyttle. New York: Atheneum, 1981. 224 pp., illus. $10.95 hb. Ages 10 up.

The story of the development of underwater archeology in the 20th century.

Wooden Ship. Jan Adkins. Boston: Houghton Mifflin, 1978. 48 pp., $6.95 hb. Ages 10 up.

Chronicle of the building of a wooden sailing vessel in 1870, woven around the mythical whaleship *Ulysses.*

The President's Car. Nancy Winslow Parker. Introduction by Betty Ford. New York: Crowell Junior Books, 1981. 64 pp., illus., append., biblio., gloss. $10.89 hb.

Presents cars and carriages used by the presidents, arranged chronologically.

Townscape and Planning

Central City/Spread City: The Metropolitan Regions Where More and More of Us Spend Our Lives. Alvin Schwartz. New York: Macmillan, 1973. 132 pp., illus., biblio., index. Ages 14 up.

An examination of inner city and suburb, their problems and strengths.

Let's Find Out About the City. Valerie Pitt. New York: Franklin Watts, 1968. Ages 5–8.

The complexities of urban life (economics, laws and city services), simply defined and attractively illustrated.

Forest, Village, Town, City. Dan Beekman. Illustrated by Bernice Loewenstein. New York: Crowell Junior Books, 1982. 32 pp., illus. $9.50 hb. Ages 8–11.

An illustrated look at the evolution of America from virgin land to skyscraper cities.

What Shall We Do with the Land: Choices for America. Laurence Pringle. New York: Crowell Junior Books, 1981. 160 pp., illus., biblio., index. $10.89 hb. Ages 10 up.

Surveys critical choices regarding farmlands, rangelands, forests, seacoasts, deserts and wild places.

Ox-Cart Man. Donald Hall. Illustrated by Barbara Cooney. New York: Viking, 1979. $12.95 hb. Ages 4–8.

Depicts the life cycle of a New England farm before the 20th century. 1979 Caldecott Award for best illustrated book.

The Story of an English Village. John S. Goodall. New York: Atheneum, 1979. 60 pp., color illus. $8.95 hb. Ages 5–12.

Detailed watercolor paintings show an English village at 100-year intervals, from a medieval clearing to a modern town.

A Tree on Your Street. Seymour Simon. New York: Holiday House, 1973. 44 pp., illus. Ages 5–8.

A child's introduction to the natural environment.

Town and Country. Alice and Martin Provensen. New York: Crown, 1985. $9.95.

Panoramic paintings of rural and urban America by two Caldecott Medalists.

Four by Weitzman

"Search as we might in the history-book lives of others we don't know, and have never known, sooner or later we will return to find that the answers to who we are and where we've been are nearby, and many of them are underfoot."

David Weitzman, *Underfoot*

My Backyard History Book. David Weitzman. Boston: Little, Brown, 1975. 128 pp., illus. $9.95 hb, $5.95 pb. Ages 9 up.

An entertaining book enlivened by sketches, cartoons and photographs designed to teach children how to trace and record their personal histories and how to use local resources—the cemetery, the Yellow Pages, elderly neighbors—to find out what the "olden days" were like in their home towns.

Underfoot: An Everyday Guide to Exploring the American Past. David Weitzman. New York: Scribner's, 1976. 192 pp., illus., biblio., index. Ages 15 up.

A handbook for learning local history from old photographs, oral history, old advertisements and buildings, among other sources.

Traces of the Past: A Field Guide to Industrial Archaeology. David Weitzman. New York: Scribner's, 1980. 229 pp., illus., biblio., index. Ages 15 up.

About railroad rights of way, old maps, bridges, factory roof trusses, iron furnaces, oil wells and a case history describing the exploration of an old bridge with children. "Through aboveground archaeology [children] experience history in an active sense, doing the work of historians. But, most important, such activities make history what it once was for children—a natural way to get a sense of place and roots."

Windmills, Bridges, and Old Machines: Discovering Our Industrial Past. David Weitzman. New York: Scribner's, 1982. $13.95 hb. Ages 10 up.

A lavishly illustrated introduction to the workings of windmills, waterwheels, canals, bridges and other industrial artifacts.

Drawing by Fermin Rocker. From *Andy's Landmark House*.

Landmark Fiction

The Landmark man was right. The whole block was going to improve.

I guess I should measure for my shelves, Andy thought, but he was too full of his own feelings to do anything but walk and think. Nothing in his life had ever made him feel as good as this. He had tried to play a part in making one block beautiful, and he would never walk down his street again without a sense of pride and a special feeling for the tradition and dignity of the five Greek Revival houses.

> Hila Colman, *Andy's Landmark House*

Andy's Landmark House. Hila Colman. New York: Parents' Magazine Press, 1969. 124 pp., illus. Ages 9–12.

Andy and friends set out to save their old neighborhood brownstones from destruction.

Big World and the Little House. Ruth Krauss. New York: Harper and Row, 1949. Ages 5–8.

A family transforms a deserted house into a home.

The Building That Ran Away. Robert Heit. New York: Walker and Company. Ages 5–8.

A six-story structure's reaction to impending demolition.

The Cable Car and the Dragon. Herb Caen. Illustrated by Barbara Ninde Byfield. Garden City, N.Y.: Doubleday, 1972. 25 pp., illus. Ages 6–8.

The youngest San Francisco cable car (a spry 60-year-old) literally goes off its trolley and takes a colorful tour of the city's landmarks.

Goodbye Dove Square. Janet McNeill. Boston: Little, Brown, 1969. Ages 11–14.

Former inhabitants of the demolished square become embroiled in a mystery.

The House on Charlton Street. Dola De Jong. New York: Scribner's, 1962. Ages 12 up.

Eleven-year-old David develops a fascination for Greenwich Village history when his family buys a mysterious old house there.

The House on East Eighty Eighth Street. Bernard Waber. Boston: Houghton Mifflin, 1962. $4.95 pb. Ages 5–8.

An amusing fantasy in which the Primm family moves into a New York brownstone rich in architectural detail.

The House on the Roof. David A. Adler. New York: Hebrew Publishing Company, 1979. 32 pp., illus. $6.95 hb. Ages 5–9.

An old man builds a Sukkah (a temporary house), as his ancestors did when they escaped from slavery into the desert, on the roof of his apartment house. His grandchildren are delighted, but the landlady takes him to court.

I Want to Be an Architect. Eugene Baker. Chicago: Children's Press, 1969. Ages 5–8.

Two boys discover that they want to be architects when Mr. Jones shows them how to plan a play house.

The Legend of New Amsterdam. Peter Spier. Garden City, N.Y.: Doubleday, 1979. 32 pp., illus. $7.95 pb. Ages 6–10.

A tantalizing twist to a colorful portrait of Manhattan life 300 years ago.

The Little House. Virginia Lee Burton. 1942. Boston: Houghton Mifflin, 1978. $12.95 hb, $4.95 pb. Ages 5–8.

A classic that tells the story of a little country house gradually engulfed by roads and buildings until it was rescued by the great-great-granddaughter of the builder, who moved it out into the country again.

Marco and That Curious Cat. John Foster. New York: Dodd, Mead, 1971.

Marco, a boy detective-hero, his cousin Lily and a curious cat live four exciting adventure-filled days in a historic Louisiana plantation home inspired by the National Trust's Shadows-on-the-Teche.

Nak. Belle Coates. Boston: Houghton Mifflin, 1981. Ages 10 up.

The story of a young Native American living on a Montana reservation whose work for a paleontologist brings him into conflict with Indian society.

Matilda Young reading a story at the Conduit Road Schoolhouse (1864), Washington, D.C. (Stephen Northrup, *Washington Post*)

Piccolo's Prank. Leo Politi. New York: Scribner's, 1965. Ages 6–8.

A slight story of an Italian organ-grinder set among Victorian gingerbread houses in an unusual community in Los Angeles.

A Small Piece of Paradise. Geoffrey Morgan. New York: Knopf, 1968. Ages 10–12.

An enchanting garden, tucked away behind Mr. Penny's London junkyard, is ripe for redevelopment.

Sparrow Song. Ben Schecter. New York: Harper and Row, 1981. 32 pp., illus. $9.95 hb. Ages 5–8.

When a house is to be torn down, a boy saves its resident sparrow and builds a birdhouse identical to the old house.

Three Wishes for Sarah. Mary Malone. New York: Dodd, Mead, 1961. Ages 9–11.

Faced with urban renewal, Sarah and friends fight city hall.

The Tiny Little House. Eleanor Clymer. New York: Atheneum, 1972. Ages 3–9.

A deserted house, dwarfed by neighboring high-rises, is put to adaptive use thanks to two little girls.

The Vandals of Treason House. Nancy Veglahn. Boston: Houghton Mifflin, 1974. 160 pp., illus. $5.95. Ages 8–12.

An education for four children sentenced to cleaning and restoring an old house after vandalizing it.

We Lived in the Almont. Eleanor Clymer. New York: E. P. Dutton, 1970. Ages 9–12.

Family and friends live comfortably in an old downtown apartment building—until the owner opts for demolition in favor of a supermarket.

What Ever Happened to the Baxter Place? Pat Ross. New York: Pantheon, 1976. 40 pp., illus. Ages 6–10.

How the Baxter farm became a shopping mall.

Seven by Macaulay

"There are any number of children's books which attempt to explain aspects of the world's workings. . . . Few, however, can match the eloquence and calm confidence of David Macaulay's. . . . And none is quite so successful at bringing the past to life, with the homely intricacies of its everyday tools and materials."

> Russell M. Griffin, "Within the Moat." *Washington Post*, November 13, 1977.

"[Macaulay's] books are so lucidly written and dramatically illustrated that they delight 8-year-olds and fascinate adults. . . . even experts on architectural history gain a fresh view."

> Wolf Von Eckardt, " 'Pyramid' and 'City': Building Blocks for Elementary Schools." *Washington Post*, February 18, 1978.

Cathedral: The Story of Its Construction. David Macaulay. Boston: Houghton Mifflin, 1973. 80 pp., illus. $5.95 pb. Ages 6 up.

The building of a French Gothic cathedral, using a fictitious example.

City: A Story of Roman Planning and Construction. David Macaulay. Boston: Houghton Mifflin, 1974. 112 pp., illus. $5.95 pb. Ages 6 up.

Another hypothetical location, this time a first-century Roman city and how it was planned and built.

Pyramid. David Macaulay. Boston: Houghton Mifflin, 1975. 80 pp., illus. $12.95 hb, $5.95 pb. Ages 13 up.

The story of your average ancient Egyptian pyramid.

Underground. David Macaulay. Boston: Houghton Mifflin, 1976. 112 pp., illus. $10.95 hb, $5.95 pb. Ages 6 up.

All about the interesting, complex and astounding things under our feet in the city.

Castle. David Macaulay. Boston: Houghton Mifflin. 1977. 80 pp., illus. $13.95 hb, $6.95 pb. Ages 6 up.

Traces the creation of an imaginary, but typical, castle and its ancillary town built to aid in the conquest of Wales in the late 13th century.

Unbuilding. David Macaulay. Boston: Houghton Mifflin, 1980. 80 pp., illus. $12.95 hb. Ages 8 up.

Dedicated "to those of us who don't always appreciate things until they are gone," this is the only slightly exaggerated tale of how the Empire State Building was sold in 1989 to Prince Ali, who had it dismantled with the intention of reconstructing it in his homeland. The reader learns about skyscraper construction, dismantling buildings and how money talks.

Mill. David Macaulay. Boston: Houghton Mifflin, 1983. 128 pp., illus., gloss. $14.95 hb.

The life of four 19th-century New England mills, tracing changes in architecture, power production and labor-management relations and ending with the mill's conversion to apartments.

Imaginary 13th-century Gothic cathedral conceived by David Macaulay. From *Cathedral: The Story of Its Construction.*

A coliseum in David Macaulay's first-century Roman city. From *City: A Story of Roman Planning and Construction.*

Children playing with giant Tinkertoys by Gabriel (CBS Toys), "Just for Fun" exhibit. (AIA Foundation)

Fun and Games

Much of the child's play is an attempt to discover, understand, and manipulate the built environment, often in a scale more manageable than that of the large-sized adult world. Building with blocks, maneuvering toy cars and trucks through imaginary streets, making models, doll houses, and sand castles—all these activities are built environment education.

Aase Ericksen, "Recent Developments in Built Environment Education." *Environmental Comment*, April 1979. Urban Land Institute.

Building blocks, miniature houses, rooms and shops, sandcastles, chocolate bricks, a house of cards, an abandoned refrigerator box, a toy windmill, a birdcage or even a cookie can, while delighting a child, influence his thinking.

Jeanne Butler Hodges, Introduction. *Just for Fun! A Celebration of Architecture.* Exhibit catalog. Christine Miles. Washington, D.C.: American Institute of Architects Foundation, 1979.

Construction Toys, Old and New

"Commercial construction toys did not find their way to the toy counters in any calculable quantity until the 1850's. Yet, by the 1870's toy manufacturers were marketing all kinds of blocks with colorful surfaces made of lithographed paper glued onto each side. Many historians credit the growing interest in the construction toy to the Kindergarten movement, implemented by Friedrick Froebel in Germany by 1840. . . ."

Christine Miles, *Just for Fun!*

"A small interior world of color and form now came within the grasp of small fingers. Color and pattern, in the flat, in the round. Shapes that lay hidden behind the appearances all about. . . . Here was something for invention to seize, and use to create."

Frank Lloyd Wright, *An Autobiography.* 1943. Reprint. New York: Horizon Press, 1976.

The Complete Block Book. Eugene F. Provenzo, Jr., and Arlene Brett. Syracuse, N.Y.: Syracuse University Press, 1984. 180 pp., illus., appends. $19.95 hb, $12.95 pb.

Froebel Blocks (1840s)

Richter Bricks (1880s)

Bauhaus Blocks (available from Museum of Modern Art)

Bristle Blocks (Milton Bradley Company)

Playskool Blocks (Milton Bradley Company)

Lincoln Logs (Milton Bradley Company)

LEGO (Lego Systems)

Tinkertoy Construction Set (CBS Toys)

Erector Set (CBS Toys)

Fischertechnik Kit (Fischerwerke, West Germany)

Cut-and-Build Models

"Build Your Own" Series. New York: Perigree, Putnam, 1981–82. $7.95–8.95 each. Ages 10 up.

Included are the Brooklyn Bridge, Chrysler Building, Empire State Building, U.S. Capitol and Washington Monument, a cable car and a windmill.

Dover Cut and Assemble Series. New York: Dover, 1977–84. 48 pp. $4.50 pb each.

Projects include an early New England village, seaport, Main Street, frontier town, Victorian houses and a farm.

Build Your Own Statue of Liberty. Bill Feeney and John Williams. New York: Dolphin, 1984. $7.95.

Build the Alamo. Mark Weakley. Austin: Texas Monthly Press, 1982. $8.95.

Good Old Houses Neighborhood: A Book of Historic Houses to Color and Cut Out. Ann Arbor, Mich.: Aristoplay, Ltd., 1981. $3.95.

Make Your Own Victorian House. Rosemary Lowndes and Claude Kailer. Boston: Little, Brown. $8.95. Ages 10 up.

The Victorian Parlor: A Cut and Color Book. Theodore Menten. New York: Dover, 1975. $2.50 pb.

Our Village Shop. Faith Jaques. New York: Philomel, Putnam, 1984. 32 pp., color illus. $8.95 pb.

Houses for Dolls

The Complete Dollhouse Building Book. Kathryn Falk and Edleycoe Griek. Indianapolis: Bobbs-Merrill, 1982. 192 pp., illus., appends.

Instructions, diagrams and photographs for re-creating historically based miniature dwellings.

The Doll's House: A Reproduction of the Antique Pop-up Book. Lothar Meggendorfer. New York: Viking, 1979. $8.95. Ages 5–8.

Unfolds to show five scenes with connecting doors; with pop-up furniture.

Victorian Doll House Book. Kristin Helberg. Sausalito, Calif.: Rainy Day Press, 1974. $5.95 spiral bound.

This sturdy cardboard book forms a stand-up dollhouse, which can be filled from the 12 sheets of furniture to color, cut out and put together.

Victorian Doll House. Harry Saffren. New York: Random House, 1982. $6.95.

The house pops up out of the book for play.

Art Deco Dollhouse Book. Kristin Helberg. Sausalito, Calif.: Rainy Day Press, 1975. $5.95 spiral bound.

A stand-up dollhouse, 1930s vintage, with printed sheets of furniture to assemble and color.

Dolls' Houses: Life in Miniature. Shirley Glubok. New York: Harper and Row, 1984. 104 pp., illus. $15.50 hb.

A tour of 26 historic miniature homes from the 17th century to the present from around the world.

Architect Hugh Newell Jacobsen constructing a classically inspired sand castle at the "Just for Fun" exhibit. (Carleton Knight III, NTHP)

Castles in the Sand

Sandcastles: The Splendors of Enchantment. Joseph Allen. Garden City, N.Y.: Doubleday, 1981. 148 pp., illus.

"Sand fantasies are doomed from their beginnings to absolute mortality—to death, to destruction, to oblivion." Photography, however, has captured these elaborate specimens of the art. The book also tells the story of real castles and gives the ambitious sculptor instructions in the art of building in sand.

Sandtiquity. Connie Simo et al. New York: Taplinger, 1980. $10.95 hb, $4.95 pb.

For serious sand sculptors, instructions on how to build, from the simple to complex. Photographs on Tibetan monasteries, pueblo villages, etc., all in sand.

Architivities

Carpenter's Lace. Judith Helm Robinson. Washington, D.C.: Smithsonian Institution, 1980. $3.50 pb. Available from SITES, 900 Jefferson Drive, S.W., Washington, D.C. 20560.

Twelve "architivity" cards designed to introduce Victorian architecture to children.

The Colonial Williamsburg Activities Book. Pat Fortunato and John Wallner. Williamsburg, Va.: Colonial Williamsburg Foundation (P.O. Box C, 23185), 1982. 48 pp., illus. $2.95. Ages 7 up.

Word hunts, word scrambles and puzzles on 18th-century life in Williamsburg.

The Metropolitan Museum of Art Activity Book. Osa Brown. New York: Metropolitan Museum of Art, 1983. 88 pp., color illus. $6.95 pb.

A compendium of models, toys, games, puzzles and crafts to put together, all based on the museum's collections.

Color a Building

American House Styles of Architecture Coloring Book. Albert G. Smith, Jr. New York: Dover, 1983. 48 pp., illus. $2.50 pb. Ages 8 up.

Victorian House Coloring Book. Kristin Helberg and Daniel Lewis. New York: Dover, 1980. 48 pp., illus. $2.25 pb. Ages 8 up.

The Victorian Seaside Hotel Coloring Book. Charles Fleischman and Kristin Helberg. New York: Dover, 1982. 48 pp., illus. $2.50 pb. Ages 8 up.

The Family Tree Coloring Book. Martha H. Griffis. New York: Scribner's, 1978. $1.98 pb. Ages 8 up.

The Victorian Wallpaper Design Coloring Book. Ramona Jablonski. Owings Mills, Md.: Stemmer House, 1981. 48 pp., illus. $3.50 pb.

The Victorian Gothic Coloring Book. Romona Jablonski. Owings Mills, Md.: Stemmer House, 1981. 48 pp., illus. $3.50 pb.

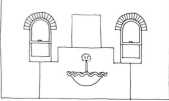

A face found on a Baltimore building. From *Color Me Baltimore.*

Color Me Baltimore. Baltimore: Neighborhood Design Center (720 East Pratt Street, 21202), 1980. $2.50 pb.

Observa-story: Portland to Cut and Color. Portland, Maine: Greater Portland Landmarks (165 State Street, 04101), 1976. $1.25 pb.

Puzzles

Good Old Houses: A Puzzle Game of Historic American Architecture. Douglas Kassabaum. Ann Arbor, Mich.: Aristoplay, Ltd. (931 Oakdale Road, 48107), 1981. $10.

Main Street: A Puzzle Game of Historic American Architecture. Douglas Kassabaum. Ann Arbor, Mich.: Aristoplay, Ltd., 1982. $10.

Houses of New England. Isabelle English. Boston: Museum of Fine Arts (Museum Shop, P. O. Box 1044, 02120). $10.

Architectural Heritage of Chicago: The Reliance Building and *The Robie House.* Chicago: ArchiCenter (330 South Dearborn Street, 60604). $4.95 each.

Board Games

Market Square. National Trust for Historic Preservation. Concord, Mass.: Heritage Games, 1983. $19.95. Ages 10 up. Available from the National Trust.

A preservation and real estate strategy game allowing players to experience the pleasures and pitfalls of rehabilitating buildings.

Made for Trade: A Game of Early American Life. Winterthur Museum and Gardens. Ann Arbor, Mich.: Aristoplay, Ltd. $16.50. Ages 8 up. Available from Winterthur Museum Shop, Winterthur, Del. 19735.

Four games can be played using the board depicting an early seaport town, providing glimpses into town life, early trade and contacts with the Indians.

Rubbings

"Rubbing is a method of reproducing the surface of a carved design by rubbing or dabbing a piece of paper or cloth with various media. Generally, colored waxes, inks, or graphite are used for this purpose. . . .

Rubbing offers the opportunity to explore the architecture, history, and peculiar art forms of any city.

Since much old stonework is rapidly eroding due to air pollution, or being destroyed by urban redevelopment, lifting a rubbing helps to keep a record of some beautiful objects that might otherwise be forgotten."

Cecily Firestein, *Rubbing Craft*

Rubbing Craft. Cecily B. Firestein. New York: Quick Fox, 1977. 95 pp., illus., biblio., index.

A brief history of rubbing, techniques and projects that are inspired by rubbings.

Early New England Gravestone Rubbings. Edmund V. Gillon, Jr. New York: Dover, 1966. 223 pp., illus. $7.95 pb.

Pictorial documentation of gravestones, with identification and style explanations plus a description of rubbing techniques and materials.

Making a rubbing of Chicago's Marquette Building. (Chicago Architecture Foundation)

Elementary and Secondary Education
Every child needs a sense of place, a way to identify personally with man-made structures, neighborhoods and communities of yesterday, as well as with the feelings and lifestyles of their inhabitants.

Richard C. Balaban and Alison Igo St. Clair, *The Mystery Tour: Exploring the Designed Environment with Children.* 1976. Reprint. Washington, D.C.: Preservation Press, 1976.

"There are many reasons to introduce historic preservation to children.

Children who understand how their neighborhoods have evolved and the style and materials of the buildings will always carry a respect for these areas and a concern for their upkeep.

When an appreciation of the built environment in addition to technical procedures of preservation is emphasized, children are likely to share this new awareness with their parents. It's a good combination—today's children become tomorrow's preservationists and their parents serve as today's supporters of preservation."

Antoinette J. Lee, "Fund Aids Education Programs." *Preservation News,* July 1979.

Teacher Resources
"The emphasis in built environment education is on active participation in the immediate environment of the school and local community. Although books can supply much background, the classroom, the playground, and the neighborhood offer an opportunity to learn through direct experience—by investigating, questioning, classifying, synthesizing, and problem solving."

Aase Eriksen and Valerie Smith, "Art Education and the Built Environment." *Art Education,* September 1978.

"Buildings are as much of a primary source for history as the Declaration of Independence."

Susan Saidenberg, Curator, Fraunces Tavern. In "Young Students Meeting Old Buildings, with Appreciation," Patricia Leigh Brown. *Christian Science Monitor,* May 23, 1980.

General

Preservation Education: Kindergarten Through Twelfth Grade. Ellen G. Kotz. Information Series, National Trust for Historic Preservation. Washington, D.C.: Preservation Press, 1979. 31 pp., append. $2 pb.

A compilation of preservation projects designed to enhance the teaching of traditional subjects for preschool through high school. Included are workbooks, games, model and map making, tours, oral histories and activities such as building preservation and placing historical markers.

The Sourcebook. Washington, D.C.: American Institute of Architects, 1981–82. $10.

An expandable teachers' reference of resources relating to the built and natural environments, updated periodically with supplements. Describes exemplary environmental education programs; reviews books and activity cards for classroom use, including evaluations by users of the materials; includes a bibliography for teachers and students; and lists resource people in environmental education.

Learning About the Built Environment. Educational Facilities Laboratories and National Association of Elementary School Principals. New York: EFL, 1974. 88 pp., illus., biblio. $3 pb. Available from NAESP, 1801 North Moore Street, Arlington, Va. 22209.

A comprehensive catalog of resources, books and teaching tools for built environment education in elementary and secondary schools.

Architects-in-Schools: Planning Workbook. Educational Futures and Attic and Cellar Studios. Philadelphia: Educational Futures, 1977. 82 pp., illus., biblio. $8 pb.

Describes the Architects-in-Schools program, approaches and materials for built environment education and documentation, and evaluation procedures for the program.

Historic Preservation Education: Curriculum Materials. Carol D. Holden, Gary L. Olsen, Michele R. Olsen and Raymond H. Lytle. Champaign, Ill.: Educational Concepts Group (315 South State Street, 61820), 1980. 155 pp., illus., gloss., biblio. $12.95 pb.

Developed for a social studies approach but also uses reading, vocabulary, mathematics, language arts and aesthetics skills. For all ages through college level, with chapters on aesthetic perception, discovering the environment, styles, development of the city, and planning for preservation.

Art, Culture and Environment: A Catalyst for Teaching. June King McFee and Rogena M. Degge. 1977. Dubuque, Iowa: Kendall/Hunt, 1980. 416 pp., illus., biblio., indexes. $14.95 pb.

The study and teaching of aesthetic awareness, design, space as design, how cities and towns evolve and the cultural meaning of art.

Environmental Encounter: Experiences in Decision-Making for the Built and the Natural Environment. Allied Professionals Education Consulting Services. Dallas: Reverchon Press (P.O. Box 19647, 75219), 1979. 168 pp., illus., biblios., index. $14.95.

For professionals and lay people of any age group. Examples emphasize the value of preservation to communities.

Art Education, September 1978. National Art Education Association (1916 Association Drive, Reston, Va. 22091). $9.

Entire issue devoted to "Art Education and the Built Environment."

"Preservation Made Elementary." Supplement to *Preservation News,* July 1979.

Articles on the teaching of preservation at the elementary and secondary levels.

Museum School Partnerships: Plans and Programs. Susan Nichols Lehman and Kathryn Igoe, eds. Center for Museum Education, George Washington University. Washington, D.C.: American Association of Museums, 1981. 139 pp. $7.25 pb.

A sourcebook describing collaborative efforts between museums and educational institutions, from planning to implementation.

K–8th Grade

Street Smart: An Educational Program on the Physical Environment. Cambridge, Mass.: Vision, Inc. (Center for Environmental Design and Education, 219 Concord Avenue, 02138). $80.

A curriculum package designed to teach elementary and middle-school children to explore and interpret their communities. Can be incorporated into language arts, social studies, drama, math, science and art classes. The program consists of a filmstrip with a sound cassette, an activity guide and a poster.

Child drawing a church as part of the Street Smart curriculum developed by the Center for Environmental Design and Education of Vision, Inc. From *Street Smart.* (Vision, Inc.)

Students-Structures-Spaces: Activities in the Built Environment. Educational Futures. Menlo Park, Calif.:Addison-Wesley, 1983. $12.50. Grades K–12.

A teacher resource book of activities to enhance students' awareness of the built environment, including neighborhoods, people spaces, styles and architectural details.

Beginning Experiences in Architecture: A Guide for the Elementary School Teacher. George E. Trogler. New York: Van Nostrand Reinhold, 1972. 141 pp., illus., biblio.

Introduces teachers to the use of art and architectural media for elementary school children, with helpful photographs.

Architecture Is Elementary. Washington, D.C.: Education Department, Corcoran Gallery of Art (17th Street and New York Avenue, N.W., 20006), 1979. 63 pp., illus., biblio. $5 pb.

A handbook on spatial relationships used by gallery docents and teachers for kindergarten and early primary-grade children.

Streets. The Architects Collaborative and Cambridge, Mass., Schools. Cambridge: TAC. $7.95. Available from Boston Society of Architects Bookshop, 66 Hereford Street, Boston, Mass. 02115.

A curriculum package for grades 3–6 that helps children understand why their street looks the way it does.

The Small Town Sourcebook. Sturbridge, Mass: Old Sturbridge Village, 1979. *Part I:* 48 pp., illus. *Part II:* 95 pp., illus. $10 pb set. Teacher's guide: *Guide for the Small Town Sourcebook.* 125 pp. $4.50 pb.

Subtitled "Reliving New England's Past through Pictures, Ads, and Personal Histories," the book is designed as a workbook for classroom use.

Essence I and *Essence II.* Robert Samples, American Geological Institute. Menlo Park, Calif.: Addison-Wesley, Innovative Division (2725 Sandhill Road, 94025). Set I, $53.16. Set II, $88.76.

Sets of 78 and 171 cards, respectively, designed to encourage environmental exploration and awareness among children. A teacher's guide accompanies each set.

Secondary School

Historic Houses as Learning Laboratories: Seven Teaching Strategies. Thomas J. Schlereth. Nashville: American Association for State and Local History, 1978. Technical Leaflet 105. 12 pp., biblio. $2 pb.

Suggestions on how teachers can use a historic house museum as a teaching tool for American history, for high school students and older.

Using Local History in the Classroom. Fay D. Metcalf and Matthew T. Downey. Nashville: American Association for State and Local History, 1982. 284 pp., illus., appends. index. $18.50 hb.

A manual for secondary and college history teachers. Organized into sections on methods and sources, content and concepts and teaching a local history course, the book provides guidance on activities and includes examples and sample forms. The projects are usable also by museums and historical societies.

Artifacts and the American Past. Thomas J. Schlereth. Nashville: American Association for State and Local History, 1981. 294 pp., illus., appends., index. $15.95 hb.

A resource for teachers of high school and college students that examines the role of artifacts as cultural statements to be interpreted in their historical context. Explains material culture study as an exercise in determining why things were made, why they took various forms and what social, functional, aesthetic and symbolic needs they serve.

Close Encounters with the Built Environment. Susan Davis. Vancouver: Evergreen Press, 1981. 54 pp., illus., append., gloss. $7.50 pb. Available from Susan J. Davis, 1940 Four Seasons Drive, Burlington, Ontario L7P 2Y1, Canada.

A sourcebook of built environment activities for secondary school students.

The Local Community: A Handbook for Teachers. Association of American Geographers. 1968. New York: Macmillan, 1971. 255 pp., illus., biblio.

A teacher's handbook for using the local environment to teach geography. Includes analysis of the built environment in a detailed, sophisticated approach.

Teaching History with Community Resources. Clifford L. Lord. New York: Teachers College Press, 1967. 82 pp. $4.95 pb.

Suggests how to research community resources, field trips, building a collection of community resources and special activities, such as dramas, fairs, historical markers, programs for adults, radio and television.

Robert Stoddard pointing out the cast-iron facade of the Grand Opera House (1871) to Wilmington, Del., students. (Grand Opera House, Inc.)

Architecture as a Primary Source for Social Studies. Daniel C. Leclerc. How to Do It Series. Series 2, no. 5. Washington, D.C.: National Council for the Social Studies (3615 Wisconsin Avenue, N.W., 20016), 1978. 8 pp., illus., biblio. $1.75 pb.

A survey of architectural forms and historical development to be used as a source of teaching methods, with general learning activities.

Periodicals

Consult *Education Index* for built environment education articles appearing in education journals such as *Today's Education, Instructor, Education Digest, Harvard Educational Review, High School Journal* and *New York Times Educational Supplement.*

Specialized education periodicals from time to time also include examples of preservation and architectural education, including *Social Studies, The History Teacher, School Arts Magazine, Journal of Geography* and *Art Teacher.*

Built Environment Education Educational Futures, Inc. 2118 Spruce Street Philadelphia, Pa. 19103

Publication suspended, but back issues are available on developments in preservation-related primary and secondary education.

Eco-News Environmental Action Coalition 417 Lafayette Street New York, N.Y. 10003

Publication suspended, but back issues are available. An environmental newsletter for young people, each issue of which focuses on a single topic such as "Rescuing Old Buildings." Includes a teacher's guide.

Environmental Education Report American Society for Environmental Education P.O. Box 800 Hanover, N.H. 03755

Directed toward the natural environment, but with useful articles on built structures.

Hands On Foxfire Fund, Inc. Rabun Gap, Ga. 30568

Published irregularly for the exchange of ideas and programs about cultural information projects, mostly oral history, in schools.

Cobblestone Cobblestone Publishing 28 Main Street Peterborough, N.H. 03458

A monthly magazine for children (8–13 years). Each issue concentrates on a single historical theme—lighthouses, Mount St. Helens, etc.

Contacts

American Institute of Architects Public Education Program 1735 New York Avenue, N.W. Washington, D.C. 20006

Provides information about using architecture in the classroom, teacher training, resource materials and architecture as a career.

Educational Futures, Inc. 2118 Spruce Street Philadelphia, Pa. 19103

Works with architects, educators, schools, state arts agencies, communities and others to provide architectural education for children. Develops built environment education programs for schools, conducts workshops and conferences, publishes newsletters, books, articles and audiovisual materials.

Massie Heritage Center student learning about Gothic arches. (Grant Compton)

Austin, Tex., student building a room during an architects-in-schools program. (Janet Felsten)

Classroom Programs: A Sampler

Teaching about the preservation of the built environment can and should take place in every classroom. Children in nursery school and kindergarten can learn to "read" their environment by observing shapes and textures and then noting their similarities and differences. Elementary school students can study their community and its history to understand the forces that have created the townscape. High school students have the ability to analyze the decision-making process which daily confronts those people who are in a position to determine the future directions of a given community.

National Trust for Historic Preservation

Learning the Big Word

" 'Renata, does old mean good?' The sober-faced six-year-old nods her head tentatively.

'Does it?' Sarah Parsons prods, turning to face a tow-headed boy in an Eton collar and dark blue tie. 'If I tell you this building is very old, Courtney, does that mean it's good?' Courtney shakes his head vigorously from side to side.

'It doesn't?' Parsons feigns astonishment. Slowly, she says, 'Well, this building is old, more than 125 years old, and it's kind of nice, isn't it?' A scattering of small heads bobs up and down. 'How many of you think old can be good?' A forest of raised hands sprouts around her. After a moment's hesitation, Courtney's hand joins the others. 'Oh, that's wonderful,' Parsons coos.

Then she addresses a dark-haired boy whose mischievous grin never leaves his face. 'But, David, if you had a hot dog 125 years old, that wouldn't be good, would it?' David giggles, and chortles break out here and there among the crowd of first graders. . . .

'No,' Sarah Parsons answers her own question. 'So, old can be good, and old can be bad.' She lowers her voice and speaks emphatically now, with great care. 'We learn to look at things and decide what is good and what is worth saving, and there's a great big old word. I wonder if you can say it: pres-er-va-tion. Can you say that big word?'

Twenty-eight little voices, in ragged unison, pipe out, 'pres-er-va-tion.' "

Bill Cutler, "When Sarah Parsons Talks, Savannah Listens." *Historic Preservation*, June 1984.

Architects-in-Schools

This is a program in which an architect spends full or part-time in a school, working with children on architectural design and city planning, teaching them to analyze their surroundings and to participate in forming their environments. Once funded nationally, the program now is sponsored by some state arts councils. Contact your state arts agency or state department of education for further information.

Massie Heritage Center

Housed appropriately in Savannah's Massie School (1856), Georgia's oldest, the Massie Heritage Interpretation Center has been teaching students and their teachers about preservation and visual awareness for eight years. Programs range from single tours to year-long courses and have welcomed students of all ages from in and out of state, incuding teachers, librarians and principals. Now part of the city's social studies curriculum, the center maintains a permanent exhibit on Savannah's architecture. Classes use the program for activities such as compiling a book on important Savannah buildings and earning extra high school credits by conducting a "scavenger hunt" for features in the Victorian District.

Massie Heritage Interpretation Center
207 East Gordon Street
Savannah, Ga. 31401

Downtown—An Outdoor Classroom

A fifth- and sixth-grade curriculum (usable for grades 4–9) developed by Marjorie White and Claire Datnow of the Birmingham Historical Society and the Junior League of Birmingham and partially funded by the National Trust. Volunteers from the historical society visit each class with a slide show to begin the unit and lead the students on Downtown Discovery Tours.

Downtown: An Outdoor Classroom. Teacher's Handbook. 1978. Rev. ed. Birmingham: Birmingham Historical Society, 1981. 76 pp., illus., append. $10 pb. Student Workbook. 44 pp., illus. $2 pb.

Downtown Birmingham: An Architectural and Historical Walking Tour Guide. 1977. Rev. ed. Birmingham: Birmingham Historical Society, 1980. 144 pp., illus. $14 hb, $7 pb.

" 'So When's History Class?' 'You Just Had It,' " Kathleen Burke. *Historic Preservation*, March–April 1979.

Describes a variety of school preservation programs, including Birmingham's and those in Colorado Springs, Colo., and Savannah, Ga.

Birmingham Historical Society
1425 22nd Street, South
Birmingham, Ala. 35205

Cub scouts discovering downtown Birmingham, Ala., through treasure hunts and a curriculum package. *(Birmingham News)*

Student in the Beaumont, U.S.A. program learning how to measure a building as part of an architectural survey. (Roy Bray)

Beaumont students getting hands-on experience with carpentry skills needed in rehabilitation work. (Roy Bray)

Beaumont, U.S.A.

Eighth-grade students combine the study of architecture and local history in this program, learning how to conduct an architectural survey and prepare a National Register application and taking field trips to observe buildings and vestiges of the past, such as trolley car tracks. An architect assigns a monthly architectural exercise. The one-year course ends with a large project chosen by the students. One class documented an endangered historic house, while another obtained a marker for a historic fire station.

Beaumont Art Museum
1111 Ninth Street
Beaumont, Tex. 77702

Neighborhood Discovery Program

A one-year program for gifted and talented fifth and sixth graders has produced a model course of study for teaching neighborhood awareness.

Neighborhood Discovery Guidebook: An Elementary Instructional Guide for the Investigation of Local History. Baltimore: Commission for Historical and Architectural Preservation, 1981. 53 pp., illus., biblio., append. $5.

Baltimore Commission for Historical and Architectural Preservation
118 North Howard Street
Room 606
Baltimore, Md. 21201

Salt Lake Awareness

Held in conjunction with fourth- and seventh-grade state history courses in the city and county schools, this program develops classroom activities based on historic buildings and architecture, laced with folklore, personalities and stories. In-service workshops also are held for teachers.

Architecture Is Elementary: Visual Thinking Through Architectural Concepts. Nathan B. Winters. Salt Lake City: Peregrine Smith, 1985. 300 pp., illus. $19.95 pb.

Utah Heritage Foundation
355 Quince Street
Salt Lake City, Utah 84103

Plantation Perspectives

Since 1977, fourth through sixth graders have combined art and the humanities by documenting, studying and drawing plantation houses in their community. The *Oak Alley Plantation Coloring Book,* researched, written and illustrated by students, was the result of one such project. Another project compared an urban Creole neighborhood with a rural Cajun community.

Lakewood Junior High School
c/o Lloyd Sensat
124 East Third Street
Luling, La. 70070

Life in Minnesota

Programs are offered in local and Minnesota history for grades 1–6, geared to the subjects the children are studying—Indians in third grade, for example. Volunteers visit the schools with traveling displays, and teachers are invited to bring classes to the society's museum, where changing exhibits highlight the topic being studied. School children and adults also can participate in "A Day at the Bunnell Home," experiencing farm life as it was in the 1850s.

Winona County Historical Society
160 Johnson Street
Winona, Minn. 55987

Walking to Learn

A multidisciplinary curriculum for grades 3–8 used in New York City schools that teaches about maps, map reading and map making by using field trips such as a history walk, tree walk and pollution walk. It is adaptable for use nationally and for other age levels.

Walking: A Realistic Approach to Environmental Education. Michael Zamm. New York: Council on the Environment of New York City, 1977. 39 pp., biblio. $2 pb.

Council on the Environment of New York City
51 Chambers Street
Room 228
New York, N.Y. 10007

Oak Alley Plantation (c. 1830), drawn by 11-year-old artist Russell Smith from the A. A. Songy, Sr., Elementary School. From *Oak Alley Plantation Coloring Book.*

Boy hugging a building in Chicago's Pullman area. (© 1982 Fred Leavitt and the City of Chicago)

Hug a Building . . . and Other Special Activities

One should not assume that children naturally have a high regard for architecture. They can take it or leave it and, given a choice, they probably prefer skateboards or movies. It is a mistake to herd large groups of children through old buildings, burdening them with canned lectures on Romanesque arches. They resist; eyes glaze, attention fades, fidgeting prevails. It is far better to give the students tools with which to see and opportunities for them to use their own skills. Then, in the long run, they will defend old buildings because they truly like them and because an initial awareness has turned to proprietary affection.

Elaine Freed, "Teaching Children to See." *Historic Preservation,* January–March 1977.

Put Your Arms Around a Building

A tour for children in grades 1–5 that teaches them to use their bodies as a basic measure of buildings, to make rubbings and to learn the relationships of technology, design and history.

Chicago Architecture
Foundation
ArchiCenter
330 South Dearborn Street
Chicago, Ill. 60604

Happy Birthday to Henry Hobson Richardson

The foundation, keeper of the Glessner House, once held a birthday party in honor of its famous architect, H. H. Richardson. Adults were charged a fee, but children's tickets were 25 rubbings per child of architectural features of their choice.

Chicago Architecture
Foundation
ArchiCenter
330 South Dearborn Street
Chicago, Ill. 60604

Adopt a Building

Each child adopts a building and gets to know it by various means: taking photographs, making rubbings, learning about its construction, making drawings of its interior and the surrounding streetscape. The children can pretend that they are the buildings and can write a story describing their feelings and experiences as a building, including what the future may hold for it. Various sponsors.

Make Way for Ducklings

Several tours emphasize architectural, environmental and social history and fit into the school curriculum as mini-units. The *"Make Way for Ducklings Tour"* is based on the route the mallard family took in the famous children's book; the "Kennedy Roots Tour" concentrates on the Irish North End. There is also a "Kid's View of the Waterfront," which emphasizes Boston as a port city.

Historic Neighborhoods
Foundation
92 South Street
Boston, Mass. 02111

The Park as School

Uses Central Park as a source to teach children to appreciate the park as a work of art, as nature and as a setting for all kinds of festivals and activities.

The Central Park Workbook: Activities for an Urban Park. Robert J. Finkelstein and Central Park Task Force "Park as School" Program. New York: Central Park Conservancy, 1980. 54 pp., illus., append., biblio. $3.95 pb.

The Arthur Ross Pinetum in Central Park: A Children's Walking Tour. Marie Ruby,. New York: Central Park Conservancy, 1980. 29 pp., illus., gloss. $.75 pb.

The Arthur Ross Pinetum in Central Park: An Adult Walking Tour. Geraldine Weinstein. New York: Central Park Conservancy, 1980. 21 pp., illus., gloss. $1 pb.

Central Park Task Force
Central Park Conservancy
830 Fifth Avenue, Room 103
New York, N.Y. 10021

Victorian Legacy

Board of education volunteers teach students to recognize and appreciate their Victorian legacy of decorated wooden buildings through classroom discussions, slide shows and a tour of various neighborhoods in which they make rubbings and search for architectural details.

City Guides Program
c/o Friends of the
San Francisco Public Library
Main Library
Civic Center
San Francisco, Calif. 94102

Boston preschoolers taking the "Kid's View of the North End" tour of historic city sites. (Elizabeth Reinhardt)

Students with their "restored" downtown block created in the Pittsburgh History and Landmarks Foundation's "Eye for Architecture" program.

Madison, Wis., students with some of the materials they made to help save the Gates of Heaven Synagogue (1863). (Bruce M. Fritz, *Capital Times*)

Participatory Preservation

Working with graduate students and teachers, area school students hold mock public hearings on preservation issues, sometimes before "mayors" and "city councils." They also conduct architectural surveys, prepare exhibits, make presentations to PTAs, lead walking tours, build models and devise town plans.

Built Environment
Education Team
Department of City and
Regional Planning
Cornell University
Ithaca, N.Y. 14853

Environmental Action

A variety of problem-solving activities for children in grades K–6, each explained in publications for children and teachers. Those available include "Rescuing Old Buildings," "City Planning" and "Building to Save Energy."

Environmental Action Coalition
417 Lafayette Street
New York, N.Y. 10003

Bookwork

A Is for Avon. Jan Brennan. Avon, Conn.: Author (153 Haynes Road, 06001), 1979. 48 pp., illus. $5 pb.

An alphabet book in which each letter stands for something important or interesting about Avon and is accompanied by photographs and a text. The first part is for an adult to read to the child, while the second is for the child to read and the third is a suggested activity.

The Durant Primer. Elizabeth M. Safanda and Janet W. Safanda. Batavia, Ill.: Restorations of Kane County, 1980. 24 pp., illus. $1.50 pb. Available from Elizabeth Safanda, 226 North Van Buren, Batavia, Ill. 60510.

A workbook for elementary school children to use in conjunction with a visit to the Durant-Peterson Homestead in Illinois. Includes matching games, puzzles, old recipes, pictures to color and opportunities for creative writing and art work.

More Than Kid Stuff

"What can a kid do? . . . All right, here you are, kids: Not just mourn the loss of worthy buildings being wrecked or carry placards in front of the wreckers. There's more to heritage than structures, however precious they may be. You can . . .

1. Inventory, identify, classify and conserve objects, memorabilia, diaries, letters that record the past history of your own family.

2. Make a historic base map of your community. . . .

3. You can organize with others who want to explore history by digging out the facts on how the community evolved. . . .

No, this isn't kid stuff, kids. It is hard work and takes careful planning and organization. But that is what learning is all about, isn't it? Most of the facts of history were recorded by those who were never historians, but it could be that the people in school are the best resource for conserving history. It's your history and your heritage."

John L. Cotter, Letter to the Editor. *Preservation News*, April 1972.

Young people learning the art of making colonial pottery at Old Sturbridge Village, Sturbridge, Mass. (Donald F. Eaton, Old Sturbridge Village)

Cornell University students developing a preservation plan for Watkins Glen, N.Y. (Russ Hamilton)

Summary Report on Historic Preservation and Higher Education. Antoinette J. Lee. Washington, D.C.: National Trust for Historic Preservation, 1980. 17 pp., append.

Summarizes the history of the National Trust's involvement in higher education, the need for professional training in preservation, current programs and the formation of the National Council for Preservation Education.

Contacts

National Council for Preservation Education P.O. Box 23 Middle Tennessee State University Murfreesboro, Tenn. 37132

Publicizes preservation education; encourages communication and coordination among educators; represents the collective concerns of its membership before governmental and private agencies; advises on the development of new educational programs; advances instructional development, research and public service programs; and formulates standards for graduate preservation programs.

Center for Preservation Training National Trust for Historic Preservation 1785 Massachusetts Avenue, N.W. Washington, D.C. 20036

Serves as a clearinghouse on education, sponsoring educational seminars, conferences and training programs; developing communication among preservation educators; and awarding modest grants for preservation education development and cosponsored conferences.

"Prior to 1962, preservation education consisted primarily of on-the-job training. Architects, historians and others who entered the preservation field had little, if any, training in interpretation, planning, building technology, legislation and other tools available to preservationists. In 1959, the architecture school at the University of Virginia initiated a course in historic preservation that covered the documentation and analysis of historic buildings and possibilities for their adaptive use or restoration. In 1962, the planning faculty at Cornell University initiated courses in preservation planning. Two years later, Columbia University, through its School of Architecture, established a graduate seminar on the restoration of American buildings. By 1966, Columbia's seminar had formed the basis of a full-fledged curriculum.

Since this formative period, more than 200 colleges and universities have instituted individual courses and degree programs in historic preservation. Reflecting the multidisciplinary nature of the preservation field today, these courses and programs are generally linked to departments or schools of history, architecture, planning, museum studies, urban studies or law. They also draw from the resources of many other academic disciplines."

National Trust for Historic Preservation

Higher Education

The restoration and preservation in our populous future of such portions of our physical past as are worth preserving can be accomplished only if the discipline and authority of learning—that is, professional education at the highest level—can be brought to bear upon the universal enthusiasm.

Report of the Committee on Professional and Public Education for Historic Preservation. Walter Muir Whitehill, Chairman. Washington, D.C.: National Trust for Historic Preservation, 1968.

University of Texas architecture students and faculty at the McGregor-Grimm House (1861), part of the Winedale Institute. (University of Texas)

Undergraduate and Graduate Degree Programs

Arkansas College
Department of History
Batesville, Ark. 72501

Ball State University
College of Architecture and
Planning
Muncie, Ind. 47306

Boston University
Preservation Studies Program
226 Bay State Road
Boston, Mass. 02215

Brigham Young University
Heritage Conservation Program
4069 HBLL
Provo, Utah 84602

Colorado State University
Department of History
Fort Collins, Colo. 80523

Columbia University
Division of Historic
Preservation
New York, N.Y. 10027

Cornell University
Graduate Program in Historic
Preservation Planning
106 West Sibley Hall
Ithaca, N.Y. 14853

Eastern Michigan University
Department of Geography and
Geology
Ypsilanti, Mich. 48197

George Washington University
Graduate Program in Historic
Preservation
Washington, D.C. 20052

Kansas State University
College of Architecture and
Design
Manhattan, Kans. 66506

Mary Washington College
Center for Historic Preservation
915 Monroe Street
Fredericksburg, Va. 22401

Michigan State University
Department of Art
East Lansing, Mich. 48824

Middle Tennessee State
University
Historic Preservation Program
P.O. Box 23
Murfreesboro, Tenn. 37132

Northern Arizona University
Department of Anthropology
Flagstaff, Ariz. 86011

Ohio State University
Department of Architecture
190 West 17th Avenue
Columbus, Ohio 43210

Educator James Marston Fitch working with graduate students in the Columbia University preservation program.

Pennsylvania State University
Graduate Program in American
Studies
Middletown, Pa. 17057

Roger Williams College
American Studies Area
Bristol, R.I. 02809

Southeast Missouri State
University
Department of History
Cape Girardeau, Mo. 63701

Texas A&M University
Department of Architecture
College Station, Tex. 77843

Chester H. Liebs and University of Vermont preservation students on a field trip to the Windsor Plantation ruins, Port Gibson, Miss. (Chester Liebs)

University of Arizona
College of Architecture
Tucson, Ariz. 85721

University of Cincinnati
Department of History
Cincinnati, Ohio 45221

University of Florida
Department of Architecture
Gainesville, Fla. 32611

University of Georgia
School of Environmental Design
Athens, Ga. 30602

University of Illinois
Department of Architecture
Chicago, Ill. 60608

University of Illinois
Department of Urban and
Regional Planning
1003 West Nevada
Urbana, Ill. 61801-3882

University of Michigan
College of Architecture and
Urban Planning
2000 Bonisteel Boulevard
Ann Arbor, Mich. 48109

University of New Orleans
School of Urban and Regional
Studies
New Orleans, La. 70148

University of Oregon
School of Architecture
and Applied Arts
Eugene, Ore. 97403

University of South Carolina
Department of History and
Department of Art History
Columbia, S.C. 29208

University of Tennessee
School of Architecture
Knoxville, Tenn. 37916

University of Texas
School of Architecture
Austin, Tex. 78712

University of Vermont
Historic Preservation Program
Department of History
Burlington, Vt. 05405

University of Virginia
Architectural History Division
Charlottesville, Va. 22903

University of Wisconsin
Department of Landscape
Architecture
Madison, Wis. 53706

Western Kentucky University
Department of Modern
Languages and Intercultural
Studies
Bowling Green, Ky. 42101

Summer Programs

Preservation Institute:
Nantucket
c/o Department of Architecture
University of Florida
Gainesville, Fla. 32611

A nine-week summer program for advanced undergraduate and graduate students in preservation research and techniques in a laboratory situation on Nantucket Island.

University of Connecticut
Courses in American Maritime
Studies
Office of Credit Programs
Storrs, Conn. 06268

Summer courses cosponsored with Mystic Seaport for advanced undergraduate and graduate students and teachers studying for a master's degree.

Williamsburg Seminar on
Historical Administration
c/o National Trust for
Historic Preservation
1785 Massachusetts Avenue, N.W.
Washington, D.C. 20036

An intensive program covering all aspects of administering historic sites, historical agencies and related organizations. Cosponsored with the American Association for State and Local History, American Association of Museums and Colonial Williamsburg.

Internships

"Among both professionals in historic preservation and college and university faculty who teach courses related to historic preservation, there seems to be general agreement that there is a need for first-hand, on-the-job practical experience in historic preservation as a supplement to formal academic training before a person is really ready to accept full-time employment in this field. . . . Interships have emerged as one way of helping students gain some first-hand, practical experience."

Norman T. Moline, "Long-Term Internships." A Report of a Preliminary Survey and a Review of Existing Internship Opportunities in Related Fields. Washington, D.C.: National Trust for Historic Preservation, 1979.

Yankee Interns

Building on 25-cent donations made by renewing *Yankee* magazine subscribers, Yankee Publishing, Inc., in 1983 initiated one of the most successful preservation intern programs in coordination with the National Trust. From applicant pools of more than 10 times the available places, students were selected to work with Trust member organizations and public agencies throughout New England. Interns helped restore the Joshua Chamberlain House in Brunswick, Maine; prepare a

Historic school building that houses the annual summer Preservation Institute on Nantucket Island, Mass. (Preservation Institute: Nantucket)

preservation plan for a downtown New Haven, Conn., historic district; and excavate an Indian burial ground in Rhode Island. One intern even called out the Army (a reserve unit) to deliver supplies in amphibious vehicles and cart off a truckload of debris as part of a project to rehabilitate the Fayerweather Island lighthouse in Bridgeport, Conn.

Contacts

National Park Service
U.S. Department of the Interior
Personnel Office
P.O. Box 37127
Washington, D.C. 20013-7127

National Trust for
Historic Preservation
Personnel Office
1785 Massachusetts Avenue, N.W.
Washington, D.C. 20036

Yankee Intern Program
Northeast Regional Office
National Trust for
Historic Preservation
45 School Street, 2nd Floor
Boston, Mass. 02108

National Building Museum
Student Intern Coordinator
440 G Street, N.W.
Washington, D.C. 20001

National Endowment
for the Arts
Fellowship Program Office
1100 Pennsylvania Avenue, N.W.
Washington, D.C. 20506

Smithsonian Institution
Office of Fellowships and Grants
955 L'Enfant Plaza
Room 3300
Washington, D.C. 20560

American Institute of Architects
National Council of
Architectural Registration Boards
1735 New York Avenue, N.W.
Washington, D.C. 20006

Conservation Foundation
Fellowship Program
1717 Massachusetts Avenue, N.W.
Washington, D.C. 20036

National Society for Internships
and Experiential Education
122 St. Mary's Street
Raleigh, N.C. 27605

US/ICOMOS
Summer Internship Program
1600 H Street, N.W.
Washington, D.C. 20006

U.S. Army amphibious vehicles landing on Fayerweather Island, Bridgeport, Conn. Yankee intern Steven Englehart devised this scheme to obtain needed restoration materials and remove trash. (Morgan Kaolian)

Restoration Crafts Training

Restoration artisans today play a small but distinctive role in the building trades. The cornerstone of their trade is a working knowledge of ancient and modern tools, ability to perform highly complicated tasks and a sensitivity to the essential qualities of an old building regardless of its architectural style. These characteristics enable artisans to perpetuate the profession of the early builders of America.

The evolution of the building tradition continues today with epoxies and sophisticated power tools supplementing traditional mortise and tenon joinery and hand planes and chisels. But the early skills and tools that built America are still viable. Many construction, reconstruction and restoration projects can be accomplished with modern power tools, but for some restoration work only an 18th or 19th-century hand tool with just the right size and shape can accomplish the job.

"The Builder's Tradition." *Historic Preservation*, July–September 1977.

Repairing deteriorated molding, one of the services offered by the National Trust's Restoration Workshop at Lyndhurst. (NTHP)

"There has been a considerable wailing and wringing of hands by those who appreciate quality craftsmanship in buildings and have seen its decline as the machine becomes increasingly dominant. It is my opinion, however, that the old crafts can be revived. What is needed for such a revival is encouragement, not necessarily the expenditure of large sums of money. The two basic ingredients of such encouragement are continuous employment and plenty of appreciation when quality results are achieved by individuals."

Charles E. Peterson, "The Role of the Architect in Historical Restorations." *Preservation and Conservation: Principles and Practices.* Washington, D.C.: Preservation Press, 1976.

"Existing education and apprenticeship programs can . . . benefit by the introduction of preservation knowledge into their classrooms and workshops. Subjects that should be brought into these programs include restoration practices, proper cleaning techniques, historic structure stabilization and building material maintenance."

Michael Leventhal, "Trust Study Surveys Apprentice Training Programs." In "Preservation Training for the Building Trades." Supplement to *Preservation News*, June 1977.

Training Programs
Restoration Workshop
National Trust for
Historic Preservation
Lyndhurst
635 South Broadway
Tarrytown, N.Y. 10591

Established in 1973 to provide on-the-job training in preservation, restoration, renovation and maintenance at National Trust properties and for other organizations. Its goal is to serve preservationists with quality restoration work at reasonable cost and to train apprentices who will return to their firms or communities with skills to share. The workshop treats the whole building, providing training in all aspects of construction and restoration.

RESTORE
19 West 44th Street
17th Floor
New York, N.Y. 10036

A 30-week course in the restoration and maintenance of masonry structures designed to upgrade the preservation skills of craftsmen, contractors and qualified people in the building industry. Involves classroom instruction and laboratory and field workshop sessions.

Durham Technical Institute
Residential Carpentry and
Preservation
Box 11307, East Durham
Station
Durham, N.C. 27703

Provides day and evening instruction in carpentry, preservation and a combination of both, plus preservation of historic structures, for people with entry-level skills.

Campbell Center for
Historic Preservation Studies
Box 66
Mount Carroll, Ill. 61053

Provides training sessions in restoration crafts such as wood carving, interior and exterior historic finishes, masonry cleaning and repair and related techniques, in addition to general preservation courses.

National Park Service
Mather Training Center
P.O. Box 77
Harpers Ferry, W. Va. 25425-0077

A one-week course on preservation maintenance problems and the basic skills of various crafts principally for Park Service and other federal employees.

National Park Service
Williamsport Preservation
Training Center
P.O. Box 106
Williamsport, Md. 21795

Three-year crafts apprenticeship program in preservation techniques for federal employees, plus a two-year program for professionals such as architects and engineers.

Helpful Organizations
AFL-CIO
Building and Construction
Trades Department
815 16th Street, N.W.
Suite 603
Washington, D.C. 20006

Associated Builders and
Contractors
729 15th Street, N.W.
Washington, D.C. 20005

Brick Institute of America
11490 Commerce Park Drive
Suite 300
Reston, Va. 22091

National Concrete Masonry
Association
2302 Horse Pen Road
Herndon, Va. 22070

Portland Cement Association
Educational Services Section
5420 Old Orchard Road
Skokie, Ill. 60077

Continuing Education

Goal: To educate citizens involved in preservation, professionals in allied fields and public officials whose work affects historic resources on new developments in the preservation field.

"Education." In *Preservation: Toward an Ethic in the 1980s.* National Trust for Historic Preservation. Washington, D.C.: Preservation Press, 1980.

"Training programs in historic preservation are evolving as educational tools designed to augment the background of professionals and nonprofessionals. These programs generally have pragmatic how-to-do-it emphasis.

The purpose of preservation training programs is to provide experiences that may not have been included in a person's education but nevertheless entail valuable skills or areas of knowledge.

In all cases, training programs offer the dual benefits of education in the subject matter and communication between senior professionals and others committed to preservation. Both the content and the setting can make participation in a well-planned training program a highlight in an individual's involvement in preservation."

Antoinette J. Lee, "Tools for Students and Professionals." Supplement to *Preservation News,* January 1978.

Annual National Conferences and Workshops

Many organizations hold annual meetings with sessions devoted to preservation-related topics. Others hold periodic workshops, seminars, lectures, recording projects, laboratories and tours—foreign and domestic—on architectural history, decorative arts, building materials conservation and technology, urban planning and neighborhood conservation, tax law and the economic benefits of preservation. The groups' publications usually publish calendars with a variety of coming events.

National Trust for
Historic Preservation
Center for Preservation Training
1785 Massachusetts Avenue, N.W.
Washington, D.C. 20036

Sponsors an annual four-day fall conference with workshops, seminars, affinity-group meetings and tours. Also holds an annual business meeting in the spring in Washington, D.C., with speakers and presentation of awards. The Trust cosponsors the Williamsburg Seminar on Historical Administration and holds a variety of workshops and special conferences on topics such as tax incentives, Main Street revitalization, neighborhoods, law, industrial reuse, landmarks commissions, maritime preservation and old and new design relationships. It also provides modest funding to support cosponsored conferences of national or regional significance. The Trust also sponsors study tours in the United States and abroad.

American Association for
State and Local History
708 Berry Road
Nashville, Tenn. 37204

Annual meeting presents discussions and speakers on current topics of interest. Also sponsors workshops and seminars each year on such subjects as interpreting history, museum exhibits and publications. Offers independent study programs (correspondence courses) for paid and volunteer historical agency personnel in areas including publications, interpretation of historic sites and school programs for museums.

American Institute of Architects
1735 New York Avenue, N.W.
Washington, D.C. 20006

Holds an annual convention with local tours, workshops and lectures. Also conducts training laboratories and seminars in various cities on topics of interest to architects, including preservation, and produces audiocassette and video programs and correspondence courses.

Preservationists dining at the Cleveland Arcade (1890, Eisenmann and Smith) during a National Trust annual conference. (Carleton Knight III, NTHP)

Association for Preservation
Technology
P.O. Box 2487, Station D
Ottawa, Ontario K1P 5W6,
Canada

Annual meeting covers aspects of preservation technology—paint chemistry, landscaping, wallpaper restoration, etc. Annual training courses for advanced levels are offered before the annual meeting.

Society of Architectural
Historians
1700 Walnut Street
Suite 716
Philadelphia, Pa. 19103

Annual meeting is a forum for discussion of architectural history, decorative arts and preservation.

Preservation Action
1700 Connecticut Avenue, N.W.
Suite 401
Washington, D.C. 20009

An annual meeting is held in Washington, timed to coincide with congressional sessions and featuring workshops, seminars, talks by legislators and government officials.

The Victorian Society in
America
219 South Sixth Street
Philadelphia, Pa. 19106

Conducts an annual meeting in May in various cities and an annual fall symposium in Philadelphia. Sponsors a three-week summer school in Great Britain and an occasional one in the United States.

Society for Industrial
Archeology
National Museum of
American History
Room 5020
Washington, D.C. 20560

Annual meeting includes lectures and tours for amateurs and professionals on industrial archeology concerns.

Society for Commercial
Archeology
National Museum of
American History
Room 5010
Washington, D.C. 20560

Sponsors an annual meeting in the late fall in areas with special concentrations of commercial landmarks, which participants tour.

American Association of
Museums
1055 Thomas Jefferson Street, N.W.
Suite 428
Washington, D.C. 20007

Holds an annual convention with sessions and exhibits of particular value to museum administrators.

Short Courses and Workshops

Seminars in American Culture
New York State Historical
Association
Lake Road, Route 80
Cooperstown, N.Y. 13326

Two one-week sessions in the summer, held since 1948 and open to the general public. Lecture courses (nondegree) on preservation, antiques, museum practices, etc., as well as workshops on crafts and skills such as book binding, hand spinning, open-hearth cooking and blacksmithing.

North Carolina Department of
Cultural Resources
Planning for Historic
Preservation
c/o Education Coordinator
109 East Jones Street
Raleigh, N.C. 27611

Held one week in the fall, for preservationists and planners, on planning for the preservation of historic sites, buildings, districts and areas.

Preservation Resource Group, Inc.
5619 Southampton Drive
Springfield, Va. 22151

Offers occasional courses on restoration and preservation for architects, preservationists and owners of old buildings.

National Preservation Institute
c/o National Building Museum
440 G Street, N.W.
Washington, D.C. 20001

Holds occasional courses for the general public on a variety of architectural and preservation-related topics.

National Park Service
Preservation Assistance
Division
P.O. Box 37127
Washington, D.C. 20013-7127

Cosponsors occasional conferences on topics such as federal tax provisions pertaining to preservation.

Society for the Preservation
of New England Antiquities
141 Cambridge Street
Boston, Mass. 02114

One-day annual meeting includes workshops for members and the general public. Also offers lectures and forums at various times during the year.

Smithsonian Institution
Workshop Series
Office of Museum Programs
Arts and Industries Building
Room 2235
Washington, D.C. 20560

Short courses for museum employees, held at the Smithsonian in Washington, on museum management, display techniques, public relations for museums, education projects, etc. Also issues a listing of museum studies programs in the United States and abroad.

Studio on historic paints held during the University of Vermont's summer institute. (Philip C. Marshall, University of Vermont)

Museums Collaborative
Continuing Professional
Education Program
15 Gramercy Park South
New York, N.Y. 10003

Holds courses concentrating on specific management problems of interest to museum administrators and related middle- and executive-level professionals.

Practising Law Institute
810 Seventh Avenue
New York, N.Y. 10019

Conducts a yearly seminar on legal aspects of preservation at several locations in the fall.

Urban Land Institute
Member Services
1090 Vermont Avenue, N.W.
Suite 300
Washington, D.C. 20005

Has semiannual conferences open to the public on various aspects of land development and economic revitalization.

Bureau of National Affairs, Inc.
1231 25th Street, N.W.
Washington, D.C. 20037

Holds numerous conferences each year in all sections of the country on legal, taxation and real estate topics. Geared to professionals (accountants, real estate developers, lawyers, stockbrokers, etc.) and the informed public.

Royal Oak Foundation
41 East 72nd Street
New York, N.Y. 10021

Sponsors lectures and conferences in the United States and a scholarship to the Attingham Summer School, in addition to the English Country House Seminar, tours of England, Wales and Scotland and the Acorn Conservation Camps. Open to preservation and museum professionals and amateurs.

**College-Sponsored Community
Education**

"Universities can . . . make a vital contribution toward fostering a society capable of responsibly managing its built environment. Through education there is the potential of engendering a national preservation ethic—an ethic reaching far beyond the cliches of the emerging preservation style—that will nurture a new national value system based on environmental maintenance rather than environmental disposal. This ethic can best be developed at the university level through the initiation of dynamic programs in broad-based community education."

> Chester H. Liebs, "University Programs Foster Community Awareness." Supplement to *Preservation News,* January 1978.

Many colleges and universities offer preservation-related courses that are open to the public, either through their adult education or extension programs or as open classes in the regular program. Some leaders:

Boston University
Preservation Studies Program
Community Education Program
226 Bay State Road
Boston, Mass. 02215

Conducts courses on various aspects of preservation and planning open to the public as well as students. Also sponsors a three-week summer institute with its American and New England Studies Programs.

Cornell University
Summer Institute on
Historic Preservation Planning
209 West Sibley Hall
Ithaca, N.Y. 14853

A one-week intensive course on preservation topics for professionals and nonprofessionals.

University of Vermont
Historic Preservation
Summer Institute
Department of History
Burlington, Vt. 05405

Series of one-week intensive courses (two credits each) for professionals and nonprofessionals on a variety of preservation topics.

Harvard Graduate School of
Design
Office of Special Programs
48 Quincy Street
Cambridge, Mass. 02138

Offers various courses each term and summer on environmental and architectural aspects of preservation for professionals and other serious students of preservation. The summer courses are accredited by the AIA.

Programs Abroad

Attingham Summer School
c/o American Friends of
Attingham
126 Jefferson Road
Princeton, N.J. 08540

Three-week course, the "Historic Houses of England," surveying the architectural and social history of country houses and their landscape settings.

Institute of Advanced
Architectural Studies
University of York
The King's Manor
York, Y01 2EP, England

Offers year-long and shorter courses for architects, architectural historians and surveyors in architectural conservation, architectural history, landscape and conservation area planning.

International Centre for the
Study of the Restoration and
Preservation of Cultural
Property
13, Via di San Michele
00153 Rome, Italy

Four courses yearly on architectural conservation, conservation of wall paintings, introduction to scientific conservation and preventive conservation in museums.

US/ICOMOS
Summer Work Projects
1600 H Street, N.W.
Washington, D.C. 20006

Varied programs for graduate students and young professionals including work on historic sites in France and internships in Britain.

Bookstores and Publishers

"The very cheapness of literature is making even wise people forget that if a book is worth reading, it is worth buying."

John Ruskin, *Sesame and Lilies.* 1865.

Numerous bookstores and book ordering services now specialize in architecture and preservation-related books. The following stores are among the most likely to have some or many of the titles included in this book. It is best to check with the store before ordering a title by mail to determine whether it is in stock and what the store's payment policy is; most will require a postage and handling fee of $2.50 to $3. Most of the stores also are open to the public. The largest selections of preservation books are available from the Preservation Shop of the National Trust, which sells all Preservation Press titles, and Urban Center Books.

The publishers listed are those that are most active in publishing preservation-related books and that are represented extensively in this book. Others can be found through *Books in Print.* An excellent source to contact for regional titles is the university press in your state or region. Publishers prefer that buyers first seek a desired title from a bookseller. If a book cannot be obtained this way, most publishers will sell it directly, with a postage and handling fee.

Bookstores

National

Preservation Shop
National Trust for
Historic Preservation
1600 H Street, N.W.
Washington, D.C. 20006
(202) 673-4200 or 673-4197

AIA Bookstore
American Institute of Architects
1735 New York Avenue, N.W.
Washington, D.C. 20006
(202) 626-7475

The National Trust's *Historic Preservation* magazine at a Washington, D.C., newsstand. (Paul Kennedy)

Planners Bookstore
American Planning Association
1313 East 60th Street
Chicago, Ill. 60637
(312) 955-9100

Superintendent of Documents
U.S. Government
Printing Office
Washington, D.C. 20402
(202) 783-3238

National Technical
Information Service
U.S. Department of Commerce
5285 Port Royal Road
Springfield, Va. 22161
(703) 487-4650

Stores by State

Southwest Parks and
Monuments Association
221 North Court
Tucson, Ariz. 85701
(602) 622-1999

Builders Booksource
1801 Fourth Street
Berkeley, Calif. 94710
(415) 845-6874

Art and Architecture Books
of the Twentieth Century
8373 Melrose Avenue
Los Angeles, Calif. 90069
(213) 655-5348

Rizzoli International Bookstore
and Gallery
South Coast Plaza
3333 Bristol
Costa Mesa, Calif. 92626
(714) 957-3331

San Francisco Chapter, AIA
790 Market Street
Third Floor
San Francisco, Calif. 94102
(415) 362-7397

William Stout
Architectural Books
804 Montgomery Street
San Francisco, Calif. 94133
(415) 391-6757

Hennessey and Ingalls, Inc.
Art and Architecture Books
1254 Santa Monica Mall
Santa Monica, Calif. 90401
(213) 458-9074

City Spirit Books
1434 Blake Street
Denver, Colo. 80202
(303) 595-0434

Tattered Cover Book Store
2930 East Second Avenue
Denver, Colo. 80206
(303) 322-7727

Parks and History Association
P.O. Box 40929
Washington, D.C. 20016
(202) 472-3083

Smithsonian Institution
Museum Shops
Capital Gallery Building
Suite 295B
600 Maryland Avenue, S.W.
Washington, D.C. 20560
(202) 287-3563

U.S. Government Printing
Office Bookstore
710 North Capitol Street, N.W.
Washington, D.C. 20402
(202) 275-2091

Architectural Book Center
Atlanta Chapter, AIA
Mall Level, Colony Square
1197 Peachtree Street, N.E.
Atlanta, Ga. 30361
(404) 873-3207

ArchiCenter
Chicago Architecture
Foundation
330 South Dearborn Street
Chicago, Ill. 60604
(312) 782-1776

Art Institute of Chicago
Michigan Avenue at
Adams Street
Chicago, Ill. 60603
(312) 443-3536

Prairie Avenue Bookshop
711 South Dearborn Street
Chicago, Ill. 60614
(312) 922-8311

Rizzoli International Bookstore
and Gallery
Water Tower Place
835 North Michigan Avenue
Chicago, Ill. 60611
(312) 642-3500

Architectural Center
Indiana Society of Architects
148 North Delaware
Indianapolis, Ind. 46204
(317) 634-3871

Iowa Chapter, AIA
512 Walnut Street
Des Moines, Iowa 50309
(515) 244-7502

Urban Design Center and
Bookstore
Baltimore Chapter, AIA
Candler Building
720 East Pratt Street
Baltimore, Md. 21218
(301) 727-6156

Architectural Bookshop
Boston Society of
Architects, AIA
66 Hereford Street
Boston, Mass. 02115
(617) 262-2727

Rizzoli International Bookstore
and Gallery
Copley Place
100 Huntington Avenue
Boston, Mass. 02116
(617) 437-0700

Michigan Society of Architects
553 East Jefferson Avenue
Detroit, Mich. 48226
(313) 965-4100

Paper Architecture
Minnesota Society of
Architects, AIA
910 Nicollet Mall
Minneapolis, Minn. 55402
(612) 333-1484

Kansas City Chapter, AIA
20 West Ninth Street
Suite B
Kansas City, Mo. 64105
(816) 221-3485

St. Louis Chapter, AIA
919 Olive Street
St. Louis, Mo. 63101
(314) 621-3484

Rizzoli International Bookstore
and Gallery
454 West Broadway
New York, N.Y. 10012
(212) 674-1616 or 674-1677

Rizzoli International Bookstore
and Gallery
31 West 57th Street
New York, N.Y. 10019
(212) 759-2424

Urban Center Books
457 Madison Avenue
New York, N.Y. 10022
(212) 935-3595

Eastern National Park
and Monument Association
339 Walnut Street
Philadelphia, Pa. 19106
(215) 597-7236

Philadelphia Chapter, AIA
117 South 17th Street
Philadelphia, Pa. 19103
(215) 569-3186

The Shops at Station Square
Pittsburgh, Pa. 15219
(412) 765-1042

Tennessee Society of Architects
223½ Sixth Avenue North
Nashville, Tenn. 37219
(615) 256-2311

Architext
Austin Chapter, AIA
1206 West 38th Street
Austin, Tex. 78705
(512) 452-4332

Dallas Chapter, AIA
2800 Routh
Suite 141
Dallas, Tex. 75201
(214) 748-4264

Rizzoli International Bookstore
and Gallery
316 Northpark Center
Dallas, Tex. 75225
(214) 739-6633

PRG, Inc.
5619 Southampton Drive
Springfield, Va. 22151
(703) 323-1407

Pacific Northwest National
Parks and Forest Association
2001 Sixth Avenue
Suite 1840
Seattle, Wash. 98121
(206) 442-7958

Peter Miller Art and
Architecture Books
1909 First Avenue
Seattle, Wash. 98101
(206) 623-5563

Publishers

Abbeville Press
505 Park Avenue
New York, N.Y. 10022

Harry N. Abrams
100 Fifth Avenue
New York, N.Y. 10011

American Association for
State and Local History
708 Berry Road
Nashville, Tenn. 37204

Center for Urban Policy
Research
P.O. Box 489
Piscataway, N.J. 08854

Chronicle Books
870 Market Street
San Francisco, Calif. 94102

Crown Publishers
One Park Avenue
New York, N.Y. 10016

Da Capo Press
233 Spring Street
New York, N.Y. 10013

Doubleday and Company
245 Park Avenue
New York, N.Y. 10167

Dover Publications
31 East Second Street
Mineola, N.Y. 11501

E. P. Dutton
Two Park Avenue
New York, N.Y. 10016

Gale Research Company
Book Tower
Detroit, Mich. 48226

Garland Publishing
136 Madison Avenue
New York, N.Y. 10016

Globe Pequot Press
Old Chester Road
Chester, Conn. 06412

David R. Godine, Publisher
306 Dartmouth Street
Boston, Mass. 02116

Stephen Greene Press
Fessenden Road
Brattleboro, Vt. 05301

Harcourt Brace Jovanovich
757 Third Avenue
New York, N.Y. 10017

Harper and Row, Publishers
10 East 53rd Street
New York, N.Y. 10022

Holt, Rinehart and Winston
521 Fifth Avenue
New York, N.Y. 10175

Houghton Mifflin Company
One Beacon Street
Boston, Mass. 02108

Alfred A. Knopf
201 East 50th Street
New York, N.Y. 10022

Lexington Books
125 Spring Street
Lexington, Mass. 02173

Little, Brown and Company
34 Beacon Street
Boston, Mass. 02106

Macmillan Publishing Company
866 Third Avenue
New York, N.Y. 10022

McGraw-Hill
1221 Avenue of the Americas
New York, N.Y. 10020

The Main Street Press
William Case House
Pittstown, N.J. 08867

The MIT Press
28 Carleton Street
Cambridge, Mass. 02142

William Morrow
105 Madison Avenue
New York, N.Y. 10016

New York Graphic Society
Books
34 Beacon Street
Boston, Mass 02106

W. W. Norton and Company
500 Fifth Avenue
New York, N.Y. 10110

The Overlook Press
12 West 21st Street
New York, N.Y. 10010

Pantheon Books
201 East 50th Street
New York, N.Y. 10022

Clarkson N. Potter
One Park Avenue
New York, N.Y. 10016

Prentice-Hall
Route 9W
Englewood Cliffs, N.J. 07632

The Preservation Press
1785 Massachusetts Avenue, N.W.
Washington, D.C. 20036

Pruett Publishing Company
2928 Pearl Street
Boulder, Colo. 80301

The Putnam Publishing Group
200 Madison Avenue
New York, N.Y. 10016

Random House
201 East 50th Street
New York, N.Y. 10022

Rizzoli International
Publications
597 Fifth Avenue
New York, N.Y. 10017

St. Martin's Press
175 Fifth Avenue
New York, N.Y. 10010

Charles Scribner's Sons
507 Fifth Avenue
New York, N.Y. 10017

Simon and Schuster
1230 Avenue of the Americas
New York, N.Y. 10020

Peregrine Smith
Box 667
Layton, Utah 84041

Peter Smith Publisher
6 Lexington Avenue
Magnolia, Mass. 01930

Technical Preservation Services
National Park Service
U.S. Department of the Interior
P.O. Box 37127
Washington, D.C. 20013-7127

University Press of Virginia
Box 3608
University Station
Charlottesville, Va. 22903

U.S. Government
Printing Office
Washington, D.C. 20402

Vance Bibliographies
P.O. Box 229
Monticello, Ill. 61856

Van Nostrand Reinhold
Company
135 West 50th Street
New York, N.Y. 10020

Viking Penguin
40 West 23rd Street
New York, N.Y. 10010

Westview Press
5500 Central Avenue
Boulder, Colo. 80301

Whitney Library of Design
Watson-Guptill Publications
1515 Broadway
New York, N.Y. 10036

John Wiley and Sons
605 Third Avenue
New York, N.Y. 10158

Acknowledgments

The Preservation Press is grateful to the authors and publishers of the many quotations used throughout this book to illustrate the important contents of various publications. In most instances, credit accompanies the quoted material or is found in the publication listing in the chapter. For longer quoted material and excerpts from other publications or broadcasts, we acknowledge special permission from the following authors and publishers to reprint excerpts from the following publications:

1. Fugitive Places

Page 11: Mrs. Norma Millay Ellis—"Second Fig," from *A Few Figs From Thistles*, by Edna St. Vincent Millay. From *Collected Poems, Edna St. Vincent Millay*. Norma Millay, ed. New York: Harper and Row, 1975.

Page 12: Harcourt Brace Jovanovich, Inc.—*Cavett*, copyright © 1974 by Richard A. Cavett and Christopher Porterfield. Reprinted by permission of Harcourt Brace Jovanovich, Inc.

Page 15: The New York Times Company—"Anatomy of a Failure," by Ada Louise Huxtable. © 1968 by The New York Times Company. Reprinted by permission. "A Vision of Rome Dies," by Ada Louise Huxtable. © 1966 by the New York Times Company. Reprinted by permission.

Page 18: The New York Times Company—"The Architectural Follies," by Ada Louise Huxtable. © 1965 by The New York Times Company. Reprinted by permission. *Washington Post*—"Building Wreckers Recall Better Days," by Lew Sichelman. © *Washington Star*, April 22, 1977. All rights reserved.

Page 26: Art Buchwald—"Save Lincoln Center," by Art Buchwald. *New York Herald Tribune*, 1962. Reprinted by permission of the author.

2. Preservation

Page 30: Alvin Toffler and Random House, Inc.—*Future Shock*, by Alvin Toffler. Copyright © 1970 by Alvin Toffler. All rights reserved. Reprinted by permission of the author and Random House, Inc. Viking Penguin, Inc.—*The Grapes of Wrath*, by John Steinbeck. Copyright 1939 by John Steinbeck. Copyright renewed 1967 by John Steinbeck. Reprinted by permission of Viking Penguin, Inc.

Page 34: The New York Times Company—"Where Ghosts Can Be at Home," by Ada Louise Huxtable. © 1968 by The New York Times Company. Reprinted by permission.

3. Looking at the Built Environment

Pages 66-67: Norval White and Alfred A. Knopf, Inc.—*The Architecture Book*, by Norval White. © 1976 by Norval White. Reprinted by permission of the author and Alfred A. Knopf, Inc.

Page 71: Doubleday and Company, Inc.—*Rewards and Fairies*, by Rudyard Kipling. Copyright 1910 by Rudyard Kipling. Reprinted by permission of the National Trust and Doubleday and Company, Inc.

Page 86: The New York Times Company—"The Skyscraper Style," by Ada Louise Huxtable. © 1974 by The New York Times Company. Reprinted by permission.

Page 94: Random House, Inc.—*The Eye of the Story: Selected Essays and Reviews*, by Eudora Welty. Copyright © 1978 by Eudora Welty. Reprinted by permission of Random House, Inc.

4. Form and Function

Page 114: Lescher and Lescher, Ltd.—*Georgia O'Keeffe*, by Georgia O'Keeffe. Copyright © 1976 by Georgia O'Keeffe. Reprinted by permission of Lescher and Lescher, Ltd.

Page 115: The New York Times Company—"Art for Money's Sake," by Ada Louise Huxtable. © 1978 by The New York Times Company. Reprinted by permission.

Page 128: Random House, Inc.—*Requiem for a Nun*, by William Faulkner. Copyright © 1951 by William Faulkner. Reprinted by permission of Random House, Inc.

Page 152: The New York Times Company—Article by Ada Louise Huxtable, *New York Times*, August 13, 1980. © 1980 by The New York Times Company. Reprinted by permission.

Page 164: The New York Times Company—"What's in a Wall?" by Ada Louise Huxtable. © 1976 by The New York Times Company. Reprinted by permission.

5. Preservationists

Page 169: Ada Louise Huxtable—*Vogue*, March 1977. Reprinted by permission of the author and *Vogue*. Copyright © 1977 by The Condé Nast Publications Inc.

6. Protecting the Past

Page 197: *Pasadena Heritage* Newsletter—"Relections of a Streetwalker," by Bunny Gould and Carol Robillard. *Pasadena Heritage*, Summer 1977. Reprinted by permission.

Page 198: California Office of Planning and Research—*Historic Preservation Element Guidelines*, California Office of Planning and Research, 1976. Reprinted by permission.

Page 199: Stanford Environmental Law Society—*Historic Preservation in California: A Legal Handbook*, by Grady Gammage, Jr., Philip N. Jones and Stephen L. Jones, 1975. Reprinted by permission of Stanford Environmental Law Society.

7. Taking Action

Page 224: The New York Times Company—"Goodbye History, Hello Hamburger," by Ada Louise Huxtable. © 1971 by The New York Times Company. Reprinted by permission.

8. Building Roots

Page 268: *Old-House Journal*—"How to Date an Old House," *Old-House Journal*, October 1976. Reprinted with permission.

9. Rehabilitation and Restoration

Page 282: The New York Times Company—"They Don't Make That Anymore," by Russell Baker. © 1975 by The New York Times Company. Reprinted by permission.

Page 300: *Old-House Journal*—"Sprucing Up Old Radiators," *Old-House Journal*, October 1978. Reprinted with permission.

10. Adaptive Use

Page 325: *The New Yorker*—"U.S. Journal: New England. Thoughts Brought On by Prolonged Exposure to Exposed Brick," by Calvin Trillin. © 1977 by The New Yorker Magazine, Inc. Reprinted by permission.

11. Historic Sites

Page 336: Alvin Toffler and Random House, Inc.—*Future Shock*, by Alvin Toffler. Copyright © 1970 by Alvin Toffler. All rights reserved. Reprinted by permission of the author and Random House, Inc.

12. Neighborhoods

Page 351: *The Christian Science Monitor*—"A Nation of Neighborhoods," by Stewart Dill McBride. Reprinted by permission from *The Christian Science Monitor*. © 1977 The Christian Science Publishing Society. All rights reserved.

Page 356: Hartford Architecture Conservancy, Inc.—Editorial, *HAC News*, Winter 1977. Reprinted by permission.

13. Main Streets

Page 367: Alfred A. Knopf, Inc.—*The American Language,* by H. L. Mencken. Copyright © 1938 by Alfred A. Knopf, Inc. Reprinted by permission. Harcourt Brace Jovanovich, Inc.—*Main Street,* by Sinclair Lewis. Reprinted by permission of Harcourt Brace Jovanovich, Inc. CBS News—"A Few Minutes with Andy Rooney." © CBS Inc. 1978. All rights reserved. Originally broadcast September 17, 1978, over the CBS Television Network as part of the "60 Minutes" program series.

Page 370: The New York Times Company—"The Fall and Rise of Main Street," by Ada Louise Huxtable. © 1976 by The New York Times Company. Reprinted by permission.

Page 373: Chamber of Commerce of the United States of America—*Downtown Redevelopment,* Chamber of Commerce of the United States of America. Copyright © 1974 Urban Strategy Center, Chamber of Commerce. Reprinted by permission. *The New Yorker*—"U.S. Journal: New England. Thoughts Brought On by Prolonged Exposure to Exposed Brick," by Calvin Trillin. Copyright © 1977 by The New Yorker Magazine, Inc. Reprinted by permission.

Page 374: The New York Times Company—"The Fall and Rise of Main Street," by Ada Louise Huxtable. © 1976 by The New York Times Company. Reprinted by permission.

Page 378: The Warren Company—"Things to Know Before Beginning Main Street Revitalization: Essential Elements, Obstacles, Leveraging Points," by Robert Porter Lynch. Reprinted by permission.

Page 372: Simon and Schuster—*The Heart of Our Cities,* by Victor Gruen. Copyright © 1964 by Victor Gruen. Reprinted by permission of Simon and Schuster.

Patterned 19th-century paving bricks in Madison, Ind., adapted as the logo of the National Main Street Center. (James L. Ballard, NTHP)

Index of Subjects

Iron gate near the Mississippi River in Louisiana. From *Archabet: An Architectural Alphabet.* (Balthazar Korab)

Other Preservation Press Books

America's City Halls. William L. Lebovich, Historic American Buildings Survey. 224 pp., illus., append., index. $18.95 pb.

A record of America's municipal architectural achievements, this book documents for the first time 114 notable examples of city and town halls. An introduction and individual essays accompany more than 300 photographs.

America's Country Schools. Andrew Gulliford. 296 pp., illus., appends., biblio., index. $18.95 pb.

The first book to examine the country school as a distinctive building type, this captures in 400 photographs the historical and architectural legacy of country schools (from dugouts and soddies to frame buildings and octagons) and provides ideas for preserving them.

America's Forgotten Architecture. National Trust for Historic Preservation, Tony P. Wrenn and Elizabeth D. Mulloy. 312 pp., illus., biblio., appends. $12.95 pb.

A lavish introduction to preservation, the book surveys in 475 photographs what is worth saving and how to do it.

Archabet: An Architectural Alphabet. Photographs by Balthazar Korab. 64 pp., illus. $12.95 hb.

Here is a new way of looking at architecture—through the eyes and imagination of an award-winning photographer in search of an alphabet in, on and around buildings. The award-winning volume juxtaposes dramatic photographs with quotations from architectural observers from Goethe to Frank Lloyd Wright.

The Brown Book: A Directory of Preservation Information. Diane Maddex, ed., with Ellen R. Marsh. 160 pp., illus., biblio., gloss., index. $17.95 spiral bound.

The first directory to provide names, addresses and telephone numbers for some 1,000 key preservation organizations and individuals, plus practical preservation tips.

Scrollwork detail on the Huntington House, Howell, Mich. From *Archabet: An Architectural Alphabet.* (Balthazar Korab)

Built in the U.S.A.: American Buildings from Airports to Zoos. Diane Maddex, ed. 192 pp., illus., biblio. $8.95 pb.

A heavily illustrated, guidebook-sized history of 42 types of American buildings, presented individually in concise essays by noted authorities. Building Watchers Series.

Fabrics for Historic Buildings. Jane C. Nylander. 3rd edition. 160 pp., illus., biblio. $9.95 pb.

A popular guide that gives practical advice on selecting and using reproductions of historic fabrics. A key feature is an illustrated catalog listing 550 reproduction fabrics. Also included are a glossary and list of manufacturers.

The History of the National Trust for Historic Preservation, 1963-1973. Elizabeth D. Mulloy. 315 pp., color illus., biblio., appends., index. $9.95 hb.

The story of preservation's rise in the 1960s as well as a record of the National Trust's role.

"I Feel I Should Warn You . . ." Historic Preservation Cartoons. Terry Morton, ed. Essay by Draper Hill. 112 pp., illus. $6.95 pb.

From Peanuts to Punch, this is a unique collection of cartoons that have nipped and nudged to keep the wreckers at bay for more than 150 years.

Old and New Architecture: Design Relationship. National Trust for Historic Preservation. 280 pp., illus., biblio., index. $25 hb, $15.95 pb.

Twenty well-known architects and preservationists tell how old and new buildings can coexist—giving their own solutions, explaining why others fail, suggesting how design review should work and addressing the legal, aesthetic and practical problems of relating old and new.

Presence of the Past: A History of the Preservation Movement in the U.S. Before Williamsburg. Charles B. Hosmer, Jr. 386 pp., illus., biblio., index. $12.95 hb.

A thorough and entertaining account of early preservationists and their landmark achievements, this classic recounts famous battles to save sites such as Mount Vernon and Monticello.

Preservation Comes of Age: From Williamsburg to the National Trust, 1926-1949. Charles B. Hosmer, Jr. 1,291 pp., illus., biblio., chron., index. 2 vols. $37.50 hb. University Press of Virginia.

A monumental history that is the standard reference work on the subject, documenting the people, projects and philosophies of the movement's formative years.

Respectful Rehabilitation: Answers to Your Questions About Old Buildings. Technical Preservation Services, U.S. Department of the Interior. Drawings by David J. Baker. 192 pp., illus., biblio., appends., gloss., index. $9.95 pb.

This unique book answers 150 questions property owners and residents most frequently ask about rehabilitating old houses and other historic buildings. The answers are based on the Secretary of the Interior's Standards for Rehabilitation, which are reprinted in full. Illustrated with 100 photographs and drawings.

Wallpapers for Historic Buildings. Richard C. Nylander. 128 pp., illus., biblio., appends. $9.95 pb.

This compact handbook shows how to select authentic reproductions of historic wallpaper and where to buy more than 350 recommended patterns. Includes a glossary, reading list and manufacturers' addresses.

What Style Is It? A Guide to American Architecture. John Poppeliers, S. Allen Chambers, Jr., and Nancy B. Schwartz, Historic American Buildings Survey. 112 pp., illus., gloss., biblio. $7.95 pb.

One of the most popular, concise books on American architectural styles, this portable guidebook discusses 22 important styles and is designed for easy identification of buildings at home or on the road. Honored by the National Endowment for the Arts. Building Watchers Series.

With Heritage So Rich. U.S. Conference of Mayors. Albert Rains and Laurence G. Henderson, eds. New introduction by Charles B. Hosmer, Jr. 232 pp., illus., appends. $18.95 pb.

A classic that helped spur passage of the 1966 preservation act, this handsome book shows in dramatic photographs and essays why America's architectural heritage should be preserved. Landmark Reprint Series.

Preservation Press Bookplates:

Cape Cod House. Package of 40. 2¾ × 5". $4.95.

Decorative sawn-wood porch on a Cape Cod house. Drawing on yellow background by Sandra Webbere-Hall.

Star Tie Rod. Package of 40. 2¾ × 5". $3.95.

Screened photograph featuring a star-shaped rod used to stabilize major beams in old masonry buildings. Brick-red design by Tom Engeman.

Victorian Fabric. Package of 40. 2¾ × 5". $4.95.

Full-color detail from Victorian Garden Glazed Chintz (c. 1850), reproduced by Brunschwig and Fils from the Winterthur Museum collection.

Victorian Storefront Facade. Package of 30. 2¾ × 5". $3.95.

Arched window detail inspired by the Germond Crandell Building (1877), part of Gallery Row in Washington, D.C. Blue and green design by Tom Engeman.

To order Preservation Press books, send the total of the book prices (less 10 percent discount for National Trust members), plus $3 postage and handling, to: Preservation Shop, National Trust for Historic Preservation, 1600 H Street, N.W., Washington, D.C. 20006. Residents of California, Massachusetts, New York and South Carolina, please add applicable sales tax. Make checks payable to the National Trust; or you may charge to VISA or MasterCard, providing your account number, expiration date and signature. (All Preservation Press titles listed in this book may be ordered from the Preservation Shop.)

When we build, let us think that we build for ever. Let it not be for present delight, nor for present use alone; let it be such work as our descendants will thank us for. . . .

John Ruskin, *The Seven Lamps of Architecture.* 1849.

All About Old Buildings was designed by Robert Wiser and Marc Alain Meadows of Meadows and Wiser, Washington, D.C.

The type was composed in Times Roman by Carver Photocomposition, Inc., Arlington, Va. The book was printed on 70-pound Warren Patina by Collins Lithographing and Printing Company, Inc., Baltimore, Md., and bound by Bookcrafters, Inc., Columbia, Md.